Thailand

THE ROUGH GUIDE

D0574034

There are more than one hundred Rough Guide titles
covering destinations from Amsterdam to Zimbabwe

Forthcoming titles include
Bangkok • Barbados • Edinburgh
Japan • Jordan • Syria

Rough Guide Reference Series
Classical Music • European Football • The Internet • Jazz
Opera • Reggae • Rock Music • World Music

Rough Guide Phrasebooks
Czech • French • German • Greek • Hindi & Urdu • Indonesian • Italian
Mandarin Chinese • Mexican Spanish • Polish • Portuguese
Russian • Spanish • Thai • Turkish • Vietnamese

Rough Guides on the Internet
http://www.roughguides.com
http://www.hotwired.com/rough

Thailand: Rough Guide Credits

Text editor:	Annie Shaw
Series editor:	Mark Ellingham
Editorial:	Martin Dunford, Jonathan Buckley, Samantha Cook, Jo Mead, Amanda Tomlin, Paul Gray, Sarah Dallas, Kate Berens, Chris Schüler, Helena Smith, Julia Kelly, Caroline Osborne, Kieren Falconer, Judith Bamber, Alan Spicer (UK); Andrew Rosenberg (US)
Online:	Kate Hands (UK); Geronimo Madrid (US)
Production:	Susanne Hillen, Andy Hilliard, Melissa Flack, Judy Pang, Link Hall, Nicola Williamson, David Callier, Helen Ostick, Maxine Burke
Finance:	John Fisher, Celia Crowley, Catherine Gillespie
Marketing and Publicity:	Richard Trillo, Simon Carloss, Niki Smith (UK), Jean-Marie Kelly, Sorelle Braun (US)
Administration:	Tania Hummel, Alexander Mark Rogers

Acknowledgments

The authors would both like to thank: Khun Peck at Bangkok TAT; Lysiane Belton and London TAT; Sukasem Chongmankhong, Pojanee Tuppasutti and Roongthip Thongwattanaporn at Premier Inter Leasing (Hertz); Jeanne Muchnick; David Leffman; Philip Cornwel-Smith; John Clewley; Ron Emmons; Colin McCarthy at the Natural History Museum and Brian Groombridge at the World Conservation Monitoring Centre; Andrew Tibber for proofreading; Susanne Hillen, Nicola Williamson and Judy Pang for production; Micromap Ltd and Melissa Flack for cartography; and most especially Jon, Annie, and David Reed. Individually, the authors would also like to thank:

Paul – Santipap Sulaiman at Sungai Kolok TAT; Pornlert Ooncharoen in Nakhon; Khun Wisut, Khun Tossaporn and Khun Preecha in Chiang Mai; Nuan Sarnsorn in Nakhon Phanom; Thepnarong Polngam and Manit Boonchim in Udon Thani; Laksana Iam-Sumang in Ayutthaya; Khun Somboon, Khun Grit and Khun Porn in Hat Yai; Khun Sarith and Khun Nongyao on Ko Samui; Sanga Namwong in Chiang Rai; Sunthorn Sidtrirueang at Doi Inthanon; Bon Satarat on Ko Tarutao; Suvan Boonthae in Nong Khai; Moo Zaikaen in Mae Hong Son; Khun Kannika in Narathiwat; Francois and Sin Benier; Shane Beary; Tamar Le Clue; Jonggon Duangsri; Soren Skibsted; Khun Jittakon; Chad; Wat; Michael Barraclough; Preecha Thitichon; Bill and Sheila Gray, Bill and Maud Hall, Jack Grassby and David Johnson, and Ruth and Sarah Derry, for their generous support and much else besides.

Lucy – Jariyathon Soohoo at Khon Kaen TAT; Renat Permpongsacharoen and Sombut Prommacharee at Kanchanaburi TAT; Sombat Panarong of Mae Sot; Nutty from Umpang and Apple from Phitsanulok; Hugh Mulcahy; Sally Burbage; Charlie and Mary for first-hand travel tips; Mark Tindall for oriental hospitality; Steven Geers for flight info; Chris Humphreys for Ko Chang insights; and to Jon, Ralph, Deb, Mark, and the Ridout family for great support and lots of extra publicity.

This second edition published 1995 by Rough Guides Ltd, 1 Mercer Street, London WC2H 9QJ.
Reprinted in April 1996, February and November 1997.

Distributed by the Penguin Group:
Penguin Books Ltd, 27 Wrights Lane, London W8 5TZ
Penguin Books USA Inc., 375 Hudson Street, New York 10014, USA
Penguin Books Australia Ltd, 487 Maroondah Highway, PO Box 257, Ringwood, Victoria 3134, Australia
Penguin Books Canada Ltd, 10 Alcorn Avenue, Toronto, Ontario, Canada M4V 1E4
Penguin Books (NZ) Ltd, 182–190 Wairau Road, Auckland 10, New Zealand

Previous edition published in the United States and Canada as *The Real Guide Thailand*.

Typeset in Linotron Univers and Century Old Style to an original design by Andrew Oliver.
Printed in the United Kingdom by Cox & Wyman Ltd (Reading).
Illustrations in Part One and Part Three by Edward Briant; Illustrations on p.1 and p.515 by Henry Iles.

608pp. includes index

A catalogue record for this book is available from the British Library.

ISBN 1-85828-140-7

Thailand

THE ROUGH GUIDE

Written and researched by
Paul Gray and Lucy Ridout

Contributors
John Clewley, John R Davies and Gavin Lewis

THE ROUGH GUIDES

LIST OF MAPS

MAP SYMBOLS

REGIONAL MAPS

+++	Railway
▬▬	Main Road
▬▬	Minor Road
-[115]-	Road number
- - - - -	Track or Trail
▬▬	River
⬭	Lake
— —	Ferry route
▬■▬■	International boundary
▬ ▬	Chapter division boundary
⩙	Mountains
▲	Peak
⯭	Waterfall
☼	Viewpoint
ⵔ	Lighthouse
◆	Ancient site

TOWN MAPS

▬▬	Railway
▪▪▪▪	Fortified wall
▨	Park
⊞	Church
⁺⁺⁺	Christian cemetery

GENERAL

☒	Mosque
▲	Temple
ⓘ	Tourist Office
✉	Post Office
▣	Accommodation
◉	Restaurant
◫	Market
ℭ	Telephone
⊞	Hospital
▦	Beach
✈	Airport

CONTENTS

Introduction viii

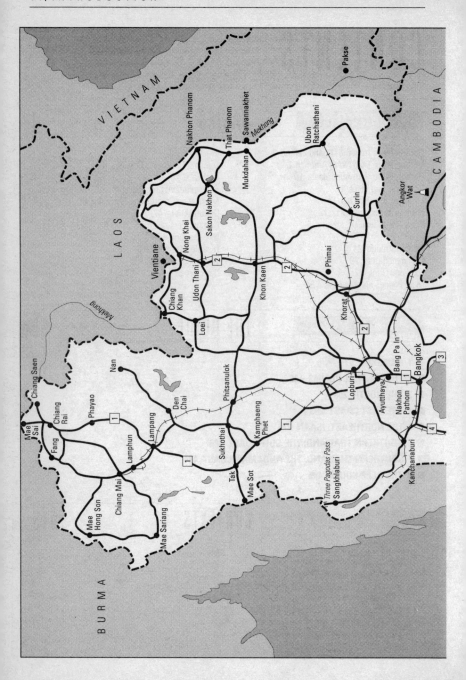

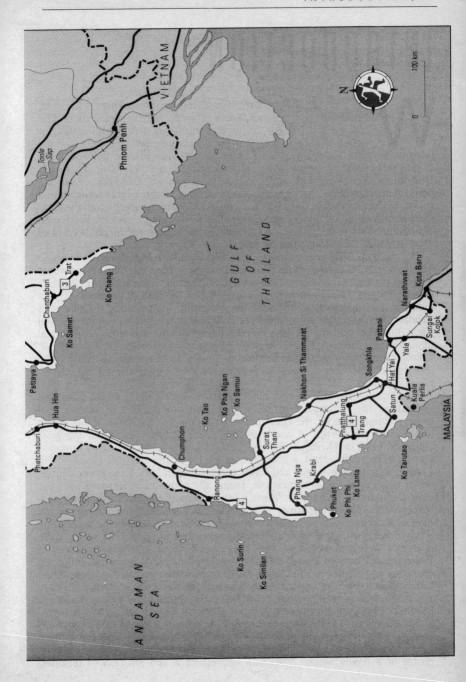

INTRODUCTION

With over five million foreigners flying into the country each year, **Thailand** has become Asia's primary holiday destination. The influx of tourist cash has played a significant part in making this one of the world's fastest growing economies, yet Thailand's cultural integrity remains largely undamaged except for the main resorts. In this country of fifty-three million people, over ninety percent are practising Theravada **Buddhists**, a unifying faith which colours all aspects of daily life – from the tiered temple rooftops that dominate every skyline, to the omnipresent saffron-robed monks and the packed calendar of festivals. Furthermore, though the high-rises and neon lights occupy the foreground of the tourist picture, the typical Thai community is the traditional **farming** village, and some ninety percent of Thais still earn their living from the land.

The clash of tradition and modernity is most intense in **Bangkok**, the first stop on almost any itinerary. Within the capital's historic core you'll find resplendent temples, canalside markets and the opulent indulgence of the eighteenth-century **Grand Palace**, while in downtown Bangkok lies the hub of the country's sex industry, the infamous strip known as **Patpong**. The political fault-lines of Thailand are inevitably most visible in Bangkok as well. Home of the revered King Bhumibol and the far less revered ministers who run this constitutional monarchy, it's the cockpit of the country's burgeoning environmental movement, whose campaigns on such inflammatory issues as the trade in endangered species and the construction of large-scale dams have regularly hit the international headlines.

After touchdown in Bangkok, much of the package-holiday traffic flows east to **Pattaya**, the country's first and most popular beach resort. Born as a rest-and-recreation base for the US military during the Vietnam War, it has grown into a concrete warren of hotels and strip joints that's just about the least authentic town in Thailand. For unpolluted beaches and clear seas, however, you have to venture just a little further afield, to the unspoilt island of **Ko Chang**, with its superb sand and idyllic bamboo beach huts. Even fewer tourists strike north from the east coast into **Isaan**, the poorest and in some ways the most traditionally Thai region. Here, a trip through the gently modulating landscapes of the **Mekhong River** valley, which defines Thailand's northern and eastern extremities, takes in archetypal agricultural villages and a fascinating array of religious sites, while the southern reaches of Isaan hold some of the country's best-kept secrets – the magnificent stone temple complexes of **Phimai** and **Phanom Rung**, both built by the Khmers of Cambodia almost ten centuries ago. Closer to the capital, in the southwestern corner of Isaan, **Khao Yai National Park** encapsulates the phenomenal diversity of Thailand's flora and fauna, which here range from wild orchids to strangling figs, elephants to hornbills, tigers to macaques.

Attractively sited at the heart of the northern uplands, **Chiang Mai** draws tourists in almost the same quantities as Pattaya, but it has preserved its looks with far greater care, and appeals to a different kind of visitor. It's the vibrant cultural centre of a region whose overriding enticement is the prospect of **trekking** through villages inhabited by a richly mixed population of tribal peoples. With Chiang Mai so firmly planted on the independent tourist trail, the ancient cities of the intervening **central plains** tend to get short shrift. Yet the elegant ruins of former capitals **Ayutthaya** and **Sukhothai** embody a glorious artistic heritage, displaying Thailand's distinctive ability to absorb influences from quite different cultures. **Kanchanaburi**, stunningly located on the **River Kwai** in the western reaches of the central plains, tells a much darker episode of Thailand's past, for it was along the course of this river that the Japanese army built the Thailand–Burma Railway during World War II, at the cost of thousands of POW lives.

Sand and sea are what most Thailand holidays are about, though, and the pick of the coasts are in southern Thailand, where the **Samui archipelago**, off the **Gulf coast** is one of the highlights: its small resorts, desolate coves and immaculate sweeping beaches draw teenage ravers and solitude seekers in equal parts. Across on the other side of the peninsula, the **Andaman coast** boasts even more exhilarating scenery and the finest **coral reefs** in the country. The largest resort, **Ko Phuket**, is packed with expensive highrises and threatens to go the way of Pattaya, but on nearby **Ko Phi Phi** the emphasis on budget travel persists, and the coral-rich sea remains an untainted azure. Neither of these, however, can match the spectacular **Ko Similan** island chain, some six hours out to sea, which ranks as one of the world's top diving destinations. Further down the Thai peninsula, in the provinces of the **deep south**, the teeming marine life and unfrequented sands of **Ko Tarutao National Marine Park** are the immediate attractions, though the edgy relationship between Thai sovereignty and Malaysian Islam – the kind of cultural brew that has characterized Thailand throughout its history – makes this region a rewarding one for the more adventurous traveller to explore.

When to go

The **climate** of most of Thailand is governed by three seasons: rainy (roughly June to October), caused by the southwest monsoon dumping moisture gathered from the Andaman Sea and the Gulf of Thailand; cool (November to February); and hot (March to May). The **rainy season** is the least predictable of the three, varying in length and intensity from year to year, but usually it gathers force between June and August, coming to a peak in September and October, when unpaved roads are reduced to mud troughs and whole districts of Bangkok are flooded. The **cool season** is the pleasantest time to visit, although temperatures

---

TRANSLITERATION OF THAI WORDS

Because there's no standard system of **transliteration** of Thai script into Roman, you're sure to find that the Thai words and proper names in this book do not always match the versions written elsewhere. Maps and street signs are the biggest sources of confusion, so where possible we've used the transliteration that's most common on the spot; in less clear instances we've stuck to the most frequent national transliteration. However, it's sometimes necessary to practise a little lateral thinking when it comes to deciphering Romanized Thai, bearing in mind that a town such as Ubon Ratchathani, for example, could come out as Ubol Rajatani, or that Ayutthaya is synonymous with Ayudhia. As for street names, a classic variant would be Ratchawithi Road or Rajvithi Road – and it's not unheard of to find one spelling posted at one end of a road, with another at the opposite end.

can still reach a broiling 30°C in the middle of the day. In the **hot season**, when temperatures rise to 40°C, the best thing to do is to hit the beach.

Within this scheme, slight variations are found from region to region. The less humid **north** experiences the greatest range of temperatures: at night in the cool season the thermometer occasionally approaches zero on the higher slopes, and this region is often hotter than the central plains between March and May. It's **the northeast** which gets the very worst of the hot season, with clouds of dust gathering above the parched fields, and humid air too. In **southern Thailand**, temperatures are more consistent throughout the year, with less variation the closer you get to the equator. The rainy season hits the **Andaman coast** of the southern peninsula harder than anywhere else in the country – heavy rainfall usually starts in May and persists at the same level until October.

One area of the country, the **Gulf coast** of the southern peninsula, lies outside this general pattern – because it faces east, this coast and its offshore islands feel the effects of the northeast monsoon, which brings rain between October and January. This area also suffers less from the southwest monsoon, getting a relatively small amount of rain between June and September.

Overall, the **cool season** is generally the **best time** to come to Thailand: as well as having more manageable temperatures and less rain, it offers waterfalls in full spate and the best of the upland flowers in bloom. Bear in mind, however, that it's also the busiest season, so forward planning is essential.

THAILAND'S CLIMATE

Average daily maximum temperatures °C (°F) and monthly rainfall (inches)

	Jan	Feb	Mar	Apr	May	June	July	Aug	Sept	Oct	Nov	Dec
Bangkok												
°C	32	34	35	36	34	33	32	32	32	32	31	31
(°F)	(90)	(93)	(95)	(97)	(93)	(91)	(90)	(90)	(90)	(90)	(88)	(88)
Inches	1	1	1	2	7	6	6	8	13	5	2	0
Chiang Mai												
°C	28	31	34	36	34	32	31	30	31	31	30	28
(°F)	(82)	(88)	(93)	(97)	(93)	(90)	(88)	(86)	(88)	(88)	(86)	(82)
Inches	1	1	1	2	6	6	7	10	10	5	1	1
Pattaya												
°C	33	33	33	34	33	33	32	32	32	32	32	32
(°F)	(91)	(91)	(91)	(93)	(91)	(91)	(90)	(90)	(90)	(90)	(90)	(90)
Inches	1	2	2	3	7	3	4	4	9	11	3	1
Ko Samui												
°C	27	27	28	29	29	28	28	28	28	27	27	26
(°F)	(81)	(81)	(82)	(84)	(84)	(82)	(82)	(82)	(82)	(81)	(81)	(79)
Inches	8	1	2	4	6	3	5	4	4	10	17	10
Ko Phuket												
°C	32	33	33	33	32	31	30	31	30	30	30	31
(°F)	(90)	(91)	(91)	(91)	(90)	(88)	(86)	(88)	(86)	(86)	(86)	(88)
Inches	1	1	2	5	12	11	12	11	14	13	7	2

PART ONE

THE
BASICS

GETTING THERE FROM THE UK AND IRELAND

The fastest and most comfortable way of reaching Thailand from the UK is to fly non-stop from London to Bangkok with either *Qantas*, *British Airways*, *EVA Airways* or *Thai International* – a journey time of about twelve hours. Many scheduled airlines operate indirect flights (ie flights with one or more connections), which usually take up to four hours longer, but work out significantly cheaper, particularly if you go with *Lauda Air* via Vienna, *Kuwait Airways* via Kuwait or *Finnair* via Helsinki. *Lauda Air* also flies London–Phuket with a change in

Vienna. There are no non-stop flights from Glasgow, Manchester, Dublin or Belfast, only flights via other European cities, and fares sometimes work out about the same as for indirect flights from London – though with flights from Ireland it may be worthwhile getting a cheap flight or ferry to England then booking your flight to Bangkok from London. If you're really determined to get rock-bottom prices, then plump for *Aeroflot* or *Tarom Romanian Air*. However, many agents refuse to deal with them because of the unreliability of their booking systems and schedules, and there has been considerable concern recently about *Aeroflot's* safety standards.

If you want to make extra use of all that flying time and **stop over** on the way there or back, you'll probably have to go with the associated national airline – for example *Air India* for stops in Delhi or Bombay. This is an option which most airlines offer at the same price as their direct flights. If you're continuing onward from Thailand, then consider buying a one-way London–Bangkok ticket (from £178 low season and £330 high season) and shopping around for the next leg of your trip once you arrive in Bangkok: because of lax governmental control, flights out of Thailand can be significantly cheaper than those bought in the West (see p.131). Remember, though, that if

MAJOR AIRLINES

Aeroflot, 70 Piccadilly, London W1 (☎0171/355 2233). Three flights a week from Heathrow via Moscow. Very cheap, no frills and not very reliable.

British Airways, 156 Regent St, London W1 (☎0181/897 4000). Daily non-stop flights from Heathrow.

EVA Airways, 231 St John St, London EC1 (☎0171/833 9610). Three non-stop flights a week from Heathrow.

Finnair, 14 Clifford St, London W1 (☎0171/408 1222). Twice weekly flights from Heathrow via Helsinki.

Kuwait Airways, 16 Baker St, London W1 (☎0171/412 0007). Three flights a week from Heathrow via Kuwait.

Lauda Air, 123 Buckingham Palace Rd, London SW1 (☎0171/630 5924). Three flights a week from

Gatwick/Heathrow via Vienna. Once a week from Heathrow to Phuket, also via Vienna.

Qantas, 182 The Strand, London W1 (☎01345/747767). Daily non-stop flights from Heathrow.

Royal Brunei, 49 Cromwell Rd, London SW7 (☎0171/584 6660). Three flights a week from Heathrow via Frankfurt and Dubai (one plane change in Frankfurt).

Tarom Romanian Air, 27 New Cavendish St, London W1 (☎0171/224 3693). Three flights a week from Stansted/Heathrow via Bucharest and Dubai (two a week in low season). Not very reliable, but very cheap.

Thai International, 41 Albemarle St, London W1 (☎0171/499 9113). Four non-stop flights a week from Heathrow, and three via Delhi.

you go into Thailand on a one-way ticket you must buy a sixty-day visa beforehand (see p.12). Alternatively, if planning a long trip with several stops in Asia or elsewhere, buying a **round-the-world ticket** makes a lot of sense: a typical one-year open ticket would depart and return to London, taking in Singapore, Bangkok, Bali, Sydney, Auckland, Tahiti, Los Angeles and New York, leaving you to cover the Singapore–Bangkok and LA–NYC legs overland.

FARES

As there are currently no APEX fares to Thailand and the scheduled airline prices show very little seasonal variation, there's little point in buying direct from the airlines unless you want the option of being able to alter your dates of departure or return. Any reliable specialist **agent** (see box below) will be able to undercut airline prices by a hefty percentage – as an indicator, *Finnair* charges in the region of £2000 return to Bangkok (at all times of the year), which is at least double the price of the same ticket bought through an agent. Thus the prices we refer to in this section are agents' prices. There's no minimum advance booking period on agency tickets, which means that theoretically you could book a discount ticket and fly out on the same day, but these discount deals nearly always carry **restrictions** on your length of stay in Thailand (generally 7–90 days) and sometimes require a fixed departure date from Thailand – check particulars with your agent.

The most expensive **times to fly** are July, August and December – you may have to book two to three months in advance for these peak periods. Check the airline's exact seasonal dates through an agent, as you could make major savings by shifting your departure date by as little as one day.

Discounted non-stop London–Bangkok return **fares** start at around £462 low season, rising to £605 during peak periods. For the cheaper indirect flights, *Finnair* flights via Helsinki usually come out among the cheapest at £440 low season, £506 high season, with *Tarom* some-

DISCOUNT FLIGHT AGENTS

UK

Bridge the World, 1–3 Ferdinand St, London NW1 (☎0171/911 0900). A wide choice of cut-price flights and other services.

Campus Travel, 52 Grosvenor Gardens, London SW1 (☎0171/730 3402); and branches in Birmingham, Bristol, Cambridge, Edinburgh, Manchester and Oxford. Student/youth travel specialists, with branches also in YHA shops and on university campuses all over Britain.

Council Travel, 28a Poland St, London W1 (☎0171/437 7767). Flights and student discounts.

South Coast Student Travel, 61 Ditchling Rd, Brighton, East Sussex BN1 4SD (☎01273/570226). Student experts but plenty to offer non-students as well, and good associate agent in Bangkok.

STA Travel, 74 Old Brompton Rd, London W7 (☎0171/581 4132); and branches in Bristol, Cambridge, Manchester. Personal callers at 117 Euston Rd, London NW1; 28 Vicar Lane, Leeds LS1 7JH; 36 George St, Oxford OX1 2OJ; and offices at the universities of Birmingham, London, Kent and

Loughborough. Discount fares, with particularly good deals for students and young people.

Trailfinders, 42–48 Earls Court Rd, London W8 (☎0171/938 3366) and194 Kensington High St, London W8 (☎0171/938 3939); and branches in Birmingham, Bristol, Glasgow and Manchester. One of the best-informed and most efficient agents, dealing with Southeast Asia among other destinations; good for RTW tickets, too.

Travel Bug, 597 Cheetham Hill Rd, Manchester M8 5EJ (☎0161/721 4000). Large range of discounted tickets.

Travel Cuts, 295a Regent St, London W1 (☎0171/255 2082). Large range of discounted tickets.

Union Travel, 93 Piccadilly, London W1 (☎0171/493 4343). Competitive airfares and agents for *Tarom*.

UniqueTravel, Dudley House, Second floor, 169 Piccadilly, London W1 (☎0171/495 4848). The main *Aeroflot* outlet.

IRELAND

Joe Walsh Tours, 8–11 Baggot St, Dublin 2 (☎01/676 3053). Discounted flight agent.

USIT, Aston Quay, O'Connell Bridge, Dublin 2 (☎01/677 8117) & 13b College St, Belfast BT1 6ET (☎0232/324073). Ireland's main outlet for discounted, youth and student fares.

times dropping to as low as £345 in low season. Some agents offer special discounts (down to £367 return) with more reputable airlines for full-time students and/or under-26s. Typical one-year open round-the-world tickets bought in London and taking in two stops in Asia, one in Australia, two in the Pacific, and one in the US, start at about £725.

Before making a final decision on who to book with, it's always worth checking out the travel sections in the Sunday papers, ITV's *Teletext* and, in London, the ads in *Time Out* and the *Evening Standard*, and free travel magazines like *TNT*. Many of the companies advertising in these publications are **bucket shops** who are able to offer extremely inexpensive deals, but there's a risk attached to companies who don't belong to official travel associations such as ABTA or IATA – if your bucket shop goes bust you'll get no refund, even on a fully paid-up ticket. With associated agents, such as those listed below, ABTA and IATA will cover any debts in the case of bankruptcy.

Bear in mind that however much your ticket costs, you'll always have to pay a B200 airport **departure tax** when leaving Thailand on an international flight (B20 on domestic flights), payable when you check in.

PACKAGE COMPANIES

Bales Tours, Bales House, Junction Rd, Dorking, Surrey RH4 3HB (☎01306/885991). High-quality escorted tours, including nine-day northern Thailand tour from £935 with flights and some meals.

British Airways Holidays, Pacific House, Hazelwick Ave, Crawley, West Sussex RH10 1NP (☎01293/611611). Beaches and cities (7 days from £717 including flights). Bookings direct or through most travel agents.

Exodus Expeditions, 9 Weir Rd, London SW12 (☎0181/675 5550). Sixteen-day Golden Triangle (£970 including flights, £595 including) and fifteen-day Classic Thailand (£1040 including flights, £595 excluding) adventure tours which cover Bangkok, Ayutthaya, Sukhothai, Chiang Mai and Ko Samet. Bookings direct or through major travel agents.

Explore Worldwide, 1 Frederick St, Aldershot, Hants, GU11 1LQ (☎01252/319448). One of the best adventure-tour operators. First-class tours, including hill-tribe trekking, island-hopping and sailing down the Mekhong, using a variety of transport and accommodation from £890 for fifteen days.

Far East Travel Centre, 33 Maddox St, London W1 (☎0171/414 8844). Beaches and cities (12 nights in 2 centres from £830 including flights and accommodation) plus optional tours.

Hayes & Jarvis, Hayes House, 152 Kings St, London W6 (☎0181/748 5050). Tours and hotel-based holidays from around £600 inclusive for two weeks.

Imaginative Traveller, 14 Barley Mow Passage, London W4 (☎0181/742 8612). Small-group adventure tours off the beaten track, including hill-tribe trekking. From £355 for nine days, excluding flights.

Kuoni Worldwide, Kuoni House, Dorking, Surrey RH5 4AZ (☎01306/740500). Specializing in two-centre holidays, including flights and accommodation: twelve nights in Bangkok and Phuket from £728, nine nights in Bangkok and northern Thailand £746. Bookings through most travel agents.

Magic Of The Orient, 2 Kingsland Court, Three Bridges Rd, Crawley, West Sussex RH10 1HL (☎01293/537700). A wide range of tailor-made packages, from all-in two-centre holidays (12 nights in Bangkok and Chiang Mai from £814) to four-wheel-drive safaris and kayaking in Phuket.

Thai Adventures, PO Box 82, Victoria St, Alderney, Channel Islands GY9 3DG (☎0481/823417). Small operator with a tailor-made approach focusing on hotel-based holidays.

Thomas Cook Holidays, PO Box 36, Thorpe Wood, Peterborough PE3 6SB (☎01733/332255). Range of flight and board deals from about £600 inclusive for five nights, plus some tours.

Travel Bag, 12 High St, Alton, Hants GU34 1BN (☎0420/80828). Thailand specialists selling tailor-made trips at varying prices direct to travellers only, not through agents.

Twickers World, *Ocean Leisure Dive Shop*, Embankment Place, London WC2 (☎0171/839 1990). Diving-tour organizers, specializing in the Similan islands – five days living aboard for £450.

World Expeditions, 7 North Rd, Maidenhead, Berks SL6 1PL (☎01628/74174). Adventure tours, such as jungle trekking and elephant safaris, as well as cultural tours. From £473 for eight days, excluding flights.

PACKAGES

Package deals come in two varieties: those offering a return flight and a week or more's accommodation, and specialist tours which organize daytime activities and escorted excursions – sometimes in addition to flights, sometimes instead of. **Flight and accommodation deals** can work out good value if you're planning to base yourself in just one or two places, starting as low as £600 for two weeks in a moderately priced hotel in Bangkok or Pattaya (see box on previous page for the main operators). **Specialist tour** packages on the other hand work out pretty expensive compared to what you'd pay if you organized everything independently (from about £1000 including flight for a 16-day trip), but they do cut out a lot of hassle and the most adventurous ones in particular often feature activities that it wouldn't be easy to set up by yourself – such as rafting or canoeing. Before booking, make sure you know exactly what's included in the price.

GETTING THERE FROM NORTH AMERICA

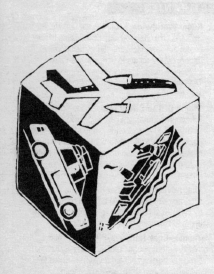

There are no non-stop flights from North America to Thailand, but *United Airlines* and *Japan Airlines* both run daily flights to Bangkok from major North American east- and west-coast cities, with one change in either Taipei, Tokyo or Seoul. Flying time is twenty two hours from New York, twenty hours from Chicago and sixteen hours from Seattle. West-coast travellers can also go with *Thai International*, which does daily Bangkok flights departing from Los Angeles, and thrice-weekly flights from Seattle, both via Tokyo or Seoul. East-coast travellers have the alternative option of flying with *Swissair* (change in Zurich; 17hr) or *Finnair* (change in Helsinki; 18hr).

Most major airlines offer "Circle Pacific" deals, which allow four **stopovers** at no extra charge if tickets are bought fourteen to thirty days in advance. If Thailand is only one stop on a longer journey, you might want to consider buying a **round-the-world ticket** . Some travel agents can sell you an "off-the-shelf" RTW ticket that will have you touching down in about half a dozen cities (Bangkok is on many itineraries); others will have to assemble one for you, which can be more tailored to your needs but is apt to be more expensive. Figure on $3000–5000 for a RTW ticket including Thailand (and also Australia/New Zealand and Africa).

FARES

Fares depend on where you're flying from and when: it's cheaper from the west coast, and weekends and peak periods (generally the Christmas and New Year season and from June through Aug) are more expensive. Prices quoted here are for round-trip tickets bought **direct from the airlines** (midweek low season–weekend high season) and don't include tax, an additional fee of about $20: **Chicago** $1423–1530; **Los Angeles** $1000–2300; **Montréal** CAN$1695–2085; **New York** $1423–1630; **San Francisco** $1124–2300; **Seattle** $1124–1252; **Toronto** CAN$1695–2055. The only reason to pay these prices, however, is if you need to travel at very short notice, or want to stay in the country for less than six days or over six months. For most tourists, the best option is to go for the much **lower** fares offered by a **specialist flight agent or consolidator** (see p.8).

SHOPPING FOR TICKETS

Whatever the airlines have on offer, any number of specialist agents set out to beat it. These are the outfits you'll see advertising in the Sunday newspaper travel sections. **Consolidators** buy up blocks of tickets from the airlines to sell at a discount. They don't normally impose advance-purchase tickets (although in busy periods you'll want to book ahead to be sure of getting a seat), but they do often charge very stiff fees for date changes; note also that airlines generally won't alter tickets after they've gone to a consolidator, so you can only make changes through the consolidator itself. Remember, as these companies' profit margins are pretty tiny, they make their money by dealing in bulk – don't expect them to entertain lots of questions. **Discount agents** also wheel and deals in blocks of tickets offloaded by the airlines, and often offer special student and youth fares and a range of other travel-related services such as travel insurance, rail passes, car rentals, tours and the like. They tend to be most worthwhile for students and under-26s (this group may be able to make even larger savings through *STA Travel,* listed in the box overleaf).

Some agents specialize in **charter flights**, which may be cheaper than anything available on a scheduled flight, but again departure dates are fixed and withdrawal penalties are high (examine the refund policy and check companies' reputations with a travel agent before paying up). If you travel a lot, **discount travel clubs** are another option – the annual membership fee may be worth it for benefits such as cut-price air tickets and car rental.

AIRLINES

Aeroflot (☎1-800/995-5555; in Canada, ☎514/288-2125). Flights from New York into Bangkok via Moscow five times a week, though flight regularity varies depending on the season.

Air Canada (in Canada, call directory enquiries, ☎1-800/555-1212, for local toll-free number; US ☎1-800/776-3000). Flies into Japan and Korea but can make arrangements for tourists to go to Thailand via other carriers. Departure points include Vancouver, Toronto and Montréal.

Air France (☎1-800/237-2747; in Canada, ☎1-800/667-2747). Flights to Bangkok via Paris.

Air New Zealand (☎1-800/262-1234; in Canada, ☎1-800/563-5494). Flights to Bangkok via Auckland only.

American Airlines (☎1-800/433-7300). Only flies to Tokyo, but with connections on another airline into Thailand.

Canadian Airlines (☎403/235-1161). Six flights a week from Vancouver via Hong Kong.

Cathay Pacific (☎1-800/233-2742; in Canada, call directory enquiries, ☎1-800/555-1212, for local toll-free number). Flights from Los Angeles to Hong Kong, then Hong Kong to Thailand.

China Air Lines (☎1-800/227-5118). Three flights a week from New York, Los Angeles and San Francisco to Tapei, with continuing service to Bangkok.

Finnair (☎1-800/950-5000; in Canada ☎416/927-7400). Twice-weekly flights from New York via Helsinki. Summertime connections only between Toronto and Helsinki, also twice a week.

Garuda Air (☎1-800/342-7832; in Canada, ☎1-800/663-2254). Flights into Bangkok from Jakarta.

Japan Air Lines (☎1-800/525-3663; in Canada ☎604/688-6611). Daily one-stop flights via Tokyo from Chicago, Los Angeles, New York and San Francisco. Three flights a week from Seattle and Toronto.

Malaysia Airlines (☎1-800/421-8641). Every day except Wed and Fri from Los Angeles to Kuala Lumpur, with continuing service to Bangkok.

Mandarin Air (☎604/682-6777). Three flights a week from Vancouver to Taipei, with continuing service to Bangkok.

Singapore Airlines (☎1-800/742-3333). Daily flights from New York, Los Angeles, San Francisco and Vancouver to Bangkok via Singapore.

Swissair (☎1-800/221-4750; in Canada ☎1-800/267-9477). Six weekly connections from Montréal, New York and Toronto via Zurich.

Thai International (☎1-800/426-5204; in Canada ☎1-800/668-8103). Daily flights from Los Angeles via either Tokyo or Seoul and three a week from Seattle via Taipei.

United Airlines (☎1-800/538-2929). Daily one-stop flights from Chicago, Los Angeles, New York, San Francisco, Seattle and Toronto via either Taipei or Tokyo; all flights routed via San Francisco.

DISCOUNT AGENTS AND CONSOLIDATORS

Air Brokers International, 323 Geary St, Suite 411, San Francisco, CA 94102 (☎1-800/883-3273). Consolidator.

Air Courier Association,191 University Blvd, Suite 300, Denver, CO 80206 (☎303/278-8810). Courier flight broker.

Council Travel, Head office: 205 E 42nd St, New York, NY 10017 (☎212/661-1450 or 1-800/743-1823). Student travel organization with branches in many US cities.

Educational Travel Center, 438 N Frances St, Madison, WI 53703 (☎1-800/747-5551). Student/youth discount agent.

Encore Travel Club, 4501 Forbes Blvd, Lanham, MD 20706 (☎1-800/444-9800). Discount travel club.

Hotline Travel, 3001 E Pershing Ave, Cheynne, WY 82001 (☎1-800/221-8139).

Interworld Travel, 800 Douglass Rd, Miami, FL 33134 (☎305/443-4929). Consolidator.

Last Minute Travel Club, 132 Brookline Ave, Boston, MA 02215 (☎1-800/LAST MIN). Travel club specializing in standby deals.

Moment's Notice, 425 Madison Ave, New York, NY 10017 (☎212/486-0503). Discount travel club.

New Frontiers/Nouvelles Frontières, Head offices: 12 E 33rd St, New York, NY 10016 (☎212/779-0600 or 1-800/366-6387); 1001 Sherbrook E, Suite 720, Montréal, H2L 1L3 (☎514/526-8444). French discount travel firm. Other branches in LA, San Francisco and Québec City.

Now Voyager, 74 Varick St, Suite 307, New York, NY 10013 (☎212/431-1616). Courier flight broker.

STA Travel, Head office: 48 E 11th St, New York, NY 10003 (☎212/477-7166 or 1-800/777-0112 nationwide). Worldwide specialist in independent travel with branches in the Los Angeles, San Francisco and Boston areas.

TFI Tours International, Head office: 34 W 32nd St, New York, NY 10001 (☎1-800/745-8000). Consolidator; other offices in Las Vegas, San Francisco, Los Angeles.

Travac, Head office: 989 Sixth Ave, New York NY 10018 (☎1-800/872-8800). Consolidator and charter broker; has another branch in Orlando.

Travel Avenue, 10 S Riverside, Suite 1404, Chicago, IL 60606 (☎1-800/333-3335). Discount travel agent.

Travel Cuts, Head office: 187 College St, Toronto, ON M5T 1P7 (☎416/979-2406). Canadian student travel organization with branches all over the country.

Travelers Advantage, 3033 S Parker Rd, Suite 900, Aurora, CO 80014 (☎1-800/548-1116). Discount travel club.

UniTravel,1177 N Warson Rd, St Louis, MO 63132 (☎1-800/325-2222). Consolidator.

Worldtek Travel, 111 Water St, New Haven, CT 06511 (☎1-800/243-1723). Discount travel agency.

Worldwide Discount Travel Club, 1674 Meridian Ave, Miami Beach, FL 33139 (☎305/534-2082). Discount travel club.

Finally, remember that all discount and charter flights require a minimum six days' and maximum six months' stay in Thailand.

PACKAGES

Relatively few operators in the US and Canada offer tours that concentrate solely on Thailand – many more feature a few places in Thailand (usually Bangkok, Chiang Mai and Phuket) as part of a two- or three-week round-Asia or round-Southeast Asia trip. Before booking, confirm exactly what expenses are included, what class of hotel you're being offered and how large a group you'll be joining.

PACKAGE TOUR OPERATORS

Abercrombie & Kent, 1520 Kensington Rd, Oak Brook, IL 60521 (☎1-800/323-7308). Top-notch seven-day tours of major Thai cities ($1500 excluding flights), plus several two- to three-week round-Asia jaunts which include a few stops in Thailand (about $4450).

Absolute Asia, 180 Varick St, New York, NY 10014 (☎212/627-1950 or 1-800/736-8187).

Adventure Center, 1311 63rd St, Suite 200, Emeryville, CA 94608 (☎1-800/227-8747).

Backroads, 1516 5th St, Suite L101, Berkeley, CA 94710 (☎1-800/462-2848).

Boulder Adventures, PO Box 1279, Boulder, CO 80306 (☎303/443-6789 or 1-800/642-2472).

Creative Adventure Club, PO Box 1918, Costa Mesa, CA 92628 (☎1-800/544-5088).

Cultural Tours, 9920 La Cienega Blvd, Suite 715, Inglewood, CA 90301 (☎310/216-1332 or 1-800/282-8898). fifteen-day inclusive packages taking in major Thai cities, ancient sites and beaches from $2666.

EastQuest, 1 Union Square W, Suite 606, New York, NY 10003 (☎212/741-1688 or 1-800/638 3449).

Exotik Tours, 1117 St Catherine W, Suite 806, Montréal, Québec H3B 1H9 (☎514/284-3324).

Globus & Cosmos, 5301 S Federal Circle, Littleton, CO 80123 (☎1-800/221-0090). Round-Asia tours, taking in Thailand, from $1508 for eleven days.

Goway Travel, 3284 Yonge St, Toronto, Ontario M4N 3M7 (☎416/322-1034).

InnerAsia, 2627 Lombard St, San Francisco, CA 94123 (☎1-800/777-8183).

Journeyworld International, 119 W 57th St, Penthouse N, New York, NY 10019 (☎1-800/635-3900).

Maupintour, 1515 St Andrew's Drive, Lawrence, KS 66044-0807 (☎913/843-1211 or 1-800/255-4266). Round-Asia tours from $4654 for two weeks.

Mindful Journeys, 1242 24th St, Santa Monica, CA 90404 (☎1-800/654-7975).

Mountain Travel-Sobek, 6420 Fairmount Ave, El Cerrito, CA 94530 (☎1-800/227-2384). Range of active adventure tours such as sixteen-day hill-tribe treks through the north of Thailand (from $2290) and nine days' mountain biking, also in the north (from $1090).

Nature Expeditions International, 474 Wilamette St, Eugene, OR 97440 (☎1-800/869-0639).

Pacific Bestour, 228 River Vale Rd, River Vale, NJ 07675 (☎1-800/688-3288).

Pacific Delight Tours, 132 Madison Ave, New York, NY 10016 (☎1-800/221-7179).

Questers Worldwide Nature Tours, 257 Park Ave S, New York, NY 10010 (☎1-800/468-8668).

Royal Orchid Holidays (☎800/426 5204). Subsidiary of *Thai International* airlines with seven- to fifteen-day tours of Thai cities and beaches from $1215.

Tourcan Vacations, 255 Duncan Mill Rd, Suite 507, Toronto, Ontario M3B 3H9 (☎416/391-0334).

Tour East, 1033 Bay St, Suite 302, Toronto, Ontario M5S 3A5 (☎416/929-0888).

Vacationland, 150 Post St, Suite 680, San Francisco, CA 94108 (☎1-800/245-0050).

Vantage Travel, 111 Cypress St, Brookline, MA 02146 (☎1-800/322-6677). Tours of Asia, including Thailand, for the more mature (55-plus) traveller.

Worldwide Adventures, 36 Finch Ave W, North York, Ontario M2N 2G9 (☎1-800/387-1483).

GETTING THERE FROM AUSTRALASIA

From eastern Australia, you can reach Bangkok directly with *Thai International* or *British Airways* (AUS$985 low season/AUS$1175 high season) or *Qantas* (AUS$1015/1205). For stopovers on the way, there's *Royal Brunei* (via Bandar Seri Begawan; AUS$996/1106), *Air New Zealand* (Auckland; AUS$1151/1366 – although there are direct ANZ flights from Brisbane only) or *Garuda* (Denpasar or Jakarta; AUS$1258/1458). Where available, flights are around ten percent less from Perth.

From New Zealand, *Thai International* offers the best overall rates (NZ$1220/1410), though *British Airways'* low-season fare is slightly cheaper (NZ$1216/1559). Alternatively you can fly there with *Garuda* via Denpasar or Jakarta for NZ$1369/1595, or *Air New Zealand* at a pricey NZ$1510/1773.

Round-the-world fares from Australasia start from around AUS$2000/NZ$2500. Student discounts for ISIC-card-holders, and sometimes the under-26s, are hard to predict as they are contracted between individual travel agents and airlines for specific routes. Where offered, you should get around nine percent off the fares above.

OVERLAND ROUTES FROM ASIA

Australia's proximity to **Indonesia** makes this country the obvious starting point for overlanding through Asia, and the cheapest fares are from Darwin to Kupang in Timor with either *Garuda* or *Merpati Airlines* (AUS$198 single/AUS$330 return). From Kupang, it takes at least a month to island-hop west by ferry and bus to Bali's international airport at Denpasar; if you can live without comforts and have a very flexible timetable, it's an exciting journey, though East Timor is currently prone to violence as the Indonesian militia suppresses protests against Jakarta's annexation of the country. Once in Denpasar there are direct flights to Bangkok, although you could trek onwards to pick up a flight from Jakarta. Indonesian sixty-day visas are available on arrival at Kupand, Denpasar and Jakarta.

Alternatively, like nearly all travellers entering Thailand overland, you can fly from Indonesia to **Singapore** or **Malaysia** and make your own way from there. Most Western tourists can pass through both these countries without having bought a visa beforehand, but remember that to get into Thailand you need either an onward ticket or a sixty-day visa with you when you arrive at the Thai border (see p.12).

From Australasia, the best deals on direct flights to Singapore or Malaysia are with *Malaysian Airlines* to Kuala Lumpur (Perth AUS$950/1045, eastern Australia AUS$1015/1116, Auckland NZ$1249/1450); *Royal Brunei Airlines* to either Singapore or Kuala Lumpur (east coast AUS$840/915, Perth $700/763, Darwin $790/861); and *Singapore Airlines* (east coast AUS$910/1000, Perth AUS$830/905, Auckland NZ$1199/1400).

A daily **train** covers the 1943km from **Singapore to Bangkok** in 34 hours at a cost of about £25/$38 second class, with a change at Kuala Lumpur and again at Butterworth or Hat Yai, and stops all the way up the line through Thailand. Considerably more expensive but ultimately luxurious is the *Eastern and Oriental Express* (a Southeast Asian version of the *Orient Express*) which shuttles between Singapore and Bangkok via Kuala Lumpur roughly once a week. The full journey takes 41 hours and costs from £760/$1150 per person, inclusive of cabin, restaurant and bar tabs, although you can join or leave the train at Kuala Lumpur and Butterworth in Malaysia. Contact *Venice Simplon-Orient-Express Ltd*, Sea Containers House, 20 Upper Ground, London SE1 (☎0171/928 6000).

AIRLINES AND AGENTS

AIRLINES

Air New Zealand, 5 Elizabeth St, Sydney (☎02/223 4666); Corner Customs and Queen streets, Auckland (☎09/366 2424).

British Airways, 64 Castlereagh St, Sydney (☎02/258 3300); Dilworth Building, corner of Customs and Queen streets, Auckland (☎09/367 7500).

Garuda, 175 Clarence St, Sydney (☎02/334 9900); 120 Albert St, Auckland (☎09/366 1855).

Malaysia Airlines (MAS), 388 George St, Sydney (☎02/231 5066 or 1-800/269 998); Floor 12, Swanson Centre, 12–26 Swanson St, Auckland (☎09/373 2741).

Merpati Airlines, 15 W Lane Arcade, Darwin (☎089/41 1030).

Qantas, International Square, Jamison St, Sydney (☎02/957 0111 or 236 3636); Qantas House, 154 Queen St, Auckland (☎09/303 2506).

Royal Brunei, Level 52, MLC Centre, 19 Martin Place, Sydney (☎02/223 1566); no New Zealand office.

Singapore Airlines, 17 Bridge St, Sydney (☎02/236 0111); Lower Ground Floor, West Plaza Building, corner Customs and Albert streets, Auckland (☎09/379 3209).

Thai International, 75–77 Pitt St, Sydney (☎02/844 0999 or 1-800 221 320); Kensington Swan Building, 22 Fanshawe St, Auckland (☎09/377 3886).

SPECIALIST AND DISCOUNT AGENTS

Accent on Travel, 545 Queen St, Brisbane (☎07/832 1777).

Adventure World, 73 Walker St, N Sydney (☎1-800/221 931); 8 Victoria Ave, Perth (☎09/221 2300).

Alma Travel Centre, Ground Floor, 150 Queen St, Melbourne (☎03/670 2288). Trekking specialists.

Anywhere Travel, 345 Anzac Parade, Kingsford, Sydney (☎02/663 0411).

Asia and World Travel, corner of George St and Adelaide St, Brisbane (☎07/229 3511).

Asian Explorer Holidays, 197 Wickham Terrace, Brisbane (☎07/832 4222).

Asian Travel Centre, 126 Russel St, Melbourne (☎03/654 8277).

Asia Specialist Travel, 40 St George Terrace, Perth (☎09/325 5411).

Asia Town and Country Travel, 21 Burwood Highway, Burwood (☎03/808 3233).

Brisbane Discount Travel, 360 Queen St, Brisbane (☎07/229 9211).

Budget Travel, PO Box 505, Auckland (☎09/309 4313).

Discount Travel Specialists, Shop 53, Forrest Chase, Perth (☎09/221 1400).

Far East Travel Centre, 50 Margaret St, Sydney (☎02/262 6414).

Flight Centres, *Australia*: Circular Quay, Sydney (☎02/241 2422); Bourke St, Melbourne (☎03/650 2899); plus other branches nationwide. *New Zealand*: National Bank Towers, 205–225 Queen St, Auckland (☎09/309 6171); Shop 1M, National Mutual Arcade, 152 Hereford St, Christchurch (☎09/379 7145); 50–52 Willis St, Wellington (☎04/472 8101); other branches countrywide.

Harvey World Travel, 7 Frederick St, Oatley, NSW (☎02/570 5677); branches across Australia.

JW Asean Travel, Suite 206, 2 Pembroke St, Epping (☎02/868 5199).

Northern Gateway, 22 Cavenagh St, Darwin (☎089/41 1394).

Passport Travel, 320b Glenferrie Rd, Malvern, Melbourne (☎03/824 7183).

STA Travel, *Australia*: 732 Harris St, Ultimo, Sydney (☎02/212 1255 or 281 9866); 256 Flinders St, Melbourne (☎03/347 4711); other offices in Townsville, Cairns and state capitals. *New Zealand*: Traveller's Centre, 10 High St, Auckland (☎09/309 9995); 233 Cuba St, Wellington (☎04/385 0561); 223 High St, Christchurch (☎03/379 9098); other offices in Dunedin, Palmerston North and Hamilton.

Thai Binh Travel, 202 Railway Parade, Cabramatta, Sydney (☎02/724 2304).

Thailand Travel, 169 Unley Rd, Unley, Adelaide (☎08/272 2010); 40 St George Terrace, Perth (☎09/325 5411).

Thailand Travel Centre, 81 York St, Sydney (☎02/299 1111); Embankment Arcade, Melbourne (☎03/629 4961); Cinema City Arcade, corner of Barrack and Murray streets, Perth (☎09/325 1288).

Thai Travel, 141 Queen St Mall, Brisbane (☎07/221 4599).

Topdeck Travel, 45 Grenfell St, Adelaide (☎08/410 1110).

Trailfinders, Hides Corner, Shield St, Cairns (☎07/041 1199).

Tymtro Travel, Suite G12, Wallaceway Shopping Centre, Chatswood, Sydney (☎02/413 1219).

A wide choice of private **buses** also enter Thailand every day from Singapore and Malaysia, the most popular of which are from Singapore (18hr; £8/$12), Kuala Lumpur (12hr; £6/$9) and Penang (6hr; £5/$8) to Hat Yai, the transport hub of southern Thailand. It's also possible to cross the Malaysian/ Thai border by taking a **boat** from Kuala Perlis or Langkawi Island to Satun and then a bus on to destinations further north (see p.499 for more on this). A full list of frontier posts can be found on p.485, and transport arrangements at each are detailed in the course of Chapter 8, *The Deep South.*

RED TAPE AND VISAS

There are three basic visa categories for entering Thailand. For stays of up to thirty days, most foreign passport holders automatically get a free non-extendable transit visa when passing through immigration at Don Muang Airport or at the Malaysian border, but must show proof of onward travel arrangements: unless you have a confirmed bus, train or air ticket out of Thailand, you may well be put back on the next plane or sent back to get a sixty-day tourist visa from the Thai Embassy in Kuala Lumpur.

Thirty-day transit visas cannot be extended under any but the most exceptional circumstances. If you think you may want to stay longer, then from the outset you should apply for a **sixty-day tourist visa** from a Thai embassy or consulate (see below), accompanying your application with your passport and two photos. In the **UK** visa applications take two working days to process (10 if applied for by post), and the sixty-day visa costs £8. In the **US** it costs $15 and takes about 24 hours to process if you go to the embassy or consulate in person, or about five days by post. In **Canada** it costs CAN$16.50 and takes three working days for personal applications, a week or more by post. In **Australia** it costs AUS$18 and takes five days to process postal applications, and you should allow extra days for postage; personal applications are sometimes handled in three to five days. Because of a reciprocal arrangement

---

THAI EMBASSIES AND CONSULATES ABROAD

Australia 111 Empire Circuit, Yarralumla, Canberra, ACT 2600 (☎06/273 1149); plus consulates in Adelaide, Brisbane, Melbourne, Perth and Sydney.

Canada 180 Island Park Drive, Ottawa, Ontario K1Y OA2 (☎613/722 4444); plus consulates in Montréal, Calgary and Toronto.

Ireland Sedgwich Dineen, 18–19 Harcourt St, Dublin 2 (☎01/781599).

Malaysia 206 Jalan Ampang, 50450 Kuala Lumpur (☎03/248 8222); plus consulates at 4426 Jalan Pengkalan Chepha, Kota Baru, Kelantan 15400 (☎099/782545) and 1 Jalan Tunku Abdul Rahman, Penang 10350 (☎04/372533).

Netherlands 1 Buitenrustweg, 2517 KD The Hague (☎070/345 2088).

New Zealand 2 Cook St, PO Box 17–226, Karori, Wellington (☎04/476 8619).

UK 29 Queens Gate, London SW7 (☎01891/600150 or 0171/589 0173); plus consulates in Birmingham, Cardiff, Glasgow, Hull and Liverpool.

US 1024 Wisconsin Ave, NW Washington, DC 20007 (☎202/944-3600 or 3608); plus consulates in New York and Los Angeles.

with Thai immigration, **New Zealanders** with a valid onward ticket get a free ninety-day visa; this is not extendable, but border-hopping enables the holder to procure another.

If entering on a sixty-day visa, you don't need to show proof of onward travel but, as in all countries, it's up to the immigration officials at the port of entry as to what expiry date they stamp on your visa, so it's always advisable to dress respectably (see p.47) when crossing borders.

Thai embassies will also accept applications for the slightly more expensive **ninety-day non-immigrant visas** as long as you produce a letter of recommendation from an official Thai source (an employer or school principal for example) that explains why you need to be in the country for three months.

As it's quite a hassle to organize a ninety-day visa from outside the country (and generally not feasible for most tourists), you're better off applying for a thirty-day **extension** to your sixty-day visa once inside Thai borders. All sixty-day tourist visas can be extended in Thailand for a further thirty days, at the discretion of officials; extensions cost B500 and are issued

over the counter at immigration offices (*kaan khao muang*) in every provincial capital – most offices ask for one or two extra photos as well, plus two photocopies of the first four pages and latest Thai visa page of your passport. If you use up the three-month quota, the quickest and cheapest way of extending your stay for a further sixty days is to head down to Malaysia and apply for another tourist visa at the embassy in Kuala Lumpur.

Immigration offices also issue **re-entry permits** (B500) if you want to leave the country and come back again within sixty days. If you **overstay** your visa limits, expect to be fined B100 per extra day when you depart Don Muang Airport, though an overstayed period of a month or more could land you in trouble with immigration officials.

STAYING ON

Unless you have work or study fixed up before you arrive, staying on in Thailand is a precarious affair. Plenty of people do – teaching English, working in resort bars and guest houses, or even unofficially buying in to tourist businesses (farangs are legally barred from

CUSTOMS REGULATIONS

To export antiques or religious artefacts – especially Buddha images – from Thailand, you need to have a licence granted by the Fine Arts Department, which you can obtain through Bangkok's National Museum on Na Phra That Road (☎02/224 1370). Applications take at least a week and need to be accompanied by two postcard-sized photos of the object, taken face on, and photocopies of the applicant's passport. Some antique shops will organize this for you.

Americans can bring home up to $400 worth of goods purchased overseas duty-free, including a litre of alcohol or wine, two hundred cigarettes and one hundred cigars. If you carry back between $400 and $1000 worth of stuff you'll have to go through the red lane and pay ten percent of the value in duty; above $1000 and the duty depends on the items.

Canadians are exempt from paying duty on up to CAN$300 worth of goods after spending seven days out of the country (or CAN$100 worth after a trip lasting 2 to 6 days). Those goods may include up to 40fl oz of spirits or wine, 24 twelve-ounce bottles of beer and two hundred cigarettes.

British citizens can bring home up to £136 worth of goods purchased outside the EU without having to pay duty, in addition to two hundred cigarettes (or 100 cigarillos or 50 cigars or 250g of tobacco) and two litres of table wine, plus one litre of alcohol over 22 percent by volume or two litres of fortified wine. Also permitted are 60ml of perfume and 250ml of toilet water.

Irish citizens can return home with IR£34 worth of goods purchased outside the EU without paying duty, plus two hundred cigarettes (or 100 cigarillos or 50 cigars or 250g of tobacco), one litre of liquor, two litres of wine, 50ml of perfume and 250ml of toilet water.

Australians can bring back AUS$200 worth of "gifts" duty free (excluding personal purchases, such as clothing, which don't incur duty) if under eighteen years of age; over-eighteens are allowed $400 worth of the same, plus two hundred cigarettes and one litre of alcohol.

New Zealanders can bring home NZ$700 worth of gifts, plus 4.5 litres of wine or beer, 1125ml of spirits, two hundred cigarettes or 250g of tobacco or fifty cigars (or a mixture of these not exceeding 250g).

owning businesses in Thailand) – but it involves frequent and expensive visa runs to Penang or Kota Baru in Malaysia, or Vientiane in Laos, and often entails hassle from the local police. All non-residents who acquire income while in Thailand should get a tax clearance certificate from the Revenue Department on Chakrapong Road in Bangkok (☎02/282 9340). Theoretically, anyone who's stayed in Thailand for over ninety days within one calendar year also needs one of these certificates. Check with TAT (see below) or the Revenue Department on your specific case, but don't be surprised if they say you don't need one.

INFORMATION AND MAPS

The efficient **Tourism Authority of Thailand (TAT)** maintains offices in several cities abroad, where you can pick up a few glossy brochures and get fairly detailed answers to specific pre-travel questions. More comprehensive local information is furnished at TAT headquarters in Bangkok and its nineteen regional branches, all open daily 8.30am to 4.30pm, which provide an array of information on everything from tennis courts and swimming pools in Bangkok to Thai rules of the road. Among their most useful stuff are the lists of TAT- and government-approved travel agents, shops and restaurants – if pressed, staff will also give you names of those places de-listed because of malpractice. In addition, all TAT offices should have up-to-date information on local festival dates and regional transport schedules, but none of them offers accommodation booking services.

Independent **tour operators** and information desks crop up in tourist spots all over the country and will usually help with questions about the immediate locality, but be on the look-out for self-interested advice, given by staff desperate for commission. As with TAT offices, independent operators won't book accommodation – unless of course they happen to have business links with specific guest-houses or hotels. For off-beat, enthusiastic first-hand advice, you can't do better than guest house **bulletin boards** – the best of these boast a whole range of travellers' tips, from anecdotal accounts of cross-country bike trips to recommendations as to where to get the perfect suit made.

TAT OFFICES ABROAD

Australia Floor 7, 56 Pitt St, Sydney (☎02/247 7549); 2 Hardy Rd, South Perth (☎09/474 3646).

Canada 250 St Claire Ave W, Suite 3306, Toronto, Ontario M4V 1R6 (☎416/925-9329).

New Zealand Floor 2, 87 Queen St, Auckland (☎09/379 8398).

UK 49 Albemarle St, London W1 (☎0171/499 7679) – also responsible for **Ireland**.

USA 303 E Wacker Drive, Suite 400, Chicago, IL 60601 (☎312/819-3990); 3440 Wilshire Blvd, Suite 1100, Los Angeles, CA 90010 (☎213/382 2353); 5 World Trade Center, Suite 3443, New York, NY 10048 (☎212/432-0433).

MAPS

One thing neither TAT nor tour operators provide is a decent **map**. For most major destinations, the maps in this book should be all you need, though you may want to supplement them with larger-scale versions of Bangkok and the whole country. Bangkok bookshops are the best scource of maps,

MAP OUTLETS

UK

London

Daunt Books, 83 Marylebone High St, W1 (☎0171/224 2295).

National Map Centre, 22–24 Caxton St, SW1 (☎0171/222 4945).

Stanfords, 12–14 Long Acre, WC2 (☎0171/836 1321).

The Travel Bookshop, 13–15 Blenheim Crescent, W11 (☎0171/229 5260).

The Travellers Bookshop, 25 Cecil Court, WC2 (☎0171/836 9132).

Edinburgh

Thomas Nelson and Sons Ltd, 51 York Place, EH1 (☎0131/557 3011).

Glasgow

John Smith and Sons, 57–61 St Vincent St, G2 5TD (☎0141/221 7472).

Maps by **mail or phone order** are available from *Stanfords* (☎0171/836 1321).

NORTH AMERICA

Chicago

Rand McNally, 444 N Michigan Ave, IL 60611 (☎312/321-1751).

Montréal

Ulysses Travel Bookshop, 4176 St-Denis (☎514/289-0993).

New York

British Travel Bookshop, 551 Fifth Ave, NY 10176 (☎1-800/448-3039 or 212/490-6688).

The Complete Traveler Bookstore, 199 Madison Ave, NY 10016 (☎212/685-9007).

Rand McNally, 150 E 52nd St, NY 10022 (☎212/758-7488).

Traveler's Bookstore, 22 W 52nd St, NY 10019 (☎212/664-0995)

San Francisco

The Complete Traveler Bookstore, 3207 Fillmore St, CA 92123 (☎415/923-1511).

Rand McNally, 595 Market St, CA 94105 (☎415/777-3131).

Santa Barbara

Pacific Traveler Supply, 529 State St, CA 93101 (☎805/963-4438; phone orders ☎805/965-4402).

Seattle

Elliot Bay Book Company, 101 S Main St, WA 98104 (☎206/624-6600).

Toronto

Open Air Books and Maps, 25 Toronto St, M5R 2C1 (☎416/363-0719).

Washington DC

Rand McNally, 1201 Connecticut Ave NW, DC 20036 (☎202/223-6751).

Vancouver

World Wide Books and Maps, 736A Granville St, V6Z 1G3 (☎604/687-3320).

Note: *Rand McNally* now has more than twenty stores across the US; call ☎1-800/333-0136 (ext 2111) for the address of your nearest store, or for **direct-mail** maps.

AUSTRALIA

Adelaide

The Map Shop, 16a Peel St, SA 5000 (☎08/231 2033).

Brisbane

Hema Maps, 239 George St, QLD 4000 (☎07/221 4330).

Melbourne

Bowyangs, 372 Little Bourke St, VIC 3000 (☎03/670 4383).

Perth

Perth Map Centre, 891 Hay St WA 6000 (☎09/322 5733).

Sydney

Rex Map Centre, 42 Castlereagh St, NSW 2000 (☎02/235 3017).

Travel Bookshop, 20 Bridge St, NSW 2000 (☎02/241 3554).

Note: In **New Zealand**, the national *Wisers* chain should be able to help.

but if you want to buy one before you get there, go for *Bartholomew*'s 1:1,500,000 map of Thailand, the most consistently accurate of those published abroad. The *Nelles* 1:1,500,000 is the other map of the country widely available outside Thailand, but this isn't nearly as reliable (for outlets, see box on previous page). Where appropriate, detailed local maps and their stockists are recommended in the relevant chapters of the *Guide*.

Published by the Roads Association of Thailand in conjunction with Shell, the large-format 1:1,000,000 *Thailand Highway Map* is especially good on **roads**, and is updated annu-

ally; it's available for B120 at most bookstores in Thailand where English-language material is sold. If you can't get hold of that one, go for the set of four 1:1,000,000 regional maps produced by the Highway Department and sold for around B65 at *DK Books* all over the country, and in Bangkok at Hualamphong station and *Central* department stores. The drawback with this series is that much of the detail is written in Thai script. **Trekking maps** are hard to come by except in the most popular national parks, where you can pick up a free handout of the main trails on arrival.

MONEY, BANKS AND COSTS

Thailand's unit of currency is the baht (abbreviated to "B"), which is divided into 100 satang. Notes come in B10 (brown), B20 (green), B50 (blue), B100 (red) and B500 (purple) denominations, inscribed with Arabic as well as Thai numerals, and increasing in size according to value. The coinage is more confusing, because new shapes and sizes circulate alongside older ones. Brass-coloured 25- and 50-satang pieces both come in two sizes but are rarely used, as most prices are rounded off to the nearest baht. Of the three silver one-baht coins, only the medium-sized one fits public call-boxes but all are legal tender; silver five-baht pieces are distinguishable from the one-baht by a copper rim; lastly, ten-baht

coins have a small brass centre encircled by a silver ring.

The baht is a stable currency, tied to the US dollar. At the time of writing, **exchange rates** averaged out at B25 to $1 and B38 to £1, with more favourable rates for travellers' cheques. Daily rates are published in the *Bangkok Post* and the *Nation*, and at all foreign exchange counters and kiosks in Thailand. Thailand has no black market in foreign currency.

Banking hours are Monday to Friday 8.30am–3.30pm, but exchange kiosks in the main tourist centres are always open till at least 5pm, sometimes 10pm, and upmarket hotels will change money 24 hours a day. The **Don Muang airport exchange counter** also operates 24 hours (and exchange kiosks at overseas airports with flights to Thailand usually keep Thai currency), so there's little point arranging to buy baht before you leave home, especially as it takes seven working days to order from most banks outside Thailand.

TRAVELLERS' CHEQUES & CREDIT CARDS

The safest way to carry your money is in **travellers' cheques** (a fee of 1 or 2 percent is usually levied when you buy them). Sterling and dollar cheques are accepted by banks, exchange booths and upmarket hotels in every sizeable Thai town, and most places also deal in a variety of other currencies. Everyone offers better rates for cheques than for straight cash and they generally charge a total of B13 in commission and duty per cheque – though kiosks and hotels in isolated places may charge extra commission. All issuers give you a list of numbers to call in the case of **lost or stolen cheques** and will refund if you can produce the original receipts and a note of your cheque numbers. Instructions in cases of loss or theft vary from issuer to issuer, but you'll usually have to notify the police first and then call the issuing company collect who will arrange a refund, usually within 24 hours, either by courier or at a local agent.

American Express, *Visa*, *Mastercard* and *Diners Club* **credit cards** and **charge cards** are accepted at top hotels as well as in some posh restaurants, department stores, tourist shops and travel agents, but surcharging of up to five per cent is rife, and theft and forgery are major industries — always demand the carbon copies and destroy them immediately, and never leave cards in baggage storage. If you have a PIN number for your card, you should also be able to **withdraw cash** from hundreds of 24-hour ATMs ("automatic teller machines" or cashpoints) around the country — call the issuing bank or credit company to find out whether your particular card works in Thailand and, if so, which Thai bank's ATMs accept it. There's usually a handling fee of 1.5 percent on every withdrawal, little different from the total amount of fees and commissions payable on travellers' cheques, but it's wise not to rely on plastic alone, which is more tempting to thieves and less easy to replace than the trusty travellers' cheque.

WIRING MONEY

Having **money wired** from home is never convenient or cheap, and should be considered a last resort. Funds can be sent via *Western Union* (in the UK ☎0800/833833; in the US and Canada ☎1-800/325-6000; in Australia (within Sydney only) ☎886 0666, or (outside Sydney) 1-800/230 100; in New Zealand ☎09/ 379 8243 or 04/499 7899) or *American Express MoneyGram* (in the UK ☎0171/839 7541; in the US and Canada ☎1-800/543-4080; in Australia (within Brisbane only) ☎229 8610 or (outside Brisbane) 1-800/649 565; in New Zealand ☎09/302 0143). Both companies' fees depend on the amount being transferred, but as an example, wiring £500 to Thailand will cost around £40/$60. The funds should be available for collection at *Amex* 's agent (*Siam Commercial Bank*, 1060 Phetchaburi Rd, Bangkok; ☎02/256 1220) or *Western Union* 's (*Central*

Department Store, 1027 Ploenchit Rd, Bangkok; ☎02/255 6955) within minutes of being sent. It's also possible to have money wired directly from a bank in your home country to a bank in Thailand, although this is somewhat less reliable because it involves two separate institutions. Your home bank will need the address of the branch bank where you want to pick up the money and the address and telex number of the Bangkok head office, which will act as the clearing house; money wired this way normally takes two working days to arrive, and costs around £20/$30 per transaction.

COSTS

You'll find Thailand an extremely inexpensive place. At the **bottom of the scale**, you could manage on a daily budget of about B300 if you're willing to opt for basic accommodation and eat, drink and travel as the locals do — spending B100 for a room (less if you share), around B100 on three meals, and the rest on travel and incidentals. With extras like air conditioning in rooms and on buses, taking tuk-tuks (see p.27) rather than buses for cross-town journeys, and a meal and a couple of beers in a more touristy restaurant, a day's outlay will rise to a minimum of B700. Staying in expensive hotels and eating in the more exclusive restaurants, you should be able to live in extreme comfort for around B2000 a day.

Travellers soon get so used to the low cost of living in Thailand that they start **bargaining** at every available opportunity, much as Thai people do. Although it's expected practice for a lot of commercial transactions, particularly at markets and when hiring tuk-tuks and taxis, bargaining is a delicate art that requires humour, tact and patience. If your price is way out of line, the vendor's vehement refusal should be enough to make you increase your offer: never forget that the few pennies you're making such a fuss over will go a lot further in a Thai's hands than in your own.

On the other hand, making a tidy sum off foreigners is sometimes official practice: at government-run museums and historical parks, for example, foreigners often pay a B20 admission charge while Thais get in for B5. A number of privately owned tourist attractions follow a similar two-tier system, posting an inflated price in English for foreigners and a lower price in Thai for locals. This is perfectly legitimate, but overcharging tourists on fixed-fare public transport is definitely not acceptable – the best way to avoid getting stung by wily conductors on buses and trains is to watch or ask fellow passengers.

Few museums or transport companies offer student reductions, but in some cases **children**

get discounts; these vary a lot, one of the more bizarre provisos being the State Railway's regulation that a child of three to twelve only qualifies for half fare if under 150cm tall – in some stations you'll see a measuring scale painted onto the ticket-hall wall.

TRAVEL INSURANCE

If you're unlucky enough to require hospital treatment in Thailand, you'll have to foot the bill – this alone is reason enough to make sure you have adequate travel insurance before you leave. Besides covering medical expenses and emergency flights home, a good policy should include insurance against loss and theft of money and personal belongings, and possibly cover for damage to rented motorbikes and cars as well. If trouble occurs, make sure you keep all medical bills, and, if possible, contact the insurance company before making any major outlay (for example, on additional convalescence expenses). If you have anything stolen, get a copy of the police report when you report the incident – otherwise you won't be able to claim. Note that many bank and charge accounts include some form of travel cover, and insurance is also sometimes included if you pay for your trip with a credit card.

UK INSURANCE

If insurance is not included with a bank or charge account or on a credit-card travel purchase, **UK citizens** can ask about policies at any bank or travel agent, or use a policy issued by a specialist travel firm like *STA* and *Campus* (see p.4 for addresses), or by the low-cost insurers *Endsleigh Insurance* (97–107 Southampton Row, London WC1; ☎0171/436 4451) or *Columbus Travel Insurance* (17 Devonshire Square, London EC2; ☎0171/375 0011). Two weeks' cover starts at around £42; a month costs from £50. For trips of up to four months, or if this is one of many short trips in one year, you may be better off with a frequent traveller policy, which offers twelve months of cover for around £100 – details from the companies listed above. Remember that certain activities, like scuba diving, mountain climbing and other dangerous sports, are unlikely to be covered by most policies, although by paying an extra premium of around £25 you can usually get added cover for the period in which these activities are taking place.

AUSTRALASIAN INSURANCE

In **Australia**, *CIC Insurance*, offered by *Cover-More Insurance Services* (Level 9, 32 Walker St, North Sydney; ☎02/202 8000; branches in Victoria and Queensland), has some of the widest cover available and can be arranged through most travel agents. It costs from AUS$140 for 31 days. In **New Zealand**, a good range of policies is offered by *STA* and *Flight Centres* (addresses given on p.11).

NORTH AMERICAN INSURANCE

As well as the perks of their bank and credit cards, travellers from the **US and Canada** should carefully check their **current insurance**

policies before taking out specific travel insurance, as you may discover that you're covered already for medical care or losses while abroad. Canadians are usually covered for medical mishaps overseas by their provincial health plans. Holders of official student/teacher/youth cards are entitled to accident coverage and hospital in-patient benefits: ISIC and Go-25 card-holders, for example, can call a 24-hour hotline in the event of a medical, legal or financial emergency, and are entitled to be reimbursed for $3000 worth of accident coverage and eighty days of in-patient benefits up to $100 a day for the period the card is valid – though this might not go far in the event of a serious setback. (The cards cost $16 for Americans and CAN$15 for Canadians; ISIC is available from *Council Travel*, *STA* and *Travel Cuts*, while Go-25 can be bought at *Council Travel* in the US and *Hostelling International* in Canada.) **Students** will often find that their student health coverage extends during the vacations and for one term beyond the date of last enrolment, while **homeowners' or renters'** insurance may cover theft or loss of documents, money and valuables while overseas.

After exhausting the possibilities above, you might want to contact a specialist **travel insurance** company; your travel agent can usually recommend one, or see the box below. Policies are comprehensive (accidents, illnesses, delayed or lost luggage, cancelled flights and so on), but maximum payouts tend to be meagre. Premiums vary, so shop around. The best deals are usually to be had through student/youth travel agencies – *ISIS* policies, for example, cost $48–69 for fifteen days (depending on coverage), $80–105 for a month, $149–207 for two months, on up to $510–700 for a year. If you're planning to do any "dangerous sports", figure on a surcharge of twenty to fifty percent. Members of *International SOS Assistance* (PO Box 11568, Philadelphia, PA 19116; in the US ☎1-800/523-8930, in Canada ☎1-800/363-0263) receive pre-trip medical referral information and are entitled to overseas emergency services.

TRAVEL INSURANCE COMPANIES IN NORTH AMERICA

Access America, PO Box 90310, Richmond, VA 23230 (☎1-800/284-8300).

Carefree Travel Insurance, PO Box 310, 120 Mineola Blvd, Mineola, NY 11501 (☎1-800/323-3149).

International Student Insurance Service (**ISIS**) – sold by *STA Travel*, which has several branches in the US (head office is 48 E 11th St, New York, NY 10003; ☎1-800/777-0112).

Travel Assistance International, 1133 15th St NW, Suite 400, Washington, DC 20005 (☎1-800/821-2828).

Travel Guard, 1145 Clark St, Stevens Point, WI 54481 (☎1-800/826-1300).

Travel Insurance Services, 2930 Camino Diablo, Suite 300, Walnut Creek, CA 94596 (☎1-800/937-1387).

HEALTH

Although Thailand's climate, wildlife and cuisine present Western travellers with fewer health worries than in many Asian destinations, it's as well to know in advance what the risks might be, and what preventive or curative measures you should take.

For a start, there's no need to bring huge supplies of non-prescription medicines with you, as Thai **pharmacies** (*raan khai yaa*; daily 8.30am–8pm) are well stocked with local and international branded medicaments, and of course they are much less expensive. All pharmacies, whatever size the town, are run by highly trained English-speaking pharmacists, who are usually the best people to talk to if your symptoms aren't acute enough to warrant seeing a doctor.

Hospital (*rong phayaabahn*) cleanliness and efficiency vary, but generally hygiene and health-care standards are good and the ratio of medical staff to patients is considerably higher than in most parts of the West. As with head pharmacists, doctors speak English. All provincial capitals have at least one hospital: ask at your accommodation for advice on and possibly transport to the nearest or most suitable. In the event of a major health crisis, get someone to contact your embassy (see p.133) or insurance company – it may be best to get yourself flown home.

INOCULATIONS

There are no compulsory **inoculation** requirements for people travelling to Thailand from the West, but it makes sense to ensure your polio and tetanus boosters are up to date (they last 5–10 years); most doctors also strongly advise vaccinations against typhoid and hepatitis A and, if you're intending to travel in rural areas, they might recommend protecting yourself against Japanese B encephalitis and rabies. If you do decide to have several injections, plan your course at least four weeks in advance, as some combinations wipe each other out if given simultaneously and others come in two parts.

In the **UK** the least costly way of getting immunized is to buy the vaccines on prescription and have them administered for free by your doctor or health-centre nurse. You also have the option of going to a specialist travel clinic: these work out expensive at between £6 and £25 a shot, but have the advantage of being staffed by tropical-disease specialists. An appointment is required at the travel clinic run by the *Hospital for Tropical Diseases* at Queen's House, 180–182 Tottenham Court Rd, London W1 (Mon–Fri 9am–5pm; ☎0171/636 6099), which also operates a recorded message service on ☎01839/337722, giving hints on hygiene and illness prevention as well as listing appropriate immunizations. A similar service is run by the *British Airways Travel Clinic*, whose main branch at 156 Regent St, London W1 (Mon–Fri 9am–4.15pm, Sat 10am–4pm; ☎0171/439 9584), can be visited without an appointment; there are also appointment-only branches at 101 Cheapside, London EC2 (☎0171/606 2977) and at the *BA* terminal in London's Victoria Station (☎0171/233 6661). *BA* has an information helpline on ☎01891/224100 and also operates other regional clinics throughout the country (call ☎0171/831 5333 to discover the one nearest to you). *Trailfinders* travel agency also runs no-appointments-necessary immunization clinics at its 194 Kensington High Street branch in London (Mon–Wed & Fri 9am–5pm, Thurs 9am–6pm, Sat 9.30am–3pm; ☎0171/938 3999) and its Glasgow branch at 254–284 Sauchiehall St (Tues & Thurs 2–5.30pm; ☎0141/353 0066).

North Americans will have to pay full whack for their inoculations, available at an immunization centre – there's one in every city of any size – or most local clinics. In the US, the doctor's consultation fee is generally $75, and the inoculations cost between $75 and $175 each. For further information, contact the *Travelers Medical Center*, 31 Washington Square, New York, NY 10011 (☎212/982-1600), which offers a consultation service on immunizations and treatment of diseases for people travelling to developing countries; or the *International Association for Medical Assistance to Travellers*, 417 Center St, Lewiston, NY 14092 (☎716/754-4883), and 40 Regal Rd, Guelph, Ontario N1K 1B5 (☎519/836-0102), a non-profit organization supported by donations, which can provide leaflets on various diseases and inoculations.

Australians and **New Zealanders** can have their jabs administered by their GP for AUS$35/

NZ$31 per visit plus the cost of the serums. In Australia, sixty percent of the consultation fee is refundable via Medicare, though you still pay for the serums, while Healthcare card-holders are excused the consultation fee and pay only AUS$2.50 for medicines. In New Zealand, nothing is refundable without medical insurance. In both countries, those who have to pay will find vaccination centres less expensive than doctors' surgeries. Australian centres include *Travel-Bug Medical and Vaccination Centre*, 161 Ward St, North Adelaide (☎08/267 3544); *Travel Health and Vaccination Clinic*, 114 William St, Melbourne (☎03/670 3871); *Travel Immunisation and Health Services*, 63 The Centreway, Mount Waverley, Melbourne (☎03/802 9898); *Travellers' Immunisation Service*, 303 Pacific Highway, Sydney (☎02/416 1348); and *Travellers' Medical and Vaccination Centre*, 428 George St, Sydney (☎02/221 7133) with branches of the last in Adelaide, Perth and Brisbane. New Zealand's main vaccination centre is *Auckland Hospital*, Park Rd, Grafton (☎07/797 440; in Auckland, use the prefix 3).

HEALTH PROBLEMS

For a comprehensive, and sobering, account of the health problems which travellers encounter worldwide, consult the regularly updated *Travellers' Health (How to stay healthy abroad)* by Dr Richard Dawood (Oxford University Press). What follows are some of the most common ailments encountered by visitors to Thailand.

MALARIA

Thailand is **malarial**, and there isn't a single, simple means of combating the disease. Malaria-bearing mosquitoes have become resistant to many of the prophylactics prescribed in the past, and, in any case, some doctors in Thailand believe that being tanked up on preventive medicines reduces the efficacy of their cures.

Current medical opinion in the UK, however, holds that some kind of prophylaxis is wise for Thailand's malaria hot spots: a prescription drug, Mefloquine, is strongly recommended for anyone travelling to provinces bordering Burma or Cambodia. If possible, start taking the pills two weeks before you leave home, because, in a small minority of people, Mefloquine produces such strong side effects that it's not worth them continuing with the course. Otherwise, start a

week before you enter one of the malarial zones, and continue the course for four weeks after you leave it; to reduce any side effects, take the pills before you go to sleep at night. Prophylaxis advice can change from year to year, so it might be worth getting the most up-to-date information from the *Malaria Reference Laboratory* in London (Mon–Fri 9.30–10.30am & 2–3pm; ☎0171/636 3924). In the US, try the *Travelers Medical Center* (see previous page for address).

The best way of combating malaria is to stop yourself getting bitten. Malarial mosquitoes are active from dusk until dawn and during this time you should smother yourself and your clothes in **mosquito repellent**, reapplying regularly: shops, guest houses and department stores all over Thailand stock the stuff, but if you want the highest-strength repellent, or convenient roll-ons or sprays, do your shopping before you leave home. At night you should either sleep under a **mosquito net** or in a room with screens across the windows. Accommodation in tourist spots always provides screens or a net, but if you're planning to go way off the beaten track or want the security of having your own mosquito net just in case, wait until you get to Bangkok to buy one, where they cost about an eighth of what you'd pay in the West. Mosquito coils – also widely available in Thailand – also help keep the insects at bay. The first **signs of malaria** are remarkably similar to flu, and may take months to appear: if you suspect anything go to a hospital or clinic immediately.

POISONOUS CUTS, BITES AND STINGS

Wearing protective clothing is a good idea when **swimming, snorkelling or diving**: a T-shirt will stop you from getting sunburnt in the water, while long trousers can guard against **coral grazes**. Should you scrape your skin on coral, wash the wound thoroughly with boiled water, apply antiseptic and keep protected until healed. Thailand's seas are home to a few dangerous creatures of which you should be wary, principally **jellyfish**, **poisonous sea snakes**, **sea urchins** and a couple of less conspicuous species – **sting rays**, which often lie buried in the sand, and **stone fish**, whose potentially lethal venomous spikes are easily stepped on because the fish look like stones and lie motionless on the sea bed.

If **stung or bitten** you should always seek medical advice as soon as possible, but there are a few ways of alleviating pain or administering your own first aid in the meantime. If stung by a **jellyfish** the priority treatment is to remove the fragments of tentacles from the skin – without causing further discharge of poison – which is easiest done by applying vinegar to deactivate the stinging capsules. In the case of a poisonous **snake bite**, don't try sucking out the poison or applying a tourniquet: immobilize the limb and stay calm until medical help arrives (all provincial hospitals in Thailand should carry supplies of antivenoms, produced by the Snake Farm in Bangkok). The best way to minimize the risk of stepping on the **toxic spines** of sea urchins, sting rays and stone fish is to wear thick-soled shoes, though these cannot provide total protection; sea-urchin spikes should be removed after softening the skin with a special ointment, though some people recommend applying urine to help dissolve the spines; for sting ray and stone fish stings, alleviate the pain by immersing the wound in very hot water – just under 50°C – while waiting for help.

DIGESTIVE PROBLEMS

By far the most common travellers' complaint in Thailand, **digestive troubles** are often caused by contaminated food and water, or sometimes just by an overdose of unfamiliar foodstuffs. Break your system in gently by avoiding excessively spicy curries and too much raw fruit in the first few days, and then use your common sense about choosing where and what to eat: if you stick to the most crowded restaurants and noodle stalls you should be perfectly safe. Furthermore, because most Thai dishes can be cooked in under five minutes, you'll rarely have to contend with stuff that's been left to smoulder and stew. You need to be a bit more rigorous about drinking the water, though: stick to bottled water, which is sold everywhere, or else opt for boiled water or tea. If you're planning on trekking independently in remote areas, you might want to invest in a water purifier (see box below).

Stomach trouble usually manifests itself as simple **diarrhoea**, which should clear up without medical treatment within three to seven days and is best combated by drinking lots of fluids. If this doesn't work, you're in danger of getting **dehydrated** and should take some kind of rehydration solution, either a commercial sachet sold in all Thai pharmacies or a do-it-yourself version which can be made by adding a handful of sugar and a pinch of salt to every litre of boiled or bottled water (soft drinks are *not* a viable alternative). Note that anti-diarrhoeal agents such as Imodium are useful for blocking you up on long bus journeys, but only attack the symptoms and may prolong infections. If diarrhoea persists for more than ten days, or if you have blood or mucus in

---

WATER PURIFICATION

Contaminated water is a major cause of sickness, the micro-organisms it contains causing diseases such as diarrhoea, gastroenteritis, typhoid, dysentery, poliomyelitis, hepatitis A, giardiasis and bilharziasis. Most travellers to Thailand need not worry about contracting these diseases from drinking water, as safe bottled water is available almost everywhere. However, those trekking independently in remote areas may find themselves without, in which case it's essential to know how to **treat your own**, whether your source is tap water or natural groundwater such as a river or stream.

There are various methods of treating water whilst travelling. **Boiling** for a minimum of five minutes is the time-honoured method, although it's not always practical and won't remove unpleasant tastes. **Chemical sterilization**, using either chlorine or iodine tablets or a tincture of iodine liquid, is a more convenient option, although chlorine tablets leave an especially unpalatable taste in the water and aren't wholly effective.

Purification, a two-stage process involving both filtration and sterilization, gives the most complete treatment. Portable water purifiers range in size from units weighing as little as 60g which can be slipped into a pocket, to 800g for carrying in a backpack. Some of the best water purifiers on the market are made in Britain by **Pre-Mac**; for suppliers contact:

Pre-Mac (Kent) Ltd, 40 Holden Park Rd, Southborough, Tunbridge Wells, Kent TN4 0ER, England (☎01892/534361).

All Water Systems Ltd, Unit 12, Western Parkway Business Centre, Lower Ballymount Rd, Dublin 12, Ireland (☎01/456 4933).

Outbound Products, 1580 Zephyr Ave, Box 56148, Hayward CA 94545-6148, USA (☎1-800/663-9262).

Outbound Products, 8585 Fraser St, Vancouver, BC V5X 3Y1, Canada (☎604/321-5464).

your stools, you may have contracted bacillary or amoebic **dysentery**, in which case go to a doctor or hospital.

HEAT PROBLEMS

Aside from the obvious considerations about restricting your exposure to the searing midday sun, using high protection-factor sun creams, and protecting your eyes with dark glasses and your head with a hat, you should avoid **dehydration** by drinking plenty of water and occasionally adding a pinch of salt to fruit shakes. To prevent and alleviate heat rashes, prickly heat and fungal infections it's a good idea to use a mild antiseptic soap and to dust yourself with prickly heat talcum powder, both of which are sold cheaply in all Thai stores.

AIDS

Aids is spreading fast in Thailand, primarily because of the widespread sex trade (see the box on the sex industry, p.110). Condoms (*meechai*) substantially lower the risk of HIV infection through sexual contact, and are sold in pharmacists, department stores, hairdressers, even on street markets. Should you need to have a hypodermic injection at a hospital, try to check that the needle has been sterilized first; this is not always practicable, however, so you might consider carrying your own syringes. Don't even consider getting yourself tattooed in Thailand. Due to rigorous screening methods, the country's **medical blood supply** is now considered safe.

A TRAVELLERS' FIRST-AID KIT

Among items you might want to carry with you – especially if you're planning to go trekking – are:

Antiseptic cream.

Antihistamine cream.

Plasters/band aids.

Lints and sealed bandages.

Knee supports.

Imodium, Lomotil or Arret for emergency diarrhoea relief.

Paracetamol/aspirin.

Multi-vitamin and mineral tablets.

Rehydration sachets.

Hypodermic needles and sterilized skin wipes.

GETTING AROUND

Travel in Thailand is both inexpensive and efficient, if not exactly speedy. For long-distance travel between major towns you nearly always have the choice of a variety of buses, and in some cases a train or plane as well. Local transport comes in all sorts of permutations, both public and chartered, with relatively little to choose in terms of cost.

LONG-DISTANCE TRANSPORT

Unless you travel by plane, long-distance journeys in Thailand can be arduous, especially if a shoestring budget restricts you to hard seats and no air conditioning. Still, the wide range of efficient transport options makes travelling around this country easier than elsewhere in Southeast Asia. Buses are fast and frequent, and can be quite luxurious; trains are slower but safer and offer more chance of sleeping during overnight trips; moreover, if travelling by day you're likely to follow a more scenic route by rail than by road. Inter-town songthaews, share taxis and air-conditioned minibuses are handy, and ferries provide easy access to all major islands.

INTER-TOWN BUSES

Buses, overall the most convenient way of getting around the country, come in two categories: **ordinary** (*rot thammadaa*) and **air-conditioned** (*rot air*), with an additional air-conditioned subsection known as **tour buses** (*rot tua*). The ordinary and air-conditioned buses are run by *Baw Kaw Saw*, the government transport company, whereas the misleadingly named tour buses are privately owned and ply the most popular long-distance routes, with no tours involved.

The orange-coloured **ordinary buses** are incredibly inexpensive and cover most short-range routes between main towns (up to 150km) very frequently during daylight hours. Each bus is staffed by a team of two or three – the driver, the fare collector and the optional "stop" and "go" yeller – who often personalize the vehicle with stereo systems, stickers, jasmine garlands and the requisite Buddha image or amulet. With an entertaining team and eye-catching scenery, journeys can be fun, but there are drawbacks. For a start, teams work on a commission basis, so they pack as many people in as possible and might hang around for thirty minutes in the hope of cramming in a few extra. They also stop so often that their average speed of 60kmh can only be achieved by hurtling along at breakneck speeds between pick-ups, often propelled by amphetamine-induced craziness.

Air-conditioned buses stop a lot less often (if at all) and cover the distances faster and more comfortably: passengers are allotted specific seats and on long journeys get blankets, snacks and non-stop videos. On the downside, they usually cost one-and-a-half times as much (though that's still a paltry amount), depart less frequently, and don't cover nearly as many routes – and make sure you have some warm clothes, as temperatures can get chilly, even with the blanket.

In a lot of cases **tour buses** are indistinguishable from air-conditioned ones, operating the busiest routes at similar prices and with comparable facilities. However, some tour buses – such as *VIP* – do offer a distinctly better service, with reclining seats and plenty of leg room. They do cost more than air-conditioned buses, but are worth every baht for mammoth journeys like Bangkok–Krabi.

Tickets for all buses can be bought from the departure terminals, but for ordinary buses it's normal to buy them on board. Air-conditioned buses often operate from a separate station, and tickets for the more popular routes should be booked a day in advance. As a rough indication of **prices**, a trip from Bangkok to Chiang Mai should cost around B190 by ordinary bus, B237 by air-conditioned bus and B304–470 by tour bus.

For a rough idea of frequency and duration of bus services between towns, check the **travel details** at the end of each chapter. **Timetables** do exist but are often ignored: for medium-length;

distances (150–300km) you can almost always turn up at a bus terminal and guarantee to be on your way within two hours. Long-distance buses often depart in clusters around the same time (early morning or late at night for example), leaving five or more hours during the day with no service at all.

SONGTHAEWS, SHARE TAXIS AND AIR-CONDITIONED MINIBUSES

In rural areas, the bus network is supplemented – or even substantially replaced – by **songthaews** (literally "two rows"), which are open-ended vans, or occasionally cattle-trucks, onto which the drivers squash as many passengers as possible on two facing benches, leaving latecomers to swing off the running board at the back. As well as their function within towns (see "Local Transport" on the next page), songthaews ply set routes from larger towns out to their surrounding suburbs and villages, and, where there's no call for a regular bus service, between small towns: some have destinations written on in Thai, but few are numbered. In most towns you'll find the songthaew "terminal" near the market; to pick one up between destinations just flag it down, and to indicate to the driver that you want to get out, the normal practice is to rap hard with a coin on the metal railings as you approach the spot. As a general rule, the cost of inter-town songthaews is comparable to that of air-conditioned buses.

In the deep south they do things with a little more style – **share taxis**, often clapped-out old limos, connect all the major towns, though they are slowly being replaced by more comfortable **air-conditioned minibuses** (for more details, see p.485).

TRAINS

Managed by the *State Railway of Thailand* (SRT), the rail network consists of four main lines and a few branch lines. The **Northern Line** connects Bangkok with Chiang Mai via Ayutthaya and Phitsanulok. The **Northeastern Line** splits into two just beyond Ayutthaya, the lower branch running eastwards to Ubon Ratchathani via Khorat and Surin, the more northerly branch linking the capital with Nong Khai via Khon Kaen and Udon Thani. You should have no reason to use the **Eastern Line**, which mainly ferries Cambodian refugees and refugee workers from Bangkok to the troubled border town of Aranyaprathet. The **Southern Line** extends to Hat Yai, where it branches to continue down the west coast of Malaysia, via Butterworth and Kuala Lumpur, to Singapore or down the eastern side of the peninsula to Sungai Kolok on the Thailand–Malaysia border (20km from Pasir Mas on Malaysia's interior railway). At Nakhon Pathom a branch of this line veers off to Nam Tok via Kanchanaburi – this is all that's left of the Death Railway, of *Bridge Over the River Kwai* notoriety.

Fares depend on the class of seat, whether or not you want air conditioning, and on the speed of the train. Hard wooden **third-class** seats cost about the same as an ordinary bus (Bangkok–Chiang Mai B121), and are fine for about three hours, after which numbness sets in. For longer journeys you'd be wise to opt for the padded and often reclining seats in **second class** (Bangkok–Chiang Mai B255, or B305 with air conditioning). On long-distance trains, you also usually have the option of **second-class berths** (for an extra B70–150, or B200–250 with air conditioning), with day seats that convert into comfortable curtained-off bunks in the evening. Travelling **first class** (Bangkok–Chiang Mai B537) means you automatically get a private two-person air-conditioned compartment (add on B500–550 per person for a sleeping berth, complete with washbasin). All long-distance trains have **dining cars**, and rail staff will also bring meals to your seat. Tourist menus are written in English but have inflated prices – ask for the similar but less expensive "ordinary" version, the *menu thammadaa*.

The speed supplements are as follows: Special Express (B50 extra), Express (B30), and Rapid (B20). The rare Special Diesel Railcars, whose speed is somewhere between Special Express and Express, operate on fares midway between those two categories.

Advance booking of at least one day is strongly recommended for second-class and first-class seats on all lengthy journeys, and for sleepers needs to be done as far in advance as possible. Recent computerization of the reservation system means that, subject to occasional glitches, it's now possible to make bookings at the station in any major town. For details on how to book trains out of Bangkok, see p.130.

The SRT publishes two clear and fairly accurate free **timetables** in English, one for the Northern, Northeastern and Eastern lines and another for the Southern and Kanchanaburi lines.

These detail types of trains and classes available on each route as well as fares and supplementary charges; the best place to get hold of them is over the counter at Bangkok's Hualamphong station or, if you're lucky, the TAT office in Bangkok. The information desk at Hualamphong also stocks more detailed local timetables covering the Bangkok–Lopburi route via Don Muang airport and Ayutthaya.

Travel agents overseas sell seven-, fourteen- and 21-day **rail passes**, covering conveyance anywhere in Thailand in second-class seats without air conditioning, but they're generally more trouble than they're worth, as the country's network is not extensive enough to make the passes pay, and many booking offices in Thailand are at a loss as to how to handle them, especially if, as is usually the case, pass-holders want to pay extra for a sleeping berth.

FERRIES

Regular **ferries** connect all major islands with the mainland, and for the vast majority of crossings you simply buy your ticket on board. In tourist areas competition ensures that prices are kept low, and fares tend to vary with the speed of the crossing: thus Surat Thani–Ko Samui costs B105 if you do it in two and a half hours or B60 for the six-hour crossing, while the two-hour Krabi–Ko Phi Phi route costs between B125 and B250. Boats generally operate a reduced service during the monsoon season – from May through October along the east coast and Andaman coast and from November through January on the Gulf coast – while the more remote spots become inaccessible in these periods. Details on island connections are given in the relevant chapters.

FLIGHTS

The domestic arm of *Thai Airways* dominates the **internal flight** network, which extends to all extremities of the country, using a total of 21 airports. *Bangkok Airways* plies four additional routes. It's unlikely that you'll be tempted by the 65-minute Bangkok–Chiang Mai flight, which costs B1650 one-way, but in some instances a flight can save you days of travelling: the flight from Chiang Mai to Phuket (B3455), for example, takes just over two hours, as against a couple of days by meandering train and/or bus.

All towns served by an airport have at least one *Thai Airways* **booking** office; flights get

booked a long way ahead, so reserve early if possible – but bear in mind it costs much less to book in Thailand than from abroad. The main Bangkok offices for *Thai* and *Bangkok Airways* are detailed on p.131, and flight durations and frequencies are listed at the end of each chapter. If you're planning to use the *Thai Airways'* internal network a lot, you can save money by buying a **"Discover Thailand Airpass"**, available only from *Thai Airways'* offices and travel agents outside of Thailand, which gives you four one-way flights in a two-month period for £153/$239 (plus up to four additional flights at £33/$50 each).

LOCAL TRANSPORT

In the midday heat, spending twenty-odd baht on local transport can be an awful lot more appealing than sweating it out on foot. In most sizeable towns you have two broad options – **fixed-route** or **chartered** transport. The former, such as buses, songthaews or even longtail boats, have set fares and routes, but not rigid timetabling: in most cases vehicles leave when they're full and run about every ten to twenty minutes. Chartered transport – tuk-tuk, samlor, motorbike, taxi or boat – is generally more expensive, but the increased cost is often so slight as to be completely offset by the added convenience. Whenever you charter a vehicle, always establish the **fare** beforehand: although drivers nearly always pitch their first offers too high, they do calculate with traffic and time of day in mind, as well as according to distance – if successive drivers scoff at your price, you know you've got it wrong.

BUSES AND SONGTHAEWS

Larger cities like Bangkok, Chiang Mai and Khorat have a **local bus** network which usually extends to the suburbs and operates from dawn till dusk (through the night in Bangkok); most are numbered in Arabic numerals, and you pay the conductor B2–7 depending on your destination. Within medium-sized and large towns, the main transport role is often played by **songthaews**; the size and shape of vehicle used varies from town to town – and in some places they're known as "tuk-tuks" from the noise they make – but all have the telltale two facing benches in the back. In some towns, especially in the northeast, songthaews follow fixed routes, in others they act as communal taxis, picking up a number of people who are going in roughly the same direction and taking each of them right to their destination. Fares within towns range between B5 and B20, depending on distance.

TUK-TUKS AND SAMLORS
Named after the noise of its excruciatingly un-silenced engine, the three-wheeled open-sided **tuk-tuk** is the classic Thai vehicle. Painted in primary colours, tuk-tuks blast their way round towns and cities on two-stroke engines, zipping around faster than any car, and taking corners on two wheels. They aren't as dangerous as they look, and can be an exhilarating way to get around, as long as you're not too fussy about exhaust fumes. They're also inexpensive: fares start at B10 (B20 in Bangkok) regardless of the number of passengers – three is the safe maxi-mum, though six is not uncommon.

Tuk-tuks are also sometimes known as samlors (literally "three wheels"), but the real **samlors** are tricycle rickshaws propelled by pedal power alone. Slower and a great deal more stately than tuk-tuks, samlors operate pretty much everywhere except in Bangkok. Forget any qualms you may have about being pedalled around by another human being: samlor drivers' livelihoods depend on having a constant supply of passengers, so your most ethical option is to hop on and not scrimp on the fare. Drivers usually charge a minimum B10 fee and add B10 per kilometre, possibly more for a heavy load.

TAXIS
Even faster and more precarious than tuk-tuks, **motorbike taxis** feature both in big towns and out-of-the-way places. In towns – where the driv-ers are identified by coloured, numbered vests – they have the advantage of being able to dodge traffic jams, but obviously they are only really suitable for the single traveller, and they aren't the easiest mode of transport if you're carrying luggage. In remote spots on the other hand, motorbike taxis are often the only alternative to hitching or walking and are especially useful for getting between bus stops on main roads and to national parks or ancient ruins. Within towns motorbike-taxi fares are comparable to those for tuk-tuks, but for trips to the outskirts the cost rises steeply – about B80–100 for a twenty-kilometre round trip. **Car taxis** are generally available only in the biggest towns, and charge fares that begin at around B40; only Bangkok has metered taxis (see p.67). In theory, some offer

the benefit of air conditioning, but clapped-out air-conditioning systems are probably more numerous than functioning ones.

LONGTAIL BOATS
Wherever there's a decent public waterway, there'll be a **longtail boat** ready to ferry you along it. Another great Thai trademark, these elegant, streamlined boats are powered by deafening diesel engines – sometimes custom-built, more often adapted from cars or trucks – which drive a propel-ler mounted on a long shaft that is swivelled for steering. Longtails carry from ten to twenty passen-gers: in Bangkok the majority follow fixed routes, but elsewhere are for hire at about B100 an hour per boat, more in tourist spots.

VEHICLE RENTAL

Take a look at the general standard of driving (dangerously reckless) and state of the roads (poor) before deciding to **rent a car or motor-bike**, and then take time to get used to the more eccentric conventions. Of these, perhaps the most notable is the fact that a major road doesn't necessarily have right of way over a minor, but that the bigger vehicle *always* has right of way. Few vehicle owners stick to the roadside, prefer-ring to hog the whole route by careering up the centre, and when it comes to lanes, speed distinctions are rarely adhered to; it's accepted practice to use your horn to warn the vehicle in front that you are overtaking. Also remember that most driving licences in Thailand are bought over the counter, so the general level of competence cannot be underestimated. The published **rules of the road** state that everyone drives on the left (which they do) and that they should keep to the speed limit of 60kmh within built-up areas and 80kmh outside them (which they don't).

Theoretically, foreigners need an international driver's licence to hire any kind of vehicle, but some companies accept national licences, and the smaller operations (especially bike rentals) may not ask for any kind of proof at all. **Petrol** (*nam man*, which also means oil) costs about B12–15 a litre; the big stations are the least costly places, but most small villages have roadside huts where the fuel is pumped out of a large barrel.

CARS
If you decide to rent a car, go to a reputable dealer, preferably a *Hertz*, *Avis* or *SMT* branch or a rental company recommended by TAT, and

CAR RENTAL AGENCIES

Britain

Avis ☎0181/848 8733.

InterRent (Thai agents *SMT*) ☎01345/222 525.

Hertz ☎0181/679 1799.

North America

Avis ☎1-800/331-1084.

Hertz in the US ☎1-800/654-3001; in Canada ☎1-800/263-0600.

National (Thai agents *SMT*) ☎1-800/227-3876.

Australasia

Avis in Australia ☎1-800/22 5533; in New Zealand: ☎09/525 1982.

Hertz in Australia ☎13/1918; in New Zealand ☎09/309 0989.

make sure you get insurance from them. Prices for a small car range from B800 to B1200 per day, depending on the quality, which is generally not bad. If appropriate, consider the safer option of hiring a driver along with the car, which you can often do for the same price on day rentals. **Jeeps** are a lot more popular with farangs, especially on beach resorts and islands like Pattaya, Ko Phuket and Ko Samui, but they're no less dangerous; a huge number of tourists manage to roll their jeeps on steep hillsides and sharp bends. Jeep rental also works out somewhere between B800 and B1200. For all cars, the renters will often ask for a deposit of at least B2000, and will always want to hold onto your passport; you could offer an airline ticket if you're not happy about this.

MOTORBIKES

One of the best ways of exploring the countryside is to rent a **motorbike**, an especially popular option in the north of the country. Two-seater **80cc** bikes with automatic gears are best if you've never ridden a motorbike before, but aren't really suited for long slogs. If you're going to hit the dirt roads you'll certainly need something more powerful, like a **125cc** trail bike, though an inexperienced rider may find these machines a handful. Trail bikes have the edge in gear choice and are the best bikes for steep slopes, but the less widely available 125cc road bikes are easier to control and much cheaper on petrol.

Rental prices for the day usually work out at somewhere between B100 (for a fairly beat-up 80cc) and B250 (for a good trail bike), though you can bargain for a discount on a long rental. As with cars, the renters will often ask for a deposit and a document as ransom. Insurance is not often available, so it's a good idea to make sure your travel insurance covers you for possible mishaps.

Before signing anything, **check the bike** thoroughly and preferably take it for a test run. Test the brakes, look for oil leaks, check the treads and the odometer, and make sure the chain isn't stretched too tight – a tight chain is likelier to break. As you will have to pay an inflated price for any damage when you get back, make a note on the contract of any defects such as broken mirrors, indicators and so on. Make sure you know what kind of petrol the bike takes as well.

As far as **equipment** goes, a helmet is essential – most rental places provide poorly made ones, but they're better than nothing. You'll need sunglasses if your helmet doesn't have a visor. Long trousers, a long-sleeved top and shoes, as well as being more culturally appropriate, will provide a second skin if you go over, which most people do at some stage. For the sake of stability, leave most of your luggage in baggage storage and pack as small a bag as possible, strapping it tightly to the bike with bungee cords – these are usually provided. Once on the road, **oil the chain** at least every other day, keep the **radiator** topped up, and fill up with oil every 300km or so.

BICYCLE

The safest and pleasantest way of conveying yourself around many towns and rural areas is by **bicycle**, except of course in Bangkok. You won't find bike rentals everywhere, but a lot of guest houses keep a few, and in certain bike-friendly tourist spots, like Kanchanaburi, Chiang Mai and Sukhothai, you'll find larger-scale rental places. They should charge around B30 a day. Mountain-biking doesn't seem to have hit Thailand in a big way yet, but there are a sprinkling of rental outlets in the north, where the average fee is B50 per day.

HITCHING

Public transport being so inexpensive, you should only have to resort to **hitching** in the most remote areas, in which case you'll probably get a lift to the nearest bus or songthaew stop quite quickly. On routes served by buses and trains hitching is not standard practice, but in other places locals do rely on regular passers-by (such as national park officials), and as a farang you can make use of this "service" too. As with hitching anywhere in the world, think twice about hitching solo, especially if you're female. Truck drivers are notorious users of amphetamines (as are a lot of bus drivers), so you may want to wait for a better offer.

ACCOMMODATION

Inexpensive accommodation can be found all over Thailand: for the simplest double room prices start at around B80 in the outlying regions and B120 in Bangkok, rising to B250 in some resorts. Tourist centres invariably offer a huge range of more upmarket choices, and you'll have little problem finding luxury hotels of international standard in these places. In most resort areas rates fluctuate according to demand, plummeting during the off-season and, in some places, rising at weekends throughout the year. In some towns, tuk-tuk and samlor drivers get a commission for bringing in customers and the extra baht will get slapped on your bill; to avoid this, either walk or make it clear to hotel or guest-house staff that you asked to be brought there.

Whatever the establishment, staff expect you to look at the room before taking it; in the budget ones especially, check for cockroaches and mosquitoes, and make sure it's equipped with a decent mosquito net or screens. En suite showers and flush toilets are the norm only in moderately priced and expensive hotels; in the less touristed places you'll be "showering" with a bowl dipped into a large water jar and using squat toilets.

GUEST HOUSES AND HOSTELS

Any place calling itself a **guest house** – which could be anything from a bamboo hut to a three-storey concrete block – is almost certain to provide inexpensive, basic accommodation

ACCOMMODATION PRICES

Throughout this guide, guest houses, hotels and bungalows have been categorized according to the price codes given below. These categories represent the minimum you can expect to pay in the high season (roughly Nov–Feb & July–Aug) for a double room – or, in the case of national park bungalows, for a multi-berth room which can be rented for a standard price by an individual or group. If travelling on your own, expect to pay anything between sixty and one hundred percent of the rates quoted for a double room. Wherever a range of prices is indicated, this means that the establishment offers rooms with varying facilities – as explained in the write-up. Wherever an establishment also offers dormitory beds, the prices of these beds are given in the text, instead of being indicated by price code.

Remember that the top-whack hotels will add seven percent tax and a ten-percent service charge to your bill – the price codes below are based on net rates after taxes have been added.

① under B100	④ B250–400	⑦ B1000–1500
② B100–150	⑤ B400–600	⑧ B1500–3000
③ B150–250	⑥ B600–1000	⑨ B3000+

specifically aimed at Western travellers and priced at around B80–150 for a sparse double room with a fan and (usually shared) bathroom. You'll find them in all major tourist centres (in their dozens in Bangkok and Chiang Mai), on beaches, where they're also called **bungalows**, and even in the most unlikely backcountry spots.

In the main towns they tend to be concentrated in cheek-by-jowl farang ghettos, but even if you baulk at the world travellers' scene that often characterizes these places, guest houses make great places to stay, with attached cafeterias, clued-up English-speaking staff and informative bulletin boards. These days, they're providing more and more services and **facilities**, such as safes for valuables, baggage-keeps, travel and tour operator desks and their own poste restantes. Staying at one out in the sticks, you'll often get involved in local life a lot more than if you were encased in a hotel.

At the vast majority of guest houses check-out time is noon, which means that during high season you should arrive to check in at about 11.30am to ensure you get a room: few places will draw up a "waiting list" and they rarely take advance bookings unless they know you already.

Upmarket guest house is almost a contradiction in terms, but there are a few that charge between B250 and B1000 for facilities that may include air conditioning, bathroom, TV and use of a swimming pool. Beware of pricey guest houses or bungalows in mega-resorts like Pattaya and Phuket, however, which often turn out to be low-quality fan-cooled establishments making a killing out of unsuspecting holidaymakers.

With fewer than ten officially registered **youth hostels** in the whole country, it's not worth becoming a YHA member just for your trip to Thailand, especially as card-holders get only about B20 discount anyway. In general, youth-hostel prices work out the same as guest-house rates and rooms are open to all ages, whether members or not.

BUDGET HOTELS

Few Thais use guest houses, opting instead for hotels offering rooms in the B80–B400 range. Beds in these places are large enough for a couple, and it's quite acceptable for two people to ask and pay for a single room (*hong diaw*). Usually run by Chinese-Thais, you'll find these three- or four-storey places in every sizeable

town, often near the bus station. They're generally clean and usually come with attached bathroom, fan (or air conditioning) and boiled water, which makes them good value in terms of facilities. Unfortunately they also tend to be grim and unfriendly, staffed by brisk non-English speakers, and generally lacking in any communal seating or eating area, which makes them lonely places for single travellers. A number of budget hotels also employ prostitutes, though as a farang you're unlikely to be offered this sideline, and may not even notice the goings-on anyway.

If the hotel's on a busy main road, as many of them are, try asking for a quiet room (*mii hong ngiap-kwaa mai* ?). Advance bookings are accepted over the phone – if you can make yourself understood – but this is rarely necessary, as such hotels rarely fill up. The only time you may have difficulty finding a budget hotel room is during Chinese New Year (a moveable 3-day period in February), when many Chinese-run hotels close and the others get booked up fast.

MODERATE HOTELS

Moderate hotels – priced between B400 and B1000 – can sometimes work out good value, offering many of the trimmings of a top-end hotel (TV, fridge, air conditioning, pool), but none of the prestige. They're often the kind of places that once stood at the top of the range, but were downgraded when the multinational luxury-class hotels hogged the poshest clientele. They make especially welcome alternatives to the budget hotels in provincial capitals, but, like upmarket guest houses, can turn out to be vastly overpriced in the resorts.

As with the budget hotels, you're unlikely to have trouble finding a room on spec in one of these places, though advance bookings are accepted by phone. Bed size varies a lot more than in the Chinese-run places, though, with some making the strict Western distinction between singles and doubles.

UPMARKET HOTELS

Many of Thailand's **upmarket hotels** belong to international chains like *Hilton*, *Holiday Inn*, *Le Meridien* and *Sheraton*, maintaining top-quality standards in Bangkok and major resorts at prices of B3000 and upward for a double – rates far lower than you'd pay for such luxury accommodation in the West. Some of the best home-grown upmarket hotels are up to B1000 cheaper for equally fine service, rooms equipped with TV, minibar and balcony, and full use of the hotel sports' facilities and swimming pools. Then of course, there's the *Oriental*, Bangkok's palatial riverside hotel, which is ranked among the best ten hotels in the world and has rooms from B5300 – nothing short of an outright bargain. All upmarket hotels can be booked in advance, an advisable measure in Chiang Mai, Phuket or Pattaya during peak season.

NATIONAL PARKS AND CAMPING

Unattractive accommodation is one of the big disappointments of Thailand's **national parks**. Generally built to a standard two-roomed format, these dismal concrete huts feature in 39 of the country's 83 parks, and cost an average B500 for four or more beds plus a probably malfunctioning shower. Because most of their custom comes from Thai family groups, park officials rarely discount these huts for lone travellers, even if you only use one bed, rendering them poor value for most farang visitors. In most parks, advance booking is unnecessary except on weekends and national holidays; if you do want to pre-book then

either pay on the spot at the Forestry Department offices near Kasetsart University on Phaholyothin Road in Bangkok's Chatuchak district (☎02/579 0529) – which can be quite a palaver, so don't plan on doing anything else that day – or book on the phone, then send a baht money order and wait for confirmation. If you turn up without booking, check in at the park headquarters – which is usually adjacent to the visitors' centre.

In a few parks, private operators have set up low-cost guest houses on the outskirts and these make much more attractive and economical places to stay. Failing that, you can usually **camp** in a national park for a minimal fee of around B10, and some national parks also rent out tents at about B60. Unless you're planning an extensive tour of national parks, though, there's little point in lugging a tent around Thailand: accommodation everywhere else is too inexpensive to make camping a necessity, and anyway there are no campgrounds inside town perimeters. Few travellers bother to bring tents for beaches either, opting for inexpensive bungalow accommodation or simply sleeping out under the stars. But camping is allowed on nearly all islands and beaches, many of which are national parks in their own right.

FOOD AND DRINK

Bangkok and Chiang Mai are the country's big culinary centres, boasting the cream of gourmet Thai restaurants and the best international cuisines. The rest of the country is by no means a culinary wasteland, however, and you can eat well and inexpensively even in the smallest provincial towns, many of which offer the additional attraction of regional specialities. In fact you could eat more than adequately without ever entering a restaurant, as itinerant food vendors hawking hot and cold snacks materialize in even the most remote spots, as well as on trains and buses, and night markets often serve customers from dusk until dawn.

Hygiene is a consideration when eating anywhere in Thailand, but being too cautious means you'll end up spending a lot of money and missing out on some real local treats. Wean your stomach gently by avoiding excessive amounts of chillies and too much fresh fruit in the first few days and by always drinking either bottled or boiled water.

You can be pretty sure that any noodle stall or curry shop that's permanently packed with customers is a safe bet, but if you're really concerned about health standards you could stick to restaurants displaying the TAT-approved symbol (also used for shops), which shows a woman seated between two panniers beneath the TAT logo. The *Thai Shell: Good Food Guide* also endorses a huge range of eating places: look for signs showing a rice bowl symbol with red, black or blue lettering underneath it.

Broad **price** categories are appended to restaurant listings throughout this guide: "inexpensive" means you can get a main course for under B40, "moderate" means B40–70, and "expensive" over B70.

WHERE TO EAT

Despite their obvious attractions, a lot of tourists eschew the huge range of Thai places to eat and opt instead for the much "safer" restaurants in **guest houses and hotels**. Almost all tourist accommodation has a kitchen, and while some are excellent, the vast majority serve up bland imitations of Western fare alongside equally pale versions of common Thai dishes. Having said that, it can be a relief to get your teeth into a processed cheese sandwich after five days' trekking in the jungle, and guest houses do serve comfortingly familiar Western breakfasts – most farangs quickly tire of eating rice three times a day.

Throughout the country most **inexpensive Thai restaurants and cafés** specialize in one general food type or preparation method – a "noodle shop", for example, will do fried noodles and noodle soups, plus a basic fried rice, but they won't have curries, meat or fish dishes. Similarly, a restaurant displaying whole roast chickens and ducks in its window will offer these sliced or with chillis and sauces and served over rice, but their menu probably won't extend to noodles or fish, while in "curry shops" your options are limited to the vats of curries stewing away in the hot cabinet.

To get a choice of low-cost food, it's sometimes best to head for the wider array at the local **night market** (*talaat yen*), a term for the gatherings of open-air night-time kitchens found in every town. Operating usually from about 6pm to 6am, they are to be found on permanent patches close to the fruit and vegetable market or the bus station, and as often as not they're the best and most entertaining places to eat, not to mention the least expensive– after a lip-smacking feast of two savoury dishes, a fruit drink and a sweet you'll come away no more than B50 the poorer.

A typical night market has some thirty-odd "specialist" pushcart kitchens jumbled together, each fronted by several sets of tables and stools. Noodle and fried-rice vendors always feature prominently, as do sweets stalls, heaped high with sticky rice cakes wrapped in banana leaves or thick with bags of tiny sweetcorn pancakes hot from the griddle – and no night market is complete without its fruit-drink stall, offering banana shakes and freshly squeezed orange, lemon and tomato juices. In the best setups you'll find a lot more besides: curries, barbecued sweetcorn, fresh pineapple, watermelon and mango, and – if the town's by a river or near the sea – heaps of fresh fish. Having decided what you want, you order from the cook or the cook's dogsbody and sit down at the nearest table; there's no territorialism about night markets, so it's normal to eat several dishes from separate stalls and rely on the nearest cook to sort out the bill.

For a more relaxing ambience, Bangkok has a range of gourmet restaurants specializing in **"royal" Thai cuisine**, which differs from standard fare mainly in the quality of the ingredients and the way the food is presented. As with the nouvelle cuisine of the West, great care is taken over how individual dishes look: they are served in small portions and decorated with carved fruit and vegetables in a way that used to be the prerogative of royal cooks, but has now filtered down to the common folk. The cost of such delights is not prohibitive, though – a meal in one of these places is unlikely to cost more than B500.

WHAT TO EAT

The repertoire of noodles, stir-fries, curries and rice dishes listed below is pretty much standard throughout Thailand. When you get out into the provinces, you'll have the chance to sample a few specialities as well, which have evolved either from the cuisines of neighbouring countries or from the crops best suited to that area. Bland food is anathema to Thais and restaurant tables everywhere come decked out with a condiment set featuring the four basic flavours: chopped chillis in watery fish sauce, chopped chillis in vinegar, sugar, and ground red pepper – and often extra bowls of ground peanuts and a bottle of chilli ketchup as well.

NOODLE AND RICE DISHES

Thais eat **noodles** (*kway tiaw* or *ba mii*) when Westerners would dig into a sandwich – for lunch, as a late-night snack or just to pass the time – and at B10–15 they're the most inexpensive hot meal you'll find anywhere, whether bought from an itinerant street vendor or ordered

in an air-conditioned restaurant. They come in assorted varieties (wide and flat, thin and transparent, made with eggs, soy-bean flour or rice flour) and get boiled up as soups (*kway tiaw nam*), doused in sauces (*kway tiaw rat na*), or stir-fried (*kway tiaw haeng* or *kway tiaw pat*). All three versions include a smattering of vegetables, eggs and meat, but the usual practice is to order the dish with extra chicken, beef, pork or shrimps. Most popular of noodle dishes is **kway tiaw pat thai** (usually abbreviated to *pat thai*), a delicious combination of fried noodles, beansprouts, egg and tofu, sprinkled with ground peanuts and the juice of half a lime, and occasionally spiked with tiny shrimps.

Fried rice (*khao pat*) is the other faithful standby, guaranteed to feature on menus right across the country. Curries that come served on a bed of rice are more like stews, prepared long in advance and eaten more as a light meal than a main one; they are usually called *khao na* plus the meat of the chosen dish – thus *khao na pet* is duck curry served over rice.

CURRIES, STIR-FRIES, FISH AND SOUPS

Thai **curries** (*kaeng*) are based on coconut milk – which gives them a slightly sweet taste and a soup-like consistency – and get their fire from chilli peppers. The best curries are characterized by a subtle blend of freshly ground herbs and spices, but only the most practised palate can discern these beneath the mouth-blasting fire of the chillies. It's often possible to request one that's "not too hot" (*mai phet*); if you do bite into a chilli, the way to combat the searing heat is to take a mouthful of plain rice – swigging water just exacerbates the sensation.

Stir-fries tend to be a lot milder, often flavoured with ginger and whole cloves of garlic and featuring a pleasing combination of soft meat and crunchy vegetables or nuts. Chicken with cashew nuts (*kai pat met mamuang*) is a favourite of a lot of farang-oriented places as is sweet and sour chicken, pork or fish (*kai/muu/plaa priaw waan*). *Pat phak bung* – slightly bitter morning-glory leaves fried with garlic in a blackbean sauce – makes a good vegetable side dish with any of these.

All seaside and most riverside restaurants rightly make a big deal out of locally caught **fish and seafood**. If you order fish it will be served whole, either steamed or grilled with ginger or chillies. Mussels often get stuffed into a viscous batter mixture and shrimps turn up in everything from soups to fried noodles.

You can't make a meal out of a Thai **soup** (*tom yam*), but it is an essential component in any shared meal, eaten simultaneously with other dishes, not as a starter. Watery and broth-like, soups are always flavoured with the distinctive tang of lemon grass and can be extremely hot if the cook adds liberal handfuls of chillies to the pot. It's best eaten in small slurps between mouthfuls of rice.

FRUIT AND SWEETS

The best way to round off a meal is with **fresh fruit** (*phonlamai*), as the country's orchards heave with an amazing variety, from papayas, mangoes, pineapples and watermelons to seventeen different types of banana, hairy red rambutans and the notoriously stinky durian. Restaurants often serve mixed platefuls of fresh fruit, while ready-peeled and cut segments are sold on the street to be taken away in bags and eaten with a toothpick.

Sweets (*khanom*) don't really figure on most restaurant menus, but a few places offer bowls of *luk taan cheum*, a jellied concoction of lotus or palm seeds floating in a syrup scented with jasmine or other aromatic flowers. **Cakes** are sold on the street and tend to be heavy, sticky affairs made from glutinous rice and coconut cream pressed into squares and wrapped in banana leaves.

REGIONAL DISHES

Many of the specialities of the **north** originated over the border in Burma; one such is *khao soi*, in which both boiled and crispy egg noodles are served with beef, chicken or pork in a curried coconut soup. Also popular around Chiang Mai are thick spicy sausages (*nam*) made from minced pork, rice and garlic left to cure for a few days and then eaten raw with spicy salad. Somewhat more palatable is the local curry *kaeng hang lay* made from pork, ginger, coconut and tamarind.

The crop most suited to the infertile lands of **Isaan** is **sticky rice** (*khao niaw*), which replaces the standard grain as the staple diet for north-easterners. Served in its own special rattan "sticky rice basket" (the Isaan equivalent of the Tupperware lunchbox), it's usually eaten with the fingers, rolled up into small balls and dipped into chilli sauces and side dishes such as the local dish *somtam*, a spicy green-papaya salad. Although you'll find basted barbecued **chicken** on a stick (*kai yang*) all over Thailand, it originated in Isaan and it's even tastier in its home

region. As with Chiang Mai, Isaan produces its own **sausages**, called *sai krog Isaan*, made from spiced and diced raw pork. Raw minced pork is also the basis of another popular Isaan and northern dish called *larb*, when it is subtly flavoured with mint and served with vegetables.

Aside from putting a greater emphasis on seafood, **southern** Thai cuisine displays a marked Malaysian and Muslim aspect as you near the border. Satays feature more down here, but the two mainstays are the thick, rich but fairly mild Muslim **beef curry** (*kaeng matsaman*) and the **chicken curry** served over lightly spiced saffron rice, known as *kaeng karii kai*. You'll find **rotis** in the south, too – pancakes rolled with sickly sweet condensed milk and sugar and sold hot from pushcart griddles.

VEGETARIAN FOOD

Although very few Thais are **vegetarian,** it's rarely impossible to persuade cooks to rustle up a vegetable-only fried rice or noodle dish, though in more out-of-the-way places that's often your only option unless you eat fish – so you'll need to supplement your diet with the nuts, barbecued sweetcorn, fruit and other non-meaty goodies sold by food stalls. In tourist spots, vegetarians can happily splurge on specially concocted Thai and Western veggie dishes, and some restaurants will come up with a completely separate menu if requested. If you're **vegan** you'll need to stress that you don't want egg when you order, as eggs get used a lot; cheese and other dairy produce, however, don't feature at all in Thai cuisine.

DRINKS

Thais don't drink water straight from the tap, and nor should you: plastic bottles of drinking **water** (*nam plao*) are sold countrywide, even in the smallest villages, for about B10. Inexpensive restaurants and hotels generally serve free jugs of boiled water which should be fine to drink, though not as foolproof as the bottles.

Night markets, guest houses and restaurants do a good line in freshly squeezed **fruit juices** such as lemon (*nam manao*) and orange (*nam som*), which often come with salt and sugar already added. The same places will usually do **fruit shakes** as well, blending bananas (*nam kluay*), papayas (*nam malakaw*), pineapples (*nam sapparot*) and others with liquid sugar or condensed milk (or yoghurt, to make *lassi*). Fresh **coconut milk** (*nam maprao*) is another great thirst-quencher – you buy the whole fruit dehusked, decapitated and chilled.

Bottled brand-name orange and lemon **soft drinks** are sold all over the place for B6–10 (on average a bit more expensive than fresh drinks), but only the big names like *Pepsi*, *Coca-Cola* and *Fanta* go by their names – the rest are known by the generic terms. Soft-drink bottles are returnable, so shops and drink stalls have an amazing system of pouring the contents into a small plastic bag (fastened with an elastic band and with a straw inserted) rather than charging you the extra for taking away the bottle. The larger restaurants keep their soft drinks refrigerated, but smaller cafés and shops add ice (*nam khaeng*) to glasses and bags. Most ice is produced commercially under hygienic conditions, but it might become less pure in transit so be wary – and don't take ice if you have diarrhoea.

Weak Chinese **tea** (*nam chaa*) makes a refreshing alternative to water and often gets served in Chinese restaurants and roadside cafés. Posher restaurants keep stronger Chinese and Western teas (*chaa*) and **coffee** (*kaafae*), which is mostly the local instant variety, blended with copious amounts of chicory.

Beer (*bia*) is one of the few consumer items in Thailand that's not a bargain – at B50–60 for a 355ml bottle it works out roughly the same as what you'd pay in the West. The most famous beer is the slightly acrid locally brewed *Singha*, but *Carlsberg* and *Kloster*, which are brewed in Thailand under licence and cost about B5–10 more than *Singha*, are easier on the tongue. Some places also stock a lighter version of *Singha* called *Singha Gold* and another beer called *Amarit*, though that's not widely distributed.

At about B40–60 a 375ml bottle, the local **whisky** is a lot better value and Thais think nothing of consuming a bottle a night. The most palatable and widely available of these is *Mekhong*, which is very pleasant once you've stopped expecting it to taste like Scotch; distilled from rice, *Mekhong* is 35 percent proof, deep gold in colour and tastes slightly sweet. Check the menu carefully when ordering a bottle of *Mekhong* from a bar in a tourist area, as they often ask up to five times more than you'd pay in a guest house or shop.

You can buy beer and whisky in food stores, guest houses and most restaurants at any time of the day; **bars** aren't really an indigenous feature as Thais rarely drink out without eating, but you'll find a fair number of Western-style drinking holes in Bangkok and tourist centres elsewhere in the country.

A FOOD AND DRINK GLOSSARY

Note: This glossary includes phonetic guidance to assist you with menu selection; a more complete guide to the Thai language appears in *Contexts* (p.567).

NOODLES (KWÁY TIĀW or BA MÌÌ)

Ba mìi	Egg noodles	*Kwáy tiāw/ba mìi*	Rice noodles/egg noodles
Kwáy tiāw (sên yài/sên lék)	White rice noodles (wide/thin)	*rât nâ (mūu)*	fried in gravy-like sauce with vegetables (and pork slices)
Ba mìi kràwp	Crisp fried egg noodles		
Kwáy tiāw /ba mìi haēng	Rice noodles/egg noodles fried with egg, small pieces of meat and a few vegetables	*Pàt thai*	Thin noodles fried with egg, beansprouts and tofu, topped with ground peanuts
Kwáy tiāw/ba mìi nám (mūu)	Rice noodle/egg noodle soup, made with chicken broth (and pork balls)	*Pàt siyú*	Wide or thin noodles fried with soy sauce, egg and meat

RICE (KHÂO) AND RICE DISHES (KHÂO RÂT NÂ)

Khâo	Rice	*Khâo niāw*	Sticky rice
Jók	Rice breakfast porridge	*Khâo pàt kài/mūu/*	Fried rice with chicken/
Khâo man kài	Slices of chicken served over marinated rice	*kûng/phàk*	pork/shrimp/vegetables
		Khâo rât kaeng	Curry over rice
Khâo nâ kài/pèt	Chicken/duck served with sauce over rice	*Khâo tôm*	Rice soup

STIR-FRIES, CURRIES (KAENG) AND SEAFOOD (AHĀAN THALEH)

Hâwy thâwt	Omelette stuffed with mussels	*Pàt phàk bûng*	Morning glory fried in garlic and bean sauce
Kaeng kài/néua/pèt/ plaa dùk/sôm	Chicken/beef/duck/ catfish/fish and vegetable curry	*Pàt phàk lāi yàng*	Stir-fried vegetables
Kài pàt nàw mái	Chicken with bamboo shoots	*Plaa (mūu) prîaw wāan*	Sweet and sour fish (pork)
Kài pàt mét mámûang	Chicken with cashew nuts	*Plaa nêung páe sá*	Whole fish steamed with vegetables and ginger
Kài pàt khĭng	Chicken with ginger	*Plaa rât phrík*	Whole fish cooked with chillies
Kûng chúp paêng thâwt	Prawns fried in batter	*Plaa thâwt*	Fried whole fish

FRUIT (PHŌNLAMÁI)

Fàràng	Guava (year-round)	*Mánao*	Lemon/lime (year-round)
Khanŭn	Jackfruit (year-round)	*Mangkùt*	Mangosteen (April–Sept)
Klûay	Banana (year-round)	*Mapráo*	Coconut (year-round)
Lamyai	Longan (July–Oct)	*Nóinà*	Custard apple (July–Sept)
Línjìì	Lychee (April–May)	*Sàppàròt*	Pineapple (year-round)
Mámûang	Mango (Jan–June)	*Sôm*	Orange (year-round)
Ngáw	Rambutan (May–Sept)	*Sôm oh*	Pomelo (Oct–Dec)
Málákaw	Papaya (year-round)	*Taeng moh*	Watermelon (year-round)
Mákhāam	Tamarind (Dec–Jan)	*Thúrian*	Durian (April–June)

THAI SWEETS (KHANŌM)

Khanŏm beuang	Small crispy pancake folded over with coconut cream and strands of sweet egg inside	*Khâo niãw thúrian/ mámûang*	Sticky rice mixed with coconut cream, and durian/mango
Khâo lāam	Sticky rice, coconut cream and black beans cooked and served in bamboo tubes	*Klûay khàek*	Fried banana
		Lûk taan chêum	Sweet palm kernels served in syrup
Khâo niãw daeng	Sticky red rice mixed with coconut cream	*Tàkôh*	Squares of transparent jelly (jello) topped with coconut cream

DRINKS (KHREÛANG DEÙM)

Bia	Beer	*Nám mánao/sôm*	Fresh, bottled or fizzy lemon/orange juice
Chaa ráwn	Hot tea	*Nám plaò*	Drinking water (boiled or filtered)
Chaa yen	Iced tea		
Kaafae ráwn	Hot coffee	*Nom jeùd*	Milk
Mâekhŏng (or anglicized "Mekhong")	Thai brand-name rice whisky	*Ohlíang*	Iced coffee
Nám klûay	Banana shake	*Sohdaa*	Soda water

ORDERING

I am vegetarian	*Phŏm (male)/diichăn (female) kin jeh*	I would like ...	*Khăw...*
		With/without	*Sài/mâi sài*
		Can I have the bill please?	*Khăw bin?*
Can I see the menu?	*Khăw duù menu?*		

MAIL, PHONES AND THE MEDIA

With its booming economy, it's hardly surprising that Thailand boasts a fast and efficient communications network. International mail services are relatively speedy, and phoning overseas is possible even from some small islands. To keep you abreast of world affairs there are several English-language newspapers, though a mild form of censorship affects the predominantly state-controlled media, even muting the English-language branches on occasion.

MAIL

Mail takes around seven days to get between Bangkok and Europe or North America, and a little longer from the more isolated areas. Almost all **main post offices** across the country operate a **poste restante** service and will hold letters for two to three months. Mail should be addressed: Name (family name underlined or capitalized), Poste Restante, GPO, Town or City, Thailand. It will be filed by surname, though it's always wise to check under your first initial as well. The smaller post offices pay scant attention to who takes what, but in Bangkok you need to show your passport, pay B1 per item received and sign for them. The poste restante at Bangkok GPO opens Monday to Friday 8am to 8pm and until 1pm on Saturday; others follow regular post office hours – Monday to Friday 8am to 4pm (some close from noon to 1pm and may stay open until 6pm) and Saturday 8am to noon.

American Express in Bangkok also offers a poste restante facility of up to sixty days to holders of *Amex* credit cards or travellers' cheques. Mail should be addressed: c/o Amex, *Sea Tours Ltd*, Siam Centre, 965 Rama I Rd, Bangkok and can be collected Monday to Friday 8.30am to noon and 1pm to 4.30pm, Saturday 8.30am to noon, from its office on the top floor of the Siam Centre, opposite Siam Square. Amex customers can also receive **faxes** here on 02/253 2960.

Post offices are the best places to buy **stamps**, though hotels and guest houses often sell them too, charging an extra baht per stamp. An airmail letter of under 10g costs B14 to send to Europe or Australia and B16 to North America; postcards cost B9, and aerogrammes B10, regardless of where they're going to. All **parcels** must be officially boxed and sealed (for about B20) at special counters within main post offices or in a private outlet just outside – you can't just turn up with a package and buy stamps for it. In tourist centres (especially at Bangkok's GPO) be prepared to queue, first for the packaging, then for the weighing and then again for the buying of stamps. The surface rate for a parcel of up to 5kg is B560 to the UK, B530 to the US and B420 for Australia, and the package should reach its destination in three months; the airmail parcel service is about twice as expensive and takes about a week.

PHONES

Every so often phone lines get jammed and a whole town becomes incommunicado for a few hours, but generally the phone system works well. Payphones are straightforward enough and generally come in three colours: red for **local calls**, blue for **long-distance calls within Thailand**, and green cardphones for either. Red phones take the medium-sized one-baht coins and will give you three minutes per B1. Blue ones gobble up B5 coins (inter-provincial rates vary with distance, but on the whole are surprisingly pricey) and are generally unreliable, so you're better off buying a phonecard (B50 or B100), available from hotels, post offices and a wide variety of shops. The least hassled way of calling across the country is to go to a **private long-distance telephone office**, generally located

---

opposite the post office, which will make the connection for you. Regional codes are given throughout the *Guide*, but note that for some large hotels and government offices we've given several line numbers – thus ☎02/431 1802–9 means that there are eight lines and that you can substitute the last digit with any number between 3 and 9. One final local idiosyncrasy: Thai phone books list people by their first, not their family names.

The least costly way of making an **international call** is to use the government telephone centre. Nearly always located within or adjacent to the town's main post office, and open daily from about 7am to 11pm (24hr in Bangkok and Chiang Mai), the government phone centres allot you an individual booth and leave you to do the dialling (in Bangkok) or call via the operator for you (in other towns). A five-minute IDD call to the UK, for example, costs B270, an operator-assisted call costs slightly more. If you can't get to one of the official places, try the slightly more expensive private international call offices in tourist areas (like Bangkok's Khao San Road), or the even pricier services offered by the posher hotels. Many guest houses on touristed islands like Ko Samet, Ko Chang and Ko Phi Phi have radiophones which guests can use to call long distance and overseas (phone numbers for these are prefixed by ☎01). A *BT* Chargecard allows British travellers to charge calls from Thailand to their home phone bill, and there's a similar system in Australia; *AT&T, MCI,* and other North American long-distance companies enable their customers to make credit-card calls from Thailand (before you leave, call your company's customer service line to find out the toll-free access code in Thailand). Collect or reverse-charge calls can be made from many guest houses and private phone offices, usually for a fee of B60.

NEWSPAPERS

Of the hundreds of Thai-language **newspapers** and magazines published every week, the sensationalist tabloid *Thai Rath* attracts the widest readership and the independent *Siam Rath* the most intellectual. Alongside these, two **daily English-language papers** – the *Bangkok Post* and the *Nation* – both adopt a fairly critical attitude to governmental goings-on and cover major domestic and international stories as well as tourist-related issues. Both detail English-language cinema programmes, TV schedules and expat social events, and are sold at most news-stands in the capital as well as in major provincial towns and tourist resorts; the more isolated places receive their few copies at least one day late. You can also pick up foreign publications such as *Newsweek, Time* and the *International Herald Tribune* in Bangkok, Chiang Mai, Phuket and Pattaya; expensive hotels sometimes carry air-freighted copies of foreign national newspapers for at least B50 a copy.

TELEVISION

Channel 9 is Thailand's major TV station, transmitting a daily eighteen-hour dosage of news, quiz shows and predominantly imported cartoons and dramas to all parts of the country. Four other networks broadcast to Bangkok – the privately run Channel 3, the military-controlled channels 5 and 7, and the Public Relations' Department Channel 11 – but not all are received in every province. The *Bangkok Post* and the *Nation* tell you which English-language programmes are dubbed in Thai; English soundtracks for some programmes are transmitted simultaneously on FM radio as follows – Channel 3: 105.5 MHz; Channel 7: 103.5 MHz; Channel 9: 107 MHz.

Many posh hotels pipe into their guest rooms five channels of *IBC* cable TV (4 of which are in

English), or Hong Kong-based *Star TV*, which includes BBC World Service TV and a sports channel. Channel 9 also broadcasts two hours of programmes in English, including the news, every day from 6am.

RADIO

Radio Thailand broadcasts in several languages on shortwave bands 9655 kHz and 11905 kHz from 7am to 2pm and 4.30 to 10pm daily, with an uninterrupted English-language slot from 6 to 11.30am and again from 6.30 to 7.30pm. Similarly, the **Voice of Free Asia** transmits in English from 10 to 10.30pm on shortwave 1575 kHz.

With a shortwave radio, you can pick up the **BBC World Service**, **Radio Australia**, **Voice of America** and various other international stations on a variety of bands (depending on the time) right across the country. Times and wavelengths can change every

three months, so get hold of a recent schedule just before you travel.

Bangkok is served by a handful of English-language FM stations. Apart from a few specialist shows, *Gold FM 95.5* pumps out non-stop upbeat chart hits; there are few pauses for chat, except for local news coverage, provided by *The Nation*, at ten minutes to the hour, and international headlines at half past. Proud to dub itself "Bangkok's premier easy listening station", *Smooth 105 FM* rarely veers from the middle of the road; international news breaks in on the hour. Bilingual *Smile Radio 4* (107FM) is aimed at the young and hip, and follows current music trends, with frequent breaks for chat, phone-ins and the like; on the hour, there's local and international news, plus information about what's on in Bangkok. At the opposite end of the taste spectrum, *Chulalongkorn University Radio* (101.5FM) plays a wide selection of Western classical music from 9.30pm to midnight every evening.

TROUBLE

As long as you keep your wits about you, you shouldn't encounter much trouble in Thailand. Theft and pickpocketing are the main problems – not surprising considering that a huge percentage of the local population scrape by on a daily wage of B100. Most travellers prefer to carry their valuables with them at all times, either in a money belt, neck pouch or inside pocket, but it's also possible to leave your valuables in a hotel or guest-house locker. Padlock your

luggage when leaving it in hotel or guest-house rooms, as well as when consigning it to storage or taking it on public transport. Padlocks also come in handy as extra security on your room, particularly on the doors of beachfront bamboo huts.

Never buy anything from **touts**, and in the case of travel agents call the relevant airline first to make sure you're holding a verified ticket before paying up. **Gem** con men prey on greedy and gullible tourists, mostly in Bangkok – for information about buying stones and avoiding stings, see p.128. On a more dangerous note, beware of **drug** scams: either being shopped by a dealer (Chiang Mai samlor drivers are notorious) or having substances slipped into your luggage – simple enough to perpetrate unless all fastenings are secured with padlocks.

Violent crime against tourists is not common, but it does occur, usually to people making an ostentatious display of their belongings. Be wary of accepting food and drink from strangers, especially on long overnight bus or train journeys: it may be drugged so as to knock you out while your bags get nicked. This might sound paranoid, but there have been enough drug-muggings for TAT to publish a specific warning about the problem. Finally, be sensible about **travelling alone** at night in a taxi or tuk-tuk and on no account risk jumping into an unlicensed taxi at Don Muang airport at any time of day: there have been some very violent robberies in these, so take the well-marked authorized vehicles instead. In the north you should be wary of motorbiking alone in sparsely inhabited and politically sensitive border regions.

Drug smuggling carries a maximum penalty of death and will almost certainly get you from five to twenty years in a Thai prison. Despite the highly publicized royal pardon granted to two British teenagers in 1993, don't expect special treatment as a farang: because of its reputation as a major source of drugs, Thailand works hard to keep on the right side of the US and in most cases makes a big show of dishing out heavy sentences. Even more alarming, drug enforcement squads are said to receive 25 percent of the market value of seized drugs, so are liable to exaggerate the amounts involved

You're more likely to read about armed struggles than experience one, but nevertheless it's advisable to travel with a guide in certain **border areas**. As these regions are generally covered in dense unmapped jungle, you shouldn't find yourself alone in the vicinity anyway, but the main stretches to watch are the Burmese border north of Three Pagodas Pass – where villages, hideaways and refugee camps occasionally get shelled either by the Burmese military or by rebel Karen or Mon forces – and the border between Cambodia and southern Isaan, which is littered with unexploded mines.

REPORTING A CRIME OR EMERGENCY

TAT has a special department for tourist-related crimes and complaints called the **Tourist Assistance Center** (TAC). Set up specifically to mediate between tourists, police and accused persons (particularly shopkeepers and tour agents), TAC has an office in the old TAT headquarters on Rajdamnoen Nok Avenue, Bangkok (daily 8.30am–4.30pm; ☎02/281 5051). In **emergencies**, always contact the English-speaking **tourist police** who maintain a toll-free nationwide line (☎**1699**) and have offices within or adjacent to many regional TAT offices – getting in touch with the tourist police first is invariably more efficient than directly contacting the local police, ambulance or fire service.

SEXUAL HARASSMENT

On the whole, Thailand is a fairly hassle-free destination for women travellers. Though unpalatable and distressing, the high-profile sex industry is relatively unthreatening for Western women, with its energy focused exclusively on farang men; it's also quite easily avoided, being contained within certain pockets of the capital and a couple of beach resorts. As for harassment from Thai men, it's hard to generalize, but most Western tourists find it less of a problem in Thailand than they do back home. Outside of the main tourist spots, you're more likely to be of interest as a foreigner rather than a woman and, if travelling alone, as an object of concern rather than of sexual aggression.

OPENING HOURS AND HOLIDAYS

Most shops open at least Monday to Saturday from about 8am to 8pm, while department stores operate daily from around 9.30am to 9pm. Private office hours are generally Monday to Friday 8am–5pm and Saturday 8am–noon, though in tourist areas these hours are longer, with weekends worked like any other day. Government offices work Monday to Friday 8.30am–noon and 1pm–4.30pm, and national museums tend to stick to these hours too, but some close on Mondays and Tuesdays rather than at weekends.

Most tourists only register **national holidays** because trains and buses suddenly get extraordinarily crowded: although banks and government offices shut down on these days, most shops and tourist-oriented businesses carry on regardless, and TAT branches continue to dispense information. The only time an inconvenient number of shops, restaurants and hotels do close is during Chinese New Year, which, though not marked as an official national holiday, brings many businesses to a standstill for several days in February. You'll notice it particularly in the south, where most service industries are Chinese-managed.

A brief note on **dates**. Thais use both the Western Gregorian calendar and a Buddhist calendar – the Buddha is said to have died (or entered Nirvana) in the year 543 BC, so Thai dates start from that point: thus 1995 AD becomes 2538 BE (Buddhist Era).

NATIONAL HOLIDAYS

January 1 Western New Year's Day.

February (day of full moon) *Maha Puja* – commemorates the Buddha preaching to a spontaneously assembled crowd of 1250.

April 6 Chakri Day – founding of the Chakri dynasty.

April (usually 13–15) *Songkhran* – Thai New Year.

May 5 Coronation Day.

early May Royal Ploughing Ceremony.

May (day of full moon) *Visakha Puja* – the holiest of all Buddhist holidays, which celebrates the birth, enlightenment and death of the Buddha.

July (day of full moon) *Asanha Puja* – commemorates the Buddha's first sermon.

July (the day after *Asanha Puja*) *Khao Pansa* – the start of the annual three-month Buddhist rains retreat, when new monks are ordained.

August 12 Queen's birthday.

October 23 Chulalongkorn Day – anniversary of Rama V's death.

December 5 King's birthday.

December 10 Constitution Day.

December 31 Western New Year's Eve.

FESTIVALS

Nearly all Thai festivals have some kind of religious aspect. The most theatrical are generally **Brahmin** in origin, honouring elemental spirits with ancient rites and ceremonial costumed parades. **Buddhist** celebrations usually revolve round the local temple, and while merit-making is a significant feature, a light-hearted atmosphere prevails, as the wat grounds are swamped with food- and trinket-vendors and makeshift stages are set up to show *likay* folk theatre, singing competitions and beauty contests.

Many of the secular festivals (like the elephant roundups and the Bridge Over the River Kwai spectacle) are outdoor local culture shows, geared specifically towards Thai and farang tourists and so slightly artificial though no less enjoyable for that. Others are thinly veiled trade fairs held in provincial capitals to show off the local speciality, which nevertheless assume all the trappings of a temple fair and so are usually worth a look.

Hardly a week goes by without some kind of local or national festival being celebrated somewhere in Thailand, and most make great entertainment for participants and spectators alike. All the festivals listed below are spectacular or engaging enough to be worth altering your itinerary for, but bear in mind that for some of the more publicized celebrations (notably those in the northeast) you'll need to book transport and accommodation a week or more in advance.

Few of the **dates** for religious festivals are fixed, so check with TAT for specifics. The names of the most touristed celebrations are given here in English, the more low-key festivals are more usually known by their Thai name (*ngan* means "festival").

A FESTIVAL CALENDAR

JANUARY–MARCH

Chaiyaphum *Ngan Phraya Phakdi* – the founder of modern Chaiyaphum is feted with parades, music and dance (mid-Jan).

Chaiyaphum *Elephant roundup* – smaller version of the more famous Surin roundup (2 days in mid-Jan, just before or after *Phraya Phakdi*).

Chiang Mai *Flower Festival* – enormous floral sculptures paraded through the streets (usually first weekend in Feb).

Nationwide, particularly Wat Benjamabophit in **Bangkok** and Wat Phra That Doi Suthep in **Chiang Mai** *Maha Puja* – a day of merit-making marks the occasion when 1250 disciples gathered spontaneously to hear the Buddha preach, and culminates with a candlelit procession round the local temple's bot (Feb full-moon day).

Phitsanulok *Ngan Phra Buddha Chinnarat* – Thailand's second most important Buddha image

is honoured with music, dance and *likay* performances (mid-Feb).

Phetchaburi *Phra Nakhon Khiri* fair – *son et lumière* at Khao Wang palace (mid-Feb).

That Phanom *Ngan Phra That Phanom* – thousands come to pay homage at the holiest shrine in Isaan, which houses relics of the Buddha (Feb).

Pattani *Ngan Lim Ko Niaw* – local goddess inspires devotees to walk through fire and perform other endurance tests in public (middle of third lunar month – Feb or March).

Nationwide, particularly Sanam Luang, **Bangkok** – *Kite fights and flying contests* (late Feb to mid-April).

Nakhon Si Thammarat *Hae Pha Khun That* – southerners gather to pay homage to the Buddha relics at Wat Mahathat, including a procession of long saffron cloth around the chedi (late Feb–early March).

Yala *ASEAN Barred Ground Dove festival* – international dove-cooing contests (first weekend of March).

Phra Phutthabat, near Lopburi *Ngan Phra Phutthabat* – pilgrimages to the Holy Footprint attract food- and handicraft-vendors and travelling players (early to mid-March).

Khorat *Ngan Thao Suranari* – nineteenth-century local heroine is honoured with parades and exhibitions (late March).

APRIL AND MAY

Mae Hong Son *Poy Sang Long* – young Thai Yai boys precede their ordination into monkhood by parading the streets in floral headdresses and festive garb (early April).

Nationwide, especially **Chiang Mai** *Songkhran* – the most exuberant of the national festivals welcomes the Thai New Year with massive waterfights, sandcastle building in temple compounds and the inevitable parades and "Miss Songkhran" beauty contests (usually April 13–15).

Phanom Rung, near Surin *Ngan Phanom Rung* – daytime processions up to the eleventh-century Khmer ruins, followed by *son et lumière* (April full-moon day).

Nationwide, particularly **Bangkok's Wat Benjamabophit** *Visakha Puja* – the holiest day of the Buddhist year, commemorating the birth, enlightenment and death of the Buddha all in one go; most public and photogenic part is the candlelit evening procession around the wat (May full-moon day).

Sanam Luang, Bangkok *Raek Na* – the royal ploughing ceremony to mark the beginning of the rice-planting season in which ceremonially clad Brahmin leaders parade sacred oxen and the royal plough, and interpret omens to forecast the year's rice yield (early May).

Yasothon *Rocket festival* (*Bun Bang Fai*) – beautifully crafted painted wooden rockets are paraded and fired to ensure plentiful rains; celebrated all over Isaan, but especially lively in Yasothon (weekend in mid-May).

JUNE–SEPTEMBER

Dan Sai, near Loei *Phi Ta Khon* – masked reenactment of the Buddha's penultimate incarnation (end of June or beginning of July).

Ubon Ratchathani *Candle Festival (Asanha Puja)* – Ubon citizens celebrate the nationwide festival to mark the Buddha's first sermon and the subsequent beginning of the annual Buddhist retreat period (*Khao Pansa*) with parades of enormous wax sculptures (July, 3 days around the full moon).

Phra Phutthabat, near Lopburi *Tak Bat Dok Mai* – another merit-making festival at the Holy Footprint, this time on the occasion of the start of *Khao Pansa*, the annual three-month Buddhist retreat period (July around full-moon day).

Nakhon Pathom *Food and fruits fair* (*Ngan Phonlamai*)– cooking and fruit-carving demonstrations and folk-theatre performances in the chedi compound (first week of Sept).

Nakhon Si Thammarat *Tamboon Deuan Sip* – merit-making ceremonies to honour dead relatives accompanied by a ten-day fair on the town field (late Sept to early Oct).

OCTOBER–DECEMBER

Phuket and Trang *Vegetarian Festival (Ngan Kin Jeh)* – Chinese devotees become vegetarian for a nine-day period and then parade through town performing acts of self-mortification (Oct).

Nationwide *Tak Bat Devo* – offerings to monks and general merrymaking to celebrate the Buddha's descent to earth from *Tavatimsa* heaven and the end of the *Khao Pansa* retreat (Oct full-moon day).

Surat Thani *Chak Phra* – the town's chief Buddha images are paraded on floats down the streets and on barges along the river (mid-Oct).

Nan and Phimai *Boat races* – long-boat races and barge parades along town rivers (mid-Oct to mid-Nov).

Nationwide *Thawt Kathin* – the annual ceremonial giving of new robes by the laity to the monkhood at the end of the rains retreat (mid-Oct to mid-Nov).

Nationwide, especially **Sukhothai and Chiang Mai** *Loy Krathong* – baskets of flowers and lighted candles are floated to honour water spirits and celebrate the end of the rainy season; accompanied by *son et lumière* in Sukhothai and the release of balloons in Chiang Mai (late Oct or early Nov).

Wat Saket, Bangkok *Ngan Wat Saket* – probably Thailand's biggest temple fair, held around the Golden Mount with all the usual festival trappings (first week of Nov).

Surin *Elephant roundup* – two hundred elephants play team games, perform complex tasks and parade in battle dress (third weekend of Nov).

Nakhon Pathom *Ngan Phra Pathom Chedi* – week-long jamboree held in the grounds of the chedi with itinerant musicians, food-vendors and fortune-tellers (Nov).

Kanchanaburi *River Kwai Bridge festival* – spectacular *son et lumière* at the infamous bridge (last week of Nov & first week of Dec).

ENTERTAINMENT AND SPORT

Most travellers confine their experience of Thai traditional culture to a one-off atten- dance at a big Bangkok tourist show, but these extravaganzas are far less rewarding than authentic folk theatre, music (see p.555) and sports performances. Traditional sport fits neatly into the same category as the more usual theatrical classifications, not only because it can be graceful, even dance-like, to watch, but because, in the case of Thai boxing, classical music plays an important role in the proceedings. Bangkok has one authentic fixed venue for dance and a couple for Thai boxing; other- wise it's a question of keeping your eyes open in upcountry areas for signs that a travelling troupe may soon turn up.

DRAMA AND DANCE

Drama pretty much equals **dance** in Thai thea- tre, and many of the traditional dance-dramas are based on the Hindu epic the *Ramayana* (in Thai, *Ramakien*), a classic adventure tale of good versus evil which is taught in all the schools. Not understanding the plots can be a major disadvan- tage, so try reading an abridged version before- hand (see "Books" in *Contexts*) and check out the wonderfully imaginative murals at Wat Phra Kaeo in Bangkok, after which you'll certainly be able to sort the goodies from the baddies, if little else. There are three broad categories of traditional Thai dance-drama – *khon*, *lakhon* and *likay* – described below in descending order of refinement.

KHON

The most spectacular form of traditional Thai theatre is **khon**, a stylized drama performed in masks and elaborate costumes by a troupe of highly trained classical dancers. There's little room for individual interpretation in these dances, as all the movements follow a strict choreography that's been passed down through generations: each graceful, angular gesture depicts a precise event, action or emotion which will be familiar to educated *khon* audiences. The dancers don't speak, and the story is chanted and sung by a chorus who stand at the side of the stage, accompanied by a classical *phipat* orchestra.

A typical *khon* performance features several of the best-known **Ramayana** episodes, in which the main characters are recognized by their masks, headdresses and heavily brocaded costumes. Gods and humans don't wear masks, but it's generally easy enough to distinguish the hero Rama and heroine Sita from the action; they always wear tall gilded headdresses and often appear in a threesome with Rama's brother Lakshaman. Monkey masks are always open- mouthed, almost laughing, and come in several colours: monkey army chief Hanuman always wears white, and his two right-hand men – Nilanol, the god of fire and Nilapat, the god of death – wear red and black respectively. In contrast, the demons have grim mouths, clamped shut or snarling out of usually green faces: Totsagan, king of the demons, wears a green face in battle and a gold one during peace, but always sports a two-tier headdress carved with two rows of faces.

Khon is performed regularly at Bangkok's *National* and *Chalermkrung Royal* theatres and nightly at various cultural shows staged by tourist restaurants in Bangkok, Chiang Mai and Pattaya. Even if you don't see a show you're bound to come across copies of the masks worn by the main *khon* characters, which are sold as sou- venirs all over the country and constitute an art form in their own right.

LAKHON

Serious and refined, **lakhon** is derived from *khon* but is used to dramatize a greater range of stories including Buddhist *Jataka* tales, local folk dramas and of course the *Ramayana*. The form you're most likely to come across is *lakhon chatri*, which is performed at shrines like Bangkok's Erawan and Lak Muang shrines as entertainment for the spirits and a token of gratitude from worshippers. Usually female, the *lakhon chatri* dancers perform as a group rather than as individ- ual characters, executing sequences which, like *khon* movements, all have minute and particular symbolism. They wear similarly decorative costumes but no masks, and dance to the music of a *phipat* orchestra. Unfortunately, as resident shrine troupes tend to repeat the same dances over and over, it's rarely the sublime display it's cracked up to be. Occasionally the *National*

Theatre features the more elegantly executed *lakhon nai*, a dance-form that used to be performed at the Thai court and often retells the *Ramayana*.

LIKAY

Likay is a much more popular derivative of *khon* – more light-hearted with lots of comic interludes, bawdy jokes and over-the-top acting and singing. Some *likay* troupes perform *Ramayana* excerpts, but a lot of them adapt pot-boiler romances or write their own. Depending on the show, costumes are either traditional as in *khon* and *lakhon*, modern and Western as in films, or a mixture of both. *Likay* troupes travel around the country doing shows on makeshift outdoor stages wherever they think they'll get an audience; temples sometimes hire them out for fairs and there's usually a *likay* stage of some kind at a festival. Performances are often free and generally last for about five hours, with the audience strolling in and out of the show, cheering and joking with the cast throughout. Televised *likay* dramas get huge audiences and always follow romantic plot-lines.

NANG

Nang or shadow plays are said to have been the earliest dramas performed in Thailand, but now are rarely seen except in the far south, where the Malaysian influence ensures an appreciative audience for *nang thalung* (see p.431). Crafted from buffalo hide, the two-dimensional *nang thalung* puppets play out scenes from popular dramas against a backlit screen, while the storyline is told through songs, chants and musical interludes. An even rarer *nang* form is the *nang yai*, which uses enormous cut-outs of whole scenes rather than just individual characters, so the play becomes something like an animated film.

FILM AND VIDEO

Fast-paced Chinese blockbusters dominate the Thai **movie** scene, serving up a low-grade cocktail of sex, spooks, violence and comedy. Not understanding the dialogue is rarely a drawback, as the storylines tend to be simple and the visuals more entertaining than the words. In the cities, Western films are also pretty big, and new releases often get subtitled rather than dubbed. All sizeable towns have a cinema or two and tickets generally start at around B40. Villagers have to make do with the travelling cinema, which sets up a mobile screen in wat compounds or other public spaces, and often entertains the whole village in one sitting.

Western **videos** come free with your evening meal in guest houses all over Thailand and dissuade many a traveller from venturing anywhere else of an evening. Even if you steer clear of them, you'll get back-to-back Chinese movies on long-distance air-conditioned buses and in some trains too.

THAI BOXING

Thai boxing (*muay Thai*) enjoys a following similar to football in Europe: every province has a stadium and whenever it's shown on TV you can be sure that large noisy crowds will gather round the sets in streetside restaurants and noodle shops. The best place to see Thai boxing is at one of Bangkok's two stadiums, which between them hold bouts every night of the week and on some afternoons as well.

There's a strong spiritual and **ritualistic** dimension to *muay Thai*, adding grace to an otherwise brutal sport. Each boxer enters the ring to the wailing music of a three-piece *phipat* orchestra, often flamboyantly attired in a lurid silk robe over the statutory red or blue boxer shorts. The fighter then bows, first in the direction of his birthplace and then to the north, south, east and west, honouring both his teachers and the spirit of the ring. Next he performs a slow dance, claiming the audience's attention and demonstrating his prowess as a performer.

Any part of the body except the head may be used as an **offensive weapon** in *muay Thai*, and all parts except the groin are fair targets. Kicks to the head are the blows which cause most knockouts. As the action hots up, so the orchestra speeds up its tempo and the betting in the audience becomes more frenetic. It can be a gruesome business, but it was far bloodier before modern boxing gloves were made compulsory in the 1930s – combatants used to wrap their fists with hemp impregnated with a face-lacerating dosage of ground glass.

TAKRAW

You're very unlikely to stumble unexpectedly on an outdoor bout of *muay Thai*, but you're sure to come across some form of **takraw** game at some point, whether in a public park, a wat compound or just in a backstreet alley. Played with a very light rattan ball (or one made of plastic to look like rattan), the basic aim of the game is to keep the ball off the ground. To do this you can use any part of your body except your hands, so a well-played *takraw* game looks extremely balletic, with players leaping and arching to get a good strike. There are at least five versions of competitive *takraw*, based on the same principles. The one featured in the Southeast Asian Games and most frequently in school tournaments is played over a volleyball net and involves two teams of three; the other most popular competitive version has a team ranged round a basketball net trying to score as many goals as possible within a limited time period before the next team replaces them and tries to outscore them. Other *takraw* games introduce more complex rules (like kicking the ball backwards with your heels through a ring made with your arms behind your back) and many assign points according to the skill displayed by individual players rather than per goal or dropped ball. Outside of school playing fields, proper *takraw* tournaments are rare, though they do sometimes feature as entertainment at Buddhist funerals.

MEDITATION CENTRES AND RETREATS

Of the hundreds of meditation temples in Thailand, a few cater specifically for foreigners by holding meditation sessions and retreats in English. The meditation taught is mostly Vipassana or "insight", which emphasizes the minute observation of internal physical sensation, and novices and practised meditators alike are welcome. To join a one- or two-hour session in Bangkok, call to check times and then just turn up; for overnight and longer visits to wats in more remote areas, you usually have to contact the monastery in advance, either directly or through the WFB (see below).

Longer retreats are for the serious-minded only. All the temples listed in the box below welcome both male and female English-speakers, but strict segregation of the sexes is enforced and many places observe a vow of silence. An average day at any one of these monasteries starts with a wake-up call at 4am and includes several hours of group meditation and chanting, as well as time put aside for chores and for personal reflection. All visitors are expected to keep the eight Buddhist precepts, however long their stay, the most restrictive of these being the abstention from food after midday and from alcohol, tobacco, drugs and sex at all times. Most wats ask for a minimal daily donation (B40–100) to cover accommodation and food costs. For more information and access details for particular temples, see the relevant sections in the *Guide*.

MEDITATION CENTRES AND RETREAT TEMPLES

House of Dhamma, 26/9 Soi Chumphon, Soi Lardprao 15, Bangkok (☎02/511 0439). Meditation instruction available in English from 9am to 6pm Monday to Friday (except Mon and Thurs afternoons); classes in English at 2pm on Sundays and regular one-day Sunday retreats. Buddhist library and small bookshop.

Wat Mahathat, Ratanakosin, Bangkok (☎02/222 6011). Meditation class in English in Section 5 of the temple, on the second and fourth Saturday of each month (4–6pm). Longer courses usually in Thai, but English instruction can be arranged.

The World Fellowship of Buddhists (WFB), 33 Sukhumvit Rd, between sois 1 and 3 (☎02/251 1188). The main information centre for advice on English-speaking retreats in Thailand. Holds meditation sessions in English on the first Sunday of every month.

Wat Khao Tham, Ban Tai, Ko Pha Ngan (no phone). Frequent ten-day retreats led by farang teachers.

Wat Ram Poeng, Canal Road, Chiang Mai (☎053/278620). Month-long courses held in English at the Northern Insight Meditation Centre.

Wat Suan Mokkh, Chaiya, Surat Thani (☎077/431552). Popular *anapanasati* meditation course held on first ten days of every month.

CULTURAL HINTS

Tourist literature has so successfully marketed Thailand as the "Land of Smiles" that a lot of farangs arrive in the country expecting to be forgiven any outrageous behaviour. This is just not the case: there are some things so universally sacred in Thailand that even a hint of disrespect will cause deep offence. TAT publishes a special leaflet on the subject, entitled *Do and Don't in Thailand* – be sure to read it before you travel.

THE MONARCHY

The worst thing you can possibly do is to bad-mouth the **royal family**. The monarchy might be a constitutional one, but almost every household displays a picture of King Bhumibol and Queen Sirikit in a prominent position, and respectful crowds amass whenever either of them makes a public appearance. When addressing or speaking about royalty, Thais use a special language full of deferentials, called *rajasap* (literally "royal language").

Aside from keeping any anti-monarchy sentiments to yourself, you should be prepared to stand when the **national anthem** is played at the beginning of every cinema programme, and to stop in your tracks if the town you are in plays the national anthem over its public address system – many small towns do this twice a day at 8am and again at 6pm. A less obvious point: as the king's head features on all Thai currency, you should never step on a coin or banknote, which is tantamount to kicking the king in the face.

RELIGION

Almost equally insensitive would be to disregard certain religious precepts. Buddhism plays an essential part in the lives of most Thais, and Buddhist monuments should be treated accordingly – which basically means wearing long trousers or knee-length skirts, covering your arms, and removing your shoes whenever you visit one.

All **Buddha images** are sacred, however small, however tacky, however ruined, and should never be used as a backdrop for a portrait photo, clambered over, placed in a position of inferiority, or treated in any manner that could be construed as disrespectful. In an attempt to prevent foreigners from committing any kind of transgression the government requires a special licence for all Buddha statues exported from the country.

Monks come only just beneath the monarchy in the social hierarchy, and they too are addressed and discussed in a special language. If there's a monk around, he'll always get a seat on the bus, usually the back one. Theoretically, monks are forbidden to have any close contact with **women**, which means, as a female, you musn't sit or stand next to a monk, or even brush against his robes; if it's essential to pass him something, put the object down so that he can then pick it up – never hand it over directly. **Nuns**, however, get treated like women rather than like monks.

THE BODY

The Western liberalism embraced by the Thai sex industry is very unrepresentative of the majority Thai attitude to the body. **Clothing** – or the lack of it – is what bothers Thais most about tourist behaviour. As mentioned above, you need to dress modestly when entering temples, but the same also applies to other important buildings and all public places. Stuffy and sweaty as it sounds, you should keep shorts and vests for the real tourist resorts, and be especially diligent about covering up and, for women, wearing bras in rural areas. Baring your flesh on beaches is very much a Western practice: when Thais go swimming they often do so fully clothed, and they find **topless and nude bathing** extremely unpalatable. It's not illegal, but it won't win you many friends.

According to ancient Hindu belief the head is the most sacred part of the **body** and the feet the most unclean. This belief, imported into Thailand, means that it's very rude to touch another person's head or to point your feet either at a human being or at a sacred image – when sitting on a temple floor, for example, you should tuck your legs beneath you rather than stretch them out towards the Buddha. These hierarchies also forbid people from wearing shoes (which are even more unclean than feet) inside temples and most private homes, and – by extension – Thais take offence when they see someone sitting on the "head", or prow, of a boat. On a more practical note, the **left hand** is used for washing after defecating, so Thais never use it to put food in their mouth, pass things or shake hands – as a farang though, you'll be assumed to have different customs, so left-handers shouldn't worry unduly.

SOCIAL CONVENTIONS

In fact, Thais very rarely shake hands anyway, using the **wai** to greet and say goodbye and to acknowledge respect, gratitude or apology. A prayer-like gesture made with raised hands, the *wai* changes according to the relative status of the two people involved: Thais can instantaneously assess which *wai* to use when, but as a farang your safest bet is to go for the "stranger's" *wai*, which requires that your hands be raised close to your chest and your fingertips placed just below your chin. If someone makes a *wai* at you, you should definitely *wai* back, but it's generally wise not to initiate.

Public displays of **physical affection** in Thailand are much more acceptable between friends of the same sex than between lovers, whether hetero- or homosexual. Holding hands and hugging is as common among male friends as with females, so if you're given fairly intimate caresses by a Thai acquaintance of the same sex, don't assume you're being propositioned.

Finally, there are three specifically Thai **concepts** you're bound to come across and which may help you to comprehend a sometimes *laissez-faire* attitude to delayed buses and other inconveniences. The first, **jai yen**, translates literally as "cool heart" and is something everyone tries to maintain – most Thais hate raised voices, visible irritation and confrontations of any kind. Related to this is the oft-quoted response to a difficulty, **mai pen rai** – "never mind", "no problem" or "it can't be helped" – the verbal equivalent of an open-handed shoulder shrug which has its base in the Buddhist notion of karma (see "Religion" in *Contexts*). And then there's **sanuk**, the wide-reaching philosophy of "fun", which, crass as it sounds, Thais do their best to inject into any situation, even work. Hence the crowds of inebriated Thais who congregate at waterfalls and other beauty spots on public holidays, and the national waterfight which takes place every April on streets right across Thailand.

OUTDOOR PURSUITS

The vast majority of travellers' itineraries take in a few days' trekking in the north and a stint snorkelling or diving off the beaches of the south. The big beach resorts of Pattaya, Ko Phuket and Ko Samui also offer dozens of other water sports, and for the well-prepared wildlife enthusiast Thailand offers plenty of national parks to explore. What follows is a guide to the essentials of the outdoor activities you might pursue in various parts of the country – except for the small-scale operations in Kanchanaburi and Mae Sot, trekking is concentrated in the north, so we've covered the practicalities of trekking in that chapter (see pp.212–221), while details of water sports at the major resorts are given in the sections on those towns.

SNORKELLING AND DIVING

Thailand has exceptionally rich marine fauna, and conditions for coral growth are ideal, with an average sea temperature of about 28°C and very clear waters, so snorkelling and diving are extremely rewarding. Each coast has at least one resort with a number of equipment-rental shops, diving schools and agencies which organize diving and snorkelling trips to outlying islands, usually at very reasonable prices in worldwide terms. You can dive all year round, too, as the coasts are subject to different monsoon seasons: the diving seasons are from November to April along the Andaman coast, from January to October on the Gulf coast, and all year round on the east coast.

Whether you're snorkelling or diving you should be aware of your effect on the fragile reef structures. The bottom line is that any human contact with the reefs damages them in some way, and that if you're really concerned about saving these delicate ecosystems you should forgo the pleasure of seeing them. Obviously few people are willing to do that, so the next best thing is to minimize your impact by not touching the reefs or asking your boatman to anchor in the middle of one. And don't buy coral souvenirs, as tourist demand only encourages local entrepreneurs to dynamite reefs.

As far as **snorkelling equipment** goes, the most important thing is that you buy or rent a mask that fits. To check the fit, hold the mask against your face, then breathe in and remove your hands – if it falls off, it'll leak water. If you're buying equipment, you should be able to kit yourself out with a mask, snorkel and fins for between B750–1000; few places rent fins, but a mask and snorkel set usually costs about B50 a day to rent, and if you're going on a snorkelling day trip they are often included in the price. When renting equipment you'll nearly always be required to pay a deposit of around B200.

Before you sign up for a **diving course** or expedition check that the diving centre has proof of membership of either **PADI** (Professional Association of Diving Instructors) or **NAUI** (National Association of Underwater Instructors) and ask other people who've done the course or expedition how they rate it. Ko Phuket and Ko Tao are the best places to learn, and dive centres at both offer a range of courses from beginner to advanced level, which all include equipment rental in the cost. The most popular are the one-day introductory or resort dive (a pep talk and escorted shallow dive fairly close to shore; from B1650), and the four- or five-day open-water course (qualifying certificate course with lessons and at least one dive a day; B5500–8000). Renting a full set of diving gear, including wet suit, from one of these dive centres costs about B600–700 a day. Insurance should be included in the price of courses and introductory dives; for qualified divers, it's available from most reputable outlets in Thailand for around B900.

NATIONAL PARKS

Over the last 35 years some 83 areas across Thailand have been singled out for conservation as **national parks**, with the dual aim of protecting the country's natural resources and creating educational and recreational facilities for the public, and these generally make the best places to observe wildlife. One of the best places for seeing larger animals is in **Khao Yai** (p.328), the most popular national park, some three hours northeast of Bangkok. If you join a night safari here, you could be rewarded with sightings of elephants, deer, civets, even tigers and leopards, while during the day you'll come across gibbons and hornbills at the very least. Bird-watchers consider the national-park mountains of **Doi Suthep** (p.241) and **Doi Inthanon** (p.258) – both close to Chiang Mai – primary observation spots. Many of southern Thailand's protected reserves are marine parks, incorporating anything from a single beach, such as the turtle-egg-laying grounds on Ko Phuket (see p.452), to an entire archipelago, such as **Ko Phi Phi** (p.474). See "Flora, Fauna and Environmental Issues" in *Contexts* for a fuller account of Thailand's wildlife.

Most parks charge an entrance fee (B5–25) and have limited public facilities such as a set of bungalows (see "Accommodation", above) and a few signposted walking trails. Not all of the parks are well served by public transport – some can take a day to reach from the nearest large town, via a route that entails several bus and songthaew changes and a final lengthy walk. This factor, combined with the expense and poor quality of most national park accommodation, means that if you're planning to do a serious tour of the parks you should consider bringing a tent (all parks allow you to pitch for about B10) and be prepared to rent your own transport.

All the national parks are administered by the Royal Forestry Department on Phaholyothin Road, Chatuchak District, Bangkok 10900 (☎02/579 0529), about forty minutes' bus ride north of Democracy Monument. To book national park bungalows in advance (advisable for weekends and public holidays) you need to pay up front.

GAY THAILAND

The most public aspect of Thailand's gay scene is the farang-oriented sex industry, which, with its tawdry floor shows and host services, bears a gruesome resemblance to the straight sex trade, and is similarly most active in Bangkok and Pattaya, with smaller zones operating in Phuket and Chiang Mai. Like their female counterparts in the hetero-sexual fleshpots, many of the boys working in the gay sex bars that dominate these districts are under age and a significant number of gay prostitutes are gay by economic necessity rather than by inclination. The result of this racket is that gay foreigners have acquired a predatory repu-tation in certain quarters: many genuine Thai gay bars and clubs are hostile to farang customers, some going so far as to post "no farangs" notices above their doors. Also, Thailand's gay scene is very heavily male: lesbians are poorly catered for and, unless otherwise specified, gay means male throughout this guide. As with the straight sex scene we've eschewed mentioning the most flagrant of the gay sex bars, so those listed in the *Guide* tend to be low-key meet-ing places for Thai and farang gay men.

For all the ill-will generated by the flesh industry, Thailand has a reputation for being open to homosexuality, exemplified by the fact that the age of consent is fifteen years old, the same as for heterosexuals. Although excessively physical displays of affection are frowned upon for both heterosexuals and homosexuals, Western gay couples should get no hassle about being seen together in public.The Thai tolerance extends to cross-dressers and you'll find trans-vestites doing ordinary jobs even in upcountry towns.

Possibly because of the overall lack of homo-phobia in the country, there's no **gay move-ment** to speak of in Thailand – the nearest equivalent to an organized gay political force is the *Fraternity for Aids Cessation in Thailand* (*FACT*), which runs Aids awareness campaigns, staffs a telephone counselling service (☎02/ 574 1100) and publishes a bilingual monthly newsletter. The recently opened *Utopia Café*, 116/1 Soi 23, Sukhumvit Rd (☎02/259 9619), with its shop, café, gallery and meeting rooms, looks set to become an important contact point. *Anjaree* is a small lesbian activists' group of around 150 members, which organizes bi-monthly meetings, newsletters and networking. Write to them at PO Box 322, Rajdamnoen, Bangkok 10200, and they will write back c/o Poste Restante, GPO, Bangkok – otherwise enclose postage for the reply.

DISABLED TRAVELLERS

Thailand makes few provisions for its disabled citizens and this obviously affects the disabled traveller. For example, wheelchair users will have a hard time negotiating the uneven pavements, which are high to allow for flooding and invariably lacking in dropped kerbs, and will find it difficult to board buses and trains. On the other hand, the country's top hotels are wising up to the need to provide decent facilities, and wherever you go there will always be people willing to help if necessary.

One way to cut down the hassle is to go with a **tour**: the extra money is often well spent if it guarantees adapted facilities throughout your stay and enables you to explore otherwise inaccessible sights. In the **UK**, both *Kuoni* and *BA Holidays* tour operators (see p.5 for addresses and phone numbers) are used to tailoring package deals to specific needs. For more general information on disabled travel abroad get in touch with the organizations listed in the box below; in Thailand, try Mr Narong Patibatsarakich, chairperson of the Council of Disabled People of Thailand (☎02/583 3031; fax 02/583 6518), who can provide limited infor-mation on the country's resources for the disabled.

For **independent travellers**, life is made a lot easier if you can afford to pay for more upmarket hotels (which should have lifts) and to shell out for taxis, the odd domestic flight and the occasional tour. Similarly, the more expensive international airlines tend to be the better equipped: *British Airways*, *Thai International* and *Qantas* all carry aisle wheelchairs and have at least one toilet adapted for disabled passengers.

CONTACTS FOR TRAVELLERS WITH DISABILITIES

UK

Holiday Care Service, 2 Old Bank Chambers, Station Rd, Horley, Surrey RH6 9HW (☎01293/774535).
Information on all aspects of travel.

Mobility International, 228 Borough High St, London SE1 (☎0171/403 5688). Information, access guides, tours and exchange programmes.

RADAR, 25 Mortimer St, London W1N (☎0171/637 5400). A good source of advice on holidays and travel abroad.

AUSTRALASIA

ACROD, PO Box 60, Curtain, ACT 2605 (☎06/682 4333).

Barrier Free Travel, 36 Wheatley St, N Bellingen, NSW 2454 (☎066/551733).

Disabled Persons Assembly, PO Box 10–138, The Terrace, Wellington (☎04/472 2626).

NORTH AMERICA

Directions Unlimited, 720 N Bedford Rd, Bedford Hills, NY 10507 (☎1-800/533-5343). Tour operator specializing in custom tours for people with disabilities.

Mobility International USA, PO Box 10767, Eugene, OR 97440 (Voice and TDD: ☎503/343-1284). Information and referral services, access guides, tours and exchange programmes. Annual membership $20 (includes quarterly newsletter).

Society for the Advancement of Travel for the Handicapped, 347 Fifth Ave, New York, NY 10016 (☎212/447-7284). Non-profit travel-industry referral service that passes queries on to its members as appropriate; allow plenty of time for a response.

Travel Information Service, Moss Rehabilitation Hospital, 1200 West Tabor Rd, Philadelphia, PA 19141 (☎215/456-9600). Telephone information and referral service.

Twin Peaks Press, Box 129, Vancouver, WA 98666; ☎206/694-2462 or 1-800/637-2256). Publisher of the *Directory of Travel Agencies for the Disabled*, listing more than 370 agencies worldwide; *Travel for the Disabled*; the *Directory of Accessible Van Rentals*, and *Wheelchair Vagabond*, loaded with personal tips.

TRAVELLING WITH KIDS

Travelling with kids can be both challenging and rewarding. Thais are very tolerant of childen so you can take them almost anywhere without restriction, and they always help break the ice with strangers.

The main problem with children, especially the very young, is their extra vulnerability. Even more than their parents, they need protecting from the sun, unsafe drinking water, heat and unfamiliar food. All that chilli in particular may be a problem, even with older kids, if they're not used to it. Remember too that diarrhoea, perhaps just a nuisance to you, could be dangerous for a child: rehydration solutions (see under "Health", p.22) are vital if your child goes down with it. Make sure too, if possible, that your child is aware of the dangers of rabies; keep children away from animals, and consider a rabies jab.

For babies, nappies (diapers) and places to change them can be a problem. For a short visit, you could bring disposable ones with you or buy them in large supermarkets in the main Thai towns; for longer, more out-of-the-way journeys, consider going over to washables. A changing mat is another necessity. If your baby is on powdered milk, it might be an idea to bring some of that: you can certainly get it in Thailand but it may not taste the same. Dried baby food, too, could be worth taking – mix it with hot (boiled) water that any hotel should be able to supply you with.

For touring, child-carrier backpacks such as the *Tommy Lightrider* are ideal, starting at around £30/$45, and can weigh less than 2kg. If the child is small enough, a fold-up buggy is also well worth packing.

DIRECTORY

Addresses Thai addresses can be immensely confusing, mainly because property is often numbered twice, firstly to show which real estate lot it stands in, and then to distinguish where it is on that lot. Thus 154/7–10 Rajdamnoen Rd means the building is on lot 154 and occupies numbers 7–10. There's an additional idiosyncrasy in the way Thai roads are sometimes named too: in large cities a minor road running off a major road is often numbered as a soi ("lane" or "alley", though it may be a sizeable thoroughfare), rather than be given its own street name. Sukhumvit Road for example – Bangkok's longest – has minor roads numbered Soi 1 to Soi 103, with odd numbers on one side of the road and even on the other; so a Sukhumvit Road address could read something like 27/9–11 Soi 15 Sukhumvit Rd, which would mean the property occupies numbers 9–11 on lot 27 on minor road number 15 running off Sukhumvit Road.

Contraceptives Condoms (known as *meechai*) are sold in all pharmacies and in many hairdressers and village shops as well. You can get the Pill from the British Dispensary, Sukhumvit Road, Bangkok, but it's advisable to bring a sufficient supply of your own brand with you.

Electricity Supplied at 220 volts AC and available at all but the most remote villages and basic beach huts.

Film The price of film in Thailand is comparable to that in the West, but developing is a lot less expensive and in the main tourist areas is done in a couple of hours, to about the same quality as you'd get in the West.

Laundry services Guest houses and hotels all over the country run low-cost same-day laundry services.

Left luggage Most major train stations have left-luggage facilities, enabling you to store your bags for up to twenty days; at bus stations you can usually persuade someone official to look after your stuff for a few hours. Many guest houses and hotels also offer an inexpensive and reliable service.

Tampons There's no need to haul boxloads of tampons into Thailand with you as you can stock up from department stores in every sizeable town and guest houses often sell them as well.

Women's groups The main political focus for Thai women is *Friends of Women* at 49 Phra Athit Rd, Bangkok (☎02/280 0429) which runs a counselling service and takes up women's rights issues, in particular fighting against the demeaning consequences of sex tourism. *More Women Travel* (Rough Guides, £9.99), an informative collection of women's independent-travel essays, includes accounts of experiences in Thailand and other Southeast Asian countries.

PART TWO

THE
GUIDE

BURMA

CHAPTER 3
THE NORTH

Chiang Mai

LAOS

Sukhothai

Udon Thani

CHAPTER 2
**THE
CENTRAL PLAINS**

CHAPTER 5
**THE NORTHEAST:
ISAAN**

Khorat

Ayutthaya

CHAPTER 1
BANGKOK

CHAPTER 4
**THE
EAST
COAST**

Pattaya

CAMBODIA

VIETNAM

*ANDAMAN
SEA*

CHAPTER 6
**SOUTHERN THAILAND:
THE GULF COAST**

Ko Samui

CHAPTER 7
**SOUTHERN THAILAND:
THE ANDAMAN COAST**

GULF OF THAILAND

Phuket

N

Hat
Yai

CHAPTER 8
THE DEEP SOUTH

0   250 km

MALAYSIA

CHAPTER ONE

BANGKOK

The headlong pace and flawed modernity of **Bangkok** match few people's
visions of the capital of exotic Siam. Spiked with high-rise buildings of
concrete and glass, it's a vast flatness which holds a population of nearly
eight million, and feels even bigger. But under the shadow of the
skyscrapers you'll find a heady mix of chaos and refinement, of frenetic markets
and hushed golden temples, of dispiriting, zombie-like sex shows and early-
morning almsgiving ceremonies. One way or another, the place will probably get
under your skin – and if you don't enjoy the challenge of slogging through jams
of buses and tuk-tuks, which fill the air with a chain-saw drone and clouds of
pollution, you can spend a couple of days on the most impressive temples and
museums, have a quick shopping spree and then strike out for the provinces.

Most budget travellers head for the **Banglamphu** district, where if you're not
careful you could end up watching videos all day long and selling your shoes
when you run out of money. It's far from having a monopoly on Bangkok accommodation, but it does have the advantage of being just a short walk from the
major sights in the **Ratanakosin** area: the dazzling ostentation of **Wat Phra**

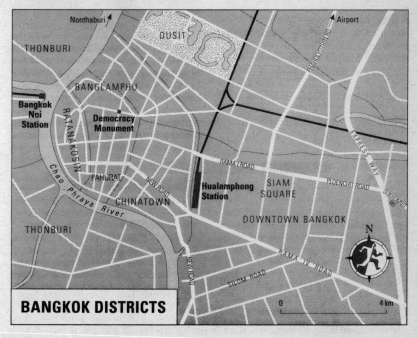

BANGKOK DISTRICTS

Kaeo, the grandiose decay of **Wat Po** and the **National Museum**'s hoard of exquisite works of art. Once those cultural essentials have been seen, you can choose from a whole bevy of lesser sights, including **Wat Benjamabophit** (the "Marble Temple"), especially at festival time, and **Jim Thompson's House**, a small, personal museum of Thai design.

For livelier scenes, explore the dark alleys of **Chinatown**'s bazaars or head for the water: the great **Chao Phraya River**, which breaks up and adds zest to the city's landscape, is the backbone of a network of **canals and floating markets** that remains fundamentally intact in the west-bank Thonburi district. Inevitably the waterways have earned Bangkok the title of "Venice of the East", a tag that seems all too apt when you're wading through flooded streets in the rainy season; indeed, the city is year by year subsiding into the marshy ground, literally sinking under the weight of its burgeoning concrete towers.

Shopping on dry land varies from ubiquitous touristic stalls selling silks, handicrafts and counterfeit watches and clothes, to completely and sometimes undesirably authentic marketplaces – notably Chatuchak, where caged animals cringe among the pots and pans. As you might expect, the city offers the country's most varied **entertainment**, ranging from traditional dancing and the orchestrated bedlam of Thai boxing, through to the sex bars of the notorious Patpong district, a tinseltown Babylon that's the tip of a dangerous iceberg. Even if the above doesn't appeal, you'll inevitably pass through Bangkok once, if not several times – not only is it Thailand's main port of entry, it's also the obvious place to sort out **onward travel**, with some of the world's best deals on international air tickets as well as a convenient menu of embassies for visas to neighbouring countries.

A little history

Bangkok is a relatively young capital, established in 1782 after the Burmese sacked Ayutthaya, the former capital. A temporary base was set up on the western bank of the Chao Phraya, in what is now **Thonburi**, before work started on the more defensible east bank, where the French had built a grand, but short-lived fort in the 1660s. The first king of the new dynasty, Rama I, built his palace at **Ratanakosin**, within a defensive ring of two (later expanded to three) canals, and this remains the city's spiritual heart.

Initially, the city was largely **amphibious**: only the temples and royal palaces were built on dry land, while ordinary residences floated on thick bamboo rafts

---

CITY OF ANGELS

When Rama I was crowned in 1782, he gave his new capital a grand 43-syllable name to match his ambitious plans for the building of the city. Since then 21 more syllables have been added. Krungthepmahanakhornbowornrattanakosinmahintarayutthaya-mahadilokpopnopparatratchathaniburiromudomratchaniwetmahasathanamornpim–anavatarnsathitsakkathattiyavisnukarprasit is Guinness-certified as the longest place name in the world and roughly translates as "Great city of angels, the supreme repository of divine jewels, the great land unconquerable, the grand and prominent realm, the royal and delightful capital city full of nine noble gems, the highest royal dwelling and grand palace, the divine shelter and living place of the reincarnated spirits". Fortunately, all Thais refer to the city simply as Krung Thep, though plenty can recite the full name at the drop of a hat. Bangkok – "Village of the Plum Olive" – was the name of the original village on the Thonburi side; with remarkable persistence, it has remained in use by foreigners since the time of the French garrison.

on the river and canals, and even shops and warehouses were moored to the river bank. A major shift in emphasis came in the second half of the last century, first under Rama IV (1851–68), who as part of his effort to restyle the capital along European lines built Bangkok's first roads, and then under Rama V (1868–1910), who constructed a new residential palace in Dusit, north of Ratanakosin, and laid out that area's grand boulevards.

Since World War II, and especially from the mid-1960s onwards, Bangkok has seen an explosion of **modernization**, which has blown away earlier attempts at orderly planning and left the city without an obvious centre. Most of the canals have been filled in, to be replaced by endless rows of cheap and functional concrete shophouses, sprawling over a built-up area of 330 square kilometres; these piles of drab boxes are now the capital's most prominent architectural feature. Most of the benefits of the **economic boom** since the 1980s have been concentrated in Bangkok, which has attracted mass migration from all over Thailand and made the capital ever more dominant: Bangkokians own four-fifths of the nation's automobiles and the population is now forty times that of the second city, Chiang Mai.

ARRIVAL AND ACCOMMODATION

Finding a place to stay in Bangkok is usually no problem: the city has a huge range of **accommodation**, from the murkiest backstreet bunk to the plushest five-star riverside suite, and you don't have to spend a lot to get a comfortable place. Getting to your guest house or hotel, however, is unlikely to put you in a good mood, for there can be few cities in the world where **transport** is such a headache. Bumper-to-bumper vehicles create fumes so bad that a recent spot check revealed forty percent of the city's traffic policemen to be in need of hospital treatment, and some days the city's carbon monoxide emissions come close to the international danger level. It's not unusual for residents to spend three hours getting to work – and these are people who know where they're going. Although two new mass-transit systems are planned for the metropolis (one underground and one overhead train network), these have been under discussion now for over thirty years, and continued squabbling between rival construction companies and the occasional successful intervention by environmentalists mean that an end to Bangkok's transport crisis is still far from imminent. Waterborne transport provides the least arduous means of hopping from one site to another, but visitors are best advised to have low expectations of how much can be done in a day, and to find accommodation in the areas where you want to spend most time.

Arriving in Bangkok

Unless you arrive in Bangkok by train, be prepared for a long slog into the centre. Most travellers' first sight of the city is the International Terminal at Don Muang airport, a slow 25km to the north. Even if you arrive by coach, you'll still have a lot of work to do to get into the centre.

By air

Once you're through immigration at **Don Muang Airport** – queues are often horrendous, owing to the availability of free short-stay visas on the spot – you'll find 24-hour exchange facilities, a TAT information desk (☎02/523 8972), a post office, a left-luggage depot (B20 per item per day for a maximum of 3 months), an emergency clinic and a variety of cafés. Note that you'll have problems checking in at some of the smaller, more budget-oriented guest houses after 10pm (night-watchmen aren't usually authorized to admit new arrivals), so if you're arriving after about 8pm either make straight for the backpackers' district of Banglamphu and hope to get lucky, or resign yourself to shelling out for a hotel room for your first night: a round-the-clock *Thai Hotels Association* **accommodation desk** can help with bookings.

The most economical way of getting into the city is by **bus**, but this can be excruciatingly slow and the invariably crowded vehicles are totally unsuitable for heavily laden travellers. The bus stop is on the main highway which runs north–south just outside the airport buildings: to find it, head straight out from the northern end of arrivals. Ordinary buses run all day and night, with a reduced service after 10pm; the slightly more expensive air-conditioned buses stop running around 8.30pm (see "City transport", p.65). The box opposite gives a rough sketch of the most useful routes – the TAT office in arrivals has further details.

Thai Airways also runs a **minibus** ("limousine") service to the *Asia Hotel* near Siam Square and the *Vieng Thai Hotel* in Banglamphu, which at B100 per person is good value; the minibuses will run to other hotels on request, but expect to pay up to half as much again.

The **train** to Hualamphong station is the quickest way into town. To reach the station at Don Muang follow the signs from arrivals to the *Airport Hotel* across the main highway, carry on through the hotel foyer and the station is in front of you. About twenty-five trains a day make the fifty-minute trip to Hualamphong for B5 third class, B10 second class and B18 first class (plus a surcharge on rapid and express trains), but they're concentrated around the early morning – after 7.30am you might have to wait over an hour. On weekdays there are two special, but illogically timed, airport shuttle trains a day, departing Don Muang at 7.40am and 7.20pm, for which you need to buy tickets at the *Thai Airways* limousine desk in arrivals.

Taxis to the centre are comfortable, air-conditioned and not too extravagantly priced, although the driving can be hairy. A wide variety is on offer, from a B350–400 *Thai Airways* limousine down to a B180 unlicensed cab – avoid the latter, as newly arrived travellers are seen as easy victims for robbery, and the cabs are untraceable. Licensed taxis are identifiable by their yellow and black numberplates: for the best service, head for the airport-regulated taxi desk at the south end of the arrivals concourse (after going through customs, walk through the barriers to your left). Here you can opt either for a pre-determined fare – B200 and up, depending on which side of town you're aiming for – or for a metered cab, which unless the traffic's exceptionally heavy is usually less expensive. That's not quite the end of the story: you'll also be expected to stump up B50 in tolls for the overhead expressways which the taxi-drivers will use to cut up to an hour off your journey.

Anyone with reservations at one of Bangkok's three plushest riverside hotels, the *Shangri-La*, the *Oriental* or the *Royal Orchid Sheraton*, can eschew the stresses of land-based transportation and take the luxurious airport **river-taxi**; this glides down the Chao Phraya River in about an hour, but its B700 seats must be reserved in advance along with your room.

If you're booked on a connecting **internal flight**, the domestic terminal at Don Muang is almost 1km away from the international terminal, soon to be connected by a covered walkway but currently accessed by a free, regular *Thai Airways* mini-bus shuttle. The **domestic departure tax** is B30. If you've got time to kill and money to spare between flights, the very upmarket *Amari Airport Hotel* (☎02/566 1020), just across the road from the international terminal, has **rooms** available for three-hour periods (8am–6pm; ⑥) as well as for overnight stays (⑨).

Finally, you can spare yourself the trip into Bangkok if you're planning to head straight to **the north or northeast** by train or bus: all trains to these parts of the country stop at Don Muang train station, and all the city buses which pass the airport (except #4 and #69) also pass the Northern Bus Terminal on Phaholyothin Road. *Thai Airways* also runs an air-conditioned bus from the airport direct to **Pattaya** three times a day for B180 per person.

By train and bus

Travelling to Bangkok by **train** from Malaysia and most parts of Thailand, you arrive at **Hualamphong Station**, which is centrally located and served by numerous city buses – the most useful being bus #53, which stops on the east side (left-hand exit) of the station and runs to the budget accommodation in Banglamphu. The station is also well placed for **longtail boats** to the area, with a stop outside the *Sri Krung Hotel* just 30m to the right of the main station

USEFUL BUS ROUTES

#3 (air-con): Northern Bus Terminal–Sri Ayutthaya Road (for National Library and guest houses)–Democracy Monument (for Banglamphu guest houses)–Sanam Luang.

#4 (air-con): Airport–Rajaprarop Road–Silom Road.

#7 (air-con): Southern Bus Terminal–Sanam Luang (for Banglamphu guest houses)–Chinatown–Rama IV Road–Sukhumvit Road.

#8 (air-con): Eastern Bus Terminal–Sukhumvit Road–Siam Square–Grand Palace–Wat Po.

#9 (air-con): Northern Bus Terminal–Democracy Monument (for Banglamphu guest houses)–Thonburi.

#10 (air-con): Airport–Northern Bus Terminal–Rajwithi Road (for National Library and guest houses)–Thonburi.

#11 (air-con): Eastern Bus Terminal–Sanam Luang (for Banglamphu guest houses)–Southern Bus Terminal.

#13 (air-con): Airport–Northern Bus Terminal–Rajaprarop Road–Sukhumvit Road–Eastern Bus Terminal.

#15 (ordinary) Phra Athit Road–Siam Square–Rajdamri Road–Silom Road–New Road–Krungthep Bridge.

#29 (air-con and ordinary): Airport–Northern Bus Terminal–Siam Square–Hualamphong Station.

#38 (ordinary): Northern Bus Terminal–Rajaprarop Road–Eastern Bus Terminal.

#39 (air-con): Airport–Northern Bus Terminal–Democracy Monument (for Khao San Road guest houses)– Sanam Luang.

#53 (ordinary): Hualamphong Station–Samsen Road and Phra Athit Road (for Banglamphu guest houses).

#59 (ordinary): Airport–Northern Bus Terminal–Sanam Luang (for Banglamphu guest houses).

#124 and #127 (ordinary): Southern Bus Terminal–Tha Pinklao (for ferry to Phra Athit and Banglamphu guest houses).

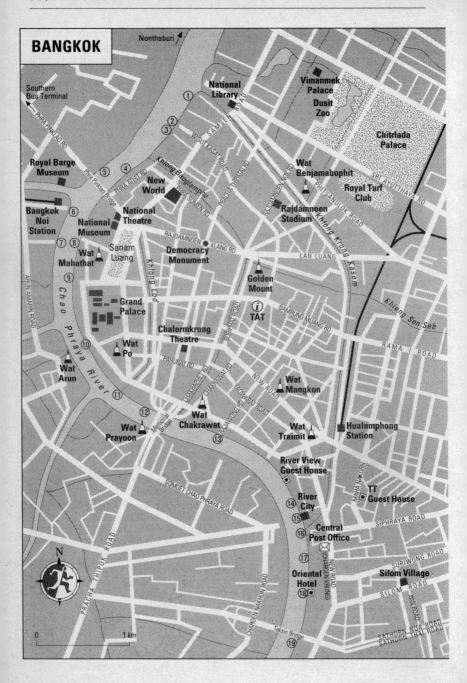

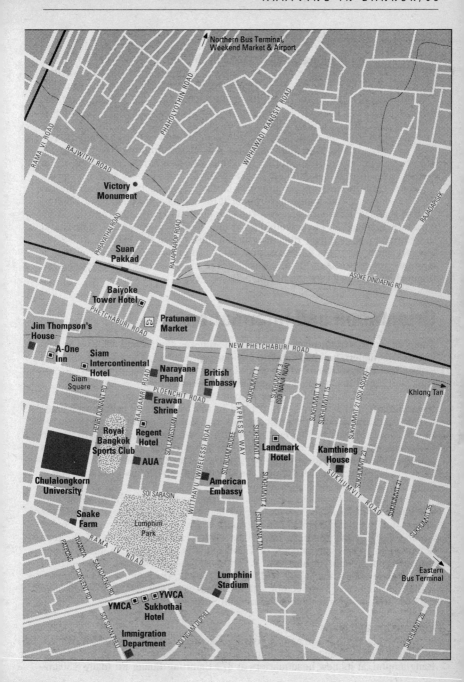

entrance – the regular service will take you to the bridge in front of Banglamphu's *New World* department store. Station facilities include a free **accommodation-booking service** offered by the State Railway's *PC & C* travel agent (daily 5am–8pm) in Room 100, close by the newspaper stands – worth a try if you can't face looking for a vacant hotel or guest-house room yourself. The **left-luggage** office (daily 4am–10.30pm) charges a hefty B30 per item per day and will keep baggage for several months at a time; a more economical alternative is the *TT Guest House* (see "Accommodation", p.72), about ten minutes' walk from the station, which provides the same service for only B5 per item per day. Trains from Kanchanaburi pull in at **Bangkok Noi Station** in Thonburi, which is on the express-boat line (see over), just across the Chao Phraya River from Banglamphu and Ratanakosin.

Buses come to a halt at a number of far-flung spots: services from Malaysia and the south use the Southern Terminal at the junction of Pinklao and Nakhon Chaisri roads in Thonburi; services from the north and northeast come in at the Northern Terminal on Phaholyothin Road (due for a temporary move soon round the corner to Kamphaeng Phet Road); and buses from the east coast use the Eastern Terminal at Soi 40, Sukhumvit Road. All of these will leave you with a long bus, tuk-tuk or taxi ride into town; for the main city bus routes serving the regional bus terminals see the box on p.61.

Orientation and information

Bangkok can be a tricky place to get your bearings as it's vast and flat, with largely featureless modern buildings and no obvious centre. The boldest line on the map is the **Chao Phraya River**, which divides the city into Bangkok proper on the east bank, and **Thonburi**, recently incorporated into Greater Bangkok, on the west.

The historical core of Bangkok proper, site of the original royal palace, is **Ratanakosin**, which nestles into a bend in the river. Three concentric canals radiate eastwards around Ratanakosin: the southern part of the area between the canals is the old-style trading enclave of **Chinatown** and Indian **Pahurat**, linked to the old palace by New Road; the northern part is characterized by old temples and the **Democracy Monument**. Beyond the canals to the north, **Dusit** is the site of many government buildings and the nineteenth-century palace, which is linked to Ratanakosin by Rajdamnoen Road.

"New" Bangkok begins to the east of the canals and beyond the main rail line, and stretches as far as the eye can see to the east and north. The main business district and most of the embassies are south of **Rama IV Road**, with the port of Khlong Toey at the southern edge. The diverse area north of Rama IV Road includes the sprawling campus of Chulalongkorn University, huge shopping centres around **Siam Square** and a variety of other businesses. Due north of Siam Square stands the tallest building in Bangkok, the *Baiyoke Tower Hotel* – with its distinctive rainbow colour scheme it makes a good point of reference. To the east lies the swish residential quarter off **Sukhumvit Road**.

Information and maps
As well as the booth in the airport arrivals concourse, the **Tourism Authority of Thailand (TAT)** maintains an information office within walking distance of Banglamphu, at its new headquarters at 372 Bamrung Ruang Rd (daily 8.30am–

4.30pm; ☎02/226 0075). This has plenty of handouts about Bangkok and the provinces, as well as a guide to TAT-approved shops. Other useful sources of information, especially about what to avoid, are the travellers' **bulletin boards** in many of the Banglamphu guest houses.

If you're staying in Bangkok for more than a couple of days and want to get the most out of the city, it's worth getting hold of *Metro*, a monthly **listings magazine** available in bookstores and hotel shops. For B80, you get coverage very similar to London's *Time Out*, including a mixed bag of cultural articles and especially useful sections on nightlife and gay life. If you don't wish to fork out for this, *Guide of Bangkok* is a free monthly entertainments **newspaper** which covers some of the same ground. The two English-language dailies, the *Nation* and the *Bangkok Post*, also give limited information about what's on across the city.

To get around Bangkok without spending much money, you'll need to buy a colour **bus map**: two similar versions, produced by rival map companies, are widely available in Bangkok, showing ordinary and air-conditioned routes, as well as the names of dozens of streets and *soi*s (side roads). Each costs around B35, although the price is hiked up at the train stations and various other places where you need it most. Serious shoppers might also want to buy a copy of **Nancy Chandler's** idiosyncratic map of Bangkok, available for B70 in most tourist areas.

City transport

The main form of transport in the city are **buses**, and once you've mastered the labyrinthine complexity of the route map you'll be able to get to any part of the city, albeit slowly. Catching the various kinds of **taxi** can make a serious dent in your budget, and you'll still get held up by the daytime traffic jams. **Boats** are obviously more limited in their range, but they're regular and as inexpensive as buses, and you'll save a lot of time by using them whenever possible – a journey between Banglamphu and the GPO, for instance, will take around thirty minutes by water, half what it would take on land. **Walking** might often be quicker than travelling by road, but the heat can be unbearable, distances are always further than they look on the map and the engine fumes are stifling.

Buses

Bangkok has three types of bus service, and it's not uncommon for one route to be served by the full trio. On the **ordinary** (non-air-conditioned) buses, fares depend on the colour of the bus rather than the distance travelled: a ride on an old blue bus or a smaller green one costs a flat fee of B2.50, while the red buses charge B3.50; however, all ordinary buses charge B5 after 10pm, regardless of colour or distance. The minimum fare on the blue, advertisement-carrying **air-conditioned** buses is B6; after the first 8km the fare rises in B2 stages to a maximum of B18, reflecting the distance travelled. As buses can only go as fast as the car in front, which at the moment is averaging 4kph, you'll probably be spending a long time on each journey, so you'd be well advised to pay the extra for cool air – and the air-conditioned buses are usually less crowded, too. Air-conditioned services stop at around 8.30pm, but most ordinary routes have a reduced service throughout the night. It's recently also become possible to travel certain routes on flashy, air-conditioned **microbuses**, which were designed with the commuter in mind and offer the use of an on-board fax, telephone and newspapers, plus the certainty of a seat (no standing allowed) for a flat B15 fare (exact money only), which is dropped into a box beside the driver's seat.

Boats

Bangkok was built as an amphibious city around a network of canals – or *khlongs* – and the first streets were constructed only in the second half of the last century. Although most of the canals have been turned into roads on the Bangkok side, the Chao Phraya River is still a major transport route for residents and non-residents alike, forming more of a link than a barrier between the two halves of the city, and used by several different kinds of boat.

EXPRESS BOATS

Two rival companies operate **express-boat** (*reua duan*) services, using large, numbered water buses to plough up and down the river.

The **Chao Phraya Express** is the longer-established service and probably the more useful for tourists, its clearly signed piers (*tha*) appearing on all Bangkok maps. Its usual route, ninety minutes in total, runs between Krung Thep Bridge in the south and Nonthaburi in the north, although some boats continue upriver as far as Pakkred (see p.115), adding an extra half-hour. They set off every ten to fifteen minutes or so from 6am to 6pm (that is, the first and last boats leave their termini at these times, with the last boat in each direction flying a blue flag).

Boats do not necessarily stop at every landing – they'll only pull in if people want to get on or off. During rush hours, certain boats fly either a **red** or a **green flag** (it is the latter that travel on to Pakkred) to indicate a limited-stop service: a correspondingly coloured flag is painted on the pier signboard to show which service stops there. The important central *Chao Phraya Express* stops are outlined in the box below and marked on our city map (see pp.62–3).

CENTRAL STOPS FOR THE CHAO PHRAYA EXPRESS BOAT

1 Thewes – for National Library and guest houses.

2 Wisut Kasat – for Samsen Road guest houses.

3 Wat Sam Phraya.

4 Phra Athit – for Khao San Road and Banglamphu guest houses.

5 Pinklao – for Thonburi shops and city buses to the Southern Bus Terminal.

6 Bangkok Noi – for trains to Kanchanaburi.

7 Prannok – for Siriraj Hospital.

8 Maharat – for Wat Mahathat.

9 Chang – for the Grand Palace.

10 Thien – for Wat Po, and the cross-river ferry to Wat Arun.

11 Ratchini (shared by *Laemthong* boats) – for Pak Khlong Talad market.

12 Saphan Phut (Memorial Bridge) – for Pahurat (and Wat Prayoon in Thonburi).

13 Rajavongse (Rajawong; shared by *Laemthong* boats) – for Chinatown.

14 Harbour Department.

15 River City shopping complex.

16 Si Phraya.

17 Wat Muang Kae – for GPO.

18 Oriental – for Silom Road.

19 Sathorn (shared by *Laemthong* boats) – for Sathorn Road.

(Numbers correspond to those on the map on pp.62–3)

The **Laemthong Express** boats, meanwhile, travel a slightly more extended route, from Pakkred to Krung Thep Bridge, and run from 6am to 7.30pm (departure times are from the termini), with the last boat in each direction flying a gold flag. Only a few piers serve both sets of boats; *Laemthong* landings are usually close to those of the competition but don't serve either Tha Thewes (for National Library and guest houses) or Tha Chang (for the Grand Palace).

Tickets for both services can be bought either at the pier or on board, and cost B4, B6 or B8 according to distance travelled. Some *Laemthong* boats offer seats in an air-conditioned cabin for a B5 supplement, while the additional Nonthaburi-to-Pakkred leg offered on *Chao Phraya* green-flag boats incurs a B7 supplement, and there's a B1 surcharge on all its red-flag services. Don't discard your ticket until you're off the boat, as the staff at some piers (such as *Chao Phraya*'s Phra Athit and Oriental) impose a B1 fine on anyone disembarking without one.

CROSS-RIVER FERRIES

Smaller than express boats are the slow **cross-river ferries** (*reua kham fak*), which shuttle back and forth between the same two points. They can be found at every express stop and plenty of other piers in between and are especially useful for connections to red- or green-flag stops during rush hours. Fares are 50 satang or B1, which you usually pay at the entrance to the pier.

LONGTAIL BOATS

Longtail boats (*reua hang yao*) ply the khlongs of Thonburi like buses, stopping at designated shelters (fares are in line with those of express boats), and are also available for individual rental here and on the river (see p.99). On the Bangkok side, Khlong Sen Seb has been opened up to longtails, which run from the Phanfa pier at the Golden Mount (handy for Banglamphu, Ratanakosin and Chinatown), and head due east to Khlong Tan, with useful stops at Phrayathai Road, Pratunam, Witthayu (Wireless) Road and Soi Nana Nua (Soi 3) off Sukhumvit Road. This is your quickest and most interesting way of getting across town, if you can stand the stench of the canal. State your destination to the conductor when he collects your fare, which will be B5 or just over. Another longtail service travels along Khlong Krung Kasem between Hualamphong train station and Tha Thewes, with some boats veering off up the Khlong Banglamphu to deposit passengers in front of *New World* department store.

Taxis

Bangkok **taxis** come in three forms, and are so plentiful that you rarely have to wait more than a couple of minutes before spotting an empty one of any description. Neither tuk-tuks nor motorbike taxis have meters so you should agree on a price before setting off, and expect to do a fair amount of haggling. Rates for all rise after midnight, and during rush hours when each journey takes far longer.

The most sedate option, Bangkok's metered, air-conditioned **taxi cabs** are also the most expensive, but well worth the extra in the heat of the day. Fares start at B35, increasing in B2 stages on a combined time/distance formula. However, this relatively new phenomenon of metering cabs is still having teething problems, largely because the drivers feel that cab-leasing fees are too high compared to the fare scale they are obliged to implement. The result is that they will often refuse long, slow, less-profitable journeys across town (especially in the middle of the afternoon, when many cabs have to return to the depot for a change of drivers), and will sometimes engage in the kind of meter-fiddling that's found in big cities across the world. If a string of metered-cab drivers don't like the sound of your destination, you'll have to try to negotiate a flat fare with one of them, or with an unmetered-cab driver, in which case avoid unlicensed cabs (white and black plates): they're no more expensive than licensed ones (yellow and black plates) and tend to be less reputable – you've got no comeback in the event of an accident – although outright rip-offs are confined mainly to the airport run.

Slightly less stable but typically Thai, **tuk-tuks** can carry three passengers comfortably and are the standard way of making shortish journeys (Banglamphu to Patpong should cost around B50). These noisy, three-wheeled, open-sided buggies fully expose you to the worst of Bangkok's pollution, but are the least frustrating type of city transport – they are a lot nippier than taxi cabs, and the drivers have no qualms about taking semi-legal measures to avoid gridlocks. Be aware, however, that tuk-tuk drivers tend to speak less English than taxi drivers – and there have been cases of robberies and attacks on women passengers late at night.

Least costly (a short trip, say from Banglamphu to Wat Po, should cost B20) and quickest of the trio are **motorbike taxis**, though these are rarely used by tourists as they carry only one passenger and are too dangerous to recommend for cross-city journeys on Bangkok's hectic roads. Even the locals use them sparingly. Still, if you've got nerves of steel, pick the riders out by their numbered, coloured vests or find their taxi rank, often at the entrance to a long soi. Crash helmets are now compulsory on all main thoroughfares in the capital and passengers should insist on wearing one (traffic police fine non-wearers on the spot), though the local press has reported complaints from people who've caught head-lice this way.

Transport rental

Renting a car is possible in Bangkok (see p.133), but is best kept for out-of-town trips – city traffic jams are just too much to cope with, and parking is impossible. As there are some novel rules of the road, it would be better to get a car with driver from a travel agent or hotel for about B1000 a day. If you really want to take your life into your hands, *Chusak Yont* at 1400 New Phetchaburi Rd (☎02/251 9225) rents out **motorbikes** from B300 per day – much more than you'll pay in most other parts of the country. **Bicycles** are rarely available for rent.

Accommodation

For double rooms under B400 your widest choice lies with the **guest houses** of Banglamphu and the smaller, dingier travellers' ghetto that has grown up around Soi Ngam Duphli, off the south side of Rama IV Road. Bangkok guest houses are tailored to the independent traveller's needs and often have genuine single rooms with prices to match, a rarity elsewhere; many also have left-luggage rooms, available at minimal cost. The most inexpensive rooms here are no-frills crash pads: small and usually windowless with thin walls and shared bathrooms. Bookings of any kind are rarely accepted by guest houses, but it's often useful to telephone just to establish whether a place is full already – note that during peak season (roughly Nov–Feb) you may have difficulty getting a room after noon.

Moderate and expensive lodgings are mainly concentrated downtown around Siam Square and in the area between Rama IV Road and New Road, along Sukhumvit Road, where the eastern suburbs start, and to a lesser extent in

ACCOMMODATION PRICES

Throughout this guide, guest houses, hotels and bungalows have been categorized according to the price codes given below. These categories represent the minimum you can expect to pay in the high season (roughly Nov–Feb & July–Aug) for a double room – or, in the case of national park bungalows, for a multi-berth room which can be rented for a standard price by an individual or group. If travelling on your own, expect to pay anything between sixty and one hundred percent of the rates quoted for a double room. Wherever a range of prices is indicated, this means that the establishment offers rooms with varying facilities – as explained in the write-up. Wherever an establishment also offers dormitory beds, the prices of these beds are given in the text, instead of being indicated by price code.

Remember that the top-whack hotels will add seven percent tax and a ten-percent service charge to your bill – the price codes below are based on net rates after taxes have been added.

① under B100   ④ B250–400   ⑦ B1000–1500
② B100–150   ⑤ B400–600   ⑧ B1500–3000
③ B150–250   ⑥ B600–1000   ⑨ B3000+

Chinatown. Air-conditioned rooms with hot-water bathrooms can be had for as little as B400, but for that you're looking at a rather basic cubicle; you'll probably have to pay more like B1000 for a place with room to breathe, smart furnishings and a swimming pool.

For **long-stay accommodation**, your most economical option is usually a room with a bathroom in an apartment building, generally advertised at around B4000 a month (with possible extra charges for hot water and TV). Good places to look include the areas around Victory Monument and Pratunam, especially the apartment buildings which line Soi Boonprarop, off Rajprarop Road just north of Pratunam. Apartment vacancies are also sometimes advertised on the bulletin boards in the AUA Language Centre on Rajdamri Road.

Banglamphu

Banglamphu, Bangkok's most inexpensive and popular accommodation centre, is within easy reach of the Grand Palace and other major sights in Ratanakosin, and all the guest houses listed lie only a few minutes' walk from one of three *Chao Phraya Express* boat stops (see the box on p.66), while public longtails also ply the three khlongs in the area. Banglamphu's main disappointment is the narrow range of evening activities it offers: entertainment options are almost entirely restricted to guest-house restaurants and their nightly video shows.

At the heart of Banglamphu is the legendary **Khao San Road** – almost a caricature of a traveller's centre, crammed with guest houses, dodgy travel agents and restaurants serving yoghurt shakes and muesli, the sidewalks lined with ethnic clothes stalls, racks of bootleg tapes, tattooists and hair-braiders. It's colourful, noisy and a good place to meet other travellers, but if you want the benefits of Khao San Road without the bustle, try the smaller, quieter roads off and around it: **Soi Chana Songkhram**, which encircles the wat of the same name; **Phra Athit**, running parallel to the Chao Phraya River and location of the most useful express-boat stop, and its continuation, **Phra Sumen**; or the residen-

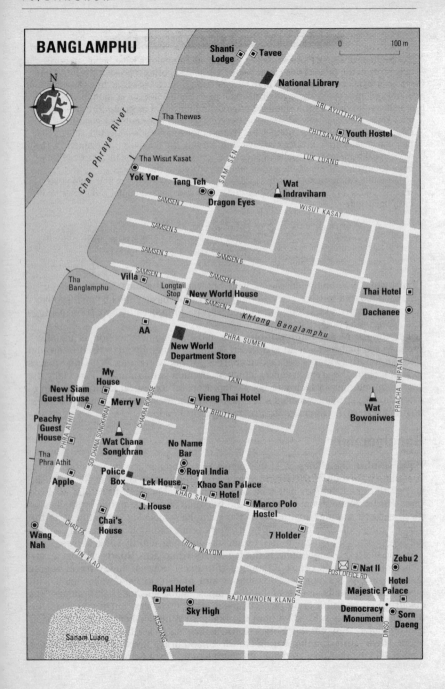

BANGLAMPHU

N

0   100 m

Shanti Lodge
Tavee
National Library
SRI AYUTTHAYA
PHITSANULOK
Youth Hostel
LUK LUANG
Tha Thewes
Chao Phraya River
SAM SEN
Tha Wisut Kasat
Yok Yor
Tang Teh
Dragon Eyes
Wat Indraviharn
WISUT KASAT
SAMSEN 7
SAMSEN 5
SAMSEN 3
SAMSEN 6
SAMSEN 1
Villa
SAMSEN 4
Tha Banglamphu
Longtail Stop
New World House
SAMSEN 2
Thai Hotel
Dachanee
Khlong Banglamphu
AA
PHRA SUMEN
New World Department Store
PRACHA THIPATAI
TANI
My House
Vieng Thai Hotel
New Siam Guest House
Merry V
RAM BHUTTRI
Wat Bowoniwes
Peachy Guest House
PHRA ATHIT
SOI CHANA SONGKHRAN
CHAKRA BONGSE
Wat Chana Songkhran
No Name Bar
Tha Phra Athit
Royal India
Apple
Police Box
Lek House
Khao San Palace Hotel
KHAO SAN
J. House
Marco Polo Hostel
Chai's House
CHAD FA
7 Holder
Wang Nah
PIN KLAO
TROK MAYOM
Nat II
Zebu 2
POST OFFICE RD
TANAO
Hotel Majestic Palace
Royal Hotel
RAJDAMNOEN KLANG
ATSADANG
Sky High
Democracy Monument
DINSO
Sorn Daeng
Sanam Luang

tial alleyways that parallel Khao San Road to the south, **Trok Mayom** and the **post office soi**. About ten minutes' walk north from Khao San Road, the **Samsen Road sois** offer a more authentically Thai atmosphere, while a further fifteen minutes' walk in the same direction will take you to **Sri Ayutthaya Road**, behind the National Library (about a 7-min walk from the Thewes express-boat stop), the newest and best-value area in Banglamphu, where rooms are larger and guest houses smaller. We've listed only the cream of what's on offer in each small area in Banglamphu: if your first choice is full there'll almost certainly be a vacancy somewhere just along the soi, if not right next door.

Banglamphu has only a few **upmarket** hotels and most of these don't live up to their price range.

Inexpensive

AA Guest House, 84–86 Phra Sumen Rd (☎02/282 9631). More like a hotel than a guest house in size (200 rooms) and facilities, this is a good place to try if everywhere else is fully booked. Air-con and shower feature at the upper end of the price bracket. ③–④.

Apple Guest House, 10/1 Phra Athit (☎02/281 6838). One of the few remaining guest houses in the capital where you actually live in a Thai family home: personal and friendly atmosphere, though rooms are small and a bit grotty. If full, try the almost identical *Apple 2* (☎02/281 1219), further north up Phra Athit Road at 11 Soi Khai Chae. Both also have B40 dorm beds. ①.

Bangkok Youth Hostel, 25/2 Phitsanulok Rd (☎02/282 0950). Mostly patronized by travelling Thai students: only open to YHA members and not really worth the money. The double rooms are equipped with bathroooms, and there are dorm beds for B50. ③.

Chai's House, 49/4–8 Soi Rongmai, between Soi Chana Songkhram and Chao Fa Road (☎02/281 4901). Large, clean, simple rooms, but a bit pricey; very good restaurant, popular with government workers. ③.

J House, 1 Trok Mayom (☎02/281 2949). Simple rooms in a traditional wooden house, located amongst real Thai homes (very unusual for Banglamphu). ②.

Lek House, 125 Khao San Rd (☎02/282 4927). Classic Khao San Road guest house: old-style with small, basic rooms, but less shabby than many others in the same price bracket. ②.

Marco Polo Hostel, 108/7–10 Khao San Rd (☎02/281 1715). Good-value rooms with air-con and shower in the heart of the ghetto, but not all have a window; the least expensive rooms of their kind in the area. ③.

Merry V, 35 Soi Chana Songkhram (☎02/282 9267). Large, efficiently run and scrupulously clean guest house, with slightly cramped, basic rooms. ②.

My House, 37 Soi Chana Songkhram (☎02/282 9263). Ethnic furnishings, bamboo walls and good food make this a popular place despite its somewhat spartan rooms. ②.

Nat II, Post Office Road. Large, clean rooms in fairly quiet location. ②.

New Siam Guest House, 21 Soi Chana Songkhram (☎02/282 4554). Comfortably kitted out, modern and well-maintained hotel-style rooms; all with fans and windows, the more expensive with hot-water showers, air-con and towels. A definite notch above the typical Banglamphu guest house. ③–⑤.

Peachy Guest House, 10 Phra Athit Rd (☎02/281 6471). Somewhat sporadic management – the office is frequently unstaffed, for instance – but clean if spartan air-con and fan-cooled rooms and a pleasant garden with bar. Popular with long-stay guests. Try to negotiate a room away from the second-floor communal area, as the TV can attract a noisy crowd of late-night viewers. ②–④.

7 Holder Guest House, 216/2–3 Khao San Rd (☎02/281 3682). Clean and modern, but its simple rooms are a little overpriced. ③.

Shanti Lodge, Soi 16, Sri Ayutthaya Rd (☎02/281 2497). Quiet, attractively furnished and comfortable rooms make this the most popular haven in the National Library area. Vegetarian restaurant. ③.

Tavee Guest House, Soi 14, Sri Ayutthaya Rd (☎02/282 5983). Good-sized rooms; quiet and friendly and the most inexpensive place in the National Library quarter. ③.

Villa, Samsen 1 (☎02/281 7009). Bangkok's most therapeutic guest house: a lovely old Thai house and garden with just 10 large rooms. Fills up quickly, but worth going on the waiting list if you're staying a long time. ③.

Moderate and expensive

Hotel Majestic Palace, 97 Rajdamnoen Klang Rd (☎02/280 5610). The best hotel in the area with fairly good facilities and a swimming pool; near Democracy Monument. ⑧.

Khao San Palace Hotel, 139 Khao San Rd (☎02/282 0578). One of several recently renovated, clean and well-appointed smallish hotels in Banglamphu: all rooms have attached bathrooms, those at the top of the range have air-con. ④–⑤.

New World House, Samsen 2 (☎02/281 5605). Good-value, large, unadorned rooms with desks, shower and air-con; popular with long-stayers as it offers one free night in every 10, but a bit soulless. ④.

Royal Hotel, 2 Rajdamnoen Klang Rd (☎02/222 9111). Most ideally located hotel in this price bracket: only a 5-min stroll across the khlong (and a couple of hectic main roads) to Sanam Luang and a further 10-min or so to the Grand Palace. Perfectly adequate facilities though not exactly plush for the price. ⑦–⑧.

Thai Hotel, 78 Pracha Thipatai Rd (☎02/282 2831). Comfortable enough, but a little overpriced, considering its slightly inconvenient location. ⑦.

Vieng Thai Hotel, Ram Bhuttri Road (☎02/280 5392). Upmarket in a faded kind of way and the only place in the immediate vicinity of Khao San Road to have a swimming pool on the premises, but a bit pricey for its age. ⑦.

Chinatown and Hualamphong Station area

Not far from the Ratanakosin sights, **Chinatown (Sampeng)** is one of the most vibrant and quintessentially Asian parts of Bangkok. Staying here, or in one of the sois around the conveniently close **Hualamphong Station**, can be noisy, but there's always plenty to look at. A couple of guest houses and a small range of moderate and expensive hotels jostle amongst a cluster of seedier places catering mainly to Thais.

Bangkok Center, 328 Rama IV Rd (☎02/238 4848). Handily placed upmarket option just across the road from the train station. ⑧–⑨.

FF Guest House, 338/10 Trok La-O, off Rama IV Road (☎02/233 4168). The closest budget accommodation to the station, but pretty basic. To get there from the station, cross Rama IV Road and walk left for 200m, and then right down Trok La-O to the end of the alley. ②.

New Empire Hotel, 572 Yaowarat Rd (☎02/234 6990). Medium-sized hotel right in the thick of the Chinatown bustle, offering average rooms with shower, air-con and use of swimming pool. ⑤.

Sri Krung Hotel, 1860 Krung Kasem Rd (☎02/225 0132). Excellent-value mid-range Chinese hotel just 50m across the khlong from the station. Rooms are spacious and all have air-con and TV. ⑤.

TT Guest House (also sometimes known as *TT2*), 516 Soi Sawang, off Maha Nakorn Road (☎02/236 2946). The best budget place in the station area, though slightly more expensive than *FF*. Clean and well run with good bulletin boards and traveller-oriented facilities, including left luggage at B5 a day. To get there from the station, cross Rama IV Road, then walk left for 250m, right down Maha Nakorn Road and left again down Soi Sawang, following the signs for *TT*. About 10-min walk from either the station or the Si Phraya express-boat stop. ③.

White Orchid Hotel, 409–421 Yaowarat Rd (☎02/226 0026). Recently renovated, this is now the plushest hotel in Chinatown, right at the hub of the gold-trading quarter. All rooms have air-con and TV, and there's an excellent *dim sum* restaurant on the premises. If you book your room through the *PC & C* travel agency in Room 100 at Hualamphong station, you should get a discount of up to 20 percent. ⑥–⑧.

Downtown: Siam Square and Ploenchit Road

Siam Square – not really a square, but a grid of shops and restaurants between Phrayathai and Henri Dunant roads – and nearby **Ploenchit Road** are as central as Bangkok gets, handy for all kinds of shopping, nightlife and Hualamphong station. There's no budget accommodation here, but a few posh guest houses have sprung up alongside the expensive hotels. Concentrated in their own "ghetto" on **Soi Kasemsan 1**, which runs north off Rama I Road just west of Phrayathai Road and is the next soi along from Jim Thompson's House (see p.104), these offer an informal guest-house atmosphere, with hotel comforts – air conditioning and en suite hot-water bathrooms – at moderate prices.

A-One Inn, 25/13 Soi Kasemsan 1, Rama I Rd (☎02/215 3029). The original posh guest house and still justifiably popular, with helpful staff and a sociable café. ⑤.

The Bed & Breakfast, 36/42 Soi Kasemsan 1, Rama I Rd (☎02/215 3004). Bright, clean and friendly, though the rooms are a bit cramped. As the name suggests, breakfast, of a continental nature, is included in the price. ⑤.

City Inn, 888/37–9 Ploenchit Rd (☎02/254 2070). Small, reliable hotel, popular with businessmen. ⑥.

Hotel Siam Inter-Continental, 967 Rama I Rd (☎02/253 0355–7). Elegant, offbeat, modern Thai building in huge, quiet gardens with a driving range and tennis. ⑨.

Jim's Lodge, 125/7 Soi Ruam Rudee (☎02/255 3100–3). Luxurious international standards on a smaller scale and at bargain prices. ⑦.

Regent, 155 Rajdamri Rd (☎02/251 6127). The stately home of Bangkok's top hotels, where afternoon tea is still served in the monumental lobby. ⑨.

Wendy House, 36/2 Soi Kasemsan 1, Rama I Rd (☎02/216 2436 or 2437). Most spartan – and marginally priciest – of this soi's upmarket guest houses, and no frills in the service either, but clean and comfortable enough. ⑤.

White Lodge, 36/8 Soi Kasemsan 1, Rama I Rd (☎02/216 8867). Well-maintained, shining white cubicles in a welcoming atmosphere, with very good continental breakfasts at the attached *Princesse Terrace*. ⑤.

Downtown: south of Rama IV Road

South of Rama IV Road, the left bank of the river contains a full cross-section of places to stay. At the eastern edge there's **Soi Ngam Duphli**, a ghetto of budget guest houses which is choked with traffic escaping the jams on Rama IV Road – the neighbourhood is generally on the slide, although the best guest houses, tucked away on quiet **Soi Saphan Khu**, compare with Banglamphu's finest. A disadvantage for lone travellers is that only *Freddy's 2* and *Madam* of the bottom-end places mentioned below offer decent single rates.

Some medium-range places are scattered between Rama IV Road and the river, ranging from the notorious (the *Malaysia*) to the sedate (the *Bangkok Christian* and the *YWCA*). The area also lays claim to the capital's biggest selection of top hotels, which are among the most opulent in the world. You're at least a long express-boat ride from the treasures of Ratanakosin, but this area is good for eating and shopping, and has a generous sprinkling of embassies for visa-hunters.

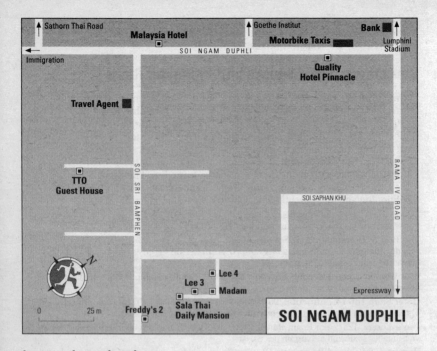

Inexpensive and moderate

Bangkok Christian Guest House, 123 Soi 2, Saladaeng (☎02/233 6303). Missionary house whose plain air-con rooms with hot-water bathrooms surround a quiet lawn. Prices at the bottom of its category, with breakfast included; good deals for singles. ⑦.

Freddy's 2, 27/40 Soi Sri Bamphen (☎02/286 7826). Popular, comfortable guest house with beer garden. Bit noisy. ③.

Lee 3 Guest House, 13 Soi Saphan Khu (☎02/286 3042). The best of the Lee family (1–4) guest houses spread around this and adjoining sois. Decent and quiet, though stuffy. ②.

Lee 4, 9 Soi Saphan Khu (☎02/286 7874). Simple, airy rooms in a dour modern tower. ③.

Madam Guest House, 11 Soi Saphan Khu (☎02/286 9289). Cleanish rooms in a warren-like wooden house. Friendly. ②.

Malaysia Hotel, 54 Soi Ngam Duphli (☎02/286 3582). Big, dilapidated rooms with air-con and hot-water bathrooms. Swimming pool (B50 per day for non-guests). Once a travellers' legend, now a sleaze pit, with probably the surliest staff in Thailand. ⑤.

Newrotel, 1216/1 New Rd, between the GPO and the *Oriental Hotel* (☎02/233 1406). Smart, clean and very good value, the price including American breakfast. ⑥.

River View Guest House, 768 Soi Panurangsri, Songvad Rd (☎02/235 8501). Great views over the bend in the river, especially from the top-floor restaurant. Large but unattractive rooms, with fan and cold water at the lower end of the range, air-con and hot water at the top. Find it through a maze of crumbling Chinese buildings: head north for 400m from River City shopping centre (on the express-boat line) along Soi Wanit 2, before following signs to the guest house to the left. ⑤–⑥.

Sala Thai Daily Mansion, 15 Soi Saphan Khu (☎02/287 1436). The pick of the area. A clean and efficiently run place at the end of this quiet, shaded alley; a roof terrace makes it all the more pleasant. ③.

TTO Guest House, 2/48 Soi Sri Bamphen (☎02/286 6783). Rough, poorly designed rooms, each with fridge, air-con and hot water, in a friendly establishment. ④.

YWCA Hostel, 13 Sathorn Thai Rd (☎02/286 1936). Bland but reliable upmarket hostel (men and women), with swimming pool, roller skating (Sun only), and an inexpensive, popular Thai café; air-con rooms with hot-water bathrooms. ⑥.

Expensive

Dusit Thani Hotel, 946 Rama IV Rd, on the corner of Silom Road (☎02/236 0450–9). Centrally placed top-class hotel, famous for its restaurants, including the *Tiara,* which has spectacular top-floor views. ⑨.

La Residence, 173/8–9 Suriwong Rd (☎02/233 3301). Above *All Gaengs* restaurant, small hotel at the lower end of its price bracket; the cutesy rooms stretch to TVs and minibars. ⑧.

Montien Hotel, 54 Surawongse Rd, on the corner of Rama IV (☎02/233 7060–9). Grand, airy and solicitous luxury hotel, famous for the astrologers who dispense predictions to Bangkok's high society in the lobby. ⑨.

Oriental Hotel, 48 Oriental Ave, off New Road (☎02/236 0400). One of the world's best. Effortlessly stylish riverside hotel, with immaculate standards of service. ⑨.

Quality Hotel Pinnacle, 17 Soi Ngam Duphli (☎02/287 0111). Bland but reliable international-standard place, with jacuzzi, fitness centre and scenic top-floor cocktail lounge. ⑧.

Sukhothai, 13/3 Sathorn Thai Rd (☎02/287 0222). The most elegant of Bangkok's top hotels, its decor inspired by the walled city of Sukhothai: low-rise accommodation coolly furnished in silks, teak and granite, around six acres of gardens and lotus ponds. Good Italian and Thai restaurants. ⑨.

Swiss Lodge, 3 Convent Rd (☎02/233 5345). Swish and friendly top-notch small hotel, just off Silom Road. Twin room designed for disabled visitors available. ⑨.

YMCA Collins International House, 27 Sathorn Thai Rd (☎02/287 1900). First-class facilities, including swimming pool, with no frills. ⑧.

Sukhumvit Road

Sukhumvit Road is Bangkok's longest – it keeps going east all the way to Cambodia – but the best accommodation is between sois 1 and 21. Although this is not the place to come if you're on a tight budget, it's a good area for mid-range hotels and small, well-appointed "inns", many of which have swimming pools and/ or include breakfast. Advance reservations are accepted at all places listed below and are recommended during high season. Staying here gives you a huge choice of restaurants, bars and shops, on Sukhumvit and the adjacent Ploenchit roads, and it's convenient for the Eastern Bus Terminal; but it does mean you're a long way from the main Ratanakosin sights, and the sheer volume of traffic on Sukhumvit means that travelling across town can take an age.

Moderate

Bangkok Inn, Soi 11 (☎02/254 4834). A friendly place whose rooms have air-con, shower, fridge and TV; rates include breakfast. ⑥.

Grand Inn, Soi 3 (☎02/254 9021). Small, very central hotel offering reasonably priced, sizeable air-con rooms with TV and fridge. ⑥.

Miami Hotel, Soi 13 (☎02/253 5611). Very popular, long-established mid-sized hotel built around a swimming pool. Large, clean, if slightly shabby rooms with shower and air-con. ⑤.

Narry's Inn, Soi 11 (☎02/254 9184). Very similar in style and facilities to the neighbouring *Bangkok Inn*: large air-con rooms with TV and fridge. ⑥.

Premier Travelodge, Soi 8(☎02/251 3031). Well-equipped hotel offering good rooms with shower, bathtub, air-con, fridge and TV. ⑥.

SV Guest House, Soi 19 (☎02/253 1747). The least expensive beds in the area, offering just about adequate rooms with shared bathroom. ④.

Uncle Rey's Guest House, Soi 4 (☎02/252 5565). The best budget option on Sukhumvit: friendly and very quiet considering its central location and proximity to the Soi Nana strip of bars; rooms are slightly shabby but clean, and all have air-con and shower. ④.

White Inn, Soi 4 (☎02/251 1662). Slightly quaint establishment at the far end of the soi which cultivates the ambience of an Alpine lodge. Fairly good rooms, most with a balcony overlooking the small swimming pool. ⑦.

Expensive

Ambassador Hotel, between sois 11 and 13 (☎02/254 0444). The largest hotel complex on Sukhumvit, with a predictably excellent range of facilities that includes over a dozen restaurants. ⑧–⑨.

Boulevard Hotel, Soi 7 (☎02/255 2930). Medium-sized, unpretentious and friendly top-notch accommodation, with fully equipped rooms and a swimming pool. ⑨.

Landmark Hotel, between sois 6 and 8 (☎02/254 0404). The most luxurious hotel on Sukhumvit, oriented towards the business traveller, with all 415 rooms linked up to a central database providing information on the stock exchange, airline schedules and so on. ⑨.

Rex Hotel, opposite Soi 49 (☎02/259 0106). Adequate rooms with all the trimmings and use of pool. Its location close to the Eastern Bus Terminal makes it convenient for east-coast connections, but too isolated from the best of Sukhumvit for a longer stay. ⑦–⑧.

THE CITY

Bangkok is sprawling, chaotic and exhausting: to do it justice and to keep your sanity, you need time, boundless patience and a bus map. The place to start is **Ratanakosin**, the royal island on the east bank of the Chao Phraya, where the city's most important and extravagant sights are to be found. On the edges of this enclave, the area around the landmark **Democracy Monument** includes some interesting and quirky religious architecture, a contrast with the attractions of neighbouring **Chinatown**, whose markets pulsate with the much more aggressive business of making money. Quieter and more European in ambience are the stately buildings of the new royal district of **Dusit**, 2km northeast of Democracy Monument. Very little of old Bangkok remains, but the back canals of **Thonburi**, across the river from Ratanakosin and Chinatown, retain a traditional feel quite at odds with the modern high-rise jungle of **downtown Bangkok**, which has evolved across on the eastern perimeter of the city and can take an hour to reach by bus from Ratanakosin. It's here that you'll find the best shops, bars, restaurants and nightlife, as well as a couple of worthwhile sights. Greater Bangkok now covers an area some 30km in diameter and though unsightly urban development predominates, an expedition to **the outskirts** is made worthwhile by several museums and the city's largest market.

Ratanakosin

When Rama I developed **Ratanakosin** as his new capital in 1782, after the sacking of Ayutthaya and a temporary stay across the river in Thonburi, he paid tribute to its precursor by imitating Ayutthaya's layout and architecture – he even shipped the building materials downstream from the ruins of the old city. Like

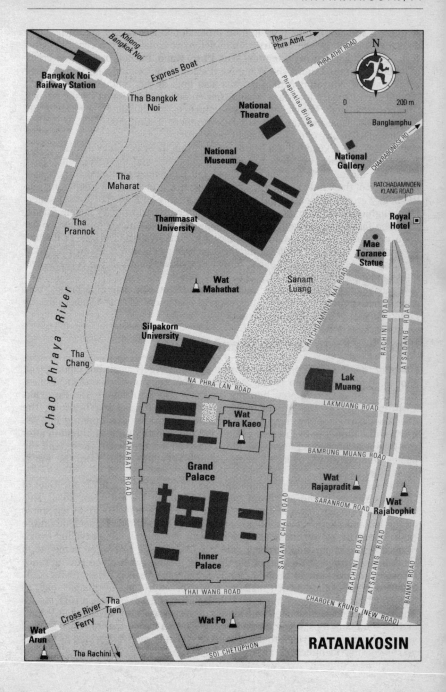

RATANAKOSIN

Ayutthaya, the new capital was sited for protection beside a river and turned into an artificial island by the construction of defensive canals, with a central **Grand Palace** and adjoining royal temple, **Wat Phra Kaeo**, fronted by an open cremation field, **Sanam Luang**; the Wang Na (Palace of the Second King), now doing service as the **National Museum**, was also built at this time. **Wat Po**, which predates the capital's founding, was further embellished by Rama I's successors, who consolidated Ratanakosin's pre-eminence by building several grand European-style palaces (now housing government institutions), Wat Mahathat, the National Theatre and Thammasat University.

Bangkok has expanded eastwards away from the river, leaving the Grand Palace a good 5km from the city's commercial heart, and the royal family have long since moved their residence to Dusit, but Ratanakosin remains the ceremonial centre of the whole kingdom – so much so that it feels as if it might sink into the boggy ground under the weight of its own mighty edifices. The heavy, stately feel is lightened by noisy markets along the riverside strip and by Sanam Luang, still used for cremations and royal ceremonies, but also functioning as a popular open park and the hub of the modern city's bus system. Despite containing several of the country's main sights, the area is busy enough in its own right not to have become a swarming tourist zone, and strikes a neat balance between liveliness and grandeur.

Ratanakosin is within easy walking distance of Banglamphu, but is best approached from the river, via the express-boat piers of Tha Chang (for the Grand Palace) or Tha Thien (for Wat Po).

Wat Phra Kaeo and the Grand Palace

Hanging together in a precarious harmony of strangely beautiful colours and shapes, **Wat Phra Kaeo** is the apogee of Thai religious art and the holiest Buddhist site in the country, housing the most important image, the **Emerald Buddha**. Built as the private royal temple, Wat Phra Kaeo occupies the northeast corner of the huge **Grand Palace**, whose official opening in 1785 marked the founding of the new capital and the rebirth of the Thai nation after the Burmese invasion. Successive kings have all left their mark here, and the palace complex now covers 61 acres, though very little apart from the wat is open to tourists.

The only **entrance** to the complex in 2km of crenellated walls is the Gate of Glorious Victory in the middle of the north side, on Na Phra Lan Road. This brings you onto a driveway with a tantalizing view of the temple's glittering spires on the left and the dowdy buildings of the Offices of the Royal Household on the right: this is the powerhouse of the kingdom's ceremonial life, providing everything down to chairs and catering, and even lending an urn when someone of rank dies. Turn left at the end of the driveway for the ticket office and entrance turnstiles: **admission** to Wat Phra Kaeo and the palace is B125 (daily 8.30–11.30am & 1–3.30pm), which includes a free brochure and invaluable map, as well as admission to the Vimanmek Palace in the Dusit area (see p.101). As it's Thailand's most sacred site, you should show respect by dressing in smart clothes – no tank tops, leggings, shorts, fisherman's trousers or flip-flops – but if your rucksack won't stretch that far, suitable gaments can be provided as long as you leave some identification as surety.

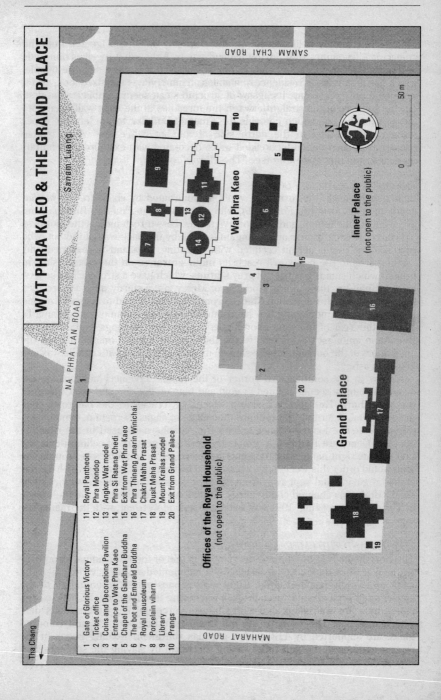

WAT PHRA KAEO & THE GRAND PALACE

Tha Chang

NA PHRA LAN ROAD

MAHARAT ROAD

SANAM CHAI ROAD

Sanam Luang

Wat Phra Kaeo

Grand Palace

Inner Palace
(not open to the public)

Offices of the Royal Household
(not open to the public)

N

0   50 m

1	Gate of Glorious Victory
2	Ticket office
3	Coins and Decorations Pavilion
4	Entrance to Wat Phra Kaeo
5	Exit from Wat Phra Kaeo
6	Chapel of the Gandhara Buddha
7	The bot and Emerald Buddha
8	Royal mausoleum
9	Porcelain viharn
10	Library

11	Royal Pantheon
12	Phra Mondop
13	Angkor Wat model
14	Phra Si Ratana Chedi
15	Exit from Wat Phra Kaeo
16	Phra Thinang Amarin Winichai
17	Chakri Maha Prasat
18	Dusit Maha Prasat
19	Mount Krailas model
20	Exit from Grand Palace

Wat Phra Kaeo

Entering the temple is like stepping onto a lavishly detailed stage set, from the immaculate flagstones right up to the gaudy roofs. Although it receives hundreds of foreign sightseers and at least as many Thai pilgrims every day, the temple, which has no monks in residence, maintains an unnervingly sanitized look, as if it were built only yesterday. Its jigsaw of structures can seem complicated at first, but the basic layout is straightforward: the turnstiles in the west wall open onto the back of the bot, which contains the Emerald Buddha; to the left, the upper terrace runs parallel to the north side of the bot, while the whole temple compound is surrounded by arcaded walls, decorated with extraordinary murals of scenes from the *Ramayana* (see "The Murals", p.82).

THE APPROACH TO THE BOT

Immediately inside the turnstiles, you'll be confronted by six-metre tall *yaksha*, gaudy demons from the *Ramayana*, who watch over the Emerald Buddha from every gate of the temple and ward off evil spirits. Less threatening is the toothless old codger, cast in bronze and sitting on a plinth by the back wall of the bot, who represents a Hindu hermit credited with inventing yoga and herbal medicine. Skirting around the bot, you'll reach its **main entrance** on the eastern side, in front of which stands a cluster of grey **statues**, which have a strong Chinese feel: next to Kuan Im, the Chinese Goddess of Mercy, are a sturdy pillar topped by a lotus flower, which Bangkok's Chinese community presented to Rama IV during his 27 years as a monk, and two handsome cows which commemorate Rama I's birth in the Year of the Cow. Worshippers make their offerings to the Emerald Buddha in amongst the statues, where they can look at the image through the open doors of the bot without messing up its pristine interior with candle wax and joss-stick ash.

Nearby in the southeastern corner of the temple precinct, look out for the beautiful country scenes painted in gold and blue on the doors of the **Chapel of the Gandhara Buddha**, a building which was crucial to the old royal rain-making ritual. Adorning the roof are thousands of nagas (serpents), symbolizing water; inside the locked chapel, among the paraphernalia used in the ritual, is kept the Gandhara Buddha, a bronze image in the gesture of calling down the rain with its right hand, while cupping the left to catch it. In times of drought the king would order this week-long ceremony to be conducted, during which he was bathed regularly and kept away from the opposite sex while Buddhist monks and Hindu Brahmins chanted continuously. Traditional methods still have their place in Thai weather reading: 1991 was said to be a good wet year, with the rain measured at "five nagas".

THE BOT AND THE EMERALD BUDDHA

The **bot**, the largest building of the temple, is one of the few original structures left at Wat Phra Kaeo, though it has been augmented so often it looks like the work of a wildly inspired child. Eight *sema* stones mark the boundary of the consecrated area around the bot, each sheltering in a psychedelic fairy castle, joined by a low wall decorated with Chinese porcelain tiles which depict delicate landscapes. The walls of the bot itself, sparkling with gilt and coloured glass, are supported by 112 golden garudas (birdmen) holding nagas in the representations of the god Indra saving the world by slaying the serpent-cloud which had swallowed up all the water. The symbolism reflects the king's traditional role as a rainmaker.

Inside the bot, a nine-metre high pedestal supports the tiny **Emerald Buddha**, a figure whose mystique draws pilgrims from all over Thailand – here especially you must act with respect, sitting with your feet pointing away from the Buddha. The spiritual power of the 60-centimetre jadeite image comes from its legendary past. Reputed to have been created in Sri Lanka, it was discovered when lightning cracked open an ancient chedi in Chiang Rai in the early fifteenth century. The image was then moved around the north, dispensing miracles wherever it went, before being taken to Laos for two hundred years. The future Rama I snatched it back when he captured Vientiane in 1779, as it was believed to bring great fortune to its possessor, and installed it at the heart of his new capital as a talisman for king and country.

To this day the king himself ceremonially changes the Buddha's costumes, of which there are three, one for each season: the crown and ornaments of an Ayutthayan king for the hot season; a gilt monastic robe dotted with blue enamel for the rainy season, when the monks retreat into the temples; and a full-length gold shawl to wrap up in the cool season. (The spare outfits are displayed in the Coins and Decorations Pavilion outside the turnstiles leading into the temple.) Amongst the paraphernalia in front of the pedestal is the small, black Victory Buddha, which Rama I always carried with him into war for luck. The two lowest Buddhas were both put there by Rama IX: the one on the left on his sixtieth birthday in 1987, the other when he became the longest-reigning Thai monarch in 1988.

THE UPPER TERRACE

The eastern end of the **upper terrace** is taken up with the **Prasat Phra Thep Bidorn**, known as the **Royal Pantheon**, a splendid hash of styles. The pantheon has its roots in the Khmer concept of *devaraja*, or the divinity of kings: inside are bronze and gold statues, precisely life-size, of all the kings since Bangkok became the Thai capital. The building is open only on special occasions, such as Chakri Day (April 6), when the dynasty is commemorated.

From here you get the best view of the **royal mausoleum**, the **porcelain viharn** and the **library** to the north, all of which are closed to the public, and, running along the east side of the temple, a row of eight bullet-like **prangs**, which Somerset Maugham described as "monstrous vegetables": each has a different nasty ceramic colour and they represent, in turn, the Buddha, Buddhist scripture, the monkhood, the nunhood, the three Buddhas to come, and finally the king.

In the middle of the terrace, dressed in deep-green glass mosaics, the **Phra Mondop** was built by Rama I to house the *Tripitaka*, or Buddhist scripture. It's famous for the mother-of-pearl cabinet and solid-silver mats inside, but is never open. Four tiny **memorials** at each corner of the mondop show the symbols of each of the nine Chakri kings, from the ancient crown representing Rama I to the present king's sun symbol, while the bronze statues surrounding the memorials portray each king's lucky white elephants, labelled by name and pedigree. A contribution of Rama IV, on the north side of the mondop, is a **scale model of Angkor Wat**, the prodigious Cambodian temple, which during his reign was under Thai rule. At the western end of the terrace, you can't miss the golden dazzle of the **Phra Si Ratana Chedi**, which Rama IV (1851–68) erected to enshrine a piece of the Buddha's breastbone.

THE MURALS

Extending for over a kilometre in the arcades which run inside the wat walls, the **murals of the Ramayana** depict every blow of this ancient story of the triumph of good over evil, using the vibrant buildings of the temple itself as backdrops, and setting them off against the subdued colours of richly detailed landscapes. Because of the damaging humidity, none of the original work of Rama I's time survives: maintenance is a never-ending process, so you'll always find an artist working on one of the scenes.

The story is told in 178 panels, labelled and numbered in Thai only, starting in the middle of the northern side: in the first episode, a hermit, while out ploughing, finds the baby Sita, the heroine, floating in a gold urn on a lotus leaf and brings her to the city. Panel 109 shows the climax of the story, when Rama, the hero, kills the ten-headed demon Totsagan, and the ladies of the enemy city weep at the demon's death. Panel 110 depicts his elaborate funeral procession, and in 113 you can see the funeral fair, with acrobats, sword jugglers, and tightrope walkers. In between, Sita – Rama's wife – has to walk on fire to prove that she has

THE RAMAYANA

The **Ramayana** is generally thought to have originated as an oral epic in India, where it appears in numerous dialects. The most famous version is that of the poet Valmiki, who as a tribute to his king drew together the collection of stories over two thousand years ago. From India, the *Ramayana* spread to all the Hindu-influenced countries of South Asia and was passed down through the Khmers to Thailand, where as the **Ramakien** it has become the national epic, acting as an affirmation of the Thai monarchy and its divine Hindu links. As a source of inspiration for literature, painting, sculpture and dance-drama, it has acquired the authority of holy writ, providing Thais with moral and practical lessons, while its appearance in the form of films and comic strips shows its huge popular appeal. The version current in Thailand was composed by a committee of poets sponsored by Rama I, and runs to three thousand pages.

The **central story** of the *Ramayana* concerns **Rama** (in Thai, Phra Ram), son of the king of Ayodhya, and his beautiful wife **Sita**, whose hand he wins by lifting and stringing a magic bow. The couple's adventures begin when they are exiled to the forest, along with Rama's good brother, **Lakshaman** (Phra Lak), by the hero's father under the influence of his evil stepmother. Meanwhile, in the city of Lanka (in Thai, Longka), the demon king **Totsagan** (also known as Ravana) has conceived a passionate desire for Sita and, disguised as a hermit, sets out to kidnap her. By transforming one of his subjects into a beautiful deer, which Rama and Lakshaman go off to hunt, Totsagan catches Sita alone and takes her back to Lanka. Rama then wages a long war against the demons of Lanka, into which are woven many battles, spy scenes and diversionary episodes, and eventually kills Totsagan and rescues Sita.

The Thai version shows some characteristic differences from the Indian. Hanuman, the loyal monkey king, is given a much more playful role in the *Ramakien*, with the addition of many episodes which display his cunning and talent for mischief, but the major alteration comes at the end of the story, when Rama doubts Sita's faithfulness after rescuing her from Totsagan. In the Indian story, this ends with Sita being swallowed up by the earth so that she doesn't have to suffer Rama's doubts any more; in the *Ramakien* the ending is a happy one, with Rama and Sita living together happily ever after.

been faithful during her fourteen years of imprisonment by Totsagan. If you haven't the stamina for the long walk round, you could sneak a look at the end of the story, to the left of the first panel, where Rama holds a victory parade and distributes thank-you gifts.

The palace buildings

The exit in the southwest corner of Wat Phra Kaeo brings you to the palace proper, a vast area of buildings and gardens, of which only the northern edge is on show to the public. Though the king now lives in the Chitrlada Palace in Dusit, the Grand Palace is still used for state receptions and official ceremonies, during which there is no public access to any part of the palace.

PHRA MAHA MONTHIEN

Coming out of the temple compound, you'll first be confronted by a beautiful Chinese gate covered in innumerable tiny porcelain tiles. The **Phra Maha Monthien**, which extends in a straight line behind the gate, was the grand residential complex of earlier kings. Only the **Phra Thinang Amarin Winichai**, the main audience hall at the front of the complex, is open to the public. The supreme court in the era of the absolute monarchy, it nowadays serves as the venue for the king's birthday speech; dominating the hall is the *busbok*, an open-sided throne with a spired roof, floating on a boat-shaped base. The rear buildings are still used for the most important part of the elaborate coronation ceremony, and each new king is supposed to spend a night there to show solidarity with his forefathers.

CHAKRI MAHA PRASAT AND INNER PALACE

Next door you can admire the facade – nothing else – of the "farang with a Thai hat", as the **Chakri Maha Prasat** is nicknamed. Rama V, whose portrait you can see over the entrance, employed an English architect to design a purely Neoclassical residence, but other members of the royal family prevailed on the king to add the three Thai spires. This used to be the site of the elephant stables: the large red tethering posts are still there and the bronze elephants were installed as a reminder. The building displays the emblem of the Chakri dynasty on its gable, which has a trident (*ri*) coming out of a *chak*, a discus with a sharpened rim.

The **Inner Palace**, which used to be the king's harem (closed to the public), lies behind the gate on the left-hand side of the Chakri Maha Prasat. The harem was a town in itself, with shops, law-courts and a police force for the huge all-female population: as well as the current queens, the minor wives and their servants, this was home to the daughters and consorts of former kings, and the daughters of the aristocracy who attended the harem's finishing school. Today, the Inner Palace houses a school of cooking, fruit-carving and other domestic sciences for well-bred young Thais.

DUSIT MAHA PRASAT

On the western side of the courtyard, the delicately proportioned **Dusit Maha Prasat**, an audience hall built by Rama I, epitomizes traditional Thai architecture. Outside, the soaring tiers of its red, gold and green roof culminate in a gilded *mongkut*, a spire shaped like the king's crown which symbolizes the thirty-three Buddhist levels of perfection. Each tier of the roof bears a typical *chofa*, a slender, stylized bird's head, and several *hang hong* (swan's tails), which represent three-headed nagas. Inside, you can still see the original throne, the **Phra Ratcha Banlang Pradap Muk**, a masterpiece of mother-of-pearl inlaid work. When a senior member of the royal family dies, the hall is used for the lying-in-state: the body, embalmed and seated in a huge sealed urn, is placed in the west transept, waiting up to two years for an auspicious day to be cremated.

To the right and behind the Dusit Maha Prasat rises a strange model mountain, decorated with fabulous animals and topped by a castle and prang. It represents **Mount Krailas**, a version of Mount Meru, the centre of the Hindu universe, and was built as the site of the royal tonsure ceremony. In former times, Thai children had shaved heads except for a tuft on the crown which, between the age of five and eight, was cut in a Hindu initiation rite to welcome adolescence. For the royal children, the rite was an elaborate ceremony that sometimes lasted five days, culminating with the king's cutting of the hair knot. The child was then bathed at the model Krailas, in water representing the original river of the universe flowing down the central mountain.

Wat Po

Where Wat Phra Kaeo may seem too perfect and shrink-wrapped for some, **Wat Po** (daily 8am–5pm; B10), covering twenty acres to the south of the Grand Palace, is lively and shambolic, a complex arrangement of lavish structures which jostle with classrooms, basketball courts and a turtle pond. Busloads of tourists shuffle in and out of the **north entrance** stopping only to gawp at the colossal Reclining Buddha, but you can avoid the worst of the crowds by using the **main entrance** on Soi Chetuphon to explore the huge compound, where you'll more than likely be approached by friendly young monks wanting to practise their English.

Wat Po is the oldest temple in Bangkok and older than the city itself, having been founded in the seventeenth century under the name Wat Potaram. Foreigners have stuck to the contraction of this old name, even though Rama I, after enlarging the temple, changed the name in 1801 to Wat Phra Chetuphon, which is how it is generally known to Thais. The temple had another major overhaul in 1832, when Rama III built the chapel of the Reclining Buddha, and turned the temple into a public centre of learning by decorating the walls and pillars with inscriptions and diagrams on subjects such as history, literature, animal husbandry and astrology. Dubbed Thailand's first university, the wat is still an important centre for traditional medicine, notably **Thai massage**, which is used against all kinds of illnesses, from backaches to viruses. Thirty-hour training courses in English, held over either ten or fifteen days, cost B4500; alternatively you can simply go and suffer a massage yourself in the ramshackle buildings on the east side of the main compound, for B180 per hour (allow two hours for the full works and note that the massage school stays open until 6pm).

The eastern courtyard

The main entrance on Soi Chetuphon is one of a series of sixteen monumental gates around the main compound, each guarded by stone **giants**, many of them comic Westerners in wide-brimmed hats – ships which exported rice to China would bring these statues back as ballast.

The entrance brings you into the eastern half of the main complex, where a courtyard of structures radiate from the bot – the principal congregation and ordi-

WAT PO

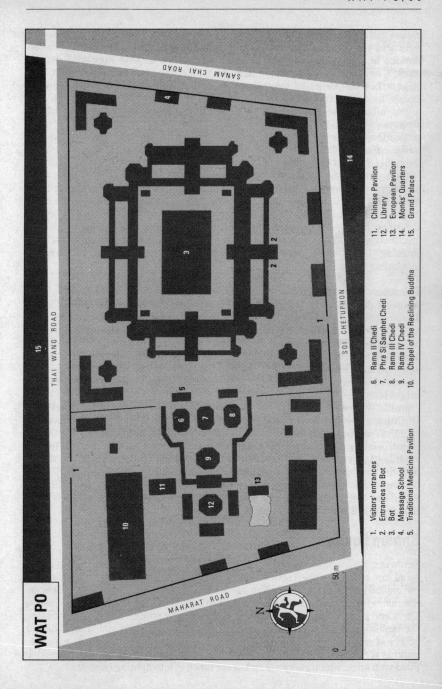

1. Visitors' entrances
2. Entrances to Bot
3. Bot
4. Massage School
5. Traditional Medicine Pavilion
6. Rama II Chedi
7. Phra Si Sanphet Chedi
8. Rama III Chedi
9. Rama IV Chedi
10. Chapel of the Reclining Buddha
11. Chinese Pavilion
12. Library
13. European Pavilion
14. Monks' Quarters
15. Grand Palace

nation hall – in a disorientating symmetry. To get to the bot at the centre, turn right and cut through the two surrounding cloisters, which are lined with 394 Buddha images, many of them covered with stucco to hide their bad state of repair – anyone can accrue some merit by taking one away and repairing it. The elegant **bot** has beautiful teak doors decorated with mother-of-pearl, showing stories from the *Ramayana* in minute detail. Look out also for the stone bas reliefs around the base of the bot, which narrate a longer version of the *Ramayana* in 152 action-packed panels. The plush interior has a well-proportioned altar on which ten statues of disciples frame a graceful Buddha image containing the remains of Rama I, the founder of Bangkok. Rama IV placed them there so that the public could worship him at the same time as the Buddha.

Back outside the entrance to the double cloister, keep your eyes open for a miniature mountain covered in statues of naked men in tall hats who appear to be gesturing rudely: they are *rishis* (hermits), demonstrating various positions of healing massage. Skirting the southwestern corner of the cloisters, you'll come to a pavilion between the eastern and western courtyards, which displays plaques inscribed with the precepts of traditional medicine, as well as anatomical pictures showing the different pressure points and the illnesses that can be cured by massaging them.

The western courtyard

Amongst the 95 chedis strewn about the grounds, the four **great chedis** in the western courtyard stand out as much for their covering of garish tiles as for their size. The central chedi is the oldest, erected by Rama I to hold the remains of the most sacred Buddha image of Ayutthaya, the Phra Si Sanphet. (All chedis are supposed to hold the ashes of the Buddha or some other important religious figure.) Later, Rama III built the chedi to the north for the ashes of Rama II and the chedi to the south to hold his own remains. Rama IV built the fourth, with bright blue tiles, for an uncertain purpose.

In the northwest corner of the courtyard stands the chapel of the **Reclining Buddha**, a 45-metre-long gilded statue of plaster-covered brick which depicts the Buddha entering Nirvana, a common motif in Buddhist iconography. The chapel is only slightly bigger than the statue – you can't get far enough away to take in anything but a surreal close-up view of the beaming five-metre smile. As for the feet, the vast black soles are beautifully inlaid with delicate mother-of-pearl showing the 108 *lakshanas* or auspicious signs which distinguish the true Buddha. Along one side of the statue are 108 bowls which will bring you good luck and a long life if you put 25 satang in each.

Sanam Luang

Sprawling across thirty acres north of the Grand Palace, **Sanam Luang** represents one of the last open spaces left in Bangkok, a bare field where residents of the capital gather in the evening to meet, eat and play. The nearby pavements are the marketplace for some exotic spiritual salesmen: on the eastern side sit astrologers and palm readers, and sellers of bizarre virility potions and contraptions; on the western side and spreading around Thammasat University and Wat Mahathat, scores of small-time hawkers sell amulets, though the range and quality are not as good as at the main market at Wat Rajnadda. In the early part of the year, the sky is filled with kites, which every afternoon are flown in kite-fighting contests.

KITE FLYING

Flying intricate and colourful **kites** is now done mostly for fun in Thailand, but it has its roots in more serious activities. Filled with gunpowder and fitted with long fuses, kites were deployed in the first Thai kingdom at Sukhothai (1240–1438) as machines of war. In the same era, special *ngao* kites, with heads in the shape of bamboo bows, were used in Brahmin rituals: the string of the bow would vibrate in the wind and make a noise to frighten away evil spirits (nowadays noisy kites are still used, but only by farmers, to scare the birds). By the height of the Ayutthayan period (1351–1767) kites had become largely decorative: royal ceremonies were enhanced by fantastically shaped kites, adorned with jingling bells and ornamental lamps.

In the nineteenth century Rama V, by his enthusiastic lead, popularized kite flying as a clean-cut and fashionable recreation. **Contests** are now held all over the country between February and April, when winds are strong and farmers have free time after harvesting the rice. These contests fall into two broad categories: those involving manoeuvrable flat kites, often in the shapes of animals; and those in which the beauty of static display kites is judged. The most popular contest of all, which comes under the first category, matches two teams, one flying star-shaped *chulas*, two-metre-high "male" kites, the other flying the smaller, more agile *pakpaos*, diamond-shaped "females". Each team uses its skill and teamwork to ensnare the other's kites and drag them back across a dividing line.

As it's in front of the Grand Palace, the field is also the venue for national ceremonies, such as royal funerals and the **Ploughing Ceremony**, held in May at a time selected by astrologers to bring good fortune to the rice harvest. The elaborate Brahmin ceremony is led by an official from the Ministry of Agriculture, who stands in for the king in case the royal power were to be reduced by any failure in the ritual. At the designated time, the official cuts a series of circular furrows with a plough driven by two oxen, and scatters rice which has been sprinkled with lustral water by the Brahmin priests of the court. When the ritual is over, spectators rush in to grab handfuls of the rice, which they then plant in their own paddies for good luck.

Lak muang

At 6.54am on April 21, 1782 – the astrologically determined time for the auspicious founding of Bangkok – a pillar containing the city's horoscope was ceremonially driven into the ground opposite the northeast corner of the Grand Palace. This pillar, the **lak muang** – all Thai cities have one, to provide a home for their guardian spirits – was made from a twelve-foot tree trunk carved with a lotus-shaped crown, and is now sheltered in an elegant shrine surrounded by immaculate gardens. It shares the shrine with the taller *lak muang* of Thonburi, which was recently incorporated into Greater Bangkok.

Hundreds of worshippers come every day to pray and offer flowers, particularly childless couples seeking the gift of fertility. In one corner of the gardens you can often see short performances of **classical dancing**, paid for by well-off families when they have a piece of good fortune to celebrate.

Mae Toranee

In a tiny park by the hectic bus stops at the northeast corner of Sanam Luang stands the abundant but rather neglected figure of **Mae Toranee**, the earth goddess, wringing the water from her ponytail. Originally part of a fountain built here by Rama V's queen, Saowaba, to provide Bangkokians with fresh drinking water, the statue illustrates a Buddhist legend featured in the murals of many temples. While the Buddha was sitting in meditation at a crucial stage of his enlightenment, Mara, the force of evil, sent a host of earthly temptations and demons to try to divert him from his path. The Buddha remained cross-legged and pointed his right hand towards the ground – the most popular pose of Buddha statues in Thailand – to call the earth goddess to bear witness to his countless meritorious deeds, which had earned him an ocean of water stored in the earth. Mae Toranee obliged by wringing her hair and engulfing Mara's demons in the deluge.

The National Museum

Near the northwest corner of Sanam Luang, the **National Museum** (Wed–Sun 9am–4pm; B20) houses a colossal hoard of Thailand's chief artistic riches, ranging from sculptural treasures in the north and south wings, to bizarre decorative objects in the older buildings, as well as occasionally staging worthwhile temporary exhibitions (details on ☎02/281 2224). The free **guided tours in English** (Wed & Thurs 9.30am) are worth making time for: they're generally entertaining and their explication of the choicest exhibits provides a good introduction to Thai religion and culture. Should you linger longer than anticipated – and most people do – the **cafeteria** there serves good, inexpensive Thai food.

History and prehistory

The building which houses the ticket office provides a quick whirl through the **history** of Thailand, a display in which are hidden a couple of gems. The first is a black stone inscription, credited to King Ramkhamhaeng of Sukhothai, which became the first capital of the Thai nation in the thirteenth century. Discovered in 1833 by the future Rama IV, it's the oldest extant inscription using the Thai alphabet. This, combined with the description it records of prosperity and piety in Sukhothai's Golden Age, has made the stone a symbol of Thai nationhood. Further on is a four-foot-tall carved *kinnari*, a graceful half-human, half-bird creature said to live in one of the Himalayan heavens. This delicate masterpiece is from the best period of Thai woodcarving, the seventeenth and early eighteenth centuries, before the fall of Ayutthaya.

The **prehistory** room is entered through a separate door at the back end of the building. Prominent here are bronze artefacts from Ban Chiang in the northeast of Thailand, one of the earliest Bronze Age cultures ever discovered, including the world's oldest socketed tool, an axe head set in a sandstone mould (3600–2300 BC).

The main collection: southern building

At the back of the compound, two large modern buildings, flanking an old converted palace, house the museum's **main collection**, kicking off on the ground floor of the **southern building**. Look out here for some historic sculptures from the rest of Asia, including one of the earliest representations of the Buddha, from Gandhara in northwest India. Alexander the Great left a garrison at Gandhara, which explains why the image is in the style of Classical Greek sculpture: for example, the *ushnisha*, the supernatural bump on the top of the head, which symbolizes the Buddha's intellectual and spiritual power, is rationalized into a bun of thick, wavy hair.

Upstairs, in the **Dvaravati** rooms (sixth to eleventh centuries), the pick of the stone and terracotta Buddhas is a small head in smooth, pink clay, whose downcast eyes and faintly smiling full lips typify the serene look of this era. You can't miss a voluptuous Javanese statue of elephant-headed Ganesh, Hindu god of wisdom and the arts, which, being the symbol of the Fine Arts Department, is always freshly garlanded. As Ganesh is known as the clearer of obstacles, Hindus always worship him before other gods, so by tradition he has grown fat through getting first choice of the offerings – witness his trunk jammed into a bowl of food in this sculpture.

Room 9 contains the most famous piece of **Srivijaya** art (seventh to thirteenth centuries), a bronze Bodhisattva Avalokitesvara found at Chaiya – according to Mahayana Buddhism, a *bodhisattva* is a saint who has postponed his passage into Nirvana to help ordinary believers gain enlightenment. With its pouting face and sinuous torso, this image has become the ubiquitous emblem of southern Thailand. The rough chronological order of the collection continues back downstairs with an exhibition of **Khmer** and **Lopburi** sculpture (seventh to fourteenth centuries), most notably some dynamic bronze statuettes and stone lintels. Look out for an elaborate lintel which depicts Vishnu reclining on a dragon in the sea of eternity, dreaming up a new universe after the old one has been annihilated in the Hindu cycle of creation and destruction. Out of his navel comes a lotus, and out of this emerges four-headed Brahma, who will put the dream into practice. Nearby, a smooth, muscular stone statue with a sweet smile and downcast eyes shows King Jayavarman VII, last of the great Khmer emperors. Such royal statues are very rare and the features borrowed from Buddha images suggest that Jayavarman believed that he was close to Buddhahood himself.

The main collection: northern building

The second half of the survey, in the northern building, begins upstairs with the **Sukhothai** collection (thirteenth to fifteenth centuries), which is short on Buddha images but has some chunky bronzes of Hindu gods and a wide range of ceramics. The **Lanna** room (thirteenth to sixteenth centuries) includes a miniature set of golden regalia, including tiny umbrellas and a cute pair of filigree flip-flops, which would have been enshrined in a chedi. An ungainly but serene Buddha head, carved from grainy, pink sandstone, represents the **Ayutthaya** style of sculpture (fourteenth to eighteenth centuries): the faintest incision of a moustache above the lips betrays the Khmer influences which came to Ayutthaya after its conquest of Angkor. A sumptuous scripture cabinet, showing a cityscape of old Ayutthaya, is a more unusual piece, one of a surviving handful of such carved and painted items of furniture.

Downstairs in the **Bangkok** rooms (eighteenth century onwards), a stiffly realistic standing bronze brings you full circle: in his zeal for Western naturalism, Rama V had the statue made in the Gandhara style of the earliest Buddha image displayed in the first room of the museum.

The funeral chariots

To the east of the northern building, beyond the café on the left, stands a large garage where the fantastically elaborate **funeral chariots** of the royal family are stored. Pre-eminent among these is the Vejayant Rajarot, built by Rama I in 1785 for carrying the urn at his own funeral. The forty-foot-high structure symbolizes heaven on Mount Meru, while the dragons and divinities around the sides – piled in five golden tiers to suggest the flames of the cremation – represent the mythological inhabitants of the mountain's forests. Weighing forty tons and pulled by three hundred men, the teak chariot was used as recently as 1985 for the funeral of Queen Rambhai Bharni, wife of Rama VII.

Wang Na (Palace of the Second King)

The central building of the compound was originally part of the **Wang Na**, a huge palace stretching across Sanam Luang to Khlong Lod, which housed the "second king", appointed by the reigning monarch as his heir and deputy. When Rama V did away with the office in 1887, he turned the "Palace of the Second King" into a museum, which now contains a fascinating array of Thai *objets d'art*. Behind heavy iron bars, the display of sumptuous rare gold pieces includes a well-preserved armlet taken from the ruined prang of fifteenth-century Wat Ratburana in Ayutthaya. Nearby, an intricately carved ivory seat turns out, with gruesome irony, to be a *howdah*, for use on an elephant's back. Among the masks worn by *khon* actors, look out especially for a fierce Hanuman, the white monkey-warrior in the *Ramayana* epic, gleaming with mother-of-pearl.

The huge and varied ceramic collection includes some sophisticated pieces from Sukhothai, while the room above holds a riot of mother-of-pearl items, whose flaming rainbow of colours comes from the shell of the turbo snail from the Gulf of Thailand. It's also worth seeking out the display of richly decorated musical instruments, where you can hear tapes of the unfamiliar sounds they produce.

The Buddhaisawan Chapel

The second holiest image in Thailand, after the Emerald Buddha, is housed in the **Buddhaisawan Chapel**, the vast hall in front of the eastern entrance to the Wang Na. Inside, the fine proportions are enhanced by painted rows of divinities and converted demons, all turned to face the chubby, glowing **Phra Sihing Buddha**, which according to legend was magically created in Sri Lanka and sent to Sukhothai in the thirteenth century. Like the Emerald Buddha, the image was believed to bring good luck to its owner and was frequently snatched from one northern town to another, until Rama I brought it down from Chiang Mai in 1795 and installed it here in the second king's private chapel. Two other images (in Nakhon Si Thammarat and Chiang Mai) now claim to be the authentic Phra Sihing Buddha, but all three are in fact derived from a lost original – this one is in a fifteenth-century Sukhothai style. It's still much loved by ordinary people and at Thai New Year is carried out onto Sanam Luang, where worshippers sprinkle it with water as a merit-making gesture.

The careful detail and rich, soothing colours of the surrounding 200-year-old **murals** are surprisingly well-preserved; the bottom row between the windows narrates the life of the Buddha, beginning in the far right-hand corner with his parents' wedding.

The National Gallery and Silpakorn University Gallery

If the National Museum hasn't finished you off, two other lesser galleries nearby might. **The National Gallery**, on the north side of Sanam Luang at 4 Chao Fa Rd (Wed–Sun 9am–4pm; B10), houses a permanent collection of largely uninspiring twentieth-century Thai art, most based on traditional

Buddhist themes or the *Ramayana*. The gallery hosts some interesting temporary exhibitions, though, as does the **Silpakorn University Gallery** on Na
Phra Lan Road, across the road from the entrance to the Grand Palace: see the
Bangkok Post or the *Nation* for details. For a less formal contemporary arts
forum, stop by at the *Na Pralan* **art gallery café** (see p.119), 20m up the street
from Silpakorn University Art College: here you'll find temporary exhibitions
of contemporary Thai art on the walls, a stack of recent exhibition catalogues
for public perusal, and a constant flow of arty young Thais traipsing through
the premises.

The Democracy Monument area

The most interesting sights in the area stretching to the south and east of
Democracy Monument – a district within walking distance of the Grand Palace
and the guest houses of Banglamphu – are its temples. Though not as spectacular as the excesses of neighbouring Ratanakosin, all have some significant idiosyncratic feature to make them worth visiting.

Democracy Monument
Midway along Rajdamnoen Klang, the avenue that connects the Grand Palace
and the new royal district of Dusit, looms the imposing **Democracy Monument**.
Begun in 1939, it was conceived as a testament to the ideals that fuelled the 1932
revolution and the changeover to a constitutional monarchy, hence its symbolic
positioning between the royal residences. Its dimensions are also significant: the
four wings tower to a height of 24m, the same as the radius of the monument –
allusions to June 24, the date the system was changed; the 75 cannons around the
perimeter refer to the year, 2475 BE (1932 AD). The monument contains a copy
of the constitution and is a focal point for public demonstrations – it was a rally-
ing-point during the pro-democracy protests of May 1992.

It was designed by Corrado Feroci, an Italian sculptor who'd been invited to
Thailand by Rama VI in 1924 to encourage the pursuit of Western art. He
changed his name to Silpa Bhirasi and stayed in Thailand until his death, producing many of Bangkok's statues and monuments – including the Rama I statue at
Memorial Bridge and Victory Monument in the Phrayathai district – as well as
founding the first Institute of Fine Arts.

Wat Rajnadda, Loh Prasat and the amulet market
Five minutes' walk southeast of Democracy Monument, at the point where
Rajdamnoen Klang meets Mahachai Road, stands the assortment of religious
buildings known collectively as **Wat Rajnadda**. It's immediately recognizable by
the dusky-pink, multi-tiered, castle-like structure called **Loh Prasat** or "Iron
Monastery" – a reference to its numerous metal spires. The only structure of its
kind in Bangkok, Loh Prasat is the dominant and most bizarre of Wat Rajnadda's
components. Each tier is pierced by passageways running north–south and east–
west (15 in each direction at ground level), with small meditation cells at each
point of intersection. The Sri Lankan monastery on which it is modelled
contained a thousand cells; this one probably has half that number. Until a couple
of years ago, the elegant facade of Loh Prasat was completely hidden by the
Chalerm Chai movie theatre; as the cinema was Thailand's first, there was some

debate as to whether it merited conservation, but eventually Loh Prasat won out and the cinema was demolished.

An adjoining compound contains Bangkok's biggest **amulet market**, where at least a hundred stalls open up daily to sell tiny Buddha images of all designs, materials and prices. Alongside these miniature charms are statues, dolls and carved wooden phalluses, also bought to placate or ward off disgruntled spirits. While the amulet market at Wat Rajnadda is probably the best in Bangkok, you'll find less pricey examples from the streetside vendors who congregate daily along the pavement in front of Wat Mahathat. Prices start as low as B10 and rise into the thousands.

The Golden Mount

The dirty yellow hill crowned with a gleaming gold chedi just across the road from Wat Rajnadda is the grandiosely named Golden Mount, or Phu Khao Tong. It rises within the compound of **Wat Saket**, a dilapidated late eighteenth-century temple built by Rama I just outside his new city walls to serve as the capital's crematorium. During the following hundred years the temple became the dumping ground for some sixty thousand plague victims – the majority of them too poor to afford funeral pyres, and thus left to the vultures.

AMULETS

To gain protection from malevolent spirits and physical misfortune, Thais wear or carry at least one **amulet** at all times. The most popular **images** are copies of sacred statues from famous wats, while others show revered holy men, kings (Rama V is a favourite), healers or a many-armed monk depicted closing his eyes, ears and mouth so as to concentrate better on reaching Nirvana – a human version of the hear-no-evil, see-no-evil, speak-no-evil monkeys. On the reverse side is often inscribed a *yantra*, a combination of letters and figures also designed to ward off evil, sometimes of a very specific nature: protecting your durian orchards from gales, for example, or your tuk-tuk from oncoming traffic. Individually hand-crafted or mass produced, amulets can be made from bronze, clay, plaster or gold, and some even have sacred ingredients added, such as the ashes of burnt holy texts. But what really determines its efficacy is its history: where and by whom it was made, who or what it represents and who consecrated it. Monks are often involved in the making of the images and are always called upon to consecrate them – the more charismatic the monk, the more powerful the amulet. In return, the proceeds from the sale of amulets contributes to wat funds.

The **belief in amulets** is thought to have originated in India, where tiny images were sold to pilgrims who visited the four holy sites associated with the Buddha's birth, enlightenment, first sermon and death. But not all amulets are Buddhist-related – there's a whole range of other enchanted objects to wear for protection, including tigers' teeth, rose quartz, tamarind seeds, coloured threads and miniature phalluses. Worn around the waist rather than the neck, the phallus amulets provide protection for the genitals as well as being associated with fertility, and are of Hindu origin.

For some people, amulets are not only a vital form of spiritual protection, but valuable **collectors' items** as well. Amulet-collecting mania is something akin to stamp collecting – there are at least six Thai magazines for collectors, which give histories of certain types, tips on distinguishing between genuine items and fakes, and personal accounts of particularly powerful amulet experiences.

The **Golden Mount** was a late addition to the compound and dates back to the early nineteenth century, when Rama III built a huge chedi on ground that proved too soft to support it. The whole thing collapsed into a hill of rubble, but Buddhist law states that a religious building can never be destroyed, however tumbledown, so fifty years later Rama V topped the debris with a more sensibly sized chedi in which he placed a few Buddhist relics, believed by some to be the Buddha's teeth.

To reach the base of the mount, follow the renovated crenellations of the old city wall, past the small bird and antiques market skulking in one of the recesses, before veering left when signposted. Climbing to the top, you'll pass remnants of the collapsed chedi and plaques commemorating donors to the temple. The **terrace** surrounding the base of the new chedi is a good place for landmark-spotting: immediately to the west are the gleaming roofs of Wat Rajnadda and the salmon-pink Loh Prasat, and behind them you should be able to see the spires of the Grand Palace and, even further beyond, the beautifully proportioned prangs of Wat Arun on the other side of the river. To the northwest, look for the controversial *Banglamphu Department Store*, whose eleven storeys contravene the local building laws, which ordain that no structure in the vicinity should compete with the Grand Palace.

Wat Saket hosts an enormous annual **temple fair** in the first week of November, when the mount is illuminated with coloured lanterns and the whole compound seethes with funfair rides, food sellers and travelling performers.

Wat Suthat and Sao Ching Cha

Located about 1km southwest of the Golden Mount, and a similar distance directly south of Democracy Monument along Thanon Dinso, **Wat Suthat** contains Bangkok's tallest **viharn**, built in the early nineteenth century to house the meditating figure of **Phra Sri Sakyamuni Buddha**. This eight-metre-high statue was brought all the way down from Sukhothai by river, and now sits on a glittering mosaic dais surrounded with surreal **murals** that depict the last twenty-four lives of the Buddha rather than the more usual ten. The courtyard and galleries around the bot are full of **Chinese statues**, most of which were brought over from China during Rama I's reign, as ballast in rice boats: check out the gormless Western sailors and the pompous Chinese scholars. Note that the viharn is often locked on weekdays.

The area just in front of Wat Suthat is dominated by the towering, red-painted teak posts of **Sao Ching Cha**, otherwise known as the **Giant Swing**, once the focal point of a Brahmin ceremony to honour Shiva's annual visit to earth. Teams of two or four young men would stand on the outsized seat (now missing) and swing up to a height of 25m, to grab between their teeth a bag of gold suspended on the end of a bamboo pole. The act of swing-

Sailor statue at Wat Suthat

ing probably symbolized the rising and setting of the sun, though legend also has it that Shiva and his consort Uma were banned from swinging in their heavenly abode because doing so caused cataclysmic floods on earth – prompting Shiva to demand that the practice be continued on earth as a rite to ensure moderate rains and bountiful harvests. Accidents were so common with the terrrestrial version that it was outlawed in the 1930s.

Wat Rajabophit

On Rajabophit Road, midway between Wat Suthat and the Grand Palace, stands **Wat Rajabophit**, one of the city's prettiest temples and another example of Chinese influence. It was built by Rama V and is characteristic of this progressive king in its unusual design, with the rectangular bot and viharn connected by a circular cloister that encloses a chedi. Every external wall in the compound is covered in the pastel shades of Chinese *bencharong* ceramic tiles, creating a stunning overall effect, while the bot interior looks like a tiny banqueting hall, with gilded Gothic vaults and intricate mother-of-pearl doors.

If you now head west towards the Grand Palace from Wat Rajabophit, you'll pass a gold **statue of a pig** as you cross the canal. The cute porcine monument was erected in tribute to one of Rama V's wives, born in the Chinese Year of the Pig.

Wat Indraviharn

North of Democracy, at the edge of the Banglamphu shopping and eating district on Wisut Kasat Road, **Wat Indraviharn** (also known as Wat In) features on some tourist itineraries by virtue of the enormous standing Buddha that dominates its precincts. Commissioned by Rama IV in the mid-nineteenth century to enshrine a Buddha relic from Sri Lanka, the 32-metre-high image certainly doesn't rate as a work of art: its enormous, overly flattened features give it an ungainly aspect, while the gold mirror-mosaic surface only serves to emphasize its faintly kitsch overtones. But the beautifully pedicured foot-long toenails peep out gracefully from beneath devotees' garlands of fragrant jasmine, and you can get reasonable views of the neighbourhood by climbing the stairways of the tower supporting the statue from behind; when unlocked, the doorways in the upper part of the tower give access to the interior of the hollow image, affording vistas from shoulder level. Elsewhere in the wat's compact grounds you'll find the usual amalgam of architectural and spiritual styles, including a Chinese shrine and statues of Ramas IV and V.

Chinatown and Pahurat

When the newly crowned Rama I decided to move his capital across to the east bank of the river in 1782, the Chinese community living on the proposed site of his palace was given no choice but to relocate downriver, to the **Sampeng** area. Two hundred years on, **Chinatown** has grown into the country's largest Chinese district, a sprawl of narrow alleyways, temples and shophouses packed between New Road (Charoen Krung) and the river, separated from Ratanakosin by the Indian area of **Pahurat** – famous for its cloth and dressmakers' trimmings – and bordered to the east by Hualamphong train station. Real estate in this part of the city is said to be the most valuable in the country, with land prices on the New and Yaowarat road arteries reputed to fetch over a million baht per square metre;

not surprisingly, there are almost a hundred gold shops in the Sampeng quarter. For the tourist, Chinatown is chiefly interesting for its markets and shophouses, its open-fronted warehouses, and remnants of colonial-style architecture, though it also has a few noteworthy temples. The following account covers Chinatown's main attractions and most interesting neighbourhoods, sketching a meandering and quite lengthy route which could easily take a whole day to complete on foot.

Easiest **access** is to take the *Chao Phraya Express* boat to Tha Rajavongse (Rajawong) at the southern end of Rajawong Road, which runs through the centre of Chinatown, or to jump on one of the longtail boats that serve Khlong Krung Kasem and connecting canals, linking Banglamphu with Hualamphong

THE CHINESE IN THAILAND

The **Chinese** have been a dominant force in the shaping of Thailand, and **commerce** is the foundation of their success. Chinese merchants first gained a toehold here in the mid-fourteenth century, when they contributed so much to the prosperity of the city-state of Ayutthaya that they were the only foreign community allowed to live within the city walls. Soon their compatriots were established all over the country, and when the capital was eventually moved to Bangkok it was to an already flourishing Chinese trading post.

The Bangkok era marked an end to the wars that had dogged Thailand and as the economy began to boom, both Rama I and Rama II encouraged Chinese immigration to boost the indigenous workforce. Thousands of migrants came, most of them young men eager to earn money that could be sent back to families impoverished by civil wars and persistently bad harvests. They saw their overseas stints as temporary measures, intending to return after a few years, though many never did. By the middle of the nineteenth century half the capital's population were of pure or mixed Chinese blood, and they were quickly becoming the masters of the new import-export trade, particularly the burgeoning tin and rubber industries. By the end of the century, the Chinese dominated Thailand's commercial and urban sector, while the Thais remained in firm control of the political domain, an arrangement that apparently satisfied both parties: as the old Chinese proverb goes, "We don't mind who holds the head of the cow, providing we can milk it."

Up until the beginning of this century, **intermarriage** between the two communities had been common, because so few Chinese women had emigrated – indeed, there is some Chinese blood in almost every Thai citizen, including the king. But in the early 1900s Chinese women started to arrive in Thailand, making Chinese society increasingly self-sufficient and enclosed. **Anti-Chinese feelings** grew and discriminatory laws ensued, including the restricting of Chinese-language education and the closing of some jobs to Chinese citizens, a movement that increased in fervour as communism began to be perceived as a threat. Since the late 1970s, strict immigration controls have been enforced, limiting the number of new settlers to one hundred per nationality per year, a particularly harsh imposition on the Chinese.

The Chinese still dominate the commercial sector, as can be witnessed over the annual three-day holiday at **Chinese New Year**, when throughout the kingdom nearly all shops, hotels and restaurants shut down. This is the community's most important festival, but is celebrated much more as a family affair than in the Chinatowns of other countries. The Vegetarian Festival in October, observed with gusto by the Chinese residents of Phuket and Trang provinces, and marked in Bangkok by the removal of meat from all dishes in the city's Chinese restaurants, is a more public celebration (see p.451).

station. This part of the city is also well served by buses from downtown Bangkok, as well as from Banglamphu and Ratanakosin. **Orientation** in Chinatown can be quite tricky: the alleys (known as *trok* rather than the more usual *soi*) are extremely narrow, their turn-offs and other road signs often obscured by the mounds of merchandise that clutter the sidewalks and the surrounding hoards of buyers and sellers. If you do get lost, remember that the parallel New and Yaowarat roads lead to Hualamphong station in the east and head towards the Chao Phraya River in the west.

Wat Traimit and the Golden Buddha

Given the confusing layout of the district, it's worth starting your explorations at the eastern edge of Chinatown, just west of Hualamphong station, with the triangle of land occupied by **Wat Traimit** (daily 9am–5pm; B10). Outwardly unprepossessing, the temple boasts a quite stunning interior feature: the world's largest solid-gold Buddha is housed here, fitting for a community so closely linked with the gold trade, even if the image has nothing to do with China's spiritual heritage. Over 3m tall and weighing five and a half tons, the **Golden Buddha** gleams as if coated in liquid metal, seated amidst candles and surrounded with offerings of lotus buds and incense. A fine example of the curvaceous grace of Sukhothai art, the beautifully proportioned figure is best appreciated by comparing it with the much cruder Sukhothai Buddha in the next-door bot, to the east.

Cast in the thirteenth century, the image was brought to Bangkok by Rama III, completely encased in stucco – a common ruse to conceal valuable statues from would-be thieves. The disguise was so good that no one guessed what was underneath until 1955 when the image was accidentally knocked in the process of being moved to Wat Traimit, and the stucco cracked to reveal a patch of gold. The discovery launched a country-wide craze for tapping away at plaster Buddhas in search of hidden precious metals, but Wat Traimit's is still the most valuable – it's valued, by weight alone, at $14 million. Sections of the stucco casing are now on display alongside the Golden Buddha.

Sampeng Lane, Soi Issaranuphap and Wat Mangkon Kamalawat

Turn right outside Wat Traimit onto Yaowarat Road, then left onto Songsawat Road, to reach **Sampeng Lane** (signposted as Soi Wanit 1), an area that used to thrive on opium dens, gambling houses and brothels, but now sticks to a more reputable trade in wholesale fabrics, shoes and household goods. Stretching southeast–northwest for about 1km, Sampeng Lane makes an interesting enough introduction to commercial Chinatown, but a right turn into **Soi Issaranuphap** (also signed in places as Soi 16), which crosses it about halfway along, launches you into a more sensual experience.

Packed with people from dawn till dusk, this long, dark alleyway, which also traverses New Road (Charoen Krung), is where you come in search of ginseng roots (essential for good health), quivering fish heads, cubes of cockroach-killer chalk, and pungent piles of cinnamon sticks. You'll see Chinese grandfathers discussing business in darkened shops, ancient pharmacists concocting bizarre potions to order, alleys branching off in all directions to gaudy Chinese temples and market squares. Soi Issaranuphap finally ends at the Plaplachai Road intersection amidst a flurry of shops specializing in paper **funeral art**. Believing that the deceased should be well provided for in their afterlife, Chinese buy miniature paper replicas of necessities to be burned with the body: especially popular are houses, cars, suits of clothing and, of course, money.

If Soi Issaranuphap epitomizes traditional Chinatown commerce, then **Wat Mangkon Kamalawat** (also known as Wat Leng Nee Yee or, in English, "Dragon Flower Temple") stands as a superb example of the community's spiritual practices. Best approached via its dramatic multi-tiered gateway 10m up New Road from the Soi Issaranuphap junction, Wat Mangkon receives a constant stream of devotees, who come to leave offerings at one or more of the small altars inside this important Mahayana Buddhist temple. As with the Theravada Buddhism espoused by the Thais, Mahayana Buddhism (see "Religion: Thai Buddhism" in *Contexts*) fuses with other ancient religious beliefs, notably Confucianism and Taoism, and the statues and shrines within Wat Mangkon cover the whole spectrum. Passing through the secondary gateway, under the glazed ceramic gables topped with undulating Chinese dragons, you're greeted by a set of four outsize statues of bearded and rather forbidding sages, each clasping a symbolic object: a parasol, a pagoda, a snake's head and a mandolin. Beyond them, a series of Buddha images swathed in saffron netting occupies the next chamber, a lovely open-sided room of gold paintwork, red-lacquered wood, lattice lanterns and pictorial wall panels inlaid with mother-of-pearl. Elsewhere in the compound are little booths selling devotional paraphernalia, a Chinese medicine stall and a fortune-teller.

Wat Ga Buang Kim, Wat Chakrawat and Nakhon Kasem

Less than 100m up New Road from Wat Mangkon, a left turn into Rajawong Road, followed by a right turn into Anawong Road and a further right turn into the narrow, two-pronged Soi Krai brings you to the typical neighbourhood temple of **Wat Ga Buang Kim**. Here, as at Thai temples upcountry, local residents socialize in the shade of the tiny, enclosed courtyard and the occasional worshipper drops by to pay homage at the altar. This particular wat is remarkable for its exquisitely ornamented "vegetarian hall", a one-room shrine with altar centrepiece framed by intricately carved wooden tableaux – gold-painted miniatures arranged as if in sequence, with recognizable characters reappearing in new positions and in different moods. The hall's outer wall is adorned with small tableaux, too – the area around the doorway at the top of the stairs peopled with finely crafted ceramic figurines drawn from Chinese opera stories. The other building in the wat compound is a stage used for Chinese opera performances.

Back on Anawong, a right turn down Chakrawat Road leads to the quite dissimilar **Wat Chakrawat**, home to several long-suffering crocodiles, not to mention monkeys, dogs and chess-playing locals. **Crocodiles** have lived in the tiny pond behind the bot for about fifty years, ever since one was brought here after being hauled out of the Chao Phraya, where it had been endangering the limbs of bathers. (Unlikely as it sounds, crocodiles still occasionally turn up: a boy was attacked recently while playing in the Chao Phraya in Nonthaburi). The original crocodile, stuffed, sits in a glass case overlooking the current generation in the pond.

Across the other side of the wat compound is a grotto housing two unusual Buddhist relics. The first is a black silhouette on the wall, decorated with squares of gold leaf and believed to be the Buddha's shadow. Nearby, the statue of a fat monk looks on. The story goes that this monk was so good-looking that he was forever being tempted by the attentions of women; the only way he could deter them was to make himself ugly, which he did by gorging himself into obesity.

Further along Chakrawat Road, away from the river, is the western limit of Chinatown and an odd assortment of shops in the square known as **Nakhon Kasem** (Thieves' Market), bordered by New and Yaowarat roads to the north and south and Chakrawat and Boriphat roads to the east and west. In the sois that crisscross Nakhon Kasem, outlets once full of illicitly acquired goods now stock a vast range of metal wares, from antique gongs to modern musical instruments and machine parts.

Pahurat

The ethnic emphasis changes west of Nakhon Kasem. Cross Khlong Ong Ang and you're in **Pahurat** – here, in the small square south of the intersection of Chakraphet and Pahurat roads, is where the capital's sizeable Indian community congregates. Curiosity-shopping is not as rewarding here as in Chinatown, but if you're interested in buying **fabrics** other than Thai silk this is definitely the place. Pahurat Road is chock-a-block with cloth merchants specializing in everything from curtain and cushion materials, through saree and sarong lengths to wedding outfits and *lakhon* dance costumes complete with accessories. Also here, at the New Road/Triphet Road intersection, is the *Old Siam Plaza*: its mint-green and cream exterior, resplendent with shutters and balustraded balconies, redolent of a colonial summer palace, and its airy, three-storey interior filled with upmarket gift, handicraft and antique shops. You'll find a few eateries and a food hall under this roof, too, but Pahurat is renowned for its **Indian restaurants**, and a short stroll along Chakraphet Road will take you past a choice selection of bona fide curry houses and street-vendors.

Thonburi

Bangkok really began across the river from Ratanakosin in the town of **Thonburi**. Devoid of grand ruins and isolated from central Bangkok, it's hard to imagine Thonburi as a former capital of Thailand, but so it was for fifteen years, between the fall of Ayutthaya in 1767 and the establishment of Bangkok in 1782. General Phrya Taksin chose to set up his capital here, strategically near the sea and far from the marauding Burmese, but the story of his brief reign is a chronicle of battles that left little time and few resources to devote to the building of a city worthy of its predecessor. When General Chao Phraya displaced the demented Taksin to become Rama I, his first decision as founder of the Chakri dynasty was to move the capital to the more defensible site across the river. It wasn't until 1932 that Thonburi was linked to its replacement by the **Memorial Bridge**, built to commemorate the one-hundred-and-fiftieth anniversary of the foundation of the Chakri dynasty and of Bangkok, and dedicated to Rama I, whose bronze statue sits at the Bangkok approach. Thonburi retained its separate identity for another forty years until, in 1971, it officially became part of Bangkok.

While Thonburi may lack the fine monuments of Thailand's other ancient capitals, it nevertheless contains some of the most traditional parts of Bangkok and makes a pleasant and evocative place to wander. As well as the imposing riverside structure of Wat Arun, Thonburi offers a fleet of royal barges and several moderately interesting temples. In addition, life on this side of the river still revolves around the khlongs, on which vendors of food and household goods paddle their boats through the residential areas, and canalside factories transport their wares

THONBURI CANAL RIDES

One of the most popular ways of seeing the sights of Thonburi is to embark on a canal tour by **chartering a longtail boat** from Tha Chang, in front of the Grand Palace. These tours follow a set route, taking in Wat Arun and the Royal Barge Museum and then continuing along Thonburi's network of small canals, and charge an average price of B250 per person. There are no official departure times: you just turn up at the pier, haggle with the boatman next in line and jump into his longtail.

A less expensive but equally satisfying alternative is to use the **public longtails** that run bus-like services along back canals from central Bangkok-side piers, departing every ten to thirty minutes and charging B10–30 a round trip. No single route is more interesting than another, but the most accessible ones include: the Khlong Bangkok Noi service from Tha Chang; the Khlong Mon service from Tha Thien, in front of Wat Po; the Khlong Bang Waek service from Tha Saphan Phut, at Memorial Bridge; and the Khlong Om service from Tha Nonthaburi.

A fixture of the upper-bracket tourist round is the **organized canal tour** to see Thonburi's Wat Sai **floating market**. This has become so commercialized and land-based that it can't be recommended in preference to the two-hour trip out to the floating market of Damnoen Saduak (see p.143), but if you're short on time and set on seeing fruit- and flower-laden paddle boats, you can join longtail Wat Sai market tours from Tha Chang or from Tha Orienten (at the *Oriental Hotel*). Tours leave at around 7am and cost from B300 per person.

to the Chao Phraya River artery. Canalside **architecture** ranges from ramshackle, makeshift homes balanced just above the water – and prone to flooding during the monsoon season – to villa-style residences where the river is kept at bay by lawns, verandahs and concrete. Modern Thonburi, on the other hand, sprawling to each side of Phra Pinklao Road, consists of the prosaic line-up of department stores, cinemas, restaurants and markets found all over urbanized Thailand.

Getting there is simply a matter of crossing the river – use one of the numerous bridges (Memorial and Phra Pinklao are the most central), take a cross-river ferry, or hop on the express ferry, which makes three stops around the riverside Bangkok Noi station, just south of Phra Pinklao Bridge. You might find yourself taking a train from Bangkok Noi station, as this is the departure point for Kanchanaburi; the Southern Bus Terminal is also in Thonburi, on Pinklao–Nakhon Chaisri Road, and all public and air-conditioned buses to southern destinations leave from here.

Wat Arun

Amost directly across the river from Wat Po rises the enormous five-pranged **Wat Arun** (daily 8.30am–5.30pm; B10), the Temple of Dawn, probably Bangkok's most memorable landmark and familiar as the silhouette used in the TAT logo. It's best seen from the river, as you head downstream from the Grand Palace towards the *Oriental Hotel*, but is ornate enough to merit stopping off for a closer look. All boat tours include half an hour here, but Wat Arun is also easily visited by yourself, although tour operators will try to persuade you otherwise: just take a cross-river ferry from Tha Thien (B2).

A wat has occupied this site since the Ayutthaya period, but only in 1768 did it become known as the Temple of Dawn – when General Phrya Taksin reputedly reached his new capital at the break of day. The temple served as his royal chapel and housed the recaptured Emerald Buddha for several years until the image was moved to Wat Phra Kaeo in 1785. Despite losing its special status after the relocation, Wat Arun continued to be revered and was reconstructed and enlarged to its present height of 104m by Rama II and Rama III.

The Wat Arun that you see today is a classic prang structure of Ayutthayan style, built as a representation of Mount Meru, the home of the gods in Khmer mythology. Climbing the two tiers of the square base that supports the **central prang**, you not only get a good view of the river and beyond, but also a chance to examine the tower's curious decorations. Both this main prang and the four minor ones that encircle it are covered in bits of broken porcelain, arranged to create an amazing array of polychromatic flowers. (Local people gained much merit by donating their crockery for the purpose.) Statues of mythical figures such as *yaksha* demons and half-bird, half-human *kinnari* support the different levels and, on the first terrace, the mondops at each cardinal point contain statues of the Buddha at the most important stages of his life: at birth (north), in meditation (east), preaching his first sermon (south) and entering Nirvana (west). The second platform surrounds the base of the prang proper, whose closed entranceways are guarded by four statues of the Hindu god Indra on his three-headed elephant Erawan. In the niches of the smaller prangs stand statues of Phra Pai, the god of the wind, on horseback.

Wat Prayoon

Downstream of Wat Arun, beside Memorial Bridge, **Wat Prayoon** is worth visiting for its unusual collection of miniature chedis and shrines, set on an artificial hill constructed on a whim of Rama III's, after he'd noticed the pleasing shapes made by dripping candle wax. Wedged in among the grottoes, caverns and ledges of this uneven mass are numerous shrines to departed devotees, forming a phenomenal gallery of different styles, from traditionally Thai chedis, bots or prangs to such obviously foreign designs as the tiny Wild West house complete with cactuses at the front door. Turtles fill the pond surrounding the mound – you can feed them with the banana and papaya sold nearby. At the edge of the pond stands a memorial to the unfortunate few who lost their lives when one of the saluting cannons exploded at the temple's dedication ceremony in 1836.

About ten minutes' walk upstream from Wat Prayoon, the Catholic church of **Santa Cruz** sits at the heart of what used to be Thonburi's **Portuguese quarter**. The Portuguese came to Thailand both to trade and to proselytize, and by 1856 had established the largest of the European communities in Bangkok: four thousand Portuguese Christians lived in and around Thonburi at this time, about one percent of the total population. The Portuguese ghetto is a thing of the distant past, but this is nonetheless an interesting patch to stroll through, comprising narrow backstreets and tiny shophouses stocked with all manner of goods, from two-baht plastic toys to the essential bottles of chilli sauce.

Royal Barge Museum

Until about fifteen years ago, the king would process down the Chao Phraya River to Wat Arun in a flotilla of royal barges at least once a year, on the occasion of Kathin, the annual donation of robes by the laity to the temple at the end of the rainy season. Fifty-one barges, filling the width of the river and stretching for almost 1km, drifted slowly to the measured beat of a drum and the hypnotic strains of ancient boating hymns, chanted by over two thousand oarsmen whose red, gold and blue uniforms complemented the black and gold craft.

The hundred-year-old boats are becoming quite frail, so such a procession is now a rare event – the last was in 1987, to mark the king's sixtieth birthday. The three elegantly narrow vessels at the heart of the ceremony now spend their time moored in the **Royal Barge Museum** on the north bank of Khlong Bangkok Noi (daily 8.30am–4.30pm; B10). Up to 50m long and intricately lacquered and gilded all over, they taper at the prow into magnificent mythical figures after a design first used by the kings of Ayutthaya. Rama I had the boats copied and, when those fell into disrepair, Rama V commissioned the exact reconstructions still in use today. The most important of the trio is *Sri Suphanahongse*, which bears the king and queen and is instantly recognizable by the fifteen-foot-high prow representing a golden swan. In front of it floats *Anantanagaraj*, fronted by a magnificent seven-headed naga and bearing a Buddha image, while the royal children bring up the rear in *Anekchartphuchong*, which has a monkey god from the *Ramayana* at the bow.

The museum is a feature of all canal tours. To get there on your own, cross the Phra Pinklao Bridge and take the first left (Soi Wat Dusitaram), which leads to the museum through a jumble of walkways and houses on stilts. Alternatively, take a ferry to Bangkok Noi station; from there follow the tracks until you reach the bridge over Khlong Bangkok Noi, cross it and follow the signs. Either way it's about a ten-minute walk.

Dusit

Connected to Ratanakosin via the boulevards of Rajdamnoen Klang and Rajdamnoen Nok, the spacious, leafy area known as **Dusit** has been a royal district since the reign of Rama V (1860–1910). The first Thai monarch to visit Europe, Rama V returned with radical plans for the modernization of his capital, the fruits of which are most visible in Dusit: notably **Vimanmek Palace** and **Wat Benjamabophit**, the so-called Marble Temple. Today the peaceful Dusit area retains its European feel, and much of the country's decision-making goes on behind the high fences and impressive facades that line its tree-lined avenues: Government House is here, and the king lives on the eastern edge of the area, in the Chitrlada Palace.

Vimanmek Palace

Vimanmek Palace, at the end of the impressive sweep of Rajdamnoen Nok (daily 9.30am–4pm; compulsory free guided tours every 30min, last tour 3pm; B50, or free if you have a Grand Palace ticket, which remains valid for one month), was built by Rama V as a summer retreat on Ko Si Chang (see p.296), from where it was transported bit by bit in 1901. Built entirely of golden teak without a single nail, the L-shaped "Celestial Residence" is encircled by verandahs that look out on to well-kept lawns, flower gardens and lotus ponds. Not surprisingly, Vimanmek soon became the king's favourite palace, and he and his enormous retinue of officials, concubines and children stayed here for lengthy periods between 1902 and 1906. All of Vimanmek's 81 rooms were out of bounds to male visitors, except for the king's own apartments, which were entered by a separate staircase.

A bronze equestrian statue of Rama V stands close to the entrance to the palace compound – walk to the right of the statue, around the Italian Renaissance-

THE ROYAL WHITE ELEPHANTS

In Thailand the most revered of all elephants are the so-called **white elephants** – actually tawny brown albinos – which are considered so sacred that they all, whether wild or captive, belong to the king by law. Their special status originates from Buddhist mythology, which tells how the previously barren Queen Maya became pregnant with the future Buddha after dreaming one night that a white elephant had entered her womb. The thirteenth-century King Ramkhamhaeng of Sukhothai adopted the beast as a symbol of the great and the divine, and ever since, a Thai king's greatness is said to be measured by the number of white elephants he owns. The present king, Rama IX, has eleven, the largest royal collection to date.

Before an elephant can be granted official "white elephant" status, it has to pass a stringent assessment of its physical and behavioural **characteristics**. Key qualities include a paleness of seven crucial areas – eyes, nails, palate, hair, outer edges of the ears, tail and testicles – and an all-round genteel demeanour, manifested, for instance, in the way in which it cleans its food before eating, or in a tendency to sleep in a kneeling position. The most recent addition to King Bhumibol's stables was first spotted in Lampang in 1992, but experts from the Royal Household had to spend a year watching its every move before it was finally given the all-clear. An elaborate ceremony takes place every time a new white elephant is presented to the king: the animal is paraded with great pomp from its place of capture to Dusit, where it's annointed with holy water before an audience of the kingdom's most important priests and dignitaries, before being housed in the royal stables.

The expression "white elephant" probably derives from the legend that the kings used to present certain enemies with one of these exotic creatures. The animal required expensive attention but, being royal, could not be put to work in order to pay for its upkeep. The recipient thus went bust trying to keep it.

style Throne Hall (home of the National Assembly until the 1970s), and a little way past the entrance to Dusit Zoo (see below). Note that the same **dress rules** apply here as to the Grand Palace (see p.78).

On display inside is Rama V's collection of artefacts from all over the world, including *bencharong* ceramics, European furniture and bejewelled Thai betel-nut sets. Considered progressive in his day, Rama V introduced many newfangled ideas to Thailand: the country's first indoor bathroom is here, as is the earliest typewriter with Thai characters, and some of the first portrait paintings – portraiture had until then been seen as a way of stealing part of the sitter's soul.

Dusit Zoo

Nearby **Dusit Zoo** (daily 8am–6pm; B20), once part of the Chitrlada Palace gardens and now a public park, is nothing special but it does have a few rare animals in its small bare cages. Look out for the Komodo dragon, the world's largest reptile, which lives only on a small part of the Indonesian archipelago and in a few zoos in other parts of the world. The Dusit resident is relatively small as these monsters go: in the wild they can grow to a length of 3m and achieve a weight of 150kg. Also on show are cage-loads of white-handed gibbons, a favourite target of Thai poachers, who make a lot of money by selling them as pets (and to zoos) via Chatuchak Weekend Market and other channels. The zoo used to house several royal white elephants, but at the time of writing they had all been returned to the stables in the grounds of Chitrlada Palace.

Wat Benjamabophit

Ten minutes' walk southeast from Vimanmek and the zoo along Sri Ayutthaya Road, **Wat Benjamabophit** (daily 7am–5pm; B10) was the last major temple to have been built in Bangkok. It's an interesting fusion of classical Thai and nineteenth-century European design, with its Carrara marble walls – hence the touristic tag "The Marble Temple" – complemented by the bot's unusual stained-glass windows, Victorian in style but depicting figures from Thai mythology. Inside, a fine replica of the highly revered Phra Buddha Chinnarat image of Phitsanulok presides over the small room containing Rama V's ashes. The courtyard behind the bot houses a gallery of Buddha images from all over Asia, set up by Rama V as an overview of different representations of the Buddha.

Wat Benjamabophit is one of the best temples in Bangkok to see religious **festivals** and rituals. Whereas monks elsewhere tend to go out on the streets every morning in search of alms, at the Marble Temple the ritual is reversed, and meritmakers come to them. Between about 6 and 7.30am, the monks line up on Nakhon Pathom Road, their bowls ready to receive donations of curry and rice, lotus buds, incense, even toilet paper and Coca-Cola. The evening candlelight processions around the bot during the Buddhist festivals of Maha Puja (in Feb) and Visakha Puja (in May) are among the most entrancing in the country.

Downtown Bangkok

Extending east from the rail line and south to Sathorn Road, **downtown Bangkok** is central to the colossal expanse of Bangkok as a whole, but rather peripheral in a sightseer's perception of the city. This is where you'll find the main financial district, around Silom Road, and the chief shopping centres, around Siam Square, in addition to the smart hotels and restaurants, the embassies and airline offices. Scattered widely across the downtown area there are just a few attractions for visitors, including the noisy and glittering **Erawan Shrine**, the **Visual Dhamma Gallery**, and three attractive museums housed in traditional teak buildings: **Jim Thompson's House**, the **Kamthieng House** and the **Suan Pakkad Palace Museum**. The infamous **Patpong** district hardly shines as a tourist sight, yet, lamentably, its sex bars provide Thailand's single biggest draw for farang men.

If you're heading downtown from Banglamphu, allow at least an hour to get to any of the places mentioned here by **bus**. To get to the southern part of the area, take an **express boat** downriver and then change onto a bus if necessary. For other parts of the downtown area, it's worth considering the regular **longtails** on Khlong Sen Seb, which runs parallel to Phetchaburi Road. They start at the Golden Mount, near Democracy Monument, and have useful stops at Phrayathai Road (for Jim Thompson's House), Pratunam (for Suan Pakkad and the Erawan Shrine) and Soi 23 off Sukhumvit Road (for Kamthieng House).

Siam Square to Sukhumvit Road

Though Siam Square has just about everything to satisfy the Thai consumer boom – big shopping centres, Western fast-food restaurants, cinemas – don't come looking for an elegant commercial piazza: the "square" is in fact a grid of small streets on the south side of Rama I Road, between Phrayathai and Henri

Dunant roads, and the name is applied freely to the surrounding area. Further east, you'll find newer, bigger and more expensive shopping malls at Erawan corner, where Rama I becomes Ploenchit Road. Life becomes less frenetic along Ploenchit, which is flanked by several grand old embassies, and starts to become suburban once you pass under the expressway flyover and enter Sukhumvit Road, the broad avenue through the heart of the wealthy farang quarter.

Jim Thompson's House

Just off Siam Square at 6 Soi Kasemsan 2, Rama I Rd, **Jim Thompson's House** (Mon–Sat 9am–5pm, last tour 4.30pm; B100, under-25s B40) is a kind of Ideal Home in elegant Thai style, and a peaceful refuge from downtown chaos. The house was the residence of the legendary American adventurer, entrepreneur, art collector and all-round character whose mysterious disappearance in the jungles of Malaysia in 1967 has made him even more of a legend among Thailand's farang community. Apart from putting together this beautiful home, Thompson's most concrete contribution was to turn traditional silk-weaving from a dying art into the highly successful international industry it is today.

The grand, rambling **house** is in fact a combination of six teak houses, some from as far afield as Ayutthaya and most over two hundred years old. Like all traditional houses, they were built in wall sections hung together without nails on a frame of wooden pillars, which made it easy to dismantle them, pile them onto a barge and float them to their new home. Although he had trained as an architect, Thompson had more difficulty in putting them back together again; in the end, he had to go back to Ayutthaya to hunt down a group of carpenters who still practised the old house-building methods. Thompson added a few unconventional touches of his own, incorporating the elaborately carved front wall of a Chinese

---

THE LEGENDS OF JIM THOMPSON

Thai silk-weavers, art dealers and conspiracy theorists all owe a debt to **Jim Thompson**, who even now, 25 years after his death, remains Thailand's most famous farang. An architect by trade, Thompson left his New York practice in 1940 to join the Office of Strategic Services (later to become the CIA), a tour of duty which was to see him involved in clandestine operations in North Africa, Europe and, in 1945, the Far East, where he was detailed to a unit preparing for the invasion of Thailand. When the mission was pre-empted by the Japanese surrender, he served for a year as OSS station chief in Bangkok, forming links that were later to provide grist for endless speculation.

After an unhappy and short-lived stint as part owner of the *Oriental Hotel*, Thompson found his calling in the struggling **silk-weavers** of the area near the present Jim Thompson House, whose traditional product was unknown in the West and had been all but abandoned by Thais in favour of less costly imported textiles. Encouragement from society friends and an enthusiastic write-up in *Vogue* convinced him there was a foreign market for Thai silk, and by 1948 he had founded the Thai Silk Company Ltd. Success was assured when, two years later, the company was commissioned to make the costumes for the Broadway run of *The King and I*. Thompson's celebrated eye for colour combinations and his tireless promotion – in the early days, he could often be seen in the lobby of the *Oriental* with bolts of silk slung over his shoulder, waiting to pounce on any remotely curious tourist – quickly made his name synonymous with Thai silk.

pawn shop between the drawing room and the bedroom, and reversing the other walls in the drawing room so that their carvings faced into the room.

The impeccably tasteful **interior** has been left as it was during Thompson's life, even down to the cutlery on the dining table, and visitors are shown around on guided tours in several languages. Complementing the fine artefacts from throughout Southeast Asia is a stunning array of Thai arts and crafts, including one of the best collections of traditional Thai paintings in the world. Thompson picked up plenty of bargains from the Thieves' Quarter (Nakhon Kasem) in Chinatown, before collecting Thai art became fashionable and expensive. Other pieces were liberated from decay and destruction in upcountry temples, while many of the Buddha images were turned over by ploughs, especially around Ayutthaya. Some of the exhibits are very rare, such as a seventeenth-century Ayutthayan teak Buddha, but Thompson also bought pieces of little value and fakes simply for their looks – a shopping strategy that's all the more sensible in the jungle of today's Thai antiques trade.

The Erawan Shrine

For a break from high culture drop in on the **Erawan Shrine**, at the corner of Ploenchit and Rajdamri roads. Remarkable as much for its setting as anything else, this shrine to Brahma, the ancient Hindu creation god, and Erawan, his elephant, squeezes in on one of the busiest and noisiest corners of modern Bangkok, in the shadow of the *Grand Hyatt Erawan Hotel* – whose existence is the reason for the shrine. When a string of calamities held up the building of the hotel in the 1950s, spirit doctors were called in, who instructed the owners to build a new home for the offended local spirits: the hotel was then finished without further mishap.

Like a character in a Somerset Maugham novel, Thompson played the role of Western exile to the hilt. Though he spoke no Thai, he made it his personal mission to preserve traditional arts and architecture at a time when most Thais were more keen to emulate the West, assembling his famous Thai house and stuffing it with all manner of Oriental *objets d'art*. At the same time he held firmly to his farang roots and society connections: no foreign gathering in Bangkok was complete without Jim Thompson, and virtually every Western luminary passing through Bangkok – from Truman Capote to Ethel Merman – dined at his table.

If Thompson's life was the stuff of legend, his **disappearance** and presumed death only added to the mystique. On Easter Sunday, 1967, Thompson, while staying with friends in a cottage in Malaysia's Cameron Highlands, went out for a stroll and never came back. A massive search of the area, employing local guides, tracker dogs and even shamans, turned up no clues, provoking a rash of fascinating but entirely unsubstantiated theories. The grandfather of them all, advanced by a Dutch psychic, held that Thompson had been lured into an ambush by the disgraced former prime minister of Thailand, Pridi Panyonyong, and spirited off to Cambodia for indeterminate purposes; later versions, supposing that Thompson had remained a covert CIA operative all his life, proposed that he was abducted by Vietnamese communists and brainwashed to be displayed as a high-profile defector to communism. More recently, an amateur sleuth claims to have found evidence that Thompson met a more mundane fate, having been killed by a careless truck driver and hastily buried.

Be prepared for sensory overload: the main structure shines with lurid glass of all colours and the overcrowded precinct around it is almost buried under scented garlands and incense candles. You might also catch a lacklustre group of tradi-

tional **dancers** performing here to the strains of a small classical orchestra – worshippers hire them to give thanks for a stroke of good fortune. To increase their future chances of such good fortune, visitors buy a bird or two from the flocks incarcerated in cages here; the bird-seller transfers the requested number of captives to a tiny hand-held cage, from which the customer duly liberates the animals, thereby accruing merit. People set on less abstract rewards will invest in a lottery ticket from one of the physically handicapped sellers: they're thought to be the luckiest you can buy.

Merit-making

Kamthieng House

Another reconstructed traditional Thai residence, the **Kamthieng House** (Tues–Sat 9am–noon & 1–5pm; B20) was moved in the 1960s from Chiang Mai to 130 Soi Asoke, off Sukhumvit Road, and set up as an ethnological museum by the Siam Society. It differs from both Suan Pakkad and Jim Thompson's House in being the home of a commoner, and although the owner was by no means poor, the objects on display give a fair representation of rural life in northern Thailand.

The house was built on the banks of the River Ping in the mid-nineteenth century and the ground-level display of farming tools and fish traps evokes the upcountry practice of fishing in flooded rice paddies to supplement the supply from the rivers. Upstairs, the main rooms of the house are much as they would have been 150 years ago – the raised floor is polished and smooth, sparsely furnished with only a couple of low tables and seating mats, and a betel-nut set to hand. Notice how surplus furniture and utensils are stored in the rafters. The rectangular lintel above the door to the inner room is a *hum yon*, carved in floral patterns that represent testicles and designed to ward off evil spirits. Walking along the open verandah between the kitchen and the granary, you'll see areca palm (betel nut) trees to your left: the garden, too, is as authentic as possible.

Next door to Kamthieng House, in the same compound, is the more recently acquired **Sangaroon House**, built here to house the folk-craft collection of Thai architect and lecturer Sangaroon Ratagasikorn. Upon his return to Thailand after studying in America under Frank Lloyd Wright, Sangaroon became fascinated by the efficient designs of rural utensils and began to collect them as teaching aids. Those on display include baskets, fishing pots and *takraw* balls, all of which fulfil his criteria of being functional, simple and beautiful, with no extraneous features.

Visual Dhamma Gallery

Also along Sukhumvit's Soi Asoke, at 44/28, stands Bangkok's most vibrant modern art gallery, **Visual Dhamma Gallery** (Mon–Fri 1–6pm, Sat 10am–5pm; free), which houses a permanent collection of paintings by major figures – such as Vasan Sitthiket, Montien Boonma and Pichai Nirand – and temporary shows of less established artists. The gallery was set up in 1981 by Austrian expat Alfred Pawlin to promote pieces with a Buddhist and mythological theme, but over the years has widened its scope to embrace the more abstract work of painters such as Thaiwijit Puangkasemsomboon, and now also functions as an important resource centre on works of the last two decades.

Northern downtown

The area above Petchaburi Road, which becomes increasingly residential as you move north, is cut through by two major roads lined with monolithic company headquarters: Phaholyothin, which runs past the Northern Bus Terminal and the weekend market, and Wiphawadi Rangsit, leading to the airport. The area's chief tourist attraction is Suan Pakkad, a museum of Thai arts and crafts set in a beautiful garden, but it also contains two of Bangkok's most famous landmarks and an important covered market.

Suan Pakkad Palace Museum

The **Suan Pakkad Palace Museum** (Mon–Sat 9am–4pm; B80), 352–4 Sri Ayutthaya Rd, stands on what was once a cabbage patch but is now one of the finest gardens in Bangkok. The private collection of beautiful Thai objects from all periods is displayed in five traditional wooden houses, which were transported to Bangkok from various parts of the country. You can either take a mediocre guided tour in English (free) or explore the loosely arranged collection yourself (some of the exhibits are labelled).

The highlight is the renovated **Lacquer Pavilion**, across the reedy pond at the back of the grounds. Set on stilts, the pavilion is actually an amalgam of two temple buildings, a *ho trai* (library) and a *ho khien* (writing room), one inside the other, which were found between Ayutthaya and Bang Pa-In. The interior walls are beautifully decorated with gilt on black lacquer: the upper panels depict the life of the Buddha while the lower ones show scenes from the *Ramayana*. Look out especially for the grisly details in the tableau on the back wall, showing the earth goddess drowning the evil forces of Mara. Underneath are depicted some European dandies on horseback, probably merchants, whose presence suggests that the work was executed before the fall of Ayutthaya in 1767.

The carefully observed details of daily life and nature are skilful and lively, especially considering the restraints which the **lacquering technique** places on the artist, who has no opportunity for corrections or touching up: the design has to be punched into a piece of paper, which is then laid on the panel of black lacquer (a kind of plant resin); a small bag of chalk dust is pressed on top so that the dust penetrates the minute holes in the paper, leaving a line of dots on the lacquer to mark the pattern; a gummy substance is then applied to the background areas which are to remain black, before the whole surface is covered in microscopically thin squares of gold leaf; thin sheets of blotting paper, sprinkled with water, are then laid over the panel, which when pulled off bring away the gummy substance and the unwanted pieces of gold leaf that are stuck to it, leaving the rest of the gold decoration in high relief against the black background.

The **Ban Chiang house** has a very good collection of elegant, whorled pottery and bronze jewellery, which the former owner of Suan Pakkad Palace, Princess Chumbot, excavated from tombs at Ban Chiang, the major Bronze Age settle-

Ban Chiang pottery

ment in the northeast. Scattered around the museum's other three traditional houses, you'll come across some attractive Thai and Khmer religious sculpture amongst an eclectic jumble of artefacts: fine ceramics as well as some intriguing kiln-wasters, failed pots which have melted together in the kiln to form weird, almost rubbery pieces of sculpture; beautiful betel-nut sets (see p.359); and some rich teak carvings, including a 200-year-old temple door showing episodes from *Sang Thong*, a folk tale about a childless king and queen who discover a handsome son in a conch shell.

Baiyoke Tower Hotel, Pratunam Market and the Victory Monument

Fifteen minutes' walk southeast of Suan Pakkad is Thailand's tallest building, the **Baiyoke Tower Hotel**, distinguished by its rainbow colour scheme and sprouting out from a small enclave of hotels and shops. Extending southeast from the tower to the corner of Rajaprarop and Phetchaburi roads, **Pratunam Market** is famous for its low-cost, low-quality casual clothes. The vast warren of stalls is becoming touristy near the tower, though there are still bargains towards the other end, amongst the amphetamine-driven sweatshops.

A good half-hour north of Suan Pakkad, the stone obelisk of the **Victory Monument** can be seen from way down the broad Phrayathai and Rajwithi streets. It was erected after the Indo-Chinese War of 1940–41, when Thailand pinched back some territory in Laos and Cambodia while the French government was otherwise occupied in World War II, but nowadays it commemorates all of Thailand's past military glories.

Southern downtown

South of Rama I Road, commercial development gives way to a dispersed assortment of large institutions, dominated by Thailand's most prestigious centre of higher learning, Chulalongkorn University, and the green expanse of Lumphini Park. Rama IV Road marks another change of character: downtown proper, centring around the high-rise American-style boulevard of Silom Road, heart of the financial district, extends from here to the river. Alongside the smoked-glass banks and offices, the plush hotels and tourist shops, and opposite Bangkok's Carmelite convent, lies the dark heart of Bangkok nightlife, Patpong.

Carrying on to the river, the strip west of New Road reveals some of the history of Bangkok's early dealings with farangs in the fading grandeur of the old trading quarter. Here you'll find the only place in Bangkok where you might be able to eke out an architectural walk, though it's hardly compelling. Incongruous churches and "colonial" buildings (the best of these is the Authors' Wing of the *Oriental Hotel*, where nostalgic afternoon teas are served) are hemmed in by the spice shops and *halal* canteens of the growing Muslim area along New Road and the outskirts of Chinatown to the north.

The Museum of Imaging Technology

Chulalongkorn University's brand-new, high-tech **Museum of Imaging Technology** (Sat & Sun 10am–4pm; B100), just south of the big entrance to the campus on the east side of Phrayathai Road, can compete with any museum of photography in the world, and is especially good for kids, with plenty of activities and things to take home. The impressive facilities have been made possible by corporate sponsors, who naturally capitalize on the PR potential of their bequests: in the Fuji Discovery Room you can set various machines going to make, process and develop a film (Fuji, of course), and the Canon Room allows you to handle the latest technology from – who else? – Canon. In addition to the activity rooms, the gallery of contemporary photography has a good permanent display, plus occasional temporary shows, of high-class works from around the world, and the gallery of Thai photography exhibits the best of local work.

The Snake Farm

The **Snake Farm**, also known as the Queen Saowaba Institute, at the corner of Rama IV and Henri Dunant roads, is a bit of a circus act, but an entertaining, informative and worthy one at that. Run by the Thai Red Cross, it has a double function: to produce snake-bite serums, and to educate the public on the dangers of Thai snakes. The latter mission involves putting on displays (Mon–Fri 10.30am & 2pm, Sat, Sun & holidays 10.30am; B70) that begin with a slick half-hour slide show illustrating, among other things, how to apply a tourniquet and immobilize a bitten limb. Things warm up with a live demonstration of snake handling, which is well presented and safe, and gains a perverse fascination from the knowledge that the strongest venoms of the snakes on show can kill in only three minutes. The climax of the display comes when, having watched a python squeezing great chunks of chicken through its body, the audience is invited to handle a docile Burmese constrictor.

SNAKE'S BLOOD AND OTHER TREATS

In Thailand's big cities you'll occasionally come across obscure stalls offering restorative glasses of warm **snake's blood**, which appeals mostly to Malaysian, Chinese and Korean visitors. Not just any snake, of course: only poisonous varieties will do, with prices ranging from B200 for a common cobra, through B2000 for a king cobra, up to B30,000 for the rare albino cobra.

Once you've selected your victim from the roadside cages, the proprietor will take the snake behind the stall, hang it up by its head and slit it open with a razor blade. The major artery yields enough blood to fill a wine glass, and when it's been mixed with the bile from the snake's gall bladder, warm whisky and a dash of honey, you down the potion in one. If this doesn't satisfy, delicacies like dried gall bladder and pickled snake genitals might tempt you. But if your health is really in a bad way, all that's left is the shock cure of drinking the **venom**, after it's been mixed with whisky and left standing for quarter of an hour.

There's no evidence to support the claims made for the **medicinal properties** of snakes' innards, but there's no proof to the contrary either. While male impotence remains the main reason for the trade's persistence, the blood is also said to be good for the eyes, for backache, for malodorous urine, and simply to "make happy".

Lumphini Park

If you're sick of cars and concrete, head for **Lumphini Park**, at the east end of Silom Road, where the air is almost fresh and the traffic noise dies down to a low murmur. Named after the town in Nepal where the Buddha was born, the park is arrayed around two lakes, where you can take out a pedalo or a rowing

THE SEX INDUSTRY

Bangkok owes its reputation as the carnal capital of the world to a highly efficient sex industry adept at peddling fantasies of cheap sex on tap. More than 1000 sex-related businesses operate in the city, but the gaudy neon fleshpots of Patpong give a misleading impression of an activity that is deeply rooted in Thai culture – the overwhelming majority of Thailand's prostitutes of both sexes (estimated at anywhere between 120,000 and 700,000) work with Thai men, not farangs.

Prostitution and polygamy have long been intrinsic to the Thai way of life. Until Rama VI broke with the custom in 1910, Thai kings had always kept a retinue of concubines around them, a select few of whom would be elevated to the status of wife and royal mother, the rest forming a harem of ladies-in-waiting and sexual playthings. The practice was aped by the status-hungry nobility and, from the early nineteenth century, by newly rich merchants keen to have lots of sons and heirs. Though the monarch is now monogamous, many men of all classes still keep mistresses, known as *mia noi* (minor wives), a tradition bolstered by the popular philosophy which maintains that an official wife (*mia luang*) should be treated like the temple's main Buddha image – respected and elevated upon the altar – whereas the minor wife is an amulet, to be taken along wherever you go. For those not wealthy enough to take on *mia noi*, prostitution is a far less costly and equally accepted option. Between 43 and 97 percent of sexually active Thai men are thought to use the services of prostitutes twice a month on average, and it's common practice for a night out with the boys to wind up in a brothel or massage parlour.

The **farang sex industry** is a relatively new development, having had its start during the Vietnam War, when the American military set up seven bases around Thailand. The GIs' appetite for "entertainment" fuelled the creation of instant redlight districts near the bases, attracting women from surrounding rural areas to cash in on the boom; Bangkok joined the fray in 1967, when the US secured the right to ferry soldiers in from Vietnam for R&R breaks. By the mid-1970s, the bases had been evacuated but the sex infrastructure remained and tourists moved in to fill the vacuum, lured by advertising that diverted most of the traffic to Bangkok and Pattaya. Sex tourism has since grown to become an established part of the Thai economy, the two million-plus foreign males who arrive each year representing a foreign-exchange earnings potential of B50 billion. Even the highly respectable *Bangkok Post* publishes a weekly column on sex-industry news and gossip, and, despite attempts by the tourist authorities to downplay the country's sleazy image, Bangkok attracts a growing international clientele, with some German and Japanese companies organizing sex tours as a reward for high productivity.

The majority of the women who work in the Patpong bars come from the poorest rural areas of north and northeast Thailand. **Economic refugees** in search of a better life, they're easily drawn into an industry where they can make in a single night what it takes a month to earn in the rice fields – in some Isaan villages, money sent home by prostitutes in Bangkok far exceeds financial aid given by the government. Small wonder then that the government remains happy enough to let rural Thai families sell their daughters into prostitution rather than come banging at the door of the agricultural subsidies department. Women from rural communities

boat (B20 per half-hour), and is landscaped with a wide variety of local trees and numerous pagodas and pavilions, usually occupied by Chinese chess players. The wide open spaces here are a popular area for gay cruising, and you might be offered dope, though the police patrol regularly – for all that, it's not an intimidating place. To recharge your batteries, make for the garden restau-

have always been expected to contribute an equal share to the family income and it's hardly surprising that many opt for a couple of lucrative years in the sex bars and brothels as the most effective way of helping to pay off family debts and improve the living conditions of parents stuck in the poverty trap. Reinforcing this social obligation there's the pervasive Buddhist notion of **karma**, which holds that your lot, however unhappy, is the product of past-life misdeeds and can only be improved by making sufficient merit to ensure a better life next time round.

While most women enter the racket presumably knowing at least something of what lies ahead, younger girls definitely do not. **Child prostitution** is rife: an estimated ten percent of prostitutes are under fourteen, some are as young as nine. They are valuable property: in the teahouses of Chinatown, a prepubescent virgin can be rented to her first customer for B5000, as sex with someone so young is believed to have rejuvenating properties. Most child prostitutes have been sold by desperate parents as **bonded slaves** to pimps or agents, and are kept locked up until they have fully repaid the money given to their parents, which may take two or more years.

Despite its ubiquity, prostitution has been **illegal** in Thailand since 1960, but sex-industry bosses easily circumvent the law by registering their establishments as bars, restaurants, barbers, nightclubs or massage parlours, and making payoffs to the police. Sex workers, on the other hand, have no legal rights and will often endure exploitation and violence from employers, pimps and customers rather than face imprisonment and fines. In an attempt to partially redress this iniquitous system, and protect the youngest prostitutes at least, a government bill has been drafted to penalize the procurers, pimps and, most radically, the clients of prostitutes under eighteen years of age instead of the girls themselves. The bill looks set to become law by the end of 1995 but, given the vast sums of money generated by the sex industry, its enforcement is by no means guaranteed.

In recent years, the spectre of **AIDS** has put the problems of the sex industry into sharp focus: according to the latest World Health Organization figures, there are around 500,000 HIV carriers in Thailand, including an estimated fourteen per cent of the country's prostitutes (although in some northern cities, like Chiang Rai, the figure is thought to be as high as 70 percent) and twelve percent of military conscripts in the provinces, where men are least likely to use condoms. The wives, girlfriends and new-born children of prostitute-visiting males now constitute the highest risk group, and 1.3 percent of pregnant women are infected.

Since 1988, the government has conducted an aggressive, WHO-approved AIDS awareness campaign, a vital component of which has been to send health officials into brothels to administer blood tests and give out condoms. The programme seems to be having some effect, and the spread of the disease has slowed from the alarming rates of the late 1980s, when HIV figures were doubling every six months. One of the major campaigning bodies in Thailand, the Population and Community Development Association (PDA) – whose director, Meechai Viravaidhya, was the inspiration for the commonest Thai word for condom, *meechai* – has revealed that between 1991 and 1994 the rate of new infections dropped by 77 percent. The WHO now estimates that Thailand has a lower per capita infection rate than the US or Australia, though this still means that around six hundred Thais are becoming HIV-positive every day.

rant, *Pop*, in the northwest corner (see p.121), or the pavement food stalls at the northern edge of the park.

Patpong

Concentrated into a small area between the eastern ends of Silom and Suriwong roads, the neon-lit go-go bars of the **Patpong** district loom like rides in a tawdry sexual Disneyland. In front of each bar, girls cajole passers-by with a lifeless sensuality while insistent touts proffer printed menus detailing the degradations on show. Inside, bikini-clad or topless women gyrate to Western music and play hostess to the (almost exclusively male) spectators; upstairs, live shows feature women who, to use Spalding Gray's phrase in *Swimming to Cambodia*, "do everything with their vaginas except have babies".

Patpong was no more than a sea of mud when the capital was founded on the marshy riverbank to the west, but by the 1960s it had grown into a flash district of nightclubs and dance halls for rich Thais, owned by a Chinese millionaire godfather who gave his name to the area. In 1969, an American entrepreneur turned an existing teahouse into a luxurious nightclub to satisfy the tastes of soldiers on R&R trips from Vietnam, and so began Patpong's transformation into a Western sex reservation. At first, the area was rough and violent, but over the years it has wised up to the desires of the affluent farang, and now markets itself as a packaged concept of Oriental decadence. The centre of the skin trade lies along the interconnected sois of **Patpong 1 and 2**, where lines of go-go bars share their patch with respectable restaurants, bookstores, a 24-hour supermarket and *Kentucky Fried Chicken*. By night, it's a thumping theme park, whose blazing neon promises tend towards self-parody, with names like *French Kiss* and *Love Nest*. Budget travellers, purposeful safari-suited businessmen and noisy lager louts throng the streets, and even the most demure tourists – of both sexes – turn out to do some shopping at the night market down the middle of Patpong 1, where hawkers sell fake watches and designer T-shirts. By day, a relaxed hangover descends on the place. Bar-girls hang out at food stalls and cafés in respectable dress, often recognizable only by their faces, pinched and strained from the continuous use of antibiotics and heroin in an attempt to ward off venereal disease and boredom. Farang men slump at the bar beers on Patpong 2, drinking and watching videos, unable to find anything else to do in the whole of Bangkok.

The small dead-end alley to the east of Patpong 2, **Silom 4** (ie Soi 4, Silom Road), hosts Bangkok's hippest nightlife, its bars, clubs and pavements heaving at weekends with the capital's brightest and most overprivileged young things. A few gay venues still cling to Silom 4, but the focus of the scene has recently shifted to **Silom 2**. In between, **Thaniya Road**'s hostess bars and one of the city's swishest shopping centres, Thaniya Plaza, cater mostly to Japanese tourists.

The outskirts

The amorphous clutter of Greater Bangkok doesn't harbour many attractions, but there are a handful of places – principally **Chatuchak Weekend Market**, the cultural theme park of **Muang Boran**, the upstream town of **Nonthaburi** and the tranquil artificial island of **Ko Kred** – which make pleasant half-day escapes.

Theoretically, you could also see any one of these sights en route to destinations north, east or west, though lumping luggage around makes negotiating city transport even more trying.

Chatuchak

Bangkok's weekly shopping extravaganza, the enormous **Chatuchak Weekend Market** (Sat & Sun 7am–6pm), is inconveniently relegated to a patch of waste ground in Chatuchak Park near the Northern Bus Terminal, but with six thousand open-air stalls to peruse, and wares as diverse as Laotian silk, Siamese kittens and buffalo-horn catapults to choose from, it's well worth the effort. To get there, catch air-conditioned **buses** #2 from Silom Road, #9 from Rajdamnoen Klang Road, #10 or #13 from Victory Monument, or #13 from Sukhumvit Road.

Though its primary customers are Bangkok residents in search of inexpensive clothes, home accessories and a strong dose of *sanuk*, Chatuchak also has some collector- and tourist-oriented **stalls** and – highly controversially – a large wildlife section. It's unlikely that you'll see any endangered species on display, though you're bound to come across fighting cocks around the back (demonstrations are almost continuous), miniature flying squirrels being fed milk through pipettes, and iridescent red and blue Siamese fighting fish, kept in individual jars and shielded from each others' aggressive stares by sheets of cardboard. Best buys include antique and unusual silks and cottons, jeans, northern crafts, silver jewel-

---

ENDANGERED SPECIES FOR SALE

In April 1991 the Worldwide Fund for Nature (WWF) denounced Thailand as "probably the worst country in the world for the illegal trade in **endangered wildlife**", and branded Chatuchak Weekend Market "the wildlife supermarket of the world". Protected and endangered species traded at Chatuchak include gibbons, palm cockatoos, golden dragon fish, Indian pied hornbills – even tiger cubs and lions. Many of the animals are smuggled across from Laos and Cambodia and then sold at Chatuchak to private animal collectors and foreign zoos, particulary in eastern Europe. Those that don't make it alive to overseas destinations usually get there in some other form: leopard and reptile skins, ivory products and tiger claws are just a few of the goods for sale not only at Chatuchak, but throughout the city.

Although Thailand is a signatory to the **Convention on International Trade in Endangered Species** (CITES), until April 1991 it had failed to honour its membership with appropriate laws and penalties. WWF subsequently launched a campaign to boycott Thailand and Thai goods, and the US banned all Thai wildlife exports. In response, stringent amendments to Thailand's outdated and ineffective 1960 Wildlife Preservation Act were passed in November 1991 (anyone caught exporting endangered-animal products, such as ivory or turtle shells, without a licence now faces a fine of up to B20,000 and a maximum jail sentence of five years; TAT publishes an English-language list of offending articles) – and CITES subsequently lifted the ban in April 1992. The Thai police have, meanwhile, become zealous in their pursuit of illegal traders, which is why you probably won't see rare species openly displayed at Chatuchak – though that doesn't mean the black market has folded. Vendors are hardly likely to forego the estimated $500,000 earned from trading wildlife at Chatuchak each year, and domestic demand will continue until it's no longer so amusing to have a cute white-handed gibbon chained to your tree or a myna bird screeching from a cage outside your front door.

lery, basketware and ceramics, particularly the five-coloured *bencharong*. If you're going there to buy, take a copy of *Nancy Chandler's Map of Bangkok*, as it shows the location of all the specialist areas within the market.

There's no shortage of **food** stalls inside the market compound, but for really good vegetarian sustenance head for *Chamlong's (Asoke)*, an open-air, cafeteria-style restaurant just outside on Kamphaeng Phet Road (across Kamphaeng Phet II Road, behind the air-conditioned bus stop), set up by Bangkok's former governor as a service to the citizenry: good, wholesome food from B5 a plate (Sat & Sun 8am–noon).

Nonthaburi

A trip to **NONTHABURI**, the first town beyond the northern boundary of Bangkok, is just about the easiest excursion you can make from the centre of the city and affords a perfect opportunity to experience a slice of rural Thailand without even having to board a bus. Nonthaburi is the last stop upriver on the *Chao Phraya Express* boat, only 45 minutes from Tha Phra Athit (every 15min; B8 from Tha Si Phraya and points south, B6 from all other stops) and is also served by the *Laemthong Express* (30min), which pulls in here before continuing northwards to its Pakkred terminus. The ride is half the fun in itself, weaving round huge, crawling rice barges and tiny canoes, and the slow pace of the boat gives you plenty of time to take in the sights on the way. Once out of the centre, you'll pass the royal boat house in front of the National Library on the east bank, where you can glimpse the minor ceremonial boats which escort the grand royal barges. The nearer you get to Nonthaburi, the less you see of the riverbanks, which are increasingly obscured by houses on stilts and houseboats – past the *Singha* brew-

---

DURIANS

The naturalist Alfred Russel Wallace, eulogizing the taste of the **durian**, compared it to "rich butter-like custard highly flavoured with almonds, but intermingled with wafts of flavour that call to mind cream cheese, onion sauce, brown sherry and other incongruities". He neglected to discuss the smell, which is so bad – somewhere between detergent and dogshit – that durians are barred from Thai hotels and aeroplanes. The different **varieties** bear strange monikers which do nothing to make them more appetizing: "frog", "golden pillow", "gibbon" and so on. However, the durian has fervent admirers, perhaps because it's such an acquired taste, and because it's considered a strong aphrodisiac. Aficionados discuss the varieties with as much subtlety as if they were vintage champagnes, and they treat the durian as a social fruit, to be shared around despite a price of up to B600 each.

Durian season is roughly April to June and the most famous durian orchards are around Nonthaburi, where the fruits are said to have an incomparably rich and nutty flavour due to the fine clay soil. If you don't smell them first, you can recognize durians by their sci-fi **appearance**: the shape and size of a rugby ball, but slightly deflated, they're covered in a thick, pale-green shell which is heavily armoured with short, sharp spikes (*duri* means "thorn" in Malay). By cutting along one of the faint seams with a good knife, you'll reveal a white pith in which are set a handful of yellow blobs with the texture of a bad soufflé: this is what you eat. The taste is best when the smell is at its highest, about three days after the fruit has dropped. Be careful when out walking: due to its great weight and sharp spikes, a falling durian can lead to serious injury, or even an ignominious death.

ery with its manicured lawns and topiary garden, you'll see a community of people who live on the huge teak vessels used to carry rice, sand and charcoal.

Disembarking at Nonthaburi, you immediately get the feeling of being out in the sticks: the pier, on the east bank of the river, is overrun by a market that's famous for the quality of its fruit; the Provincial Office across the road is covered in rickety old wooden latticework; and the short promenade, its lampposts hung with models of the town's famous durian fruit, lends a seaside atmosphere.

Two sights – a riverside wat and an oddball museum dedicated to Thai crime and punishment – will repay a few hours' wandering in the vicinity. To break up your trip with a slow, scenic drink or lunch, you'll find a floating restaurant at the end of the prom which, though a bit overpriced, is quiet and breezy. If you're thirsty for more cruising on the water, take a longtail boat from the pier up **Khlong Om** (round trip 45min, B10): the canal, lined with some grand suburban mansions, traditional wooden houses, temples and durian plantations, leads almost out into open country.

Wat Chalerm Phra Kiat

Set in relaxing grounds on the west bank of the river, elegant **Wat Chalerm Phra Kiat** injects a splash of urban refinement amongst a grove of breadfruit trees. From the Nonthaburi pier, you can either squeeze into one of the regular longtails going upriver (a 5-min ride) or take the ferry straight across the Chao Phraya then walk up the river bank for fifteen minutes. The beautifully proportioned temple, which has been lavishly restored, was built by Rama III in memory of his mother, whose family lived in the area. Entering the high, white walls of the temple compound, you feel as if you're coming upon a stately folly in a secret garden, and a strong Chinese influence shows itself in the unusual ribbed roofs and elegantly curved gables, decorated with pastel ceramics. The restorers have done their best work inside: look out especially for the simple, delicate landscapes on the shutters.

Museum of the Department of Corrections

Ghouls and social anthropologists might want to take a look at the **Museum of the Department of Corrections** (Mon–Fri 9am–4pm; free), a small collection of torture and execution instruments that's a ten-minute walk from the river. Take the road straight ahead from Nonthaburi pier, then turn first left – you'll then walk along the front of Bangkwang Central Prison on your right and find the museum signposted on the left. The display kicks off with pictures of grisly methods of execution used at Ayutthaya, such as scalping and burning. Even the game of *takraw*, a kind of foot-volleyball which you'll see played on any patch of open ground in Thailand, had its ugly side: an outsized version of the wicker *takraw* ball, with spikes inside, is on display here, into which an offender was placed before being thrown to the elephants for a kickaround. Numerous butchers' hooks and headsmen's axes are here to turn your stomach even more, along with photographs of recent executions: Thailand still has capital punishment, by machine gun, though it's rarely carried out.

Ko Kred

About 7km north of Nonthaburi, the tiny island of **KO KRED** lies in a particularly sharp bend in the Chao Phraya, cut off from the east bank by a waterway created to make the cargo route from Ayutthaya to the Gulf of Thailand just that little bit faster. This artificial island is something of a time capsule: a little oasis of village life completely at odds with the metropolitan chaos just ninety minutes downriver. Roughly ten square kilometres in all, Ko Kred has no roads, just a concrete path that circles its circumference, with a few arterial walkways branching off towards the interior. Villagers, the majority of whom are Mons (see p.162), use the fifteen-strong fleet of motorbike taxis to cross their island, but as a sight-seer you're much better off on foot: a round-island walk takes less than an hour and a half and it's practically impossible to get lost.

There are no sights as such on Ko Kred, but its lushness and comparative emptiness make it a perfect place in which to wander. You'll no doubt come across one of the island's potteries and kilns, which churn out the regionally famous earthenware flower-pots and small water-storage jars and employ a large percentage of the village workforce. The island's clay is also very rich in nutrients and therefore excellent for fruit-growing, and banana trees, coconut palms, pomelo, papaya and durian trees all grow in abundance on Ko Kred, fed by an intricate network of irrigation channels that crisscrosses the interior. In amongst the orchards, the Mons have built their wooden houses, mostly in traditional style and raised high above the marshy ground on stilts. A couple of attractive riverside wats, a school and a few diminutive general stores complete the picture.

The **access** point for Ko Kred is **Pakkred**, the terminus for all *Laemthong Express* boats, as well as for a few rush-hour green-flag *Chao Phraya Express* boats (see "City transport", p.66), the latter docking 50m south of the former. The **direct** *Laemthong* boats from **Bangkok** take at least an hour and cost B13. Alternatively, you can take a *Chao Phraya Express* boat to Nonthaburi (see above) and travel on to Pakkred from here on a *Laemthong* boat: the half-hour journey costs B7. From Pakkred, which is on the east bank of the Chao Phraya, the easiest way of getting across to the island is to hire a longtail boat for B10–20 per person, although B1 shuttle boats operate at the river's narrowest point at Wat Sanam Nua, about 1km's walk or a B5–10 samlor-ride south of the Pakkred boat piers.

Ko Kred is definitely not on the tourist trail and farang visitors are a rarity here, but the riverside *Song Fung* **restaurant**, beside the *Chao Phraya Express* pier in Pakkred, offers a detailed English-language menu, with over 170 Chinese, Thai and seafood dishes from which to choose.

Muang Boran Ancient City

The brochure for **Muang Boran Ancient City** (daily 9am–5pm; B50), 33km southeast of the city, sells the place as a sort of cultural fast-food outlet – "a realistic journey into Thailand's past in only a few hours, saving you the many weeks of travel and considerable expense of touring Thailand yourself". The open-air museum is a considerably more authentic experience than its own publicity makes out, showcasing past and present Thai artistry and offering an enjoyable introduction to the country's architecture. To get there from Bangkok, take air-conditioned **bus** #8 or #11 or regular bus #25 to **Samut Prakan** on the edge of built-up Greater Bangkok, then a songthaew.

Some of the 89 buildings are **originals**, such as the rare scripture library rescued from Samut Songkhram. Others are painstaking **reconstructions** from contemporary documents (the Ayutthaya-period Sanphet Prasat palace is a particularly fine example) or **scaled-down copies** of famous monuments such as the

Grand Palace. A sizeable team of restorers and skilled craftspeople maintains the buildings and helps keep some of the traditional techniques alive; if you come here during the week you can watch them at work. Muang Boran also publishes a quarterly journal of the same name (in Thai and English) on Thai art, which is available from its Bangkok office on Rajdamnoen Klang Avenue, at the southwest corner of Democracy Monument.

A couple of kilometres east of Samut Prakan, the **Crocodile Farm** (daily 7am–6pm; B300) figures on tour-group itineraries, but is a depressing place. The thirty thousand reptiles kept here are made to "perform" for their trainers in hourly shows (daily 9, 10 & 11am & 2, 3 & 4pm) and are subsequently turned into handbags, shoes, briefcases and wallets, a selection of which are sold on site. Songthaews run from Samut Prakan.

Human Imagery Museum

Thirty-one kilometres west of Bangkok on Highway 4, the **Human Imagery Museum** (Mon–Fri 9am–5.30pm, Sat & Sun 8.30am–6pm; adults B140, kids B70) is a Thai version of Madame Tussaud's Wax Museum, but with a less global perspective than its London counterpart. The lifelike **figures**, complete with glistening tongues and dewy eyes, are skilfully cast in fibreglass – wax would melt – and for the most part represent key characters in Thailand's history. Aside from a group portrait of the first eight kings of the Chakri dynasty, there's a strong emphasis on revered monks, as well as several wry interpretations of everyday life in the kingdom. The upper floor is given over to temporary exhibitions on unusual aspects of Thai history – such as the story of slavery here – with informative English-language captions.

The regular **buses** from Bangkok's Southern Bus Terminal to Nakhon Pathom will drop you outside the entrance, but to flag one down for the return journey you might have to enlist the help of the museum's car-park attendant.

On the way to the Human Imagery Museum you'll see signposts for the nearby **Rose Garden Country Resort**, accessible only on tours from Bangkok, and a very synthetic experience. The lushly landscaped riverside resort makes big bucks from its hotel and golf course, but its main draw is the **Thai Village Cultural Show** (every afternoon; B220), an all-in-one cultural experience of Thai boxing, cockfighting, a wedding ceremony, elephant training and classical and hill-tribe dancing.

FOOD, ENTERTAINMENT, SHOPPING – AND MOVING ON

As you'd expect, nowhere in Thailand can compete with Bangkok's diversity when it comes to eating and entertainment, and although prices are generally higher here than in the provinces, it's still easy to have a good time while on a budget.

Bangkok boasts an astonishing fifty thousand **places to eat** – that's almost one for every hundred citizens – ranging from grubby streetside noodle shops to the most elegant of restaurants. Despite this glut, though, an awful lot of tourists venture no further than their guest house's front doorstep, preferring the dining-room's ersatz Thai or Western dishes to the more adventurous fare to be found in even the most touristed accommodation areas. The section below is a run-through on the best of the city's indigenous eateries, with a few representatives of the capital's numerous ethnic minorities.

Except among the men who've come to Bangkok for the sex on sale in Patpong, guest-house inertia is prevalent when it comes to **nightlife** as well, with many travellers settling for an evening of videos. It's true that Bangkok's drinking bars and clubs have not always been the city's strongest suit, but a vibrant house and techno scene has now emerged around the fringes of Patpong. Getting back to your lodgings is no problem in the small hours: most bus routes run a reduced service throughout the night, and tuk-tuks and taxis are always at hand – though it's probably best for unaccompanied women to avoid using tuk-tuks late at night.

Introductions to more traditional elements of Thai culture are offered by the raucous ambience of the city's **boxing arenas**, its **music and dancing** troupes and its profusion of **shops**, stalls and markets – all of them covered here. This section concludes with an overview of the options for **moving on from the city** – not only to elsewhere in Thailand, but to other countries too, as Bangkok is one of Asia's bargain counters when it comes to buying flights.

Eating

Thai restaurants of all types are found all over the city. The air-conditioned **standard Thai** places, patronized by office workers and middle-class families, almost always work out excellent value, with massive menus of curries, soups, rice and noodle dishes and generally some Chinese dishes as well; the Banglamphu and Democracy areas have an especially high concentration of these. The best **gourmet Thai** restaurants operate from the downtown districts around Sukhumvit and Silom roads, proffering wonderful royal, nouvelle and traditional cuisines that definitely merit an occasional splurge. At the other end of the scale there are the **night markets** and **street stalls**, so numerous in Bangkok that we can only flag the most promising areas – but wherever you're staying, you'll hardly have to walk a block in any direction before encountering something edible.

Of the non-Thai cuisines, Chinatown naturally rates as the most authentic district for pure **Chinese** food; likewise neighbouring Pahurat, the capital's Indian enclave, is best for unadulterated **Indian** dishes – though here, as in Chinatown, most establishments are nameless and transient, so it's hard to make recommendations.

Fast food comes in two forms: the mainly Thai version, which stews canteen-style in large tin trays on the upper floors of department stores all over the city, and the old Western favourites like *McDonald's* and *Kentucky Fried Chicken* that mainly congregate around Siam Square and Ploenchit Road – an area that also has its share of good Thai and foreign restaurants.

The restaurants listed below are graded by three general price categories based on the cost of a main dish: inexpensive (under B40), moderate (B40–70) and expensive (over B70). In the more expensive restaurants you may have to pay a service charge and seven percent government tax. All the restaurants have English menus unless stated; telephone numbers are given for the most popular, where bookings are advisable.

Banglamphu and Democracy area

Dachanee, 18/2 Pracha Thipatai Rd, near *Thai Hotel*. Standard Thai fare such as fiery *tom yam*, plus tasty extras like tofu- and beansprout-stuffed *khanom buang* (crispy pancakes), in air-con restaurant. Inexpensive to moderate.

Dragon Eyes, Samsen Road, on the corner of Wisut Kasat Road. Small restaurant popular with young Thai couples. Stylish renditions of standard Thai dishes – try the *khao pat* with added fruit and nuts, or the chilli-fried chicken with cashews. Huge selection of bar drinks as well, and, as you'd expect from a place managed by a *Bangkok Post* music critic, a fine range of music. Open 6.30pm–midnight, closed Sun. Moderate.

Isaan restaurants, behind the Rajdamnoen Boxing Stadium on Rajdamnoen Nok Road. At least 5 restaurants in a row serving northeastern fare to hungry boxing fans: take your pick for hearty plates of *kai yang* and *khao niaw*. Inexpensive.

Lotus Café, Khao San Road. Archetypal travellers' haven, with only a few tables, an emphasis on wholesome ingredients, and yoga posters on the walls. Delicious home-made brown bread and yoghurt. Inexpensive.

Na Pralan, almost opposite the Gate of Glorious Victory, Na Phra Lan Road. Technically in Ratanakosin but very close to Banglamphu, this tiny art gallery café, only a couple of doors up the street from the Silpakorn University Art College, is ideally placed for refreshment before or after your tour of Wat Phra Kaeo and the Grand Palace. Its temporary exhibitions make it a very pleasant place to while away half an hour or so. The small menu offers a tasty selection of aesthetically presented rice and fish dishes and a range of international coffee blends. Mon–Sat 10am–10pm. Moderate.

New World Food Centre, top floor of *New World* department store, corner of Chakra Bongse and Phra Sumen roads. Buy lunches and choose from Thai, Chinese and vegetarian food stalls; a bit school-dinnerish but a bargain. Very inexpensive.

Royal India, signposted off Khao San Road. Excellent Indian food in copious quantities at this popular branch of the Pahurat original. Inexpensive to moderate.

Shogun, Phra Sumen Road, behind *New World* department store. *Sukiyaki* a speciality, and the place has a family atmosphere. Some Chinese dishes, too. Inexpensive.

Sky High, Rajdamnoen Klang Road, not far from the *Royal Hotel*. Large menu of tasty Thai dishes, with both streetside and indoor seating. Inexpensive to moderate.

Sorn Daeng, southeast corner of Democracy Monument. Standard Thai dishes including unadulterated southern curries like the rich sweet beef *kaeng matsaman*. Inexpensive.

So Ying Thai, at the Tanao Road/Bamrung Muang Road intersection. Popular family restaurant, serving up family-sized portions of Thai standards such as chicken and bamboo shoots, plus less common ones, like fried frog in curry sauce. Inexpensive to moderate.

Tang Teh, corner of Samsen and Wisut Kasat roads. Unusual, quality Thai restaurant, with contemporary art on the walls and high-class food on the menu. Fried catfish with cashews and chilli sauce recommended, as are the superb fishcakes; also home-made ice cream. Moderate.

Wang Nah, Phra Athit Road, under Phra Pinklao Bridge. Sizeable seafood menu, riverside location. Inexpensive to moderate.

Yok Yor, Tha Wisut Kasat, Wisut Kasat Road. Riverside restaurant in two sections, which sends a boatload of diners down to Rama IX Bridge and back every evening: departs 8pm, returns 10pm. The food is definitely nothing special – there's more choice before the boat sets off and leaves the main kitchen behind – but it's the most inexpensive of a host of similar operations, and the floodlit views of Wat Arun, Wat Phra Kaeo and others are worth the B50 cover charge. Moderate.

Chinatown and Pahurat

Chong Tee, 84 Soi Sukon 1, Traimit Rd, between Hualamphong station and Wat Traimit. Delicious pork satay and sweet toast. Inexpensive.

Royal India, just off Chakraphet Road. Serves the same excellent curries as its Banglamphu branch, but attracts an almost exclusively Indian clientele. Inexpensive to moderate.

White Orchid Hotel, 409–421 Yaowarat Rd. Great-value *dim sum*, with bamboo baskets of prawn dumplings, spicy spare ribs, stuffed beancurd and the like, served in 3 different portion sizes at B25, B35 and B45. *Dim sum* 11am–2pm & 5–10pm. Inexpensive to moderate.

Silom and New roads

Akane Japanese Noodle, 236 Silom Rd, between sois 16 and 18, next to the *Narai Hotel*. Deliciously authentic *soba*, *udon, ramen* and *sushi* dishes in unpretentious café-style surrounds. Moderate.

All Gaengs, 173/8–9 Suriwong Rd. Large menu of tasty curries (*gaeng* or *kaeng*) served in cool, modern surrounds. Closed Sat & Sun lunch-times. Moderate.

Ban Chiang, 14 Srivieng Rd, between Silom and Sathorn roads (☎02/236 7045). Fine Thai cuisine in an elegant wooden house. Moderate to expensive.

Bussaracum, 35 Soi Pipat 2, Convent Rd (☎02/235 8915). Superb classical Thai cuisine. Expensive, but well worth it.

Chai Karr, opposite *Holiday Inn*, Silom Road. No English name but easily recognized by its traditional-style wooden exterior. Good place for standard Thai and Chinese dishes, followed by liquor coffees and ice creams. Inexpensive to moderate.

Charuvan, 70–2 Silom Rd, near Patpong. Specializing in inexpensive and tasty duck on rice; the beer's a bargain too.

Himali Cha-Cha, 1229/11 New Road, just south of GPO (☎02/235 1569). Fine north Indian restaurant founded by a character who was chef to numerous Indian ambassadors, now run by his son; good vegetarian selection. Moderate.

Laicram, second floor, Thaniya Plaza, east end of Silom Road. Small, proficient restaurant offering some unusual specialities from around Thailand, plus loads of veggie dishes and traditional desserts. Moderate to expensive.

Ratree Seafood, opposite Thaniya Plaza, Soi 1, Silom Rd. Famous street stall with 20 or so tables, serving up all manner of fresh seafood (barbecued fish a speciality) and noodle soup. Evenings only. Inexpensive.

Ratstube, Goethe Institut, 18/1 Soi Ngam Duphli (in fact, round the corner on Soi Attakarn Prasit; ☎02/286 4528). Delicious, but pricey German food in elegant surroundings. There's also a good, inexpensive Thai cafeteria (daytime only) in the grounds outside.

Savoury, 60 Pan Rd, above the *Artist's Gallery* (☎02/236 4830). Excellent European food, recommended for a splurge; closed Sun. Expensive.

Tip Top, Patpong 1. Comfy air-con diner serving reliable Thai and Western food 24hr a day. Inexpensive to moderate.

Trattoria Da Roberto, Patpong Plaza (first floor), Patpong 2. Informal haven at the epicentre of sleaze-land which somehow retains an easy-going family atmosphere. Pizzas and pastas wouldn't win any prizes, but palatable enough for the area. Moderate.

Siam Square and Ploenchit Road

Bali, 15/3 Soi Ruam Rudee (☎02/250 0711). Top-notch Indonesian food in a cosy nook; closed Sun lunch. Moderate to expensive – blow out on 7-course *rijstaffel* for B160.

Ban Khun Phor, 458/7–9 Soi 8, Siam Square. Rustic atmosphere and traditional music with good Thai specialities; food spiced to order. There's another branch on Sukhumvit Road (see facing page). Moderate to expensive.

Chancharas, 34/1 Soi Langsuan. A very good bet in this price range: even the appetizers and the rice and noodle dishes are thoughtfully prepared and presented. Moderate.

Kirin Restaurant, 226/1 Soi 2, Siam Square. Swankiest and best of many Chinese restaurants in the area. Expensive.

Kroissant House, ground floor of *World Trade Centre*, corner of Rama I and Rajdamri roads. Fine Italian ice creams and cakes.

Kub Khum, 208 Soi 1, Siam Square. Good Thai favourites with tacky, folksy decor. Moderate.

Mah Boon Krong Food Centre, sixth floor of *MBK* shopping centre, corner of Rama I and Phrayathai roads. Increase your knowledge of Thai food: ingredients, names and pictures of dishes (including some vegetarian ones) from all over the country are displayed at the various stalls. Inexpensive.

Phai-boon, 219–223 Chulalongkorn Soi 50, near corner of Rama IV and Phrayathai roads. Busy, no-frills air-con restaurant serving mostly seafood. Interesting combination dishes. Moderately priced.

Pop, northwest corner of Lumphini Park. Garden restaurant popular for breakfasts and *dim sum* lunches. Inexpensive.

Sarah Jane's, 36/2 Soi Langsuan. Unfussy restaurant, popular with Bangkok's Isaan population, serving excellent, simple northeastern food. Inexpensive.

Talat Samyarn (Samyarn Market), set back on the west side of Phrayathai Road, near the corner of Rama IV. Fruitful area for stall-grazing, always busy with Chulalongkorn University students. Inexpensive.

TCBY – The Country's Best Yoghurt, Soi 7, at the east end of Siam Square. Consumer colonialism at its most bizarre: fat-free frozen yoghurt ("All the pleasure, none of the guilt").

Whole Earth, 93/3 Soi Langsuan. The best veggie restaurant in Bangkok, serving interesting and varied Thai food (plus some dishes for carnivores); twee but relaxing atmosphere. Moderate.

Sukhumvit Road

Ambassador Hotel Asian Food Centre, inside the *Ambassador Hotel* complex, between sois 11 and 13. Street-level canteen with about 30 stalls selling Japanese, Vietnamese, Chinese, Korean and regional Thai dishes; also vegetarian fare, both Thai and European. Food bought with coupons, sold (and refunded) from a booth at the entrance. Inexpensive.

Bangkapi Terrace, on the edge of the *Ambassador Hotel* complex, between sois 11 and 13. Streetside 24-hr coffee-shop, billed as Bangkok's most popular after-hours meeting place. Workaday rice, noodle and Western standards. Inexpensive to moderate.

Ban Khun Phor, 212/16–17 Sukhumvit Plaza, Soi 12. Same name, same formula as in Siam Square (see facing page). Moderate to expensive.

Cabbages and Condoms, Soi 12. Run by the Planned Parenthood Association of Thailand: safe eating in the Condom Room or the Vasectomy Bar. Good, authentic Thai food. Moderate.

Haus München, Soi 15. German food, from pigs' knuckles to *bratwurst*. Moderate.

Jools Bar and Restaurant, Soi 4, Sukhumvit Rd, a short walk from the Soi Nana go-go strip. Hearty British fare of the meat-and-two-veg variety dished out in the upstairs room of a popular British-run pub. Moderate.

Lemongrass, Soi 24. Scrumptious Thai nouvelle cuisine in a converted traditional house; vegetarian menu on request. Moderate to expensive.

Nipa, third floor of Landmark Plaza, between sois 6 and 8. Menu features an adventurous range of traditional Thai dishes, including a sizeable vegetarian selection; set meals are good value. Classical Thai music in the evening. Moderate to expensive.

Seafood Market, 89 Soi 24. More of a pink-neon supermarket than a restaurant: you pick your fish off the racks ("if it swims, we have it") and then choose how you want it cooked. Go for the novelty and choice rather than the atmosphere or fine cuisine. Moderate.

Suda Restaurant, Soi 14. Unpretentious locals' hangout, patronized by office workers at lunch-time, but open till midnight. Standard rice and noodle dishes, plus some fish: fried tuna with cashews and chilli recommended. Inexpensive to moderate.

Thai Ruam Ros, Soi 1. Mexican food a speciality – and it's not at all bad. Thai and European dishes also available and a large vegetarian menu. A good place for lunch. Inexpensive to moderate.

Yong Lee, corner of Soi 15. One of the few unpretentious and refreshingly basic rice-and-noodle shops on Sukhumvit. Inexpensive, considering the competition.

Nightlife and entertainment

For many of Bangkok's visitors, nightfall in the city is the signal to hit the **sex bars**, the neon sumps that disfigure three distinct parts of town: along Sukhumvit Road's Soi Cowboy (between sois 21 and 23) and Nana Plaza (Soi 4), and, most notoriously, in the two small sois off the east end of Silom Road known as Patpong 1 and 2. But within spitting distance of the beer bellies flopped onto Patpong's bars lies **Silom 4**, Bangkok's most happening after-dark haunt, pulling in the cream of Thai youth and tempting an increasing number of travellers to stuff their party gear into their rucksacks: Soi 4, the next alley off Silom Road to the east of Patpong 2, started out as a purely gay area but now offers a disorienting range of styles, from punk rock through transvestite cabarets to the newest, hardest dance grooves, in gay, mixed and straight pubs, dance bars and clubs. This is also the best place to hear about the occasional "underground" raves that take place, usually at the weekend, at the few other Bangkok pubs and clubs to have embraced party culture.

For a more casual drink, join the less adventurous Thai youth and yuppie couples who pack out the **music bars** concentrated around Soi Langsuan and Sarasin Road on the north side of Lumphini Park, and scattered randomly over the rest of the city. The atmosphere in these places is as pleasant as you'll find in a Bangkok bar, but don't expect anything better than Western covers and bland jazz from the resident musicians. Look out for inflated drink prices in the popular bars – a small bottle of *Mekhong* whisky can cost up to five times what a guest house would charge.

Away from the cutting edge of imported sounds, Bangkok has its fair share of **discos** which churn out Thai and Western chart hits. Besides those listed on the following page, most of the de luxe hotels – notably the *Ambassador, Dusit Thani* and *Montien* – have nightclubs; all charge an admission price which often includes a couple of free drinks. The city's main **gay** areas are Silom 4, the more exclusive Silom 2 (towards Rama IV Road), and the rougher, mostly Thai bars of Sutthisarn Road near the Chatuchak Weekend Market. As with the straight scene, the majority of gay bars feature go-go dancers and live sex shows. Those listed here do not.

On the cultural front, **Thai dancing** is the most accessible of the capital's performing arts, particularly when served up in bite-size portions on tourist restaurant stages. **Thai boxing** is also well worth watching: the live experience at either of Bangkok's two main national stadiums far outshines the TV coverage.

Bars

For convenient drinking, we've split the most recommended of the city's bars into three central areas. The most happening Thai venue of the moment – *Beurak Mai Thai* at Soi 30 (Soi Aladin), Phaholyothin Road – boasts "country" design, live political folk/rock and inexpensive drinks, but is miles from anywhere in north Bangkok.

BANGLAMPHU

Gypsy Pub, west end of Phra Sumen Road. Friendly, medium-sized bar attracts a youthful and predominantly Thai clientele with its nightly live music (of varying quality). Closed Sun.

Jai Yen, next to Tha Phra Athit. A good place for an early evening drink after 6pm, when the express boats stop running; riverside location, inexpensive beer, but the food is better for snacking.

No Name Bar, Khao San Rd. Small, low-key upstairs drinking-spot at the heart of the back-packers' ghetto. Dim lighting, a more varied than average tape selection and competitively priced beer.

Zebu 2, just north of Democracy Monument on Thanon Dinso. Cavernous youth-oriented beer hall with live Thai pop; not overly popular, but worth checking out for the original local bands. Expensive beer.

DOWNTOWN BANGKOK

Blue's Bar, 231/16 Soi Sarasin. Long-standing, friendly haunt where creative types drink to British indie sounds.

Bobby's Arms, first floor of Patpong 2 car park. Naff imitation of an English pub (darts and horse brasses), but a quiet and inexpensive place for a draught beer. Dixieland band Sun nights.

Brown Sugar, 231/19–20 Soi Sarasin. Chic, pricey but lively bar, acknowledged as the capital's top jazz venue.

Hard Rock Café, Soi 11, Siam Square. Genuine outlet of the famous chain, better for drink than food. Big sounds, brash enthusiasm, bank-breaking prices.

Old West, 231/17 Soi Sarasin. Slightly expensive but buzzing saloon with nightly live music from local bands: country and western from Sat through Tues, rock 'n' roll Wed through Fri; popular with Thai yuppies (mobile phones much in evidence).

Redwood, 76 Soi 4, Silom Rd. Dark, packed and punky inside, sweeping views over Silom 4 high life from the tables on the alley outside.

Round Midnight, 106/2 Soi Langsuan. Gimmicky decor and generally uninspiring live jazz and blues (nightly from 9pm), but the atmosphere is unpretentious and the drinks are moderately priced.

Saxophone, 3/8 Victory Monument (southeast corner), Phrayathai Rd. Lively second-floor bar hosts nightly blues, folk and rock bands and attracts a good mix of Thais and farangs; relaxed drinking atmosphere and reasonable prices. There's a pool table on the first floor and a more sedate ground-floor bar with innocuous jazz bands.

SUKHUMVIT ROAD

Imageries By The Glass, Soi 24, Sukhumvit Rd. Usually packed out with Thai yuppies, but nothing special; nightly music from jazz-fusion band. Moderately priced drinks.

Jools Bar and Restaurant, Soi 4, Sukhumvit Rd, a short walk from the Soi Nana go-go strip. Easy-going British-run pub, popular with expat drinkers (photos of regular customers plaster the walls). The cosy downstairs bar is mainly standing room only, and traditional British food – roast beef and Yorkshire pudding, ploughman's lunch etc – is served at tables upstairs.

Manet Club, Renoir Club, Van Gogh Club, Soi 33, Sukhumvit Rd. Three very similar, unexciting, not-at-all-Parisian bars, all almost next door to each other, that are best visited during happy hour (4–8pm).

Old Dutch, Soi 23, Sukhumvit Rd, at the mouth of the Soi Cowboy strip. Cool, dark, peace-ful oasis at the edge of Sukhumvit's frenetic sleaze; reasonable basic menu and a big stock of current US and European newspapers make this an ideal daytime or early evening watering hole.

Clubs and discos

Calypso Cabaret, *Ambassador Hotel* complex, between sois 11 and 13, Sukhumvit Rd. Fairly tame transvestite show in theatre setting; B400.

Speed, 82 Soi 4, Silom Rd. Currently Bangkok's funkiest dance venue: small, heaving upstairs room, spray-painted Day-glo, which features house, hardcore and techno flown in hot off the presses from London and the States; B50.

King's Lounge, Patpong 1, above *King's Corner* go-go bar. No-nonsense chart-sound dance club, popular with travellers and Thais. Free; moderate drink prices.

Nasa Spacedrome, 999 Ramkhamhaeng Rd. Said to be Asia's largest disco, designed like an enormous spacecraft and featuring the nightly "lift-off" of a space capsule from the edge of the dance floor. B150 (B200 Fri & Sat), including 3 drinks. Open until 3am.

Phoebus, Ratchadapisek Rd, opposite *Yaoham*. Enormous disco complex with awesome lights and mainstream sounds.

Rome Club, 90–96 Soi 4, Silom Rd. Once the city's leading gay nightclub, then its most fashionable mixed venue, now aiming itself exclusively at straight yuppies. B200 including 2 drinks (B300 Fri & Sat).

The Cave and **The Zulu-Teque**, fifth floor, United Center Building (above *Popeye's*), 323 Silom Rd. The famed *FM228* premises (climb the tower building through a car park and shoe shop) have recently reawoken with a split personality: hippest sounds from the States and Europe for Silom 4 trendies in one room, Africa-theme disco and chart dance hits in the other; sporadic raves in the former go, too. B150.

Gay scene

Babylon, Soi Nantha, Sathorn Thai Rd (next to Austrian Embassy). The least sleazy, most luxurious sauna complex in Thailand, with bar, restaurant, steam room, plunge pool and well-endowed gym. Weekdays 5–11pm (B180), weekends noon–11pm (B200).

Disco Disco, Soi 2, Silom Rd. Small, new, well-designed bar/disco, with reasonably priced drinks, playing kitsch standards for a fun crowd. Daily 10pm–3am.

Divine, 98–104 Soi 4, Silom Rd. Slick, suave 3-floor dance club above *Sphinx*, with cabaret and regular theme nights, which pulls in a young Thai and farang crowd. Daily 10pm–4am; expensive drinks.

DJ Station, Soi 2, Silom Rd. Highly fashionable disco, packed at weekends, attracting a happy mix of gays and straights, Thais and farangs; midnightly cabaret show. Daily 10pm–4am; B100 weekdays including one drink, B200 weekends including two drinks.

Jet Set, Soi 21 (Soi Asoke), Sukhumvit Rd. Predominantly gay Thai karaoke bar, with informal, laid-back atmosphere. Daily until 3am.

JJ Park, 8/3 Sol 2, Silom Rd. Classy, Thai-oriented bar/restaurant, for socializing rather than raving, with live music and karaoke. Daily 3pm–4am.

Khrua Silom, 60/10–11 Silom Rd (in soi beside *Hong Kong and Shanghai Bank*). Unpretentious and fun club/café, thronged with gay Thai students. Daily 9pm–3am; B70 including one drink.

Sphinx, 98–104 Soi 4, Silom Rd. Chic decor, terrace seating and good food attract a young, fashionable crowd to this ground-floor bar and restaurant. Weekdays 7pm–12.30am, weekends 7pm–1am.

Telephone Bar, 114/11–13 Soi 4, Silom Rd. Smart eating and drinking venue with good Thai cuisine and a terrace on the alley, popular with older men; each table has a telephone with a clearly displayed number so you can call up other customers. Daily 8pm–3am.

Utopia, 116/1 Soi 23 (Soi Sawadee), Sukhumvit Rd (☎02/259 9619). Bangkok's first gay and lesbian community venue, comprising a shop, gallery, café, guest rooms, and a bar with weekly women-only nights. Daily noon–10pm.

Culture shows

Only in Bangkok can you be sure to catch a live display of non-tourist-oriented traditional dance or theatre; few of the outlying regions have resident troupes, so authentic performances elsewhere tend to be sporadic and may not coincide with your visit. The main venue is the *National Theatre* (☎02/221 0173) next to the National Museum on the northwest corner of Sanam Luang, which puts on special medley shows of **drama and music** from all over the country, performed by students from the attached College of the Performing Arts. These take place on the last Friday and Saturday of every month (more regularly Nov–May); tickets start at B40. Spectacular and authentic, the performances serve as a tantalizing introduction to the theatre's full-length shows, which include *lakhon* (classical) and *likay* (folk) theatre and the occasional *nang thalung* (shadow-puppet play). Tickets for these start at around B100 and programme details can be checked by calling the theatre or TAT.

The recently restored *Chalermkrung Royal Theatre* (☎02/222 1352) at 66 New Rd (on the intersection with Triphet Road in Pahurat, next to *Old Siam Plaza)* shows contemporary Thai drama and comedy most of the week, but on Tuesday and Thursday nights puts on the *Khon Light and Sound Spectacular* (B500) especially for the tourists. Essentially a high-tech interpretation of the traditional masked drama, the show presents the best bits of the *Ramayana* story, performed in classical costume and set against glorious Technicolor backdrops.

Many tourist restaurants feature nightly **culture shows** – usually a hotchpotch of Thai dancing and classical music, with a martial-arts demonstration thrown in. Worth checking out are *Baan Thai*, a traditional teak house on Soi 32, Sukhumvit Road, where diners are served a set meal during the show (performances at 9pm), and the outdoor restaurant in *Silom Village* on Silom Road, which does a nightly half-hour show (8pm) to go with its à la carte menu.

Thai dancing is performed for its original ritual purpose, usually several times a day, at the Lak Muang Shrine behind the Grand Palace and the Erawan Shrine on the corner of Ploenchit Road. Both shrines have resident troupes of dancers who are hired by worshippers to perform *lakhon chatri*, a sort of *khon* dance-drama, to thank benevolent spirits for answered prayers. The dancers are always dressed up in full gear and accompanied by musicians, but the length, number of dancers and complexity of the dance depends on the amount of money paid by the supplicant: a price list is posted near the dance area. The musicians at the Erawan Shrine are particularly highly rated, though the almost comic apathy of the dancers there doesn't do them justice.

Cinemas

Central Bangkok has over twenty **cinemas**, many of which show recent American and European releases with their original dialogue and Thai subtitles. Programmes are detailed every day in the *Nation* and *Bangkok Post*, and cinema locations are printed on *Nancy Chandler's Map of Bangkok*; seats start at about B30. The *Bata* cinema in the department store complex on Phra Pinklao Road in Thonburi is convenient for Banglamphu and there are four massive movie theatres in Siam Square. Western films are also occasionally shown at the Japan Cultural Centre, Goethe Institut and Alliance Française: check the English-language press for details.

Thai Boxing

Thai boxing

The violence of the average **Thai boxing** match may be offputting to some, but spending a couple of hours at one of Bangkok's two main stadiums can be immensely entertaining, not least for the enthusiasm of the spectators and the ritualistic aspects of the fights.

Bouts are held in the capital every night of the week at the **Rajdamnoen Stadium**, next to the TAT office on Rajdamnoen Nok Avenue (Mon & Wed 6pm; Thurs 6pm & 9pm; Sun 3pm & 7pm), and at **Lumphini Stadium** on Rama IV Road (Tues & Fri 6pm; Sat 5pm & 9pm). Tickets go on sale one hour before and, unless the boxers are big stars, start at around B150. You might have to queue for a few minutes, but there's no need to get there early unless there's a really important fight on. Sessions feature ten bouts, each consisting of five three-minute rounds (with 2-min rests in between each round), so if you're not a big fan it may be worth turning up an hour late, as the better fights tend to happen later in the billing. It's more fun if you buy one of the less expensive standing tickets, enabling you to witness the wild gesticulations of the betting aficionados at close range.

Shopping

Bangkok has a justifiably good reputation for **shopping**, particularly for silk, tailored clothes and gems, where the range and quality is streets ahead of other Thai cities, and of many other Asian capitals as well. Antiques and handicrafts are good buys too, and some shops stock curiosities from the most remote regions of the country alongside the more typical standards. But as always, watch out for old, damaged goods being passed off as antiques: if you're concerned about the quality or authenticity of your purchases, stick to TAT-approved shops. Bangkok can also claim a healthy range of English-language bookshops.

For travellers, spectating, not shopping, is apt to be the main draw of Bangkok's neighbourhood **markets** – notably the bazaars of Chinatown and the massive Chatuchak Weekend Market (see p.113). If you're planning on some serious market exploration, get hold of *Nancy Chandler's Map of Bangkok*, an enthusiastically annotated creation which includes special sections on the main areas of interest. With the chief exception of Chatuchak, most markets operate daily from dawn till early afternoon; early morning is often the best time to go to beat the heat and crowds.

Fabrics and clothes

Thai silk became internationally recognized only about forty years ago after the efforts of American Jim Thompson (see p.104). Noted for its thickness and sheen, much of it comes from the northeast, but you'll find the lion's share of outlets and

COUNTERFEIT CULTURE

Faking it is big business in Bangkok, a city whose copyright regulations carry about as much weight as its anti-prostitution laws. Forged **designer clothes** and accessories are the biggest sellers; street vendors around the *Oriental Hotel* pier and along Silom, Sukhumvit and Khao San roads will flog you a whole range of inexpensive lookalikes, including Louis Vuitton bags, Armani jeans, Levi 501s, Ray-ban sunglasses, and Lacoste shirts – even YSL underpants.

Along Patpong, after dark, plausible would-be **Rolex and Cartier watches** from Hong Kong and Taiwan go for about B500 – and are fairly reliable considering the price. If your budget won't stretch to a phony Rolex Oyster, there's plenty of opportunities for smaller expenditure at the stalls concentrated on Khao San Road, where pirated **music and video cassettes** are sold at a fraction of their normal price. Quality is usually fairly high but the choice is often less than brilliant, with a concentration on mainstream pop and rock albums. Finally, a couple of holes-in-the-wall along Khao San Road even make up passable international **student and press cards** – though travel agencies and other organizations in Bangkok aren't so easily fooled.

---

tailoring facilities in the capital. Prices start at about B250 per yard for single-ply silk, B500 for four-ply. *Jim Thompson's Thai Silk Company* at 9 Suriwong Rd is a good place to start looking, or at least to get an idea of what's out there – silk by the yard and ready-made items from dresses to cushion covers are well designed and of good quality, but pricey. *Khanitha*, with branches at 111/3–5 Suriwong Rd, the *River City* shopping complex (which has its own express-boat pier near New Road) and the *Regent* hotel, home in on women's eveningwear, for which Thai silk is probably best suited.

Traditional fabrics from the north and the northeast, as well as from Laos and Cambodia, are the speciality of *Prayer Textile Gallery*, at 197 Phrayathai Rd, on the corner of Rama I Road. The selection is good, but prices for these textiles are getting surprisingly high, particularly those now classified as antiques.

Bangkok can be a great place to have **tailored clothes** made: materials don't cost much, and work is often completed in only 24 hours. On the other hand, you may find yourself palmed off with artificial silk and a suit that falls apart in a week. Inexpensive silk and tailoring shops crowd Silom, Sukhumvit and Khao San roads, but many people opt for hotel tailors, preferring to pay more for the security of an established business. Be wary of places offering ridiculous deals – when you see a dozen garments advertised for a total price of less than $200, you know something's fishy – and look carefully at the quality of samples before making any decision. If you're staying in Banglamphu, keep an eye on guest-house bulletinboards for cautionary tales from other travellers.

Designer fashions from big names as well as lesser-known labels are particularly good in the Siam Centre, across the road from Siam Square, while the nearby *Mah Boon Krong (MBK)* shopping centre (at the Rama I/Phrayathai intersection) houses hundreds of small shops both upmarket and inexpensive. The most exclusive designer wear fills the boutiques of Amarin Plaza on Ploenchit Road, Peninsula Plaza on Rajdamri Road and Thaniya Plaza on Silom Road. Khao San Road is lined with stalls selling low-priced **ready-mades**: the tie-dyed shirts, baggy cotton trousers, fake Levi's and ethnic-style outfits are all aimed at backpackers and New Age hippies; the stalls around *New World* department store have the best range of inexpensive Thai fashions in this area. **Shoes** and **leather**

goods are good buys in Bangkok, being generally hand-made from high-quality leather and quite a bargain: check out the "booteries" along Sukhumvit Road or the shoe and bag shops at *MBK*.

Gems and stones

Bangkok boasts the country's best **gem and jewellery** shops, and some of the finest lapidaries in the world, making this *the* place to buy cut and uncut stones such as rubies, blue sapphires and diamonds. The most exclusive gem outlets are scattered along Silom Road, but many tourists prefer to buy from hotel shops, where reliability is assured.

While it's unusual for established jewellers to fob tourists off with glass and paste, a common sales technique is to charge a lot more than what the gem is worth based on its carat weight. Get the stone tested on the spot, and ask for a written guarantee and receipt. Be extremely wary of touts and the shops they recommend. Unless you're an experienced gem trader, don't even consider buying gems in bulk to sell at a supposedly vast profit elsewhere: many a gullible traveller has invested thousands of baht on a handful of worthless multi-coloured stones. If you want independent professional advice or precious stones certification, contact either the *Asian Institute of Gemological Sciences* at 484 Rajadapisek Rd (☎02/513 2112) or the *Geological Survey Division, Department of Mineral Resources* on Rama VI Road (☎02/246 1694).

The tiny *House of Gems* at 1218 New Rd, near the GPO, deals almost exclusively in **fossils**, minerals and – no kidding – dinosaur droppings. Ranging from sixty million to two hundred million years old, these petrified droppings (properly known as coprolite) were unearthed in the mid-1980s in Thailand's Isaan region; weighing from 150g to 8kg, they are sold at B2 per gramme. Also on sale here, from B60 each, are **tektites**, pieces of glassy rock found in Thai fields and thought to be the 750,000-year-old products of volcanic activity on the the moon.

Handicrafts

Samples of nearly all regionally produced **handicrafts** end up in Bangkok, so the selection is phenomenal, if not quite exhaustive. Competition keeps prices in the city at upcountry levels, with the main exception of household objects – particularly wickerware and tin bowls and basins – which get palmed off relatively expensively in Bangkok.

Sukhumvit Road is full of touristy souvenir outlets, but one of the most interesting handicraft-antique shops is *Krishna's*, between sois 9 and 11. The four-storey building is crammed full of artefacts from all over Asia: many are unique and expensive collector's items, but there are also plenty of small curios for all budgets, including Balinese masks, Indian bedspreads, Thai and Burmese carvings and Nepalese jewellery. More specifically Thai is *Rasi Sayam* (closed Sun) a ten-minute hike down Soi 23, opposite *Le Dalat* restaurant, which specializes in eclectic and fairly pricey decorative and folk arts such as tiny betel-nut sets woven from *lipao* fern. Less exclusive crafts and souvenirs are sold in the *Tourist Centre* under the expressway which divides Sukhumvit Road from Ploenchit Road.

On **Ploenchit Road**, on the second floor of Amarin Plaza (the *Sogo* building), *The Legend* stocks a small selection of well-made Thai handicrafts, from wood and wickerware to fabrics, at reasonable prices. Around the corner at 127 Rajdamri Rd, *Narayana Phand*, a government souvenir centre set up to ensure the preservation of traditional crafts and to maintain standards of quality, is the place to head for last-minute presents: packed under one roof is a huge assortment of goods from all over the country at very reasonable prices, including *khon* masks and shadow puppets, musical instruments and kites, nielloware and celadon, and hill-tribe crafts.

On the ground floor of the *YMCA* hotel, towards the eastern end of **Sathorn Thai Road**, the non-profitmaking *Thai Craft* handles a small but well-chosen range of mostly hill-tribe handicrafts. *Silom Village*, at 286/1 **Silom Rd**, just west of Soi Decho, is a complex of wooden houses that attempts to create a relaxing, upcountry atmosphere as a backdrop for its pricey fabrics and occasionally unusual souvenirs. In the **River City shopping complex**, the second-floor *Hyacinth Shop* focuses on high-quality crafts, including decorative boxes and quirky cushion covers, at reasonable prices.

Handicraft sellers in **Banglamphu**, particularly on Khao San Road, tend to tout a limited range compared to the shops downtown, but if you're interested in masks, try the shop on Chakrabongse Road, between Khao San and Rajdamnoen Klang roads.

Antiques

Bangkok is the entrepôt for the finest Thai, Burmese and Cambodian **antiques**, but the market has long been sewn up, so don't expect to happen upon any undiscovered treasure. Even experts admit that they sometimes find it hard to tell real antiques from fakes, so the best policy is just to buy on the grounds of attractiveness. The *River City* shopping complex devotes its third and fourth floors to a bewildering array of pricey treasures and holds an auction on the first Saturday of every month (viewing during the preceding week). The other main area for antiques is the stretch of New Road that runs between the GPO and the bottom of Silom Road. Here you'll find a good selection of reputable individual businesses specializing in wood carvings, bronze statues and stone sculptures culled from all parts of Thailand and neighbouring countries as well. Remember that most antiques require an export permit (see p.13).

Books

English-language **bookstores** in Bangkok are always well stocked with everything to do with Thailand, and most carry fiction classics and popular paperbacks. *Asia Books*, an exclusively English-language Bangkok chain, covers all the usual bases and keeps a good range of coffee-table tomes and reference works: there are branches on Sukhumvit Road between sois 15 and 19 and in Landmark Plaza between sois 4 and 6; in Peninsula Plaza on Rajdamri Road; and in Thaniya Plaza near Patpong off Silom Road. *DK (Duang Kamol) Books*, one of Thailand's biggest chains (the central Bangkok branches are on the third floor of the *MBK* shopping centre, corner of Rama I and Phrayathai roads; at 244–6 Soi 2, Siam Square; and at 180/1 Sukhumvit Rd between sois 8 & 10), is especially good for maps and books on Thailand; the company has recently splashed out on the *DK International Book Forum* (miles from the centre in the Seacon Square shopping complex, 904 Moo 6, Srinakarin Rd), Southeast Asia's largest bookstore, which stocks half a million titles in English and hosts exhibitions, meet-the-author sessions and other literary events. *Central* department stores – the most convenient is on Silom Road – sell paperback fiction, maps and reference books in English.

The capital's few **second-hand** bookstores are surprisingly poor value, but you might turn up something worthwhile – or earn a few baht by selling your own cast-offs – in the shops and stalls along Khao San Road.

Travel from Bangkok

Despite Bangkok's numerous attractions, most travellers feel like getting out of it almost as soon as they arrive – and the city is full of tour operators and travel agents encouraging you to do just that. What's more, on any tour of Thailand you're bound to pass through the capital, as it's the terminus of all major highways and rail lines – there are no through Chiang Mai–Surat Thani links, for example. Fortunately, public transport between Bangkok and the provinces is inexpensive and plentiful, if not particularly speedy. This is also an unrivalled place to make arrangements for onward travel from Thailand – the city's travel agents can offer some amazing flight deals and all the major Asian embassies are here, so getting the appropriate visas should be no problem.

Travel within Thailand

Having to change trains or buses in Bangkok might sound a tiresome way to travel the country, but it has its advantages – breaking up what would otherwise be an unbearably long trip, and giving the chance to confirm plane tickets and stock up on supplies not so widely available elsewhere. It also means that you can store unwanted clothes in a guest house or hotel – very useful if coming from Chiang Mai (where you might need jumpers and walking boots) and going on to Ko Samui or Ko Phi Phi (T-shirts and swimwear).

Trains

All trains depart from **Hualamphong Station** except the daily service to Kanchanaburi, and two of the Hua Hin trains, which leave from **Bangkok Noi Station** in Thonburi. **Tickets** for overnight trains and other busy routes should be booked at least a day in advance, either from the desk at Hualamphong (daily 8.30am–4pm) or through an authorized train ticket agency, the most convenient being the *Trade Travel Service* at the *Vieng Thai Hotel* on Ram Bhuttri Road, Banglamphu (☎02/282 8670–1), and *Boon Vanit* at 420/9–10 Soi 1, Siam Square (☎02/251 0526–7). Some hotels and guest houses will also book tickets for a commission of about B50.

Buses

Bangkok's three main bus terminals are distributed around the outskirts of town. The **Northern Bus Terminal** (*sathaanii moh chit*), on Phaholyothin Road near Chatuchak Weekend Market, is the departure point for northern and northeastern towns; there are plans to spruce up this terminal, during which time the buses will depart from nearby Kamphaeng Phet Road. The **Eastern Bus Terminal** (*sathaanii ekamai*), at Soi 40, Sukhumvit Rd, serves east-coast destinations. The **Southern Bus Terminal**, on Pinklao Road in Thonburi, handles departures to all points south and west of the capital. Regular and air-conditioned buses leave from different sections of the same terminals.

Regular buses don't need to be **booked** in advance, but air-conditioned ones should be reserved ahead of time either at the relevant bus station or through an agent – much more widespread than train agencies, they can be found in many hotels and guest houses. Agencies sometimes provide transport to the bus station for an additional charge.

Planes

Domestic **flights** should be booked as far in advance as possible. *Thai Airways* flies to most major destinations; its main offices are at 485 Silom Rd (☎02/234 3100–19) and at 6 Larn Luang Rd near Democracy Monument (☎02/280 0070). *Bangkok Airways* (☎02/229 3456), at Queen Sirikit Convention Center, New

TRAVEL AGENTS

Diethelm Travel, Kian Gwan Building II, 140/1 Witthayu (Wireless) Rd (☎02/255 9150–70).

Educational Travel Centre, c/o *Royal Hotel*, 2 Rajdamnoen Rd (☎02/224 0043).

Exotissimo, 755 Silom Rd (☎02/235 9196); and 21/17 Soi Nana Tai, Sukhumvit Rd (☎02/254 0838).

Pamela Tours and Travels, 888/18 Ploenchit Rd (☎02/255 7066).

STA Travel, c/o *Thai Hotel*, 78 Pracha Thipatai Rd, Banglamphu (☎02/281 5314–5); and fourteenth floor, Wall Street Tower, 33 Suriwong Rd (☎02/233 2633).

Trade Travel Service, c/o *Vieng Thai Hotel*, Ram Bhuttri Rd, Banglamphu (☎02/282 8670–1).

INTERNATIONAL AIRLINES

Aeroflot Regent House, 183 Rajdamri Rd (☎02/251 0617–18).

Air France Charn Issara Tower, 942/51 Rama IV Rd (☎02/233 9477).

Air India Amarin Plaza, 500 Ploenchit Rd (☎02/256 9614–8).

Air Lanka Charn Issara Tower, 942/34–35 Rama IV Rd (☎02/236 4981).

Biman Bangladesh Airlines Chongkolnee Building, 56 Suriwong Rd (☎02/235 7643–4).

British Airways Charn Issara Tower, 942/81 Rama IV Rd (☎02/236 8655–8).

Cambodia International Airlines Queen Sirikit Convention Centre, New Rajadapisek Rd (☎02/229 3387–9).

Canadian Airlines Maneeya Centre, 518/5 Ploenchit Rd (☎02/251 4521).

Cathay Pacific Ploenchit Tower, 898 Ploenchit Rd (☎02/263 0606).

China Airlines Peninsula Plaza, 153 Rajdamri Rd (☎02/253 4242–3).

Egyptair CP Tower, 313 Silom Rd (☎02/231 0505–8).

Finnair Maneeya Centre, 518/2 Ploenchit Rd (☎02/251 5012).

Garuda Lumphini Tower, 1168/77 Rama IV Rd (☎02/285 6470–3).

Gulf Air Maneeya Building, 518/5 Ploenchit Rd (☎02/254 7931–4).

Japan Airlines 254/1 Rajadapisek Rd (☎02/274 1411–25).

KLM Maneeya Centre, 518/5 Ploenchit Rd (☎02/254 8325–7).

Korean Air Kongboonma Building, 699 Silom Rd (☎02/235 9221–6).

Lao Aviation Silom Plaza, Silom Rd (☎02/236 9822–3).

Lauda Air Wall Street Tower, 33/37 Suriwong Rd (☎02/233 2565–6).

Lufthansa Q-House, Soi 21 Sukhumvit Rd (☎02/264 2400).

Malaysia Airlines Ploenchit Tower, 898 Ploenchit Rd (☎02/263 0565–71).

Myanmar Airlines Charn Issara Tower, 942/48 Rama IV Rd (☎02/236 8309).

Northwest Peninsula Plaza, 153 Rajdamri Rd (☎02/254 0781–99).

Pakistan International (PIA) 52 Suriwong Rd (☎02/234 2961–5).

Philippine Airlines Chongkolnee Building, 56 Suriwong Rd (☎02/233 2350–2).

Qantas Airways Charn Issara Tower, 942/51 Rama IV Rd (☎02/236 9193–5).

Royal Nepal Sivadon Building, 1/4 Convent Rd (☎02/233 3921–4).

Singapore Airlines Silom Centre, 2 Silom Rd (☎02/236 0440).

Swissair FE Zuellig Building, 1 Silom Rd (☎02/233 2930–9).

Thai International 485 Silom Rd (☎02/233 3810).

United Airlines Regent House, 183 Rajdamri Rd (☎02/253 0558).

Ratchadapisek Rd, Klong Toey, seems to change its routings almost by the month, but for the moment it covers Bangkok–Hua Hin, Bangkok–Ko Samui, U-Tapao (for Pattaya)–Ko Samui, and Ko Samui–Phuket.

Tours

Many Bangkok outfits offer budget package **"tours"** to major tourist destinations (Chiang Mai, Phuket, Ko Samui, Ko Phi Phi), which typically consist of a minibus ride to the train or bus station, a return ticket to your destination on standard public transport, and possibly a night's accommodation thrown in. It might be worth paying the extra if you haven't got time to make your own arrangements or can't face the hassle – and trips to the east-coast islands of Ko Samet and Ko Chang are particularly good value, with fast, comfortable journeys and good connections – but always be wary of unbelievably good deals: the free accommodation often has small print attached or is miles from anywhere. **Day trips** to outlying destinations tend to be better value as they combine several places which would otherwise take a couple of days to see on your own: the most popular itinerary takes in Damnoen Saduak, Nakhon Pathom and Kanchanaburi.

Tour operators open up and go bust all the time, particularly in the Khao San Road area, so ask around for recommendations or make your arrangements through a reputable hotel or guest house; never hand over any money until you see the ticket.

Leaving Thailand

Whether you're moving on within Asia or just trying to get home, Bangkok is one of the best places in the world to buy **low-priced international air tickets**, and there are hundreds of travel agents to buy them from. You'll get the rock-bottom deals from agents who don't belong to the Association of Thai Travel Agents (ATTA), but as with their Western counterparts many of these are transient and not altogether trustworthy. Khao San Road is a notorious centre of such fly-by-night operations, some of which have been known to flee with travellers' money overnight: if you buy from a non-ATTA outlet it's a good idea to ring the airline and check your reservation yourself – don't hand over any money until you've done that and have been given the ticket. The slightly more expensive ATTA agencies still work out good value by international standards: to check if an agency is affiliated either get hold of the TAT list, ask for proof of membership or call the ATTA office (☎02/252 0069). The box on the previous page lists some tried and tested companies.

All major airline offices are in downtown Bangkok, with a particularly dense concentration in the multi-storey office buildings along Ploenchit and Rajdamri roads and along Rama IV and Suriwong roads. There's absolutely no advantage in buying tickets directly from the airlines – their addresses and phone numbers are listed so you can check reservations and confirm bookings.

Visas for other Asian countries

All foreign embassies and consulates with offices in Thailand are based in downtown Bangkok; the following list covers those countries that figure most frequently in onward Asian itineraries (North American, Australasian and European embassies are detailed in "Listings", on the following pages.) Before heading off to the embassy, ring ahead to check on the opening hours (usually very limited), documentation, payment and number of photos you'll need for your visa application, the probable waiting period and any restrictions on your itinerary within the country.

Entry formalities for Thailand's near neighbours (other than Malaysia) have undergone radical transformations over the past few years, and may well change again. At the time of writing, visas for a month's independent travel in **Laos** were available through just about any travel agent in Bangkok for around B2200, and you had to allow five working days for "processing" (see p.374 for an overview of the current situation, including lower-priced or quicker alternatives at the border towns). **Vietnamese** visas also take five working days and provide a month's independent travel, but are readily available from their embassy for B1200. **Burma** (Myanmar) now issues four-week tourist visas for B470 – apply to the embassy and collect the next day. Given the present security situation, trips to **Cambodia,** which currently doesn't have an embassy in Bangkok, are not recommended, but if you're determined to go, it's best to hitch up with a tour organized by an experienced and reliable travel agency, such as *Diethelm Travel* (see box, p.131). Finally, note that **China** and **India** also run consulates in Chiang Mai (see p.239) – visa formalities are the same as in Bangkok, but the Chiang Mai offices are less busy and more accessible.

Burma (Myanmar) 132 Sathorn Nua Rd (☎02/233 2237).
China 57/2 Rajdapisek Rd (☎02/245 7032).
India 46 Soi 23, Sukhumvit Rd (☎02/258 0300–6).
Indonesia 600–602 Phetchaburi Rd (☎02/252 3135–40).
Korea 23 Thiam-Ruammit Rd (☎02/237 7537–9).
Laos 193 Sathorn Thai Rd (☎02/287 3963).
Malaysia 35 Sathorn Thai Rd (☎02/286 1390–2).
Nepal 189 Soi 71, Sukhumvit Rd (☎02/391 7240).
Pakistan 31 Soi 3, Sukhumvit Rd (☎02/253 0288–90).
Philippines 760 Sukhumvit Rd, opposite Soi 47 (☎02/259 0139–40).
Singapore 129 Sathorn Thai Rd (☎02/286 2111).
Sri Lanka 48/3 Soi 1, Sukhumvit Rd (☎02/251 2788–9).
Vietnam 83/1 Witthayu (Wireless) Rd (☎02/251 5835).

Listings

Airport enquiries International departures ☎02/535 1254; international arrivals ☎02/535 1301; domestic services ☎02/535 1253.

American Express C/o *Sea Tours*, Room 436, Siam Centre (opposite Siam Square), 965 Rama I Rd, Bangkok 10330 (☎02/251 4862–9). Amex credit card- and travellers' cheque-holders can use the office (Mon–Fri 8.30am–noon & 1–4.30pm, Sat 8.30am–noon) as a poste restante, but mail is only held for 60 days. They will also receive faxes for Amex customers on ☎02/253 2960. To report lost cards or cheques call toll-free (☎02/088 227312).

Astrologers Mezzanine floor of the *Montien Hotel*, 54 Suriwong Rd (☎02/233 7060–9); astrology, palm- and tarot-reading available in English for B400 per half-hour.

Car rental *Avis*, Head Office, 2/12 Witthayu (Wireless) Rd (☎02/255 5300–4), and *Amari Airport Hotel*, Don Muang International Terminal (☎02/566 1020–1); *Hertz*, Head Office, 420 Soi 71, Sukhumvit Rd (☎02/382 0293–5), and Don Muang Domestic Terminal (☎02/535 3004–5); *SMT Rent-A-Car (Inter Rent)*, 931/11 Rama I Rd (☎02/216 8020); plus numerous others on Sukhumvit and Ploenchit roads.

Embassies and consulates *Australia*, 37 Sathorn Thai Rd (☎02/287 2680); *Canada*, Boonmitr Building, 138 Silom Rd (☎02/237 4126); *UK*, 1031 Wireless Rd (☎02/253 0191–9);

Ireland, United Flour Mill Building, 205 Rajawong Rd (☎02/223 0876); *Netherlands*, 106 Witthayu (Wireless) Rd (☎02/254 7701–5); *New Zealand*, 93 Witthayu (Wireless) Rd (☎02/ 251 8165); *US*, 95 Witthayu (Wireless) Rd (☎02/252 5040–9). For visas to Asian countries, see p.132.

Emergencies For all emergencies, call the tourist police on ☎195 or 1699.

Exchange The airport exchange desk and those in the upmarket hotels are open 24hr; many other exchange desks stay open till 8pm, especially along Khao San, Sukhumvit and Silom roads.

Hospitals and clinics *Bangkok Adventist Hospital*, 430 Phitsanulok Rd (☎02/281 1422); *Bangkok Christian Hospital*, 124 Silom Rd (☎02/233 6981); *Bangkok Nursing Home*, 9 Convent Rd (☎02/233 2610–9); *British Dispensary*, between sois 5 and 7, Sukhumvit Rd (☎02/252 8056); *Clinic Banglamphu*, 187 Chakrabongse Rd (☎02/282 7479); *Dental Polyclinic*, 211–3 New Phetchaburi Rd (☎02/314 5070); *Pirom Pesuj Eye Hospital*, 117/1 Phaya Thai Rd (☎02/252 4141); *VD International*, 588 Ploenchit Rd (☎02/250 1969).

Immigration office About 1km down Soi Suan Plu, off Sathorn Thai Rd (Mon–Fri 8am–noon & 1–4pm; ☎02/287 3101–10). Visa extension takes about an hour.

Language Courses *AUA*, 179 Rajdamri Road (☎02/252 8170) runs regular Thai language courses.

Laundries If you don't want to entrust your clothes to a guest-house laundry service, there are a couple of self-service laundries on Khao San Road.

Left luggage Both Don Muang airport and Hualamphong train station have left-luggage facilities (B20 per day); most hotels and guest houses will store bags by the week at much more reasonable rates.

Libraries *The National Library* at the junction of Samsen and Sri Ayutthaya roads (Mon–Sat 9am–4.30pm) has a large collection of English-language books, as do *AUA* at 179 Rajdamri Rd (Mon–Fri 8.30am–6pm, Sat 9am–1pm) and the *British Council* in Siam Square (Tues–Fri 10am–7pm, Sat 10am–5pm).

Meditation *World Fellowship of Buddhists*, between sois 1 and 3, 33 Sukhumvit Rd (☎02/251 1188) holds a monthly meditation session in English; *Wat Mahathat* in Ratanakosin (☎02/ 222 6011) has classes twice a month; *House of Dhamma*, 26/9 Soi Chumphon, Soi Lardprao 15, Bangkok (☎02/511 0439) has meditation instruction available in English throughout the week (see p.46 in *Basics*, for more details).

Pharmacies English-speaking staff at the *British Dispensary*, between sois 5 and 7, Sukhumvit Rd (☎02/252 8056).

Post The GPO is on New Road, just northeast of Wat Muang Kae express-boat stop. Poste restante can be collected Mon–Fri 8am–8pm, Sat & Sun 8am–1pm; letters are kept for 3 months. The parcel packing service at the GPO operates Mon–Fri 8am–4.30pm, Sat 9am–noon.

Telephones The least expensive places to make international calls are the public telephone offices in or adjacent to post offices. The largest and most convenient of these is across Soi Praysanii from the New Road GPO (open 24hr); the post offices at Hualamphong station and off Khao San Road in Banglamphu also have international telephone offices attached, but these close at 10pm.

travel details

Trains

Bangkok Hualamphong Station to: Aranyaprathet (2 daily; 5hr); Ayutthaya (20 daily; 1hr 30min); Butterworth (daily; 21hr 10min); Chiang Mai (6 daily; 12hr 25min–14hr 15min); Chumphon (9 daily; 6hr 45min–8hr 20min); Hat Yai (4 daily; 16hr); Hua Hin (9 daily; 3–4hr); Khon Kaen (5 daily; 7–8hr); Khorat (9 daily; 4–5hr); Lampang (6 daily; 11hr); Lamphun (6 daily; 13hr); Lopburi (12 daily; 2hr 30min–3hr); Nakhon Pathom (9 daily; 1hr 20min); Nakhon Si Thammarat (2 daily; 15hr); Nong Khai (3 daily; 11–12hr); Pak Chong, for Khao Yai National Park (7 daily; 3hr 30min); Phatthalung (4 daily; 15hr); Phitsanulok (12 daily; 5hr 25min–9hr 30min); Surat Thani (8 daily; 9hr–11hr 30min); Surin (7 daily; 8–10hr); Trang (2 daily; 13hr 40min); Ubon Ratchathani (6 daily; 10hr 20min–13hr 15min); Udon Thani (5 daily; 10hr); Yala (3 daily; 18hr).

Bangkok Noi Station to: Hua Hin (2 daily; 4hr–4hr 30min); Nakhon Pathom (3 daily; 1hr 20min); Nam Tok (daily; 4hr 35min), via Kanchanaburi (2hr 40min).

Buses

Eastern Bus Terminal to: Ban Phe, for Ko Samet (10 daily; 3hr); Pattaya (every 30min; 2hr 30min); Si Racha, for Ko Si Chang (every 30min; 2–3hr); Trat, for Ko Chang (14 daily; 6–8hr).

Northern Bus Terminal to: Ayutthaya (every 15min; 2hr); Chiang Mai (28 daily; 9–10hr); Chiang Rai (15 daily; 12hr); Khon Kaen (23 daily; 6–7hr); Khorat (every 20min; 3–4hr); Lampang (10 daily; 8–9hr); Loei (15 daily; 9hr); Lopburi (every 15min; 3hr); Mae Hong Son (2 daily; 18hr); Mae Sai (8 daily; 13hr); Mukdahan (13 daily; 11hr); Nakhon Phanom (17 daily; 12hr); Nan (13 daily; 13hr); Nong Khai (18 daily; 10hr); Pak Chong, for Khao Yai National Park (every 15min; 3hr); Phitsanulok (up to 19 daily; 5–6hr); Sakhon Nakhon (11 daily; 11hr); Sukhothai (17 daily; 6–7hr); Surin (up to 20 daily; 8–9hr); Ubon Ratchathani (19 daily; 10–12hr); Udon Thani (34 daily; 9hr).

Southern Bus Terminal to: Chumphon (9 daily; 7hr); Damnoen Saduak (every 20min; 2hr); Hat Yai (9 daily; 14hr); Hua Hin (every 25min; 3–3hr 30min); Kanchanaburi (every 15min; 2–3hr); Krabi (at least 5 daily; 12–14hr); Nakhon Pathom (every 10min; 40min–1hr 20min); Nakhon Si Thammarat (12 daily; 12hr); Narathiwat (3 daily; 17hr); Pattani (2 daily; 16hr); Phang Nga (4 daily; 11hr–12hr 30min); Phatthalung (4 daily; 13hr); Phuket (at least 10 daily; 14–16hr); Ranong (7 daily; 9–10hr); Satun (2 daily; 16hr); Sungai Kolok (3 daily; 18hr); Surat Thani (11 daily; 12hr); Trang (8 daily; 14hr); Yala (3 daily; 16hr).

Flights

Bangkok to: Chiang Mai (7–10 daily; 1hr 5min); Chiang Rai (4–5 daily; 1hr 25min); Hat Yai (4–6 daily; 1hr 25min); Hua Hin (1 daily; 25min); Khon Kaen (3–4 daily; 55min); Khorat (1–2 daily; 40min); Ko Samui (8 daily; 1hr 20min); Lampang (2 daily; 2hr); Nakhon Si Thammarat (4 weekly; 2hr); Nan (1 daily; 2hr); Phitsanulok (2–3 daily; 50min); Phuket (8–13 daily; 1hr 15min); Sakhon Nakhon (1 daily; 1hr); Surat Thani (2–3 daily; 1hr 10min); Trang (3 weekly; 2hr 5min); Ubon Ratchathani (1–2 daily; 1hr); Udon Thani (3 daily; 1hr).

CHAPTER TWO

THE CENTRAL PLAINS

N orth and west of the capital, the unwieldy urban mass of Greater Bangkok peters out into the vast, well-watered **central plains**, a region that for centuries has grown the bulk of the nation's food and been a tantalizing temptation for neighbouring power-mongers. The most densely populated region of Thailand, with sizeable towns sprinkled among patchworks of paddy and sugarcane fields, the plains are fundamental to Thailand's emergence as one of Southeast Asia's healthiest economies. Its rivers are the key to this area's fecundity, especially the Nan and the Ping, whose waters flow from the Chiang Mai hills to irrigate the northern plains before merging to form the Chao Phraya, which meanders slowly south through Bangkok and out into the Gulf of Thailand.

West of Bangkok, beyond the extraordinary religious site of **Nakhon Pathom**, the riverside town of **Kanchanaburi** has long attracted visitors to the notorious Bridge over the River Kwai and is now acquiring a reputation as a budget-travellers' hangout, for its unique and unpretentious raft-house accommodation. Few tourists venture further west except as passengers on the remaining stretch of the **Death Railway** – the most tangible wartime reminder of all – but the remote and tiny hilltop town of **Sangkhlaburi** holds enough understated allure to make the extra kilometres worthwhile.

On the plains north of Bangkok, the historic heartland of the country, the major sites are ruined ancient cities which cover the spectrum of Thailand's art and architecture. Closest to Bangkok, **Ayutthaya** served as the country's capital for the four centuries prior to the 1782 foundation of Bangkok, and its ruins evoke an era of courtly sophistication. A short hop north of here, the remnants of **Lopburi** hark back to an earlier time when the predominantly Hindu Khmers held sway over this region, building a constellation of stone temples across central and northeastern Thailand and introducing a complex grammar of sacred architecture that still dictates aspects of wat design today.

A separate nucleus of sites in the northern neck of the plains centres on **Sukhothai**, birthplace of the Thai kingdom in the thirteenth century. The buildings and sculpture produced during the Sukhothai era are the acme of Thai art, and the restored ruins of the country's first official capital are the best place to appreciate them, though two satellite cities – **Si Satchanalai** and **Kamphaeng Phet** – provide further incentives to linger in the area. West of Sukhothai, on the Burmese border, the town of **Mae Sot** makes a therapeutic change from ancient history and is most easily reached from the northern plains, though it also forges a less predictable link between the northern plains and the far north.

Chiang Mai makes an obvious next stop after exploring the sights north of Bangkok, chiefly because the Northern Rail Line makes connections painless. A less common itinerary branches east into Isaan by bus from Lopburi, Sukhothai or Phitsanulok. Most people treat Kanchanaburi as a mini-break from Bangkok, but to avoid gratuitous exposure to the capital's traffic, it's possible to cut across from Kanchanaburi to Ayutthaya, with a change of buses at Suphanburi.

WEST OF BANGKOK

Although the enormous chedi of **Nakhon Pathom** and the floating markets of **Damnoen Saduak** are easily seen in a day trip from the capital, the region west of Bangkok really merits a more extended stay, with at least a couple of nights spent on a raft house in **Kanchanaburi**. All tourist itineraries in this predominantly budget-traveller territory are dictated by the rivers – in particular the Kwai Noi, route of the Death Railway. At Kanchanaburi you reach the outer range of package tours from Bangkok, and following the Kwai Noi to its headwaters at **Sangkhlaburi** takes you into a forested and sparsely populated hill region that fifteen years ago was considered too dangerous to visit. These days it makes an attractive, unhyped retreat worth a stay of a day or two, offering the possibility of a sidetrip to the nearby Burmese border at **Three Pagodas Pass** as well as visits to nearby Mon and Karen settlements and the chance to trek in a relatively uncharted area.

Highway 323 is the main artery of the region, branching northwest off Highway 4 just beyond Nakhon Pathom and running the length of the Mae Khlong and Kwai Noi valleys as far as Sangkhlaburi and the Burmese border, a journey of some 400km from Bangkok. **Buses** bound for Nakhon Pathom and Kanchanaburi leave Bangkok's Southern Bus Terminal several times an hour; from there onwards services dwindle a little but never run less than once every two hours during daylight. The first 200km out of the capital is accessible by **train** along the remaining stretch of the Thailand–Burma station from Bangkok Noi to Nam Tok, via Nakhon Pathom and Kanchanaburi. Southbound trains also pass through Nakhon Pathom on their way to Phetchaburi, Surat Thani and eventually Malaysia.

Nakhon Pathom

Even if you're just passing through, you won't miss the star attraction of **NAKHON PATHOM**: the enormous **Phra Pathom Chedi** dominates the skyline from every direction, and forms the calm centre around which wheels the daily bustle of this otherwise unexceptional provincial capital, 56km west of Bangkok. Eye-catching in sunlight and floodlight, and imposing in all weathers, the chedi is well worth stopping off for, but there's little else to detain you here. Most people move on from Nakhon Pathom the same day, heading south to Damnoen Saduak to catch the next morning's floating markets or continuing west to Kanchanaburi and the River Kwai.

The only time you might want to stay overnight in Nakhon Pathom would be during either of its two annual **festivals**: for a week in early September the town hosts a food and fruits fair, featuring produce from Thailand's most fertile region and demonstrations of cooking and fruit-carving; then in mid-November the week-long Phra Pathom Chedi fair brings together itinerant musicians, food vendors and fortune-tellers.

Nakhon Pathom (derived from the Pali for "First City") is probably Thailand's oldest town and is thought to be the point at which **Buddhism** first entered the region now known as Thailand, over two thousand years ago. Then the capital of a sizeable Mon kingdom, the settlement was deemed important enough to rate a visit from a pair of missionaries dispatched by King Ashoka of India, one of

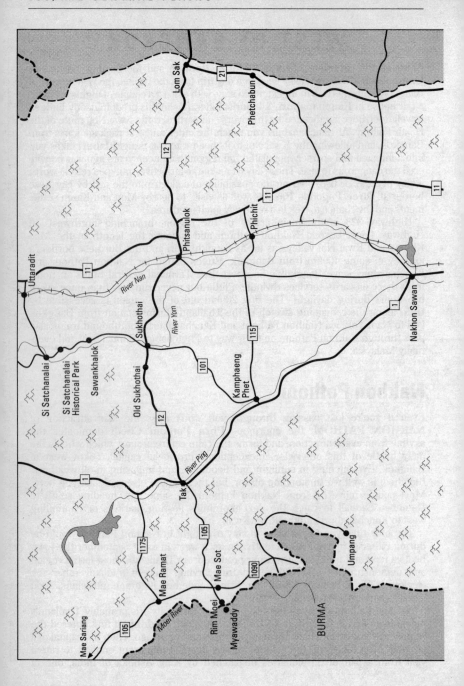

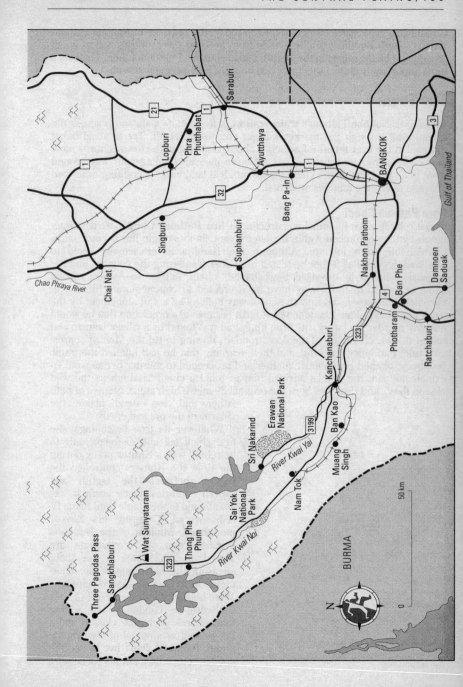

Buddhism's great early evangelists. Even today, the province of Nakhon Pathom retains a high Buddhist profile – aside from housing the country's holiest chedi (reputed to be the tallest in the world), it also contains Phuttamonthon, Thailand's most important Buddhist sanctuary and home of its supreme patriarch.

The Town

Arriving at Nakhon Pathom's **train station**, a five-minute walk south across the khlong and through the market will get you to the chedi. Try to avoid being dumped at the **bus terminal**, which is about 1km east of the town centre – most buses circle the chedi first, so get off there instead. Finding your way around town is no problem as the chedi makes an ideal landmark: everything described below is within ten minutes' walk of it.

Phra Pathom Chedi

Twice rebuilt since its initial construction, **Phra Pathom Chedi**'s earliest fragments remain entombed within the later layers, and its origin has become indistinguishable from folklore. Although the Buddha never actually came to Thailand, legend has it that he rested here after wandering the country, and the original Indian-style (inverted bowl-shaped) chedi, similar to Ashoka's great stupa at Sanchi in India, may have been erected to commemorate this. Local chronicles, however, tell how the chedi was built as an act of atonement by the patricidal Phraya Pan. Abandonded at birth because of a prediction that he would one day murder his father, the Mon king, Pan was found by a village woman and raised to be a champion of the downtrodden. Vowing to rid the Mon of oppressive rule, Pan killed the king, and then, learning that he had fulfilled the tragic prophecy, blamed his adoptive mother and proceeded to murder her as well. To expiate his sin, the monks advised him to build a chedi "as high as the wild pigeon flies", and thus was born the original 39-metre-high stupa. Statues of both father and son stand inside the viharns of the present chedi.

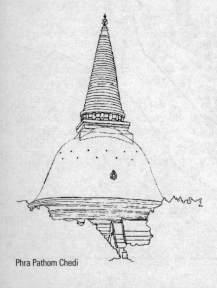

Phra Pathom Chedi

Whatever its true beginnings, the first chedi fell into disrepair, only to be rebuilt with a **Khmer** prang during the time the Khmers controlled the region, between the eighth and twelfth centuries. Once again it was abandoned to the jungle until Rama IV rediscovered it during his 27-year monkhood. Mindful of the Buddhist tradition that all monuments are sacred, in 1853 Rama IV set about encasing the old prang in the enormous new plunger-shaped **chedi** – 120m high, it stands as tall as St Paul's Cathedral in London – and adding four viharns, a circular cloister and a bot as well as a model of the original prang. Rama IV didn't live to see the chedi's completion, but his successors

A STUPA IS BORN

One of the more colourful explanations of the origin of the Buddhist **stupa** – chedi in Thai – comes from a legend describing the death of the Buddha. Anxious about how to spread the Buddha's teachings after his death, one of his disciples asked for a symbol of the Dharma philosophy. Notoriously lacking in material possessions, the Buddha assembled his worldly goods – a teaching stick, a begging bowl and a length of cloth – and constructed the stupa shape using the folded cloth as the base, the inverted bowl as the central dome and the stick as the spire.

Upon the Buddha's death, disciples from all over Asia laid claim to his **relics**, burying many of them in specially constructed stupa structures. In Thailand, the temples containing such chedis were given the title Wat Phra Mahathat (Temple of the Great Relic) and each royal city had one – today you'll find a Wat Phra Mahathat in Ayutthaya, Lopburi, Phetchaburi, Phitsanulok, Sukhothai, Nakhon Si Thammarat and Bangkok, all enjoying a special status although the presence of a genuine piece of the Buddha in each is open to question.

Stupa design has undergone many changes since the Buddha's makeshift example, and there are chedis in Thailand reflecting the architectural style of every major historical period. The **Sukhothai** chedi (thirteenth to fifteenth centuries), for example, is generally an elegant reworking of the original Sri Lankan model: early ones are bell-shaped (the bell symbolizing the ringing out of the Buddha's teachings), while the later, slimmer versions evoke the contours of a lotus bud. **Ayutthayan** architects (fourteenth to eighteenth centuries) owed more to the Khmers, elongating their chedis and resting them on a higher square platform, stepped and solid. Meanwhile, the independent **Lanna** kingdom (thirteenth to sixteenth centuries) of northern Thailand built some stupas to a squat pyramidal design that harked back to the seventh century, and other more rotund ones that drew on Burmese influences.

Twentieth-century chedi-builders have tended to combine historical features at will, but most still pay some heed to the traditional **symbolism** of each stupa component. In theory, the base or platform of the chedi structure should be divided into three layers to represent hell, earth, and heaven. The dome usually supports the cube-shaped reliquary, known as a *harmika* after the Sanskrit term for the Buddha's seat of meditation. Crowning the structure, the "umbrella" spire is graded into thirty-three rings, one for each of the thirty-three Buddhist heavens.

Over the centuries, Thailand's chedis have been used to house the ashes of kings and important monks and, in the last two hundred years or so, as reliquaries and memorials for anyone who can afford to have one erected.

covered it in golden-brown tiles from China and continued to add statues and murals as well as new buildings. The most recent restoration was completed in 1981, when cracks were discovered in the dome, a job which clocked up a bill of over B24 million.

AROUND THE CHEDI

Approaching the chedi from the main (northern) staircase you're greeted by the eight-metre-high Buddha image known as **Phra Ruang Rojanarit**, recast in 1913 from a broken statue found among the ruins of Si Satchanalai near Sukhothai, and installed in front of the north viharn. Each of the viharns – there's one at each of the cardinal points – has an inner and an outer chamber containing tableaux of the life of the Buddha. The figures in the outer chamber of the **north viharn** depict two princesses paying homage to the newly born Prince Siddhartha (the future Buddha), while the inner one shows a monkey and an elephant offering honey and water to the Buddha at the end of a forty-day fast.

Proceeding clockwise around the chedi – as is the custom at all Buddhist monuments – you can weave between the outer promenade and the inner cloister by climbing through the red-lacquered Chinese **moon windows** that connect them. The promenade is dotted with **trees** – many of religious significance, such as the bodhi tree (*ficus religiosa*) under which the Buddha was meditating when he achieved enlightenment – and shaded seating areas, making it a pleasant and peaceful place to relax a while; the inner cloister is filled with the desks, chairs and whiteboards used at night by young monks learning the ancient Buddhist script of Pali. Moving on, you'll come to the **east viharn**, painted on whose wall is a clear cross-section of the chedi construction showing the encased original. Flanking the staircase which leads up to the **south viharn** you can see a three-dimensional replica of the original chedi with Khmer prang (east side) and a model of the venerated chedi at Nakhon Si Thammarat (west side). The **west viharn** houses two reclining Buddhas: a sturdy, nine-metre-long figure in the outer chamber and a more delicate portrayal in the inner one.

THE MUSEUMS

Two museums within the chedi compound vie for visitors' attention and, confusingly, both call themselves **Phra Pathom Museum**. The newer, more formal setup is clearly signposted from the bottom of the chedi's south staircase (Wed–Sun 9am–noon & 1–4pm; B5). It displays a good collection of Dvaravati-era (sixth to eleventh centuries) artefacts excavated nearby, including Wheels of Law – an emblem introduced by Theravada Buddhists before naturalistic images were permitted – and Buddha statuary with the U-shaped robe and thick facial features characteristic of Dvaravati sculpture.

For a broader, more contemporary overview, hunt out the other magpie's nest of a collection found near the east viharn (Wed–Sun 9am–noon & 1–4pm; free). More a curiosity shop than a museum, the small room is an Aladdin's cave of Buddhist amulets, seashells, gold and silver needles, Chinese ceramics, Thai musical instruments, world coins and banknotes, gems and ancient statues.

Sanam Chan Palace

A ten-minute walk west of the chedi along Rajdamnoen Road takes you through a large park to the **Sanam Chan Palace** complex. Built as the country retreat of Rama VI in 1907, the palace and pavilions were designed to blend Western and Eastern styles. Several of the elegant wooden structures still stand, complete with graceful raised walkways and breezy verandahs. The main palace building has been converted into local government offices and so is officially off-limits to tourists, but you can have a quick gander at the still sumptuous interior by going in to ask for a local (though not very useful) map. In the grounds, Rama VI erected a memorial statue of his favourite dog and a small shrine to the Hindu god Ganesh.

Practicalities

Nakhon Pathom's sights only merit half a day, and at any rate **accommodation** here is no great shakes. If you have to stay the night, probably the quietest of the budget places is *Mitrsampant Hotel* (☎034/242422; ②), on the

---

ACCOMMODATION PRICES

Throughout this guide, guest houses, hotels and bungalows have been categorized according to the price codes given below. These categories represent the minimum you can expect to pay in the high season (roughly Nov–Feb & July–Aug) for a double room – or, in the case of national park bungalows, for a multi-berth room which can be rented for a standard price by an individual or group. If travelling on your own, expect to pay anything between sixty and one hundred percent of the rates quoted for a double room. Wherever a range of prices is indicated, this means that the establishment offers rooms with varying facilities – as explained in the write-up. Wherever an establishment also offers dormitory beds, the prices of these beds are given in the text, instead of being indicated by price code.

Remember that the top-whack hotels will add seven percent tax and a ten-percent service charge to your bill – the price codes below are based on net rates after taxes have been added.

① under B100	④ B250–400	⑦ B1000–1500
② B100–150	⑤ B400–600	⑧ B1500–3000
③ B150–250	⑥ B600–1000	⑨ B3000+

---

corner opposite the west gate of the chedi compound at the Lang Phra/ Rajdamnoen intersection, which has fan-cooled rooms and showers. Rooms at the *Mit Thawon* (☎034/243115; ②), next to the train station, are similarly priced – but don't take the one next to the generator. Rajvithee Road, which starts at the southwestern corner of the chedi compound, leads to the unbearably noisy *Muang Thong* and, further along, two much more comfortable hotels: *Nakorn Inn Hotel* (☎034/251152; ⑥) is the town's best, while *Whale Hotel* (☎034/251020; ⑤), down Soi 19 and signposted from the main road, offers good-value mid-range rooms, plus disco.

Both the posh hotels have **restaurants** – the *Whale* does terrific American breakfasts – but for inexpensive Thai and Chinese dishes try *Thai Food*, on Phraya Gong Road just south across the khlong from the train station, or one of the garden restaurants along Rajdamnoen Road, which runs west from the chedi's west gate. Night-time food stalls next to the *Muang Thong Hotel* specialize in noodle broth and chilli-hot curries, and during the day the market in front of the station serves up the usual takeaway goodies, including reputedly the tastiest *khao laam* (bamboo cylinders filled with steamed rice and coconut) in Thailand. Alternatively, buy noodles or *khao pat* from one of the vendors that set up in the chedi compound, and eat out under the trees.

Damnoen Saduak floating markets

To get an idea of what shopping in Bangkok used to be like before all the canals were tarmacked over, make an early-morning trip to the **floating markets** (*talat khlong*) of **DAMNOEN SADUAK**, 60km south of Nakhon Pathom. Vineyards and orchards here back onto a labyrinth of narrow canals thick with paddle boats overflowing with fresh fruit and vegetables: local women ply these waterways every morning between 6 and 11am, selling their produce to each other and to the residents of weatherworn homes built on stilts along the banks. Many wear the deep-blue jacket and high-topped straw hat traditionally favoured by Thai farmers. It's all richly atmospheric, which naturally makes it a big draw for tour groups – but you can avoid the crowds if you leave before they arrive, at about 9am.

The target for most groups is the main **Talat Khlong Ton Kem**, 2km west of the tiny town centre at the intersection of Khlong Damnoen Saduak and Khlong Thong Lang. Many of the wooden houses here have been expanded and converted into warehouse-style souvenir shops and tourist restaurants, dangerously diverting trade away from the khlong vendors and into the hands of large commercial enterprises. But, for the moment at least, the traditional water trade continues, and the two bridges between Ton Kem and **Talat Khlong Hia Kui** (a little further south down Khlong Thong Lang) make rewarding and unobtrusive vantage points. Touts invariably congregate at the Ton Kem pier to hassle you into taking a **boat trip** around the khlong network (asking an hourly rate of anything from between B25 per person to B200 for the whole boat) and while this may be worth it to get to the less accessible **Talat Khlong Khun Phitak** to the south, there are distinct disadvantages in being propelled between markets at top speed in a noisy motorized boat. For a less hectic and more sensitive look at the markets, explore the walkways beside the canals.

Practicalities

One of the reasons why Damnoen Saduak hasn't yet been totally ruined is that it's a 109-kilometre, two-hour **bus** journey from Bangkok. To make the trip in a day you'll have to catch one of the earliest #78 buses from Bangkok's Southern Bus Terminal (departures every 20min from 5am) or outside the *Nakorn Inn Hotel* on Rajvithee Road in Nakhon Pathom (from 6am onwards; about 1hr). From Kanchanaburi, take bus #461 to **Ban Phe** (every 15min from 5.25am onwards; 1hr 15min), then change to the #78. Many tours from Bangkok combine the floating markets with a day trip to Phetchaburi (p.387), about 40km further south: to get from Damnoen Saduak to Phetchaburi by public bus, you'll have to change at **Samut Songkhram**. To get to Damnoen Saduak from Phetchaburi or any points further south, catch any Bangkok-bound bus and, depending on which route it takes, change either at Samut Songkhram or at the **Photharam** intersection.

Damnoen Saduak's **bus terminal** is just north of Thanarat Bridge and Khlong Damnoen Saduak. Songthaews cover the 2km to Ton Kem, but walk if you've got the time: a walkway follows the canal, which you can get down to from Thanarat Bridge, or you can cross the bridge and take the road to the right (Sukhaphiban 1 Road, but unsignposted) through the orchards. The small **tourist information** office on the corner of this road keeps random hours and nobody there speaks much English.

The best way to see the markets is to **stay overnight** in Damnoen Saduak and get up before the buses and coach tours from Bangkok arrive – and, if possible, explore the khlongside walkways the evening before. The only **place to stay** in town is the *Little Bird Hotel* (☎032/241315; ②), whose sign is clearly visible from the main road and Thanarat Bridge. Although it's a motel with a trade in "short-stay" customers (note the condom display in the lobby), the rooms are good value: enormous, clean and all with en suite bathrooms.

Kanchanaburi and around

Set in a landscape of limestone hills 65km northwest of Nakhon Pathom, the provincial capital of **KANCHANABURI** unfurls along the left bank of the River Kwai Yai to reveal its most attractive feature: a burgeoning number of raft houses and riverside guest houses, any of which makes a wonderful place to unwind for a few days. With most of these catering mainly for modest budgets, Kanchanaburi has blossomed into quite a bustling independent travellers' centre. There's plenty to occupy several days here – the surrounding area offers numerous caves, waterfalls, wats and historical sites to explore, some of them easily reached by bicycle, and organized trekking and rafting trips to destinations further afield are also becoming popular.

Kanchanaburi's more official attractions, however, relate to its World War II role as a POW camp and base for construction work on the Thailand–Burma Railway. Day-trippers and tour groups descend in their hundreds on the infamous **Bridge over the River Kwai**, the symbol of Japanese atrocities in the region – though the town's main **war museum** and **cemeteries** are much more moving. Many veterans returning to visit the graves of their wartime comrades are understandably resentful that others have in some cases insensitively exploited the POW experience – the commercial paraphernalia surrounding the bridge is a case in point. On the other hand, the JEATH War Museum provides a shockingly instructive account of a period not publicly documented elsewhere.

Kanchanaburi's history, of course, begins a lot further back – in the Stone Age – when small communities established themselves in the fertile river basin near the present-day town, an era documented in the **Ban Kao Museum** west of town. Several millennia later, the people of this area probably paid allegiance to the Mon kings of Nakhon Pathom and subsequently to the Khmers, whose sphere of influence spread north from what is now Cambodia – the temple sanctuary at **Muang Singh**, not far from Ban Kao, stands as a fine example of twelfth-century Khmer architecture. Over the next five hundred years, Kanchanaburi's proximity to Thailand's aggressive Burmese neighbours gained it kudos as a key border stronghold; Rama III built walls around the town in 1743, and a small chunk of these can still be seen towards the western end of Lak Muang Road.

Arrival and accommodation

Trains from Bangkok Noi (2hr 40min) or Nakhon Pathom (1hr 10min) are the most scenic way to get to Kanchanaburi, if not always the most convenient – there are only two trains daily in each direction. The State Railway also runs special day trips from Bangkok's Hualamphong station which include short stops at Nakhon Pathom, the Bridge over the River Kwai and Nam Tok, the terminus of the line (Sat, Sun & holidays only; advance booking is essential, see p.130). The station is on Saeng Chuto Road, about 2km north of the town centre – convenient for riverside lodgings along Soi Rong Heeb and Maenam Kwai Road, but a bit of a hike from Song Kwai Road accommodation. Samlor drivers armed with sheaves of guest-house cards always meet the trains so you'll have no problem finding a ride, though getting to the guest house of your choice may take some firm negotiation.

Faster than the train are non-stop air-conditioned **buses** (about 2hr) from Bangkok's Southern Bus Terminal; slower regular services stop at Nakhon

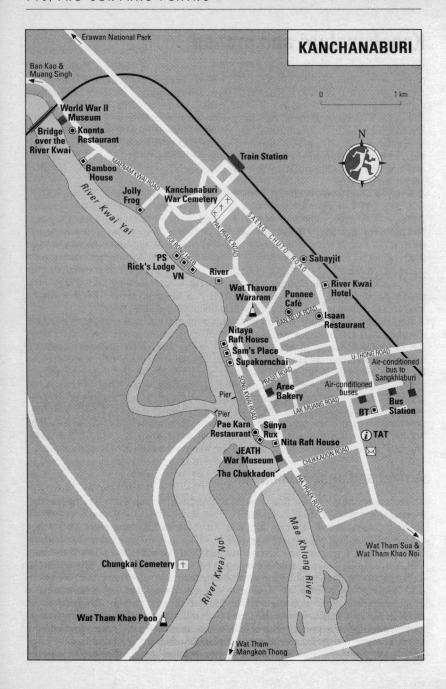

Pathom and several smaller towns en route. From Lopburi or points further north, you'll have to return to Bangkok or change buses at **Suphanburi**, about 70km north of Kanchanaburi. Arriving at the bus station at the southern edge of the town centre, it's a five-minute walk around the corner to the TAT office (daily 8.30am–4.30pm) and a ten- to twenty-minute walk, B10 motorbike taxi ride or B20 samlor ride down Lak Muang Road to the raft houses off Song Kwai Road.

Accommodation

To get the best out of Kanchanaburi, you'll want to stay on or near the river, in either a raft house or a guest house. Most **raft houses** are little more than rattan and cane huts, partitioned into two or three sparsely furnished rooms and balanced on a raft of planks and logs moored close to the river bank. There's nothing romantic about sleeping in them, but the uninterrupted views of the river set against the blue silhouettes of the craggy hills can be magnificent. Not all **riverside guest houses** can offer such perfect vistas, but having solid ground beneath you provides the option of an attached bathroom and sometimes the bonus of a grassy area on which to loll about. There's really little point in coming to Kanchanaburi and staying on dry land, but the town does have some non-aquatic accommodation options, a couple of which we've detailed below.

The river accommodation divides into two distinct areas. The noisier, brasher stretch near **Song Kwai Road** is where holidaying Thais come – about half the rafts along here cater specifically for Thai families and package tours – so a party atmosphere prevails and it's not the place for peace and quiet. Development here has just about reached full capacity: karaoke bars, patronized primarily by Thais although stray farangs are welcome enough, line the road proper, while the river bank is crowded during the daytime with covered one- and two-storey rafts, most of which are for group-hire only and set off upriver in the late afternoon. Several hundred metres upriver, the accommodation along **Soi Rong Heeb and Maenam Kwai Road** offers a greater sense of isolation. The former is little more than a narrow village lane with a handful of pleasant raft-house places, where bicycles and dogs constitute the main traffic and the home-owners sell a few groceries from their front rooms. Maenam Kwai Road is a bit more of a thorough-fare, stretching 2km from Soi Rong Heeb to the bridge, but the guest houses here are at the river-end of sois branching off it.

Despite Kanchanaburi's increasing popularity, you're unlikely to have a problem finding a room except during the crazy ten days of the annual Bridge Festival (late Nov to early Dec) when every inch of floor space seems to be taken.

SONG KWAI ROAD AREA

Nita Raft House (☎034/514521). Kanchanaburi's most inexpensive accommodation option is set away from the main Song Kwai Road fray, near the museum. Offers both very basic floating rooms, and some better ones with river view and shower. Superb views can also be enjoyed from the relaxed seating/eating area. Friendly management, well-organized day trips and tourist information. ①–②.

Nitaya Raft House (☎034/513341). Some overpriced rooms, with air-con and shower, on the riverfront; less costly fan-cooled ones further back. ②–⑤.

Sam's Place (☎034/513971). Attractively designed range of raft houses – the best with their own small terrace and shower, but all with some kind of river view. Very pleasant communal seating and eating areas. ①–③.

Supakornchai Raft (☎034/512055). Fairly basic raft houses, the least value for money in this area. ③.

SONG RONG HEEB AND MAENAM KWAI ROAD AREA

Bamboo House, down Soi Vietnam off the bridge end of Maenam Kwai Road (☎034/512532). Kanchanaburi's most secluded and peaceful accommodation, if a little inconvenient for shops and restaurants. A large and luscious lawn (good for kids) slopes down to simple floating huts; also a few air-con rooms in the chalet-style house. ②–⑤.

Jolly Frog Backpackers, Soi China, just off the southern end of Maenam Kwai Road (☎034/514579). Sizeable 2-storey complex of comfortable bamboo huts, some with attached bathroom, ranged around a riverside garden. The friendly and informative staff organize day trips and treks. ①–②.

PS Guest House, Soi Rong Heeb (☎034/513039). Simple, inexpensive huts away from the river, and some raft houses. ①–②.

Rick's Lodge, Soi Rong Heeb (☎034/514831). Unusual, 2-storey, A-frame bamboo huts with sleeping quarters in the roof section; rates are a bit steep, but negotiable. ③–④.

River Guest House, Soi Rong Heeb (☎034/512491). Beautifully located set of simple raft houses moored 30m from the river bank. ①.

VN Guest House, Soi Rong Heeb (☎034/514082). Well-run and attractively designed riverside huts with some of the thickest mattresses in town. The managers organize treks in the Sangkhlaburi area. ②.

SAENG CHUTO ROAD AREA

BT Guest House, near the bus terminal, just east off Saeng Chuto Road (☎034/511967). Fairly grotty, characterless rooms, but convenient for onward travel. ②.

River Kwai Hotel (aka *Rama of River Kwai*), 284/3–16 Saeng Chuto Rd (☎034/511184). The town's top hotel is nowhere near the river, but all rooms have air-con, and facilities include a swimming pool and nightclub. ⑦.

The Town

Strung out along the east bank of the River Kwai Yai, at the point where it joins the River Kwai Noi to become Maenam Mae Khlong, Kanchanaburi is a long, narrow ribbon of a town measuring about 5km from north to south. The war sights are sandwiched between the river and the busy main drag, Saeng Chuto Road, which along with the area around the bus station forms the commercial centre of Kanchanaburi. If you have the time, start with the JEATH War Museum at the far southern end (not to be confused with the inappropriately named World War II Museum near the bridge), and work your way northwards via the Kanchanaburi cemetery to the bridge, returning to one of the piers on Song Kwai Road for the ferry to the town's outlying tourist attractions.

A samlor

Walking around Kanchanaburi's main sights can be exhausting. By far the best way to see them, and the surrounding countryside, is by **bicycle**; most guest houses rent out bikes for about B20 per day, and several also have **motorbikes** and jeeps for hire. Other outlets include *Punnee Bar and Café* on Ban Neua Road, the shop opposite *Aree Bakery* on Pak Praek Road, the house across from *VN Guest House* on Soi Rong Heeb, and *BT Travel*, on the ground floor of the guest house of the same name. Alternatively, flag down a **samlor** or **motorbike** taxi or make use of the frequent **songthaew** service that runs along Saeng Chuto Road between the bus terminal and the bridge.

The JEATH War Museum

The **JEATH War Museum** (daily 8.30am–6pm; B20) gives the clearest introduction to local wartime history, putting the notorious sights of the Death Railway in context and painting a vivid picture of the gruesome conditions suffered by the POWs who worked on the line. JEATH is an acronym of six of the countries involved in the railway: Japan, England, Australia, America, Thailand and Holland. Notably lacking, though, is any real attempt to document the plight of the conscripted Asian labour force.

Set up by the chief abbot of the adjacent Wat Chaichumpon, the museum is housed in a reconstructed Allied POW hut of thatched palm beside the Mae Khlong, about 200m from the TAT office or a fifteen-minute walk southwest of the bus station. It's run by monks from the wat, so in accordance with Buddhist etiquette, women should remember to put the entrance fee on the table and not directly into the monk's hand (see "Cultural Hints" in *Basics*).

The most interesting **exhibits** are the newspaper articles, paintings and photographs recording conditions in the camps. When things got really bad, photography was forbidden and any sketches had to be done in secret, on stolen scraps of toilet paper; some of those sketches, many by English POW Jack Chalker, were

---

THE DEATH RAILWAY

Shortly after entering World War II in December 1941, Japan, fearing an Allied blockade of the Bay of Bengal, began looking for an alternative supply route to connect its newly acquired territories that now stretched from Singapore to the Burma–India border. In spite of the almost impenetrable terrain, the River Kwai basin was chosen as the route for a new **Thailand–Burma Railway**, the aim being to join the existing terminals of Nong Pladuk in Thailand (51km southeast of Kanchanaburi) and Thanbuyazat in Burma – a total distance of 415km.

About 60,000 Allied POWs were shipped up from captured Southeast Asian territories to work on the link, their numbers later augmented by as many as 200,000 conscripted Asian labourers. Work began at both ends in June 1942. Three million cubic metres of rock were shifted and nine miles of bridges built with little else but picks and shovels, dynamite and pulleys. By the time the line was completed, fifteen months later, it had more than earned its nickname, the **Death Railway**: an estimated 16,000 POWs and 100,000 Asian labourers died while working on it.

The appalling conditions and Japanese brutality were the consequences of the samurai code: Japanese soldiers abhorred the disgrace of imprisonment – to them, ritual suicide was the only honourable option open to a prisoner – and considered that Allied POWs had forfeited any rights as human beings. Food rations were meagre for men forced into backbreaking eighteen-hour shifts, often followed by night-long marches to the next camp. Many suffered from beri-beri, many more died of dysentry-induced starvation, but the biggest killers were cholera and malaria, particularly during the monsoon. It is said that one man died for every sleeper laid on the track.

The two lines finally met at Konkuita, just south of present-day Sangkhlaburi. But as if to underscore its tragic futility, the Thailand–Burma link saw less than two years of active service: after the Japanese surrender on August 15, 1945, the Thais cut up the line between Nam Tok and Three Pagodas Pass and sold the rails as scrap.

later reproduced as paintings. The simple drawings and paintings of torture methods are the most harrowing of all the evidence.

The Kanchanaburi War Cemetery

Thirty-eight Allied POWs died for each kilometre of track laid on the Thailand–Burma Railway, and many of them are buried in Kanchanaburi's two war cemeteries. Of all the region's war sights, the cemeteries are the only places to have remained completely untouched by the tourist trade. Opposite the train station on Saeng Chuto Road, the **Kanchanaburi War Cemetery** (daily 8am–4pm; free) is the bigger of the two, with 6982 POW graves laid out in straight lines amidst immaculately kept lawns and flowering shrubs. Many of the identical stone memorial slabs state simply "A man who died for his country", others, inscribed with names, dates and regiments, indicate that the overwhelming majority of the dead were under 25 years old. A commemorative service is held here every year on April 25, Anzac Day. (The second cemetery, Chungkai, is just outside the town on the banks of the Kwai Noi – see facing page.)

Asian labourers on the Death Railway – who died in far higher numbers than the Allies – are remembered with rather less ceremony. In November 1990 a **mass grave** of Asians was discovered beneath a sugar cane field on the edge of town. The digging started after a nearby resident dreamt that the dead couldn't breathe and were asking for his help. The skeletons, many of them mutilated, have since been given a proper burial service, but the new graves are not for public viewing – aside from those rather tastelessly displayed in the World War II Museum (see facing page).

The Bridge over the River Kwai

For most people the plain steel arches of the **Bridge over the River Kwai** come as a disappointment: as a war memorial it lacks both the emotive punch of the JEATH museum and the perceptible drama of spots further up the line, and as a bridge it looks nothing out of the ordinary – certainly not as awesomely hard to construct as it appears in David Lean's famous film of the same name. But it is the film, of course, that draws tour buses here by the dozen, and makes the bridge approach seethe with trinket-sellers and touts. For all the commercialization of the place, however, you can't really come to the Kwai and not see it. To get here either take any songthaew heading north up Saeng Chuto Road, hire a samlor, or cycle – it's 5km from the bus station.

The fording of the Kwai Yai at the point just north of Kanchanaburi known as Tha Makkham was one of the first major obstacles in the construction of the Thailand–Burma Railway. Sections of a steel bridge were brought up from Java and reassembled by POWs using only pulleys and derricks. A temporary **wooden bridge** was built alongside it, taking its first train in February 1943; three months later the steel bridge was finished. Both bridges were severely damaged by Allied bombers in 1944 and 1945; only the stumps of the wooden bridge remain, but the steel bridge was repaired after the war and is still in use today. In fact the best way to see the bridge is by taking the train over it: the Bangkok–Kanchanaburi–Nam Tok train crosses it twice a day in each direction.

Some of the original World War II **railway engines** used on this stretch have been spruced up and parked beside the bridge; nearby, a memorial stone commemorates the Japanese soldiers who died while overseeing the construction work.

The bridge forms the dramatic centrepiece of the annual *son et lumière* **River Kwai Bridge Festival**, held over ten nights from the end of November to commemorate the first Allied bombing of the bridge on November 28, 1944. The hour-long show uses spectacular effects to sketch the history of the region's wartime role, liberally lacing the commentary with a stodgy anti-war message that doesn't quite square with the climactic go-get-'em pyrotechnics. Tourists of all nationalities, including Thais, flock here for the show, and the area around the bridge turns into an enormous funfair. Book accommodation and air-conditioned buses well in advance, or join one of the many special tours operating out of Bangkok.

World War II Museum

Whilst at the bridge, you can't fail to see the signs for the nearby **World War II Museum** (daily 8am–6pm; B30), 30m south along Maenam Kwai Road. Not to be confused with the JEATH War Museum (see p.149), this is a new and privately owned collection that cynically uses the war to pull in curious coach parties, but it is nevertheless worth visiting for the sheer volume and bizarre eclecticism of its contents. The war section is housed on the lower floors of the building to the left of the entrance, and comprises a very odd mixture of memorabilia (a rusted bombshell, the carpet used by the local Japanese commander), reconstructed tableaux featuring emaciated POWs, and sanctimonious quotes from local dignitaries – a marked contrast from the first-hand accounts at JEATH. Although barely educative, these displays are at least inoffensive, unlike the museum's glass tomb containing the remains of over one hundred of the Asian conscripts found locally in a mass grave.

Elsewhere in the same building are more light-hearted and less unseemly displays, among them stamp and banknote collections, a ceiling painted with illustrations of Thai proverbs, and a top-floor gallery of selected "Miss Thailand" portraits from 1934 to 1992. Across the courtyard, a second building seeks to present an overview of Thailand's most venerated institutions with the help of specially commissioned wall paintings: Buddhism on the ground floor, prime ministers and kings on the middle storeys, and family portraits of the museum's founders – the Chansiris – right at the top.

Chungkai Cemetery and Wat Tham Khao Poon

Several of Kanchanaburi's other sights lie some way across the river, and are best reached by bike (or by longtail boat, organized through your guest house). For Chungkai Cemetery and Wat Tham Khao Poon, on the left bank of the Kwai Noi, take the two-minute ferry ride (for pedestrians and bikes) from the pier at the confluence of the two rivers on Song Kwai Road and follow the road on the other side. After about 2km you'll reach **Chungkai**, a peaceful cemetery built on the banks of the Kwai Noi at the site of a former POW camp. Some 1750 POWs are buried here; most of the gravestone inscriptions include a name and regimental insignia, but a number remain unnamed – at the upcountry camps, bodies were thrown onto mass funeral pyres, making identification impossible.

One kilometre on from Chungkai Cemetery, at the top of the road's only hill, sits the cave temple **Wat Tham Khao Poon** (daily 8am–6pm; donation). This labyrinthine Santa's grotto is presided over by a medley of religious icons – the star being a Buddha reclining under a fanfare of flashing lights. The scenery around here is a strong argument for continuing along the road for another few kilometres; once over the hill, the prospect widens to take in endless square miles of sugar cane plantation (for which Kanchanaburi has earned the title "sugar capital of Thailand") fringed by dramatically looming limestone crags. Aside from the odd house, the only sign of human life along here is at the agricultural college in Somdech Phra Srinagarindra Park, 6km south of the temple.

Wat Tham Mangkon Thong (Floating Nun Temple)

The impressive scenery across on the right bank of the River Kwai Noi makes for an equally worthwhile bike trip, but the cave temple on this side – **Wat Tham Mangkon Thong**, otherwise known as the **"Floating Nun Temple"** – is fairly tacky. The attraction here is an elderly Thai nun who, clad in white robes, will get into the temple pond and float there, meditating – if tourists give her enough money to make it worth her while. It's difficult not to be cynical about such a commercial, and unspectacular, stunt, though Taiwanese visitors are said to be particularly impressed. The floating takes place on a round pond at the foot of the enormous naga staircase that leads up to the temple embedded in the hillside behind. The temple comprises an unexceptional network of low, bat-infested limestone caves, punctuated at intervals with Buddha statues.

To **get to** Wat Tham Mangkon Thong, cross the bridge over the River Mae Khlong at the bottom of Chukkadon Road (near the museum) and then follow the road on the other side for about 4km.

Eating

All of Kanchanaburi's guest houses and raft houses have **restaurants**, so independent eateries specializing in similar Western and toned-down Thai dishes have to be pretty outstanding to survive. Local food is, of course, less expensive and more authentic: tasty **noodle shops** abound, particularly down Pak Praek Road, and at night there's the ever-reliable gastronomic delights of the **night market**, which sets up alongside Saeng Chuto Road near the air-conditioned bus stop – the roar of the traffic is complemented by the jukebox that gets wheeled out every evening. For **seafood** try out the land-based restaurants between *Sunya Rux's* and *Supakornchai* on Song Kwai Road: the **floating restaurants** opposite are overpriced, uninspired and cater for hapless tour groups, though the views are impressive; the same goes for the vast open-air restaurant next to the bridge.

Aree Bakery, near the corner of Pak Praek and Khu Muang roads. Especially popular for its German-made, home-baked cakes; sandwiches, coffee and ice cream also served and there's usually a fluctuating pile of second-hand books to peruse or buy. Closes around 4pm. Inexpensive to moderate.

Isaan, Saeng Chuto Road, 50m south of the *River Kwai Hotel*, on the other side of the road. Typical northeastern fare, including the excellent barbecued chicken (*kai yang*), sticky rice (*khao niaw*) and spicy papaya salad (*somtam*). Inexpensive to moderate.

Koonta Restaurant, about 75m south of the Bridge over the River Kwai on Maenam Kwai Road. The quietest, most reasonably priced and least touristed place to eat in the vicinity of the bridge, and pleasantly set in a flower garden. Simple menu of *khao pat* and *tom yum* dishes. Inexpensive.

Pae Karn, just north of *Sunya Rux* on Song Kwai Road. The best of the touristy floating restaurants, worth checking out day or night for its vistas, if not for its unexceptional seafood. Moderate.

Punnee Bar and Café, Ban Neua Road. English/Thai-run eatery serving up Thai, Western and Laotian food, and reasonably priced drinks. The owner, Danny, also sells second-hand books, changes money outside banking hours and deals in sapphires. Inexpensive to moderate.

Sabyjit, just north of *River Kwai Hotel* on Saeng Chuto Road. Unsigned in English, but directly opposite the unmistakable wood-panelled *Apache Saloon*, this place boasts a large and tasty menu of sweet-and-sour soups, curries, spicy salads, wontons and noodle dishes. Moderate.

Around Kanchanaburi

The optimum way of getting to the main sights in the Kanchanaburi countryside – the temples of **Tham Sua** and **Tham Khao Noi**, the **Ban Kao Museum** and **Erawan National Park** – is by hiring a motorbike from one of the guest houses: the roads are good, but the public transport in the immediate vicinity of town is sporadic and wearisome at best. Alternatively, most guest houses in Kanchanaburi organize reasonably priced day trips to caves, waterfalls and historical sights in the surrounding area, as well as more adventurous and lengthier expeditions (see box below).

Wat Tham Sua and Wat Tham Khao Noi

A twenty-kilometre ride from the town centre gets you to the modern hilltop wats of **Tham Sua** and **Tham Khao Noi**, examples of the sort of rivalry that exists within all religious communities, even Buddhist ones. Take Highway 323 in the direction of Bangkok and follow signs for Wachiralongkorn Dam; cross the dam – at this point you should be able to see the wats in the distance – and turn right at the T-junction. If you have to rely on public transport, a tuk-tuk from the centre shouldn't cost more than B100.

DAY TRIPS, TREKKING AND RAFTING

Excursions to Erawan National Park are the most popular organized **day tours** from Kanchanaburi and they usually include transport to Phrathat Cave as well as the boat ride to Huay Khamin Falls; at about B100 per person, the day trips run by *Nita Raft House, Jolly Frog Backpackers* and *VN Guest House* are all recommended. *Punnee Bar and Café* (☎034/513503) on Ban Neua Road does an interesting day trip that begins with a walk along Hellfire Pass (see p.158) and a segment of the now overgrown route of the Death Railway, before visiting the Khmer temple ruins at Muang Singh (see p.156) and the archaeological museum at Ban Kao (see p.154) – a full day's itinerary that would be impossible to cover without your own transport. It costs about B500 per person (depending on the size of the group), including lunch and entrance fees.

For **treks** and other outings slightly further afield, contact *Kanchanaburi Trekking Tour* (☎034/513909), which has an office close by *Jolly Frog* at the Soi China intersection with Maenam Kwai Road and leads one-, two- and three-day treks up the Kwai Noi, the longer ones going as far as Sangkhlaburi (see p.160), and all of them including rafting and jungle walking. Prices are all-inclusive and range from B800 to B2000 according to duration of trek. Some guest houses, such as *Jolly Frog* and *VN*, also do two- and three-day treks up to Sangkhlaburi at comparable rates.

Except during the rainy season, *Nita Raft House* runs three-day **rafting** excursions up the Kwai Noi. Participants pole their own rafts, food is cooked over campfires and overnight accommodation is in tents. You can now also paddle your own **canoe** up the River Kwai: *Jolly Frog* rents them out at B50 an hour.

Designed by a Thai architect, **Wat Tham Sua** was conceived in typical grandiose style around a massive chedi covered with tiles similar to those used at Nakhon Pathom. More than a quarter of a century on, it is still unfinished, but alongside it has emerged the Chinese-designed **Wat Tham Khao Noi**, a fabulously gaudy, seven-tiered Chinese pagoda whose more advanced state is an obvious indication of the differences in wealth between the Thai and Chinese communities. The differences between the temple interiors are equally pronounced: within Wat Tham Khao Noi, a laughing Buddha competes for attention with a host of gesturing and grimacing stone and painted characters, while next door a placid seated Buddha takes centre stage, his huge palms raised to show the Wheels of Law inscribed like stigmata across them. Common to both temples is the expansive view you get from their top storeys, which look down over the river valley and out to the mountains beyond.

Ban Kao Museum

Thirty-five kilometres west of Kanchanaburi, the **Ban Kao Museum** (daily 8.30am–4.30pm; B25) throws up some stimulating hints about an advanced prehistoric civilization that once settled along the banks of the Kwai Noi. The first evidence that a Stone Age community lived around here was uncovered during World War II, by the Dutch POW and former archeologist H R van Heekeren. Recognizing that the polished stone axes he found might be several millennia old, he returned to the site in 1961 with a Thai–Danish team which subsequently excavated a range of objects covering the period from around 8000 to 1000 BC. Many of these finds are now displayed in the museum.

One of the most interesting discoveries was a group of some fifty **skeletons**, which had been buried with curiously designed pots placed significantly at the heads and feet. The graves have been dated to around 1770 BC and the terracotta pot shards reassembled into tripod-shaped vessels of a kind not found elsewhere – they are thought to have been used for cooking over small fires. Polished stone tools from around 8000 BC share the display cabinets with inscribed bronze pots and bangles transferred from a nearby bronze culture site, which have been placed at around 1000 BC – somewhat later than the bronze artefacts from Ban Chiang in the northeast (see p.361). The hollowed-out tree trunks just in front of the museum are also unusual: they may have been used as boats or as coffins – or possibly as a metaphorical combination of the two.

There's no public **transport** to the museum, so unless you join a tour (see box on previous page) your best option is to hire a motorbike from Kanchanaburi, which also means that you can easily combine Ban Kao with a visit to Prasat Muang Singh, 8km west (see over).

Erawan National Park

Chances are that when you see a poster of a waterfall in Thailand, you'll be looking at a picture of the falls in **Erawan National Park**, 65km northwest of Kanchanaburi. The seven-tiered waterfall, topped by a triple cascade, is etched into the national imagination not solely by its beauty but also by its alleged resemblance to a three-headed elephant – this elephant (*erawan* in Thai) is the former national symbol and the usual mount of the Hindu god Indra. It makes a lovely setting for a picnic, especially just after the rainy season, and on Sundays and holidays Thais flock here to eat, drink and take family photographs against the falls; weekdays are generally a more peaceful time to come.

Access is along the well-maintained Highway 3199, which follows the River Kwai Yai upstream, taking in fine views along the way. Buses stop at **Srinakarind** market, from where it's a one-kilometre walk to the national park **headquarters** and the trailhead. Although the park covers an area of 550 square kilometres, the only official trail is the one to the waterfalls. It's a fairly easy walk, though if you're aiming for the seventh and final level (2km), you'll have to negotiate a few dilapidated bridges and ladders, so wear strong shoes. Each level comprises a waterfall feeding a pool of invitingly clear water partly shaded by bamboos, rattans, lianas and other clotted vegetation – like seven sets for a Tarzan movie. The best pools for swimming are levels two and seven, though these inevitably get the most crowded.

If you follow the road from Srinakarind market for another 10km you'll reach Wat Phrathat, from where it's a 500-metre walk to **Phrathat Cave**. A songthaew from the market to the wat costs B200: buses don't come this far. The stalactite cave has several large chambers, but is of interest to geologists for the fault lines which run under the Kwai Noi and are clearly visible in the disjointed strata.

The Kwai Yai is dammed a few kilometres north of the turn-off to Erawan and broadens out into the scenic **Srinakarind Reservoir**, now a popular recreation spot and site of several resorts. From the dam you can hire boats to make the two-hour journey across the reservoir to **Huay Khamin Falls**, but as the boats cost at least B100 per person, you'd probably be better off joining a tour from Kanchanaburi. The falls, which are said to be the most powerful in the district, reputedly gets the name "Turmeric Streak" from the ochre-coloured limestone rockface.

PRACTICALITIES

Buses to Erawan (#8170) leave Kanchanaburi every fifty minutes between 8am and 4pm and take two hours; if you miss the 4pm ride back you'll probably be there for the night. **Accommodation** is plentiful enough along the Kwai Yai valley, if a little select, most so-called "resorts" being fairly isolated communities of upmarket raft houses. The *Erawan Resort* (☎034/513568; ⑥) is only ten minutes' drive from the park, while the nearby *Kwai Yai Hilton Park* (☎02/421 3179; ⑤) and *Pha Daeng Resort* (☎034/513349; ⑤) both offer attractive lakeside accommodation. It's also possible to stay in the Erawan national park bungalows, but these are pretty grim and cost a minimum of B500 for a two-bedroom hut that sleeps four. There are several **food** stalls, restaurants and shops selling snacks near the trailhead.

The Death Railway: to Nam Tok

The two-hour rail journey from Kanchanaburi to Nam Tok is one of Thailand's most scenic, and most popular. Leaving Kanchanaburi via the Bridge over the River Kwai, the train chugs through the Kwai Noi valley, stopping frequently at country stations decked with frangipani and jasmine to pick up villagers who tout their wares in the carriages before getting off at the nearest market. There are three **trains** daily in both directions, which means it's possible to make day trips from Kanchanaburi to Muang Singh and Nam Tok if you get the timing right: Kanchanaburi TAT keeps up-to-date timetables. Frequent **buses** also connect Kanchanaburi with Nam Tok via Highway 323.

Prasat Muang Singh

Eight hundred years ago, the Khmer empire extended west as far as Muang Singh (City of Lions), an outpost strategically sited on the banks of the River Kwai Noi, 43km west of present-day Kanchanaburi. Thought to have been built at the end of the twelfth century, the temple complex of **Prasat Muang Singh** (daily 9am–5pm; B20) follows Khmer religious and architectural precepts (see p.337), but its origins are obscure – the City of Lions gets no mention in any of the recognized chronicles until the nineteenth century. If you're coming by train, get off at **Tha Kilen** (1hr 15min from Kanchanaburi), walk straight out of the station for 500m, turn right at the crossroads and continue for another 1km. If you have your own transport, Muang Singh combines well with a trip to the Ban Kao Museum, 8km east of here (see p.154); both sites are on minor road 3445 which forks off from Highway 323 just north of Kanchanaburi.

Prasat Muang Singh covers eighty acres, bordered by moats and ramparts which probably had cosmological as well as defensive significance, but unless you fancy a long stroll, you'd be wise to stick to the enclosed **shrine complex** at the heart of it all. Restoration work on this part has been sensitively done to give an idea of the crude grandeur of the original structure, which was constructed entirely from blocks of rough russet laterite.

Avalokitesvara

As with all Khmer prasats, the pivotal feature of Muang Singh is the main prang, as always surrounded by a series of walls and a covered gallery, with gateways marking the cardinal points. The prang faces east, towards Angkor, and is guarded by a fine sandstone statue of **Avalokitesvara**, one of the five great *bodhisattvas* of Mahayana Buddhism, would-be Buddhas who have postponed their entrance into Nirvana to help others attain enlightenment. He's depicted here in characteristic style, his eight arms and torso covered with tiny Buddha reliefs and his hair tied in a top-knot. In Mahayanist mythology, Avalokitesvara represents mercy, while the other statue found in the prasat, the female figure of **Prajnaparamita**, symbolizes wisdom. When wisdom and mercy join forces, enlightenment ensues.

Just visible on the inside of the north wall surrounding the prang is the only intact example of the stucco carving that once ornamented every facade. Other fragments and sculptures found at this and nearby sites are displayed beside the north gate; especially tantalizing is the single segment of what must have been a gigantic face hewn from several massive blocks of stone.

Nam Tok

Shortly after Tha Kilen the most hair-raising section of track begins: at **Wang Sing**, also known as Arrow Hill, the train squeezes through ninety-foot solid rock cuttings, dug at the cost of numerous POW lives; 6km further, it slows to a crawl at the approach to the **Wang Po viaduct**, where a 300-metre trestle bridge clings to the cliff face as it curves with the Kwai Noi – almost every man who worked on this part of the railway died. A couple of raft house operations have capitalized on the drama of this stretch of the river: on the viaduct side, *River Kwai Cabin* (☎034/591073; ⑥) offers upmarket bungalow accommodation; on the other bank, *River Kwai Jungle House* (☎034/561052; ⑥) has well-positioned raft houses.

Half an hour later, the train reaches **NAM TOK**, a small town that thrives chiefly on its position at the end of the line. Few foreign travellers stay here – day-trippers leave when the train begins its return journey, while those on package tours are whisked downriver to pre-booked raft resorts. Nam Tok **train station** is at the top of the town, 3km from the river and 500m north of Highway 323; **buses** usually stop near the T-junction of the highway and the station road.

On rainy-season weekends, Thais flock to the town's roadside **Sai Yok Noi waterfall**, but if you're filling time between trains, you'd be better off stretching your legs on the short trek to the nearby Wang Badan cave or taking a boat trip from Pak Saeng pier to Tham Lawa and Sai Yok Yai Falls (see below and p.159).

Best-value **accommodation** in town are the *Sai Yok Noi Bungalows* (☎034/512279; ②); to get there, turn northwest at the T-junction, walk five minutes and then turn right again. Or you can sleep in a floating room, comfortably kitted out with attached bathroom and verandah, beside Pak Saeng pier, at *Kitti Raft* (☎034/591106; ⑤). The biggest resort on this section of the river is *River Kwai Jungle Rafts* (☎02/245 3069; ⑥), about forty minutes upstream from Pak Saeng pier. A company called *River Kwai Floatel* runs the resort, organizing overnight packages starting from Bangkok, which include transport, trips along the river, French and Thai meals and raft accommodation. A two-day package costs B2300 per person; packages with only meals and accommodation cost B650 per person per day.

For **eating**, try the large open-air *Raena Restaurant* opposite the T-junction, which serves good food but sometimes caters to tour groups so is a little over-priced; the very friendly restaurant (no English sign) across the road offers the usual range of standard Thai dishes and is particularly lively in the evening.

Around Nam Tok

Impressive stalactites, fathomless chambers and unnerving heat make **Tham Wang Badan** (8.30am–4.30pm), one of the most exciting undergound experiences in the region. Located at the western edge of Erawan National Park (see p.154), the cave is reached by a trail that begins from Highway 323 about 1500m northwest of the T-junction (towards Sangkhlaburi). About 1km into the trail, you'll reach the park warden's office where you can rent feeble torches; better to bring your own or to pay the warden at least B50 to accompany you and turn on the generator – it's worth the money. From the office it's 2km of easy walking to the cave, but the descent should be made with care and sturdy shoes.

Longtail boats can be hired from Pak Saeng pier for the upstream **boat ride** to **Tham Lawa**, the largest stalactite cave in the area and home to three species of bat. To get to the pier from the T-junction, turn left towards Kanchanaburi, then take the first road on your right. The return journey to the cave takes roughly two hours, including half an hour there, and should cost about B550 for the eight-seater boat. Add on at least four more hours and another B750 if you want to continue on to Sai Yok Yai Falls.

Nam Tok to Three Pagodas Pass

Although the rail line north of Nam Tok was ripped up soon after the end of the war, it casts its dreadful shadow all the way up the Kwai Noi valley into Burma. The remnants of track are most visible at **Hellfire Pass**, while many of the villages in the area are former POW sites – locals frequently stumble across burial sites, now reclaimed by the encroaching jungle. Small towns and vast expanses of impenetrable mountain wilderness characterize this stretch, a landscape typified by the dense monsoon forests of **Sai Yok National Park**. Most travellers drawn here will continue, via the market town of Thong Pha Phum, a further 160km to the border territory around **Sangkhlaburi**, 20km short of the actual border at **Three Pagodas Pass**, a notorious port of entry for smuggled goods and site of occasional skirmishes between Karen, Mon, Burmese and Thai factions. However, even if you have a visa you won't be allowed to enter Burma here, other than for the designated one-kilometre border stroll.

The only access to this region is via Highway 323, which runs all the way to the border, past the massive **Khao Laem reservoir**, along a course dominated by the Tenasserim mountains to the west and the less extensive Mae Khlong range to the east. All **buses** originate in Kanchanaburi, and run every half-hour between Nam Tok and Thong Pha Phum, in both directions, with four a day continuing up to Sangkhlaburi (the last of these through buses leaving Kanchanaburi at 1.15pm), so it's quite feasible to stop off for a couple of hours at either Hellfire Pass or Sai Yok National Park before resuming your trip northwards. As there's nowhere to stay at Hellfire Pass and the budget accommodation at Sai Yok fills up fast, it's advisable to set off from Nam Tok reasonably early and aim to spend the night in Sangkhlaburi – though Thong Pha Phum has a couple of bungalow outfits if you get stuck.

Hellfire Pass

To keep the Death Railway level through the uneven course of the Kwai valley the POWs had to build a series of embankments and trestle bridges and, at dishearteningly frequent intervals, gouge deep cuttings through solid rock. The most concentrated digging was at **Konyu**, 18km beyond Nam Tok, where seven separate cuttings were made over a 3.5-kilometre stretch. The longest and most brutal of these was **Hellfire Pass**, which got its name from the hellish lights and shadows of the fires the POWs used when working at night – a job which took three months of round-the-clock labour with the most primitive tools.

Hellfire Pass has now been turned into a **memorial walk** in honour of the POWs who worked and died on it. The ninety-minute circular trail follows the old rail route through the eighteen-metre-deep cutting and on to Hin Tok creek – then forded by a trestle bridge so unstable that it was nicknamed the Pack of Cards Bridge – along a course relaid with some of the original narrow-gauge track. The trail doubles back on itself, passing through bamboo forest and a viewpoint that gives some idea of the phenomenal depth of rock the POWs had to dig through. To get to the trailhead, take any Nam Tok–Thong Pha Phum–Sangkhlaburi bus and ask to be dropped off at the Army farm (*suan thahaan*) – Hellfire Pass is signposted on the left-hand side of Highway 323 as you face Sangkhlaburi.

Sai Yok National Park

Ten kilometres further up Highway 323, **Sai Yok National Park** also retains some evidence of World War II occupation, but the chief attractions here are caves, waterfalls and teak forests. The park covers 500 square kilometres of uninhabited land stretching west of Highway 323 as far as the Burmese border, but the public has access only to the narrow strip between the Kwai Noi and the road, an area crisscrossed by short trails and dotted with caves and freshwater springs. It makes a refreshing resting point between Nam Tok and Sangkhlaburi, particularly if you have your own transport; accommodation and restaurant facilities are available, but cater primarily for Thai family groups.

Any of the Kanchanaburi–Sangkhlaburi **buses** will stop at the road entrance to Sai Yok (marked by the 104-kilometre stone), from where it's a three-kilometre walk to the **visitors' centre**, trailheads and river. The last buses in both directions pass the park at about 7.30pm. Motorbike taxis sometimes hang around the road entrance waiting to transport visitors, but a more scenic way of visiting the park would be to join a longtail excursion from Nam Tok (see p.157).

All the trails start from near the visitors' centre, and are clearly signposted from there as well as being marked on the map available from the centre. As in most of Thailand's national parks, Thais themselves come here for a waterfall. In this case it's the much-photographed **Sai Yok Yai Falls**, which tumbles right into the Kwai Noi in a powerful cascade – you can shower under it and bathe in the pools nearby, or gaze at it from the suspension bridge. If you come by longtail from Nam Tok, the boatman will probably also take you another 5km upstream to the stalactite-filled **Daowadung Caves**, a two-kilometre walk west of the river bank.

However, Sai Yok's most unusual feature is its dominant forests of **teak**, an endangered species in Thailand as a consequence of rapacious logging. During the war all the teak in this area was felled for rail sleepers – the present forests were replanted in 1954. The park's other rarity is the smallest known mammal in the world, the hognosed or **bumblebee bat**, discovered in 1973 and weighing only 1.75g, with a wingspan of 1.6cm. The bats live in twenty limestone caves in the Kanchanaburi area, of which Sai Yok's **bat cave** is the most accessible. Don't get too excited, though: it's almost impossible to see the bats unless you venture quite far inside with a powerful flashlight, and even then you'll need a fair amount of luck. On the way to the cave along the signposted trail, you might stumble across a few disintegrating rail sleepers which, together with the pile of bricks identified as the "Japanese cooking facility", constitute the park's only visible World War II remains. Although the camp kitchen is not worth making the effort for, follow its signposts from the visitors' centre for some secluded bathing spots in the crystal clear **natural springs** nearby.

Sai Yok has quite a few national park **bungalows**, which house a minimum of five people for B500. More inviting are the *Sai Yok Falls* (☎034/511964; ⑤) raft houses near the waterfall; get there early if you want to be sure of a room. The raft house serves **food** and there are plenty of fried rice and noodle stalls near the visitors' centre.

The Khao Laem reservoir and Wat Sunyataram

From Sai Yok, Highway 323 continues northwest, following the course of the Kwai Noi. Forty kilometres along the road is **THONG PHA PHUM**, a market town whose prosperity owes much to the tin and silver mines on the nearby

Burmese border. There's not much more than a collection of market stalls and missed bus connections to keep you here; if you do have to stay over, a couple of inexpensive bungalow-hotels right in the town centre – *Som Chai Nuk* (☎034/599067; ②) and *Sri Thong Pha Phum* (☎034/599058; ②–③) – offer decent enough accommodation.

Immediately north of Thong Pha Phum is the vast **Khao Laem reservoir** (also known as the Kreung Kra Wia reservoir), the creation of which, in the early 1980s, flooded every village in the vicinity. The former villagers have been rehoused along the reservoir's banks, and the road twists along its eastern shore, affording increasingly spectacular views of the waterlogged valley as it climbs through the remaining swathes of montane rainforest.

Halfway along the route from Thong Pha Phum to Sangkhlaburi, a sign at kilometre-marker 32 points you to **Wat Sunyataram Forest Monastery**, a retreat and meditation centre (at which foreigners are welcome: details from the wat or through *P Guest House* in Sangkhlaburi) run under the auspices of the renowned charismatic monk Phra Yantra Amaro Bhikku, currently under investigation for alleged sexual misconduct (see "Religion: Thai Buddhism" in *Contexts*, p.543).

Sangkhlaburi

Right at the reservoir's northernmost tip, **SANGKHLABURI**, at the end of Highway 323 and 160km from Sai Yok, overlooks an eerily beautiful post-holocaust scene of semi-submerged trees. One of those unassuming backwaters where there's nothing much to do except enjoy the scenery and observe everyday life, it has the rough feel of a mountain outpost and is a charming place to hang out for a few days.

Because of its proximity to the border, Sangkhlaburi's **ethnic mix** is particularly marked: Mon, Karen and Burmese townspeople and traders mingle with indigenous Thais at the central early morning market. Many wear the checked *longyis* favoured across the border, and the Burmese face powder used as protection against the elements. The older villagers have the hardy, weathered bearing of mountain people: in the cool season, when mist blankets the place until late morning, they make their transactions wrapped in woolly hats and jumpers, sarongs and denim jackets.

Other than people-watching, you could spend a pleasant afternoon **boating** across the reservoir in search of the all-but submerged spires of Wat Sam Phrasop, a former village temple. *P Guest House* lends rowing boats to guests for this purpose, and rents them to non-guests. It also runs one-day **excursions**, featuring elephant riding and some jungle walking, into wilderness slightly further afield; Sangkhlaburi's other guest house, the *Burmese Inn*, offers more idiosyncratic, customized itineraries.

Ban Waeng Ka

The Mon village of **Ban Waeng Ka**, divided from the rest of Sangkhlaburi by the reservoir, grew up in the late 1940s after the outbreak of civil war in Burma when the emergence of an intolerant nationalist regime prompted the country's ethnic minorities to flee across the border (see box over). Illegal immigrants in Thailand, their presence was permitted but not officially recognized, so that thirty years later when the dam was constructed and the valley villages flooded, the Mon refugees weren't entitled to compensation. Despite this, an influential local

Mon abbot, Pa U Thama, managed to secure the right to relocate five hundred submerged households to the northwest shore of the reservoir, a settlement which mushroomed into the 1000-household village of Waeng Ka. Although most now have official Sangkhlaburi residency, the Mon still have limited rights: they must apply for expensive seven-day permits if they wish to travel out of the district, a system which lends itself to corruption.

To explore the village, you can rent a motorbike from one of Sangkhlaburi's guest houses and cross the spider's web of a wooden bridge spanning the lake: said to be the longest handmade wooden bridge in the world, it's open to pedestrian and motorbike traffic only; cars use the more solid structure a few hundred metres further north. Once across the bridge, turn left at the cinema to get into the village – a sprawling collection of traditional wooden houses lining a network of steep dirt tracks, with a lively dry-goods market at its heart; smaller but much less touristy than the market at Three Pagodas Pass (see p.164), this is a good place to pick up sarongs, *longyis* and locally crafted bone jewellery.

Wat Wiwekaram, Ban Waeng Ka's most dramatic sight, stands at the edge of the village, its massive, russet-coloured chedi clearly visible from Sangkhlaburi. Built in a composition of Thai, Indian and Burmese styles, the imposing square-sided stupa is modelled on the centrepiece of India's Bodh Gaya, the sacred site of the Buddha's enlightenment, and is hugely popular with Buddhist pilgrims from all over Thailand. Devotees donate enormous sums of money in honour of the octogenarian Pa U Thama, now the wat's abbot, whose photograph is displayed in the temple compound, and the astonishing opulence of the wat buildings is testimony to this munificence. The wat is spread over two compounds, with the gleaming new bot, viharn and monks' quarters about 1km away from the chedi, at the end of the right-hand fork in the road.

Practicalities

If you're coming to Sangkhlaburi direct from Kanchanaburi, the most pleasant way to travel is by air-conditioned **minibus** (hourly every day from 7.30am to 4.30pm; 3hr), which departs from the office in the far southeastern corner of Kanchanaburi bus station. It's worth reserving your seat in advance, especially for the first or last minibus of the day, from either terminus. The four daily **regular buses** are less expensive but may take twice as long: if you're coming from Nam Tok or Sai Yok, though, these are your only viable option, as the minibus only picks up passengers at Thong Pha Phum. In Sangkhlaburi, the minibuses terminate in front of the *Sreedaeng Hotel* on the eastern edge of town, and the regular buses stop a couple of blocks further west, opposite *No Name Restaurant*.

Not many foreign tourists make it here, but those who do all seem to head for one of the town's two inexpensive **guest houses**, both run by friendly and informative managers, with mountain bikes and motorbikes for rent. *Burmese Inn* (☎034/595146; ①), 800m from either bus terminal (follow the clearly posted signs, or take a motorbike taxi), has a range of comfortable huts strung across the hillside, with excellent views of the wooden bridge and Ban Waeng Ka across the lake. The Austrian manager, Armin, is a font of local knowledge, including current border politics, and will arrange excursions into uncharted national park territory on request. A few hundred metres further down the same road (also well signposted), *P Guest House* (☎034/595061; ①) is spectacularly sited on the sloping banks of the reservoir, and offers fairly basic accommodation and good food at its hillside restaurant. Manager Darunee organizes one-

THE MON

Dubbed by some "the Palestinians of Asia", the **Mon** people – numbering around four million in Burma and three million in Thailand (chiefly in the western provinces of Kanchanaburi and Ratchaburi, and in the regions of Nonthaburi and Pathum Thani just north of Bangkok) – have endured centuries of persecution, displacement and forced assimilation.

Ethnologists speculate that the Mon originated either in India or China, travelling south to settle on the western banks of the Chao Phraya valley in the first century BC. Here they founded the **Dvaravati kingdom** (sixth–eleventh centuries AD), building centres at U Thong, Lopburi and Nakhon Pathom and later consolidating a northern kingdom in Haripunchai (modern-day Lamphun). They probably introduced Theravada Buddhism to the region, and produced some of the earliest Buddhist monuments, particularly Wheels of Law and Buddha footprints.

Over on the Burmese side of the border, the Mon kingdom had established itself around the southern city of Pegu well before the Burmese filtered into the area in the ninth century, but over the next nine hundred years consistent harassment from the Burmese forced thousands to **flee** to Thailand. (As Burma was also engaged in an endless series of territorial battles with Thailand, the Mon got their own back by acting as spies and informers for the Thais.) Eventually, in the mid-eighteenth century, the Burmese banned the use of the Mon language in Burma, segregated Mon men and women by force, and decreed that they should be known as Talaings, a pejorative term implying bastardy. Stripped of their homeland, the Mon were once again welcomed into Thailand as a useful source of labour – in 1814, the future Rama IV arrived at the Kanchanaburi border with three royal warboats and a guard of honour to chaperone the exiles. Whole areas of undeveloped jungle were given over to them, many of which are still Mon-dominated today.

The persecution of Burmese Mons has continued right through the **twentieth century** although both the Mons and the Karen (see p.204) have thus far

day treks to nearby Karen and Burmese villages, and also has rowing boats available for anyone who wants to paddle off in search of the sunken chedis. If the guest houses are full, the central *Sreedaeng Hotel* (☎034/512996; ③), just behind the market and opposite the army camp, has large clean rooms with attached bathrooms.

Round the corner from *Sreedaeng* are several noodle shops, but the most popular **restaurant** is *No Name Restaurant*, which serves good, inexpensive Thai dishes under friendly management; it's on the road down to the guest houses, across from the regular bus and songthaew terminal. *P*'s kitchen dishes up a tasty range of travellers' fare, including Western breakfasts and Thai and Burmese curries. Travellers' cheques and dollars can be changed at the bank, which is close to the market in the town centre; the post office is near *Sreedaeng*.

Three Pagodas Pass

Four kilometres before reaching Sangkhlaburi, a road branches off Highway 323 to **Three Pagodas Pass** (Sam Phra Chedi Ong), winding its way through cloud-capped, forested hills and passing a few Karen and Mon settlements before reaching the border terminus 18km further on. Songthaews leave Sangkhlaburi bus station every forty minutes from 6am to 6pm, cost B30 and take forty minutes.

refused to capitulate to Rangoon's demands for ceasefires. In December 1993, the governing State Law and Order Restoration Council (SLORC) launched its most recent offensive in an attempt to round up the labour supply for two infrastructure projects: the extension of the Rangoon–Ye rail line as far south as Tavoy, and the construction of a gas pipeline connecting Burmese waters with Kanchanaburi. International human rights organizations have reported that hundreds of thousands of Mon, Karen and Muslim men, women and children have been press-ganged into unpaid labour; furthermore, deaths from malnutrition, malaria and cholera have been reported, as have beatings and gang rapes. Other captive workers are used as human land-mine detectors, and as porters to transport arms for the Burmese attacks on their own rebel army. Not surprisingly, Mons have been fleeing these atrocities in droves, the majority ending up in Sangkhlaburi, the established home to a large community of Mon people. The Thai government, however, now sees great economic benefit in good relations with Burma's junta, and has made attempts to force the recent refugees back across the border.

Political expediency looks like reversing what had previously been centuries of successful assimilation into Thai society. Like Thais, the Mon are a predominantly Buddhist, rice-growing people, but they also have strong animist beliefs. All Mon families have totemic **house spirits**, such as the turtle, snake, chicken or pig, which carry certain taboos; if you're of the chicken spirit family, for example, the lungs and head of every chicken that you cook have to be offered to the spirits, and although you're allowed to raise and kill chickens, you must never give one away. Guests belonging to a different spirit group from their host are not allowed to stay overnight. Mon **festivals** also differ slightly from Thai ones – at Songkhran (Thai New Year), the Mon spice up the usual water-throwing and parades with a special courtship ritual in which teams of men and women play each other at bowling, throwing flirtatious banter around with their wooden discs.

All **border trade** for hundreds of kilometres north and south has to come through Three Pagodas Pass: textiles, sandals, bicycles and medical supplies go out to Burma, in return for cattle and highly profitable teak logs – the felling of which has been illegal in Thailand since 1989. Over the last half-century, the Mon, the Karen and the Burmese government have vied with each other constantly for supremacy at the pass, the rebels relying on the tax on smuggled goods to finance their insurgency campaigns, and the government desperate to regain its foothold in rebel territory. Until 1990, an offensive was launched every dry season against the current holder of the pass, but that year the power wrestle ended with the Burmese government gaining command from the Mon, a situation that has so far remained unchallenged.

It must be the romantic image of a hilltop smuggling station that attracts the few foreign tourists to the 1400-metre-high pass, because there's nothing substantial to see here. The **pagodas** themselves are diminutive whitewashed structures unceremoniously encircled by a roundabout, though traffic is not exactly heavy up here. They are said to have been erected in the eighteenth century by the kings of Burma and Thailand as a symbolic commitment to peace between the traditionally warring neighbours. (During the Ayutthayan period, Burmese troops would regularly thunder through here on elephant-back on their way to attack the capital.) Each supposedly built a chedi on his own side of the border and, at the foot of the central, borderline pagoda they signed an agreement never to war with each other again.

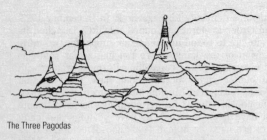

The Three Pagodas

All three are now on Thai soil, at the edge of Ban Sam Phra Chedi Ong, a tiny village comprising not much more than a few food stalls, a songthaew stop, a wat and a "souvenir hall". Burmese land starts 50m away, at the newly prosperous village of **Payathonzu**. At the time of writing, you are allowed to **cross the border**, but only after relinquishing your passport to the Thai officials and then paying a whopping B130 "tax" to the Burmese government officials in the next-door hut; Thais pay only B10 to cross. Once over the border you can explore just 1km of the village – a few dusty streets lined with wooden shophouses, many of which are given over to Payathonzu's main industry, the manufacture, polishing and varnishing of heavy teak furniture. The **market** at the far end of Payathonzu sells an impressive range of cloth, including Thai sarongs, batik from Indonesia, Burmese *longyis*, and gorgeous embroidered Indian bedspreads. Jade and sapphires, bone jewellery, Burmese face powder and cheroots are also good buys here. All this legal commercial activity is a relatively new development for Payathonzu; until 1990, the continual struggles over the pass meant that the village was almost always being rebuilt, and much of the weekly trade passed through after dark. Whether the Burmese military will hold on to this crucial outpost is by no means a certainty, though in the last five years there's been massive investment in a bid to stabilize the area.

As somewhere to hang out for a few days, Three Pagodas Pass doesn't compare to the more scenic and essentially more congenial Sangkhlaburi, but it is possible to **stay** on the Thai side of the border, at *Three Pagodas Resort* (☎02/ 412 4159; ⑤) whose selection of fairly upmarket bungalows is set round a garden on the edge of Ban Sam Phra Chedi Ong.

AYUTTHAYA AND THE CHAO PHRAYA BASIN

Bisected by the country's main artery, the **Chao Phraya River**, and threaded by a network of tributaries and canals, the fertile plain to the north of the capital retains a spectrum of attractions from just about every period of the country's history. The monumental kitsch of the nineteenth-century palace at **Bang Pa-In** provides a sharp contrast with the atmospheric ruins at the former capital of **Ayutthaya**, where ancient temples, some crumbling and overgrown, others alive and kicking, are arrayed in a leafy, riverine setting. **Lopburi**'s disparate remains, testimony to more than a millennium of continuous settlement, are less compelling, but you'll get a frenetic, noisy insight into Thai religion if you visit the nearby **Wat Phra Phutthabat** (Temple of the Buddha's Footprint), still Thailand's most popular pilgrimage site after three and a half centuries.

Each of the attractions of this region can be visited on a day trip from the capital – or, if you have more time to spare, you can slowly work your way through them before heading north or northeast. **Trains** are the most useful means of getting around, as plenty of local services run to and from Bangkok (note that the State Railway's *Northern, Northeastern and Eastern Lines* English-language timetable does not list all the short-distance trains – phone Hualamphong station on ☎02/223 7010 or 7020 for more comprehensive information). The line from the capital takes in Bang Pa-In and Ayutthaya before forking at Ban Phachi: the northern branch heads for Lopburi and goes on to Phitsanulok and Chiang Mai; the northeastern branch serves Isaan. **Buses** between towns are regular but slow, while Bang Pa-In and Ayutthaya can also be reached on scenic, but usually expensive **boat** trips up the Chao Phraya.

Bang Pa-In

Little more than a roadside market, the village of **BANG PA-IN**, 60km north of Bangkok, has been put on the tourist map by its extravagant and rather surreal **Royal Palace** (daily 8.30am–3.30pm; B50), even though most of the buildings can be seen only from the outside. King Prasat Thong of Ayutthaya first built a palace on this site, 20km downstream from his capital, in the middle of the seventeenth century and it remained a popular country residence for the kings of Ayutthaya. The palace was abandoned a century later when the capital was moved to Bangkok, only to be revived in the middle of the last century when the advent of steamboats shortened the journey time upriver. Rama IV (1851–68) built a modest residence here, which his son Chulalongkorn (Rama V), in his passion for Westernization, knocked down to make room for the eccentric mélange of European, Thai and Chinese architectural styles visible today.

Set in manicured grounds on an island in the Chao Phraya River, and based around an ornamental lake, the palace complex is flat and compact – a free brochure from the ticket office gives a diagram of the layout. On the north side of the lake stand a two-storey, colonial-style residence for the royal relatives and the Italianate **Warophat Phiman** (Excellent and Shining Heavenly Abode), which housed Chulalongkorn's throne hall and still contains private apartments where the present royal family sometimes stays. A covered bridge links this outer part of the palace to the **Pratu Thewarat Khanlai** (The King of the Gods Goes Forth Gate), the main entrance to the inner palace, which was reserved for the king and his immediate family. The high fence which encloses half of the bridge allowed the women of the harem to cross without being seen by male courtiers. You can't miss the photogenic **Aisawan Thiphya-art** (Divine Seat of Personal Freedom) in the middle of the lake: named after King Prasat Thong's original palace, it's the only example of pure Thai architecture at Bang Pa-In. The elegant tiers of the pavilion's roof shelter a bronze statue of Chulalongkorn.

In the inner palace, the **Uthayan Phumisathian** (Garden of the Secured Land) was Chulalongkorn's favourite house, a Swiss-style wooden chalet painted in bright two-tone green. After passing the **Ho Withun Thasana** (Sage's Lookout Tower), built so that the king could survey the surrounding countryside, you'll come to the main attraction of Bang Pa-In, the **Phra Thinang Wehart Chamrun** (Palace of Heavenly Light). A masterpiece of Chinese design, the mansion and its contents were shipped from China and presented as a gift to

Chulalongkorn in 1889 by Chinese merchants living in Bangkok. You're allowed to take off your shoes and feast your eyes on the interior, which drips with fine porcelain and embroidery, ebony furniture inlaid with mother-of-pearl and fantastically intricate woodcarving. This residence was the favourite of Rama VI, whose carved and lacquered writing table can be seen on the ground floor.

The simple marble **obelisk** behind the Uthayan Phumisathian was erected by Chulalongkorn to hold the ashes of Queen Sunandakumariratana, his favourite wife. In 1881, Sunanda, who was then 21 and expecting a child, was taking a trip on the river here when her boat capsized. She could have been rescued quite easily, but the laws concerning the sanctity of the royal family left those around her no option: "If a boat founders, the boatmen must swim away; if they remain near the boat [or] if they lay hold of him [the royal person] to rescue him, they are to be executed." Following the tragedy, King Chulalongkorn became a zealous reformer of Thai customs and strove to make the monarchy more accessible.

Turn right out of the main entrance to the palace grounds and cross the river on the small cable car, and you'll come to the greatest oddity of all: **Wat Nivet Dhamapravat**. A grey Buddhist viharn in the style of a Gothic church, it was built by Chulalongkorn in 1878, complete with wooden pews and stained-glass windows.

Practicalities

There's nowhere to stay in the village, but it can easily be visited on a day trip from Bangkok or Ayutthaya. The best way of getting to Bang Pa-In **from Bangkok** is by early-morning **train** from Hualamphong station (departures at 7.05am and 8.30am). The journey takes just over an hour and all trains continue to Ayutthaya, with half going on to Lopburi. From Bang Pa-In station (notice the separate station hall built by Chulalongkorn for the royal family) it's a two-kilometre hike to the palace, or you can take a samlor for about B20. Slow **buses** leave Bangkok's Northern Terminal every twenty minutes and stop at Bang Pa-In market, a samlor ride from the palace.

Every Sunday, the *Chao Phraya Express* boat company runs a **river tour** to Bang Pa-In, taking in a shopping stop at a folk arts and handicrafts centre. The boat leaves Bangkok's Maharat pier at 8am, stopping also at Phra Athit pier, and returns at 5.30pm. Tickets, available from the piers, are B180, not including lunch and admission to the palace. Luxury cruises to Ayutthaya (see p.170) also stop here.

From Ayutthaya, buses leave Chao Phrom Road every half-hour for the thirty-minute journey to Bang Pa-In market; irregular trains from Ayutthaya's inconveniently located station are less useful for this short hop.

Ayutthaya

In its heyday as the booming capital of the Thai kingdom, **AYUTTHAYA** was so well endowed with temples that sunlight reflecting off their gilt decoration was said to dazzle from three miles away. Wide, grassy spaces today occupy most of the atmospheric site 80km north of Bangkok, which now resembles a graveyard for temples: grand, brooding red-brick ruins rise out of the fields, satisfyingly evoking the city's bygone grandeur while providing a soothing contrast to the brashness of modern temple architecture. A few intact buildings help form an image of what the capital must have looked like, while three fine museums flesh out the picture.

The core of the ancient capital was a four-kilometre-wide **island** at the confluence of the Lopburi, Pasak and Chao Phraya rivers, which was once encircled by a twelve-kilometre wall, crumbling parts of which can be seen at the Phom Phet fortress in the southeast corner. A grid of broad roads now crosses the island, with recent buildings dotted about uneasily: the main part of the small, grim and lifeless modern town rests on the northeast bank of the island around the corner of U Thong and Chao Phrom roads, although the most recent development is off the island to the east.

Some history

Ayutthaya takes its name from Ayodhya (Sanskrit for "invincible"), the city of Rama, hero of the *Ramayana* epic (see p.82). It was founded in 1351 by U Thong – later King Ramathibodi I – after Lopburi was ravaged by smallpox, and rose rapidly through exploiting the expanding trade routes between India and China. Stepping into the political vacuum left by the decline of the Khmer empire at Angkor and the first Thai kingdom at Sukhothai, Ayutthaya by the mid-fifteenth century controlled an empire covering most of the area of modern-day Thailand. Built entirely on canals, few of which survive today, Ayutthaya grew into an enormous amphibious city, which by 1685 had one million people – roughly double the population of London at the same time – living largely on houseboats in a 140-kilometre network of waterways.

Ayutthaya's great wealth attracted a swarm of foreign traders, especially in the seventeenth century. At one stage forty different nationalities, including Chinese, Portuguese, Dutch, English and French, were settled here, many of whom lived in their own ghettos and had their own docks for the export of rice, spices, timber and hides. With deft political skill, the kings of Ayutthaya maintained their independence from outside powers, while embracing the benefits of their cosmopolitan influence: they employed foreign architects and navigators, used Japanese samurai as royal bodyguards, and even took on outsiders as their prime ministers, who could look after their foreign trade without getting embroiled in the usual court intrigues.

In 1767, this 400-year-long golden age of stability and prosperity came to an abrupt end. After over two centuries of recurring tensions, the Burmese captured and ravaged Ayutthaya, taking tens of thousands of prisoners back to Burma with them. With even the wats in ruins, the city had to be abandoned to the jungle, but its memory endured: the architects of the new capital on Ratanakosin island in Bangkok perpetuated Ayutthaya's layout in every possible way.

Arrival and accommodation

The best way of getting to Ayutthaya **from Bangkok** is by **train** – there are twenty a day, concentrated in the early morning and evening; trains continue on to the north and the northeast, making connections to Chiang Mai (5 daily), Nong Khai (3 daily) and Ubon Ratchathani (6 daily). To get to the centre of town from the station on the east bank of the Pasak, take the one-baht ferry from the jetty 100m west of the station (last ferry 8pm); it's then a five-minute walk to the junction of U Thong and Chao Phrom roads. The station has a left-luggage service (5am–10pm; B5 per piece per day) and, helpfully, sells onward first- or second-class tickets (9am–noon & 1–4pm).

Though frequent, **buses** to Ayutthaya are slower and much less convenient, as they depart from Bangkok's remote Northern Terminal. A small lane off Chao

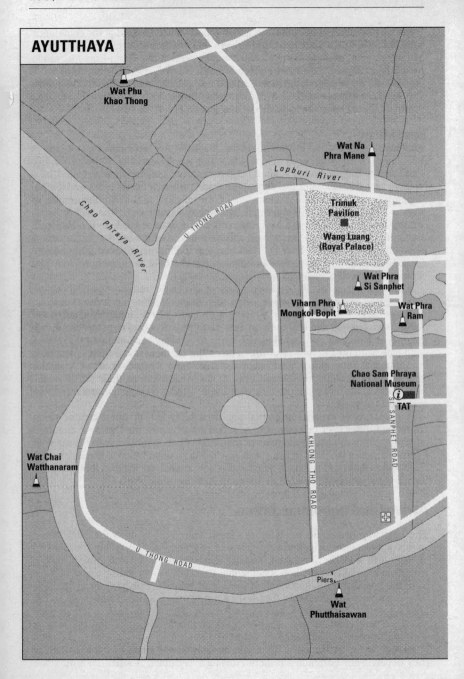

AYUTTHAYA

Wat Phu
Khao Thong

Wat Na
Phra Mane

Lopburi River

Chao Phraya River

U THONG ROAD

Trimuk
Pavilion

Wang Luang
(Royal Palace)

Wat Phra
Si Sanphet

Viharn Phra
Mongkol Bopit

Wat Phra
Ram

Chao Sam Phraya
National Museum

TAT

SI SANPHET ROAD

Wat Chai
Watthanaram

KHLONG THO ROAD

U THONG ROAD

Piers

Wat
Phutthaisawan

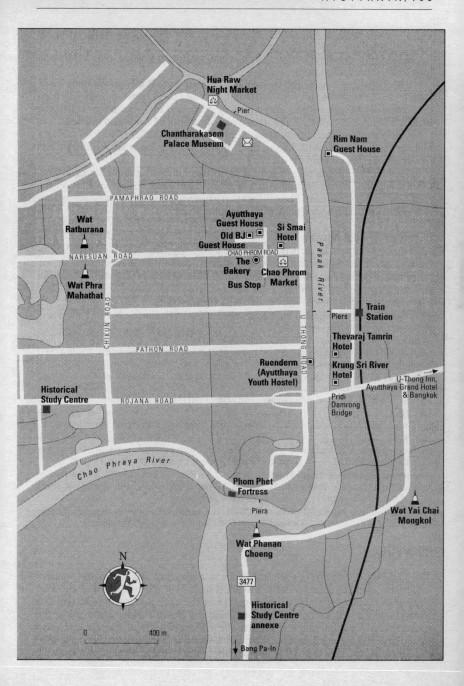

Phrom Road, right in the centre of Ayutthaya new town, acts as the stop for Bangkok, Lopburi, Suphanburi and other local buses (long-distance services use the bus terminal by the *Ayutthaya Grand Hotel* on Rojana Road, connected by tuk-tuks to the centre, 2km to the west).

It's also possible to get here by scenic **boat tour** from Bangkok via Bang Pa-In Palace: the *Oriental Hotel* (☎02/236 0400), among others, runs swanky day trips for around B1000 per person, and a plushly converted teak rice barge called the *Mekhala* (☎02/256 7168 or 7169) does exorbitantly priced overnight cruises.

From Kanchanaburi, it's possible to bypass the Bangkok gridlock by taking a bus to Suphanburi (every 30min; 2hr), then changing onto an Ayutthaya bus (every 30min; 1hr 40min).

Once in Ayutthaya, the helpful **TAT office** (daily 8.30am–4.30pm; ☎035/246076 or 246077) can be found in a beautiful traditional house on stilts on the west side of the Chao Sam Phraya National Museum – though it's due for a move at some stage to the opposite side of Si Sanphet Road.

Hotels and guest houses

Although Ayutthaya is usually visited on a day trip, there is a slim choice of **budget** accommodation for those who want to make a little more of it. A few more upmarket options offer fancier facilities, although two of these, *U-Thong Inn* and *Ayutthaya Grand Hotel*, are a fair distance from town. Avoid *Si Smai Hotel* on Chao Phrom Road – it's uncomfortable and overpriced.

Ayutthaya Grand Hotel, 55/5 Rojana Rd (☎035/335483–91). Upscale but way out east of town, with hot water and air-con. ⑥.

Ayutthaya Guest House, 16/2 Chao Phrom Rd (☎035/251468). This friendly place, on a quiet lane in the town centre, has decent rooms and an outdoor bar/restaurant, and is a good source of local information. ①.

Krung Sri River, 27/2 Moo 11, Rojana Rd (☎035/244333). Ayutthaya's newest and most upmarket accommodation is a grand affair, with swanky lobby and attractive pool, occupying a prime, but noisy, position at the eastern end of the Pridi Damrong Bridge. ⑧.

Old BJ Guest House, NG16/7 Naresuan Rd (☎035/251526). Next door but one to the *Ayutthaya Guest House*, with much the same to offer, though it's a little more cramped. ①.

Rim Nam Guest House, 90 Wat Pa Kho Rd, on the east bank of the Pasak River, 1km north of the train station. A traditional riverside compound with peaceful rooms. It's a long way from the island by road, but you can nip straight across by boat for B3. ①.

Ruenderm (Ayutthaya Youth Hostel), 48 Moo 2 Tambon Horattanachai, U Thong Rd, just north of Pridi Damrong Bridge (☎035/241978). Large, simple rooms, with shared but plentiful cold-water bathrooms, in a shambolic riverside teak house. ③.

U-Thong Inn, 210 Rojana Rd (☎035/242236–9). Hot water and air-con in all rooms. Similar to, and as far out of town as, *Ayutthaya Grand Hotel* but not quite as good value. ⑥.

The City

The majority of Ayutthaya's ancient remains are spread out across the western half of the island in a kind of large historical park: **Wat Phra Mahathat** and **Wat Ratburana** stand near the modern centre at the park's eastern edge, while a broad band runs down its middle, containing the **Royal Palace** and temple, the most revered Buddha image at **Viharn Phra Mongkol Bopit,** and the two main **museums**. To the north of the island you'll find the best-preserved temple, **Wat Na Phra Mane,** and **Wat Phu Khao Thong**, the "Golden Mount", while to the southeast lie the giant chedi of **Wat Yai Chai Mongkol** and **Wat Phanan Choeng**, still a vibrant place of worship.

Busloads of tourists descend on the sights during the day, but the area covered by the old capital is large enough not to feel swamped. Distances are deceptive, so it's best not to walk everywhere if you're doing a full visit: **bicycles** can be hired at the guest houses for B50 per day (*Old BJ* also has a moped for B300 a day), or it's easy enough to hop on a **tuk-tuk** – B3 for a short, popular journey if you're sharing, B20 if you're on your own. If you're short on time you could hire a tuk-tuk for a whistle-stop tour of the old city for around B150 an hour, either from the train station or from Chao Phrom market.

Big tour **boats** can be chartered from the pier outside the Chantharakasem Palace. A two-hour trip will take in Wat Phanan Choeng and a couple of overgrown temples (B300 for the boat). Because of the lack of bridges, small **ferries** also ply across the river at specific points, such as at Wat Phanan Choeng, charging around B1 and leaving as soon as they have passengers.

Wat Phra Mahathat and Wat Ratburana

Heading west out of the new town centre along Chao Phrom Road (which becomes Naresuan Road), the first ruins you'll come to, after about 1km, are a pair of temples on opposite sides of the road. The overgrown **Wat Phra Mahathat**, on the left (daily 8.30am–4pm; B20), is the epitome of Ayutthaya's nostalgic atmosphere of faded majesty. The name "Mahathat" (Great Relic) indicates that the temple was built to house remains of the Buddha himself: according to the royal chronicles – never renowned for historical accuracy – King Ramesuan (1388–95) was looking out of his palace one morning when ashes of the Buddha materialized out of thin air here. A gold casket containing the ashes was duly enshrined in a grand 38-metre-high prang. The prang later collapsed, but the reliquary was unearthed in the 1950s, along with a horde of other treasures including a gorgeous marble fish which opened to reveal gold, amber, crystal and porcelain ornaments – all now on show in the Chao Sam Phraya National Museum (see over).

You can climb what remains of the prang to get a good view of the broad, grassy complex, with dozens of brick spires tilting at impossible angles and headless Buddhas scattered around like spare parts in a scrapyard – and look out for the serene head of a stone Buddha which has become nestled in the embrace of a bodhi tree's roots. To the west you'll see a lake where Ramathibodi I discovered an auspicious conch shell, symbol of victory and righteousness, which confirmed his choice of site for his new city. Nowadays you can hire pedalos for B50 per hour from the western side of the lake, behind the crumbling remains of Wat Phra Ram.

Across the road from Wat Phra Mahathat, the towering **Wat Ratburana** (daily 8.30am–4pm; B20) was built in 1424 by King Boromraja II to commemorate his elder brothers Ay and Yi, who managed to kill each other in an elephant-back duel over the succession to the throne, thus leaving it vacant for Boromraja. Four elegant Sri Lankan chedis lean outwards as if in deference to the main prang, on which some of the original stucco work can still be seen, including fine statues of garudas swooping down on nagas. It's possible to go down steep steps inside the prang to the crypt, where on two levels you can make out fragmentary murals of the early Ayutthaya period. Several hundred Buddha images were buried down here, most of which were snatched by grave robbers, although some can be seen in the Chao Sam Phraya Museum. They're in the earliest style that can be said to be distinctly Ayutthayan – an unsmiling Khmer expression, but on an oval face and elongated body that show the strong influence of Sukhothai.

Wat Phra Si Sanphet and the Wang Luang (Royal Palace)

Further west you'll come to **Wat Phra Si Sanphet** (8.30am–4.30pm; B20), built in 1448 by King Boromatrailokanat as his private chapel. Formerly the grandest of Ayutthaya's temples, and still one of the best preserved, it took its name from one of the largest standing metal images of the Buddha ever known, the **Phra Si Sanphet**, erected here in 1503. Towering 16m high and covered in 173kg of gold, it did not survive the ravages of the Burmese, though Rama I rescued the pieces and placed them inside a chedi at Wat Po in Bangkok. The three remaining grey chedis in the characteristic style of the old capital were built to house the ashes of three kings and have now become the most hackneyed image of Ayutthaya.

The site of this royal wat was originally occupied by Ramathibodi's wooden palace, which Boromatrailokanat replaced with the bigger **Wang Luang (Royal Palace)**, stretching to the Lopburi River on the north side. Successive kings turned the Wang Luang into a vast complex of pavilions and halls with an elaborate system of walls designed to isolate the inner sanctum for the king and his consorts. The palace was destroyed by the Burmese in 1767 and plundered by Rama I for its bricks, which he needed to build the new capital at Bangkok. Now you can only trace the outlines of a few walls in the grass and inspect an unimpressive wooden replica of an open pavilion – better to consult the model of the whole complex in the Historical Study Centre (see below).

Viharn Phra Mongkol Bopit and the cremation ground

Viharn Phra Mongkol Bopit (8.30am–5pm), on the south side of Wat Phra Si Sanphet, attracts tourists and Thai pilgrims in about equal measure. The pristine hall – a replica of a typical Ayutthayan viharn with its characteristic chunky lotus-capped columns around the outside – was built in 1956, with help from the Burmese to atone for their flattening of the city two centuries earlier, in order to shelter the revered **Phra Mongkol Bopit**, one of the largest bronze Buddhas in Thailand. The powerfully plain jet-black image, with its flashing mother-of-pearl eyes, was cast in the fifteenth century, then sat exposed to the elements from the time of the Burmese invasion until its new home was built. During restoration, the hollow image was found to contain hundreds of Buddha statuettes, some of which were later buried around the shrine to protect it.

The car park in front of the viharn used to be the **cremation site** for Ayutthayan kings and high-ranking members of the royal family. Here, on a propitious date decided by astrologers, the embalmed body was placed on a towering *meru* (funeral pyre), representing Mount Meru, the centre of the Hindu-Buddhist universe. These many-gabled and pinnacled wooden structures, which had all the appearance of permanent palaces, were a miracle of architectural technology: the *meru* constructed for King Phetracha in 1704, for example, was 103m tall and took eleven months to raise, requiring thousands of tree trunks and hundreds of thousands of bamboo poles. The task of building at such great heights was given to *yuan-hok*, a special clan of acrobats who used to perform at the top of long poles during special festivals. Their handiwork was not consigned to the flames: the cremation took place on a pyramid erected underneath the central spire, so as not to damage the main structure, which was later dismantled and its timber used for building temples. The cremation ground is now given over to a picnic area and a clutch of souvenir and refreshment stalls.

The museums

A ten-minute walk south of the viharn brings you to the largest of the town's three museums, the **Chao Sam Phraya National Museum** (Wed–Sun 9am–4pm; B10), where most of the movable remains of Ayutthaya's glory – those which weren't plundered by treasure-hunters or taken to the National Museum in Bangkok – are exhibited. Apart from numerous Buddhas, it's bursting with gold treasures of all shapes and sizes – betel-nut sets and model chedis, a royal wimple in gold filigree, a model elephant dripping with gems and the original relic casket from Wat Mahathat. A second gallery, behind the main hall, explores foreign influences on Thai art and is particularly good on the origins of the various styles of Buddha images. This room also contains skeletons and artefacts from the site of the Portuguese settlement founded in 1540 just south of the town on the banks of the Chao Phraya. The Portuguese were the first Western power to establish ties with Ayutthaya, when in 1511 they were granted commercial privileges in return for supplying arms.

The **Historical Study Centre** (Wed–Fri 9am–4.30pm, Sat & Sun 9am–5pm; B100), five minutes' walk away along Rotchana Road, is the town's showpiece, with a hefty admission charge to go with it. The visitors' exhibition upstairs puts the ruins in context, dramatically presenting a wealth of background detail through videos, sound effects and reconstructions – temple murals and model ships, a peasant's wooden house and a small-scale model of the Royal Palace – to build up a broad social history of Ayutthaya. The centre's annexe (closes half an hour earlier, otherwise same times, same ticket), 500m south of Wat Phanan Choeng on the road to Bang Pa-In, also merits a visit despite its remoteness: built with Japanese money on the site of the old Japanese settlement, it tells the fascinating story of Ayutthaya's relations with foreign powers, through similar multimedia effects and maps, paintings and documents prised from venerable museums around the world.

In the northeast corner of the island, the museum of the **Chantharakasem Palace** (Wed–Sun 9am–noon & 1–4pm; B10) was traditionally the home of the heir to the Ayutthayan throne. The Black Prince, Naresuan, built the first *wang na* (palace of the front) here in about 1577 so that he could guard the area of the city wall which was most vulnerable to enemy attack. Rama IV (1851–68) had the palace rebuilt and it now displays many of his possessions, including a throne platform overhung by a white *chat*, a ceremonial nine-tiered parasol which is a vital part of a king's insignia. The rest of the museum is a jumble of beautiful ceramics, Buddha images and random artefacts.

Wat Na Phra Mane

Wat Na Phra Mane, on the north bank of the Lopburi River opposite the Wang Luang, is Ayutthaya's most rewarding temple, as it's the only one from the town's golden age which survived the ravages of the Burmese. The story goes that when the Burmese were on the brink of capturing Ayutthaya in 1760, a siege gun positioned here burst, mortally wounding their king and prompting their retreat; out of superstition, they left the temple standing when they came back to devastate the city in 1767.

The main **bot**, built in 1503, shows the distinctive features of Ayutthayan architecture – outside columns topped with lotus cups, and slits in the walls instead of windows to let the wind pass through. Inside, underneath a rich red and gold coffered ceiling representing the stars around the moon, sits a powerful six-metre-high Buddha in the disdainful, overdecorated royal style characteristic of the later Ayutthaya period.

In sharp contrast is the dark green **Phra Khan Thavaraj** Buddha which dominates the tiny viharn behind to the right. Seated in the "European position", with its robe delicately pleated and its feet up on a large lotus leaf, the gentle figure conveys a reassuring serenity. It's advertised as being from Sri Lanka, the source of Thai Buddhism, but more likely is a Mon image from Wat Phra Mane at Nakhon Pathom dating from the seventh to ninth centuries.

Wat Phu Khao Thong

Head 2km northwest of Wat Na Phra Mane and you'll be in open country, where the fifty-metre chedi of **Wat Phu Khao Thong** rises steeply out of the ricefields. In 1569, after a temporary occupation of Ayutthaya, the Burmese erected a Mon-style chedi here to commemorate their victory. Forbidden by Buddhist law from pulling down a sacred monument, the Thais had to put up with this galling reminder of the enemy's success until it collapsed nearly two centuries later, when King Borommakot promptly built a truly Ayutthayan chedi on the old Burmese base – just in time for the Burmese to return in 1767 and flatten the town. This "Golden Mount" is now cracked, overgrown and grey, but you can still climb 25m of steps to the top of the base to look out over the countryside and the town, a view that's best appreciated in the wet season, when the paddies are flooded. In 1956, to celebrate 2500 years of Buddhism, the government placed on the tip of the spire a ball of solid gold weighing 2500g, of which there is now no trace.

Wat Yai Chai Mongkol

To the southeast of the island, if you cross the suspension bridge over the Pasak River and the rail line, then turn right at the major roundabout, you'll pass through Ayutthaya's new business zone and some rustic suburbia before reaching the ancient but still functioning **Wat Yai Chai Mongkol**, nearly 2km from the bridge

(B20). Surrounded by decidedly un-Asian formal lawns and flower beds, the wat was established by King Ramathibodi in 1357 as a meditation site for monks returning from study in Sri Lanka. King Naresuan put up the celebrated **chedi** to mark the decisive victory over the Burmese at Suphanburi in 1593, when he himself had sent the enemy packing by slaying the Burmese crown prince in a duel. Built on a colossal scale to outshine the Burmese Golden Mount on the opposite side of Ayutthaya, the chedi has come to symbolize the prowess and devotion of Naresuan and, by implication, his descendants down to the present king.

Reclining Buddha

By the entrance, a **reclining Buddha**, now gleamingly restored in toothpaste white, was also constructed by Naresuan; elsewhere in the grounds, the wat maintains its contemplative origins with some highly topical maxims pinned to the trees such as, "Cut down the forest of passion not real trees".

Wat Phanan Choeng

In Ayutthaya's most prosperous period the docks and main trading area were located near the confluence of the Chao Phraya and Pasak rivers, to the west of Wat Yai Chai Mongkol. This is where you'll find the oldest and liveliest working temple in town, **Wat Phanan Choeng** (and the annexe to the Historical Study Centre – see p.173). If you can get here during a festival, especially Chinese New Year, you'll be in for an overpowering experience. The main viharn is filled with the sights, sounds and smells of an incredible variety of merit-making activities, as devotees burn huge pink Chinese incense candles, offer food and rattle fortune sticks. It's even possible to buy tiny golden statues of the Buddha to be placed in one of the hundreds of niches which line the walls, a form of votive offering peculiar to this temple.

The nineteen-metre-high Buddha, which almost fills the hall, has survived since 1324, shortly before the founding of the capital, and tears are said to have flowed from its eyes when Ayutthaya was sacked by the Burmese. However, the reason for the temple's popularity with the Chinese is to be found in the early eighteenth-century shrine by the pier, with its image of a beautiful Chinese princess who drowned herself here because of a king's infidelity: his remorse led him to build the shrine at the place where she had walked into the river.

Eating

Ayutthaya has a dearth of decent **places to eat**, so for inexpensive evening dining your best bet is the Hua Raw night market, near the northernmost point of U Thong Road. Riverside restaurants in Ayutthaya are slightly expensive and generally disappointing: the most popular, attached to the sprawling *Thevaraj Tamrin Hotel*, south of the train station, has live singers, lousy service and a floating terrace; the most atmospheric is *Ruenderm* at the youth hostel, which serves reasonable food in some weird combinations, amidst gnarled wooden furniture and curios. The bakery (its sign advertises evening "karaoke" sessions) by the bus station at 9/3 Chao Phrom Rd does good cakes, ice cream and breakfasts. Around the central ruins are a few pricey restaurants if you're in need of air conditioning with your lunch.

Lopburi and around

Mention the name **LOPBURI** to a Thai and the chances are that he or she will start telling you about monkeys – the central junction of this tidy provincial capital, 150km due north of Bangkok, swarms with them. So beneficial are the beasts to the town's tourist trade that a local hotelier treats six hundred of them to a sit-down meal every year, complete with menus, waiters and napkins, as a thank you for the help. In fact, the monkeys can be a real nuisance, but at least they add some life to the town's central **Khmer buildings**, which, though historically important, are rather unimpressive sights. More illuminating is the **Narai National Museum**, housed in a partly reconstructed palace complex dating from the seventeenth century, and distant Wat Phra Phutthabat, a colourful eye-opener for non-Buddhists.

Originally called Lavo, Lopburi is one of the longest-inhabited towns in Thailand, and was a major centre of the Mon (Dvaravati) civilization from around the sixth century. It maintained a tenuous independence in the face of the advancing Khmers until as late as the early eleventh century, when it was incorporated into the empire as the provincial capital for much of central Thailand. Increasing Thai immigration from the north soon tilted the balance against the Khmers and Lopburi was again independent from some time early in the thirteenth century until the rise of Ayutthaya in the middle of the fourteenth. Thereafter, Lopburi was twice used as a second capital, first by King Narai of Ayutthaya in the seventeenth century, then by Rama IV of Bangkok in the nine-teenth, because its remoteness from the sea made it less vulnerable to European expansionists. Rama V downgraded the town, turning the royal palace into a provincial government office and museum; Lopburi's modern role is as the site of several huge army barracks.

As it's on the main line north to Chiang Mai, Lopburi is best reached by **train**. Twelve trains a day, concentrated in the early morning and evening, run from

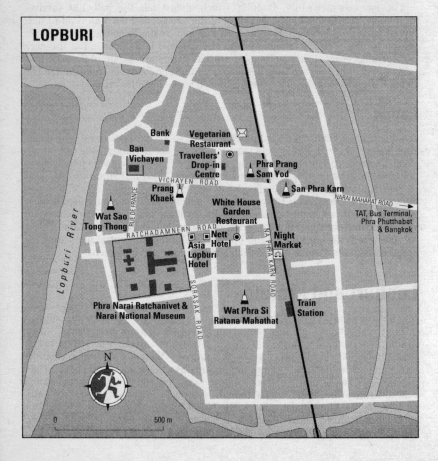

Bangkok (3hr) via Ayutthaya (1hr 30min): a popular option is to arrive in Lopburi in the morning, leave your bags at the conveniently central station while you look around the town, then catch one of the night trains to the north. **Buses** from Ayutthaya take up to three hours, as do services from Bangkok's Northern Terminal (every 15min). The long-distance bus terminal is on the south side of the huge Sakeo roundabout, 2km east of the town centre: a city bus or a song-thaew will save you the walk.

The Town

The centre of Lopburi sits on an egg-shaped island between canals and the Lopburi River, with the rail line running across it from north to south. Most of the hotels and just about everything of interest lie to the west of the line, within walking distance of the train station. The main street, Vichayen Road, crosses the rail tracks at the town's busiest junction before heading eastwards through the newest areas of development to Highway 1. If you're tempted by a gleaming samlor, it'll cost you about B100 per hour to get around the sights.

Wat Phra Si Ratana Mahathat

Coming out of the train station, the first thing you'll see are the sprawled grassy ruins of **Wat Phra Si Ratana Mahathat** (daily 8.30am–4pm; B20), where the impressive centrepiece is a laterite prang in the Khmer style of the twelfth century, decorated with finely detailed stucco work and surrounded by a ruined cloister. Arrayed in loose formation around this central feature are several more rocket-like Khmer prangs and a number of graceful chedis in the Ayutthaya style, among them one with a bulbous peak and faded bas-reliefs of Buddhist saints. On the eastern side of the main prang, King Narai added to the mishmash of styles by building a "Gothic" viharn, now roofless, which is home to a lonely, headless stone Buddha, draped in photogenic saffron.

Phra Narai Ratchanivet (King Narai's palace)

The imposing gates and high crenellated walls of the **Phra Narai Ratchanivet**, a short walk northwest of the ruins, might promise more than the complex delivers, but the museum in its central courtyard is outstanding, and the grounds are a green and relaxing spot. King Narai built the heavily fortified palace in 1666 as a precaution against any possible confrontation with the Western powers, and for the rest of his reign he was to spend eight months of every year here, entertaining foreign envoys and indulging his love of hunting. After Narai's death, Lopburi was left forgotten until 1856, when Rama IV – worried about British and French colonialism – decided to make this his second capital and lavishly restored the central buildings of Narai's palace.

THE OUTER COURTYARD
The main **entrance** to the palace complex (free) is through the Phayakkha Gate on Sorasak Road. You'll see the unusual lancet shape of this arch again and again in the seventeenth-century doors and windows of Lopburi – just one aspect of the Western influences embraced by Narai. Around the **outer courtyard**, which occupies the eastern half of the complex, stand the walls of various gutted buildings – twelve warehouses for Narai's treasures, stables for the royal hunting elephants, and a moated reception hall for foreign envoys.

THE CENTRAL COURTYARD AND THE NARAI NATIONAL MUSEUM
Straight ahead from the Phayakkha Gate another arch leads into the **central courtyard**, where the typically Ayutthayan **Chanthara Phisan Pavilion** contains a fascinating exhibition on Narai's reign – check out the pointed white cap typical of those worn by noblemen of the time, which increased their height by no less than 50cm.

To the left is the colonial-style Phiman Mongkut Hall, now the **Narai National Museum** (Wed–Sun 9am–noon & 1–4pm; B10), whose exhibits span the whole of Lopburi's existence, from simple, elegant prehistoric pottery to modern Thai abstract painting. On the ground floor, a rubbing taken from a Dvaravati bas-relief, showing the Buddha preaching to Shiva and Vishnu, eloquently illustrates how Buddhism lived side by side with Hinduism in Thailand in the second half of the first millennium. Details of Arab costume in some fragments of eighth-century architectural decoration show the extent of Lopburi's early trade routes – from the third century onwards the town had links with the Middle East as well as with China. Inevitably there's a surfeit of Buddhas, most of them fine examples of the Khmer style and the distinctive **Lopburi style**, which emerged in the thirteenth and fourteenth centuries, mixing traditional Khmer elements – such as the conical *ushnisha* or flame on the crown of the Buddha's head – with new features such as a more oval face and slender body.

On the south side of the museum lies the shell of the **Dusit Sawan Hall**, where foreign dignitaries came to present their credentials to King Narai. Inside you can still see the niche, raised 3.5m above the main floor, where the throne was set. The whole building is divided in two around the throne: the front half has "foreign" doors and windows with pointed arches; the rear part, from where the king would have made his grand entrance, has traditional Thai openings. The hall used to be lined with French mirrors, in imitation of Versailles, with Persian carpets and a pyramidal roof of golden glazed tiles rounding off the most majestic building in the palace.

THE PRIVATE COURTYARDS
King Narai's private courtyard, through whose sturdy walls only the trusted few were admitted, occupied the southwest corner of the complex. During Narai's time, hundreds of lamps used to be placed in niches around the walls of this courtyard by night, shedding a fairy-like light on the palace. Now there's not much more than the foundations left of his residence, the **Sutha Sawan Hall**, and its bathing ponds and artificial grotto.

Rama IV's private courtyard was built to house his harem in the northwest corner of the grounds, behind the present site of the museum. In what used to be the kitchen there's now a small folk museum, containing a bamboo house, a loom and various pieces of farming and fishing equipment. In front, you can consult a crude model of the palace as it looked in Narai's time.

Wat Sao Tong Thong and Ban Vichayen
The north entrance to the palace is called the Vichayen Gate after Constantine Phaulkon, who took the title *ookya vichayen* (prime minister) under King Narai. It leads directly to the aptly named Rue de France, the approach to the remains of his grand residence. Halfway along this road, set back on the left, you'll pass a building whose plain terracotta roof tiles and whitewashed exterior give it a strangely Mediterranean look. This is in fact the viharn of **Wat Sao Tong**

Thong, and is typical of Narai's time in its combination of Thai-style tiered roof with "Gothic" pointed windows. Erected as either a Christian chapel or a mosque for the Persian ambassador's residence, it was later used as a Buddhist viharn and has now been tastefully restored, complete with brass door-knockers and plush red carpet. Inside there's an austere Buddha image of the Ayutthaya period and, in the lamp niches, some fine Lopburi-style Buddhas.

The complex of **Ban Vichayen** (daily 8.30am–4pm; B20) was built by Narai as a residence for foreign ambassadors, complete with a Christian chapel incongruously stuccoed with Buddhist flame and lotus-leaf motifs. Though now just a nest of empty shells, it still succeeds in conjuring up the atmosphere of court intrigue and dark deeds which, towards the end of Narai's reign, centred on the colourful figure of **Constantine Phaulkon**. A Greek adventurer who had come to Ayutthaya with the English East India Company in 1678, Phaulkon entered the royal service as interpreter and accountant, rapidly rising to the position of Narai's prime minister. It was chiefly due to his influence that Narai established close ties with Louis XIV of France, a move which made commercial sense but also formed part of Phaulkon's secret plan to turn Narai and his people to Christianity with the aid of the French.

Two missions were sent from Versailles, but both failed in their overt aim of signing a political alliance and their covert attempt at religious conversion. (It was around this time that the word for Westerner, *farang*, entered the Thai language, derived from *français*, which the Thais render *farangset*.) In 1688, a struggle for succession broke out, and leading officials persuaded the dying Narai to appoint as regent his foster brother, Phetracha, a great rival of Phaulkon's. Phetracha promptly executed Phaulkon on charges of treason, and took the throne himself when Narai died. Under Phetracha, Narai's open-door policy towards foreigners was brought to a screeching halt and the Thai kingdom returned to traditional, smaller-scale dealings with the outside world.

East of Narai's palace

By the northeast corner of the palace, the junction of Vichayen and Sorasak roads is marked by an unusual traffic island, on which perch the three stubby red-brick towers of **Prang Khaek**, a well-preserved Hindu shrine possibly dating from as early as the eighth century. The nearby **Phra Prang Sam Yod**, at the top of Na Phra Karn Road, seems also to have been a Hindu temple, later converted to Buddhism under the Khmers. The three chunky prangs, made of dark laterite with some restored stucco work, are Lopburi's most photographed sight, though they'll only detain you for a minute or two – at least check out some carved figures of seated hermits at the base of the door columns. The shrine's grassy knoll, a popular meeting place for Lopburians, is good for monkey-watching – they run amok all over this area, so keep an eye on your bags and pockets. Across the rail line at **San Phra Karn**, there's even a monkey's adventure playground for the benefit of tourists, beside the base of what must have been a huge Khmer prang.

Wat Phra Phutthabat (Temple of the Buddha's Footprint)

Seventeen kilometres southeast of Lopburi along Highway 1 stands the most important pilgrimage site in central Thailand, **Wat Phra Phutthabat**, which is believed to house a footprint made by the Buddha. From Lopburi, any of the frequent buses to Saraburi or Bangkok from Lopburi's Sakeo roundabout will get you there in half an hour. The souvenir village around the temple, which is on the western side of Highway 1, includes plenty of food stalls for day-trippers.

The **legend** of Phra Phutthabat dates back to the beginning of the seventeenth century, when King Song Tham of Ayutthaya sent some monks to Sri Lanka to worship the famous Buddha's footprint of Sumankut. To the monks' surprise, the Sri Lankans asked them why they had bothered to travel all that way when, according to the ancient Pali scriptures, the Buddha had passed through Thailand and had left his footprint in their own backyard.

As soon as Song Tham heard this he instigated a search for the footprint, which was finally discovered in 1623 by a hunter named Pram Bun, when a wounded deer disappeared into a hollow and then emerged miraculously healed. The hunter pushed aside the bushes to discover a foot-shaped trench filled with water, which immediately cured him of his terrible skin disease. A temple was built on the spot, but was destroyed by the Burmese in 1765 – the present build- ings date from the Bangkok era.

A staircase flanked by nagas leads up to a marble platform, where pilgrims make a cacophony by whacking the bells with walking sticks, many of them bought from the stalls below. It's said that if you ring all 93 bells, and count them correctly, you will live that number of years. In the centre of the platform, a gaudy mondop with mighty doors inlaid with mother-of-pearl houses the **footprint**, which in itself is not much to look at. Sheltered by a mirrored canopy, the stone print is five feet long and is obscured by layers of gold leaf presented by pilgrims; people also throw money into the footprint, some of which they take out again as a charm or merit object. The hill behind the shrine, which you can climb for a fine view over the gilded roofs of the complex to the mountains beyond, is covered in a plethora of shrines. The small bot, which elsewhere would be the centrepiece of a temple, is where pilgrims go for a nap.

During the dry season in January, February and March – the free time in the rice-farming calendar, between harvesting and sowing – a million pilgrims from all over the country flock to the **Ngan Phrabat** (Phrabat Fair), when other pilgrims are making their way to the other major religious sites at Doi Suthep, Nakhon Si Thammarat and Nakhon Phanom. During the fair, the stalls selling souvenirs and traditional medicines around the entrance swell to form a small town, and traditional entertainments, magic shows and a Ferris wheel are laid on. The fair is still a major religious event, but before the onset of industrialization it was the highlight of social and cultural life for all ages and classes. It was an important place of courtship, for example, especially for women at a time when their freedom was limited. Another incentive for women to attend the fair was the belief that visiting the footprint three times would ensure a place in heaven – for many women, the Phrabat Fair became the focal point of their lives, as Buddhist doctrine allowed them no other path to salvation. Up to the reign of Rama V (1868–1910) even the king used to come, performing a ritual lance dance on elephant-back to ensure a long reign.

Practicalities

Lopburi has a poor choice of **accommodation**. Na Phra Karn Road is a mine-field of seedy hotels (①), but a far better option are the en suite rooms at the clean and friendly *Nett Hotel*, 17/1–2 Ratchadamnern Rd (☎036/411738; ②). Opposite the entrance to the Royal Palace, the *Asia Lopburi Hotel* (☎036/

411892) has good-value rooms with fan and bathroom (③), or with air conditioning and hot water (⑤). A long trek east of the centre, the air-conditioned rooms at the *Lopburi Inn*, 28/9 Narai Maharat Rd (☎036/412300; ⑤–⑧), are as posh as Lopburi gets.

For **food**, good breakfast doughnuts and coffee are served on the corner of Na Phra Karn and Ratchadamnern roads; later in the morning, up to 1pm, the simple vegetarian restaurant at 26/47 Soi Manora is well worth seeking out – inventive Thai food at very low prices. The surprisingly clean night market on Na Phra Karn Road is the best place to eat in the evening. At about 6pm, the stallholders don their blue aprons and chef's hats to rustle up a wide variety of popular dishes – *khanom beuak* (a kind of veggie omelette), *pat thai* and *hawy thawt* (mussels in batter omelette). For a classier meal, try the open-air *White House Garden Restaurant*, on Praya Kumjud Road (parallel to and south of Ratchadamnern), which specializes in rich seafood dishes at moderate prices.

TAT has a temporary, but enthusiastic, office (Mon–Fri 8.30am–4.30pm; ☎036/422768 or 422769) 1km east again from the bus terminal, in the provincial hall by the King Narai monument on Narai Maharat Road. Another useful source of information is the *Travellers' Drop-In Centre* on Ratchadamnern Rd, Soi 3, which doubles as a language school. The owner of the school has a wealth of local knowledge and encourages travellers to come into his classes to speak English; the students also enjoy taking foreigners out sightseeing or for a meal.

THE NORTHERN PLAINS

Most tourists bypass the lush northern reaches of the central plains, fast asleep in an overnight train from Bangkok to Chiang Mai, yet it was here, during the thirteenth, fourteenth and fifteenth centuries, that the kingdom of Thailand first began to cohere and assume its present identity. Some of Thailand's finest buildings and sculpture were produced in **Sukhothai**, once the most powerful city in Thailand. Abandoned to the jungle by the sixteenth century, it has now been extensively restored, the resulting historical park making an attractive open-air museum. Less complete renovations have made Sukhothai's satellite cities of **Si Satchanalai** and **Kamphaeng Phet** worth visiting, both for their relative wildness and lack of visitors.

With so many ruins on offer, it's sensible to interweave days of history with days out in the wilds. The nearest hills in which to clear the cobwebs are in the rugged Phu Hin Rongkla National Park (see p.367), but to get there you'll need to hire a motorbike or base yourself in **Phitsanulok**. By public transport from Sukhothai an easier option is the longer expedition to the Burmese border town of **Mae Sot**, which offers excellent trekking.

Phitsanulok stands at the hub of an efficient **transport** network that works well as a transit point between Bangkok, the far north and Isaan. Nearly every Bangkok–Chiang Mai train stops here, and assorted buses head east towards the Isaan towns of Loei, Khon Kaen and Chaiyaphum. It's also possible to fly in and out of the northern plains, through the tiny airstrips at Phitsanulok, Tak and Mae Sot. Within the region, local buses and songthaews ferry tourists between sights, though a less time-consuming way of doing things would be to hire a car or motorbike from Phitsanulok or Sukhothai.

Phitsanulok

Heading north from Lopburi, road and rail plough through Thailand's "rice bowl", a landscape of lurid green paddies interrupted only by the unwelcoming sprawl of **Nakhon Sawan**, sited at the confluence of the Ping and the Nan. A prosperous city of about 100,000 predominantly Chinese inhabitants, Nakhon Sawan plays a vital role as the region's main market and the distribution centre for rice, but about the only reason you'd ever want to set foot in the place would be to change buses for Kamphaeng Phet, Phitsanulok or Chaiyaphum. The bus station is in the town centre and there are a couple of passable budget hotels close by as a last resort. All Bangkok–Chiang Mai trains stop here, but as the station is 10km out of town, with skeletal local transport and no station hotels, breaking your journey 130km further north at Phitsanulok makes much more sense.

Well equipped with hotels and pleasantly located on the east bank of the River Nan, **PHITSANULOK** makes a handy base for exploring the historical centres of Sukhothai and Kamphaeng Phet. Phitsanulok itself, however, has been basically a one-temple town since fire destroyed most of its old buildings thirty-odd years ago: the country's second most important Buddha image is housed here in Wat Mahathat, drawing pilgrims from all over Thailand. This modest town harks back to a heyday in the late fourteenth and early fifteenth centuries when, with Sukhothai waning in power, it rose to prominence as the favoured home of the crumbling capital's last rulers. After supremacy was finally wrested by the emerging state of Ayutthaya in 1438, Phitsanulok was made a provincial capital, subsequently becoming a strategic army base during Ayutthaya's wars with the Burmese and adoptive home to Ayutthayan princes.

Arrival, information and accommodation

Nine **trains** a day pass through Phitsanulok on their way between Bangkok and Chiang Mai; the train station is in the town centre. **Buses** are more frequent, but you'll need to catch a local bus into town from the bus station, 2km east on Highway 12. If you're short on time you could even **fly** here: by air, Phitsanulok is fifty minutes from Bangkok, Chiang Mai or Mae Sot, and just 35 minutes from Lampang. **Local buses** all start from the city bus centre on Ekathosarot Road, a few hundred metres south of the train station, and cover five main routes: #1 serves Wat Mahathat and the regional bus station, #2 goes to villages on the southeastern edge of town, #3 heads west over the river, #4 is the airport shuttle and goes via the youth hostel, and #5 runs to *Topland Plaza* hotel and shopping centre and *Green House* guest house.

Should you need to contact Phitsanulok's efficient **TAT** (daily 8.30am–4.30pm; ☎055/252742), it's on Sithamtraipidok Road, east off Boromtrailoknat Road, in a row of travel businesses that includes *Thai Airways* (☎055/258020) and **car hire** companies *Golden House* (☎055/259627) and *Able Tour and Travel* (☎055/242206). To rent a (low-powered) **motorbike**, go to *Landi Motor* on Phra Ong Dum Road (☎055/242687).

Accommodation

There's a fair spread of **places to stay** in Phitsanulok, from simple guest houses to top-end hotels. The two least expensive options, the *Phitsanulok Youth Hostel*

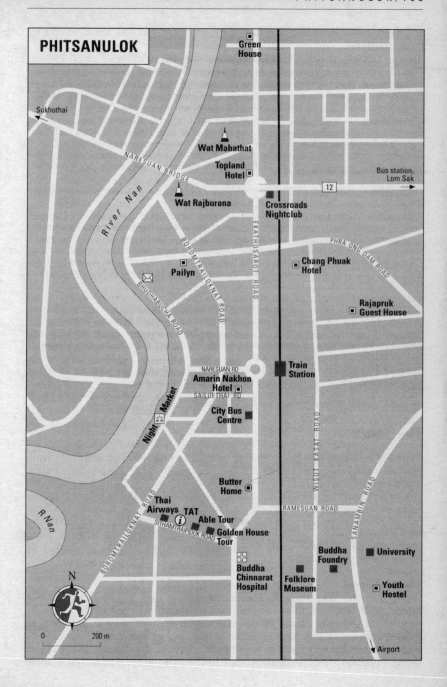

PHITSANULOK

Green House

Sukhothai

NARESUAN BRIDGE

River Nan

Wat Mahathat

Topland Hotel

Bus station, Lom Sak

12

Wat Rajburana

Crossroads Nightclub

BOROMTRAILOKNAT ROAD

EKATHOSAROT ROAD

PHRA ONG DAM ROAD

BHUDHABUCHA ROAD

Pailyn

Chang Phuak Hotel

Rajapruk Guest House

NARESUAN RD

Amarin Nakhon Hotel

SAILUETHAI RD

Train Station

Night Market

City Bus Centre

WISUT KASAT ROAD

SANAMBIN ROAD

Butter Home

RAMESUAN ROAD

Thai Airways

TAT

Able Tour

SITHAMTRAIPIDOK ROAD

Golden House Tour

BOROMTRAILOKNAT ROAD

R Nan

Buddha Chinnarat Hospital

Buddha Foundry

University

Folklore Museum

Youth Hostel

N

0   200 m

Airport

and *Green House*, are a long way from the town centre, but both are accessible by public transport.

Amarin Nakhon Hotel, 3/1 Chaophraya Rd, near the train station (☎055/258588). Centrally located mid-range business hotel, lacking in character but fine for the price. ⑥–⑧.

Chang Phuak Hotel, next to the rail line at 63/28 Phra Ong Dam Rd (☎055/252822). In a similar vein and price range to the *Rajapruk Guest House* (see below), but a cut beneath. Large, slightly shabby rooms with attached bathroom, and fan or air-con. ③–④.

Green House, 11/12 Ekathosorat Rd (☎055/252803). The friendliest and most relaxed of Phitsanulok's inexpensive options, with just a handful of fairly simple rooms in a traditional wooden house. A fair trek from the train station and town centre: a 30-min (2km) walk or a B40 tuk-tuk ride, though you can take local bus #5 (takes 6-min, get off about 2-min after the *Topland Plaza* roundabout); from the regional bus station take a #1 to the city bus centre, then a #5. ①.

Pailyn Hotel, 38 Boromtrailoknat Rd (☎055/252411). Luxurious but good value, with many rooms offering river views, and 2 restaurants. ⑦–⑧.

Phitsanulok Youth Hostel, 38 Sanambin Rd (☎055/242060). Occupies a lovely old wooden building furnished with carved beds and chairs and featuring a communal eating/sitting area on ground level; there are more rooms here than at *Green House*, and IYHA members get a small discount. Its location on a busy major thoroughfare means it's seriously noisy, and it's a 1.5-km walk from the centre: take bus #4 from the city bus centre; from the regional bus station take a #1, #8, or #10 to the technical college, then a #4. Bikes can be borrowed from the hostel. ②.

Rajapruk Guest House, just east of Wisut Kasat Road at 99/9 Phra Ong Dam Rd (☎055/258788). The name is misleading, as this place is a scaled-down version of the adjoining *Rajapruk Hotel*, offering relatively upmarket, hotel-style rooms with adjoining bathroom. ③.

Rajapruk Hotel, just east of Wisut Kasat Road at 99/9 Phra Ong Dam Rd (☎055/258788). Well-equipped but rather soulless rooms, all wth air-con, hot water and fridge. Swimming pool and nightclub on the premises. ⑥–⑧.

Topland Plaza, 68/33 Ekathosarot Rd (☎055/247800). Phitsanulok's newest and swankiest top-of-the-range option: all rooms have en suite marble bathrooms, and you can land a helicopter on the rooftop. There's a swimming pool, Chinese restaurant and beer garden on the premises, and the *Topland Plaza* shopping centre downstairs. ⑧–⑨.

The Town

Typically for a riverside town, "Phi-lok" is long and narrow, and while the centre is small enough to cover on foot, the two main sights lie at opposite extremities. You'd be hard pressed to find more than a half-day's worth of attractions to detain you here, though an evening stroll along the river – past the ramshackle houseboats which are illegal everywhere but Phitsanulok – and the prospect of a fresh fish dinner eaten on its banks may entice you. And now that the town boasts two exceptionally friendly, traveller-oriented places to stay, the *Phitsanulok Youth Hostel* and *Green House*, many people find themselves hanging out here a lot longer than they'd intended.

Wat Mahathat

Officially called **Wat Phra Si Ratana Mahathat** (and known locally as Wat Mahathat or Wat Yai), this fourteenth-century temple was one of the few buildings to miraculously escape Phitsanulok's great fire. Standing at the northern limit of town on the east bank of the River Nan (bus #1 from the city bus centre), it receives a constant stream of worshippers eager to pay homage to the highly revered Buddha image inside the viharn. Because the image is so sacred, a **dress**

code is strictly enforced – shorts and skimpy clothing are forbidden – and there's an entrance fee of B10.

Delicately inlaid mother-of-pearl doors mark the entrance to the viharn, opening onto the low-ceilinged interior, painted mostly in dark red and black and dimly lit by narrow slits along the upper walls. In the centre of the far wall sits the much-cherished **Phra Buddha Chinnarat**: late Sukhothai in style, and probably cast in the fourteenth century, this gleaming, polished-bronze Buddha is one of the finest of the period and, for Thais, second in importance only to the Emerald Buddha in Bangkok. Tales of the statue's miraculous powers have fuelled the devotion of generations of pilgrims – one legend tells how the Buddha wept tears of blood when Ayutthayan princes arrived in Phitsanulok to oust the last Sukhothai regent. The Phra Buddha Chinnarat stands out among Thai Buddha images because of its *mandorla*, the flame-like halo that frames the upper body and head like a chair-back, tapering off into nagas at the arm rests, which symbolizes extreme radiance and makes any reproductions immediately recognizable. Not surprisingly, the image has spawned several copies, including an almost perfect replica commissioned for Bangkok's Marble Temple by Rama V in 1901. Every February, Phitsanulok honours the Phra Buddha Chinnarat with week-long festivities, which include *likay* folk theatre performances and dancing.

Behind the viharn, the gilded mosaic **prang** houses the holy relic that gives the wat its name (Mahathat means "Great Relic") – though which particular remnant lies entombed here is unclear – and the cloister surrounding both structures contains a gallery of Buddha images of different styles. As in all such popular pilgrimage spots, the courtyard is crammed with amulet stalls, trinket sellers and lottery-ticket vendors.

Also spared by the fire was the nearby **Wat Rajburana**, just south of Naresuan Bridge and five minutes' walk from Wat Mahathat. Recognizable by the dilapidated brick-based chedi that stands in the compound, the wat is chiefly of interest for the *Ramayana* murals (see p.82) that cover the bot's interior walls. Quite well preserved, they were probably painted in the mid-nineteenth century.

The Folklore Museum and Buddha foundry

Across town on Wisut Kasat Road, southeast of the train station, the **Dr Thawi Folklore Museum** (daily 8.30am–4.30pm; donation) puts a different slant on the region's culture with an engaging display of crude but ingenious traditional farm implements and domestic tools. The collection belongs to former sergeant-major Dr Thawi, who has pursued a lifelong personal campaign to preserve and document a way of life that's gradually disappearing. Among the exhibits, his roomful of traps is unparalleled in any other ethnology museum in Thailand – it showcases an amazing assortment of specialized contraptions designed to ensnare everything from cockroaches to birds perched on water buffaloes' backs. Amongst the home accessories, check out the masochistic aid for "improving blood circulation" and the range of simple wooden games.

Cross the road from the museum for a rare chance to see Buddha images being forged at the **Buranathai Buddha Bronze-Casting Foundry**. The foundry, which also belongs to Dr Thawi, is open during working hours and anyone can drop in to watch the stages involved in moulding and casting a Buddha image. It's a fairly lengthy procedure, based on the lost-wax method, and best assimilated from the illustrated explanations inside the foundry. Images of all sizes are made here, from thirty-centimetre-high household icons the size of sporting trophies to mega-models destined for wealthy temples. The Buddha business is quite a profitable one: worshippers can earn a great deal of merit by donating a Buddha statue, particularly a precious one, to their local wat, so demand rarely slackens.

Eating

Good, inexpensive Thai, Chinese and European **food** features on the meticulously coded menu at *Butter Home*, a couple of blocks south of the station on Ekathosarot Road, and if that doesn't appeal, you only have to walk back up the same road to pass five or six curry and noodle shops. In the evening, the place to head for is the lively **night market** along the east bank of the river, which gets started at about 6pm: fish and mussels are a speciality – along with cassette tapes, souvenirs and clothes. If you want to eat on the water and don't mind paying for the privilege, try the cruising **restaurant boats** run by *Song Kwae* and *Tharn Thip*, which leave fairly regularly throughout the day from near the post office and travel upriver and back for an hour or two at a time. The nearby floating restaurants also overcharge for their unexceptional food, but – if you miss the boats – it's probably worth forking out the extra money for the breezy riverside location. Restaurants serving **"flying vegetables"** are also perennial crowd-pullers: the vegetable in question is the strong-tasting morning-glory (*phak bung*), which is stir-fried before being tossed flamboyantly in the air towards the plate-wielding waiter or customer. Several restaurants around the *Rajapruk Hotel* on Phra Ong Dam Road do the honours, and stall-holders at the night market put on occasional performances – look out for the specially adapted, stationary two-tiered trucks.

Sukhothai

For a brief but brilliant 150 years (1238–1376), the walled city of **SUKHOTHAI** presided as the capital of Thailand, creating the legacy of a unified nation of Thai peoples and a phenomenal artistic heritage. Now an impressive assembly of elegant ruins, **Muang Kao Sukhothai (Old Sukhothai)**, 58km northwest of Phitsanulok, has been designated a historical park and has grown into one of Thailand's most visited ancient sites.

There are a couple of good hotels near the historical park, but little in the way of entertainment, so most travellers stay in **"New" Sukhothai** (see p.193), a small and friendly town 12km to the east, which is also better for restaurants and travel connections. Aside from the necessities, the new town has little of interest, but makes a peaceful base for visiting not only the historical park but also the outlying ruins of Si Satchanalai and Kamphaeng Phet. Reasonably priced **tours** (from B2000) can be arranged through *Sky Tour* (☎055/612237) on Prasertpong Road, the *Chinawat Hotel* or any of the town's guest houses.

Sukhothai can be done as a day trip from Phitsanulok easily enough, with **buses** to New Sukhothai running every half-hour. From Bangkok it's a six- or seven-hour journey; from Chiang Mai it takes between five and six hours. Frequent **songthaews** shuttle between the new and old towns, departing from behind the police box on Charodvithitong Road, west of the river.

Some history

Prior to the thirteenth century, the land now known as Thailand was divided into a collection of petty principalities, most of which owed their allegiance to the Khmer empire and its administrative centre Angkor (in present-day Cambodia). With the Khmers' power on the wane, two Thai generals joined forces in 1238 to oust the Khmers from the northern plains, founding the kingdom of **Sukhothai** ("Dawn of Happiness" in Pali) under the regency of one of the generals, Intradit. In short order they had extended their control over much of present-day Thailand, including parts of Burma and Laos.

The third and most important of Sukhothai's eight kings, Intradit's youngest son **Ramkhamhaeng** (c. 1278–1299) laid the foundations of a unique Thai identity by establishing Theravada (Hinayana) Buddhism as the common faith and introducing the forerunner of the modern Thai alphabet; of several inscriptions attributed to him, the most famous, known as Ramkhamhaeng's Stele and housed in Bangkok's National Museum, tells of a utopian land of plenty ruled by a benevolent monarch. Ramkhamhaeng turned Sukhothai into a vibrant spiritual and commercial centre, inviting Theravada monks from Nakhon Si Thammarat and Sri Lanka to instruct his people in the religion that was to supplant Khmer Hinduism and Mahayana Buddhism, and encouraging the growth of a ceramics industry with the help of Chinese potters. By all accounts, Ramkhamhaeng's successors lacked his kingly qualities and, paying more attention to religious affairs, squandered much of Sukhothai's political capital. By the second half of the fourteenth century, Sukhothai had become a vassal state of the newly emerged kingdom of Ayutthaya and finally, in 1438, was forced to relinquish all vestiges of its independent identity.

Traditionally, the **Sukhothai era** has always been viewed as the golden age of Thai history: the beginning of the kingdom of Thailand as we know it, the cornerstone of all things Thai, and a happy and prosperous time for all. Recently, however, the importance of Ramkhamhaeng's Stele, upon which this rose-tinted view is based, has been reappraised. Some historians consider the stele's inscription a fake or at best an outrageous exaggeration, but whatever the authenticity of the stele, Sukhothai-era ruins provide compelling evidence of a time of great prosperity, strong Buddhist faith and a refined artistic sensibility.

Old Sukhothai: Sukhothai Historical Park

In its prime, **OLD SUKHOTHAI** boasted some forty separate temple complexes and covered an area of about seventy square kilometres between the River Yom and the low range of hills to the west. At its heart stood the walled royal city, protected by a series of moats and ramparts. **Sukhothai Historical Park** (daily 6am–6pm) covers all this area and is divided into five zones, each costing B20 to enter. All of the most important temples lie within the central zone, as does the museum (which charges a separate admission fee); the ruins outside the city walls are spread out over a sizeable area and divided into north, south, east and west zones. There's an official entrance gate for the central zone, but in the other zones you generally buy your ticket at the first temple you visit.

With the help of UNESCO, the Fine Arts Department has restored the most significant ruins and replaced the retreating jungle with lawns, leaving some trees for shade, unclogging a few ponds and moats, and clearing pathways between the

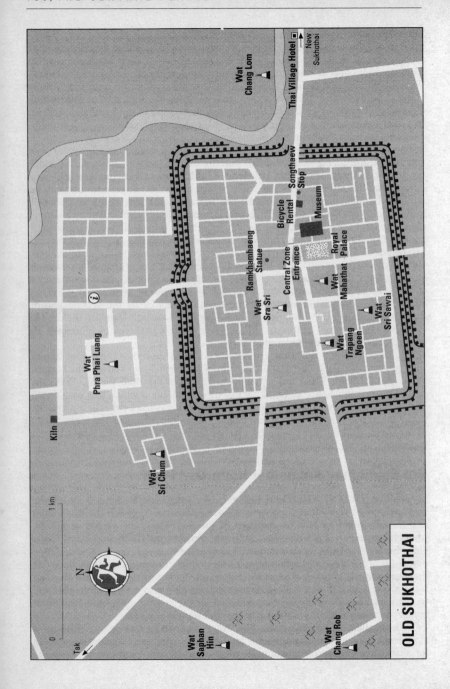

Wat
Chang Lom

Thai Village Hotel

New
Sukhothai

Songthaew
Stop

Bicycle
Rental

Museum

Ramkhamhaeng
Statue

Royal
Palace

Central Zone
Entrance

Wat
Sra Sri

Wat
Mahathat

Wat
Sri Sawai

Wat
Trapang
Ngoen

Wat
Phra Phai Luang

Kiln

Wat
Sri Chum

1 km

0

N

Tak

Wat
Saphan
Hin

Wat
Chang Rob

OLD SUKHOTHAI

wats. The result reveals the original town planners' keen aesthetic sense, especially their astute use of water to offset and reflect the solid monochrome contours of the stone temples. Nevertheless, there is a touch of the too perfectly packaged theme park about the central zone, and while some critics have detected an overly liberal interpretation of the thirteenth-century design, it still takes a determined imagination to visualize the ancient capital as it must once have looked. Noticeably absent are the houses and palaces which would have filled the spaces between the wats: like their Khmer predecessors, the people of Sukhothai constructed their secular buildings from wood, believing that only sacred structures merited such a durable and costly material as stone.

Songthaews from New Sukhothai stop about 300m inside the east walls, close to the museum and central zone entrance point. The best way to avoid being overwhelmed (or bored) by so many ruins is to hire a **bicycle** from one of the numerous outlets near the museum. Paths crisscross the park and circle most of the ruins, particularly in the central zone, which means you'll be able to appreciate some of the more spectacular settings from all angles without having to explore every individual site – and you'll have a jump on the tour groups.

If you want to **eat** inside the park, try the large (and pricey) restaurant near the museum, or buy cold drinks and snacks from the vendors who congregate under the trees near Wat Mahathat. Tour groups all eat at *Thai Village Hotel*, just east of the city walls on the road to New Sukhothai – enough said. **Accommodation** at *Thai Village Hotel* (☎055/611049; ⑤) is much better value than the food, however, with attractive, air-conditioned wooden bungalows in the landscaped garden behind the restaurant. The only other place fairly near the park is the top-class *Pailyn Hotel* (☎055/613310; ⑥–⑦), 4km east along the New Sukhothai road.

THE SUKHOTHAI BUDDHA

The classic Buddha images of Thailand were produced towards the end of the Sukhothai era. Ethereal, androgynous figures with ovoid faces and feline expressions, they depict not a Buddha meditating to achieve enlightenment – the more usual representation – but an already **enlightened Buddha**: the physical realization of a philosophical abstract. Though they produced mainly seated Buddhas, Sukhothai artists are renowned for having pioneered the **walking Buddha**, one of four postures described in ancient Pali texts but without precedent in Thailand. These texts also set down a list of the marks of greatness by which future Buddhas could be recognized; of all Thai schools of art, Sukhothai sculptors stuck the most literally to these precepts, as you can see by checking the **features** below against any Sukhothai statue:

Legs like a deer's.

Thighs like the trunk of a banyan tree.

Shoulders as massive as an elephant's head.

Arms tubular like an elephant's trunk, and long enough to touch each knee without bending.

Hands like lotus flowers about to bloom.

Fingertips turned back like petals.

A head shaped like an egg.

A flame to signify fiery intellect.

Hair like scorpion stings.

A chin like a mango stone.

A nose like a parrot's beak.

Eyebrows like drawn bows.

Eyelashes like a cow's.

Earlobes elongated by the heavy earrings worn by royalty.

Skin so smooth that dust couldn't stick to it.

The central zone

Only four of the eleven ruins in the **central zone** are worth dwelling on, and of these Wat Mahathat should definitely not be missed. The area covers three square kilometres: a bike is recommended, but not essential.

Just outside the entrance to the central zone, the **Ramkhamhaeng National Museum**'s (daily 9am–4pm; B10) collection of locally found artefacts is neither particularly inspiring nor informatively displayed, but if you haven't already seen King Ramkhamhaeng's famous stele in Bangkok, you might want to look at the copy kept here. A modern **statue** of the great man sits to the right just inside the zone entrance: cast in bronze, he holds a palm-leaf book in his right hand – a reference to his role as founder of the modern Thai alphabet. Close by stands a large bronze **bell**, a replica of the one referred to on the famous stele (also reproduced here), which told how the king had the bell erected in front of his palace so that any citizen with a grievance could come by and strike it, whereupon the king himself would emerge to investigate the problem.

WAT MAHATHAT

Turn left inside the gate for Sukhothai's most important site, the enormous **Wat Mahathat** compound, packed with the remains of scores of monuments and surrounded, like a city within a city, by a moat. This was the spiritual epicentre of the city, the king's temple and symbol of his power; eager to add their own stamp, successive regents restored and expanded it so that by the time it was abandoned in the sixteenth century it numbered ten viharns, one bot, eight mondops and nearly two hundred small chedis.

Looking at the wat from ground level, it's hard to distinguish the main structures from the minor ruins. Remnants of the viharns and the bot dominate the present scene, their soldierly ranks of pillars (formerly supporting wooden roofs) directing the eye to the Buddha images seated at the far western ends.

The one component you can't overlook is the principal chedi complex, which houses the Buddha relic (*mahathat*): it stands grandly – if a little cramped – at the heart of the compound, built on an east–west axis in an almost continuous line with two viharns. Its elegant centrepiece follows a design termed **lotus-bud chedi** (after the bulbous finial ornamenting the top of a tower), and is classic late Sukhothai in style. This lotus-bud reference is no mere whimsy but an established religious symbol: though Sukhothai architects were the first to incorporate it into building design – since when it's come to be regarded as a hallmark of the era – the lotus bud had for centuries represented the purity of the Buddha's thoughts

Wat Mahathat

battling through the clammy swamp and finally bursting out into flower. The chedi stands surrounded by eight smaller towers on a square platform decorated with a procession of walking Buddha-like monks, another artistic innovation of the Sukhothai school, here depicted in stucco relief. The two square mondops flanking the chedi were built for the colossal standing Buddhas still inside them today.

The grassy patch across the road from Wat Mahathat marks the site of the former palace, of which nothing now remains.

AROUND WAT MAHATHAT

A few hundred metres southwest of Wat Mahathat, the triple corn-cob-shaped prangs of **Wat Sri Sawai** make an interesting architectural comparison. Just as the lotus-bud chedi epitomizes Sukhothai aspirations, the prang represents Khmer ideals – Wat Sri Sawai was probably conceived as a Hindu shrine several centuries before the Sukhothai kingdom established itself here. The stucco reliefs decorating the prangs feature a few weatherworn figures from both Hindu and Buddhist mythology, which suggests that the shrine was later pressed into Buddhist service; the square base inside the central prang supported the Khmer Shiva lingam (phallus), while the viharn out front is a later, Buddhist addition.

Just west of Wat Mahathat, the particularly fine lotus-bud chedi of **Wat Trapang Ngoen** rises gracefully against the backdrop of distant hills. Aligned with the chedi on the symbolic east–west axis are the dilapidated viharn and, east of that, on an island in the middle of the "silver pond" after which the wat is named, the remains of the bot. It's worth walking the connecting plank to the bot to appreciate the setting from the water. North of the chedi, notice the fluid lines of the walking Buddha mounted onto a brick wall – a classic example of Sukhothai sculpture.

Taking the water feature one step further, **Wat Sra Sri** commands a fine position on two connecting islands north of Wat Trapang Ngoen. The bell-shaped chedi with a tapering spire and square base shows a strong Sri Lankan influence,

LOY KRATHONG: THE FESTIVAL OF LIGHT

Every year on the evening of the full moon of the twelfth lunar month (between late Oct and mid-Nov), Thais celebrate the end of the rainy season with the festival of **Loy Krathong**. One of the country's most beautiful festivals, it's held to honour the spirits of the water at a time when all the fields are flooded and the khlongs and rivers are overflowing their banks. To thank and appease Mae Khong Kha, the goddess of water, Thais decorate **krathong** – miniature basket-boats fashioned from banana leaves – with flowers, load them with burning incense sticks, lighted candles and coins, and set them afloat on the nearest body of water. The bobbing lights of thousands of floating *krathong* make a fantastic spectacle.

Loy Krathong is celebrated all over Thailand, but nowhere more magically than on the ponds of Old Sukhothai. It is here that the festival is said to have originated seven hundred years ago, when the consort of a Sukhothai king adapted the ancient Brahmin custom of paying homage to the water goddess, and began the tradition of placing *krathong* on the lotus ponds. In recent history, Sukhothai has magnified the original "festival of lights" so that, for the three nights around the full moon, not only are the pond surfaces aglow with candles, but the ruins are wreathed in lights and illuminated during a nightly *son et lumière* performance, and spectators are dispatched home amidst a massive panoply of fireworks.

and the black replica of a freestanding walking Buddha displays many of the "marks of greatness" as prescribed in the Pali texts (see box on p.189).

The outer zones

There's a much less formal feel to the ruins in the four **outer zones**: herds of cows trample nonchalantly through the remains and farming families have built their houses amongst them, growing rice on every available patch of land. You'll need a bicycle or car to get around these zones, but the routes aren't strenuous and all sites are clearly signposted from the city-wall boundaries. The north zone is the closest and most rewarding, followed by the east zone just off the road to New Sukhothai. If you're feeling energetic, head for the west zone, which requires a much longer bike ride and some hill climbing. The ruins to the south just aren't worth the effort.

THE NORTH ZONE
Continuing north of Wat Sra Sri, cross the city walls into the **north zone** and follow the signs for the **information centre** (daily 6am–6pm; free) 500m further on. The centre's breezy pavilions make a pleasant resting place if you're on a bike, and its scale model of Old Sukhothai illustrates the aesthetic awareness of the original planners.

Across the road from the information centre stands **Wat Phra Phai Luang**, one of the ancient city's oldest structures. The three prangs (only one of which remains intact) were built by the Khmers before the Thais founded their own kingdom here and, as at the similar Wat Sri Sawai, you can still see some of the stucco reliefs showing both Hindu and Buddhist figures. It's thought that Phra Phai Luang was at the centre of the old Khmer town and that it was as important then as Wat Mahathat later became to the Thais. When the shrine was converted into a Buddhist temple, the viharn and chedi were built to the east of the prangs: the reliefs of the (now headless and armless) seated Buddhas are still visible around the base of the chedi. Also discernible among the ruins are parts of a large reclining Buddha and a mondop containing four huge standing Buddhas in different postures.

About 500m west from Wat Phra Phai Luang, **Wat Sri Chum** boasts Sukhothai's largest surviving Buddha image. The enormous brick and stucco seated Buddha, measuring over 11m from knee to knee and almost 15m high, peers through the slit in its custom-built mondop. Check out the elegantly tapered fingers, complete with gold-leaf nail varnish and mossy gloves. A passageway – rarely opened up, unfortunately – runs inside the mondop wall, taking you from ground level on the left-hand side to the Buddha's eye level and then up again to the roof, affording a great bird's-eye view of the image. Legend has it that this Buddha would sometimes speak to favoured worshippers, and this staircase would have enabled tricksters to climb up and hold forth, unseen; one of the kings of Sukhothai is said to have brought his troops here so as to spur them on to victory with encouraging words from the Buddha.

THE EAST ZONE
About 1km east of the city walls, the only temple of interest in the **east zone** is **Wat Chang Lom**, just off the road to New Sukhothai, near *Thai Village Hotel*. Chang Lom, which also transliterates as Chang Rob, means "Surrounded by Elephants": the main feature here is a large, Sri Lankan-style, bell-shaped chedi encircled by a frieze of elephants.

THE WEST ZONE

Be prepared for a long haul out to the **west zone**, in the forested hills off the main road to Tak. Marking the western edge of Old Sukhothai almost 5km west of the city walls, the hilltop temple of **Wat Saphan Hin** should – with sufficiently powerful telescopic lenses – afford a fantastic panorama of the old city's layout, but with the naked eye conjures up only an indistinct vista of trees and stones. If you make it this far, chances are you'll share the view only with the large standing Buddha at the top. The wat is reached via a steep pathway of stone slabs (hence the name, which means "Stone Bridge") that starts from a track running south from the Tak road. This is the easiest approach if you're on a bike as it's completely flat; the shorter route, which follows a lesser, more southerly, road out of the old city, takes you over several hills and past the elephant temple of **Wat Chang Rob**, 1km short of Saphan Hin, where it joins the other track.

New Sukhothai practicalities

Straddling the River Yom, **NEW SUKHOTHAI** offers a good selection of **budget accommodation** options, most no more than ten minutes' walk from the water. Gangs of guest-house touts meet the buses at all the main arrival points, vying with each other for your custom; though a bit unnerving, this does keep the prices competitive and sometimes means you get a free lift as well. There's not a comparable spread at the upper end of the spectrum, with just one upmarket option to speak of, albeit a reasonably priced one; most well-heeled guests stay either at *Pailyn Hotel* on the road to Old Sukhothai (see p.189) or in Phitsanulok. All accommodation gets packed out during the Loy Krathong festival (see box on p.141), so book in advance if you plan to visit at this time, unless you're willing to sleep sardine-style on a guest-house floor.

You're not exactly spoilt for choice when it comes to places to eat, either, although the food on offer will appeal to a range of palates. For al fresco eating, the **night market** near the *Dream Café* on Ramkhamhaeng Road offers the usual spread of soups, curries, rice and noodle dishes.

Accommodation

Ban Thai Guest House, 38 Pravetnakorn Rd (☎055/610163). On the west bank of the Yom, this comfortable budget option has a few simple rooms in a small purpose-built house, plus some plusher bungalows around the back. ①.

Chinawat Hotel, 1–3 Nikhon Kasem Rd (☎055/611031). On the east side of the River Yom, this is a popular place offering adequate rooms with fan and shower. Has a good restaurant, too, although it's only open for dinner. ②.

Northern Palace, 43 Singhawat Rd (☎055/611193). At the top of the range, this luxurious hotel has facilities including pool tables and a swimming pool. You can sometimes negotiate a discounted room rate. ⑥.

Number 4 Guest House, Soi Panitsan, at 234/6 Charodvithitong Rd (☎055/610165). Situated just beyond the songthaew stop for the old city, this lovely old teak house has large, comfortable rooms and walls plastered with useful travellers' information. There's another branch of *Number 4* at 170 Ratchathani Rd, but it's not as nice. ①.

Old Thai Guest House, 25/4 Rajuthit Rd (☎055/612853). Makeshift but welcoming homestay, very much a family enterprise. Simple rooms with fan. ①.

Sawaddipong Hotel, 56/2–5 Singhawat Rd (☎055/611567). Comparatively swish accommodation offering sizeable, clean rooms with attached bathroom, some with air-con. ③.

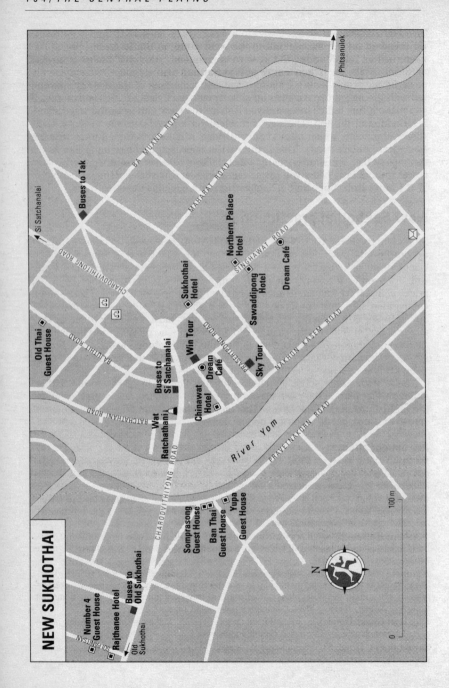

NEW SUKHOTHAI

Phitsanulok

Si Satchanalai

Buses to Tak

BA MUANG ROAD

MAHARAT ROAD

Northern Palace
Hotel

SINGHAWAT ROAD

Sawaddipong
Hotel

Dream Café

Sukhothai
Hotel

Old Thai
Guest House

CHAROD VITHITONG ROAD

RAJUTHIT ROAD

Win Tour

Buses to
Si Satchanalai

Dream
Café

PRASERTPONG ROAD

Sky Tour

NAKHON KASEM ROAD

Chinawat
Hotel

Wat
Ratchathani

RATCHATHANI ROAD

CHAROD VITHITONG ROAD

River Yom

PRAVETNAKORN ROAD

Somprasong
Guest House

Ban Thai
Guest House

Yupa
Guest House

Number 4
Guest House

Rajthanee Hotel

Buses to
Old Sukhothai

SOI PANISAN

Old
Sukhothai

N

100 m

0

Somprasong Guest House, 32 Pravetnakorn Rd (☎055/611709). Adjacent to the *Ban Thai* and across from *Chinawat*, this large wooden house has sizeable rooms and affords good views from its riverfront balcony. The affable managers are valuable sources of local information. ①.

Sukhothai Hotel, 5/5 Singhawat Rd (☎055/611133). Another good option: standard Chinese/Thai hotel rooms, all with bathroom. ②.

Yupa Guest House, 44/10 Pravetnakorn Rd (☎055/612578). Completing the trio of guest houses on this road, this converted family home has large, slightly sparse-looking rooms, some with balconies. ①.

Eating

The *Chinawat Hotel*'s **restaurant** sports a large menu of good Thai and Western fare (dinner only) that runs the range from *pla rat prik* (fish grilled with chillis) down to cheese sandwiches. Next door, *Dear House* serves up the standards: *pat thai*, *kwetiaw ratna* and *khao pat kai*. Further down Nikhon Kasem Road, *Duck Restaurant* (aka *Kho Jung Hong*) specializes, as you'd expect, in duck meals, cooked to Chinese recipes such as the stewed and mildly spiced *pet phalo*, or the roasted *pet yang*, and to Thai specifications as in the thick *kaeng pet* curries. The cosy *Dream Café*, with branches on Ramkhamhaeng Road and Singhawat Road opposite the *Bangkok Bank*, fosters a coffee-shop atmosphere with its walls and windowsills of curios and knick-knacks, and a menu of espressos and ice creams, but it also does hearty savoury plates of curries, omelettes and seafood, making a pleasant place to while away an evening until 10pm closing.

Si Satchanalai and around

In the mid-thirteenth century, Sukhothai cemented its power by establishing several satellite towns, of which the most important was **SI SATCHANALAI**, 57km upriver from Sukhothai on the banks of the Yom. Now a historical park, the restored ruins of **Muang Kao Si Satchanalai** have a quieter ambience than the grander models at Old Sukhothai, and the additional inducements of the riverside wat in nearby Chalieng and the Sawankhalok pottery kilns in Bang Ko Noi combine to make the area worth exploring.

Si Satchanalai is for all intents and purposes a day trip from Sukhothai as local accommodation is thin on the ground. Don't attempt to do Si Satchanalai and Sukhothai in a single day – a lot of tour outfits offer this option, but seeing so many dilapidated facades in seven or eight hours is mind-numbing. Half-hourly buses bound for Si Satchanalai depart from opposite the *Chinawat Hotel* on Charodwithitong Road in New Sukhothai: get off at the signpost for Muang Kao Si Satchanalai (1hr) and follow the track southwest over the River Yom for about 500m to a **bicycle rental** place, conveniently planted at the junction for the historical park (1500m northwest) and Chalieng (1km southeast); the kilns are a further 2km north of the park. Renting a bike makes sense as even the walk to the park can be exhausting in the heat; the park itself is fairly compact. If cycling isn't your cup of tea, you could either rent a motorbike next to the *Chinawat Hotel* in New Sukhothai or join a half-day tour from there.

The historical park stands pretty much on its own with only a couple of hamlets in the vicinity, where you'll be able to buy cold drinks but won't get much in the way of food or a place to stay. If you're really determined to see Muang Kao Si

Satchanalai on your way elsewhere (like Phrae or Lampang, for example), you could stay at *Wang Yom Resort* (☎055/611179; ⑤–⑦), which has a range of upmarket bungalows (and a crafts centre) set around an attractive garden 300m south of the park entrance on Highway 101. Alternatively, if you proceed to the old city's modern counterpart at Si Satchanalai proper, 11km north along Highway 101 and the terminus of the Sukhothai buses, you'll find inexpensive accommodation at the *Kruchang Hotel* (②) near the *Bangkok Bank* in the town centre.

Muang Kao Si Satchanalai

Muang Kao Si Satchanalai (daily 8.30am–4.30pm; B20) was built to emulate its capital, but Si Satchanalai is much less hyped than Sukhothai, sees fewer tourists and, most significantly, has escaped the sometimes over-zealous landscaping of the more popular sight. It's also a lot less strung out, though lacking in the watery splendour of Sukhothai's main temples.

The ruins are numbered and it makes sense to do them in order. Begin with the elephant temple of **Wat Chang Lom**, whose centrepiece is a huge, Sri Lankan-style, bell-shaped chedi set on a square base which is studded with 39 life-sized elephant buttresses. Many of the elephants are in good repair, with most of their stucco flesh still intact; others now have their laterite skeletons exposed. According to a contemporary stone inscription, the chedi was built to house sacred Buddhist relics originally buried in Chalieng. Contrary to the religious etiquette of the time, King Ramkhamhaeng of Sukhothai put the relics on display for a year before moving them – a potentially blasphemous act that should have been met with divine retribution, but Ramkhamhaeng survived unscathed and apparently even more popular with his subjects.

Across the road from Wat Chang Lom, **Wat Chedi Jet Taew**'s seven rows of small chedis are thought to enshrine the ashes of Si Satchanalai's royal rulers, which makes this the ancient city's most important temple. One of the chedis is a scaled-down replica of the hallmark lotus-bud chedi at Sukhothai's Wat Mahathat; some of the others are copies of other important wats from the vicinity.

Following the road a short way southeast of Chedi Jet Taew you reach **Wat Nang Phya**, remarkable for the original stucco reliefs on its viharn wall that remain in fine condition. The balustraded wall has slit windows and is entirely covered with intricate floral motifs. Stucco is a hardy material which sets soon after being first applied, and becomes even harder when exposed to rain – hence its ability to survive seven hundred years in the open. To the right on the way back to Wat Chang Lom, **Wat Suan Utayan Noi** contains one of the few Buddha images still left in Si Satchanalai.

North of Chang Lom, the hilltop ruins of Wat Khao Phanom Pleung and Wat Khao Suan Khiri afford splendid aerial views of different quarters of the ancient city. The sole remaining intact chedi of **Wat Khao Phanom Pleung** sits atop the lower of the hills and used to be flanked by a set of smaller chedis built to entomb the ashes of Si Satchanalai's important personages – the ones who merited some special memorial, but didn't quite make the grade for Wat Chedi Jet Taew. The temple presumably got its name, which means "mountain of sacred fire", from the cremation rituals held on the summit. **Wat Khao Suan Khiri**'s huge chedi, which graces the summit 200m northwest, has definitely seen better days, but the views from its dilapidated platform – south over the main temple ruins and north towards the city walls and entrance gates – are worth the climb.

Chalieng

Before Sukhothai asserted control of the region and founded Si Satchanalai, the Khmers governed the area from **CHALIENG**, just over 2km to the east of Si Satchanalai. Cradled in a bend in the River Yom, all that now remains of Chalieng is a single temple, **Wat Phra Si Ratana Mahathat**, the most atmospheric of all the sights in the Sukhothai area. Left to sink into graceful disrepair, the wat has escaped the perfectionist touch of restorers and now serves both as playground to the kids from the hamlet across the river and grazing patch for their parents' cows.

Originally a Khmer temple and later adapted by the kings of Sukhothai, Wat Phra Si Ratana Mahathat forms a compact complex of two ruined viharns aligned east–west each side of a central chedi. Of the western viharn only two Buddha images remain, seated one in front of the other on a dais overgrown with weeds, and staring folornly at the stumps of pillars that originally supported the roof over their heads: the rest has long since been buried under grass, efficiently grazed by the cows. A huge standing Buddha, similar to the two in Sukhothai's Wat Mahathat, gazes out from the nearby mondop. The more important viharn adjoins the central Sri Lankan-style chedi to the east, and is surrounded by a sunken wall of laterite blocks. Entering it through the semi-submerged eastern gateway, you pass beneath a sizeable carved lintel, hewn from a single block of stone. The seated Buddha in the centre of the western end of the viharn is typical Sukhothai style, as is the towering stucco relief of a walking Buddha to the left, which is regarded as one of the finest of its genre.

The Sawankhalok kilns

Endowed with high-quality clay, the area around Si Satchanalai – known as Sawankhalok during the Ayutthayan era – commanded an international reputation as a ceramics centre from the mid-fourteenth to the end of the fifteenth century, producing pieces still rated among the finest in the world. More than two hundred kilns have been unearthed in and around Si Satchanalai to date, and it's estimated that there could once have been a thousand in all. Two kilometres upstream of Muang Kao Si Satchanalai in **Ban Ko Noi**, the **Sawankhalok Kiln Preservation Centre** (daily 9am–noon & 1–4pm; B20) showcases an excavated production site, with a couple of kilns roofed over as museum pieces.

Unfortunately, there are no English signs to explain how the kilns worked, though a small display of **Sawankhalok ceramics** gives an idea of the pieces that were fired here. Works fall into three broad categories: domestic items such as pots, decorated plates and lidded boxes; decorative items like figurines, temple sculptures and temple roof tiles; and items for export, particularly to Indonesia and the Philippines, where huge Sawankhalok storage jars were used as burial urns. Most Sawankhalok ceramics were glazed

Sawankhalok dish

– the grey-green celadon, probably introduced by immigrant Chinese potters, was especially popular – and typically decorated with fish or chrysanthemum motifs. Several of Thailand's major museums feature collections of ceramics from both Si Satchanalai and Sukhothai under the umbrella label of Sawankhalok.

Kamphaeng Phet

KAMPHAENG PHET, 77km south of Sukhothai, was probably founded in the fourteenth century by the kings of Sukhothai as a buffer city between their capital and the increasingly powerful city-state of Ayutthaya. Its name, which translates as "Diamond Wall", refers to its role as a garrison town. Strategically sited 100m from the east bank of the Ping, the ruined old city has, like Sukhothai and Si Satchanalai before it, been partly restored and opened to the public as a historical park. The least visited of the three, it should nevertheless rival Si Satchanalai for your attentions, mainly because of the eloquently weathered statues of its main temple. A new city has grown up on the southeastern boundaries of the old, the usual commercial ugliness offset by a riverside park, plentiful flowers and traditional wooden houses.

Highway 1, the region's main north–south route, skirts Kamphaeng Phet on the western side of the river – the town is served by direct **buses** from Bangkok and Chiang Mai, but most travellers come here as a day trip from Sukhothai or Phitsanulok. Arriving from either of these two, you'll enter from the east and should ask to be dropped off inside the old city walls rather than wait to be dumped across the river at the terminal 2km west of town on Highway 1. If you are coming from the bus terminal, you'll need to hop on a town songthaew, which will take you to the Tesa Road roundabout just east of the river (the most convenient disembarkation point for the ruins), or further into the town centre for most of the hotels and restaurants.

Muang Kao Kamphaeng Phet

Ruins surround modern Kamphaeng Phet on all sides, but **Muang Kao Kamphaeng Phet** (daily 8.30am–4.30pm; B20) takes in the two most interesting areas: the oblong zone inside the old city walls and the forested area just north of that. A tour of both areas involves a five-kilometre round trip; there's no public transport, so if you don't feel like walking you'll have to strike a deal with a samlor driver or rent a motorbike from the shop on the road between the Tesa Road roundabout and the old city walls.

The ruins that dot the landscape west of the roundabout, across the Ping River, belong to the even older city of Nakhon Chum, but are now too overgrown, tumbledown and difficult to reach to be worth the effort.

Inside the city walls

Parts of the **city walls** that gave Kamphaeng Phet its name are still in good condition, though Highway 101 to Sukhothai now cuts through the enclosed area and a few shops have sprung up along the roadside, making it hard to visualize the fortifications as a whole.

Approaching from the Tesa Road roundabout, you enter the compound from the western side and come in at the back end of **Wat Phra Kaeo**. Built almost

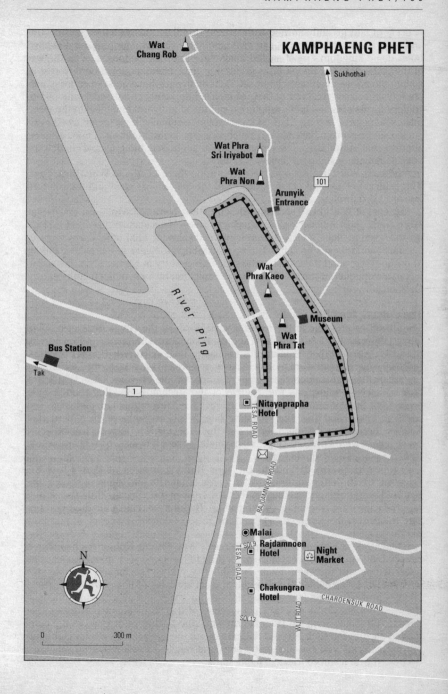

Wat
Chang Rob

KAMPHAENG PHET

Sukhothai

Wat Phra
Sri Iriyabot

Wat
Phra Non

101

Arunyik
Entrance

Wat
Phra Kaeo

River Ping

Museum

Wat
Phra Tat

Bus Station

Tak

1

Nitayaprapha
Hotel

TESA ROAD

RAJDAMNOEN ROAD

Malai

Rajdamnoen
Hotel

SOI 9

TESA ROAD

Night
Market

Chakungrao
Hotel

WUTHI ROAD

CHAROENSUK ROAD

SOI 13

N

0   300 m

entirely of laterite and adorned with laterite Buddhas, this was the city's central and most important structure, and given the name reserved for temples that have housed the kingdom's most sacred image: the Emerald Buddha, now in the wat of the same name in Bangkok, is thought to have been set down here to rest at some point. Seven centuries later, the Buddha images have been worn away into attractive abstract shadows of their originals, often aptly compared to the pitted, spidery forms of Giacometti sculptures, and the slightly unkempt feel to the place makes a perfect setting. The statues would originally have been faced with stucco, and restorers have already patched up the central tableau of one reclining and two seated Buddhas. The empty niches that encircle the principal chedi were once occupied by statues of bejewelled lions.

Adjoining Wat Phra Kaeo to the east are the three chedis of **Wat Phra That**. The central bell-shaped chedi is typical of the Sri Lankan style and was built to house a sacred relic.

Just east of Wat Phra That, **Kamphaeng Phet National Museum** (Wed–Sun 10am–4pm; B10) houses a clear, succinct survey of Thailand's major art periods on the ground floor and a comprehensive display of Sukhothai-era sculpture, ceramics and utensils upstairs. The prize exhibit is the very fine bronze standing Shiva on the ground floor: cast in the sixteenth century in Khmer style, the statue has had a chequered history, including decapitation by a keen nineteenth century German admirer.

The arunyik temples

The dozen or so ruins in the forested area north of the city walls – east 100m along Highway 101 from behind Wat Phra Kaeo, across the moat and up a track to the left – are all that remains of Kamphaeng Phet's **arunyik** (forest) temples, built here by Sukhothai-era monks in a wooded area to encourage meditation.

Passing through the entrance gate, the first temple on your left is **Wat Phra Non**, otherwise known as the Temple of the Reclining Buddha, though little remains of the enormous Buddha figure save for a few chunks helpfully labelled "neck", "head" and the like. Gigantic laterite pillars support the viharn that houses the statue; far more ambitious than the usual brick-constructed jobs, these pillars were cut from single slabs of stone from a nearby quarry and would have measured up to 8m in height.

A relic's throw to the north, the four Buddha images of **Wat Phra Sri Iriyabot** are in better condition. With cores of laterite and skins of stucco, the restored standing and walking images tower over the viharn, while the seated (south-facing) and reclining (north-facing) Buddhas remain indistinct masses. The full-grown trees rooted firmly in the raised floor are evidence of just how old the place is.

Follow the path around the bend to reach **Wat Chang Rob**, crouched atop a laterite hill 1km from the entrance gate. Built to the same Sri Lankan model as its sister temples of the same name in Sukhothai and Si Satchanalai, this "temple surrounded by elephants" retains only the square base of its central bell-shaped chedi. Climb one of its four steep staircases for a view out over the mountains in the west, or just for a different perspective of the 68 elephant buttresses that encircle the base. Sculpted from laterite and stucco, they're dressed in the ceremonial garb fit for such revered animals; along the surfaces between neighbouring pachyderms you can just make out floral reliefs – the lower level was once decorated with a stucco frieze of flying birds.

Practicalities

Few travellers spend the night in Kamphaeng Phet, but if you do want to **stay**, *Nitayaprapha Hotel* (☎055/711381; ①) has the edge in price and convenience. The rambling old wooden building has no English sign, but is prominently positioned over a restaurant on the southwest corner of the Tesa Road roundabout; rooms are basic but all come with fan and shower. Nearer the new town centre, on the corner of Soi 9 and Rajdamnoen Road, *Rajdamnoen Hotel* (☎055/711029; ②–③) has a range of reasonable fan-cooled and air-conditioned rooms. *Chakungrao Hotel* (☎055/711315; ④), between sois 11 and 13 on Tesa Road, is the poshest choice in town, though the large air-conditioned rooms are a touch shabby for the price.

Food in Kamphaeng Phet rarely rises above the noodles-and-curry level, but *Malai*, just north of Soi 9 on Tesa Road, serves up a reliable range of northeastern food – *khao niaw, kai yang* and *somtam* – at very reasonable prices. (There's no English sign, or menu, but you can recognize the place by the enormous sticky-rice baskets hanging up outside.) Otherwise you're best off with the noodle shops near *Nitayapraphya Hotel* or seeking out the **night market** on Wijit Road. The big outdoor restaurants along Tesa Road are the kind that have singers-with-synthesizers as evening-long entertainment and menus tailored for large Thai groups, which work out expensive for individuals.

West of Sukhothai

Highway 12 heads west from Sukhothai, crossing the westernmost reaches of the northern plains before arriving at the provincial capital of **TAK** (79km), on the east bank of the Ping River. Historically important only as the birthplace of King Taksin of Thonburi (who appended the name of his hometown to the one he was born with), Tak is of little interest to tourists except as a place to change **buses** for continuing north to Lampang and Chiang Mai, south to Kamphaeng Phet and Bangkok, or west to Mae Sot and the Burmese border. You might also find yourself touching down here on a **flight** between Phitsanulok and Chiang Mai – four flights a week make the journey via Tak and Mae Sot. The bus terminal and airfield are both about 3km east of the town centre. If you need to break your journey overnight, try the *Mae Ping* at 231 Mahattai Bamroong Rd (☎055/511807; ①) or *Sa Nguan Thai* at 619 Taksin Rd (☎055/511265; ①) **hotels**, both of which are near the lively central market.

Better to hold out for Mae Sot, reached by either of two roads through the stunning western mountain range that divides the northern plains from the Burmese border. Highway 105, the more direct route, is served by cramped government minibuses that leave Tak every half an hour between 6.30am and 6pm and take ninety minutes; on the way, look out for the section of the road known as "Magic Hill" (marked in English, 14km east of Mae Sot), so-called because cars are supposed to be able to climb the hill with the engine disengaged and the gears in neutral. Rickety but roomy regular buses take twice as long to ply Route 1175, which follows a winding and at times hair-raising course across the thickly forested range, affording great views over the valleys on either side and passing through makeshift roadside settlements built by hill tribes. (Returning along either of these routes to Tak, most public vehicles are stopped at an army checkpoint in an attempt to prevent Burmese entering Thailand illegally.) Much of this whole area is conserved as a national park, the most accessible stretch of which falls within **Langsang National Park** and is signposted off Highway 105, 20km west of Tak.

Route 1175 eventually descends into the valley of the **River Moei** – which forms the Thai–Burmese border here – and joins the new northbound section of Highway 105 (formerly Route 1085) at the lovely, traditional village of **Mae Ramat** before continuing south to Mae Sot. Highway 105 carries on northwards, reaching Mae Sariang (see p.260) after a five-hour songthaew ride – a bumpy but extremely scenic journey through rugged border country where law enforcement is intermittent at best. Heading south from Mae Sot, the same road becomes Route 1090, nicknamed the Sky Highway because of its panoramic vistas, and eventually winds up in the appealing village of Umpang.

Mae Sot and the border

Located 100km west of Tak and only 6km from the Burmese border, **MAE SOT** boasts a rich ethnic mix (Burmese, Karen, Hmong and Thai), thriving trade (legal and illegal) and a laid-back atmosphere. There's little to see in the small town apart from several glittering Burmese-style temples, but it's a relaxed place to hang out, and the short ride to the border market provides additional, if low-key, entertainment. Most travellers use the town as a resting spot along the border-hugging route that connects Mae Hong Song in the north with Sukhothai and the central plains, but there are enough **waterfalls** within day-tripping distance, like Nam Tok Mae Kasa (20km north of town) and Nam Tok Phra Charoen (41km south), to merit a stay of two or three days. Mae Sot's greatest attraction, however, is as a departure point for **organized treks**. This region sees so few tourists that these trips are genuine wilderness experiences, and some – such as those to the remote village of Umpang, about 160km south (see 206) – are unmissable.

Trekking

There are currently two specialist trekking companies based in Mae Sot, both offering routes that can be altered to suit individual specifications. *SP Tour* (☎055/531409), the largest and longest established, operates from the *Mae Sot Travel Centre* on the northern outskirts of town at 14/21 Asia Highway (Highway 105); it offers seven basic itineraries, most of which can include rafting, elephant-riding, jungle-walking, bird-watching and overnight stays in either refugee camps or Mon or Karen villages. Its treks north of Mae Sot stretch as far as Mae Sariang, taking in Mae Salid, while those to the south generally focus on the Umpang area and include the Tee Lor Su waterfall. Prices are all-inclusive and start at about B2500 per person for three days and two nights (the more people per trip, the less expensive it is).

Treks organized by *Mae Sot Conservation Tour* (☎055/532818), next to *Pim Hut* at 415/17 Tang Kim Chang Rd, concentrate on the Umpang and Tee Lor Su route, feature similar outdoor activities and cost about the same. It's also possible to make your own way to Umpang and arrange a trek with guides in the village (see p.206 for details). Finally, if you're staying at *Mae Sot Guest House* (see "Accommodation" p.204), you can arrange your own trek with the manager,

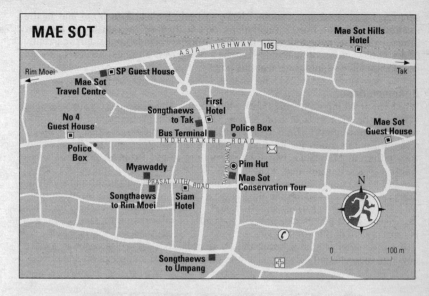

Khun Too. He offers basic routes north and south, with customized itineraries and activities; again, prices are competitive.

Shopping and Rim Moei border market

Mae Sot is also a great place for **shopping**, particularly for gems, jade and lacquerware – some of it contraband, smuggled across the border into Mae Sot at night to avoid Thai taxes. Its **gem and jade shops** in particular, clustered around *Siam Hotel* on Prasat Vithi Road, offer a larger and less expensive selection than the stalls at the Rim Moei border market (see below), and even if you don't intend to buy, just watching the performance-like haggling is half the fun. A couple of blocks west, opposite the Rim Moei songthaew stop on Prasat Vithi Road, *Myawaddy* stocks some of the most exquisite **lacquerware** in Thailand. It's all imported from Pagan in Burma and the range of patterns and designs is quite phenomenal; prices start at around B40 for a tiny cup, through B200 for trays and large bowls, up to B7000 for chests that take a year to complete (goods are shipped overseas on request). The same intricate process is used on all pieces, however small: it involves the layer-by-layer application of lacquer onto woven bamboo, followed by a delicate incising to reveal patterns of the colour underneath.

Frequent songthaews ferry Thai traders and a meagre trickle of tourists the 6km from Mae Sot to the border at **RIM MOEI**, where a large and thriving market for Burmese goods has grown up on the banks of the River Moei. It's a bit tacky, and the gems and jade on display are pricier than those in town, but it's not a bad place to pick up Burmese **handicrafts**, particularly lacquerware, checked *longyis*, silverware and jewellery. The nearby restaurants also provide an opportunity to sample genuine Burmese cuisine.

Burmese currency is accepted at the border and at some places in Mae Sot, and Burmese villagers from **Myawaddy**, on the opposite bank of the River Moei, seem to be granted unquestioned leave to trade both at Rim Moei and in the markets of Mae Sot. Border regulations look set to ease even further in the near future, with the completion of the Thai-Burma Friendship Bridge, currently under construction a few hundred metres downriver. Farangs, however, are on no account allowed into Burma at this point.

Accommodation

While the trekking companies both offer **rooms**, these are only really useful as stopovers on the way to or from a trek: *SP* (①) is inconveniently far out of town, while the more central *B&B* (③), above the *Mae Sot Conservation Tour* office, charges far too much for its spartan rooms. Fortunately, you won't go wrong with either of Mae Sot's two longest-running **guest houses**. *Mae Sot Guest House* (①–③), ten minutes' walk east of the bus terminal on Indharakiri Road, has the most comfortable good-value rooms, some with air conditioning. At the other, western, end of Indharakiri Road (15min walk from the bus terminal), *No. 4 Guest House* (①) is shabbier and not as welcoming, but slightly less expensive. Both places can provide a wealth of information on the scenic and political shape of the area.

If you'd rather stay in a **hotel**, the *Siam* (☎055/531376; ②) is centrally located amongst the gem and jade shops at 185 Prasat Vithi Rd and offers sizeable, clean

---

THE BURMESE JUNTA AND THE KAREN

With a population of five million, the **Karen** are Burma's largest ethnic minority, but their numbers have offered no protection against persecution by the Burmese. This mistreatment has been going on for centuries, and entered a new phase after World War II, when the Karen remained loyal to the British. As a reward, they were supposed to have been granted a special settlement when the British left, but were instead left to fend for themselves. Fifteen years after the British withdrawal, the **Burmese army** took control, setting up an isolationist state run under a bizarre ideology compounded of militarist, socialist and Buddhist principles. In 1988, opposition to this junta peaked with a series of pro-democracy demonstrations which were suppressed by the slaughter of thousands.

The army subsequently felt obliged to hold elections, which resulted in an overwhelming majority for the **National League for Democracy**, led by **Aung San Suu Kyi**, recipient of the 1991 Nobel Peace Prize. In response, the military placed Aung San Suu Kyi under house arrest (where she remained for six years, until freed in July 1995) and declared all opposition parties illegal. The disenfranchised MPs then joined the thousands who, in the face of the savagery of the Burmese militia against the country's minorities, had fled east to the **refugee villages** set up north and south of Mae Sot.

It is in this area that the Karen's armed struggle for their **independent state of Kawtulay** has been focused, with the Burmese army sporadically launching headline-making assaults on the Karen strongholds just across the border. Up until January 1995, the most important of these strongholds was at **Manerplaw**, upriver from Mae Sot on the Burmese bank of the River Moei. Armed by the Karen guerrillas, all resistance activities of the anti-Rangoon coalition, the Democratic Alliance of Burma, were centred on this jungle camp, which was home to the democratically elected National Coalition Government of the Union of Burma, and command centre of the Karen National Union. However, following an amnesty campaign by

rooms; *SP Tour* also has a trekking desk here. *First Hotel* (☎055/531233; ③), just north of Indharakiri Road, where Tak-bound songthaews leave from, has similar, slightly pricier rooms. *Mae Sot Hills Hotel* (☎055/532601; ⑥), away from the centre at 100 Asia Highway (Highway 105), seems incongruously upmarket for such an isolated town: all rooms are air-conditioned and there's a swimming pool on the premises, which non-guests can use for B25.

Eating

For good Thai and Western **food** at very reasonable prices – and certainly the biggest menu in town, with everything from green curries to pizzas – head for *Pim Hut* on Tang Kim Chang Road, which is popular with locals as well as Thai and farang tourists. You could also try out the two large open-air restaurants near *Mae Sot Guest House* which, wreathed in strings of coloured light bulbs and loud with the wails of teenage singers, entertain partying groups of Thais with slightly pricey menus of mostly *tom yam*, fish-and-meat-over rice dishes, and vast quantities of *Mekhong* whisky. If you're desperate for a genuine (imported) cheese sandwich – and are willing to pay for it – then stop by at the Thai/American-run café inside the *Myawaddy* lacquerware shop, opposite the Rim Moei songthaew shop on Prasat Vithi Road. Along this road you'll also find noodle shops and night-market stalls offering authentically Thai, inexpensive, no-frills meals.

the Burmese junta that exploited the rift between the Buddhist and Christian Karen, large numbers of Buddhist Karen reportedly left the camp, leaving it inadequately defended; when the Burmese army duly moved in the remaining six thousand or so Christian Karen fled to Thailand, joined within days by up to four thousand compatriots forced out of other newly vanquished strongholds.

Following these disasters, the KNU was, at the time of writing, preparing to change its tactics and take up guerrilla warfare within Burma, and had shifted its command centre to Mae Thami, a camp just across the border from Kanchanaburi and traditional headquarters of the KNU's crack 4th Brigade.

The war for democracy and a Karen homeland is locked into a cycle to which no imminent end is visible. Every dry season the Burmese army makes territorial gains, but when the rains arrive in June, the Karen recapture most of their strongholds, ready for the next round of battles in October. Although the **Thai government** used to tolerate the rebel camps, even sending in the troops whenever the Burmese army sneaked across the border to try and attack Manerplaw from Thai soil, official attitudes towards Rangoon are softening (see *Contexts*, p.529), and Thailand anticipates great economic benefit from its policy of "constructive engagement" with Burma. Just two days after Karen refugees from Manerplaw started pouring over the border, Bangkok signed a major deal with Rangoon, agreeing to buy gas from Burma for the next thirty years, even though the specially constructed pipeline will cross areas of Karen-controlled and Mon-held territory (see p.162).

Meanwhile, in the Burmese heartlands the murderers and rapists wreak their frustrated revenge on unarmed villagers, and every year, half of Burma's GNP is spent on weaponry. The entrenched virulence of the Burmese attitude to the Karen – and by extension, their allies – can be gauged by the recent comment of a senior Burmese soldier: "I want my country to be at peace; I want to extinguish all the minority peoples."

(For more on the Karen, see p.217.)

Umpang

Even if you don't fancy joining a trek from Mae Sot (see p.202), consider making the spectacular trip 160km or so south to the village of **UMPANG**, both for the stunning mountain scenery you'll encounter along the way, and for the buzz of being in such an isolated and typically rural part of Thailand. Umpang-bound songthaews leave Mae Sot from a spot one block south of Prasat Vithi Road, about 200m west of the hospital, departing approximately every hour between 7am and the early afternoon. The drive can take anything from three and a half to five hours and for the first hour proceeds in a fairly gentle fashion through the maize, cabbage and banana plantations of the Moei valley. The fun really begins when you start climbing into the mountains and the road – accurately dubbed the **"Sky Highway"** – careers round the edges of endless steep-sided valleys, undulating like a fairground rollercoaster (if you're prone to car-sickness take some preventative tablets before setting out). Karen, Akha and Lisu people live in the few hamlets along the route, many growing cabbages along the cleared lower slopes with the help of government incentives (part of a national campaign to steer upland farmers away from the opium trade).

Surrounded by mountains and sited at the confluence of the Mae Khlong and Umpang rivers, Umpang itself is quiet and sleepy, made up of little more than a thousand or so wooden houses, a few tiny general stores, a post office, a police station, a primary school and a wat. It won't take you long to explore the minute grid of dusty tracks that dissects the village, but as tourists are rare you'll spend a lot of time with interested locals.

As for **things to do**, the village has its own year-round trekking operation, *Yai and Dick Jungle Tour*, which operates from Yai's house close to the wat at 172 Prawet Prai Wan Rd, along the road from the songthaew stop. A three-day/two-night trek should cost around B2000 per person and will take in the three-tiered **Tee Lor Su Waterfall**, said to be the sixth largest falls in the world; during the dry season you can get halfway there by road, but otherwise it's reached by a combination of rafting and walking.

Practicalities

Most of the **accommodation** in Umpang is geared towards groups of trekkers accompanied by Thai guides, but independent travellers, though unusual, are welcome. The two best places to stay are at the far end of the village, 500m southwest of the songthaew stop, on either side of the Mae Khlong River. *Umphang Hill Resort* (☎055/561063; ②–⑤) is beautifully set in a flower garden on a grassy slope leading down to the water, with fantastic views of the surrounding mountains. The choice here ranges from simple but attractive "ox-cart" huts arranged pioneer-style round a camp fire, to upscale, air-conditioned chalets with huge verandahs. Across the river, the friendly *Boonyaporn Garden Huts* (☎055/561093; ②–③) has both simple and mid-range huts as well as a restaurant. Closer to the heart of the village, *Umphang House* (☎055/561073; ②) has a series of inexpensive but unsightly concrete bunker-like rooms and a few more atmospheric four-person huts. Trekkers sometimes stay at *Gift* (①), which is 2km out of Umpang, on the road to Mae Sot, but there's little point staying here unless you've got your own transport or you're with an organized trip.

All the above places to stay serve **food** to their guests, and the *Boonyaporn Garden Hut* restaurant is open to non-residents as well. Alternatively, there are half a dozen tiny eateries in the village centre and a bigger restaurant, serving meat-and-curry-over-rice dishes, right next to the songthaew stop.

travel details

Trains

Ayutthaya to: Bangkok Hualamphong (20 daily; 1hr 30min); Chiang Mai (5 daily; 12hr); Lopburi (12 daily; 1hr–1hr 30min); Nong Khai (3 daily; 9hr 30min); Phitsanulok (9 daily; 5hr); Ubon Ratchathani (6 daily; 8hr 30min–10hr).

Kanchanaburi to: Bangkok Noi (2 daily; 2hr 40min); Nam Tok (3 daily; 2hr).

Lopburi to: Bangkok Hualamphong (12 daily; 2hr 30min–3hr), via Ayutthaya (1hr–1hr 30min); Chiang Mai (5 daily; 11hr); Phitsanulok (9 daily; 4hr).

Nakhon Pathom to: Bangkok Hualamphong (10 daily; 1hr 20min); Bangkok Noi (3 daily; 1hr 10min); Nakhon Si Thammarat (up to 9 daily; 15hr), via Phetchaburi (2hr 50min–3hr 15min) and Surat Thani (9hr–11hr 30min); Nam Tok (2 daily; 4hr 20min–4hr 50min), via Kanchanaburi (1hr 25min).

Nam Tok to: Bangkok Noi (2 daily; 4hr 35min).

Phitsanulok to: Bangkok Hualamphong (9 daily; 6hr 15min–9hr 30min); Chiang Mai (4 daily; 7hr 10min–8hr).

Buses

Ayutthaya to: Bangkok (every 15min; 2hr); Bang Pa-In (every 30min; 30min); Chiang Mai (12 daily; 8hr); Lopburi (every 30min; 3hr); Phitsanulok (9 daily; 4–5hr); Sukhothai (6 daily; 6hr); Suphanburi (every 30min; 1hr 40min).

Bang Pa-In to: Bangkok (every 20min; 2hr).

Damnoen Saduak to: Bangkok (every 20min; 2hr).

Kamphaeng Phet to: Tak (hourly; 1hr).

Kanchanaburi to: Bangkok (every 15min; 2–3hr); Sai Yok (every 30min; 2hr 30min), via Nam Tok (1hr 30min); Sangkhlaburi (14 daily; 3–5hr); Suphanburi (every 30min; 2hr).

Lopburi to: Bangkok (every 15min; 3hr), via Wat Phra Phutthabat (30min); Khorat (every 30min; 3hr).

Mae Sot to: Phitsanulok (1 daily; 5hr); Tak (every 30min; 1hr 30min–3hr); Umpang (at least 5 daily; 3hr 30min–5hr).

Nakhon Pathom to: Bangkok (every 10min; 40min–1hr 20min); Damnoen Saduak (every 20min; 1hr); Kanchanaburi (every 10min; 1hr 20min).

Nam Tok to: Sangkhlaburi (5 daily; 3hr 30min).

Phitsanulok to: Bangkok (up to 19 daily; 5–6hr); Chiang Mai (up to 18 daily; 5–6hr); Chiang Rai (9 daily; 6–7hr); Kamphaeng Phet (hourly; 3hr); Khon Kaen (13 daily; 5hr); Khorat/ Nakhon Ratchasima (10 daily; 6–7hr); Loei (9 daily; 4hr); Phrae (hourly; 3hr); Sukhothai (every 30min; 1hr); Tak (hourly; 2–3hr).

Sukhothai to: Bangkok (up to 17 daily; 6–7hr); Chiang Mai (up to 16 daily; 5–6hr); Kamphaeng Phet (hourly; 2hr); Si Satchanalai (every 30min; 1hr); Tak (every 90min; 2hr).

Tak to: Mae Sot (every 30min; 1hr 30min–3hr).

Flights

Mae Sot to: Chiang Mai (4 weekly; 50 min); Phitsanulok (4 weekly; 45min).

Phitsanulok to: Bangkok (2–3 daily; 50min); Chiang Mai (daily; 2hr), via Mae Sot (4 weekly; 45min) or Nan (3 weekly; 55min).

CHAPTER THREE

THE NORTH

T ravelling up through the central plains, there's no mistaking when you've reached the **north** of Thailand: somewhere between Uttaradit and Den Chai, the train slows almost to a halt, as if approaching a frontier post, to meet the abruptly rising mountains, which continue largely unbroken to the borders of Burma and Laos. Beyond this point the climate becomes more temperate, nurturing the fertile land which gave the old kingdom of the north the name of **Lanna**, "the land of a million ricefields". Although only one-tenth of the land can be used for rice cultivation, the valley ricefields here are three times more productive than those in the dusty northeast, and the higher land yields a great variety of fruits, as well as beans, groundnuts, tobacco and, notoriously, opium.

Until the beginning of this century, Lanna was a largely independent region. On the back of its agricultural prosperity, it developed its own styles of art and architecture, which can still be seen in its flourishing temples and distinctive handicraft traditions. The north is also set apart from the rest of the country by its exuberant way with festivals, a cuisine which has been heavily influenced by Burma and a dialect quite distinct from central Thai. Northerners proudly call themselves *khon muang*, "people of the principalities", and their gentle sophistication is admired by the people of Bangkok, whose wealthier citizens build their holiday homes in the clean air of the north's forested mountains.

Chiang Mai, the capital and transport centre of the north, is a place to relax before setting off into the hills. For many travellers, this means joining a trek to visit one or more of the **hill tribes**, who comprise one-tenth of the north's population and are just about clinging on to the ways of life which distinguish them from each other and the Thais around them. For those with qualms about the exploitative element of this ethnological tourism, there are plenty of other, more independent options. To the west, the trip to **Mae Hong Son** takes you through the most stunning mountain scenery in the region into a land with its roots across the border in Burma. Heading north from Chiang Mai brings you to **Chiang Rai**, which is making a bid to rival Chiang Mai as a base for exploring the countryside. Above Chiang Rai, the northernmost tip of Thailand is marked by the fascinating, schizophrenic border town of **Mae Sai**, and the junction of Laos and Burma at **Sop Ruak**. Fancifully dubbed the "Golden Triangle", Sop Ruak is a must on every bus party's itinerary – you're more likely to find peace and quiet among the ruins of nearby **Chiang Saen**, set on the leafy banks of the Mekhong River. Few visitors backtrack south from Chiang Mai, even though the towns of **Lamphun** and **Lampang** are packed with artistic and historical goodies. Further out on a limb to the east, **Nan** is even less popular, but combines rich mountain scenery with eclectic temple art.

The forecast explosion of trade and tourism across the northern frontiers, forming a "Golden Quadrangle" of Thailand, Burma, China and Laos, remains for now a mere squib, as Thailand, with only limited success, tries to cajole the others into relaxing their entry restrictions. Setting aside crossings to Laos from

Isaan, your options for leaving Thailand in this direction are currently restricted to expensive and often arduous trips to Burma and China, from Mae Sai and Chiang Saen (although trips from the latter are organized in Chiang Rai), and twice-weekly flights from Chiang Mai to Kunming (B3540 single, B4960 return).

Transport routes in northern Thailand are necessarily roundabout and bus services often slow, though frequent: in some cases, it's worth considering hopping over the mountains by plane. To appreciate the landscape fully, many people take to the open roads on rented **motorbikes**, which are available in most northern towns and relatively inexpensive – Chiang Mai has the best choice, followed by Chiang Rai. You should be cautious about biking in the north, however. The border police may stop you from venturing into an area that's considered too dangerous, but don't ride alone on any remote trails – there have been incidents where lone riders have been shot.

Some history

The first civilization to leave an indelible mark on the north was **Haripunjaya**, the Mon (Dvaravati) state which was founded at Lamphun in the ninth century. Maintaining strong ties with the Mon kingdoms to the south, it remained the cultural and religious centre of the north for four centuries. The Thais came onto the scene after the Mons, migrating down from China between the seventh and the eleventh centuries and establishing small principalities around the north. The prime mover for the Thais was **King Mengrai** of Ngon Yang, who shortly after the establishment of a Thai state at Sukhothai in the middle of the thirteenth century, set to work on a parallel unified state in the north. By 1296, when he began the construction of Chiang Mai, which has remained the capital of the north ever since, he had brought the whole of the north under his control and at his death in 1317 he had established a dynasty which was to oversee a 200-year period of unmatched prosperity and cultural activity.

However, after the expansionist reign of Tilok (1441–87), a series of weak, squabbling kings came and went, while Ayutthaya increased its unfriendly advances. But it was the **Burmese** who finally snuffed out the Mengrai dynasty by capturing Chiang Mai in 1558, and for most of the next two centuries, they controlled Lanna through a succession of puppet rulers. In 1767, the Burmese sacked the Thai capital at Ayutthaya, but the Thais soon regrouped under King Taksin, who with the help of **King Kawila** of Lampang gradually drove the Burmese northwards.

Kawila was succeeded as ruler of the north by a series of incompetent princes for much of the nineteenth century, until colonialism reared its head. After the British took control of Upper Burma, **Rama V** of Bangkok began to take an interest in the north to prevent its annexation. He forcibly moved large numbers of ethnic Thais northwards, in order to counter the British claim of sovereignty over territory occupied by Thai Yai (Shan), who also make up a large part of the population of Upper Burma. In 1877 Rama V appointed a high commissioner in Chiang Mai, and since then the north has built on its agricultural richness to become relatively prosperous. However, the recent economic boom has been concentrated, as elsewhere in Thailand, in the towns, due in no small part to the increase in tourism. The eighty percent of Lanna's population who live in rural areas, of which the vast majority are subsistence farmers, are finding it increasingly difficult to earn a living off the soil, due to rapid population growth and land speculation for tourism and agro-industry.

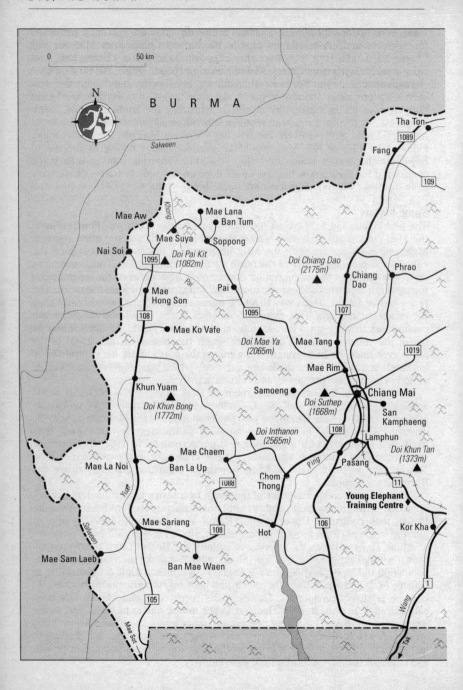

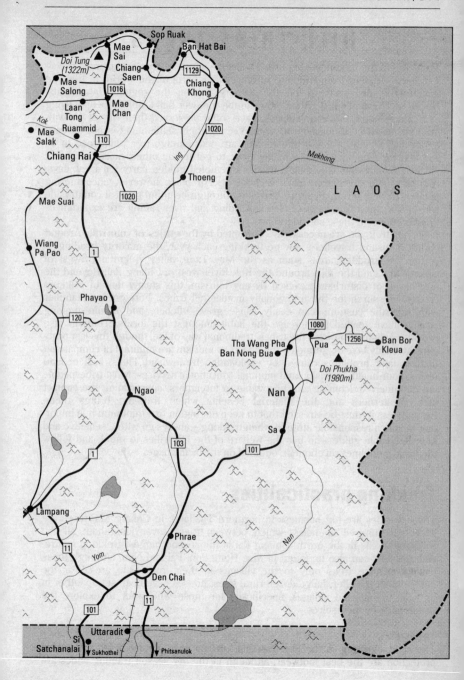

HILL-TRIBE TREKS

Trekking in the mountains of north Thailand – which is what brings most travellers here – differs from trekking in most other parts of the world, in that the emphasis is not primarily on the scenery but on the region's inhabitants. Northern Thailand's **hill tribes**, now numbering over half a million people living in as many as ten thousand villages, have so far preserved their way of life with little change over thousands of years. Visiting their settlements is not an easy enterprise, as only a few of the villages are near enough to a main road to be reached on a day trip from a major town: to get to the other, more traditional villages usually entails joining a hastily assembled guided party for a few days, roughing it in a different place each night. For most, however, encountering peoples of so different a culture, travelling through beautiful tropical countryside and tasting the excitement of elephant riding and river rafting are experiences that far outweigh these considerations.

On any trek you are necessarily confronted by the **ethics** of your role. Around eighty thousand travellers now go trekking each year, the majority heading to certain well-trodden areas such as the Mae Tang valley, 40km northwest of Chiang Mai, and the hills around the Kok River west of Chiang Rai. Beyond the basic level of disturbance caused by any tourism, this steady flow of trekkers creates pressures for the traditionally insular hill tribes. Foreigners unfamiliar with hill-tribe customs can easily cause grave offence, and opium-smoking farangs have tended to increase the habit amongst the locals. Tourism also provides a distraction from the tribes' traditional way of life, though this last problem can easily be exaggerated – the effects of tourism are minimal in comparison to the major problems caused by exploitation by lowland Thais, lack of land rights, poor health provision and minimal educational services. Most tribespeople are genuinely welcoming and hospitable to foreigners, appreciating the contact with Westerners and the material benefits which trekking brings them. Nonetheless it must be stressed that to keep disruption to a minimum it is important to take a responsible attitude when trekking – always go with a sensitive and knowledgeable guide who has the welfare of the hill tribes in mind, and follow the basic guidelines on etiquette outlined on the facing page.

Trekking practicalities

The hill tribes are big business in northern Thailand: in Chiang Mai there are over two hundred agencies, which between them cover just about all the trekkable areas in the north. Chiang Rai is the second biggest trekking centre, and agencies can also be found in Mae Hong Son, Pai and Nan, although these usually arrange treks only to the villages in their immediate area. For the independent traveller, half a dozen rural guest houses have been set up either in or near to hill-tribe villages, specifically for those who want to explore the countryside by themselves.

The basics

The right **clothing** is the first essential on any trek. Strong boots with ankle protection are the best footwear, although in the dry season training shoes are

TREKKING ETIQUETTE

As the guests, it's up to farangs to adapt to the customs of the hill tribes and not to make a nuisance of themselves. Apart from keeping an open mind and not demanding too much of your hosts, a few simple rules should be observed.

● Dress modestly, in long trousers or skirt and a T-shirt or shirt.

● Loud voices and boisterous behaviour are out of place. Smiling and nodding establishes good intent.

● Most hill-tribe houses contain a religious shrine. Do not touch or photograph this shrine, or sit underneath it.

● Some villagers like to be photographed, most do not. Point at your camera and nod if you want to take a photograph. Never insist if the answer is an obvious "no". Be particularly careful with pregnant women and babies – most tribes believe cameras affect the soul of the foetus or new-born.

● Taking gifts is dubious practice: writing materials for children are very welcome, but sweets and cigarettes may encourage begging.

● Smoking opium on a trek is a big attraction for many travellers, but there is evidence of increased addiction rates among hill-tribe villagers who are regularly visited by trekkers.

adequate. Long trousers should be worn, to protect against thorns and, in the wet season, leeches. Wear thin, loose clothing and a hat, and cover your arms if prone to sunburn. Antiseptic, antihistamine, anti-diarrhoea **medicine** and insect repellant are essential, and a mosquito net is a good idea. At least two changes of clothing are needed, plus a sarong or towel.

If you're going on an organized trek, **water** is usually provided by the guide, as well as a small backpack. **Blankets** are also supplied, but rarely enough in the cool season, when night-time temperatures can dip to freezing – you should bring a sleeping bag, and a sweater, to be sure of keeping the chill off.

It's wise not to take anything valuable with you – most banks in the north have safe-deposit boxes in which you can leave small items (though in Chiang Mai these are difficult to obtain. Trekkers have occasionally been robbed by bandits, although the Border Patrol Police have recently increased their activities in trekking areas to provide better security. If there is a robbery attempt, don't resist.

Organized treks

Organized treks can be as short as two days or as long as fifteen, but are typically of three days' duration. Each trek usually follows a regular itinerary established by the agency, although they can sometimes be customized, especially for smaller groups and with agencies in the smaller towns. Some itineraries are geared towards serious hikers while others go at a much gentler pace, but on all treks much of the walking will be up and down steep forested hills, often under a burning sun, so a minimum fitness level is required. Many treks now include a ride on an elephant and a trip on a bamboo raft – exciting to the point of being dangerous if the river is running fast. The typical trek costs about B1500 in Chiang Mai, often less in other towns, and much less without rafting and elephant riding.

Between eight and ten people is a standard size for a trekking group, but a **party of four** is preferable, enabling you to strike a more informative relationship with your guides and with the villagers. Everybody in the group usually sleeps on a bamboo floor or platform in the headman's hut, with a guide cooking communal meals, the ingredients for which are generally brought from outside, since the effects of hill-tribe food are unpredictable.

When **choosing a trek**, there are several features to look out for. If you want to trek with a small group, get an assurance from your agency that you won't be tagged onto a larger group. A trek should have at least two guides – a leader and a back-marker; tourists have got lost for days by losing touch with the rest of the group. Ask about transport from base at the beginning and end of the trek, since sometimes the trip can entail a long public bus ride. Meet the guides, who should speak reasonable English and know about hill-tribe culture, especially the details of etiquette in each village. Finally, ask what food will be eaten, check how much walking is involved per day, and get a copy of the route map to gauge the terrain.

Recommending particular **agencies** is difficult, as names change and standards rise and fall. However, you should check whether the guide has a licence – and a certificate which he or she should be able to show you – from the Tourism Authority of Thailand: this ensures at least a minimum level of training, and provides some comeback in case of problems. TAT further recommends using agencies which are members of local clubs such as the Jungle Tour Club of Chiang Mai; alternatively, word of mouth is often the best recommendation, so if you hear of a good one, try it. Each trek should be **registered** with the Tourist Police, stating the itinerary, the duration and the participants, in case the party encounters any trouble – it's worth checking with the tourist police that your agency has done this before departure.

Independent trekking

Unfortunately, the options for independent trekking are limited, chiefly by the poor mapping of the area. Only Hongsombud's *Guide Map of Chiang Rai* (Bangkok Guides) offers anything like adequate detail, as it includes 1:1000 maps of the more popular chunks of the province. For other areas of the north, you can consult the maps at the **Hill Tribe Research Institute** at Chiang Mai University (Mon–Fri 9am–noon & 1–4pm), between Huai Kaeo and Suthep roads, which mark the villages where people can stay.

For most independent travellers, the only feasible approach is to use as a base one of the half-dozen or so **guest houses** specifically geared for farangs in various parts of the north. They're generally set deep in the countryside, within walking range of several hill-tribe villages, about which the owner can give information in English. Conditions in these guest houses are usually spartan, but the food should be safe to eat. All these guest houses are covered in the relevant parts of this chapter, and listed in the box below.

If you're confident about finding your way round, it's possible to find **accommodation in hill-tribe villages**. It helps if you speak some Thai, but most villagers, if

---

GUEST HOUSES FOR INDEPENDENT TREKKING

Between Mae Hong Son and Pai: *Wilderness Lodge* near Mae Suya; *Mae Lana Guest House* at Mae Lana; *Cave Lodge* at Ban Tum.

Between Chiang Mai and Chiang Rai: *Trekker House* near Ban Sop Pong.

North of Chiang Rai: *Laan Tong Lodge* between Mae Chan and Tha Ton.

you hang around for any time, will ask if you want to stay with the usual "sleep" gesture. It is usual to stay in the headman's house on a guest platform, but increasingly villages are building small guest houses. Expect to pay B50 per night – for this, you will often be offered dinner and breakfast. It's safe to accept plain rice, boiled drinks and food that's boiled or fried in your presence, but you're taking a risk with anything else, as it's not unusual for foreigners to suffer food poisoning.

Most villages are safe to stay in, but trekking this way leaves you particularly vulnerable to armed bandits who sporadically rob foreigners. If possible check with the Hill Tribe Research Institute, and with local guides and the district police in the area where you intend to trek. Furthermore, the lone trekker will learn very little without a guide as intermediary, and is far more likely to commit an unwitting offence against the local customs.

The hill tribes

Originating in various parts of China and Southeast Asia, the hill tribes are often termed Fourth World people, in that they are migrants who continue to migrate without regard for established national boundaries. Most arrived in Thailand during this century, and many of the hill peoples are still also found in other parts of Southeast Asia – in Vietnam, for example, where the French used the *montagnards* in their fight against communism.

Called **chao khao** (mountain people) by the Thais, the tribes are mostly pre-literate societies, whose sophisticated systems of customs, laws and beliefs have developed to harmonize relationships between individuals and their environment. In recent years, with the effects of rapid population growth and ensuing competition for land, of discrimination and exploitation by lowland Thais, and of tourism, their ancient culture has come under threat, but the integrity of their way of life is as yet largely undamaged, and what follows is the briefest of introductions to an immensely complex subject. If you want to learn more, the small museum and library at the Hill Tribe Research Institute in Chiang Mai (see previous page) are worth a visit, as is the *Hill Tribe Museum and Handicrafts Shop* in Chiang Rai.

Agriculture
Although the hill tribes keep some livestock such as pigs, poultry and elephants, the base of their economy is **slash-and-burn farming**, a crude form of shifting cultivation also practised by many Thai lowland farmers. At the beginning of the season an area of jungle is cleared and burned, producing ash to fertilize rice, corn, chillies and other vegetables, which are replanted in succeeding years until the soil's nutrients are exhausted. This system is sustainable with a low population density, which allows the jungle time to recover before it is used again. However, with the increase in population over the last thirty years, ever greater areas are being exhausted and the decreasing forest cover is leading to erosion and micro-climatic change.

As a result, many villages have taken up the large-scale production of **opium** to supplement the traditional subsistence crops. With some success the government has attempted to stamp out opium cultivation, but the cash crops which have been introduced in its place have often led to further environmental damage, as these low-profit crops require larger areas of cultivation, and thus greater deforestation. Furthermore, the water supplies have become polluted with chemical pesticides, and although more environmentally sensitive agricultural techniques are being introduced, they have yet to achieve widespread acceptance. Meanwhile, progress towards long-term solutions is hindered by the resentment of neighbouring Thais against whatever projects are set up to help the hill tribes, and the uncertainty of the tribes' legal position: few have identity cards, and without citizenship they have no rights to the land they inhabit.

Religion and festivals

Although some have taken up Buddhism and others – especially among the Karen, Mien and Lahu – have been converted by Christian missionaries bringing the material incentives of education and modern medicine, the hill tribes are predominantly **animists**. In this belief system, all natural objects are inhabited by spirits, which, along with the tribe's ancestor spirits and the supreme divine spirit, must be propitiated to prevent harm to the family or village. Most villages have two religious leaders, a priest who looks after the ritual life of the community, and a shaman who has the power to mediate with the spirits and prescribe what has to be done to keep them happy. If a member of the community is sick, for example, the shaman will be consulted to determine what action has insulted which spirit, and will then carry out the correct sacrifice.

The most important festival, celebrated by all the tribes, is at **New Year**, when whole communities take part in dancing, music and rituals particular to each tribe: Hmong boys and girls, for instance, take part in a courting ritual at this time, while playing catch with a ball. The New Year festivals are not held on fixed dates, but at various times during the cool-season slack period in the agricultural cycle from January to March.

Costumes and handicrafts

The most conspicuous characteristics of the hill tribes are their exquisitely crafted **costumes** and adornments, the styles and colours of which are particular to each group. Although many men and children are adopting Western clothes for everyday wear, most women still wear the traditional attire at all times, and it's the women who make the clothes – most still spin their own cotton, but some Hmong, Lisu and Mien women are prosperous enough to buy materials from itinerant traders. Other distinctive hill-tribe artefacts – tools, jewellery, weapons and musical instruments – are the domain of the men, and specialist **blacksmiths** and **silversmiths** have such high status that some attract business from villages many kilometres away. Jewellery, the chief outward proof of a family's wealth, is displayed most obviously by women at the New Year festivals, and is commonly made from silver melted down from Indian and Burmese coins, though brass, copper and aluminium are also used.

Clothing and handicrafts were not regarded as marketable products until the early 1980s, when cooperatives were set up to manufacture and market these goods, which are now big business in the shops of Thailand. The hill tribes' deep-dyed coarse cloth, embroidered with simple geometric patterns in bright colours, has become popular among middle-class Thais as well as farang visitors. Mien material, dyed indigo or black with bright snowflake embroidery, is on sale in many shops, as is the simple but very distinctive Akha work – coarse black cotton, with triangular patterns of stitching and small fabric patches in rainbow colours, usually made up into bags and hats. The Hmong's much more sophisticated embroidery and appliqué, added to jacket lapels and cuffs and skirt hems, is also widely seen – Blue Hmong skirts, made on a base of indigo-dyed cotton with a white geometric batik design and embroidered in loud primary colours, are particularly attractive.

Besides clothing, the hill tribes' other handicrafts, such as knives and wooden or bamboo musical pipes, have found a market amongst farangs, the most saleable product being the intricate engraving work of their silversmiths, especially in the form of chunky bracelets. For a sizeable minority of villages, handicrafts now provide the security of a steady income to supplement what they make from farming.

The main tribes

Within the small geographical area of northern Thailand there are at least ten different hill tribes, many of them divided into distinct sub groups – the following are the main seven, listed in order of population and under their own names, rather than the sometimes derogatory names used by Thais. (The Thai Yai – or Shan – the dominant group in most of the west of the region, are not a hill tribe, but a subgroup of Thais.) Beyond the broad similarities outlined above, this section sketches their differences in terms of history, economy and religion, and describes elements of dress by which they can be distinguished.

Karen

The **Karen** (called Kaliang or Yang in Thai) form by far the largest hill-tribe group in Thailand with a population of about 300,000, and are the second oldest after the

Lawa, having begun to arrive here from Burma and China in the seventeenth century. The Thai Karen, many of them refugees from Burma (see p.204), mostly live in a broad tract of land west of Chiang Mai, which stretches along the border from Mae Hong Son province all the way down to Kanchanaburi, with scattered pockets in Chiang Mai, Chiang Rai and Phayao provinces.

The Karen traditionally practise a system of rotating cultivation which is ecologically far more sensitive than slash-and-burn in the valleys of this region and on low hills. Their houses are small (they do not live in extended family groups) and are very similar to those of lowland Thais: built on stilts and made of bamboo or teak, they're often surrounded by fruit gardens and neat fences. As well as farming their own land, they often hire out their labour to Thais and other hill tribes, and they keep a variety of livestock including elephants, which used to be employed in the teak trade but are now often found giving rides to trekking parties.

Unmarried Karen women wear loose white or undyed V-necked blouses, decorated with grass seeds at the seams. Married women wear blouses and skirts in bold colours, predominantly red or blue. Men generally wear blue, baggy trousers with red or blue shirts, a simplified version of the women's blouse.

Karen woman

Hmong

Called the Meo by the Thais (a term meaning "barbarian"), the **Hmong** (free people) originated in central China or Mongolia and are now found widely in northern Thailand. There are two subgroups: the **Blue Hmong**, who live around and to the west of Chiang Mai; and the **White Hmong**, who are found to the east. A separate group of White Hmong live in refugee camps along the border with Laos: they fled from Laos after the end of the Vietnam War, during which they had sided with the Americans. Their overall population in Thailand is about seventy thousand, making them the second-largest hill-tribe group.

Of all the hill tribes, the Hmong have been the quickest to move away from subsistence farming. Many villages grow opium for sale, although many others have eagerly embraced the newer cash crops. Hmong clothing has become much in demand in Thailand, and Hmong women will often be seen at markets throughout the country selling their handicrafts. The women, in fact, are expected to do most of the work on the land and in the home.

Hmong villages are usually built at high altitudes, below the crest of a protecting hill. Although wealthier families sometimes build the more comfortable Thai-style houses, most stick to the traditional house, with its dirt floor and a roof descending almost to ground level. They live together in extended families, with two or more bedrooms and a large guest platform.

Hmong child

The Blue Hmong dress in especially striking clothes. The women wear intricately embroidered pleated skirts decorated with parallel horizontal bands of red, pink, blue and white; their jackets are of black satin, with wide orange and yellow embroidered cuffs and lapels. White Hmong women wear black baggy trousers and simple jackets with blue cuffs. Men of both groups generally wear baggy black pants with colourful sashes round the waist, and embroidered jackets closing over the chest with a button at the left shoulder. All the Hmong are famous for their chunky silver jewellery, which the women wear every day and the men only on special occasions: they believe silver binds a person's spirits together, and wear a heavy neck ring to keep the spirits weighed down in the body.

Lahu

The **Lahu** originated in southwest China and have migrated into Thailand from northern Burma since the end of the last century. They're called Muser, from the Burmese word for "hunter", by the Thais, because many of the first Lahu to reach northern Thailand were professional hunters. Most of their settlements are concentrated close to the Burmese border, in Chiang Rai, northern Chiang Mai and Mae Hong Son provinces, but families and villages change locations frequently. The Lahu language has become the *lingua franca* of the hill tribes, since the Lahu often hire out their labour. About one-third of Lahu have been converted to Christianity, and many have abandoned their traditional way of life as a result. The remaining animist Lahu believe in a village guardian spirit, who is often worshipped at a central temple that is surrounded by banners and streamers of white and yellow flags. Ordinary houses are built on high stilts with walls of bamboo or wooden planks, thatched with grass.

Some Lahu women wear a distinctive black cloak with diagonal white stripes, decorated in bold red and yellow at the top of the sleeve, but traditional costume has been supplanted by the Thai shirt and sarong amongst many Lahu groups. The tribe is famous for its richly embroidered *yaam* (shoulder bags), which are widely available in Chiang Mai.

Mien

The **Mien** (called Yao in Thai) consider themselves the aristocrats of the hill tribes. Originating in southern China, where they used to have such power that at one time a Mien princess was married to a Chinese emperor, the Mien are now widely scattered throughout the north, with concentrations around Nan, Phayao and Chiang Rai. The Mien are the only hill tribe to have a written language, and a codified religion based on medieval Chinese Taoism, although in recent years there have been many converts to Christianity and Buddhism.

In general, the Mien strike a balance between integration into Thai life and maintenance of their separate cultural base. Many earn extra cash by selling exquisite embroidery and religious scrolls, painted in bold Chinese style, and the number of villages which grow opium is declining rapidly, as the Mien begin to adopt new cash crops.

Mien villages, which are never sited below those of other tribes, are not especially distinctive: their houses are usually built of wooden planks on a dirt floor, with a guest platform of bamboo in the communal living area. The clothes of the women, however, are instantly recognizable: long black jackets with lapels of bright scarlet wool, heavily embroidered loose trousers in intricate designs which can take up to two years to complete, and a similarly embroidered

Mien woman

black turban. The caps of babies are also very beautiful, richly embroidered with red or pink pom-poms. On special occasions, women and children wear silver neck rings, with silver chains decorated with silver ornaments extending down the back.

Akha

The poorest of the hill tribes, the **Akha** (Kaw or Eekaw in Thai) migrated from Tibet over two thousand years ago to Yunnan in China, where at some stage they had an organized state and kept written chronicles of their history – these chronicles, like the Akha written language, are now lost. From the 1910s the tribe began to settle in Thailand, mostly in Chiang Rai and northern Chiang Mai province.

The Akha are less open to change than the other hill tribes, and have maintained their old agricultural methods – though many Akha villages grow opium

OPIUM AND THE GOLDEN TRIANGLE

The production of **opium** has been illegal in Thailand since 1959, and with concerted attempts by the government to eliminate it, the size of the crop has been reduced by eighty percent in the last decade, to around 20 tonnes per year. Opium nevertheless remains an important cash crop of the Hmong, Yao, Lahu and Lisu hill tribes, and Thailand has now become an important conduit for opium from Burma and Laos, where production stands at 2500 tonnes per year and is still rising.

For the hill farmers, the attractions of the opium poppy are difficult to resist. It's an easy crop to grow, even on almost barren land; it's a highly productive plant, with each flower pod being tapped several times for its sap; and it yields a high value for a small volume – around B500 per kilo at source. Refined into heroin and transported to the US – the world's biggest market – the value of the powder is as much as ten thousand times greater.

The small-scale heroin refineries in the lawless region on the borders of Thailand, Burma and Laos have become so successful that the area has earned the nickname the "**Golden Triangle**". Two "armies" operate most of the trade within this area. The **Shan United Army**, which is fighting the Burmese government for an independent state for the Shan people, funds its weapons and manpower from the production of heroin. Led by the notorious warlord Khun Sa, the Shan United Army attempted to extend their influence inside Thailand during the 1960s, where they came up against the **Kuomintang** (KMT). These refugees from China, who fled after the communist takeover there, were at first befriended by the Thai and Western governments, who were pleased to have a fiercely anti-communist force patrolling this border area. The Kuomintang were thus able to develop the heroin trade, while the authorities turned a blind eye.

The Kuomintang and Shan armies were once powerful enough to operate unhindered. In the last ten years, though, the danger of communist incursion into Thailand has largely disappeared, and the government has been able to concentrate on the elimination of the crop. In 1983 the Shan United Army was pushed out of its stronghold at Ban Hin Taek near Mae Salong, and over the border into Burma, and the Kuomintang in the surrounding area have been put on a determined "pacification" programme. With the destruction of huge areas of poppy fields, it has been necessary for the Thai government to give the hill tribes an alternative livelihood through the introduction of more legitimate cash crops. Yet opium cultivation continues in remote valleys, hidden from the Thai authorities, and opium abuse among the hill tribes themselves is if anything getting worse: over thirty percent of Hmong men, for example, are addicted.

for their own consumption, creating a major problem of addiction, especially amongst the older men. The Akha's form of animism – *Akhazang*, "the way of life of the Akha" – has also survived in uncompromised form. As well as spirits in the natural world, *Akhazang* encompasses the worship of ancestor spirits: some Akha can recite the names of over sixty generations of forebears.

Every Akha village is entered through ceremonial gates decorated with carvings of human activities and attributes – even cars and aeroplanes – to indicate to the spirit world that beyond here only humans should pass. To touch any of these carvings, or to show any lack of respect to them, is punishable by fines or sacrifices. The gates are rebuilt or replaced every year, so many villages have a series of gates, the older ones in a state of disintegration. Another characteristic of all Akha villages is its giant swing, used every August in a swinging festival in which the whole population takes part.

Akha houses are recognizable by their low stilts and steeply pitched roofs. Even more distinctive is the elaborate headgear which women wear all day: it frames the entire face and usually consists of a conical wedge of white beads interspersed with silver coins and topped with plumes of red taffeta. The rest of their heavy costume is made up of hooped leggings, a short black skirt with a white beaded centrepiece, and a loose fitting black jacket with heavily embroidered cuffs and lapels.

Lisu

The **Lisu** (Lisaw in Thai), who originated in eastern Tibet, first arrived in Thailand in 1921 and are found mostly in the west, particularly between Chiang Mai and Mae Hong Son, but also in western Chiang Rai, Chiang Mai and Phayao provinces. Whereas the other hill tribes are led by the village headman or shaman, the Lisu are organized into patriarchal clans which have authority over many villages, and their strong sense of clan rivalry often results in public violence. Many Lisu villages are involved in the opium trade, but addiction rates are declining and the Lisu are turning increasingly to alternative cash-crop production.

The Lisu live in extended families at moderate to high altitudes, in houses built on the ground, with dirt floors and bamboo walls. Both men and women dress colourfully. The women wear a blue or green parti-coloured knee-length tunic, split up the sides to the waist, with a wide black belt and blue or green pants. At New Year, dazzling outfits are worn by the women, including waistcoats and belts of intricately fashioned silver and turbans with multicoloured pom-poms and streamers. Men wear green, pink or yellow baggy pants and a blue jacket.

Lawa

The history of the Lawa people (Lua in Thai) is poorly understood, but it seems very likely that they have inhabited Thailand since at least the eighth century and they were certainly here when the Thais arrived eight hundred years ago. The Lawa believe that they migrated from Cambodia, but some archaeologists think that their origins lie in Micronesia, which they left perhaps two thousand years back.

This lengthy cohabitation with the Thais has produced large-scale integration, so that most Lawa villages are indistinguishable from Thai settlements and most Lawa speak Thai as their first language. However, in an area of about 500 square kilometres between Hot, Mae Sariang and Mae Hong Son, the Lawa still live a largely traditional life, although even here the majority have adopted Buddhism and Thai-style houses. The basis of their economy is subsistence agriculture, with rice grown on terraces according to a sophisticated rotation system.

Unmarried Lawa women wear distinctive strings of orange and yellow beads, loose white blouses edged with pink, and tight skirts in parallel bands of blue, black, yellow and pink. After marriage, these brightly coloured clothes are replaced with a long fawn dress, but the beads are still worn. All the women wear their hair tied in a turban, and the men wear light-coloured baggy pants and tunics or, more commonly, Western clothes.

Lawa woman

CHIANG MAI

Although rapid economic progress in recent years – due largely to tourism – has brought its share of problems, **CHIANG MAI** manages to preserve some of the atmosphere of an overgrown village alongside its urban sophistication. A population of two hundred thousand makes this the country's second city, but the contrast with the maelstrom of Bangkok could scarcely be more pronounced: the people are famously easy-going and even speak more slowly than their cousins in the capital, while the old quarter, set within a two-kilometre-square moat, has retained many of its traditional wooden houses and quiet, leafy gardens. Chiang Mai's elegant temples are the primary tourist sights, but these are no pre-packaged museum pieces – they're living community centres, where you're quite likely to be approached by monks keen to chat and practise their English. Inviting craft shops, rich cuisine and riverside bars further enhance the city's allure, making Chiang Mai a place that detains many travellers longer than they expected.

Chiang Mai – "New City" – was **founded** as the capital of Lanna in 1296, on a site indicated by the miraculous presence of deer and white mice, and it has remained the north's most important city ever since. Lanna's golden age under the Mengrai dynasty, when most of the city's notable temples were founded, lasted until the Burmese captured Chiang Mai in 1556. Two hundred years passed before the Thais pushed the Burmese back beyond Chiang Mai to roughly where they are now, and the **Burmese influence** is still strong – not just in art and architecture, but also in the rich curries and soups served here, which are better "Burmese" food than you can find in modern-day Burma. After the recapture of the city, the *chao* (princes) of Chiang Mai remained nominal rulers of the north until 1939, but with communications rapidly improving from the beginning of this century, Chiang Mai was brought firmly into Thailand's mainstream as the region's administrative and service centre. Plans for the city's **700th anniversary** in 1996 look set to include a Thai and English *son et lumière* on the history of Chiang Mai in April, the most important month of the celebrations.

In the past few years, concern has grown about Chiang Mai's traffic jams and fumes, and a solution whereby the city would be split in two is being seriously considered; most businesses would move out to a new site (Lamphun is the current frontrunner) while the present town and its ancient temples would be preserved as a tourist enclave. As it is, the city remains bounded by a huge ring road, the Superhighway, and divides roughly into two main parts: the **old town**, bounded by the well-maintained moat and occasional remains of the city wall, where you'll find most of Chiang Mai's traditional wats, and the **new town centre**, between the moat and the Ping River to the east, for hotels, shops and travel agents. The main concentration of guest houses and restaurants hangs between the two, centred on the landmark of Pratu Tha Pae (**Tha Pae Gate**) in the middle of the east moat.

The main tourist activities in Chiang Mai – apart from eating, drinking and relaxing – are visiting the **temples** and **shopping** for handicrafts, pursuits which many find more appealing here than in the rest of Thailand. A pilgrimage to **Doi Suthep**, the mountain to the west of town, should not be missed, however, to see the sacred temple and the views over half of northern Thailand. Beyond the city limits, a number of other day trips can be made, such as to the ancient temples of Lamphun or to the orchid farms and elephant shows of the Mae Sa valley – and, of course, Chiang Mai is the main centre for hill-tribe **trekking**.

Arrival, information and transport

Most people **arrive** at the **train station** on Charoen Muang Road, just over 2km from Tha Pae Gate on the eastern side of town, or at the Arcade **bus station** on Kaeo Nawarat Road, 3km out to the northeast. Getting from either of these to the centre is easy by bus, songthaew or tuk-tuk (see "Transport" below). Coming south from Fang or Tha Ton, you'll wind up at the Chang Phuak bus station on Chotana Road, 2km north of Tha Pae Gate. If you plan to travel with one of the low-cost private bus companies on Bangkok's Khao San Road, find out exactly where you'll be dropped in Chiang Mai before making a booking: many of these companies' buses stop on a remote part of the Superhighway, where they "sell" their passengers to various guest-house touts. There's no obligation to go with the touts, but if you try to duck out you'll have a hard job getting downtown and you'll certainly come in for a lot of hassle. The better guest houses – and certainly those listed below – don't involve themselves in such shenanigans.

Arriving at the **airport**, 3km southwest of the centre, you'll find banks, a post office with an overseas phone, and a TAT office. A *Thai Airways* minibus to any destination in town should cost B40 per person, while a taxi will run to B80 for the car. The #6 bus, which stops outside the airport compound, follows a tedious route around the outskirts.

Information

TAT operates out of a swish **information** office (daily 8.30am–4.30pm; ☎053/ 235334) at 105/1 Chiang Mai–Lamphun Rd, on the east bank of the river just south of Nawarat Bridge, where you can pick up various handouts and a simple free **map** of the city. An important resource for trekkers is the **Hill Tribe Research Institute** at Chiang Mai University (Mon–Fri 9am–noon & 1–4pm), between Huai Kaeo and Suthep roads, where you can consult detailed maps and get clued up on the cultures of the north.

Nancy Chandler's Map of Chiang Mai, sold in many outlets all over the city (B70), is very handy for a detailed exploration: like her Bangkok map, it highlights a personal choice of sights, shops, restaurants and various oddities, as well as local transport information. *The Book of What, Where & How* (B95) acts as a local Yellow Pages, listing over a thousand farang-oriented businesses by category and marking them on detailed city maps.

Transport

Although you can comfortably walk between the most central temples, **bicycles** are the best way of looking round the old town and, with a bit of legwork, getting to the attractions outside the moat. Trusty sit-up-and-beg models (B30 a day) and mountain bikes (B50) are available at many outlets on the roads along the eastern moat. If you don't fancy pedalling through the heat and pollution, there are plenty of **motorbikes** for rent, though these really come into their own for exploring places around Chiang Mai and in the rest of the north (see p.240 for addresses of outlets).

The most economical form of public transport is the fleet of small, often crowded **buses** (B3–6), though their routes are sometimes eccentric (see box on p.226). The most useful services are #1, #2 and #3, which all pass Tha Pae Gate at some stage. One or two air-conditioned buses (B5) follow the same routes and sport the same numbers, but they're too irregular to rely on.

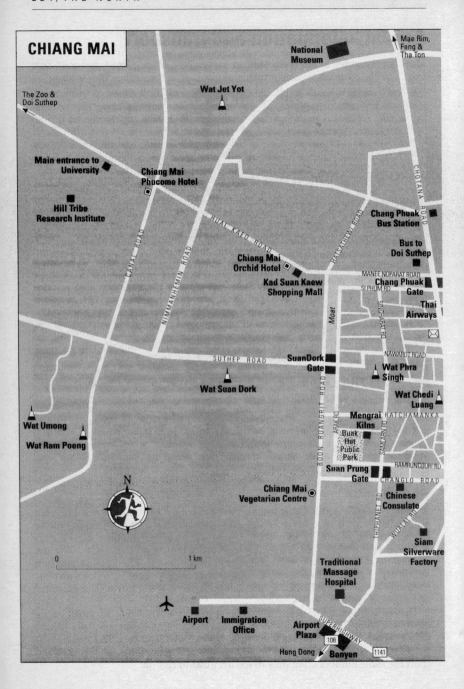

CHIANG MAI

National Museum

Mae Rim, Fang & Tha Ton

Wat Jet Yot

The Zoo & Doi Suthep

Main entrance to University

Chiang Mai Phucome Hotel

CHOTANA ROAD

Chang Phuak Bus Station

Hill Tribe Research Institute

Bus to Doi Suthep

HUAI KAEO ROAD

BALSAHEW ROAD

Chiang Mai Orchid Hotel

MANEE NOPARAT ROAD

Chang Phuak Gate

SI PHUM RD.

Kad Suan Kaew Shopping Mall

Thai Airways

CANAL ROAD

NIMMANHEMIN ROAD

SINGHARAT RD

Moat

SUTHEP ROAD

NAWAROT ROAD

SuanDork Gate

Wat Phra Singh

Wat Suan Dork

Wat Chedi Luang

RATCHAMANKA

Mengrai Kilns

Wat Umong

ARAK RD

Buak Hat Public Park

SAMLANG RD

Wat Ram Poeng

BOON RUANGRIT ROAD

RAMRUNGQURI RD.

Suan Prung Gate

CHANGLO ROAD

Chiang Mai Vegetarian Centre

Chinese Consulate

THIPHANET RD.

WUALAI RD.

Siam Silverware Factory

0   1 km

N

Traditional Massage Hospital

Airport

Immigration Office

Airport Plaza

SUPERHIGHWAY

108

Hang Dong   Banyen

1141

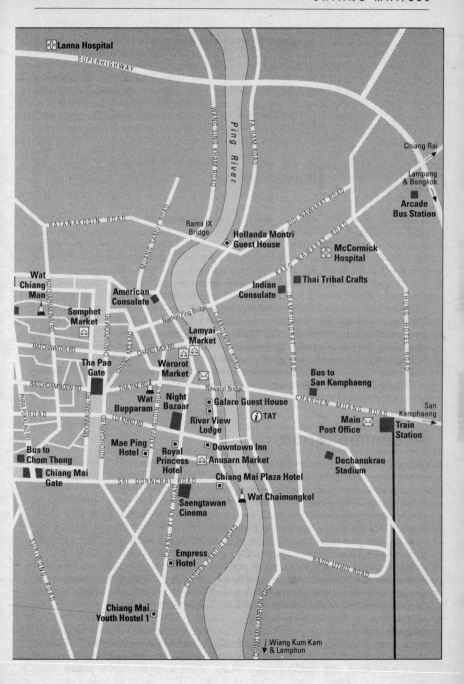

BUS ROUTES

#1 Charoen Muang Road train station–Tha Pae Gate–Wualai Road–Phra Pokklao Road –northwest corner of the moat–Suthep Road.

#2 Chotana Road–Chang Phuak bus station–Tha Pae Gate–Chang Klan Road–Charoen Prathet Road–Chiang Mai-Lamphun Road.

#3 Train station–Arcade bus station–Tha Pae Gate–Wat Phra Singh–Huai Kaeo Road.

#5 Rama IX Bridge–Charoen Prathet Road–Tha Pae Road–Kotchasarn Road–Changlo Road–Boon Ruangrit Road–Manee Noparat Road–Rama IX Bridge.

#6 Train station–southern leg of Superhighway–airport; airport–Boon Ruangrit Road–Suthep Road–Canal Road–Huai Kaeo Road–northern leg of Superhighway–train station.

Quicker and more efficient are the red **songthaews** (other colours serve outlying villages) which act as shared taxis within the city, picking up a number of people headed in roughly the same direction and taking each to their specific destination. They charge according to how far you're going – expect to pay B10 for a medium distance, say from the train station to Tha Pae Gate.

Chiang Mai is also stuffed with **tuk-tuks**, for which heavy bargaining is expected – allow around B30 for getting from the train station to Tha Pae Gate. They're quick and useful on arrival and departure, and work out quite reasonable if you're in a group. You can hire a tuk-tuk for a day for as little as B100, but there are strings attached: half the day will be spent sightseeing, the other half shopping along the San Kamphaeng Road at stores chosen by the driver, where he'll pick up a commission for bringing you there.

The town still has a few inexpensive **samlors**, but they're really too dangerous in Chiang Mai's fast traffic, and the drivers are notorious for dealing dope to farangs and then shopping them to the police.

Accommodation

Chiang Mai is well stocked with all kinds of **accommodation** and usually there are plenty of beds to go around, but many places fill up from December to February and at festival time (there will be extra pressure when the city hosts the Southeast Asian Games in December 1995, and during the 700th anniversary celebrations in 1996). For expensive hotels you'll need a booking at these times, and for guest houses it's a good idea to phone ahead – you may not be able to book a place, but you can save yourself a journey if the place is full. Many touts at the bus and train stations offer a free ride if you stay at their guest house, but you'll probably find that the price of a room is bumped up to pay for your ride. Be sure that you can trust your proprietor before you leave valuables in one of the **left-luggage rooms** while you go off trekking, and make a detailed inventory signed by both parties, because the hair-raising stories of theft and credit-card abuse are often true.

Inexpensive

In all ways that matter, the choice of **budget guest houses** is better in Chiang Mai than in Bangkok: they're generally more comfortable, friendly and quiet, and often have their own outdoor cafés. Many of the least expensive places make their money from hill-tribe trekking, which can be convenient, as a trek often needs a lot of organizing beforehand.

Most low-cost places are gathered around the eastern side of the old moat, and on the surprisingly quiet sois around Tha Pae Gate. This puts you between the old city and the new shopping centre, in the middle of a larder of Thai and travellers' restaurants.

C & C Teak House, 29 Bamrung Rat Rd (☎053/246966). Decent rooms in a friendly, family-run atmosphere. East of the centre, but free bicycles available. ①.

Chiang Mai Youth Hostel 1, 21/8 Chang Klan Rd (☎053/276737). Very clean, quiet and reliable, but 1500m from the night bazaar. Dorm beds B50; rooms have hot showers and fans or air-con. ③–④.

Chiang Mai Youth Hostel 2, 63 Bamrung Buri Rd (☎053/272169). Inexpensive and adequate, with dorm beds for B35. Reductions for IYHA members. ②.

Hollanda Montri, 365 Charoenrat Rd (☎053/242450). Clean rooms with hot-water bathrooms and friendly service in a spacious modern building by the river. ③.

Julie Guest House, 7/1 Soi 5, Ratchaphakinai Rd (☎053/274355). On a peaceful soi in the old town. Offers compact, modern cubicles with hot-water bathrooms beneath a good roof-garden restaurant, or clean rooms sharing facilities in a wooden house. ①–③.

Kent Guest House, 5 Soi 1, Ratchamanka Rd (☎053/278578). Clean, quiet and well run, with en suite rooms in a concrete building overlooking a small garden. Minimum stay 2 nights. ②.

Lek House, 22 Chaiyapoom Rd (☎053/252686). Central and set back from the road, with clean rooms round a shaded garden. ①.

Libra House, 28 Soi 9, Moonmuang Rd (☎053/210687). Excellent modern guest house with a few traditional trimmings and keen service. Hot water en suite or in shared bathrooms. ②.

Pha Thai House, 48/1 Ratchaphakinai Rd (☎053/278013). Efficiently run modern building with a quiet patio and solar-heated water in all rooms. Phone for free pick-up. ③.

Rendezvous Guest House, 3/1 Soi 5, Ratchdamnoen Rd (☎053/213763). Large, attractive modern rooms over a quiet garden courtyard. ②.

Rose Garden, 25/2 Soi 1, Ratchawithi Rd (☎053/217929). Small, spartan rooms with shared hot showers in a quiet wooden house. ①.

ACCOMMODATION PRICES

Throughout this guide, guest houses, hotels and bungalows have been categorized according to the price codes given below. These categories represent the minimum you can expect to pay in the high season (roughly Nov–Feb & July–Aug) for a double room – or, in the case of national park bungalows, for a multi-berth room which can be rented for a standard price by an individual or group. If travelling on your own, expect to pay anything between sixty and one hundred percent of the rates quoted for a double room. Wherever a range of prices is indicated, this means that the establishment offers rooms with varying facilities – as explained in the write-up. Wherever an establishment also offers dormitory beds, the prices of these beds are given in the text, instead of being indicated by price code.

Remember that the top-whack hotels will add seven percent tax and a ten-percent service charge to your bill – the price codes below are based on net rates after taxes have been added.

① under B100	④ B250–400	⑦ B1000–1500
② B100–150	⑤ B400–600	⑧ B1500–3000
③ B150–250	⑥ B600–1000	⑨ B3000+

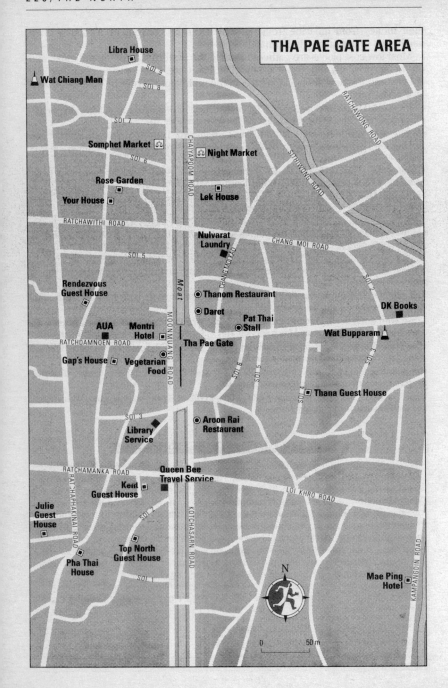

THA PAE GATE AREA

Libra House

Wat Chiang Man

Somphet Market

Night Market

Rose Garden

Your House

Lek House

RATCHAWITHI ROAD

Nulvarat
Laundry

CHANG MOI ROAD

Rendezvous
Guest House

Thanom Restaurant

Daret

DK Books

AUA   Montri
Hotel

Pat Thai
Stall

RATCHDAMNOEN ROAD

Tha Pae Gate

Wat Bupparam

Gap's House   Vegetarian
Food

Thana Guest House

Aroon Rai
Restaurant

Library
Service

RATCHAMANKA ROAD

Queen Bee
Travel Service

Kent
Guest House

LOI KHRO ROAD

Julie
Guest
House

Top North
Guest House

Pha Thai
House

N

Mae Ping
Hotel

0   50 m

SOI 9
SOI 8
SOI 7
SOI 6
SOI 5
SOI 3
SOI 2
SOI 1

CHAIYAPOOM ROAD
SITHIWONG ROAD
RATCHAWONG ROAD
MOONMUANG ROAD
CHANG MOI KAO
Moat
RAT CHAPHAKINAI ROAD
KOTCHASARN ROAD
KAMPANGDIN ROAD

Thana Guest House, 27/8 Soi 4, Tha Pae Rd (☎053/279794). One of several popular rowdy hangouts on this soi. Clean rooms with hot showers. ②.
Your House, 8 Soi 2, Ratchawithi Rd. (☎053/217492). A welcoming atmosphere and good food in an old-town teak house. Shared hot-water bathrooms. B40 for a dorm bed. ② .

Moderate

For a little over B300 for a double, you can buy yourself considerably more comfort than the bottom-bracket accommodation provides. By far the best of these **moderate** places are the upmarket guest houses and lodges, which as well as providing good facilities (hot water and often air conditioning) do a good line in decor and atmosphere. Chiang Mai is also scattered with dozens of bland, no-frills hotels in the same price range, of which the best few are included here.

Chiang Mai Phucome, 21 Huai Kaeo Rd (☎053/211026). Relaxed hotel with basic luxury facilities, popular with businessmen. ⑤.
Downtown Inn, 172/1–11 Loi Khro Rd (☎053/270662). Western-style comforts without the extras of the big luxury hotels; quiet considering its central location. ⑦.
Galare Guest House, 7 Charoen Prathet Rd (☎053/273885). Smart, popular place with terrace and shady lawn overlooking river. ⑤.
Gap's House, 3 Soi 4, Ratchdamnoen Rd (☎053/278140). Best deal in town, especially welcoming to lone travellers. Plush air-con rooms with hot showers in a relaxing, leafy compound strewn with antiques. Price of a double includes American breakfast. ④.
Montri Hotel, 2–6 Ratchdamnoen Rd (☎053/211069 or 211070). Smart, clean and good value. Beside noisy Tha Pae Gate, so ask for a back room. ⑤.
River Ping Palace, 385/2 Charoen Prathet Rd (☎053/274932). Camp nostalgia in a traditional house with riverside garden on the south side of town. ⑦.
River View Lodge, 25 Soi 2, Charoen Prathet Rd (☎053/271109 or 271110). Tasteful alternative to international-class hotels, with beautiful riverside garden, swimming pool and bags of character. ⑦.
Top North Guest House, 15 Soi 2, Moonmuang Rd (☎053/278900; Bangkok ☎02/251 8448). Modern, unpretentious place with a swimming pool, in a quiet enclave of guest houses. Fan-cooled and air-con rooms available. ④–⑤.

Expensive

Clustered around the night bazaar, and out towards Doi Suthep, Chiang Mai's **expensive hotels** aren't quite up to Bangkok's very high standards, but the best of them lay on all the expected luxuries plus traditional Lanna architectural touches. In general, top-end room prices are more reasonable here than in Bangkok.

Chiang Mai Orchid, 100 Huai Kaeo Rd (☎053/222091–9; Bangkok ☎02/245 3973). Grand, tasteful hotel with efficient service and a health club, inconveniently located on the northwest side of town. ⑨.
Chiang Mai Plaza, 92 Sri Dornchai Rd (☎053/270036–50; Bangkok ☎02/253 1276). Sprawling and impersonal central hotel, ragged at the edges, whose facilities run to a health club and a popular disco. ⑧.
Empress, 199 Chang Klan Rd (☎053/270240; Bangkok ☎02/251 0324 or 0325). Grand international-class hotel conveniently placed on the south side of town: within walking distance of the night bazaar, but far enough removed to get some peace and quiet. ⑧.
Mae Ping Hotel, 153 Sri Dornchai Rd (☎053/270160–80; Bangkok reservations ☎02/235 1350). Massive and characterless luxury hotel, popular with Asian tourists, in an ugly highrise building in the former red-light area. ⑧.
Royal Princess, 112 Chang Klan Rd (☎053/281033–43; Bangkok reservations ☎02/281 3088). Tidy, centrally located hotel with elegant rooms, fine restaurants and impeccable standards of service. ⑨.

CHIANG MAI'S FESTIVALS

Chiang Mai is the best and busiest place in the country to see in the Thai New Year, **Songkhran**, which takes over the city between April 13 and 16. The most obvious role of the festival is as an extended "rain dance" in the driest part of the year, when huge volumes of canal water are thrown about in a communal water fight that spares no one a drenching. The other elements of this complex festival are not as well known but no less important. Communities get together to build sand castles in the shape of chedis in the temple compounds, which they cover with coloured flags – this bestows merit on any ancestors who happen to find themselves in hell and may eventually release them from their torments, and also shows an intent to help renovate the wat in the year to come. Houses are given a thorough spring-clean to see out the old year, while the Buddha images are cleaned, polished and sprinkled with lustral water, before being ceremonially carried through the middle of the water fight, to give everyone the chance to throw water on them and receive the blessing of renewal. Finally, younger family members formally visit their elders during the festival to ask for their blessings, while pouring scented water over their hands.

Loy Krathong, on the night of the full moon in November, has its most showy celebration at Sukhothai, but Chiang Mai is not far behind. While a spectacular but unnerving firework fiesta rages on the banks, thousands of candles are gently floated down the Ping River in beautiful lotus-leaf boats. People hope in this way to float away any sins or ill luck they have incurred, and give thanks for the rainy season to Mae Kong Kha, the ancient water goddess. In northern Thailand, the parallel event of **Loy Khome** takes place during the daytime, when brightly coloured paper hot-air balloons (*khome fai*), often with fireworks attached, are released to carry away problems and bad luck, and honour the Buddha's top-knot, which he cut off when he became an ascetic. According to legend, the top-knot is looked after by the Buddha's mother in heaven.

Chiang Mai's brilliantly colourful **flower festival**, usually on the first weekend of February, also attracts huge crowds. The highlight is a procession of floats, modelled into animals, chedis, and even scenes from the *Ramayana* (see p.82), which are then covered in flowers.

The City

Chiang Mai feels less claustrophobic than most large towns in Thailand, being scattered over a wide plain and broken up by waterways: in addition to the moat encircling the temple-strewn old town, the gentle Ping River brings a breath of fresh air to the eastern side of the pungent food markets above Nawarat Bridge, and the modern, hectic shopping area around Chang Klan Road. To make the most of the river, take a **boat trip** in a covered longtail out through the suburbs into open countryside: *Mae Ping River Cruises* (☎053/274822), based at Wat Chaimongkol on Charoen Prathet Road, charges B300 per person for the two-hour jaunt, stopping 8km upstream from the centre for refreshments and a look round a farmer's fruit, vegetable, spice and rose gardens.

Wat Phra Singh

If you see only one temple in Chiang Mai it should be **Wat Phra Singh**, at the far western end of Ratchdamnoen Road in the old town (bus #3), perhaps the single most impressive array of buildings in the city. The largest structure, a colourful modern viharn fronted by naga balustrades, hides from view a rustic wooden bot, a chedi constructed in 1345 to house the ashes of King Kam Fu, and the beautiful **Viharn Lai Kam**, the highlight of the whole complex. This wooden gem from the early nineteenth century is a textbook example of Lanna architecture, with its squat, multi-tiered roof and exquisitely carved and gilded pediment: if you feel you're being watched as you approach, it's the sinuous double arch between the porch's central columns, which represents the Buddha's eyebrows.

Naga at Wat Phra Singh

Inside sits one of Thailand's three **Phra Singh** (or Sihing) Buddha images (see p.430), a portly, radiant and much-revered bronze in a fifteenth-century Lanna style. The image's setting is enhanced by the colourful **murals** of action-packed tableaux, which give a window on life in the north a hundred years ago: courting scenes and piggyback fights, merchants, fishermen and children playing. The murals illustrate two different stories: on the right-hand wall is an old folk tale, the *Sang Thong*, about a childless king and queen who are miraculously given a beautiful son, the "Golden Prince", in a conch shell; those on the left, which have been badly damaged by water, show the story of the mythical swan Suwannahong, who forms the magnificent prow of the principal royal barge in Bangkok. Incidentally, what look like Bermuda shorts on the men are in fact **tattoos**: in the last century, all boys in the north were tattooed from navel to kneecap, an agonizing ordeal undertaken to show their courage and to make themselves beautiful to women.

Wat Chedi Luang

From Wat Phra Singh a ten-minute walk east along a quiet stretch of Ratchadamnoen Road brings you to **Wat Chedi Luang** on Phra Pokklao Road, where an enormous chedi, toppled from 90m to its present 60m by an earthquake in 1545, presents an intriguing spectacle – especially in the early evening when the resident bats flit around. You'll need a titanic leap of the imagination, however, to picture the chedi as it was in the fifteenth century, when it was covered in bronze plates and gold leaf, and housed the Emerald Buddha. In an unprepossessing modern building by the main entrance stands the city's navel pillar, the *lak muang*, sheltered by a stately eucalyptus tree which, the story has it, will stand for as long as the city's fortunes prosper.

If you've got time, pop in on **Wat Pan Tao** next door to see the wonderfully gnarled wooden viharn, a classic of graceful Lanna architecture.

Wat Chiang Man

From Wat Chedi Luang, the old town's main commercial street, Phra Pokklao Road, heads north past a monument to King Mengrai, the founder of Chiang Mai, and the conspicuous old provincial office, set in its own small piazza. Turn right along Wiang Kaeo Road to reach the oldest temple in Chiang Mai, **Wat Chiang Man**, fifteen minutes' walk from Chedi Luang.

Erected by Mengrai on the site where he first pitched camp, the wat is most notable for two dainty and very holy Buddha images housed in the viharn to the right of the entrance: the **Phra Sila**, a graceful stone work carved in northern India in the sixth century BC, stands in the typical *tribunga* or hipshot stance; its partner, the **Phra Setangamani** (or Crystal Buddha), made four centuries later probably in Lavo (modern Lopburi), is much revered by the inhabitants of Chiang Mai for its rain-making powers and is carried through the streets during the Songkhran festival to help the rainy season on its way. Neither image is especially beautiful, but a powerful aura is created by making them difficult to see, high up behind three sets of iron bars. Check out the chedi at the back of the compound, for the herd of stone elephants on whose backs it sits.

Chiang Mai National Museum

For a fuller picture of Lanna art and culture, head for the grand **National Museum** (Wed–Sun 9am–4pm; B20), on the northwestern outskirts of Chiang Mai: leave the old town through Chang Phuak Gate on the northern moat, then go up Chotana Road, a crowded shopping street, for 2km, before turning left along the Superhighway to reach the museum after about 1km. The #2 bus will get you to the junction of Chotana and the Superhighway, where you could switch to the #6 bus or start walking (about 15min); otherwise bike it, or charter a tuk-tuk or songthaew from the centre of town.

The museum's neat lawns and impressive architecture, mixing modern materials with traditional stylistic elements, contrast palatially with the tedium of the Superhighway. Inside, the airy rooms are cool enough for a long browse, and the collection, though it doesn't quite match the grandness of its setting, is engrossing and liberally labelled. The ground floor supports a wide range of beautiful **Buddha images**, including a humble, warmly smiling sandstone head from Haripunjaya (Lamphun), representing the earliest northern style, and many statues from the golden age of Lanna sculpture in the fifteenth and sixteenth centuries, when images were produced in two contrasting styles.

One group, which resembles images from northern India, has been called the "**lion-type**", after the Shakyamuni (Lion of the Shakyas) archetype at the great Buddhist temple at Bodhgaya, the site of the Buddha's enlightenment. It's been conjectured that a delegation sent by King Tilok to Bodh Gaya in the 1450s brought back not only a plan of the temple to be used in the building of Wat Jet Yot, but also a copy of the statue, which became the model for hundreds of Lanna images. These broad-shouldered and plump-bellied Buddhas are always seated with the right hand in the touching-the-earth gesture, while the face is well rounded with pursed lips and a serious, majestic demeanour: typical of this style is the massive bronze head with chubby cheeks and disdainfully hooded eyes which dominates one end of the downstairs hall. The second type is the "**Thera Sumana**" style named after the monk Mahathera Sumana, who came from Sukhothai in 1369 to establish his Sri Lankan sect in Lanna. The museum is well stocked with this type of image – though confusingly, they're labelled "late Chiang Saen" – which show strong Sukhothai influence, with an oval face and a flame-like *ushnisha* on top of the head. A number of crude wooden Buddhas round off the story of Lanna styles – they were carved after 1556, when, under Burmese domination, the region's sculpture became little more than popular folkcraft.

Also on this floor there's a fine exhibition of **ceramics**, including simple wares for everyday use, some dainty porcelain and Sawankhalok-style celadon (see p.197) –

much of it produced at the local kilns near San Kamphaeng – the latter typified by a muddy green plate decorated with wriggling fish. And if you've ever wondered what the **relics** enshrined in Thailand's chedis look like, the answer is revealed here in a humble brass bowl containing some highly venerable black pellets. Upstairs, a free-form "local history" room contains everything from early photos of the town and giant ceremonial drums to intricately carved opium weights and musty hill-tribe costumes.

Wat Jet Yot

Set back from the Superhighway ten minutes' walk west of the museum, the peaceful garden temple of **Wat Jet Yot** is named after the "seven spires" of its unusual chedi, which lean together like brick chimneys at crazy angles. The temple was built in 1455 by King Tilok, to represent the seven places around Bodh Gaya in India which the Buddha visited in the seven weeks following his enlightenment. Around the base of the chedi, delicate stuccos portray cross-legged deities serenely floating in the sky, a role model for all yogic fliers; their faces are said to be those of King Tilok's relatives.

The zoo and arboretum

About 1km beyond Wat Jet Yot, the Superhighway ends at the junction with Huai Kaeo Road, a broad avenue of posh residences and hotels, which starts out from the northwest corner of the moat and ends at the foot of Doi Suthep. Bus #3 runs up Huai Kaeo, past the sprawling campus of Chiang Mai University to **Chiang Mai Zoo** (daily 9am–6pm; B20 adults, B10 children), at the base of the mountain. Started as a menagerie of a missionary family's pets, the zoo now extends over an attractive 36-acre park, run by the municipality. Despite a disorienting layout, it makes a diverting visit, especially for kids: housed in modern, relatively comfortable conditions is a huge collection of colourful Asian birds, monkeys and larger mammals, including the most popular attraction, Thai elephants.

An unprepossessing park next door, where you'll often see joggers toiling in the heat and itinerant monks sleeping or meditating under their parasols, is in fact a small **arboretum**, with name tags stuck to the plants and trees, so you can mug up on them before going upcountry.

Wat Umong

More of a park than a temple, **Wat Umong** makes an unusual, charming place for a stroll in the western suburbs. If you're coming from the zoo, it's best to take a tuk-tuk or songthaew around the university campus. From the centre of town, you can take bus #1 along Suthep Road for about 2km; ask for the wat and, from where you're dropped off, it's a fifteen-minute walk down a winding lane to the left.

According to legend the wat was built in the 1380s by King Ku Na for a brilliant but deranged monk called Jan, who was prone to wandering off into the forest to meditate. Because Ku Na wanted to be able to get Jan's advice at any time, he founded this wat and decorated the **tunnels** (*umong*) beneath the chedi with paintings of trees, flowers and birds to simulate the monk's favoured habitat. Some of the old tunnels can still be explored, where obscure fragments of paintings and one or two small modern shrines can be seen. Above the tunnels, frighteningly lavish nagas guard the staircase up to the overgrown **chedi** and a grassy platform supporting a grotesque black statue of the fasting Buddha, all ribs and veins: it shows him during his six years of self-mortification, before he realized that he should avoid extremes along the Middle Path to enlightenment. Behind the chedi, the ground slopes away

Fasting Buddha

to a **lake** inhabited by hungry carp, where locals come to study and talk. On a tiny island here, reached by a concrete bridge, stands a statue of Buddhadasa Bhikkhu, whose eclectic philosophy is followed at Wat Umong. Meditation classes in English are sometimes held here on Sunday afternoons, when a German monk is in residence.

Throughout the tranquil wooded grounds, the temple's diverse philosophy comes stridently alive: educational signs are pinned to nearly every tree, displaying outrageous cartoons of sinning dogs and simple Buddhist maxims. Colourful and surreal didactic paintings also cover the modern hall near the entrance. At the entrance gate, handicrafts are sold by the community of disabled people who have a house and workshop in the wat.

Wat Suan Dork

From the turn-off to Wat Umong, Suthep Road heads back towards town, meeting the western moat at Suan Dork Gate. Halfway along this stretch of the road, the *Hill Tribe Products Foundation* (see p.236) sits in front of **Wat Suan Dork**, the "Flower Garden Temple", which was later surrounded by walls as part of Chiang Mai's fortifications. Legend says that Mahathera Sumana, when he was invited to establish his Sri Lankan sect here in 1369, brought with him a miraculous glowing relic. The king of Chiang Mai ordered a huge chedi – the one you see today – to be built in his flower garden, but as the pea-sized relic was being placed inside the chedi, it split into two parts: one half was buried here, the other found its way to Doi Suthep, after more miracles.

The brilliantly whitewashed chedi now sits next to a garden of smaller, equally dazzling chedis containing the ashes of the Chiang Mai royal family – framed by Doi Suthep to the west, this makes an impressive and photogenic sight, especially at sunset. Standing in the way of a panoramic shot of all the chedis, the huge, open-sided viharn on the east side has been crudely restored, but the bot at the back of the dusty compound is more interesting – decorated with lively *Jataka* murals, it enshrines a 500-year-old Buddha.

Wat Bupparam

On the east side of town at the mid-point of the main shopping drag, Tha Pae Road, **Wat Bupparam** makes for a mildly interesting stroll from the main guesthouse area around Tha Pae Gate. The new wedding-cake structure at the centre of the temple houses a magnificent black Buddha, which was apparently made for King Naresuan of Ayutthaya nearly four hundred years ago from a single piece of teak. The **temple well** (off-limits for women) was used for watering the Buddha relics enshrined in the chedi and is also Chiang Mai's representative in the *murathaphisek* ceremony, when holy waters are gathered from Thailand's most auspicious localities for the ritual bathing of a new king.

Shopping

Shopping is an almost irresistible pastime in Chiang Mai, a hotbed of traditional cottage industries whose prices are low and standards of workmanship generally high. Two main shopping areas, conveniently operating at different times of the day, sell the full range of local handicrafts.

The **road to San Kamphaeng**, which extends due east from the end of Charoen Muang Road for 13km, is the main daytime strip, lined with every sort of shop and factory, where you can usually watch the craftsmen at work. The biggest concentrations are at Bo Sang, the "umbrella village", 9km from town, and at San Kamphaeng itself, once important for its kilns but now dedicated chiefly to silk-weaving. Red and white **buses** to San Kamphaeng leave Chiang Mai every thirty minutes from in front of the *Bangkok Bank* on Charoen Muang Road. Numerous **tuk-tuk** drivers offer inexpensive (B100 or less) excursions, but the catch is that you go to the shops they choose, where they'll pick up a commission.

The other shopper's playground is the **night bazaar** on Chang Klan Road, which starts up at around 5pm. It's an unatmospheric modern shopping centre, surrounded by department stores and bumper-to-bumper street stalls, but it sells just about anything produced in Chiang Mai, plus crafts from other parts of Thailand and counterfeit designer goods. You're more likely to get ripped off or palmed off with junk or fakes here, but then again it's one of the few things to do at night in Chiang Mai.

Fabrics and clothes

The **silk** produced out towards **San Kamphaeng** is richly coloured and hard-wearing, with an attractively rough texture. Bought off a roll, the material is generally less costly than in Bangkok, though more expensive than in the north-east – prices start from around B300 a metre for two-ply (for thin shirts and skirts) and B400 a metre for four-ply (suitable for suits). Ready-made clothes and made-to-measure tailoring, though inexpensive, are generally staid and more suited to formal wear. With branches 5km out of Chiang Mai and in San Kamphaeng itself, *Piankusol* is the best place to follow the silk-making process right from the cocoon. If you've got slightly more money to spend on better quality silk, head for *Shinawatra* (branches 7km out and in San Kamphaeng), which was once graced by no less a personage than Princess Diana.

Shops in San Kamphaeng and Chiang Mai sell the coarse, pale-coloured **cotton** made around Pasang, near Lamphun, starting at B80 per metre, which is nice for furnishings: *Leerawat Pah Fai* on the third floor of the Chiang Inn Plaza, Chang Klan Road, has an especially good selection. Chiang Mai is also awash with geometric *mut mee* cloth and Technicolor Thai Lue weaves, but both are far better and much less expensive in their place of origin: the former in the north-east, the latter around Chiang Khong and Nan.

At the top end of the market, *The Loom*, at 27/3 Ratchamanka Rd, specializes in gorgeous and very pricey "antique" silk and cotton weaves from the north, the northeast and Laos. Also worth a root around is *Pa Ker Yaw*, 180 Loi Khro Rd, a weather-beaten wooden shophouse stuffed with a similar selection of rich fabrics, as well as folksy jewellery and other crafts. For the all-over ethnic look, *Classic Lanna Thai*, on the first floor of the night bazaar and on Moonmuang

Road, sells ready-to-wear **clothes**, made from local fabrics by traditional northern methods. If you just need to replenish your rucksack, *Gagamo* at 1/1 Kotchasarn Rd opposite Tha Pae Gate sells ordinary casual clothes of reasonable quality at low prices.

For responsible consumerism, take your custom to one of the **non-profit-making shops**, whose proceeds go to the hill tribes. These include *The Hill Tribe Products Foundation*, on Suthep Road in front of Wat Suan Dork, which sells beautiful lengths of cotton and silk and a variety of hill-tribe gear, and *Thai Tribal Crafts*, 204 Bamrungrat Rd off Kaeo Nawarat Road – *yaam*, the embroidered shoulder bags popular with Thai students, are particularly good here (around B250).

Woodcarving

Chiang Mai has a long tradition of **woodcarving**, which expresses itself in everything from salad bowls to half-size elephants. In the past the industry has relied on the cutting of Thailand's precious teak, but manufacturers are now beginning to use other hardwoods, while bemoaning their inferior quality.

The best place for carving is *Chiangmai Banyen Company*, 201 Wualai Rd at the junction with the Superhighway: the workmanship is topnotch and the wood is treated to last, although prices are quite high – a statue of a chubby, reclining boy of the kind found all over Chiang Mai will set you back B250 here. With refreshing honesty, the proprietors explain that a lot of their stuff is left outside for a few rainy seasons to give it a weathered look – elsewhere, pieces that have been weathered in this way are often passed off as antiques. *Banyen* also has an absorbing folk museum of wooden objects collected from around the north. If you're a real aficionado and have your own transport, head for Ban Tawai, a large village of shops and factories where prices are low and you can watch the woodworkers in action – to get there, follow Highway 108 south from Chiang Mai 13km to Hang Dong, then head east for 2km.

Lacquerware

Lacquerware can be seen in nearly every museum in Thailand, most commonly in the form of betel-nut sets, which used to be carried ceremonially by the slaves of grandees as an insignia of rank and wealth (see p.359). Betel-nut sets are still produced in Chiang Mai according to the traditional technique, whereby a woven bamboo frame is covered with layers of rich red lacquer and decorated with black details. A variety of other objects, such as trays and jewellery boxes, are also produced, some decorated with gold leaf on black gloss. Just about every other shop in town sells lacquerware: *Laitong*, 6km towards San Kamphaeng, is a good place to see the intricate process of manufacture, though prices are lower elsewhere.

Celadon

Celadon, sometimes known as greenware, is a delicate variety of stoneware which was first made in China over two thousand years ago and was later produced in Thailand, most famously at Sukhothai and Sawankhalok. Several kilns in Chiang Mai have revived the art, the best of them being *Mengrai Kilns* at 79/2 Soi 6, Samlarn Rd. Sticking to the traditional methods, *Mengrai* produces beautiful handcrafted vases, boxes and plates, thrown in elegant shapes and covered with transparent green and blue glazes, from as little as B200.

Umbrellas and paper

The village of **Bo Sang** bases its fame on souvenir **umbrellas** – made of silk, cotton or mulberry paper and decorated with bold, painted colours (from about B100 for a kid's parasol) – but the artists who work here will also paint a small motif on your bag or camera in two minutes flat. The grainy mulberry (*sa*) **paper**, which makes beautiful writing or sketching pads, is sold almost as an after-thought in many of Bo Sang's shops.

Jade

Chinese soft **jade** and nine colours of hard jade from Burma are worked into a great variety of objects, from chopsticks (B3000) to large Buddha images (B30,000), but the finest, translucent, hard jade is reserved for jewellery, usually deep green in colour, which is supposed to bring the wearer good health. *Chamchuree Lapidary*, about 8km towards San Kamphaeng, is reliable and boasts a wide selection – but for the very best workmanship and prices you need to visit Mae Sai on the Burmese border (see p.285).

Silver

Of the traditional craft quarters, only the **silversmiths'** area on Wualai Road remains in its original location. The *Siam Silverware Factory* on Soi 3, a ramshackle and sulphurous compound loud with the hammering of hot metal, gives you a whiff of what this zone must have been like in its heyday. The end results are repoussé plates, bowls and cups, and attractive, chunky jewellery (bracelets from B250).

Eating

The main difficulty with eating in Chiang Mai is knowing when to stop. All over town there are inexpensive and enticing restaurants serving typically northern food, which has been strongly influenced by Burmese cuisine, especially in curries such as the spicy *kaeng hang lay* (usually translated on menus as "Chiang Mai curry"), made with pork, ginger and coconut cream, often with added tama-rind. Another favourite local dish is Chiang Mai *nam*, spicy pork sausage – although the uncooked, fermented varieties are probably not a wise move. At lunchtime the thing to do is to join the local workers in one of the simple cafés that put all their efforts into producing just one or two special dishes – the tradi-tional meal at this time of day is *khao soi*, a thick broth of curry and coconut cream, with egg noodles and a choice of meat.

None of the Western food in Chiang Mai is brilliant, and it's generally more expensive than Thai, but sometimes it's very hard to resist. Easier to refuse are the restaurants which lay on touristy **cultural shows** with *khan toke* dinners, a selection of northern dishes eaten on the floor off short-legged lacquer trays. There are better places to sample the region's food, and the hammy dancing displays, often with embarrassing audience participation, are a dubious diversion.

Thai

Anusarn Market, Chang Klan Rd. Happy night-time hunting ground of open-air stalls and restaurants. One-dish operators (mussel omelettes fried up with great panache, *khao soi*, or very good *pat thai*) square up to each other across a shared courtyard of tables; beyond lie *halal* restaurants specializing in barbecued chicken with honey, and several good seafood places including the old favourite *Fatty's*. Inexpensive to moderate.

Aroon Rai, 43 Kotchasarn Rd. Excellent northern food in popular no-frills restaurant, one of many open-air places on this stretch. Inexpensive to moderate.

Chiang Mai Vegetarian Centre, Boon Ruangrit Road. Run by the Santi Asoke group, like the café at Bangkok's Chatuchak Market: a cavernous traditional *sala* serving good veggie dishes on rice, and desserts. Inexpensive.

The Gallery, 25 Charoenrat Rd. Refined eaterie on soothing riverside terraces, behind a gallery for local artists. Interesting selection, big portions, slow service. Moderate to expensive.

Heuan Phen, 112 Ratchamanka Rd. Probably Chiang Mai's most authentic northern restaurant; not yet on the tourist trail, so no English sign. Moderate.

New Lamduon Fahharm Khao Soi, 352/22 Charoenrat Rd. Excellent *khao soi* prepared to a secret recipe, which was once cooked for King Bhumibo, no less. Also satay, waffles and *som tam* (spicy papaya salad). Way up the east bank of the river; open 9am–3pm only. Inexpensive.

Pat Thai stall, alleyway on Tha Pae Rd, near *Roong Ruang Hotel*. Best *pat thai* in town, prepared with flaming theatricality. Worth queuing for. Open 6–9pm. Inexpensive.

Sala Kai, 41 Nawarot Rd, off Phra Pokklao Road. Delicious and very popular satay and *khao man kai* – boiled chicken breast served with broth and garlic rice. This and the surrounding cafés are especially handy if you're looking round the old town. Open 5am–2pm. Inexpensive.

Suthasinee, 164/10 Chang Klan Rd. Great, creamy *khao soi*, and good *som tam* ordered from the stall outside. Lunchtime only. Inexpensive.

Ta-krite Restaurant, 17 Soi 1, Samlarn Rd, on the south side of Wat Phra Singh. Delicious and varied cuisine, in a maze of rooms and balconies around a green and pleasant courtyard. Inexpensive to moderate.

Thanom Restaurant, Chaiyapoom Rd, near Tha Pae Gate. Great introduction to northern Thai and Burmese-style cooking, in startlingly clean surroundings. Closes 8pm. Moderate.

Vegetarian Food, on the corner of Ratchdamnoen and Moonmuang roads. Noisy and dingy, but interesting veggie dishes. Inexpensive.

Whole Earth, 88 Sri Dornchai Rd. Mostly veggie dishes, from Thailand and India; soothing atmosphere with occasional live mood music in a traditional Lanna house. Moderate.

European and all-rounders

Daret, 4 Chaiyapoom Rd. The definitive budget travellers' hang-out with outdoor trestles and a friendly buzz. Famous fruit shakes, good breakfasts and back-home staples; pass over the Thai food. Inexpensive to moderate.

JJ Coffee Shop and Bakery, *Montri Hotel*, corner of Ratchadamnoen and Moonmuang roads. All kinds of food, but best for breakfast, with bread and croissants baked in front of your eyes. Sanitized atmosphere with air-con and camp indoor garden. Smaller branch at Chiang Inn Plaza, Chang Klan Rd. Moderate to expensive.

Julie Guest House, 7/1 Soi 5, Ratchaphakinai Rd. Carefully prepared French food, including good-value set menus, plus less costly Thai dishes, all served in a breezy roof garden. Wine by the glass or carafe at reasonable prices. Inexpensive to expensive.

L'Orient Express, 23/2 Charoen Prathet Rd. Neat, simple, French-run restaurant dishing up good French and Thai food. Moderate to expensive.

Pensione La Villa, 145 Ratchdamnoen Rd. Relaxing barn-style restaurant with good salads and the best pizzas in town. Closed Tues. Expensive but good value.

Piccola Roma, 3/2–3 Charoen Prathet Rd. The genuine article, with especially good pasta, which would stand the test back in Italy, though don't expect too much of the wines. Phone for free pick-up. Very expensive.

Tanya, 25 Ratchawithi Rd. Good steaks, pastas and salads, as well as beautifully presented Thai dishes in bright and neat surroundings. Moderate to expensive.

Nightlife

Although there's a clutch of hostess bars bordering the east moat and a few gay bars offering sex shows scattered around the outskirts, Chiang Mai's **nightlife** generally avoids Bangkok's excesses – most of the places below are bar-restaurants with no admission fees, geared to a relaxing night out. If your heart's set on dancing, some of the big hotels have predictable, Westernized night clubs: *Bubbles* at the *Porn Ping* on Charoen Prathet Road, *Crystal Cave* at the *Empress*, *The Wall* at *Chiang Inn*, and *Plaza* at the *Chiang Mai Plaza* all charge about B100 admission, including one drink.

Baritone, Kad Suan Kaew Shopping Mall, Huai Kaeo Rd. One of the country's top jazz venues, slickly designed and featuring US-trained guitarist Teh Intaranan, his band, *The Jazzliners*, and occasional guests.

Brasserie, 37 Charoenrat Rd. Good restaurant with pretty riverside terraces, more famous as the venue for some of the city's best live blues and rock.

Old West, 326/3 Manee Noparat Rd. Popular bar with young Thais. Lively scene, with rock bands and sprawling outdoor terraces.

The Pub, 88 Huai Kaeo Rd. Homely, relaxing ex-pat hangout, rated by *Newsweek* as one of the world's best bars. As the name suggests: draught beer, darts, old-fashioned landlord.

The River, 239/1 Charoenrat Rd. Outside, tables on an unappealing stretch of river; inside, typical Thai nightclub till 4am – dark and friendly, with an impossibly loud MOR band.

Riverside, 9 Charoenrat Rd. Archetypal farang bolthole: candlelit terraces by the water, reliable Western and Thai food (moderate to pricey), extensive drinks list and inexpensive draught beer. Live bands perform slavish folk-rock covers. *Rim Ping* next door is an extension, with mostly Thai clientele. Usually packed.

Listings

Airlines *Thai Airways*, 240 Phra Pokklao Rd (☎053/210042).

Banks Dozens of banks are dotted around Tha Pae Road and Chang Klan Road, many staying open for evening shoppers.

Books *Suriwong* at 54/1 Sri Dornchai Rd and *DK* at 234 Tha Pae Rd have a wide selection of English-language publications, including novels, books about Thailand and maps. The *Library Service* at 21/1 Soi 2, Ratchamanka Rd (nearer Moonmuang Road) trades second-hand books as well as giving advice on motorbike trekking. The owner, David Unkovich, has also written *The Pocket Guide to Motorcycle Touring in Northern Thailand*.

Car rental Many outlets around Tha Pae Gate rent out cars and 4-wheel drives, from around B800 a day, but for comprehensive insurance and back-up it's probably worth paying the full whack (B1000–1300 a day) at *Hertz*, 90 Sri Dornchai Rd (☎053/270184–7); *AVIS*, 14/14 Huai Kaeo Rd (☎053/221316); or *SMT* (*Inter-rent*), *Amari Rincome Hotel*, 301 Huai Kaeo Rd (☎053/221044).

Cinemas Thai and Hong Kong romantic action comedies are standard fare at the *Saengtawan*, on the corner of Sri Dornchai and Chang Klan roads, but for American films, the English soundtrack is relayed into a separate room at the back of the auditorium. The *Vista* chain also shows some English-language films at its shopping complex branches: the *Chiang Inn Plaza* on Chang Klan Road, Kad Suan Kaew on Huai Kaeo Road, and the *Airport Plaza* on the Superhighway. French films with English subtitles are screened at the *Alliance Française*, 138 Charoen Prathet Rd (☎053/275277), usually on Fri at 8pm.

Consulates Useful visa stops for China (111 Chang Lo Rd; Mon–Fri 9–11am; ☎053/272197) and India (113 Bamrung Rat Rd; Mon–Fri 9am–noon; ☎053/243066). The US (387 Witchayanon Rd; ☎053/252629–31) and Japan (12/1 Boonruangrit Rd; ☎053/221451) also have full consulates, while the UK (54 Moo 2, Suthep Rd; ☎053/211474), France (*Alliance Française*, 138 Charoen Prathet Rd; ☎053/281466) and Sweden (YMCA, Sroemsuk Rd; ☎053/221820) have honorary consuls.

Cooking lessons *Chiang Mai Thai Cookery School*, 1–3 Moonmuang Rd (☎053/278033), holds 1-day courses (B600 with home-made recipe book to take away) covering traditional Lanna and common Thai dishes, including vegetarian options and substitute ingredients available in the West.

Directory enquiries (in English) ☎13 for Chiang Mai, ☎183 for other areas.

Hospitals *Lanna*, at 103 Superhighway (☎053/211037–41 or 215020–2), east of Chotana Road, has a 24-hr emergency service and dentistry department. *McCormick* (☎053/241107) is also used to farangs and is nearer, on Kaeo Nawarat Road.

Immigration On the southern leg of the Superhighway, 300m before the airport on the left (☎053/277510).

Laundry *Nulvarat*, 29/1 Chang Moi Kao (behind Chaiyapoom Road), which has machines and charges by the kilo, is affordable and reliable.

Meditation *Northern Insight Meditation Centre*, at Wat Ram Poeng (aka Wat Tapotaram) on Canal Road near Wat Umong (☎053/278620), offers month-long *vipassana* courses and has a resident farang instructor.

Motorbike rental Motorbikes of all shapes and sizes are available, starting from about B100 per day for an old 80cc step-through. The reliable *Queen Bee Travel Service*, 5 Moonmuang Rd (☎053/275525) can also offer limited insurance. (See also "Books", on previous page.)

Post and telephones The GPO is on Charoen Muang Rd near the rail station. Poste restante and other postal services are available downstairs at the usual times (private packing services operate outside on Charoen Muang Road); an overseas phone and fax service upstairs is open until 8pm every day. The main office for calling abroad is the new Chiang Mai Telecommunication Center (open 24hr) on the Superhighway, just south of the east end of Charoen Muang Road. Many private agencies in town, for example in the basement of the night bazaar, sell overseas calls, but at a higher rate. Other post offices are on Charoen Prathet Road by Nawarat Bridge, on Phra Pokklao Road at the junction with Ratchawithi Road, at 195/8–9 Chotana Rd, and at the airport.

Thai boxing Dechanukrau Stadium, Khong Say Rd (off Charoen Muang Road); Fri & Sat 7pm.

Tourist Police 105/1 Chiang Mai–Lamphun Rd (☎053/248974; or nationwide helpline ☎1699).

Traditional massage *Traditional Hospital*, 78/1 Soi Moh Shivagakomarpaj, off Wualai Rd opposite the *Old Chiang Mai Cultural Center* (daily 8.30am–4.30pm; ☎053/275085): B200 for 2hr, plus highly respected 11-day courses in English (B2770).

Around Chiang Mai

You'll never feel cooped up in Chiang Mai, as the surrounding countryside is dotted with day-trip options in all directions. Dominating the skyline to the west, **Doi Suthep** and its eagle's-nest temple are hard to ignore, and a wander around the pastoral ruins of **Wiang Kum Kam** on the southern periphery has the feel of fresh exploration. Further south, the quiet town of **Lamphun** offers classic sightseeing in the form of historically and religiously significant temples and a museum. In sharp contrast to the north, the **Mae Sa valley** is a kind of rural theme park and too artificial and exploitative for many tastes – for honest, unabashed commerce, head for the shopping strip which stretches east towards San Kamphaeng (see p.235). All the trips described here can be done in half a day; longer excursions are dealt with later in the chapter.

Doi Suthep

A jaunt up **DOI SUTHEP**, the mountain which rises steeply at the city's western edge, is the most satisfying brief trip you can make from Chiang Mai,
chiefly on account of beautiful **Wat Phra That Doi Suthep**, which dominates
the hillside and gives a towering view over the goings-on in town. This is the
north's holiest shrine, which takes its pre-eminence from a magic relic
enshrined in its chedi and the miraculous legend of its founding. The original
chedi here was built by King Ku Na at the end of the fourteenth century, after
the glowing relic of Wat Suan Dork had self-multiplied just before being
enshrined. A place had to be found for the clone, so Ku Na put it in a travelling
shrine on the back of a white elephant and waited to see where the sacred
animal would lead: it eventually climbed Doi Suthep, trumpeted three times,
turned round three times, knelt down and died, thereby indicating that this was
the spot. Ever since, it's been northern Thailand's most important place of
pilgrimage, especially for the candlelit processions on **Maha Puja**, the anniversary of the sermon to the disciples, and **Visakha Puja**, the anniversary of the
Buddha's birth, enlightenment and death.

Frequent **songthaews** leave the corner of Manee Noparat and Chotana roads
for the sixteen-kilometre trip up the mountain (B30 to the wat). The road, although
steep in places, is paved all the way and well suited for **motorbikes**. At the end of
Huai Kaeo Road, a statue of Khruba Srivijaya, the monk who organized the gargantuan effort to build the road from here to the wat, points the way to the temple.

A checkpoint halfway up is about the only sign that Doi Suthep is a **national
park**: despite the nearness of the city, its rich mixed forests support 330 species
of birds, and the area is a favoured site for nature study, second in the north only
to the larger and less disturbed Doi Inthanon National Park. On the higher slopes

---

KHRUBA SRIVIJAYA

Khruba Srivijaya, the most revered monk in northern Thailand, was born in 1877
in a small village 100km south of Chiang Mai. His birth coincided with a supernatural thunderstorm and earthquake, after which he was named In Fuan, "Great Jolt",
until he joined the monkhood. A generous and tireless campaigner, he breathed life
into Buddhist worship in the north by renovating over a hundred religious sites,
including Wat Phra That Haripunjaya in Lamphun and Wat Phra That Doi Tung
near Mae Sai. His greatest work, however, was the construction in 1935 of the
paved road up to Wat Phra That Doi Suthep, which beforehand could only be
reached after a climb of at least five hours. The road was constructed entirely by
the voluntary labour of people from all over the north, using the most primitive
tools. The project gained such fame that it attracted donations of B20 million, and
on any one day as many as four thousand people worked on it. So that people didn't
get in each other's way, Khruba Srivijaya declared that each village should contribute 15m of road, but as more volunteers flocked to Chiang Mai, this figure had to
be reduced to 3m. After just six months, the road was completed and Khruba
Srivijaya took the first ride to the temple in a donated car.

When Khruba Srivijaya died in 1938, Rama VIII was so moved that he sponsored
a royal cremation ceremony, which was held in 1946. The monk's relics were
divided up and are now enshrined at Wat Suan Dork in Chiang Mai, Wat Phra Kaeo
Don Tao in Lampang and at many other holy places throughout the north.

near park headquarters (☎053/248405) there's a **campsite** and simple, twelve-berth **bungalows** (⑦), which can only be reached if you have your own transport – ask for a map at the checkpoint.

About 1km beyond the checkpoint, a good unpaved road on the right leads 3km to **Mon Tha Than Falls**, a beautiful and rarely visited spot, believed by some to be home to evil spirits. Camping is possible beside the pretty lower cascade, where a refreshment stall is open during the day. The higher fall is an idyllic five-metre drop into a small bathing pool, completely overhung by thick, humming jungle.

Wat Phra That Doi Suthep

Opposite a car park and souvenir village, a flight of three hundred naga-flanked steps is the last leg on the way to Wat Phra That Doi Suthep – a nearby funicular (B10 donation) provides a welcome alternative. From the temple's **lower terrace**, the magnificent views of Chiang Mai and the surrounding plain, 1000m below, are best in the early morning or late afternoon, though peaceful contemplation of the view is frequently shattered by people sounding the heavy, dissonant bells around the terrace – it's supposed to bring good luck.

Before going to the **upper terrace** you have to remove your shoes – and if you're showing a bit of knee or shoulder, the temple provides wraps to cover your impoliteness. This terrace is probably the most harmonious piece of temple architecture in Thailand, a dazzling combination of red, green and gold in the textures of carved wood, filigree and gleaming metal – even the tinkling of the miniature bells and the rattling of fortune sticks seem to keep the rhythm. A cloister, decorated with gaudy murals, tightly encloses the terrace, leaving room only for a couple of small minor viharns and the altars and ceremonial gold umbrellas which surround the central focus of attention, the **chedi**. This dazzling gold-plated beacon, a sixteenth-century extension of Ku Na's original, was modelled on the chedi at Wat Phra That Haripunjaya in Lamphun – which previously had been the region's most significant shrine – and has now become a venerated emblem of northern Thailand.

A small *hong*, or swan, on a wire stretching to the pinnacle is used to bless the chedi: a cup in the swan's beak is filled with water, a pulley draws the swan to the spire where the water is tipped out over the sides of the chedi. Look out also for a wooden statue at the northwestern corner of the chedi, showing a cockerel which used to peck the feet of visitors who entered with their shoes on.

Beyond the wat

Songthaews continue another 4km up the paved road to **Phuping Palace**, the residence for the royals when they come to visit their village development projects in the north. A viewpoint over the hills to the south, a rose garden and some pleasant trails through the forest are open to the public when the family is not in residence, but only from Friday to Sunday and on public holidays (9am–5pm).

About 3km from the palace along a dirt side road, **Ban Doi Pui** is a highly commercialized Hmong village, only worth visiting if you don't have time to get out into the countryside – seeing the Hmong is about all you'll get out of it.

Wiang Kum Kam

The well-preserved and rarely visited ruins of the ancient city of **WIANG KUM KAM** – traditionally regarded as the prototype for Chiang Mai – are hidden away in the picturesque, rural fringe of town, 5km south of the centre.

According to folklore, Wiang Kum Kam was built by King Mengrai as his new capital of the north, but was soon abandoned because of inundation by the Ping River. Recent excavations, however, have put paid to that theory: Wiang Kum Kam was in fact established much earlier, as one of a cluster of fortified satellite towns that surrounded the Mon capital at Lamphun. After Mengrai had conquered Lamphun in 1281, he resided at Kum Kam for a while, raising a chedi, a viharn and several Buddha statues before moving on to build Chiang Mai. Wiang Kum Kam was abandoned sometime before 1750, probably as a result of a Burmese invasion.

The ancient city, which is about 3km square, can only be explored on a bicycle or a motorbike. The best way to approach it without getting lost is from Highway 1141, the southern leg of the Superhighway, which links the airport to Highway 11: immediately to the east of the Ping River bridge, take the signposted turning to the south.

About half of Wiang Kum Kam's 22 known temple sites have now been uncovered, along with a unique stone slab (now housed in the Chiang Mai National Museum) inscribed in a unique forerunner of the Thai script and a hoard of terracotta Buddha images. It's easiest to head first for **Chedi Si Liam**, reached 1km after the Ping River bridge, which provides a useful landmark: this much-restored Mon chedi, in the shape of a tall, squared-off pyramid with niched Buddha images, was built by Mengrai on the model of Wat Kukut in Lamphun, and is still part of a working temple.

Backtracking along the road you've travelled down from Chiang Mai, take the first right turn, turn right again and keep left through a scattered farming settlement to reach, after about 2km, **Wat Kan Thom** (aka Chang Kham), the centre of the old city and still an important place of worship. Archaeologists were only able to get at the site after much of it had been levelled by bulldozers building a playground for the adjacent school, but they have managed to uncover the brick foundations of Mengrai's viharn. The modern spirit house next to it is where Mengrai's soul is said to reside. Also in the grounds are a white chedi and a small viharn, both much restored, and a large new viharn displaying fine craftsmanship.

The real joy now is to head off along the trails through the thick foliage of the longan plantations to the northwest of Wat Kan Thom, back towards Chedi Si Liam. You'll come across surprisingly well-preserved chedis and the red-brick walls of Wiang Kum Kam's temples in a handful of shady clearings, with only a few stray cows and sprouting weeds for company.

Lamphun

Though capital of its own province, **LAMPHUN** is a small, disconsolate place, living in the shadow of the tourist attention (and baht) showered on Chiang Mai, 26km to the north. The town's largely drab architecture is given some character by the surrounding waterways, beyond which stretch lush ricefields and *lam yai* (longan) plantations – the sweetness of the local variety is celebrated every year in early August at the **Ngan Lam Yai** (Longan Festival), when the town comes alive with processions of fruity floats, a drum-beating competition and a Miss Lam Yai beauty contest. In welcome contrast with the rest of downtown Lamphun, however, the ancient but lively working temples of Wat Phra That Haripunjaya and Wat Kukut are worth aiming for on a half-day trip from Chiang Mai.

Lamphun's history dates back to the early ninth century, when the ruler of the major Dvaravati centre at Lopburi sent his daughter, Chama Thevi, to found the Buddhist state of **Haripunjaya** here. Under the dynasty established by Chama Thevi, Haripunjaya flourished as a link in the trade route to Yunnan in southwest China, although it eventually came under the suzerainty of the Khmers at Angkor, probably in the early eleventh century. In 1281, after a decade of scheming, King Mengrai of Chiang Mai conquered Lamphun and integrated it once and for all into the Thai state of Lanna, which by then covered all of the north country.

The Town

Chama Thevi's planners are said to have based their design for the town on the shape of an auspicious conch shell. The rough outcome is a rectangle, narrower at the north end than the south, with the Khuang River running down its kilometre-long east side, and moats around the north, west and south sides. The main street, Inthayongyot Road, bisects the conch from north to south, while the road to Wat Kukut (Chama Thevi Road) heads out from the middle of the west moat.

One of the north's grandest and most important temples, **Wat Phra That Haripunjaya** (Wat Hari for short) has its rear entrance on Inthayongyot Road and its bot and ornamental front entrance facing the river. The earliest guess at the date of its founding is 897, when the king of Haripunjaya is said to have built a chedi to enshrine a hair of the Buddha. More certain is the date of the main rebuilding of the temple, under King Tilokaraja of Chiang Mai in 1443, when the present ringed chedi was erected in the then-fashionable Sri Lankan style (later copied at Doi Suthep and Lampang). Clad in brilliant copper plates, it has since been raised to a height of 50m, crowned by a gold umbrella.

The plain open courtyards around the chedi contain a compendium of religious structures in a jarring mix of styles and colours. On the north side, the tiered Haripunjaya-style pyramid of **Chedi Suwanna** was built in 1418 as a replica of the chedi at nearby Wat Kukut. You get a whiff of southern Thailand in the open space beyond the Suwanna chedi, where the **Chedi Chiang Yan** owes its resemblance to a pile of flattened pumpkins to the Srivijayan style. On either side of the viharn (to the east of the main chedi) stand a dark red **belltower**, containing what's claimed to be the world's largest bronze gong, and a weather-beaten **library** on an ochre-coloured base. Just to add to the temple's mystique, an open pavilion at the southwestern corner of the chedi shelters a stone indented with four overlapping **footprints**, which are believed by fervent worshippers to confirm an ancient legend that the Buddha once passed this way. Next to the pavilion can be seen the **Phra Chao Tan Jai**, a graceful standing Buddha, and a small **museum**, which houses bequests to the temple, including some beautiful Buddha images in the Lanna style.

Across the main road from Wat Hari's back entrance, the **National Museum** (Wed–Sun 9am–noon & 1–4pm; B10) contains a well-organized but not quite compelling collection of religious finds, and occasionally stages some interesting temporary exhibitions. The terracotta and bronze Buddha images here give the best overview of the distinctive features of the Haripunjaya style: large hair curls above a wide, flat forehead, bulging eyes, incised moustache and enigmatic smile.

Art-history buffs will get the most out of **Wat Kukut** (aka Wat Chama Thevi), though they'll bemoan the neon lights which decorate the tiers of the main chedi.

Queen Chama Thevi is supposed to have chosen the site by ordering an archer to fire an arrow from the city's western gate – to retrace his epic shot, follow the road along the National Museum's southern wall to the west gate at the city moat, and keep going for nearly 1km along Chama Thevi Road. The two brick **chedis**, dated to 1218, are the only complete examples not just of Haripunjaya architecture, but of the whole Dvaravati style. The main chedi – Suwan Chang Kot – is tiered and rectangular, the smaller one octagonal, and both are inset with niches sheltering beautiful, wide-browed Buddha images in stucco, typical of the Haripunjaya style. Suwan Chang Kot, believed to enshrine Chama Thevi's ashes, lost its pinnacle at some stage, giving rise to the name Wat Kukut, the "topless" wat.

Practicalities

The direct (and scenic) route from Chiang Mai to Lamphun is Highway 106, for much of the way a stately avenue lined by thirty-metre-tall *yang* trees. Frequent white and blue **buses** from Lamyai Market on Charoen Prathet Road make the journey (45min), stopping outside the back entrance of Wat Hari. If you turn up at Lamphun by **train**, it's a half-hour walk or a samlor ride southwest to the town centre.

An attractive nineteenth-century teak house and the former residence of the prince of Lamphun, *Khum Ton Kaew*, behind the National Museum on Wangsai Road, now contains an expensive handicrafts shop downstairs and a good but overpriced **restaurant** on the balcony and in the garden. Basic inexpensive Thai food is served at cafés on Inthayongyot Road to the south of Wat Hari. It's unlikely you'll want to **stay overnight** in Lamphun, especially as the town's only hotel, *Sri Lamphun*, 50m south of Wat Hari's back entrance at 51/2 Inthayongyot Rd (☎052/511176; ②), is noisy and grubby.

The Mae Sa valley

On the north side of Chiang Mai, Chotana Road turns into Highway 107, which heads off through a flat, featureless valley, past a golf course and an army camp, before reaching the small market town of Mae Rim after 16km. Turn left at Mae Rim to enter the **Mae Sa valley**, a twenty-kilometre strip of touristy sideshows, including a snake farm, several upmarket "hill station" resorts and a couple of unexciting waterfalls. The most interesting attractions are the orchid nurseries and the elephant camp, where you can see logging shows in the morning and take an expensive elephant ride into the countryside (B200 an hour). If any of this takes your fancy, it's best to go on a tour from one of Chiang Mai's many travel agents, or on a rented motorbike.

EAST OF CHIANG MAI

From Chiang Mai, visitors usually head west to Mae Hong Son or north to Chiang Rai, but a trip eastwards to the ancient city-states of Lampang and Nan can be just as rewarding, not only for the dividends of going against the usual flow, but also for the natural beauty of the region's upland ranges and its eccentric variety of Thai, Burmese and Laotian art and architecture. Congenial **Lampang** contains Thai wats to rival those of Chiang Mai for beauty – in Wat Phra That Lampang Luang it has the finest surviving example of traditional northern architecture anywhere – and is further endowed with pure Burmese temples and some fine old city architecture. More difficult to reach but a more intriguing target is **Nan**, with its heady artistic mix of Thai and Laotian styles and steep ring of scenic mountains.

A few major **roads**, served by regular through buses from Chiang Mai, cross the region: Highway 11 heads southeast through Lampang and the junction town of Den Chai, before plummeting south to Phitsanulok; from Lampang Highway 1 heads north to Chiang Rai, and from Den Chai Highway 101 carries on northeast to Nan, almost on the border with Laos. The northern **rail line** follows a course roughly parallel with Highway 11 through the region, and although trains here are generally slower than buses, the Lampang and Den Chai stations are useful if you're coming up from Bangkok.

Lampang and around

Slow passes and long tunnels breach the narrow, steep belt of mountains between Chiang Mai and **LAMPANG**, 100km to the southeast. The north's second largest town and an important transport hub – Highway 11, Highway 1 and the northern rail line all converge here – Lampang's attractions are undeniably low-key, and nearly all travellers sail through it on their way to the more trumpeted sights further north. But unlike most provincial capitals, it has the look of a place where history has not been completely wiped out: houses, shops and temples survive in the traditional style, and the town makes few concessions to tourism. Out of town, the beautiful complex of Wat Phra That Lampang Luang is the main event in these parts, but while you're in the neighbourhood you could

also stop by to watch a logging show at the Young Elephant Training Centre, on the road from Chiang Mai.

Founded as Kelang Nakhon by the ninth-century Haripunjaya queen Chama Thevi, Lampang became important enough for one of her two sons to rule here after her death. After King Mengrai's conquest of Haripunjaya in 1281, Lampang suffered much the same ups and downs as the rest of Lanna, enjoying a burst of prosperity as a **timber** town at the end of the last century, when it supported a population of twenty thousand people and four thousand working elephants. Many of its temples are financially endowed by the waves of outsiders who have settled here: refugees from Chiang Saen (who were forcibly resettled here by Rama I at the beginning of the last century), Burmese teak-loggers and workers, and, more recently, rich Thai pensioners attracted by the town's sedate charm.

The whole town can be covered on foot without trouble, though to get out to Wat Phra Kaeo Don Tao you might want to hop on one of the many **songthaews** which cruise the streets. **Horse-drawn carriages**, which have become a hackneyed symbol of Lampang, can be hired in the centre (starting from B50 for 15min).

The Town

The modern centre of Lampang sprawls along the south side of the Wang River, with its most frenetic commercial activity taking place along Boonyawat and Robwiang roads near Ratchada Bridge, where you'll find stalls and shops selling the famous local pottery, a kitsch combination of whites, blues and browns, made from the area's rich kaolin clay. The town's few sights are well scattered, the best place to start being the leafy suburbs on the north side of the river – the site of the original Haripunjaya settlement – which today contain the most important and interesting temple, **Wat Phra Kaeo Don Tao**, an imposing, rather forbidding complex on Phra Kaeo Road, 1km northeast of the Ratchada Bridge (B10 admission fee for farangs). The temple was founded in the fifteenth century to enshrine the Phra Kaeo Don Tao image, now residing at Wat Phra That Lampang Luang (see over), and for 32 years also housed the Emerald Buddha – which local stories aver to be a copy of Phra Kaeo Don Tao – when an elephant carrying the holy image from Chiang Rai to Chiang Mai made an unscheduled and therefore auspicious halt here in 1436.

The clean, simple lines of the white **chedi**, which is reputed to contain a hair of the Buddha, form a shining backdrop to the wat's most interesting building, a Burmese **mondop** stacked up in extravagantly carved tiers. A Thai prince, whose British-style coat of arms can be seen on the ceiling inside, employed craftsmen from the local Burmese community to build the mondop in 1909. The interior decoration, all gilt and gaudy coloured glass, is a real fright, mixing Oriental and European influences, with some incongruously cute little cherubs on the ceiling. The mondop's boyish bronze centrepiece has the typical features of a Mandalay Buddha, with its jewelled headband, inset black and white eyes, and exaggerated, dangling ears, which denote the Buddha's supernatural ability to hear everything in the universe. The image in front of the Buddha, dripping with gold-leaf offerings, is of Khruba Srivijaya, the north's most venerated monk (see p.241). A small, gloomy **museum** opposite the mondop displays some dainty china and a humorous *nagadan*, a carved supporting panel showing a man being given a piggyback to hold up the roof.

The Burmese who worked on Wat Phra Kaeo Don Tao were brought to Lampang in the late nineteenth century when, after the British conquest of Upper Burma, timber companies expanded their operations as far as northern Thailand. Fearing that the homeless spirits of fallen trees would seek vengeance, the Burmese logging workers often sponsored the building of temples, most of which still stand, to appease the tree sprites and gain merit. Unfortunately the spirits, though they have had to wait nearly a century, seem to have got their revenge: due to a short circuit in some dodgy wiring, Wat Sri Chum, the most important and beautiful Burmese temple, five minutes' walk south of Robwiang Road, recently burnt to the ground. None of the remaining wats are of outstanding architectural merit, but to get a flavour of Burma try **Wat Sri Rong Muang**, towards the west end of Takrao Noi Road, which presents a dazzling ensemble: the crazy angles of its red and yellow roof shelter more Mandalay Buddhas and several extravagantly carved gilt sermon thrones, swimming in a glittering sea of coloured-glass wall tiles.

If you've had your fill of temples, the streets of the **Talat Khao**, the "Old Market" (also known as Talat Jiin, "Chinese Market") around Tipchang Road are good for a stroll, especially in the evening. It's now a quiet area of shophouses and mansions, which show a mixture of Burmese, Chinese and European influence, with intricate balconies, carved gables and unusual sunburst designs carved over some of the doors. Small lanes on the north side of the Talat Khao lead down to the Wang River, whose waters are as green as its overgrown banks – what used to be the main thoroughfare for trading boats and huge rafts of felled timber has been reduced almost to stagnation by an upriver dam.

Practicalities

Buses from Nawarat Bridge in Chiang Mai run to Lampang every half-hour for most of the day, some of which then trundle on up Highway 1 to Phayao and Chiang Rai. Ten buses a day from Chiang Mai's Arcade station also stop at Lampang on their way to Nan. Only six **trains** a day stop here in each direction, though if you're coming from Bangkok the train is more convenient than direct buses to Lampang. The train and bus stations lie to the southwest of town, but many buses also stop on Phaholyothin Road in the centre. The small, primitive **tourist information** centre (Mon–Fri 9am–noon & 1–4pm) at the Provincial Office, at the corner of Boonyawat and Pakham roads, can help with advice on excursions to the elephant training centre and the like.

Despite receiving few visitors, accommodation prospects in Lampang have improved markedly with the recent opening of several **guest houses**. In a leafy spot one street north of the river, *No. 4 Guest House*, 54 Phamaikhed Rd (②), occupies a gorgeous wooden house in a large garden: rooms are simply furnished but the shared bathrooms have hot water. About 4km from the centre on the right-hand side of Highway 1 towards Chiang Rai, *Bann Fai* (☎054/224602; ③) is most useful for those with their own transport. Named "Cotton House" for the spinning and weaving which you can watch in a small workshop, the complex also comprises a good handicrafts shop and an attractive outdoor restaurant, as well as rooms in a wooden house at the back, sparsely but tastefully decorated with low antique dressing tables and triangular "axe" pillows. Run by the owners of the eponymous restaurant (see facing page), *Riverside Guest House*, 286 Talat Khao Rd (☎054/227005; ④), is a peaceful traditional compound of elegantly decorated rooms, some with balconies overlooking the river: on a riverfront lane to the east of the restaurant, it's quite hard to find as there's no sign – look for the house number in Arabic numerals. The town's lowest-priced **hotels**, which queue up to the west of the centre along Boonyawat Road, are generally dismal, dirty affairs. Best of them is *9 (Kao) Mithima Hotel*, far out and set back from the road at 285 Boonyawat Rd (☎054/217438; ②). For a little more cash, standards improve markedly: rooms with air conditioning and hot water at the *Asia Hotel*, 229 Boonyawat Rd (☎054/217844; ④), are clean, comfortable and good value. At the top end is the tacky luxury of the *Tipchang Hotel*, to the west at 54/22 Takrao Noi Rd (☎054/226501; ⑥), which has a swimming pool.

The **place to eat and drink** is the *Riverside* at 328 Tipchang Rd, a cosy, relaxing spot on terraces overlooking the water. A wide variety of excellent Thai and Western food (moderate to expensive) is served to the strains of live acoustic music. To catch passing trade on Highway 1, there's a similar offshoot, *Riverside Hill*, 3km northeast of the centre.

Wat Phra That Lampang Luang

If you've made it as far as Lampang, a visit to **Wat Phra That Lampang Luang**, a grand and well-preserved capsule of beautiful Lanna art and architecture, is a must. However, although the wat is a busy pilgrimage site, **getting there** without your own transport isn't easy: catch a songthaew from Lampang's Sri Chum Road (south of the junction with Boonyawat Road) for **Kor Kha**, 10km southwest on Highway 1; songthaews covering the last 5km from there to the wat are rare, so you'll probably have to hire a motorbike taxi (about B50 round trip) or walk (cross the bridge over the Mae Nam Wang and turn right, heading north on a paved road).

The wat was built early in the Haripunjaya era as a *wiang* (fortress), one of a satellite group around Lampang – you can still see remains of the threefold ramparts in the farming village around the temple. Getting into the *wiang* is easier nowadays: a naga staircase leads you up to a wedding cake of a gatehouse, richly decorated with stucco, which is set in the original brick boundary walls. Just inside, the oversized **viharn** is open on all sides in classic Lanna fashion, and shelters a spectacular centrepiece: known as a *ku*, a feature found only in the viharns of northern Thailand, this gilded brick tower looks like a bonfire for the main Buddha image sitting inside, the Phra Chao Lan Thong. Watch your head on the panels hanging from the low eaves, which are decorated with attractive early nineteenth-century paintings of battles, palaces and nobles in traditional Burmese gear.

This central viharn is snugly flanked by three others. In front of the murky, beautifully decorated viharn to the left, look out for a wooden *tung chai* carved with flaming, coiled nagas, which was used as a heraldic banner for northern princes. The battered, cosy **Viharn Nam Tame**, second back on the right, is possibly the oldest wooden building in Thailand, dating back to the early sixteenth century. Its drooping roof configuration is archetypal: divided into three tiers, each of which is divided again into two layers, it ends up almost scraping the ground. Under the eaves you can just make out fragments of panel paintings, as old as the viharn, illustrating a story of one of the exploits of the Hindu god Indra.

Hundreds of rainy seasons have turned the copper plates on the wat's huge central **chedi** into an arresting patchwork of greens, blues and purples: safe inside are supposed to be a hair of the Buddha and ashes from his right forehead and neck. By the chedi's northwest corner, a sign points to a drainage hole in the wat's boundary wall, once the scene of an unlikely act of derring-do: in 1736, local hero Thip Chang managed to wriggle through the tiny hole and free the *wiang* from the occupying Burmese, before going on to liberate the whole of Lampang.

A gate in the south side of the boundary wall leads to a spreading **bodhi tree** on crutches: merit-makers have donated hundreds of supports to prop up its drooping branches. The tree, with its own small shrine standing underneath, is believed to be inhabited by spirits, and the sick are sometimes brought here in search of a cure.

Don't miss the small, unimpressive viharn to the west of the bodhi tree – it's the home of **Phra Kaeo Don Tao**, the much-revered companion image to Bangkok's Emerald Buddha, and the wat's main focus of pilgrimage. Legend has it that the statuette first appeared in the form of an emerald found in a watermelon presented by a local woman to a venerated monk. The two of them tried to carve a Buddha out of the emerald, without much success, until the god Indra appeared and fashioned the marvellous image, at which point the ungrateful townsfolk accused the monk of having an affair with the woman and put her to death, thus bringing down upon the town a series of disasters which confirmed the image's awesome power. In all probability, the image was carved at the beginning of the fifteenth century, when its namesake wat in Lampang was founded. Peering through the dim light and the rows of protective bars inside the viharn, you can just make out the tiny meditating Buddha – it's actually made of jasper, not emerald – which on special occasions is publicly displayed wearing a headdress and necklace. To cash in on its supernatural reputation, a dusty shop in the viharn sells monkeys' skulls, turtle shells and other exotic charms.

Young Elephant Training Centre

The **Young Elephant Training Centre** (shows daily 9.30 & 11am; B40), 25km west of Lampang on Highway 11, is the most authentic place to see elephants being trained for logging work and, being more out of the way, is less touristy than the elephant showgrounds to the north of Chiang Mai. It's best visited en route from Chiang Mai to Lampang: ask the bus conductor for Suan Pa (Forest Park) Thung Kwian, 70km from Chiang Mai. On a day trip from Lampang, a bus towards Lamphun or Chiang Mai should get you there in around half an hour. Note that the centre closes for every conceivable religious holiday, of which there are about fifty a year, so you'd do well to check with TAT in Chiang Mai or the tourist information centre in Lampang before setting off.

Run by the veterinary section of the Thai forestry organization, the training centre was the earliest of its kind in Thailand and is now home to around a hundred elephants. The daily **shows** put the young elephants through their paces with plenty of amusing showmanship and loud trumpeting for their audience: after some photogenic bathing, they walk together in formation and go through a long routine of pushing, dragging, carrying and piling logs. If you want to get a closer look, bring some bananas or sugar cane to feed the animals.

THE ELEPHANT IN THAILAND

To Thais the **Asian elephant** has profound **spiritual significance**, derived from both Hindu and Buddhist mythologies. Carvings and statues of **Ganesh**, the Hindu god with an elephant's head, feature on ancient temples all over the country and, as the god of knowledge and remover of obstacles, Ganesh has been adopted as the symbol of the Fine Arts Department – and is thus depicted on all entrance tickets to historical sights. The Hindu deity Indra rarely appears without his three-headed elephant mount **Erawan**, and miniature devotional elephant effigies are sold at major Brahmin shrines, such as Bangkok's Erawan shrine. In Buddhist legend, the future **Buddha's mother** was able to conceive only after she dreamt that a white elephant had entered her womb: that is why elephant balustrades encircle many of the Buddhist temples of Sukhothai, and why the rare white elephant is accorded royal status (see p.102) and regarded as a highly auspicious animal.

The **practical** role of the elephant in Thailand is almost as great as its symbolic importance. The kings of Ayutthaya relied on elephants to take them into battle against the Burmese – one king assembled a trained elephant army of three hundred – and during the last century King Rama IV offered Abraham Lincoln a male and a female to "multiply in the forests of America" and to use in the Civil War. In times of peace, the phenomenal strength of the elephant has made it invaluable as a beast of burden: elephants hauled the stone from which the gargantuan Khmer temple complexes of the north and northeast were built, and for centuries they have been used to clear forests and carry timber.

By a terrible irony, the **timber industry** has been the animal's undoing. Mechanized logging has destroyed their preferred river-valley habitats, forcing them into isolated upland pockets. As a result, Thailand's population of wild elephants is perhaps only half the size of the domesticated population of five thousand, many of which are trained for environmentally less damaging forms of logging. Most are bred in captivity, spending the first three years of their lives with their mothers (who get five years' maternity leave), before being forcibly separated and raised with other calves in training schools. From the age of three each elephant is assigned its own **mahout** – a trainer, keeper and driver rolled into one – who will stay with it for the rest of its working life. Training begins gently, with mahouts taking months to earn the trust of their charge; over the next thirteen years the elephant is taught about forty different commands, from simple "stop" and "go" orders to complex instructions for hooking and passing manoeuvres with the trunk. By the age of sixteen an elephant is ready to be put to work and is expected to carry on working until it reaches fifty or so. Today, however, the domesticated elephant is becoming less useful. The government ban on teak logging has reduced the role of the working elephant to such an extent that training schools concentrate as much on perfecting shows for tourists as on honing their practical skills.

Nan

From Lampang, most travellers head north for Chiang Rai, but remote and little-visited Nan – recently designated a tourist development area for its historic hybrid temples and stunning mountainous countryside – provides a strong incentive to carry on eastwards. **Buses** from Lampang follow Highway 11 to the junction town of Den Chai (Bangkok–Chiang Mai trains also stop here), 83km to the southeast, then veer northeastwards on Highway 101

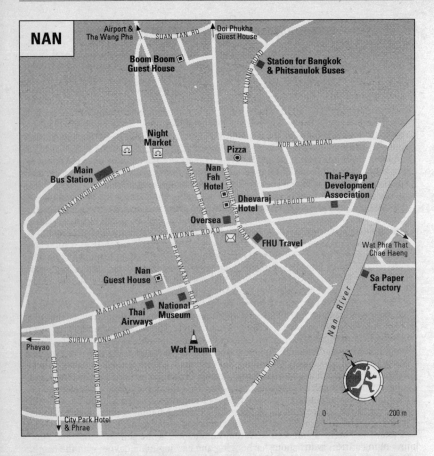

through the tobacco-rich Yom valley, dotted with distinctive brick curing houses. Phrae, 20km on, is famous for woodcarving and the quality of its *seua maw hawm*, the deep-blue, baggy working shirt seen all over Thailand. After leaving the Yom, the highway gently climbs through rolling hills of cotton fields and teak plantations to its highest point, framed by limestone cliffs, before descending into the high, isolated valley of the Nan River, one of the two great tributaries of the Chao Phraya. Coming direct from Chiang Mai, you might want to weigh up the seven-hour bus journey to Nan (B83 non-air-con) against the one-hour **flight** (B510).

Ringed by high mountains, the sleepy but prosperous provincial capital of **NAN**, 225km east of Lampang, rests on the grassy west bank of the Nan River, where traditional floating houses moored to the bank add to the rustic ambience. This stretch of river really comes alive during the **Lanna boat races**, usually held in the second week of October, when villages from around the province send teams of up to fifty oarsmen here to race in long, colourfully decorated canoes with dragon prows. The lush surrounding valley is noted for its cotton-weaving, sweet oranges and the attractive grainy paper made from the bark of local *sa* (mulberry) trees.

Although it has been kicked around by Burma, Laos and Thailand, Nan province has a history of being on the fringes, distanced by the encircling barrier of mountains. Rama V brought Nan into his centralization programme at the turn of the century, but left the traditional ruling house in place, making it the last province in Thailand to be administered by a local ruler (it remained so until 1931). During the troubled 1970s, communist insurgents holed up in this twilight region and proclaimed Nan the future capital of the liberated zone, which only succeeding in bringing the full might of the Thai Army down on them. Though the insurgency faded after the government's 1982 offer of amnesty, roadside checkpoints betray a continued large military presence in the province. Nan still has a slight reputation for lawlessness, but most of the bandits nowadays are illegal loggers.

The Town

Nan's unhurried centre comprises a disorienting grid of crooked streets, around a small core of shops and businesses where Mahawong and Anantaworarichides roads meet Sumondhevaraj Road. The best place to start an exploration is to the southwest at the **National Museum** (Wed–Sun 9am–noon & 1–4pm; B10), located in a tidy palace with superb teak floors, which used to be home to the rulers of Nan. Informative, user-friendly displays give you a bite-sized introduction to Nan, its history and its peoples. The prize exhibit is a talismanic elephant tusk with a bad case of brown tooth decay, which is claimed to be magic black ivory. The tusk was discovered over three hundred years ago and now sits on a colourful wooden *khut*, a mythological eagle. The museum also houses elegant pottery and woodcarving, gorgeously wrought silverware and some rare Laotian Buddhas.

Nearby on Phakwang Road, **Wat Phumin** will grab even the most over-templed traveller. Its 500-year-old centrepiece is an unusual cruciform building, combining both the bot and the viharn, which balances some quirky features in a perfect symmetry. Two giant nagas pass through the base of the building, with their tails along the balustrades at the south entrance and their heads at the north, representing the sacred oceans at the base of the central mountain of the universe. The doors at the four entrances, which have been beautifully carved with a complex pattern of animals and flowers, lead straight to the four Buddha images arranged around a tall altar in the centre of the building – note the Buddhas' piercing onyx eyes and pointed ears, showing the influence of Laos, 50km away. What really sets the bot apart are the recently restored **murals**, whose bright, simple colours seem to jump off the walls. Executed in 1857, the paintings take you on a whirlwind tour of heaven, hell, the Buddha's previous incarnations, local legends and incidents from Nan's history, and

A khut

include stacks of vivacious, sometimes bawdy, detail, which provides a valuable pictorial record of that era.

Wat Phra That Chae Haeng, on the opposite side of the river 2km southeast of town, is another must, as much for its setting on a hill overlooking the Nan valley as anything else. The wat was founded in 1300, at a spot determined by the Buddha himself when he passed through this way – or so local legend would have it. The nagas here outdo even Wat Phumin's: the first you see of the wat across the fields is a wide driveway flanked by monumental serpents gliding down the slope from the temple. A magnificent gnarled bodhi tree with hundreds of spreading branches and roots guards the main gate, set in high boundary walls. Inside the walls, the highlight is a slender, 55-metre-high golden chedi, surrounded by four smaller chedis and four carved and gilded umbrellas, as well as small belfries and stucco lions. Close competition comes from the viharn roof, which has no less than fifteen Laotian-style tiers, stacked up like a house of cards and supported on finely carved *kan tuei* (wood supports) under the eaves.

Crafts and shops

Loyalty to local traditions ensures the survival of several good **handicrafts shops** in Nan, most of which are found on Sumondhevaraj Road north of the junction with Anantaworarichides. Right on this junction, *Nan Silverware* has locally made **silver** ornamental bowls and cups, as well as attractive belts and jewellery, priced at around B10 per gramme. Traditional lengths of **cotton** (mostly *pha sin*, used as wraparound skirts) are sold at *Pha Nan*, 21/2 Sumondhevaraj Rd, and *Jantragun*, at nos. 304–306 (see also Ban Nong Bua, p.256); the latter also has a good selection of *seua maw hawm*, Phrae's famous blue working shirts, and a few notebooks made from **sa paper**. You can watch the smelly, sticky, fascinating process of making this paper on the south bank of the Nan River just west of the town bridge. Look out for what appears to be a field of solar panels as you cross the bridge: the *sa* bark is softened and milled in water to form a gluey soup, into which these finely meshed frames are gently dunked before drying on the river bank. The resulting coarsely grained white sheets can be bought here at the factory for B5 each.

The *Thai-Payap Development Association*, which has a shop at 288 Sumondhevaraj Rd and a showroom at its head office at 24 Jetaboot Rd, is a **non-profitmaking organization**, set up to bring surplus income to local hill tribes. On sale are bags, basketware, woodcarving, honey, and all manner of fabrics, even Hmong baby-carriers.

Transport, accommodation and eating

The main **bus station** is on Anantaworarichides Road on the west side of town, but Bangkok and Phitsanulok services use a smaller station to the east of the centre on Kha Luang Road; arriving at either leaves a manageable walk or a samlor ride to the central accommodation area. A free *Thai Airways* minibus runs passengers from the **airport** on the north side of town to the hotels. For exploring Nan, *Oversea*, at 488 Sumondhevaraj Rd, rents out decent **bicycles** (B20–50 a day) and **mopeds** (B150).

Nan's **guest-house** scene boasts two great places, both on the north side of town. *Doi Phukha Guest House*, 94/5 Soi 1, Sumondhevaraj Rd (☎054/771422; ①), occupies a beautiful wooden house in a quiet compound; simple rooms share hot showers, and there's an informative noticeboard and excellent maps of the province. Closer to the centre at 6/1 Soi 5, Sumondhevaraj Rd, *Boom Boom House* (②) can also help with local information and serves good food; its four bedrooms, with shared hot-water bathrooms, are clean and quiet. If both of the above are full, *Nan Guest House*, 57/16 Mahaphom Rd (☎054/771849; ①), is adequate. Among the mid-range **hotels**, the *Dhevaraj*, 466 Sumondhevaraj Rd (☎054/710094–6; ④–⑤)), has slightly dingy rooms, with fan or air conditioning, but rates are reasonable for the facilities provided. The best in town is the new *City Park Hotel*, 99 Yantarakit Koson Rd (☎054/710376; ⑦), 2km from the centre on Highway 101 to Phrae; tasteful rooms in low-rise buildings give onto balconies overlooking a large swimming pool.

The night market and plenty of simple Thai **restaurants** line Anantaworarichides Road, but Nan's big culinary surprise is *Pizza* (*Tiptop 2*), further east along this road opposite the main cinema. Trained by a Swiss-Italian chef, the present cook produces fine pastas, pizzas and the like, as well as very good bread and Thai dishes, all at reasonable prices. *Pin Pub*, in an airy ground-floor room of the *Nan Fah Hotel* on Sumondhevaraj Road, is a lively, popular night-time hangout, which offers live bands playing Thai pop and American standards, and good, moderately priced Thai food.

Around Nan

The remote, mountainous countryside around Nan runs a close second to the headlong scenery of Mae Hong Son province, but its remoteness means that Nan has even worse transport and is even more poorly mapped. However, it's worth making the effort. Your easiest option is to head for the reliable *FHU Travel*, the only fixer in town at 453/4 Sumondhevaraj Rd (☎054/710636), which organizes slightly pricey but popular and enjoyable guided tours and trekking trips. One-day **tours** to Wat Nong Bua, Doi Phukha (see below) and several minor sights cost B1800 for two to three people or B500 per person for four to six people, including transport, driver/guide and lunch. **Treks** of two days (B1100 per person) or three days (B1500) head west, through tough terrain of thick jungle and high mountains, visiting at least one Phi Tong Luang village (see box, below) and nearby Hmong and Mien villages where they work, as well as settlements of Htin, an upland Mon-Khmer people most of whom have migrated into Nan province since the communist takeover of Laos in 1975. You may have to hang around for a few days to assemble the minimum quota of four people for a trek; alternatively, if you have the cash, this area could be seen on an expensive one-day tour.

If you want to go it alone, the bus service is sketchy, but *Oversea* (see facing page) rents out motorbikes. The easiest and most varied day trip out of Nan is to the north, heading first for **BAN NONG BUA**, site of a famous muralled temple of the same name. If you're on a bike, ride 40km up Highway 1080 to the southern outskirts of the town of **Tha Wang Pha**, where signs in English point you left across the Nan River to Wat Nong Bua, 3km away; buses from Nan's main bus station make the hour-long journey to Tha Wang Pha roughly hourly – then either rent a motorbike taxi in the town centre, or ask on the bus for Ban Nong Bua and walk the last 3km.

Wat Nong Bua stands behind the village green on the west side of the unpaved through road. Its beautifully gnarled viharn was built in 1862 in typical Lanna style, with low, drooping roof tiers surmounted by stucco finials – here you'll find horned nagas and tusked *makaras* (elephantine monsters), instead of the garuda finial which invariably crops up in central Thai temples. The viharn enshrines a pointy-eared Laotian Buddha, but its most outstanding features are the remarkably intact **murals** which cover all four walls. Executed between 1867 and 1888, probably by the Wat Phumin painters, they depict, with much humour and vivid detail, scenes from the *Chanthakhat Jataka* (the story of one of the Buddha's previous incarnations, as a hero called Chanthakhat). This is a particularly long and complex *Jataka* (although a leaflet, available from the monks in return for a small donation to temple funds, outlines the story in English), wherein our hero gets into all kinds of scrapes, involving several wives, sundry other liaisons, some formidably nasty enemies, and the god Indra transforming himself into a snake. The crux of the tale comes on the east wall (opposite the Buddha image): in the bottom left-hand corner, Chanthakhat and the love of his life, Thewathisangka, are shipwrecked and separated; the distraught queen wanders through the jungle, diagonally up the wall, to the hermitage of an old woman, where she shaves her head and becomes a nun; Chanthakhat travels through the wilderness along the bottom of the wall, curing a wounded naga-king on the way, who out of gratitude gives him a magic crystal ball, which enables our hero to face another series of perils along the south wall, before finally rediscovering and embracing Thewathisangka in front of the old woman's hut, at the top right-hand corner of the east wall.

Ban Nong Bua and the surrounding area are largely inhabited by Thai Lue people, distant cousins of the Thais, who've migrated from China in the past 150 years. They produce beautiful cotton garments in richly coloured geometric patterns; walk 200m behind the wat and you'll find weavers at work under the stilted sky-blue house of Khun Chunsom Prompanya, who sells the opulent fabrics in the shop behind. The quality of design and workmanship is very high here, and prices, though much the same as in Nan, are often discounted.

SPIRITS OF THE YELLOW LEAVES

Inhabiting the remote hill country west of Nan, the **Phi Tong Luang** – "Spirits of the Yellow Leaves" – represent the last remnant of nomadic hunter-gatherers in Thailand, and their way of life, like that of so many other indigenous peoples, is rapidly passing. Believing that spirits will be angered if the tribe settles in one place, grows crops or keeps animals, the Phi Tong Luang build only temporary shelters of branches and wild banana leaves and move on to another spot in the jungle as soon as the leaves turn yellow, thus earning their poetic Thai name. They call themselves Mrabri – "Forest People" – and traditionally eke out a hard livelihood from the forest, hunting with spears, trapping birds and small mammals, digging roots and collecting nuts, seeds and honey.

Recent deforestation by logging and slash-and-burn farming have eaten into the tribe's territory, however, and many of the Phi Tong Luang have been forced to sell their labour to Hmong and Mien farmers (the spirits apparently do not get angry if the tribe settles down and works the land for other people). They are paid only with food – because of their docility and their inability to understand and use money, they often get a raw deal for their hard work. They are also particularly ill-equipped to cope with curious and often insensitive tourists, although one of the American missionaries working with the tribe believes that occasional visits help the Phi Tong Luang to develop by teaching them about people in the outside world. Their susceptibility to disease (especially malaria) is high and life expectancy low, however, and at the last count there were only ninety members of the tribe alive.

Beyond Tha Wang Pha, Highway 1080 curves east towards the town of Pua, on whose southern outskirts Highway 1256, the spectacular access road for **DOI PHUKHA NATIONAL PARK**, begins its journey eastwards and upwards. It's difficult to get into the park on public transport, and you'll have to stay the night: hourly buses run from Nan's main station to Pua, from where one unreliable songthaew a morning (usually between 8am and 9am) serves the handful of villages along Highway 1256. Best tackled on a bike – though watch out for loose chippings on the bends – the access road climbs up a sharp ridge, through occasional stands of elephant grass and bamboo, towards Doi Dong Ya Wai (1939m), providing one of the most jawdroppingly scenic drives in Thailand: across the valleys to north and south stand rows of improbably steep mountains (including the 1980-metre Doi Phukha itself, far to the south), covered in lush vegetation with scarcely a sign of human habitation. At park headquarters, 24km up the road, simple bamboo huts (②) and sturdy six- to fifteen-berth bungalows with bathrooms and stoves (⑤–⑥) are available, and there's a campsite and an inexpensive daytime cafeteria. The park has no marked trails, but **guides** can be hired at HQ for B100 a day (a proportion of which is given to the local hill tribes) to lead visitors to Hmong and Htin villages and up the arduous slope to the nearest summit, Dong Khao (1305m).

THE MAE HONG SON LOOP

Two roads from Chiang Mai head over the western mountains into Mae Hong Son, Thailand's most remote province, offering the irresistible prospect of tying them together into a 600-kilometre loop. The towns en route give an appetizing taste of Burma to the west, but the journey itself, winding over implausibly steep forested mountains and through tightly hemmed farming valleys, is what will stick in the mind.

The southern leg of the route, Highway 108, first passes **Doi Inthanon National Park**, with its lofty views over half of northern Thailand and enough waterfalls to last a lifetime, then **Mae Sariang**, an important town for trade across the Burmese border. The provincial capital, **Mae Hong Son**, at the midpoint of the loop, still has the relaxing atmosphere of a big village and makes the best base for exploring the area's mountains, rivers and waterfalls. The northern leg, Highway 1095, heads northeast out of Mae Hong Son into an area of beautiful caves and stunning scenery around **Mae Lana** and **Soppong**: staying at one of the out-of-the-way guest houses here will enable you to trek independently around the countryside and the local hill-tribe villages. **Pai**, halfway back towards Chiang Mai from Mae Hong Son, is a cosy travellers' hang-out with some gentle walking trails in the surrounding valley.

We've taken the loop in a clockwise direction here only because Doi Inthanon is best reached direct from Chiang Mai – apart from that consideration, you could just as easily go the other way round. Travelling the loop is straightforward, although the mountainous roads go through plenty of bends and jolts. Either way, Mae Hong Son is about eight hours' travelling time from Chiang Mai by **bus**, although services along the newly paved northern route are slightly less frequent. The one-hour **flight** to Mae Hong Son is surprisingly inexpensive (B345), and is worth considering for one leg of the journey, especially if you're short on time. Above all, though, the loop is made for **motorbikes** and **jeeps**: the roads are quiet (but watch out for huge logging trucks) and you can satisfy the inevitable craving to stop every five minutes and admire the mountain scenery.

Highway 108: Chiang Mai to Mae Hong Son

Bus drivers who ply **Highway 108** are expected to have highly sharpened powers of concentration and the landlubber's version of sea legs – the road negotiates almost two thousand curves in the 349km to Mae Hong Son, so if you're at all prone to travel sickness plan to take a breather in Mae Sariang. Buses to Mae Sariang and Mae Hong Son depart from Chiang Mai's Arcade bus station; services to Chom Thong (for Doi Inthanon National Park) leave from the bottom of Phra Pokklao Road (Chiang Mai Gate).

Doi Inthanon National Park

Covering a huge area to the southwest of Chiang Mai, **DOI INTHANON NATIONAL PARK**, with its hill-tribe villages, dramatic waterfalls and panoramas over rows of wild, green peaks to the west, gives a pleasant, if sanitized, whiff of northern countryside, its attractions and concrete access roads kept in good order by the Thai Forestry Department. The park, named after the highest mountain in the country and so dubbed the "Roof of Thailand", is geared mainly to wildlife conservation but also contains a hill-tribe agricultural project producing strawberries, apples and flowers for sale. Often shrouded in mists, Doi Inthanon's temperate forests shelter a huge variety of flora and fauna, which make this one of the major destinations for naturalists in Southeast Asia. The park supports about 380 bird species, the largest number of any site in Thailand – among them the ashy-throated warbler and a species of the green-tailed sunbird, both unique to Doi Inthanon – and, near the summit, the only red rhododendrons in Thailand (in bloom Dec–Feb) and a wide variety of ground and epiphytic orchids. The waterfalls, birds and flowers are at their best in the cool season, but night-time temperatures sometimes drop below freezing, making warm clothing a must.

Getting there

The gateway to the park is **Chom Thong**, 58km southwest of Chiang Mai on Highway 108, a drab town with little to offer apart from the attractive **Wat Phra That Si Chom Thong**, whose impressive brass-plated chedi dates from the fifteenth century. The nearby bo tree has become an equally noteworthy architectural feature: dozens of Dalí-esque supports for its sagging branches have been sponsored by the devoted in the hope of earning merit. Inside the gnarled sixteenth-century viharn, a towering, gilded *ku* housing a Buddha relic just squeezes in beneath the ceiling, from which hangs a huge, sumptuous red and green umbrella. Weaponry, gongs, umbrellas, thrones and an elephant-tusk arch carved with delicate Buddha images all add to the welcoming clutter.

The main road through the park leaves Highway 108 1km north of Chom Thong, winding generally northwestwards for 48km to the top of Doi Inthanon (after 8km, by Mae Klang Falls, a checkpoint collects **entrance fees** of B25 per person, plus B10 per motorbike, and B30 per car, including driver); a second paved road forks left 10km before the summit, reaching the riverside market of Mae Chaem, southwest of the park, after 20km. For a detailed park map, bird lists and other information, stop at the **visitors' centre**, 9km up the main road, or the **park headquarters**, a further 22km on. Sticking to public transport, you'll be limited to the **songthaews** that shuttle between Chom Thong and Mae Chaem along the mountain's lower slopes – to get to the summit you'll have to hitch the last 10km (generally manageable). By **motorbike** or jeep you could do the park justice in a day trip from Chiang Mai, or treat it as the first stage of a longer trip to Mae Hong Son, following the newly paved Highway 1088 south from Mae Chaem to pick up Highway 108 again 20km west of Hot.

The park

Three sets of waterfalls provide the main roadside attractions on the way to the park headquarters: overrated **Mae Klang Falls**, 8km in, which with its picnic areas and food vendors gets overbearingly crowded, especially at weekends; **Vachiratharn Falls**, a misty long drop down a granite escarpment 11km beyond; and the twin cascades of **Siriphum Falls**, backing the park headquarters a further 11km on. With your own wheels you could reach a fourth and much more beautiful cataract, **Mae Ya**, which is believed to be the highest in Thailand – the winding, newly paved fourteen-kilometre track to it heads west off the main park road 2km north of Highway 108. Another unpaved side road, dubbed the **Karen Village Circuit Road**, takes a roundabout but culturally more enlightening route to the headquarters, leaving the main road 3km beyond Vachiratharn Falls and takes in three traditional and unspoilt Karen villages before rejoining the main road at the more developed Hmong village of **Ban Khun Klang**, 500m before the HQ.

For the most spectacular views in the park, continue 11km along the summit road or trek up the steep trail (about 4hr – ask for a guide at the HQ) to the sleek, modern **Napamaytanidol Chedi**, looming incongruously over the misty green hillside: on a clear day you can see the mountains of Burma to the west. Starting a short distance up the road from the chedi, the rewarding **Gew Mae Pan Trail**, a two-hour circular walk, wanders through sun-dappled forest and open savannah as it skirts the steep, western edge of Doi Inthanon, where violent-red rhododendrons are framed against open views over the canyoned headwaters of the Pan River; a signpost on the summit road marks the trailhead, and the well-cut path from there is easy to follow.

Doi Inthanon's **summit** (2565m), 6km beyond the chedi, is a big disappointment – from the car park you can see little beyond the radar installation. A small, still-revered stupa on the right contains the ashes of King Inthanon of Chiang Mai (after whom the mountain was renamed): at the end of the last century he was the first to recognize the importance of this watershed area in supplying the Ping River and ultimately the Chao Phraya, the queen of Thailand's rivers. One hundred metres back down the road, it's an easy walk to the bog which is the highest source of these great waterways, and one of the park's best birdwatching sites. The cream and brown sphagnum mosses which spread underfoot and hang off the trees give a creepy, primeval atmosphere, offset by the brash rhododendrons.

The paved **Mae Chaem road** skirts yet another set of waterfalls, 7km after the turnoff: look for a steep, unpaved road to the right, leading down to a ranger station and, just to the east, the dramatic long drop of **Huai Sai Luaeng Falls**. A circular two-hour trail from the ranger station takes in creeks and small waterfalls as well as **Mae Pan Falls**, a series of short cascades in a peaceful, shady setting. Continuing southwest, the paved road affords breathtaking views as it helter-skelters down to the sleepy valley of Mae Chaem. Hardy bikers can take on a tough, unpaved route towards Mae Hong Son from here, heading north up Route 1088 then west along 1263, before joining Highway 108 north of Khun Yuam; for saner souls, the southern 45-kilometre stretch of Highway 1088 is now paved, bringing you out on Highway 108 20km west of Hot.

Practicalities

Accommodation in the park is not as rough and ready as you might expect. Sturdy, four-berth national park bungalows (④), set in a pleasant wooded compound near the headquarters, come with electricity, cold showers, mattresses and bedding – these are sometimes booked up at weekends, but at other times you should be all right turning up on the day. Elsewhere, the *Little Home Guest House and Restaurant*, 7km along the main park road from Chom Thong (☎053/311475; ③–④), has clean, breeze-block, fan-cooled or air-conditioned huts with inside bathrooms.

Camping, an often chilly alternative, is permitted in the headquarters compound and at Mae Pan Falls (B5 per person per night). Two-person tents can be rented at the headquarters for B40 per night, as can blankets at B10 each per night.

Daytime **food** stalls operate at Mae Klang Falls and at the headquarters, and the restaurant in the national park bungalow compound serves inexpensive evening meals as long as you request them earlier in the day.

West to Mae Sariang and Mae Sam Laeb

Highway 108 parallels the Ping River downstream as far as **Hot**, a dusty, forgettable place 27km from Chom Thong, before bending west and weaving through pretty wooded hills up the valley of the Chaem River. If you're ready for a stopover at this point, the twee *Hot Resort* (☎053/461070; ④), 4km west of Hot, has well-appointed chalets with hot water. The resort's riverside restaurant does tasty food at moderate prices.

Another 13km brings you to **Ob Luang Gorge National Park**, billed with wild hyperbole as "Thailand's Grand Canyon" (entrance fee B15). A wooden bridge over the short, narrow channel lets you look down on the Chaem River bubbling along 50m below; upstream from the bridge, you can relax at the roadside food stalls and swim in the river when it's not too fast, and the shady park contains a campsite (B5 to pitch your own tent; B100 to hire a tent and blankets). West of Ob Luang the highway gradually climbs through pine forests, the road surface deteriorating and the countryside becoming steeper and wilder. A tranquil **guest house** at Ban Mae Waen, in a pretty valley 6km south of the highway, *Pan's House* (①) offers basic wooden rooms with electricity and mosquito nets, and inexpensive, simple food. The owner, Khun Pan, can arrange guided **trekking** to Karen and Lawa villages, and elephant-riding trips. To reach the guest house, take a largely downhill track signposted from the highway 68km from Hot, which takes nearly an hour to walk but is navigable on a motorbike (if you're travelling by bus, ask for Ban Mae Waen).

Mae Sariang

After a nerve-wracking hairpin descent into the broad, smoky valley of the Yuam River, Highway 108's westward progress ends at **MAE SARIANG**, 183km from Chiang Mai, a quietly industrious market town showing a marked Burmese influence in its temples and its rows of low wooden shophouses. If you need a stopover between Chiang Mai and Mae Hong Son, this is an obvious place as it's halfway along the southern route. From here you can make an intriguing day trip to the trading post of Mae Sam Laeb on the river border with Burma, and it's also possible to strike off south on a bone-rattling journey to Mae Sot. Buses enter Mae Sariang from the east along the town's main street, Wiang Mai Road, and

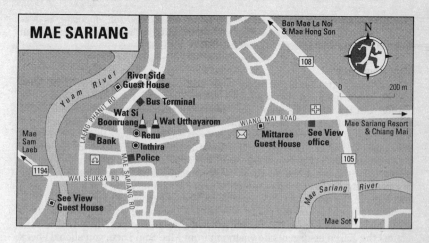

pull in at the terminal on Mae Sariang Road, one of two north–south streets; the other, Laeng Phanit Road, parallels the Yuam River to the west.

Apart from soaking up the atmosphere, there's nothing pressing to do in this border outpost, which is regularly visited by local hill tribes and dodgy traders from Burma. If you want something more concrete to do, stroll around a couple of temples off the north side of Wiang Mai Road, whose Burmese features provide a glaring contrast to most Thai temples. The first, **Wat Si Boonruang**, sports a fairy-tale bot done out in lemon, ochre and red, with an intricate, tiered roof piled high above. Topped with lotus buds, the unusual *sema* stones, which delineate the bot's consecrated area, look like old-fashioned street bollards. The open viharns here and next door at the lop-sided **Wat Utthayarom** are mounted on stilts, with broad teak floors that are a pleasure to get your feet onto. Both enshrine the hard-faced white Buddhas of Burma.

PRACTICALITIES

The best **place to stay** in town is the *See View Guest House* (☎053/681556; ①–②), run by a young and friendly staff, with a choice of big, comfortable, concrete rooms, each with a hot-water bathroom, or simple, well-designed wooden cubicles, sharing facilities. It's located across the river from the town centre, but call in at the office at 70 Wiang Mai Rd and they'll take you from there. Running a close second is Mae Sariang's other travellers' hang-out, the *River Side Guest House* at 85 Laeng Phanit Rd (☎053/681188; ②). Rooms are slightly dingy, but they and the popular terrace restaurant occupy a choice position above the curving river; B60 dorm beds are also available. Located 50m east of the post office on Wiang Mai Road (15min from Laeng Phanit Road by foot), the *Mittaree Guest House* (☎053/681109; ③–④) is as noisy as accommodation gets in Mae Sariang, but it offers clean rooms with attached baths and air-conditioning or fan, some with views. Outside of town, the *Mae Sariang Resort* (③) has simple chalets in an idyllic riverside setting – to get there, go 2km out towards Chiang Mai, then follow the signs to the left for a further 1km.

When it's time for **food**, don't be put off by the shabby appearance of the *Inthira Restaurant* on Wiang Mai Road – it's the locals' favourite, and dishes up excellent Thai dishes at moderate prices. *Renu Restaurant*, opposite, is less highly favoured but less expensive, and specializes in "wild food" such as nut hatch curry and wild boar.

Mae Sam Laeb

Mae Sariang's attractions are pretty tame stuff compared to a trip to **MAE SAM LAEB**, about 50km to the southwest on the Salween River, which forms the border with Burma at this point. Songthaews for the ninety-minute journey (B50) are sporadic, and only leave when they have a full complement of passengers – you can usually catch one at around 8am from the bridge over the River Yuam in Mae Sariang, but it's best to get the latest information from one of the town's guest houses first. Mae Sam Laeb is no more than a row of bamboo stores and restaurants (though a budget guest house is planned in the near future), ending in a gambling den by the river, which swarms with smuggling traffic and floating teak logs. In the dry season, it's possible to hire an expensive longtail boat (figure on B300 for an hour) on the rocky river to view the steep, wooded banks on both sides of the frontier. As the Burmese army has in the past mounted attacks against the Karen insurgents downstream from Mae Sam Laeb, you should check that all is quiet before leaving Mae Sariang.

South from Mae Sariang: Highway 105 to Mae Sot

Highway 105, which drops south for 230km to Mae Sot, makes a scenic and quiet link between the north and the central plains, though it has some major drawbacks. Setting off through the Yuam valley, the road winds over a range of hills to the Burmese border, formed here by the Moei River, which it then hugs all the way down to Mae Sot; along the way, you'll pass through traditional Karen villages which still keep some working elephants, and dense forests with occa- sional forlorn stands of teak.

The major deterrent against travelling this way is the standard of public transport: though the route is now paved, it's covered only by hourly **songthaews**, with a jour- ney time of five hours or more – really too much on a rattling bench seat – at a cost of B150 per person. In addition to the discomfort, this border area is rather remote and lawless, and the scene of occasional **skirmishes** between the Burmese army and the opposition freedom fighters – most of the fighting is conducted on the Burmese side, but check that the coast is clear before leaving Mae Sariang.

North to Mae Hong Son

North of Mae Sariang, wide, lush valleys alternate with tiny, steep-sided glens – some too narrow for more than a single rice paddy – turning Highway 108 into a winding roller coaster. With your own transport, an attractive detour can be made by turning right on the south side of **Ban Mae La Noi**, 32km from Mae Sariang, onto Highway 1266. This all-weather unpaved road climbs sharply eastwards, against a stunning backdrop of sawtoothed, forested mountains, speckled here and there with incongruous grids of bright-green cabbage patches. After 25km, the friendly Lawa settlement of **Ban La Up** appears, strung along a razor-blade ridge, where the village elephant, if not on agricultural duty, can be hired for a two-hour round trip to the pretty Pang Tai waterfall.

The market town of **KHUN YUAM**, 95km north of Mae Sariang, is a popular resting place, especially for bikers who've taken the gruelling direct route over the mountains from Mae Chaem. The *Ban Farang* **guest house** here, just off the main thoroughfare, Rajaburana Road, at the north end of town (③) and well signposted, can put you up in fine style: each of the smart twin rooms has duvets and a cold-water bathroom, with access to a shared hot shower. The restaurant serves up good Thai and French food, including home-made bread, at reasonable prices. Less pricey rooms can be had at the simple but friendly *Mitkhunyuam Hotel*, 115 Rajaburana Rd (☎053/691057; ①–②).

Ten kilometres north of Khun Yuam, the landscape broadens for the river crossing at **Ban Mae Surin**, gracefully complemented by a typical Burmese temple and chedi. A steep, paved side road, 35km north of Khun Yuam, leads 10km to **BAN MAE KO VAFE** (a distortion of "microwave" – a reference to the radio mast on the peak above the settlement), perched high in the mountains to the east. This Hmong village of low, wooden houses, with one or two poppy fields dotted around, commands breathtaking views of layer upon layer of forested mountains stretching across to Burma in the west. The villagers are used to tourists by now and it's possible to stay with the headman, but the only way to get there is by motorbike or jeep, or on a tour from Mae Hong Son.

After the side road to Mae Ko Vafe, Highway 108 climbs for 10km to a **viewing area**, with fine vistas of the sheer, wooded slopes and the Pha Bong Dam in the valley far below, before making a dramatic, headlong descent towards Mae Hong Son. Twelve kilometres north of the viewing area (10km before Mae Hong Son), the **Ban Pha Bong** hot springs have been turned into a small spa complex, with showers, toilets and a restaurant – swimming is now discouraged, so you're expected to haul out buckets full of the healing waters with which to douse yourself.

Mae Hong Son and around

MAE HONG SON, capital of Thailand's northwesternmost province, sports more nicknames than a town of six thousand people seems to deserve. In Thai, it's Muang Sam Mok, the "City of Three Mists": set deep in a mountain valley, Mae Hong Son is often swathed in mist, the quality of which differs according to the three seasons (in the hot season it's mostly composed of unpleasant smoke from slash-and-burn agriculture). In former times, the town, which wasn't connected to the outside world by a paved road until 1968, was known as "Siberia" to the troublesome politicians and government officials who were exiled here from Bangkok. Nowadays, thanks to its mountainous surroundings, it's increasingly billed as the "Switzerland of Thailand": eighty percent of Mae Hong Son province is on a slope of more than 45 degrees.

To match the hype, Mae Hong Son has become one of the fastest-developing tourist centres in the country, sporting dozens of backpacker guest houses and more latterly, for Thais and farangs who like their city comforts, luxury hotels. Most travellers come here for **trekking** and day-hiking in the beautiful countryside, others just for the cool climate and lazy upcountry atmosphere. The town is still small enough and sleepy enough to hole up in for a quiet week, but there's no telling how long this can last – if local civic boosters had their way, Mae Hong Son would reverberate every week with the lucrative sounds of explosions and machine-gun fire, as it did during the 1994 filming of *Dumbo Drop*, starring Danny Glover.

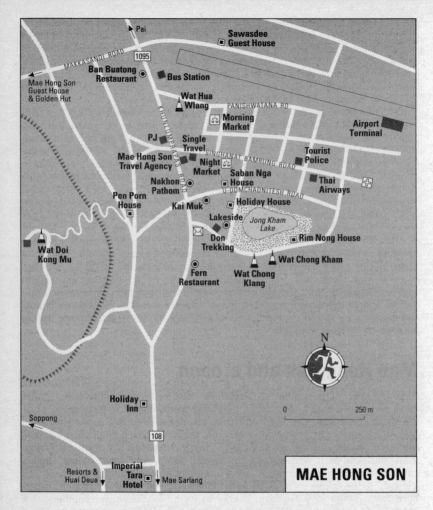

MAE HONG SON

Mae Hong Son was founded in 1831 as a training camp for elephants captured from the surrounding jungle for the princes of Chiang Mai (Jong Kham Lake, in the southeastern part of the modern town, served as the elephants' bathing spot). The hard work of hunting and rearing the royal elephants was done by the **Thai Yai**, who account for half the population of the province and bring a strong Burmese flavour to Mae Hong Son's temples and festivals. The other half of the province's population is made up of various hill tribes (a large number of Karen, as well as Lisu, Hmong and Lawa), with a tiny minority of Thais concentrated in the provincial capital.

The latest immigrants to the province are **Burmese refugees**: as well as rural Karen, driven across the border when the Burmese army razed their villages (see

POY SANG LONG

Mae Hong Son's most famous and colourful festival is **Poy Sang Long**, held at the beginning of April, which celebrates the ordination into the monkhood, for the duration of the schools' long vacation, of Thai Yai boys between the ages of seven and fourteen. Similar rituals take place all over Thailand at this time, but the Mae Hong Son version is given a unique flavour by its Thai Yai elements. On the first day of the festival, the boys have their heads shaved and are anointed with turmeric and dressed up in the gay colours of a Thai Yai prince, with traditional accessories: long white socks, plenty of jewellery, a headcloth decorated with fresh flowers, a golden umbrella and heavy face make-up. They are then announced to the guardian spirit of the town and taken around the temples. The second day brings general merry-making and a spectacular parade, headed by a drummer and a richly decorated riderless horse, which is believed to carry the town's guardian spirit. The boys, still in their finery, are each carried on the shoulders of a chaperone, accompanied by musicians and bearers of traditional offerings. In the evening, the novices tuck into a sumptuous meal, waited on by their parents and relatives, before the ordination ceremony in the temple on the third day.

p.204), many urban students and monks, who formed the hard core of the brutally repressed 1988 uprising, have fled to this area to join the resistance forces; the latter are susceptible to malaria and generally suffer most from the harsh jungle conditions here. Many refugees live in camps between Mae Hong Son and the border, but these do not encourage visitors as they've got quite enough on their plates without having to entertain onlookers.

The Burmese army has been known to attack villages and camps along the border, and there is occasional fighting over opium on the northern frontier beyond Mae Aw, so if you're planning any trips other than those described below, you should check with the **tourist police** on Singhanat Bamrung Road (☎053/611812) first.

Arriving at Mae Hong Son's **bus station** towards the north end of Khunlumprapas Road puts you within walking distance of the guest houses. Tuk-tuks run from the **airport** to the centre, or if you're booked into a resort or hotel you can arrange for a car to pick you up. Motorbike taxis also operate in and around the town: the local transport hub is the north side of the morning market.

Accommodation

At the lower end of the accommodation spectrum, Mae Hong Son has a healthy roster of **guest houses**, most of them being good-value, rustic affairs built of bamboo or wood and set in their own quiet gardens; many have ranged themselves around Jong Kham Lake in the southeast corner of town, which greatly adds to their scenic appeal. If you've got a little more money to spend, you can get out into the countryside to one of several self-contained **resorts** on the grassy banks of the Pai River, though staying at one of these is not exactly a wilderness experience – they're really designed for weekending Thais travelling by car. Finally, two **luxury hotels** on the southern edge of town have latched onto the area's meteoric development, offering all the usual international-standard facilities.

One hindrance to the farang traveller is that many of Mae Hong Son's guest houses, restaurants and travel agents don't advertise themselves with English signs, as this would incur extra local taxes – you'll just have to refer to the map to home in on them.

GUEST HOUSES

Golden Hut, 253/1 Moo 11, Makkasandi Rd (☎053/611544). Simple en suite A-frames thatched with *tong teung* leaves, or brightly designed concrete rooms with hot water, in a sloping garden on the northwest side of town facing open country. ③–④.

Holiday House, 23 Pradit Jongkham Rd. Clean and friendly, with shared hot-water bathroom and its own small garden overlooking the lake. ②.

Mae Hong Son Guest House, 295 Makkasandi Rd (☎053/612510). Relaxing old-timer that's moved out to the suburbs for a view over the town. Choice of bare wooden rooms, clean and simple huts, or bungalows with their own cold-water bathrooms; all have access to shared hot showers. ①–③.

Pen Porn House, 16/1 Padunomuaytaw Rd (☎053/611577). Smart, motel-like doubles with hot showers. ④.

Rim Nong House, on the south side of the lake at 4 Chamnansathit Rd. The most economical bed in town is in the cosy dorm here (B40); also has cramped but decent bungalows with shared hot showers. ②.

Saban Nga House, 14 U-Dornchaonitesh Rd (☎053/612280). Clean, friendly and central with shared hot showers. ②.

Sawasdee Guest House, 18 Khunlumprapas Rd (☎053/612023). Homely traditional wooden house in a small garden on the north side of the airport runway; clean rooms with all the basic equipment and shared hot showers. ①.

RESORTS

Golden Pai Resort, 6km north of town, signposted to the left of the road towards Pai (☎053/612265). Clean, well-appointed air-con chalets arranged around a smart swimming pool. ⑥.

Mae Hong Son Resort, 6km south of town, on the road to Huai Deua (☎053/611406, or 251217–22 in Chiang Mai). Poshest of the resorts – a friendly and quietly efficient place, with chalets by the river or rooms in the grounds behind. Price includes cooked breakfast. ⑥ .

Rim Nam Klang Doi, 5km along the road to Huai Deua (☎053/612142). The best situated of the resorts, with rambling gardens sloping down to the Pai River and swimming, fishing and boating. Comfortable, well-maintained rooms with hot-water bathrooms (or 2-person tents on the banks of the Pai for B140). ⑤.

HOTELS

Holiday Inn, 114/5–7 Khunlumprapas Rd (☎053/611390; Bangkok reservations ☎02/254 2614). At the south end of town on the road out towards Mae Sariang. Has a swimming pool, tennis courts, snooker club and a karaoke bar. ⑧.

Imperial Tara Hotel, 149 Moo 8, Tambon Pang Moo (☎053/611021–6; Bangkok reservations ☎02/261 9000 ext. 4102–4). Further out by the turn-off for Huai Deua, this grand building is set in pretty landscaped gardens, with a swimming pool. ⑧.

The Town

Running north to south, laid-back shops and businesses line Mae Hong Son's main drag, Khunlumprapas Road, intersected by Singhanat Bamrung at the only traffic lights in the region (a landmark which locals are very proud of). Beyond the typical concrete boxes around the central junction, the town sprawls lazily across the valley floor and up the lower slopes of Doi Kong Mu to the west, with trees and untidy vegetation poking through at every possible opportunity to remind you that open country is only a stone's throw away. Plenty of traditional Thai Yai buildings remain – wooden shophouses with balconies, shutters and corrugated-iron roof decorations, homes thatched with *tong teung* leaves and fitted with herringbone-patterned window panels – though they take a severe beating from the weather and may eventually be replaced by inexpensive, all-engulfing concrete.

Mae Hong Son's classic picture-postcard view is of its twin nineteenth-century Burmese-style temples from the opposite bank of Jong Kham Lake, their gleaming white chedis and the multi-tiered spires of their viharns reflected in the lily-strewn water. In the viharn of **Wat Chong Kham** you'll find a huge, intricately carved sermon throne, decorated with the *dharmachakra* (Wheel of Law) in coloured glass on gold; the pink building on the left has been built around the temple's most revered Buddha image, the benign, inscrutable Luang Pho To. Next door, **Wat Chong Klang** is famous for its crude paintings on glass, displayed over three walls on the left-hand side of the viharn: the first two walls behind the monks' dais (on which women are not allowed to stand) depict *Jataka* stories from the Buddha's previous incarnations in their lower sections, and the life of the Buddha himself in their upper, while the third wall is devoted entirely to the Buddha's life. A small room beyond houses an unforgettable collection of **teak statues**, brought over from Burma in the middle of the last century. The dynamically expressive, often humorous figures are characters from the *Vessantara Jataka*, but the woodcarvers have taken as their models people from all levels of traditional Burmese society, including toothless emaciated peasants, butch tattooed warriors and elegant upper-class ladies.

The town's vibrant, smelly **morning market**, just south of the bus station, is worth dragging your bones up at dawn to see. People from the local hill tribes often come down to buy and sell, and the range of produce is particularly weird and wonderful, including, in season, porcupine meat, displayed with quills to prove its authenticity. Next door, the many-gabled viharn of **Wat Hua Wiang** shelters, under a lace canopy, one of the most beautiful Buddha images in northern Thailand, the **Chao Palakeng**. Copied from a famous statue in Mandalay, the strong, serene bronze has the regal clothing and dangling ears typical of Burmese Buddhas.

For a godlike overview of the area, especially at sunset, climb up to **Wat Doi Kong Mu** on the steep hill to the west: from the temple's two chedis, which enshrine the ashes of respected nineteenth-century monks, you can look down on the town and out across the sleepy farming valley north and south. Behind the chedis, the dilapidated viharn contains an unusual and highly venerated white marble image of the Buddha, surrounded in gold flames. If you've still got the energy, trek up to the new lemon-coloured bot on the summit, where the view extends over the Burmese mountains to the west.

Around Mae Hong Son

Once you've exhausted the few obvious sights in town, the first decision you'll have to grapple with is whether to visit the **"long-neck" women** – our advice is don't, though many travellers do. Less controversial, **boat and raft trips** on the babbling Pai River are fun, and roaring **Pha Sua Falls** and the Kuomintang village of **Mae Aw** make a satisfying day out. If all that sounds too easy, Mae

LONG-NECK WOMEN

The most famous – and notorious – of the Mae Hong Son area's spectacles is its contingent of **"long-neck" women**, members of the tiny Padaung tribe of Burma who have come across to Thailand to escape Burmese repression. Though the women's necks appear to be stretched to 30cm and more by a column of brass rings, the "long-neck" tag is a technical misnomer: a *National Geographic* team once X-rayed one of the women and found that instead of stretching out her neck, the pressure of eleven pounds of brass had simply squashed her collarbones and ribs. Girls of the tribe start wearing the rings from about the age of six, adding one or two each year up to the age of sixteen or so. Once fastened, the rings are for life, for to remove a full stack would cause the collapse of the neck and suffocation – in the past, removal was a punishment for adultery. Despite the obvious discomfort, and the laborious daily task of cleaning and drying the rings, the tribeswomen, when interviewed, say that they're used to their plight and are happy to be continuing the tradition of their people.

The **origin** of the ring-wearing ritual remains unclear, despite an embarrassment of plausible explanations. Padaung legend says that the mother of their tribe was a dragon with a long, beautiful neck, and that their unique custom is an imitation of her. Tour guides will tell you the practice is intended to enhance the women's beauty. In Burma, where it is now outlawed as barbaric, it's variously claimed that ring-wearing arose out of a need to protect women from tiger attacks or to deform the wearers so that the Burmese court would not kidnap them for concubines.

In spite of their handicap (they have to use straws to drink, for example), the women are able to carry out some kind of an ordinary life: they can marry and have children, and they're able to weave and sew, although these days they spend most of their time posing like circus freaks for photographs. Only half of the Padaung women now lengthen their necks; left to its own course, the custom would probably die out, but the influence of tourism may well keep it alive for some time yet.

Hong Son is now Thailand's third largest centre for **trekking**. Other feasible targets include the hot springs at Ban Pha Bong and the hilltop village of Mae Ko Vafe (see p.263) and, at a push, Tham Lot (see p.272).

Local transport, in the form of songthaews from the morning market, is thinly spread and unreliable, so for all of these excursions it's best to rent your own vehicle or join an organized tour. **Mopeds** can be hired from *PJ*, 51 Khunlumprapas Rd (B120–150 a day), while the helpful and reputable *Single Travel*, at no. 5/5 (in fact, round the corner on Singhanat Bamrung Road; ☎053/612388 or 612389), has **four-wheel drives** for B1000 a day (no insurance). Mae Hong Son's travel agents (see box on p.270) do some good deals on **tours**: *Single Travel*, for instance, can lay on unusual activities like horse riding and landscape painting, as well as organizing packages from Mae Hong Son with Pai's *Thai Adventure Rafting* (see p.273).

Nai Soi

The original village of long-neck Padaung women in the Mae Hong Son area, **NAI SOI**, 25km northwest of town, has effectively been turned into a human zoo for snap-happy tourists, with an entrance fee of B250 per person. The "long necks" pose in front of their huts and looms, every now and then getting it together to stage a good-luck song – all a visitor can do is stand and stare in embarrassed silence or click away with a camera. All in all it's a disturbing spectacle, offering no opportunity to discover anything about Padaung culture. At least, contrary to many reports, the "long necks" are not held as slaves in the village: the entrance fee is handled by the Karenni National People's Party, to whom the Padaung, in their precarious plight as refugees, have offered their services (the KNPP is fighting for the independence of Burma's Kayah state, where the Padaung come from). Much of the fee is used to support the KNPP, and some goes to help improve conditions in the village, while the "long necks" themselves are each paid a living wage of B1100 per month.

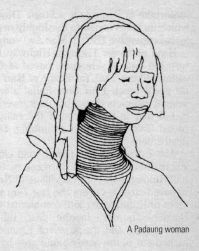

A Padaung woman

Without your own transport, you'll have to hitch up with an expensive tour (about B700 per person, including entrance fee) from a travel agent in town. By motorbike, head north along Highway 1095 and turn left at the police box (5km from the traffic lights) into **Tung Kong Moo**; beyond the village, the paved road becomes a trail before crossing a narrow suspension bridge (*saphan khwaen*) at **Ban Khun Klang**, and widening out again to lead to Nai Soi.

Trips on the Pai River

Scenic **boat trips** on the Pai River start from Huai Deua, 7km southwest of town near the *Mae Hong Son Resort*. No need to go on an organized tour: take a motorbike taxi, tuk-tuk or one of the infrequent songthaews from Mae Hong Son market to Huai Deua and approach the owners at the boat station. Twenty minutes downriver from Huai Deua will get you to **Huai Phu Kaeng**, where a dozen or so "long-neck" women display themselves in a set-up similar to Nai Soi (B400, plus B250 admission charge to the village). You're better off enjoying the river for its own sake, as it scythes its way between cliffs and forests to the Burmese border, another ten minutes beyond (B400), or travelling upriver to **Soppong** (B350), a pretty, quiet Thai Yai village 5km due west of Mae Hong Son (not to be confused with the Soppong on Highway 1095, northeast of Mae Hong Son). **Elephant rides** into the surrounding jungle, for B400 per hour for two people, can be arranged at the *Mae Hong Son Resort*, or, on the north side of town, at the unmarked farm by the suspension bridge in Ban Khun Klang (for directions, see "Nai Soi" above).

A small stretch of the Pai River between **Sop Soi**, 10km northwest of Mae Hong Son, and Soppong is clear enough of rocks to allow safe clearance for bamboo **rafts**. The journey takes two hours at the most, as the rafts glide down the gentle river, partly hemmed in by steep wooded hills. Most of Mae Hong Son's travel agents can fix this trip up for you, including travel to Sop Soi and from Soppong, charging around B300 per person.

Pha Sua Falls and Mae Aw

North of Mae Hong Son, a trip to Pha Sua Falls and the border village of Mae Aw takes in some spectacular and varied countryside. Your best options are to rent a motorbike or join a tour – *Single Travel*, for example, charges B300 per person, which includes a visit to the highly overrated Fish Cave – as there are only occasional expensive (B80 to Mae Aw) songthaews from the market in the morning.

Head north for 17km on Highway 1095 and then, after a long, steep descent, turn left onto a side road, paved at first, which passes through an idyllic rice valley and the Thai Yai village of **Ban Bok Shampae**. About 9km from the turn-off you'll reach **Pha Sua Falls**, a wild, untidy affair, which crashes down in several cataracts through a dark, overhung cut in the limestone. The waterfall is in full roar in October after the rainy season, but has plenty of water all year round. Take care when swimming, as several people have been swept to their deaths here.

Above the falls the paved road climbs precipitously, giving glorious, broad vistas of both Thai and Burmese mountains, before reaching the unspectacular half-Hmong, half-Thai Yai village of **Naphapak** after 11km. A decent, largely flat, unpaved stretch covers the last 7km to **MAE AW** (aka Ban Ruk Thai), a settlement of Kuomintang anti-communist Chinese refugees (see p.283), right on the Burmese border. In the past, this area has seen fighting between the Kuomintang and the army of Khun Sa, the opium warlord who, having been kicked out of the Mae Salong area by the Thai army in 1983, set up his present base somewhere in the uncharted mountains across the border northeast of Mae Aw. The road up here was recently built by the Thai military to help the fight against the opium trade and all has been quiet for a couple of years, but it might be worth checking in Mae Hong Son before setting out. Mae Aw is the highest point on the border which visitors can reach, and provides a fascinating window on Kuomintang life. The tight ring of hills around the village heightens the feeling of being in another country: delicate, bright-green tea bushes line the slopes, while Chinese ponies wander the streets of long, unstilted bamboo houses. In the central marketplace on the north side of the village reservoir, shops sell great bags of the Oolong and Chian Chian tea, as well as dried mushrooms, and rustle up simple noodle dishes for visitors.

TREKKING AROUND MAE HONG SON

There's no getting away from the fact that **trekking** up and down Mae Hong Son's steep inclines is tough, but the hill-tribe villages are generally unspoilt and the scenery is magnificent. To the west, trekking routes tend to snake along the Burmese border, occasionally nipping over the line for a quick thrill, and can sometimes get a little crowded as this is the more popular side of Mae Hong Son. Nearly all the hill-tribe villages here are Karen, interspersed with indigenous Thai Yai settlements. To the east of Mae Hong Son the Karens again predominate, but by travelling a little further you'll also be able to visit Hmong, Lisu and Lahu — many villages here are very traditional, having little contact with the outside world. If you're very hardy, you might want to consider the five-day route to Pai, which by all accounts has the best scenery of the lot.

About a dozen guest houses and travel agencies run treks out of Mae Hong Son, among which the *Mae Hong Son Guest House, Single Travel, Don Trekking* (77/1 Khunlumprapas Rd) and *Mae Hong Son Travel Agency* (18/1 Singhanat Bamrung Rd, though in fact on Khunlumprapas Road; ☎053/611621) are known to be reliable; charges range from B300 to B500 per person per day, depending on how far into the more remote, interesting areas the trek ventures.

Eating and drinking

Nobody comes to Mae Hong Son for the **food** – the available options are limited, although a few good restaurants have sprung up in order to cater specifically to foreigners.

If you fancy a change from guest-house **breakfasts**, head for the morning market, where a stall on the south side rustles up good *roti* (pancakes with condensed milk and sugar) for B6 a throw. The night market on Singhanat Bamrung Road does the standard **Thai dishes** at negligible prices, and is a good place to meet other travellers. For excellent, simple restaurant meals that won't burn a hole in your money belt, try *Nakhon Pathom* on Khunlumprapas Road, which specializes in tasty pork on rice and noodle soup, or, slightly upmarket, the very popular *Kai Muk* on U-Domchaonitesh Road. For a bit of posh, try *Fern*, at 87 Khunlumprapas Rd, a showy, tourist-oriented eatery with a nice candlelit terrace. At 34 Khunlumprapas Rd, *Ban Buatong* does the best **Western food** in town, with an especially wide range of veggie dishes from around the world, all at surprisingly reasonable prices. A good place for a **drink** – and some tasty Thai dishes – is *Lakeside Bar and Restaurant*, 2/3 Khunlumprapas Rd, where you can relax to the gentle strains of an acoustic guitar, on a terrace overlooking Jong Kham Lake and the fairy lights on the temples behind.

Highway 1095: Mae Hong Son to Chiang Mai

Highway 1095, the 243-kilometre northern route between Mae Hong Son and Chiang Mai, is every bit as wild and scenic as the southern route through Mae Sariang – if anything it has more mountains to negotiate, with a greater contrast between the sometimes straggly vegetation of the slopes and the thickly cultivated valleys. Much of the route was established by the Japanese army to move troops and supplies into Burma after its invasion of Thailand during World War II. The labour-intensive job of paving every hairpin bend has only recently been completed, but ongoing repair work can still give you a nasty surprise if you're riding a motorbike. If you're setting off along this route from Chiang Mai by public transport, catch either a bus to Pai and change, or one direct to Mae Hong Son, from Chiang Mai's Arcade Station.

Mae Suya and Mae Lana

The first stretch north out of Mae Hong Son weaves up and down the west face of Doi Pai Kit (1082m), giving great views over the lush valley to the north of town. Beyond the turn-off for Mae Aw (see facing page) and the much-touted but pretty useless Fish Cave, the highway climbs eastward through many hairpin bends before levelling out to give tantalizing glimpses through the trees of the Burmese mountains to the north, then passes through a hushed valley of paddy fields, surrounded by echoing crags, to reach the Thai Yai/Kuomintang village of **MAE SUYA**, 40km from Mae Hong Son. Take the left turning 3km east of the village to reach *Wilderness Lodge* after a further 1km of dirt road; set in wild countryside, the friendly guest house offers primitive bungalows (①) and dorm beds in the barn-like main house (B40), and does a wide range of vegetarian and meat-based Thai food, as well as baking its own bread, cakes and pizzas.

The owner of the lodge can give you directions and maps for cave exploration and beautiful wilderness day walks to hill-tribe villages. Two hours' walk to the north, **Tham Nam Pha Daeng** is a pretty, 1600-metre-long cave which, like Tham Lot (see below), is dotted with unexplained coffins; apart from a few low crawls, the journey through the cave is relatively easy (Nov to May only). To the south beyond Highway 1095, **Tham Nam Lang**, one of the most capacious caves in the world, has a towering entrance chamber which anyone can appreciate, although the spectacular 9km beyond that demand full-on caving, again in the dry season only, and the proper equipment (available at the lodge).

Two further remote guest houses lie in the sleepy valley of **MAE LANA**, a Thai Yai village 6km north of the highway, reached by a dirt road which branches off to the left 56km from Mae Hong Son and leads uphill through dramatic countryside. The clean and cosy *Mae Lana Guest House* (①), by a stream on the edge of the village, knocks spots off the more central but cramped *Top Hill Guest House*, and serves good Thai food. The village is within easy walking distance of Lahu villages, plus **Tham Mae Lana**, with its white-water flows and phallic formations, and several other caves. A three-hour walk along easy-to-follow tracks through beautiful mountain scenery will also save you the fare to Ban Tum (see below).

Soppong, Ban Tum and Tham Lot

The small, lively market town of **SOPPONG**, 68km from Mae Hong Son, gives access to the area's most famous cave, **Tham Lot**, 9km north in **BAN TUM** (or Ban Tham). There's no public transport along the gentle forest road to the village, so if you haven't got your own wheels, you'll have to hitch, walk or rent a motorbike taxi (B40).

Turn right in the village to find the entrance to the Forestry National Park recently set up to look after the cave, where you can hire a guide with lantern for B100. A short walk through the forest brings you to the entrance of Tham Lot, where the Lang River begins a 600-metre subterranean journey through the cave, requiring you to wade across the flow half a dozen times (the height of the water varies with the seasons), but if you don't fancy getting your feet wet, bamboo rafts can be hired (at B100 per group of 1 to 5) for all or part of the journey. Two hours should allow you enough time for travelling through the broad, airy tunnel, and for the main attraction, climbing up into the sweaty caverns in the roof.

The first of these, **Column Cavern**, 100m from the entrance on the right, seems to be supported by the metre-thick stalagmites which snake up towards the ceiling. Another 50m on the left, bamboo ladders lead up into **Crystal Cave**, which has a glistening, pure white wall and a weird red and white formation shaped like a Wurlitzer organ. Just before the vast exit from the cave, wooden ladders on the left lead up into **Coffin Cave**, named after the remains of a dozen crude burial caskets discovered here, one of them preserved to its full length of 5m. Hollowed out from tree trunks, they are similar to those found in many of the region's caves: some are raised 2m off the ground by wooden supporting poles, and some still contain bones, jewellery and other artefacts. The coffins are between 1200 and 2200 years old, but anthropologists are at a loss to explain the custom. Local people attribute them to *phi man*, the cave spirits. It's worth hanging round the cave's main exit at sunset, when thousands upon thousands of tiny black chirruping fork-tailed swifts pour into the cave in an almost solid column, to find their beds for the night.

Practicalities

Cave Lodge (②), on the other side of Ban Tum from the cave, makes an excellent and friendly base for exploring the area. The owners, a former trekking guide and her Australian husband, have plenty of useful information about Tham Lot and some of the two hundred other caves in the region, and organize occasional guided trips through the more interesting ones. Walking to local Karen, Lahu and Lisu villages from the lodge is possible, as well as elephant riding at a nearby Karen village (B200 per person per hour). Dorm beds here are B40, and the simple wooden bungalows, with shared hot showers, are scattered over the overgrown hillside.

On the main road at the western end of Soppong, *Jungle Guest House* is the most popular of several places in town, and can give advice on local walks to Lisu villages or organize inexpensive trekking trips to Lisu, Lahu and Karen settlements further to the south. Accommodation here is in simple huts with shared hot showers (①) or on a dormitory basis (B40), and the food is great. A short walk east of Soppong's bus stop and a little upmarket, *Lemonhill Guest House* (☎01/510 1366; ②–③) has chalets with or without their own hot-water bathrooms, in a pretty garden sloping down to the Lang River.

Pai and beyond

Beyond Soppong, the road climbs through the last of Mae Hong Son province's wild landscape before descending into the broad, gentle valley of **PAI**, 43km from Soppong. There's nothing special to do in Pai, but the atmosphere is relaxing and the guest houses and restaurants have tailored themselves to the steady trickle of travellers who make the four-hour bus journey out from Chiang Mai. The small town's traditional buildings spread themselves liberally over the west bank of the Pai River, but everything's still within walking range of the bus station at the north end.

Several undemanding **walks** can be made around Pai's broad, gently sloping valley. The easiest – one hour there and back – takes you across the river on the east side of town and up the hill to Wat Mae Yen, which commands a great view over the whole district (the much-touted hot springs, 7km south of the wat, are a big disappointment). To the west of town, an unpaved road (accessible by motorbike) heads out from Pai hospital, passing, after 3km, Wat Nam Hu, whose Buddha image has an unusual hinged top-knot containing holy water, before gradually climbing through comparatively developed Kuomintang, Lisu and Lahu villages to Mo Pang Falls, about 10km west of Pai.

Pai makes a good base for **trekking**, which can be arranged inexpensively through the guest houses. Karen, Lisu and Lahu villages are within range, and the terrain has plenty of variety: jungles and bamboo forests, hills and flat valleys. The area north of town, where trekking can be combined with **bamboo rafting** and **elephant riding**, can get rather touristy, but the countryside to the south is very quiet and unspoilt, with a wider range of hill tribes: hardened walkers could arrange a trek to Mae Hong Son, five days away to the southwest. With a little more cash to spare, you could strike up with the French-run *Thai Adventure Rafting*, on Rungsiyanon Road (☎053/699111), for a **rubber-raft trip** south down the Khong

River from Mae Suya, then west along the Pai River, before finishing up just north of Mae Hong Son where Highway 1095 crosses the river. Sturdier than bamboo rafts, these craft can negotiate the exciting Hin Mong rapids, and will also take you through the Pai Kit gorges and past Suza Waterfalls, a series of twenty travertine falls cascading from a jungle delta, which make a good place for swimming. The journey takes two days, including a night under canvas by the river, and costs B1500 per person (4 people minimum); the season runs from July to December, with the highest water in September, and participants must be able to swim.

Practicalities

Opposite the bus station at the north end of town, *Duang Guest House*, 5 Rungsiyanon Rd (☎053/699101; ①) is a welcoming, relaxing **place to stay**, though in a rather cramped compound. On the river bank to the east of *Duang*, *Pin's Huts* has simple bamboo huts (①) in a quiet, shady spot and offers home-baked bread. *Charlie's Guest House* at 9 Rungsiyanon Rd (☎053/699039; ①–③), the main street running south from the bus station, offers a variety of rooms, including a kitsch honeymoon suite, set around a lush garden, all of them clean (Charlie is the district health officer) with access to hot showers; it also has B40 dorm beds. In a beautiful setting by the river to the east of the bus station, *Rim Pai Cottage*, 17 Moo 3 Viang Tai (☎053/699133; ④), is as posh as Pai gets; first choice among its rustic but comfortable log cabins, all with hot showers, is the riverside treehouse. On the road to Mo Pang, 1km before the falls, *Pai Mountain Lodge* (☎053/699068; ④) has large chalets with proper fireplaces (a great boon in the cool season) in a flower-strewn upland bowl.

Best of the travellers' **restaurants** is *Thai Yai* at 12 Rungsiyanon Rd, where the Scottish chef rustles up generous portions of back-home favourites at surprisingly low prices. On Ratchadamrong Road, which leads to the bridge, *Own Home Vegetarian Restaurant* is also popular, serving good, moderately priced Western and Thai food.

Northern Green, by the bus station, rents out small **motorbikes** for B150 a day, while *Duang Guest House* has a few ropey **mountain bikes** (B30).

Beyond Pai

Once out of the Pai valley, Route 1095 climbs for 35km of hairpin bends, with beautiful views north to 2175-metre Doi Chiang Dao at each turn. Once over the 1300-metre pass, the road steeply descends the south-facing slopes in the shadow of Doi Mae Ya (2065m), before working its way along the narrow, more populous lower valleys. Mokfa Falls makes an appealing setting for a break – it's 2km south of the main road, 76km from Pai. At Mae Ma Lai, you'll turn right onto the busy Route 107 for the last 34km across the wide plain of rice paddy to Chiang Mai.

CHIANG RAI AND THE BORDERS

The northernmost tip of Thailand, stretching from the Kok River and **Chiang Rai** to the border, is a schizophrenic place, split in two by Highway 110, the continuation of Thailand's main north–south road. In the western half, rows of wild, shark's-tooth mountains jut into Burma, while to the east, low-lying rivers flow through Thailand's richest rice-farming land to the Mekhong River, which forms the border with Laos here. In anticipation of Burma and Laos throwing open their frontiers to tourism, the region is well connected and has been thoroughly kitted out for visitors. Chiang Rai now has well over two thousand hotel rooms, catering mostly to upmarket fortnighters, who plough through the countryside in air-conditioned Scenicruisers in search of quaint, photogenic primitive life. What they get – fairground rides on boats and elephants, a sanitized presentation of the Golden Triangle's opium fields, and colourfully dressed hill people performing artificial folkloric rituals – generally satisfies expectations, but has little to do with the harsh realities of life in the north.

Chiang Rai itself pays ever less attention to independent travellers, so although you have to pass through the provincial capital, you should figure on spending most of your time in the border areas to the north, exploring the dizzy mountain heights, frenetic border towns and ancient ruins. Trekking, the prime domain of the backpacker, has also taken the easy route upmarket, and is better embarked on elsewhere in the north.

Chiang Mai to Chiang Rai

From Chiang Mai you can choose from three main approaches to Chiang Rai. The quickest and most obvious is Highway 1019, a fast, 185-kilometre road that swoops through rolling hill country. Tourist buses make the run in three hours, and most travellers end up passing this way once – it's best saved for the return journey, when you may well want to speed back to the comforts of Chiang Mai. For do-it-yourself **trekking**, this route has the benefit of running close to the primitive *Trekker House*, set in a beautiful landscape among a plethora of hill-tribe settlements: get off at the signpost 64km from Chiang Mai, just before Ban Sob Pong, and then it's a seven-kilometre walk up a dirt road. But unless you're in a desperate hurry getting to and from Chiang Rai, you'll probably opt for one of the scenic routes to Chiang Rai described below. The westerly of the two follows Highway 107 to **Tha Ton** and then completes the journey by longtail boat or bamboo raft down the **Kok River**. The other heads east as far as Lampang (see p.246) before barrelling north on Highway 1 via **Phayao**.

Tha Ton and the Kok River

You should set aside two days for this road and river journey along the **Kok River**, allowing for the almost inevitable overnight stay in Tha Ton. **Buses** between Chiang Mai's northern Chang Phuak bus station and Tha Ton take about five hours, but many buses go only as far as Fang, 23km and an hour short of Tha Ton, in which case you'll have to do the final leg by songthaew. The standard **boat** trip takes the better part of the following afternoon. If you're on a motorbike, once at Tha Ton you have the choice of stowing your bike on the longtail for Chiang Rai, or pushing on northeastwards to Mae Chan or Mae Salong.

Chiang Mai to Fang

From Chiang Mai the route heads north along Highway 107, retracing the Mae Hong Son loop in the early going and, after 56km, passing an **elephant training centre** on the right, which puts on logging shows daily at 9am and 10am (June–April; B40). It's a tourist trap, though – you're better off visiting the less hyped equivalent near Lampang. **Chiang Dao**, an oversized market village, stretches on and on along the road around the 72km marker, as the crags and forests of the mountain after which the village is named loom up on the left. Before descending into the flat plain around Fang and the Kok River, the road shimmies over a rocky ridge, which marks the watershed separating the catchment areas of the Chao Phraya River to the south and the Mekhong River ahead.

It would be nice to give the ugly frontier outpost of **Fang**, 153km from Chiang Mai, a miss altogether but you'll probably have to change buses here. The town has a few cheap and nasty hotels, but you're far better off pushing on to Tha Ton for somewhere to stay. If you're travelling by bike you can cut east 5km before Fang on Highway 109 for Chiang Rai (125km), but this route misses out the beautiful Kok valley and is no easy option as much of it is unpaved.

Tha Ton

The tidy, leafy settlement of **THA TON**, 176km north of Chiang Mai, huddles each side of a bridge over the Kok River, which flows out of Burma 4km upstream. The main attractions here are boat and raft rides, but if you've got a morning to kill while waiting to go downriver, the ornamental gardens of **Wat Tha Ton**, endowed with colossal golden and white Buddha images and an equally huge statue of Chao Mae Kuan Im, the Chinese goddess of mercy, are well worth the short climb and the B20 entrance fee. From any of the statues, the views up the narrow green valley towards Burma and downstream across the sun-glazed plain are heady stuff.

Thip's Traveller House (☎053/459312; ②), on the south side of the bridge, is the best budget **place to stay**, with decent en suite rooms in a crowded compound, and good food. The formidable Mrs Thip can fix packages to Chiang Rai, combining the raft trip down the Kok with trekking to the wide variety of hill-tribe villages nearby and elephant riding, as well as scenic longtail-boat trips to the Burmese border (20min upstream). If *Thip's* is full, *Garden Home* (③), 300m from the bridge on the north side of the river, is next best: the attractive en suite bungalows (one with hot water) shelter under an orchard of lychees and mangoes.

With its own gardens and fine restaurant nearer to the bridge on the same bank, *Mae Kok River Lodge* (☎053/459328; ⑥) is Tha Ton's best **upmarket choice**. A traditional teak building houses guests in well-designed comfort, with a cooked breakfast included in the price, and the owner, Shane Beary, organizes a wide variety of **soft adventure tours**, taking visitors off the well-trodden trekking trails in a measure of luxury (around B1500 per day, depending on itinerary).

Around Tha Ton

Beyond Tha Ton, the newly paved but drab Highway 1089 heads to Mae Chan and Highway 110, with an exciting roller coaster of a side road after 20km, also freshly paved, north to Mae Salong (see p.283). Yellow songthaews leave the north side of the bridge in Tha Ton for the one-and-a-half-hour trip to Mae Salong (every 30min in the morning); for Mae Chan, change onto a green songthaew at the turn-off for the side road to Mae Salong. Mrs Thip has opened a second guest house (②–⑤) 4km along Highway 1089 on a rise above the Kok valley, with a restaurant and a wide variety of comfortable rooms – ask at her Tha Ton headquarters for a lift out there.

About 40km from Tha Ton, and 13km short of Mae Chan, the *Laan Tong Lodge* (☎053/772049; ②–⑤) has opened up the Chan valley to independent travellers. Set in an idyllic riverside meadow, the lodge's bungalows are variously modelled on the traditional dwellings of the region's hill-tribe and lowland peoples, some with an extra injection of luxury. With a map from the lodge, you can walk to Lisu, Akha, Mien and Lahu settlements and a small waterfall with a quiet bathing pool, while Mae Salong is a hard day's walk to the northwest. If you're coming from the opposite direction, take any northbound bus from Chiang Rai along Highway 110 to Mae Chan, and then board one of the songthaews that head west towards Tha Ton every half-hour – the whole operation should take a little over one hour.

Along the Kok River

Travelling down the hundred-kilometre stretch of the **Kok River** to Chiang Rai gives you a chance to soak up a rich diversity of typical northern landscapes, which you never get on a speeding bus. Heading out of Tha Ton, the river traverses a flat valley of ricefields and orchards, where it's flanked by high reeds inhabited by flitting swallows – be sure to take a look back for the best view of Wat Tha Ton's beacon-like Buddhas, which remain in sight for at least the first half-hour of the trip. About the same time as the statue disappears, you'll pass the 900-year-old **Wat Phra That Sop Fang**, with its small hilltop chedi and a slithering naga staircase leading up from the river bank. After a five-minute break in **Mae Salak**, 20km from Tha Ton, where dozens of Akha women and children beg and hawk necklaces, the river starts to meander between thickly forested slopes. From amongst the banana trees and giant wispy ferns, kids come out to play, adults to bathe and wash clothes, and water buffalo emerge simply to enjoy the river.

About two hours out of Tha Ton the hills get steeper and the banks rockier, leading up to a half-hour stretch of small but feisty rapids, where you might well get a soaking. Here and there, denuded slopes studded with burnt tree stumps attest to recent deforestation. Beyond the rapids, crowds of boats suddenly appear, ferrying camcorder-toting tour groups from Chiang Rai to the Karen village of **Ruammid**, 20km upstream, for elephant riding. From here on, the landscape deteriorates as the bare valley around Chiang Rai opens up.

The best time of year to make this trip is in the cool season (roughly Nov–Feb), when the vegetation is lushest and the rapids most exciting; between March and June services are sometimes suspended because the water level falls too far – phone *Thip's* (see facing page) to check. Canopied **longtail boats** leave from the south side of the bridge in Tha Ton every day at 12.30pm for the trip to Chiang Rai, which takes around four hours. The fare is B160, with motorbikes an extra B300. The slower, less crowded journey upriver (B170 per person) gives an even better chance of appreciating the scenery – the longtails leave Chiang Rai at 10.30am.

If you have more time, the **bamboo rafts** which glide downriver to Chiang Rai in two days almost make you part of the scenery. Rafts can fit up to six paying passengers – there are usually plenty of travellers to hitch up with during the high season, when you shouldn't have to wait more than a day for a full complement – and the price (B4000) includes mats, sleeping bags and food. Each party is accompanied by two steersmen, who recycle the raft in Chiang Rai by selling the bamboo off as building material. Raft trips can be organized through *Taton Tour* (☎053/459441) by the longtail pier, but only when the river is high enough in the rainy and cool seasons – roughly July to February.

River boats used to be easy pickings for bandits – an English woman was shot dead in a longtail in 1987 – but the police have clamped down by setting up riverside checkpoints. The most important is at Mae Salak, where you'll be asked to show your **passport**.

To Chiang Rai via Phayao

The only substantial reason to consider the old 337-kilometre route from Chiang Mai to Chiang Rai along highways 11 and 1 is to stop off at Lampang (see p.246), as the full journey takes around seven hours, over twice as long as the newer Highway 1019. Northeast of Lampang, Highway 1 winds over a forested range, after 50km passing through the narrow gulley called **Pratu Pa** (Gateway of the Cliffs), where bus drivers invariably honk at a small spirit shrine. Beyond, the road descends to the unremarkable junction town of **Ngao**, before speeding over a low pass to Phayao.

Facing the 1800-metre peak of Doi Bussaracum, the ancient town of **PHAYAO**, 140km from Lampang, is worth a break in the journey to visit its bizarre wat or to have lunch on the east bank of its hyacinth-strewn lake. Buses pull in at the station on the north side of town off Phaholyothin Road; the town's best budget hotel is the central *Tharn Thong*, 55 Donsanam Rd (✆054/431302; ③–④), which has clean, reasonably quiet rooms with hot water and fan or air conditioning.

According to legend, the lakeside position of **Wat Sri Khom Kham** – a twenty-minute walk or a songthaew ride north along Phaholyothin Road from the bus station – was chosen by the Buddha himself, when, wilting in the notorious Phayao heat, he received shelter from a tree which miraculously sprouted from a seed planted by a passing bird. The main object of worship here is the Phra Chao Ton Luang, a huge pointy-nosed Buddha in the crude, angular local style of the fifteenth century. Outside the central image hall, various Buddha bits in crumbling sandstone are forlornly piled together on the grass like a spare-parts shop. Their limelight has been stolen by a gruesome modern **statue garden** at the north end of the temple: standing next to a children's playground, the supposedly educational statues, which look like special-effects models from a particularly nasty fright movie, are inspired by the Buddhist scriptures and represent the torments of hell. In contrast to these horrors, a modern **viharn**, which has been built on stilts over the lake at the south end of the wat, is all elegance and good taste. The interior has been vibrantly decorated with murals by Angkarn Kalyanapongsa, a famous artist and poet, who has followed traditional Lanna styles and included typically homely comic detail but added a sharp, modern edge.

Chiang Rai

Having lived in the shadow of Chiang Mai for all but thirty years of its existence, **CHIANG RAI** – sprawled untidily over the south bank of the Kok River – is now coming up on the rails to make a challenge as an upmarket tourist centre, with all the hype and hustle that goes with it. The long arm of the package-tour industry has reached this northern outpost, bringing snap-happy bus-bound tourists and well-heeled honeymooners, who alight for a couple of days of excursions and then shoot off again. Paradoxically, this leaves the town to get on with its own business during the day, when the trippers are out on manoeuvres, but at night the neon lights flash on and souvenir shops and ersatz Western restaurants are thronged. Meanwhile, the town keeps up its reputation as a dirty-weekend destination for Thais, a game given away by just a few motels and carports – where you drive into the garage and pay for a discreet screen to be pulled across behind you. Budget travellers have been side-lined, but they still turn up for the trekking and for the excellent handicraft shopping.

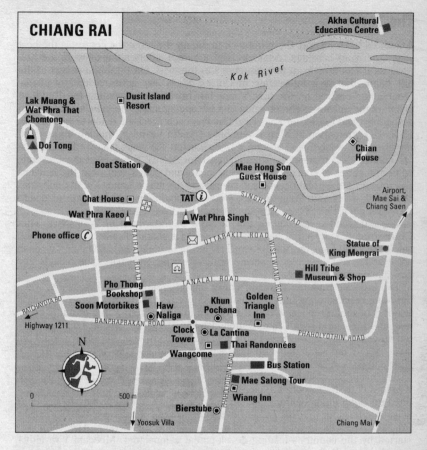

CHIANG RAI

Chiang Rai is most famous for the things it had and lost. It was founded in 1263 by King Mengrai of Ngon Yang who, having recaptured a prize elephant he'd been chasing around the foot of Doi Tong, took this as an auspicious omen for a new city. Tradition has it that Chiang Rai prevailed as the capital of the north for thirty years, but historians now believe Mengrai moved his court directly from Ngon Yang to the Chiang Mai area in the 1290s. Thailand's two holiest images, the Emerald Buddha (now in Bangkok) and the Phra Singh Buddha (now perhaps in Bangkok, Chiang Mai or Nakhon Si Thammarat, depending on which story you believe), also once resided here before moving on – at least replicas of these can be seen at Wat Phra Kaeo and Wat Phra Singh.

Arriving at the **bus station** on Phaholyothin Road on Chiang Rai's south side leaves a long walk to most of the guest houses, so you might want to bundle into a samlor (around B20), the main form of transport around town. Longtails from Tha Ton dock at the **boat station**, situated at the top end of Trairat Road north-west of the centre and handy for the best guest houses. Taxis run into town from the **airport**, 8km northeast, for B150.

The Town

A walk up to **Doi Tong**, the hummock to the northwest of the centre, is the best way to get your bearings and, especially at sunset, offers a fine view up the Kok River as it emerges from the mountains to the west. On the highest part of the hill stands the most interesting of Chiang Mai's few sights, a kind of phallic Stonehenge centred on the town's new **lak muang**, representing the Buddhist layout of the universe. The erection of a *lak muang* marks the official founding of a Thai city, and in Chiang Rai's case this has been precisely dated to January 26, 1263. To commemorate King Bhumibol's sixtieth birthday, this *lak muang* and the elaborate stone model around it were erected 725 years later to the day. The *lak muang* itself represents Mount Sineru (or Meru), the axis of the universe, while the series of concentric terraces, moats and pillars represent the heavens and the earth, the great oceans and rivers, and the major features of the universe. Sprinkling water onto the garlanded *lak muang* and then dabbing your head with the water after it has flowed into the basin below brings good luck.

The old wooden *lak muang* can be seen in the viharn of **Wat Phra That Chomtong**, the city's first temple, which sprawls shambolically over the eastern side of the hill. Look out for the small teetering prang, the old-fashioned wooden spirit house and the Chinese shrine, with which the wat shares the hillside in a typically ecumenical spirit.

The Emerald Buddha, Thailand's most important image, was discovered when lightning cracked open the chedi (since restored) at **Wat Phra Kaeo** on Trairat Road. A beautiful replica, which was carved in China from 300kg of milky green jade and presented by a Chinese millionaire in 1991, can now be seen here. It's not an exact copy, however: according to religious protocol, the replica could not have exactly the same name, materials or appearance as the original. At 47.9cm wide and 65.9cm high, the model is millimetres smaller.

As Chiang Rai is surrounded by such a variety of hill tribes and visited by such a weight of tourists, there are plenty of **handicraft shops**, though most of those lined up along Phaholyothin Road are merely trinket stalls. For a more authentic selection, head for the *Hill Tribe Museum and Handicrafts Shop* at 620/25 Tanalai Rd, which stocks tasteful and well-made hill-tribe handicrafts. The shop was started by the country's leading development campaigner, Meechai Viravaidya, and all proceeds go to village projects. The upstairs museum is a good place to learn about the hill tribes before going on a trek – ask to see the slick, informative slide show (a donation of B50 is requested to cover costs). The *Akha Cultural Education Centre* on the north bank of the river (take the left turn 200m after the bridge on the Mae Sai Road and then it's down a lane to the left after 1km; Mon–Fri 9am–5pm) sells a small but inexpensive range of bags and clothes in characteristic black and red patterns, and the profits are used to help Akha students. The *Handicraft Centre*, 2km north of town on the Mae Sai Road, is the biggest souvenir shop, but it's pricey and the quality isn't up to much.

Practicalities

What Chiang Rai lacks in sights it more than makes up for with accommodation, if only in terms of quantity. That said, one or two guest houses compare with Chiang Mai's finest, and in the *Dusit* it boasts one of the north's finest hotels. You can eat well in Chiang Rai too, as long as you're prepared to shell out a bit. **TAT**

TREKKING FROM CHIANG RAI

Communities from all the hill tribes have settled around Chiang Rai and the region offers the full range of terrain for **trekking**, from gentle walking trails near the Kok River to tough mountain slopes further north towards the Burmese border. The Kok River both to the west and the east of town is deep enough for rafts, and elephant-riding is also included in most treks. However, this natural suitability has attracted too many agencies and trekkers, and many of the hill-tribe villages, especially between Chiang Rai and Mae Salong, have become weary of the constant to-ing and fro-ing. Some of the agencies in Chiang Rai have recently widened their net to include the rest of the province, such as Chiang Khong, where there's a large population of Hmong and Mien, and other provinces like Nan, 270km to the southeast. All guest houses in Chiang Rai can fix you up with a trek – *Chat, Chian* and *Mae Hong Son* are responsible and reliable.

For comprehensive and accurate coverage of trails and hill-tribe villages in Chiang Rai province, the widely available *Guide Map of Chiang Rai* by V. Hongsombud (Bangkok Guides) is essential.

has a helpful office, shared by the **tourist police**, at 448/16 Singakai Rd near Wat Phra Singh (☎053/717433). *Pho Thong,* 201 Tanalai Rd, has a small range of **books** on Thailand in English, as well as maps and popular fiction.

Currently, the only agency running **boat trips** (albeit infrequent and extremely expensive ones) up the Mekhong to China, departing from and returning to Chiang Saen, is Chiang Rai's *Mae Salong Tour,* 882–4 Phalolythin Rd, (☎053/712515; Fax 053/711011).

Accommodation

Chiang Rai is overstuffed with **places to stay** of all categories, but many offer poor quality for the price – the ones listed below are those that stand out. Much of the more expensive accommodation is clustered around the commercial centre on Phaholyothin Road, while the guest houses can be found along the south bank of the river and on the fringes.

INEXPENSIVE AND MODERATE

Chat House, 3/2 Soi Sangkaew, Trairat Rd (☎053/711481). Located behind its own garden café, this is Chiang Rai's longest-running and best travellers' hang-out. ①.

Chian House, 172 Sri Boonruang Rd (☎053/713388). Pleasant en suite rooms in a lively, ramshackle compound around a small swimming pool. ②.

Golden Triangle Inn, 590 Phaholyothin Rd (☎053/711339). Large, tastefully decorated rooms in a garden compound in the heart of town. ⑥.

Mae Hong Son Guest House, 126 Singhakai Rd. A quiet, laid-back establishment with decent rooms sharing hot showers. ①.

YMCA, 70 Phaholyothin Rd (☎053/713785 or 713786). Ever reliable with comfortable rooms, some with air-con, in a modern building on the northern edge of town. There's a swimming pool, too. Dorm beds for B70. ④–⑤.

Yoosuk Villa, 952/13 Ruamjitthawai Rd (☎053/711913). A good deal in the moderate price range: neat rooms with air-con, TV, fridge and hot water. ④.

EXPENSIVE

Dusit Island Resort Hotel, 1129 Kraisorasit Rd (☎053/715777). Set on a 10-acre island in the Kok River, with unbeatable views of the valley, this is the top of the top end. Facilities include a health club, tennis courts, swimming pool and children's playground, with high standards of service. ⑧.

Rim Kok Resort, 6 Moo 4, Chiang Rai–Tha Ton Rd (☎053/716445–60). Palatial luxury hotel in sprawling grounds on the quiet north side of the river. ⑧.

Wangcome, 869/90 Pemavipat Rd (☎053/711800). Chintzy hotel, not quite up to international 5-star standards. ⑦.

Wiang Inn, 893 Phaholyothin Rd (☎053/711543). Almost identical to the *Wangcome*, but with a swimming pool and Chiang Rai's premier nightspot, *The Hill Discotheque*. ⑧.

Eating

Chiang Rai's restaurants congregate along Banphaprakan and Phaholyothin roads, with a growing number of unimpressive Western places scattered around, and a largely disappointing bunch of Thai budget options. There are some good places, though, and they're listed below.

Bierstube, south of the *Wiang Inn* at 897/1 Phaholyothin Rd. A well-run and easy-going watering hole, with inexpensive draught beer and good German food, including its own smoked sausages and pickles. Expensive.

La Cantina, 528/20 Banphaprakan Rd, on a southerly soi just east of the clock tower. The Italian owner rustles up a long menu of good pastas, pizzas and veggie options, accompanied by home-baked bread. Expensive.

Chiang Rai Island Restaurant, in the grounds of the *Dusit Island Resort*, 1129 Kraisorasit Rd. An elegant, open-sided pavilion well worth a splurge for its wide range of delicious Thai cuisine. Expensive.

Haw Naliga, 402/1–2 Banphaprakan Rd. To the west of the clocktower after which it's named, this eaterie is a touch upmarket, but justifiably popular for its varied Thai menu. Moderate.

Khun Pochana, by the clocktower at 529/4–5 Banphaprakan Rd. A popular, rough-hewn night-time restaurant which serves tasty Thai and Chinese standards. Inexpensive.

Salungkhum, 843 Phaholyothin Rd (between King Mengrai's statue and the river). Rated by locals as serving the best food for the price in town, and has a garden at the back for evening dining; there's no sign in English, but look out for the *Cosmo* petrol station on the opposite side of the road. Moderate.

North of Chiang Rai

At a push, any one of the places described in this section could be visited on a day trip from Chiang Rai, but if you can devote three or four days, you'd be better off moving camp to make a circuit of **Mae Salong** with its mountaintop Chinese enclave, **Mae Sai**, an intriguing border town, and **Chiang Saen**, whose atmospheric ruins by the banks of the Mekhong contrast sharply with the commercialism of nearby **Sop Ruak**. Given more time and patience, you could also stop over on the way to Mae Sai at *Laan Tong Lodge* (see p.276) for walks to the nearby hill-tribe villages, and at **Doi Tung** to look down over Thailand, Laos, Burma and China, and continue beyond Chiang Saen to the sleepy, little-visited town of **Chiang Khong** on the banks of the Mekhong.

Chiang Rai province is unique in being so well mapped, which opens it up to independent exploration: the *Guide Map of Chiang Rai* (see box on previous page) is indispensable for getting the most out of a rented motorbike, and even if you're not on a bike might well give you some ideas for day walks away from the major attractions. For renting a **motorbike**, *Soon* at 197/2 Trairat Rd

(☎053/714068) is the most reliable place in Chiang Rai and has the best choice. **Four-wheel drives** are available for B1000–1200 a day at *Avis* in the *Dusit Island Resort* (☎053/715777), *SMT* (*Inter-rent*) at the airport (☎01/213 6815), and at the reliable *Thai Randonnées*, in front of the *Wangcome Hotel* at 869/112 Pemavipat Rd (☎053/711893), which also organizes expensive car and motorbike tours in the area. If you just want to hop around the main towns by **public transport**, the set-up is straightforward enough: frequent buses to Mae Sai run due north up Highway 110; to Chiang Saen, they start off on the same road before forking right onto Highway 1016; for most other places, you have to make one change off these routes onto a songthaew.

Mae Salong (Santikhiri)

Perched 1300m up on a ridge with commanding views of sawtoothed hills, the Chinese Nationalist outpost of **MAE SALONG** lies 36km along a roller coaster of a road that ploughs into the harsh border country west of Highway 110. Songthaews make the dizzying ninety-minute journey frequently, starting from **Ban Pa Zang**, 32km north of Chiang Rai on Highway 110. A few marginally interesting attractions might tempt you to hop off en route – notably the Hill Tribe Training Centre, 12km from Ban Pa Zang, where local minorities are taught how to farm cash crops other than opium, and a couple of Mien and Akha souvenir villages – and you should have no trouble flagging down another pickup when you're done.

Mae Salong is the focal point for the area's fourteen thousand **Kuomintang**, who for two generations now have held fast to their cultural identity, if not their political cause. The ruling party of China for 21 years, the Kuomintang (Nationalists) were swept from power by the communist revolution of 1949 and fled in two directions: one group, under party leader Chiang Kai-shek, made for Taiwan, where it founded the Republic of China; the other, led by General Li Zongren, settled in northern Thailand and Burma. The Nationalists' original plan to retake China from Mao Zedong in a two-pronged attack never came to fruition, and the remnants of the army in Thailand became major players in the heroin trade. Over the last ten years, the Thai government has worked hard to "pacify" the Kuomintang by a mixture of force and more peaceful methods, such as crop programmes to replace opium. Around Mae Salong at least, its work seems to have been successful, as evidenced by the slopes to the south of the settlement, which are covered with a carpet of rich green tea bushes. Since its rehabilitation, Mae Salong is now officially known as **Santikhiri** (Hill of Peace).

The Town and beyond

Though it has a new temple, a church, a wat and a mosque, it's the details of Chinese life in the back streets – the low-slung bamboo houses, the pictures of Chiang Kai-shek, ping pong tables, the sounds of Yunnanese conversation punctuated with throaty hawking – that make the village absorbing. Mae Salong gets plenty of Thai visitors, especially at weekends, who throng the main street's souvenir stalls to buy such delicacies as sorghum whisky (pickled with ginseng, deer antler and centipedes) and locally grown Chinese tea and herbs. If you want to sample the wares for yourself in a less commercialized environment, take the left fork, which skirts along the hill towards the western end of the main street to reach the **traditional medicine shop**, on the right 50m before *Shin Sane Guest House*. Mr Soo Ton, the ancient teacher who runs it, will explicate in wild sign language the teas, pellets and biscuits which are good for the various parts of the body. It's also worth braving the dawn chill to get to the **morning market**, held on the basketball court by the *Shin Sane Guest House* between 6 and 7.30am, which pulls them in from the surrounding Akha, Lisu and Mien villages.

The right fork, which passes the wat at the west end of town, leads after an hour to a clutch of very traditional and conservative **Akha villages** – notably Ban Mae Do – whose inhabitants moved here from Burma only in the last few years. The Kuomintang live up to their Thai nickname – *jiin haw*, meaning "galloping Chinese" – by offering treks on horses, a rare sight in Thailand. Trips can be arranged at the *Mae Salong Guest House* (see below) from B300 for three hours.

Beyond Mae Salong, newly paved roads let you nip the back way to Tha Ton; half-hourly songthaews cover the distance in ninety minutes. North of Mae Salong lies **Ban Therd Thai**, although to get to it by road you'd have to back-track down the main road 12km to Sam Yaek and then make your own way up a nasty side road a further 13km into the hills. In its former incarnation as Ban Hin Taek, this mixed village was the opium capital of the notorious Khun Sa (see p.220): the Thai army drove Khun Sa out after a pitched battle in 1983, and the village has now been renamed and "pacified" with the establishment of a market, school and hospital, but it's still not considered safe enough to visit.

Practicalities

The best of Mae Salong's budget **accommodation** is *Shin Sane Guest House* (☎053/765026; ②–③), a friendly guest house on the west side of the main fork in the road, which has small rooms in the funky wooden main building and smart bungalows in the yard behind, plus B50 dorm beds. If that's full, the shabby rooms of *Mae Salong Guest House* (☎053/765102; ②) are a stone's throw away up the bank. Of the upmarket places, *Mae Salong Villa* (☎053/765114–9; ⑥–⑧) on the main road at the eastern end of the village offers most value, with a choice of functional rooms or comfy wooden bungalows with balconies facing the Burmese mountains, all with hot-water bathrooms. The terrace **restaurant** shares the same view and cooks up the best food in town, including delicious but expensive Chinese specialities like *het hawm* (wild mushrooms) and *kai dam* (black chicken).

Doi Tung

Steep, wooded hills rise abruptly from the plains west of Highway 110 as it approaches the Burmese border. Crowned by a thousand-year-old wat, the central peak here, 1300-metre **DOI TUNG**, makes a worthwhile outing just for the journey. A broad paved road runs up the mountainside, beginning 32km north of Chiang Rai on Highway 110, just before **Ban Huai Khrai**. It's best to have your own vehicle for the trip, as public transport to the summit is irregular – you might be lucky enough to find a songthaew in Ban Huai Khrai ferrying villagers up the mountain (better in the morning), but your only other options are to hitch (easy at weekends) or to charter a whole songthaew for B600.

The summit road ascends past Thai Yai, Chinese, Akha and Lahu villages, shimmies over a precarious saddle with some minor temple buildings and refreshment stalls 2km before the top, and finally climbs through a tuft of thick woods to **Wat Phra That Doi Tung** – look out for the strange collection of small Indian, Chinese and Thai statues, brought as offerings by pilgrims, in a rocky glade just before you reach the main temple buildings. Pilgrims to the wat earn themselves good fortune by clanging the rows of dissonant bells around the temple compound and by trying to throw coins into the gaping belly-button of a giant Chinese Buddha: even if they miss they earn merit, because an attendant monk scoops up the misdirected money for temple funds. For non-Buddhist travellers, the reward for getting this far is the stunning view out over the cultivated slopes and half of northern Thailand. The wat's most important structures are its twin **chedis**, erected to enshrine relics of the Buddha in 911. When the building of the chedis was complete, King Achutaraj of Ngon Yang ordered a giant flag (*tung*), reputedly 2km long, to be flown from the peak, which gave the mountain its name.

More recently, Doi Tung has become the country seat of the Princess Mother (mother of the present king, who was never queen herself, but is affectionately known as *Mae Fa Luang*, "great mother of mankind"); the palace buildings, 12km up the summit road then 2km left up a side road, are closed to visitors, but the immaculate ornamental gardens below (daily 6am–6pm; B20) throng with snap-happy day-trippers at weekends. The Princess Mother's hill-tribe project has helped to develop local villages by introducing new agricultural methods: the slopes which were formerly blackened by the fires of slash-and-burn farming are now used to grow teak and pine, and crops such as strawberries and coffee, which are sold in the shop by the entrance to the gardens.

A steep **back road** north to Mae Sai (22km) begins at the saddle beneath the peak, by the refreshment stalls. This area has been the scene of conflict among the Kuomintang, the hill tribes and others involved in the opium trade, but with the development of Doi Tung under the Princess Mother's project it should now be safe. After 4km of asphalt, you'll reach the chedi and arboretum at the pinnacle of **Doi Chang Moob**, an even higher and better viewpoint than Doi Tung – on a clear day, you can make out the Mekhong River and the triangular outline of 2600-metre Loi Pangnao, on the border between Burma and China. A difficult track (soon to be paved) then follows the sharp ridge north before snaking down to **Ban Pha Mee**, an Akha village where you can get refreshments. From Ban Pha Mee, a paved road descends directly to Mae Sai after 7km.

Mae Sai

MAE SAI, with its hustling tourist trade and bustling border crossing, is not to everyone's taste, but it can be an intriguing place to watch the world go by, and with some good-value guest houses it can also be used as a base for exploring Doi Tung or Sop Ruak. Thailand's most northerly town lies 61km from Chiang Rai at the dead end of Highway 110, which forms the town's single north–south street and is the site of the bus stop. Wide enough for an armoured battalion, this ugly boulevard still has the same name – Phaholyothin Road – as at the start of its journey north in the suburbs of Bangkok.

Phaholyothin Road ends at a short but commercially important **bridge** over the Mae Sai River, which forms the border with Burma. During daylight hours, Thais have long been allowed to travel up to 5km into Burmese territory, but this dubious pleasure is now also open to farangs, upon payment of a US$5 note

– no visa is required, just leave your passport at the Thai immigration check-point at the southern end of the bridge and take photocopies of the important pages (copying service conveniently available next to Thai immigration) across to Burmese immigration. Prospering on the back of growing cross-border trade, **Thakhilek**, the Burmese town opposite, looks remarkably similar to the concrete boxes of Mae Sai, one of the few obvious differences being that traffic in Burma is rather perversely made to drive on the right (a snook cocked at the British after the overthrow of colonial rule, though most vehicles in the country are still right-hand drive). Thakhilek's handful of temples have next to nothing of architectural interest, the town's big draw being, for farangs and for the hundreds of Thai day-trippers who crowd the narrow streets, a frenzy of **shopping**. The huge market on the right after the bridge is an entrepôt for a bizarre diversity of goods from around the world – from Jacob's Cream Crackers to bears' paws and tigers' intestines – but its main thrust is to cater to the everyday demands of Thai customers, with a selection of ordinary, inexpensive clothes and bedding. The array of Burmese handicrafts – tatty Pagan lacquerware and crude woodcarving – is disappointing.

Shopping is the main activity in Mae Sai, too: from the central morning market crowded with purposeful Burmese, to the stores around the bridge which hawk "Burmese" handicrafts – mostly made in the factories of Chiang Mai, though slightly better quality than in Thakhilek – and coloured glass posing as gems. On the left 100m before the bridge, *Village Product* offers more interesting stuff, such as hill-tribe fabric and clothes from both Thailand and Burma. *Thong Tavee*, further south at 17 Phaholyothin Rd, is the place to buy good quality jade and to watch the delicate process of cutting, decorating and polishing the stone in the workshop behind.

Climb up to the chedi of **Wat Phra That Doi Wao**, five minutes' walk from the bridge (behind the *Top North Hotel*), for a better perspective on the town. As well as Doi Tung to the south and the hills of Laos in the east, you get a good view up the steep-sided valley and across the river to Thakhilek.

Most travellers staying in Mae Sai end up making **day trips** out to Doi Tung (see previous pages) and Sop Ruak (opposite). A third, less compelling choice would be **Tham Luang**: this "Royal Cave" has an impressive entrance cavern, flooded with natural light, and 7km of low, sweaty passageways beyond (guides and weak lanterns can be hired by the entrance for B20 plus a "donation for cleaning"). Without a bike you'll have to hop on a bus south on Highway 110 for 5km, to where a row of roadside stalls sell strawberries in the cool season; the cave is a signposted 3km from there. On the way, look out for the elaborate mausoleums of Mae Sai's Chinese cemetery, 2km south of town.

At the time of writing, pricey and uncomfortable package tours into Burma and China were newly available, arranged (with at least a week's notice) through *Chad Guest House* (see facing page), *Ananda*, 22 Moo 7 Phaholythin Rd (☎053/731038; Fax 053/731749) and *Five Chiang*, 381/3 Phaholythin Rd (☎053/642130; Fax 053/642131).

Practicalities

A handful of **inexpensive guest houses** are strung out along the river bank west of the bridge. The best of these is the furthest away: *Mae Sai* (☎053/732021; ②) is a beautiful, relaxing place to stay with a wide variety of bungalows, wedged between a steep hill and the river, fifteen minutes from the main road. *Chad Guest House* on Soi Wiangpan – look out for the signpost on the left, 1km before the bridge – scores low for location but is the classic travellers' rest (☎053/732054; ①): the family is welcoming and well informed about the area (B20 for maps and information for non-guests), the food is good and it's an easy place to meet people. It also has B50 dorm beds, and **motorbikes** for rent, from B150 a day.

The *Wang Tong*, on the east side of the bridge at 299 Phaholyothin Rd (☎053/733388–95; ⑦), is Mae Sai's best **hotel**, with a huge, ornate lobby, a swimming pool and sloppy service. Much less pretentious and better value is the *Mae Sai Hotel* at 125/5 Phaholyothin Rd (☎053/731462; ③–④), which has simple, clean rooms with attached bathrooms, some with air conditioning.

Mae Sai's top **place to eat** is *Rabieng Kaew*, a wooden house with an open-air terrace, opposite the *Krung Thai Bank* on Phaholyothin Road – the menu lists a wide choice of excellent Thai cuisine, though it's not inexpensive by local standards. The terrace of the *Rim Nam* (*Riverside*), under the western side of the bridge, is crowded during the day with tourists watching the border action, but the Thai dishes are surprisingly good and generous, and not too pricey. The night market, across the main road from the *Sri Wattana Hotel*, is inexpensive and very popular. *JoJo*, 233 Phaholyothin Rd (daytime only), serves up decent Western breakfasts, Thai fast food and fancy ice creams at a price.

Sop Ruak

The Golden Triangle, which actually denotes a huge opium-producing area spreading across Burma, Laos and Thailand, has, for the benefit of tourists, been artificially concentrated into the precise spot where the borders meet, 57km northeast of Chiang Rai. Don't come to the village of **SOP RUAK**, at the confluence of the Ruak and Mekong rivers, expecting to run into sinister drug-runners, addicts or even poppy-fields – instead you'll find souvenir stalls, pay toilets, an opium museum and a huge sign saying "Golden Triangle" which pops up in a million photo albums around the world.

The meeting of the waters is undeniably monumental, but to get an unobstructed view of it you need to climb up to **Wat Phra That Phu Khao**, a 1200-year-old temple perched on a small hill above the village: to the north, beyond the puny Ruak (Mae Sai), the mountains of Burma march off into infinity, while eastwards across the mighty Mekhong spread the hills and villages of Laos. The scene is slowly being transformed, however, as building work has started on a Thai luxury hotel, over on the uninhabited strip of Burmese land immediately upstream of the confluence. The attached casino will bypass Thai laws against gambling, and the usually strict border formalities will be waived for visitors coming from Thailand.

For B300, you can have the thrill of stepping on Laotian soil. A longtail boat from the pier in the centre of the village will give you a kiss-me-quick tour of the "Golden Triangle", including five minutes on a sand bar in the Mekhong which belongs to Laos.

To get to Sop Ruak you'll have to go via Chiang Saen or Mae Sai. **From Chiang Saen** you can go by regular songthaew (departing from in front of the school on the west side of the T-junction), rented bicycle (an easy 14-km ride on a paved road, though not much of it runs along the river bank) or longtail boat up the Mekhong (B400 round trip). **From Mae Sai**, songthaews make the 45-minute trip from the side of the *Sri Wattana Hotel* on Phaholyothin Road (they leave when they're full); longtails are a pricey alternative (B1000), if the Mae Sai River is high enough.

Practicalities

For budget travellers, there's nowhere to **stay** in Sop Ruak. With more cash to spare for a bit of comfort, try *MP World Villa* at the south end of the village (☎053/784101 or 784102; ⑥), whose rustic bungalows have verandahs overlooking the river. For all the luxury you'll ever want, *Le Meridien Baan Boran* (☎053/784084; Bangkok reservations ☎02/254 8147–59; ⑧), 1km north out of Sop Ruak, is probably northern Thailand's finest hotel. Tastefully designed in impeccable traditional style, all the rooms and the swimming pool have great views over the countryside to the Mekhong.

Chiang Saen

Combining tumbledown ruins with sweeping Mekhong River scenery, **CHIANG SAEN**, 60km northeast of Chiang Rai, makes a rustic haven and a good base camp for the border region east of Mae Sai. The town's focal point, where the Chiang Rai road meets the main road along the banks of the Mekhong, is a lively junction thronged by buses, songthaews and longtails, with a small day market on its south side. Turning left at this junction will soon bring you to Sop Ruak, but you may well share the road with the tour buses that sporadically thunder through; very few tourists turn right in Chiang Saen along the rough road to Chiang Khong, even though this is the best way to appreciate the slow charms of the Mekhong valley.

The region around Chiang Saen, originally known as Yonok, seems to have been an important Thai trading crossroads from some time after the seventh century. The much-romanticized chronicles of the region maintain that Chiang Saen ruled as the capital of northern Thailand from the twelfth century, but most historians now reserve that distinction for the lost principality of Ngon Yang. The city whose remains you see now was founded around 1328 by the successor to the renowned King Mengrai of Chiang Mai, Saen Phu, who gave up his throne to retire here. Coveted for its strategic location, guarding the Mekhong, Chiang Saen was passed back and forth between the kings of Burma and Thailand for nearly three hundred years until Rama I razed the place to the ground in 1804. The present village was established only in 1881, when Rama V ordered a northern prince to resettle the site with descendants of the old townspeople mustered from Lamphun, Chiang Mai and Lampang.

Buses from Chiang Rai and **songthaews** from Sop Ruak stop just short of the T-junction of Phaholyothin Road and the river road, a short walk or a samlor ride from Chiang Saen's main guest houses. **Longtail boats** from Sop Ruak dock just south of this junction. If you're travelling by **bike or car**, follow Highway 110 north as far as **Mae Chan** (30km), then bear northeastwards along a secondary route (Highway 1016) for the last 30km to Chiang Saen. To get around the ruins and the surrounding countryside, **bicycles** can be rented at *Gin's Guest House* (B20 a day), while *JS Guest House* has **mopeds** for B160 a day.

The Town

The layout of the old, ruined city is defined by the Mekhong River running along its east flank; a tall rectangle, 2.5km from north to south, is formed by the addition of the ancient ramparts, now fetchingly overgrown, on the other three sides. The grid of leafy streets inside the ramparts is now too big for the modern town, which is generously scattered along the river road and across the middle on Phaholyothin Road. For serious temple explorers, a **tourist information centre** opposite the National Museum has free detailed **maps** of the town.

The **National Museum** (Wed–Sun 9am–4pm; B10), announced by the primitive stone bell at the western end of Phaholyothin Road, makes an informative starting point. As well as a disparate collection of exhibits from elsewhere, including unusual silver Buddhas and a transparent phallic *lingam*, the museum houses some impressive Buddha images and architectural features rescued from the surrounding ruins. The art of northern Thailand was once dubbed "Chiang Saen style" because the town had an important school of bronze casting. The more appropriate name "Lanna style" is now preferred, though you'll still come across the traditional term. As in many of Thailand's museums, the back end is given over to a curious jumble of folk objects, one highlight being the beautiful wooden lintel carved with *hum yon* (floral swirls representing testicles), which would have been placed above the front door of a house to ward off evil. **Wat Phra That Chedi Luang**, originally the city's main temple, is worth looking in on next door for its imposing octagonal chedi, now decorated with weeds and a huge yellow ribbon.

Beyond the ramparts to the west, **Wat Pa Sak**'s brick buildings and laterite columns have been excavated and restored by the Fine Arts Department, making it the most accessible and impressive of Chiang Saen's many temples (there's an entrance fee of B20 whenever the custodian is about). The wat's name is an allusion to the thousand (or so) teak trees which Saen Phu planted in the grounds when he built the chedi in 1340 to house some Indian Buddha relics. The central chedi owes its eclectic shape largely to the grand temples of Pagan in Burma: the square base is inset with niches housing alternating Buddhas and *deva* (angels) with flowing skirts, and above rises the tower for the Buddha relic, topped by a circular spire. Beautiful carved stucco covers much of the structure, showing intricate floral scrolls and stylized lotus patterns as well as a whole zoo of mythical beasts.

The open space around modern Chiang Saen, which is dotted with trees and another 140 overgrown ruins (both inside and outside the ramparts), is great for a carefree wander. A spot worth aiming for is the hapless leaning chedi of **Wat Phra That Chom Kitti**, which gives a good view of the town and the river from a small hill outside the northwest corner of the ramparts.

Practicalities

The best of a handful of **guest houses** in the town itself is the hospitable, Swiss/Thai-owned *JS*, 303 Praisanee Rd (☎053/777060; ②), behind the post office on the north side of Phaholyothin Road: clean rooms in a modern family house share an equally clean bathroom with solar-heated water (beds are also available on a dormitory basis for B50 per person). Outside the ramparts, 2km north of the T-junction, *Gin's Guest House* (☎053/650387; ③) is run by an informative teacher, who presents the choice of large, jerry-built A-frame bungalows in a lychee orchard, or decent rooms in the main house, all with at least access to hot water; it also has B50 dorm beds. Upmarket but out on the town's western bypass, *Ban Suan* (☎053/650419; ④), with the same owners as *JS*, adopts a motel style to catch passing trade on the way to Sop Ruak; large, well-designed rooms with solar-heated water are ranged around a sloping garden. **Eat** standard travellers' fare at your guest house or Thai food at the cosy *Sala Thai Pub Restaurant*, just south of the T-junction.

East to Chiang Khong

Several routes lead from Chiang Saen to Chiang Khong, 70km downriver, a peaceful and rarely visited backwater which is the only other town on the Mekhong before it enters Laos. The most scenic way to get there is by **motorbike**, following the northward kink in the river for three hours along bumpy, partly paved roads. An exciting but expensive alternative – about B1200 – is to run the rapids on a hired **longtail boat**, which will also take about three hours. Public transport between the two towns is limited to two **songthaews** a day, which head off along the river before cutting across country on Highway 1129 to reach Chiang Khong after two hours. If you're going straight to Chiang Khong from Chiang Rai, direct **buses** leaving every 45 minutes cover the ground in two hours.

Heading out of Chiang Saen by the river road, you'll pass through tobacco fields and, after 4km, see the brick gate of **Wat Phra That Pha Ngao** on the right. The tenth-century temple contains a supposedly miraculous chedi perched on top of a large boulder, but the real attraction is the view from the new chedi on the hillside above: take the one-kilometre paved track which starts at the back of the temple and you can't miss the lumbering **Chedi Ched Yod**, designed by an American in the style of a concrete bunker and built over and around a ruined brick chedi. From here the panorama takes in Chiang Saen's ruins, the wide plain and the slow curve of the river. To the east, the Kok River, which looks so impressive at Chiang Rai, seems like a stream as it pours into the mighty Mekhong.

Twenty-three kilometres from Chiang Saen, turn left off Highway 1129 to follow the course of the Mekhong, reaching after 9km the Thai Lue settlement of **Ban Hat Bai**. Signposts will lead you to *Sukhawadee* in the heart of the village, a small unkempt shop selling a wide selection of the beautifully coloured cotton for which the Thai Lue are famous – if you ask you'll be taken to see the old women of the village weaving (*tor pha*) at their looms in the space beneath their stilted houses. Beyond Hat Bai, the hills close in and the river enters a stretch of rocky rapids, forcing the road to climb up the valley side and making for some dramatic vantage points.

Chiang Khong

CHIANG KHONG achieved its greatest fame among travellers as the starting point for the old Laotian loop, lost after the Pathet Lao government closed the country in 1975, but coming back to prominence with the current loosening of attitudes towards tourism. Chiang Khong is currently one of five places where it's possible for farangs to **cross to Laos** (the others are Nong Khai, Nakhon Phanom, Mukdahan and Chang Mek in the northeast). At the north end of town is Chiang Khong's main pier, **Hua Wiang**. The departure point for frequent passenger ferries to **Ban Huai Sai** across the border, it is being showered with money to

GIANT CATFISH

The **giant catfish** (*pla buk*), found only in the Mekhong, is said to be the largest freshwater fish in the world, measuring up to 3m in length and weighing in at 300kg. Chiang Khong is the catfish capital of the north, attracting fish merchants and restaurateurs from Chiang Rai and Chiang Mai – the tasty meat of the *pla buk* is prized for its fine, soft texture and can fetch up to B400 a kilo. The hunting season is officially opened at the port of Ban Hat Khrai on April 18 with much pomp, including an elaborate ceremony to appease Chao Por Pla Buk, the giant catfish god. Around a hundred fishing boats then set out, as they do every morning before dawn for the rest of the season, from both the Thai and Laotian banks, vying with each other to see who can make the first catch. Gone is the old challenge and excitement of harpooning the fish, however: the fishermen now trawl the river over several kilometres of its course with 250-metre nylon nets. The season's haul is usually between thirty and sixty fish all told, but recent years have been so disappointing that Thailand's Fishery Department has begun an artificial spawning programme.

develop it into a major port for trade with Laos and China. For fishing boats, the port is **Ban Hat Khrai**, just south of town, which springs to life during the annual giant catfish hunt: at this time the good but pricey restaurant above the port is the place to sample catfish. In between the two ports, Chiang Khong is strung out along a single north–south street, Sai Klang Road, on a high, steep bank above the river. If you're not crossing to Laos, once you've admired the elevated view of the traffic on the Mekhong and the turrets of the French-built Fort Carnot across in Huai Sai, there's little to do but relax and enjoy the fact that none of the hustle is directed at you.

If you do decide to cross over into Laos, there are several possibilities for onward travel once over the border. From Ban Huai Sai daily cargo boats glide down the scenic Mekhong, taking two days to reach Luang Prabang and charging B300 per passenger; uncomfortable longtails cover the same stretch in six hours for B600 per person. As an alternative to buses on Laos' appalling road system, thrice-weekly flights leave Huai Sai for Luang Prabang and Vientiane, while travelling overland or up the Mekhong to China should be possible in the near future.

PRACTICALITIES

Chiang Khong's sole **guest house**, *Ban Tam-Mi-La*, at 113 Sai Klang Rd (☎ & Fax 053/791234; ①), is a welcome relief if you've made the tough trip down from Chiang Saen. Easy-going and restful, the restaurant and tasteful, well-designed wooden bungalows are set on a wooded slope with ringside views over the water. Wat, the helpful and reliable owner, is the best person to approach in Chiang Khong for **visas to Laos** and information about transport on the other side. At the moment, Wat can obtain a visa the day after you arrive (not including Sun) for B2000, but is hoping to bring this price down; he's also working on a longer, more complex system for about B1000 – telephone him from Bangkok at least ten days before you want to enter Laos for further details (see p.374 for information about other means of getting a Laotian visa). Note, however, that Wat may have to move his bungalows if the local authorities get round to building a planned concrete embankment along the river – if that happens, he's a familiar enough character that you could find him by asking around town.

travel details

Trains

Chiang Mai to: Bangkok (6 daily; 13hr).

Den Chai to: Bangkok (8 daily; 9hr); Chiang Mai (6 daily; 4hr).

Doi Khun Tan to: Bangkok (5 daily; 12hr); Chiang Mai (5 daily; 1hr).

Lampang to: Bangkok (6 daily; 11hr); Chiang Mai (6 daily; 2hr).

Lamphun to: Bangkok (4 daily; 13hr); Chiang Mai (4 daily; 20min).

Buses

Chiang Khong to: Bangkok (3 daily; 13–14hr); Chiang Mai (5 daily; 6hr).

Chiang Mai to: Bangkok (28 daily; 10–11hr); Chiang Khong (5 daily; 6hr); Chiang Rai (29 daily; 3–4hr); Chiang Saen (4 daily; 5hr); Chom Thong (every 30min; 1hr); Fang (every 30min; 3hr); Khon Kaen (10 daily; 11–12hr); Khorat (8 daily; 11–12hr); Lampang (every 30min; 2hr); Lamphun (every 30min; 45min); Loei (4 daily; 9–10hr); Mae Hong Son (9 daily via Mae Sariang, 4 daily via Pai; 8hr); Mae Sai (11 daily; 4–5hr); Mae Sot (4 daily; 5–6hr); Nan (10 daily; 7hr); Pai (6 daily; 4hr); Phayao (14 daily; 3hr); Phitsanulok (10 daily; 5–6hr); Rayong (7 daily; 15hr); San Kamphaeng (every 30min; 30min); Sukhothai (12 daily; 5–6hr); Tak (4 daily; 4hr); Tha Ton (5 daily; 4hr); Ubon (6 daily; 15–17hr); Udon Thani (4 daily; 11–12hr).

Chiang Rai to: Bangkok (15 daily; 12hr); Chiang Khong (every 45min; 3hr); Chiang Saen (every 15min; 1hr 30min); Khon Kaen (5 daily; 12hr); Khorat (3 daily; 13hr); Mae Sai (every 15min; 1hr 30min); Nakhon Phanom (3 daily; 16hr); Nan (1 daily; 7hr); Pattaya (3 daily; 16hr); Phayao (21 daily; 2hr); Phitsanulok (5 daily; 7hr); Sukhothai (5 daily; 6hr); Udon Thani (3 daily; 13hr).

Lampang to: Bangkok (10 daily; 8hr); Chiang Rai (21 daily; 5hr); Nan (10 daily; 5hr); Phayao (21 daily; 3hr).

Mae Hong Son to: Bangkok (2 daily; 18hr).

Mae Sai to: Bangkok (8 daily; 13hr).

Nan to: Bangkok (13 daily; 13hr).

Pai to: Mae Hong Son (6 daily; 4hr).

Phayao to: Nan (3 daily; 5hr).

Flights

Chiang Mai to: Bangkok (8–11 daily; 1hr); Chiang Rai (2 daily; 40min); Kunming, China (2 weekly; 3hr); Mae Hong Son (5 daily; 40min); Mae Sot (4 weekly; 1hr); Nan (3 weekly; 1hr); Phitsanulok (1 daily; 2hr); Phuket (3 weekly; 2hr); Surat Thani (2 weekly; 2hr); Tak (4 weekly; 2hr).

Chiang Rai to: Bangkok (4 daily; 1hr 20min).

Lampang to: Bangkok (2 daily; 2hr); Phitsanulok (2 daily; 35min).

Nan to: Bangkok (1 daily; 2hr); Phitsanulok (3 weekly; 1hr).

CHAPTER FOUR

THE EAST COAST

B illed optimistically by tour operators as Thailand's riviera, the **east coast** is a five-hundred-kilometre string of predominantly dull, grey beaches blotched with expensive, over-packaged family resorts. Worse still, the discovery of oil and natural gas fields in these coastal waters has turned pockets of the first hundred-kilometre stretch into an unsightly industrial landscape of refineries and depots. Offshore, however, it's an entirely different story, with island beaches as peaceful and unsullied as many of the more celebrated southern retreats.

The first worthwhile stop comes 100km east of Bangkok at **Si Racha**, a less than scintillating town but the point of access for diminutive **Ko Si Chang**, whose dramatically rugged coastlines and low-key atmosphere make it a restful haven. In complete contrast, **Pattaya**, just half an hour south, is Thailand's number-one package-tour destination, its customers predominantly middle-aged Western males enticed by the resort's sex-market reputation and undeterred by its notoriety as the country's most polluted beach. Things soon look up, though, as the coast veers sharply eastwards towards Ban Phe, revealing the island of **Ko Samet**, the loveliest of all the beach resorts within comfortable bus-ride range of Bangkok. Geared primarily towards budget travellers, Samet strikes a perfect balance between unspoilt rough living and well-equipped comfort.

East of Ban Phe, the landscape starts to get more lush and hilly as the coastal highway nears **Chanthaburi**, the dynamo of Thailand's gem trade and one of only two provincial capitals in the region worth visiting. The other appealing inland city is **Trat**, 68km further along the highway and an important departure point for **Ko Chang**, a huge, still largely unspoilt island with long, fine beaches. Ko Chang marks the easternmost limit of the tourist trail: although it looks tantalizingly easy to **cross into Cambodia** from this part of Thailand, it's illegal to do so and involves a long, potentially dangerous journey to the capital – in the light of recent tourist kidnappings, you'd be well advised to fly out of Bangkok instead.

Highway 3 extends almost the entire length of the east coast – beginning in Bangkok as Sukhumvit Road, and known as such when cutting through towns – and hundreds of **buses** ply the route, connecting all major mainland destinations. Buses from Bangkok's Eastern Bus Terminal serve all the provincial capitals and tourist spots, but it's also possible to travel between the east coast and the northeast without doubling back through the capital. The most direct routes into **Isaan** start from Pattaya, Rayong and Chanthaburi, and all pass through fairly spectacular upland scenery, crossing the two ranges of invariably cloud-capped mountains which mark the climatic and geological divide between the fertile, fruit-growing east coast and the almost barren scrublands of the Khorat plateau.

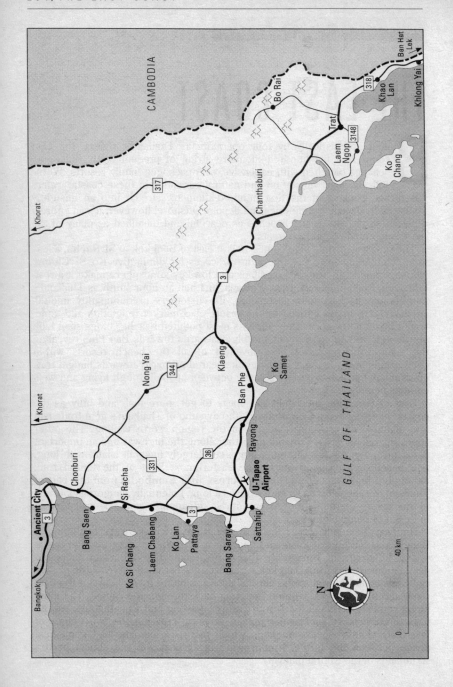

Si Racha: the approach to Ko Si Chang

Almost 30km southeast of Bangkok, Highway 3 finally emerges from the urban sprawl at the fishing town of Samut Prakan. It then follows the edge of the plain for a further 50km before reaching the prosperous but dull provincial capital of **Chonburi**, whose single annual attraction is its October bout of buffalo-racing. The road forks here, Route 344 making a diagonal short cut to the coastal stretch between Rayong and Chanthaburi, and Highway 3 continuing to hug every kilometre of the L-shaped coastline to Rayong. Thai holidaymakers are very keen on the expensive beach resort of Bang Saen, 10km south of Chonburi, particularly as a day-trip break from Bangkok. As an off-the-beaten-track experience, however, the nearby island of Ko Si Chang (see below) is much more rewarding.

Access to Ko Si Chang is from the fishing port and refinery town of **SI RACHA**, famous throughout Thailand as the home of *nam phrik Si Racha*, the orange-hued, chilli-laced ketchup found on every restaurant and kitchen table in the country. You'll probably only find yourself wanting to stay here if you miss the last boat to the island, though the idiosyncratic seafront hotels make this an unexpectedly enjoyable experience, and the town is not without charm, especially at twilight, when the rickety, brightly painted fishing boats load up with ice and nets before setting off into the night.

Buses to the town leave Bangkok every 25 minutes and take about two hours: air-conditioned buses stop near *Laemtong* department store on Sukhumvit Road, from where you'll need to take a samlor to the pier for ferries to Ko Si Chang, whereas most regular buses stop nearer the waterfront, on Chermchompon Road. Strung out along the wooden jetties are the simple, cabin-like rooms of three pleasant waterfront **hotels**, all of which are on Chermchompon Road, within five minutes' walk of the pier. The English-speaking managers give a slight advantage to *Sri Wattana* on the (unmarked) Soi 8 (☎038/311307; ①–③), but the adjacent *Siwichai* (☎038/311212; ①–③) is just as pleasant, as is the *Samchai* at the end of the signposted Soi 10 (☎038/311134; ①–③). For **eating**, try any of the seafood restaurants along Chermchompon Road, especially the Chinese-style *Chua Lee* between sois 8 and 10, or the night-market stalls by the clocktower further up the road.

Ferries to Ko Si Chang

Ferries leave five times a day (last one at 5pm) from the pier at the end of Soi 14, Chermchompon Road, though occasionally they set off instead from Wat Ko Loi, the "island temple" at the end of the very long causeway 400m further along. The hop across to Ko Si Chang should take about forty minutes, but this varies according to how many passengers need to be transferred to and from the cargo ships between which the ferries weave.

Ko Si Chang

The unhurried pace and the absence of consumer pressures make tiny, rocky **KO SI CHANG** a satisfying place to hang out for a few days. Unlike most other east-coast destinations, it offers no real beach life – fishing is the major source of income, and there's little to do here but explore the craggy coastline and gaze at the horizon. Yet there is some night-time action: the island caters for the crews of the cargo ships which choke the deep channel between Ko Si Chang and the mainland, hence the transformation after dark, when the apparently unsophisticated village is enlivened by the strains of singing hostessess.

On arrival, you'll probably dock at Tha Bon pier, the more northern of the two piers on the east coast, though some boats pull in at Tha Lang pier, and all departing boats stop off at the latter on their way back to the mainland. Both piers connect with Asadang Road, a small ring road on which you'll find the market, shops, bank (with exchange facilities), post office and most of the island's houses. The rest of the island is accessible only by paths and tracks.

It's easy enough to walk from place to place, the simplest point of reference for **orientation** being *Tiew Pai Guest House*, which stands at the southwest "corner" of Asadang Road, about 750m from Tha Lang. Alternatively, you can jump in one of the bizarrely elongated, ridiculously powerful motorbike samlors which, as there are probably fewer than ten private cars on Ko Si Chang, virtually monopolize the roads. A tour of the island in one of these 1200cc-engined contraptions will only set you back between B150 and B250, and as a few of the drivers speak good English, you can learn about the island while you ride.

The **southern part** of the island is the more interesting area. From *Tiew Pai* a road veers south, passing the Marine Research Centre before coming to an end at pebbly **Hat Tha Wang**, which is fine for picnics but useless for swimming. If you follow the path west from here, uphill through trees, you'll see the overgrown foundations of **Rama V's summer palace**, built here in the 1890s but moved piece by piece to Bangkok in 1901, and reconstructed there as Vimanmek Palace (see p.101). Aside from the stone steps and balustrades which still cling to the shallow hillside, the only structure on the site to survive intact is the circular **Wat Asadang Nimitr**, right at the top and surmounted by a crumbling chedi. The whole complex is currently under renovation, however, and when the water channels and ornamental ponds are finally unclogged, the elegance of the original royal retreat should become more apparent.

The path splits just beyond the old palace. One branch heads south to what used to be the island's most swimmable beach, **Hat Sai Kaew** (about 2km from *Tiew Pai*); at the time of writing, however, a quarrying project had rendered this

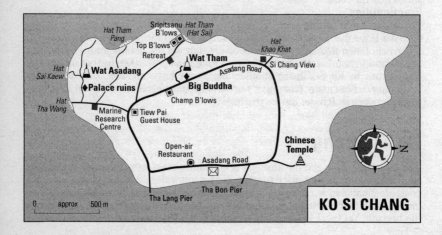

sandy and secluded spot out of bounds. The other track snakes through grass-land, affording glimpses of the rugged western coastline, but giving no direct access to it; this quiet part of the island was once a good place to observe wildlife, particularly butterflies and yellow squirrels – until the quarrying project scalped the south-facing beachside cliffs of their vegetation.

The main beach on the southern stretch of the **west coast** is **Hat Tham Pang** – a great place to perch on the clifftops and watch the seagulls, but again, too rocky for swimming, and in the monsoon season too slimy with algae. You can only get there via the unmetalled road opposite the Marine Research Centre, a half-hour walk.

The central stretch of the west coast is reached via a fork off Asadang Road opposite *Tiew Pai*. This minor road, off which you'll find a Vipassana meditation retreat centre, comes to an abrupt end at **Hat Tham** (sometimes called Hat Sai), a tiny, rocky cove with an unprepossessing beach, overlooked by a couple of dramatically situated guest houses.

Back down on the ring road, continuing northwards from *Tiew Pai*, you'll soon pass beneath the gaze of the large yellow Buddha of **Wat Tham Chakrapong**. The temple itself is built into the cliffside, accessible via a steep and winding side road; the upper levels are given over to public altars and offertory paraphernalia, with a cluster of monks' meditation cells in the labyrinthine passage below. It's well worth the vertiginous ascent, not least for the views out over Thailand's east coast; looking out from the terraces, down over a Gulf congested with cargo boats from Ayutthaya and Bangkok, you'll see the tiny island of Ko Khram and, clearly visible on the horizon, the Si Racha coast.

Spectacular views can also be enjoyed from the rocky **northwest** headland of **Khao Khat**, a few hundred metres further along Asadang Road. The uninter-rupted panorama of open sea makes this a classic sunset spot, and it's safe enough for cliffside scrambling. From here the road heads east to reach the gaudy, multi-tiered **Chinese Temple**, stationed at the top of a steep flight of steps and commanding a good view of the harbour and the mainland coast. Boatloads of Chinese pilgrims make their way here, particularly over Chinese New Year.

Practicalities

There's a surprising range of **accommodation** on Ko Si Chang, including some places with superb sea views. Most backpackers stay in the centrally located *Tiew Pai Guest House* (☎038/216084; ①–④), where rooms range from the simple to the comparatively plush. The restaurant serves a good range of food, the friendly managers speak English, and there's nightly karaoke-style enter-tainment from teenage Thai girls. Further up Asadang Road, below the hillside Buddha, *Champ Bungalows* (☎038/216105; ④) has more of a resort feel, with fairly well-appointed bungalows and an open-air bar and restaurant which also features adolescent crooners. If you prefer a coastal spot, and are willing to pay a bit more, then your first choice should be *Sripitsanu* (☎038/216034; ⑤–⑥), which has just half a dozen comfortably furnished bungalows almost right at the edge of the Hat Tham cliff. Set a little way back from the same cliffside, *Top Bungalows* (⑤) is similar, though a bit overpriced considering that it only enjoys a partial view of the water. Further along the coast, at Khao Khat, *Si Chang View Resort* (☎038/216210; ⑤–⑥) occupies another prime spot, though

ACCOMMODATION PRICES

Throughout this guide, guest houses, hotels and bungalows have been categorized according to the price codes given below. These categories represent the minimum you can expect to pay in the high season (roughly Nov–Feb & July–Aug) for a double room – or, in the case of national park bungalows, for a multi-berth room which can be rented for a standard price by an individual or group. If travelling on your own, expect to pay anything between sixty and one hundred percent of the rates quoted for a double room. Wherever a range of prices is indicated, this means that the establishment offers rooms with varying facilities – as explained in the write-up. Wherever an establishment also offers dormitory beds, the prices of these beds are given in the text, instead of being indicated by price code.

Remember that the top-whack hotels will add seven percent tax and a ten-percent service charge to your bill – the price codes below are based on net rates after taxes have been added.

① under B100	④ B250–400	⑦ B1000–1500
② B100–150	⑤ B400–600	⑧ B1500–3000
③ B150–250	⑥ B600–1000	⑨ B3000+

sadly you can't see the rugged coastline clearly from the otherwise very attractive rooms. For the very best and personally selected sea views, nothing can beat **camping** on your chosen spot: the cliffs at Khao Khat are a particularly popular site, though quite exposed.

Aside from the **nightlife** on offer at *Tiew Pai* and *Champ*, there's a lively open-air restaurant south of Tha Bon; to the north of here, near the Chinese Temple, an outdoor *likay* stage is a venue for frequent performances by travelling folk-theatre players.

Pattaya

Voted by *Which Holiday* magazine in 1992 as one of the world's ten worst beach resorts, **PATTAYA** – 30km south of Si Racha – is the epitome of exploitative tourism gone mad. Visibly polluted sea, narrow, rubbish-strewn beaches and streets packed with high-rise hotels combine to make it visually Thailand's least attractive holiday spot. But most of Pattaya's visitors don't mind that the place looks like Torremolinos nor that most buildings dump their sewage straight into the bay – what they are here for is **sex**. The town swarms with male and female prostitutes, spiced up by a sizeable population of transvestites (*katoey*), and planeloads of Western men flock here to enjoy their services in the rash of go-go bars and massage parlours for which "Patpong-on-Sea" is notorious. It has the largest **gay scene** in Thailand, too, with several exclusively gay hotels and a whole area given over to gay sex bars.

Pattaya's evolution into sin city began with the Vietnam War, when Pattaya got fat on selling sex to American servicemen. Tempted by the dollars, outside investors moved in, local landowners got squeezed out, and soon the place was unrecognizable as the fishing village it once was. When the soldiers and sailors left in the mid-Seventies, Western tourists were enticed to fill their places, and as the seaside Sodom and Gomorrah boomed, ex-servicemen returned to run the sort of

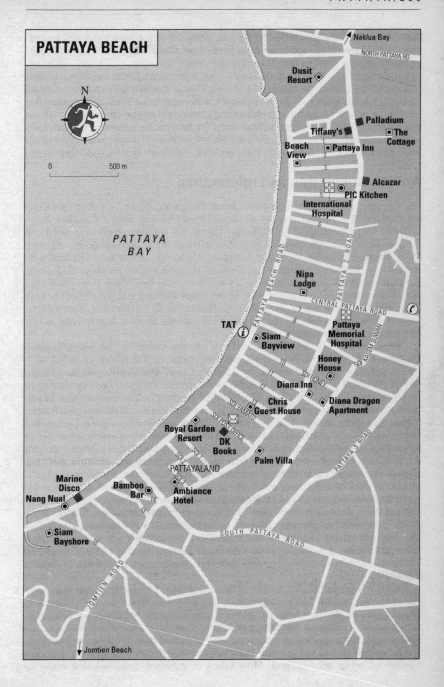

PATTAYA BEACH

N

0   500 m

PATTAYA
BAY

Naklua Bay

NORTH PATTAYA RD.

Dusit
Resort

Palladium

Tiffany's

The
Cottage

Beach
View

Pattaya Inn

Alcazar

PIC Kitchen

International
Hospital

Nipa
Lodge

PATTAYA BEACH ROAD

CENTRAL PATTAYA ROAD

PATTAYA 2 ROAD

TAT

Siam
Bayview

Pattaya
Memorial
Hospital

KASEM SUWAN

Honey
House

SOI HONEY

Diana Inn

Chris
Guest House

SOI YAMATO

Diana Dragon
Apartment

SOI POST OFFICE

Royal Garden
Resort

DK
Books

Palm Villa

PATTAYALAND

SOI 1

PATTAYA 3 ROAD

Marine
Disco

Nang Nual

Bamboo
Bar

Ambiance
Hotel

SOUTH PATTAYA ROAD

Siam
Bayshore

JOMTIEN ROAD

Jomtien Beach

joints they had once blown their dollars in. Almost half the bars, cafés and restaurants are Western-run, specializing in home-from-home menus of English breakfasts, sauerkraut and bratwurst, hamburgers and chips.

Yet Pattaya does have its good points even if you don't fit the lecherous profile of the average punter, as attested by the number of families who choose to spend their packaged fortnights here. Pattaya's water-sports facilities are among the best in the country, and though holidaying here might not be inexpensive – there are no makeshift, low-budget bamboo huts for backpackers and few bargain food stalls – there are several relatively low-cost hotels with their own pools. You won't learn much about Thailand in Pattaya, but you could have quite a good time here.

Arrival, orientation and information

Most people **arrive** in Pattaya direct **from Bangkok**, either by public bus from the Eastern Bus Terminal, or by air-conditioned tour bus from a Bangkok hotel or Don Muang airport. All public buses stop at the station just north of Soi 1, off Pattaya Beach Road in North Pattaya; tour buses have drop-off points all over town. **From Si Racha** it's a thirty-minute ride in one of the frequent buses or songthaews and you'll probably get dropped just east of the resort on Sukhumvit Road, from where Pattaya songthaews will ferry you into town; a few Si Racha songthaews will take you all the way. Buses **from Rayong** and points further east generally drop passengers on Sukhumvit Road as well. It's also possible to get to Pattaya direct **from Isaan** – buses leave Khorat four times a day, arriving at the bus station in North Pattaya.

Pattaya comprises three separate bays. At the centre is the four-kilometre **Pattaya Beach**, the noisiest, most unsightly zone of the resort, crowded with yachts and tour boats and fringed by a sliver of sand. **Pattaya Beach Road** runs the length of the beach and is connected to the parallel Pattaya 2 Road by a string of sois numbered from 1 in the north to 17 in the south. The core of this block, between sois 6 and 13, is referred to as **Central Pattaya** and is packed with hotels, restaurants, bars, fast-food joints, souvenir shops and tour operators. During the day this is the busiest part of the resort, but after dark the neon zone south of Soi 13 – **South Pattaya** – takes over. Known locally as "the strip", this is what Pattaya's really about, with sex for sale in go-go bars, discos, massage parlours and "bar beers". The town's enclave of gay sex bars is here too, focused mainly on the inter-linked network of small lanes numbered as Pattayaland sois 1, 2 and 3, between the wider Beach Road sois 13 and 14. **North Pattaya**, between Central Road and North Pattaya Road, also has its "bar beers", but is a more sedate, upmarket district.

The southerly bay, **Jomtien Beach**, though fronted by enormous high-rises, is the only one where swimming and sunbathing are actually enjoyable. Fourteen kilometres long, it is cleaner and safer than Pattaya Beach, and is considered Thailand's number one windsurfing spot. The northernmost end has become a gay cruising beach.

Naklua Bay, around the northerly headland from Pattaya Beach, is the quietest of the three, and has managed to retain its fishing harbour and indigenous population despite the onslaught of condominiums and holiday apartments. On the downside, much of the accommodation is so far off the main road that it's inaccessible for tourists without private transport, and there's no decent beach.

The easiest way to **get around** Pattaya is by **songthaew** – though on all routes beware of being overcharged. Most follow a standard anti-clockwise route up

Pattaya 2 Road as far as North Pattaya Road and back down Pattaya Beach Road, for a fixed fee of B5 per person. Songthaews to Jomtien leave from the junction between Pattaya 2 Road and South Pattaya Road and cost B5 to the beginning of the beach, B10 beyond. To get to Naklua you need to negotiate with your driver to take you further up Pattaya 2 Road. The alternative is to rent your own transport: Pattaya Beach Road is full of **motorbike and jeep** rental places.

The **TAT** office at 382/1 Beach Rd, Central Pattaya (daily 8.30am–4.30pm), has lots of information on the area, including up-to-date price lists, and will give you trustworthy advice on pollution levels. The **tourist police** headquarters is next door (☎038/429371). The **post office** is, not surprisingly, on Soi Post Office, where you'll also find Pattaya's branch of *DK Books* (daily 8am–11pm). This store's phenomenal selection of English-language **books** rivals even the choice you get in Bangkok, and is particularly strong on anecdotal literature of the "farang in Thailand" and "confessions of a bar girl" ilk. You'll also find a huge range of international newspapers, magazines and periodicals at nearly all mini-markets and postcard shops.

Accommodation

Most of Pattaya's inexpensive and moderately priced hotels offer similar facilities, notably swimming pools or the use of those in neighbouring hotels – an essential asset considering the dreadful beaches. Those listed below as "moderate" are the best of the under-B600 range; there's no point paying more than that unless you're looking for the plush facilities of the top-end hotels, which start at around B1500 (though prices plummet by up to 50 percent when demand is slack). Bear in mind that the sex industry ensures that all rooms have beds large enough for at least two people; rates quoted here are for "single" rooms with one big double bed (a "double" room will have two big double beds and cost more). Though hotels are easy-going about gay couples, we've listed a few exclusively gay hotels as well, for which it may be worth paying over B500.

None of the places detailed below has rooms for less than B200, so if your budget can't stretch to that you'll have to resort to one of the less pricey "rooms for rent" advertised in the shops along Pattaya 2 Road between Soi 11 and Soi Post Office, along Soi Post Office itself, and on Soi Yamato. These tend to be grotty back rooms, and operate only until the owner finds something more lucrative to do with the premises.

Moderate

Beach View, Soi 2, Pattaya Beach Rd, North Pattaya (☎038/422660). Medium-sized mid-range high-rise just across the road from the beach; many rooms have sea view. Extremely reasonable for its class. ⑤.

Chris Guest House, Soi 13, Pattaya Beach Rd (☎038/429586). Small, friendly establishment run by a congenial British expat, offering a dozen remarkably good value air-con rooms set around a small courtyard; very peaceful despite its central location. ④.

The Cottage, Pattaya 2 Rd, North Pattaya (☎038/425660). Excellent-value, well-appointed bungalows, attractively designed and pleasantly located in a quiet garden compound a good distance off the main road. Facilities include two small swimming pools, a bar and a restaurant. ⑤.

Diana Dragon Apartment, 198/16 Soi Buakhao, off Pattaya 2 Road at the end of the soi opposite Soi 11, Central Pattaya (☎038/429550). Enormous rooms with fridge, and use of the pool at *Diana Inn*, 100m away; favoured by long-stay tourists. Very good value. ③.

Diana Inn, 216/3–9 Pattaya 2 Rd, opposite Soi 11, Central Pattaya (☎038/429675). Upmarket hotel atmosphere, central location and good rooms. ⑤.

Honey House, Soi Honey, opposite Soi 10, Pattaya 2 Rd, Central Pattaya (☎038/424396). Small, welcoming budget hotel, with large, fan-cooled rooms with attached bathrooms. ③.

Palm Villa, 485 Pattaya 2 Rd, opposite Soi Post Office, Central Pattaya (☎038/429099). Peaceful haven close to the nightlife, with small garden and sizeable rooms. ④.

Expensive

Asia Pattaya, 325 Cliff Rd, South Pattaya (☎038/250602–6). Attractively placed in private bay between the *Royal Cliff* and Jomtien Beach. Extensive facilities including nine-hole golf course, tennis courts, swimming pool and snooker tables. ⑧.

Dusit Resort, 240/2 Pattaya Beach Rd, North Pattaya (☎038/425616). In the thick of the high-rises; has an excellent reputation for high-quality service and facilities, such as 2 pools, a gym and tennis courts. ⑨.

Royal Cliff, Royal Cliff Bay, between South Pattaya and Jomtien (☎038/421421). Pattaya's most luxurious retreat, with landscaped gardens, private bay, 3 pools and tennis courts. ⑨.

Royal Garden Resort, 218 Pattaya Beach Rd, South Pattaya (☎038/428126). Facilities include floodlit tennis courts, a huge pool, a tropical garden and a certified dive centre. Well-equipped, relatively good-value rooms at the less expensive end of this price range. ⑧–⑨.

Siam Bayshore, 559 Pattaya Beach Rd, South Pattaya (☎038/428678). Set in a secluded wooded spot overlooking the beach; many rooms with balconies and sea view. Two pools, tennis courts, snooker, table tennis and badminton facilities. At the less expensive end of this price range. ⑧.

Gay hotels

Ambiance Hotel, 325/91 Pattayaland Soi 3, South Pattaya (☎038/424099). Right in the heart of the gay area. Well-appointed rooms. ⑥.

Homex Inn, 157/24–30 Pattaya Naklua Rd, North Pattaya (☎038/429039). Small hotel built around a pool in quiet part of town. ⑤.

Pattaya Inn, 380 Soi 2, North Pattaya (☎038/428400). Lots of facilities and good rooms. ⑤.

Daytime activities

Most tourists in Pattaya spend the days recovering from the night before: not much happens before midday, breakfasts are served until early afternoon, and the hotel pool generally seems more inviting than a tussle with water-skis. But the energetic are well catered for, with a massive range of water sports, particularly at Jomtien Beach, and a fair choice of land-based activities.

Water sports

Jomtien Beach is the place for windsurfing, water- and jet-skiing and parasailing: you can either book up in the outlets along Beach Road or head down to Jomtien itself and sign up there. Average prices start at about B1000 per hour for water-skiing, B200 for windsurfing, and B250 for parasailing.

Snorkelling and **scuba diving** are also big here, though if you've got the choice between diving here or off the Andaman Coast (see p.434), go for the latter – the waters are a lot more spectacular. TAT-approved dive shops that run certificate courses and diving expeditions include *Dave's Divers Den* (☎038/221860) on Soi 6, Pattaya Beach Rd, *Steve's Dive Shop* (☎038/428392) on Soi 4, Pattaya Beach Rd, *Dolphin Diving Centre* (☎038/427185) on Soi Post Office, and *Seafari Sports Center* (☎038/428126) at the *Royal Garden Resort* hotel (see facing page). One-day introductory dives start at about B2000, and four-day open-water courses average out at B9000. Be careful when signing up for a dive course or expedition: unqualified instructors and dodgy equipment are a fact of life in Pattaya, and it's as well to question other divers about all operators, TAT-approved or not (see *Basics*, p.48, for more guidelines). Several companies along Pattaya Beach Road run snorkelling trips to nearby Ko Larn and Bamboo Island, though mass tourism has taken its toll on the coral and the islands.

Land-based activities

All top-end hotels have **tennis courts** and some offer badminton and gym facilities too, though these are generally only open to guests. The *Pattaya Bowl*, just north of Soi 5, Pattaya 2 Rd, has twenty **bowling** lanes (B30 per game) and ten **snooker** tables (B100 per hour) and opens daily from 10am to 2am; if you're more of a gung-ho type, head for the **shooting range** at *Tiffany's* on Pattaya 2 Road, North Pattaya (daily 9am–9pm; B120), or the **go-kart circuit** in Jomtien (daily 10am–6pm; B50–200 for 12min). And at weekends there's always the prospect of watching a **speedway race** at the Bira International Circuit, 14km northeast of Pattaya on Route 36 (B80–150).

Mini Siam and day trips

If you're really stuck for something to do, you could visit **Mini Siam**, just north of the North Pattaya Road/Sukhumvit Road intersection, which is just what it sounds like: two hundred of Thailand's most precious monuments reconstructed to 1:25 scale. Mini Europe is coming soon. Alternatively, **Nong Nooch Village**, 18km south of Pattaya off Sukhumvit Road, serves life-sized Thai culture in the form of traditional dancing and elephant rides against the backdrop of an attractively landscaped park. It's on all tour-group itineraries, but it's worth coming here if you're into flowers: the **orchid garden** is said to be the world's largest.

Plenty of agents fix up day trips to tourist spots further afield, like Ko Samet (B650), the River Kwai (B2400) and Bangkok (B1200), though for all these the journey times are so long as to make them hardly worth the effort.

Eating

The scores of expat restaurateurs in Pattaya have made Western food the resort's primary dining option, a generally dismal situation worsened by the host of fast-food joints along Pattaya Beach Road – *Shakey's, Kentucky Fried Chicken, Mr Donut* and so on. For inexpensive **Thai food**, hunt out the curry and noodle vendors on Soi Kasem Suwan – they are concentrated between Central Pattaya Road and Soi Honey, but might pitch up anywhere. Top-quality Thai restaurants are a bit thin on the ground – not surprisingly, given the setting, there's more of an emphasis on seafood than on classical cuisine, though the *PIC Kitchen* (see over) ranks alongside the best of Bangkok's restaurants.

Blue Parrot, Soi 2 Pattayaland, Central Pattaya. Mexican café and bar, good for lunch-time tacos, enchiladas and chilli. Moderate.

Café India, Soi Post Office, Central Pattaya. Authentic Indian standards at moderate prices.

Dolf Riks, signposted just north of Soi 5, off Pattaya 2 Road, North Pattaya. High-class international cuisine, with Indonesian food a speciality. The *rijstaffel* – a set of 18 different dishes – is well worth B190; some vegetarian dishes too. Moderate to expensive.

Flying Vegetable, opposite Welcome Plaza on Pattaya 2 Road. Named after the speciality dish from Phitsanulok – stir-fried greens tossed theatrically from the pan to the customer's plate. Also on offer are standard Thai rice, noodle and curry dishes. Inexpensive.

Nang Nual, Pattaya Beach Rd, South Pattaya. Pattaya's most popular seafood restaurant, where you get to choose your fish from the iceblocks out front before eating it on the seafront terrace. Moderate.

PIC Kitchen, Soi 5, North Pattaya. One of Pattaya's finest traditional Thai restaurants, set in a stylish series of teak buildings. Mouthwatering menu of elegantly presented curry, seafood, rice, noodle and vegetarian dishes. A classical dance show is sometimes included. Moderate.

Schwarzwaldstübe, Soi 15, Central Pattaya. Hearty Swiss and German dishes with lots of steak and an unusually good cheese selection. Moderate.

Yamato, Soi Yamato, Central Pattaya. Good-value Japanese fare including sushi, soba and udon dishes, tempura and sashimi. Inexpensive to moderate.

Nightlife

Entertainment is Pattaya's *raison d'être* and the **nightlife** is what most tourists come for – as do oilfield workers from the Gulf and US marines on R&R – "Pattaya Suffers Mother of all Hangovers" was one of the *Bangkok Post*'s more memorable Gulf War headlines. Of the four hundred-odd **bars** in Pattaya, the majority are the so-called "bar beers", relatively innocent open-air drinking spots staffed by hostesses whose primary job is to make you buy beer not bodies. However, sex makes more money than booze in Pattaya – depending on who you believe, there are between six and twenty thousand Thais working in Pattaya's sex industry, a workforce that includes children as young as ten years old. It's an all-pervasive trade: the handful of uninspiring discos depend more on prostitutes than on ravers, while the transvestite cabarets attract audiences of thousands.

Bars

Pattaya's often nameless outdoor "**bar beers**" group themselves in clusters all over North, Central and South Pattaya. The set-up is the same in all of them: the punters – usually lone males – sit on stools around a brashly lit circular bar, behind which the hostesses keep the drinks, bawdy chat and well-worn jokes flowing. Beer is generally quite inexpensive at these places, the atmosphere low-key and good-humoured, and couples as well as single women drinkers are almost always made welcome.

Drinks are a lot more expensive in the bouncer-guarded **go-go bars** on the South Pattaya "strip" where near-naked hostesses serve the beer and live sex shows keep the boozers hooked through the night. The scene follows much the same pattern as in Patpong, with the women dancing on a small stage in the hope they might be bought for the night – or the week. Go-go dancers, shower shows and striptease are also the mainstays of the **gay scene**, centred on Pattayaland Soi 3, South Pattaya.

There's not a great deal of demand for bars where the emphasis is on simple companiable drinking, but those listed below are comparatively subtle and welcoming. Most are open-sided streetside joints, with a few bar stools and a number of chairs set out around low tables in the front. Even here, bartenders are nearly always young and female, and many of them earn extra money by occasionally sleeping with customers.

Bamboo Bar, seafront end of South Pattaya Road. An exuberant in-house band pulls in a sizeable crowd. No hostesses, no cover charge, no sleaze.

Green Bottle, adjacent to *Diana Inn*, Pattaya 2 Rd. A cosy, air-con, pub-style bar which has forged a studiously unsleazy atmosphere. Serves food.

Saloon Bar, close by the *Marine Disco*, Pattaya Beach Rd, South Pattaya. Pattaya's most youthful joint, a laid-back, underground watering hole where a local band plays heavy rock covers nightly from 10pm until around 2am. Drinkers are mainly farang couples and female tourists.

Shamrock, Pattayaland 2. The British-run bar is a good place to catch local expat gossip. The manager sometimes entertains customers on his banjo, though his collection of folk-music tapes is also worth listening out for. On the edge of the gay district, but attracts a very mixed crowd.

Wild Chicken, Soi Post Office (Pattaya 2 Rd end). Attracts a friendly expat crowd, including the local Hash House Harriers. Discreet hostesses and amiable managers.

Wonderful Bar, Soi Yamato. Genial enough watering hole, which deserves its name for the generous "happy hour" it operates daily from 7am to 7pm.

Discos

Pattaya's **discos** tend to be pick-up joints with few frills, no admission charges, relatively inexpensive beer, and a large number of unattached women hanging round the edges. The rave scene hasn't hit the discos yet, so expect old Western hits rather than sophisticated club sounds. The huge and sleazy *Marine Disco*, in the heart of "the strip", is the ultimate meat market, with its cramped upstairs dancefloor encircled by ringside seats, and a more official boxing ring downstairs, starring prepubescent boys. The more hi-tech *Pattaya Palladium*, at the intersection of Soi 1 and Pattaya 2 Road in North Pattaya, boasts a more salubrious ambience, but is not exactly intimate – it's supposed to have a capacity of six thousand and is popular with tour groups.

Cabarets

Tour groups – and families – also constitute the main audience at the **transvestite cabarets**. Glamorous and highly professional, these shows are performed three times a night at two theatres in North Pattaya: *Alcazar*, opposite Soi 4 on Pattaya 2 Road, and *Tiffany's*, north of Soi 1 on Pattaya 2 Road. Each theatre has a troupe of sixty or more transvestites who run through twenty musical-style numbers in fishnets and crinolines, ball gowns and leathers, against ever more lavish stage sets. All glitz and no raunch, the shows cost from B300.

Pattaya to Ko Samet

South of Pattaya, buses race along Highway 3 past the turn off to the deep-sea fishing port of **Bang Saray**, before stopping to offload returning sailors at **Sattahip**, site of the Thai Navy headquarters. This stretch of shoreline is out of bounds to the general public, with the few beaches in the vicinity not clogged up with naval shipyards reserved for holidaying sailors and their families. The nearby **U-Tapao** air base also belongs to the military, though some international charter flights are permitted to drop their Pattaya-bound package tourists off here.

Few farang travellers choose to stop for longer than they have to in the busy provincial capital of **RAYONG**, but you may find yourself changing buses here (if travelling between the east coast and the northeast, for example). There's absolutely nothing worth seeing in a town known only for producing the national condiment *nam plaa* – a sauce made from decomposed fish – and for the pineapples and durian grown in the provincial orchards. In the unlikely event that you get stuck here overnight, there are three passable moderately priced **hotels** within walking distance of the bus terminal, a few hundred metres east along Sukhumvit Road. All three offer fan-cooled and air-conditioned rooms with attached bathroom; the least costly but dingiest rooms belong to the *Asia Hotel* at no. 84 (☎038/611022; ①–④), otherwise try the *Rayong Hotel* at no. 65/1 (☎038/611073; ③–④) or the *Rayong Otani* at no. 69 (☎038/611112; ③–⑤).

If you prefer a sea view, you could stay at one of the new high-rise hotels or family bungalows along the **Rayong coast** that are finding increasing favour with Thai weekenders, despite the superiority of beaches elsewhere in the vicinity. Sandwiched between the seafront and the Rayong River estuary, a couple of kilometres southwest of Sukhumvit Road and the bus terminal, *Rayong Seaview* at 46 Beach Rd (☎038/611364; ⑤) is the most moderately priced, while the *PMY Beach Hotel*, along the road at no. 147 (☎038/614980; ⑦–⑨) has a swimming pool, fitness centre and snooker club.

Ko Samet

With its sparkling seas, bamboo huts and limited electricity and water supply, **KO SAMET**, 80km southeast of Pattaya, is the east coast's high spot. Backpackers and Thai students flock to the island for low-budget fun, attracted by its proximity to Bangkok and its powdery white sand – the island's former name, Ko Kaew Phitsadan, means "the place with sand of crushed crystal". Only 6km long, Ko Samet was declared a **national park** in 1981, but typically the ban on building has been ignored and there are now over forty bungalow operations here, albeit unobtrusive one-storey affairs. Since 1990 the authorities have been flexing their muscles a bit, periodically closing the island to overnight visitors, and fining bungalow managers as they see fit. Tourist ventures now pay rent to the Royal Forestry Department, and foreign visitors are charged a B50 national park entrance fee on arrival (B25 for children). There's unlikely to be an overnight closure in the near future, but it may be worth checking the current situation with TAT all the same.

Samet's **beaches** fall into three broad categories: the popular backpackers' bays along the northern stretch of the east coast; the upmarket resort-oriented area in the middle of the east coast; and the increasingly isolated retreats towards the southern tip. All beaches get packed on weekends and national holidays, so you'd be sensible to take the first available **room** and if necessary change early the following day. Many bungalow managers raise their rates by fifty percent during such peak periods, but at most times there's a lot of low-cost space in simple **bamboo huts**. Usually containing a large well-worn mattress, a blanket and mosquito net, these huts cost from around B70; the more upmarket you go, the more solid – but not necessarily more attractive – your hut will be. If all affordable accommodation is booked up, you can always **camp** – in accordance with national park rules, camping is permissible on any of the beaches, despite what you might be told. Samet has no fresh water, but water is trucked in from the mainland, and most sets of bungalows offer at least a few huts with attached bathroom. Electricity in the more basic places is rationed for evening consumption only, but even these outfits have video shows after dark to help keep the beer flowing.

Until a few years ago, Samet was considered to be **malarial**, but has now been pronounced safe. Despite this, bungalows are still routinely sprayed with DDT, and the Na Dan health centre continues to dispense advice and blood tests to those who suspect they've come down with it.

Getting to the island

The mainland departure point for Ko Samet is the tiny fishing port of **Ban Phe**, about 200km from Bangkok. Ten regular **buses** make the daily three-hour journey from the Eastern Bus Terminal to the Ban Phe pier. Buses from Pattaya also leave ten times a day and take ninety minutes. Coming by bus from points further east (Chanthaburi and Trat, for example), you'll most likely be dropped at the Ban Phe junction on the Sukhumvit Road, from where a songthaew or motorbike taxi (B15) will take you the remaining 5km to the pier.

Boats leave at least every two hours between 8am and 4pm, take thirty minutes to get to Samet and charge B30 one way. Some boats are owned by individual resorts and ferry both pre-paid package tourists and fare-paying independent travellers, others make the crossing as soon as they have enough passengers or sufficient cargo to make it worth their while; during peak periods there can be as many as eight boats a day, and during high season some will make the crossing after dark as well. It should also be possible to charter a boat across to Samet at any time of day: prices start at around B800 per boat to **Na Dan** pier, more to beaches further south. Na Dan's proximity to Hat Sai Kaew, the most popular beach, means that all boats stop here, after which the resort boats continue to their bungalows at the more central Ao Cho and Ao Wong Deuan. Your best option is to take the first available boat – if it terminates at Na Dan and you want to go further you'll be able to hop on one of the island's **songthaews**, which meet the boats and drive down the centre of the island as far as Wong Deuan, charging B10 to Hat Sai Kaew, B20 to Tub Tim, and B30 to Wong Deuan.

Several tour operators organize **through-trips** from Bangkok to Ko Samet: the fares include the air-conditioned minibus journey from your Bangkok guest house to Ban Phe and the boat trip, and are good value at about B300 return, especially considering that the minibuses are timed to link up with resort-boat departures. *Sea Horse Tours* (☎02/280 2643), bookable through most low-budget Bangkok tour operators, offer a good deal whereby you can part-exchange your return ticket for an onward ticket to Ko Chang (see p.320).

The island

Most of the islanders not associated with the tourist trade live in the **northeast** of the island, near Na Dan, where there are a few shops and food stalls, as well as the island's only school, health centre and wat. Samet's best **beaches** are along the **east coast**, and this is where you'll find most of the bungalow resorts. A rough track connects some of them, otherwise it's a question of walking along the beach at low tide or over the low, rocky points at high water. Long stretches of the **west coast** are well-nigh inaccessible, though at intervals the coastal scrub has been cleared to make way for a track. The views from these clifftop clearings can be magnificent, particularly around sunset time, but you can only safely descend to sea level at the bay up near the northwest headland.

A few narrow tracks cross the island's forested central ridge to link the east and west coasts, but much of the **interior** is dense jungle, home of hornbills, gibbons,

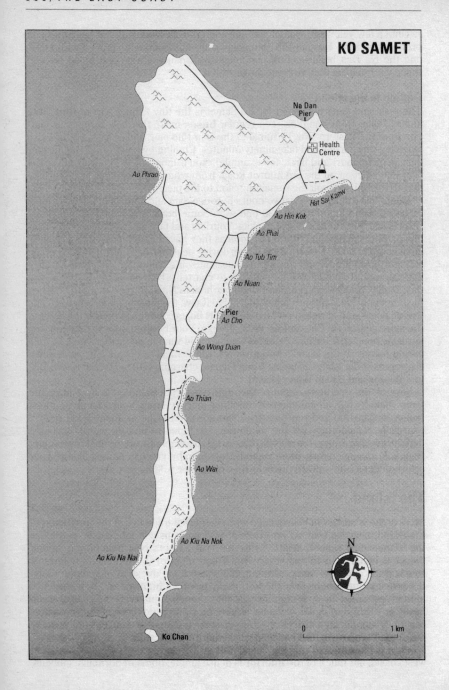

KO SAMET

Na Dan Pier

Health Centre

Ao Phrao

Hat Sai Kaew

Ao Hin Kok

Ao Phai

Ao Tub Tim

Ao Nuan

Pier
Ao Cho

Ao Wong Duan

Ao Thian

Ao Wai

Ao Kiu Na Nok

Ao Kiu Na Nai

N

Ko Chan

0   1 km

spectacular butterflies, and of course the ubiquitous **gecko**. Even if you don't venture inland, you'll see and hear geckos in every beachfront restaurant, and more than likely a few will turn up in your bungalow as well. The gecko's most astonishing characteristic is its ability to scale almost any surface – even glass. Such tenacity is made possible by the hundreds of microscopic hairs that cover the undersides of the gecko's flattened toes; they catch at even

Tokay gecko

the tiniest irregularities and enable the reptile to stick around for hours at a time. Ko Samet harbours a huge population of the largest and most vociferous gecko, the **tokay**, named after the disconcertingly loud sound it makes. Tokays can grow to an alarming 35cm, but they are completely harmless to humans – in fact they're welcomed by most householders, as they devour insects and mice, and Thais consider it auspicious if a baby is born within earshot of a crowing tokay.

Samet has no large or spectacular coral reefs of its own, so you'll have to take a boat trip to the islands of Ko Kuti and Ko Thalu, off the northeast coast, to get good **snorkelling**. At least one bungalow outfit on each of the main beaches runs daily excursions for about B250, including mask and lunch.

Hat Sai Kaew

Arriving at **Na Dan** pier, a ten-minute walk south along the track, past the health centre and school, will bring you to **HAT SAI KAEW** or Diamond Beach, named after its beautiful long stretch of luxuriant sand, so soft and clean it squeaks underfoot – a result, apparently, of its unusually high silicon content, which also makes it an excellent raw material for glass-making. The most popular beach on Samet, this is the only part of the island where the beachfront is lined with bungalows, restaurants, beachwear stalls, deck chairs and parasols. Holidaying Thais and farang flock here in pretty much equal numbers, especially at weekends and on public holidays, and the Thai influence lends a very particular atmosphere; itinerant *kai yang* and *kwetiaw nam* vendors set up their stalls under the palm trees, huge family groups of *Mekhong*-drunk adults sprawl nearby, and their offspring splash about playing *takraw* in the water. Meanwhile, islanders stroll up and down Hat Sai Kaew, selling cold drinks, massages and makeovers to the tourists, or hunting for buried treasures with metal-detectors.

Diamond Resort, which covers a long expanse at the far northern end of the strand (☎01/321 0814; ③–⑦), is the largest and most appealing **bungalow** operation on Hat Sai Kaew. Its less expensive huts are good value: attractive wooden structures pleasantly set in a garden away from the fray – some afford uninterrupted sea views as well, a rare bonus on this beach. Huts belonging to the other six operations on Hat Sai Kaew are uncomfortably cramped together, but slightly less expensive than *Diamond Resort*, and generally of an adequate standard; there's little to distinguish between them, and most fall within the ②–④ price brackets. The **restaurant** attached to *White Sand* serves good fish dishes and *Toy*'s restaurant is a popular place to hang out in the evening. Those who

SUNTHORN PHU AND PHRA ABHAI MANI

Over thirty thousand lines long and written entirely in verse, the nineteenth-century romantic epic **Phra Abhai Mani** tells the story of a young prince and his adventures in a fantastical land peopled not only by giants and mermaids, but also by gorgeous women with whom he invariably falls in love. Seduced by an ogress who lives beneath the sea, and kept captive by her for several months, Phra Abhai Mani pines for dry land and eventually persuades a mermaid to help him escape. Naturally, the two fall in love, and decide to spend some time together on the nearby island of Ko Samet (hence the mermaid statue on Ao Hin Kok). But the prince soon tires of the mermaid's charms, and leaps aboard a passing ship in pursuit of another ill-fated affair, this time with a princess already engaged to someone else. And so it goes on.

Widely considered to be one of Thailand's greatest ever poets, **Sunthorn Phu** (1786–1856) is said to have based much of his work on his own life, and the romantic escapades of *Phra Abhai Mani* are no exception. By all accounts, the man was a colourful character – a commoner alternately in and out of favour at Bangkok's Grand Palace, where he lived and worked for much of his life. The child of a broken marriage, he was taken to the palace as a baby when his mother got a job as wet nurse to a young princess (his father had returned to his home town of Klaeng in Rayong province). His first brush with court officialdom came sometime before his twentieth birthday, when he was temporarily imprisoned for having an affair with a court lady. Soon pardoned, the couple married, and Sunthorn Phu was employed as the court poet. By the time Rama II ascended the throne in 1809, he was an established royal favourite, acting as literary aide to the king. However, he took to the bottle, was left by his wife, and participated in a drunken fight that landed him in jail again. It was during this stint inside (estimated to be around 1821) that he started work on *Phra Abhai Mani*. The poem took twenty years to complete and was rented out in instalments to provide the poet with a modest income – necessary as royal patronage had ceased with the ascent to the throne of Rama III (1824–1851), whose literary efforts Sunthorn Phu had once rashly criticized. In desperation, the poet became a monk, and was only reinstated at court a few years before his death when Rama IV (1851–1868) was crowned.

Aside from authoring several timeless romances, Sunthorn Phu is remembered as a significant **poetic innovator**. Up until the end of the eighteenth century, Thai poetry had been the almost exclusive domain of high-born courtiers and kings, written in an elevated Thai incomprehensible to most of the population, and concerned mainly with the moral Hindu epics the *Mahabarata* and the *Ramayana* (see p.82). Sunthorn Phu changed all that by injecting huge doses of realism into his verses. He wrote of love triangles, thwarted romances and heartbreaking departures, and he also composed travel poems, or *nirat*, about his own journeys to well-known places in Thailand. Most crucially, he wrote them all in the common, easy-to-understand language of everyday Thai.

Not surprisingly, he's still much admired. In Bangkok, the centenary of his death was celebrated by the publication of several new anthologies and translations of his work. And in the province of Rayong, he's the focus of a special memorial park, constructed, complete with statues of his most famous fictional characters, on the site of his father's home in Klaeng.

don't want to spend all night watching videos in their bungalow restaurant usually gravitate towards the string of laid-back small bars, mini-discos and karaoke huts along the track that connects Hat Sai Kaew with the pier at Na Dan.

Ao Hin Kok and Ao Phai

Separated from Hat Sai Kaew by a low promontory on which sits a mermaid statue – a reference to Sunthorn Phu's early nineteenth-century poem, *Phra Abhai Mani* (see box above) – **AO HIN KOK** is smaller and less cluttered than its neighbour. There are only two bungalow outfits here, both looking over the beach from the grassy slope on the far side of the track. The friendly, English-run *Naga* (☎01/321 0732; ①) has simple huts and a restaurant which not only has a good vegetarian selection on its menu, but also specializes in home-made bread and cakes, serves cocktails, and houses the island's only **poste restante**. Next door, *Little Hut* (☎01/323 0264; ②) offers slightly less basic bungalows.

Beach life gets a little more active around the next collection of rocks on **AO PHAI**, where evenings are enlivened by the outdoor bar and an occasional disco. Straddling the rocky divide between the two beaches, *Ao Phai Hut* (☎01/353 2644; ②–⑤) occupies a lovely position and offers both slightly dilapidated fan-cooled huts as well as a few more salubrious air-conditioned ones. *Sea Breeze* (☎01/321 1397; ②–③) is the largest set of bungalows on Ao Phai, with a cross-section of huts, plus an overseas telephone service, boat tickets, windsurfing equipment and money-exchange facilities. *Samed Villa* (④) has the most attractive accommodation on this beach: sturdy chalet-style bungalows, a little too close together but scenically sited along the rocks and up the slope behind the restaurant.

Ao Tub Tim

Also known as Ao Pudsa, **AO TUB TIM** is a lovely white-sand bay sandwiched between rocky points, partly shaded with palms and backed by a wooded slope. It feels secluded and peaceful, but is only a short stroll from Ao Phai and the other beaches further north, so you get the best of both worlds. Of the two bungalow operations here, *Tub Tim* (☎01/321 1425; ①–④) offers the greatest choice of accommodation, from simple, rather run-down bamboo huts through to sizeable concrete bungalows. Huts at the adjacent *Ao Pudsa* (②–③) are fairly basic, but the restaurant occupies a superb site, extending out onto the sand, with several tables fixed under the palm trees. *Ao Pudsa* also organizes boat trips, sells ferry tickets and operates money-exchange facilities.

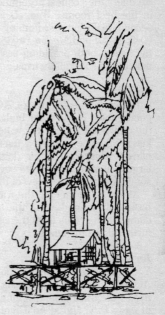

Ao Tub Tim

Ao Nuan

Clamber up over the next headland (which gives you a panoramic take on the expanse of Hat Sai Kaew) to reach Samet's smallest beach, **AO NUAN**. The atmosphere here teeters somewhere between hippy and New Age, but it's relaxed and friendly, and the mellow restaurant of the *Ao Nuan* – decked out with huge floor cushions and shell mobiles – has some of the best veggie food on the island. The huts, too, are idiosyncratic (②–③), each built to a slightly different design (some circular, some A-frame, all thatched), and dotted across the slope that drops down to the bay. Although not brilliant for swimming, the rocky shore reveals a good patch of sand when the tide withdraws, and Tub Tim is only five minutes' walk away.

Ao Cho and Ao Wong Deuan

A five-minute walk south along the track from Ao Nuan brings you to the unappealing **AO CHO**: the sand's not so good and the sea gets packed with supply boats, so there's not a vast amount of pleasure to be had here. But if everywhere else is booked up, you've got the choice between the timbered huts at *Wonderland Resort* (also known as *Ao Lung Wang*; ③–④) and the well-designed but overpriced *Tantawan* (☎01/321 0682; ④–⑤).

The horseshoe bay of **AO WONG DEUAN**, round the next headland, is dominated by bungalow resorts with prices pitched just beyond the backpackers' range. Although the beach isn't bad, it suffers revving jet-skis and an almost continual stream of crowds, and the shorefront is consequently fringed with a rash of beachwear stalls and tourist shops. *Wong Deuan Villa* (☎01/321 0789; ⑥–⑧) offers the poshest accommodation, complete with mini-golf, snooker and TVs in the best rooms. *Wong Deuan Resort* (☎01/321 0731; ⑥–⑧) comes a close second, featuring a swimming pool and flower garden; while *Seahorse* (☎01/323 0049; ④–⑤) and *Malibu* (☎038/651292; ④–⑥) are the least expensive options on the beach, both providing passable huts and a range of facilities including boat tickets and snorkelling trips.

Ao Thian

Off nearly all beaten tracks, **AO THIAN** (also known as Candlelight Beach) is a good choice if you want budget-conscious seclusion: backpackers who eschew the crowds of Hat Sai Kaew head straight here, with the knowledge that upmarket indulgence is only a ten-minute walk away, on Wong Deuan. Ao Thian's narrow white-sand bay is dotted with wave-smoothed rocks and partitioned by larger outcrops that create several distinct beaches; as it curves outwards to the south you get a great view of the east coast.

At the northern end, the friendly *Candlelight Beach* (①–②) has a dozen or so basic huts ranged along the shorefront slope and a simple restaurant; its only competition comes from the comparatively inferior *Lung Dum Hut* (①–②), much further down the beach.

Ao Kiu

You have to really like the solitary life to plump for Samet's most isolated beach, **AO KIU**, over an hour's walk south of Ao Thian through unadulterated wilderness – the track begins behind *Wong Deuan Resort* and can be joined at the back of *Lung Dum Hut* at Ao Thian. It's actually two beaches: Ao Kiu Na Nok on the east coast and Ao Kiu Na Nai on the west, separated by a few hundred metres of scrub and coconut grove. The few bungalows here belong to *Coral Beach* (☎01/321 1231; ②), and most are set in among the palms on the east shore, although a couple look down on the tiny west-coast coral beach. The most convenient way of getting here is by direct boat from the mainland; at least one *Coral Beach* boat makes the run daily – call to check departure times.

Ao Phrao

Across on the west coast, the rugged, rocky coastline only softens into beach once and that's at the run-down **AO PHRAO**, misleadingly known as Paradise Bay, on the northwestern stretch, some 4km north of Ao Kiu Na Nai. The most direct route from the east coast beaches is via the inland track from behind *Sea Breeze* on Ao Phai, though the track from the back of *Tub Tim* on Ao Tub Tim will also get you there. Ao Phrao gets nowhere near as many overnight visitors as the other beaches, perhaps because its view over the mainland is marred by the Rayong skyscrapers peeping between the cliffs. What accommodation exists is largely overpriced; your best bets are *Ratana* (②), which has the lowest-priced and most basic accommodation on Ao Phrao, or the more upmarket *Ao Phrao Resort* (☎01/941 8652; ④–⑤) at the far northern end of the beach.

Chanthaburi

For over five hundred years precious stones have drawn prospectors and traders to the provincial capital of **CHANTHABURI**, 80km east of Ban Phe, and it's the town's pivotal role within Thailand's most lucrative **gem-mining** area that makes it one of the most appealing of all the east-coast towns. Seventy percent of the country's gemstones are mined in the hills of Chanthaburi and Trat provinces, a fruitful source of sapphires and Thailand's only known vein of rubies. Since the fifteenth

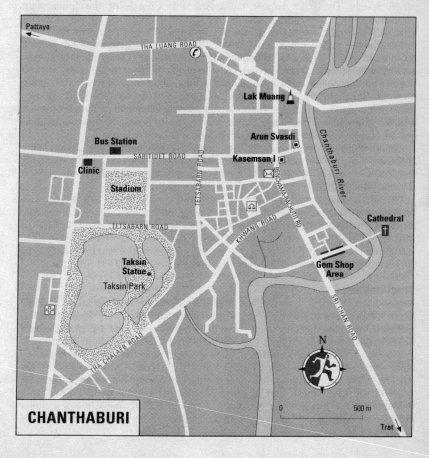

century, hopefuls of all nationalities have flocked here, particularly the Shans from Burma, the Chinese and the Cambodians, many of them establishing permanent homes in the town. The largest ethnic group, though, are Catholic refugees from Vietnam, vast numbers of whom have arrived here since the eighteenth century. The French, too, have left their mark: during their occupation of Chanthaburi from 1893 to 1905, when they held the town hostage against the fulfilment of a territorial treaty on the Laotian border, they undertook the restoration and enlargement of the town's Christian cathedral.

This cultural diversity makes Chanthaburi an engaging place, even if there's less than a day's worth of sights here. Built on the wiggly west bank of the Maenam Chanthaburi, the town fans out westwards for a couple of kilometres, though the most interesting parts are close to the river, in the district where the Vietnamese families are concentrated. Here, along the soi running parallel to the river, the town presents a mixture of pastel-painted, colonial-style housefronts and traditional wooden shophouses, some with finely carved latticework.

Continuing south along this soi, you'll reach a footbridge on the other side of which stands Thailand's largest **cathedral**: the Church of the Immaculate Conception. There's thought to have been a church on this site ever since the first Christians arrived in town, though the present structure was revamped in French style in the late nineteenth century. West of the bridge, the **gem dealers' quarter** begins, where shopkeepers sit sifting through great mounds of tiny coloured stones, peering at them through microscopes and classifying them for resale. Some of these shops also cut, polish and set the stones: Chanthaburi is as respected a cutting centre as Bangkok, and Thai lapidaries are considered amongst the most skilled – not to mention most affordable – in the world. Most of Chanthaburi's market-trading is done on weekend mornings, when buyers from Bangkok descend in their hundreds to sit behind rented tables and haggle with local dealers.

Chanthaburi has a reputation for high-grade fruit too, notably durian, rambutan and mangosteen, all grown in the orchards around the town and sold in the daily **market**, a couple of blocks northwest of the gem quarter. Basketware products are also good buys here, mostly made by the Vietnamese.

West of the market and gem quarter, the landscaped **Taksin Park** is the town's recreation area and memorial to King Taksin of Thonburi, the general who reunited Thailand between 1767 and 1782 after the sacking of Ayutthaya by the Burmese. Chanthaburi was the last Burmese bastion on the east coast – when Taksin took the town he effectively regained control of the whole country. The park's heroic bronze statue of Taksin is featured on the back of the B20 note.

Practicalities

Buses from Bangkok, Ban Phe and Trat all arrive at the bus station on Saritidet Road, about 750m northwest of the town centre and market. Chanthaburi also makes a handy connection point between the east coast and Isaan: eight daily buses make the scenic six-hour Chanthaburi–Khorat journey in both directions.

The two best **accommodation** options are both near the river. The small and basic *Arun Svasdi* at 239 Sukha Phiban Rd (☎039/311082; ①), down a soi off the eastern end of Saritidet Road, has quiet rooms with fan and bathroom and is in the heart of the Vietnamese part of town. Around the corner at 98/1 Benchama-Rachutit Rd, the much larger *Kasemsan 1* (☎039/312340; ③–④) offers a choice between the sizeable, clean rooms with fan and bathroom on the noisy streetside,

RUBIES AND SAPPHIRES

As long ago as the fifteenth century, European travellers noted the abundance of precious stones in Chanthaburi and Trat, but the first **gem-mining rush** happened in 1857, when stories of farmers ploughing up cartloads of rubies and fishermen trawling precious stones from the sea bed brought in hundreds of prospectors from ruby-rich Burma. Before long they had been joined by Cambodians and Vietnamese, and then the British mine companies from Burma came over to organize the industry. By 1900, *Sapphires and Rubies of Siam Ltd* had bought up nearly all the mining fields in eastern Thailand, but it proved an unwise move, as most immigrant miners refused to work for the colonials and moved on elsewhere. When Thailand lost many of its best sapphire mines in a border dispute with Cambodia, the company decided to pull out, leaving the Chanthaburi fields once more to independent self-employed miners.

The next great transformation came half a century later, as a consequence of the upheavals in Burma, which until then had been the world's main supplier of **corundum** – the term for all crystalline forms of aluminium oxide, such as ruby and sapphire. In 1962 the Burmese effectively sealed their country against the outside world, ousting all foreign companies and ceasing all external trade. The Thai dealers promptly muscled in to fill the gap in the world corundum market, and rapidly achieved their current dominant status by forcing the government to ease import and export duties.

Locally produced stones account for a small fraction of the total trade in and around Chanthaburi, whose mines have now been exploited for so long that high-cost mechanical methods are the only viable way of getting at the rocks. Self-employed panhandlers have rushed to work on new veins in Cambodia, while Thai dealers pull the strings in Vietnam's embryonic industry, and regularly buy up the entire annual production of some of Australia's gem fields.

Though artificially produced stones are now used where formerly only the genuine article would do – the glasses of most high-quality watches are nowadays made from synthetic sapphire – the demand for top-notch natural stones from jewellers and watchmakers is virtually limitless. In view of the profits to be made – an uncut 150-carat ruby sold for $1.2 million in 1985 – it's inevitable that sharp practice should be commonplace.

Doctoring the classification of a stone is a common act of skulduggery. A low-quality rough stone from Africa might emerge from the cutter's workshop with a label identifying it as Burmese or Kashmiri, the top rank in the gem league. But perhaps the most prevalent form of fraud involves **heating the stones** to enhance their colour, a cosmetic operation recorded as long ago as the first century, when Pliny the Elder described the technique of enhancing the quality of agate by "cooking" it. Trace elements are what give corundums their colour – in the case of blue sapphires it's titanium and iron that create the hue. To convert a weakly coloured sapphire into an expensive stone, factories now pack the low-grade rocks with titanium and iron oxide, heat the lot to within a whisker of 2050°C – the melting point of sapphire – and thereby fuse the chemicals into the surface of the stone to produce an apparently flawless gem. As long as the cutter and polisher leave the new "skin" intact when they do their work, only an expert will be able to tell whether the highly priced end product is a sham. It takes a lot less effort to fool the gullible Westerners who reckon they can make a killing on the Chanthaburi market: tumble the red glass of a car tail-light in a tub of gravel, and after an hour or two you've got a passable facsimile of a ruby.

and the similar but more expensive air-conditioned ones in the quieter section. The **restaurant** next door to *Kasemsan 1*, called *Chanthon Pochana* (no English sign), serves a range of standard rice and seafood dishes. Otherwise, check out the food stalls in the market and along the riverside soi for Vietnamese spring rolls (*cha gio*) served with sweet sauce, and for the locally made Chanthaburi rice noodles (*kwetiaw Chanthaburi*).

Trat and around

Most travellers who find themselves in and around the minor provincial capital of Trat are heading for Ko Chang, via the tiny fishing port of Laem Ngop. However, as the increasing number of tourists testifies, Trat is worth lingering in for a while, chiefly on account of its access to some lovely countryside. The best of it lies to the east of the town, along the coast road through the port of Khlong Yai and the duty-free border market at Hat Lek, a route that also passes the Khao Lan refugee camp museum, a testament to one of the bleakest episodes of recent local history.

Trat

The small and pleasantly unhurried market town of **TRAT**, 68km east of Chanthaburi, is the perfect place to stock up on essentials, change money, make long-distance telephone calls or extend your visa before striking out for the idyllic isolation of Ko Chang. The town is served by regular buses from Bangkok and Chanthaburi, which arrive on the main Sukhumvit Road, one block away from the central commercial area.

Guest houses open and close with little warning in this town, and the tourist market is distinctly seasonal, but you should be able to count on the very welcoming *Foremost Guest House* (☎039/511923; ①), a short signposted walk southeast of the bus stop, at 49 Thoncharoen Rd. The rooms are basic but large, and the Swedish manager, Lars, is a mine of information on local attractions and issues, including the vagaries of the Ko Chang ferry schedules and the current state of border formalities; he also runs trips to Hat Lek. Just around the corner, in the narrow Soi Luang off Soi Sukhumvit, *Max and Tick's* (☎039/520799; ②) occupies an elegantly renovated traditional teak-wood house; rooms here are quite small and sparsely furnished but very spruce, and the downstairs eating area is a pleasant place to hang out. Close by, the tiny *Windy Guest House* (①) at 63 Thoncharoen Rd is perfectly situated right on the khlong, though the three rooms and one dormitory have fallen into disrepair and the management is a trifle haphazard. Another alternative is *NP Guest House* at 952 Nern Tamaew Rd (☎039/512564; ②), about twenty minutes' walk east of the bus stop; it's inconveniently far from the town centre, but the owners are friendly and the rooms both sizeable and comfortable. Finally, if all guest-house rooms are full, the *Muang Trat Hotel* close to the night market (☎039/511091; ②–⑥) offers standard fan rooms as well as fairly plush air-conditioned ones.

The best **places to eat** in Trat are at the day market, on the ground floor of the Sukhumvit Road shopping centre, and the night market, between Soi Vichidanya and Soi Kasemsan, east of Sukhumvit Road. Otherwise, you should check out *Kiew Wan* restaurant (no English name, but recognizable by its "Food/

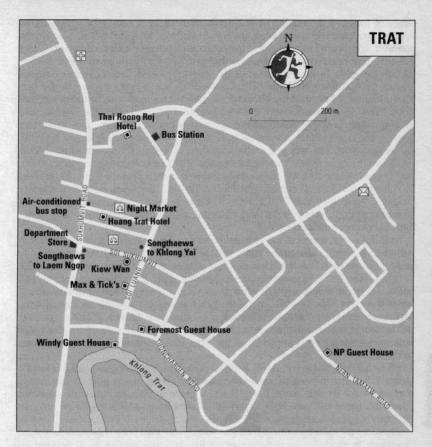

Beverage" sign) across from the day market on Soi Sukhumvit. Not only is its Thai food excellent, you can also get Western breakfasts and beer, and the English-speaking managers can supply tourist information and rent out motorbikes, jeeps and tents. A further option is *Golf Pub and Restaurant* near the bus stop which serves breakfasts and good northeastern dishes and is popular with young Thai couples in the evening.

The road to the border

From Trat, the obvious land-based excursion is a trip as far as the Cambodian border. **Songthaews** to the small, thriving fishing port of Khlong Yai, 74km east, leave Trat about every thirty minutes from behind the shopping centre; they all travel via Khao Lan, take an hour and a quarter and cost B27. From Khlong Yai it's just a short journey on to Ban Hat Lek and the border.

The journey into this narrow tail of Thailand passes through some of the most enthralling countryside in the region, with sea views to the south and a continuous range of forested mountains to the north, pierced by a couple of waterfalls so mighty you can see them from the road. Midway to Khlong Yai, you might consider stopping off for an hour at the **Khao Lan refugee camp museum** (daily 8.30am–4pm; donation); ask the songthaew driver for *"phipitapan Khao Lan"* – though it's easy to spot because of the enormous Red Cross symbol outside. During the last few months of 1978, Cambodians started pouring across the Ban That mountains into eastern Thailand, desperate to escape the brutalities of Pol Pot's "Year Zero" mania and the violence that erupted with the Vietnamese invasion. Trat province received the heaviest influx of refugees, and Khao Lan became the largest of the six camps in Thailand, eventually comprising a hospital, an orphanage and an arts and crafts workshop as well as thousands of makeshift dwellings. In its nine years of operation, this Red Cross camp served as a temporary home to some 200,000 people. By the time it ceased operation in 1987, most of its refugees had been resettled, and Thailand's last Cambodian refugee camp was closed in April 1993. The Thai government now brands any Cambodians refusing to return to their former homeland as illegal immigrants, a curious policy in the light of Pol Pot's re-emergence.

Nothing now remains of the original Khao Lan camp: the museum is housed in a modern building close to the road, and the few other new structures on the site were purpose-built for the Thai soldiers stationed here. The contents of the museum are disappointingly sparse, offering only a sketchy historical and political context, spiced up with a few photos and a couple of waxwork tableaux of life in the camp. The overall tone of the place seems inappropriately ingratiating, with each exhibit presented more as a memorial to Queen Sirikit's gracious patronage of the camp than as a testimony to the resilience of its displaced residents – the queen is president of the Thai Red Cross and made several visits to the Khao Lan site.

Forty kilometres up the road, **Khlong Yai** boasts a great setting, the town's long pier juttling way out to sea, partly flanked by rows of stilt houses that form a shelter for the fishing boats. It's a dramatic place to visit during rough weather, when the turbulent seas lash against the housefronts and the end of the pier disappears beneath low-lying storm clouds.

There's little point venturing all the way on to **Ban Hat Lek** unless you're desperate to stock up on duty-free cigarettes and alcohol (up to 30 percent off Bangkok airport prices) at the border market here. You might, of course, be tempted to try your luck at **crossing the border** here, but this is illegal, potentially dangerous and entails a long and complicated journey; *Foremost* guest house in Trat (see p.316) has up-to-date advice, but at the time of writing the trip into Cambodia from Hat Lek involved an eighteen-hour haul on a cargo boat and a couple of lengthy share-taxi rides – and because the entry papers issued here are unofficial, holders had to leave Cambodia via the same route.

Laem Ngop

The departure point for Ko Chang is **LAEM NGOP**, 17km southwest of Trat and served by songthaews every twenty minutes or so (B10). If you do miss the boat or the seas are too rough to negotiate, it's no great hardship to be stuck in this tiny port, which consists of little more than a wooden pier, one main road, and a small collection of traditional houses inhabited mainly by fisherfolk, a number of them Muslim. If you happen to be in the area between January 13 and 17, it may be worth staying here anyway for the festival commemorating the repulse of French forces from Laem Ngop in 1941.

Although it still retains its small-town atmosphere, Laem Ngop has started to capitalize on the burgeoning Ko Chang tourist trade: a cluster of partisan **tourist information** booths has emerged around the pier head at which you can buy Ko Chang ferry tickets and reserve accommodation on the island – definitely worthwhile in peak season. There's also an official TAT office (daily 8.30am–4.30pm) close by, which offers independent though not always clued-up advice on the island. You can change money at the Thai Farmers' Bank five minutes' walk back down the main road from the pier, and extend your visa at the Laem Ngop Immigration Office if necessary. Your best bet for **accommodation** is *Chut Kaew* (☎039/597088; ①), close to the bank on the main road, a guest house with fairly good rooms and some useful information on Trat and Ko Chang.

For details of boat services from here to Ko Chang, see "Getting to Ko Chang", over.

Ko Chang

Part of a national marine park archipelago of 52 islands, **KO CHANG** offers miles of beaches as yet fronted only by bamboo and wooden huts, and a hilly interior of barely penetrable virgin forest. It's Thailand's third-largest island, 30km north to south and 8km across, but has just three thousand inhabitants, most of whom make their living from fishing and reside in the hamlets scattered around the fringes of the island. As a tourist destination, Ko Chang is only now emerging from its infancy, attracting travellers who are happy just to swim, trek, and down the odd bottle of *Mekhong* on a moonlit beach. During peak season, accommodation on the island's main beaches tends to fill up very quickly, but a fair few places close down between May and October, when fierce storms periodically render whole chunks of the southern part of the island completely inaccessible – on the plus side, those that do stay open offer heavily discounted rates. Either ask other travellers in Trat for current recommendations, or opt for Hat Sai Khao (see p.321) where you're guaranteed to find at least three or four places operating, whatever the weather.

Although a wide concrete road now runs almost all the way round the island, leaving only the southeastern and southwestern coasts out of bounds to vehicles, **getting round** Ko Chang is still quite time-consuming, so it makes life a lot easier if you decide which beach you want to stay on before leaving the mainland, and catch the most direct boat.

Several of the other much **smaller islands** in the archipelago have been built on, but most are the domain of expensive resorts patronized by Thai businessmen; if you can get to them, though, camping is allowed on any island within the national marine park. A number of bungalow outfits on Hat Sai Khao and Hat Bang Bao run one-day snorkelling trips out to some of these islands (Ko Lao Nai, Ko Lao Klang and Ko Wai are all popular destinations) for around B350 per person including lunch and equipment and will drop you off there if asked; four-hour fishing trips (B150) are also an option. Some places also arrange overnight **"island-hopper"** tours to Ko Lao Nai and Ko Lao Klang, and to Ko Whai, Ko Mai Si Lek and Ko Mak, with one night spent on Ko Kud: these cost around B600 excluding food and accommodation. It's also sometimes possible to get to the islands from Laem Ngop, either on the occasional direct boat, or by hitching a ride with a fishing boat or on one of the coconut boats which come up the canal into Trat (check at *Foremost* guest house). One island that is easily accessible, Ko Mak, is detailed on p.324.

Getting to Ko Chang

Boat departures **from Laem Ngop** vary according to the day, the tide, and the time of year, but during **peak season** there should be five to ten boats crossing every day between 9am and 4pm, many of them run by bungalow operations and none of them costing more than B100. The majority of these boats go to the west-coast beaches, dropping passengers off into longtails just off Hat Sai Khao (1hr 45min), before continuing on to Hat Khlong Phrao and Hat Kai Bai (2–3hr). There are also services to Ao Saparot (40min) on the northeastern coast, to Hat Sai Tong (45min) and Hat Sai Yao (1hr 45min) on the east coast, and to Hat Bang Bao on the far southwestern tip – these are not so frequent and may only run once a day even during peak season.

During the **monsoon season** (May–Oct), you'd be lucky indeed to find a boat going all the way round to the west coast: most will only go as far as Ao Saparot, from where songthaews ferry passengers to Hat Sai Khao and beyond, road conditions permitting.

If schedules run according to plan, it's possible to do the whole **Bangkok** to Ko Chang trip in a day, catching the earliest public bus from the Eastern Bus Terminal at 7am, arriving in Trat about 1pm, and making the short connection to Laem Ngop in time for the afternoon west-coast boats. Budget tour operators in Bangkok also offer **air-conditioned minibus** rides from Khao San Road through to Laem Ngop (6hr) for B200 (B400 return) which are timed to catch the afternoon boats (drivers usually radio ahead if necessary); *Sea Horse Tours* (see page 307) does Ko Samet to Laem Ngop minibus connections as well.

The island

Ko Chang's **west coast** has the best beaches and is the more developed, with Hat Sai Khao (White Sand Beach) pulling in the largest crowds, though the further south down the coast you go the less crowded the resorts become. The **east coast** is closer to the mainland and less exposed to storms, but only has three beaches, two of which are very small, the other extremely remote.

Much of the island's pot-holed, undulating roadway is more suitable for scrambling than for a quiet afternoon's bike ride, but most bungalows rent out **motorbikes** at the inflated rate of B90 per hour or B300–500 per day. Several places on Hat Sai Khao also rent out **mountain bikes** for around B120 a day. If you don't fancy braving the route yourself, **motorbike taxis** will take you to most points, but again prices are not good value: for example, the trip from Hat Sai Khao in the northwest across to Hat Sai Tong on the northeast coast costs B150. Alternatively, a **songthaew** service usually meets the ferries at Ao Saparot and transports passengers down to Hat Sai Khao and Hat Kai Bai. During high season, a minibus runs most mornings between the east-coast *Ko Chang Cabana* and the west-coast *Ko Chang Resort* on Hat Khlong Phrao, charging non-guests B50. The other quite feasible way of travelling between west-coast beaches in high season is to make use of the Laem Ngop **ferries**, which pass Hat Sai Khao, Hat Khlong Phrao and Hat Kai Bai several times a day.

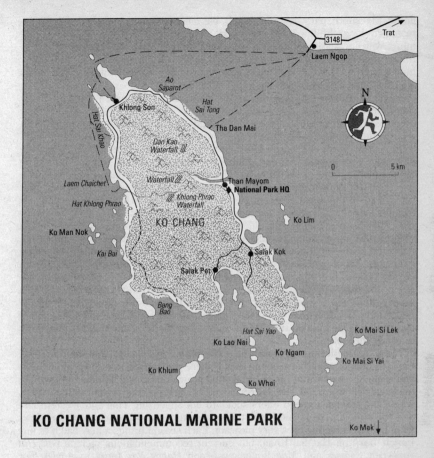

KO CHANG NATIONAL MARINE PARK

There are money-exchange facilities on the island, but no bank and few shops, so buy any necessities before you leave Trat. These should include mosquito repellent and a net, as the island is notoriously **malarial**. (Ko Chang, Laem Ngop and Trat all have malaria clinics.) Sand fleas are also a problem, but there's not a lot you can do about them except soothe your bites with calamine; apart from that, watch out for **jellyfish**, which plague the west coast in April and May, and for **snakes** sunbathing on the overgrown paths into the interior.

Khlong Son and Hat Sai Khao

Built mainly on stilts in the deep bay carved out of the island's northwestern tip, **KHLONG SON** village has no beach to speak of, though if you want to break a long round-island trek, try putting up at *Mannee Guest House* (①), tucked away alongside the more rickety of the two piers, which offers tasty home-cooking and simple rooms.

The closest beach, **HAT SAI KHAO** (White Sand Beach) is also the island's longest, busiest and most attractive, with a dozen different bungalow operations lining the shore plus the odd beach bar and seafront restaurant. Bungalow managers keep the fine white sand very clean, and the beach is ideal for swimming, with its sparkling aquamarine water, sandy bottom and sloping shore. A thick fringe of coconut palms and casuarinas provides good shade as well. Many huts along here have neither electricity nor running water, so it's paraffin lamps after dark and Thai-style bathing in the mornings.

At the northern end, the efficiently managed, if not overly friendly *White Sand Resort* (aka *Hat Sai Khao Resort*; ☎02/234 7294; ②–④) is about ten minutes' walk from the nearest set of **bungalows** and thus quite secluded. The resort offers simple bamboo huts and more upmarket ones with attached bathroom – most have sea views. More conveniently located just to the south, the large and very popular *KC* (②) dominates a long stretch of beach – huts here are simple but enjoy a sea view, and the price is very reasonable. There's not a great deal to choose between the more central bungalows, all of which offer basic huts in the ①–② price range, but *Mak Bungalows* (②–③) is particularly friendly and also boasts some more upmarket seafront bungalows. *Bamboo Huts* (①–②) are smaller and older but occupy a lovely wide stretch of beach with fine views, as does the adjacent *Apple* (①–②), which has new huts at the back and a volleyball net by the sea. Further south, off the end of the beach on a raised piece of land between the road and the sea, *Sun Sai* (①–⑤) is far from ideally placed, but offers a wide range of accommodation – prices reflect the age of the huts as well as the facilities. A few hundred metres beyond, set on a grassy plot even further from the beach, the German-run *Plaloma Cliff Resort* (☎01/323 0164; ④–⑦) is the poshest place on Hat Sai Khao, with attractive if overpriced basic huts on the cliff side, and some better-value deluxe bungalows down by the water.

Every night during high season, *Fisherman's Restaurant* (between *KC* and *Cookies*) puts on nightly barbeque feasts where you can **eat** your fill of grilled fish and seafood – barracuda, shark, tuna, king prawns, crab and squid – for anything between B40 and B150. Hat Sai Khao's other most popular restaurant is *Cookies*, where the extensive menu offers standard but appetizing Thai and Western fare and the atmosphere is laid back, the service quick and friendly, and the views from the raised eating area very pleasant. Each season brings a new batch of tiny **beach bars** on Hat Sai Khao, but current recommendations include *Nut Hut* (between *Cookies* and *Mak* bungalows), and *Happy Bar* (next to *Apple*). For sundowners, head up to the northern end of Hat Sai Khao, to *Jungle Pub* (between *White Sand Resort* and *KC*), where the bar perches on a small promontory overlooking the beach.

Along the west coast

Following the track south for another 4km or so, you come to **Laem Chaichet**, a small cape topped by the simple huts that comprise *Chaichet Bungalows* (②). The boats dock at the pier just around the cape, at the northernmost stretch of **HAT KHLONG PHRAO** (Coconut Beach), a pretty sweep of fine, clean sand with only a few bungalows. Closest to the pier, *Coconut Beach* (☎01/329 0432; ②–④) has both rattan huts and more solid wooden ones with bathroom attached. The nearby *Ko Chang Resort* (☎039/597212; ⑧) offers the island's most exclusive accommodation, in the shape of thirty luxury air-conditioned bungalows set around a verdant beachfront garden, plus some hotel-style rooms and a reasonably priced restaurant. An estuary cuts the beach in half; cross it by boat (for B5) to get to *Magic* (☎01/329 0408; ②–④), which has good food and fair huts; and *Chog Dii* (①–②), which has better huts but poorer food.

Ko Chang's loveliest waterfall, **Nam Tok Khlong Phrao**, is only a few kilometres inland from Hat Khlong Phrao and easily accessible either on foot or by mountain bike. To get there, follow the road south of the Khlong Phrao estuary for about 500m and then turn left (east) onto a narrow, signposted track. The route fords a shallow stream and cuts through pineapple fields and shady tropical forest before emerging at the falls 2–3km further on. Twenty-odd metres high, the Khlong Phrao plunges into an invitingly clear pool defined by a ring of smooth rocks which are ideal for sunbathing.

The rocky **HAT KAI BAI**, an hour's walk south around the headland from Hat Khlong Phrao, is lined with half a dozen indistinguishable bungalow outfits strung out between the estuaries at each end. Some are set back from the beach and all offer basic huts in the ①–③ range: the friendly *Nan Muang* has notably good huts for the price, but avoid *Kai Bai Beach Bungalows*, as it backs onto a mosquito-ridden, stagnant pond. Swimming's not so good here – head south for about twenty minutes along the path behind *Siam Bay* restaurant at the southernmost end of Kai Bai to get to a more secluded, sandy and nameless beach.

From Kai Bai, the track narrows down into a path, which worms its way through inland forest until, three hours' walk later, it reaches the southernmost beach of **HAT BANG BAO** and its village. Boats sometimes come direct here from Laem Ngop, otherwise you'll have to walk. Three sets of bungalows share this isolated, clean and sandy stretch. Near the village, *Bang Bao Viewside* (②) and *Bang Bao Cottage* (②) both offer quite good huts. Across on the other end of the beach, *Bang Bao Beach Bungalows* (③) is slightly better; staff here sometimes organize boat trips to the islands of Ko Khlum, Ko Rung and Ko Mak.

The east coast

There's little reason to visit the tiny northernmost beach of **AO SAPAROT**, unless you get dropped here by the Ko Chang boat – a likely possibility during the monsoon season. Aside from the few houses that make up the hamlet, there's not much to do and, currently, nowhere to stay. Better to get yourself a ride round to the livelier and better-equipped west-coast beaches.

During peak season, a daily boat docks a little way further down the east coast, about fifteen minutes' walk north of **HAT SAI TONG**. Close by the pier, the upmarket *Ko Chang Cabana* (⑥) offers overpriced fan-cooled bungalows and, because this coast is fairly grotty, runs a daily minibus service to west-coast beaches in accordance with demand. The one set of bungalows at Hat Sai Tong itself, also called *Hat Sai Tong* (②), has comfortable huts ranged around a garden-cum-menagerie, complete with caged squirrels, monkeys and an aviary.

There's little to entice you into undertaking the two-and-a-half-hour trek down to **THAN MAYOM**, site of the national park office and unattractive national park bungalows, except perhaps the prospect of a long walk along the base of a forested hillside punctuated by occasional sea views. South of Than Mayom the track continues another 4km to the equally unattractive south-coast **HAT SALAKPET**, cutting inland and bypassing the whole southeast headland.

The southeast headland holds the best beach on this coast, **HAT SAI YAO** (also known as Long Beach), but the only access is via direct boat from Laem Ngop. Another fine, isolated spot, Hat Sai Yao is excellent for swimming and has some coral close to shore. Depending on the sea conditions, some boats will take you directly into Hat Sai Yao, while others will drop you just around a small promontory close to *Tantawan House* (①), which has a couple of very basic huts. For slightly better accommodation, follow the path westwards for ten minutes to the beachfront *Long Beach Bungalows* (②), whose large huts are equipped with fans and electric lights.

Ko Mak

The tiny island of **KO MAK**, off the south coast of Ko Chang, can be reached (Nov–April only) on the daily 3pm boat from Laem Ngop, a journey of three hours. To date, Ko Mak has but one budget bungalow operation, *Lazy Days* (☎02/281 3412; ①), which receives a steady trickle of backpacking travellers – though some have complained about the package policy that obliges you to eat all your meals there – plus a more upmarket resort called *TK Hut* (☎01/329 0333; ⑥).

travel details

Buses

Ban Phe to: Bangkok (10 daily; 3hr); Chanthaburi (6 daily; 1hr 30min); Trat (6 daily; 3hr).

Chanthaburi to: Bangkok (18 daily; 5–7hr); Khorat (8 daily; 6hr); Trat (every 90min; 1hr 30min).

Pattaya to: Bangkok (every 40min; 2hr 30min); Ban Phe (10 daily; 1hr 30min); Chanthaburi (6 daily; 3hr); Khorat (4 daily; 5–6hr); Trat (6 daily; 4hr 30min).

Si Racha to: Bangkok (every 25min; 2hr); Ban Phe (10 daily; 2hr); Chanthaburi (6 daily; 3hr 30min); Pattaya (every 20min; 30min); Trat (6 daily; 5hr).

Trat to: Bangkok (16 daily; 6–8hr).

Ferries

Ban Phe to: Ko Samet (4–8 daily; 30min).

Laem Ngop to: Ko Chang (at least 2 daily; 45min–3hr).

Si Racha to: Ko Si Chang (5 daily; 40min).

CHAPTER FIVE

THE NORTHEAST: ISAAN

Bordered by Laos and Cambodia on three sides, the tableland of **northeast Thailand** – known as **Isaan**, after the Hindu god of death and the northeast – comprises a third of the country's land area and is home to nearly a third of its population. This is the least-visited region of the kingdom, and the poorest: eighty percent of Isaan villagers earn less than the minimum wage of B100 a day. Farming is the livelihood of virtually all northeasterners, despite appallingly infertile soil – the friable sandstone contains few nutrients and retains little water – and long periods of drought punctuated by downpours and intermittent bouts of flooding. In the 1960s, government schemes to introduce hardier crops set in motion a debt cycle that has forced farmers into monocultural cash-cropping to repay their loans for fertilizers, seeds and machinery. With so much time and energy going into raising the cash crops, little is left over for growing and making everyday necessities, which farmers then have to buy. For many families, there's only one way off the treadmill: each January and February, Bangkok-bound trains and buses are crammed with northeasterners leaving in search of seasonal or short-term work; of the twenty million who live in Isaan, an average of two million seasonal economic refugees leave the area every year, and northeasterners now make up the majority of the capital's lowest-paid workforce.

Most northeasterners speak a dialect that's more comprehensible to residents of Vientiane than Bangkok, and Isaan's historic allegiances have tied it more closely to Cambodia and Laos than to Thailand. Between the eleventh and thirteenth centuries, the all-powerful **Khmers** covered the northeast in magnificent stone temple complexes, the remains of which constitute the region's most satisfying tourist attractions. During subsequent centuries the territories along the Mekong River changed hands numerous times, until the present border with Laos was set at the end of World War II. In the 1950s and 1960s, **communist insurgents** played on the northeast's traditional ties with Laos; a movement to align Isaan with the Marxists of Laos gathered some force, and the Communist Party of Thailand, gaining sympathy amongst poverty-stricken northeastern farmers, established bases in the region. At about the same time, major US air bases for the **Vietnam War** were set up in Khorat, Ubon Ratchathani and Udon Thani, fuelling a sex industry that has plagued the region ever since. When the American military moved out, northeastern women turned to the tourist-oriented Bangkok flesh trade instead, and nowadays the majority of prostitutes in the capital come from Isaan.

These cities, like Isaan's other major population centres, are chaotic, exhausting places, with precious little going for them apart from accommodation and onward transport. **Khorat** (officially called Nakhon Ratchasima), the inescapable and unprepossessing hub of southern Isaan, is nevertheless worth enduring as a springboard for the majestic Khmer ruins of **Prasat Hin Phimai**, which adorns an otherwise insignificant outlying village, and **Prasat Hin Khao Phanom Rung**, perched on a hilltop miles from anywhere. Congenial guest houses make the provincial capitals of **Surin** and **Chaiyaphum** rewarding targets at any time of year, especially in

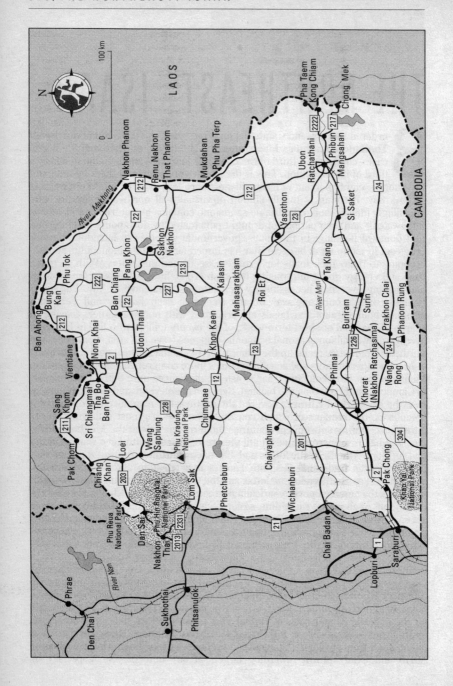

November (in the case of Surin) and January (Chaiyaphum), when they host their flamboyant, though inevitably touristy, "elephant round-ups". Festivals also put two other Isaan cities on the map: **Ubon Ratchathani**, focal point of the extravagant candle festival in July, and **Yasothon**, with its bawdy rocket festival in May.

Isaan's only mountain range of any significance divides the uninspiring town of **Loei** from the central plains and offers some stiff walking, awesome scenery and the possibility of spotting unusual birds and flowers in the **national parks** which spread across its heights. Due north of Loei, the **Mekhong River** begins its leisurely course around Isaan with a lush stretch where a sprinkling of guest houses have opened up the river countryside to travellers. Marking the eastern end of this upper stretch, the fast-developing border town of **Nong Khai** is surrounded by possibly the most outlandish temples in Thailand. The grandest and most important religious site in the northeast, however, is **Wat Phra That Phanom**, way downstream beyond **Nakhon Phanom**, a town which affords some of the finest Isaan vistas.

The most comfortable **time of year** in Isaan is the cool season (Nov–Feb), which is also when the waters of the Mekhong are highest and the scenery greenest – but if you want to catch the region's most exciting festivals you'll have to brave the hotter months, when temperatures can soar to 40°C. Many travellers **approach Isaan** from the north, either travelling directly from Chiang Mai to Loei, a nine-hour bus ride, or stopping off at Phitsanulok, in the northern reaches of the central plains, and crossing into Isaan via the Phetchabun hills, arriving at Khon Kaen or Chaiyaphum. But there are a number of other equally viable routes into Isaan: a regular and efficient bus service connects the east-coast towns of Pattaya (5hr), Rayong (4hr) and Chanthaburi (6hr) with Khorat, and direct bus services run from Bangkok to all major northeastern centres. It's also possible to arrive by train from Bangkok: two rail lines cut through Isaan, one extending eastwards across the south of the region, the other pursuing the northern route up as far as the Laotian border. **Getting around** Isaan can be time-consuming, as northeastern bus drivers are particularly nonchalant about timetables, but most sizeable places are connected by public transport.

Many of the roads through Isaan were built in the 1960s and 1970s by a government desperate to quash the spread of communism in these hitherto isolated parts; the United States helped with much of the finance, and was also responsible for the so-called Friendship Highway (Highway 2), which connects Bangkok with the **Laotian border** at Nong Khai. More recently, Australia funded the construction of the Thai-Australia Friendship Bridge, completed in 1994, that now spans the Mekhong River at Nong Khai, providing easy road access to the Laotian capital, Vientiane, and making the town the main legal entry point into Laos. For more information about trips to Laos via Nong Khai and the other crossing points along the Mekhong River see p.374.

SOUTHERN ISAAN

For tourists, Isaan divides conveniently into three regions, dictated primarily by transport routes. **Southern Isaan**, described in this section, more or less follows one of two branches of the northeastern rail line as it makes a beeline towards the eastern border, skirting the edge of Khao Yai National Park before entering Isaan proper to link the major provincial capitals of Khorat, Surin and Ubon

Ratchathani. The rail line is handy enough for entering the region, but once here it's as well to follow a route that takes in smaller towns and villages wherever possible, which means switching to buses and songthaews.

Even if your time is limited, you shouldn't leave this part of Isaan without visiting at least one set of **Khmer ruins**: Prasat Hin Phimai and Prasat Hin Khao Phanom Rung are the most accessible examples. Relics of an even earlier age, prehistoric **cliff paintings** also draw a few visitors eastwards to the border town of Kong Chiam, but crowds only mass for southern Isaan's spectacular calendar of **festivals**, most notably Surin's elephant round-up, Ubon Ratchathani's candle festival and Yasothon's Bun Bang Fai rocket festival. To get the best out of Isaan you need to meet English-speaking locals – the small **guest houses** in Surin, Phimai and Kong Chiam are some of the friendliest in the country.

Khao Yai National Park

About 120km northeast of Bangkok, the unrelieved cultivated lushness of the central plains gives way to the thickly forested Phanom Dongrek mountains. A 2168-square-kilometre chunk of this sculpted limestone range has been conserved as **KHAO YAI NATIONAL PARK**, one of Thailand's most rewarding preserves, and certainly its most popular. Spanning five distinct forest types, Khao Yai (Big Mountain) sustains three hundred bird and twenty large land-mammal species, and offers a plethora of waterfalls and several undemanding walking trails.

Although Khao Yai can be done as a day trip from Bangkok, it really deserves an overnight stop, as night safaris are a highlight here (although a recent crackdown on land encroachment means there's only very limited, camping accommodation within the park itself and most people stay outside). Try to avoid visiting at weekends and holidays, when trails and waterfalls get ridiculously crowded and the animals make themselves scarce. Even at quiet times, don't expect it to be like a safari park – patience, a soft tread and a keen-eyed guide are generally needed, and it's well worth bringing your own binoculars if you have them. Finally, be prepared for patches of fairly rough terrain, and pack some warm clothes, as the air can get quite cool at the higher altitudes in the park, especially at night.

Getting to Khao Yai

If you're travelling to Khao Yai by public transport, you'll almost certainly be deposited at **Pak Chong**, 37km north of the park visitors' centre along Highway 2. Most Bangkok–Khorat **trains** (7 daily; 3hr 30min) and **buses** (every 15min; 2hr 30min–3hr) stop here. An irregular songthaew service will get you into the park; otherwise you'll have to rent an expensive motorbike taxi or tuk-tuk, or try hitching – nearly all cars travelling up the road to Khao Yai will stop. The other option is to take the daily **direct bus** service from Bangkok's Northern Bus Terminal, which bypasses Pak Chong and goes straight to the park visitors' centre, departing at 9am and returning at 3pm (3hr; B79 one way). On weekends and holidays, you can pick up **rail excursions** from Bangkok that include a day-return to **Prachinburi** (50km south of the visitors' centre), connecting transport to the park, and lunch; trains leave Hualamphong at 6am and the fare is B150.

Accommodation and tours

The most popular, and rewarding, way to explore the park is to join a **guided tour**. Most backpackers opt for the package offered by the Swedish/Thai-run *Jungle Adventure Tours* and guest house (☎044/313836; ②), at Soi 1 Kongvasin Rd in Pak Chong. For B650, you get a one-and-a half-day tour of the park, including transport into and around it, guided day-time treks and a night safari, but the two nights' accommodation in the guest house comes extra. Rooms here are spartan but clean, and rates include breakfast; in low season, it's sometimes possible to earn free bed and breakfast in exchange for giving English conversation lessons to local townspeople. *Jungle Adventure* is midway between the train station and the bus stop; from Highway 2, walk a few metres down the (signposted) Tessaban Soi 16 then turn left down Soi 1 Kongvasin, following the signs.

The other recommended tour operates out of *Garden Lodge* (☎044/313567; ②–⑥), a beautifully designed bungalow resort 12km out of Pak Chong, on the access road (known as Thanon Thanarat) to Khao Yai, at kilometre stone 7. To get here from Pak Chong, either try for a songthaew, take a taxi, or call the manager, the very congenial and well-informed Klaus, who will send someone to pick you up. Klaus's tailor-made Khao Yai tours start at around B600 a day, with guests paying extra for their choice of accommodation, which ranges from the basic to the plush. He also does one-and-a-half-day "backpackers" tours similar in style to *Jungle Adventure*'s at B850 per person including accommodation and breakfast.

The final, most exclusive option is to stay in one of Khao Yai's **luxury resorts**, close to the park entrance on Thanon Thanarat, and organize private tours when you're there. The small and well-equipped *Juldis Khao Yai Resort*, at kilometre stone 17 (☎02/255 2480, ext 413; ⑧), offers upmarket accommodation, plus a swimming pool and tennis courts; *Sophanaves*, at kilometre stone 22 (☎044/311347; ⑤–⑦), doesn't boast parallel facilities, but is comfortable enough and less expensive. Both places will arrange transport from Bangkok.

The main advantage that **independent exploration** of the park has over a guided tour is its cost – and the fact that you can base yourself inside the park.

ACCOMMODATION PRICES

Throughout this guide, guest houses, hotels and bungalows have been categorized according to the price codes given below. These categories represent the minimum you can expect to pay in the high season (roughly Nov–Feb & July–Aug) for a double room – or, in the case of national park bungalows, for a multi-berth room which can be rented for a standard price by an individual or group. If travelling on your own, expect to pay anything between sixty and one hundred percent of the rates quoted for a double room. Wherever a range of prices is indicated, this means that the establishment offers rooms with varying facilities – as explained in the write-up. Wherever an establishment also offers dormitory beds, the prices of these beds are given in the text, instead of being indicated by price code.

Remember that the top-whack hotels will add seven percent tax and a ten-percent service charge to your bill – the price codes below are based on net rates after taxes have been added.

① under B100	④ B250–400	⑦ B1000–1500
② B100–150	⑤ B400–600	⑧ B1500–3000
③ B150–250	⑥ B600–1000	⑨ B3000+

For a nominal fee, you can camp near the visitors' centre if you have your own tent, or sleep in a makeshift hut close by if you don't, store your bags inside the visitors' centre, and set off on a different trail every day. It's quite easy to trek around the park by yourself, as long as you stick to the colour-coded trails (see below), but as some of the park's best features – like its waterfalls, caves and viewpoints – are as much as 20km apart, without transport you'll find yourself missing out. The restaurant next door to the visitors' centre serves reasonable standard rice dishes, so you don't need to carry lots of food with you.

If you want to explore the remoter parts, hire a guide from the park headquarters (next to the visitors' centre) for B300–500 a day. Night safaris should not be undertaken without a guide.

The park

During the daytime you're bound to hear some of the local wildlife even if you don't catch sight of them. Noisiest of all are the white-handed (or lar) and crowned **gibbons**, and the long-tailed and pig-tailed **macaques**, which hoot and whoop from the tops of the tallest trees. **Hornbills** also create quite a racket, calling attention to themselves by flapping their enormous wings; Khao Yai harbours large flocks of four different hornbill species, which makes it one of the best places in Southeast Asia to observe these creatures. The great hornbill in particular is an incredibly beautiful bird, with brilliant yellow and black undersides; the equally magnificent Indian pied hornbill boasts less striking black and white colouring, but is more commonly seen at close range because it swoops down to catch fish, rats and reptiles. You might also see silver pheasants, woodpeckers and Asian fairy-bluebirds, and – from November to March – several species of **migrant birds**, including the yellow-browed warbler from North Asia and the red-breasted flycatcher from Europe.

Great hornbill

Night safaris, organized by the hotels and guest houses, are definitely worth the time and money for the excitement of following trails of tiger tracks, fresh elephant dung, or whatever else you happen to come across – but be sure to wear warm clothes. A herd of about two hundred Asian **elephants** lives in the park and its members are often seen at night – this is the only place in Thailand where you have much likelihood of spotting wild elephants. Khao Yai is also thought to harbour Thailand's largest population of **tigers**; sightings are rare but not mythical – you're about as likely to encounter one of the park's two dozen tigers as you are to see one of the park's **leopards**. However, you're almost certain to spot **civets**, and you might come across a **slow loris**, while barking **deer** and sambar deer are less nervous after dark. **Bats** assemble en masse at sunset, especially at the cave entrance on Khao Roobchang (Elephant Head Mountain), which every evening disgorges millions of them on their nightly forage.

Several well-worn **trails** – originally made by elephants and other park species, and still used by these animals – radiate from the area around the visitors' centre at kilometre stone 37, and a few more branch off from the roads that traverse the park. Although the Bangkok TAT office stocks a sketchy trail map of the park, don't rely on finding copies of it at the park visitors' centre; you shouldn't need a map anyway, as paths in the central area are well signposted and colour-coded.

The two most popular trails, **Kaeng Kaeo** (about 1km one way) and **Haew Sawat** (a further 6km), start just beside the visitors' centre and pass through tropical forest and grassland. Even on the short trek east to Kaeng Kaeo you may encounter gibbons, woodpeckers and kingfishers, and the route on to Haew Sawat runs close to an area used by roosting hornbills from June to August. The more rewarding **Beung Phai/Khlong E Taw** trail is a circular trek of 11km (beginning north of the visitors' centre near kilometre stone 32) that takes you west through a forested area thick with large strangling figs, across the Beung Phai grasslands, over Khlong E Taw and eventually to the **Nong Pak Chee observation tower**. The tower stands just 1km west of the road, linked by a trail which starts between kilometre stones 35 and 36. The fruits of the figs attract all manner of birds and animals, including hornbills, barbets and mynah birds, macaques and palm civets, while barking deer come to graze the grassland. Khlong E Taw also entices birds such as the rarely glimpsed silver pheasant, but only the observation tower gives you the cover necessary for several hours' of wildlife-spotting: stay here long enough and you'll see needletails dive-bombing the nearby pond and maybe some otters playing in the water; elephants and gaurs sometimes come to drink here, too, and you're almost certain to see deer and hornbills – possibly a tiger, too.

Khorat (Nakhon Ratchasima) and around

Beyond Pak Chong, Highway 2 and the rail line diverge to run either side of picturesque Lam Takhong Reservoir, offering a last taste of undulating, forested terrain before gaining the largely barren Khorat Plateau. They rejoin at **KHORAT** (officially renamed **Nakhon Ratchasima**) – literally, "Frontier Country" – which is still considered the gateway to the northeast.

If this is your first stop in Isaan, it's not a particularly pleasant introduction: Khorat's streets are far too narrow for the traffic they're expected to cope with, the town seems constantly under construction, and there's little that merits the term "tourist attraction". But Khorat is at the centre of a good transport network and makes an obvious base for exploring the potteries of Ban Dan Kwian; the Khmer ruins of Phimai, Phanom Rung and Muang Tham are also within striking distance.

Khorat can be a confusing place to get to grips with: the commercial centre used to be contained within the old city moat, at the eastern end of town, but it has spilt over westwards and there are shops and markets as well as hotels and restaurants in both areas. Regular **buses** stop at the main bus station just off Suranari Road, close to the town centre and most hotels; the terminus for air-conditioned buses is on Mittraphap Road (Highway 2), ten minutes' walk to the northwest. Aside from serving Bangkok and all the main centres within Isaan, Khorat's bus network also extends south along Highway 304 to the east coast, enabling you to travel directly to Pattaya, Rayong and Chanthaburi without going through the capital. Arriving at the **train** station on Mukkhamontri Road, you're midway between the commercial centre to the east (1km) and the town's best

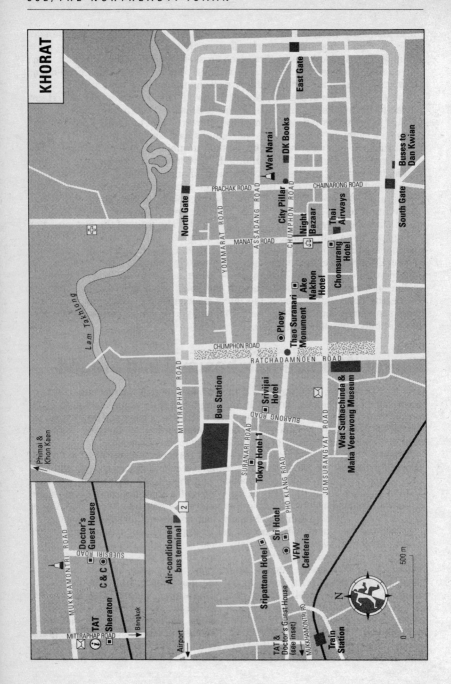

KHORAT

North Gate

Wat Narai
DK Books
East Gate

PRACHAK ROAD

City Pillar
Night Bazaar
Chomsurang Hotel
Thai Airways
CHAINARONG ROAD

Buses to Dan Kwian

South Gate

YOMMARAT ROAD
ASADANG ROAD
CHUMPHON ROAD

MANAT ROAD

Ake Nakhon Hotel

Ploey
Theo Suranari Monument

CHUMPHON ROAD

RATCHADAMNOEN ROAD

Bus Station

Srivijai Hotel

MITTRAPHAP ROAD

BUARONG ROAD

Wat Sutthachinda & Maha Veeravong Museum

JOMSURANGYAT ROAD

SURANARI ROAD

Tokyo Hotel 1

PHO KLANG ROAD

Phimai & Khon Kaen

Air-conditioned bus terminal

Sri Hotel

VFW Cafeteria

Sripattana Hotel

TAT & Doctor's Guest House (see inset)

MUKKHAMONTRI RD

Train Station

Airport

500 m

N

Lam Takhlong

Doctor's Guest House

MUKKHAMONTRI ROAD
SUEBSIRI ROAD

C & C

TAT

Sheraton

MITTRAPHAP ROAD

Bangkok

guest house, *Doctor's*, to the west (1km). It's also possible to **fly** to Khorat from Bangkok; the airport is about 5km southwest of town on Highway 304.

Local buses travel most of the main roads and cost B3 a ride within the town (the exact money is required on some of the most ancient buses). The most useful routes are #1, which heads west along Chumphon Road, past the train station and out to *Doctor's Guest House* and returns east via Yommarat Road, and #2, which runs between the main TAT office in the west and beyond the *lak muang* (city pillar) to the east.

The City

Sights are thin on the ground in Khorat, but if you spend more than a couple of hours in the city you're bound to come across the landmark statue at the western gate of the old city walls. This is the much-revered **Thao Suranari Monument**, erected to commemorate the heroic actions of the wife of the deputy governor of Khorat, during an attack by the kingdom of Vientiane – capital of modern-day Laos – in 1826. Local chronicles proffer several versions of her feat: some say she organized a feast for the Laotian army and enticed them into bed, where they were then slaughtered by the Thais; another tells how she and the other women of Khorat were carted off as prisoners to Vientiane, whereupon they attacked and killed their guards with such ferocity that the Laotians retreated out of fear that the whole Thai army had arrived. At any rate, Thao Suranari saved the day and is still feted by the citizens of Khorat, who lay flowers at her feet, light incense at her shrine and even dance around it. At the end of March, the town holds a week-long **festival** in her honour, with parades through the streets and the usual colourful trappings of Thai merry-making.

The closest Khorat has to a public **park** is the strip of grass that runs north and south of the monument, between Chumphon and Ratchadamnoen roads. It's a great place for hanging out with the local populace: all sorts of things happen here, from haircuts and massages to chess tournaments and picnics. Otherwise, check out the city's **Maha Veeravong Museum** (Wed–Sun 9am–4pm; B5), which houses a small and unexceptional collection of predominantly Dvaravati- and Lopburi-style Buddha statues found at nearby sites. It's in the grounds of Wat Suthachinda, on Ratchadamnoen Road.

Tourist shops and crafts outlets don't really feature in Khorat, but if you're not going further east to Surin, or north to Chaiyaphum, this is a good place to buy **silk**, much of which is produced in Pak Tong Chai, an uninteresting and over-exploited town 32km south of Khorat on Highway 304; the specialist shops along Chumphon Road sell at reasonable prices and stock a bigger range than places in the town of origin. The reverse is true of **ceramics**: there's far more choice at the local pottery village of **Dan Kwian** (see p.335) than at Khorat's night bazaar.

Practicalities

There's a small tourist information booth at the train station, but if you're basing yourself in Khorat for more than a night you'd do well to trek out to the main **TAT office** (daily 8.30am–4.30pm; ☎044/243751), on the western edge of town, to pick up a free map of the convoluted city bus network and get advice on transport to sights out of town. A branch of *DK Books* east of the *lak muang* on Chumphon Road stocks the whole range of regional Survey Department maps, plus a number of English-language novels and reference books.

Accommodation

Khorat isn't short of **accommodation**, but apart from a couple of notable exceptions recommended here, the city's budget places currently rate as pretty poor value. Noise is the main problem in the more economical central hotels – best to request a room away from the main road. If you're planning a visit to Phimai, consider staying in the lovely old guest house there, rather than commuting from Khorat.

Ake (Ek) Nakhon Hotel, 120 Chumphon Rd (☎044/242504). Typical Thai–Chinese hotel with noisy but adequate fan-cooled rooms in a central location. ②.

Chomsurang Hotel, 2701/2 Mahathai Rd, near the night bazaar (☎044/257088). One of Khorat's affordable best, and the usual choice of businesspeople and better-off tourists. All rooms have air-con; the pricier ones have TV and mini bar. Facilities include a swimming pool. ⑥–⑨.

Doctor's Guest House, 78 Soi 4, Suebsiri Rd, near TAT (☎044/255846). Friendliest and most peaceful place in town, with a quaint B&B atmosphere, mounds of local information and a garden seating area; only 6 rooms and a dorm. About 10min from the central bus station: local bus #1 stops opposite the soi entrance (ask for "thanon Suebsiri soi sii"), while #2 passes the Suebsiri Road junction, so get off at the huge "American Standard" billboard across from the ornate Wat Mai Amphawan. Buses from Bangkok or Khao Yai can drop you outside the *Sheraton*, around 1km before the central bus stations. ①–②.

Sima Thani Sheraton Hotel, next to the TAT office on Mittraphap Road (☎044/243812). The city's most luxurious accommodation, with all the usual *Sheraton* trimmings. Buses from Bangkok or Khao Yai can drop you at the door en route to Khorat town. ⑧–⑨.

Sri Hotel, 167–168 Pho Klang Rd (☎044/242831). More central than *Doctor's* and a viable alternative; surprisingly quiet and spacious rooms with fan and shower, plus some less expensive ones near the road. ②–④.

Sripattana Hotel, 355/1 Suranari Rd (☎044/242883). Reasonably priced for the facilities, which include air-con in all rooms, TV and mini bar in some, and a swimming pool on site. ⑤–⑧.

Srivijai Hotel, 9–11 Buarong Rd (☎044/242194). Very noisy streetside location near the regular bus station. Rooms with fan or air-con. ③–⑤.

Tokyo Hotel I, 329–333 Suranari Rd, 30m from the main bus station (☎044/242873). The most conveniently located budget option; clean and friendly. ②.

Eating

Khorat's time as a US airbase during the Vietnam War has left a legacy of night-clubs, massage parlours and Western **restaurants**. But the "night bazaar" – as Khorat's rather small night market is ambitiously named – along the *Chomsurang Hotel* end of Mahathai Road is the place to come for low-priced Isaan specialities like *kai yang* (barbecued chicken), *khao niaw* (sticky rice) and *somtam* (raw papaya salad), not to mention all manner of spicy sausages. If it's good old *pat thai* you're after, there are inexpensive and tasty roadside noodle stalls opposite the train station.

C&C (Cabbages and Condoms), next to the Soi 4 intersection on Suebsiri Road, close to the *Doctor's Guest House* and TAT. High-quality traditional Thai fare, managed along the same lines as its sister restaurant in Bangkok, with all proceeds going to the Thai family planning association. Moderate.

The Emperor, inside the *Sima Thani Sheraton Hotel* on Mittraphap Road, next to TAT. Khorat's best Chinese restaurant, with superb food. Very expensive.

Ploey, on the corner of Chumphon and Poklang roads. Family restaurant and bakery serving pizzas and other Western food, as well as Thai standards and the local speciality, *mii Khorat* (actually not much different from *pat thai)*. Inexpensive to moderate.

Veterans of Foreign Wars (VFW) Cafeteria, next to the *Sri Hotel* on Pho Klang Road. A combination of greasy spoon and local pub, this welcoming and laid-back place, set up by and for the GIs who've settled in the city, dishes up hearty helpings of steak and fries, pork chops, pizzas and sandwiches (drinks only after 7pm). Inexpensive.

Dan Kwian

Some of the most sought-after modern pottery in Thailand is produced by the potters of **DAN KWIAN**, a tiny village 15km south of Khorat on Route 224. Buses to the village leave frequently from Khorat's southern city gate; get off as soon as you see the roadside pottery stalls. Inevitably, the popularity of the highly distinctive Dan Kwian ceramics has made the village something of a tourist trap, but the place remains remarkably untacky (and the wares underpriced). The roadside stalls display the whole range of products, from inexpensive sunbaked clay necklaces to traditional urn-shaped water jars; in the background the potters work the clay without much regard for curious onlookers.

Characteristic of **Dan Kwian pottery** is its unglazed metallic finish. The local clay, dug from the banks of the Mun, has a high iron content, which when fired in wood-burning kilns combines with ash to create the shimmering end result. Different shades are achieved by cramming the pots into the kiln to achieve uneven firing: the greater their exposure to heat, the darker the finish. The usual technique consists of building the pots through the continuous addition of small pieces of clay. From this method comes the most typical Dan Kwian motif, the geometrical latticework pattern, which is incorporated into all sorts of designs, from incense burners and ashtrays to vases and storage jars. The potters also mould clay into sets of ceramic tiles and large-scale religious and secular murals – increasingly popular decorations in modern wats and wealthy city homes.

First settled by Mons in the mid-eighteenth century, Dan Kwian has always been a convenient resting place for travellers journeying between the Khorat plateau and Cambodia – hence its name, which means "Cart Place" or "Wagon Station". The tag still applies, as the village is now home to the only **cart museum** in Thailand (always open; free), a ramshackle **outdoor collection** of traditional vehicles and farming implements assembled at the back of the pottery stalls. Look out for the monster machine with two-metre wheels, designed to carry two tons of rice, and the covered passenger wagons with their intricately carved shafts. The exhibits aren't all as archaic as they look – Isaan farmers still use some of the sugar-cane presses on display, and the fish traps and lobster pots are a common sight in this part of the country.

Phimai

Hemmed in by its rectangular old city walls and encircled by tributaries of the River Mun, the tiny modern town of **PHIMAI**, 60km northeast of Khorat, is completely dominated by one of the most impressive Khmer sites in Thailand – the exquisitely restored temple complex of **Prasat Hin Phimai**. No one knows for sure when the prasat was built or for whom, but as a religious site it probably dates back to the reign of the Khmer king Suriyavarman I (1002–49); the complex was connected by a direct road to Angkor and oriented southeast, towards the Khmer capital. Over the next couple of centuries Khmer rulers made

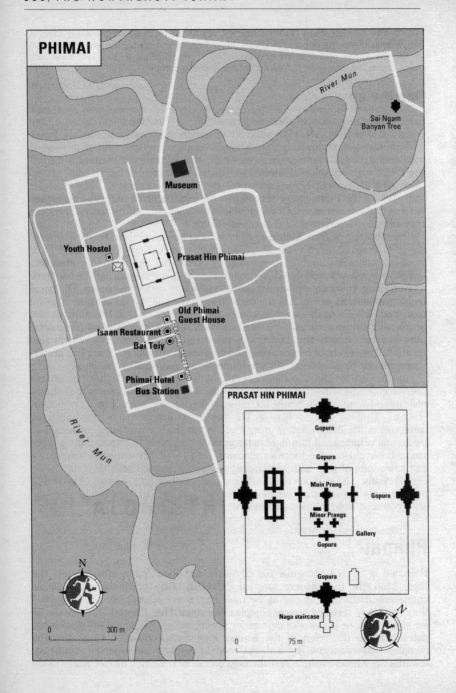

PHIMAI

River Mun

Sai Ngam
Banyan Tree

Museum

Youth Hostel

Prasat Hin Phimai

Old Phimai
Guest House

Isaan Restaurant

Bai Teiy

CHOMSUDASADETROAD

Phimai Hotel
Bus Station

River Mun

N

0   300 m

PRASAT HIN PHIMAI

Gopura

Gopura

Main Prang

Gopura

Minor Prangs

Gallery

Gopura

Gopura

Naga staircase

N

0   75 m

substantial modifications, and by the end of Jayavarman VII's reign (1181–1220) Phimai had been officially dedicated to Mahayana Buddhism. Phimai's other claim to fame is **Sai Ngam** (Beautiful Banyan), reputedly the largest banyan tree in Thailand, still growing a couple of kilometres beyond the temple walls.

Phimai's ruins attract a constant trickle of (mostly Thai) tourists throughout the year, but crowds only really congregate here for the annual **boat races**, held on the Mun's tributaries over a weekend in late October or early November. In common with many other riverside towns throughout Thailand, Phimai marks the end of the rainy season by holding fiercely competitive longboat races on the well-filled waterways, and putting on lavish parades of ornate barges done up to emulate the Royal Barges of Bangkok.

The ruins

Built mainly of dusky pink and greyish white sandstone, **Prasat Hin Phimai** (daily 7.30am–6pm; B20) is a seductive sight for so solemn a set of buildings. Even from a distance, the muted colours give off a far from austere glow; closer inspection reveals a mass of intricate carvings.

KHMER RUINS

To make sense of the **Khmer ruins** of Thailand, it's essential to identify their common architectural features. The history of the Khmers in Thailand is covered in *Contexts*; what follows is a brief rundown of the layout of their temple complexes.

At the centre of the rectangular temple compound is always the **main prang**, a pyramidal or corn-cob-shaped tower built to house the temple's most sacred image. Each prang has four entrance chambers or **gopura**, the most important of which (usually the eastern one, facing the dawn) is often extended into a large antechamber. The **lintels** and **pediments** above the gopura are carved with subjects from relevant mythology: typical Hindu reliefs show incidents from the *Ramayana* epic (see p.82) and lively portraits of the Hindu deities Shiva and Vishnu, while Buddhist scenes come from the lives of the Buddha and other *bodhisattva*s. **Antefixes** on the roof of the prang are often carved with the Hindu gods of direction, some of the most common being: east, Indra on the three-headed elephant; south, Yama on a buffalo; west, Varuna on a naga or a *hamsa* (sacred goose); north, Brahma on a *hamsa*; and northeast, Isaana on a bull.

Originally, the prang would have sheltered a **shiva lingam**, continuously bathed by lustral water dripping from a pot suspended over it; the water then flowed out of the inner chamber by means of a stone channel, a process which symbolized the water of the Ganges flowing from the Himalayan home of Shiva. In most prasats, however, the lingam has disappeared or been replaced with Hindu or Buddhist statues.

One or two **minor prangs** usually flank the main prang: often these were added at a later date to house images of less important gods, though in some cases they predate the main structure. Concentric sets of walls shield these shrines within an inner courtyard. In many temples, the innermost wall – the **gallery** – was roofed, either with wood (none of these have survived) or stone, and some galleries have gopuras at their cardinal points. These gopuras also have carved lintels and pediments and are usually approached by staircases flanked with **naga balustrades**; in Khmer temples, nagas generally appear as symbolic bridges between the human world and that of the gods. Most prangs enclose ponds between their outer and inner walls, and many are surrounded by a network of moats and reservoirs: historians attribute the Khmers' political success in part to their skill in designing highly efficient irrigation systems.

From the main southeastern gate, a staircase ornamented with classic naga balustrades leads to a gopura in the **outer walls**, which are punctuated on either side by false balustraded windows – a bit of sculptural sleight-of-hand to jazz up the solid stonework without piercing the defences. A raised pathway bridges the space between these walls and the inner gallery that protects the prangs of the **inner sanctuary**. The minor prang to the right, made of laterite, is attributed to the megalomaniac twelfth-century King Jayavarman VII, and the statue enshrined within it is of him, a copy of the original which was found in the same location, but is now kept in the National Museum in Bangkok. The pink sandstone prang to the left, which is connected to a Brahmin shrine where seven stone linga were found, was probably built around the same time.

After more than twenty years of archaeological detective work and painstaking reassembly, the magnificent **main prang** has now been restored to its original cruciform groundplan and conical shape, complete with an almost full set of carved lintels, pediments and antefixes, and capped with a stone lotus bud. The **carvings** around the outside of the prang depict predominantly Hindu themes. Shiva – the Destroyer – dances above the main entrance to the southeast antechamber: his destruction dance heralds the end of the world and the creation of a new order, a supremely potent image that warranted this place over the most important doorway. Most of the other external carvings pick out momentous episodes from the *Ramayana* (see p.82), starring heroic Rama, his brother Lakshaman, and their band of faithful monkeys in endless battles of strength, wits and magical powers against Ravana, the embodiment of evil. Inside, more sedate Buddhist scenes give evidence of the conversion from Hindu to Buddhist faith, and the prasat's most important image, the Buddha sheltered by a seven-headed naga, sits atop a base that once supported a Hindu shiva lingam.

The souvenir stalls inside the prasat compound sell some quite evocative miniature **reproduction sandstone carvings** of the most famous lintels found here at Phimai and at Phanom Rung (see p.341). They are sculpted from local yellow and pink sandstone, much as the originals were, and subjects include "Shiva's

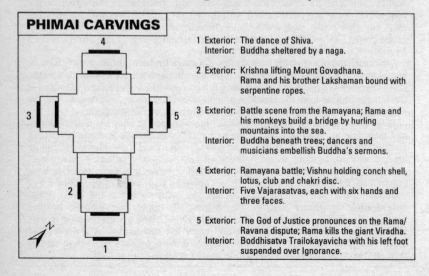

PHIMAI CARVINGS

1 Exterior: The dance of Shiva.
Interior: Buddha sheltered by a naga.

2 Exterior: Krishna lifting Mount Govadhana.
Rama and his brother Lakshaman bound with serpentine ropes.

3 Exterior: Battle scene from the Ramayana; Rama and his monkeys build a bridge by hurling mountains into the sea.
Interior: Buddha beneath trees; dancers and musicians embellish Buddha's sermons.

4 Exterior: Ramayana battle; Vishnu holding conch shell, lotus, club and chakri disc.
Interior: Five Vajarasatvas, each with six hands and three faces.

5 Exterior: The God of Justice pronounces on the Rama/Ravana dispute; Rama kills the giant Viradha.
Interior: Boddhisatva Trailokayavicha with his left foot suspended over Ignorance.

Dance" (Phimai) and "Reclining Vishnu Asleep on the Milky Sea of Eternity" (Phanom Rung); prices start at under B50. For more on these legends, see "Art and Architecture" in *Contexts* (p.534).

Much of the ancient carved stonework discovered at Phimai but not fitted back into the renovated structure can be seen at the open-air **museum** (Wed–Sun 8am–4.30pm; free) northeast of the ruins, just inside the old city walls. They're easier to appreciate here, being at eye-level, well labelled and backed up by a photographic lesson on the evolution of the different styles.

Sai Ngam

Two kilometres northeast of the museum – get there by bicycle (see below) or samlor – **Sai Ngam** is a banyan tree so enormous that it's reputed to cover an area about half the size of a football pitch (approximately 2300 square metres). It might look to you like a grove of small banyans, but Sai Ngam is in fact a single *ficus bengalensiss* whose branches have dropped vertically into the ground, taken root and spawned other branches, thereby growing further and further outwards from its central trunk. Banyan trees are believed to harbour animist spirits and you can make merit here by releasing fish into the artificial lake which surrounds Sai Ngam. The tree has become a popular recreation spot, and several restaurants have sprung up alongside it. If you go by bike you'll pass a large-scale model of the Thungsunrit Irrigation Project, an indication of the northeast's dependence on a well-regulated water supply.

Practicalities

Regular direct **buses** to Phimai from Khorat's main bus station take about an hour and a half and stop within sight of the ruins (the last return bus departs at 6pm). It's also feasible, if somewhat troublesome, to visit Phimai en route to points east or west without having to pass through Khorat. Coming from Surin or anywhere further east, take an ordinary or "rapid" (read slow) Khorat-bound **train** to **Hin Dat**, a tiny station 25km from Phimai; from here you can catch a songthaew (infrequent in this direction, but timed to link up with east-bound trains coming back; check with the *Old Phimai Guest House*, listed below, for current timetables), splash out on an expensive motorbike taxi or try hitching straight there.

Once in Phimai, the best way to get about is by **bicycle**, although this isn't permitted inside the ruins. *Bai Teiy* restaurant, listed over, has bicycles for rent and issues free maps of cycling routes around town, while the guest house has bicycles for guests only. Aside from the ride out to Sai Ngam, the area just west of the ruins, beyond the post office and youth hostel, is especially rewarding – many of the traditional wooden houses here double as workshops, and you'll often see householders weaving cane chairs in the shade beneath the buildings.

ACCOMMODATION

Though most people visit the ruins as a day trip, Phimai has two inexpensive **places to stay** as well as an unpretentious hotel, and makes a much more attractive and peaceful overnight stop than Khorat. Your first choice should be the *Old Phimai Guest House* (☎044/471918; ①–②), a lovely old wooden house with a roof garden and sun rooms, just off Chomsudasadet Road and only a couple of minutes from the ruins; YHA members get a slight discount on room rates, and there are also inexpensive dorm beds available. It's also an excellent source of information, with a big noticeboard and full details of local travel connections. Even if you're just passing through and need somewhere to leave your luggage for a few hours, this is the place to ask. The other option in this category is an official *Youth Hostel* (☎044/471446; ①–②) just west of the ruins on Araksuksit Road. Slightly more upmarket but nowhere near as atmospheric as any of the budget places, the *Phimai Hotel* (☎044/471306; ③–④), next to the bus station, is worth considering only if you're desperate for air conditioning.

EATING
Bai Teiy on Chomsudasadet Road, the town's most popular **restaurant**, serves tasty Thai dishes, including fresh fish from the river; it also runs a tourist information desk where you can pick up a bus timetable. For typical northeastern fare try around the corner at *Isaan Excellent Taste*, but if you prefer a meal with a view go to the string of interchangeable restaurants alongside Sai Ngam – their food is good enough, though prices are pitched high because of the location.

Phanom Rung and Muang Tham

East of Khorat the bleached plains roll blandly on, broken only by the occasional small town and, if you're travelling along Highway 24, the odd tantalizing glimpse of the smoky Phanom Dongkrek mountain range above the southern horizon. That said, it's well worth jumping off the Surin-bound bus for a detour to the fine Khmer ruins of **Prasat Hin Khao Phanom Rung** and **Prasat Muang Tham**. Built during the same period as Phimai, and for the same purpose, the temple complexes form two more links in the chain that once connected the Khmer capital with the limits of its empire. Sited dramatically atop an extinct volcano, Phanom Rung has now been beautifully restored, while the still wild ruins of Muang Tham lie on the plains below.

Buses plying between Khorat and Surin will let you off at **Ban Tako**, roughly midway between the two towns on Highway 24; from there it's 12km south to Phanom Rung and another 8km south to Muang Tham. There's no public transport direct to the ruins, so unless you hitch you'll have to rent a **motorbike taxi**, which should cost B80–100 per person for a return trip with as much time as you like at both prasats. It's worth the money, especially for the exhilarating views as you climb up to Phanom Rung and then drop down again to Muang Tham. Most people do the ruins as a day trip from Khorat or Surin, but if you need to stay the night there's a simple **guest house**, *Little Home* (①–②) in Prakhon Chai, the village closest to Phanom Rung on Route 24.

Prasat Hin Khao Phanom Rung

Prasat Hin Khao Phanom Rung (daily 8am–5pm; B20) stands as the finest example of Khmer architecture in Thailand, its every surface ornamented with exquisite carvings and its buildings so perfectly aligned that on the morning of April's full-moon day you can stand at the westernmost gopura and see the rising sun through all fifteen doors. This day marks Songkhran, the Thai New Year, which is celebrated with a day-long **festival** of huge parades all the way up the hill to the prasat – a tradition believed to go back eight hundred years. As at most Khmer prasats, building at Phanom Rung was a continuous process that spanned several reigns: the earliest structures are thought to date to the beginning of the tenth century and final additions were probably made three hundred years later, not long before it was abandoned. Restoration work, started in 1971, was completed in 1988.

A false window

The **approach** to the temple compound is one of the most dramatic of its kind. Symbolic of the journey from earth to the heavenly palace of the gods, the ascent to the inner compound is freighted with metaphorical import: by following the 200-metre-long avenue, paved in laterite and sandstone and flanked with lotus-bud pillars, you are walking to the ends of the earth. Ahead, Mount Meru, home of the gods, looms large above the gallery walls, accessible only via the first of three **naga bridges**, a raised cruciform structure with sixteen naga balustrades, each naga having five heads. You have now crossed the abyss between earth and heaven. A series of stairways ascends to the eastern entrance of the celestial home, first passing four small ponds, thought to have been used for ritual purification. A second naga bridge crosses to the **east gopura**, entrance to the inner sanctuary, which is topped by a lintel carved with Indra (god of the east) sitting on a lion throne. The gopura is the main gateway through the **gallery** which runs right round the inner compound and has one main and two minor entranceways on each side. Part of the gallery has been restored to its original covered design, with arched roofs, small chambers inside and false windows. The chambers may have been used for exhibiting as well as storing artefacts.

Phanom Rung is surprisingly compact, so the east gopura leads almost directly into the **main prang**, separated from it only by a final naga bridge. A dancing Shiva, nine of his ten arms intact, and a lintel carved with a relief of a **reclining Vishnu** preside over the eastern entrance to the prang. The Vishnu image has a somewhat controversial history: stolen from the site in the early 1960s, it mysteriously reappeared as a donated exhibit in the Art Institute of Chicago; for over ten years the curators refused to return it to Thailand, but as restoration work on Phanom Rung neared completion in 1988, the public took up the cause and the Institute finally relented. The relief depicts a common Hindu creation myth, known as "Reclining Vishnu Asleep on the Milky Sea of Eternity", in which Vishnu dreams up a new universe, and Brahma (the four-faced god perched on the lotus blossom that springs from Vishnu's navel) puts the dream into practice. (See p.534 for more on the Hindu legends.) Of the other recurring figures decorating the prang, one of the most important is the lion head of Kala, also known as Kirtimukha, symbolic of both the lunar and the solar eclipse and – because he's able to "swallow" the sun – considered far superior to other planetary gods. Inside the prang you can still see the base of the once all-powerful shiva lingam, for which the prang was originally built.

Two rough-hewn laterite libraries stand alongside the main prang, in the northeast and southeast corners, and there are remains of two early tenth-century brick prangs just northeast of the main prang. The unfinished **prang noi** (little prang) in the southwest corner now contains a stone Buddha footprint, which has become the focus of the merit-making that underlies the annual April festivities, thus neatly linking ancient and modern religious practices.

Prasat Muang Tham

Tumbledown and dishevelled **Prasat Muang Tham** (daily 8am–5pm; B20) makes a wonderful counterpoint to Phanom Rung – at least until the Fine Arts Department gets to work on it. Like Phanom Rung, it was probably built in stages between the tenth and thirteenth centuries, but it hasn't weathered nearly so well. Walls and windows lean gracefully at 45-degree angles, balustrades lie in collapsed heaps, and blocks of carved sandstone litter the grassy compound. At the heart of the prasat, the main prang has crumbled into a forlorn pile, but the four smaller prangs surrounding it are sturdier and almost complete; parts of the gallery protecting them remain recognizable, too, pierced by shaky gopuras displaying some of their original carvings. Between the gallery and the outer wall, the four L-shaped ponds still hold water, though the stone rims are slipping beneath the surface. Having seen Phanom Rung, it's quite easy to make out the layout from this partial evidence, but it's an evocative site even without an imaginative effort to reconstruct it.

Surin province

Best known for its highly hyped elephant round-up, the provincial capital of **SURIN**, 197km east of Khorat, is an otherwise typical northeastern town, a good place to absorb the easy-going pace of Isaan life, with the bonus of some atmospheric Khmer ruins nearby. The elephant tie-in comes from the local Suay people, whose prowess with pachyderms is well known and can be seen first-hand in the nearby village of Ta Klang (see p.346). Thais, Laotians and Khmers make up the remainder of the population of Surin province – the Khmer population was boosted during the Khmer Rouge takeover of Cambodia in the 1970s, when many upper-class Cambodians fled here.

Surin's **elephant round-up**, held every year on the third weekend of November, draws some forty thousand spectators to watch elephants play soccer, engage in tugs of war, and parade in full battle garb. These shows give both trainers and animals the chance to practise their skills, but however well controlled the elephants appear, you should always approach them with caution – an American woman was trampled to death in 1991 when her camera flash frightened one. If you miss the Surin show, you might catch one of the lesser round-ups in Chaiyaphum or Ayutthaya – or better still, take a trip out to Ta Klang.

Nine **trains** a day make the Bangkok–Surin connection (though only 3 arrive at a sensible hour), stopping at the station on the northern edge of town, less than ten minutes' walk from the central market area on Krungsrinai Road. The **bus** terminal is one block east of the rail station. Extra trains and buses are laid on to cope with the crowds that flock here for the elephant round-up and these can be booked through TAT; alternatively you could join one of the overnight packages organized by Bangkok tour agencies (see p.132).

Surin town

Surin's only official sight is its **museum** (Mon–Fri 8.30am–4.30pm; free), a tiny one-room exhibition on Chitramboong Road featuring stacks of carved antefixes and, more interestingly, several sacred elephant ropes formerly used by the Suay in their hunts to capture wild elephants for taming. Made of buffalo hide and measuring up to 100m, these ropes were considered so special by the men who handled them that women weren't allowed to touch them and, as the essential tools of the hunt, they were blessed by ancestral spirits before every expedition. As added protection the hunters wore the specially inscribed protective clothing on display here: the *yantra* designs are produced by combinations of letters and numbers arranged in such a way as to invoke magic and ward off evil.

You won't find "magic" clothing on sale in Surin, but the local **silk** weave is famous for its variety: seven hundred designs are produced in Surin province alone, many of them of Cambodian origin, including the locally popular rhomboid pattern. A shop opposite the *Ubon Hotel* on Tannasarn Road stocks a huge selection of silks and cottons, though prices are of course cheaper on the street; there

---

SILKWORMS

Most hand-woven **Thai silk** is produced by Isaan village women, some of whom oversee every aspect of sericulture, from the breeding of the silkworm through to the dyeing of the fabric. "Silk-tours" give you a good insight into the weaving and subsequent processes, but guides rarely dwell on the fascinating stages that precede them.

A principal reason for Isaan's pre-eminence in the silk industry is that its soils are particularly suitable for the growth of mulberry trees, the leaves of which are the silkworms' favoured diet. The cycle of production commences with the female silk-moth, which lives just a few days but lays around 300–500 eggs in that time. In three to four weeks each egg expands from a microscopic speck into a six-centimetre-long silkworm – gorging itself on mulberry leaves, it finally attains a weight ten thousand times its original size, ready for the cocoon-building **pupal** stage.

The silkworm constructs its **cocoon** from a single white or yellow fibre that it secretes from its mouth at a rate of 12cm a minute, sealing the filaments with a gummy substance called sericin. The metamorphosis of the pupa into a moth may take as few as two days or as many as seven, but the sericulturist must anticipate the moment at which the new moth is about to break out of the cocoon, in order to prevent the destruction of the precious fibre – which at this stage is often 900m. At the crucial point the cocoon is dropped into boiling water, killing the moth and softening the sericin, so that the unbroken filament can be unravelled. The fibres from several cocoons are "reeled" into a single thread, and two or three threads are subsequently twisted or "thrown" into the yarn known as **raw silk**. (Broken threads from damaged cocoons are worked into a second-rate yarn called "spun silk".) In most cases, next comes the "degumming process", in which the raw silk is soaked in soapy water to entirely dissolve the sericin, reducing the weight of the thread by as much as thirty percent and leaving it soft and lustrously semi-transparent.

Extremely absorbent and finely textured, finished silk is the perfect material for dyeing. It's also one of the strongest natural textiles, able to sustain a dead weight of as much as 28 grammes on a single fibre – which is why it's used to make parachutes as well as £700 shirts from Gianni Versace.

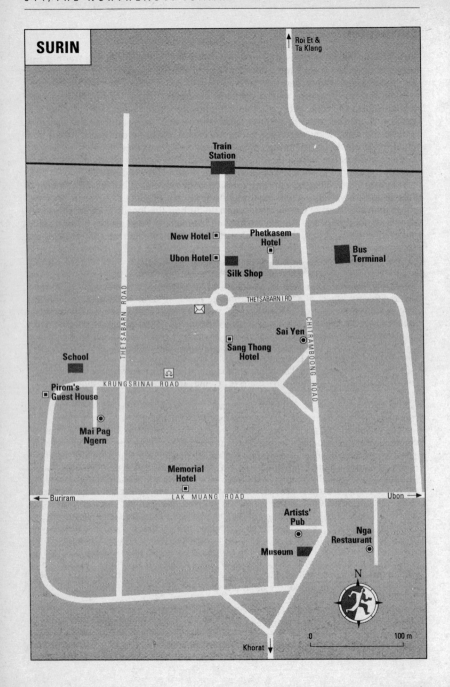

SURIN

Roi Et &
Ta Klang

Train
Station

New Hotel

Phetkasem
Hotel

Ubon Hotel

Silk Shop

Bus
Terminal

THETSABARN I RD

Sai Yen

Sang Thong
Hotel

School

CHILRAMBOONG ROAD

THETSABARN ROAD

Pirom's
Guest House

KRUNGSRINAI ROAD

Mai Pag
Ngern

Memorial
Hotel

Buriram

LAK MUANG ROAD

Ubon

Artists'
Pub

Nga
Restaurant

Museum

N

Khorat

0   100 m

are usually four or five women selling their wares around the Tannasarn–Krungsrinai intersection. Most of these women come from surrounding villages, and while it is possible to visit these villages, you'll need to go with a guide, not only to understand the weavers' explanations of what they do, but also to get a more behind-the-scenes look at the less obvious aspects of the process, like the breeding of the silkworms and the extracting of the thread; *Pirom's Guest House*, listed below, should be able to arrange a guide for you.

Timing is also important if you want to see the weavers in action: the best months to see them are between November and June, when the women aren't required to work day and night in the fields.

Practicalities

During the elephant round-up, **accommodation** in Surin gets extremely tight and rates double, but at other times you'll have no trouble finding a place to stay. First choice has to be *Pirom's Guest House* (☎044/515140; ①), one block west of the market at 242 Krungsrinai Rd: quintessentially Thai in its stylish simplicity, it's one of the best establishments in Isaan, and almost a reason in itself to stop off in Surin. Pirom himself is a highly informed social worker who genuinely enjoys conversing with foreigners and leading informal tours around the area; he also has plans for "village tours" further afield.

Phetkasem Hotel at 104 Chitramboong Rd (☎044/511274; ⑥) offers much more conventional accommodation, with sizeable air-conditioned rooms and a swimming pool. Other less luxurious hotels offering clean rooms with fan and shower include *New Hotel*, near the station at 22 Tannasarn Rd (☎044/511341; ②); *Sang Thong Hotel*, near the post office at 155–161 Tannasarn Rd (☎044/512099; ③); and *Memorial Hotel*, at 186 Lak Muang Rd (☎044/511288; ③). Bottom of the range, and a last resort, is the *Ubon Hotel* at 156 Tannasarn Rd (☎044/511133; ①).

For the best in Isaan **food**, make for *Sai Yen* on Chitramboong Road, which serves a constant stream of local office workers and families in traditional style: roll the sticky rice into little balls and dip them into assorted chilli sauces, *larb* curries and spicy *somtam* salads. Try the (unsigned) *Mai Pag Ngern* restaurant, off the western end of Krungsrinai Road, for good food from central Thailand – curries, noodle soups and the like – and inexpensive beer in a garden setting. The *Nga* restaurant off Lak Muang Road, instantly recognizable by the two huge tusks outside its gates, offers a much more touristy and expensive experience, with weekend dinner shows featuring – you guessed it – performing elephants. Surin's lively **night market** on Krungsrinai Road is one of Isaan's best, boasting a remarkably large and tasty selection of local food. More prosaically, the restaurant and bowling alley in the forecourt of the *Phetkasem Hotel* specializes in ice creams and Western food.

Aspiring local rock **musicians** and their friends hang out in the *Artist's Pub* down a small soi just north of the museum, where the atmosphere is laid-back and welcoming, if not always exactly bustling, and the beer is a bargain. For more traditional music, it's well worth checking out the *Phetkasem Hotel* bar on a Friday or Saturday evening, as Cambodian ensembles play a regular slot here, performing their particular brand of Khmer folk music known as *kantrum* (see "Music" in *Contexts*, p.559, for more on this). Not surprisingly, given the ethnic make-up of Surin, there are quite a few *kantrum* bands in the town, and although they don't have fixed venues you could well stumble across a group if you try out two or three local bars of an evening.

Ta Klang

Some 50km north of Surin, the "elephant village" of **TA KLANG** is the main settlement of the Suay people and training centre for their elephants. One out of every two Ta Klang families owns its own elephant, using it as a Western farmer would a tractor, but otherwise treating it as a much-loved pet. A visit to the village could be worthwhile if you time it right: although Suay mahouts and their herd now spend most of their time doing shows around the country, they are likely to be home during the rice-growing season from July to October and for the period just before the Surin round-up on the third weekend in November. For the ten days prior to the Surin show they train intensively in their village and then walk to Surin for the round-up; you'll see them in a healthier state if you make the trip just before the big weekend rather than after.

Traditionally regarded as the most expert hunters and trainers of elephants in Thailand, the **Suay** tribe migrated to the region from Central Asia before the rise of the Khmers in the ninth century. It was the Suay who masterminded the use of elephants in the construction of the great Khmer temples, and a Suay chief who in 1760 helped recapture a runaway white elephant belonging to the king of Ayutthaya, earning the hereditary title "Lord of Surin". Surin was governed by members of the Suay tribe until Rama V's administrative reforms of 1907.

The role of the elephant has diminished with the advent of modern machinery and the 1989 ban on teak logging, but other Asian governments occasionally ask for their help as hauliers, and one of the stranger Thai superstitions provides the Suay with a handy money-spinner. Many Thais believe that it's good luck to walk under an elephant's belly (pregnant women who do so are guaranteed an easy birth), so it's not unheard of for a Suay mahout to walk his elephant the 450km from Surin to Bangkok, charging around B20 per limbo en route.

Local **buses** to Ta Klang depart approximately hourly from the Surin terminal and take about two hours. Although there are no hotels in Ta Klang, **overnight visits** can be arranged through *Pirom's Guest House* – even if you don't want to stay, it might be a good idea to get advice on timing.

Ta Muen Toj, Prasat Ta Muen Tam and Bay Kream

The cluster of Khmer ruins called **Ta Muen Toj**, **Prasat Ta Muen Tam** and **Bay Kream**, close to the Cambodian border east of Surin, are best visited on a tour from *Pirom's Guest House*, for this is not a zone to explore unguided. The two-hour drive to the frontier area passes through several checkpoints along the way, and as the road nears Phanom Dongrek – the mountains that divide Thailand from Cambodia – it runs through villages whose inhabitants live under the daily threat of unexploded land mines whenever they go fishing in remote parts of the river or wood-cutting off the main forest paths. These legacies from the war in Cambodia continue to claim lives and limbs, and not a village in this area is without its disabled victims. The pathways to the ruins have of course been cleared, but when you arrive at Ta Muen Toj an armed escort joins the tour – with tensions still unresolved in Cambodia, the area is a sensitive one, and if there happens to be fighting in the immediate locality you won't be able to get anywhere near.

It's thought that the tiny **Ta Muen Toj** was a resting place for worshippers at the nearby **Prasat Ta Muen Tam**, a walled temple compound in the clutches of enormous trees – a testament to the age of the place and to the durability of the materials with which the temple was built. A kilometre or so further, **Bay Kream** stands on a mound, like an island in the suffocating jungle. This is the largest and the most recognizable of the three sites, with carved lintels and large stone blocks strewn between the dilapidated walls; piled-up earth now fills many of the rooms to ceiling height and the window frames have subsided beneath ground level, giving the whole complex a wonderful air of decomposition. Beyond Bay Kream, the unconquered Cambodian jungle stretches to the horizon, a vista accompanied by the sound of sporadic shelling.

Ubon Ratchathani

East of Surin, Highway 226 and the rail line run in tandem through desiccated, impoverished plains before coming to a halt at **UBON RATCHATANI** (Royal City of the Lotus), a provincial capital which, despite its name, is of neither regal nor botanical distinction. Almost always referred to simply as Ubon – not to be confused with Udon (Udon Thani) to the north – Thailand's fifth-largest city holds little in the way of atmosphere or attraction beyond a couple of wats, a decent museum and a lingering hangover from its days as a US airbase site. It's only really worth visiting in order to make trips out: eastwards to the prehistoric cliff paintings at Pha Taem (see p.351), or southwest to the ruins of Khao Phra Viharn (see p.353).

If you're near Ubon in early July, you should definitely consider coming into town for the local **Asanha Puja** festivities, an auspicious Buddhist holiday celebrated all over Thailand to mark the beginning of Khao Pansa (the annual 3-month Buddhist retreat). Ubon's version of this festival is the most spectacular in the country: local people make huge wooden or plaster sculptures, coat them in orange beeswax and then carve intricate decorations in the wax. The sculptures are mounted on floats around enormous candles and paraded through the town – hence the tourist name for the celebrations, the **Ubon Candle Festival** – before being presented to various wats. In most wats the candle is kept burning throughout the retreat period.

The most painless way to get to Ubon from Bangkok (and most places in between) is by **train** – the line terminates at **Warinchamrab**, Ubon's suburban alter ego just across the sluggish Maenam Mun. City buses #1, #2, #3, #6 and #7 will get you across the river to Ubon, #2 and #7 carrying on to Kaenthani and Auparat roads for the main hotels and TAT office. Regular long-distance **buses** from Bangkok and points west, and Kong Chiam to the east, pull into the Warinchamrab terminal, one block east of the train station; those from the north (Yasothon, Khon Kaen, Udon) arrive at a terminal north of Ubon's town centre on Jaengsanit Road. The several air-conditioned bus companies connecting Ubon with other cities (Bangkok, Chiang Mai, Phitsanulok, Khorat, Surin) have various arrival and departure points near TAT on Kaenthani Road and opposite the Monument of Merit on the parallel Phalorangrit Road.

The City

Aside from its confusing number of arrival points, central Ubon is easy enough to negotiate. The main hotel and eating area is confined to a fairly compact area between Sumpasit Road in the north and the Maenam Mun in the south. Of the city's eight main wats, **Wat Thung Si Muang**, in the middle of this zone near the post office, is the most noteworthy, mainly for its unusually well-preserved teak

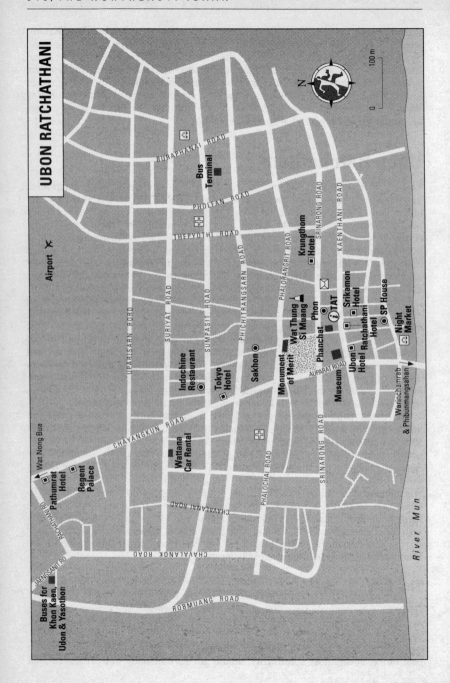

UBON RATCHATHANI

Airport ✈

N

100 m

0

BURAPHANAI ROAD

Bus Terminal

PHOLFAN ROAD

THEPYOTHI ROAD

SRINARONG ROAD

KAENTHANI ROAD

PHALORANGRIT ROAD

Krungthom Hotel

Srikamon Hotel

SP House

UPARISARN ROAD

SURIYAT ROAD

SUMPASIT ROAD

PHICHITRANGSARN ROAD

Wat Thung Si Muang

Phon Phanchat

TAT

Ubon Ratchathani Hotel

Night Market

Indochine Restaurant

Tokyo Hotel

Sakhon

Monument of Merit

AUPARAT ROAD

Museum

Warinchamrab & Phibunmangsahan

Wat Nong Bua

CHAYANGKUN ROAD

Wattana Car Rental

PHALOCHAI ROAD

SRINARONG ROAD

Pathumrat Hotel

Regent Palace

RACHATHANI RD

CHAVALANAI ROAD

River Mun

JAENSANIT RD

Buses for Khon Kaen, Udon & Yasothon

CHAVALANOK ROAD

ROBMUANG ROAD

library – raised on stilts over an artificial pond to keep book-devouring insects at bay. The murals in the bot, to the left of the library, have also survived remarkably well: the lively scenes of everyday nineteenth-century life include musicians playing *khaen* pipes and devotees performing characteristic Isaan merit-making dances, as well as conventional portraits of city life in Bangkok.

Off Chayangkun Road at the northern edge of town, the much more modern **Wat Nong Bua** (city bus #2 or #3) is modelled on the stupa at Bodh Gaya in India, scene of the Buddha's enlightenment. The whitewashed replica is carved with scenes from the *Jataka* and contains a scaled-down version of the stupa covered in gold leaf. Of more interest, especially if you don't happen to be here during the candle festival, is the wax float kept in a small building behind the chedi.

For an overview of all things to do with southern Isaan, pay a visit to the **museum** (Wed–Sun 8.30am–4.30pm; free) housed in the blue and grey building opposite the *Ubon Hotel* on Kaenthani Road. This is a real something-for-everyone offering, with thematic displays on the region's geology, ancient history, folk crafts, musical instruments and more, most with informative descriptions in English. Particularly worth looking out for are a ninth-century Khmer statue of Ganesh, examples of the star-embroidered fabric that is a speciality of Ubon, and a pre-fourth-century bronze bell and ceremonial drum found in the vicinity. Also on show is a serviceable reproduction of the Pha Taem cliff paintings – much easier to get to than the originals, though hardly as atmospheric.

Silk, cotton and silverware are all good buys in Ubon. Several shops along Kaenthani Road specialize in clothes made from the stripey rough **cotton** weaves peculiar to the Ubon area, while the silver handicrafts shop on Ratchabut Road (just north of *SP House* near the riverside night market) has a good selection of the Laotian-style **silver filigree** belts and accessories currently fashionable with middle-class Thai women, as well as lots of other jewellery. The best place for **northeastern crafts** is *Phanchat*, which has two branches along Ratchabut Road (50m east of the museum, off Kaenthani Road) – the larger, unsigned in English but next to a motorbike showroom, is at no. 158, the smaller, also unsigned, is 100m south. Both specialize in fine-quality regional goods, like triangular "axe" pillows (*mawn khwan*), lengths of **silk** and clothes made to local designs, and also stock antique farm and household implements.

Practicalities

Ubon's choice of hotels is fair enough, though to date there are no guest houses within the city to act as a focal point for travellers. Staff at the **TAT office** on Kaenthani Road (daily 8.30am–4.30pm) will help you out with specific queries on bus and train departures, but all their local information is in Thai. If you're thinking of going out to the cliff paintings, then consider renting a **motorbike** (B350 per day) or **car** (B1000 per day with or without a driver) from *Wattana* (☎045/242202) at 269 Suriyat Rd.

Accommodation

Chumrat Hotel, Chayangkun Road (☎045/241501). One of Ubon's top 2 hotels, this is some way out, on the northern edge of town, close to the bus terminal. Still, it's well equipped, with air-con rooms and a swimming pool. ⑤.

Krungthom Hotel, 24 Sri Narong Rd (☎045/241609). Centrally located near the post office, with spacious rooms and a hotel bar. ④.

Ratchathani Hotel, 229 Kaenthani Rd (☎045/254599). Very central with large, but over-priced, average rooms. ④.

Regent Palace, 256 Chayangkun Rd (☎045/255529). Similar to the equally upmarket neighbour, *Chumrat Hotel*, but with no pool. ⑦.

Srikamon Hotel, 22 Ubonsak Rd (☎045/241136). Comfortable rooms right in the heart of downtown Ubon, much more convenient than the city's top 2 hotels stuck out on the edge of town. ⑥.

Suriyat Hotel, 302 Suriyat Rd (☎045/241144). Dirt-cheap but dingy. One to avoid unless everywhere else is full. ①–②.

Tokyo Hotel, 178 Auparat Rd (☎045/241739). About a 5-min walk north of the museum, this is the best and friendliest of Ubon's budget hotels. Although rooms here are a little shabby, all are adequate and equipped with fan and shower. ②.

Ubon Hotel, 333 Kaenthani Rd (☎045/254952). In the same vein as the *Ratchathani*, this centrally located place has unremarkable rooms for unjustifiable prices. ④.

Eating

One of Ubon's more interesting **eating** experiences is the *Indochine Restaurant* on Sumpasat Road – there's no English sign, but it's easily recognizable by the photos of speciality dishes on the walls. The predominantly Vietnamese food is based around stuffed rice-noodle pancakes with spicy sauces and lashings of fresh mint. A set meal of two or three dishes costs about B70; unfortunately the place closes at 6pm. Also reasonably priced, the air-conditioned *Phon Restaurant* (no English sign), round the corner from TAT, serves a large range of Thai and Chinese dishes – the ribs in black-bean sauce are a treat. Northeastern specialities are an obvious option in Ubon: try *Sakhon* on Pha Daeng Road for some of the best regional food. The café-style *Chiokee,* across from the museum on Kaenthani Road, seems to get the most breakfast business – farangs come for the ham and eggs, local office workers for rice gruel – but it serves a daytime menu of Thai and Western staples until nightfall. If it's coffee, cakes and ice-cream sundaes you're after, head for *SP House*, round the corner from the *Ratchathani Hotel* near the river on Ratchabut Road. The Maenam Mun makes a great setting for Ubon's main **night market**, which serves particularly good *hawy thawt* (mussel omelettes), among other standard fare; a smaller market sets up next to the *Tokyo Hotel* every evening.

Around Ubon

On the whole, the area **around Ubon** is a lot more interesting than the metropolitan hub, particularly if you venture eastwards towards the Mekhong River and the Laotian border or (political tensions permitting) southwestwards to the stunning Khmer temple at the Cambodian border. Nearly all the routes detailed on the following pages can be done as a day trip from Ubon – most comfortably with your own transport, but manageable on buses and songthaews if you set off very early in the morning – though there's a lot to be said for taking things more slowly and spending a night or two in the rural reaches of Ubon Ratchathani province.

East of Ubon: the roads to the Laotian border

There are several routes east out of Ubon, but they all begin with Highway 217, which starts in Ubon's southern suburb of Warinchamrab and then follows the River Mun eastwards for 45km before splitting into two at the town of Phibun

Mangsahan. From here, Highway 217 continues in a southeasterly direction to the border at **Chong Mek**, passing through **Kaeng Tana National Park**; the northeasterly fork out of Phibun, called Route 2222, follows the course of the Mun to its confluence with the Mekhong at **Kong Chiam** – an appealing riverside village worth a trip in its own right, as well as for the nearby prehistoric paintings at **Pha Taem**.

Sited at the turbulent point of the Mun called Kaeng Saphue (*kaeng* means rapids), there's little more to **Phibun Mangsahan** (known locally as Phibun) than a chaotic central bus station and a sprawling market that caters for the riverine catchment area, but for travellers it's an inevitable interchange on any eastbound journey. Phibun's one exceptional sight stands on the western outskirts of town and is signposted off Highway 217. This is **Wat Phokakaew**, an unusually attractive modern wat, worth a look for its eye-catchingly tiled exterior and its interior reliefs of twelve of Thailand's most revered wats, including the Golden Mount in Bangkok and Nakhon Pathom's monumental chedi.

To get to Phibun from Ubon, you'll need to first take **city bus** #1, #3 or #6 across the river to the Warinchamrab bus station, and then change onto a **local bus** bound for Phibun (every 10min until 4.30pm). These terminate in Phibun's town centre from where it's a ten-minute walk through town to the songthaew stop beside the Kaeng Saphue bridge – the departure point for all public transport east along Highway 217 and Route 2222.

Route 2222: Kong Chiam and the Pha Taem paintings

Thirty kilometres northeast of Phibun, along Route 2222, the small riverside village of **KONG CHIAM** is a popular destination for day-tripping Thais, who drive out here to see the somewhat fancifully named "two-coloured river" for which the village is nationally renowned. Created by the merging of the muddy brown Mun with the muddy brown Mekhong at "the easternmost point of Thailand", the water is hardly an irresistible attraction. The village, however, even though it comprises little more than a collection of wooden houses, the requisite post office, school and police station, three guest houses and a couple of wats, has a certain appeal and makes a very pleasant stopover point.

The cliffside **Wat Tamkohasawan**, located at the point where Route 2222 turns into Kong Chiam, is unprepossessing, with a huge and ugly modern Buddha image staring down on the villagers below, but **Wat Kong Chiam** is far more charming. Built at the rivers' confluence, it appears to stand on an island, and a small *sala* (open-sided pavilion) in the grounds provides a peaceful spot for waterside contemplation. Elsewhere in the compound, look out for the old wooden bell tower, its ornamental paintwork faded gracefully with age.

Kong Chiam's sights are thin on the ground, but you can rent a bicycle (B50) or motorbike (B150) from any of the guest houses for the day and explore the area, or take a B5 **longtail ride across the Mekhong River** into Laos: there's nothing to do in the village on the other side, and you can't use it as an entry port, however many official bits of paper you have with you, but the river crossing is pleasant enough.

The most rewarding trip from Kong Chiam, though, is a visit to the **PHA TAEM PAINTINGS** 18km up the Mekhong. Clear proof of the antiquity of the fertile Mekhong Valley, these are believed to be between three thousand and four thousand years old. The work of rice-cultivating settlers who lived in huts rather than caves, the bold and childlike paintings cover a 170-metre stretch of cliff face.

Protected from the elements by an overhang, the red paint – a mixture of soil, tree gum and fat – has kept its colour so well that the shapes and figures are still clearly discernible. Human forms and geometric designs appear in groups alongside massive depictions of animals and enormous fish – possibly the prized catfish still caught in the Mekhong. Most awesome of all is a thirty-metre string of hand prints, giving an uncannily emphatic sense of prehistoric human presence.

Pha Taem (Taem Cliff) is clearly signposted from Kong Chiam. If you're lucky, you might get a ride on one of the infrequent Ubon-bound buses as far as the Pha Taem turn-off, from where you can try and hitch the rest of the way (about 8km), but otherwise, unless you rent a motorbike, you'll have to hitch all the way or charter a tuk-tuk or taxi from the village – ask at *Apple Guest House* (listed below) for advice. The road ends at the cliff, passing weird, mushroom-shaped sandstone rock formations known as Sao Chaliang; from the car park, follow the unsigned path down the cliff face and along the shelf in the rock to the paintings. If you continue along the path past the paintings, you'll eventually climb back up to the top of the cliff again, taking in fine views of the fertile Mekhong valley floor and glimpses of hilly western Laos. Having reached surface level again, double back across the rocky scrub to reach the car park, a couple of kilometres away.

PRACTICALITIES

Kong Chiam-bound **songthaews** leave Phubon's Kaeng Saphue bridge every half-hour throughout the morning and then hourly until 4.30pm, and take sixty to ninety minutes. There are a few daily **buses** that go directly from Ubon to Kong Chiam, but these are painfully slow, taking a convoluted backroad route and stopping for long breaks along the way. If you have your **own transport**, you can also get to Kong Chiam from Kaeng Tana National Park – see opposite for details.

Kong Chiam is well off the beaten track, and rarely do you get the opportunity to stay in such a well-appointed **guest house** in so typical a Thai village. The best place to stay is the convivial *Apple Guest House* (☎045/351160; ①), opposite the post office on Kaewpradit Road, about five minutes' walk from the bus stop and the river bank. Rooms are squeaky clean with good beds, and there's a traveller-oriented restaurant and a useful noticeboard. In the unlikely event that you find *Apple* full, try *Kong Chiam Guest House* (☎045/351074; ①), one block further south (away from the river) on Phukamchai Road, where rooms are slightly less comfortable and not as attractive in design, but fine nonetheless. The other option is *Pio* (☎045/351091; ①), 75m from the bus stop, which offers only a few rooms in the family home and tends to get filled up with Thai students.

For **restaurants** you're limited to a string of similar riverside places, which are reasonably priced if not very exciting, though you might be lucky enough to coincide with a good fish catch, in which case you should ask if they have any *pla duk*, the catfish which is very much a local speciality. Otherwise, check out the travellers' staples at *Apple*, or order *khao pat* at the locals' restaurant attached to the cook's house at the western end of the river bank, in front of the District Office.

Highway 217: Kaeng Tana National Park and Chong Mek

The less popular but more scenic route east of Phibun continues along the course of **Highway 217** and passes through Kaeng Tana National Park (at which point you can loop northwards to reach Kong Chiam) before hitting the Laotian border at Chong Mek 46km away. To see this area by public transport, you'll have to rely on the Phibun–Chong Mek **songthaews**, which leave approximately hourly from the songthaew stop beside Phibun's Kaeng Saphue bridge and take about one and a quarter hours to reach the border. It's a pretty restrictive mode of transport, so if you're planning on doing some exploring along the way, you should definitely consider renting or chartering your own.

After travelling about 30km east of Phibun along Highway 217, you'll come to the **Srindhorn Dam**, which holds in one of the largest reservoirs (measuring some 43km north to south) in Isaan. The landscape around here has changed drastically over the last few years, thanks to the construction of the hydroelectric **Pak Mun dam** across the River Mun, a few kilometres north of the highway. Completed in 1994, its creation was bitterly contested, not only by the two thousand-plus families whose homes and livelihoods were to be severely affected, but also by environmental pressure groups and NGOs across the world (see "Environmental Issues" in *Contexts*, p.552, for more on this). The former residents and fishermen lost out, and 117 square kilometres of previously farmed and inhabited land were flooded, but the environmentalists gained a partial victory: their concern about the movement of fish between the Mekhong and the Mun rivers has resulted in the dam incorporating a ground-breaking "fish ladder", which facilitates just this.

KAENG TANA NATIONAL PARK headquarters are 7km down a dirt track signposted off Highway 217 just northwest of Sirindhorn Dam. Although the park offers only a couple of short trails (starting from the headquarters), through predominantly scrubby vegetation to waterfalls and caves, it does make a pleasant excursion. The best picnic spot is beside **Kaeng Tana**, a much wilder set of rapids than those at Kaeng Saphue, less than 1km beyond the headquarters. If desperate you can also stay here: six-berth national park bungalows go for B700 but, during daylight hours, it's quite possible to continue **on to Kong Chiam** instead, without having to go back via Phibun. There are no bridges across the Mun at this point, so you'll have to cross the river by vehicle ferry, which pulls in about 4km away from the headquarters – ask there for directions. Once on the other bank, follow the road until the signpost for Kong Chiam, a couple of kilometres further.

Highway 217 finally peters out 15km southeast of the Sirindhorn Dam, at the border town of **CHONG MEK**, Thais and Laotians can cross freely here, with access to a limited but workable radius, but day-tripping farangs are restricted to the duty-free shops in Ban Mai Sing Amphon. To proceed any further, you must be in possession of a Laotian visa (for information on how to arrange this see the box on p.374) which specifies Chong Mek as your entry point; Ban Mai Sing Amphon is about three hours by road from the southern Laotian centre of Pakse. At the time of writing, the border itself closes at 3pm every day.

Khao Phra Viharn and Wat Pa Nanachat Beung Rai

Perched atop a 547-metre-high spur of the Dongkrek mountains about 80km southwest of Ubon, the eleventh-century Khmer ruins of **KHAO PHRA VIHARN** (daily 8am–4pm; B200) surpass even the spectacularly set Phanom Rung. A magnificent avenue over 500m long rises to the sanctuary, lined at intervals with naga balustrades and punctuated by four pavilions which afford views from each cardinal point – east and west over jungle-clad hills, north to Thailand, and south up to the main temple sited right on the cliff edge.

Accessible only by this promenade, which starts just inside Thailand's southern border, the central sanctuary of the Khao Phra Viharn complex nevertheless stands on Cambodian land – and until January 1992 it was officially out of bounds, due both to the territorial struggles between the two neighbours and the continuing fighting in Cambodia. Although the international disputes have by now been pretty much resolved (when open, half the entrance fee goes to each national government), Khao Phra Viharn has become something of a trophy in the internal war between the Khmer Rouge and the Phnom Penh regime, making it far too dangerous a place to visit; check with any TAT office before setting off – even if the ruins are open, you may need to obtain written permission from the Ubon police beforehand. **Buses** from Ubon's Warinchamrab station will get you as far as **Kantharalak** (1hr 30min) – from there you'll have to arrange a motorbike taxi to the ruins.

Seventeen kilometres west of Ubon, a short walk off Highway 226, a group of foreign monks have established the forest monastery of **WAT PA NANACHAT BEUNG RAI** specifically for farangs who want to immerse themselves in meditation. Short- and long-term visitors are welcome, but the atmosphere is serious and intense and not for curious sightseers. Nearly all west-bound buses from the Warinchamrab station in Ubon pass close by the monastery; ask to be let out at the village of **Beung Rai** and follow the signs for the wat. (For general information on meditation centres, see p.46.)

Yasothon and Roi Et

By the beginning of May, Isaan is desperate for rain; there may not have been significant rainfall for six months and the rice crops need to be planted. In northeastern folklore, rain is the fruit of sexual encounters between the gods, so at this time villagers all over Isaan hold the bawdy **Bun Bang Fai** – a merit-making **rocket festival** – to encourage the gods to get on with it. The largest and most public of these festivals takes place in **YASOTHON**, 98km northwest of Ubon, on a weekend in mid-May. Not only is the firework display a spectacular affair, but the rockets built to launch them are superbly crafted machines in themselves, beautifully decorated and carried proudly through the streets before blast-off. Up to 25kg of gunpowder may be packed into the nine-metre-long rockets and, in keeping with the fertility theme of the festivities, performance is everything. Sexual innuendo, general flirtation and dirty jokes are essential components of Bun Bang Fai; rocket builders compete to shoot their rockets the highest, and anyone whose missile fails to leave the ground gets coated in mud as a punishment. At other times of the year, Yasothon is a dud, with a faceless high street full of motorbike-part shops and not even a worthwhile wat to look at.

All Khon Kaen-bound **buses** from Ubon stop in Yasothon, as do some heading for Chaiyaphum. If you want to **stay** here during festival time, book well in advance and be prepared to pay double what the room's worth. *Yot Nakhon* at 141–143 Uthai Ramrit Rd (☎045/711122; ②–③) is the biggest hotel in town and has both fan and air-conditioned rooms. Otherwise, there's not much to choose between the following, which all offer adequate rooms with fan and shower at competitive prices: *Udomphon*, 82/3 Uthai-Ramrit Rd (☎045/711564; ①); *Surawet Watthana*, 128/1–3 Jaengsanit Rd (☎045/711690; ①); and *Suk Niran*, 278–286 Jaengsanit Rd (☎045/711196; ①).

If Yasothon's booked out you could commute from either Ubon or **ROI ET**, a pleasant if unarresting town 71km further northwest and also on the Ubon–Khon Kaen bus route. The best value here is the large *Si Chumphon* on Haisok Road (☎043/511741; ③–⑤), where all rooms are air-conditioned. The more central *Banchong*, 99–101 Suriyadet Bamrung Rd (☎043/511235; ①–②) has reasonable enough rooms for the price, and the nearby *Sai Thip* at 133 Suriyadet Bamrung Rd (☎043/511365; ③) is also convenient but slightly overpriced. *Mai Thai*, 99 Haisok Rd (☎043/511136; ⑤–⑥), is Roi Et's poshest hotel.

CENTRAL ISAAN

The more northerly branch of the northeastern rail line bypasses Khorat, heading straight up through **central Isaan** to the Laotian border town of Nong Khai via Khon Kaen and Udon Thani, paralleling Highway 2 most of the way. West of these arteries, the smaller Highway 201 is shadowed by the thickly wooded Phetchabun hills and Dong Phaya Yen mountain range, the westernmost limits of Isaan, chunks of which have been turned into the **national parks** of Phu Kradung, Phu Reua and Phu Hin Rongkla. But hills play only a minor part in central Isaan's landscape, most of which suffers from poor-quality soil that sustains little in the way of profitable crops and, quite apart from what it does to the farmers who work it, makes for drab views from the bus or train window. Nevertheless, there are a handful of towns worth stopping off at: **Chaiyaphum**, where guest houses provide the opportunity to visit silk weavers in a nearby village; **Khon Kaen**, for its excellent museum of local history; **Udon Thani**, a departure point for the Bronze Age settlement of **Ban Chiang**; and **Loei**, for its access to the mountainous national parks.

Trains connect only the larger towns, but **buses** link all the above centres, also conveniently servicing the town of Phitsanulok (see p.182) – via a spectacularly hilly route through the rounded contours of Phetchabun province – the springboard for a tour of the ruins of Sukhothai and a junction for onward travel to Chiang Mai.

Chaiyaphum

The few travellers who stop off at **CHAIYAPHUM** generally come for the organized silk tours, but even if you're not interested in cocoons, dye vats and hand looms, you could spend a couple of enjoyable days here. It's a relaxing town, compact enough to walk easily from end to end in half an hour, and only gets really lively in January, when it holds a week-long celebration in honour of Phraya Phakdi Chumphon, the nineteenth-century founder of the modern town, whose statue graces the main roundabout at its southern end. Recently an **elephant round-up** has been held on the two days preceding the festival – a scaled-down version of the famous Surin show that's a lot less crowded than its prototype.

The only notable sight in town is **Prang Ku**, a ruined Khmer temple probably built in the late twelfth century at the site of a resting place along the route between Phimai and northern outposts of the Khmer empire. All that's left here is the central prang, now housing a sandstone Dvaravati-era Buddha, and the remnants of a surrounding wall. Prang Ku is on Bannakarn Road, about 2km east of the main roundabout. If you go by bike (rentable from the guest houses) you can make a pleasant round trip by continuing past the prang, through rice fields interspersed with villages, eventually ending up on Niwet Rat Road, 1km east of the bus station at the northern edge of the town centre.

While it's easy enough to cover the 15km west to the **silk-weaving** villages of **Ban Khwao** and **Ban Tawn** by songthaew from Nonmuang Road (on the west side of town), you're likely to have a much more rewarding time if you go with a tour from one of the two guest houses. These cost about B80 per person and include an overview of the whole process from breeding through spinning, dyeing and weaving (see box on p.343). Buying silk direct from the weavers makes economic sense for both parties as it cuts out the middle merchants – 6m of good-quality plain-coloured silk can cost as little as B1200–1500. Tailors in Chaiyaphum will make up the cloth for you, but for complicated designs you should wait until you reach the savvy stitchers of Chiang Mai or Bangkok.

Finally, for a therapeutic shower and peaceful jungle picnic you could head out to one of two waterfalls in the area. The most impressive is the multi-tiered, fifty-metre-wide **Nam Tok Thad Tone**, 21km north of Chaiyaphum in the small Thad Tone National Park off the end of Route 2051. To get there from Chaiyaphum take a songthaew from the bus station on Niwet Rat Road (3 daily 10am, 11am and noon) to **Ban Nam Tok Thad Tone**, the falls village at the end of the road, and then walk the 2km to the waterfall. Coming back, you'll have to rely on hitching a lift, which shouldn't be too difficult. Alternatively, make the trip to **Nam Tok Pa Eung**, 26km to the northwest. From the bus station take a songthaew bound for **Nong Bua Daeng** and ask to get out at the waterfall, 45 minutes on. Follow the dirt track on the right to a car park (1500m), cross the river and continue for 1km to the next pair of bridges – the falls are just beyond.

Practicalities

From Bangkok, **buses** to Chaiyaphum leave at least once an hour and take about six hours. There are also connections from Phitsanulok in the central plains, Chiang Mai and Chiang Rai in the north, and Khorat, Surin, Ubon, Khon Kaen, Loei and Chiang Khan in Isaan. All ordinary buses stop at the station on Niwet Rat Road at the eastern edge of town; air-conditioned tour buses stop on Nonmuang Road at the western edge.

There's not much to choose between Chaiyaphum's two basic but quiet, friendly and laid-back **guest houses**. *Yin's Guest House* (①), the longer established, is haphazardly run but none the less agreeable for that, and Yin herself is very welcoming. She offers simple but comfortable rooms in a traditional wooden house by a swampy lake just five minutes' walk from the ordinary bus terminal (cross Niwet Rat Road and head straight down the soi next to the "boat noodle shop" for about 250m). *Chaiyaphum Guest House* (①), at 447 Nonmuang Rd, near the air-conditioned-bus terminal, has a large garden and cooking facilities, but sometimes closes down from May to October. If you prefer a **hotel**, try the typical Thai-Chinese *Sirichai Hotel* (☎044/811461; ③) just south of *Chaiyaphum Guest House* at 565 Nonmuang Rd, or the *Lert Nimit* (☎044/811522; ③–⑤) opposite the ordinary bus station at 447 Niwet Rat Rd, which has better rooms for the price, and some with air conditioning.

For value and variety the best place to **eat** is, as usual, the **night market**, which starts from about 6pm along the roads running east and west one block south of the main roundabout; alternatively, the **curry stalls** in front of the department store on Ratchathani Road serve through the evening and during most of the day as well. If you prefer to eat inside, there are **noodle shops** on Ratchathani and Nonmuang roads, including the "boat noodle" place at the end of *Yin's* soi on Niwet Rat Road, where *kwetiaw reua* (noodles cooked in a dark, strong-tasting broth) are served from a traditional wooden sampan stationed in the dining area.

Khon Kaen

Geographically at the virtual centre of Isaan, **KHON KAEN** has been the focus of government plans to regenerate the northeast, and is now the base of a highly respected university as well as the Channel 5 television studios; its province, however, still has the lowest per capita income in the country, at just B4000 per year. Considering its size and importance, the city is surprisingly uncongested and spacious, and there's a noticeably upbeat feel to the place, underlined by its apparently harmonious combination of traditional Isaan culture – huge markets and hordes of street-vendors – and flashy shopping plazas and world-class hotels. Its location, 188km northeast of Khorat on the Bangkok–Nong Khai rail line and Highway 2, makes it a convenient resting point, even though the provincial museum is just about the only sight here: the farangs staying in the city tend to be businesspeople or university teachers, not tourists.

In keeping with its status as a university town, Khon Kaen has several fine collections in its **museum**, two blocks north of the bus station on Lung Soon Rachakarn Road (daily 8.30am–4.30pm; B10). The star attraction on the ground floor is a *sema* carved with a sensuous depiction of Princess Bhimba wiping the Buddha's feet with her hair on his return to Kabilabasad after years of absence in search of enlightenment. In the same room, the scope of the **Ban Chiang** collection of reassembled pots, bronze tools and jewellery rivals those held in Bangkok's National Museum and at Ban Chiang itself (see p.361), and is put into context by a map showing the distribution of contemporaneous settlements in the region. The display of **folk art** in one of the smaller ground-floor galleries includes traditional fish traps and animal snares, and a selection of betel trays that run the gamut of styles from crude wooden vessels carved by Isaan farmers to more intricate silver sets given by the better-off as a dowry. Upstairs, the displays of Buddha sculptures feature the most perfect small bronze Lanna-style images outside of northern Thailand.

If you have an evening to fill, you could take a samlor tour of **Beung Kaen Nakhon** (about B100 from the *Kaen Inn*), the artificial lake 1500m south of the bus station on the southern outskirts of town, and then eat at one of the lakeside restaurants. Aside from a couple of wats and some upmarket residences on its shores, there's nothing else much here, but it's the nearest Khon Kaen has to a public park and as such attracts families and kids on weekends and holidays. You can walk the perimeter in an hour and a half.

The other moderately interesting way of killing a few hours in Khon Kaen is to make a trip out into the countryside north of town, to visit the revered *that* (reliquary tower) which gave the town and province its name, and to take in some typical northeastern hamlets. The monument, called **Phra That Kham Kaen**, is located within the compound of Wat Chediyaphum in a hamlet of **Nan Pong**, 30km north of Khon Kaen, and large yellow songthaews make the ninety-minute

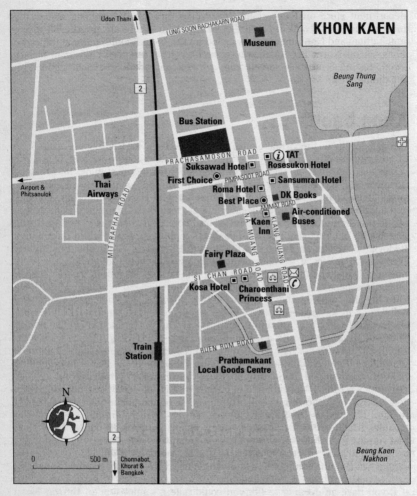

KHON KAEN

Udon Thani

LUNG SOON RACHAKARN ROAD

Museum

Beung Thung Sang

2

Bus Station

PRACHASAMOSON ROAD

TAT

Suksawad Hotel   Rosesukon Hotel

First Choice   PIMPASOOT ROAD   Sansumran Hotel

Airport & Phitsanulok

Thai Airways

Roma Hotel

Best Place   DK Books

AMMAT ROAD   Air-conditioned Buses

Kaen Inn

Fairy Plaza

SI CHAN ROAD

Kosa Hotel   Charoenthani Princess

RUEN ROM ROAD

Train Station

Prathamakant Local Goods Centre

N

2

0   500 m   Chonnabot, Khorat & Bangkok

Beung Kaen Nakhon

journey from Khon Kaen bus station about every half-hour. On the way you'll pass through a string of settlements consisting of little more than a few wooden houses raised on stilts to provide shelter for livestock and storage space for looms and ox-carts, and surrounded by small groves of banana and areca palm trees. Outside every house you'll see at least one enormous *ohng*, the all-important water storage jars that are left to collect rainwater for use during the debilitating annual drought. The journey to Nan Pong is more rewarding than the arriving: the whitewashed *that* looks too inconsequential to merit such a signifi-cant place in local mythology. The story goes that two monks once rested here beneath a dead tamarind tree (*kham*); when they returned to the spot a couple of months later it had sprung back into life, so they had the miraculous tree enshrined – and the name Khon Kaen followed from the Kham Kaen shrine.

BETEL

Betel-chewing is a habit indulged in all over Asia, and in Thailand nowhere more enthusiastically than in the northeast, where the three essential ingredients for a good chew – **betel leaf**, **limestone ash** and **areca palm fruit** – are found in abundance. You chew the coarse red flesh of the narcotic fruit (best picked when small and green-skinned) first, before adding a large heart-shaped betel leaf, spread with limestone ash paste and folded into manageable size. For a stronger kick, you can include tobacco and/or marijuana at this point. It's an acquired and bitter taste that numbs the mouth and generates a warm feeling around the ears. Less pleasantly, constant spitting is necessary: in traditional houses you spit through any hole in the floorboards, while in more elegant households a spittoon is provided. It doesn't do much for your looks either: betel-chewers are easily spotted by their rotten teeth and lips stained scarlet from the habit.

When travelling long distances, chewers carry basketloads of the ingredients with them; at home, guests are served from a **betel set**, comprising at least three small covered receptacles, and sometimes a tray to hold these boxes and the knife or nut-cracker used to split the fruit. Betel-chewing today is popular mainly with elderly Thais, particularly northeastern women, but it used to be a much more widespread social custom, and a person's betel tray set was once a Thai's most prized possession and an indication of rank: royalty would have sets made in gold, the nobility's would be in silver or nielloware, and poorer folk wove theirs from rattan or carved them from wood. Betel sets still feature as important dowry items in Isaan, with tray-giving processions forming part of northeastern engagement ceremonies.

Practicalities

Khon Kaen is easily reached by road or rail from Bangkok and most other major towns in the northeast. **Trains** from Bangkok leave five times daily, taking between seven and eight hours; two of these go via Khorat and continue as far as Udon Thani; the other three bypass Khorat en route to the end of the line at Nong Khai. The **train station** is just off Highway 2 on the southwestern edge of town, about fifteen minutes' walk from the main hotel area. More than twenty air-conditioned **buses** come from Bangkok daily , taking six to seven hours; regular bus connections also serve Chaiyaphum, Nong Khai via Udon Thani, Khorat, Ubon and Phitsanulok. The main **bus station** is on Prachasamoson Road, a five-minute walk northwest of the Klang Muang Road hotels; the air-conditioned-bus terminal is right in the town centre, at the junction of Ammat and Klang Muang roads. Three daily **flights** make the Bangkok–Khon Kaen trip, in both directions, taking fifty minutes, and there are three *Thai Airways* flights a week from Khon Kaen to Sakhon Nakhon and back (35min); the **airport** is 6km west of the city centre. If you want to **rent your own transport**, you're looking at around B1200 a day for a smallish car (excluding petrol): try either *Air Booking Centre* at 403 Si Chan Rd (☎043/244482) or *Kaen Koon Car Rent* at 54/1-2 Klang Muang Rd (☎043/239458). For help with car rental or any other local queries, call in at the welcoming, well-informed **TAT** office (☎043/244498) on Prachasamoson Road, about five minutes' walk east of the bus station.

Accommodation

Accommodation in Khon Kaen is plentiful and reasonably priced, with most of the hotels along Klang Muang Road. Best value in the budget category is *Suksawad* (☎043/236472; ①–②): set back from the road, it's quiet, and all rooms have fan and shower. Rooms at *Sansumran* (☎043/239611; ②) are fairly similar, while *Roma* (☎043/236276; ③–⑤) has fairly well-maintained fan-cooled rooms and slightly better air-conditioned ones. *Kaen Inn* (☎043/236866; ⑥) is the biggest and most upmarket place along this road: all rooms are air-conditioned and come with shower, TV and fridge. Khon Kaen's newest and poshest hotel is a little further south on Si Chan Road: *Charoenthani Princess* (☎043/220400; ⑦–⑧) has the works – bars, restaurants, a nightclub and a range of moderately luxurious rooms.

Shopping

Khon Kaen is great for **shopping**, its stores boasting a huge range of regional **arts and crafts**, including high-quality Isaan silk of all designs and weaves. One of the best outlets is the cavernous *Prathamakant Local Goods Centre* at the southern end of town at 81 Ruen Rom Rd. Although aimed squarely at tourists, the selection here is quite phenomenal: hundreds of gorgeous *mut mee* (see p.374) cotton and silk weaves, as well as clothes, furnishings, triangular axe pillows of all sizes, *khaen* pipes and silver jewellery. Itinerant vendors, who wander the main streets with panniers stuffed full of silk and cotton lengths, also offer competitive prices, and though the choice is restricted you can be sure most of the money will go to the weavers. Klang Muang Road, lined with small but often specialized shops and a huge covered fresh- and dry-goods market, is another good area for local products. *DK Books,* across the road from *Roma*, stocks some English-language **books** and a fair selection of regional **maps**, while there's a smaller books outlet in the *Fairy Plaza*, the glitzy air-conditioned shopping centre on Si Chan Road.

Khon Kaen also makes a reasonable base from which to explore the local **silk-weaving centre** of **Chonnabot**, about 54km southwest of the city. Traditionally a cottage industry, this small town's silk production has become centralized over the last few years, and weavers now gather in small workshops in town, each specializing in just one aspect of the process. You can walk in and watch the women (it's still exclusively women's work) at their wheels, looms or dye vats, and then buy from the vendors in the street out front. To get to Chonnabot from Khon Kaen take any ordinary Khorat-bound bus to **Ban Phae** (every 30min), and then a songthaew for the final 10km to Chonnabot.

Eating

Khon Kaen has a reputation for very **spicy food**, particularly sausages, *sai krog isaan*, which are served with cubes of raw ginger, onion, lime and plenty of chilli sauce, at stalls along Klang Muang Road between the *Suksawad* and *Kaen Inn*. You can also sample these and other local favourites – such as pigs' trotters, roast duck and shellfish – at the stalls along the northern edge of Bueng Kaen Nakhon. There's quite a choice of restaurants around the lake as well, including one that actually juts out over it, which makes a pleasant spot to spend the evening. For inexpensive *pat thai* and *khao pat*, with air conditioning, go to *Coffee Break*, west of Klang Muang Road off Sri Chan Road. *First Choice*, opposite *Khon Kaen Hotel* on Pimpasoot Road, is another farang-friendly restaurant, offering air-conditioned premises and an English-language menu detailing a large range of moderately priced Thai, Western and Japanese options, plus a sizeable vegetarian selection. For take-away food, *Neam Lap La* at the top end of Klang Muang Road, just north of *Roma Hotel,* is the place to buy spicy sausages, sugar-coated beans and other Khon Kaen specialities.

Udon Thani and Ban Chiang

Economically important but charmless, **UDON THANI** looms for most travellers as a misty, early-morning sprawl of grey cement seen from the window of the overnight train to Nong Khai. The capital of an arid rice-growing province, 137km north of Khon Kaen, Udon was given an economic shot in the arm during the Vietnam War with the siting of a huge American military base nearby, and despite the American withdrawal in 1976, the town has maintained its rapid industrial and commercial development. The only conceivable reason to alight here would be to satisfy a lust for archaeology at the excavated Bronze Age settlement of **BAN CHIANG**, 50km to the east in sleepy farming country, though plenty of travellers avoid spending time in Udon by visiting Ban Chiang on a day trip from the much preferable base of Nong Khai (2–3hr each way).

The village of Ban Chiang is unremarkable nowadays, though its fertile setting is attractive. It achieved worldwide fame in 1966, when a rich seam of archaeological remains was accidentally discovered: clay pots, uncovered in human graves alongside sophisticated **bronze** objects, were dated to around 3000 BC, implying the same date for the bronze pieces; Ban Chiang was immediately hailed as the vanguard of the Bronze Age, seven hundred years before Mesopotamia's discovery of the metal. Unfortunately the archaeologists' triumph was spiked by a later, more accurate test that set the date at around 2000 BC. Nevertheless Ban Chiang stands as one of the world's earliest bronze producers, its methods of smelting showing no signs of influence from northern China and other neighbouring bronze cultures, which suggests the area was the birthplace of Southeast Asian civilization.

The present village's fine **National Museum** (Tues–Sun 9am–4pm; B10) displays some of the choicest finds from Ban Chiang and provides a richly informative commentary. It also contains the country's best collection of characteristic late-period Ban Chiang clay pots, with their red whorled patterns on a buff background – although not of prime historical significance, these have become an attractive emblem of Ban Chiang, and freely adapted by local souvenir producers – and takes you through the stages of manufacturing them. A single room in the museum is dedicated to the modern village; the tale it tells, of the rapid disappearance of traditional ways, is an all-too-familiar lament in Thailand. The story, however, doesn't quite end there: the recent influx of tourists has encouraged local farming villages to turn to their looms again, producing especially rich and intricate lengths of silk and cotton *mut mee* for sale in the souvenir shops around the museum.

In the grounds of **Wat Pho Si Nai**, on the south side of the village, part of an early dig has been canopied over and opened to the public (same times and ticket as the museum). Two burial pits have been left exposed to show how and where artefacts were found.

Practicalities

Buses pull into Udon Thani at a variety of locations, depending on where they've come from: Loei, Phitsanulok and Chiang Mai services use the terminal on the town's western bypass; Nong Khai buses also stop here, though their main station is at Talat Langsina (Langsina market, also used by Ban Phu buses) on the north side of town; Bangkok and Khorat services arrive at Wattana Road, northeast of the

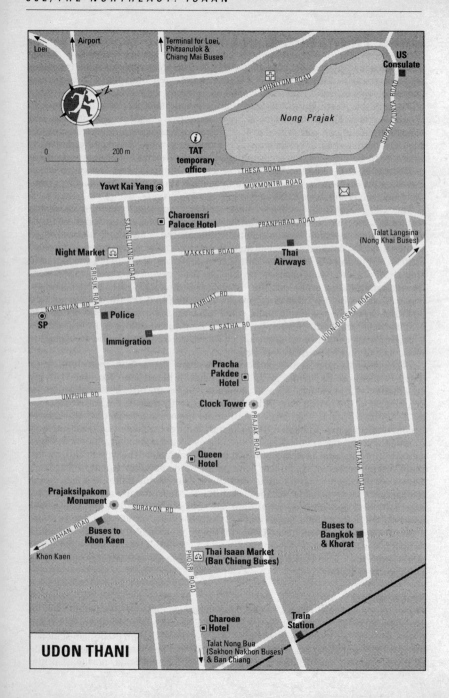

Airport
Loei
Terminal for Loei,
Phitsanulok &
Chiang Mai Buses

US
Consulate

POHNIYOM ROAD

Nong Prajak

SUPAKITJUNYA ROAD

0   200 m

i
TAT
temporary
office

THESA ROAD

Yawt Kai Yang

MUKMONTRI ROAD

Charoensri
Palace Hotel

PRANPHRAD ROAD

Talat Langsina
(Nong Khai Buses)

SAENGLUANG ROAD

MAKKENG ROAD

Thai
Airways

Night Market

SRISUK ROAD

NARESUAN RD

TAMRUAT RD

SP

Police

SI SATHA RD

UDON-DUSSADI ROAD

Immigration

Pracha
Pakdee
Hotel

UMPHUR RD

Clock Tower

PRAJAK ROAD

WATTANA ROAD

Queen
Hotel

Prajaksilpakom
Monument

SURAKON RD

THAHAN ROAD

Buses to
Khon Kaen

Khon Kaen

Buses to
Bangkok
& Khorat

PHOSRI ROAD

Thai Isaan Market
(Ban Chiang Buses)

Charoen
Hotel

Train
Station

Talat Nong Bua
(Sakhon Nakhon Buses)
& Ban Chiang

UDON THANI

centre; east of the centre, Ban Chiang buses base themselves at the morning market, Talat Thai Isaan, on Phosri Road, which changes its name further out to Nityo Road before passing Talat Nong Bua (Sakhon Nakhon services); on the south side of town, Khon Kaen buses stop on Thahan Road, south of the Prajaksilpakom Monument. Arriving by **train** is no more convenient, as the station lies a good 2km east of the town centre. The best way of connecting these points is in a **skylab**, Udon's version of a tuk-tuk (B15 and upwards per journey). From the **airport**, 3km west of the centre, *Thai Airways'* air-conditioned minibuses run passengers downtown (B30 per person) and direct to Nong Khai (B100 per person).

To **get to Ban Chiang** from Udon, either take a direct bus (hourly until 2pm), or catch a Sakhon Nakhon-bound bus (every 25min) and then a tuk-tuk (B10 per person) for the last 5km or so from the main road to the village.

Udon has a friendly **TAT office** (☎042/241968), which also covers Nong Khai and Loei provinces; housed at the moment in Phosri Road's Provincial Education Office, on the south side of Nong Prajak, a lake and park to the northwest of the centre, it's scheduled to move soon to Thesa Road on the east side of the lake. A small **US consulate** overlooks the northern side of Nong Prajak, at 35/6 Supakitjunya Rd (☎042/244271).

ACCOMMODATION AND EATING

There's no accommodation in Ban Chiang, but you can get a simple fried lunch at one of the village cafés. In Udon, the *Prachapakdee Hotel* at 156/7–9 Prajak Rd (☎042/221804; ②) is your best budget bet, with reasonably clean rooms set back from the road overlooking a yard; the *Queen Hotel*, 6–8 Udon–Dussadi Rd (☎042/221451; ②), also has a central location and decent rooms. Moving upmarket, the *Charoensri Palace Hotel*, 60 Phosri Rd (☎042/242611–3; ⑤), is a popular businessmen's haunt which offers large, clean bedrooms with air conditioning and hot water. Several luxury hotels, including the Imperial Group's *Charoensri* (271/5 Prajak Rd; ☎042/242777), are in the offing, but for the moment Udon's finest remains the *Charoen Hotel* at 549 Phosri Rd (☎042/248155, Bangkok ☎02/476 8837–40; ⑦), which has air-conditioned rooms with hot showers and TVs, and a swimming pool outside.

Delicious *kai yang* (barbecued chicken) and *khao niaw* (sticky rice) are served at several inexpensive **restaurants** around the junction of Prajak and Pranphrao roads, and at the larger *Yawt Kai Yang* on the corner of Phosri and Mukmontri roads, which also offers a good *som tam* (spicy mango salad). For a greater variety of low-priced comestibles – Thai, Chinese and Vietnamese – head for the night market on Makkeng Road between Saengluang and Srisuk roads. A hangover from Nam days is *SP* at 63/2 Naresuan Rd, which rustles up good steaks, pizzas, burgers and french fries.

Loei and around

Most people carry on from Udon Thani straight north to Nong Khai (see p.372), but making a detour via **LOEI**, 147km to the west, takes you within range of three towering national parks and sets you up for a lazy tour along the Mekhong River. The capital of a province renowned for the unusual shapes of its stark, craggy mountains, Loei is, more significantly, the crossroads of one of Thailand's least tamed border regions; from Laos come all manner of illegal goods and

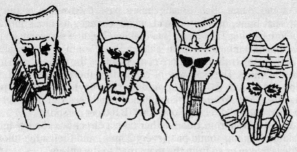

Phi Ta Kon masks

refugees, especially Hmong tribespeople, who are still punished for siding with the Americans during the Vietnam War by the communist Pathet Lao, who seized control of Laos at the end of the war in 1975. The border area to the northwest remains sensitive after a major skirmish with Laos in 1987 over disputed territory, and Thai soldiers are often to be seen around Loei town.

Despite its frontier feel, the town, lying along the west bank of the small Loei River, is generally friendly and offers legitimate products of its own: tamarind paste and pork sausages are sold in industrial quantities along Ararree Road (off Charoenrat Road, Loei's main street, which runs roughly parallel to the river), while local quilts and lengths of silk and cotton in strong, simple designs are available at *Dork Fai*, 138/2 Charoenrat Rd, and at the more refined *Chao Sakul*, 4 Ararree Rd.

One reason to make a special trip to this region is to attend the unique rain-making festival of **Phi Ta Kon**, held either at the end of June or the beginning of July in **Dan Sai**, 80km southwest of Loei. In order to encourage the heavens to open, young men dress up as spirits in patchwork rags and fierce, brightly painted wooden masks, and then parade the town's most sacred Buddha image round the streets, while making fun of as many onlookers as they can and generally having themselves a whale of a time. The carnival can be visited in a day from Loei, though rooms are hard to come by at this time; a tamer version of the procession is tacked onto the otherwise uninspiring Cotton Blossom Festival, held in Loei town in February.

Practicalities

Beyond its meagre attractions, Loei is really only useful as a transport hub. **Buses** run here from Udon Thani and Khon Kaen every thirty minutes, from Phitsanulok in the central plains seven times a day and from Bangkok (via Chaiyaphum) seventeen times a day. Half-hourly songthaews link the town to Chiang Khan, an hour to the north at the start of the Mekhong River route, while little green buses run hourly in the mornings to Sang Khom (3hr, bypassing Chiang Khan) and all the way to Nong Khai (6–7hr) – though it's quicker to catch a bus to Udon and change if you're going straight from Loei to Nong Khai. All of these arrive and depart at the **bus terminal** on Ruamjai Road, the main cast–west street, about 300m west of the intersection with Charoenrat Road.

ACCOMMODATION AND EATING

Unless it's festival time, finding a decent **place to stay** in Loei shouldn't be a problem. Turn left out of the bus station towards the river and left again into an unmarked soi to reach the town's only guest house, *Muang Loei*, 103/72 Ruamjai

Rd (☎042/832839; ①), where cubicles in a modern building contain a double bed, mosquito net and not much else. The bubbly owner can give some help with local information, and rents out bikes and motorbikes at a daily rate of B40 and B200 respectively. Comfortable and centrally placed, *Thai Udom Hotel*, at 122/1 Charoenrat Rd (☎042/811763; ③–④), has rooms with fan or air conditioning, all with hot-water bathrooms. The newer, quieter *Muang Fai* (*Cotton Inn*), south of the centre at 191/1–9 Charoenrat Rd (☎042/811302), offers the same choice of facilities at marginally lower rates.

The **food** at the *Nawng Neung Restaurant*, next to the Thai Military Bank at 8/22 Ruamjai Rd, is delicious and very economical – *khao man kai* and *khao moo daeng* (chicken rice and pork rice) and noodle soup are specialities – but it's only open until 3pm. The central night market, on the east side of Charoenrat Road, serves up the usual budget eats, as well as the distinctly uncommon local delicacy, *khai ping* – barbecued eggs on skewers, which taste like coarse, salty soufflés. *Savita Bakery* at 137 Charoenrat Rd does cakes, Western breakfasts, ice cream and good coffee, plus an inexpensive buffet and a wide-ranging menu of Thai food.

Phu Kradung National Park

The most accessible of the parks in Loei province, **PHU KRADUNG NATIONAL PARK**, about 80km south of Loei, protects a grassy 1300-metre plateau whose temperate climate supports a number of tree, flower and bird species not normally found in tropical Thailand. Walking trails crisscross much of sixty-square-kilometre Phu Kradung (Bell Mountain), and you ought to reckon on spending three days here if you want to explore them fully – at a minimum you'll have to spend one night, as the trip from Loei to the top of the plateau and back can't be done in a day. The park is closed during the rainy season (June–Sept), due to the increased risk of mud-slides and land-slips.

Access and accommodation

To get to the park, take any bus between Loei and Khon Kaen and get off at the village of **Phu Kradung** (1hr 30min), then hop on a B7 songthaew for the remaining 7km to the **visitors' centre**, where you can pick up a trail map and pay the B25 admission fee.

The park's primitive **accommodation** is up on the plateau; you can leave your gear at the visitors' centre, or hire a porter to tote it to the top for B8 per kilo. At park headquarters, 8km from the visitors' centre, the least costly room (④) in a national park bungalow has enough mattresses and blankets for ten; tents can be hired for B40 per day, blankets (needed on cool-season nights) for B10. A private concern, *Phu Kradung House*, operates on the south side of the plateau, 7km from the visitors' centre (Bangkok reservations ☎02/271 3737; ③). Small A-frame huts, equipped with a light mattress and a decent blanket, squeeze together in holiday-camp rows. A simple **restaurant** there competes with several at park headquarters and at the rim of the plateau, all of which can rustle up inexpensive, tasty food from limited ingredients, so there's no need to bring your own provisions.

The park

The gruelling main **trail** leads from the visitors' centre 5km up the eastern side of Phu Kradung, passing occasional refreshment stalls; most people take at least three hours, including rest stops. The path becomes steeper and rockier in the last 1km, with wooden steps over the most difficult parts, but it's worth it for the unbelievable view as your head peeps over the rim: flat as a playing field, the broad plateau is dotted with odd clumps of pine trees, thinned by periodic lightning fires, which give it the appearance of a country park. Several feeder trails fan out from here, including a twelve-kilometre path along the precipitous southern edge that offers sweeping views of Dong Phaya Yen, the untidy range of mountains to the southeast that forms the unofficial border between the northeast and the central plains. Another trail heads along the eastern rim for 2.5km to Pha Nok An – also reached by a two-kilometre path due east from the headquarters – which looks down on neat ricefields and matchbox-like houses in the valley below, an outlook that's especially breathtaking at sunrise.

The attractions of the mountain come and go with the **seasons**. October is muddy after the rains, but the waterfalls which tumble off the northwestern edge of the plateau are in full cascade and the main trail is green and shady. December brings out the maple leaves, but by February the waterfalls have disappeared and the vegetation on the lower slopes has been burnt away. April is good for the rhododendrons and wild roses, which in Thailand are only found at such high altitudes as this.

Among the park's **wildlife**, mammals such as elephants, sambar deer and gibbons can be seen very occasionally, but they generally confine themselves to the evergreen forest on the northern part of the plateau, which is out of bounds to visitors. In the temperate pines, oaks and beeches that dot the rest of the plateau you're more likely to spot resident **birds** such as jays, sultan tits and snowy-browed flycatchers if you're out walking in the early morning and evening.

Phu Reua National Park

About 50km west of Loei, **PHU REUA NATIONAL PARK** gets the name "Boat Mountain" from its resemblance to an upturned sampan, with the sharp ridge of its hull running southeast to northwest. The highest point of the ridge (1365m) offers one of the most spectacular panoramas in Thailand: the land drops away sharply on the Laos side, allowing views over toytown villages to countless green-ridged mountains spreading towards Luang Prabang. To the northwest rises Phu Soai Dao (2102m) on Laos' western border; to the south are the Phetchabun mountains.

Access and accommodation

The Tourism Authority of Thailand has recently sponsored a nine-kilometre paved road north from Highway 203 to the summit, so the park can get crowded at weekends though during the week you'll probably have the place to yourself. The snag is that there's no organized **public transport** up the steep summit road – regular Lom Sak and Phitsanulok buses from Loei will drop you at the turn-off to the park on Highway 203, but then you'll have to walk/hitch or ask at the small supermarket on the west side of the turn-off for a ride (about B100 by motorbike, B150 by pick-up). The easiest thing would be to **rent a motorbike** at *Muang Loei Guest House* in Loei (see p.364). Once on the summit road, you'll have to pay B20 admission at a checkpoint, before reaching the **visitors' centre** after 4km, which has a trail map and wildlife photos labelled in English, several simple restaurants with erratic opening hours, and, in the pretty, pine-shaded grounds, standard-issue, five-berth national park **bungalows** (④). **Tents** are available for a minimal fee at the visitors' centre and can be pitched at the campsite (4km further up the mountain and 1500m along a dirt road from the summit road), where food stalls also set up shop at weekends. Warm clothes are essential on cool-season nights – the lowest temperature in Thailand (-4°C) was recorded here in 1981 – and even by day the mountain is usually cool and breezy.

The park

A day's worth of well-marked trails fan out over the meadows and pine and broad-leaved evergreen forests of Phu Reua, taking in gardens of strange rock formations, the best westerly viewpoint, Phu Kut, and, during and just after the rainy season, several waterfalls. The park's population of barking deer, wild pigs and pheasants has declined over recent years – rangers' attempts to stop poaching by local villagers have been largely unsuccessful and have resulted in occasional armed clashes – but you may be lucky enough to spot one of 26 bird species, which include the crested serpent-eagle, green-billed malkoha, greater coucal, Asian fairy bluebird, rufescent prinia and white-rumped munia, as well as several species of babbler, barbet, bulbul and drongo.

Phu Hin Rongkla National Park

Thailand's densely forested hills and mountains have always harboured bandits and insurgents, and the rugged 300-square-kilometre tract of highland known as **PHU HIN RONGKLA NATIONAL PARK** is no exception: for over a decade these mountains, straddling Phitsanulok, Phetchabun and Loei provinces, were the stronghold of the **Communist Party of Thailand**. Founded in 1942 and banned ten years later, the CPT went underground and by 1967 had established a self-contained command centre in Phu Hin Rongkla, complete with a hospital, library and a printing press that even issued birth and death certificates. Despite assaults on the Phu Hin Rongkla base from government forces, numbers swelled in the wake of the murderous suppression of Bangkok pro-democracy demonstrations in 1973 and 1976. Then, in 1978, a policy of amnesty in return for the surrender of weapons was extended to the students and others who had fled to the hills; over the next few years, as CPT members returned to the cities, the party began to crumble. As the threat of insurgence diminished, the government built roads through Phu Hin Rongkla and other inaccessible parts of Isaan; finally, in 1982, Phu Hin Rongkla was declared a national park.

The park's history is a significant part of its appeal but for most visitors Phu Hin Rongkla is principally a refreshing change of scenery – and temperature – from the plains to the east and west. At an elevation that rises to about 1800m, much of the park's vegetation is typical of a tropical mountain forest, with trees growing much further apart than they do in the valleys, leaving occasional expanses of exposed rock peppered by low-lying scrub and montane flowers. Walking through these open forests is relatively easy, and the park's few short trails take you across some of the most attractive parts of the stony terrain.

Access and accommodation

Getting to Phu Hin Rongkla by public transport is a hassle, involving uncertain connections and lengthy journeys. **From Loei**, take a Phitsanulok-bound bus to either **Nakhon Thai** (130km southwest on the junction of routes 2013 and 2331), or **Lom Sak** (140km down Highway 203); **from Phitsanulok**, take an hourly bus direct to Nakhon Thai. Route 2331 is the main access road through the park and about three songthaews make the daily 20km run from Nakhon Thai to the park visitors' centre and back. From Lom Sak you'll have to hire a motorbike taxi to take you the 30km to the vistors' centre (about B100).

All in all, considering you have to trek fair distances along Route 2331 to get between trail heads once you're in the park, you're much better off renting your own transport from either Phitsanulok or Loei. If travelling by **car** or **motorbike** from Loei, your quickest route is west via Route 203, then south on 2013 to Nakhon Thai, and southeast on 2331. From Phitsanulok, follow Highway 12 eastwards towards Lomsak for 68km, then north along Route 2013 to Nakhon Thai.

About 10km after entering the park gates via Nakhon Thai on Route 2331, you'll reach the **visitors' centre**, alongside the park headquarters and a rudimentary restaurant. The centre doubles as a small CPT **museum** and provides free maps giving trail distances and routes. There's not really enough in the park to merit an **overnight stay**, but if you do get stuck, there are bungalows here for B100 per person and two-person tents for B40. It's also possible to stay in Lom Sak: *Pen Sin 1* at 33/8 Wachi Rd (☎056/701545; ①–②) and *Sawang Hotel* at 147/6 Samakkichai Rd (☎056/701642; ①–②) are both within a few minutes' walk of the bus station.

The park

The best of the park's trails is the 3.5-kilometre **Lan Hin Pum** (One Million Knotty Rocks), which starts about 5km east of the visitors' centre. It runs through a superb natural rock garden that's particularly pretty in the rainy season when wild orchids and all kinds of hardy flowers bloom amongst the mosses, ferns and lichen. Halfway through the circuit you come to a precipice overlooking dense jungle, usually with plenty of mist to heighten the atmosphere; the route also passes the office of the Communist Party's headquarters, as well as Pha Chu Thong, the so-called "flag-raising cliff" where the red flag was unfurled after every CPT victory.

A less dramatic 1500-metre walk across **Lan Hin Daeg** (One Million Broken Rocks) begins 3km west of the visitors' centre. The rocks here are so deeply fissured that at times it feels like picking your way across a stegosaurus's back; clogged with ferns and mosses, the well-camouflaged crevices made ideal natural hideouts and air-raid shelters for the CPT – with full command of terrain like this, it's hardly surpring that the CPT withstood some fifteen years of persistent battery from the government forces.

ALONG THE MEKHONG

Having descended from its Tibetan sources through China, Burma and Laos, with a brief stint along Thailand's northern frontier, the mighty **Mekhong River** reappears on the scene in Isaan to form 750km of the border between Thailand and Laos. Word is beginning to get out about this remote and dramatic margin, and as Laos opens further border crossings to visitors, the Mekhong will become more of a busy transport link and less of a forbidding barrier.

The guest houses along the upper stretch, east from **Chiang Khan**, are geared towards relaxation and gentle exploration of the rural way of life. **Nong Khai**, the terminus of the rail line from Bangkok and the principal jumping-off point for trips to the Laotian capital of Vientiane, is the pivotal town on the river, but has lost some of its restful charm since the building of the massive Thai-Australian

Friendship Bridge and the ensuing increase in cross-border trade. East of Nong Khai you're into wild country. The unique natural beauty of **Wat Phu Tok** is well worth the hefty detour, and your Mekhong journey wouldn't be complete without seeing **Wat Phra That Phanom**, a place of pilgrimage for 2500 years. Sights get sparse beyond that, although by continuing south through **Mukdahan** you'll be able to join up with the southern Isaan route at Ubon Ratchathani (see p.347).

A road, served by very slow **buses** and **songthaews**, runs beside or at least parallel to the river as far as Mukdahan. If you've got the time (allow at least a week to do it any sort of justice) you could make the entire marathon journey described in this section, although realistically you'll probably start in Nong Khai and work your way either upstream or downstream from there. **Motorbike** rental may provide another incentive to base yourself in Nong Khai: having your own transport will give you more freedom of movement in this region, and the roads are quiet and easy to negotiate. There's no long-distance **boat** transport along this stretch of the river – you'll have to settle for brief forays by chartered boat or inner tube.

Chiang Khan to Tha Bo

Rustic "backpackers' resorts" – and the travelling between them – are the chief draw along the reach of the Mekhong between Chiang Khan and Tha Bo. Highway 211 covers this whole course: songthaews take you as far as Pak Chom, from where buses complete the journey, stopping at all towns en route.

Chiang Khan

The Mekhong route starts promisingly at **CHIANG KHAN**, a friendly town that happily hasn't been converted to concrete yet. Rows of wooden shophouses stretch out in a two-kilometre-long ribbon parallel to the river, which for much of the year runs red with what locals call the "blood of the trees": rampant deforestation on the Laotian side causes the rust-coloured topsoil to erode into the river. The town has only two streets – the main through route (Highway 211, also known as Sri Chiang Khan Road) and the quieter Sai Khong Road on the waterfront – with a line of sois connecting them numbered from west to east. Songthaews from Loei and Pak Chom stop at the west end of town near the junction of Highway 201 (the road from Loei) and Highway 211.

Arguably the most enjoyable thing you can do here is to hitch up with other travellers for a **boat trip** on the river, organized through one of the guest houses. If you opt to go **upstream**, you'll head west towards the lofty mountains of Khao Laem and Khao Ngu on the Thai side and Phu Lane and Phu Hat Song in Laos, gliding round a long, slow bend to **Tha Dee Mee**, 20km from Chiang Khan, where the Mekhong is joined by the Heuang River, which forms the border to the west of this point; stops can be arranged at the Ban Khok Mat Queen's Project to see silk and cotton weaving and an agricultural experiment area, and at Hat Sai Kaew, a sandy beach for swimming. Trips cost between B400 and B570 per boat depending on how far you venture. A ride **downstream to Pak Chom** will take you through some of the most beautiful scenery on the Thai Mekhong: hills and cliffs of all shapes and sizes advance and recede around the winding flow, and outside the rainy season, the rapids are dramatic without being dangerous (best between Dec and April), and the shores and islands are enlivened by neat grids of market gardens. This jaunt costs around B1000 for the boat, and takes around six hours, including an hour in Pak Chom, if you go both ways.

It's also worth taking a walk towards the eastern end of the river road to **Wat Tha Khok**, by Soi 20, for its unobstructed view across the majestic Mekhong. The Laotian viharn shows some odd French influences in its balustrades, rounded arches and elegantly coloured ceiling. Continuing another 2km east along the main highway, a left turn back towards the river will bring you to **Wat Tha Khaek**, a formerly ramshackle forest temple which, on the back of millions of bahts' worth of donations from Thai tourists, has embarked on an ambitious building programme in a bizarre mix of traditional and modern styles. One kilometre further along this side road lies the reason for the influx of visitors: at this point, the river runs over rocks at a wide bend to form the modest rapids of **Kaeng Kut Khu**. Set against the forested hillside of imaginatively named Phu Yai (Big Mountain), it's a pretty enough spot, with small restaurants and souvenir shops shaded by trees on the river bank.

Practicalities

When it comes to **accommodation**, the *Nong Sam Guest House* (☎042/821457; ②) has the most relaxing and scenic spot in town: smart brick rooms with ceiling fans and mosquito screens are strewn around a quiet, ramshackle compound by the Mekhong, 1km west of the centre. The owners rent out bicycles (B50 per day) and can advise on local exploration. *Zen Guest House* (①), which has clean, simple wooden rooms on quiet Soi 12, advertises a range of activities, including massages, herbal steam baths and bicycle rental (B30–50 per day); there's also a borrowing library strong on spiritual matters, and a fully equipped kitchen – but smoking is not allowed anywhere on the premises. *Poonsawat Guest House*, 251/2 Soi 9 (☎042/821114; ①), weighs in as Chiang Khan's most affordable option, with cleanish rooms in an old wooden building; the kitchen's open to budding Thai chefs, the unusual luxury of a hot shower can be had for B10, and a motorbike can be rented for B150 per day. A more traditional wooden hotel is the *Souksomboon Hotel* (☎042/821064; ②), built around a courtyard on Sai Khong Road between sois 8 and 9, with a café and its best rooms overlooking the river. If you want more in the way of luxury, the unwelcoming *Chiang Khan Hill Resort* (☎042/821285; ⑤– ⑥) has fan-cooled and air-conditioned rooms in a pretty garden at Kaeng Kut Khu.

The most fruitful hunting grounds for **food** are the day market, on the south side of Sri Chiang Khan Road between sois 9 and 10, and the night market (6– 8pm), between sois 18 and 19 on the same road. For a hearty *pat thai*, head for *Lom Look* on the east side of Soi 9.

Pak Chom, Sang Khom and Wat Hin Ma Beng

Half-hourly songthaews from Chiang Khan cover the beautiful, winding route to **PAK CHOM**, 41km downriver, where you can pick up a bus from Loei to continue your journey towards Nong Khai. Pak Chom used to be the site of a refugee camp for fifteen thousand Laotian Hmong, who in 1992 were moved to Chiang Rai province; its array of largely redundant administrative buildings has something of the air of a ghost town, offering little incentive to stay. If you get stuck, the *Pak Chom Guest House* (②), at the west end of town, is at least set in leafy grounds, with primitive bungalows on stilts overlooking the river.

Beyond Pak Chom the road through the Mekhong valley becomes flatter and straighter. After 50km, a sign in English points down a side road to **Than Tip Falls**, 3km south, which is well worth seeking out. The ten-metre-high waterfall splashes down into a rock pool overhung by jungle on three sides; higher up, a bigger waterfall has a good pool for swimming, and if you can face the climb you can explore three higher levels.

Staying in idyllic, tree-shaded **SANG KHOM**, 63km east of Pak Chom, puts you in the heart of an especially lush stretch of the river within easy **biking** distance of several backroad villages and temples. You can rent bicycles (B30–60 per day) and a motorbike (B180) at *Bouy Guest House* (☎042/441605; ①), which enjoys the best location of the village's **"backpackers' resorts"**: decent bamboo huts with beautiful views out over the river are set in a spacious compound, half of it on a spit of land reached by a wooden bridge over a small tributary. The owners also have inner tubes, dugout canoes and fishing boats to get you onto the Mekhong, and if that sounds too strenuous, there's a herbal sauna or you can get yourself massaged. Further downstream, *River Huts* (☎042/441012; ①) occupies a smaller patch of shady river bank, with bungalows that run to tables, chairs and verandahs. As well as herbal saunas, a motorbike and bicycles – for travellers with their own bikes, the owner is a dab hand at repairs – the establishment offers good food, a large library and an inflatable kayak. On the eastern side of the village, the oldest guest house in Sang Khom, *TXK* (①), was almost obliterated in the heavy rainy season of 1994, when the Mekhong washed away most of its land and bungalows. The ebullient owner, Mama, is looking for new premises, but for the moment clings onto the steep river bank with a handful of primitive huts. Compensations are as much free sticky rice and bananas as you can eat, a dugout canoe, and the least costly bed in Sang Khom, if you're prepared to sleep in an open-sided sala.

Another 19km east on Route 211, **Wat Hin Ma Beng** is a famous meditation temple, popular with Thai pilgrims and rich donors. The long white boundary wall and huge modern buildings are evidence of the temple's prosperity, but its reputation is in fact based on the asceticism of the monks, who keep themselves in strict poverty and allow only one meal a day to interrupt their meditation. The flood of merit-makers, however, proved too distracting for the founder of the wat, Luang Phu Thet, who before his death in 1994 decamped to the peace and quiet of Wat Tham Kham near Sakhon Nakhon. Visitors have the opportunity to revere an unnervingly lifelike waxwork of the great monk that has been set up next to the river, near a large statue of a tiger, the symbol of hermits. Across the narrow stretch of water here, you can get a good look at a much less prosperous Laotian forest wat.

Sri Chiangmai and Wat Nam Mong

Unprepossessing it may be, but **SRI CHIANGMAI**, 38km east of Sang Khom, is known in Chinese catering circles as one of the world's leading manufacturing centres of spring-roll wrappers: if the weather's fine, production of these rice-flour discs, which you can see drying on bamboo racks around the town and taste in local restaurants, hits 200,000 pieces per day. Outside of the rainy season, the resourceful burghers of Sri Chiangmai also reclaim vast tracts of land from the Mekhong to grow tomatoes, which has led to the establishment of Thailand's largest ketchup factory and a jolly tomato festival, featuring messy tomato-eating contests, in February. Many of these tomato growers and spring-roll-wrapper makers are Vietnamese, victims of the upheavals caused by World War II and two

Indochina wars since, who have fled across Laos to safe haven in Thailand. The town also offers the unique opportunity of gazing at the backstreets of Vientiane, directly across the Mekong, without having to go through all the expensive red tape to get there. It looks quite unappealing and lifeless, replicating the same concrete architecture as on the Thai side.

Here again, one outstanding **guest house** makes the town accessible to farangs who want to experience its daily life. *Tim Guest House* (☎042/451072; ①) has clean, quiet rooms at 553 Moo 2 Rimkhong Rd (the riverfront road), and spoils homesick guests with ham, pâté, French bread and good coffees, as well as dishing up some tasty Thai food. The Swiss manager is hospitable and informative, and, as well as herbal saunas and massages, can arrange bicycle (B30 a day) and motorbike (B150) rental – the guest house is a handy jumping-off point for **Ban Phu** (see p.378), 40km south. **Boat trips** (B500 per boat), past the suburbs of Vientiane, river islands and swimming beaches to Wat Hin Ma Beng, are also on offer, when you might be lucky enough to see gold panners and fishermen at work, wild ducks, herons and kingfishers.

Thanks to ketchup and spring-roll traffic, the condition of Highway 211 and the frequency of buses improve noticeably east of Sri Chiangmai. **Wat Nam Mong** can be seen across the fields on the west side of the road, 12km out of Sri Chiangmai and 3km before **Tha Bo**. A slender Laotian-style viharn makes the perfect setting for the gaunt Phra Ong Thu image inside. Stern but handsome, the 300-year-old bronze image is the brother of a more famous Buddha in Laos – it's much revered, especially by Laotian emigrants, some of whom even send their sons from the United States to serve as monks here.

Nong Khai and around

The major border town in these parts is **NONG KHAI** (population 25,000), still a backwater but developing fast since the construction of the huge Thai-Australian Friendship Bridge over the Mekong on the west side of town. Occupying a strategic position at the end of Highway 2 and the northeastern rail line, and just 24km from Vientiane, Nong Khai acts as a conduit for goods bought and sold by Thais and Laotians, who are allowed to pass between the two cities freely for stays of up to three days. For the souvenir markets that have sprung up around the main pier, Tha Sadet, and the slipway to the bridge, the Laotians bring across silver, wood and cane items, and sundry goods from the old Soviet bloc, such as vacuum cleaners and samovars. They return with noodles, soap powder, ketchup, warm clothes and toilet rolls.

As with most of the towns along this part of the Mekong, the thing to do in Nong Khai is just to take it easy, enjoying the riverside atmosphere and the peaceful settings of the good-value guest houses. Before you lapse into a relaxation-induced coma, though, try joining an evening river tour, or make a day trip out to see the sculptures and rock formations in the surrounding countryside. Nong Khai is also the major overland jumping-off point for visits to Laos, and the quickest place to get kitted up with a visa (see over).

From the capital, you'll most likely be coming to Nong Khai by night **train**, arriving just after dawn at the station 2km west of the centre. Day **buses** from all points in Isaan and night buses from further afield pull in at the terminal on the east side of town off Prajak Road.

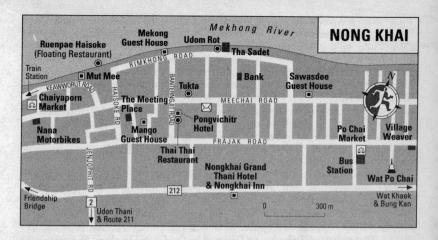

The Town

Nong Khai lays itself out along the south bank of the Mekhong in a four-kilometre band which is never more than 500m deep. Running from east to west, Meechai Road dominates activity: the main shops and businesses are plumb in the middle around the post office, with more frenetic commerce to the east at the Po Chai day market by the bus station, and to the west at the Chaiyaporn night market. Although most of the buildings have been replaced by concrete boxes, a few weather-beaten wooden houses remain, their attractive balconies, porticoes and slatted shutters showing the influence of colonial architecture, which was imported from across the river before the French were forced out of Laos in 1954.

The most pleasant place for a stroll, however, is the riverside area, which, although built-up in the centre around Tha Sadet, becomes rustic and leafy around the fringes, which are often busy with people bathing, washing their clothes and fishing, especially in the early morning and evening. The largest freshwater fish in the world, the *pla beuk* or **giant catfish**, which can weigh in at 300kg, lives in the Mekhong: instead of the old method of harpooning, fishermen now trawl the river with nets during the catfish season (April–June), when you can occasionally see them struggling with these leviathans on the river bank. If you're lucky, you might also catch sight of a sunken chedi, **Phra That Nong Khai**, which slipped into the river in 1847 and has since subsided so far that it's only visible in the dry season.

To catch the best of life on the river, take the **boat trip** which sets out from the *Ruenpae Haisoke* floating restaurant behind the temple at the top of Haisoke Road every evening at 5.30pm. At B20 it's the least expensive way of getting onto the Mekhong in Thailand, and runs up and down the length of Nong Khai for an hour, sticking to the Thai side. Drinks are available, as is food if you order twenty minutes before the boat leaves, all at reasonable prices. There's no stunning scenery, but plenty of activity on both river banks as the sun sets behind the Friendship Bridge. The **bridge** itself has also become a tourist attraction for some, and between 3 and 6pm on Fridays, Saturdays and Sundays, you're permitted to sidestep passport control and walk its span.

The main temple of the region is **Wat Po Chai** at the east end of Prajak Road. The cruciform viharn with its complex and elegant array of Laotian tiers shelters a venerated solid gold image, the Phra Sai Buddha. Prince Chakri, the future Rama I, is said to have looted the image from Vientiane along with the Emerald Buddha, but the boat which was bringing back the Phra Sai overturned and sank in the Mekhong. Later, the statue miraculously rose to the surface and the grateful people of Nong Khai built this great hangar of a viharn to house it, where the present king, Chakri's descendant, comes every year to pay his respects. It's worth a visit for the Buddha's stagey setting, in front of a steep, flame-covered altar, dazzlingly lit from above and below in green. The solid gold is so highly polished that you have to peer carefully to make out the Sukhothai influence in its haughty expression and beaked nose.

Five minutes' walk east of Wat Po Chai at 786 Prajak Rd, *Village Weaver* (☎042/ 411236) specializes in **mut mee**, the northeastern method of tie-dyeing which produces geometrical patterns on a coloured base. White on indigo is the simplest, most traditional form, but the shop also carries a wide range of more richly patterned lengths of silk and cotton, as well as ready-made clothes, bags and axe pillows. Through a self-help project initiated by the Good Shepherd Sisters to help local farmers earn cash, the work is produced in nearby villages and in the yard behind the shop, where you're welcome to watch the weaving process.

Practicalities

As everything in Nong Khai is so spread out, you might want to consider hopping on a **tuk-tuk** (B10 for a medium journey such as Chaiyaporn Market to Tha Sadet) for getting around. To get to some of the area's remoter spots, **motorbikes** (B150–200

TRIPS TO LAOS

As **Laos** has loosened its attitudes towards tourism in recent years, the means of getting a tourist visa for independent travel have changed almost by the month, and can be expected to continue changing just as rapidly. What follows is an outline of the options at the time of going to press, and some pointers as to how things might develop.

Theoretically, you should be able to get a fifteen-day tourist visa at the Laotian embassy in Bangkok for B300 within five working days. However, a semi-official system of palm-greasing prevents that from happening in practice: if you ring up the Bangkok embassy, you will be given the names of two travel agents in Bangkok who can "arrange" your visa. There's no need to restrict yourself to these two because in fact nearly all travel agents in **Bangkok**, as well as many in **Chiang Mai** and other major tourist centres, know how to push the right knobs, charging the punter B2100–2500 to get a visa, via the Laotian embassy in Bangkok, in about a week.

Before the travel agent sends your passport off to the Bangkok embassy, you need to specify your chosen **point of entry** into Laos. It's possible to fly from Bangkok to Vientiane, and there are currently five permissible overland crossing points: Chiang Khong in northern Thailand, and Nong Khai, Nakhon Phanom, Mukdahan and Chong Mek in Isaan.

At the moment, visas can also be obtained at three of these crossing points without having to go through a travel agent:

At **Chiang Khong**, the reliable Wat, owner of the *Ban Tam-Mi-La* guest house (see p.39), can obtain a visa the day after you arrive for B2000. Wat is hoping to bring this price down and is working on a longer, more complex system for about B1000 – telephone him from Bangkok at least ten days before you want to enter Laos for further details.

for a moped, B400–500 for a 400cc) can be hired at *Nana Motorbikes*, 1160 Meechai Rd, opposite Chaiyaporn Market (☎042/411998), while *Village Weaver* (see facing page) offers **four-wheel drives** (B1000 per day including insurance); for local exploration, **bicycles** are available at *Mut Mee* and *Sawasdee* guest houses (listed below and over). If time's running out on your Thai tourist visa, you should be able to get an extension at the **immigration office** by Tha Sadet. *Wasambe*, 1121 Keawworut Rd (on *Mut Mee Guest House*'s driveway), stocks a reasonable selection of **books** in English, especially on spiritual matters, and buys and sells cast-offs.

Accommodation

Nong Khai has a good choice of inexpensive **places to stay**, the best among which are *Mut Mee* and *Sawasdee*. In the wake of the Friendship Bridge has come a rash of luxury developments, of which more are to be expected.

Holiday Inn Mekong Royal Nongkhai, 222 Jommanee Beach (☎042/420024; Bangkok ☎02/271 3125). The name's a mouthful, but the standard's just what you'd expect from a *Holiday Inn* franchise. No beach, but a large swimming pool in the riverside grounds west of town. Twin room designed for disabled visitors available. ⑧.

Mango Guest House, Soi Wat Sri Chom Chuen. Large, airy modern house on a quiet soi to the south of Wat Sri Chom Chuen. Smart rooms, hammocks in the garden and a kitchen for guests' use. ②.

Mekong Guest House, Rimkhong Road by Tha Sadet (☎042/412119). Good for watching the bustle at the pier, but noisy. Clean, basic rooms. ①.

Mut Mee Guest House, 1111 Keawworut Rd. The attractive riverside terrace is a magnet for travellers; well-kept rooms and bamboo huts sprawl around it. Bathrooms are either shared or en suite, and B60 dorm beds are available. Home of the Nong Khai Alternative Center for irregular yoga, meditation and Tai Ch'i workshops. Bicycles are for rent at a rate of B40–60 a day. ②–③.

In **Nong Khai**, most travel agents get visas through the Bangkok embassy in around a week as outlined above; however, *Meeting Place*, 1117 Soi Chuenchitt (☎ and Fax 042/421233), which like *Ban Tam-Mi-La* deals largely with expats wanting to go to Laos to renew their Thai visas, can get you across the same day, if you arrive in Nong Khai in the morning, for B2800, including transport and escort across the bridge.

It's also currently possible to turn up at **Mukdahan**, catch a ferry across the Mekhong, and pay B1500 directly to the Sawannakhet immigration officers for a fifteen-day visa, but it can't be long before local travel agents muscle in on the act.

The **transport** options for crossing to Laos are much simpler. From Bangkok, there are daily flights to Vientiane for B5100, and regular public ferries traverse the Mekhong from Chiang Khong, Nakhon Phanom and Mukdahan, while at Chong Mek it's just a question of walking between the two border posts. The ferry service from Nong Khai is now reserved for Thais and Laotians, so farangs have to use the Thai-Australian Friendship Bridge. From downtown Nong Khai, take a tuk-tuk to the foot of the bridge (about B30), then a minibus (B10) across the span itself, before catching a bus (B10–20) or a taxi (about B400) to Vientiane, 24km away. An air-conditioned minibus meets incoming passengers at Udon Thani airport to carry them to the Laotian side of the bridge for B100.

Looking to the **future**, it seems likely that sooner or later, under pressure from the Thai government and businesses in the border region, the Laotian government will make B300 visas available in practice. These may be obtainable from new Laotian consulates planned for Nong Khai and Khon Kaen. Plans are also afoot for a new bridge across the Mekhong either at Nakhon Phanom or Mukdahan – though a seemingly insoluble squabble between the two provinces over which should be favoured is holding everything up – and eventually the river will also be spanned at Loei and at Ubon.

Nongkhai Grand Thani Hotel and Nongkhai Inn, 589 Moo 5 Nongkhai–Phonpisai Rd (☎042/420033; Bangkok ☎02/237 6809–12). On the southern bypass, a luxury hotel with the *Dusit Thani* group's usual high standards of service; and in the building above the nightclub behind, a moderately priced "inn" – clean, large rooms with air-con, hot water and access to the hotel's swimming pool. ⑥–⑨.

Pongvichitr Hotel, 1244/1–2 Banterngjit Rd (☎042/411583). Bland, but clean and efficient concrete building. All rooms with cold-water bathrooms; some with fan, others with air-con. ③–⑤.

Sawasdee Guest House, 402 Meechai Rd (☎042/412502). A well-equipped, grand old wooden house round a pleasant courtyard, with helpful management: late luggage storage and showers available for those catching a night train or bus. Fan-cooled rooms sharing cold-water bathrooms (try to avoid those overlooking the noisy main road), and air-con rooms with en suite hot showers. Bikes B30 a day. ②–④.

Eating

The most popular **restaurants** in Nong Khai, amongst locals and tourists alike, are the handful of moderately priced riverside terraces clustered around the pier on Rimkhong Road. *Udom Rot* here has particularly good food and atmosphere, specializing in *paw pia yuan* (Vietnamese spring rolls), *plaa raat phrik* (whole fish cooked in chillies and garlic) and *kai lao daeng* (Laotian-style chicken cooked in red wine), and occasionally serving up fresh giant catfish in season. The *Ruenpae Haisoke* behind Wat Haisoke is also justifiably popular: as well as the boat trip mentioned on p.373, it has a floating restaurant that is permanently moored to the bank, where you can enjoy large, moderately priced portions of standard Thai dishes. For honest, inexpensive Thai food, try the *Thai Thai Restaurant* on Banterngjit Road; the menu in English is limited, but you can point out anything else you fancy on the impressive display counter. The *Tukta Bakery* on Meechai Road opposite the post office is a clean and businesslike café, which serves Thai and Western food including cakes and good breakfasts – it closes at 9pm.

Around Nong Khai

By far the easiest and most popular day trip out of Nong Khai takes in **Wat Khaek**, with its weird artificial setting, a short songthaew hop to the east. To the southwest of town and also fairly easy to get to, **Wat Phra That Bang Phuan** offers classic temple sightseeing, while the natural rock formations at **Ban Phu** require much more effort and a full day out. Some of the sights upstream along the Mekhong described on the previous pages are also within day-tripping distance, and it's quite possible to get to Ban Chiang and back in a day – change buses at Udon Thani – without having to stay in drab Udon.

Wat Khaek

Just off the main highway 5km east of Nong Khai, **Wat Khaek** is best known for its bizarre sculpture garden, which looks like the work of an artistic giant on acid. Its proper name is Phutthamamakasamakhom, but even locals have a hard time getting their mouths around that – if you're getting there by songthaew, ask to be let off at **Sala Kaeokoo**, the stop on the highway five minutes' walk north of the wat.

The temple was founded by **Luang Phu Boonlua Surirat**, an unconventional Thai holy man who studied under a Hindu guru in Vietnam and preached in Laos until he was thrown out by the communists in the late 1970s. His charisma –

those who drink water offered by him will, it's rumoured, give up all they own to the temple – and heavy emphasis on morality have attracted many followers among the farmers of Nong Khai. Luang Phu's popularity has suffered, however, since his recent spell in prison for insulting King Bhumibol, a crime alleged by jealous neighbours and probably without foundation.

Viewed to the accompaniment of saccharine piped music, the **sculpture garden** bristles with Buddhist, Hindu and secular figures, all executed in concrete with imaginative abandon by unskilled followers under Luang Phu's direction. The religious statues, in particular, are radically modern. Characteristics that marked the Buddha out as a supernatural being – tight curls and a bump on the crown of the head called the *ushnisha* – are here transformed into beehives, and the *rashmis* on top (flames depicting the Buddha's fiery intellect) are depicted as long, sharp spikes. The largest statue in the garden shows the familiar story of the kindly naga king, Muchalinda, sheltering the Buddha, who is lost in meditation, from the heavy rain and floods: here the Buddha has shrunk in significance and the seven-headed snake has grown to 25m, with fierce, gaping fangs and long tongues.

Many of the statues illustrate **Thai proverbs**. Near the entrance, an elephant surrounded by a pack of dogs symbolizes integrity, "as the elephant is indifferent to the barking dogs". The nearby monster with the moon in his mouth – Rahoo, the cause of eclipses – serves as an injunction to oppose all obstacles, just as the people of Isaan and Laos used to ward off eclipses by banging drums and firing guns. In the corner furthest from the entrance, you enter the complex Circle of Life through a huge mouth representing the womb, inside which a policeman, a monk, a rich man, a beggar and even a farang represent different paths in life. A man with two wives is shown beating the older one because he is ensnared by the wishes of the younger one, and an old couple who have made the mistake of not having children now find they have only each other for comfort.

The disturbingly vacant, smiling faces of the garden Buddhas bear more than a passing resemblance to Luang Phu himself, whose picture you can see in the **temple building** – he's the one with the bouffant hairdo, dressed in white. This featureless, two-storey building contains similar, smaller statuary, a random collection of sculpture from all over Southeast Asia and a greenhouse full of prize cacti.

Wat Phra That Bang Phuan

More famous as the site of a now concealed 2000-year-old Indian chedi than for its modern replacement, rural **Wat Phra That Bang Phuan** remains a highly revered place of pilgrimage. The wat is in the hamlet of **Ban Bang Phuan**, southwest of Nong Khai on Highway 211 – buses west from Nong Khai no longer pass this way (they use the newly paved road along the river bank to Tha Bo), so you'll have to take an Udon-bound service 12km down Highway 2 to Ban Nong Song Hong, then change onto an Udon–Sri Chiangmai bus for the remaining 12km. If you fancy breaking the journey in Nong Song Hong, *Visachol*, on the east side of Highway 2 south of the police checkpoint, sells a wide selection of attractive cotton next to its posh restaurant.

The original **chedi** is supposed to have been built by disciples of the Buddha to hold 29 relics – pieces of chest bone – brought from India. A sixteenth-century king of Vientiane piously earned himself merit by building a tall Laotian-style chedi over the top of the previous stupa; rain damage toppled this in 1970, but it was restored in 1977 to the fine, gleaming white edifice you can see now. The unkempt compound also contains a small museum, crumbling brick chedis and some large open-air Buddhas.

Ban Phu

Deep in the countryside 61km southwest of Nong Khai, the wooded slopes around **BAN PHU** are dotted with strangely eroded sandstone formations which have long exerted a mystical hold over people in the surrounding area. Local wisdom has it that the outcrops, many of which were converted into small temples from the seventh century onwards, are either meteorites – believed to account for their burnt appearance – or, more likely, were caused by under-sea erosion some fifteen million years ago. Together with a stupa enshrining a Buddha footprint that is now an important pilgrimage site (especially during its annual festival, held between March 11 and 15), the rock formations have been rounded up under the auspices of the 1200-acre **Phu Phra Bat Historical Park** (daylight hours; free).

Such charming rural isolation is, however, difficult to reach for those relying on **public transport**. The fastest way of getting there from Nong Khai is to take an Udon Thani-bound bus for about 35km to Ban Ngoi, where you can change onto one of the half-hourly buses from Udon to Ban Phu; from Ban Phu, it's another 13km west to the historical park, which makes a difficult hitch or a hairy ride on a motorbike taxi. The total journey takes a couple of hours. Ten kilometres out of Ban Phu, a right fork in the road leads to the main park entrance, which the Fine Arts Department has helpfully sprinkled with site maps.

A well-signposted network of **paths** has been cleared from the thin forest to connect 25 of the outcrops, which would take a good five hours to explore. Among the most interesting are **Tham Wua** and **Tham Khon**, two natural shelters whose paintings of oxen and human stick figures suggest that the area was first settled at least six thousand years ago.

A local legend accounts for the name of nearby **Kok Ma Thao Barot** (Prince Barot's Stable), a broad platform overhung by a huge slab of sandstone. A certain Princess Ussa, banished by her father to these slopes to be educated by a hermit, sent out an SOS which was answered by a dashing prince, Barot. The two fell in love and were married against the wishes of Ussa's father, prompting the king to challenge Barot to a distinctly oriental sort of duel: each would build a temple, and the last to finish would be beheaded. The king lost. Kok Ma Thao Barot is celebrated as the place where Barot kept his horse when he visited Ussa.

More spectacular is **Hor Nang Ussa** (Ussa's Tower), a mushroom formed by a flat slab capping a five-metre-high rock pillar. Under the cap of the mushroom, a shelter has been carved out and walled in on two sides. The *sema* found scattered around the site, and the square holes in which others would have been embedded, indicate that this was a shrine, probably in the Dvaravati period (seventh to tenth centuries). Finally, a huge rock on a flimsy pivot miraculously balances itself against a tree at **Wat Por Ta** (The Father's Temple); the walls and floor have been evenly carved out to form a vaguely rectangular shrine, with Dvaravati Buddha images dotted around.

The left fork on the way to the park entrance leads to **Wat Phra Bat Bua Bok**: a crude chedi built in imitation of Wat Phra That Phanom (see p.382), it's decorated with naive bas-reliefs of divinities and boggle-eyed monsters, which add to the atmosphere of simple, rustic piety. In a gloomy chamber in the tower's base, the only visible markings of the sandstone **Buddha footprint** show the Wheel of Law. Legend has it that the Buddha made the footprint here for a serpent which had asked to be ordained as a monk, but had been refused because it was not human. Higher up the slope, a smaller *that* perches on a hanging rock that seems to defy gravity.

Downstream to Mukdahan

East of Nong Khai, the land on the Thai side of the Mekhong becomes gradually more arid, while jagged forest-covered mountains loom on the Laos side. Few visitors make it this far, to the northeast's northeast, though the attractions are surprisingly varied, ranging from painterly riverscapes to Isaan's major religious site, **Wat Phra That Phanom**.

Transport along Highway 212 out of Nong Khai is fairly straightforward: sixteen buses a day from Nong Khai run to Bung Kan (2hr), four of which continue to Nakhon Phanom (6hr), where you have to change onto one of the hourly buses to get to That Phanom (1hr) and Mukdahan (2hr).

Ban Ahong and Wat Phu Tok

Just over 100km east of Nong Khai, at Isaan's northernmost point, **BAN AHONG** is a traditional farming village of eight hundred inhabitants which would go unnoticed but for a newly opened guest house, catering for travellers who want to drop out and experience rural daily life. "Welcome to the middle of nowhere" is the slogan of *Hideaway Guest House* (②), run by the English- and German-speaking Saksil, who also cooks the vegetarian and meaty communal food. Sited at the eastern end of the village, its bamboo huts with mosquito nets and fans sit among banana trees on a beautiful winding stretch of the river opposed by lofty hills on the Laos side. Apart from chilling out, you can explore the forest wat set among huge boulders next door, inhabited by a single "monk-herbalist", take a boat ride to islands and beaches on the river, hire a bicycle (B20 a day), even join in the daily football game in the village, and Wat Phu Tok is an easy day trip away on public transport. Any bus between Nong Khai and Bung Kan will drop you at Ban Ahong, and it's then a fifteen-minute walk to the guest house.

Ban Ahong's nearest town, **Bung Kan**, 137km from Nong Khai, is a reasonably prosperous riverside settlement, but dusty and ugly. Since the opening of *Hideaway Guest House*, there should be no reason to endure one of its cheap and nasty hotels, but you'll almost certainly have to change buses here to get to the area's most compelling destination, the extraordinary hilltop retreat of **Wat Phu Tok**. One of two sandstone outcrops which jut steeply out of the plain 35km southeast of Bung Kan, Phu Tok has been transformed in the past few years into a meditation wat, its fifty or so monks building their scattered huts on perches high above breathtaking cliffs.

Getting there isn't easy – the location was chosen for its isolation, after all – but the trip out gives you a slice of life in remote countryside. Coming from Nong Khai, change at Bung Kan and catch one of the half-hourly buses south along Route 222 towards Pang Khon; get off at **Ban Siwilai**, from where songthaews make the hour-long, 25-kilometre trip east to Phu Tok when they have a full complement of passengers (services are more frequent in the morning). The outcrop comes into sight long before you get there, its sheer red face sandwiched between green vegetation on the lower slopes and tufts of trees on the narrow plateau above. As you get closer, the horizontal white lines across the cliffs reveal themselves to be painted wooden walkways, built to give the temple seven levels to represent the seven stages of enlightenment.

In an ornamental garden at the base, an elegant, incongruously modern marble chedi commemorates **Phra Ajaan Juen**, the famous meditation master who founded the wat in 1968 and died in a plane crash ten years later. His books and other belongings, and diamond-like fragments of his bones, are preserved in a small museum. The first part of the ascent takes you to the third level up a series of long, sometimes slippery, wooden staircases, the first of many for which you'll need something more sturdy than flip-flops. A choice of two routes – the left fork is more interesting – leads to the fifth and most important level, where the **Sala Yai** houses the temple's main Buddha image in an airy, dimly lit cavern.

The artificial ledges which cut across the northeast face are not for the faint-hearted, but they are one way of getting to the dramatic northwest tip: here, on the other side of a deep crevice spanned by a wooden bridge, a monk has built a shelter under a huge anvil rock. This spot affords stunning **views** over a broad sweep of countryside and across to the second, uninhabited outcrop. The flat top of the hill forms the seventh level, where you can wander along overgrown paths through thick forest.

It's possible to **stay** overnight at Phu Tok, and in fact a monk will often approach when you arrive offering somewhere to sleep in the temple buildings. You should make a small donation to the temple (about B50 a night), and the monks will usually invite you to share – at a respectable distance – in a hearty breakfast, the only meal they eat each day. Bring your own provisions for other meals. The monks don't speak English, but sign language suffices.

Nakhon Phanom

Beyond Bung Kan, the river road rounds the hilly northeastern tip of Thailand before heading south through remote country where you're apt to find yourself stopping for buffalo as often as for vehicles. The Mekhong can only be glimpsed occasionally until you reach **NAKHON PHANOM**, 302km from Nong Khai, a clean and prosperous town which affords the finest view of the river in northern Isaan, framed against the giant ant hills of the Laotian mountains opposite.

The town makes a pleasant place to hang out, its broad streets lined with some grand old public buildings, colonial-style houses and creaking wooden shop-houses. During the Indochina wars, Nakhon Phanom was an important gateway for thousands of Vietnamese refugees, whose influence can be seen in the dilapidated and atmospheric hybrid, **Wat Or Jak**, opposite the pier for Laos at the northern end of the riverside promenade. The ferry (B30) from this pier to Khammouan in Laos can be used by farangs, as long as they have a visa, of course – and at the time of writing, visas were not available anywhere in Nakhon Phanom, so you would have to equip yourself with one before you left Bangkok. If that all sounds like too much hassle, the closest you can get to Laos is to take an hour-long, circular **boat trip** (B30) on the *Mae Nam Khong Princess*, which leaves the pier every evening at 5pm, providing the best perspective on the beautiful riverscape. The biggest Buddha in Isaan is at **Wat Phra Yai**, but the image is an unattractive 25-metre-high architectural feature covered in rust-coloured tiles, which forms the roof of a small viharn, squeezed in underneath its crossed legs. To reach the temple, take a tuk-tuk or walk west of town on the road to Udon Thani (Highway 22) for 2km, then turn left down the western bypass for another 2km.

TAT has a new office at 2/16 Salaklang Rd (☎042/513490–1), at the north end of the promenade, which also covers Sakhon Nakhon and Mukdahan provinces. The friendly and informative *River Inn* (☎042/511305; ②–④) at 137 Suntorn Vichit Rd has the best location of Nakhon Phanom's budget **hotels**, as well as a good riverside restaurant: quiet, air-conditioned rooms overlook the river; fan rooms face the road. At the luxury end, *Mae Nam Khong Grand View*, 527 Suntorn Vichit Rd (☎042/513564–70; ⑦), lives up to its name, at least from its riverside rooms, but not its price, although you get a cooked breakfast thrown in – it would be worth asking for a discount. A few small, reasonable **restaurants** with riverside terraces, specializing in Mekhong giant catfish dishes, are clustered around the pier and the clocktower, at the corner of Suntorn Vichit and Sri Thep roads.

Sakhon Nakhon

Ninety kilometres to the west on Highway 22, unappealing **SAKHON NAKHON** only justifies a detour off the Mekhong River route if you're interested in temples – though if you're travelling by bus from Udon Thani or Khon Kaen to Nakhon Phanom or That Phanom you'll have to pass through here in any case. Separated from the heart of Isaan by the forested Pan mountains, Sakhon Nakhon has developed only recently, and you can still see the fields out of which the town grew in the empty lots and partly paved roads of the town centre.

Top of the wats is **Wat Phra That Choeng Choom**, near Nong Harn Lake, where the angular, white Laotian chedi has been built around and on top of a Khmer laterite prang dating from the eleventh century. The chedi affords glimpses of the prang through its three outer doors and can be entered through a door at the back of the adjacent viharn. Legend has it that the chedi was built to enshrine four pairs of footprints made by the Buddha in his different manifestations. Elsewhere in the spacious grounds is a tower with a huge wooden bell, hollowed from a single tree trunk.

A small, well-restored Khmer prang, **Wat Phra That Narai Cheng Weng** lies 6km northwest of town, 100m to the left off Highway 22 opposite the turning for Nakhon Phanom. The laterite prang, set among coconut palms on a grassy knoll, is said to contain ashes of the Buddha. The lintel above the eastern doorway displays a well-preserved bas-relief of twelve-armed Shiva, dancing a jig to destroy the universe. On the northern pediment is shown the next stage in the never-ending cycle of destruction and rebirth, with Vishnu reclining on a dragon dreaming up the new creation. An umbilical cord topped by a lotus extends from his navel, but the figure of Brahma on top of the lotus, whose job it is to put Vishnu's dream into practice, has been eroded. Beneath is a lively carving of Krishna, one of the incarnations of Vishnu, locked in combat with a toothy lion.

Accommodation in Sakhon Nakhon is pokey, though comparatively inexpensive. Large, shabby rooms with en suite bathrooms at the *Krong Thong Hotel*, 645/2 Charoen Muang Rd (☎042/711235; ①), are your best bet in the budget range, but if you're stuck in Sakhon you might well feel like upgrading to the much cleaner and more comfortable *Dusit Hotel*, 1784 Yuvapatana Rd (☎042/711198 or 711199; ④), where all rooms have air conditioning and hot water.

That Phanom

Fifty kilometres south of Nakhon Phanom, **THAT PHANOM**, a green and friendly village of weather-beaten wooden buildings, sprawls around Isaan's most important shrine. Popularly held to be one of the four sacred pillars of Thai religion (the other 3 are Chiang Mai's Wat Phra That Doi Suthep, Wat Mahathat in Nakhon Si Thammarat, and Wat Phra Phuttabat near Lopburi), **Wat Phra That Phanom** is a fascinating place of pilgrimage – especially at the time of the Ngan Phra That Phanom, usually in February, when thousands of people come to pay homage and enjoy themselves in the holiday between harvesting and sowing. That Phanom is only an hour away from Nakhon Phanom, Sakhon Nakhon and Mukdahan, and served by frequent **buses** from each, which stop on Chayangkun Road, immediately outside the wat. The centre of the village is 200m due east of here, clustered around the pier on the Mekhong.

This far-northeastern corner of Thailand may seem like a strange location for one of the country's holiest sites, but the wat used to serve both Thais and Laotians, as evidenced by the ample boat landing in the village, now largely disused – since the Pathet Lao took over in 1975, Laotians have only been allowed to cross the river for the Monday and Thursday morning markets and for the Ngan Phra That Phanom. The temple reputedly dates back to the eighth year after the death of the Buddha (535 BC), when five local princes built a simple brick chedi to house bits of his breastbone. It's been restored or rebuilt seven times, most recently after it collapsed during a rainstorm in 1975; the latest incarnation is in the form of a Laotian *that*, 57m high, modelled on the That Luang in Vientiane.

The best approach is from the river: a short ceremonial way leads directly from the pier, under a Disneyesque victory arch erected by the Laotians, through the temple gates to the chedi itself, which, as is the custom, faces water and the rising sun. A brick and plaster structure covered with white paint and gold floral decorations, the **chedi** looks like nothing so much as a giant, ornate table leg turned upside down. From each of the four sides, an eye forming part of the traditional flame pattern stares down, and the whole thing is surmounted by an umbrella made of 16kg of gold with precious gems and gold rings embedded in each tier. The chedi sits on a gleaming white marble platform, on which pilgrims say their prayers and leave every imaginable kind of offering to the relics. Look out for the brick reliefs in the shape of four-leaf clovers above three of the doorways in the base: the eastern side shows Vishnu mounted on a garuda; on the western side, the four guardians of the earth putting offerings in the Buddha's alms bowl; and above the south door, a carving of the Buddha entering Nirvana. At the corners of the chedi, brick plaques, carved in the tenth century but now heavily restored, tell the stories of the wat's princely founders.

That Phanom's outstanding **accommodation** choice is the welcoming *Niyana Guest House* (①), 73 Soi Withi Sawrachon, one block north of the pier on an east–west lane. The owner, Niyana, is a fund of local information, and rustles up excellent Thai and Western food, as well as renting out bicycles (B25 a day) and organizing occasional boat trips. Rooms in Niyana's quiet modern house share cold-water bathrooms, and she has recently taken over the nearby *Esan Guest House*, where there's a B40 dorm. If Niyana can't put you up, try the *Sang Thong Hotel* (①), south of the victory arch at 34 Phanom Phanarak Rd, a wooden house around a family courtyard offering basic rooms with their own bathrooms.

From That Phanom regular songthaews run to the weaving village of **Renu Nakhon**, 17km northwest. The wat at the centre of the village has a smaller, stubbier imitation of the Phra That Phanom, crudely decorated with stucco carvings and brown paint. Around the wat, stalls and shops sell a huge variety of reasonable cotton and silk, much of it in simple, colourful *mut mee* styles.

Mukdahan – and beyond

Fifty kilometres downriver of That Phanom, **MUKDAHAN** is the last stop on the Mekhong trail before Highway 212 heads off inland to Ubon Ratchathani, 170km to the south. You're really in the Wild East out here: rutted dirt roads and makeshift buildings of wood and corrugated iron bear witness to the fact that this is the country's newest province. However, it's also one of the fastest developing, due to increasing friendship between Laos and Thailand and the proximity of Sawannakhet, the second biggest Laotian city, just across the water. Very few farang visitors make it this far, though the B30 ferry trip is an officially sanctioned crossing to Laos (see p.375).

Half-hourly buses from That Phanom and Ubon Ratchathani stop on Samut Sakdarak Road, the main north–south street. In the heart of town to the east of this road, the main river pier serves the cross-border trade, which accounts for a large part of the local economy. By the pier, a pleasant tree-lined promenade overlooks Sawannakhet, and a market, which spills over into the compound of Wat Sri Mongkon, sells household goods and inexpensive ornaments, such as Vietnamese mother-of-pearl and Chinese ceramics, brought over from Laos.

To **stay**, try the large, cleanish rooms of the *Hua Nam Hotel* at 20 Samut Sakdarak Rd (☎042/611197; ②). If you want a little more comfort, turn south off the main east–west street, Pitakpanomkhet Road, at the town's largest traffic circle, onto Phitak Santirat Road, where you'll find *Saensuk Bungalows* (☎042/611214; ④) at no. 2, 100m down on your right: clean air-conditioned rooms, some with hot water, are ranged around a tidy courtyard. Further west at 40 Pitakpanomkhet Rd, *Ploy Palace Hotel* (☎042/611329; ⑦), a grand pink edifice with an overblown lobby and tasteful bedrooms, is Mukdahan's top luxury option. **Restaurants** dot the riverside promenade, Somranchaikhong Road, best – and priciest – of which is *Riverside*, 1km south of the pier, which serves excellent food on a pretty terrace over the Mekhong.

Mukdahan National Park

If you're tired of concrete Isaan towns, you can stretch your legs exploring the strange rock formations and beautiful waterfalls of **MUKDAHAN NATIONAL PARK** (aka Phu Pha Terp), down a minor road along the Mekhong southeast of Mukdahan. Regular songthaews pass the turning for the park 14km out of town, and from there it's a two-kilometre walk uphill to the park headquarters. If he's free, the bustling English-speaking park ranger will guide you around the park for no charge. Just above the headquarters is a hillside of bizarre rocks, eroded into the shapes of toadstools and crocodiles, which is great for scrambling around. The hillside also bears two remnants of the area's prehistory: the red finger-painting under one of the sandstone slabs is reckoned to be four thousand years old, while a small cage on the ground protects a 75-million-year-old fossil. Further up, the bare sandstone ridge seems to have been cut out of the surrounding forest by a giant lawnmower, but in October it's brought to life with a covering of grasses and wildflowers. A series of ladders leads up a cliff to the highest point, on a ridge at the western end of the park, which affords a sweeping view over the rocks to the forests and paddies of Laos. Halfway up the cliff is a cave in which villagers have enshrined scores of Buddha images, and nearby, at least from July to November, you'll find the park's most spectacular waterfall, a thirty-metre drop through thick vegetation.

The park, which can be readily visited on a day trip from Mukdahan or That Phanom, has no official accommodation, but the simple **food** stalls near HQ will keep you going with fried rice and noodles.

travel details

Trains

Khon Kaen to: Bangkok (5 daily; 7–8hr); Nong Khai (3 daily; 2hr 45min); Udon Thani (5 daily; 1hr 40min).

Khorat to: Ayutthaya (7 daily; 3hr 30min); Bangkok (9 daily; 4–5hr); Khon Kaen (2 daily; 3hr); Si Saket (7 daily; 4hr–5hr 30min); Surin (7 daily; 2hr 30min–3hr 40min); Ubon Ratchathani (7 daily; 5hr–6hr 40min); Udon Thani (2 daily; 4hr 30min).

Nong Khai to: Bangkok (3 daily; 11hr), via Udon Thani (1hr), Khon Kaen (3hr) and Ayutthaya (10hr).

Pak Chong to: Bangkok (7 daily; 3hr 30min); Ubon Ratchathani (7 daily; 6hr 50min–8hr 40min), via Khorat (1hr 30min–2hr) and Surin (4hr 25min–5hr 40min).

Prachinburi to: Bangkok (7 daily; 2hr 30min); Aranyaprathet (2 daily; 2hr 20min).

Surin to: Bangkok (9 daily; 8–10hr); Buriram (7 daily; 55min); Sikhoraphum (6 daily; 30–55min); Si Saket (7 daily; 1hr 35min–2hr 10min); Ubon Ratchathani (7 daily; 2hr 30min–3hr 30min).

Ubon Ratchathani to: Bangkok (7 daily; 10hr 20min–13hr 15min); Si Saket (7 daily; 1hr 10min).

Udon Thani to: Ayutthaya (3 daily; 9hr); Bangkok (5 daily; 9–10hr); Khon Kaen (5 daily; 2hr); Khorat (2 daily; 4hr 30min); Nong Khai (3 daily; 1hr).

Buses

Bung Kan to: Nakhon Phanom (5 daily; 4hr); Nong Khai (16 daily; 2hr); Sakhon Nakhon (hourly; 3hr); Udon Thani (every 70min; 4hr).

Chaiyaphum to: Bangkok (hourly; 6hr); Khon Kaen (10 daily; 2–3hr); Khorat (about every 30min; 2hr); Phitsanulok (6 daily; 3hr); Surin (5 daily; 4hr); Ubon Ratchathani (5 daily; 6–7hr).

Chiang Khan to: Bangkok (5 daily; 11hr); Loei (every 30min by songthaew; 1hr); Pak Chom (every 30min by songthaew; 1hr).

Khon Kaen to: Bangkok (23 daily; 6–7hr); Chaiyaphum (hourly; 2–3hr); Khorat (hourly; 2hr 30min–3hr); Loei (every 30min; 4hr); Nong Khai (10 daily; 2–3hr); Phitsanulok (hourly; 5hr); Sri Chiangmai (6 daily; 3hr); Ubon Ratchathani (15 daily; 6hr); Udon Thani (10 daily; 1hr 30min–2hr).

Khorat to: Bangkok (every 15min; 3–4hr); Chaiyaphum (every 30min; 2hr); Chanthaburi (12 daily; 6hr); Chiang Mai (7 daily; 9–11hr); Khon Kaen (hourly; 2hr 30min–3hr); Lopburi (11 daily; 3hr 30min); Nakhon Phanom (3 daily; 8hr); Nong Khai (3 daily; 6hr); Pattaya (4 daily; 5hr); Phimai (every 30min; 1hr–1hr 30min); Phitsanulok (7 daily; 5–7hr); Rayong (18 daily; 4hr); Sri Chiangmai (6 daily; 6hr 30min); Surin (every 30min; 4–5hr); Ubon Ratchathani (17 daily; 5hr); Udon Thani (every 45min; 3hr 30min–5hr).

Loei to: Bangkok (15 daily; 10hr); Chiang Khan (every 30min by songthaew; 1hr); Chiang Mai (4 daily; 9hr); Chiang Rai (2 daily; 11hr); Khon Kaen (every 30min; 4hr); Nong Khai (7 daily; 6–7hr); Pak Chom (hourly songthaew; 2hr 30min); Phitsanulok (6 daily; 4hr); Sang Khom (7 daily; 3hr); Udon Thani (every 30min; 3hr).

Mukdahan to: Bangkok (13 daily; 11hr); Nakhon Phanom (hourly; 2hr); Sakhon Nakhon (2 daily; 2hr); Ubon Ratchathani (every 30min; 2–3hr); Udon Thani (5 daily; 4hr–4hr 30min).

Nakhon Phanom to: Bangkok (17 daily; 12hr); Chiang Rai (2 daily; 16hr); Khorat (3 daily; 8hr); Loei (2 daily; 7hr); Nong Khai (4 daily; 6hr); Phitsanulok (2 daily; 10hr); Ubon Ratchathani (2 daily; 4hr); Udon Thani (11 daily; 5–7hr).

Nong Khai to: Bangkok (18 daily; 10hr); Bung Kan (16 daily; 2hr); Loei (7 daily; 6–7hr); Nakhon Phanom (4 daily; 6hr); Sang Khom (7 daily; 3–4hr); Udon Thani (every 30min; 1hr).

Pak Chom to: Chiang Khan (every 30min by songthaew; 1hr); Loei (hourly songthaew; 2hr 30min); Nong Khai (7 daily; 5hr).

Pak Chong to: Bangkok (every 15min; 3hr); Khorat (every 20min; 1hr 30min).

Sakhon Nakhon to: Bangkok (11 daily; 11hr); Chiang Rai (1 daily; 12hr); Khon Kaen (6 daily; 4hr); Khorat (6 daily; 7hr); Mukdahan (hourly; 3hr); Nakhon Phanom (every 30min; 2hr); That Phanom (every 30min; 1hr 30min); Ubon Ratchathani (9 daily; 5hr); Udon Thani (every 30min; 3hr).

Sang Khom to: Loei (7 daily; 3hr); Nong Khai (7 daily; 3–4hr).

Sri Chiangmai to: Bangkok (7 daily; 12hr); Khon Kaen (6 daily; 3hr); Khorat (6 daily; 6hr 30min); Loei (7 daily; 5hr); Nong Khai (hourly; 2hr); Udon Thani (every 30min; 1hr 30min).

Surin to: Bangkok (up to 20 daily; 8–9hr); Chaiyaphum (5 daily; 4–5hr); Khorat (every 30min; 4hr); Ta Klang (hourly; 2hr); Ubon Ratchathani (at least 12 daily; 2hr 30min–3hr); Yasothon (hourly; 2–3hr).

That Phanom to: Nakhon Phanom (every 30min; 1hr).

Ubon Ratchathani to: Bangkok (19 daily; 10–12hr); Chaiyaphum (5 daily; 6–7hr); Chiang Mai (5 daily; 9hr); Kantharalak (8 daily; 1hr 30min); Khon Kaen (16 daily; 6hr); Khorat (17 daily; 5hr); Phibun Mangsahan (every 25min; 1hr); Rayong (7 daily; 9hr); Roi Et (16 daily; Surin (12 daily; 2hr 30min); 2hr 30min–3hr); Udon Thani (11 daily; 5–7hr); Yasothon (18 daily; 1hr 30min–2hr).

Udon Thani to: Ban Chiang (hourly; 1hr 30min); Bangkok (38 daily; 9hr); Ban Phu (every 45min; 1hr); Bung Kan (every 70min; 4hr); Chiang Mai (6 daily; 11–13hr); Chiang Rai (4 daily; 12–14hr); Khon Kaen (every 20min; 1hr 30min–2hr); Khorat (every 45min; 3hr 30min–5hr); Loei (every 30min; 3hr); Nakhon Phanom (11 daily; 5–7hr); Nong Khai (every 30min; 1hr); Phitsanulok (5 daily; 8hr); Rayong (11 daily; 12hr); Sakhon Nakhon (every 30min; 3hr); Sri Chiangmai (every 30min; 1hr 30min); Ubon Ratchathani (11 daily; 5–7hr).

Yasothon to: Khon Kaen (hourly; 3hr–3hr 30min); Roi Et (hourly; 1hr).

Flights

Khon Kaen to: Bangkok (4 daily; 50min).

Khorat to: Bangkok (1–2 daily; 40min).

Nakhon Phanom to: Bangkok (1 daily; 1hr 20min).

Sakhon Nakhon to: Bangkok, via Nakhon Phanom (1 daily; 2hr 15min).

Ubon Ratchathani to: Bangkok (2 daily; 1hr).

Udon Thani to: Bangkok (3 daily; 1hr).

CHAPTER SIX

SOUTHERN THAILAND:
THE GULF COAST

The major part of southern Thailand's **Gulf coast**, gently undulating from Bangkok to Nakhon Si Thammarat, 750km away, is famed above all for the **Samui archipelago**, three small idyllic islands lying off the most prominent hump of the coastline. This is the country's most popular seaside venue for independent travellers, and a lazy stay in a Samui beachfront bungalow is so seductive a prospect that most people overlook the attractions of the mainland, where the sheltered sandy beaches and warm clear water rival the top sunspots in most countries. Added to that you'll find scenery dominated by forested mountains that rise abruptly behind the coastal strip, and a sprinkling of historic sights – notably the crumbling temples of ancient **Phetchaburi**, which offer an atmospheric if less grandiose alternative to the much-visited attractions at Ayutthaya and Lopburi, on the other side of the capital. The stretch of coast south of Phetchaburi, down to the traditional Thai resorts of **Cha-am** and **Hua Hin**, is handy for weekenders escaping the oppressive capital, while the nearby **Khao Sam Roi Yot National Park** is one of Thailand's most rewarding bird-watching spots. **Chumphon**, 450km down the coast from Bangkok, has little to offer in its own right, but is the most convenient departure point for direct boats to Ko Tao.

Southeast of Chumphon lies **Ko Samui**, by far the most beautiful of the islands, with its pure white sands, limpid blue waters, and arching fringes of palm trees. The island's beauty has not gone unnoticed by tourist developers of course, but this has marred it only slightly and means you can buy a little extra comfort if you've got the cash. In recent years the next island out, **Ko Pha Ngan**, has drawn increasing numbers of backpackers away from its neighbour: its simple rustic bungalows cost less than Ko Samui's, and it offers a few stunning beaches with a more laid-back atmosphere. **Hat Rin** is the distillation of all these features, with back-to-back white sands, relaxed resident hippies and T'ai Chi classes – though after dusk it swings into action as Thailand's rave capital, a reputation cemented by its farang-thronged monthly "full moon" parties. For real solitude and the primitive life, you have to go right out to the small rugged, outcrop of **Ko Tao**, where you can explore a network of hilly trails and scramble down to isolated rocky coves. The variety of its coral and fish has also turned it into a well-equipped scuba-diving centre, but this doesn't disturb the island's peace and quiet.

Tucked away beneath the islands, **Nakhon Si Thammarat**, the cultural capital of the south, is well worth a short detour from the main routes down the centre of the peninsula – it's a sophisticated city of grand old temples, delicious cuisine, and highly finished handicrafts, which are found nowhere else in Thailand. With its small but significant Muslim population, and machine-gun dialect, Nakhon begins the transition into Thailand's deep south.

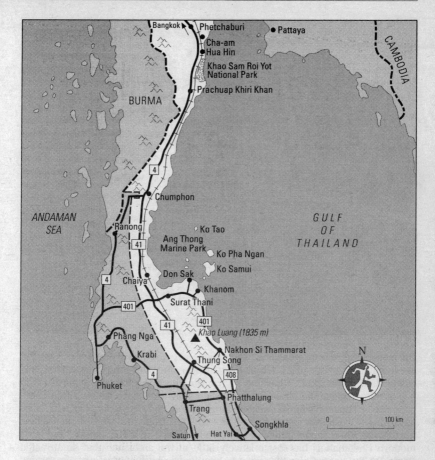

The **train** from Bangkok connects all the mainland towns, and **bus** services, along highways 4 (also known as the Phetkasem Highway, or, usually, Phetkasem Road when passing through towns) and 41, are frequent. Daily boats run to the islands from two jumping-off points: **Surat Thani**, 650km from Bangkok, has the best choice of routes, but the alternatives from **Chumphon** get you straight to the tranquillity of Ko Tao.

Phetchaburi

Straddling the River Phet about 120km south of Bangkok, the provincial capital of **PHETCHABURI** (aka Phetburi) has been settled ever since the eleventh century, when the Khmers ruled the region, but only really got going six hundred years later, when it began to flourish as a trading post between the Andaman Sea ports, Burma and Ayutthaya. Despite periodic incursions from the

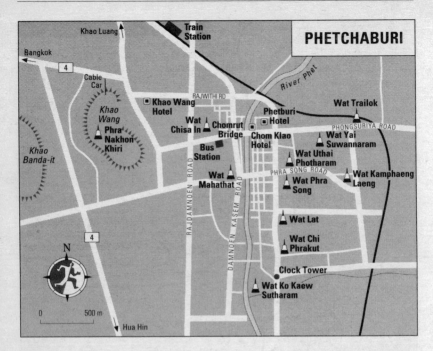

Burmese, the town gained a reputation as a cultural centre – as the ornamentation of its older temples testifies – and after the new capital was established in Bangkok it became a favourite country retreat of Rama IV, who had a hilltop palace built here in the 1850s. Today the town's main claim to fame is as one of Thailand's finest sweet-making centres, the essential ingredient for its assortment of *khanom* being the sugar extracted from the sweet-sapped palms that cover Phetchaburi province. This being very much a cottage industry, modern Phetchaburi has lost relatively little of the ambience that so attracted Rama IV: the central riverside area is hemmed in by historical wats in varying states of disrepair, and wooden rather than concrete shophouses still line the river bank.

Yet despite the obvious attractions of its old quarter, Phetchaburi gets few visitors and accommodation is poor – most visitors return to Bangkok for the night. It's also possible to combine a day in Phetchaburi with an early morning expedition from Bangkok to the floating markets of Damnoen Saduak, 40km north (see p.143); budget tour operators in the Khao San Road area offer this option as a day-trip package for about B300 per person.

Arriving by **bus** from Bangkok, you'll be dropped either at the bus station on Phongsuriya Road, a few minutes' walk west of the town centre or – if it's a bus to Hua Hin and Chumphon – a bit further out, on Rajdamnoen Road. **Trains** pull in on the northern outskirts of town, not far from the hilltop palace of Khao Wang, about 1500m or a B10 samlor ride from the main sight area. Phetchaburi's town centre might look compact, but to see the major temples in a day and have sufficient energy left for climbing Khao Wang and exploring the lesser sights, you're best off hiring a **samlor** for a couple of hours (about B60 per hour) – also, samlor drivers have no qualms about riding through wat compounds, so you can get close-up views of the crumbling facades without getting out.

The Town

The pinnacles and rooftops of the town's thirty-odd wats are visible in every direction, but only a few have particular historic or artistic significance. Of this group the most attractive is the still-functioning seventeenth-century **Wat Yai Suwannaram** on Phongsuriya Road, about 700m east of the bus station, across the river. On your right as you enter the compound, the fine old teak *sala* or hall has elaborately carved doors, bearing a gash said to have been made by the Burmese in 1760 as they plundered their way towards Ayutthaya. Across from the *sala*, the windowless Ayutthayan-style bot contains a remarkable set of murals, depicting Indra, Brahma and other lower-ranking divinities ranged in five rows of ascending importance. The bot overlooks a pond in the middle of which stands a well-preserved scripture library or *ho trai*: such structures were built on stilts over water to prevent ants and other insects destroying the precious documents.

The five tumbledown prangs of **Wat Kamphaeng Laeng**, ten minutes' walk south from Wat Yai, mark out Phetchaburi as the probable southernmost outpost of the Khmer empire. Built to enshrine Hindu deities and set out in a cruciform arrangement facing east, the "corncob" prangs were later adapted for Buddhist use, as you can see from the two which now house Buddha images. These days worshippers congregate in the modern whitewashed wat behind these shrines, leaving the decaying prangs to chickens, stray dogs and the occasional tourist.

Continuing west from Wat Kamphaeng Laeng, across the river, you reach Phetchaburi's most fully restored and important temple, **Wat Mahathat**. Boasting the "Mahathat" title only since 1954, when the requisite Buddha relics were donated by the king, it was probably founded in the fourteenth century, but suffered badly at the hands of the Burmese. The five landmark prangs at its heart are adorned with stucco figures of mythical creatures, though these are nothing compared with those on the roofs of the main viharn and the bot. Instead of tapering off into the usual serpentine *chofa* finials, the gables are studded with miniature *thep* and *deva* figures (angels and gods), which add an almost mischievous vitality to the place. In a similar vein, a couple of gold-embossed crocodiles snarl above the entrance to the bot, and a caricatural carving of the writer and former prime minister Kukrit Pramoj – bare-chested, grimacing and wearing thick-rimmed glasses – rubs shoulders with mythical giants in a relief around the base of the gold Buddha housed in a separate mondop nearby.

Dominating the western outskirts, about thirty minutes' walk from Wat Mahathat, stands Rama IV's hilltop palace, a stew of mid-nineteenth-century Thai and European styles known as **Khao Wang**. During his day, the royal entourage would struggle its way up the steep brick path to the summit, but now there's a **cable car** (Mon–Fri 8am–5.30pm, Sat & Sun 8am–6pm; B35 return including museum entrance) which starts from the base of the hill on Highway 4. Up top, the wooded hill is littered with wats, prangs, chedis, whitewashed gazebos and lots more, in an ill-assorted combination of architectural idioms – the prang-topped viharn, washed all over in burnt sienna, is possibly the ugliest religious building in the country. Whenever the king came on an excursion here, he stayed in the airy summer house, **Phra Nakhon Khiri** (Wed–Sun 9am–4pm;

B20 without cable-car ticket), with its Mediterranean-style shutters and verandahs. Now a museum, it houses a moderately interesting collection of ceramics, furniture and other artefacts given to the royal family by foreign friends. Besides being cool and breezy, Khao Wang also proved to be a good star-gazing spot, so Rama IV had an open-sided, glass-domed observatory built close to his sleeping quarters. The king's amateur astronomy was not an inconsequential recreation: in August 1868 he predicted a solar eclipse almost to the second, thereby quashing the centuries-old Thai fear that the sun was periodically swallowed by an omnipotent lion god.

If you've got energy to spare, the two cave wats out on the western edges of town make good time-fillers. **Khao Banda-it**, a couple of kilometres west of Khao Wang, comprises a series of stalactite caves filled with Buddha statues and a 200-year-old Ayutthayan-style meditation temple. A bizarre story goes with this wat, attempting to explain its design faults as an intentional whim. The money for the three wat buildings was given by a rich man and his two wealthy wives: the first wife donated the bot, the second wife gave the viharn and the husband stuck the chedi in the middle. The chedi, however, leans distinctly southwards towards the viharn, prompting local commentators to point this out as subtle public acknowledgement of the man's preferences. Five kilometres north of Khao Wang, the caves of **Khao Luang** have the distinction of being a favourite royal picnic spot, and have also been decorated with various Buddha images.

Practicalities

The town's three main **hotels** all offer fairly large, clean rooms of just passable standard. The best-placed is *Chom Klao* at 1–3 Phongsuriya Rd, beside Chomrut Bridge (☎032/425398; ②), where some of the rooms give out onto the riverside walkway. Alternatively, try the *Phetburi Hotel*, at 39 Phongsuriya Rd (☎032/425315; ②) or, right over the other side of town, near the base of Khao Wang, the *Khao Wang Hotel*, at 174/1–3 Rajwithi Rd (☎034/425167; ②–③).

ACCOMMODATION PRICES

Throughout this guide, guest houses, hotels and bungalows have been categorized according to the price codes given below. These categories represent the minimum you can expect to pay in the high season (roughly Nov–Feb & July–Aug) for a double room – or, in the case of national park bungalows, for a multi-berth room which can be rented for a standard price by an individual or group. If travelling on your own, expect to pay anything between sixty and one hundred percent of the rates quoted for a double room. Wherever a range of prices is indicated, this means that the establishment offers rooms with varying facilities – as explained in the write-up. Wherever an establishment also offers dormitory beds, the prices of these beds are given in the text, instead of being indicated by price code.

Remember that the top-whack hotels will add seven percent tax and a ten-percent service charge to your bill – the price codes below are based on net rates after taxes have been added.

① under B100	④ B250–400	⑦ B1000–1500
② B100–150	⑤ B400–600	⑧ B1500–3000
③ B150–250	⑥ B600–1000	⑨ B3000+

Most of Phetchaburi's **restaurants** are near Chomrut Bridge, the best and closest being the open-fronted *Rabieng*, 50m east along Phongsuriya Road from Chomrut Bridge, easily recognized by its glass-topped tables. Popular with young locals, the food here is good, inexpensive standard Thai, with an English menu for the smattering of farang customers. The nearby *Sri Taleun*, on the corner at 18/7–8 Thanon Surinluechai, is a bit more basic but does a good line in duck and sausage dishes. The best thing about the nameless riverside restaurant is its location on Chomrut Bridge, which makes it a scenic spot for a beer. If you fancy sampling one of the local **sweet snacks**, such as *khanom maw kaeng (*sweet egg custard), you won't have to look far: almost half the shops in the town centre stock the stuff, as do many of the stalls crowding the base of Khao Wang.

South to Chumphon

Continuing south from Phetchaburi, road and rail pass through the seaside towns of **Cha-am** (41km), **Hua Hin** (70km) – the latter worth a visit primarily for its proximity to **Khao Sam Roi Yot National Park** – and **Prachuap Khiri Khan** (158km) before arriving at Chumphon, 340km down the coast. In the early 1900s, the royal family "discovered" this stretch of the coast, making summer expeditions here to take the sea air and to go deer- and tiger-hunting in the inland jungle. It soon became a fashionable resort area for the lower echelons of Thai society, and Cha-am and Hua Hin are now very popular weekend holiday spots, while Prachuap Khiri Khan is famed for its seafood if not for its sand. But rampant building is beginning to ruin the shoreline and pollute the sea around Cha-am and Hua Hin, and visually the area is not a patch on seafronts further down the coast, so the towns have little to offer sun-worshipping farang travellers, except perhaps as places to break a long journey south.

Cha-am and the coast

CHA-AM is a typically Thai resort: almost empty during the week, it gets packed with families on weekends and holidays, when beach life tends to revolve around eating and drinking rather than sunbathing and swimming – Cha-am's beach is long and pleasantly shaded, but disappointingly grey.

Half-hourly **buses** from Bangkok stop in the tiny town centre on Highway 4, 1km west of the beach; **trains** (8 daily) drop passengers at the station one block further west. The local **TAT** office (daily 8.30am–4.30pm; ☎032/471502) is on Highway 4, about 1km south of the intersection with the access road to the beach. Most of the **accommodation** is on the beachfront Ruamchit Road and is geared towards family groups. For non-familial travellers, the best options include *Arunthip* (☎032/471503; ③), which has large rooms with showers, and the overpriced but adequate rooms at *Nirindhorn* (☎032/471038; ④).

Over the last few years, the **stretch of coastline** between Cha-am and Hua Hin has become a coastal conurbation, thanks to the development of a new highrise satellite resort. Accommodation in this strip is upmarket and package-tour-oriented, with the emphasis on resort facilities rather than a beautiful beach or an authentic Thai atmosphere. *Beach Garden Hotel* (☎032/471350; ⑧–⑨), about 8km south of Cha-am at 249/21 Phetkasem Rd, is one of the more attractive: just three storeys high, with some bungalow accommodation, it's right on the beach, has its own pool and boasts water-sports, tennis and golf facilities. A couple of kilometres further along, at no. 853/1, the comparable but high-rise *Golden Sands* (☎032/471985–8; ⑨) has rooms with private balconies and sea view and is set in pleasantly landscaped gardens. The most luxurious spot on this stretch of coast is further south still, 3–4km before the palace: the elegant *Dusit Resort and Polo Club* at 1349 Phetkasem Rd (☎032/520009; ⑨) has five restaurants, a huge pool and all manner of sporting facilities – including a polo field – and cultural entertainments.

Phra Ratchaniwet Marukhathaiyawan

Midway between Cha-am and Hua Hin lies the lustrous seaside palace of Rama VI, **Phra Ratchaniwet Marukhathaiyawan** (daily 8am–4pm; by donation), a rarely visited place despite the easy access – the half-hourly buses from Bangkok to Hua Hin stop within a couple of kilometres' walk of the palace: just follow the track through the army compound.

Designed by an Italian architect and completed in just sixteen days in 1923, the golden teak building was abandoned to the corrosive sea air after Rama VI's death in 1925. Restoration work began in the 1970s and most of the structure now looks as it once did: a stylish composition of verandahs and latticework painted in pastel shades of beige and blue, with an emphasis on cool simplicity. The spacious open hall in the north wing, hung with chandeliers and encircled by a first-floor balcony, was once used as a theatre, and the adjacent upstairs rooms, now furnished only with a few black-and-white portraits from the royal family photo album, were given over to royal attendants. The king stayed in the centre, with the best sea view and access to the promenade, while the south wing (still not fully restored) contained the queen's apartments.

Hua Hin

Thailand's oldest beach resort, **HUA HIN** used to be little more than an over-grown fishing village with one exceptionally grand hotel, but now the grotty beachfront flounders under a jungle of half-built upmarket hotels and high-rise condominiums, while the numerous farang-managed bars make Hua Hin a favourite weekend haunt of expatriate Western men. With the far superior beaches of Ko Samui, Krabi and Ko Samet so close at hand, there's little here to draw the sunseeker, but it's nonetheless a convivial place in which to drink and enjoy superb seafood – and unlike Pattaya across the Gulf, it's as yet free of go-go bars and neon architecture. In addition, the town boasts a glut of tour agencies, making it a convenient base for **day trips** to Khao Sam Roi Yot National Park, 63km south.

Around the turn of the century, **royalty** were Hua Hin's main visitors, but the place became more widely popular in the 1920s, when the opening of the Bangkok–Malaysia rail line made short excursions to the beach much more viable. The Victorian-style *Railway Hotel* was built soon after to cater for the leisured classes, and in 1926 Rama VII had his own summer palace, Klai Klangwon (Far from Worries), erected at the northern end of the beach. It was here, ironically, that Rama VII was staying in 1932 when the coup was launched in Bangkok against the system of absolute monarchy. The royals still come down to the palace for summer breaks – you'll know if they are in town, because the streets get decked with enormous hand-painted billboard portraits of the king and queen, and all the shops hang out the national flag.

If you're not here for the beer, you've been to the park, and there are no royals to be seen, the only reason to visit Hua Hin is to stay in the former **Railway Hotel**, down by the beach at the eastern end of Damnern Kasem Road. Now called the *Hotel Sofitel Central Hua Hin* (☎032/512021; Bangkok ☎02/233 0980; ⑨), the hotel remains a classic of colonial-style architecture, with cool, high ceilings, heavy-bladed ceiling fans, polished wood-panelling and wide sea-view balconies. All is much as it was seventy years ago, except for the swimming pools and tennis courts which were built especially for the filming of *The Killing Fields* – the *Railway Hotel* stood in as Phnom Penh's plushest hotel.

Practicalities

If you do find yourself staying here but can't afford the *Railway Hotel*'s prices, check in at one of the pretty wooden **guest houses** squashed into the sois behind the seafront, bearing in mind that all rooms are more expensive at weekends. *Phuen Guest House* on Soi Binthabat (☎032/512344; ②–③), has smallish rooms, some giving onto a quaint streetfront balcony, while *Sunee* at 156 Naretdamri Rd (②–③) is more spacious. Alternatively, the guest houses at the northern end of Naretdamri Road are strung out along wooden jetties, so you can hear the waves even if you can't afford a room overlooking them. The best of these is *Mod Guest House* at no. 116 (☎032/512296; ②–⑤), which has some very good rooms and some fairly basic ones, plus a great seafront terrace-restaurant and seating area. The adjacent *Sea Breeze* (②–④) also has a seafront terrace, though rooms here are slightly inferior. In the **mid-range** bracket, the sprucely kept and comfortable *Jed Pee Nong* on the main Damnern Kasem artery (☎032/512381; ⑤–⑥) has a pool, which makes it pretty good value, while the Italian-run *Fresh Inn* at 132 Naretdamri Rd (☎032/511389; ⑤–⑥) enjoys a friendly, cosy atmosphere. Finally, if you want extreme luxury but for some reason don't fancy the old *Railway Hotel*, the *Melia Hua Hin* at 33 Naretdamri Rd (☎032/512879; ⑨) is the obvious alternative; bang in the centre of Hua Hin's beachfront, its high-rise profile disfigures the local skyline, but the facilities are extensive and the views fine.

The best places to sample locally caught fish and seafood are the seafront **restaurants** at the north end of Naretdamri Road, the larger among them, like *Seaside Restaurant* in the heart of the port, fairly pricey but recommended. Of the string of smaller places further south along Naretdamri, the unpretentious but very palatable *Khun Daeng's Restaurant,* near Damnern Kasem Road, serves tasty Thai, Western and vegetarian dishes at reasonable prices. More affordable still, and authentically Thai, are the **night-market stalls**, in the streets around the train station, which start frying at dusk. Finally, the small, farang-run bars along almost every soi between Highway 4 and the seafront comfort homesick Westerners with fish and chips, baked beans and German sausage.

For **excursions** to Khao Sam Roi Yot National Park, try the Thai/English *Toodtoo Tours* (☎032/512209), opposite the *Melia Hotel* at 128 Naretdamri Rd. The **tourist information** desk at the local government office (daily 8.30am–4.30pm; ☎032/511047), on the corner of Damnern Kasem Road and Highway 4 (about 50m east of the train station), also offers advice on getting there and stocks bus and train timetables. Alternatively, you can rent your own transport – bicycles (B60 a day) and motorbikes (B150–600) – from several places on Damnern Kasem Road.

Khao Sam Roi Yot National Park

With a name that translates as "the Mountain with Three Hundred Peaks", the magnificent **KHAO SAM ROI YOT NATIONAL PARK**, 63km south of Hua Hin, boasts a remarkable variety of terrain, vegetation and wildlife within its 98 square kilometres. The dramatic **limestone crags** after which it is named are indeed its dominant feature, looming up to 650m above the Gulf waters and the forested interior, but perhaps more significant are the mudflats and freshwater marsh which attract and provide a breeding ground for thousands of migratory birds. **Bird-watching** is the major draw, but great caves, excellent forest and coastal trails and a couple of secluded beaches provide strong competition. Pick up a **park map** from Hua Hin's tourist information desk before you go – it's sketchy but better than nothing.

Access and accommodation

Like most of Thailand's national parks, Khao Sam Roi Yot's chief drawback is also the secret of its appeal – it's hellishly hard to get to by public transport. You need to take a local **bus** (every 20min; 40min) to Pranburi (23km) and then either charter a songthaew or a motorbike taxi (B150–250) to the park headquarters. But even once you're there, it's difficult to get about without wheels, as the sights, all accessible by park road, are spread all over the place – Hat Laem Sala and Tham Phraya Nakhon are 16km from HQ, Tham Sai is 8km, and the marsh at Rong Jai is 32km away. You can bypass the headquarters altogether and go directly to the beach at Laem Sala and the cave of Phraya Nakhon; hourly songthaews from Pranburi market go to the fishing village of **Bang Phu**, then it's a thirty-minute boat ride (B150 return for the whole boat) or a steep twenty- to thirty-minute trek from Bang Phu's temple – note that the last return songthaew leaves Bang Phu at 1pm.

Your best bet is to **rent your own transport from Hua Hin**: follow Highway 4 south to **Pranburi** (23km), turn left at Pranburi's main intersection and drive another 23km to the park checkpoint, carry on past the turn-off to Laem Sala, and continue 13km to the **park headquarters and visitors' centre**, near the village of Khao Daeng. Alternatively, you could join a one-day **tour** from Hua Hin for about B650, though these tend to focus on the caves and beaches rather than the birds and animals.

The park's **accommodation** sites are around the headquarters and at Laem Sala; at both places it's a choice between camping, at B10 per person, or staying in one of the national park bungalows (③–⑤), which sleep up to twenty people.

The park

Wildlife-spotting is best begun from the **visitors' centre**, which has easy access to the mudflats along the shore, and is the starting-point for the park's two official **nature trails** – the "Horseshoe Trail", which takes in the forest habitats of monkeys, squirrels and songbirds, and the "Mangrove Trail", which leads through the swampy domiciles of crabs, mudskippers, monitor lizards and egrets (for more on mangrove habitats, see p.553). When hungry, the **long-tailed (crab-eating) macaque** hangs around the mangrove swamps, but is also quite often spotted near the park headquarters, along with the **dusky langur** or leaf monkey (also know as the spectacled langur because of the distinctive white skin around its eyes); the nocturnal **slow loris** (very furry and brown, with a dark ring around each eye, and a dark stripe along its back) is a lot shyer and rarely seen. The park's forested crags are home to the increasingly rare **serow** (a black ungulate that looks like a cross between a goat and an antelope), as well as hordes of monkeys. Eminently spottable are the small, tawny-brown **barking deer** and **palm civets; dolphins** are also sometimes seen off the coast.

The park hosts up to **three hundred species of bird**. Between September and November, the mudflats along the park's shoreline are thick with migratory shore birds from Siberia, China and northern Europe – some en route to destinations further south, others here for the duration. The freshwater marsh near the village of **Rong Jai** is a good place for observing **waders** and **songbirds** and is one of only two places in the whole country where the **purple heron** breeds. Pick up a photocopied "bird-watchers' guide" – and a pair of binoculars – from the visitors' centre.

The park also has a number of trails leading to **caves**, **beaches** and **villages**, the most popular heading to the area around **Hat Laem Sala**, a sandy, casuarina-fringed bay shadowed by limestone cliffs (see opposite for access). Nearby, the huge, roofless **Tham Phraya Nakhon** is also quite a draw: it houses an elegant wooden pavilion constructed here by Rama V in 1890, and subsequent kings have left their signatures on the limestone walls. A three-hour trek from Phraya Nakhon, **Tham Sai** is a genuine dark and dank limestone cave, complete with stalactites, stalagmites and petrified waterfalls. The trek offers some fine coastal views, but a shorter alternative is the twenty-minute trail from **Khung Tanot** village (accessible by road), where you can rent a (very necessary) flashlight.

Prachuap Khiri Kan

Between Hua Hin and Chumphon there's only one place that makes a decent way-station on the route south, and that's **PRACHUAP KHIRI KHAN**, 90km beyond Hua Hin. It has attractive streets of brightly painted wooden houses and vibrant bougainvillea and hibiscus blossoms, as well as a very good night market serving delicious fresh fish, set up alongside the otherwise dismal beach. Prachuap is only 12km east of the Burmese border, and you can see the Burmese mountains clearly if you climb the 417 steps up the monkey-infested Khao Chong Krajok at the northern end of town. For overnight stops, try the *Yutichai Hotel* (☎032/611055; ②) near the train station or the *Inthira Hotel* (②) around the corner near the market square; the better appointed *Tesaban Bungalows* (☎032/611150; ④) on Susuk Rd, sleep four and have sea views.

Chumphon and around

South Thailand officially starts at **CHUMPHON**, where the main road splits into west- and east-coast branches, and inevitably the provincial capital saddles itself with the title "gateway to the south". Yet only recently has Chumphon begun to sell itself to tourists, an area of economic potential that assumed vital significance after November 1989, when Typhoon Gay – the worst typhoon to hit Thailand in recent decades – crashed into Chumphon province, killing hundreds of people and uprooting acres of banana, rubber and coconut plantations. With the mainstays of the

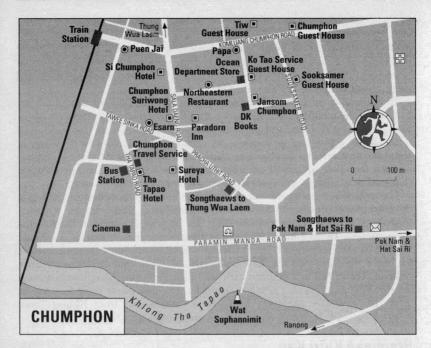

CHUMPHON

region's economy in ruins, TAT and other government agencies began billing the beaches 12km east of town as a diving centre for the February to October season, when west-coast seas get too choppy. More recently, the town has started to profit from its proximity to **Ko Tao** (see p.425 for details of getting there), successfully marketing itself as the up-and-coming island's most convenient departure point.

Chumphon's arrival on the backpackers' circuit has resulted in the frenzied development of a service-based infrasructure. But although the single diving base, *Chumphon Cabana* (see p.398), offers competitive prices and trips to unpolluted offshore reefs, the town is simply not in the same league as neighbouring Ko Samui (see p.403). It's relaxed and friendly for sure, and not yet overrun with farangs, but the beaches are twenty minutes out of town and the resorts there seemingly unwilling to accommodate the budget visitor. And so it is still the case that most travellers stop by Chumphon for a night, take the boat to Ko Tao, and spend another night here on their way back north.

Arrival and accommodation

Buses from Bangkok arrive at the terminal on Tha Tapao Road, one block west of Chumphon's main thoroughfare, Sala Daeng Road; **trains** stop at the station about 500m further north.

As with most other Thai towns, Chumphon's **guest houses** are the friendliest places to stay, if not exactly the last word in comfort, and they're all geared up for travellers, with farang-friendly menus, bikes for hire and plenty of local information. The **hotels** in town are generally less pricey than those on the beaches, but nothing special.

Chumphon's guest houses are used to accommodating Ko Tao-bound travellers, so it's generally no problem to check into a room for half a day before catching the night boat. Most places will also store luggage for you until your return to the mainland.

Chumphon Guest House, 73 Komluang Chumphon Rd (☎077/501242). Small, scruffy and only worth considering if everywhere else is full. ②.

Chumphon Suriwong, 125/27–29 Sala Daeng Rd (☎077/511397). Large and characterless, but scrupulously clean, with both fan-cooled and air-con rooms with shower. ③–④.

Jansom Chumphon, off Sala Daeng Road (☎077/502502). Chumphon's swanky, top-of-the-range hotel offers air-con, TV and all the usual trimmings. ⑥–⑦.

Ko Tao Service Guest House, on the *Papa Restaurant* soi off Komluang Chumphon Road, opposite the side entrance to *Ocean Department Store* (☎077/511606). A simple but welcoming place, efficiently flagged from the station. ②.

Paradorm Inn, 180/12 Paradorm Rd, east off Sala Daeng Road (☎077/511597). The best value of the town's mid-range hotels: all rooms have air-con, and there's a pool and restaurant. ⑤.

Si Chumphon, 127/22–24 Sala Daeng Rd (☎077/511379). Very similar to neighbouring *Chumphon Suriwong*, with no ambience but faultless hygiene. ③.

Sooksamer Guest House, 118/4 Sooksamer Rd (☎077/502430). Located on a very peaceful street, this is Chumphon's most appealing budget option, with comfortable rooms in a traditional house and a communal seating area in the breezy space beneath. ②.

Sureya Hotel, 125/24–25 Sala Daeng Rd (☎077/511444). Boasting the least pricey beds in town, it's slightly grotty but not as bad as *Chumphon Guest House*. ①.

Tha Tapao Hotel, 66/1 Tha Tapao Rd (☎077/511479). Only slightly less costly than the *Paradorm* but notably shabbier, this mid-range hotel's redeeming feature is its proximity to the bus station. ④–⑤.

Tiw Guest House, Komluang Chumphon Soi 1 (☎077/502900). Clearly signposted all the way from the train station (about a 5-min walk away), this guest house offers smallish rooms in a house on a quiet, residential soi. Friendly and well-informed staff. ②.

Eating

There are a couple of very good northeastern **restaurants** in town – the one next to the *Ocean Department Store* off Sala Daeng Road serves *kai yang*, *somtam* and sticky rice all day, the other, *Esarn* on Tawee Sinka Road, has basic Thai dishes in the daytime and northeastern fare in the evening. For freshly caught seafood, try the large, open-air *Papa* on Komluang Chumphon Road (close to *Ko Tao Guest House)*, or the similar *Puen Jai*, an upmarket garden restaurant across from the train station. Simple standard Thai fare is the speciality of *Tiw Restaurant* at the Tawee Sinka/Sala Daeng intersection, run by the friendly managers of *Tiw Guest House*. After dark, the night market sets up along both sides of Sala Daeng Road. For Western food, check out the breakfasts at *Paradorm Inn*, the coffee bar on the third floor of the *Ocean Department Store*, which stocks ten different coffee blends, or the pizzas in the food centre on the same floor.

Beaches, islands and day trips

Chumphon's best beach is **THUNG WUA LAEM**, 12km north and served by frequent songthaews from halfway down Pracha Uthit Road, about ten minutes' walk southeast of the Sala Daeng Road hotels. The long sandy stretch is as yet undeveloped, with only a couple of resorts and a handful of seafood restaurants. *Chumphon Cabana* (☎077/501990; ⑤–⑥) offers a selection of well-appointed bungalows at the southern end of the beach, and also runs Chumphon's only **dive centre**, running trips to nearby islands and offering NAUI-certificated five-day courses for around B7500. About 700m further up the beach, *Chuan Phun Resort* (☎01/726 0201; ⑤–⑦) has a range of attractively furnished seafront bungalows and a terrace restaurant.

If you're keen to go diving or snorkelling independently, then you should make for **HAT SAI RI**, 21km south of town and reached by frequent songthaews from Paramin Manda Road. Though dirtier and busier than Thung Wua Laem, this is the best place to hire boats to the tiny offshore **islands**, some of the best of which are visible from the beach: it's well worth exploring the reefs around **Ko Mattra** and **Ko Rat** (the one shaped like a half-submerged rhino), and although nearby **Ko Lang Ka Chiu** is out of bounds because of its birds'-nest collecting business, it's permissible to dive in the surrounding waters. Further afield, about 18km offshore, the reefs of **Ko Ngam Yai** and **Ko Ngam Noi** are the usual destination of the *Chumphon Cabana* diving expeditions. A day's boat ride around all or some of these islands should cost about B1600 per ten-person boat (excluding any diving or snorkelling equipment); either negotiate directly with the fishermen on Hat Sai Ri or enlist the help of the amenable manager of *Sai Ri Lodge* (☎077/ 521212; ⑤–⑦) at the southern end of the beach.

Most organized **day-trip** itineraries take in a selection of waterfalls and caves around Chumphon, and end with a quick swim at Thung Wua Laem – ask at *Ko Tao Service Guest House* or *Chumphon Information Centre* for details. For longer, more adventurous trips, check out the **treks** run by *Tri Star Adventure Tours* (contactable at *Sooksamer Guest House*) whose packages include jungle walking, rafting and camping, island-hopping and caving.

Chaiya and around

About 140km south of Chumphon, **CHAIYA** was the capital of southern Thailand under the Srivijayan empire, which fanned out from Sumatra between the eighth and thirteenth centuries. Today there's little to mark the passing of the Srivijayan civilization, but this small, sleepy town has gained new fame as the site of Wat Suan Mokkh, a progressively minded temple whose meditation retreats account for the bulk of Chaiya's farang visitors. There's nowhere to stay in town, so unless you're interested in one of the retreats the town is best visited on a day trip, either as a break in the journey south, or as an excursion from Surat Thani.

Chaiya is 3km from Highway 41, the main road down this section of the Gulf coast: **buses** from Chumphon to Surat Thani will drop you off on the highway, from where you can catch a motorbike taxi or walk into town; from Surat Thani's local bus station, hourly buses take an hour to reach Chaiya. Although the town lies on the main southern rail line, most **trains** arrive in the middle of the night. Only the evening trains from Bangkok are useful, getting you to Chaiya first thing in the morning.

The Town
The main sight in Chaiya is **Wat Phra Boromathat** on the western side of town, where the ninth-century chedi – one of very few surviving examples of Srivijayan architecture – is said to contain relics of the Buddha himself. Hidden away behind the viharn in a pretty, red-tiled cloister, the chedi looks like an over-sized

wedding cake surrounded by an ornamental moat. Its unusual square tiers are spiked with smaller chedis and decorated with gilt, in a style similar to the temples of central Java.

The **National Museum** (Wed–Sun 8am–4pm; B10) on the eastern side of the temple is a disappointment. Although the Srivijaya period produced some of Thailand's finest sculpture, much of it discovered at Chaiya, the best pieces have been carted off to the National Museum in Bangkok. Replicas have been left in their stead, which are shown alongside fragments of some original statues and an exhibition of local handicrafts. The best remaining piece is a serene stone image of the Buddha from **Wat Kaeo**, an imposing chedi on the south side of town. Heading towards the centre from Wat Phra Boromathat, you take the first paved road on the right, which brings you first to the brick remains of Wat Long, and then after 1km to Wat Kaeo, enclosed by a thick ring of trees. Here you can poke around the murky antechambers of the chedi, taking care not to trip over the various dismembered stone Buddhas that are lying around.

Ban Phum Riang

If you've got some time on your hands, you could take one of the regular songthaews to **BAN PHUM RIANG**, 5km east of Chaiya, a Muslim crab-fishing village of wooden stilted houses clustered around a rickety mosque. The weavers here are famous for their original designs of silk and cotton: although the cottage industry is on the decline, you might still be able to pick up a bargain in the village's handful of shops.

Wat Suan Mokkh

The forest temple of **Wat Suan Mokkh** (Garden of Liberation), 6km south of Chaiya on Highway 41, was founded by **Buddhadasa Bhikkhu**, southern Thailand's most revered monk until his death in 1993 at the age of 87. His back-to-basics philosophy, encompassing Christian, Zen and Taoist influences, lives on and continues to draw Thais from all over the country to the temple, as well as thousands of farangs. It's not necessary to sign up for one of the wat's retreats to enjoy the temple, however – all buses between Chaiya and Surat Thani pass the wat, and there are songthaews and motorbike taxis too, so it's easy to drop by for a quiet stroll through the wooded grounds.

The layout of the wat is centred on the Golden Hill: scrambling up between trees and monks' huts, you'll reach a hushed clearing on top of the hill which is the temple's holiest meeting-place, a simple open-air platform decorated with nothing more than a stone Buddha with the Wheel of Law. At the base of the hill, the outer walls of the Spiritual Theatre are lined with bas-reliefs, replicas of originals in India, which depict scenes from the life of the Buddha. Inside, every centimetre is covered with colourful didactic painting, executed by resident monks and visitors in a jumble of realistic and surrealistic styles.

MEDITATION RETREATS

The **meditation retreats** are held by farang and Thai teachers over the first ten days of every month at the International Dharma Heritage, a purpose-built compound 1km from the main temple. Large numbers of farang travellers, both novices and experienced meditators, turn up for the retreats, which are intended as a challenging exercise in mental development – it's not an opportunity to relax and live at low cost for a few days. Conditions imitate the rigorous lifestyle of a *bhikkhu* (monk) as far as possible, each day beginning before dawn with meditation according to the *anapanasati* method, which aims to achieve mindfulness by focusing on the breathing process. Although talks are given on *dharma* (the doctrines of the Buddha – as interpreted by Buddhadasa Bhikkhu) and meditation technique, most of each day is spent practising *anapanasati* in solitude. To aid concentration, participants maintain a rule of silence, broken only by daily chanting sessions, although supervisors are available for individual interviews if there are any questions or problems. Men and women are segregated into separate dormitory blocks, and, like monks, are expected to help out with chores.

The fee is B600 per person, which includes two vegetarian meals a day and accommodation in simple cells. Bring a flashlight (or buy one outside the temple gates) and any other supplies you'll need for the ten days – participants are encouraged not to leave the premises during the retreat. Each course has space for about one hundred people – turn up at the information desk in Wat Suan Mokkh by early afternoon on the last day of the month to enrol, or telephone the temple (☎077/431552) for further information.

Surat Thani

Uninspiring **SURAT THANI**, 60km south of Chaiya, is generally worth visiting only as the jumping-off point for the Samui archipelago (see p.403, p.416 and p.422), though it might be worth a stay when the Chak Phra Festival is in swing, or using as a base for seeing the nearby historic town of Chaiya.

Strung along the south bank of the Tapi River, with a busy port for rubber and coconuts near the river mouth, the town is experiencing rapid economic growth and paralyzing traffic jams. Its sole attraction is the **Monkey Training College** (daylight hours; B100), a half-hour trip out of town to the east, where young monkeys are trained to pick coconuts from trees which are too tall for humans to reach.

Coconut-picking monkey

To get there, charter a songthaew, or take a local bus 6km east towards Kanchanadit and Don Sak and then walk the last 2km, following the signpost south from the main road. For anyone who turns up, the owner will put on an exploitative hour-long coconut-picking display with his champion pig-tailed macaque, although the serious business of the college is undoubtedly worthy, for coconuts are the province's most important crop, providing a much-needed cash livelihood for small farmers. At the end of the display, the owner will show you the stable at the back where the most laborious parts of the training take place. Graduates of the three-month course are worth B3000 and can farm up to one thousand coconuts a day.

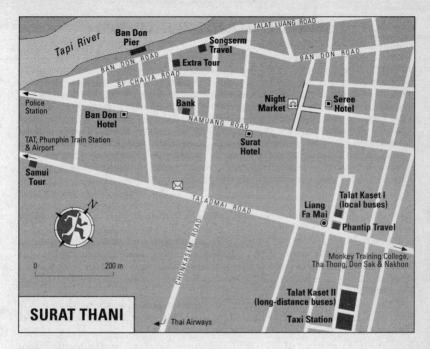

Map labels:

Tapi River
Ban Don Pier
TALAT LUANG ROAD
Songserm Travel
BAN DON ROAD
Extra Tour
SI CHAIYA ROAD
BAN DON ROAD
Police Station
Bank
Night Market
Seree Hotel
Ban Don Hotel
NAMUANG ROAD
TAT, Phunphin Train Station & Airport
Surat Hotel
Samui Tour
TALADMAI ROAD
Talat Kaset I (local buses)
Liang Fa Mai
Phantip Travel
CHONKASEM ROAD
0   200 m
Monkey Training College, Tha Thong, Don Sak & Nakhon
Talat Kaset II (long-distance buses)
SURAT THANI
Thai Airways
Taxi Station

Practicalities

All **buses** to Surat Thani arrive at Taladmai Road in the centre of town, either at Talat Kaset I on the north side of the road (local buses) or opposite at Talat Kaset II (long-distance buses). Arriving by **train**, however, means arriving at Phunphin, 13km to the west, from where buses run every ten minutes between 6am and 7pm and share-taxis leave when full (B10 per person or B60 to charter the whole car). It's also possible to buy express-boat and vehicle-ferry tickets to Ko Samui and Ko Pha Ngan from the train station, including a connecting bus to the relevant pier, Tha Thong or Don Sak. If you're planning to leave by train, booking tickets at *Phantip Travel*, in front of Talat Kaset I at 442/24–25 Taladmai Rd (☎077/272230), will save an extra trip to Phunphin.

Phunphin and the bus stations are teeming with **touts** offering to escort you onto their employer's service to **Ko Samui or Ko Pha Ngan** – they're generally reliable but make sure you don't get talked onto the wrong boat. If you manage to avoid getting hustled, you can buy tickets from Surat's major travel agents: *Songserm Travel*, on Ban Don Road opposite the night-boat pier (☎077/286340 or 286341), handles the express boats to Samui and Pha Ngan, and the vehicle ferry to Pha Ngan; *Samui Tour*, 326/12 Taladmai Rd (☎077/282352), handles the vehicle ferry to Samui.

Arriving by **air**, you can take a B35 *Thai Airways* minibus for the 27-kilometre journey south into Surat Thani, or a B150 combination ticket (express boat or vehicle ferry) to Ko Samui; if you're flying out of Surat, you can catch the minibus from town to the airport at the *Thai Airways* office, south of the centre at 3/27–28

THE CHAK PHRA FESTIVAL

At the start of the eleventh lunar month (September or October) the people of Surat Thani celebrate the end of Buddhist Lent with the Chak Phra Festival (Pulling the Buddha), which symbolizes the Buddha's return to earth after a monsoon season spent preaching to his mother in heaven. On the Tapi River, tug-boats pull the town's principal Buddha image on a raft decorated with huge nagas, while on land similar floats are hauled across the countryside and through the streets on sleigh-like floats bearing Buddha images and colourful flags and parasols. As the monks have been confined to their monasteries for three months, the end of Lent is also the time to give them generous offerings in the *kathin* ceremony, of which Surat Thani has its own version, called Thot Pha Pa, when the offerings are hung on tree branches planted in front of the houses before dawn. Longboat races, between teams from all over the south, are also held during the festival.

Karoonrat Rd, off Chonkasem Road (☎077/272610), or at the *Wangtai Hotel,* listed below.

If you're coming from points south by **air-conditioned minibus**, you should be deposited at the door of your destination; when leaving Surat, tickets are booked and passengers collected from travel agents such as *Extra Tour,* located on an unnamed lane between Ban Don and Si Chaiya roads opposite the Ban Don pier (☎077/282112).

TAT has a helpful office, shared by the **tourist police**, at the western end of town at 5 Taladmai Rd (daily 8am–4pm; ☎077/288818 or 288819), which stocks free, sketchy maps.

Accommodation and eating

Most budget **accommodation** in Surat Thani is noisy, grotty and overpriced – you'd probably be better off on a night boat to Ko Samui or Ko Pha Ngan. *Surat Hotel* at 496 Namuang Rd (☎077/272243; ①) is admittedly inexpensive but has pokey doubles; a much better choice, at the lower end of its price bracket, is the *Ban Don Hotel,* above a restaurant at 168 Namuang Rd (☎077/272167; ③), where clean rooms with en suite bathrooms are set back from the noise of the main road. *Seree Hotel,* 2/2–5 Tonpor Rd (☎077/272279; ③–④), is also clean and quiet but a little further upmarket, with fan-cooled and air-conditioned rooms. At the western end of town, *Wangtai Hotel,* 1 Taladmai Rd (☎077/283020–39; Bangkok reservations ☎02/253 7947; ⑥), is Surat Thani's luxury option, and reasonably good value with large, smart rooms around a swimming pool.

For good, inexpensive Thai and Chinese **food**, try the *Jarng Pochana* at the top end of Don Nok Road – head west on Taladmai Road past *Samui Tour* and turn left at the *Siam Thara Hotel.* The *Liang Fa Mai,* outside the local bus station at 293/41 Taladmai Rd, does inexpensive and tasty duck, chicken and pork on rice (7am–5pm only). The night market between Si Chaiya and Ban Don roads displays an eye-catching range of dishes; a smaller offshoot by Ban Don pier offers less choice but is handy if you're taking a night boat. The fare at *Steak Roy Yim,* a kitsch, air-conditioned eaterie opposite TAT at 50–1 Taladmai Rd, will not quite raise the hundred smiles its name suggests, but far outshines what passes for Western food elsewhere in Surat.

Ko Samui

An ever-widening cross-section of visitors, from globetrotting backpackers to suit-case-toting fortnighters, come to southern Thailand just for the beautiful beaches of **KO SAMUI**, 80km from Surat – and at 15km across and down, Samui is large enough to cope, except during the rush at Christmas and New Year, and in July and August. The paradisal sands and clear blue seas have kept their good looks, which are enhanced by a thick fringe of palm trees that gives a harvest of three million coconuts each month. Development behind the beaches, however, which has brought the islanders far greater prosperity than the crop could ever provide, speeds along in a messy, haphazard fashion with little concern for the environment; a local bye-law limits new construction to the height of a coconut palm, but the island's latest and largest hotel complex basks in the shade of some suspiciously lofty trees, said to be brought in from northern Thailand.

For most visitors, the days are spent indulging in a few water sports or just lying on the beach waiting for the next drinks seller, hair braider or masseur to come along. For a day off the sand, you should not miss the almost supernatural beauty of the **Ang Thong National Marine Park**, which comprises many of the eighty islands in the Samui archipelago. A motorbike day trip on the fifty-kilometre round-island road will throw up plenty more gorgeous beaches, and night-time entertainment will be provided by a growing number of bars and discos. Buffalo fighting, once a common sport on the island, is now restricted to special festivals such as Thai New Year; the practices and rituals are much the same as those of bullfighting in Hat Yai (see p.502).

The island's most appealing beaches have seen the heaviest development and are now the most expensive places to stay, while quieter beaches such as Maenam are generally less attractive. **Choeng Mon** in Samui's northeast corner makes a good compromise: the beaches are nothing to write home about but views of the bay are, the seafront between the handful of upmarket hotels is underdeveloped, and Chaweng's nightlife is within easy striking distance. **Accommodation** on the island is generally in bungalow resorts, from the primitive to the swish: at the lower end of the scale, expect to pay at least B150 per bungalow for an en suite bathroom and some degree of comfort, while for the more upmarket places at Chaweng and Lamai, the most beautiful but most developed beaches, you can pay over B1500. The price codes on the following pages are based on high-season rates, but out of season – roughly April, May, June, October and November – dramatic reductions are possible. Many of these resorts have **restaurants** which are good, inexpensive and strong on seafood.

No particular **season** is best for coming to Ko Samui. The northeast monsoon blows heaviest in November, but can bring rain at any time between October and January, and sometimes makes the sea on the east coast too choppy for swimming. (The north coast is generally calm enough for swimming all year round.) January is often breezy, March and April are very hot, and between May and October the southwest monsoon blows mildly onto Samui's west coast and causes a little rain.

Ko Samui has around a dozen **scuba-diving** companies, offering trips for qualified divers and a wide variety of courses throughout the year. Although the coral gardens at the north end of Ang Thong National Marine Park offer good diving between October and April, most trips for experienced divers head for the waters

around Ko Tao (see p.424), which contain the best sites in the region; a day's outing costs upwards of B2200, though if you can make your own way to Ko Tao, you'll save money and have more time in the water. The most established and reliable outfit is *Samui International Diving School*, which has branches on the waterfront south of the piers in Na Thon (☎077/421465), at the *Malibu Resort* towards the north end of Central Chaweng (☎077/422386), in the centre of Lamai (☎077/424395), and at *Baan Taling Ngam Resort*. The prices and range of courses are generally comparable to what's on offer at Ko Tao.

Getting to the island

The most obvious way of getting to Ko Samui is on a boat from the Surat Thani area. Of these the least expensive is the ferry which leaves Ban Don pier in **Surat Thani** itself for Na Thon – the main port on Samui – at 11pm every night (6hr); tickets, priced at B60 for the lower deck and B80 for the less claustrophobic upper deck, are sold at the pier on the day of departure.

From **Tha Thong**, 5km east of Surat, two express boats a day, handled by *Songserm Travel* (see p.401) run to Na Thon for most of the year, increased to three in peak season (2hr 30min); the B105 ticket includes bus transport through Surat or Phunphin train station to the pier. Vehicle ferries, handled by *Samui Tour* (see p.401) run five times a day between **Don Sak** pier, 68km east of Surat, and Thong Yang, 8km south of Na Thon (1hr 30min); a combination ticket including the bus trips from Surat or Phunphin to Don Sak and from Thong Yang to Na Thon costs B70 for ordinary buses, B90 for air-conditioned buses (the total journey time is much the same as on an express boat, and if the sea is turbulent, the shorter voyage on a vehicle ferry can be a blessing). Note that points of departure from the mainland are sometimes switched around due to the prevailing weather and tides – and Khanom, a commercial port 30km southeast of Don Sak, is occasionally used – but as most tickets include bus transport to the boat, this should not be a worry.

From Bangkok, the State Railway does train-bus-boat packages through to Ko Samui which cost almost exactly the same as organizing the parts independently – about B350 if you travel in a second-class reclining seat. Overnight bus-boat packages are especially inexpensive on Khao San Road, from around B250, but the vehicles used are often sub-standard and several thefts have been reported on these services. At the top of the range, you can get to Ko Samui direct **by air** on *Bangkok Airways* (in Bangkok ☎02/229 3456 or 229 3434; at Samui airport ☎077/425011 or 425012); seven eighty-minute flights a day leave Bangkok, and there are even daily flights from Phuket (40min) and U-Tapao, near Pattaya (1hr). Minibuses meet incoming flights (and connect with departures) at the **airport** in the northeastern tip of the island, and run to the north coast, Choeng Mon and Chaweng for B60, Na Thon and Lamai for B80; the rustic terminal has a reservations desk for some of the island's moderate and expensive hotels, currency exchange facilities, restaurants, and a *Hertz* car rental branch (☎077/425011–2 or 425029–30).

Finally, it's possible to hop to Ko Samui from **Ko Pha Ngan**: two boats a day (3 in high season) do the 45-minute trip from Thong Sala to Na Thon (B60), while from Hat Rin two boats a day take an hour to reach either Bangrak or Hat Bophut, depending on the prevailing weather (B60). Between January and September, if there are enough takers and the weather's good enough, one boat a day starts at Thong Nai Pan, on Ko Pha Ngan's east coast, and calls at Hat Rin before crossing to Maenam.

Na Thon

The island capital, **NA THON**, at the top of the long western coast, is a frenetic half-built town which most travellers use only as a service station before hitting the sand: though most of the main beaches now have post offices, currency exchange amenities, supermarkets, travel agents and clinics, the biggest and best concentration of amenities is to be found here. The town's layout is simple: the two piers come to land at the promenade, Chonvithi Road, which is paralleled first by narrow Ang Thong Road, then by Taweeratpakdee Road, aka Route 4169, the round-island road; the two main cross-streets are Na Amphoe Road, just north of the piers, and Preeda Road, to the south.

Accommodation and eating
If you really need a **place to stay** in Na Thon, the best budget option is the clean and friendly *Seaview Guest House*, housed in a modern building at 67/15

Taweeratpakdee Rd (☎077/236098; ③), which, though it fails to provide views of the sea, has quiet rooms at the rear. For something further upmarket, try the *Palace Hotel* towards the southern end of the waterfront, at 152 Chonithi Rd (☎077/421079; ④), where some of the large en suite rooms do overlook the sea, or, more comfortable still, *Dumrong Town Hotel* (☎077/420471; ⑤), set back from Taweeratpakdee Road at the north end of town, which offers well-designed rooms with hot water, air conditioning, TV and minibar. If you do find yourself staying, don't miss the *Garden Home Health Center*, 2km north along Route 4169 in Ban Bang Makham – it dispenses the best massages and herbal saunas on the island.

Several stalls and small cafés purvey inexpensive, unexceptional Thai **food** along Taweeratpakdee and Ang Thong roads, and there are plenty of Western-oriented places clustered around the pier. Justifiably popular, especially for breakfast, are the two branches of *RT Bakery* – one opposite the market on Taweeratpakdee Road, the other at 31/32 Na Amphoe Road – which supply bread to bungalows and restaurants around the island and also serve Thai food. In the evening, travellers and expats tend to hang out at *The Pier Pub/ Restaurant* on Na Amphoe Road, playing pool or tucking into Western food in front of the video.

Facilities

The major **travel agents**, *Phanthip* (☎077/421221 or 421222) and *Songserm* (☎077/421316–9), are based on Chonvithi Road opposite the piers; some of the **banks** have automatic teller machines, late-night opening and safe-deposit boxes; the supermarkets and department stores are geared up for beachside needs, and many stock *Samui Today*'s detailed, accurate **map** of Surat and the archipelago (B35); there's a **post office** at the northern end of the promenade with poste restante, and an IDD (international direct dialling) telephone service upstairs that's open daily from 7am to 10pm; and tourist visas may be extended at the **immigration office**, 25/3 Moo 3, Na Amphoe Rd (☎077/ 421069). **TAT** run a small but helpful booth (daily 8.30am–4.30pm; ☎077/ 420504) opposite the post office, and *Buayeng*, on Na Amphoe Road, is the best secondhand English-language **bookstore** in this part of Thailand. For emergencies, **clinics** operate on Ang Thong and Taweeratpakdee roads, while the less costly **hospital** (☎077/421230 or 421531) is 3km south of town off Route 4169. The **tourist police** (☎077/421281) also have their base south of town, 2km down Route 4169.

Transport around the island

For **getting around the island**, Na Thon is well served with songthaews: Lamai and Ao Phangka songthaews leave from just south of the piers, songthaews for the other main beaches from just north, with fares ranging from B10 to B20 (it's planned that all songthaews will soon start using the car park between the two piers). Chaweng songthaews head off clockwise on Route 4169, Lamai song-thaews anti-clockwise, their routes meeting, but not crossing, at a roadside shelter at the south end of Chaweng Noi. You can **rent** a motorbike from B150 in Na Thon, but it's hard to find a decent new bike in the capital, so it's probably safer, and more convenient, to rent at one of the main beaches – and dozens are killed on Samui's roads each year, so proceed with caution.

Ang Thong National Marine Park

Even if you don't get your buns off the beach for the rest of your stay, it's worth taking at least a day out to visit the beautiful **ANG THONG NATIONAL MARINE PARK**, a lush, dense group of 41 small islands strewn like dragon's teeth over the deep blue Gulf of Thailand, 31km west of Samui. Once a haven for pirate junks, then a Royal Thai Navy training base, the islands and their coral reefs, white sand beaches and virgin rainforest are now preserved under the aegis of the National Parks Department. Erosion of the soft limestone has dug caves and chiselled out fantastic shapes which are variously said to resemble seals, a rhinoceros, a Buddha image and even the temple complex at Angkor.

The surrounding waters are home to dolphins, wary of humans because local fishermen catch them for their meat, and *pla thu* (short-bodied mackerel), part of the national staple diet, which gather in huge numbers between February and April to spawn around the islands. On land are found long-tailed macaques, leopard cats, common wild pig, sea otters, squirrels, monitor lizards and pythons, as well as dusky langurs which, because they have no natural enemies here, are unusually friendly and easy to spot. Around forty bird species have had confirmed sightings, including the white-rumped shama noted for its singing, the brahminy kite, black baza, little heron, Eurasian woodcock, several species of pigeon, kingfisher and wagtail, as well as common and hill myna; island caves shelter swiftlets, whose homes are stolen for bird's nest soup (see p.479).

The largest land mass in the group is **KO WUA TALAB** (Sleeping Cow Island) where the park headquarters shelters in a hollow behind the small beach. From there it's a steep four-hundred-metre climb to the island's peak to gawp at the panorama, which is especially fine at sunrise and sunset: in the distance, Ko Samui, Ko Pha Ngan and the mainland; nearer at hand, the jagged edges of the surrounding archipelago; and below the peak, a secret cove on the western side and an almost sheer drop to the clear blue sea to the east. Another climb from the beach at headquarters, only 200m but even harder going, leads to Tham Buabok, a cave set high in the cliff face. Some of the stalactites and stalagmites are said to resemble lotuses, hence the cave's appellation, "Waving Lotus". If you're visiting in September, look out for the white, violet-dotted petals of **lady's slipper orchids**, which grow on the rocks and cliffs.

The feature which gives the park the name Ang Thong, meaning "Golden Bowl", is a landlocked lake, 250m in diameter, on **KO MAE KO** to the north of Ko Wua Talab. A well-made path leads from the beach to the rim of the cliff wall which encircles the lake, affording another stunning view of the archipelago and the shallow, green water far below, which is connected to the sea by a natural underground tunnel.

Clown fish

Practicalities

Apart from chartering your own boat at huge expense, the only way of **getting to Ang Thong** is on an organized day trip. From Na Thon, boats leave every day at 8.30am, returning at 5pm. In between, there's lunch on the beach at Ko Wua Talab and time to explore the island, some cruising through the archipelago, a visit to the viewpoint over the lake on Ko Mae Ko and a snorkelling stop. Tickets cost B300 per person, available from agencies around Na Thon pier and on Samui's main beaches. Similar trips run from Ban Bophut on Ko Samui and from Thong Sala pier on Ko Pha Ngan, but less frequently; *Seaflower*, at Ao Chaophao on Ko Pha Ngan's west coast, does three-day "treks" (see p.422).

If you want to **stay at Ko Wua Talab**, the National Parks Department maintains eight simple four- to fifteen-berth bungalows (⑤–⑥) at the headquarters. To book accommodation, contact the Ang Thong National Marine Park Headquarters (☎077/286931), the park office at PO Box 29, Surat Thani 84000 (☎077/286052), or the Forestry Department in Bangkok (see p.50). Camping is also possible in certain specified areas, and tents can be hired for B50 a night. If you do want to stay, you can go over on a boat-trip ticket – it's valid for a return on a later day. For getting around the archipelago from Ko Wua Talab, you should be able to charter a motor boat from the fishermen who live in the park; the best snorkelling, with the highest density and diversity of living coral, is off the west side of Ko Sam Sao or "Tripod Island", so named after its towering rocky arch. There's no public restaurant or shop in the park, so overnighters can either bring their own supplies or eat three meals with the park staff for B230 per day.

Maenam

The most westerly of the beaches on the north coast is **MAENAM**, 13km from Na Thon and now Samui's most popular destination for shoestring travellers. The exposed four-kilometre bay is not the island's prettiest, being more of a broad dent in the coastline, and the sloping beach is relatively narrow and coarse. But Maenam has the lowest rates for bed and board on the island, unspoilt views of fishing boats and Ko Pha Ngan, and, despite the recent opening of a luxury hotel, is the quietest of the major beaches. Jet-skis give way to windsurfing here (there's a rental "school" in the centre of the beach) and there's no sign of anything resembling nightlife – though if you want to go on the razzle, late-night songthaews run to and from Chaweng and Lamai. The main road is set back far from the beach amongst the trees, and runs through the sizeable fishing village of Ban Maenam, in the centre of the bay. This has some inexpensive restaurants, a clinic, and a small post office with poste restante facilities, and is one of the few places on Samui where there's more to life than tourism.

Accommodation

As well as one or two upmarket resorts, Maenam has over twenty inexpensive bungalow complexes, most offering a spread of accommodation. There's little to choose between these places, although the best of the bunch are at the far eastern end of the bay.

Cleopatra's Palace, at the eastern end of the bay, 1km from the village. A variety of clean wooden and concrete bungalows, all with fans and bathrooms, stand in an orderly though rather cramped compound. ①–④.

Friendly, about 500m east of *Cleopatra's Palace*. Easy-going place with helpful staff. All the bungalows are very clean and have their own bathrooms, though the place feels exposed with no trees to provide shade. ②–③.

Home Bay, at the far western end of Maenam. Overlooking its own large stretch of untidy beach, tucked in beside a small cliff, and set in a quiet, spacious coconut grove. Sleeping options range from primitive huts on the beach, through smart wooden bungalows with mosquito screens, to big, concrete family cottages. ①–⑤.

Maenam Resort, 500m west of the village, just beyond *Santiburi Dusit Resort* (☎077/425116). A moderately priced beachfront resort in tidy grounds, with a clean restaurant. The rooms and large bungalows, some with verandahs and air-con, offer good-value comfort. ④–⑥.

Rose, next door to *Friendly* at the eastern end of the bay. Laid-back old-timer that has resisted the urge to upgrade: basic wooden huts in a shady compound have mosquito nets but no fans, and electricity still comes from a generator (lights out 11pm). ①.

Santiburi Dusit Resort, 500m west of the village (☎077/425031–8; Bangkok reservations ☎02/236 0450–9). Maenam's only luxury hotel is also the island's most expensive, spread around a huge freshwater swimming pool and stream like a small housing estate. Accommodation is mostly in Thai-style villas, inspired by Rama IV's summer palace at Phetchaburi, each with a large bathroom and separate sitting area, furnished in luxurious traditional design. Facilities include watersports on the private stretch of beach, a health centre, an *Avis* car-rental desk, and an excellent "royal" cuisine restaurant, the *Sala Thai*. ⑨.

Shangrilah, west of *Maenam Resort*, served by the same access road (☎077/425189). A disorderly, flower-strewn compound which sprawls onto the nicest, widest stretch of sand along Maenam. Accommodation ranges from simple beachside shacks to very smart new bungalows with decent furniture and ceiling fans, and the restaurant serves good Thai food. ①–④.

Bophut

The next bay to the east is **BOPHUT**, which has a similar look to Maenam but shows a marked difference in atmosphere and facilities. The quiet two-kilometre beach attracts as many families as young travellers, and Ban Bophut, at the east end of the bay, is well geared to tourists – most of them French – with a bank, two nursing clinics, a scuba-diving outlet, a bookstore, travel agents and super-markets crammed into its two narrow streets. The part of the beach which stretches from *Peace* to *World* bungalows, at the west end of the bay, is the nicest, but again the sand is slightly coarse by Samui's high standards.

Active pursuits are amply catered for, with sailboards available at *Chai Had*, next door to *Peace*, and jet-skis and speedboats for rent in Ban Bophut; the *Samui Kart Club*, a **go-karting** track on the main road 1km west of the village, offers everyone the chance to let off steam without becoming another accident statistic on the roads of Samui (daily noon–10pm; from B230 for 12min).

Accommodation

Among Bophut's twenty or so resorts, the moderately priced bungalows offer best value. A handful of places cluster together on the west side of Ban Bophut, but the rest are well spaced out along the length of the beach.

Peace, at the mid-point of the beach (☎077/425357). This large, well-run concern concentrates more on the bottom end of the scale, but may be too much like a holiday camp for some. Bungalows range from old beachside huts with mosquito nets, showers and fans, to motel-style air-con chalets; the restaurant serves good food from Thailand and Europe, and the safe-deposit boxes are free. ②–⑤.

Samui Palm Beach Resort, next-door-but-two west of *Peace* (☎077/425494 or 425495; Bangkok reservations ☎02/245 0840). Expensive but good value, with American breakfast and airport transfers included in the price. Cottages are elegant, with air-con, hot water and hints of southern Thai architecture, and there's a small jacuzzi and swimming pool. ⑧.

Smile House, at the western end of the village (☎077/425361). Firmly in the moderate range, *Smile* has a reliable set of chalets grouped around a small, clean swimming pool. At the bottom end of the range you get a clean bathroom, mosquito screens and a fan, at the top, plenty of space and air-con. ④–⑦.

World, at the western fringe of the beach (☎077/425355 or 425356). A wide range of inexpensive and moderately priced rooms and a long menu of facilities: behind the café and beauty salon on the main road stretches a colourful garden containing a fair-sized swimming pool and a *pétanque* pitch. All of the 30-plus bungalows in the garden have verandahs and their own bathrooms, and the best are spacious and bright with hot water, air-con and cane furniture. ③–⑥.

Ziggy Stardust, at the western end of the village, near *Smile House* (☎077/425410). Welcoming mid-range place with small huts under the palm trees, and large wooden chalets with traditional gabled roofs and kitsch interiors, equipped with hot-water baths (some also have air-con). There's a good, lively beachside restaurant to boot. ④–⑦.

Bangrak

Beyond the sharp headland with its sweep of coral reefs lies **BANGRAK**, sometimes called Big Buddha Beach, after the colossus which gazes sternly down on the sun worshippers from its island in the bay. The beach is no great shakes, especially during the northeast monsoon, when the sea retreats and leaves a slippery mudflat, but Bangrak still manages to attract the water-sports crowd.

The **Big Buddha** is certainly big and works hard at being a tourist attraction, but is no beauty despite a recent face-lift. A short causeway at the eastern end of the bay leads across to a clump of souvenir shops and food stalls in front of the temple, catering to day-tripping Thais as well as farangs. Ceremonial dragon-steps then bring you up to the covered terrace around the Big Buddha, from where there's a fine view of the sweeping north coast.

Bangrak's **bungalows** are squeezed together in a narrow, noisy strip between the road and the shore, underneath the airport flight path. The best of a disappointing bunch is *LA Resort* (☎077/425330; ③), a welcoming family-run place with clean and sturdy en suite bungalows.

The northeastern cape

After Bangrak comes the high-kicking boot of the **northeastern cape**, where quiet, rocky coves, like Hat Thong Son, overlooking Ko Pha Ngan and connected by sandy lanes, are fun to explore on a motorbike. Songthaews run along the paved road to the largest and most beautiful bay, **CHOENG MON**, whose white sandy beach is lined with casuarina trees which provide shade for the bungalows and upmarket resorts.

Accommodation

Most of the accommodation on the northeastern cape is found around Choeng Mon. The tranquillity and prettiness of this bay have attracted two of Samui's most expensive hotels, but the rest of the seafront is comparatively underdeveloped and laid-back.

Boat House Hotel, south side of Choeng Mon (☎077/425041–52, Bangkok reservations ☎02/261 9004–7). One of two luxury resorts on Choeng Mon run by the reliable *Imperial* group, *Boat House* is named after the 2-storey rice barges which have been converted into suites in the grounds. It also offers luxury rooms in more prosaic modern buildings, often filled by package tours. Beyond the boat-shaped pool, a beachfront restaurant does especially good Italian fare, and the full gamut of water sports are drawn up on the sands. There's an *Avis* car-rental desk at reception. ⑧–⑨.

Choeng Mon Bungalows, north of *Boat House* on Choeng Mon (☎077/425372). A relaxing, shady compound with a good restaurant and a big choice of beds: the least costly wooden rooms have fans and en suite showers, while top-of-the-range bungalows have air-con and cold-water bathrooms. ②–⑥.

Imperial Tongsai Bay Hotel, north side of Choeng Mon (☎077/425015–28, Bangkok reservations ☎02/261 9004–7). Easy-going *Imperial* establishment with the air of a country club, with silent tuk-tuks to chauffeur you around the grounds. The luxurious red-tiled cottages command beautiful views over a secluded private beach (again plenty of water sports), a vast saltwater swimming pool and the whole bay. There's an *Avis* car rental desk, too. The very fine hotel restaurant specializes in improvising Thai dishes from the day's freshest ingredients, and, for what it's worth, was recently named by British TV personality and chef Keith Floyd as one of his top ten in the world. ⑨.

PS Villas, next door to *Choeng Mon Bungalows* (☎077/425160 or 425161). There's very little to choose between this friendly place and its neighbour, as it has a comparable range of bungalows in similarly large, beachfront grounds. ③–⑥.

Sun Sand Resort, on the southern headland of Choeng Mon (☎077/425404). Its position on a palm-clad hillside affords greater seclusion and better views over the bay than its rivals, the management is friendly and easy-going, the large, well-designed bungalows have just enough comforts (verandahs, fans and hot water, though there's no electricity during the day), the price includes American breakfast, and you can wade or swim across to a small island for exploration and snorkelling. ⑤.

Chaweng

For sheer natural beauty, none of the other beaches can match **CHAWENG**, with its broad, gently sloping strip of white sand sandwiched between the limpid blue sea and a line of palm trees. Such beauty has not escaped attention, which means, on the plus side, that Chaweng can provide just about anything the active beach bum demands – from parascending and water-skiing to thumping nightlife. The negative angle is that the new developments are ever more expensive, building work is always in progress and there's no certainty that it will look lovely when the bulldozers retreat.

The six-kilometre bay is framed between the small island of Ko Matlang at the north end and the three-hundred-metre high headland above Coral Cove in the south. From **Ko Matlang**, where the waters provide some colourful snorkelling, an often exposed coral reef slices southwest across to the mainland, marking out a shallow lagoon and **North Chaweng**. This S-shaped part of the beach has some ugly pockets of development, but at low tide it becomes a wide, inviting playground, and from October to January the reef shelters it from the worst of the northeast winds. South of the reef, the idyllic shoreline of **Central Chaweng** stretches for 2km in a dead straight line, the large village of amenities concealed behind the treeline. Around a low promontory is **Chaweng Noi**, a little curving beach in a rocky bay, which is quiet in its northern part, away from the road. South of Chaweng, the road climbs and dips into **Coral Cove**, a tiny isolated beach of coarse sand hemmed in by high rocks, with some good coral for snorkelling. It's well worth making the trip to the *Beverly Hills Café*, towards the tip of the headland which divides Chaweng from Lamai, for a jaw-dropping view over Chaweng and Choeng Mon to the peaks of Ko Pha Ngan.

Accommodation

Over fifty sets of bungalows at Chaweng are squeezed into thin strips running back from the beachfront at right angles. In the **inexpensive and moderate** range, prices are generally over the odds, although a few places, all of them listed below, offer reasonable value. More and more **expensive** places are sprouting up all the time, offering sumptuous accommodation at top-whack prices.

INEXPENSIVE TO MODERATE

Arabian, in the south of Central Chaweng, opposite *Santa Fe* nightclub (☎077/421379). Big bungalows with bathrooms, set around a lush garden. ⑤.

Blue Horizon, on the hillside above Coral Cove (☎077/422426). One of several resorts clinging to the steep hillside. A well-ordered place, where some of the sturdy, balconied bungalows have air-con and hot water. ⑤–⑥.

Charlie's Huts, in the heart of Central Chaweng. The four branches of the *Charlie's* chain, one of which is also known as *Viking*, offer Chaweng's rock-bottom accommodation, but don't expect any character or room to breathe. ①–③.

Dew Drop Huts, at the top end of Central Chaweng (☎077/422238). Secluded among dense trees, *Dew Drop* ignores the surrounding flash development to offer old-fashioned primitive huts and a friendly, laid-way-back ambience. Also on offer are herbal saunas and massages for B100 each, and reggae at the attached *Jah Dub Pub*. ②.

Hi Coral Cove, on the hillside above Coral Cove (☎077/422495). Next door to *Blue Horizon*, the bungalows here, all with en suite bathrooms, have large verandahs to make the most of their panorama over the sea; the less expensive ones offer better value. ③–④.

IKK, around the point at the far north end of North Chaweng. Comfortable en suite bungalows on an unusually spacious and peaceful stretch of sand. ③.

The Island, in the middle of North Chaweng (☎077/230941). A real find, but often full. A spread of well-designed accommodation – some of it qualifying for the upper price category – with en suite bathrooms encompasses simple rooms at the back of the compound as well as beachside, air-con cottages with hot water. A good restaurant and easy-going beach bar are turning this into a popular hang-out. ③–⑤.

Moon, at the top end of North Chaweng (☎077/422167). A lively set-up, with shaded wooden bungalows and concrete air-con rooms. ②–④.

EXPENSIVE

Chaweng Regent, at the bottom end of North Chaweng (☎077/286910; Bangkok reservations ☎02/418 4066). Elegant bungalows with all mod cons, though conditions are a little cramped. ⑧.

Coral Cove Chalets, above Coral Cove (☎077/422260 or 422261; Bangkok reservations ☎02/275 4049). Especially good-value and stylish place with bright, tasteful bungalows, each with balcony, TV and minibar, grouped around an attractive pool and jacuzzi. ⑧.

Imperial, on a small rise above Chaweng Noi (☎077/422020–36; Bangkok reservations ☎02/261 9004–7). The longest-established luxury hotel on Samui is a grand but lively establishment with a Mediterranean feel, set in leafy grounds. There's an *Avis* car-rental desk at reception. ⑨.

Eating, drinking and other practicalities

It's hard to find good inexpensive Thai **food** here, but if you're determined, head for *Mr Chin's* at the north end of Central Chaweng, which claims to stay open 24 hours a day. *Royal Thai Cuisine*, 20m up the road, is at the other end of the price

scale, but the delicious food, including a fair range of vegetarian dishes, is carefully prepared and beautifully presented, and costs less than the second-rate
Western food peddled in most places. The restaurant at *The Island* bungalows on
North Chaweng is also worth the journey for slightly pricey Western and Thai
food and good breakfasts. Prepare for culture shock if you go to *Drop-In*, a great
barn of a restaurant on the main road through North Chaweng: to the strains of a
turgid band mixing Country and Western with Neapolitan ballads, you'll find
excellent home-made pasta and choose-your-own seafood.

If you're looking for a decent place to **drink**, go to the *Rock Island Pub* on the
pretty stretch of beach in front of *The Island* bungalows, which makes a good
place to start the evening and is host to all-night bashes, usually on a Saturday.
Also on the beach, *Jah Dub* at *Dew Drop Huts* specializes in reggae, and holds
parties on Friday nights. *The Club*, at the northern end of Central Chaweng, is a
popular meeting place with good sounds, a pool table and a relaxed ambience.

Bang in the heart of Central Chaweng but set well back from the beach, *The
Reggae Pub* is not just a **nightclub**, but a venerable Samui institution, with food
and jewellery stalls, a restaurant, a message board, and an upstairs snooker club.
Chaweng's other long-standing dance venue, *Green Mango*, is set to move into a
similar multi-purpose complex at the north end of Central Chaweng in the near
future. The title of Samui's best club now goes to the recently opened *Santa Fe*, at
the south end of Central Chaweng: a Native American theme – totem-like statues,
huge corral gates and a mosaic-decorated dance floor – has resulted in a surprisingly sophisticated decor, and there are good pool tables if you need a break from
the latest imported sounds.

Small **banks** and supermarkets can be found at several locations along the
main drag, including the *Black Cat* complex, near the middle of Central
Chaweng, which also boasts a **post office** with poste restante. Opposite *The Club*
on Central Chaweng, *KL Samui* is a recommended **travel agen**t, while *Anon*, at
the north end of North Chaweng, is a reliable place to hire **motorbikes**, from
B150 a day. **Four-wheel drives** are available from *Hertz* at the *Chaweng Blue
Lagoon Hotel* on North Chaweng (☎077/422037–40; from B1100 per day with
unlimited mileage), and from *Avis* at the *Imperial Samui Hotel* on Chaweng Noi
(☎077/421390–4; from B1200 per day). The original village of Ban Chaweng, 1km
inland of Central Chaweng beach on the round-island road, has a **police station**,
a **post office** with poste restante, and a small **clinic**; about 2km north of the
village on Route 4169, *Bandon International* (☎077/425382 or 425383) is a smart,
private **hospital** with a 24-hour emergency service.

Lamai

Samui's nightlife is most intense at messily over-developed **LAMAI**, which keeps
planeloads of European package tourists happy with go-go shows and dozens of
open-air hostess bars, where the clientele sink buckets of booze slumped in front
of boxing videos. Running roughly north to south for 4km, the white palm-fringed
beach is, fortunately, still a picture – though it doesn't quite match Chaweng – and
it's possible to avoid the boozy, cruisy mayhem by staying at the quiet extremities
of the bay, where the backpackers' resorts have a definite edge over Chaweng's.
At the northern end, the spur of land which hooks eastward into the sea is perhaps
the prettiest spot: it has more rocks than sand, but the shallow sea behind the
coral reef is protected from the high seas of November, December and January.

The action is concentrated into a farang toytown of bars, clubs and Western restaurants that has grown up behind the centre of the beach, packed cheek-by-jowl along the noisy, rutted back roads. Crowded among them are supermarkets, clinics, banks and travel agents. The original village of Ban Lamai, set well back at the northern end, remains aloof from these goings-on, and its wat contains a small museum of ceramics, agricultural tools and other everyday objects. Most visitors get more of a buzz from **Hin Yay** (Grandmother Rock) and **Hin Ta** (Grandfather Rock), small rock formations on the bay's southern promontory, which never fail to raise a giggle with their resemblance to the male and female sexual organs. If the excitement gets too much for you, head for *The Spa Resort* (☎077/424126) at the far north end of the beach: its "Rejuvenation Menu" covers everything from colonic irrigation to a sound-and-light mind-enhancing device, along with more traditional treatments such as Thai massage (B150 per hour) and herbal saunas (B100), and activities such as trekking and mountain-biking tours.

Accommodation

Lamai's accommodation is generally less cramped and slightly better value than Chaweng's, though it presents fewer choices at the top end of the market. The far southern end of the bay towards the Grandparent Rocks has the tightest concentration of budget bungalows.

Bay View Villa, on the bay's northern headland (☎077/230769). Neat, simple huts with verandahs and en suite bathrooms, and great sunset views of the beach from the restaurant. ③.

Bill Resort, at the far southern end of the bay (☎077/424403). An efficient and orderly set-up, with a swimming pool on the hill above, and clean bungalows with en suite bathrooms, some with air-con. ③–⑥.

Comfort, on the bay's northern headland, next door to *Bay View Villa* (☎077/424110). The large, shady compound feels a little like a holiday camp; wooden bungalows by the beach are a better deal than the rows of uninspiring concrete rooms. ④–⑤.

Lamai Inn 99, on the beach by the tourist village's main crossroads (☎077/424427). A friendly and surprisingly spacious place, which runs the full gamut of bungalow styles and sizes. If you want to be near the throbbing heart of Lamai's nightlife, this is your place. ③–⑥.

Pavilion, on the central stretch of Lamai (☎077/232083–90; Bangkok reservations ☎02/238 0195). Lamai's best upmarket choice: just far enough from the pubs and clubs to get some peace, the atmosphere is friendly and lively with a good beachside pool and restaurant. Most of the accommodation is in comfortable concrete rooms, but if your purse will stretch that far, go for one of the huge octagonal thatched cottages. ⑧.

Rocky, beyond the headland, at the far southern end of the bay (☎077/424326). Crams as much as it can into its beachside strip: a small swimming pool, a restaurant, and a wide choice of rooms and bungalows, all with their own bathrooms, some with hot water and air-con. ③–⑥.

Spa Resort, at the far north end of the beach, next to *Weekender Villa* (☎077/424126). Cosy, well-constructed rooms, decorated with shells and other bric-a-brac, though they're often full with people being rejuvenated (see above). ③.

Swiss Chalets, beyond the headland, at the far southern end of the bay (☎077/424321). Next door to *Rocky*, and dotted over a lawn which slopes down to a private beach, the chalets are fully furnished and large enough to sleep three. ⑤.

Weekender Villa, between the main road and the beach to the east of Ban Lamai (☎077/424116). Despite its location this is a quiet spot, except when it occasionally hosts a rave. The people are friendly and the large, well-equipped bungalows shelter in an airy coconut grove. ②.

White Sand, at the far southern end of the bay. Long-established and laid-back budget place with around 50 simple beachside huts which attract plenty of long-term travellers. ①.

Eating and nightlife

To tempt you away from your guest-house kitchen, there are several good Italian **restaurants**, such as *Tempio, La Casa* and *Drop-In,* a short way north of the tourist village's main crossroads, and, a couple of hundred metres on, the German-run *Verandah* at *Mui Bungalows,* which serves excellent, well-presented international and Thai food. To work up an appetite, walk to the northern end of the bay where *Pizza Garden,* on the headland above *Comfort,* bakes excellent pizzas and baguettes.

Lamai's **nightlife** is all within spitting distance of the central crossroads. Apart from the hostess bars, *Bauhaus* is the main draw, a rough and ready entertainment complex with pool, darts, a big screen showing satellite sport, and a dance floor (Friday is party night). The formerly sophisticated *Mix Club* has gone to the dogs: the sound system churns out hits from the pop charts, and a hilariously amateurish transvestite show is staged every night for the camcorders.

The south and west coasts

Lacking the long beaches of the more famous resorts, the **south and west coasts** rely on a few charming, isolated spots with peaceful accommodation, which can usually only be reached by renting a motorbike. Heading south from Lamai, you come first to the Muslim fishing village at **BAN HUA THANON**: *Cosy Resort* (②), 1km south of the village, has some attractive wooden bungalows in a big, grassy coconut grove, though the beach is nothing to write home about. Half a kilometre down the beach, the *Samui Orchid Resort* (☎077/424017 or 424018; ⑤–⑦) offers a touch of luxury at a good price: fitted with air conditioning and hot water, the rooms, bungalows and apartments are set around two large and attractively designed swimming pools.

The gentle but unspectacular coast beyond is lined with a good reef for snorkelling, which can be explored most easily from the fishing village of **BAN BANGKAO**. Snorkellers rave about the coral around **Ko Mad Sum**, 4km offshore: an all-day tour from Ban Bangkao or the next village to the west, Ban Thongkrut, including mask, snorkel and lunch, will set you back B350 per person. About 5km inland, near Ban Thurian, the **Na Muang** falls make a popular outing as they're not far off the round-island road. The lower fall splashes and sprays down a twenty-metre wall of rock into a large bathing pool; the more spectacular, shaded cascade of the upper fall is reached by a 1500-metre path which begins 300m back along the road from the lower fall. Best place to stay hereabouts is the welcoming *Diamond Villa* (①–④), in a secluded beachside coconut grove 1km west of Ban Bangkao, where you can choose either a wooden shack, with or without bathroom, or a smart concrete hut.

At the base of the west coast, **AO PHANGKA** (Emerald Cove) is a pretty horseshoe bay, sheltered by the high headland which forms Samui's southwestern tip and by a coral reef which turns it into a placid paddling pool. The beach is poor and often littered with flotsam but, like the whole of the west coast, gives fine views of the tiny offshore islands of Ko Si Ko Ha with the sun setting over the larger Ang Thong archipelago behind. The best place to stay here is *Seagull* (①–④) on the north shore of the bay, where a wide variety of clean bungalows, all with showers, are spread out on a flowery slope.

Further up the coast, the flat beaches are unexceptional but make a calm alternative when the northeast winds hit the other side of the island. In a gorgeous hillside setting near the village of the same name, *Baan Taling Ngam*

(☎077/423019–22; Bangkok reservations ☎02/254 5335 or 5336; ⑨) is the newest branch of the *Mandarin Oriental* group. Two swimming pools – one at the top of the hill with a negative edge set against the Gulf of Thailand, the other beachside – are separated by balconied rooms on the resort's steep slope, luxuriously decorated in traditional style. The excellent main restaurant, *Lom Talay*, offers an adventurous mix of Thai and Western cuisines, service is near-immaculate, and the hotel lays on the largest array of activities, sports and water-sports facilities on the island. A rather less expensive alternative is *Cococabana* (③), 1500m south of the vehicle ferry pier at Thong Yang, which has big thatched bungalows and a long stretch of beach to itself.

Ko Pha Ngan

In recent years backpackers have begun moving over to Ko Samui's little sibling, **KO PHA NGAN**, 20km to the north, but the island still has a simple atmosphere, mostly because the lousy road system is an impediment to the developers. With a dense jungle covering its inland mountains and rugged granite outcrops along the coast, Pha Ngan lacks the huge, gently sweeping beaches for which Samui is famous, but it does have plenty of coral to explore and some beautiful, sheltered bays: **Hat Khuat** on the north coast; **Thong Nai Pan** and half a dozen remote, virgin beaches on the east coast; and, on an isolated neck of land at the southeast corner, **Hat Rin**, a pilgrimage site for travellers. Most of Pha Ngan's development, however, has plonked itself along the less attractive south and west sides, linked by the only coastal roads on the island, which fan out from Thong Sala, the capital.

Pha Ngan's **bungalows**, like most of the buildings, are made of coconut tree trunks and bamboo; all now have running water and electricity (on the remoter beaches, only in the evenings and from individual generators), and most offer the choice of shared or en suite bathrooms. The 170 or so resorts generally have more space to spread out than on Ko Samui and the cost of living is lower – the prices given on the following pages are standard for most of the year, but in slack periods you'll be able to negotiate discounts, and Pha Ngan's bungalow owners are canny enough to raise the stakes at the very busiest times, especially in December and January. As on Ko Samui, nearly all the bungalow resorts have inexpensive, traveller-oriented **restaurants**.

Ko Pha Ngan isn't a great base for **scuba diving**: getting to the best sites around Ko Tao (see p.424) involves time-consuming and expensive voyages, and there aren't as many dive companies here as on Ko Samui or Ko Tao – of those that exist, *Samui International Diving School* (☎01/723 1016) on the Sunset side of Hat Rin is recommended.

Getting to Ko Pha Ngan

The least expensive **ferry** from the Gulf coast leaves Ban Don pier in **Surat Thani** at 11pm every night for the ferry pier at Thong Sala (7hr); tickets, costing B80 for the lower deck and B100 for the less claustrophobic upper deck, are available from the pier on the day of departure. The misleadingly named *Speed Ferry*, a vehicle ferry handled by *Songserm Travel* in Surat Thani (see p.401), leaves once a day from **Tha Thong**, 5km east of Surat (5–6hr): a combination ticket including the bus trip to Tha Thong pier, either from Phunphin train station or from Surat, costs

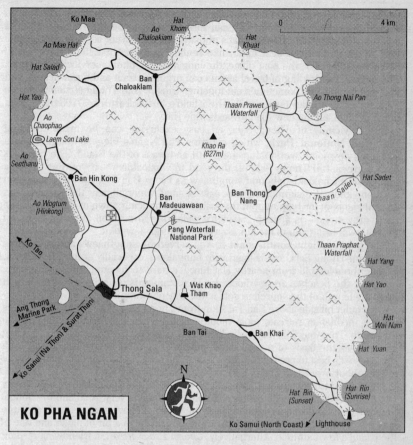

KO PHA NGAN

B105. Two *Songserm* express boats a day also run from Tha Thong to Thong Sala (4hr; B120 including transport to the pier) via **Ko Samui** (45min; B60). Small boats also shuttle between Samui and the eastern side of Pha Ngan (see p.405). An expensive high-speed service on the *Island Jet*, run by *Pha Ngan Central Hotel* (listed over), is planned for the Tha Thong–Ko Samui–Ko Pha Ngan route.

One boat a day comes **from Ko Tao** (3hr; B150), though from roughly June to November this service is occasionally cancelled due to bad weather.

From Bangkok, bus and train packages similar to those for getting to Ko Samui are available (see p.405).

Thong Sala and the south coast

Like the capital of Samui, **THONG SALA** is a port of entrance and little more, where the incoming ferries are met by touts sent to escort travellers to bunga-lows elsewhere on the island. In front of the pier, transport to the rest of the island (songthaews, jeeps and motorbike taxis) congregates by a dusty row of banks, travellers' restaurants, supermarkets and scuba-diving outfits. If you go straight ahead from the pier, you can turn right onto the town's high street, a leafy mix of shops and houses that's ghostly and windswept at night. Here you'll find laundries and the best motorbike rental places (from B150 a day) – and, 500m from the pier, the post office, the long-distance phone service and a clinic. Thong Sala's sprinkling of travel agents can organize train and plane tickets, and visa extensions, and sometimes put together trips to Ang Thong National Marine Park for B350 a head (see p.407). The island's hospital (☎077/377034) lies 3km north of town, on the new road towards Mae Hat.

In the vicinity of Thong Sala, an easy excursion can be made to **Pang Waterfall National Park**, which contains Pha Ngan's biggest waterfall and a stunning viewpoint overlooking the south and west of the island. The park lies 4km northeast of Thong Sala off the road to Chaloaklam – if you don't have a bike, take a Chaloaklam-bound songthaew as far as Ban Madeuawaan, and then it's a one-kilometre signposted walk east. A small waterfall near the entrance has an artificial pool for bathing, but the main fall – bouncing down in stages over the hard, grey stone – is a steep 250-metre walk up a forest trail. Another 200m up the path will bring you to the fantastic mountaintop viewpoint.

The long, straight **south coast** is well served by songthaews and motorbike taxis from Thong Sala, and is lined with bungalows, especially around **Ban Khai**, to take the overspill from nearby Hat Rin. It's hard to recommend staying here, however: the beaches are mediocre by Thai standards, and the coral reef which hugs the length of the shoreline gets in the way of swimming.

On a quiet hillside above Ban Tai, 4km from Thong Sala, **Wat Khao Tham** holds ten-day meditation retreats most months of the year, usually beginning on the thirteenth. The American and Australian teachers emphasize compassion and loving kindness as the basis of mental development. Only forty people can attend each retreat, so it's best to pre-register in person or by post; for further information, write to The Abbot, Wat Khao Tham, Ko Pha Ngan, Surat Thani 84280.

If you need to **stay** around Thong Sala, walk 800m north out of town to *Siriphun* (☎077/377140; ②–④). The owner is helpful, the food is very good and the bungalows are clean and well-positioned along the beach; all have showers and mosquito screens on the windows, and an extra wad of baht buys a bit of plush and one of the island's few bathtubs. Alternatively, *Charm Beach Resort*, a friendly, sprawling place only 1500m southeast of Thong Sala (☎077/377165; ①–⑤), has a variety of bungalows and good Thai food. The incongruous white high-rise overshadowing Thong Sala's pier is the *Pha Ngan Central Hotel* (☎077/377068 or 377069; ⑥), which makes a fair stab at international-standard luxuries, with air conditioning, warm water and, in some rooms, TVs, mini-bars and sea-view balconies. Worth mentioning among the handful of tourist **restaurants** in Thong Sala is *The Meeting Point*, at the only corner in the high street, which serves decent Thai food at reasonable prices and has a terrace overlooking the sea at the back.

Hat Rin

HAT RIN has been getting quite a name for itself as a rave venue over the past few years, especially among British clubbers: the main season at the "new Ibiza" is December and January, but every month of the year people flock in for the "full moon" party – something like *Apocalypse Now* without the war. There's a more sedate side to Hat Rin's alternative scene, too, with old- and new-age hippies packing out the t'ai chi, yoga and meditation classes, and helping consume the drugs that are readily available here. Drug-related horror stories are common currency round here, and many of them are true: dodgy Ecstasy, MDMA omelettes, speed punch, happy pills, and special teas containing the local fungus, *hed khi kwai,* put an average of two farangs a month into hospital for psychiatric treatment. The local authorities have started trying to clamp down on the trade, drafting scores of police in on full-moon nights – it doesn't seem to have dampened the fun, only made partygoers more circumspect.

Hat Rin occupies the neck of Pha Ngan's southeast headland, which is so narrow that the resort comprises two back-to-back beaches, joined by transverse roads at the north and south ends. The eastern beach, usually referred to as **Sunrise** or Hat Rin Nok (Outer Hat Rin), is what originally drew visitors here and you can see why. It's a classical curve of fine white sand between two rocky slopes, where the swimming's good and there's even some coral at the southern end to explore. This is the centre of the action, with a solid line of beachside bars, restaurants and bungalows tucked under the palm trees. **Sunset** beach, which for much of the year is littered with flotsam, looks ordinary by comparison but has plenty of quieter accommodation. The flat neck between is crammed with small shops and businesses: there are clinics, a post office, secondhand bookstores, travel agents, offices with expensive overseas phone facilities, a bank, even photo-developers and tattooists.

The awkwardness of **getting to Hat Rin** has in the past helped to maintain its individuality, but this may change with the promised development of the road from Ban Khai. For the moment, the often muddy road, covered by songthaews from Thong Sala, is a rollercoaster ride from hell. It's much more comfortable to take one of the longtail boats which meet incoming ferries at Thong Sala's main pier. The easiest approach of all, however, if you're coming from Ko Samui, or even Surat Thani, is by direct boat from Samui's north coast: two boats a day (currently 10.30am and 3.30pm) head for Sunset beach from either Bangrak or Bophut, depending on the prevailing weather, and occasional longtails cover the Maenam–Hat Rin–Thong Nai Pan route (for further details, see p.405).

Accommodation

For most of the year, Hat Rin has enough bungalows to cope, but on **full-moon nights** as many as seven thousand revellers turn up. As there are less than three thousand rooms on the whole island, your options are either to arrive early, to forget about sleep altogether, or to hitch up with one of the many party boats organized by guest houses and restaurants on Ko Samui, which usually leave at 9pm and return around dawn, for about B250 a head. Even at other times, staying on **Sunrise** is often expensive and noisy, though a few places can be recommended. On **Sunset**, the twenty or more resorts are laid out in orderly rows, and are especially quiet and inexpensive between June and September.

Crystal Palace, towards the north end of Sunset. Friendly and spacious, with slightly shabby, tiled concrete cottages, with or without their own bathrooms. ②–④.

Lighthouse Bungalows, on the far southeastern tip of the headland, a 20-min walk from the back of *Paradise* on Sunrise, the last section along a wooden walkway over the rocky shoreline. A friendly haven where wooden bungalows, sturdily built to withstand the wind, either share bathrooms or have their own. The restaurant food is varied and tasty. ①–③.

Palita, at the quieter northern end of Sunrise. En suite bungalows give onto the beach, and large, simple, better-value bungalows stand among the coconut palms behind. The food gets rave reviews. ②–③.

Palm Beach, on and around the tiny head marking the centre of Sunset. Typical of the bungalows here, but with a little more room as it spreads over the headland. Clean, sturdy wooden bungalows, most of them fronting the sand, either share bathrooms or have their own. ①–③.

Paradise, spread over the far southern end of Sunrise and up the slope behind. Some of the en suite bungalows have fine views over the bay from their verandahs, and the restaurant does good food. ③.

Seaview, at the quieter northern end of Sunrise. On a big plot of land, this is a similar set-up to next-door neighbour *Palita*: huts with shared bathrooms at the back, en suite bungalows (more attractive than *Palita*'s) beachside. ②–③.

Sun Cliff, high up on the tree-lined slope above the south end of Sunset. Friendly place with great views of the south coast and Ko Samui, and a wide range of bright, recently refurbished bungalows. ②–④.

Eating and nightlife

As well as good simple Thai fare at some of the bungalows, Hat Rin sports an unnerving choice of world **foods** for somewhere so remote. All-day breakfasts at the bakery behind the southern end of Sunrise are especially popular, and vegetarians are unusually well provided for in most places. Worth seeking out are *The Shell* on the southern transverse, for reasonably priced pasta, and the Indian food at *Namaste* on the northern transverse.

Nightlife normally centres around *Cactus Club* and *Tribal Club*, at the south end of Sunrise, which pump out imported music onto their indoor dance floors and low-slung beach tables. On full-moon night, *Paradise* styles itself as the party host, but the mayhem spreads itself along most of Sunrise, fuelled by hastily erected drinks stalls and sound systems.

The east coast

North of Hat Rin, the rocky, exposed **east coast** stretches as far as Thong Nai Pan, the only centre of development. No roads run along this coast, only a rough, steep, fifteen-kilometre trail, which starts from *Hillside Bungalows* on Hat Rin's northern transverse road and runs reasonably close to the shore, occasionally dipping down into pristine sandy coves.

Steep, desolate **HAT SADET**, 12km up the trail, has a handful of ramshackle bungalow operations, sited here because of their proximity to **Thaan Sadet**, a boulder-strewn brook which runs out into the sea here. The spot was popularized by various kings of Thailand who came here to walk, swim and vandalize the huge boulders by carving their initials on them. A rough road has been bulldozed through the woods above and parallel to Thaan Sadet to connect with the main road from Thong Sala to Thong Nai Pan, which is a bumpy nightmare of a dirt track winding its way for 12km over the steep mountains from Ban Tai on the south coast. Jeeps connect with incoming and outgoing boats at Thong Sala every day, but if there's heavy rain they don't chance it. The weather similarly affects the daily boat service from Thong Sala via Hat Rin.

THONG NAI PAN is a beautiful, semicircular bay backed by steep, green hills, which looks as if it's been bitten out of the island's northeast corner, leaving a tall hump of land dividing the bay into two parts. The southern half has the better sand and a hamlet which now sports a few farang bars and shops, though it's still peaceful enough; the northern half is very quiet, disturbed only by the little bit of surf which squeezes in. Both halves are sheltered and deep enough for swimming, and there's good snorkelling around the central headland and along the outer rim of the bay's southern half.

Half a dozen resorts line the southern half of the bay, where the friendly *Pingjun* (②) has large bungalows with verandahs and hammocks on a broad stretch of beach. But with most of the northern beach to itself, *Thong Tapan Resort* (①–③) gets the nod as Thong Nai Pan's best budget choice: very clean bungalows, with en suite or shared bathrooms, line the sand and the scenic cliff behind. The beautiful setting on the steep slopes of the central outcrop has been monopolized by *Panviman* (☎077/377048; Bangkok reservations ☎02/587 8491–2; ④–⑧), Ko Pha Ngan's only attempt at a luxury resort. The comfortable en suite huts at the inexpensive end of their tariff are reasonably good value, but in their hotel-style rooms and fan-cooled or air-conditioned cottages you're paying more for the fine location than the quality of accommodation. For non-guests it's worth making the climb up here for the view from the restaurant perched over the cliff edge.

The north coast

The village at **CHALOAKLAM**, the largest bay on the **north coast**, has long been a famous R & R spot for fishermen from all over the Gulf of Thailand, with sometimes as many as a hundred trawlers littering the broad and sheltered bay. Nowadays it is slowly being turned into a low-key tourist resort, as it can easily be reached from Thong Sala, 10km away, by songthaew or motorbike taxi along the island's best road. Facilities include a travel agency, a motorbike rental shop, a clinic, an international phone service and a scuba outfit – the best diving is at **Hat Khom**, a tiny cove dramatically tucked in under the headland to the east, with a secluded strip of sand and good coral. For **accommodation**, try *Fanta* (①–④) at the eastern end of Chaloaklam village, a homely and well-run place with a wide spread of clean bungalows and good food. Or walk out to the basic, flimsy bungalows of *Coral Bay* (①), which perches on the promontory dividing Hat Khom from the rest of Chaloaklam, and has the beautiful cove all to itself.

If the sea is not too rough, longtail boats run twice a day from Chaloaklam to secluded **HAT KHUAT** (Bottle Beach), the best of the beaches on the north coast, sitting between steep hills in a perfect cup of a bay. The nicest of half a dozen resorts are the friendly and helpful *Bottle Beach* and *Bottle Beach II* (①–③), which have smart beachfront bungalows, tightly packed huts behind, and highly recommended food.

The west coast

Pha Ngan's **west coast** has almost as much development as the south coast, though the landscape is nothing special and most of the sheltered bays are enclosed by reefs which keep the sea too shallow for a decent swim, especially between April and October. The minor roads from Thong Sala as far as Ao Chaophao, and from Ban Chaloaklam to Mae Hat, are usually in decent condition, and a good, new, so far unpaved road runs roughly parallel to the coast as far as the west side of Chaloaklam. Unfortunately, the side routes down to Hat Yao and Hat Salad have not as yet been similarly upgraded, and are quite testing if you're on a bike. Motorbike taxis run as far as Seethanu; songthaews, jeeps or even boats cover the rest.

The first bay north of Thong Sala, **WOGTUM** (aka Hinkong), yawns wide across a featureless expanse which turns into a mudflat when the sea retreats behind the reef barrier at low tide. If you're really counting the baht, the primitive shacks of *Kiet* (①), in a shady setting at the south end, are the island's least expensive. Beyond the headland, the nondescript bay of **SEETHANU** is home to *Loy Fa* (①–③), a well-run place which commands good views from its perch on top of the steep southern cape, and offers decent snorkelling and swimming from the rocks; lodgings range from simple huts with mosquito nets and little else, to concrete en suite cottages with verandahs and chairs.

Continuing north, there's a surprise in store in the shape of **Laem Son Lake**, a beautiful, tranquil stretch of clear water cordoned by pines which spread down to the nearby beach. Under the shade of the pines, the rudimentary en suite huts of *Bovy Resort* (①) can only be recommended for their beachfront peace and quiet. *Seethanu Bungalows* (☎077/250348; ①–②), actually round the next headland on the small bay of **CHAOPHAO**, is a lively spot with a popular restaurant: opt for a basic shack and share a bathroom, or go en suite and get a verandah, fan and mosquito screens on the windows thrown in. Next door, *Seaflower* (①–③) is quieter and more congenial: bungalows with their own bathrooms vary in price according to their size and how far you have to roll out of bed to land on the beach, the veggie and meaty food is excellent, and there's a beach bar to relax in between the well-tended garden and the sands. Snorkelling gear is available to explore the nearby reef, or if you're feeling more adventurous, ask the owner about three-day longtail-boat treks to Ang Thong National Marine Park (see p.407), which involve more snorkelling, caving, catching your own seafood, and sleeping in hammocks or rough shelters (B500 per person per day, with a minimum of 8 people).

Beyond Chaophao, **HAT YAO** offers a long, gently curved beach and a non-stop line of decent bungalows. Good bets here are *Ibiza* (②–③), with smart, airy bungalows with or without clean bathrooms in a spacious garden, and the friendly *Bay View* (①–③), which offers good food and views from a wide range of bungalows on the quiet northern headland. The only bay to the north of that, **HAT SALAD**, is probably the best of the bunch: it's pretty and quiet, and snorkelling off the northern tip is highly recommended. *My Way* (①) is a relaxing place for chilling out: primitive bamboo bungalows are set in a colourful garden, and the owner brings a boat down to Hat Yao every day to pick travellers up.

On the island's northwest corner, **MAE HAT** is good for swimming and snorkelling amongst the coral which lines the sand causeway to the tiny islet of Ko Maa. The bay also supports several decent bungalow resorts, including *Island View Cabana* (☎077/377019; ②), a lively place with a good restaurant, a snooker table and shaded, well-designed bungalows.

Ko Tao

KO TAO (Turtle Island) is so named because its outline resembles a turtle nose-diving towards Ko Pha Ngan, 40km to the south. The rugged shell of the turtle, to the east, is crenellated with secluded coves where one or two bungalows hide among the rocks. On the western side, the turtle's underbelly is a long curve of classic beach, facing Ko Nang Yuan, a beautiful Y-shaped group of islands offshore, also known as Ko Hang Tao (Turtle's Tail Island). The 21 square kilometres of granite in between is topped by dense forest on the higher slopes and

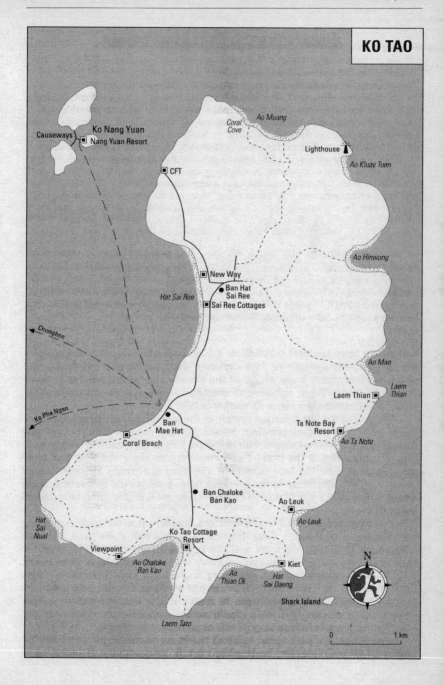

KO TAO

Causeways
Ko Nang Yuan
Nang Yuan Resort

CFT

Ao Muang
Coral Cove
Lighthouse
Ao Kluay Tuen

Chumphon

Ao Hinwong

New Way
Ban Hat Sai Ree
Sai Ree Cottages
Hat Sai Ree

Ko Pha Ngan

Ao Mao

Laem Thian
Laem Thian

Ban Mae Hat
Coral Beach

Ta Note Bay Resort
Ao Ta Note

Ban Chaloke Ban Kao

Ao Leuk
Ao Leuk

Hat Sai Nual

Ko Tao Cottage Resort

Viewpoint
Ao Chaloke Ban Kao

Kiet
Hat Sai Daeng

Ao Thian Ok

Shark Island

N

Laem Tato

0   1 km

SCUBA DIVING OFF KO TAO

Some of the best **dive sites** in Thailand are found in the seas around Ko Tao. The island is blessed with outstandingly clear waters, with visibility of up to 25m, providing near-perfect conditions for a wide range of coral species. On top of that, there's a kaleidoscopic array of marine life, and you may be lucky enough to encounter whale sharks, barracudas, leatherback turtles or dolphins. Diving is possible at any time of the year, with sheltered sites on one or other side of the island in any season – the changeover from southwest to northeast monsoon in November is the worst time, while visibility is best from April to June, in September and October.

To meet demand, Ko Tao has around a dozen **dive companies**, most of them based at Mae Hat. Competition is stiff, so prices fluctuate, with the highest rates usually between December and April, the busiest time of the year. The most popular course for beginners, PADI's four-day "Openwater", costs between B5500 and B6500; one-day introductions to diving are also available, as is the full menu of PADI courses, up to "Instructor"; for qualified divers, a two-dive package costs around B1000, rising to B4000 for ten dives, with small discounts if you bring your own gear.

Six companies – *Ko Tao Divers, Big Blue, Master Diver, Ko Nang Yuan, Ban Diving* and *Carabao* – have formed the Ko Tao Diving Association, which promotes environmental awareness and organizes clean-ups of beaches and dive sites. The longest-established company, *Samui International Diving School*, was recently nominated a PADI Five-Star Dive Center, which, among other stringent conditions, requires them to carry out similar work in the local community.

dotted with huge boulders that look as if they await some Easter Island sculptor. It's fun to spend a couple of days exploring the network of rough trails, after which you'll probably know all 750 of the island's inhabitants. Ko Tao is also a magnet for scuba divers, with several companies at Mae Hat, the main village and arrival point; see the box above for further details.

The island is the last and most remote of the archipelago which continues the line of Surat Thani's mountains into the sea. Because of the difficulties in getting there, life is still close to nature, with no sign of bars or nightclubs. There were 42 sets of **bungalows** at the latest count, concentrated along the west and south sides: most provide the bare minimum, with plain mattresses for beds, shared bathrooms, and electricity in the evenings only, from private generators. **Food** can be a little pricey and limited in range because most of it is brought across on the ferry boats.

You can **get around** easily enough on foot, but there is a road of sorts, running from the southern beaches along the west coast, and motorbike taxis, and even rental mopeds (B150 a day), are available in Mae Hat, if you feel the need. To explore the coastline fully, many bungalows lay on **round-island boat tours**, with stops for snorkelling and swimming, including a visit to Ko Nang Yuan (usually about 5hr; B100 a head). If you're just **arriving**, it might be a good idea to go with one of the touts who meet the ferries at Mae Hat, with pick-up or boat on hand, since at least you'll know that his or her bungalows aren't full or closed – the former is possible in January, the latter from June to August.

The **weather** is much the same as on Pha Ngan and Samui, but being that bit further off the mainland, Ko Tao feels the effect of the southwest monsoon more:

DIVE SITES

Ko Nang Yuan. Perfect for beginners; hard coral, sponges and granite boulders.

White Rock (Hin Khao). Sarcophyton leather coral turns the granite boulders here white when seen from the surface; also wire, antipatharian and colourful soft corals, and gorgonian sea fans. Plenty of fish, including titan triggerfish.

Shark Island. Large granite boulders with acropora, wire and bushy antipatharian corals, sea whips, gorgonian sea fans and barrel sponges. Reef fish include angelfish, parrotfish and groupers.

Hinwong Pinnacle. Similar scenery to White Rock, over a larger area. A wide range of fish, including blue-spotted fantail stingrays and large groupers.

Chumphon or **Northwest Pinnacle**.   A granite pinnacle, over 30m in depth, with the possibility of exceptional visibility. Barrel sponges, tree and antipatharian corals at deeper levels; a wide variety of fish, in large numbers, attract local fishermen.

Southwest Pinnacle. Probably the top site in terms of visibility, scenery and marine life. A huge pinnacle rising to 6m below the surface, its upper part covered in anemones; at lower levels, granite boulders, barrel sponges, sea whips, bushy antipatharian and tree corals. Big groupers and snappers; occasionally, large stingrays, leopard and sand sharks, swordfish, finback whales and whale sharks.

Sail Rock (Hin Bai). Visibility of up to 25m, and a ten-metre-deep underwater chimney. Antipatharian corals, both bushes and whips, and carpets of anemones. Large groupers, snappers and fusiliers, bright blue-ringed angelfish, curious batfish and juvenile clown sweetlips; occasional whale sharks.

June to October can have strong winds and rain, with a lot of debris blown onto the windward coasts.

Getting to Ko Tao

From Chumphon, boats to the island leave twice daily from the port at Pak Nam, 14km southeast of the town centre; the B400 **express boat** pulls out at 8am, arriving at Ko Tao's Mae Hat at 9.40am, while the B200 **slow boat** departs around midnight, arriving at 6am. Tickets can be bought at any of Chumphon's guest houses (listed on p.397), or from the following Chumphon **information centres**: *Chumphon Travel* (☎077/501880) opposite the bus terminal, next to the *Tha Tapao Hotel* on Tha Tapao Road; *Puen Jai Restaurant* across from the train station on Komluang Chumphon Road; or *Chumphon Information Centre* (☎077/503857) across from the *Jansom Chumphon Hotel* off Sala Daeng Road. (Songthaews to the pier run during daylight hours only, departing by the post office on Paramin Manda Road. Alternatively, book a minibus ride (B40) to the port with one of the ticket agents, and you'll be picked up at your accommodation.)

One boat a day makes the trip to Ko Tao **from Ko Pha Ngan** (3hr; B150), late enough for people who have taken an early morning boat from Surat or Samui to catch (there are also plans for a direct high-season service from Ban Don pier in Surat, a trip of about 7hr).

The express boat is often cancelled due to rough seas, but all services to and from Ko Tao are at the mercy of the weather, especially between June and November; plenty of travellers have missed onward connections through being stranded on the island, so it's better not to plan to visit at the end of your holiday.

The west coast and Ko Nang Yuan

All boats to the island dock at **MAE HAT**, a small, lively village with most of the scuba-diving operations, a few seafront restaurants, clinics, expensive currency exchange and postal facilities, as well as seaside necessities.

For somewhere **to stay** near Mae Hat, try *Coral Beach* (①–③), which occupies a good position on the lower slopes of the headland, ten minutes' walk south of the village; the well-run and friendly resort offers reliable bungalows with or without bathroom, and, another ten minutes beyond, there's a sandy, palm-sheltered cove for secluded sunbathing and swimming.

North of Mae Hat, beyond a blip of a promontory, you'll find **HAT SAI REE**, Ko Tao's only long beach. The strip of white sand stretches for 2km in a gentle curve, backed by a smattering of coconut palms. Nearly a dozen bungalow resorts have set up shop here, and more are sure to squeeze in; at the moment, you're better off heading for the quieter, more spacious northerly stretch. *Sai Ree Cottages* (①–④), a twenty-minute walk from Mae Hat, has primitive huts in a flower-strewn garden and sturdy en suite bungalows by the beach, and serves excellent grub. Good food is also to be had a couple of hundred metres further up the beach at *New Way* (①–②), a small, easy-going place with simple huts, where your only choice is between sharing or having your own bathroom. The road ends beyond Hat Sai Ree, at the basic shacks of *CFT* (①) on the rocky northwest flank of the island; there's no beach here, but the views over to Ko Nang Yuan are something else.

One kilometre off the northwest of Ko Tao, **KO NANG YUAN**, a close-knit group of three tiny islands encircled by a ring of coral, provides the most spectacular beach scenery in these parts, thanks to the three-legged causeway of fine white sand which joins up the islands. Longtail boats scheduled for day-trippers leave Mae Hat in the morning, returning in the late afternoon. A long-tail will also meet incoming and outgoing ferries at Mae Hat, for people staying at the *Nang Yuan Resort* (☎01/726 0085; ③–⑥), which exacts a heavy premium for its beautiful location – bungalows range from a bit of thatch over your head to swanky cottages, and snorkelling sets are B100 a day, whether you're a guest or a day-tripper.

The east and south coasts

The sheltered inlets of the **east coast**, few of them containing more than one set of bungalows, are best reached by boat, though each is served by at least one path through the forest. In the middle of the coast, the dramatic tiered promontory of **Laem Thian** shelters a tiny beach and a colourful reef on its south side. With the headland to itself, *Laem Thian* (①) offers simple shacks, decent food and a remote, castaway feel. Laem Thian's coral reef stretches down as far as **Ta Note**, a craggy horseshoe bay with the best snorkelling just north of the bay's mouth. The better of the two resorts here is *Ta Note Bay Resort* (①–③), which has a wide range of wooden bungalows, and is well equipped with snorkelling gear. The last bay carved out of the turtle's shell, **Ao Leuk**, has a white sandy beach fringed with palms and a handful of primitive huts (①).

The **southeast corner** of the island sticks out in a long, thin mole of land, which shelters the sandy beach on one side if the wind's coming from the northeast, or the rocky cove on the other side if it's blowing from the southwest.

Straddling the headland is *Kiet* (①–③), a popular, well-equipped place with a good kitchen; its pleasantly idiosyncratic bungalows, with or without bathrooms, enjoy plenty of elbow room and good views.

The **south coast** is sheltered from the worst of both monsoons, but consequently the main bay here, **Ao Chaloke Ban Kao**, is being developed into a messy, crowded resort. Most of the accommodation options here deserve to be given a wide berth – you might as well be on one of the larger islands – but *Viewpoint* (③) stands out from the crowd. Run by a friendly young bunch, the well-built, clean bungalows have bathrooms inside and verandahs overlooking the sunset from the bay's western headland. *Ko Tao Cottage Resort* (☎01/725 0662; ⑤–⑥) is the island's only stab at luxury and worth a splurge, especially if you're considering scuba diving with *Samui International Diving School*, which maintains a branch on the premises. The cottages, which have verandahs, mosquito screens on the windows, ceiling fans and plain, smart decor, are all of the same design; prices only vary between "Sea View", in the shady garden by the beach, and "Mountain View", up the slope behind the restaurant with little in the way of a view, mountainous or otherwise.

Nakhon Si Thammarat

NAKHON SI THAMMARAT, the south's second largest town, occupies a blind spot in the eyes of most tourists, whose focus is fixed on Ko Samui, 100km to the north. Its neglect is unfortunate, for in its way Nakhon is as absorbing a place as Chiang Mai, although it doesn't have the accommodation and facilities to match. The south's major pilgrimage site, it's a relaxed, self-confident and sophisticated place, well known for its excellent cuisine and traditional handicrafts – the stores on Thachang Road are especially good for local nielloware (*kruang tom*), household items elegantly patterned in gold or silver on black, and *yan lipao*, sturdy basketware made from intricately woven fern stems of different colours. Nakhon is also the only place in the country where you can see how Thai shadow plays work, at Suchart Subsin's workshop.

The town is recorded under the name of Ligor (or Lakhon), the capital of the kingdom of Lankasuka, as early as the second century, and classical dance-drama, *lakhon*, is supposed to have been developed here. Well placed for trade with China and southern India, Nakhon was the point through which the Theravada form of Buddhism was imported from Sri Lanka and spread to Sukhothai, the capital of the new Thai state, in the thirteenth century.

Known as *muang phra*, the "city of monks", Nakhon is still the religious capital of the south, and the main centre for **festivals**. The most important of these are the **Tamboon Deuan Sip**, held during the waning of the moon in the tenth lunar month (either September or October), and the **Hae Pha Khun That** in the third lunar month (either February or March). The purpose of the former is to pay homage to dead relatives and friends. It is believed that during this fifteen-day period all *pret* – ancestors who have been damned to hell – are allowed out to visit the world, and so their relatives perform a merit-making ceremony in the temples, presenting offerings from the first harvest to ease their suffering. A huge ten-day fair takes place on Sanam Na Muang, the town field, at this time, as well as processions, shadow plays and other theatrical performances. The Hae Pha Khun That also attracts people from all over the

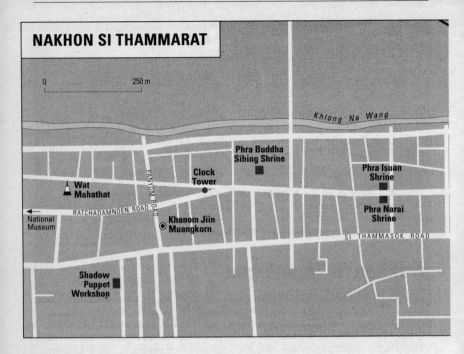

south, to pay homage to the relics of the Buddha at Wat Mahathat. The ceremonial centrepiece of this festival is the Pha Phra Bot, a strip of yellow cloth many hundreds of metres long, which is carried in a spectacular procession around the chedi.

The Town

The **town plan** is simple, but puzzling at first sight: it runs in a straight line for 7km from north to south, paralleled by the jagged peaks of 1835-metre-high Khao Luang to the west, and is never more than a few hundred metres wide, a layout dictated by the availability of fresh water. The modern centre for businesses and shops sits at the north end around the train station. To the south, centred on the elegant, traditional mosque on Karom Road, lies the old Muslim quarter, where pictures of the Thai king take their place alongside the Ayatollah Khomeini. South again is the start of the old city walls, of which a few crumbling remains can be seen, and the historic centre, with the town's main places of interest now set in a leafy residential area.

Songthaews ply up and down Ratchadamnoen Road, which links the whole length of the town, for B4 a ride.

Wat Mahathat

Missing out **Wat Mahathat** (daily 8.30am–4pm) would be like going to Rome and not visiting St Peter's, for the Buddha relics in the vast chedi make this the south's most important shrine.

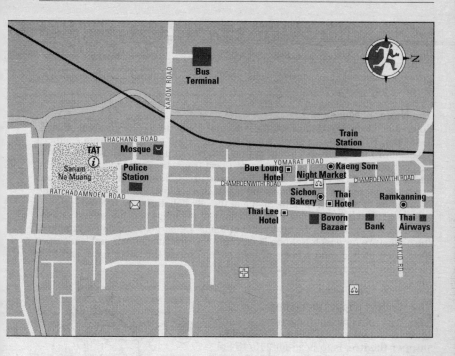

Inside the temple cloisters, which have their main entrance facing Ratchadamnoen Road about 2km south of the modern centre, the courtyard looks like a surreal ornamental garden, with row upon row of smaller chedis, spiked like bayonets, each surrounded by a box hedge in the shadow of the main chedi, the **Phra Boromathat**. This huge, stubby Sri Lankan bell supports a slender, ringed spire, which is in turn topped by a shiny pinnacle said to be covered in 600kg of gold leaf. According to the chronicles, relics of the Buddha were brought here from Sri Lanka two thousand years ago by an Indian prince and princess and enshrined in a chedi. It's undergone plenty of face-lifts since: an earlier Srivijayan version, a model of which stands at one corner, is encased in the present twelfth-century chedi. The most recent restoration work, funded by donations from all over Thailand, rescued it from collapse, although it still seems to be leaning dangerously to the southeast. Worshippers head for the north side's vast enclosed stairway, framed by lions and giants, which they liberally decorate with gold leaf to add to the shrine's radiance and gain some merit. In the left-hand shrine at the foot of the stairs here, look out for some fine stuccos of the life of the Buddha.

The **Viharn Kien Museum** (hours irregular, but usually daily 8.30am–noon & 1–4pm), which extends north from the chedi, is an Aladdin's cave of bric-a-brac, said to house fifty thousand artefacts donated by worshippers, ranging from ships made out of seashells to gold and silver models of the Bodhi Tree. At the entrance to the museum, you'll pass the Phra Puay, an image of the Buddha giving a gesture of reassurance. Women pray to the image when they want to have children, and the lucky ones return to give thanks and to leave photos of their chubby progeny.

Outside the cloister to the south is the eighteenth-century **Viharn Luang**, raised on elegant slanting columns, a beautiful example of Ayutthayan architecture. The interior is austere at ground level, but the red coffered ceiling shines with carved and gilded stars and lotus blooms. Elsewhere in the spacious grounds, cheerful, inexpensive stalls peddle local handicrafts such as shadow puppets, bronze and basketware.

The National Museum

South again from Wat Mahathat, the **National Museum** (Wed–Sun 9am–noon & 1–4.30pm; B10) houses a small but diverse collection of artefacts from southern Thailand. In the prehistory room downstairs, two impressive ceremonial bronze kettledrums, topped with chunky frogs (local frogs are the biggest in Thailand and a prized delicacy), typify the culture around the fifth century BC. Next door are some interesting Hindu finds and many characteristic Buddha images made in imitation of the Phra Buddha Sihing at the city hall, the most revered image in southern Thailand. Amongst the collections of ceramics and household articles upstairs, you can't miss the seat panel of Rama V's barge, a dazzling example of the nielloware for which Nakhon is famous – the delicate animals and landscapes have been etched onto a layer of gold which covers the silver base, and then picked out by inlaying a black alloy into the background.

The shadow puppet workshop

The best possible introduction to *nang thalung*, southern Thailand's **shadow puppet theatre**, is to head for 110/18 Soi 3, Si Thammasok Rd, ten minutes' walk east of Wat Mahathat: here Suchart Subsin, one of the south's leading exponents of *nang thalung*, has opened up his workshop to the public, and, for a small fee (usually around B50), he'll show you a few scenes from a shadow play in the small open-air theatre. You can also see the intricate process of making the leather puppets and can buy the finished products as souvenirs: puppets sold here are of much better quality and design than those usually found on southern Thailand's souvenir stalls.

Nang thalung puppet

Other shrines and temples

In the chapel of the City Hall on Ratchadamnoen Road sits the **Phra Buddha Sihing**, which according to legend was magically created in Sri Lanka in the second century. In the thirteenth century it was sent by ship to the king of Sukhothai, but the vessel sank and the image miraculously floated on a plank to Nakhon. Two other images, one in the National Museum in Bangkok, one in Wat Phra Singh in Chiang Mai, claim to be the authentic Phra Buddha Sihing, but none of the three is in the Sri Lankan style, so they are all probably derived from a lost original. Although similar to the other two in size and shape, the image in

SHADOW PUPPETS

Found throughout southern Asia, **shadow puppets** are one of the oldest forms of theatre, featuring in Buddhist literature as early as 400 BC. The art form seems to have come from India, via Java, to Thailand, where it's called *nang*, meaning "hide": the puppets are made from the skins of water buffalo or cows, which are softened in water then pounded until almost transparent, before being carved and coloured to represent the characters of the play. The puppets are then manipulated on sticks in front of a bright light, to project their image onto a large white screen, while the story is narrated to the audience.

The grander version of the art, **nang yai** – "big hide", so called because the figures are life-size – deals only with the *Ramayana* story (see p.82). It's known to have been part of the entertainment at official ceremonies in the Ayutthayan period, but has now almost died out. The more populist version, **nang thalung** – *thalung* is probably a shortening of the town name, Phatthalung, where this version of the art form is said to have originated – is also in decline now: performances are generally limited to temple festivals, marriages and ordinations, lasting usually from 9pm to dawn. As well as working the sixty-centimetre-high *nang thalung* puppets, the puppet master narrates the story, impersonates the characters, chants and cracks jokes to the accompaniment of flutes, fiddles and percussion instruments. Not surprisingly, in view of this virtuoso semi-improvised display, puppet masters are esteemed as possessed geniuses by their public.

At big festivals, companies often perform the *Ramayana*, sometimes in competition with each other; at smaller events they put on more down-to-earth stories, with stock characters such as the jokers Yor Thong, an angry man with a pot belly and a sword, and Kaew Kop, a man with a frog's head. Yogi, a wizard and teacher, is thought to protect the puppet master and his company from evil spirits with his magic, so he is always the first puppet on at the beginning of every performance.

In an attempt to halt their decline as a form of popular entertainment, the puppet companies are now incorporating modern instruments and characters in modern dress into their shows, and are boosting the love element in their stories. They're fighting a battle they can't win against television and cinemas, although at least the debt owed to shadow puppets has been acknowledged – *nang* has become the Thai word for "movie".

Nakhon has a style unique to this area, distinguished by the heavily pleated flap of its robe over the left shoulder, a beaky nose and harsh features, which sit uneasily on the short, corpulent body. The image's plumpness has given the style the name *khanom tom* – "banana and rice pudding".

You're bound to pass the small, red-roofed Hindu shrines of **Phra Isuan** and **Phra Narai** on Ratchadamnoen Road, legacies of Nakhon's ancient commercial links with India (hours irregular, but usually Mon–Fri 8.30am–4pm, with a break for lunch). The former houses a *lingam*, a phallic representation of Shiva worshipped by women who want to conceive, and in its grounds there's a ritual swing, a smaller version of the Sao Ching Cha at Wat Suthat in Bangkok; the latter shelters a life-size image of Vishnu. The Brahmin community based at these shrines supplies astrologers to the royal court and priests for the Ploughing Ceremony, held every May in Bangkok.

Practicalities

TAT has a very helpful office on Sanam Na Muang (daily 8.30am–4.30pm; ☎075/346515 or 346516). Though most of Nakhon's limited number of **hotels** are dingy and soulless, there are enough exceptions to get by. For inexpensive accommodation, the plain, clean rooms of the *Thai Lee Hotel* at 1130 Ratchadamnoen Rd (☎075/356948; ②) are a good deal. The central but quiet *Bue Loung Hotel*, at 1487/19 Soi Luang Muang, Chamroenwithi Rd (☎075/341518; ③–④), gets the thumbs-up from visiting businessmen, with a choice of fan or air conditioning. Top of the range at the moment – a new five-star place, the *Southern BM Hotel*, is due to open in 1995 – is the *Thai Hotel*, 1375 Ratchadamnoen Rd (☎075/341509; ③–⑥), a large institutional high-rise, with clean, reliable, fan-cooled and air-conditioned rooms.

Nakhon is a great place for inexpensive **food**. Most famous, and justifiably so, is *Khanom Jiin Muangkorn* (10am–3pm) on Panyom Road near Wat Mahathat: the rough-and-ready outdoor restaurant dishes up one of the local specialities, *khanom jiin*, noodles topped with hot, sweet or fishy sauce served with *pak ruam*, a platter of crispy raw vegetables. Also boasting rock-bottom prices is *Krua Nakhon* (9am–3pm) in the Bovorn Bazaar on Ratchadamnoen Road, a big, rustic pavilion with good *khanom jiin* and other local dishes: *kaeng som*, a mild yellow curry, *kaeng tai plaa*, fish stomach curry, and various *khanom wan*, coconut milk puddings. The *Sichon Bakery*, opposite the main entrance of the *Thai Hotel*, does decent foreign breakfasts.

In the evening, the busy market on Chamroenwithi Road near the *Bue Loung Hotel* is great for inexpensive food and people-watching. In the old Muslim quarter, many stalls near the corner of Karom and Yomarat roads sell good Muslim food, such as *roti* (sweet pancake) and chicken with curried rice. *Kaeng Som* (aka *The Yellow Curry House*), by the train station at 1465 Yomarat Rd, aims for a bistro atmosphere and has a wide menu of interesting Thai dishes, especially seafood. On the corner of Watkid and Ratchadamnoen roads, *Ramkanning* is one of many affordable, popular restaurants with pavement tables in the area. Nakhon's youths while away their nights in the Bovorn Bazaar, eating *roti kluay* (banana pancakes) from a street stall, sipping speciality coffees at *Hao Coffee*, or supping beer and whisky at *99% Rock*, a wooden open-air bar.

travel details

Trains

Bangkok to: Nakhon Si Thammarat (2 daily; 15hr); Surat Thani (9 daily; 12hr).

Cha-am to: Bangkok (8 daily; 3hr 10min–3hr 40min); Hua Hin (8 daily; 25min); Surat Thani (7 daily; 7hr 10min–8hr 25min) via Chumphon (4hr 10min–4hr 55min).

Chumphon to: Bangkok (8 daily; 7hr 30min–8hr); Surat Thani (7 daily; 3–4hr).

Hua Hin to: Bangkok (8 daily; 3hr 35min–4hr 5min); Surat Thani (7 daily; 6hr 45min–8hr) via Chumphon (3hr 45min–4hr 30min).

Phetchaburi to: Bangkok (8 daily; 2hr 45min–3hr 15min); Hua Hin (8 daily; 40min) via Cha-am (20min); Surat Thani (7 daily; 7hr 30min–8hr 45min) via Chumphon (4hr 30min–5hr 15min).

Surat Thani to: Butterworth, Malaysia (1 daily; 11hr); Hat Yai (4 daily; 5hr); Nakhon Si Thammarat (2 daily; 3hr 30min); Sungai Kolok (2 daily; 9hr); Trang (2 daily; 4hr).

Buses

Bangkok to: Nakhon Si Thammarat (13 daily; 12hr); Surat Thani (15 daily; 11hr).

Cha-am to: Bangkok (every 30min; 2hr 45min–3hr 15min); Chumphon (every 2hr; 4hr 10min–5hr 10min); Hua Hin (every 30min; 40min).

Chumphon to: Bangkok (6 daily; 7hr); Ranong (hourly; 2hr).

Hua Hin to: Bangkok (every 30min; 3hr 15min–3hr 45min); Chumphon (every 40min; 3hr 30min–4hr 30min); Pranburi (every 20min; 40min); Surat Thani (17 daily; 12hr).

Ko Samui (Na Thon) to: Bangkok (3 daily; 15hr).

Nakhon Si Thammarat to: Hat Yai (12 daily; 3hr); Ko Samui (1 daily; 5hr); Phatthalung (every 30min; 3hr); Phuket (8 daily; 7hr); Songkhla (every 30min; 3hr); Surat Thani (every 30min; 3hr 30min); Trang (4 daily; 3hr).

Phetchaburi to: Bangkok (every 20min; 2hr–2hr 30min); Chumphon (about every 2hr; 5hr–6hr); Hua Hin (1hr 30min) via Cha-am (50min).

Surat Thani to: Chaiya (hourly; 1hr); Chumphon (every 30min; 3–4hr); Hat Yai (7 daily; 5hr); Krabi (22 daily; 3hr–3hr 30min); Narathiwat (2 daily; 7hr); Phuket (10 daily; 6hr); Phunphin (every 10min; 30min); Trang (2 daily; 3hr).

Ferries

Chumphon to: Ko Tao (2 daily; 1hr 40min–6hr).

Don Sak to: Ko Samui (5 daily; 1hr 30min).

Ko Pha Ngan to: Ko Samui (4–5 daily; 45min–1hr); Ko Tao (1 daily; 3hr).

Surat Thani to: Ko Pha Ngan (1 daily; 7hr); Ko Samui (1 daily; 6hr).

Tha Thong to: Ko Pha Ngan (3 daily; 4–6hr); Ko Samui (2–3 daily; 2hr 30min).

Flights

Bangkok to: Ko Samui (7 daily; 1hr 20min); Nakhon Si Thammarat (4 weekly; 1hr); Surat Thani (2–3 daily; 1hr 10min).

Ko Samui to: U-Tapao (1 daily; 1hr).

Phuket to: Ko Samui (1 daily; 40min); Nakhon Si Thammarat (3 weekly; 1hr 40min); Surat Thani (3 weekly; 35min).

CHAPTER SEVEN

SOUTHERN THAILAND: THE ANDAMAN COAST

A s Highway 4 switches from the east flank of the Thailand peninsula to the **Andaman coast** it enters a markedly different country: nourished by rain nearly all the year round, the vegetation down here is lushly tropical, with forests of trees reaching up to 80m in height, and massive rubber and coconut plantations replacing the mundane rice and sugar cane fields of central Thailand. In this region's heartland the drama of the landscape is enhanced by sheer limestone crags, topographical hallmarks that spike every horizon and make for stunning views from the road. Even more spectacular – and the main crowd-puller – is the Andaman Sea itself: translucent turquoise and in some places so clear that you can see to a depth of 30m, it harbours the country's largest **coral reefs** and is far and away the top diving area in Thailand.

Unlike the Gulf coast, the Andaman coast is hit by the **southwest monsoon** from May to October, when the rain and high seas render some of the outer islands inaccessible. However, conditions aren't generally severe enough to ruin a holiday on the other islands, while the occasional cloudburst you'll get on the mainland is offset by the advantages of notably less expensive and crowded accommodation. Although some bungalows at the smaller resorts shut down entirely during low season, every beach detailed in this chapter keeps at least one place open.

Eager to hit the high-profile beaches of Phuket and Krabi, most people either fly over the first 300-kilometre stretch of the west coast or pass through it on an overnight bus, thereby missing out on the lushly forested hills of **Ranong** province and bypassing several gems: the **Ko Surin** and **Ko Similan** island chains, whose reefs rate alongside the Maldives and the Great Barrier Reef; the rarely visited **Khao Sok National Park**, where you can stay in a treehouse beneath the shadows of looming limestone outcrops; and the tiny, embryonic resort of **Khao Lak** on the edge of Khao Lak National Park, a little-known jungle retreat on the rugged mainland coast. Tourism begins in earnest on **Ko Phuket**, Thailand's largest island and the best place to learn to dive. The high-rises and consumerist gloss of Phuket don't appeal to everyone, however, and many travellers opt instead for the less mainstream but very popular beaches around the former fishing village of **Krabi**. Nearby **Ko Phi Phi** attracts a lot of attention considering its size, yet the island's natural beauty remains pretty much intact both on land and underwater. Solitude seekers have moved on again, searching out hideaways on **Ko Lanta** and bringing custom to the tiny retreats of **Ko Jum** and **Ko Bubu**.

Getting to Andaman coast destinations is made easy by Highway 4, also known as the Phetkasem Highway – and usually called Phetkasem Road when it passes through towns. The road runs from Bangkok to the Malaysian border, and frequent air-conditioned and ordinary **buses** ply this route, connecting all major – and most minor – mainland tourist destinations. There is no rail line down the Andaman coast, but as the numerous cross-peninsula roads are served by frequent buses, many travellers take the **train** from Bangkok to the Gulf coast, enjoy the region's splendours for a while, and then nip over to the Andaman coast by bus before proceeding southwards. **Ferries** to the most popular islands usually leave several times a day (with reduced services during the monsoon season), but for more remote destinations you may have to charter your own or wait for islanders' trading boats to pick you up. Alternatively, you can also **fly** direct to the Andaman coast, landing at the international airport on Ko Phuket.

Ranong and Ko Pha Yam

Highway 4 hits the Andaman coast at **Kraburi**, where a signpost welcomes you to the **Kra Isthmus**, the narrowest part of peninsular Thailand. At this point just 22km separates the Gulf of Thailand from the inlet where the River Chan flows into the Andaman Sea, west of which lies the southernmost tip of mainland Burma. For decades now, Thai governments and foreign investors have been keenly interested in this slender strip of land, envisaging the creation of a canal which would cut some 1500km off shipping routes between the Indian Ocean (Andaman Sea) and the South China Sea (the Gulf of Thailand). Despite a number of detailed proposals, no agreement has yet been reached, not least because of the political implications of such a waterway: quite apart from accentuating the divide between prosperous southern Thailand and the rest of the country, it would vastly reduce Singapore's role in the international shipping industry.

Seventy kilometres south of the contentious isthmus, the channel widens out at the small port town of **RANONG**, which thrives – not entirely legitimately – on its proximity to Thailand's neighbour. A black-market economy specializing in timber flourishes alongside the legal import businesses, and the town occasionally makes headlines when its fishing fleet gets caught poaching in Burmese waters. Rumours of racketeering are frequent, too, but on the surface Ranong is an unexceptional trading town, its population of Thais, Chinese, Malays and Burmese supplemented by tourists who come here for the health-giving properties of the local spring water.

The **geothermal springs** are the focus of a small leisure park just off Phetkasem Road, ten minutes' walk north of the bus terminal or 1km southeast of the town centre – take songthaew #2 from the central Ruangrat Road or a motorbike taxi. You can't submerge yourself in the water here, but you can buy eggs to boil in the sulphurous 65°C water, or paddle in the cooler pools that have been siphoned off from the main springs. Picnickers throng here at weekends, but to properly appreciate the springs you need to soak in them: *Jansom Thara Hotel*, five minutes' walk away, channels the mineral waters into its public bath (B50 for non-guests).

Ranong practicalities

All **buses** from Bangkok to Phuket or Krabi pass through Ranong, stopping at the bus terminal on Highway 4 (Phetkasem Road), 1500m southeast of the centre; a few buses continue on into the tiny nucleus of the town, clustered on each side of Ruangrat Road.

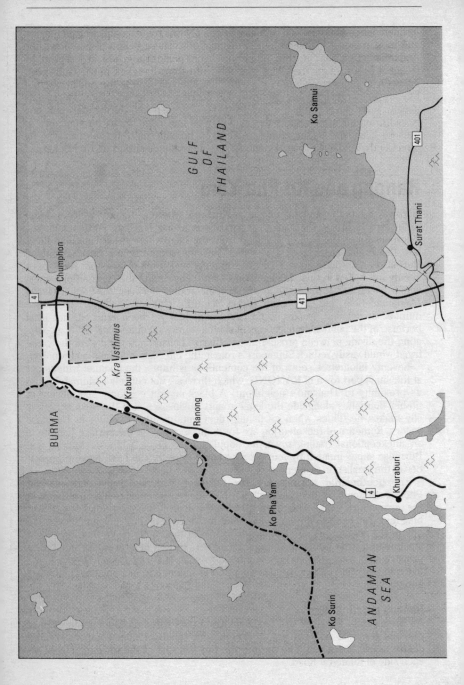

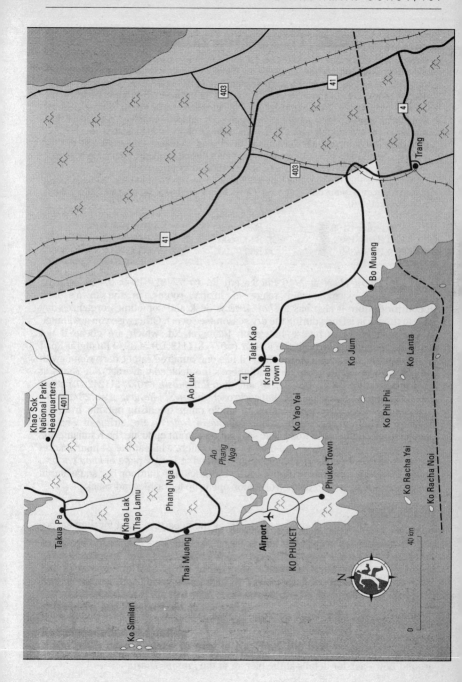

ACCOMMODATION PRICES

Throughout this guide, guest houses, hotels and bungalows have been categorized according to the price codes given below. These categories represent the minimum you can expect to pay in the high season (roughly Nov–Feb & July–Aug) for a double room – or, in the case of national park bungalows, for a multi-berth room which can be rented for a standard price by an individual or group. If travelling on your own, expect to pay anything between sixty and one hundred percent of the rates quoted for a double room. Wherever a range of prices is indicated, this means that the establishment offers rooms with varying facilities – as explained in the write-up. Wherever an establishment also offers dormitory beds, the prices of these beds are given in the text, instead of being indicated by price code.

Remember that the top-whack hotels will add seven percent tax and a ten-percent service charge to your bill – the price codes below are based on net rates after taxes have been added.

① under B100	④ B250–400	⑦ B1000–1500
② B100–150	⑤ B400–600	⑧ B1500–3000
③ B150–250	⑥ B600–1000	⑨ B3000+

Jansom Thara Hotel at 2/10 Phetkasem Rd (☎077/811513–9; ⑦–⑨), with its mineral baths, jacuzzis and range of luxury rooms, is the town's best **accommodation**; it also has a *Thai Airways* desk and sometimes organizes day trips to the Surin islands during the dry season (see over). Otherwise you are limited to the rash of Thai-Chinese hotels on Ruangrat Rd, which are cheap if not particularly cheerful. First choice is *Asia* (☎077/811113; ②) at 39/9 Ruangrat Road (the southern end): clean and friendly, it has one hundred rather dark rooms with fan and shower. Heading up the road, there's the decidedly average *Sin Thawi* at 81/1 Ruangrat Rd (☎077/822771; ③), and then *Rattanasin* (☎077/811242; ②) at no. 226. Avoid the superficially plush but cockroach-ridden *Sin Ranong* at no. 26/23–24.

Ranong's ethnic diversity ensures an ample range of **eating** options, from the Muslim restaurant just south of the *Rattanasin Hotel* to the string of Chinese pastry shops on Ruangrat Road. The seafood restaurant opposite the Kamlangsap/Ruangrat intersection serves up the day's local catch, while at the 24-hour market across from *Sin Ranong Hotel*, you're guaranteed at least a plate of *khao pat* or a bowl of *kwetiaw nam* day or night. In the evenings, the outdoor bar squashed in between *Sin Ranong* and the petrol station opens up for drinks and snacks.

Ko Pha Yam

For travellers, Ranong is of interest chiefly as the departure point for the beaches and coral reefs of **KO PHA YAM**, a small island whose few inhabitants make a tenuous living by growing cashew nuts. At the time of writing there was only one resort here: the mid-range *Ko Pha Yam Resort* (☎077/822244; ⑤), but as it only has nine rooms, you'd be wise to check availability first. Otherwise, you can camp on any of the island's beaches; you'll need to take your own fresh water and food supply across with you.

Boats to Ko Pha Yam go from **Saphan Pla**, 8km west of Ranong: song-thaews between Ruangrat Road and Saphan Pla run regularly throughout the day. Boats can be chartered for about B1500 each way, but the less expensive alternative is to get a ride on the thrice-weekly supply boats; the two-hour journey costs around B50 – ask for details at the pier, or at the *Jansom Thara*.

Ko Surin

Sticking close to the coast, but just out of sight of it, Highway 4 speeds south from Ranong between densely forested hills to the east and a strip of mangrove swamps, rubber plantations and casuarina groves to the west, much of it preserved as **Laem Son National Park**. The hillsides are streaked with waterfalls which are, of course, seen to their best advantage during the rainy season – though because Ranong province is the wettest in the whole of Thailand (annually soaking up over 5000mm of rain), the effect is staggering at almost any time of year. The most impressive is the enormous **Nam Tok Ngao**, 12km south of Ranong, which cascades almost all the way down the eastern hillside, in full view of Highway 4.

One hundred and ten kilometres south of Ranong, the road reaches the coastal town of **Khuraburi**, the closest (though not necessarily the most convenient) departure point for the national park of **KO SURIN**, a group of five small islands around 60km offshore, just inside Thai waters. The spectacular shallow reefs around these islands offer some of the best snorkelling and diving on the Andaman coast.

The most beautiful and easily explored of the reefs are those surrounding the two main islands in the group, Ko Surin Nua (north) and Ko Surin Tai (south), which are separated only by a narrow channel. **SURIN NUA**, slightly the larger at about 5km across, holds the national park headquarters, visitors' centre and park bungalows on its southwest coast. The water is so clear here, and the reefs so close to the surface, that you can make out a forest of sea anemones while sitting in a boat just 10m from the park headquarters' beach. Visibility off the east and west coasts of both islands stretches to a depth of 40m.

Across the channel, **SURIN TAI** is the long-established home of a community of *chao ley* (see p.462) who divide their time between boat-building and fishing. Every April, as part of the Songkhran New Year festivities, hundreds of *chao ley* from nearby islands (including those in Burmese waters) congregate here to celebrate with a cere-mony which involves, among other rites, the release of several hundred turtles, a symbol of longevity and especially precious to Thai and Chinese people, into the sea.

Practicalities

Because the islands are so far out at sea, Ko Surin is effectively out of bounds during the monsoon season, when the sixty-kilometre trip becomes a potentially suicidal undertaking. During the rest of the year, **getting to Ko Surin** can be both time-consuming and expensive.

The least troublesome way to reach the islands is to join an **organized over-night expedition**. At the time of writing, the least costly and most informal pack-age was the one offered by *Sea Dragon Dive Centre* (☎01/723 1418) at Khao Lak (see p.443), about 40km south of Khuraburi. The managers have been running trips to the more accessible Similan islands for several years; their new five-day Ko Surin package costs around B10,000 for divers (including equipment) and B4000 for non-divers, including food, accommodation and inter-island boat trips. The only other organized overnight tours are those included in the itineraries of some of the Phuket dive centres; these are pricey, but you get fairly luxurious on-board accommodation and the trips leave Phuket at least once a week during the diving season. The long-established *South East Asia Divers* on Patong Beach (☎076/340406), for instance, does seven-day cruises around Ko Similan and Ko Surin from \$980 (approximately B24,500) per person; prices include tanks and weights, all meals, and three dives per day.

Otherwise, Ranong's *Jansom Thara Hotel* (see p.438) occasionally organizes weekend **day trips**; these leave Ranong in the early morning and take three hours each way, giving you about five hours on the islands for around B1000 all-in. If you want to stay over on the islands, you should be able to negotiate a return trip on another day.

Finally, if you're determined to see the islands independently, you could catch one of the **national park boats** that sail from **Ban Hin Lat** pier, a five-kilometre, B30 motorbike taxi ride from Khuraburi. These boats take from three to five hours and cost B800 return; ask at the pier's national park office (☎076/ 491378) for details. It's also possible to **charter** your own fishing boat from Ban Hin Lat for around B6000 a day (journey time 4–5hr): unless you speak fluent Thai the best way to arrange this is either by calling the provincial governor's office (☎076/411140) or enquiring at the national park office. As boats tend to leave very early in the morning, you'll probably have to spend at least one night in a Khuraburi **hotel**: go for either the fairly seedy *Rungtawan* (②), next to the bus station, or the newer and more salubrious bungalows at *Tararin Resort* (④) a couple of kilometres out of town.

Once you're on the islands, you can **charter a longtail** to explore the coasts: a four-hour cruise is priced at around B400. For **accommodation** you have the choice of renting one of the expensive six-person national park bungalows on Surin Nua (⑤, but deals for couples may be negotiable), settling for a dorm bed (B100) in the nearby longhouse, or opting for a B60 two-person national park tent. Otherwise, you can camp in your own tent in the vicinity of the park buildings. Unless you take your own **food** to the islands, you'll be restricted to the three set meals a day served at the restaurant on Surin Nua for B250 (vegetarian and other special meals can be supplied if requested in advance).

Khao Sok National Park

Forty kilometres south of Khuraburi, Highway 4 reaches the junction town of **Takua Pa**. Highway 401, which cuts east from here, is the route taken by all Surat Thani-bound buses from Phuket and Krabi, and it's a spectacular journey across the mountains that stretch the length of the peninsula, a landscape of limestone crags and jungle, scarred only by the single, and at times perilous, road. Most of what you see belongs to **KHAO SOK NATIONAL PARK**, a tiny part of which – entered 40km east of Takua Pa – is set aside for overnight stays. Few visitors to south Thailand consider even briefly foregoing the delights of the coast, but Khao Sok definitely merits a couple of days: waking up to the sound of hooting gibbons and the sight of thick white mist curling around the karst formations is an experience not quickly forgotten.

Practicalities

The park entrance is less than an hour by **bus** from Takua Pa or two hours from Surat Thani. Buses run every ninety minutes or so in both directions; ask to be let off at the park and chances are there'll be someone from one of its bungalow outfits waiting to meet the bus and give you a free lift to the park headquarters and accommodation area, 3km away.

The grimly functional national park bungalows (⑤) are supplemented by three much more pleasant **accommodation** options, all within easy walking distance of the park headquarters and trail heads, yet each managing to feel quite isolated. *Treetops* (☎076/421155, radio extn 107; ④) is the most exclusive and caters primarily to tour groups pre-booked from abroad, so its riverside huts may be full. You should have no problem getting into the other two, though, as few travellers break their journey here. *Art's Jungle House* (☎076/421155, extn 205; ②–⑤), dramatically located in the lee of a huge karst formation, has several inexpensive huts as well as two superb "treehouses", large wooden huts built on seven-metre stilts overlooking the river. The food is good as well, and there's plenty of information on getting around the park. Simplest but friendliest of the three, *Bamboo House* (②) stands fifteen minutes' walk from *Art's* in a similarly scenic location beside the river. It's run by the family of the park warden, who proffer endless quantities of food, jokes and information. Bungalows are rustic but fine, and food costs B100 per person per day for three generous and delicious meals.

If you don't have the time or energy to organize a Khao Sok trip by yourself, consider joining an excursion out of Phuket: *Santana Adventure Tours* on Ao Patong (☎076/340360), for instance, offers three-day **canoeing tours** of Khao Sok for B7500 all-inclusive.

The park

Two well-defined **trails** radiate from the park headquarters and visitors' centre; they are marked by blank wooden signposts and the centre has photocopied maps, though these are not exactly a model of accuracy. Both trails follow the course of the stream that flows through the park and take you past beautiful waterfalls and pools, through forests of thirty-metre-high bamboos rife with gibbons, geckoes and frogs. The more energetic trek is the one to **Ton Sai** waterfall, over 10km away, which gets quite rugged towards the end, from where the only route back involves retracing your steps.

Longer and less well-tramped forays into the jungle interior can be arranged through your accommodation, for which you'll need a guide (B100 per person per day); if you want to make it a two- or three-day trek, you can borrow a tent. These itineraries usually take in the park's eleven-tiered waterfall, several bathing pools and a couple of stalactite caves, and occasionally feature a **night safari**, when you might be lucky enough to see some of the park's rarer inhabitants, like elephants, tigers, clouded leopards and pony-sized black and white tapirs. A northwestward trek will eventually get you to Rajaphraba lake, 40km from the headquarters, surrounded by crags and home to a number of fishing families; a shorter trek northeast from the central park area leads to an enormous bat cave.

Khao Lak National Park

Thirty kilometres south from Takua Pa, Highway 4 passes alongside the scenic strip of beach at **KHAO LAK**, whose understated ambience and nascent role as a departure point for Ko Similan (see over) and Ko Surin (see p.439) are slowly beginning to attract a few visitors. There's no village to speak of at Khao Lak, just a handful of houses and restaurants strung out along the roadside, and a track through the rubber plantations leading a smattering of beachfront bungalows. It's very much a traveller-oriented retreat, so secluded that it can feel like an island, and a welcome respite from the relentless party atmosphere of nearby Phuket and Phi Phi. Fringed by a dense growth of casuarina, palm and mangrove, the bronze-coloured beach sweeps out into rocky promontories, a picture made even more dramatic during the monsoon, when the crashing waves and squelchy mud can make Khao Lak seem almost wintry; although several bungalow operations close down for the duration, you should be able to get a room somewhere (try *Nang Thong* first).

Aside from snorkelling and diving trips out to Ko Similan, the surrounding area also holds a few points of interest. If you rent a motorbike (B200 a day from any bungalow outfit), you're within easy reach of a couple of **waterfalls** – Nam Tok Chongfah, 5km to the north, and Nam Tok Lumphi, 20km south. From

TURTLES IN THAILAND

Thailand is home to four species of **marine turtle**: the green, the leatherback, the Olive Ridley and the hawksbill; the loggerhead turtle also once swam in Thai waters, until the consistent plundering of its eggs rendered it locally extinct. Of the remaining four species, the **green turtle** is the commonest, a mottled brown creature named not for its appearance but for the colour of the soup made from its flesh. Adults weigh up to 180kg and are herbivorous, subsisting on sea grass, mangrove leaves and algae. The **leatherback**, encased in a distinctive ridged shell, is the world's largest turtle, weighing in at between 250kg and 550kg; it eats nothing but jellyfish. The small **Olive Ridley** weighs up to 50kg and feeds mainly on shrimps and crabs. The **hawksbill** is named for its peculiar beak-like mouth, but is prized for its spectacular carapace (the sale of which was banned by CITES in 1992); it weighs up to 75kg and lives off a type of sea sponge.

The survival of the remaining four species is by no means assured – prized for their meat, their shells and their eggs, and the frequent victims of trawler nets, all types of marine turtle are now **endangered species**. The worldwide population of female turtles is thought to be as small as 70,000 to 75,000, and only around fifty percent of hatchlings reach adulthood. As a result, several of the Thai beaches most favoured by egg-laying turtles have been protected as **marine parks**, and some equipped with special hatcheries. The breeding season usually starts in October or November and lasts until February, and the astonishing egg-laying ritual can be witnessed, under national park rangers' supervision, at Thai Muang (see facing page), Hat Mai Khao on Phuket (p.452), Ko Surin Tai (p.439) and Ko Tarutao (p.495).

Broody female turtles of all species always return to the beach on which they were born to lay their **eggs**, often travelling hundreds of kilometres to get there – no mean feat of memory, considering that females can wait anything from twenty to fifty years before reproducing. Once in situ, the turtles lurk in the water and wait for a cloudy night before wending their laborious way onto and up the beach: at 180kg, the green turtles have a hard enough time, but the 550kg leatherbacks endure an almost impossible uphill struggle. Choosing a spot well above the high-tide mark, each turtle digs a deep nest in the sand into which she lays ninety eggs or more; she then packs the hole with the displaced sand and returns to sea. Tears often stream down the turtle's face at this point, but they're a means of flushing out sand from the eyes and nostrils, not a manifestation of grief.

Many females come back to land three or four times during the nesting season, laying a new batch of ninety-plus at every sitting. Incubation of each batch takes from fifty to sixty days, and the temperature of the sand during this period determines the sex of the hatchling: warm sand results in young females, cooler sand in young males. When the **baby turtles** finally emerge from their eggshells, they immediately and instinctively head seawards, guided both by the moonlight on the water – which is why any artificial light, such as flashlight beams or camera flashes, can disorientate them – and by the downward gradient of the beach.

November through July, you may also have the chance to see **marine turtles** on the long stretch of national park beach in **Thai Muang**, 30km south. Almost every night between November and February, crowds of green and leatherback turtles waddle out of the sea here, settling on the beach to lay their eggs; months later, from March through to July, the beach comes alive with hundreds of young hatchlings. Visitors pay B20 to witness – under ranger supervision – the night-time laying and hatching activities.

Practicalities

All the regular **buses** running between Phuket and Ranong, Takua Pa and Surat Thani pass the turn-off to Khao Lak; if you're coming from Krabi or Phang Nga you should take a Phuket-bound bus as far as **Khokkloi** bus terminal and switch to a Takua Pa or Rayong bus. Whichever bus you're on, get off at the shelter with the large "Nang Thong Resort" sign on its roof; from here it's a 500-metre walk down the signed track to the sea and the bungalows.

The best of Khao Lak's inexpensive **bungalows** are at *Nang Thong Bay Resort* (☎01/723 1181; ②–④), which also acts as a bus-ticket agent and rents out jeeps and motorbikes. Its comfortably furnished wooden huts, most with a sea view and all with balconies, sit in a pleasant flower garden that leads right down to the water, where the restaurant serves delicious food. The whitewashed concrete huts at neighbouring *Garden Beach Resort* (☎01/723 1179; ③–④) are less attractive, but not bad. A short walk up the beach, *Khao Lak Bungalows* (☎01/723 1197; ②–⑥) has a few inexpensive rooms, but is much more notable for its luxurious traditional-style "pavilions" ranged around a casuarina-fringed lagoon. The managers here run snorkelling and diving trips to Ko Similan, open to non-guests too, as do those at another set of bungalows (closed May–Oct) at **Thap Lamu**, a tiny settlement 5km south of Khao Lak. Called *Poseidon* (☎01/723 1418; ①–④), this superbly located place has a good restaurant and bungalows on a wild and rocky shore surrounded by jungle and rubber plantations. In addition to its excellent and inexpensive trips to Ko Surin and Ko Similan (see p.439 and over), it also runs the *Sea Dragon* **dive centre**, offering introductory and certificated dive courses, and short trips out to nearby reefs. To get to *Poseidon*, ask to be dropped off the bus at Thap Lamu; from here it's a two-kilometre walk or motorbike taxi ride to the bungalows. *Sea Dragon* dive centre is on the main road in Khao Lak.

Ko Similan

Rated by *Skin Diver* magazine as one of the world's top ten spots for both above-water and underwater beauty, the nine islands that make up **KO SIMILAN** are perhaps the most exciting **diving** destination in Thailand. Massive granite boulders set magnificently against turquoise waters give the islands their distinctive character, but it's the thirty-metre visibility that draws the flipper brigade. The underwater scenery is nothing short of overwhelming here: the reefs teem with a host of coral fish, from the long-nosed butterfly fish to the black-, yellow- and white-striped angel fish, and the ubiquitous purple and turquoise parrot fish, which nibble so incessantly at the coral that they are held responsible for much of the fine white sand that rings the Similans. A little further offshore, magnificent mauve and burgundy crown-of-thorns starfish stalk the seabed, gobbling chunks of coral as they go – and out here you'll also see turtles, manta rays, moray eels, red grouper and quite possibly white-tip sharks, barracuda and enormous tuna.

As well as suffering from indigenous predators, the Similan reefs also attract idiots who lob home-made bottle bombs to kill the fish and break off the coral for sale as souvenirs. To date, though, the damage to the reefs has been limited and, thanks to their relative inaccessibility and national park protection, the islands themselves – except for the two which are inhabited – remain almost undisturbed by tourism.

Practicalities

Getting to the Similans independently can be a lengthy business, involving waiting around at **Thap Lamu pier**, the closest mainland departure point to the islands 40km offshore. Supply boats leave fairly regularly from here, usually docking at Ko Similan and sometimes at Ko Miang, the two islands with accommodation; alternatively, you could try hitching a ride on a boat that's already been chartered. Hiring your own fishing boat will cost about B11,000 for three days.

There is, however, a fair choice of **organized trips** to the Similans. The informal and well-run **three-day trips** offered by *Sea Dragon* dive centre at Khao Lak (see previous page) cost B6800 for divers (including equipment) and B3000 for non-divers, including food, live-aboard accommodation and several shuttles between the islands. Excursions **out of Phuket** (see box on p.446) are more expensive, but correspondingly more luxurious: *Phuket International Diving Centre* (*PIDC*) does an all-inclusive, three-day "live aboard" cruise to the Similans for B8500 for non-divers, while divers pay B10,000 for unlimited dives, tanks and weights, food and accommodation, and B18,000 for a six-day/seven-night trip. Alternatively, you can join the regular **day trips** operated by *Songserm* from Phuket. Its express boat does the journey in three hours, and the B2000 package deal includes lunch and snorkelling gear, but leaves you with only a few hours to explore the phenomenal underwater scenery. If you want to stay on the Similans and be picked up on the next trip, you should be able to negotiate a one-way ticket for B500.

As for accommodation on the islands, Ko Miang hosts the national park headquarters, several **bungalows** (④), **tent** accommodation (B80) and a restaurant. As these islands aren't really a destination for the independent traveller, it's unlikely that you'll stray from Ko Miang without the support of a well-equipped guide, but should you decide to go it alone come well prepared as there's no drinking water available outside Ko Miang and campfires are prohibited on all the islands. Inter-island shuttles, the only way of getting from place to place, are expensive at B200 per person per trip.

KO PHUKET

Thailand's largest island and a province in its own right, **Ko Phuket** has been a well-off region since the last century, when Chinese merchants got in on its tin-mining and sea-borne trade, before turning to the rubber industry. Phuket remains the wealthiest province in Thailand, with the highest per capita income, but what mints the money nowadays is **tourism**: with an annual influx that tops one million, Ko Phuket ranks second in popularity only to Pattaya, and the package-tour traffic has wrought its usual transformations. Thoughtless tourist developments have scarred much of the island, particularly along the west coast, and

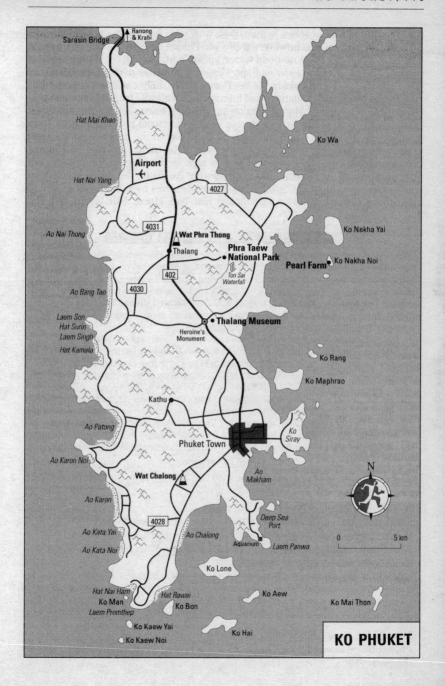

Ranong & Krabi
Sarasin Bridge

Hat Mai Khao

Ko Wa

Airport

Hat Nai Yang

4027

Ao Nai Thong

4031

Ko Nakha Yai

Wat Phra Thong

Thalang

Phra Taew National Park

Ko Nakha Noi

Pearl Farm

402

Ton Sai Waterfall

Ao Bang Tao

4030

Laem Son
Hat Surin
Laem Singh
Hat Kamala

Thalang Museum

Heroine's Monument

Ko Rang

Ko Maphrao

Kathu

Ao Patong

Ko Siray

Phuket Town

Ao Karon Noi

Ao Makham

Wat Chalong

Ao Karon

N

4028

Ao Kata Yai

Ao Chalong

Deep Sea Port

Ao Kata Noi

Aquarium   Laem Panwa

0   5 km

Ko Lone

Hat Nai Ham
Ko Man
Laem Promthep

Hat Rawai

Ko Bon

Ko Aew

Ko Mai Thon

Ko Kaew Yai

Ko Kaew Noi

Ko Hai

KO PHUKET

the trend on all the beaches is upmarket, with very few budget possibilities. As mainstream resorts go, however, those on Phuket are just about the best in Thailand, offering a huge range of **water sports** and magnificent **diving** facilities to make the most of the clear and sparkling sea. Remoter parts of the island are still attractive, too, particularly the interior: a fertile, hilly expanse dominated by rubber and pineapple plantations and interspersed with wild tropical vegetation.

Ko Phuket's capital, Muang Phuket or **Phuket town**, lies on the southeast coast, 42km south of the Sarasin Bridge linking the island to the mainland. Most people pass straight through the town on their way to the beaches on the **west coast**, where three big resorts corner the bulk of the trade: high-rise **Ao Patong**, the most developed and expensive, with a nightlife verging on the seedy; similarly unappealing **Ao Karon**; and neighbouring **Ao Kata**, the quietest and least spoilt of the trio. Most of the other west-coast beaches have been taken over by one or two upmarket hotels, specifically **Hat Nai Harn**, **Hat Surin** and **Hat**

DIVING AND SNORKELLING

The reefs and islands within sailing distance of Phuket rate amongst the most spectacular in the world, and the desire to dive off the Andaman coast draws hordes of visitors to the resort. This is where you'll find Thailand's largest concentration of **dive centres**, offering a variety of certificated courses and trips. All the dive centres listed below offer PADI- and/or NAUI-certificated **diving courses**. Average costs are from B1500–2500 for a one-day introductory course and B7000–8500 for a four-day open-water course, including equipment.

The numerous centres run **day trips** to the reefs (from about B800 to B1500 for divers, including two dives, all equipment and food), but by far the most popular – and most satisfying – way of exploring them is to join a **live-aboard** cruise. Staffed by highly qualified instructors, these last anything from three to fourteen days and cost from B10,000 to B18,000 inclusive – and most should give you at least two dives a day. Unless you're a qualified diver, you can only join fun half-day trips and introductory courses. **Snorkellers**, however, can usually join longer live-aboard cruises and many of the listed dive centres' excursions, at slightly reduced rates.

Be careful when signing up for any course or expedition: check the equipment and staff credentials carefully and try to get first-hand recommendations from other divers.

DIVE CENTRES

All these centres offer a variety of itineraries and cruises, with schedules depending on weather conditions and the number of divers.

Ao Patong

Fantasea Divers, next to *Holiday Inn* at the southern end of Patong (☎076/340088).

Holiday Diving Club, at *Patong Beach Hotel*, south of Soi Bangla (☎076/341235).

Phuket International Diving Centre (PIDC), on Thavee Wong Road (☎076/381219).

Santana, 92/18 Sawatdirak Rd (☎076/340360).

South East Asia Divers, 116/1 Thavee Wong Rd (☎076/340406).

Ao Karon/Ao Kata

Marina Divers, next to *Marina Cottages* on the headland between Ao Karon and Ao Kata (☎076/330625).

Siam Diving Centre, opposite *Marina Divers* (☎076/330936).

Phuket International Diving Centre (PIDC), at *Le Meridien Hotel*, on Ao Karon Noi (☎076/321480).

Bang Tao; the northerly **Hat Nai Yang** and **Hat Mai Khao**, on the other hand, are relatively untarnished national park beaches. In complete contrast, the south and east coasts hold one of Thailand's largest seafaring *chao ley* communities, but the beaches along these shores have nothing to offer tourists, having been polluted and generally disfigured by the island's tin-mining industry.

Although the best west-coast beaches are connected by road, to get from one beach to another by **songthaew** you nearly always have to go back into Phuket town; songthaews run regularly throughout the day and cost between B10 and B20 from town to the coast. **Tuk-tuks** do travel directly between major beaches, but charge at least B150 a ride. However, almost everyone on Phuket rides **motorbikes** (some of which would be more accurately described as mopeds), and you might consider saving time, money and aggravation by doing likewise. All the main resorts rent out motorbikes for B150–250 per day (be sure to ask for a helmet as well); alternatively, rent a **jeep** for B700–1000.

Phuket Town
Phuket Aquatic Safari, 62/9 Rasda Centre, Rasda Rd (☎076/216562).
Phuket Divers, 31/1 Poonpon Rd (☎076/215738).

DIVE SITES
The major **dive sites** visited from Phuket are listed below. In these waters you'll find a stunning variety of coral and a multitude of fish species, including sharks, oysters, puffer fish, stingrays, groupers, lion fish, moray eels and more. For more information on marine life see "Flora, Fauna and Environmental Issues" in *Contexts*, p.550; for detailed ratings and descriptions of Andaman coast dive sites, consult the **handbook** *Diving In Thailand*, by Collin Piprell and Ashley J. Boyd (Asia Books, B495).

Shark Pont (Hin Mu Sang), 24km east of Laem Panwa. Protected as a marine sanctuary. Visibility up to 10m.

Ko Racha Noi and **Ko Racha Yai**, about 33km and 28km south of Ao Chalong respectively. Visibility up to 25m.

Ko Phi Phi, 48km east of Ao Chalong. Visibility up to 30m.

Ko Rok Nok and **Ko Rok Nai**, 100km southeast of Ao Chalong, south of Ko Lanta (see p.480). Visibility up to 18m.

Hin Daeng, 26km southwest of Ko Rok Nok. Fifty-metre reef wall. Visibility up to 30m.

Ko Similan, 96km northwest of Phuket. One of the world's top ten diving spots. Visibility up to 30m.

Ko Surin, 174km northwest of Phuket. Shallow reefs particularly good for snorkelling.

Burma Banks, about 250km northwest of Phuket. A series of submerged "banks", and well away from any land mass and very close to the Burmese border. A recent feature on a few itineraries. Visibility up to 25m.

SNORKELLING TRIPS
Several ferry operators run **snorkelling** day trips to Ko Phi Phi, which include stops at Phi Phi Le and Phi Phi Don, an hour's snorkelling (mask, fins and snorkel provided) and a seafood lunch. Prices average out at around B1000, or B750 for children. These outfits also offer day trips to Ko Similan. Otherwise, you can join one of the trips run by the companies listed above.

Seatran Travel, 6 Phang Nga Rd (☎076/211809).
Songserm Travel, 51 Satoon Rd (☎076/222570).

Getting to the island

All direct **air-conditioned buses** from **Bangkok** make the journey overnight, leaving at approximately half-hourly intervals between 5.30pm and 7pm and arriving about fourteen hours later, giving you just enough early-morning daylight hours to appreciate the most scenic section of the trip. Pre-booking at least a day in advance is essential, and can be done either at the bus station or, for a commission, through booking agents in some guest houses and hotels. Unless you get a kick out of hard seats, taking the **ordinary bus** from Bangkok only makes sense if you're desperate to see all the intervening countryside.

From more **local towns**, ordinary buses are often the only way to get to Ko Phuket: eight buses make the daily trip **from Ranong** (6hr) via Takua Pa (3hr); hourly buses connect the island with **Krabi** (4hr); and eight buses make the journey from **Surat Thani** (6hr).

All buses arrive at the **bus station** at the eastern end of Phang Nga Road in Phuket town, from where it's a ten-minute walk or a short tuk-tuk ride to the central hotel area, slightly further to the departure point for the beaches in front of the fruit and vegetable market on Ranong Road.

If you're coming to Phuket from Ko Phi Phi, the quickest and most scenic option is to take the **boat**. During peak season, up to four ferries a day make the inter-island trip, taking between ninety minutes and two and a half hours and docking at the deep sea port on Phuket's southeast coast; during low season, there's at least one ferry a day in both directions. Boat tickets should include minibus transfer to Phuket town and the major west-coast beaches, but if you do get dumped at the port it's easy enough to hop on a songthaew.

Thai Airways operates up to thirteen **flights** from Bangkok (1hr 15min) every day, though at B2000 a throw that's almost five times the price of the plushest bus. For similar rates, *Thai Airways* also connects the island with Chiang Mai (B3455), Hat Yai (B780), Nakhon Si Thammarat (B690), Surat Thani (B475), and Trang (B435); and *Bangkok Airways* does one daily run between Ko Phuket and Ko Samui (B605). *Thai Airways* runs a "limousine" (minibus) service between the **airport** and the town (B70), 32km to the southeast – more reliable than the inexpensive but very infrequent songthaews. The only way of getting directly from the airport to the west-coast beaches is to take a taxi (about B350), or air-conditioned minivan to Ao Patong or Ao Karon (B150 per person).

Phuket town

Though it has plentiful hotels and restaurants, **PHUKET TOWN** stands distinct from the tailor-made tourist settlements along the beaches as a place geared primarily towards its residents. Customers for the diving centres account for a fair proportion of the few tourists who linger here – most visitors hang about just long enough to jump on a beach-bound songthaew. Nevertheless, if you're on a tight budget it can make sense to base yourself in town, as accommodation and food come a little less expensive, and you can get out to all the beaches with relative ease. Bear in mind, though, that the town offers little in the way of nightlife, and as public transport to and from the more lively beaches stops at dusk, you'll have to spend a lot of money on tuk-tuks.

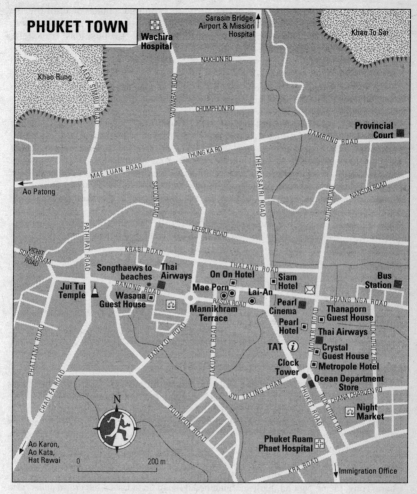

Aside from a manically bustling market on Ranong Road there's not a great deal to see, though a two-hour wander around the streets will take you past several dilapidated colonial-style residences built by Chinese merchants at the turn of the century. Recognizable by their doors and shutters painted in pastel pinks, blues and greens, a string of these faded mansions lines Yaowarat Road, and others remain on Ranong Road (the *Thai Airways* office), Phang Nga Road (the *On On Hotel*) and Damrong Road, where the town hall stood in for the US embassy in Phnom Penh in the film *The Killing Fields*.

Accommodation

Not only does Phuket town offer a better range of budget accommodation than any of the beach resorts, its rooms fill up slower during peak periods – so you might find yourself staying here either through economic choice or until there's space at your preferred beach. But the mid-range and upmarket places in town, catering mainly to short-term package tourists and to business travellers, compare much less favourably with their counterparts on the coast.

INEXPENSIVE AND MODERATE

Crystal Guest House, 41/16 Montri Rd (☎076/222774). One of several good, clean guest houses in the town centre; all rooms have attached bathroom, the more expensive have air-con and TV as well. ③–④.

On On Hotel, 19 Phang Nga Rd (☎076/211154). Attractive, colonial-style 1920s building with basic but adequate fan-cooled rooms, some with attached bathroom and air-con. ①–④.

Pacific Inn, 328 Phuket Rd (☎076/214838). Appealing toy-town building near the night market with only two dozen fan and air-con rooms. ③–④.

Siam Hotel, 13–15 Phuket Rd (☎076/212328). Above a cassette shop, so noise could be a problem, but otherwise good, spacious singles and doubles with fan and shower. ②–③.

Thanaporn Guest House, 41/7 Montri Rd (☎076/216504). Good-value, well-appointed rooms with fan and air-con. ④.

Wasana Guest House, 159 Ranong Rd (☎076/211754). Opposite *Thai Airways* and very convenient for songthaews to the beaches; comfortable enough and good value, with fan and shower included. ③.

EXPENSIVE

The Metropole, 1 Montri Rd (☎076/215050). The poshest, priciest and by far the largest place in town. ⑧–⑨.

Pearl Hotel, 42 Montri Rd (☎076/211044). Top-class hotel favoured by Asian package tourists; facilities include rooftop restaurant and swimming pool. ⑦–⑨.

Phuket Merlin, 158/1 Yaowarat Rd (☎076/212866). Swimming pool, nightclub and all the rest. ⑦–⑨.

Eating and nightlife

For authentically inexpensive and tasty Thai **food** hit any one of the noodle shops along Rasda or Takua Pa roads, or check out the curries, soups and stews at the no-frills food centre on the top floor of the Montri Road *Ocean Department Store* (10am–10pm). Alternatively, there's always the night market which materializes around the square off Tilok Uthit 1 Road every evening at about 6pm. Food stalls are also set up at night opposite TAT on Phuket Road, but the prices here are inflated because of the English-language menu. The best of the town's less than stunning array of restaurants are listed below.

Cham Tong, Phang Nga Rd. Early-morning noodle-soup breakfasts a big crowd-puller; also good for *kanom jiin* and sweet rice confections wrapped in banana leaves. Inexpensive.

Kanda Bakery, Rasda Rd. The brown bread, cakes and croissants make satisfying if pricey breakfasts and coffee-break snacks, but the full-blown Thai meals are significantly overpriced. Moderate.

Lai-An, 58 Rasda Rd. Large, busy, air-con Chinese restaurant offering a huge array of dishes, including some Thai standards. Moderate.

Mannikhram Terrace, 20 Rasda Rd. Air-con restaurant, with tasteful dark-wood interior and slightly formal service. Sizeable selection of traditional Thai fare and seafood dishes, with set meals also available. Moderate.

Phuket View Restaurant, near the top of Khao Rung, the wooded hill on the northwestern outskirts of town. Middle-class Phuketians drive up to this slightly formal eaterie for outdoor seafood with a view. Bring mosquito repellent. Moderate.

NGAN KIN JEH – THE VEGETARIAN FESTIVAL

For nine days every October or November, at the start of the ninth lunar month, the streets of Phuket are enlivened by **Ngan Kin Jeh** – the Vegetarian Festival – which culminates in the unnerving spectacle of men and women parading about with steel rods through their cheeks and tongues. The festival marks the beginning of **Taoist lent**, a month-long period of purification observed by devout Chinese all over the world, but celebrated most ostentatiously in Phuket, by devotees of the island's five Chinese temples. After six days' abstention from meat, alcohol and sex, the white-clad worshippers flock to their local temple, where drum rhythms help induce a trance state in which they become possessed by spirits. As proof of their new-found superiority to the physical world they skewer themselves with any available sharp instrument – fishing rods and car wing-mirrors have done service in the past – before walking over red-hot coals or up ladders of swords as further testament to their otherworldliness. In the meantime there's much singing and dancing and almost continuous firework displays, with the grandest festivities held at Wat Jui Tui on Ranong Road in Phuket town.

The ceremony dates back to the mid-nineteenth century, when a travelling Chinese opera company turned up on the island to entertain emigrant Chinese working in the tin mines. They had been there almost a year when suddenly the whole troupe, together with a number of the miners, came down with a life-endangering fever. Realizing that they'd neglected their gods somewhat, the actors performed expiatory rites which soon effected a cure for most of the sufferers. The festival has been held ever since, though the self-mortification rites are a later modification, possibly of Hindu origin.

Tung Ka Café, just above *Phuket View* and very similar. Renowned for its seafood, mixed grills and panoramic views. Moderate.

Apart from the **discos** in the big hotels and the fair smattering of **bars** with hostess service, your choice of **nightlife** is virtually confined to the *Pearl* cinema just off Montri Road, which has English-soundtrack headphones.

Listings

Banks and exchange All the main banks have branches on Phang Nga or Rasda roads, with adjacent exchange facilities open till at least 7pm.

Car rental *Avis*, opposite Phuket international airport (☎076/327358); *Hertz*, Phuket international airport (☎076/327230–5).

Hospitals The private *Mission Hospital*, about 1km north of TAT on Thep Kasatri Road (☎076/212386), has Phuket's best and most expensive facilities; also in town are *Wachira Hospital* on Yaowarat Road (☎076/211114) and *Phuket Ruam Phaet* on Phuket Road (☎076/212950).

Immigration At the southern end of Phuket Road, near Ao Makham (☎076/212108; Mon–Fri 8.30am–4.30pm).

Post office Montri Road, with poste restante.

TAT 73–75 Phuket Rd; daily 8.30am–4.30pm (☎076/212213).

Telephones For international calls use the 24-hr public phone office on Phang Nga Road. For long-distance calls within Thailand, go to the private office across the road.

Thai Airways International branch at 41/33 Montri Rd (☎076/212400); domestic branch at 78 Ranong Rd (☎076/211195).

Tourist Police In the TAT office on Phuket Road (☎076/212213).

Around the island

This account of the island starts at the top of Ko Phuket's most appealing coast and follows an anti-clockwise route around the perimeter, through the chief tourist centres. The west coast boasts a series of long sandy beaches punctuated by sheer rocky headlands, unprotected from the monsoons and consequently quite rough and windswept from May to October, but nevertheless heavily developed and packed with Ko Phuket's best hotels and facilities. Shadowed by the mainland, the east coast is much more sheltered and thus makes a convenient docking point for ships, but there's not a single commendable beach along its entire length. Finally, the interior remains fairly untouched either by industry or by the tourist trade, and can make a refreshing break from the beaches.

Hat Mai Khao and Hat Nai Yang

Phuket's northwest coast kicks off with the island's longest and least-visited beach, the twelve-kilometre **HAT MAI KHAO**, which starts 3km southwest of the airport and 30km northwest of Phuket town, and remains completely unsullied by any touristic enticements, with not a single hut or restaurant standing on its shores. Together with Hat Nai Yang immediately to the south, Hat Mai Khao constitutes a **national park**, chiefly because giant marine turtles come ashore here between October and February to lay their eggs (see box on p.442). Mai Khao is also a prime habitat of a much-revered but non-protected species – the sea grasshopper or sea louse, a tiny crustacean that's considered a great delicacy.

Sheltered by feathery casuarina trees and fronted only by a sandy track, a collection of wooden souvenir stalls and several makeshift open-air restaurants, **HAT NAI YANG** is very much a Thai beach resort, a particular favourite with families, who come here to picnic in the shade, eat seafood and go windsurfing or jet-skiing. It's not as unadulterated as Hat Mai Khao, but neither has it been developed to anything like the extent of the farang-oriented resorts further down this coast: the handful of condominium and hotel buildings that have somehow managed to sneak their way past national park building regulations are discreetly screened by the trees.

Practicalities

An infrequent **songthaew** service runs between Phuket town and Hat Nai Yang via the airport; to get to Mai Khao you have to walk up the beach. **Accommodation** is only available on Hat Nai Yang, where you're limited to four-person national park bamboo huts (☎076/327407; ⑤), B60 two-person tents, or rooms in one of the exceedingly expensive hotels: of the last, the *Pearl Village Hotel* (☎076/327006; ⑨) is the most attractive, complete with swimming pool, tennis courts, and its own small zoo. However, you can pitch your own tent anywhere on both Nai Yang and Mai Khao if you ask for permission at the park headquarters on Hat Nai Yang (daily 8.30am–4.30pm). **Food** options are also confined to Hat Nai Yang, with its half-dozen small open-air seafood restaurants and clutch of itinerant vendors hawking their wares beneath the casuarinas.

Hat Bang Tao, Hat Surin and Hat Kamala

Large hotel complexes dominate each of the three beaches south of Hat Nai Yang, **HAT BANG TAO, HAT SURIN** and **HAT KAMALA**; each has bought up its respective beachfront, leaving the shorelines free of the shops, bars and restaurants that make the resorts further south so frenetic. What's more, the hotels cannot legally restrict access to their strips of sand, so even if you can't afford to stay on these stretches they make good day-trip destinations – though beware of the undertow off the coast here, which confines most guests to the hotel pools. Hat Bang Tao is only accessible via a four-kilometre branch road, but a coastal road links the adjacent Hat Surin and Hat Kamala, running via Laem Singh, a very scenic headland which divides the two.

Practicalities

Songthaews from Phuket town to these beaches (about 24km) run every thirty minutes or so; from Hat Bang Tao it's also possible to charter a minivan for the round-trip journeys to Phuket town (around B150) and Ao Patong (B300).

All the **accommodation** on **Hat Bang Tao** comes under the *Laguna Resort* umbrella: the complex of five adjoining upmarket hotels shares facilities (swimming pools, restaurants, tennis courts) and dominates the beachfront. Room prices are all in the same category, but *Sheraton Grande Laguna* (☎076/324101–7; ⑨) is the most exclusive; otherwise try *Dusit Laguna* (☎076/324320–32; ⑨) or *Pacific Island* (☎076/324023–30; ⑨). **Hat Surin** (also sometimes known as Ao Pansea) boasts Phuket's most indulgent resort, the *Amanpuri* (☎076/324333–8; ⑨), part of the super-exclusive, Hong Kong-based *Aman* chain; luxuries here include a personal attendant, a private Thai-style pavilion and unlimited use of the black marble swimming pool. On **Ao Kamala**, *Kamala Beach Estate* (☎01/723 0379; ⑨) is more for long-term guests as it specializes in top-notch service apartments, while *Phuket Kamala Resort* (☎01/723 0010; ⑧–⑨) is a smaller and more typical upmarket hotel.

Ao Patong

The most popular and developed of all Phuket's beaches, **AO PATONG** – 5km south of Ao Kamala and 15km west of Phuket town – is where the action is: the broad, three-kilometre beach offers good sand, safe sea and plenty of shade beneath the casuarinas, plus the densest concentration of top hotels and the island's biggest choice of water sports and diving centres. On the downside, a congestion of high-rise hotels and souvenir shops disfigures the beachfront, pollution is becoming a problem as the big hotels persist in dumping their sewage straight into the sea, and limpet-like touts are everywhere. Signs are that things can only get worse: a huge government-sponsored billboard stating "Because We Care, Use Condom Please" welcomes you to Patong, a resort whose hostess bars and strip joints make it the most active scene between Bangkok and Hat Yai, attracting an increasing number of single Western men. Before long, this might be a second Pattaya.

Already close to saturation point, Patong just keeps on growing outwards and upwards, which can make it hard to orient yourself. But essentially, the resort is strung out along the two main roads – **Thavee Wong** and **Raja Uthit** – that run

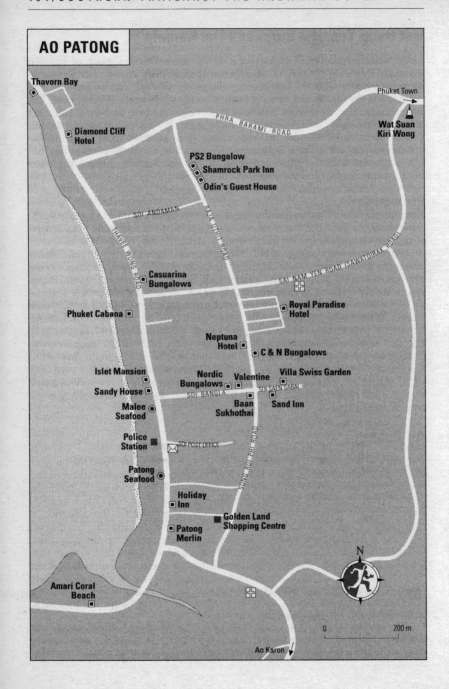

AO PATONG

Thavorn Bay

Phuket Town

Diamond Cliff
Hotel

PHRA BARAMI ROAD

Wat Suan
Kiri Wong

PS2 Bungalow
Shamrock Park Inn
Odin's Guest House

SOI ANDAMAN

RAMA UTHIT ROAD

THAVEE WONG ROAD

SAI NAM YEN ROAD (SAWATDIRAK) ROAD

Casuarina
Bungalows

Royal Paradise
Hotel

Phuket Cabana

Neptuna
Hotel

C & N Bungalows

Islet Mansion

Nordic
Bungalows

Valentine

Villa Swiss Garden

Sandy House

SOI BANGLA

SOI SAEN SABAI

Malee
Seafood

Baan
Sukhothai

Sand Inn

Police
Station

SOI POST OFFICE

SONG ROI PHI ROAD

Patong
Seafood

Holiday
Inn

Golden Land
Shopping Centre

Patong
Merlin

N

Amari Coral
Beach

0   200 m

Ao Karon

parallel to the beachfront, spilling over into a network of connecting sois which in turn have spawned numerous pedestrian-only "plazas". It's along the two major thoroughfares that you'll find most of the accommodation, while the two landmark sois connecting them have become established entertainment zones: **Soi Bangla** and its offshoots throb away at the heart of the nightlife district, while the more sedate **Soi Post Office** is dominated by tailors' shops and small cafés and restaurants.

Accommodation

Moderately priced accommodation on Patong is poor value by usual Thai standards: because demand is so great, rudimentary facilities cost twice as much here as they would even in Bangkok. If by any chance you find every central place full, head for the far northern end of Raja Uthit Road, beneath the hill-road that brings everyone in from town. Because this part of Patong is a 750-metre walk from the central shopping, eating and entertainment area (though only 100m from the sea itself), prices are noticeably lower, and rooms and bungalows larger into the bargain.

In general, Patong's **upmarket** hotels are better value, and many occupy prime beachfront sites on Thavee Wong. Officially, the beach itself is a building-free zone, but somehow a sizeable knot of developments has sprung up along the sand, confined as yet to a small central stretch close to Soi Bangla.

MODERATE

C&N Bungalows, 50/20 Raja Uthit Rd (☎076/340745). Good-value, spacious bungalows with fridge and bathroom, set in a garden (though beware the night-long din from the nearby *Titanic* disco). Quieter, more upmarket accommodation in the main building. ③–⑤.

Islet Mansion, 87/29 Thavee Wong Rd (☎076/341562). Only 10 bungalows, and one of the few outfits right on the beach. ⑥.

Nordic Bungalows, 82/25 Soi Bangla (☎076/340284). Bungalows and use of swimming pool in conveniently central location, at the far eastern end of this busy soi. ④.

Odin's Guest House, 78/59 Raja Uthit Rd (☎076/340732). One of several budget options at the far northern end of the resort, with 2-storey rows of very acceptable bungalows, all with attached bathroom. ④.

PS2 Bungalow, 78/54 Raja Uthit Rd (☎076/342207). Close by *Odin's*, so also a fair walk from the main attractions. Large, good-value bungalows with attached bathroom. ③–④.

Sand Inn, 93/95 Soi Saen Sabai (☎076/340275). Spotless, well-appointed air-con rooms, a little on the compact side, east off the bar-packed Soi Bangla. ⑥.

Sandy House, 87/14 Thavee Wong Rd (☎076/340458). Right on the beach; two good rooms with beachfront view, plus several others with no view at all. ④–⑥.

Shamrock Park Inn, 17/2 Raja Uthit Rd (☎076/340991). Near *Odin's* and *PS2*; offering pleasant rooms with shower, many with balconies, in 2-storey complex. There's a roof garden, too. ④–⑤.

Valentine, 82/46 Soi Bangla (☎076/340260). Simple bungalows in a quiet garden in the heart of the nightlife zone. ④–⑤.

Villa Swiss Garden, 84/24 Soi Saen Sabai (☎076/ 341120). East across Raja Uthit from Soi Bangla, this place has enormous air-con rooms, comfortably furnished with TV, fridge and ghetto blaster. ⑥.

EXPENSIVE

Amari Coral Beach Resort, 104 Traitrang Rd (☎076/340106–14). Occupies a secluded spot on a cliff at the southernmost end of the beach; supremely luxurious, with all facilities. ⑨.

Baan Sukhothai, eastern end of Soi Bangla (☎076/340195). Lavishly done-out traditional wooden bungalows, set in a landscaped garden. An excellent restaurant, too. ⑨.

Casuarina Bungalows, 92/2 Thavee Wong Rd (☎076/340123). Individual bungalows set in tree-covered grounds; just across the road from the sea, but in the least congested part of the resort. ⑨.

Holiday Inn Phuket, 86/11 Thavee Wong Rd (☎076/340608). International standard accommodation and facilities at the southern end of this road. ⑨.

Neptuna Hotel, 82/49 Raja Uthit Rd (☎076/340824). Bungalows with all the trimmings in a pleasantly manicured if slightly congested garden. Excellent location, protected from the bustle, but only 200m walk from Soi Bangla. ⑨.

Patong Merlin, 99/2 Thavee Wong Rd (☎076/340037). Top-quality rooms and service in large chain hotel at the southern end of the road. Popular with tour groups. ⑨.

Phuket Cabana, 94 Thavee Wong Rd (☎076/340138). Gorgeous collection of thoughtfully designed bungalows (equipped with air-con, TV and fridge) set around a garden swimming pool. Right on the beach and definitely the choice option of its price bracket. ⑨.

Eating and drinking

At night, an awful lot of people eat in their hotels, the best of which, gastronomically speaking, is the *Baan Sukhothai* (see previous page), which serves fine "Royal Thai" dishes, a sort of *nouvelle cuisine*. The Western-oriented cafés squashed in amongst the high-rises and shops are popular for daytime snacks, with Italian food and seafood big favourites; after dark the night market sets up along Raja Uthit Road, between Soi Bangla and Soi Sai Nam Yen. A selection of Patong's eateries appears below.

Malee Seafood Village, close to the Soi Bangla/Thavee Wong intersection. A deservedly popular, open-air restaurant which serves all manner of locally caught fish and seafood, particularly Phuket lobster, cooked to both Thai and Western recipes. Moderate.

Patong Seafood Restaurant, on the central stretch of Thavee Wong Road at no. 98/2. Another seafood place, with a good if pricey range at around B150 for a main dish.

Roma de Mauro e Franco, 89/15 Soi Post Office. Fresh pasta served amid checked table-cloths, candles and an intimate ambience. Inexpensive to moderate.

Vecchia Venezia, 82/16 Soi Bangla. Another Italian place, this one specializing in authentic-tasting pizzas. Inexpensive to moderate.

Nightlife

Patong's **nightlife** is packed into the strip of neon-lit open-air bar beers along Soi Bangla and the tiny sois that lead off it, where a burgeoning number of go-go bars add a seamier aspect to the zone. If the nightclubs in the big hotels don't appeal, you're otherwise limited to the cavernous *Titanic Disco* at 89/17 Raja Uthit Rd, which plays Western and Thai pop and shows videos on its huge screen, or *Maxim's* gay bar at 32/9 Raja Uthit Rd, which puts on a nightly transvestite cabaret to a mixed crowd.

Ao Karon

Twenty kilometres southwest of Phuket town, **AO KARON** is only about 5km south from Patong, but a lot less congested. Although the central stretch of beachfront is dominated by large-capacity hotels, the beach is, as yet, completely free of developments, and elsewhere you'll only find low-rise guest houses and bungalows, many set around gardens, interspersed with stretches of undeveloped grassland. With the recent emergence of a cluster of café-bars, restaurants and inexpensive guest houses on the headland at the far southern end of Ao Karon, this resort looks set to cream off the younger couples and mid-budget backpackers from the increasingly manic Ao Patong.

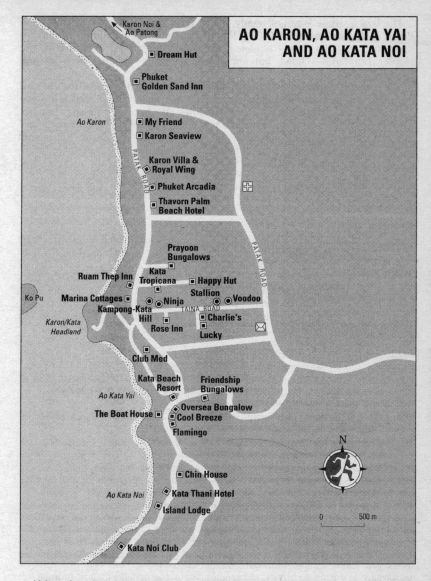

AO KARON, AO KATA YAI AND AO KATA NOI

Karon Noi & Ao Patong

Dream Hut

Phuket Golden Sand Inn

Ao Karon

My Friend

Karon Seaview

Karon Villa & Royal Wing

Phuket Arcadia

Thavorn Palm Beach Hotel

Prayoon Bungalows

Ruam Thep Inn

Kata Tropicana

Happy Hut

Stallion

Ko Pu

Marina Cottages

Ninja

Voodoo

Kampong-Kata Hill

Charlie's

Karon/Kata Headland

Rose Inn

Lucky

Club Med

Kata Beach Resort

Friendship Bungalows

Ao Kata Yai

Oversea Bungalow

The Boat House

Cool Breeze

Flamingo

N

Chin House

Ao Kata Noi

Kata Thani Hotel

Island Lodge

0   500 m

Kata Noi Club

Although swimming off any part of Karon can be quite dangerous during the monsoon season, when the undertow gets treacherously strong (look out for the red flags), there's plenty of scope for water sports here; windsurfing is good all year round, and the reefs around the tiny island of Ko Pu, just off the headland separating Karon from neighbouring Ao Kata Yai to the south, make for enjoyable snorkelling.

The beach, while long and sandy, offers very little in the way of shade and almost disappears at high tide. The tiny bay just north of Ao Karon – known as Karon Noi or Relax Bay – is almost exclusively patronized by guests of the swanky *Le Meridien* hotel, but non-guests are quite welcome to swim and sunbathe here.

The resort is encircled by a ring road, called Patak Road, which branches off the main access route to Phuket town. Karon's main commercial areas are confined to two smallish knots: one straddles the landmark *Phuket Arcadia*, halfway down the beach, and is where you'll find the banks, supermarkets and the post office; the other, spread along Taina Road on the Karon/Kata headland, is a little tourist village full of tailors, beachwear outlets, craft shops, minimarts and café-bars. **Songthaews** from Phuket town run to the north end of Karon along the outer section of Patak Road before doubling back along the beachfront and continuing south over the headland as far as *Kata Beach Resort* on Ao Kata Yai.

Accommodation

Karon is less pricey than Patong, but during peak season you'd be lucky indeed to find any **accommodation** in the ① and ② categories, with most places only dropping their rates below ③ on weekdays during the monsoon season. One of the best places to search for budget hotels is on the Karon/Kata headland, particularly along Taina Road, which bisects the road to Kata Yai. Not only are most guest houses here significantly less expensive than those on Karon proper, they're also convenient for bars, restaurants and shops, and yet less than ten minutes' walk from the beach.

INEXPENSIVE AND MODERATE

Charlie's, Taina Rd (☎076/330855). Very friendly, and the most inexpensive place on Karon. Room quality varies a lot: some have street-front balconies, others just have "wall" views; all rooms have a bathroom, though, which makes them excellent value. If *Charlie's* is full, try the adjacent and very similar *Lucky*. ①–②.

Dream Hut, far north end of the beach. Basic bungalows some way off the seafront, but still only a 10-min walk from the beach. ③.

Happy Hut, up the hill from *KataTropicana* at the southern end of Karon. Pleasantly located in a grassy dip some 300m from the beach. ③.

Karon Seaview Bungalow, 36/9 Patak Rd (☎076/396912). Slightly grotty bungalows with attached bathroom, ranged either side of a tree-lined walkway just across the road from the beach in this central area. Fine as a budget alternative if *Tropicana* is full. ③.

Kata Tropicana, far southern end of Karon (☎076/330408). Budget travellers' first stop, and a deservedly popular place. Range of well-spaced bungalows (some with air-con) on a pleasant grassy slope, nearly all with (long-distance) sea views. Two minutes' walk from the beach, and within walking distance of Taina Road's bars, restaurants and shops. ③–⑤.

Lucky, Taina Road. Very similar to the adjacent *Charlie's*, offering just a handful of basic but inexpensive rooms, some with attached bathroom. ①–②.

My Friend, 36/6 Patak Rd. Basic terraced huts in the northern central beach area. ④–⑤.

Phuket Golden Sand Inn, northern end of Ao Karon (☎076/396493). Medium-sized hotel, one of the least costly of its kind, with most rooms qualifying for the moderate price category. ⑤–⑦.

Prayoon Bungalows, up a gentle rise at the southern end of Ao Karon. Huts ranged across a grassy slope a little way off the beach. ③–④.

Rose Inn, Taina Rd (☎076/330582). Rooms are a bit dark, but not at all bad for the price and the area. Only five minutes' walk from Karon beach. All rooms with bathroom, some with air-con. ③–④.

Ruam Thep Inn, far southern end of beachfront Patak Road (☎076/330281). Small collection of very good bungalows, fully equipped and just 20m from the beach. Superbly situated restaurant terrace jutting out over the sea. ⑤–⑦.

EXPENSIVE

Karon Villa, Karon Royal Wing, 36/4 Patak Rd(☎076/381139). The most attractive place on Ao Karon: a self-contained village in the central beach area. Disparately designed bungalows bask in lovely gardens, with even more luxurious accommodation provided in the main "Royal Wing" building. Numerous restaurants and bars, plus a pool and fitness club. ⑧–⑨.

Le Meridien, on Karon Noi, north Karon (☎076/321480). Has the tiny bay all to itself. Facilities include a huge, lake-style swimming pool (with islands), squash and tennis courts and private woods. ⑨.

Marina Cottages, 120 Patak Rd, far southern end of Ao Karon, on the Karon/Kata headland (☎076/330625). Full range of luxurious cottages in a gorgeous tropical garden that leads right down to the beach. Good value considering the quality service and upmarket ambience. Convenient for bars and restaurants. ⑧–⑨.

Thavorn Palm Beach Hotel, halfway down the beachfront stretch of Patek Road, in the central beach area (☎076/381034–7). Top-quality high-rise accommodation in large chain hotel, fully equipped with swimming pool and tennis courts. ⑨.

Eating and nightlife

Many of Karon's best **restaurants** and bars are sprinkled along Taina Road on the Karon/Kata headland; here you'll find a fair selection of Thai, seafood and Western menus at reasonable prices. Despite names such as *Stallion* and *Voodoo Bar*, the **bars** seem fairly tame, certainly when compared to the nocturnal dens of Ao Patong, though none the less appealing for that. Most of them are designed along similar lines, with just five or six sets of easy chairs arranged around low tables, some of them out front on the street, others close to the bar inside. With continuous Western and Thai pop on the cassette decks and a range of enticing happy hour promotions, they're comfortable, hassle-free joints in which to while away a few hours, whether in company or alone.

RESTAURANTS

Dan Kwian, 30m up Taina Road. Specializes in northeastern fare, but also offers fresh seafood, which can be eaten at the outdoor streetside tables or under cover. Moderate.

Kampong-Kata Hill Restaurant, Taina Road. Next door to *Ninja* but significantly more upmarket, this place occupies a superb position on a steep slope just off the main road, its winding, flower-lined walkway lit up with fairylights after dark. As you'd expect, the food is fairly high-class, too, with quality Thai dishes a speciality. Moderate to expensive.

Maxim's, central beach area near the *Thavorn Palm Beach Hotel* on Ao Karon. Large-capacity seafood restaurant where you can select your fish from the day's catch. Barbecued fish a speciality. Moderate.

Ninja, 30m up Taina Road, across from *Dan Kwian*. Workaday Thai and Western standards, the former toned down for the tourists, with a relaxed and friendly atmosphere that makes it a pleasant place to hang out, whether you're eating or having a beer. Inexpensive.

Praichart Seafood Inn, *Karon Villa*, 36/4 Patak Rd. High-quality fish dishes served in plush surroundings. Expensive.

Ao Kata Yai and Ao Kata Noi

Tree-lined and peaceful, **AO KATA YAI** (Big Kata Bay) is only a few minutes' drive around the headland from Karon, but both prettier and safer for swimming thanks to the protective rocky promontories at either end. The northern stretch of Kata Yai is completely given over to the unobtrusive buildings of the *Club Med* resort, and then it's a lengthy trek down to the rest of the accommodation at the southern end. A small headland at the southernmost point divides Ao Kata Yai from **AO KATA NOI** (Little Kata Bay), a smaller and less attractive beach, currently undergoing a major redevelopment.

Practicalities

Most **songthaews** from Phuket go past *Club Med* as far as *Kata Beach Resort* on the headland between Kata Yai and Kata Noi; to get to Kata Noi, continue walking over the hill for about ten minutes.

There is no budget **accommodation** on **Kata Yai**. *Friendship Bungalows* (☎076/330499; ④–⑥) has very adequate bungalows in a garden, about ten minutes' walk from the southern end of the beach. Otherwise, you could try the nearby *Oversea Bungalow* (④–⑥), *Cool Breeze* (☎076/330484; ④–⑤) or *Flamingo* (④–⑥), all of which have a range of bungalows, many with sea view, on a roadside slope. In the more expensive categories, the very large *Kata Beach Resort*, also at the southern end of Kata Yai (☎076/330530; ⑦), has a swimming pool and lots of water sports facilities, while the exclusive *The Boat House* (☎076/330015; ⑨) has only 36 rooms and maintains a high standard of personal service.

Down on **Kata Noi**, the best spot on the beach is occupied by the fifteen rattan huts of the low-budget *Island Lodge* (②–④). At the base of the Kata Yai/Kata Noi hill, *Chin House and Bungalow* (③–④) has bungalows – some good, some less so – along the incline. Pricier options are the mid-range bungalows at *Kata Noi Club* (⑥), right at the end of the beach, or a de luxe room in the attractive, sprawling *Kata Thani Hotel* at the north end of the beach (☎076/330417; ⑧), where a sea view is guaranteed and there's a swimming pool on the premises.

Hat Nai Harn and Laem Promthep

Around the next headland south from Kata Noi, **HAT NAI HARN** – 18km southwest of Phuket town – is generally considered to be one of the loveliest beaches on the island, given character by a sparkling saltwater lagoon. Lording it over the beach and yacht-filled bay is the luxurious *Phuket Yacht Club*, which for the last few years has sponsored a King's Cup Regatta in early December, attracting high-rollers from all over Asia.

Follow the coastal road 2km south and you'll get to a small bay which has coral reefs very close to the shore, though the currents are strong and the sewage pipes uncomfortably close. A further 1km on, you reach the southernmost tip of Ko Phuket at the sheer headland of **Laem Promthep**. Wild and rugged, jutting out into the deep blue of the Andaman Sea, the cape is one of the island's top beauty spots: at sunset, busloads of tour groups get shipped in to admire the scenery – and just to ensure you don't miss the spectacle, a list of year-round sunset times is posted at the viewpoint. Several reefs lie just off the cape, but it's safer to snorkel from a boat rather than negotiating the rocky shore.

Practicalities

Songthaews bypass Laem Promthep and follow the direct inland road between Nai Harn and Hat Rawai instead, so you may have to do the lengthy climb round the promontory on foot. It's a popular spot though, so it should be easy enough to hitch.

At the time of writing, only a couple of sets of budget **bungalows** were in operation on or near Nai Harn. *Coconut Bungalows* (②), on the northern cliffside, shares the same view as the *Yacht Club* and offers inexpensive basic huts. To find anything else in this range, you have to trudge to the bay 2km south of Nai Harn, where you'll find the simple but friendly *Nai Harn Ya Noi Bungalows* (③–④). Otherwise, moderately priced accommodation is limited to condominium developments further back off the beach along the access road. The internationally acclaimed *Phuket Yacht Club* (☎076/381156–63; ⑨) is one of the most exclusive places on the whole island, offering superb rooms and exquisite service. If this is beyond your means but you want a bit of comfort, continue a little further round the headland to the minuscule Ao Sane, site of the *Jungle Beach Resort* (☎076/ 381108; ④–⑧), which has mainly mid-range rooms, some with air conditioning, and a lovely private location.

Hat Rawai and its islands

The eastern side of Laem Promthep curves round into **HAT RAWAI**, Phuket's southernmost beach and the first to be exploited for tourist purposes. Twenty-five years on, the developers have moved to the softer sands of Kata and Karon and returned Rawai to its former inhabitants, the *chao ley*. A few bungalow outfits still operate here, but most visitors come either to eat seafood with Phuket's townspeople in one of the nameless open-air seafood restaurants on the beachfront or to hire a longtail out to the **islands** offshore. Of these, Ko Lone, Ko Hai (aka Coral Island), Ko Racha Yai, Ko Racha Noi and Ko Mai Thon are good for snorkelling and diving – the visibility and variety of the reefs around **Ko Racha** in particular compare with those off Ko Similan further up the Andaman coast, and make a popular destination for Phuket's diving centres (see box on p.446). You should be able to charter a boat for a day trip to one or more of these islands for between B500 and B1000: ask at the pier.

Hat Rawai boasts an idiosyncratic monument in the shape of the *Henry Wagner*, a very ordinary twelve-metre longtail boat set back from the road just west of the pier. In June 1987, five disabled men set off in this boat to pioneer a course across the Isthmus of Kra, and in just six weeks they navigated the rivers connecting the Andaman Sea to the Gulf of Thailand, without the aid of accurate charts. The captain and inspiration behind the enterprise was Welsh-born 64-year-old amputee Tristan Jones, veteran adventurer and campaigner for the disabled, who told the story of the trip in his book, *To Venture Further*.

Practicalities

Songthaews from Phuket town pass through Rawai on their way to and from Nai Harn. Unless you're keen on desolate beaches, Rawai makes a pretty dismal place to stay. *Rawai Garden Resort* (☎076/381292; ④), beyond the far western edge of the beach where the road forks to Laem Promthep and Hat Nai Harn, is the most attractive option, with bungalows in a garden. Much closer to the pier, *Porn Sri* (③–⑤) has a range of bungalows, and *Rawai Plaza* (☎076/381346; ⑤–⑥) offers the poshest accommodation on the beach.

THE CHAO LEY

Sometimes called sea gypsies, the **chao ley** or *chao nam* ("people of the sea" or "water people") earn their living from the seas around the west coast of the Malay peninsula, some of them living in established communities, many preferring to move on when the catch dries up or the season changes. The *chao ley* are expert **divers** and make most of their money from **pearls** and **shells**, attaching stones to their waists to dive to depths of 6km with only an air-hose connecting them to the surface; sometimes they fish in this way, too, taking down enormous nets into which they herd the fish as they walk along the sea bed. Their agility and courage make them good **birds'-nesters** as well (see p.479).

Very dark-skinned and with a reddish tinge to their hair because of constant exposure to the sun, the *chao ley* probably originated in Indonesia. They speak their own language and follow animistic beliefs: for example, at the beginning and end of each fishing season, they launch miniature boats filled with tiny weapons onto the sea to placate the spirits of the deep. If the boat returns to the same village it's considered a bad omen and the inhabitants may move to a new location.

As well as being kicked off territory that has been theirs for centuries, the *chao ley* have been subjected to attempts to get them to adopt a recognized religion, and to such insensitive aid schemes as the building of communal toilets close to eating and sleeping areas – shockingly unclean in the eyes of the *chao ley*. As if that weren't enough, busloads of tourists race through *chao ley* settlements trading cute photo poses for coins and sweets, setting in motion a cycle of dependancy that threatens the very basis of the *chao ley* way of life.

The east coast

Tin mines and docks take up a lot of Phuket's east coast, which is thus neither scenic nor swimmable. East of Rawai, the sizeable offshore island of **Ko Lone** protects the broad sweep of **Ao Chalong**, where many a Chinese fortune was made from the huge quantities of tin mined in the bay. Ao Chalong tapers off eastwards into **Laem Panwa**, at the tip of which you'll find the **Phuket Aquarium** (daily 10am–4pm; B10), 9km south of Phuket town and accessible by frequent songthaews. Run by the island's Marine Research Centre, it makes a poor substitute for a day's snorkelling, but not a bad primer for what you might see on a reef. The research centre is also involved in the protection of marine turtles (see box on p.442); there's a hatchery on the premises, although it's out of bounds to casual vistors.

Around the other side of Laem Panwa, the island's main port of **Ao Makham** is dominated by a smelting and refining plant, bordered to the north by **Ko Siray** (4km east of Phuket town), just about qualifying as an island because of the narrow canal that separates it from Ko Phuket. Tour buses always stop off here to spy on Phuket's largest and longest-established *chao ley* community, an example of exploitative tourism at its worst.

The interior

If you have your own transport, exploring the lush, verdant **interior** makes a good antidote to lying on scorched beaches. All the tiny backroads – some too small to figure on tourist maps – eventually link up with the arteries connecting Phuket town with the beaches, and the minor routes south of Hat Nai Yang are especially picturesque, passing through monsoon forest which once in a while opens out into spikey pineapple fields or regimentally ordered **rubber plantations**. Thailand's first rubber trees were planted in Trang in 1901, and Phuket's sandy soil proved to be especially well suited to the crop. All over the island you'll see cream-coloured sheets of latex hanging out to dry on bamboo racks in front of villagers' houses.

North of Karon, Phuket's minor roads eventually swing back to the central Highway 402, also known as Thep Kasatri Road after the landmark monument that stands on a roundabout 12km north of Phuket town. This **Heroines' Monument** commemorates the repulse of the Burmese army by the widow of the governor of Phuket and her sister in 1785: the two women rallied the island's womenfolk who, legend has it, cut their hair short and rolled up banana leaves to look like musket barrels to frighten the Burmese away. All songthaews to Hat Surin and Hat Nai Yang pass the monument (as does all mainland-bound traffic), and this is where you should alight for **Thalang Museum** (Wed–Sun 8.30am–4pm; B20), five minutes' walk east of here on Route 4027. Phuket's only museum, it has a few interesting exhibits on the local tin and rubber industries, as well as some colourful folkloric history and photos of the masochistic feats of the Vegetarian Festival (see p.451).

Eight kilometres north of the Heroines' Monument, just beyond the crossroads in the small town of **Thalang**, stands **Wat Phra Thong**, one of Phuket's most revered temples on account of the power of the Buddha statue it enshrines. The solid gold image is half-buried and no one dares dig it up for fear of a curse that has struck down excavators in the past. After the wat was built around the statue, the image was encased in plaster to deter would-be robbers.

The road east of the Thalang intersection takes you to **Phra Taew National Park**, 3km away. Several undemanding paths cross this small hilly enclave, taking you through the forest habitat of gibbons and macaques, to the waterfalls of Nam Tok Ton Sai and Nam Tok Bang Pae.

KO PHI PHI AND THE KRABI COAST

East around the mainland coast from Ko Phuket's Sarasin Bridge, the limestone pinnacles that so dominate the landscape of southern Thailand suddenly begin to pepper the sea as well, making **Ao Phang Nga** one of the most fascinating bays in the country. Most travellers, however, head straight for the hub of the region at **Krabi**, springboard for the spectacular mainland beaches of **Laem Phra Nang** and the even more stunning – and very popular – **Ko Phi Phi**. If it's tropical paradise minus the crowds that you're after, opt instead for the sizeable but barely developed **Ko Lanta Yai** or the smaller **Ko Jum**.

All the major islands are served by frequent **ferries** from Krabi except during the rainy season (May–Oct), when convoluted routes via other mainland ports are sometimes possible. Buses and songthaews connect all mainland spots whatever the weather, and you can rent motorbikes in Krabi.

Ao Phang Nga

Protected from the ravages of the Andaman Sea by Ko Phuket, **AO PHANG NGA** has a seascape both bizarre and beautiful. Covering some four hundred square kilometres of coast between Ko Phuket and Krabi, the mangrove-lined bay is littered with limestone karst formations of up to 300m in height, jungle-clad and craggily profiled. The bay is thought to have been formed about twelve thousand years ago when a dramatic rise in sea level flooded the summits of mountain ranges which over millions of years had been eroded by an acidic mixture of atmospheric carbon dioxide and rainwater.

Bay tours and boat rental

The best and most affordable way of seeing the bay is to join an **organized tour** from the town of **Phang Nga** – you can go from Ko Phuket or Krabi, but the Phuket boats are relatively expensive and generally too big to manoeuvre the more interesting areas, and Krabi tours go via Phang Nga anyway.

The best of the budget tours are the **longtail boat trips** operated by the popular and long-established *Sayan Tour* (☎076/411521), housed in the tourist information office inside the bus station (see below), or the similar ones organized by the *Ratanapong Hotel*. Both sets of day tours leave at 7.30am, priced at B150 for a five-hour jaunt, which will have you back in town by about 12.30pm; B300 overnight tours, featuring a night on the unusual village of **Ko Panyi**, leave at 4.30pm and join up with the day tours the following morning, getting back to town at the same time. Tours leave from the two "offices" but will pick up from the town's hotels if booked in advance; people staying at **Tha Don**, 9km south and the departure point for trips around Ao Phang Nga, can join the tours at the pier.

You could **charter a longtail boat** for upwards of B600 per day from the pier at Tha Don, but this is only really an advantage if your Thai is good enough to specify your preferred itinerary, otherwise you'll probably end up covering the same ground as the tours.

If you have the money, the best way to see the bay is by **sea canoe**. *Phuket Sea Canoe Center* (PO Box 276; ☎076/392237) runs day trips around the bay in its vast "sea explorer" canoes for B2500 per person. Everyone gets full paddling instruction and each canoe is piloted by an English-speaking guide and canoeing expert; the special features of these tours are the exploration of lagoons hidden inside the karst outcrops, and of course the chance to see the bay without the constant roar of an engine to scare away the seabirds, kingfishers, crab-eating macaques, mudskippers, fiddler crabs and other wildlife that haunt the mangrove-fringed shores. *Santana Adventure Tours,* also based on Ko Phuket at 92/18 Sawatdirak Rd, Ao Patong (☎076/340360), offers similar canoeing expeditions for around the same price.

Phang Nga town and Tha Don

All buses from Phuket and Takua Pa to Krabi pass through nondescript little **PHANG NGA** about midway along their routes, dropping passengers at the bus station on Phetkasem Road within five minutes' walk of the clearly signposted budget hotels. If you want to go straight to the bay, change onto a songthaew bound for the pier at **THA DON**. The **tourist information** office at the bus station is run by the bay tour-guide Mr Sayan (see above); his staff will help you with bus connections and store your baggage for a few hours.

Phang Nga's four **budget hotels** are all within 100m of each other, two on each side of Phetkasem Road. Of the four, *Thawisuk Hotel* (①–②) gets the most custom, offering large, clean rooms and a rooftop terrace. The very similar *Ratanapong Hotel* (☎076/411247; ②) has adequate rooms and an informal restaurant on street level. On the other side of the road, *Muang Tong* (☎076/411132; ②–

③) has fan-cooled and air-conditioned rooms, all with attached bathroom, while *Rak Phang Nga* (①), about 30m along, has the lowest priced and least comfortable rooms in town. If you're after more **upmarket** accommodation, head to Tha Don, where the *Phang Nga Bay Resort* (☎076/411201; ⑦) boasts a swimming pool and good facilities, but has disappointing views considering the bayside location.

For **eating**, check out the *Phing Kan Restaurant* under the *Ratanapong Hotel*, where you can choose from a variety of noodle and rice standards detailed on the English-language menu. The well-established streetside restaurant nearby also has an English menu and a large selection of rice, noodle and fish dishes. Otherwise, plenty of noodle stalls line the Phetkasem Road day and night.

The bay

The standard itinerary follows a circular or figure-of-eight route around the bay, passing extraordinary karst silhouettes that change character with the shifting light – in the eerie glow of an early-morning mist it can be a breathtaking experience. Many of the formations have nicknames suggested by their weird outlines – like **Khao Machu**, which translates as "Pekinese Rock", and **Khao Tapu** or Nail Rock. Others have titles derived from other attributes – **Tham Nak** (Naga Cave) gets its name from the serpentine stalagmites inside; and a close inspection of **Khao Kien** (Painting Rock) reveals a cliff wall decorated with paintings of elephants, monkeys, fish, crabs and hunting weapons, believed to be between three thousand and five thousand years old.

Ao Phang Nga's most celebrated feature, however, earned its tag from a movie: the cleft **Khao Ping Gan** (Leaning Rock) is better known as **James Bond Island**, after doubling as Scaramanga's hideaway in *The Man With the Golden Gun*. Every boat stops off here and the rock crawls with trinket vendors.

From Khao Ping Gan most boats return to the mainland via the eye-catching settlement of **KO PANYI**, a Muslim village built almost entirely on stilts around the rock that supports the mosque. Nearly all boat tours stop here for lunch, so the island's become little more than a tourists' shopping and eating arcade. If you want to eat here, avoid the expensive and noisy seafood restaurants out front, and head towards the locals' food stalls around the mosque. The overnight tours, which include an evening meal and dormitory-style accommodation on the island, offer a more tranquil experience and a chance to watch the sun set and rise over the bay, though there's little to do in the intervening hours and you're confined to the village until a boat picks you up after breakfast.

At some point on your trip you should pass several small brick **kilns** on the edge of a mangrove swamp – once used for producing charcoal from mangrove wood – before being ferried beneath **Tham Lod**, a photogenic archway roofed with stalactites and opening onto spectacular limestone and mangrove vistas.

Krabi

The compact size and relatively peaceful atmosphere of **KRABI** belie this small fishing town's role as provincial capital and major hub for onward travel to some of the region's most popular islands. Apart from an early-morning flurry when the Bangkok and Surat Thani buses arrive to connect with island-bound boats, the town stays relatively empty of tourists for most of the day, and so efficient are the trans-

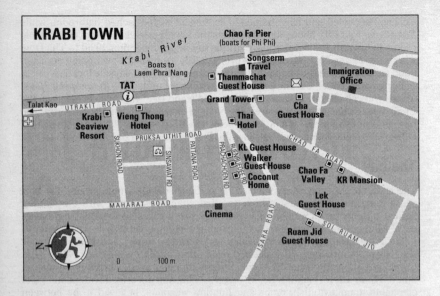

port links you don't really need to stop here. It's an attractive spot, though: strung out along the west bank of the Krabi estuary, it provides mangrove-lined shorelines to the east, a harbour filled with rickety old fishing vessels, and looming limestone outcrops on every horizon. There are plenty of guest houses, so it's possible to base yourself here and make day trips to the Krabi beaches 45 minutes' boat- or song-thaew-ride away, though most people prefer to stay at the beaches.

The main Utrakit Road runs north–south along the estuary, veering slightly inland just north of the Tha Reua Chao Fa (Chao Fa boat pier) and forming the eastern perimeter of the tiny **town centre**. Most of the banks on Utrakit Road have exchange facilities, several shops stock a sizeable range of snorkelling equipment, and the post office runs an efficient poste restante.

Arrival and information

Direct **air-conditioned and VIP buses from Bangkok** leave the southern bus terminal at staggered intervals between 6.30pm and 8pm; they take at least twelve hours and should be booked one day ahead. Seven air-conditioned buses make the daily connection with **Surat Thani**, taking three hours. Air-conditioned buses stop in front of the TAT office on Utrakit Road, less than ten minutes' walk north of the Chao Fa pier and five minutes' east of the town centre; touts for guest houses and boat tickets always meet these buses, offering free transport to the pier or guest house, regardless of what you decide, so if you're feeling weary after the long journey, you may as well take advantage of the ride. Arriving by **ordinary bus** from Phang Nga, Phuket or Surat Thani, you'll be dropped at the bus terminal 5km north of town in the village of **Talat Kao**, which stands at the intersection of Utrakit Road and Highway 4. From here there's a frequent song-thaew service into Krabi. **Ferries** from Ko Phi Phi and Ko Lanta generally dock at the main Chao Fa pier, but sometimes pull in at the pier closer to TAT, where the **longtails** from Laem Phra Nang arrive.

Krabi's only independent **tourist information** service is the small TAT branch (Mon–Sat 8.30am–noon & 1–4.30pm; ☎075/611381) housed in a lone white-washed hut on the river side of Utrakit Road. Staff here provide maps, bus timetables and hotel lists, but will send you elsewhere for beach and island accommodation bookings and ferry tickets; there's no shortage of private booking agents in town, and nearly every guest house has its own travel centre as well. There's actually no need to buy ferry tickets in advance as none of the boats have reserved seats, but it may be worth booking your first night's island or beach accommodation through one of these agents, as Ko Phi Phi especially gets packed out during peak season.

Accommodation

There's a fair spread of accommodation in town, much of it of a standard nature and price. The least expensive guest houses offer rock-bottom accommodation, often cramped and windowless but perfectly adequate for one night, while a couple of moderate hotels provide more comfortable options.

Chao Fa Valley, a 5-min walk west along Chao Fa Road from the pier (☎075/612499). By far the prettiest of the town's guest houses, with spacious bungalows arranged around a colourful flower garden; all the bungalows have attached bathroom and some have air-con, but their recent slide into shabbiness now makes the rates seem a little steep. ③–④.

Cha Guest House, opposite the post office on Utrakit Road. Hard-core budget travellers tend to head for this garden compound, which offers the most inexpensive huts in town. ①.

Coconut Home, Ruenruedee Rd (☎075/612601). One of 3 indistinguishable guest houses along this road. No frills but fair enough. ①–②.

Grand Tower Guest House, at the corner of Utrakit and Chao Fa roads (☎075/611741). Comparable to *KR Mansion*, with similarly spruce rooms for the same prices, but not so congenial.

KL Guest House, Ruenruedee Rd (☎075/612511). Like the others on this road, a standard budget option . ①–②.

KR Mansion, a 5-min walk west along Chao Fa Road from the pier (☎075/612761). In better condition than the next-door *Chao Fa Valley* and exceedingly popular with travellers; though sparse, the rooms are clean and well kept, and the staff extremely welcoming. ①–③.

Thai Hotel, Issara Road (☎075/611122). Moderate hotel, a little more luxurious than *Vieng Thong*. ⑤.

Vieng Thong, Utrakit Road (☎075/611188). Efficiently run, good value and unassuming. ④.

Walker Guest House, Ruenruedee Rd (☎075/612756). Basic budget place, with nothing to set it apart from its rivals on the same road. ①–②.

Eating

Most people eat in the guest-house **restaurants**, which serve the standard travellers' fare of milk shakes, pizzas, hamburgers, fish and chips and of course *pat thai* and *khao pat*. It might have grotty rooms, but the *Thammachat Guest House* near Chao Fa pier has the best menu in town and is particularly strong on unusual Thai and adventurous vegetarian dishes; prices are inexpensive to moderate. Alternatively, check out the *Tamarind Tree*, the restaurant attached to *KR Mansion* on Chao Fa Road, which does a full range of slap-up Thai and Western fare at prices both inexpensive and moderate. For a truly inexpensive Thai meal in a more authentic setting, eat at the **night market**, which is set up around the pier head every evening from about 6pm. The river views are the best thing about Krabi's floating restaurant, just south of the TAT office off Utrakit Road: the food is expensive and nothing special.

Day trips from Krabi

With time on your hands you'll soon exhaust the possibilities in Krabi, but there are a couple of trips to make out of town apart from the popular excursion to Ao Phang Nga. Most Krabi guest houses and tour companies rent out **motorbikes** for about B250 per day, or you can use public or chartered transport.

THE MANGROVES

For about B100 per hour, the boatmen who hang around near the floating restaurant will take you deep into the **mangrove swamps** that infest the Krabi River estuary, giving you a close-up view of the wildlife and stopping off at a couple of riverside caves on the way. It's best to set off at fairly low tide when the mangroves are at their creepiest, their aerial roots fully exposed to form gnarled and knotted archways above the muddy banks. Not only are these roots essential parts of the tree's breathing apparatus, they also reclaim land for future mangroves, trapping and accumulating water-borne debris into which the metre-long mangrove seedlings can fall. In this way, mangrove swamps also fulfill a vital ecological function: stabilizing shifting muds and protecting coastlines from erosion and the impact of tropical storms.

Mangrove swamp mud harbours some interesting creatures too, like the instantly recognizable **fiddler crab**, named after the male's single outsized reddish claw, which it brandishes for communication and defence purposes – the claw is so powerful it could open a can of baked beans. If you keep your eyes peeled you should be able to make out a few **mudskippers**; these specially adapted fish can absorb atmospheric oxygen through their skins as long as they keep their outsides damp, which is why they spend so much time slithering around in the sludge. As you'd imagine from the name, on land they move in tiny hops by flicking their tails, aided by their extra-strong pectoral fins. Of the bigger creatures who patrol the mangrove swamps in search of food, you might well come across **kingfishers** and white-bellied **sea eagles**, but you'd be very lucky indeed to encounter the rare crab-eating macaque.

To date, the Krabi mangroves have escaped the **environmentally damaging** attentions of the prawn-farming industry that has so damaged the swamps around Kanchanaburi (see "Environmental Issues" in *Contexts*, p.553, for more on this). But mangrove wood from this area has been used to make commercial **charcoal**, and on any boat trip around the Krabi estuary you'll almost certainly pass the remains of old tiny brick kilns near cleared patches of swamp.

WAT THAM SEUA

Beautifully set amidst limestone cliffs 12km northeast of Krabi, the tropical forest of **Wat Tham Seua** (Tiger Cave Temple) can be reached by songthaew from Utrakit Road, which should take about twenty minutes. The main bot – on your left under the cliff overhang – might come as a bit of a shock: alongside portraits of the abbot, a renowned teacher of Vipassana meditation, close-up photos of human entrails and internal organs are on display – reminders of the impermanence of the body. Any skulls and skeletons you might come across in the compound serve the same educative purpose.

The most interesting part of Wat Tham Seua lies beyond the bot, past the large, tacky statue of the Chinese fertility goddess Kuan Im, where a staircase takes you over the cliff and down into a deep dell encircled by high limestone walls. Here the monks have built themselves self-sufficient meditation cells, linked by paths through the lush ravine, which is home to squirrels and monkeys as well as a pair of remarkable trees with overground **buttress "roots"** over 10m high. Triangular buttress roots are quite a common sight in tropical forests such as this, where the overhead canopy is so dense that it blocks out most of the sunlight, starving the soil of the nutrients necessary to sustain such enormous trees and rendering subterranean roots ineffective; these lateral extensions to the trunk both absorb foodstuff from the forest floor, in the form of fallen leaves and fungi, and act as the tree's anchor.

SUSAAN HOI

Thais make a big deal out of **Susaan Hoi** (Shell Cemetery), 17km west around the coast from Krabi, but it's hard to get very excited about a shoreline of metre-long beige-coloured rocks that could easily be mistaken for concrete slabs. Nevertheless, the facts of their formation are impressive: these stones are 75 million years old and made entirely from compressed shell fossils. You get a distant view of them from any longtail boat travelling between Krabi and Ao Phra Nang; for a closer look take a songthaew from Utrakit Road.

THAN BOKKHARANI

Fifty kilometres northwest of Krabi, on the road to Phang Nga, the botanical gardens of **Than Bokkharani** make a small-scale contrast to the severe and rugged drama of Krabi's powerful limestone landscapes. Called Than Bok for short, the tiny park is a glade of emerald pools, grottoes and waterfalls enclosed in a ring of lush forest, and lies 1km south of **Ao Luk**. All west-bound songthaews stop here and the journey takes about an hour; from the Ao Luk intersection either walk or take a songthaew. Chances are that if you come here during the week you'll have the place to yourself, but because it's so small Than Bok quickly gets congested on holidays. Tours to Ao Phang Nga from Krabi sometimes take in Than Bok on the return journey.

Krabi beaches

Although the two mainland beach areas west of Krabi can't compete with the local islands for snorkelling or seclusion, the stunning headland of **Laem Phra Nang** is accessible only by boat, so staying on one of its three beaches can feel like being on an island, albeit a crowded one. In contrast, a road runs right along the **Ao Nang** beachfront, which has enabled an upmarket resort to thrive around its far from exceptional beach. Don't bother coming to Ao Nang between May and October, when the beach gets covered in sea-borne debris and most accommodation is closed. The Laem Phra Nang beaches, on the other hand, don't change much year-round, though a few places close up for the rainy season.

Laem Phra Nang

Seen from the close quarters of a longtail boat, the combination of sheer limestone cliffs, pure white sand and emerald waters at **LAEM PHRA NANG** is spectacular – and would be even more so without the hundreds of other admirers gathered on its beaches. Almost every centimetre of buildable land on the cape has now been taken over by bungalows, but at least high-rises don't

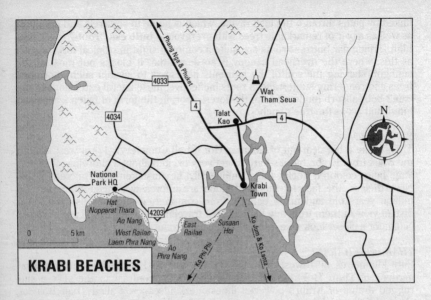

KRABI BEACHES

feature yet, and developers have so far favoured natural materials over concrete. The scene here is laid-back, but by no means comatose; it's as popular with backpackers as it is with young families, and the accommodation and entertainment facilities reflect this. Even if you don't want to stay, it's worth coming for the day to gawp at the scenery and scramble down into the lushly vegetated area around the cape's enclosed lagoon.

Longtail **boats** to Laem Phra Nang depart from beside the floating restaurant on the Krabi riverfront (45min; B45), leaving throughout the day as soon as they fill up. From November to April the boatmen pull in at Ao Phra Nang, on the tip of the cape, and can usually be persuaded to continue round to west Railae; during the rainy season they'll only go as far as east Railae. Except during the monsoon season, longtails connect Ao Nang, further west around the coast, with west Railae (10min; B20).

Several bungalows on Laem Phra Nang organize **snorkelling trips** (about B200 including equipment) to the nearby islands of Hua Kwan and Ko Poda. So-called **nautical treks** are also becoming popular: often led by *chao ley*, these are three-day snorkelling and shell-hunting forays around islands, with campfire meals and nights under the stars, all for an average of B1000 per person. A number of bungalows also run **diving trips** to nearby islands – some even venturing as far as the unrivalled reefs around Ko Similan; *Viewpoint* on east Railae (see p.473) offers PADI-certificated diving courses as well. Given the topography, there's huge potential for **rock climbing**, **caving** and even **abseiling** at Laem Phra Nang: *Phra Nang Rock Climbing Club* at *Ya Ya Bungalows*, also on east Railae, organizes all sorts of expeditions in the locality, providing equipment and tuition.

Longtail **boats** to Laem Phra Nang depart from beside the floating restaurant on the Krabi riverfront (45min; B45), leaving throughout the day as soon as they fill up. From November to April the boatmen pull in at Ao Phra Nang, on the tip of the cape, and can usually be persuaded to continue round to west Railae; during the rainy season they'll only go as far as east Railae. Except during the monsoon season, longtails connect Ao Nang, further west around the coast, with west Railae (10min; B20).

The beaches

The headland has three beaches within ten minutes' walk of each other: **Ao Phra Nang** graces the southwestern edge, and is flanked by **Hat Railae**, technically one bay but in fact composed of distinct **east** and **west** beaches.

AO PHRA NANG

Set against a magnificent backdrop of cliffs and palms, diminutive **AO PHRA NANG** (aka Hat Tham Phra Nang) is, despite the noisy longtail traffic, the loveliest spot on the cape, attracting sunbathers to its luxuriously soft sand and snorkellers to the reefs some 200m offshore. Of the three beaches, it alone has no bungalows visible from the shore, just a couple of makeshift beachfront café-bars. Screened from the beach is just one luxury resort, with the sole means of direct access to Ao Phra Nang.

The beach and cape are named after a princess (*phra nang* means "revered lady"), whom the local fisherfolk believe lives here and controls the fertility of the sea. If you walk past the entrance to **Tham Phra Nang** (Princess Cave), hollowed out of the huge karst outcrop at the eastern edge of the bay, you'll see a host of red-tipped wooden phalluses stacked as offerings to her, by way of insurance for large catches.

The numerous passageways and rocks around the cave are fun to clamber over, but getting down into **Sa Phra Nang** (Princess Lagoon) is more of a challenge. Buried deep inside the same rock, the lagoon is accessible only via a steep 45-minute descent that starts at the "resting spot" halfway along the wooden walkway connecting the east edge of Ao Phra Nang with east Railae. After an initial ten-minute clamber, negotiated with the help of ropes, the path forks: go left for a panoramic view over the east and west bays of Hat Railae, or right for the lagoon. (For the strong-armed, there's the third option of hauling yourself up ropes to the top of the cliff for a bird's-eye view.) Taking the right-hand fork, you'll pass through the tropical dell dubbed "big tree valley" before eventually descending to the murky lagoon. The muddy banks have spawned a lagoonside gallery of clay models fashioned by visitors.

Tham Phra Nang

EAST RAILAE

The least attractive of the cape's beaches, **EAST RAILAE** (also known as Nam Mao) is not suitable for swimming because of its fairly dense mangrove growth, a tide that goes out for miles, and sand that's littered with leftover building rubble. Still, there's a greater concentration of inexpensive bungalows here, and none is more than ten minutes from the much cleaner sands of west Railae and Ao Phra Nang. To get to east Railae from Ao Phra Nang, follow the wooden walkway from the eastern edge; from west Railae walk through the *Railae Bay* bungalow compound.

The northern end of east Railae backs onto a rocky hillside which, behind *Diamond Cave* bungalows, hides another set of caves. Referred to as **Tham Phra Nang Nai** (Inner Princess Cave) or Diamond Cave, these are said to shimmer with stalactite formations, but at the time of writing a tour operator had grabbed the keys to the entrance gate and would only open up for certain groups.

WEST RAILAE

Sometimes known as Sunset Beach, **WEST RAILAE** comes a close second to Ao Phra Nang, with similarly impressive karst scenery, crystal-clear water and a much longer stretch of good sand. There's some shade here, too, and you only have to walk a few hundred metres to get beyond the beachfront diners' line of vision.

Longtails do sometimes dock here, but otherwise you can walk from Ao Phra Nang via the walkway to east Railae, cutting across to west Railae beside the *King Head* bar.

Accommodation, eating and nightlife

Aside from the budget-blowing opulence of the *Dusit Rayavadee* resort, **accommodation** on the headland is of a fairly uniform standard. The places on east Railae are perhaps more budget-friendly than those on west Railae, but most operations offer a range of choices, priced to reflect flimsiness of hut or nature of view, though bear in mind that no room on the cape is more than 200m from the sea.

All the bungalow operations have **restaurants** where food is pricey and unremarkable. Evening **entertainment** consists either of watching the restaurant videos – most places have twice-nightly screenings – or patronizing one of the relaxed beachfront bars on east Railae. *King Head,* beside *Railae Bay,* is one of the longest established and most popular, but other enjoyable watering holes are *Reggae* at *Viewpoint* or *Blue Bar* at the neighbouring *Diamond Cave Bungalows.*

AO PHRA NANG

Dusit Rayavadee, right at the tip of the cape (☎02/238 4790–4). Set in a grassy compound bordering all 3 beaches, and the only place affording direct access to Ao Phra Nang, this exclusive resort is essentially an unobtrusively designed small village of private 2-storey pavilions, offering the full range of facilities. The lack of beachfront accommodation is more than compensated for by a swimming pool with sea view. ⑨.

EAST RAILAE

Coco House, in the centre of the beach. Simpler than neighbouring *Ya Ya* but none the worse for that, offering pleasant huts in a small garden compound. ②–⑤.

Diamond Cave Bungalows, at the far eastern end of the beach. Some small and basic huts with shared bathroom, others slightly larger and self-contained. ②–⑤.

Sunrise Bay Bungalows, towards the western (Laem Phra Nang) end of the beach (☎075/612728). Similar range of huts to that offered by *Diamond Cave Bungalows.* Centrally located and very convenient for the beach at west Railae. ②–⑤.

Viewpoint, over the hill, at the far eastern end of east Railae. The poshest accommodation on the beach: many of its glass-windowed bungalows look out over the bay, and guests are treated to a dawn chorus of whooping gibbons from the forested ridge beyond. The terrace restaurant also affords great vistas of the mangrove and karst-dotted seascape, and is worth a visit from non-guests as well. ③–⑤.

Ya Ya Bungalows in the centre of the beach (☎075/612728, extn 30). The most unusual accommodation on east Railae has rooms in quaint 3-storey bamboo towers, with shared bathrooms on the ground floor and excellent views from upstairs. ①–④.

WEST RAILAE

Railae Bay (☎075/611789). A competitively priced range of accommodation options: from inexpensive makeshift rattan constructions through to thoughtfully designed top-end bungalows with sea-view verandahs. Some of the lower-priced huts are closer to east than west Railae. ③–⑤.

Railae Village (☎075/612728). Not much to choose between the bungalows here or at *Railae Bay* and *SandSea*, as it offers similar facilities. This one has the least expensive and most convivial beachfront restaurant, though. ③–⑤.

SandSea (☎075/611944). Completes the trinity of Identikit operations on this beach. Same facilities as the others, including beachfront restaurant, tour agency and shop selling beach gear and postcards. ③–⑤.

Ao Nang and Hat Nopparat Thara

The scene at **AO NANG** (sometimes confusingly referred to as Ao Phra Nang), just around the rocky outcrop from west Railae, is much more middle-aged than at Laem Phra Nang, with the emphasis on air-conditioned opulence rather than beach life. Developers have moved in en masse, so the narrow and unprepossessing beach has a road running right along its length, with the resort area stretching back over 1km from the shore along Route 4203. Yet the expansive seaward view of crystal-clear water dotted with limestone monoliths remains pretty awesome, and it's easy enough to escape when the atmosphere gets too stifling – a short walk takes you to the unadulterated stretch of Hat Nopparat Thara, and it's an impressive ten-minute boatride to the beaches of Laem Phra Nang. Access is easy, as songthaews run from Krabi regularly throughout the day, taking about 45 minutes, and in terms of facilities Ao Nang is quite well set up, with diving equipment rental close to the beachfront at *Baby Shark Divers* and a couple of official money-exchanges just off the beach. Seafront restaurants and small bars proliferate, too, making a visit here a worthwhile lunch-time outing.

Continue for about 1km along the road west and you come to the eastern end of two-kilometre-long **Hat Nopparat Thara**. Invariably deserted, this beach is part of the national marine park that encompasses Ko Phi Phi, with the park headquarters about halfway along. At low tide it's almost impossible to swim here, but the sands are enlivened by millions of starfish and thousands of hermit crabs, and you can walk out to the small offshore island if you tire of the supine life.

Accommodation and eating

Although **budget accommodation** may at first glance appear thin on the ground at Ao Nang, several inexpensive and moderate places do exist, the best of them just across the beachfront road, only 50m from the sea. Because of its national park status, isolated **Hat Nopparat Thara** has only a collection of the usual grim

national park bungalows (⑤), dismal when you're cut off from the other bungalows and restaurants of Ao Nang. However, a couple of commercial operations
have sprung up on a quiet stretch of sand just around the estuary from its westernmost end and are listed below; to get there, take any Ao Nang-bound songthaew from Krabi and ask to be dropped at the park's headquarters, then hop in a
longtail taxi to cross the estuary to the bungalows on the other side. Otherwise
you are quite free to **camp** anywhere on the beach, though there's very little shelter, and the road is visible along most of it.

As for **eating**, the French-inspired menu at *Gift* is a delight, especially for fish
dishes and home-baked cakes. For seafood with an uninterrupted view of the
waves, try any of the small restaurants clustered together at the western end of the
beachfront road.

AO NANG

Ao Nang Beach Bungalow, beachfront road. Good-value accommodation considering its
location. Selection of fairly basic rooms, the more expensive with attached bathrooms. ②–④.

Ao Nang Villa, just off the beach, next to *Phra Nang Inn* (☎075/612431). A relatively upmarket resort-style operation with attractive air-con bungalows just off the beach. ④.

Gift, beachfront road (☎01/723 1128). Budget operation offering simple huts, some with
attached bathroom. Friendly staff and a great French-inspired menu at the restaurant. ②–④.

Green Park Bungalow, 200m up Route 4203 (☎01/722 0102). Comparable to *Jungle Hut*,
although its accommodation is more robust and less striking. ①–③.

Jungle Hut, 150m up Route 4203 (☎01/722 0110). Charming if slightly flimsy treehouses and
bungalows. ①–③.

Krabi Resort, just north of the main beachfront, on the road to Hat Nopparat Thara (☎075/
612160). Set in a large tropical garden in a tiny bay, this is the poshest place on Ao Nang with
both top-class bungalows and rooms in a low-rise hotel. ⑧.

Phra Nang Inn, on the main beachfront, (☎075/612173). Outstandingly elegant wooden
hotel with spacious, well-equipped rooms and a swimming pool. ⑧.

Sea Breeze, beachfront road. Adjacent to *Gift* and offering similar accommodation. ②–④.

HAT NOPPARAT THARA

Emerald Bungalows, across the estuary from the national park headquarters. Good,
comfortable traveller-oriented bungalows, with the accent, as you'd expect, very much on
relaxation and low-key beach activities. ①–③.

Krabi Andaman Inn, across the estuary from the national park headquarters (☎075/
612351).Very similar to *Emerald*, isolated from the Ao Nang action, but comfortable enough
for that not to matter. ①–④.

Ko Phi Phi

Now well established as one of southern Thailand's most popular destinations for
budget travellers, the two **KO PHI PHI** islands lie 40km south of Krabi and 48km
east of southern Phuket, encircled by water so clear that you can see almost to the
sea bed from the surface, easily making out the splayed leaves of cabbage coral and
the distinctively yellow-striped tiger fish from the boat as you approach the islands.
The action is concentrated on the larger **Ko Phi Phi Don**, packed with bungalow
operations and tourist enterprises serving the burgeoning ranks of divers, snorkellers and sybarites who just come to slump on the long white beaches. No less stunning is the uninhabited sister island of **Ko Phi Phi Leh**, whose sheer cliff faces get
national marine park protection, on account of the lucrative birds' nest business.

Inevitably, both islands have started to suffer the negative consequences of their outstanding beauty. Some of the beaches are now littered with plastic bottles and cigarette ends, and on Phi Phi Don piles of stinking rubbish lie rotting behind the ranks of bungalows. Even more worrying, eighty percent of Phi Phi Don's wells are said to be contaminated with sewage. The most effective way for travellers to register their disgust at the defilement of the islands is to withold their dollars and avoid visiting the area altogether. If that's too hard, you should at least boycott those bungalows which continue to dump their refuse.

Getting to the islands

During peak season, **ferries** to Ko Phi Phi Don run at least three times daily **from Krabi** (1hr 30min–2hr) and from **Ko Phuket** (1hr 30min–2hr 30min). In the rainy season the service from both is reduced to once or twice daily. From November to May, there are also once-daily boats to Phi Phi Don from **Ao Nang** (2hr; B135) and **Ko Lanta Yai** (1hr 30min). The only way you can get to Phi Phi Leh is by longtail from Phi Phi Don or as part of a tour.

If you're short of time, you could join one of the **day cruises** run by Phuket-based ferry companies. *Songserm Travel Center* at 51 Satoon Rd (☎076/222570), and *Seatran Travel* at 6 Phang Nga Rd (☎076/211809) both offer similar deals, offering one or two hours' snorkelling (masks, fins and snorkels provided), visits to Phi Phi Don and Phi Phi Leh and lunch – the main disadvantage being that the ferries are huge. They are priced at around B1000, or B750 for under-12s.

DIVING AND SNORKELLING OFF KO PHI PHI

More accessible than Ko Similan and Ko Surin, Ko Phi Phi and its neighbouring islands rate very high on the list of Andaman coast **diving and snorkelling** spots, offering depths of up to 35m, visibility touching 30m, and the possibility of seeing white-tip sharks, moray eels and stingrays. **Diving centres** on Ko Phuket run daily excursions here (see p.447), and there are centres closer to hand, at Ao Ton Sai and at lots of bungalows as well, all of which rent equipment, organize excursions and run courses. Recommended ones include *Moskito Diving* in the Ao Ton Sai village (☎01/723 0361), and *Siam Diving* at *Phi Phi Palm Hotel* on Laem Tong (☎076/214654). Prices are slightly lower than at Phuket – about B1500 for an introductory one-day diving course and B7500 for the certificated four-day open water course. Be careful when signing up for any course or expedition: check the equipment and the staff credentials and try to get some first-hand recommendations from other divers.

Nearly all the bungalow operations on Phi Phi Don organize day and half-day **snorkelling** trips. Prices vary slightly, but they average out at B200 for a day trip including lunch and snorkelling gear. In the case of snorkelling, the longtails that run from Ko Phi Phi are better than the cruise ships that make day trips from Phuket, which are so popular you can rarely see the fish for the swimmers.

Diving and snorkelling **tours** generally take in the same reefs and islands. At uninhabited **Ko Pai** (or Bamboo Island), off the northeast coast of Phi Phi Don, much of the reef lies near the shore and close to the surface, and gives you a chance of seeing the occasional turtle and possibly the odd silver- and black-striped banded sea snake – which is poisonous but rarely aggressive. Fewer day-trippers are brought to the adjacent **Ko Yung**, whose offshore reef plunges into a steep-sided and spectacular drop. Off the west coast of Phi Phi Don, **Ao Yongkasame** also has good reefs as do the tranquil waters at **Ao Maya** on the west coast of Phi Phi Leh.

Ko Phi Phi Don

KO PHI PHI DON would itself be two islands were it not for the tenuous palm-fringed isthmus that connects the hilly expanses to east and west, separating the stunningly symmetrical double bays of Ao Ton Sai to the south and Ao Loh Dalum to the north. So steep is the smaller western half that the small population lives in isolated clusters across the slopes of the densely vegetated eastern stretch, while the tourist bungalows stick mainly to the intervening sandy flats, with a few developments on the beaches fringing the cliffs east and north of the isthmus.

All boats dock at **Ao Ton Sai**, the busiest bay on the island. From here you can catch a longtail to any of the other beaches or walk – there are no roads or vehicle tracks on Phi Phi Don, just a series of paths across the steep and at times rugged interior, at points affording superb views over the bays. **Accommodation** on Phi Phi Don ranges from the exclusive to the tacky, but in all categories you should reckon on paying up to fifty percent more than you'd pay on the mainland.

Ao Ton Sai

The constantly expanding village at **AO TON SAI** has the feel of a pop-festival shanty town, and it's the liveliest place to stay on the island. Makeshift stalls selling everything you could possibly need for a few days on a beach form convoluted rows alongside money changers, diving schools, bars and restaurants serving the gamut of tourist fare – and at the western end there's even an open-air arena for weekly bouts of Thai boxing. The island's **health centre** is on Ton Sai as well, at the western end, close by *Tonsai Resort*; and there's a doctor's surgery in amongst the bars at the heart of the village itself. Eastwards and northwards the village merges with residential areas, and the port gives way to sunbathing spots.

Most of the **accommodation** around here is packed between the Ao Ton Sai and Ao Loh Dalum beaches and at the foot of the hills to the east and west. In the last few years, this central inland stretch has been subjected to massive redevelopment, with one new luxury hotel complex – *Phi Phi Hotel*, 50m from the pier but cleverly screened by remnants of the original coconut grove (☎01/712 0138; ⑧) – already up and running and at least one more under construction, yet it's still just possible to find inexpensive rooms here. *Chong Khao Bunglaows* (①), over towards the western end of Ao Ton Sai, is both peaceful and comfortable for the price, and offers simple huts with attached bathroom. In the thick of the inland residential scrum, *Twin Palm Guest House* (①–②) scrapes by with a handful of thin-walled small rooms. Close by but slightly more costly, the *Ruen Tai* bungalows (③) are only just about worth the price, or you could try the nearby *Tara Inn* (②–⑤). Ten minutes east of the pier at the edge of the village, *Chao Ko* (③–⑤) has beachfront bungalows with bathroom. The most luxurious bungalows on Ao Ton Sai itself belong to *Phi Phi Tonsai Resort* (☎075/611496; ⑧), set in a pretty flower garden that stretches along the far western end of the beach.

East along the coast from *Chao Ko*, between Ton Sai and the promontory known as **Laem Hin**, *Phi Phi Don Resort* (②–⑤) and the neighbouring *Phi Phi Andaman* (②–⑤) both offer a large choice of bungalows – some with sea view and bathroom, others with neither. Just east of here, the beautifully appointed bungalows of *Bay View Resort* (☎01/723 1134; ⑥–⑦) are superbly positioned high on the Laem Hin cliffside, its massive windows affording unbeatable views.

New **restaurants** spring up as old ones fold, but at the time of writing the seafront *Siam Seafood*, next to the jetty, was serving delicious red snapper, tuna

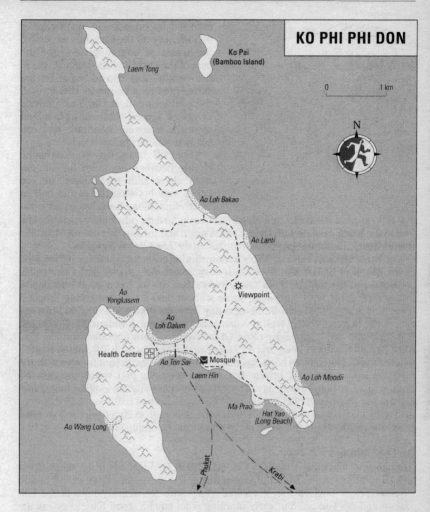

KO PHI PHI DON

Ko Pai
(Bamboo Island)

Laem Tong

0   1 km

N

Ao Loh Bakao

Ao Lanti

Ao
Yongkasem

Viewpoint

Ao
Loh Dalum

Health Centre

Ao Ton Sai   Mosque

Laem Hin

Ao Loh Moodii

Ma Prao

Hat Yao
(Long Beach)

Ao Wang Long

Phuket

Krabi

and shark, and French-run *Mama's*, on the main track from the pier, was offering high-quality seafood meals and good cakes, at a price. Less expensive but just as good are the typically Thai noodle shops at the heart of the village. Small **bars** proliferate here too, adorned with hand-painted signboards (*"Crazy Horse"*, *"Full Moon Bar"*) and throbbing to the usual Bob Marley and Euro-pop standards .

Hat Yao

With its de luxe sand and large reefs packed with polychromatic marine life just 20m offshore, **HAT YAO** (Long Beach) is the best of Phi Phi's three main beaches. Unperturbed by the longtail traffic, shoals of golden butterfly fish, turquoise and purple parrot fish, and hooped angel fish scour the coral for food,

Parrot fish

escorted by brigades of small cleaner fish who live off the parasites trapped in the scales of larger species. For the best of the coral and the biggest reef in the vicinity, you should make for the submerged rock known as **Hin Pae** off the southern end of Hat Yao – novice divers get ferried out there by boat, but if you're a strong swimmer you can easily reach it from the beach.

Longtail boats do the ten-minute shuttle between here and Ao Ton Sai from about 8am to 10.30pm, or you could walk between the two in half an hour, either along the hillside path or, at low tide, around the rocks and along the beach. Several other paths connect Hat Yao to the beaches of Ao Loh Dalum to the north and the tiny bay of Loh Moodii to the northeast: the trails start behind the last of the *Long Beach Bungalows*.

The most attractive of Hat Yao's **accommodation** is tucked away in two little coves just west of Hat Yao itself, with easy access via a rocky path. The small, secluded and friendly *Ma Prao* (aka *Funny Land*; ①–④), has a good selection of bungalows, some with bathroom, some without, and a pleasant eating area out front. Just around the rocks in the next tiny cove sits *Viking* (①–④), Phi Phi's last remaining homage to the typical Asian beach experience: rudimentary facilities, laid-back staff and inexpensive rates. Of the two bungalow operations on Hat Yao, most budget travellers head first for *Long Beach Bungalows* (②–⑤), which has the whole range of huts, from back-row places with shared bathroom to ones with sea view, mosquito nets and private bathroom; electricity and water supplies are limited to a few hours every day. The larger but more spartan-looking bungalows at *Paradise Pearl* (☎01/723 0484; ③–⑥) all have attached bathrooms. Prices here also reflect proximity to the sea, though none is more than 20m from the water and front-row residents get the worst of the noise from incoming longtails.

Ao Loh Dalum

Though less attractive than Hat Yao, **AO LOH DALUM** affords a magnificent wraparound panorama from the **viewpoint** at the far eastern edge of the beach. Photographers slog up the steep half-hour climb for sunset shots of Ao Loh Dalum and Ao Ton Sai, but early morning is an equally good time to go, as the summit's *Mountain View Café* serves simple breakfasts as well as cold drinks. From the viewpoint you can descend the rocky and at times almost sheer path to **Ao Lanti**, a tiny bay on the east coast with choppy surf and a couple of resident *chao ley*. Theoretically, it should also be possible to reach the northeastern bay of Ao Loh Bakao (see facing page) by path from near the viewpoint, but the two-kilometre route is unsignposted and overgrown.

Accommodation on Ao Loh Dalum is becoming increasingly posh: at least one new hotel building is under construction, but pending its completion three almost indistinguishable upmarket resorts dominate the beach, all with a selection of bars and restaurants. *Phi Phi Pavilion* (⑤–⑧) and *Phi Phi Princess* (☎01/723 0504; ⑤–⑧) both have some lovely wooden chalets with verandahs and sea view, and some less plush ones further back, while the piles of rubbish and building rubble dumped between its more inland huts spoil the long-established and otherwise pleasant *Phi Phi Charlie Resort* (☎01/723 0495; ⑤–⑧). Strung out across the hillside at the eastern edge of Ao Loh Dalum are the attractive but pricey bungalows of *Viewpoint Bungalows* (☎076/611318; ⑤–⑦), which boast great views out over the bay.

Ao Loh Bakao and Laem Tong

Far removed from the hustle of Ao Ton Sai and its environs, a few exclusive resorts have effectively bought up the secluded northern beaches of Phi Phi Don. This is primarily package-holiday territory – you're unlikely to find a room free if you turn up unannounced. There are no regular boats from Ao Ton Sai, but long-tail boats will take you for about B200; the trip takes around an hour to Ao Loh Bakao and a further half-hour north to Laem Tong.

Just over halfway up the coast, plush, air-conditioned chalets on stilts at *Phi Phi Island Village* (☎076/215014; ⑦) have the beach of **Ao Loh Bakao** all to themselves. At the northernmost tip, **Laem Tong** has three exclusive resorts on its shores: the top-of-the-range *Phi Phi International* (☎076/214297; ⑧), whose cruises in fully kitted-out old-fashioned sailing junks are a speciality; the similarly first-class *Phi Phi Palm Beach* (☎076/214411; ⑧), which has an outdoor jacuzzi as well as a swimming pool, dive centre and tennis courts; and the slightly more affordable *Phi Phi Coral* (⑧), which is a smaller, less opulent operation, but shares the same lovely beach.

Ko Phi Phi Leh

More rugged than its twin Ko Phi Phi Don, and a quarter the size, **KO PHI PHI LEH** is home only to the **sea swift**, whose valuable nests are gathered by intrepid *chao ley* for export to specialist Chinese restaurants all over the world. Tourists descend on the island not only to see the nest-collecting caves but also

---

BIRD'S NESTING

Prized for its aphrodisiac and energizing qualities, **bird's nest soup** is such a delicacy in Taiwan, Singapore and Hong Kong that ludicrous sums of money change hands for a dish whose basic ingredients are tiny twigs glued together with bird's spit. Collecting these nests is a lucrative but life-endangering business: sea swifts build their nests in rock crevices hundreds of metres above sea level, often on sheer cliff faces or in cavernous hollowed-out karst. **Nest-building** begins in January and the harvesting season usually lasts from February to May, during which time the female sea swift builds three nests on the same spot, none of them more than 12cm across, by secreting an unbroken thread of saliva which she winds round as if making a coil pot. **Gatherers** will only steal the first two nests made by each bird, prizing them off the cave walls with special metal forks. Gathering the nests demands faultless agility and balance, skills that seem to come naturally to the *chao ley*, whose six-man teams bring about 400 nests down the perilous bamboo scaffolds each day, weighing about 4kg in total. At a market rate of B20–50,000 per kilo, so much money is at stake that a government franchise must be granted before any collecting commences, and armed guards often protect the sites at night. The *chao ley* themselves seek spiritual protection from the dangers of the job by making offerings to the spirits of the cliff or cave at the beginning of the season; in the Viking Cave, they place buffalo flesh, horns and tail at the foot of one of the stalagmites.

to snorkel off its sheltered bays, and the anchoring of their boats has damaged much of the coral in the best spots. Most snorkelling trips out of Phi Phi Don include Phi Phi Leh, which is only twenty minutes south of Ao Ton Sai, but you can also get there by renting a longtail from Ao Ton Sai or Hat Yao (B200–400 per 6-person boat). If you do charter your own boat, go either very early or very late in the day, to beat the tour-group rush.

Most idyllic of all the bays in the area is **Ao Maya** on the southwest coast, where the water is still and very clear and the coral extremely varied – a perfect snorkelling spot and a feature of most day trips. Unfortunately the discarded lunch boxes and water bottles of day-trippers now threaten the health of the marine life in **Ao Phi Leh**, an almost completely enclosed east-coast lagoon of breathtakingly turquoise water. Not far from the cove, the **Viking Cave** gets its misleading name from the scratchy wall paintings of Chinese junks inside, but more interesting than this 400-year-old graffitti is the **bird's-nesting** that goes on here: rickety bamboo scaffolding extends hundreds of metres up to the roof of the cave, where the harvesters spend the day scraping the tiny sea-swift nests off the rock face.

Ko Lanta Yai, Ko Bubu and Ko Jum

East and southeast of Ko Phi Phi, three of the more inhabitable of the 130 islands lying off the Krabi coast have started to divert budget travellers from the crowds on Ko Phi Phi. Much closer to the mainland, neither **Ko Lanta Yai**, **Ko Bubu** nor **Ko Jum** can compete with Phi Phi's stupendous scenery or its prolific reef life, but they do offer good sandy beaches, safe seas, and the much greater likelihood of solitude and seclusion. Of the three, Ko Lanta Yai is by far the largest – some 25km long as compared with Phi Phi's 8km – and the most tourist-oriented, with fifteen bungalow operations to date. The minuscule Ko Bubu, only 7km off Lanta Yai's east coast, is the preserve of just one bungalow outfit, but in contrast to many one-resort islands, this is not an exclusive upmarket operation. The same is true of Ko Jum, which is slightly larger than Phi Phi Don but nevertheless offers only one accommodation option.

Ko Lanta Yai

Development on **KO LANTA YAI** is still fairly low key, and has so far been confined to the west-coast beaches; as a result the island still feels like it belongs to its residents (something which can't be said of Ko Phi Phi, Ko Phuket or Ko Samui), the majority of whom are mixed-blood Muslim descendants of Malaysian and *chao ley* peoples. Aside from fishing, many of the islanders support themselves by cultivating the land between the beaches and the forested ridges that dominate the central and eastern parts of Lanta Yai.

The local *chao ley* name for the island is *Paulao Satak*, "Island of Long Beaches", an apt description of the six beaches of the rocky western coast. The northerly ones tend to be the more developed, but deserted spots are not hard to find and they all offer good sand and clear water, while the bungalow outfits advertise day trips to reefs off the islands further south, where the snorkelling is better than on Ko Lanta Yai itself. Much of the east coast is fringed with mangrove swamps and unsuitable for swimming.

There's no regular songthaew service on Ko Lanta, so once you're established on the island you either have to hire a motorbike from your accommodation or hitch – which is pretty easy, though you'll probably be expected to pay.

Getting to the island

From November to May **ferries** run **from Krabi to Ban Sala Dan** on the northern tip of Ko Lanta Yai (3 daily; 2hr 30min). During the rest of the year, the rainy season, you can get the daily ferry from **Bo Muang**, about 80km southeast of Krabi, to the village of **Lanta** on the island's east coast (1hr), from where motorbike taxis will take you to the beaches. If the weather's not too bad, the boat will weave its way up the mangrove-fringed inlet between Lanta Noi and Lanta Yai and drop you at the much more convenient Ban Sala Dan. You should be able to get a direct songthaew or minibus from Krabi to Bo Muang: check with Krabi tour agencies about the songthaew and boat departure times.

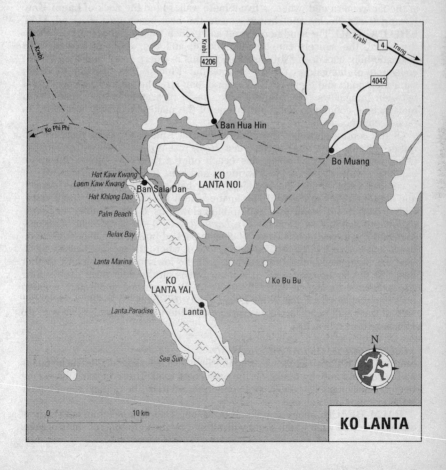

Around the island

Although several hundred farang tourists must pass through **BAN SALA DAN** every day during high season, it remains surprisingly intact as a Muslim fishing port, where concessions to the tourist trade don't stretch much further than a money exchange (poor rates) and a French restaurant. Vociferous touts always meet the boats, competing to take you from the village to your chosen bungalows free of charge, but be prepared for the price bracket you agreed on to be suddenly unavailable. Remember, too, that south of **Hat Khlong Dao** (Golden Sand Bay), the beaches are strung out at quite wide intervals, with only sporadic transport between them, and most of the beaches further south have just one set of bungalows.

HAT KAW KWANG AND HAT KHLONG DAO

The tip of the northwest coast, 500m west of Ban Sala Dan, begins with the island's least picturesque beach, **HAT KAW KWANG**, whose two-kilometre stretch of grey shoreline turns mostly to mud at low tide. But things get better at the far western end, where a five-minute walk round the neck of **Laem Kaw Kwang** (Deer Neck Cape) brings you to the best beach on the island, **HAT KHLONG DAO**. The sand here is soft and golden, palms and casuarinas shade the shore, the sunsets can be magnificent, and the whole is framed by a dramatic hilly backdrop. Not surprisingly, this is where you'll find the densest collection of bungalows on the island, but Khlong Dao has yet to reach saturation point and there are still several long stretches of undeveloped forest between bungalows. The nightlife, too, has a pleasantly low-key tenor, with most people content to hang out at one of the makeshift beach bars close to their accommodation.

Of the central cluster of **bungalows** on Hat Khlong Dao, the bamboo and rattan A-frame huts at *Lanta Garden Home* (①–③) are the least expensive. Otherwise, most places along this beach offer a range of options, the more expensive with sea views, glass windows and fans. *Golden Bay Cottages* (①–③) occupies a fantastic spot in the middle of the bay, with expansive vistas to north and south. *Lanta Sea House*, 100m further south (①–③), is equally good value, with a variety of wood and rattan bungalows, as is the simpler but well-maintained *Lanta Bungalow* (①–③); *Lanta Royal* (②–⑤) is redolent of a housing estate, with regimented rows of closely packed huts. The plushest place on the beach is *Lanta Villa* (☎075/620629; ②–⑥), where the most expensive pavilions are staggered along the seafront, and the lower-priced ones lurk further back. At the far northern end of Khlong Dao – on the deer neck itself – *Kaw Kwang Beach Bungalow* (☎01/722 0106; ②–④) has some good-value wooden huts in a cultivated garden, while *Deer Neck* (☎075/612487; ③–⑤), on the other side of the small headland, is overpriced considering its charmless view of Ko Lanta's grottiest beach.

BEACHES SOUTH OF HAT KHLONG DAO

South of Hat Khlong Dao lies a string of silken beaches separated by rocky points and accessible only by tracks off the west-coast road. These beaches have long been officially nameless, most commonly referred to by the original set of bungalows operating on each one.

PALM BEACH, about 2km south of Khlong Dao, is a beautiful long strip of almost deserted white sand, slightly disfigured by the ugly concrete huts of *Palm*

Beach Bungalows (①–④) among the palm trees at the back; you can pitch your own tent here for a small fee.

A couple of kilometres further down the coast, the German-run *Relax Bay Tropicana* (☎01/722 0089; ④–⑥) occupies its own small bay, its seventy-odd attractively designed bungalows built entirely from natural materials; a dive centre operates from here, too. Three kilometres south, you'll find the bamboo huts of *Lanta Marina* (①–③), built to a traditional A-frame design and well spaced in the thick of a coconut grove.

A further 6km on are the fine sands of **PARADISE BEACH**, where the *Lanta Paradise* (☎01/723 0528; ②–④) bungalows are packed uncomfortably close together but feel spacious inside. Another 5km on, almost at the southernmost end of Lanta Yai, *SeaSun* (①–③) has an attractive backdrop of hills and trees, but ruins the effect with ugly huts. The nearby *Waterfall Bungalows* (④–⑤) shares the setting, but offers more pleasing and comfortable accommodation.

Ko Bubu

The only reason to venture round to Lanta Yai's east coast would be to make the short hop across to **KO BUBU**, a minuscule dot of an island about twenty minutes' chartered longtail ride from the small town of **Lanta**. With a radius of not much more than 500m, wooded Ko Bubu has room for just one set of thirty bungalows (③–④); if all the rooms are full you should be allowed to pitch your own tent here.

You can also reach Ko Bubu direct **from Krabi**, by following the rainy-season route for Ko Lanta Yai and chartering a longtail from Bo Muang. Krabi's *Thammachat Guest House* (see p.467) acts as an agent for the Ko Bubu bungalow resort and might be persuaded to organize through-transport from Krabi.

Ko Jum

Situated halfway between Krabi and Ko Lanta Yai, **KO JUM** (or Ko Pu) is the sort of laid-back and simple spot that people come to for a couple of days then can't bring themselves to leave. Its mangrove-fringed east coast holds the island's only fishing village and a beachfront school, while across on the sandy west coast there's just one small bungalow operation down towards the southern tip; much of the north is made inaccessible by the breastbone of forested hills. So there's little to do here except hunt for shells, stroll the kilometre across the island to buy snacks in the village or roast on the beach and then plunge into the sea. The sole **places to stay** are the bamboo huts of *Joy Bungalows* (③–④), or you can camp for a small fee. At night the paraffin-lit **restaurant** serves food that's expensive but surprisingly varied considering the distance it has to come.

Joy Bungalows sends a **longtail** out to meet the Krabi–Ko Lanta ferries as they pass the west coast (1hr 30min from Krabi); in the rainy season it sometimes organizes a daily songthaew and longtail to cover the alternative mainland route, which runs from Krabi via the pier at **Laem Kruat**, 40km southeast, from where the boat takes you out to Ko Jum's east coast – ask any Krabi tour operator for songthaew departure times.

travel details

Buses

Krabi to: Bangkok (at least 3 daily; 12–14hr); Hat Yai (2 daily; 4hr); Nakhon Si Thammarat (8 daily; 3hr); Surat Thani (hourly; 3–4hr); Trang (8 daily; 3hr).

Phang Nga to: Bangkok (4 daily; 11hr–12hr 30min); Krabi (every 30min; 1hr 45min); Phuket (6 daily; 2hr–2hr 30min).

Phuket to: Bangkok (at least 10 daily; 14–16hr); Hat Yai (7 daily; 7–8hr); Krabi (hourly; 4hr) via Phang Nga (2hr); Nakhon Si Thammarat (8 daily; 8hr); Surat Thani (9 daily; 5–6hr); Trang (8 daily; 6hr).

Ranong to: Bangkok (7 daily; 9–10hr); Chumphon (every 90min; 2hr); Phuket (8 daily; 6hr) via Khuraburi (2hr) and Takua Pa (2hr 30min–3hr).

Ferries

Ko Phi Phi Don to: Ao Nang (Nov–May 1 daily; 2hr); Ko Lanta Yai (Nov–May 1 daily; 1hr 30min).

Krabi to: Ko Lanta Yai (Nov–May 3 daily; 2hr 30min), via Ko Jum (1hr 30min); Ko Phi Phi Don (2–4 daily; 1hr 30min–2hr).

Phuket to: Ko Phi Phi Don (2–4 daily; 1hr 30min–2hr 30min); Ko Similan (Nov–May 2 weekly; 3hr).

Ranong to: Ko Surin (Nov–May 3 weekly; 3hr).

Flights

Phuket to: Bangkok (8–13 daily; 1hr 15min); Chiang Mai (4 weekly; 2hr 5min); Hat Yai (1–2 daily; 55min); Ko Samui (1 daily; 40min); Nakhon Si Thammarat (3 weekly; 1hr 40min); Surat Thani (1 daily; 35min); Trang (2 weekly; 45min).

CHAPTER EIGHT

THE DEEP SOUTH

The frontier between Thailand and Malaysia carves across the peninsula six degrees north of the equator, but the cultures of the two countries shade into each other much further north. According to official divisions the southern Thais – the *thai pak tai* – begin around Chumphon, and as you move further down the peninsula you'll see ever more sarongs, yashmaks and towering mosques, and hear with increasing frequency a staccato dialect that baffles many Thais. In **Trang** and **Phatthalung** – the most northerly of the distinctly different southern provinces – the Muslim population is generally accepted as being Thai, but the inhabitants of the four southernmost provinces – **Satun**, **Pattani**, **Yala** and **Narathiwat** – are ethnically more akin to the Malaysians: most of the 1,500,000 followers of Islam here speak Yawi, an old Malay dialect, and many yearn for secession from Thailand. And to add to the ethnic confusion, the deep south has a large urban population of Chinese, whose comparative wealth stands them out sharply from the Muslim farmers and fishermen.

On a journey south, the first thing you might be tempted by is an atmospheric boat trip through the **Thale Noi Waterbird Park** near Phatthalung. The easiest route after that is to hop across to the great natural beauty of the **west coast**, with its sheer limestone outcrops, pristine sands and fish-laden coral stretching down to the Malaysian border. The spread of tourism around from Phuket has halted at Ko Lanta for the moment, so from **Trang** southwards – where the peaceful and spectacular islands of **Ko Tarutao National Park** are the most obvious attraction – you'll get the beaches and islands to yourself, though you'll have to work harder to get there and stay there.

On the less attractive **east** side of the peninsula, you'll probably pass through the ugly, modern city of **Hat Yai** at some stage, as it's the transport capital for the south and for connections to Malaysia, but a far more sympathetic place to stay is the old town of **Songkhla**, half an hour away on the seashore. The region southeast of here is where you'll experience Malay Muslim culture at its purest, though there's nothing compellir.g to do there.

As well as the usual bus services and the rail line, which forks at Hat Yai to Butterworth and Kuala Lumpur on the Malaysian west coast and Sungai Kolok on the eastern border, the deep south is the territory of **share taxis** – often grand old 1950s Mercs, which connect all the major towns for about twice the fare of ordinary buses. Each town has several taxi ranks, divided according to destination, and the cars leave when they're full, which usually means six passengers, with, quite possibly, babes-in-arms and livestock. They are a quick way of getting around and you should get dropped off at the door of your journey's end. A more recent phenomenon, running on almost exactly the same principles at similar prices, are **air-conditioned minibuses**; the differences are that you'll be more comfortable, with a seat to yourself, and most of the various ranks publish a rough timetable – though the minibuses tend to leave as soon as they're full.

There are eight **border crossings** to Malaysia – two by sea from Satun, the rest by land from Wang Prachan, Padang Besar, Sadao, Betong, Sungai Kolok, and Ban

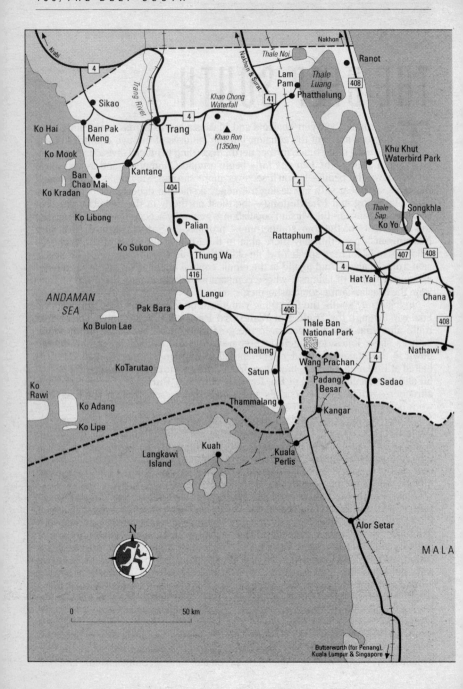

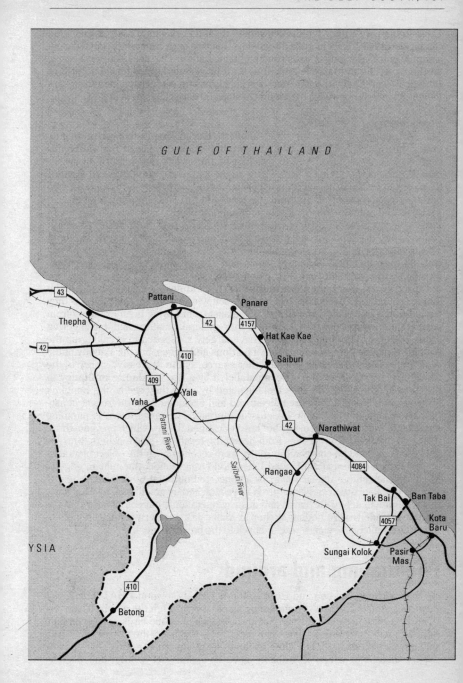

Taba – which are outlined in the relevant parts of this chapter. At any of them you can nip across and back to get a fifteen-day Thai visa or to begin the second part of a double-entry visa; longer visas can be obtained at the Thai consulates at Penang on the west side of Malaysia and Kota Baru on the east side (details on p.12 of *Basics*). Beware that although each overland crossing is officially open from 6am to 6pm, it's not unknown for the guards to slope off early if business is slow.

Some history

The central area of the Malay peninsula first entered Thai history when it came under the rule of Sukhothai, probably around the beginning of the fourteenth century. Islam was introduced to the area by the end of that century, by which time Ayutthaya was taking a firmer grip on the peninsula. **Songkhla** and **Pattani** then rose to be the major cities, prospering on the goods passed through the two ports across the peninsula to avoid the pirates in the Straits of Malacca between Malaysia and Sumatra. More closely tied to the Muslim Malay states to the south, Pattani began to **rebel** against the central power of Ayutthaya in the sixteenth century, but the fight for self-determination only weakened Pattani's strength. The town's last rebellious fling was in 1902, and seven years later Pattani was isolated from its allies, Kedah, Kelantan and Trengganu, when they were transferred into the suzerainty of the British in Malaysia.

During World War II the **Communist Party of Malaysia** made its home in the jungle around the Thai border to fight the occupying Japanese. After the war they turned their guns against the British colonialists, but having been excluded from power after independence, descended into general banditry and racketeering around Betong. The Thai authorities have largely succeeded in breaking up the bandit gangs through a combination of pardons and bribes, but the stability of the region now faces disruption from another source, as the aggressive stance of the Muslim rulers of Malaysia has been paralleled by a rise in **Islamic militancy** in the deep south. Many Muslims feel alienated by what they see as the Bangkok government's colonial-style prejudices, and feel excluded from the recent consumer boom and the economic benefits of tourism. The government is pumping money into development projects but hasn't changed the law which prevents those educated in Muslim universities from becoming teachers. Thai teachers, who are paid danger money to come to the south, have recently been the object of attacks by separatists of the Pattani United Liberation Organization, the militant edge of Muslim disaffection. August 1993 saw a concerted outburst of violence, when 34 schools in Yala, Pattani and Narathiwat were attacked by arsonists. The Thai army reacted immediately with search-and-destroy operations, but complained that the separatist leaders were finding shelter in Malaysia's northern states; attempts to solve the conflict have since switched back to the political arena.

Phatthalung and around

Halfway between Nakhon and Hat Yai, the hot, dusty town of **PHATTHALUNG** is worth a stop only if you're tempted by a boat trip through the nearby Thale Noi Waterbird Park, a beautiful watery landscape, rich in exotic birds and vegetation. Although its setting among limestone outcrops is dramatic, the town itself is drab and unwelcoming: its only claims to fame are *nang thalung*, the Thai shadow puppet theatre to which it probably gave its name (see p.431), and bandits, though it's cleaned up its act in recent years.

Phatthalung is served by frequent buses from north and south and from Trang, 57km to the west, and is on the major rail line, which crosses the main street, Ramet Road, in the centre of town. Most buses stop near the train station, which is on the north side of Ramet Road; through buses only stop at the junction of highways 4 and 41, to the west, leaving a short song-thaew hop into town.

Rice planting

Going to the waterbird park is the main reason for coming to Phatthalung, but if you've got time to kill before or after a visit there, head for **Khao Hua Taek** or "Broken-Headed Mountain", the limestone outcrop with a dent in its peak which rises abruptly out of the west end of the centre. **Wat Kuha Sawan**, on the east side, has been built around a large, cool cave in the base of the outcrop, where a crude Buddha image is sheltered by a model of the Bodhi Tree hung with delicate brass leaves. Climb the concrete steps to the right of the cave, then follow the path to the left to reach the summit, where you'll get a good view over Phatthalung and the surrounding rice fields. To the east, you'll also be able to see **Khao Ok Taloo**, "Broken-Hearted Mountain", so called because of the natural tunnel through its peak: according to legend, Hua Taek and Ok Taloo were the wife and the mistress of a third mountain to the north, **Khao Muang**, over whom they had a fierce fight, leaving them with these wounds.

If a visit to Khao Hua Taek still leaves you with time on your hands, you could make a short trip out of town towards the resort of Lam Pam, half an hour away to the northeast: take one of the frequent songthaews from the rail crossing on Ramet Road. About 6km out on the right-hand side, stop off at the two-hundred-year-old bot of **Wat Wang** to see a series of elegant and dynamic murals depicting the life of the Buddha – ask a monk for the key to the formidable cloisters which surround it. Two former **governor's palaces**, appealing examples of traditional southern Thai architecture, overlook a picturesque canal 200m beyond Wat Wang on the same side of the road. Nearer to the road, the "old" residence, Wang Khao, which dates from the middle of the last century, is built entirely of wood on inward-sloping stilts, a design whose tensile properties mean that it can be held together with tongue-and-groove joints rather than nails. In the so-called "new palace", Wang Mai, built in 1889 with a raised stone courtyard around a large tree, look out for the intricate traditional carvings on the main house, especially the "sunrise" gable, sometimes called the "crest of a monk's robe" because it resembles the edge of the robe gathered into pleats by a monk's hand.

At **LAM PAM** itself there's nothing to do but eat and drink at minimal cost, while relaxing in a deck chair on the shady banks of the Thale Luang, the lagoon adjoining Thale Noi (see over). An inexpensive way of getting onto the lake is to

ACCOMMODATION PRICES

Throughout this guide, guest houses, hotels and bungalows have been categorized according to the price codes given below. These categories represent the minimum you can expect to pay in the high season (roughly Nov–Feb & July–Aug) for a double room – or, in the case of national park bungalows, for a multi-berth room which can be rented for a standard price by an individual or group. If travelling on your own, expect to pay anything between sixty and one hundred percent of the rates quoted for a double room. Wherever a range of prices is indicated, this means that the establishment offers rooms with varying facilities – as explained in the write-up. Wherever an establishment also offers dormitory beds, the prices of these beds are given in the text, instead of being indicated by price code.

Remember that the top-whack hotels will add seven percent tax and a ten-percent service charge to your bill – the price codes below are based on net rates after taxes have been added.

① under B100   ④ B250–400   ⑦ B1000–1500
② B100–150   ⑤ B400–600   ⑧ B1500–3000
③ B150–250   ⑥ B600–1000   ⑨ B3000+

take one of the morning boats across to Ranot, two hours away, which is connected to Songkhla and Nakhon by half-hourly buses.

Practicalities

Out of a poor selection of **hotels**, best value is the friendly *Thai Hotel*, at 14 Disara Sakarin Rd, behind the *Bangkok Bank* on Ramet Road (☎074/611636; ③–④); rooms with attached bathrooms and a choice of fan or air conditioning are clean and reasonably quiet. *Koo Hoo*, at 9 Prachabamrung Rd (parallel to and south of Ramet), is an excellent, moderately priced **restaurant** – try the chicken with lemon sauce on a bed of fried seaweed.

Thale Noi Waterbird Park

Thale Noi Waterbird Park isn't just for bird-spotters – even the most recalcitrant city-dweller can appreciate boating through the bizarre freshwater habitat formed at the head of the huge lagoon that spills into the sea at Songkhla. Here, in the "Little Sea" (Thale Noi), the distinction between land and water breaks down: the lake is dotted with low, marshy islands, and much of the intervening shallow water is so thickly covered with water vines, lotus pads and reeds that it looks like a field. But the real delight of this area are the hundreds of thousands of birds which breed here – brown teals, loping purple herons, white cattle egrets, and nearly two hundred other species. Most are migratory, arriving here from January onwards from as far away as Siberia – March and April provide the widest variety of birds, whereas from October to December you'll spot just a small range of native species. Early morning and late evening are the best times to come, when the heat is less searing and when, in the absence of hunters and fishermen, more birds are visible.

To get from Phatthalung to **BAN THALE NOI**, the village on the western bank, take one of the frequent **songthaews** from Nivas Road, which runs north off Ramet Road near the station – they take one hour. If you're coming from Nakhon or points further north by bus, you can save yourself a trip into Phatthalung by getting out at **Ban Chai Khlong**, 15km from Ban Thale Noi, and waiting for a songthaew there. Look out for the water-reeds being dried by the side of the road: the locals weave them into mats, bags, fans and hats, which are on sale in Ban Thale Noi's souvenir shops – a good buy, as the sun on the lake is fierce.

Longtail boats can be hired at the pier in the village: for B150, the boatman will give you a two-hour trip around the lake, taking in the best spotting areas and, usually, a spur of land where a local artist has built a thoroughly modern spirit house from found materials. If you want to get a dawn start, ask around in the souvenir shops about renting a simple private room (②) in the village.

Trang province

From Phatthalung, Highway 4 heads south for 100km to Hat Yai, but if you want to have a thorough look around the deep south, with as little backtracking as possible, it's easiest first to visit Trang, 60km west. From there you can go down the west coast, with its pristine beaches and unspoilt islands, before heading across to Hat Yai to begin your journey down the east coast. The attractive route to Trang, served by half-hourly buses, climbs out of Phatthalung's plain of rice fields to a pass over the Khao Ron range of mountains, before descending a series of hairpin bends through forest and rubber plantations past the **Khao Chong waterfall**, 18km from Trang. A three-kilometre walk through the park on the south side of the road leads to the bathing pool and the cascades, which cut a broad path down the hillside through thick, humming jungle. The fall has only a weak flow of water from around January to July but is spectacular during and after the rainy season.

A detour at **Ban Na Yong Neua**, 10km east of Trang, will take you to **BAN NA MUEN SRI**, a famous weaving village, 5km to the north (motorbike taxis wait at the crossroads). The women of the village use a wide variety of colours but stick to intricate traditional patterns, each of which has its own name: *lai look khaew*, a diagonal weave which is used for women's and men's scarves and other accessories, is the best known. The cloth is sold at low prices in the village shop at the bend in the road.

Trang town

The town of **TRANG** (aka Taptieng), which prospers on rubber, oil palms and fisheries, is a sociable place whose wide, clean streets are dotted with crumbling, wooden-shuttered houses. In the evening, restaurant tables sprawl onto the main Rama VI Road and Wisetkul Road, and during the day, many of the town's Chinese inhabitants hang out in the cafés, drinking the local *Khao Chong* coffee. Trang's Chinese population makes the **Vegetarian Festival** at the beginning of October almost as frenetic as Phuket's (see p.451) – and for veggie travellers it's an opportunity to feast at the stalls set up around the temples.

Getting there is easy, as Trang is ninety minutes from Phatthalung and well served by **buses** from all the surrounding provinces. Most of these arrive at the terminal on Huay Yod Road, to the north of the centre; buses from Satun and Palian stop on Ratsada Road, which runs south from the eastern end of Rama VI Road. *Thai Airways* has **flights** to the airport every day from Bangkok, and one overnight **train** from the capital runs down a branch of the southern line to Trang, stopping at the station at the western end of Rama VI Road.

Practicalities

Hotels in Trang are concentrated along Rama VI Road and the busy V-shaped street just above it, Ratchadamnoen Road. The latter has the least costly option – the *Phet Hotel*, at no. 152 (☎075/218002; ①), a decaying place with no frills, where the only choice is between en suite and corridor bathrooms. The best budget choice, though, is the *Ko Teng Hotel* at 77–79 Rama VI Rd (☎075/218622; ②), with large, clean en suite rooms. The friendly family which runs the hotel can help with local information, and the restaurant downstairs is a meeting place for any travellers in town. The pick of the moderate range, *Trang Hotel*, 134/2–5 Wisetkul Rd, at the junction with Rama VI Road overlooking the clock tower (☎075/218944; ⑤), has large, comfortable twin rooms with air conditioning, hot water and television. *Thumrin Hotel* (☎075/211011; ⑥), on Rama VI near the station, used to be the town's only deluxe option, but is now looking down-at-heel. Top spot has been decisively usurped by the *Clarion MP Resort Hotel*, 2km east of the centre at 184 Trang–Phatthalung Rd (☎075/214230–45; Bangkok reservations ☎02/251 4200 or 4201; ⑦), a striking white edifice built to resemble a cruise ship. In a backwater like Trang, everything about the hotel seems larger than life, from the towering lobby dripping with chandeliers, to the plush, high-tech rooms and the long-as-your-arm menu of facilities (pool, gym, driving range, French, Chinese and Thai restaurants, and more).

Trang's **food** comes into its own in the evenings, when two good **night markets** open for business. One is in the station square, serving a mean *pat thai* with fresh prawns; the other is on Wisetkul Road north of the clock tower, where you can try very inexpensive *khanom jiin*, soft noodles topped with hot, sweet or fishy sauces and eaten with crispy greens. *Khao Tom Phui*, 1/11 Rama VI Rd, is a very popular and reasonable pavement restaurant on the north side of the street. For something posher, head for *Namui* on the opposite side at no. 130, a large, clean institution specializing in good seafood.

Diagonally opposite *Thumrin Hotel* on Rama VI, *Bo Daeng* serves the ubiquitous *Khao Chong* coffee with *patongkoh* (Chinese doughnuts) and *ahaan det diap*, plates of assorted tasty titbits such as spring rolls, baby corn and sausage. For good breakfasts, ice cream and cakes, try *Richy Restaurant and Bakery*, a slightly pricey and pretentious place at 126 Ratchadamnoen Rd.

Small **motorbikes** can be rented for B180 a day from the *Thai Pharmacy* at 44 Rama VI Rd (☎075/218473).

The Trang coast

From Ban Pak Meng, 40km due west of Trang town, to the mouth of the Trang River runs a thirty-kilometre stretch of gorgeous **beaches**, broken only by dramatic limestone outcrops which are pitted with explorable caves. If you're just looking for a day at the beach, go to Pak Meng, the most accessible part of the coast and a popular weekend picnic spot for Thais; if you want a good root around the quietest beaches, you'll have to get a motorbike or taxi in Trang, try your luck at hitching along the quiet coastal lanes, or be prepared for some long walks.

Most of the **islands** off this coast – the most notable among them Hai, Mook and Kradan – are blessed with blinding white beaches, fantastic coral and amazing marine life, and with only one or two resorts on each, have that illusory, desert-island atmosphere which better-known places like Phuket and Samui lost long ago. This remoteness comes at a price: accommodation and food are generally more expensive than on more developed islands, and boat services from the mainland are irregular. Resorts also sometimes fill up with Thais at weekends and on national holidays. The secret of success is to phone ahead, either to the place you want to stay at or its agent in Trang town (detailed below and over), to check there's a vacancy and to sort out transport – during high season (roughly from November to May), there are boats nearly every day from Pak Meng to each island, and at other times the resort you're interested in may well be willing to despatch a longtail to pick you up.

If you just fancy a day exploring the islands, *Trang Travel*, opposite *Thumrin Hotel* on Rama VI Road (☎075/219598 or 219599), organizes day trips on its own boat, taking in Ko Kradan, Ko Mook and Ko Cheuak ("Robe Island", so named after its limestone folds), for B500 including lunch. Snorkelling equipment can be rented and the boat will drop you off at one of the islands if you wish.

Pak Meng

The beach at **PAK MENG** is typical of the area, a long, gently curving strip strewn with small shells, which has a fine outlook to the headlands and islands to the west. Getting there takes about an hour on one of the hourly air-conditioned minibuses from the northwestern end of Ratchadamnoen Road in Trang. Plenty of drink and food stalls line the back of the beach, and the congenial *Pakmeng Resort* (☎075/210321; ②–④) occupies a quiet, pretty spot at the south end. The bungalows in this casuarina-shaded garden get better and pricier the closer they are to the beach: at the back, bamboo huts with mosquito nets and shared bathrooms; towards the sea, a variety of pleasingly decorated concrete bungalows, with clean toilets, ceiling fans, chairs and bedside lights. Longtail trips to Ko Hai, Ko Mook and Ko Kradan can be organized for B350 a head including lunch (minimum 4 people) and snorkels, masks and fins can be rented.

The unpaved road south from Pak Meng passes Hat Chang Lang, which is famous for its oysters, before reaching the headquarters of **Hat Chao Mai National Park** after 7km. For B60 a night, two-person tents can be rented here, which you can pitch under the casuarina trees at the back of the sandy beach. You can use the bathrooms here, but bring your own food.

Ko Hai

Of all the Trang islands, **KO HAI** (aka Ko Ngai), 16km southwest of Pak Meng, offers the best combination of accommodation and scenery. When they're running, **boats** leave Pak Meng for the one-hour voyage at 10.30am, charging B100 one-way.

Ko Hai's action, such as it is, centres on the east coast: two resorts, and an unobtrusive *chao ley* (see p.462) hamlet, enjoy a dreamy panorama of jagged limestone outcrops, whose crags glow pink and blue against the setting sun, stretching across the sea to the mainland behind. A two-kilometre-long beach of fine, white sand has a gentle slope that's ideal for swimming, and there's some good snorkelling in the shallow water off the southeast tip – though be careful of sea urchins and the sharp stag coral. For the best snorkelling in the region you can rent a longtail on Ko Hai to get to Ko Cheuak, Ko Maa and Ko Waen, just off Ko Hai to the east, where you can swim into caverns and explore a fantastic variety of multicoloured soft coral.

Of the two **resorts**, the more affordable is *Ko Hai Villa* (☎01/721 0174; Trang office at 112 Rama VI Rd, ☎075/210496; ④), which has the beach much to itself. Simple, well-organized bamboo bungalows on a nice grassy plot boast verandahs, small toilets and mosquito nets; the restaurant is run by friendly staff, though the menu is limited. *Ko Hai Resort* (☎075/211045; Trang office at 205 Sam Yaek Mohwith on the Phatthalung road, ☎075/210137; Bangkok reservations ☎02/316 3577; ④–⑦) occupies a sandy cove by the island's jetty; the restaurant is good and the wide spread of rooms ranges from basic huts on the rocks to air-conditioned beachside bungalows with wooden verandahs and spacious bathrooms.

Ko Mook

KO MOOK, about 8km southeast of Ko Hai, lies closest of the islands to the mainland, and supports a comparatively busy fishing village on its east coast. Boats leave Pak Meng for the one-hour trip to the island most days in high season at 11pm, charging B60 per person one-way; otherwise longtails can be chartered at Pak Meng for around B300.

Ko Mook's main source of renown is **Tham Morakhot**, the beautiful "Emerald Cave" on the west coast, which can only be reached by boat – longtails can be rented at *Ko Mook Resort* for B200, as well as at the resorts on Ko Hai and Ko Kradan. At low tide, boats can sail into the cave – at other times it's a short swim – to emerge at an inland beach of powdery sand open to the sky, at the base of a natural chimney whose walls are coated with dripping vegetation. Farang Beach, south of Tham Morakhot and a thirty-minute walk from the island village, is the best strip of sand, good for swimming and snorkelling; the other beaches, on the eastern side, are disappointing, often reduced to dirty mudflats. On this coast just north of the village, *Ko Mook Resort* (☎075/212613; Trang office at *Stone Graphic*, 45 Rama VI Rd, ☎075/222296; ②–④) has the least expensive **rooms** on the Trang islands, as well as big, new wooden bungalows with bathrooms, fans and mosquito screens on the windows, arrayed on shady slopes around a decent restaurant.

Ko Kradan

About 6km to the southwest of Ko Mook, KO KRADAN is the remotest of the inhabited islands off Trang. Boats come here less often than to Ko Hai and Ko Mook; phone the island's resort or its Trang office in advance to be picked up at Pak Meng for the ninety-minute voyage (B120 a head).

An institutional complex on the easterly coast, *Kradan Island Resort* (☎075/211367; Trang office next to the station at 25/36 Sathani Rd, ☎075/211391; Bangkok reservations ☎02/392 0635; ⑤–⑥) is Ko Kradan's only sign of life. If you don't fancy roughing it in a rented tent (B150), choose either a simple en suite room in a hotel-style building at the back or an attractive wooden bungalow with bath, fan and mosquito-screened windows. The friendly staff speak good English and can arrange fishing trips and longtail tours of the surrounding islands. Swim at the long, narrow beach of steeply sloping, powdery sand in front of the resort, or at Sunset Beach, in a small bay ten minutes' walk away on the other side of the island; there's good snorkelling among a great variety of hard coral in the clear waters off the island's southern tip.

Ban Chao Mai

The mainland beaches around **BAN CHAO MAI** just shade Pak Meng for beauty and, if anything, are even quieter, although getting there requires a rented motorbike or a taxi from Trang. This Muslim village, a straggle of simple thatched houses on stilts, exists on fishing, especially for crabs, and has a few shops where visitors can buy food and drink. On the canal running behind the village you'll find mangrove swamps and a large cave containing huge rock pillars and a natural theatre, its stage framed by rock curtains. **Hat Yao** (Long Beach) runs north in a broad five-kilometre strip that's exposed enough to see occasional high surf; immediately beyond comes **Hat Yong Ling**, an attractive convex beach with another large cave, which you can swim into at high tide or walk into at low tide.

Ko Tarutao National Marine Park

The unspoilt **KO TARUTAO NATIONAL MARINE PARK** is probably the most beautiful of all Thailand's accessible beach destinations. Occupying 1400 square kilometres of the Andaman Sea, the park covers 51 mostly uninhabited islands, of which three – Ko Tarutao, Ko Adang and Ko Lipe – are easy to reach and offer accommodation for visitors. The area's forests and seas support an incredible variety of **fauna**: langurs, crab-eating macaques and wild pigs are common on the islands, which also shelter several unique subspecies of squirrel, tree shrew and lesser mouse deer; among the hundred-plus bird species found here, reef egrets and horn-bills are regularly seen, while white-bellied sea eagles, frigate birds and pied impe-rial pigeons are more rarely encountered; and the park is the habitat of about 25 percent of the world's fish species, as well as marine mammals such as the dugong, sperm whale and dolphins. The islands are also an important site for **turtle egg-laying** (see p.442): Olive Ridley, green, hawksbill and leatherback turtles lay their eggs on Ko Tarutao's sands between September and April, green turtles on Ko Adang (Sept–Dec); park rangers try to keep an eye on the nests and are generally happy to share the information with visitors. A currently bearable level of tourism keeps the park's delicate environment stable; it will be disastrously disturbed if proposals to set up regular boat connections with the highly developed Malaysian resort on Langkawi Island, 8km from Ko Tarutao, are acted upon.

The park is officially closed to tourists from May 19 to November 19, when storms can make the sea passage hazardous. However, even in the open season, especially at its beginning or end, boats won't leave if there aren't enough passen-gers to break even; on the other hand, travellers have been known to find depar-tures, and sometimes accommodation in the park, in the closed season – phone

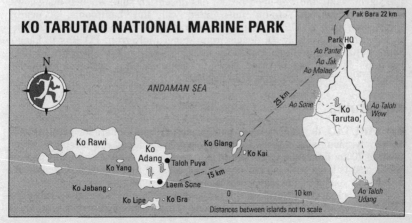

KO TARUTAO NATIONAL MARINE PARK

Pak Bara 22 km

N

ANDAMAN SEA

Park HQ
Ao Pante
Ao Jak
Ao Malae

25 km

Ao Sone
Ko Tarutao

Ao Taloh Wow

Ko Rawi

Ko Adang
Ko Yang
Taloh Puya

Ko Glang
Ko Kai

Ko Jabang

Ko Lipe
Ko Gra
Laem Sone

15 km

0   10 km

Ao Taloh Udang

Distances between islands not to scale

park headquarters on Tarutao (☎074/711383) or the Pak Bara visitors' centre (☎074/781285) for the latest. You should have no problem finding somewhere to stay except at the three New Years (Thai, Chinese and the end of December), when it's best to book ahead in Bangkok (see p.50). The *Traveler's Adventure Handbook* to Tarutao is a must-buy at only B10, though sometimes out of print – try the visitors' centres at Pak Bara on the mainland and Ao Pante on Ko Tarutao.

North of the national park, the privately run bungalows of **Ko Bulon Lae** present a slightly less regimented alternative. The small, little-known island attracts fewer crowds, there's a long and beautiful beach and some interesting snorkelling, and the food beats the institutional cooking on Tarutao.

Getting to Tarutao and Bulon Lae

In season, boats leave **PAK BARA**, 60km north of Satun, at 10.30am and 3pm (B250 round trip) for the ninety-minute voyage to Ao Pante on Ko Tarutao. The only way to reach the park's two other principal islands – Ko Adang and Ko Lipe, 40km west of Ko Tarutao – is on the mail boat which, from January to April, is scheduled to leave Ao Pante three times a week for the three-hour journey (B360 round trip). Even during these months, the service can be unreliable, and for the rest of the year there is no schedule at all, though you can count on at least one departure a week.

Boats for Ko Bulon Lae leave Pak Bara at 2pm (1hr 30min; B80 one way). They're scheduled to run only from November to June, but will sometimes set off in the low season (contact *Udom Tours* on ☎074/781435 in Pak Bara for on-the-spot information, or *First Andaman Travel* in Trang: (see p.498).

To get to Pak Bara **from Trang**, take a Satun-bound bus (2hr 30min) or a share taxi (1hr 30min) to the inland town of **Langu** and change to a red songthaew for the ten-kilometre hop to the port. From **Hat Yai**, three buses a day from the *Plaza Cinema* (at 7am, 11am and 3pm; 2hr 30min) and faster air-conditioned minibuses from an office near the *Krung Thai* bank at the north end of Niphat Uthit 1 go all the way through to Pak Bara in two and a half hours – otherwise take a share taxi to Langu, or a Satun-bound bus to **Chalung** and change onto a Satun–Trang bus to get to Langu. From **Satun**, frequent buses and taxis make the fifty-kilometre trip to Langu.

Pak Bara has simple **accommodation** for people who miss the boats. *Marena* (③), 500m along the tree-lined beach, has decent en suite wooden bungalows, and the corrugated A-frame huts, fitted with tiny bathrooms, of nearby *Krachomsai* (☎074/781231; ③) present a strange but clean alternative. *Gahsing Island Retreat* (probably ⑥; details from Maggi McKerron, PO Box 9, Langu, Satun 9110, or limited information on ☎02/260 9202), due to open late in 1995, will offer luxury, and assorted New Age courses, on a secluded beach ten minutes' boat ride up the coast from Pak Bara.

Ko Tarutao

KO TARUTAO, the largest of the national park's islands, offers the greatest natural variety: mountains covered in semi-evergreen rainforest rise steeply to a high point of 700m; limestone caves and mangrove swamps dot the shoreline; and the west coast is lined with perfect beaches for most of its 26-kilometre length. It's also where you'll find the park's best facilities for visitors.

Boats dock at **Ao Pante**, on the northwestern side of the island, where the admission fee (B50) is collected and where the **park headquarters** is situated.

Here you'll find the only shop on the island, selling basic supplies, as well as a visitors' centre and a well-stocked library. The **bungalows** (⑤–⑥), which are spread over a large, quiet park behind the beach, are national park standard issue with cold-water bathrooms. **Beds** in the bamboo longhouses cost B80 per person, and two-person **tents** can be rented for B100 a night (campers with their own gear are charged B10 per person per night). Ao Pante has two Thai **eateries**: the café does inexpensive, simple dishes, while the restaurant has a more varied and pricey menu.

Behind the settlement, the steep, half-hour climb to **To-Boo Cliff** is a must, especially at sunset, for the view of the surrounding islands and the crocodile's-head cape at the north end of the bay. A fun one-hour boat trip (B150; contact the visitor centre) can also be made near Ao Pante, up the canal which leads 2km inland from the pier, through the lush leaves and dense roots of a bird-filled mangrove swamp, to the entrance to **Crocodile Cave** – where you're unlikely to see any of the big snappers, reported sightings being highly dubious.

A half-hour walk south from Ao Pante will bring you to the two quiet bays of **Ao Jak** and **Ao Malae**, fringed by coconut palms and filled with fine white sand. Behind the house at the south end of Ao Malae, a road leads over the headland to **Ao Sone** (2hr from Ao Pante), where a pretty freshwater stream runs past the ranger station at the north end of the bay, making this a good place for peaceful camping. A favourite egg-laying site for sea turtles, the main part of the bay is a three-kilometre sweep of flawless sand, with a ninety-minute trail leading up to a waterfall in the middle and a mangrove swamp at the far south end.

On the east side of the island, **Ao Taloh Wow** is a rocky bay with a ranger station, connected to Ao Pante by a twelve-kilometre road through old rubber plantations and evergreen forest. If you have a tent, you might want to set off along the overgrown, five-hour trail beyond Taloh Wow, which cuts through the forest to **Ao Taloh Udang**, a sandy bay on the south side. Here the remnants of a penal colony for political prisoners are just visible: the plotters of two failed coup attempts were imprisoned here in the 1930s before returning to high government posts. The ordinary convicts, who used to be imprisoned at Ao Taloh Wow, had a much harsher time, and during World War II, when supplies from the mainland dried up, prisoners and guards ganged together to turn to piracy. Pirates and smugglers still occasionally hide out in the Tarutao archipelago, but the main problem now is illegal trawlers fishing in national park waters.

Ko Adang and Ko Lipe

At **KO ADANG**, a wild, rugged island covered in tropical rainforest, the boat pulls in at the **Laem Sone** park station on the southern shore, where the beach is steep and narrow and backed by a thick canopy of pines. **Beds** in the bamboo longhouses here are B80 per person (2 berths per room, with single travellers sharing at busy times). Campers can pitch their own **tents** for B10 per person per night, and the **restaurant** is limited and a bit pricey. The half-hour climb to **Sha-do** cliff on the steep slope above Laem Sone gives good views over the sand spit of the harbour and Ko Lipe to the south. About 2km west along the coast from the park station, the small beach is lined with coconut palms and an abandoned customs house, behind which a twenty-minute trail leads to the small **Pirate Waterfall**. For more ambitious explorations, the author of the park handbook recommends **"snork-hiking"**, an amphibious method of reaching distant attractions (bring your own snorkelling gear). Up the east coast, you can make such a day trip to **Rattana Waterfall**, 3km from the park station, and to the *chao ley* village of **Taloh Puya**, 1km further, which has a fine coral reef directly offshore and a nice beach to the north.

KO LIPE, 2km south of Adang, makes a busy contrast to the other islands. A small, flat triangle, it's covered in coconut plantations and inhabited by *chao ley* (see p.462), with shops, a school and a health centre in the village on the eastern side – from where longtail boats come out to meet the mail boat. By rights, such a settlement should not be allowed within the national park boundaries – and relations with park rangers are strained, sometimes to the point of armed clashes – but the *chao ley* on Lipe are well entrenched: Satun's governor forced the community to move here from Ko Lanta between the world wars, to reinforce the island's Thai character and prevent the British rulers of Malaya from laying claim to it. The *chao ley* have opened several simple **bungalow** outfits (③) in the village, all of which have B80 dorm beds: the best of the bunch is *Suan Sone* at the north end, which has bamboo bungalows by the beach under shady pine trees. The owner has longtail boats if you want to visit the coral reefs around Ko Jabang and Ko Yang, on the west side of Adang, but there's rewarding water around tiny **Ko Gra**, 200m out to sea from the village, which has a beautiful coral reef. **Pattaya Beach**, about 1km from the village on the south side of the island, has two similar sets of bungalows and a good offshore reef to explore.

Ko Bulon Lae

The scenery of tiny **KO BULON LAE**, 20km west of Pak Bara, is not as beautiful as that of the national marine park, but it's not at all bad: a two-kilometre strip of fine white sand runs the length of the casuarina-lined east coast, while *chao ley* fishermen make their ramshackle homes in the tight coves of the western fringe. A reef of curiously shaped hard coral closely parallels the eastern beach, while **White Rock**, a ten-minute, B800 charter boat ride to the south of the island, has beautifully coloured soft coral and equally dazzling fish. **Snorkelling** gear, as well as boats for the trip to White Rock, can be rented at *Pansand*, the island's largest and best **resort** (☎01/722 0279; ②–⑥), where accommodation ranges from simple longhouse rooms to swanky clapboard cottages with bathrooms, fans and mosquito screens on the windows. On the beach side of the spacious, shady grounds, the sociable **restaurant** serves up good seafood and other Thai dishes. To book a room or find out about boats in the off season, contact *First Andaman Travel*, opposite *Queens Hotel* at 82–84 Wisetkul Rd in Trang (☎075/218035). A young, long-stay crowd tends to hang out at *Bulone Resort* (①), ten minutes' walk north of *Pansand* along the beach, which can offer beds with mosquito nets, verandahs and shared bathrooms. If these two resorts are full, your only options are two rather dismal places run by the *chao ley* on the less attractive west coast, *Tamarind* and *Ko Bulon* (both ③).

Satun and around

Remote **SATUN** nestles in the last wedge of Thailand's west coast and is served by just one road, Highway 406, which approaches the town through forbidding karst outcrops. Set in a green valley bordered by limestone hills, the town is leafy and relaxing but not especially interesting: the boat services to and from Malaysia are the main reason for farangs to come here, though some use the town as an approach to Ko Tarutao or Thale Ban National Park (see below).

Frequent **buses** depart from Ratsada Road in Trang, and regular buses also come from Hat Yai and from Phatthalung – if you don't get a direct bus from Phatthalung to Satun, it's easy to change at **Rattaphum**, on the junction of highways 4 and 406. The bus depot is at the north end of town, but most buses also make a stop in the centre; share taxis and air-conditioned minibuses are centrally based around the junction of Saman Pradit Road, the main east–west thoroughfare, and Sulakanukul Road.

Rian Thong, by the town pier at 4 Saman Pradit Rd (☎074/711036; ②), is the best budget **hotel** in Satun; the owners are friendly and speak English, and some of the clean, well-furnished rooms overlook the canal. *Farm Gai* (②), more or less in open country ten minutes' west of the centre (take a motorbike taxi), is run by a Swiss who was once a pioneering bungalow-builder on Ko Samui. The comfortable, well-designed huts and rooms sit in a quiet, somewhat overgrown garden; the family prefers guests who will stay for a while to sample Thai country life, but don't insist on it. In complete contrast, *Wangmai Hotel*, out towards the bus depot at 43 Satun Thani Rd (☎074/711607; ⑤), is a typical "de luxe" hotel with air-conditioned rooms in a modern concrete building. For **food**, try *Yim Yim* on Saman Pradit Road by the Chinese temple, a clean and popular restaurant which serves good, simple Chinese food.

An informal but useful **"tourist information centre"** is operated by the teachers and students of the English school next door to *Rian Thong*.

Crossing the border

For travel across the border, longtail boats make regular morning trips (B30 per person) to **Kuala Perlis** on Malaysia's northwest tip, from where there are plentiful transport connections down the west coast. When Khlong Bambang is high enough, the boats can reach the pier in the town centre, but usually they start the half-hour voyage from **Thammalang** pier, 10km south at the mouth of the river. Three ferry boats a day (4 at peak times) are scheduled to cross to the Malaysian island of **Langkawi** from Thammalang in ninety minutes; buy tickets (B150) from the town's main travel agent, *Satun Travel and Ferry Service*, opposite the *Wangmai Hotel* at 45/16 Satun Thani Rd (☎074/711453), and check on departures, as they are sometimes cancelled if there are too few takers. Frequent songthaews and motorbike taxis run to Thammalang from the town centre in around half an hour. If you are entering the country by sea from Malaysia, be sure to report to the **immigration office**, either at Thammalang pier or in the centre of Satun on Burivanit Road, to have your passport stamped, otherwise you may have problems on your eventual departure from Thailand.

Thale Ban National Park

Spread over rainforested mountains along the Malaysian border, **THALE BAN NATIONAL PARK** is a pristine nature reserve which shelters a breathtaking variety of wildlife: from gibbons, tapirs, Malayan sun bears and a few rarely sighted elephants and tigers, to butterflies and unusual birds such as bat hawks, booted eagles and flamboyant argus pheasants, to butterflies, which proliferate in March. Unfortunately for naturalists and casual visitors alike, few trails have been marked out through the jungle, but the lush, peaceful setting and the views and bathing pools of the Yaroy Waterfall are enough to justify the trip.

Hourly songthaews leave from opposite *Rian Thong* hotel in Satun, reaching Thale Ban headquarters (☎074/797073) in an hour; if you're coming from Hat Yai, you can change onto one of these songthaews at **Ban Khwan Sator**, 19km north of Satun on Highway 406, for the twenty-kilometre journey south to the park headquarters. The songthaews continue 2km beyond headquarters to **Wang Prachan** on the border with Malaysia; at **Buket Hetam** on the other side, share taxis wait to ferry you south to Alor Setar or Penang.

Hemmed in by steep, verdant hills and spangled with red water lilies, the **lake** by the headquarters is central to the story that gives the park its name. Local legend tells how a villager once put his *ban* (headscarf) on a tree stump to have a rest; this caused a landslide, the lake appeared from nowhere, and he, the stump and the *ban* tumbled into it. The water is now surrounded by **bungalows** (⑤), for which lower rates can be negotiated on weekdays, when business is slow. A decent open-air **canteen** also overlooks the lake.

The most interesting **jungle walk** runs east along the border to the summit of **Khao Chin**, 12km away, but the trail is overgrown and easy to lose – someone at headquarters might be free to guide you. A less strenuous trip is the one to **Tham Tondin**, a low, sweaty stalactite cave which gradually slopes down for 800m to deep water. It's about 2km north of headquarters back along the road to Khwan Sator – look out for the wooden sign in Thai, on the west side of the main road just north of the 18km post, then climb 30m up the slope to see the tiny entrance at your feet. If you time your visit so that you emerge just before dusk, you'll see hundreds of bats streaming out of the hole for the night. It's best to consult the detailed map at headquarters before you visit the cave, and you'll need a flashlight.

The one essential jaunt, though, is to **Yaroy Waterfall** – bring swimming gear for the pools above the main fall. Take the main road north from the headquarters through the narrow, idyllic valley for 6km (beyond the village of Wang Prachan) and follow the sign to the right. After 700m, you'll find the main, lower fall set in screeching jungle. By climbing the path on the left side, you reach what seems like the top, with fine views of the steep, green peaks to the west. However, there's more: if you carry on up the stream, you'll find a series of gorgeous shady pools, where you can bathe and shower under the six-metre falls.

Hat Yai

HAT YAI, the transport axis of the region, was given a dose of instant American-style modernization in the 1950s, since when it's commercially usurped its own provincial capital, Songkhla. The resulting concrete mess, reminiscent of Bangkok without the interesting bits, attracts half a million tourists a year, nearly all of them Malaysians who nip across the border to shop and get laid. On any extended tour of the south you are bound to end up in Hat Yai, and you may as well take the opportunity to call in at the main **TAT** office for the deep south at 1/1 Soi 2, Niphat Uthit Rd 3 (☎074/243747). The **tourist police** have their main office at Sripoovanart Road on the south side of town (☎074/246733), but maintain a convenient booth near the *Odean* department store on Niphat Uthit 3. If the concrete and the sleaze turn you off a protracted stay, remember that Songkhla is only 25km away.

If you're leap-frogging into the deep south via Hat Yai **airport** you'll arrive 12km from town, then be shuttled into the centre on the *Thai Airways* minibus to its

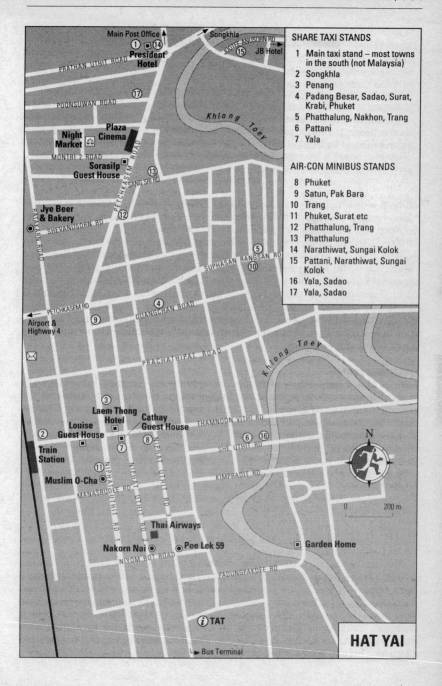

SHARE TAXI STANDS

1 Main taxi stand – most towns in the south (not Malaysia)
2 Songkhla
3 Penang
4 Padang Besar, Sadao, Surat, Krabi, Phuket
5 Phatthalung, Nakhon, Trang
6 Pattani
7 Yala

AIR-CON MINIBUS STANDS

8 Phuket
9 Satun, Pak Bara
10 Trang
11 Phuket, Surat etc
12 Phatthalung, Trang
13 Phatthalung
14 Narathiwat, Sungai Kolok
15 Pattani, Narathiwat, Sungai Kolok
16 Yala, Sadao
17 Yala, Sadao

Main Post Office
Songkhla
LOUISE ANUSORN RD
JB Hotel
PRATHAN UTHIT ROAD
President Hotel
POONSUWAN ROAD
Khlong Toey
Plaza Cinema
Night Market
MONTRI 2 ROAD
Sorasilp Guest House
PETCHKASEM ROAD
SANG SRI RD
Jye Beer & Bakery
IRATAKARN ROAD
SHEVANUSORN RD
SUPHASAN RANGSAN RD
PETCHKASEM RD
Airport & Highway 4
DUANGCHAN ROAD
Khlong Toey
PRACHATHIPAT ROAD
Laem Thong Hotel
Louise Guest House
Cathay Guest House
THAMNOON VITHI RD
Train Station
NIPHAT UTHIT RD
SHE UTHIT RD
Muslim O-Cha
MANASRUDEE RD
NIPHAT UTHIT RD
KIMPRADIT RD
NIPHAT UTHIT RD 3
Thai Airways
Nakorn Nai
Pee Lek 59
NIYOM ROT ROAD
Garden Home
PADUNGPAKDEE RD
N
0   200 m
TAT
Bus Terminal

HAT YAI

BULLFIGHTING IN HAT YAI

Hat Yai is one of the south's major centres for **bullfighting**, which in its Thai version involves bull tussling with bull, the winner being the one which forces the other to retreat. Fights can last anything from a few seconds to half an hour, in which case the frantic betting of the audience becomes more interesting than the deadlock in the ring. On the first Saturday of every month, a day-long competition, beginning at 10am, is held at the Khlong Wa stadium 8km south of town on the road to Sadao. It's best to get there in the early afternoon as the big fights, involving prize money of up to B200,000, are lower down the card. A special entrance fee of B100 is charged to farangs; to get there charter a songthaew and ask for *sanam chon wua* (bullfighting stadium).

---

office at 166/4 Niphat Uthit Rd 2 (☎074/245851 or 245852); the smooth passage of Malaysian and Singaporean dirty-weekenders is now facilitated by regular flights between Hat Yai and Johore Baru (*MAS*; B2400), Kuala Lumpur (*MAS* and *Thai*; B1900–2100)and Singapore (*MAS*, *Thai* and *Silk Air*; B2400–2900). The **train station** is on the west side of the centre at the end of Thamnoon Vithi Road, and contains a useful left-luggage office (6am–7pm; B5 per piece per day); the **bus terminal** is far to the southeast of town on Kanchanawanit Road, leaving you with a songthaew ride to the centre, but most buses make a stop at the *Plaza Cinema* on Petchkasem Road, on the north side of the centre. **Share taxis** and **air-conditioned minibuses** should drop you off at your destination; for departure, they have a number of different ranks around town (marked on the map) according to where you want to go.

Accommodation

Hat Yai has a huge range of **hotels**, none of them very good value and most worked by prostitutes. A few in the budget range are geared to travellers: the friendly *Cathay Guest House* at 93 Niphat Uthit Rd 2 (☎074/243815; ②) is falling apart, but the movable parts are reasonably clean, B60 dorm beds are available, and the information board is a guide book in itself. On the upper floors of a modern building beside the *Plaza Cinema*, *Sorasilp Guest House*, 251/7–8 Petchkasem Rd (☎074/232635; ②) is also friendly and clean, though a little noisy.

The best of many typical Chinese hotels around the three central Niphat Uthit roads (which are known locally as *sai neung, sai sawng* and *sai saam*) is the large, efficiently run *Laem Thong*, 46 Thamnoon Vithi Rd (☎074/244433; ③–④), with a choice of fan-cooled or air-conditioned rooms. For more comfort at much the same price, head for *Louise Guest House*, by the train station at 21–23 Thamnoon Vithi Rd (☎074/220966; ③–④), where you can settle for fans and carpets, or splash out on air conditioning and hot water.

Moving up a notch, *Garden Home*, southeast of the centre at 51/2 Hoi Mook Rd (☎074/234444; ④), a pastiche of a grand mansion built around a plant-filled courtyard, offers very good value; large bedrooms show some sense of decor and boast a good range of facilities (air conditioning, hot water, TV and minibar). Hat Yai's best hotel is *JB Hotel*, 99 Jootee-Anusorn Rd (☎074/234300–28; ⑦), which furnishes quite enough luxury to justify the price – among the highlights are a large swimming pool, a top-class Chinese restaurant, and the *Jazz Bistro*, a civilized place for Thai and Western fare or just a drink.

Eating and nightlife

Hat Yai's **restaurants** offer a choice of Thai, Chinese, Muslim and Western food. At the junction with Niyom Rot Road, the welcoming *Pee Lek 59*, 185/4 Niphat Uthit 3, gets the thumbs-up for moderately priced seafood in Thai style – try *gataa rawn*, a sizzling dish of mixed marine life. *Muslim O-Cha*, at 117 Niphat Uthit 1 (closes 8.30pm), is a simple, clean restaurant which serves curried chicken and rice and other inexpensive Muslim food in small portions. A reasonable place for all-day breakfasts, Western food and some interesting Thai dishes is the cool and comfortable *Nakorn Nai* at 166/7 Niphat Uthit 2. If you want to splurge out, the *Jye Beer and Bakery* on Ratakarn Road does posh Thai and American food in a cosy, rustic atmosphere. Finally, the sprawling night market, behind the *Plaza Cinema* on Montri 2 Road, has something for everyone: seafood and beer, Thai curries, deep-fried chicken, and the Muslim speciality *khao neua daeng*, tender cured beef in a sweet red sauce.

For a quiet **drink**, head for *Sugar Rock*, 114 Thamnoon Vithi Rd, a pleasant café bar with low-volume Western music. To get away from it all, the mini-theatre at *Odean* department store, on the corner of Niphat Uthit 3 and Thamnoon Vithi roads, shows Western **movies**, with the English soundtrack relayed into a separate sound room.

Crossing the border

Hat Yai is only 50km from the border with **Malaysia**. The fastest way of getting across is to take a **share taxi** to **Penang**, where you can renew your visa at the Thai consulate; taxis depart every morning for about B220. Tickets for the more comfortable and slightly less expensive **air-conditioned buses** can be bought at travel agents, such as *Magic Tour* (☎074/236119), under the *Cathay Guest House*. These buses depart every day for Penang (6hr), as well as Alor Setar (3hr), Butterworth (5hr), Kuala Lumpur (12hr) and Singapore (18hr). More comfortable again are the **trains**, though they're not very convenient: six a day run to Sungai Kolok on the east-coast border, one a day heads via the frontier at Padang Besar to Butterworth (for the ferry to Penang), and one gets you all the way to Kuala Lumpur in fourteen hours. The least expensive but most time-consuming method is to catch a **bus** to Padang Besar (every 30min; 1hr 30min), walk 800m across the border and take a share taxi to Kuala Perlis (30min) or Alor Setar (1hr) – avoid the obvious route straight down Highway 4 to Sadao, because there's a long stretch between the opposing border posts which there's no inexpensive way of covering.

Songkhla and around

Known as the "big town of two seas" because it sits on a north-pointing peninsula between the Gulf of Thailand and the Thale Sap lagoon, **SONGKHLA** provides a sharp contrast to Hat Yai. A small, sophisticated provincial capital, it retains many historic buildings – such as the elegant Wat Matchimawat and the Chinese mansion that now houses the national museum – and its broad, quiet streets are planted with soothing greenery. When you add some fine restaurants and decent accommodation, and the proximity to the wonderful Southern Folklore Museum at Ko Yo, Songkhla makes a stimulating place to hole up in for a few days.

The settlement was originally sited on the north side of the mouth of the Thale Sap, where a deepwater port has now been built, and flourished as a **trading port** from the eighth century onwards. The shift across the water came after 1769, when a Chinese merchant named Yieng Hao was granted permission by the Thai ruler, Taksin, to collect swallows' nests from Ko Si Ko Ha – now part of Khu Khut Waterbird Park. Having made a packet from selling them for their culinary and medicinal properties, he was made governor of Songkhla by Taksin and established the city on its present site. For seven generations the **Na Songkhla dynasty** he founded kept the governorship in the family, overseeing the construction of many of the buildings you see today. The town is now an unhurried administrative centre, which maintains a strong central Thai feel – most of the province's Muslim population live in the hinterland.

Most **buses** arrive at the major junction of Ramwithi Road with Jana and Platha roads. People usually come here straight from Hat Yai, 25km southwest, but buses also run direct from Nakhon and Chana. **Taxis** for these towns and places further afield congregate on the south side of the main bus stop, just off Ramwithi Road.

The Town

The town which the Na Songkhlas built has expanded to fill the headland, and makes a great place for strolling around, although if the heat gets to you, songthaews (B4 per person) and motorbike taxis (B5–20) cruise the streets. The western side, where the town first developed, shelters a fishing port which presents a vivid, smelly scene in the mornings. Two abrupt hills – **Khao Tung Kuan** and the smaller **Khao Noi** – border the north side of the centre, while in the heart of town lie the main tourist attractions, the **National Museum** and the extravagantly decorated **Wat Matchimawat**. Sitting on the fringe of town at the bottom end of Hat Samila – the 8km of beach along the eastern shore – **Khao Saen** is an impoverished but vibrant fishing village, whose multicoloured boats provide Songkhla's most hackneyed postcard image.

Khao Tung Kuan

To get your bearings, preferably in the cool of the morning or evening, climb up **Khao Tung Kuan** at the northwestern end of town. From Laem Sai Road, on the western side of the hill, steps rise past simple monks' huts which surround what looks like a red-brick Wendy house – Rama V ordered the pavilion to be built at the height of his Westernization programme, but the local artisans clearly couldn't get their heads round the monarch's conception. From the chedi at the top of the hill, you can look south over the town and the fishing port, and west over the Thale Sap to the island of Ko Yo. Further up Laem Sai Road, you can visit **Laem Sai Fort**, with its low walls and cannon, which was built by the French in the seventeenth century, when they held favour with the kings of Ayutthaya.

Songkhla National Museum

The **Songkhla National Museum** (Wed–Sun 9am–noon & 1–4pm; B10) on Jana Road, the main east–west street, is worth a visit for its architecture alone. Built in 1878 in south Chinese style, this graceful mansion was first the residence of the governor of Songkhla and Nakhon, then the city hall, and later the local poorhouse before being converted into a museum in the 1970s. Its best side faces the

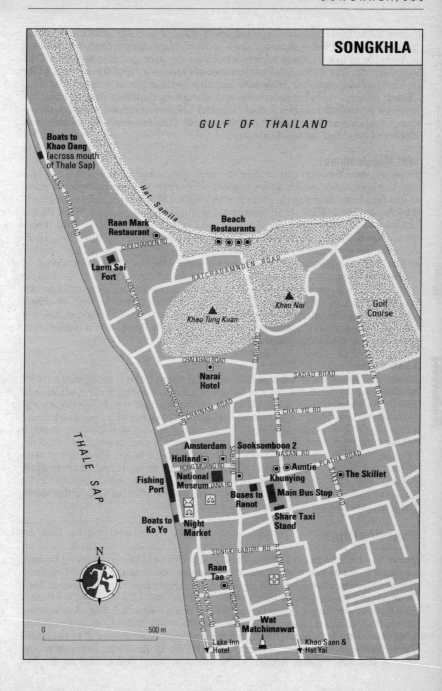

SONGKHLA

GULF OF THAILAND

Boats to
Khao Dang
(across mouth
of Thale Sap)

LANG PRARAM ROAD

Hat Samila

Raan Mark
Restaurant

Beach
Restaurants

CHOLCHAROEN RD.

RATCHADAMNDEN ROAD

Laem Sai
Fort

LAEM SAI ROAD

Khao Noi

Golf
Course

Khao Tung Kuan

SUKHLM RD.

RATCHADAMNEN ROAD

CHAI KHAO ROAD

SADAO ROAD

VICHANCHOM RD.

Narai
Hotel

CHAINAM ROAD

SISODA RD.

CHAI YO RD.

THALE SAP

Amsterdam   Sooksomboon 2

Holland   NASAN RD.

RONG MUANG RD.

SAIBURI RD.

PLATHA ROAD

Auntie
Khunying

The Skillet

Fishing
Port

National
Museum   JANA RD.

SAKET ROAD

Buses to
Ranot

Main Bus Stop

Boats to
Ko Yo

Night
Market

Share Taxi
Stand

SONGKHLABURI RD.

RAMWITHI ROAD

N

Raan
Tae

NAKHON NAI ROAD

NANG NGAM ROAD

Wat
Matchimawat

0   500 m

Lake Inn
Hotel

Khao Saen &
Hat Yai

NAKHON NAVY ROAD

garden at the back: from here you can see how the ornamental staircases and the roof were constructed in shapely curves to disorientate straight-flying evil spirits.

A jumble of folk exhibits, such as masks for the *manohra* (the southern Thai dance-drama) and agricultural implements, are strewn around the garden, while inside the wildly diverse collection includes well-preserved examples of Ban Chiang pottery, early Hindu statues and Mahayana Buddhist images from the Srivijaya period, and a selection of beautiful Chinese ceramics. Upstairs everything is upstaged by overblown Chinese and Thai furniture, all lacquer and mother-of-pearl and bas-relief carving.

Wat Matchimawat

From the museum, you can explore the atmospheric old streets of Nakhon Nai and Nakhon Nawk, which show European influence in their colonnaded pavements and crumbling stucco, on your way south to **Wat Matchimawat**, a grand, attention-grabbing affair set in ornamental grounds on Saiburi Road. What stands out most of all is the bot, a florid mixture of Chinese and Thai styles, which was apparently modelled on Wat Phra Kaeo in Bangkok. Fetching stone bas-reliefs decorate the low walls around the bot, depicting leafy scenes from *The Romance of The Three Kingdoms*, a Chinese historical novel which served as a handbook of manners and morals in the middle of the nineteenth century, when the temple was built. Every centimetre of the lofty interior is covered with colourful *Jataka* murals, telling of the previous lives of the Buddha, mixed in with vivacious tableaux of nineteenth-century Songkhla life. The bot is usually locked, but you can get the key from the adjacent museum (daily 9am–4pm), which is filled with ceramics, votive tablets, stuffed animals and other clutter.

Khao Saen

To see the best of the Muslim shanty village of **Khao Saen** – set against a rocky headland on the southern edge of Songkhla's tide of development – you should visit in the late afternoon, when the boisterous fish market is in full swing (except Fri). Songthaews from Saiburi Road, south of the junction with Jana Road, make the trip in fifteen minutes. The crowded, rotting shacks of the village make a bleak contrast with the objects for which Khao Saen is most celebrated – its decorated prawn-fishing vessels. Drawn up in rows on the beach, these immaculate small boats have dragon prows wrapped in lucky garlands and hulls brightly painted with flags and intricate artwork. These pictures, which mostly depict mosques and idyllic landscapes, are the work of an artist at Saiburi, further down the coast, and cost each fisherman a month's income.

Practicalities

Narai, at 14 Chai Khao Rd (☎074/311078; ②), is Songkhla's outstanding bottom-end **hotel**, situated in a quiet, rambling wooden house at the foot of Doi Tung Kuan. More expensive but still decent value, *Amsterdam Guest House*, at 15/3 Rong Muang Rd on the north side of the museum (☎074/314890; ③), is an easy-going place with large, bright, clean rooms in a modern building. A few doors down, *Holland Guest House*, 27 Rong Muang Rd (☎074/312716; ③), contains four cosy bedrooms, but does not welcome backpackers. *Sooksomboon 2*, at 18 Saiburi Rd, is divided in two: the old wing (☎074/311149; ③) has clean, ordinary rooms in a cavernous wooden house, while the new wing (☎074/323808; ④) has comfortable air-conditioned rooms, all with hot-water bathrooms, and provides better value. Air conditioning and hot water are also offered at the *Lake Inn Hotel*, 301 Nakhon Nawk Rd (☎074/321044; ⑤); half of this high-rise's tastefully furnished rooms, the ground-floor restaurant and the rooftop beer garden face the lake. A luxury hotel, the *New Pavilion*, is under construction on Platha Road, but for the moment Songkhla's top hotel lies across the mouth of the Thale Sap, 6km along the road to Nakhon: the swish, upmarket *Haad Kaew Princess Resort* (☎074/331059–67; Bangkok reservations ☎02/249 9305) has mod-con bungalows and a swimming pool, and gives onto an attractive beach.

For daytime eating, pull up a deck chair and relax at the shaded beach **restaurants** which congregate at the northern end of Sukhum Road and at the east end of Platha Road; or try a plate of *khanom jiin* (soft noodles with a choice of sauces) at the well-scrubbed *Khunying*, on Sisuda Road by the junction with Platha Road. Where Hat Samila starts curving to the north near the top of Laem Sai Road, you'll find a posh open-air restaurant, *Raan Mark*, which dishes up good seafood day and night. Songkhla's most famous restaurant, *Raan Tae*, at 85 Nang Ngarm Rd, is spotlessly clean and justly popular, serving especially good seafood – but it closes at 8pm. The **night market**, south of the post office on Nakhon Nai Road, is the place for budget-conscious travellers. A ghetto of Westernized bars and restaurants on Saket, Sisuda and Sadao roads caters to the good ole boys who work on the offshore oil rigs: places such as *The Skillet* ("vittles and stuff"), on Saket Road near Platha, and *Auntie*, 62/1 Sisuda Rd, serve good American-style food and ice-cold beers, at a price.

Ko Yo

KO YO, the small island in the Thale Sap to the west of Songkhla, has long been a destination for day-trippers, and the road link with the land on both sides of the lagoon has accelerated the transformation of **Ban Nok** – the island's main settlement – into a souvenir market. Here you'll find durian cakes, an amazing variety of dried and treated seafood, and the high-quality fabrics – mostly cotton, but sometimes with small amounts of silk woven in – for which Ko Yo is famous; if you're around in the morning, you can fork left off the main road in the village to watch the weavers at work in their houses.

The best way of **getting there from Songkhla** is to take one of the frequent Ranot-bound buses from Jana Road, which take half an hour to get to Ko Yo, and then continue to Khu Khut Waterbird Park. If you fancy a more scenic but costly route, longtail boats from the pier behind the post office on Nakhon Nai Road cost B100 per person. If you're coming **from Hat Yai**, there's no need to go into Songkhla first: take a Songkhla-bound bus but get off on the edge of the suburbs at the junction with Highway 408, and catch a songthaew or bus across the bridge to Ko Yo.

The chief appeal of Ko Yo is the **Southern Folklore Museum** (daily 8am–6pm; B10 with a free pamphlet in English), which sprawls over twelve acres of hillside on the northern tip of Ko Yo just before the northern bridge. Giving stunning views over the water to Songkhla and of the fishing villages on the western side of the island, the park is strewn with all kinds of boats and wooden reproductions of traditional southern houses, in which the collections are neatly set out. The exhibits inside, such as the shadow-puppet paraphernalia and the *kris* – long knives with intricately carved handles and sheaths – show the strong influences of Malaysia and Indonesia on southern Thailand. Also on show are the elaborate dance costumes for the *manohra*, but probably the most fascinating objects are the *lek kood* or coconut scrapers, which are set into seat-blocks carved into an offbeat variety of shapes – rabbits, elephants, phalluses, beauty queens. The museum's **shop** has the island's finest selection of fabrics.

One hundred metres south of the museum, a short slip road leads up to an excellent **restaurant**, *Suan Kaeo*, in a breezy spot overlooking the Thale Sap and Songkhla – try *hor mok thalay*, mixed fresh seafood in a chilli and coconut sauce.

Khu Khut Waterbird Park

About 40km up Highway 408 from Songkhla, a left turn by the police station leads after 3km to the headquarters of **Khu Khut Waterbird Park**, a conservation area on the Thale Luang where over 140 species of mostly migratory birds are found. The park is similar to Thale Noi near Phatthalung, though not as impressive and more expensive, but if you're not planning to visit Phatthalung, it's worth coming here on a day trip from Songkhla. A longtail trip to view the birds costs B150 for forty minutes, while for B300 you get a two-hour jaunt across the shallow lake, weaving between water reeds and crayfish traps, to **Ko Si Ko Ha**, the dramatic limestone islands where birds' nests are gathered for Chinese gourmets. You won't be able to set foot on the islands as the concession-holders jealously guard their hugely profitable business from spies and thieves.

Pattani

PATTANI, the traditional centre of the Muslim south, is a rather forbidding town, but presents a fascinating cultural clash embodied by the discord between its polychrome Chinese temples and the remains of its sixteenth-century mosque. Founded around the beginning of the fifteenth century, not long after the introduction of Islam to the area, Pattani soon became an important port for trade in the Gulf of Thailand. From the time of its founding, Pattani owed allegiance to the Thai kings at Ayutthaya, and after the capital was moved to Bangkok the city state was fully integrated into Thailand. However, having close ties with fellow Islamic states to the south, it has always chafed against the central power and is even now the focus of Muslim antipathy towards the Thai government. Although the port has declined, the industry and fisheries which in recent years have been established around the town have turned it into a busy, though rather ugly, commercial centre.

Pattani is also home to a sizeable Chinese community, whose rivalry with Islam is enshrined in the town's most famous legend. In the 1570s a certain Lim Toh Khiem, a notorious Chinese pirate, married a local woman and was converted to Islam. To show his conviction in his new faith, he began a mosque – at which point, legend has it, his sister Lim Ko Niaw sailed from China to persuade him to renounce Islam and return to his homeland. When her mission failed she hanged herself from the nearest cashew-nut tree, which was later carved into a statue of her, preserved at the **San Jao Lim Ko Niaw** on Arnoaru Road, a side street off the northern stretch of Yarang Road, the main north–south street. It's a gaudy, dimly lit shrine, groaning with rich offerings and grimy with the soot of endless joss-sticks, with the doll-like image of Lim Ko Niaw as its centrepiece. During the annual Lim Ko Niaw festival, held in the mini-stadium opposite in the middle of the third lunar month (usually March), the image is carried through a raging bonfire by entranced devotees, who by this and other masochistic feats seek to prove their purity to their heroine goddess.

Lim Ko Niaw's suicide put a curse on her brother's mosque, the **Masjid Kreu Se**, which confounded his and his successors' attempts to finish it. Located 5km east of town towards Narathiwat, the roofless brick shell was recently renovated by the Thai authorities as a historical and touristic site, causing great offence among the local population – in May 1990 ten thousand people gathered here to vent their anger. An unofficial Muslim guard is now stationed near the entrance at all times, to prevent non-Muslims from walking onto the holy ruins. Next door to the mosque the Chinese have built an ostentatious shrine around the horseshoe burial mound of Lim Ko Niaw. The mosque can be visited by songthaew or bus from Ramkomud Road, the eastern continuation of Rudee Road, whose intersection with Yarang Road marks the centre of town.

Facilities for visitors are very limited, though at a pinch the town could be visited on a long day trip from Hat Yai or as a break in the journey south; the bus station is towards the south end of Yarang Road. The pick of a pitiful choice of **hotels** in Pattani is the central *Palace*, on Preeda Road, between Pipit and Rudee roads (☎073/349171; ②–④), which has reasonably clean fan-cooled and air-conditioned rooms. The best place to **eat** is the busy night market on the north side of Pipit Road.

South to Yala and the border

From Pattani, Highway 410 heads due south to Yala, a dull but efficient town 43km across the coastal plain, then on for 140km through the mountains to Betong, the most southerly point on the Thai-Malaysian border. This makes a quiet, scenic route into Malaysia but otherwise has little to offer.

Yala

YALA is the business and education centre of the Muslim border provinces, a town of tree-lined boulevards that's won awards as the cleanest town in Thailand. An uninspiring place, its liveliest time is during the **ASEAN Barred Ground Dove Festival**, usually in the first weekend of March, when hundreds of competitors flock here from all over Southeast Asia. The breeding of luck-bringing Java doves is an obsession among the Muslim population of the south, where most houses have a cage outside and many villages feature fields of metal poles on which to hang the cages during the competition season, which is normally March and April. The birds are judged on the pitch, melody and volume of their cooing and on their appearance, and the most musical specimens change hands for as much as two million baht at the Yala jamboree.

Though staunchly Islamic, Yala attracts busloads of Buddhist pilgrims, who come to revere the 25-metre-long reclining Buddha at **Wat Khuhaphimuk** (Wat Na Tham), 8km out of town on the road to Yaha and Hat Yai. The image's aura of holiness comes from its atmospheric setting in a broad, dank cave, and from its great age: it's said that the image was constructed and the temple founded by a king of Palembang (Sumatra), some time around the end of the eighth century. To get there, take a bus from behind the *Thepvimarn* hotel, listed over, which will leave you with a five-hundred-metre walk south to the temple.

The train station, opposite which share taxis and air-conditioned minibuses congregate, is on the east side of the centre; buses from Pattani stop on Siriros Road, north of the station and east of the tracks – those from Hat Yai stop 500m west on the same road. If you need somewhere **to stay**, the best budget deal is *Thepvimarn* at 31 Sribumrung Rd (☎073/212400; ②–④), which has large, clean fan-cooled and air-conditioned rooms; coming from the train station, it's the first left off Pipitpakdee Road. For an evening **meal** of simple, reasonable seafood, try the popular *Talat Restaurant* at the corner of Sribumrung and Pipitpakdee roads.

Betong

Perched on the tip of a narrow tongue of land reaching into Malaysia, **BETONG** is only worth considering if you're heading out of the country – the town is notorious for its fog, and most of Betong's visitors come across the border for shopping and brothel-creeping. The mountainous route from Yala is largely the preserve of share taxis and air-conditioned minibuses, which cover the ground in three hours, as the one sluggish bus a day takes around six hours. From here you can **cross the border** by taxi to Keroh in Malaysia, which gives access to Sungai Petani and the west coast.

Along the coast from Pattani

The coastal region between Pattani and the Malaysian border is one of the least developed areas of the deep south, but it contains a couple of stunning beaches and its towns – **Saiburi** and **Narathiwat** – are appealingly ramshackle. The best way of getting around within this area is on the regular local buses, although the train stations at the border crossing of Sungai Kolok and at Tanyongmat (for Narathiwat) are useful if you're coming into the region from the north.

Saiburi and around

SAIBURI, 50km from Pattani on the bus route to Narathiwat, is a relaxing, leafy town sprinkled with evidence of its former importance as a trading port – ancient Chinese shophouses, dilapidated wooden mansions, and the brick shell of a four-hundred-year-old mosque, Masjid Khao, preserved in landscaped gardens. About 2km from the centre, across the Saiburi River and behind the fishing port, the quiet, tree-lined beach of **Hat Wasukri** is serviced by a handful of restaurants and *Ton Tan Resort* (③), the town's only accommodation, whose basic concrete bungalows are equipped with fans and bathrooms.

The best of this area, however, lies along the minor road (4157) back up the coast towards **Panare**. The remote riverside village of **Ban Pasey Yawo** (Ban Bon), 2km up the road, is renowned as the biggest and best centre for the manufacture of **korlae** boats, the beautifully decorated smacks used by Muslim fishermen all along this coast, and visitors are welcome to watch the craftsmen at work in the shade of the village's coconut plantation. The intricacy and extent of their decoration is what makes these boats unique – floral motifs and pastoral scenes cover every centimetre, from the bird-of-paradise figurehead to the *singtoh* lion god at the stern, thought to protect the fishermen from the spirits of the sea. Each boat is entirely handmade, takes four months to complete and sells for over B50,000, although B1000–3000 replicas are produced as a sideline.

About 15km further up towards Panare, you'll come to **Hat Kae Kae**, an idyllic seaside hamlet which gets its onomatopoeic name from the sound the sea makes when it hits the smooth boulders on the small, steeply sloping beach. To get this far, you'll need to take a songthaew bound for Panare – ask to be let off at Hat Kae Kae and you'll be left with a five-hundred-metre walk over a low rocky rise to reach the seashore. Among the shady palm trees, two sturdy **bungalows** (③) can usually be rented, though fresh water is sometimes a problem, and there's a beachside restaurant.

Narathiwat and around

NARATHIWAT, 50km on from Saiburi, feels like an outsized village, with goats and cows roaming its quiet, potholed streets, but the violently modern mosque which casts a huge shadow over the northern end gives away the town's status as the provincial capital. An easy-going place in which to soak up the atmosphere for a couple of days, Narathiwat also offers the opportunity of a day at the beach and an excursion to the beautiful **Wat Chonthara Sing He**, and has a decent range of hotels and restaurants.

The town is set on the west bank of the slowly curving Bang Nara River, at the mouth of which, just five minutes' walk north of the centre, sits a shanty fishing village fronted by *korlae* boats (see facing page). It's worth getting up early on a Friday morning for the bustling, colourful **market** which sprawls over the north end of Thanon Na (the main riverbank road). Local batiks are sold here, as well as all kinds of food, including the local replacement for fish sauce, a beige concoction called *budu*: it's made from lemon, chilli, onion and raw sugar.

Just beyond the fishing village, peaceful deck-chair restaurants overlook Hat Narathat, a beach too dangerous for swimming. Fortunately, the best **beach** in the area, **Ao Manao**, 3km south towards Tak Bai, then 3km left down a paved side road, is within easy motorbike-taxi reach. Known as Lemon Bay due to the long, gentle curve of its coastline, this beautiful stretch is lined with trees and dotted with seafood restaurants.

Narathiwat's two main streets run from north to south: Thanon Na (aka Puphapugdee Road) and the inland Pichit Bamrung Road, where most **buses** make a stop to the south of the clock tower – though the bus terminal is on the southwest side of town. **Trains** on the line to Sungai Kolok stop at **Tanyongmat**, a half-hour bus ride from the centre. Hat Yai, Sungai Kolok and Ban Taba air-conditioned minibuses are based at a small office at 308/5 Pichit Bamrung Rd; share taxis hang around further north on the same road.

The best of the town's budget **hotels**, *Narathiwat*, at 341 Thanon Na (☎073/511063; ①), occupies a characterful wooden building overlooking the river. On a cross street towards the north end of town, the friendly and comfortable *Tanyong Hotel* at 16/1 Sopapisai Rd (☎073/511477–9; ④) is highly recommended for a splurge. The top **restaurant** is the swish *Mankornthong* at 433 Thanon Na, fronted by Chinese dragons with a floating platform at the back – the varied food is pricey but very good. If you're counting your baht, head for the small night market behind the *Bang Nara Hotel* on Pichit Bamrung Road. For **lunch**, try the *kai ko lay* (chicken in a mild thick curry) at the inexpensive restaurant opposite the *Tanyong Hotel*.

Wat Chonthara Sing He

One of the finest bots in Thailand lies about 30km further down the coast in **TAK BAI**, which can either be visited as an easy day trip from Narathiwat or on your way to the border – frequent buses bound for Sungai Kolok or Ban Taba pass through the small town. (About 7km into the hour long trip, you can't miss the **Taksin Ratchaniwet**, the king's palace, which stands on a wooded hill overlooking the sea.)

Standing in a sandy, tree-shaded compound by the river, the bot at **Wat Chonthara Sing He** (Wat Chon) was built in the middle of the last century, as an emblem of Thai sovereignty to prove that Narathiwat was an integral part of Thailand, at a time when the British were claiming the area as part of Malaya. The building's brightly coloured fifteen-tiered roof exemplifies the fashion for curvaceous Chinese styles, here mixed with typical southern Thai features, such as the spiky white nagas, to produce an elegant, dynamic structure. Ask a monk for the key and look at the lively, well-preserved murals which completely cover the interior, portraying bawdy love scenes as well as many typical details of southern life – bull- and goat-fighting, and men dressed in turbans and long sarongs.

Crossing the border

South of Narathiwat, you can cross to Malaysia at one of two frontier posts, both of which are well connected to Kota Baru, the nearest town on the other side. Frequent buses from Narathiwat make the ninety-minute trip to the riverside frontier post of **BAN TABA**, a village 5km beyond Tak Bai with a couple of mediocre hotels in case you're really stuck. From here a B5 ferry will shuttle you across to the Malaysian town of Pengalan Kubur, which has frequent taxis and buses to Kota Baru.

Coming from points north of Narathiwat, transport connections are likely to draw you inland to **SUNGAI KOLOK**, a seedy brothel town popular with Malaysian weekenders. The longer established of the border posts, Sungai Kolok is the end of the rail line from Bangkok, its station in the northern part of town a mere kilometre west of the frontier bridge; motorbike taxis and samlors cover the ground if you can't face the walk. Hat Yai, Narathiwat, Yala and Pattani airconditioned minibuses are based opposite the station, and most buses stop to set down or pick up there, too. From Rantau Panjang on the other side, frequent taxis and buses head for Kota Baru. There should be no reason for you to stay in Kolok, but if you need a **hotel**, the best of the town's many budget places is the *Thanee*, at 4/1 Cheunmanka Rd (☎073/611241; ②), five minutes' walk south from the train station down Charoenkhet Rd (turn right at the *Merlin Hotel*) – like most of Kolok's hotels, it doubles up as a brothel, but the rooms are clean enough and the staff reasonably helpful. **TAT** maintains a small office, with responsibility for the provinces of Narathiwat, Yala and Pattani, right beside the frontier checkpoint (☎073/612126).

travel details

Trains

Bangkok to: Butterworth, Malaysia (1 daily; 21hr); Hat Yai (4 daily; 16hr); Nakhon (1 daily; 5hr); Padang Besar (1 daily; 17hr); Phatthalung (4 daily; 15hr); Sungai Kolok (2 daily; 20hr); Trang (1 daily; 16hr); Yala (3 daily; 18hr).

Hat Yai to: Bangkok (4 daily; 16hr); Butterworth, Malaysia (1 daily; 5hr); Kuala Lumpur (1 daily; 14hr); Padang Besar (2 daily; 1–3hr); Phatthalung (9 daily; 2hr); Sungai Kolok (6 daily; 3hr 30min– 5hr); Surat (6 daily; 6hr–7hr 30min); Yala (7 daily; 2–3hr).

Sungai Kolok to: Bangkok (2 daily; 20hr); Hat Yai (6 daily; 3hr 30min–5hr); Nakhon (1 daily; 9hr); Phatthalung (5 daily; 7hr); Surat (3 daily; 12hr); Yala (5 daily; 2hr 30min).

Buses

Bangkok to: Hat Yai (13 daily; 14hr); Narathiwat (3 daily; 17hr); Pattani (2 daily; 16hr); Phatthalung (4 daily; 13hr); Satun (2 daily; 16hr); Sungai Kolok (3 daily; 20hr); Trang (8 daily; 14hr); Yala (3 daily; 16hr).

Hat Yai to: Chumphon (5 daily; 9hr); Krabi (11 daily; 4–5hr); Ko Samui (1 daily; 7hr); Nakhon (16 daily; 3–4hr); Narathiwat (8 daily; 3–4hr); Padang Besar (every 30min; 1hr 30min); Pak Bara (3 daily; 2hr 30min); Pattani (every 30min; 2–3hr); Phatthalung (every 30min; 1hr 30min); Phuket (11 daily; 7–9hr); Satun (every 15min; 1hr 30min); Songkhla (every 15min; 30min); Sungai Kolok (5 daily; 4hr); Surat Thani (9 daily; 5hr); Trang (hourly; 3hr); Yala (every 30min; 2–3hr).

Narathiwat to: Ban Taba (every 30min; 1hr 30min); Pattani (every 30min; 2hr); Sungai Kolok (every 30min; 2hr); Tak Bai (every 30min; 1hr).

Songkhla to: Chana (every 30min; 30min); Nakhon (every 30min; 3hr); Pattani (2 daily; 2hr); Ranot (every 30min; 1–2hr).

Sungai Kolok to: Hat Yai (5 daily; 4hr); Narathiwat (hourly; 1hr); Pattani (4 daily; 2hr); Surat Thani (3 daily; 9–10hr); Tak Bai (hourly; 30min).

Trang to: Krabi (hourly; 2hr); Nakhon Si Thammarat (hourly; 2hr); Phatthalung (hourly; 1hr); Phuket (11 daily; 4hr 30min); Satun (every 30min; 3hr).

Yala to: Betong (1 daily; 4hr).

Flights

Bangkok to: Hat Yai (4–6 daily; 1hr 30min); Trang (3 weekly; 2hr).

Hat Yai to: Johore Baru, Malaysia (3 weekly; 4hr); Kuala Lumpur (7 weekly; 1hr); Phuket (2 daily; 1hr); Singapore (14 weekly; 1hr 30min–4hr).

Phuket to: Narathiwat (3 weekly; 1hr 15min); Trang (4 weekly; 40min).

PART THREE

THE

CONTEXTS

THE HISTORICAL FRAMEWORK

BEGINNINGS

As long as forty thousand years ago, Thailand was inhabited by **hunter-gatherers** who lived in semi-permanent settlements and used tools made of wood, bamboo and stone. By the end of the last Ice Age around ten thousand years ago, these groups had become **farmers**, keeping chickens, pigs and cattle, and – as evidenced by the seeds and plant husks which have been discovered in caves in northern Thailand – cultivating rice and beans. This drift into an agricultural society gave rise to further technological developments: the earliest **pottery** found in Thailand has been dated to 6800 BC, while the recent excavations at **Ban Chiang** in the northeast have shown that **bronze** was being worked at least as early as 2000 BC, putting Thailand on a par with Mesopotamia, which has traditionally been regarded as the earliest Bronze Age culture. By two thousand years ago, the peoples of Southeast Asia had settled in small villages among which there was regular communication and trade, but they had split into several broad families, differentiated by language and culture. At this time, the ancestors of the Thais, speaking proto-Thai languages, were still far away in southeastern China, whereas Thailand itself was inhabited by Austroasiatic speakers, among whom the Mon were to establish the region's first distinctive civilization, Dvaravati.

DVARAVATI AND SRIVIJAYA

The history of **Dvaravati** is ill-defined to say the least, but the name is applied to a distinctive culture complex which shared the **Mon** language and **Theravada Buddhism**. This form of religion probably entered Thailand during the second or third centuries BC, when Indian missionaries were sent to Suvarnabhumi, "land of gold", which seems to correspond to the broad swathe of fertile land stretching from southern Burma across the north end of the Gulf of Thailand.

From the discovery of monastery boundary stones (*sema*), clay votive tablets and Indian-influenced Buddhist sculpture it's clear that Dvaravati was an extensive and prosperous Buddhist civilization which had its greatest flourishing between the sixth and ninth centuries AD. No strong evidence has turned up, however, for the existence of a single capital – rather than an empire, Dvaravati seems to have been a collection of city states, which, at least in their early history, came under the lax suzerainty of **Funan**, a poorly documented kingdom centred in Cambodia. Nakhon Pathom, Lopburi, Si Thep and Muang Sema were among the most important Dvaravati sites, and their concentration around the Chao Phraya valley would seem to show that they gained much of their prosperity, and maintained religious and cultural contacts with India, via the **trade route** from the Indian Ocean over the Three Pagodas Pass.

Although they passed on aspects of their heavily Indianized art, religion and government to later rulers of Thailand, these Mon city states were politically fragile and from the ninth century onwards succumbed to the domination of the invading Khmers from Cambodia. One northern outpost, the state of **Haripunjaya** centred on Lamphun, which had been set up on the trade route with southern China, maintained its independence probably until the beginning of the eleventh century.

Meanwhile, to the south of Dvaravati, the shadowy Indianized state of Lankasuka had grown up in the second century, centred on Ligor (now Nakhon Si Thammarat) and covering an area of the Malay peninsula which included the important trade crossings at Chaiya and Trang. In the eighth century, it came under the control of the **Srivijaya** empire, a Mahayana Buddhist state centred on Sumatra which had strong ties with India and a complex but uneasy relationship with neighbouring Java. Thriving on seaborne trade between Persia and China, Srivijaya extended its influence as far north as Chaiya, its regional capital, where discoveries of temple remains and some of the finest stone and bronze statues ever produced in Thailand have borne witness to the cultural vitality of this crossroads empire. In the tenth century the northern part of Lankasuka, under the name **Tambralinga**, regained a measure of independence, although it seems still to have come under the influence of Srivijaya as well as owing some form of allegiance to Dvaravati. By the beginning of the eleventh century, however, peninsular Thailand had come under the sway of the Khmer empire, with a Cambodian prince ruling over a community of Khmer settlers and soldiers at Tambralinga.

THE KHMERS

The history of central Southeast Asia comes into sharper focus with the emergence of the **Khmers**, vigorous empire-builders whose political history can be pieced together from the numerous stone inscriptions they left. Originally vassal subjects of Funan, the Khmers of **Chenla** – to the north of Cambodia – seized power in the latter half of the sixth century during a period of economic decline in the area. Chenla's rise to power was knocked back by a punitive expedition conducted by the Srivijaya empire in the eighth century, but was reconsolidated during the watershed reign of **Jayavarman II** (802–50), who succeeded in conquering the whole of Kambuja, an area which roughly corresponds to modern-day Cambodia. In order to establish the authority of his monarchy and of his country, Jayavarman II had himself initiated as a *chakravartin* or universal ruler, the living embodiment of the **devaraja**, the divine essence of kingship – a concept which was adopted by later Thai rulers. Taking as the symbol of his authority the phallic *lingam*, the king was thus identified with the god Shiva, although the Khmer concept of kingship and thus the religious mix of the state as a whole was not confined to Hinduism – elements of ancestor worship were also included, and Mahayana Buddhism gradually increased its hold over the next four centuries.

It was Jayavarman II who moved the Khmer capital to **Angkor** in northern Cambodia, which he and later kings, especially after the eleventh century, embellished with a series of prodigiously beautiful temples. Jayavarman II also recognized the advantages of the lakes around Angkor for irrigating ricefields and providing fish, and thus for feeding a large population. His successors developed this idea and gave the state a sound economic core with a remarkably complex system of **reservoirs** (*baray*) and water channels, which were copied and adapted in later Thai cities.

In the ninth and tenth centuries, Jayavarman II and his imperialistic successors, especially **Yasovarman I** (889–900), confirmed Angkor as the major power in Southeast Asia. They pushed into Vietnam, Laos, southern China and into northeastern Thailand, where the Khmers left dozens of Angkor-style temple complexes, as seen today at Prasat Phanom Rung and Prasat Hin Phimai. To the west and northwest, Angkor took control over central Thailand, with its most important outpost at Lopburi, and even established a strong presence to the south on the Malay peninsula. As a result of this expansion, the Khmers were masters of the most important trade routes between India and China and indeed nearly every communications link in the region, from which they were able to derive huge income and strength.

The reign of **Jayavarman VII** (1181–1219), a Mahayana Buddhist who firmly believed in his royal destiny as a *bodhisattva*, a Buddha-to-be, sowed the seeds of Angkor's downfall. Nearly half of all the extant great religious monuments of the empire were erected under his supervision, but the ambitious scale of these building projects and the upkeep they demanded – some 300,000 priests and temple servants of 20,000 shrines consumed 38,000 tons of rice per year – along with a series of wars against Vietnam, terminally exhausted the economy.

In subsequent reigns, much of the life-giving irrigation system around Angkor turned into malarial swamp through neglect, and the rise of the more democratic creed of Theravada Buddhism undermined the divine authority which the Khmer kings had derived from the hierarchical Mahayana creed. As a result of all these factors, the Khmers were in no position to resist the onslaught between the thirteenth and fifteenth centuries of the vibrant new force in Southeast Asia, the Thais.

THE EARLIEST THAIS

The earliest traceable history of the **Thai people** picks them up in southern China around the fifth century AD, when they were squeezed by Chinese and Vietnamese expansionism into sparsely inhabited northeastern Laos and neighbouring areas. The first entry of a significant number of Thais onto what is now Thailand's soil seems to have happened in the region of Chiang Saen, where it appears that some time after the seventh century the Thais formed a state in an area then known as **Yonok**. A development which can be more accurately dated and which had immense cultural significance was the spread of Theravada Buddhism to Yonok via Dvaravati around the end of the tenth century, which served not only to unify the Thais but also to link them to Mon civilization and give them a sense of belonging to the community of Buddhists.

The Thais' political development was also aided by **Nan-chao**, a well-organized military state comprising a huge variety of ethnic groups, which established itself as a major player on the southern fringes of the Chinese empire from the beginning of the eighth century. As far as can be gathered, Nan-chao permitted the rise of Thai *muang* or small principalities on its periphery, especially in the area immediately to the south known as **Sipsong Panna**.

Thai infiltration continued until, by the end of the twelfth century, they seem to have formed the majority of the population in Thailand, then under the control of the Khmer empire. The Khmers' main outpost, at Lopburi, was by then regarded as the administrative capital of a land called "Syam" (possibly from the Sanskrit *syam*, meaning swarthy) – a mid-twelfth-century bas-relief at Angkor Wat portraying the troops of Lopburi preceded by a large group of self-confident Syam Kuk mercenaries, shows that the Thais were becoming a force to be reckoned with.

SUKHOTHAI

By the middle of the thirteenth century, the Thais, thanks largely to the decline of Angkor and the inspiring effect of Theravada Buddhism,

were poised on the verge of autonomous power. The final catalyst was the invasion by Qubilai Khan's Mongol armies of China and Nan-chao, which began around 1215 and was completed in the 1250s. Demanding that the whole world should acknowledge the primacy of the Great Khan, the Mongols set their hearts on the "pacification" of the "barbarians" to the south of China, which obliged the Thais to form a broad power base to meet the threat.

The founding of the first Thai kingdom at **Sukhothai**, now popularly viewed as the cornerstone of the country's development, was in fact a small-scale piece of opportunism which almost fell at the first hurdle. At some time around 1238, the princes of two small Thai principalities in the upper Chao Phraya valley joined forces to capture the main Khmer outpost in the region at Sukhothai. One of the princes, **Intradit**, was crowned king, but for the first forty years Sukhothai remained merely a local power, whose existence was threatened by the ambitions of neighbouring princes. When attacked by the ruler of Mae Sot, Intradit's army was only saved by the grand entrance of Sukhothai's most dynamic leader: the king's nineteen-year-old son, Rama, held his ground and pushed forward to defeat the opposing commander, earning himself the name **Ramkhamhaeng**, "Rama the Bold".

When Ramkhamhaeng came to the throne around 1278, he saw the south as his most promising avenue for expansion and, copying the formidable military organization of the Mongols, seized control of much of the Chao Phraya valley. Over the next twenty years, largely by diplomacy rather than military action, Ramkhamhaeng gained the submission of most of the rulers of Thailand, who entered the **new empire**'s complex tributary system either through the pressure of the Sukhothai king's personal connections or out of recognition of his superior military strength and moral prestige. To the east, Ramkhamhaeng pushed as far as Vientiane in Laos; by marrying his daughter to a Mon ruler to the west, he obtained the allegiance of parts of southern Burma; and to the south his vassals stretched down the peninsula at least as far as Nakhon Si Thammarat. To the north, Sukhothai concluded an alliance with the parallel Thai states of Lanna and Phayao in 1287 for mutual protection against the Mongols – though it appears that Ramkhamhaeng managed to pinch several *muang* on their eastern periphery as tribute states.

Meanwhile **Lopburi**, which had wrested itself free from Angkor sometime in the middle of the thirteenth century, was able to keep its independence and its control of the eastern side of the Chao Phraya valley – having been first a major cultural and religious centre for the Mons, then the Khmers' provincial capital, and now a state dominated by migrating Thais, Lopburi was a strong and vibrant place mixing the best of the three cultures, as evidenced by the numerous original works of art produced at this time.

Although the empire of Sukhothai extended Thai control over a vast area, its greatest contribution to the Thais' development was at home, in cultural and political matters. A famous **inscription** by Ramkhamhaeng, now housed in the Bangkok National Museum, describes a prosperous era of benevolent rule: "In the time of King Ramkhamhaeng this land of Sukhothai is thriving. There is fish in the water and rice in the fields . . . [The King] has hung a bell in the opening of the gate over there: if any commoner has a grievance which sickens his belly and gripes his heart . . . he goes and strikes the bell . . . [and King Ramkhamhaeng] questions the man, examines the case, and decides it justly for him." Although this plainly smacks of self-promotion, it seems to contain at least a kernel of truth: in deliberate contrast to the Khmer god-kings, Ramkhamhaeng styled himself as a **dhammaraja**, a king who ruled justly according to Theravada Buddhist doctrine and made himself accessible to his people. To honour the state religion, the city's temples were lavishly endowed: as original as Sukhothai's political systems were its religious **architecture and sculpture**, which, though bound to borrow from existing Khmer and Sri Lankan styles, shows the greatest leap of creativity at any stage in the history of art in Thailand. A further sign of the Thais' new self-confidence was the invention of a new **script** to make their tonal language understood by the non-Thai inhabitants of the land.

All this was achieved in a remarkably short period of time. After the death of Ramkhamhaeng around 1299, his successors took their Buddhism so seriously that they neglected affairs of state. The empire quickly fell apart, and by 1320 Sukhothai had regressed to being a kingdom of only local significance.

LANNA

Almost simultaneous with the birth of Sukhothai was the establishment of a less momentous but longer-lasting kingdom to the north, called **Lanna**. Its founding father was **Mengrai**, chief of Ngon Yang, a small principality on the banks of the Mekhong near modern-day Chiang Saen. Around 1259 he set out to unify the squabbling Thai principalities of the region, first building a strategically placed city at Chiang Rai in 1262, and then forging alliances with Ngam Muang, the Thai king of Phayao, and with Ramkhamhaeng of Sukhothai.

In 1281, after ten years of guileful preparations, Mengrai conquered the Mon kingdom of Haripunjaya based at Lamphun, and was now master of northern Thailand. Taking advice from Ngam Muang and Ramkhamhaeng, in 1292 he selected a site for an impressive new capital of Lanna at **Chiang Mai**, which remains the centre of the north to the present day. Mengrai concluded further alliances in Burma and Laos, making him strong enough to successfully resist further Mongol attacks, although he was eventually obliged to bow to the superiority of the Mongols by sending them small tributes from 1312 onwards. When Mengrai died after a sixty-year reign in 1317, supposedly struck by a bolt of lightning, he had built up an extensive and powerful kingdom. But although he began a tradition of humane, reasonable laws, probably borrowed from the Mons, he had found little time to set up sound political and administrative institutions. His death severely destabilized Lanna, which quickly shrank in size and influence.

It was only in the reign of **Ku Na** (1355–85) that Lanna's development regained momentum. A well-educated and effective ruler, Ku Na enticed the venerable monk Sumana from Sukhothai in 1369, to establish an ascetic Sri Lankan sect in Lanna. Sumana brought a number of Buddha images with him, inspiring a new school of art that flourished for over a century, but more importantly his sect became a cultural force that had a profound unifying effect on the kingdom. The influence of Buddhism was further strengthened under

King Tilok (1441–87), who built many great monuments at Chiang Mai and cast huge numbers of bronze seated Buddhas in the style of the central image at Bodhgaya in India, the scene of the Buddha's enlightenment. Tilok, however, is best remembered as a great warrior, who spent most of his reign resisting the advances of Ayutthaya, by now the strongest Thai kingdom.

Under continuing pressure both from Ayutthaya and from Burma, Lanna went into rapid decline in the second quarter of the sixteenth century. For a short period after 1546, Chiang Mai came under the control of Setthathirat, the king of Lan Sang (Laos), but, unable to cope with Lanna's warring factions, he then abdicated, purloining the talismanic Emerald Buddha for his own capital at Luang Prabang. In 1558, Burma decisively captured Chiang Mai and the Mengrai dynasty came to an end. For most of the next two centuries, the Burmese maintained control through a succession of puppet rulers, and Lanna again became much as it had been before Mengrai, little more than a chain of competing principalities.

AYUTTHAYA

While Lanna was fighting for its place as a marginalized kingdom, from the fourteenth century onwards the seeds of a full-blown Thai nation were being sown to the south at **Ayutthaya**. The city of Ayutthaya itself was founded on its present site in 1351 by U Thong, "Prince Golden Cradle", when his own town, Lopburi, was ravaged by smallpox. Taking the title **Ramathibodi**, he soon united the principalities of the lower Chao Phraya valley, which had formed the western provinces of the Khmer empire. When he recruited his bureaucracy from the urban elite of Lopburi, Ramathibodi set the **style of government** at Ayutthaya – the elaborate etiquette, language and rituals of Angkor were adopted, and, most importantly, the conception of the ruler as *devaraja*. The king became sacred and remote, an object of awe and dread, with none of the accessibility of the kings of Sukhothai: when he processed through the town, ordinary people were forbidden to look at him and had to be silent while he passed. This hierarchical system also provided the state with much-needed manpower, as all freemen were obliged to give up six months of each year to the Crown either on public works or military service.

The site chosen by Ramathibodi turned out to be the best in the region for an international port and so began Ayutthaya's rise to prosperity, based on its ability to exploit the upswing in **trade** in the middle of the fourteenth century along the routes between India and China. Flushed with economic success, Ramathibodi's successors were able to expand their control over the ailing states in the region. After a long period of subjugation, Sukhothai became a province of the Kingdom of Ayutthaya in 1438, six years after Boromraja II had powerfully demonstrated Ayutthaya's pre-eminence by capturing the once-mighty Angkor, enslaving large numbers of its subjects and looting the Khmer royal regalia. (The Cambodian royal family were forced to abandon the palace forever and to found a new capital near Phnom Penh.)

Although a century of nearly continuous warfare against Lanna was less decisive, success generally bred success, and Ayutthaya's increasing wealth through trade brought ever greater power over its neighbouring states. To streamline the functioning of his unwieldy empire, **Trailok** (1448–88) found it necessary to make reforms of its administration. His **Law of Civil Hierarchy** formally entrenched the inequality of Ayutthayan society, defining the status of every individual by assigning him or her an imaginary number of rice fields – for example, 25 for an ordinary freeman and 10,000 for the highest ministers of state. Trailok's legacy is found in today's unofficial but fiendishly complex status system, by which everyone in Thailand knows his place.

Ramathibodi II (1491–1529), almost at a loss as to what to do with his enormous wealth, undertook an extensive programme of public works. In the 1490s he built several major religious monuments and between 1500 and 1503 cast the largest standing metal image of the Buddha ever known, the Phra Si Sanphet, which gave its name to the temple of the Royal Palace. By 1540, the Kingdom of Ayutthaya had grown to cover most of the area of modern-day Thailand.

BURMESE WARS AND EUROPEAN TRADE

In the sixteenth century recurring tensions with Burma led **Chakkraphat** (1548–69) to improve his army and build brick ramparts around the capital. This was to no avail, however: in 1568 the Burmese besieged Ayutthaya with a huge army, said by later accounts to have consisted of 1,400,000 men. The Thais held out until August 8, 1569, when treachery within their own ranks helped the Burmese to break through the defences. The Burmese looted the city, took thousands of prisoners and installed a vassal king to keep control.

The decisive character who broke the Burmese stranglehold twenty years later and re-established Ayutthaya's economic growth was **Naresuan** (1590–1605), who defied the Burmese by amassing a large army to defend Ayutthaya. The enemy sent a punitive expedition which was conclusively defeated at Nong Sarai near modern-day Suphanburi on January 18, 1593, Naresuan himself turning the battle by killing the Burmese crown prince. Historians have praised Naresuan for his personal bravery and his dynamic leadership, although the chronicles of the time record a strong streak of tyranny – in his fifteen years as king he had 80,000 people killed, excluding the victims of war. A favoured means of punishment was to slice off pieces of the offender's flesh, which he was then made to eat in the king's presence.

The period following Naresuan's reign was characterized by a more sophisticated engagement in **foreign trade**. In 1511 the Portuguese had become the first Western power to trade with Ayutthaya, and Naresuan himself concluded a treaty with Spain in 1598; relations with Holland and England were initiated in 1608 and 1612 respectively. For most of the seventeenth century, European merchants flocked to Thailand, not only to buy Thai products, but also to gain access to Chinese and Japanese goods on sale there. The role of foreigners at Ayutthaya reached its peak under **Narai** (1656–88), but he overstepped the mark in cultivating close links with Louis XIV of France, who secretly harboured the notion of converting Ayutthaya to Christianity. On Narai's death, relations with Westerners were severely cut back.

Despite this reduction of trade and prolonged civil strife over the succession to the throne whenever a king died – then, as now, there wasn't a fixed principle of primogeniture – Ayutthaya continued to flourish for much of the eighteenth century. The reign of **Borommakot** (1733–58) was particularly prosperous, producing many works of drama and poetry. Furthermore, Thai Buddhism had by then achieved such prestige that Sri Lanka, from where the Thais had

originally imported their form of religion in the thirteenth century, requested Thai aid in restoring their monastic orders in 1751.

However, immediately after the death of Borommakot the rumbling in the Burmese jungle to the north began to make itself heard again. Alaunghpaya of Burma, apparently a blindly aggressive country bumpkin, first recaptured the south of his country from the Mons, then turned his attentions on Ayutthaya. A siege in 1760 was unsuccessful, with Alaunghpaya dying of wounds sustained there, but the scene was set. In February 1766 the Burmese descended upon Ayutthaya for the last time. The Thais held out for over a year, during which they were afflicted by famine, epidemics and a terrible fire which destroyed ten thousand houses. Finally, in **April 1767**, the walls were breached and the city taken. The Burmese razed everything to the ground and tens of thousands of prisoners were led off to Burma, including most of the royal family. The king, Suriyamarin, is said to have escaped from the city in a boat and starved to death ten days later. As one observer has said, the Burmese laid waste to Ayutthaya "in such a savage manner that it is hard to imagine that they shared the same religion with the Siamese." The city was abandoned to the jungle, but with remarkable speed the Thais regrouped and established a new seat of power, further down the Chao Phraya River at Bangkok.

THE EARLY BANGKOK EMPIRE

As the bulk of the Burmese army was obliged by war with China to withdraw almost immediately, Thailand was left to descend into banditry. Out of this lawless mess several centres of power arose, the most significant being at Chanthaburi, commanded by **Phraya Taksin**. A charismatic, brave and able general who had been unfairly blamed for a failed counter-attack against the Burmese at Ayutthaya, Taksin had anticipated the fall of the besieged city and quietly slipped away with a force of five hundred men. In June 1767 he took control of the east-coast strip around Chanthaburi and very rapidly expanded his power across central Thailand.

Blessed with the financial backing of the Chinese trading community, to whom he was connected through his father, Taksin was crowned king in December 1768 at his new capital of Thonburi, on the opposite bank of the river from modern-day Bangkok. One by one the new king defeated his rivals, and within two years he had restored all of Ayutthaya's territories. More remarkably, by the end of the next decade Taksin had outdone his Ayutthayan predecessors by bringing Lanna, Cambodia and much of Laos into a huge new empire. During this period of expansionism, Taksin left most of the fighting to Thong Duang, an ambitious soldier and descendant of an Ayutthayan noble family, who became the *chakri*, the military commander, and took the title **Chao Phraya Chakri**.

However, by 1779 all was not well with the king. Being an outsider, who had risen from an ordinary family on the fringes of society, Taksin became paranoid about plots against him, a delusion that drove him to imprison and torture even his wife and sons. At the same time he sank into religious excesses, demanding that the monkhood worship him as a god. By March 1782, public outrage at his sadism and dangerously irrational behaviour had reached such fervour that he was ousted in a coup.

Chao Phraya Chakri was invited to take power and had Taksin executed. In accordance with ancient etiquette, this had to be done without royal blood touching the earth: the mad king was duly wrapped in a black velvet sack and struck on the back of the neck with a sandalwood club. (Popular tradition has it that even this form of execution was too much: an unfortunate substitute got the velvet sack treatment, while Taksin was whisked away to a palace in the hills near Nakhon Si Thammarat, where he is said to have lived until 1825.)

RAMA I

With the support of the Ayutthayan aristocracy, Chakri – reigning as **Rama I** (1782–1809) – set about consolidating the Thai kingdom. His first act was to move the capital across the river to Bangkok, a better defensive position against any Burmese attack from the west. Borrowing from the layout of Ayutthaya, he built a new royal palace and impressive monasteries, and enshrined in the palace wat the Emerald Buddha, which he had snatched during his campaigns in Laos.

As all the state records had disappeared in the destruction of Ayutthaya, religious and legal texts had to be written afresh and historical chronicles reconstituted – with some very sketchy guesswork. The monkhood was in such a state of crisis that it was widely held that moral decay had been partly responsible for Ayutthaya's downfall. Within a month of becoming king, Rama I issued a series of religious laws and made appointments to the leadership of the monkhood, to restore discipline and confidence after the excesses of Taksin's reign. Many works of drama and poetry had also been lost in the sacking of Ayutthaya, so Rama I set about rebuilding the Thais' literary heritage, at the same time attempting to make it more cosmopolitan and populist. His main contribution was the *Ramakien*, a dramatic version of the Indian epic *Ramayana*, which is said to have been set to verse by the king himself, with a little help from his courtiers, in 1797. Heavily adapted to its Thai setting, the *Ramakien* served as an affirmation of the new monarchy and its divine links, and has since become the national epic.

In the early part of Rama I's reign, the Burmese reopened hostilities on several occasions, the biggest attempted invasion coming in 1785, but the emphatic manner in which the Thais repelled them only served to knit together the young kingdom. Trade with China revived, and the king addressed the besetting problem of manpower by ordering every man to be tattooed with the name of his master and his town, so that avoiding royal service became almost impossible. On a more general note, Rama I put the style of government in Thailand on a modern footing: while retaining many of the features of a *devaraja*, he shared more responsibility with his courtiers, as a first among equals.

RAMA II AND RAMA III

The peaceful accession of his son as **Rama II** (1809–24) signalled the establishment of the **Chakri dynasty**, which is still in place today. This Second Reign was a quiet interlude, best remembered as a fertile period for Thai literature. The king, himself one of the great Thai poets, gathered round him a group of writers including the famous Sunthorn Phu, who produced scores of masterly love poems, travel accounts and narrative songs.

In contrast, **Rama III** (1824–51) actively discouraged literary development – probably in reaction against his father – and was a vigorous defender of conservative values. To this end, he embarked on an extraordinary redevelopment of Wat Po, the oldest temple in Bangkok. Hundreds of educational inscriptions and mural paintings, on all manner of secular and religious subjects, were put on show, apparently to preserve traditional culture against the rapid change which the king saw corroding the country. In foreign affairs, Rama III faced a serious threat from the vassal states of Laos, who in 1827 sent an invading army from Vientiane, which got as far as Saraburi, only three days' march from Bangkok. The king's response was savage: having repelled the initial invasion, he ordered his army to destroy everything in Vientiane apart from Buddhist temples and to forcibly resettle huge numbers of Lao in Isaan. Shortly after, the king was forced to go to war in Cambodia, to save Buddhism and its traditional institutions from the attentions of the newly powerful, non-Buddhist Vietnamese. A series of campaigns in the 1830s and 1840s culminated in the peace treaty of 1845–46, which again established Thailand as the dominant influence in Cambodia.

More significant in the long run was the danger posed by the increase in Western influence which began in the Third Reign. As early as 1825, the Thais were sufficiently alarmed at British colonialism to strengthen Bangkok's defences by stretching a great iron chain across the mouth of the Chao Phraya River, to which every blacksmith in the area had to donate a certain number of links. In 1826 Rama III was obliged to sign a limited trade agreement with the British, the **Burney Treaty**, by which the Thais won some political security in return for reducing their taxes on goods passing through Bangkok. British and American missions in 1850 unsuccessfully demanded more radical concessions, but by this time Rama III was seriously ill, and it was left to his far-sighted and progressive successors to reach a decisive accommodation with the Western powers.

MONGKUT AND CHULALONGKORN

Rama IV, more commonly known as **Mongkut** (1851–68), had been a Buddhist monk for 27 years when he succeeded his brother. But far from leading a cloistered life, Mongkut had travelled widely throughout Thailand, had maintained scholarly contacts with French and American missionaries, and, like most of the country's new generation of leaders, had taken an interest in Western learning, studying English, Latin and the sciences. He had also turned his mind to the condition of Buddhism in Thailand, which seemed to him to have descended into little more than popular superstition; indeed, after a study of the Buddhist scriptures in Pali, he was horrified to find that Thai ordinations were probably invalid. So in the late 1830s he set up a rigorously fundamentalist sect called *Thammayutika*, the "Order Adhering to the Teachings of the Buddha", and as abbot of the order he oversaw the training of a generation of scholarly leaders for Thai Buddhism from his base at Bangkok's Wat Bowonniwet, which became a major centre of Western learning.

When his kingship faced its first major test, in the form of a threatening British mission in 1855 led by **Sir John Bowring**, Mongkut was able to deal with it confidently. Realizing that Thailand was unable to resist the military might of the British, the king reduced import and export taxes, allowed British subjects to live and own land in Thailand and granted them freedom of trade. Of the **government monopolies**, which had long been the mainstay of the Thai economy, only that on opium was retained. After making up the loss in revenue through internal taxation, Mongkut quickly made it known that he would welcome diplomatic contacts from other Western countries: within a decade, agreements similar to the Bowring Treaty had been signed with France, the United States and a score of other nations. Thus by skilful diplomacy the king avoided a close relationship with only one power, which could easily have led to Thailand's annexation.

While all around the colonial powers were carving up Southeast Asia amongst themselves, Thailand suffered nothing more than the weakening of its influence over Cambodia, which in 1863 the French brought under their protection. As a result of the open-door policy, foreign trade boomed, financing the redevelopment of Bangkok's waterfront and, for the first time, the building of paved roads. However, Mongkut ran out of time for instituting the far-reaching domestic reforms which he saw were needed to drag Thailand into the modern world.

THE MODERNIZATION OF THAILAND

Mongkut's son, **Chulalongkorn**, took the throne as Rama V (1868–1910) at the age of only fifteen, but he was well prepared by an excellent education which mixed traditional Thai and modern Western elements – provided by Mrs Anna Leonowens, subject of *The King and I*. When Chulalongkorn reached his majority after a five-year regency, he set to work on the reforms envisioned by his father. One of his first acts was to scrap the custom by which subjects were required to prostrate themselves in the presence of the king, which he followed up in 1874 with a series of decrees announcing the gradual abolition of slavery. The speed of his financial and administrative reforms, however, proved too much for the "**Ancients**" (*hua boran*), the old guard of ministers and officials inherited from his father. Their opposition culminated in the Front Palace Crisis of 1875, when a show of military strength almost plunged the country into civil war, and although Chulalongkorn skilfully defused the crisis, many of his reforms had to be quietly shelved for the time being.

An important administrative reform which did go through, necessitated by the threat of colonial expansionism, concerned the former kingdom of Lanna. British exploitation of teak had recently spread into northern Thailand from neighbouring Burma, so in 1874 Chulalongkorn sent a commissioner to Chiang Mai to keep an eye on the prince of Chiang Mai and make sure that he avoided any collision with the British. The commissioner was gradually able to limit the power of the princes and integrate the region more fully into the kingdom.

In the 1880s prospects for reform brightened as many of the "Ancients" died or retired. This allowed Chulalongkorn to **restructure the government** to meet the country's needs: the Royal Audit Office made possible the proper control of revenue and finance; the Department of the Army became the nucleus of a modern armed services; and a host of other departments were set up, for justice, education, public health and the like. To fill these new positions, the king appointed many of his younger brothers, who had all received a modern education, while scores of foreign technicians and advisers were brought in to help with everything from foreign affairs to rail lines.

Throughout this period, however, the Western powers maintained their pressure on the region. The most serious threat to Thai sovereignty was the **Franco-Siamese Crisis** of 1893, which culminated in the French, based in Vietnam, sending gunboats up the Chao Phraya

River to Bangkok. Flouting numerous international laws, France claimed control over Laos and made other outrageous demands, which Chulalongkorn had no option but to concede. In 1907 Thailand was also forced to relinquish Cambodia to the French, and in 1909 three Malay states fell to the British. In order to preserve its independence, the country ceded almost half of its territory and forewent huge sums of tax revenue. But from the end of the Fifth Reign, the frontiers were fixed as they are today.

By the time of the king's death in 1910, Thailand could not yet be called a modern nation state – corruption and nepotism were still grave problems, for example. However, Chulalongkorn had made remarkable advances, and, almost from scratch, had established the political institutions to cope with twentieth-century development.

THE END OF ABSOLUTE MONARCHY

Chulalongkorn was succeeded by a flamboyant, British-educated prince, **Vajiravudh** (1910–25), who was crowned as Rama VI. The new king found it difficult to shake the dominance of his father's appointees in the government, who formed an extremely narrow elite, comprised almost entirely of members of Chulalongkorn's family. In an attempt to build up a personal following, Vajiravudh created, in May 1911, the **Wild Tigers**, a nationwide paramilitary corps recruited widely from the civil service. However, in 1912 a group of young army lieutenants, disillusioned by the absolute monarchy and upset at the downgrading of the regular army in favour of the Wild Tigers, plotted a **coup**. The conspirators were easily broken up before any trouble began, but this was something new in Thai history: the country was used to in-fighting amongst the royal family, but not to military intrigue from men from comparatively ordinary backgrounds.

Vajiravudh's response to the coup was a series of modernizing **reforms**, including the introduction of compulsory primary education and an attempt to better the status of women by supporting monogamy in place of the widespread practice of polygamy. His huge output of writings invariably encouraged people to live as modern Westerners, and he brought large numbers of commoners into high positions in government.

Nonetheless, he would not relinquish his strong opposition to constitutional democracy.

When **World War I** broke out in 1914, the Thais were generally sympathetic to the Germans out of resentment over their loss of territory to the French and British. The king, however, was in favour of neutrality, until the United States entered the war in 1917, when Thailand followed the expedient policy of joining the winning side and sent an expeditionary force of 1300 men to France in June 1918. The goodwill earned by this gesture enabled the Thais, between 1920 and 1926, to negotiate away the unequal treaties which had been imposed on them by the Western powers. Foreigners on Thai soil were no longer exempted from Thai laws, and the Thais were allowed to set reasonable rates of import and export taxes.

Yet Vajiravudh's extravagant lifestyle – during his reign, royal expenditure amounted to as much as ten percent of the state budget – left severe financial problems for his successor. Vajiravudh died without leaving a son, and as three better-placed contenders to the crown all died in the 1920s, **Prajadhipok** – the seventy-sixth child and last son of Chulalongkorn – was catapulted to the throne as Rama VII (1925–35). Young and inexperienced, he responded to the country's crisis by creating a Supreme Council of State, seen by many as a return to Chulalongkorn's absolutist "government by princes".

Prajadhipok himself seems to have been in favour of constitutional government, but the weakness of his personality and the opposition of the old guard in the Supreme Council prevented him from introducing it. Meanwhile a vigorous community of Western-educated intellectuals had emerged in the lower echelons of the bureaucracy, who were increasingly dissatisfied with the injustices of monarchical government. The final shock to the Thai system came with the Great Depression, which from 1930 onwards ravaged the economy. On **June 24, 1932**, a small group of middle-ranking officials, led by a lawyer, Pridi Phanomyong, and an army major, Luang Phibunsongkhram, staged a **coup** with only a handful of troops. Prajadhipok weakly submitted to the conspirators, or "Promoters", and 150 years of absolute monarchy in Bangkok came to a sudden end. The king was sidelined to a position of symbolic significance and in 1935 he abdicated in favour of his ten-year-old nephew, **Ananda**, then a schoolboy living in Switzerland.

TO THE 1957 COUP

The success of the 1932 coup was in large measure attributable to the army officers who gave the conspirators credibility, and it was they who were to dominate the constitutional regimes that followed. The Promoters' first worry was that the French or British might attempt to restore the monarchy to full power. To deflect such intervention, they appointed a government under a provisional constitution and espoused a wide range of liberal Western-type reforms, including freedom of the press and social equality, few of which ever saw the light of day.

The regime's first crisis came early in 1933 when **Pridi Phanomyong**, by now leader of the government's civilian faction, put forward a socialist economic plan based on the nationalization of land and labour. The proposal was denounced as communistic by the military, Pridi was forced into temporary exile and an anticommunist law was passed. Then, in October, a royalist coup was mounted which brought the kingdom close to civil war. After intense fighting, the rebels were defeated by Lieutenant-Colonel **Luang Phibunsongkhram** (or Phibun), so strengthening the government and bringing Phibun to the fore as the leading light of the military faction.

Pridi was rehabilitated in 1934 and remained powerful and popular, especially among the intelligentsia, but it was Phibun who became prime minister after the decisive **elections of 1938**, presiding over a cabinet dominated by military men. Phibun encouraged a wave of nationalistic feeling with such measures as the official institution of the name Thailand in 1939 – Siam, it was argued, was a name bestowed by external forces, and the new title made it clear that the country belonged to the Thais rather than the economically dominant Chinese. This latter sentiment was reinforced with a series of harsh laws against the Chinese, who faced discriminatory taxes on income and commerce.

WORLD WAR II

The outbreak of **World War II** gave the Thais the chance to avenge the humiliation of the 1893 Franco-Siamese Crisis. When France was occupied by Germany in June 1940, Phibun seized the opportunity to invade western Cambodia and the area of Laos lying to the west of the Mekhong River. In the following year, however, the threat of a Japanese attack on Thailand loomed. On December 8, 1941, almost at the same time as the assault on Pearl Harbour, the Japanese invaded the country at nine points, most of them along the east coast of the peninsula. The Thais at first resisted fiercely, but realizing that the position was hopeless, Phibun quickly ordered a ceasefire. Meanwhile the British sent a force from Malaysia to try to stop the Japanese at Songkhla, but were held up in a fight with Thai border police. The Japanese had time to establish themselves, before pushing down the peninsula to take Singapore.

The Thai government concluded a military alliance with Japan and declared war against the United States and Great Britain in January 1942, probably in the belief that the Japanese would win the war. However, the Thai minister in Washington, Seni Pramoj, refused to deliver the declaration of war against the US and, in cooperation with the Americans, began organizing a resistance movement called **Seri Thai**. Pridi, now acting as regent to the young king, furtively coordinated the movement under the noses of the occupying Japanese, smuggling in American agents and housing them in a European prison camp in Bangkok.

By 1944 Japan's final defeat looked likely, and Phibun, who had been most closely associated with them, was forced to resign by the National Assembly in July. A civilian, Khuang Aphaiwong, was chosen as prime minister, while *Seri Thai* became well established in the government under the control of Pridi. At the end of the war, Thailand was forced to restore the annexed Cambodian and Lao provinces to French Indochina, but American support prevented the British from imposing heavy punishments for the alliance with Japan.

POSTWAR UPHEAVALS

With the fading of the military, the election of January 1946 was for the first time contested by organized political parties, resulting in Pridi's becoming prime minister. A new constitution was drafted and the outlook for democratic, civilian government seemed bright.

Hopes were shattered, however, on June 9, 1946, when King Ananda was found dead in his bed, with a bullet wound in his forehead. Three palace servants were hurriedly tried and executed, but the murder has never been satisfactorily explained, and public opinion attached at least indirect responsibility for the killing to Pridi, who had in the past shown strong anti-royalist feeling. He resigned as prime minister, and in April 1948 the military made a decisive return: playing on the threat of communism, with Pridi pictured as a red bogey man, Phibun took over the premiership.

After the bloody suppression of two attempted coups in favour of Pridi, the main feature of Phibun's second regime was its heavy involvement with the United States. As communism developed its hold in the region, with the takeover of China in 1949 and the French defeat in Indochina in 1954, the US increasingly viewed Thailand as a bulwark against the red menace. Between 1951 and 1957, when its annual state budget was only about $200 million a year, Thailand received a total $149 million in American economic aid and $222 million in military aid. This strengthened Phibun's dictatorship, while enabling leading military figures to divert American money and other funds into their own pockets.

In 1955, his position threatened by two rival generals, Phibun experienced a sudden conversion to the cause of democracy. He narrowly won a general election in 1957, but only by blatant vote rigging and coercion. Although there's a strong tradition of foul play in Thai elections, this is remembered as the dirtiest ever: after vehement public outcry, **General Sarit**, the commander-in-chief of the army, overthrew the new government in September 1957.

TO THE PRESENT DAY

Believing that Thailand would prosper best under a unifying authority, an ideology that still has its supporters, Sarit set about re-establishing the monarchy as the head of the social hierarchy and the source of legitimacy for the government. Ananda's successor, **King Bhumibol** (Rama IX), was pushed into an active role while Sarit ruthlessly silenced critics and pressed ahead with a plan for economic development. These policies achieved a large measure of stability and prosperity at home, although from 1960 onwards the international situation worsened. With the Marxist Pathet

Lao making considerable advances in Laos, and Cambodia's ruler, Prince Sihanouk, drawing into closer relations with China, Sarit turned again to the United States. The Americans obliged by sharply increasing military aid and by stationing troops in Thailand.

THE VIETNAM WAR

Sarit died in 1963, whereupon the military succession passed to **General Thanom**, closely aided by his deputy prime minister, **General Praphas**. Neither man had anything of Sarit's charisma and during a decade in power they followed his political philosophies largely unchanged. Their most pressing problem was the resumption of open hostilities between North and South Vietnam in the early 1960s – the **Vietnam War**. Both Laos and Cambodia became involved on the side of the communists by allowing the North Vietnamese to supply their troops in the south along the Ho Chi Minh Trail, which passed through southern Laos and northeastern Cambodia. The Thais, with the backing of the US, quietly began to conduct military operations in Laos, to which North Vietnam and China responded by supporting antigovernment insurgency in Thailand.

The more the Thais felt threatened by the spread of communism, the more they looked to the Americans for help – by 1968 around 45,000 US military personnel were on Thai soil, which became the base for US bombing raids against North Vietnam and Laos, and for covert operations into Laos and beyond.

The effects of the **American presence in Thailand** were profound. The economy swelled with dollars, and hundreds of thousands of Thais became reliant on the Americans for a living, with a consequent proliferation of corruption and prostitution. What's more, the sudden exposure to Western culture led many to question the traditional Thai values and the political status quo.

THE DEMOCRACY MOVEMENT AND CIVIL UNREST

At the same time, poor farmers were becoming disillusioned with their lot and during the 1960s many turned against the Bangkok government. At the end of 1964, the **Communist Party of Thailand** and other groups formed a **broad left coalition** which soon had the support of several thousand insur-

gents in remote areas of the northeast. By 1967, the problem had spread to Chiang Rai and Nan provinces, and a separate threat had arisen in southern Thailand, involving **Muslim dissidents** and the Chinese-dominated **Communist Party of Malaysia**, as well as local Thais.

Thanom was now facing a major security crisis, especially as the war in Vietnam was going badly. In 1969 he held elections which produced a majority for the government party but, still worried about national stability, the general got cold feet and in November 1971 he reimposed repressive military rule. However, the 1969 experiment with democracy had heightened expectations of power-sharing among the middle classes, especially in the universities. **Student demonstrations** began in June 1973, and in October as many as 500,000 people turned out at Thammasat University in Bangkok to demand a new constitution. Clashes with the police ensued but elements in the army, backed by King Bhumibol, prevented Thanom from crushing the protest with troops. On October 14, 1973, Thanom and Praphas were forced to resign and leave the country.

In a new climate of openness, **Kukrit Pramoj** managed to form a coalition of seventeen elected parties and secured a promise of US withdrawal from Thailand, but his government was riven with feuding. Meanwhile, the king and much of the middle class, alarmed at the unchecked radicalism of the students, began to support new, often violent, right-wing organizations. In **October 1976**, the students demonstrated again, protesting against the return of Thanom to Thailand to become a monk at Wat Bowonniwet. This time there was no restraint: supported by elements of the military and the government, the police and reactionary students launched a massive assault on Thammasat University. On October 6, hundreds of students were brutally beaten, scores were lynched and some even burnt alive; the military took control and suspended the constitution.

GENERAL PREM

Soon after, the military-appointed prime minister, **Thanin Kraivichien**, imposed rigid censorship and forced dissidents to undergo anti-communist indoctrination, but his measures seem to have been too repressive even for

RELATIONS WITH CAMBODIA AND BURMA

Under Prem and successive leaders, Thailand has taken a characteristically pragmatic attitude to the troubles of its neighbours, paying scant attention to world opinion. In 1979, the Vietnamese invaded **Cambodia** to oust the brutal Khmer Rouge, and continued to fight them in the 1980s, crossing into Thailand to attack their bases. In response to this perceived threat to national security, Prem supported and supplied the Khmer Rouge and a wide variety of other Cambodian guerrilla groups sheltering on Thai soil, while backing the United Nations and the Association of Southeast Asian Nations (ASEAN) in their attempts to persuade the Vietnamese to withdraw their troops. These attempts paid off with the 1991 Paris peace accords: Vietnamese forces withdrew, refugees on Thai soil were repatriated, and elections were held in Cambodia in May 1993 under UN auspices. The Khmer Rouge, however, obstructed the peace plan and continue to fight Phnom Penh's shaky coalition government; and since China's withdrawal of support for the murderous faction, Thailand has been seen as the Khmer Rouge's main ally and financier (Thai–Khmer Rouge trade in gems and timber, backed by Thai army commanders on the border, has been estimated at over US$1 million dollars a month), despite the recent and seemingly genuine attempts of the Bangkok government and army chiefs to sever the link.

Thailand's policy towards **Burma** has been even more contentious. Despite brutal repression by the Burmese military dictatorship (SLORC) of pro-democracy demonstrations in 1988, despite its refusal to hand over power to Aung San Suu Kyi's elected opposition, and despite irrefutable evidence of its heinous human rights abuses, Bangkok has drawn its ASEAN partners into a policy of "constructive engagement" with the military regime in Rangoon. This has allowed Thai businessmen and army officers to derive huge benefit from the devastation of Burmese teak forests and the exploitation of fishing grounds and mineral resources. Criticism of Bangkok's stance has come from the US, which, with the European Union in agreement, favours adding full sanctions against Burma to the continuing military sanctions – although it is feared that full economic isolation would give the Burmese generals the excuse to heap yet worse suffering on their people.

---

the military, who forced him to resign in October 1977. General Kriangsak Chomanand took over, and began to break up the insurgency with shrewd offers of amnesty. His power base was weak, however, and although Kriangsak won the elections of 1979, he was displaced in February 1980 by **General Prem Tinsulanonda**, who was backed by a broad parliamentary coalition.

Untainted by corruption, Prem achieved widespread support, including that of the monarchy, which was to prove crucial. In April 1981, a group of disaffected military officers seized government buildings in Bangkok, forcing Prem to flee the capital. However, the rebels' attempt to mobilize the army was hamstrung by a radio message from Queen Sirikit in support of Prem, who was easily able to retake Bangkok. Parliamentary elections in 1983 returned the military to power and legitimized Prem's rule.

Overseeing a period of strong foreign investment and rapid economic growth, Prem maintained the premiership until 1988, with a unique mixture of dictatorship and democracy sometimes called Premocracy: although never standing for parliament himself, Prem was asked by the legislature after every election to become prime minister. He eventually stepped down because, he said, it was time for the country's leader to be chosen from among its elected representatives.

THE 1992 DEMONSTRATIONS

Prem's wishes on his resignation in 1988 were respected, and the new prime minister was indeed an elected MP. **Chatichai Choonhavan**, a retired general with a long civilian career in public office, pursued a vigorous policy of economic development, filling his cabinet with businessmen and encouraging rampant foreign investment. The resultant economic boom, however, fostered widespread corruption, in which members of the government were often implicated. Following an economic downturn and Chatichai's attempts to downgrade the political role of the military, the armed forces staged a bloodless **coup on February 23, 1991**, led by Supreme Commander **Sunthorn** and General **Suchinda**, the army commander-in-chief.

Perhaps recognizing that coups were no longer a viable means of seizing power in Thailand, Sunthorn and Suchinda immediately installed a civilian caretaker government, led by a former diplomat, **Anand Panyarachun**, and promised elections within six months. A poll was eventually held on March 22, 1992, but the new constitution permitted the unelected Suchinda to barge his way to the premiership, at the head of a five-party pro-military coalition dubbed the "devils" by the Thai press. Democracy found its supporters in the shape of the four main opposition parties – the "angels" – and organized groups of academics, professionals and social activists; their campaign for the prime minister's resignation centred around **Chamlong Srimuang**, a popular former governor of Bangkok and head of the strongly Buddhist Palang Dharma party, who went on hunger strike. When Suchinda appeared to renege on earlier promises to make democratic amendments to the constitution, including a requirement that the prime minister be an elected MP, hundreds of thousands of ordinary Thais poured onto the streets in **mass demonstrations** between May 17 and 20. Hopelessly misjudging the mood of the country, Suchinda brutally crushed the protests, leaving hundreds dead or injured in the bloodiest chapter in Thai politics since 1976 – official figures proclaimed 52 deaths, but by the end of 1992 as many as two hundred others were still listed as missing. Having justified the massacre on the grounds that he was protecting the king from communist agitators, Suchinda was forced to resign when King Bhumibol expressed his disapproval in a ticking-off that was broadcast on world television. Anand was again invited to form an interim government, and quickly moved to restructure the armed forces.

THE RISE AND FALL OF CHUAN

Elections scheduled for September 13, 1992, were seen as the acid test – would Thais opt for a democratic form of government, or would they continue to sell their votes to the "traditional" politicians? In the event, vote-buying was still widespread, especially in rural areas, but the "angel" Democrat Party, led by **Chuan Leekpai**, a nine-time minister and noted upholder of democracy and the rule of law, gained the largest number of parliamentary seats. Chuan duly became prime minister, at the head of a coalition largely comprised of the parties who had opposed Suchinda's rise to power.

After the turmoil of the previous year, 1993 was relatively quiet, though Chuan suffered from a rather lacklustre image, held responsible for the government's inability to sort out Bangkok's nightmarish traffic problems – Chuan failed to deal with the inaction of the many competing government bodies responsible for traffic management, and the capital's gridlock remains a drain on the country's booming economic growth.

Against the background of a vague programme to spread wealth to rural areas, to provide "social justice for all" and to raise education standards, Chuan's popularity received two shots in the arm in 1994. In the middle of the year, the opposition was discredited when two of its MPs were refused visas to the US, on the grounds that they were suspected of drug trafficking – one of them a former deputy minister who was thought to have been involved in the heroin trade for over twenty years. Then Chuan took decisive action in the **Saudi gems case**, a saga dating back to 1989, when a Thai servant stole twenty million dollars' worth of jewellery from the Jeddah palace of Prince Faisal, son of Saudi Arabia's King Fahd-al-Aziz. Back in Thailand, the servant went on a rather obvious spending spree, was arrested and sentenced to two years in prison. The story didn't end there, however: over half of the gems returned to Prince Faisal were found to be fake, and the Thai press enjoyed itself immensely, publishing photos of policemen's and politicians' wives and challenging readers to "spot the real Saudi jewellery". In 1990, three Saudi embassy officials were murdered in Bangkok in mysterious circumstances, almost certainly because of their links to the case. The Thai authorities, however, made no progress in getting to the bottom of the affair, thus souring relations with the Saudis, who put a freeze on visas for Thais wanting to work in their country and banned Saudi tourists from visiting Thailand. When, in July 1994, the wife and son of a Thai gems dealer thought to have handled some of the missing stones were found dead, Chuan stepped in over the heads of the dithering Interior Ministry: two police generals were arrested for ordering the murders, and investigations into three former police chiefs were instigated. Considering the rank of the police officers involved, it seems unlikely that the full facts of the case will ever emerge, but Chuan scored points by being seen to take firm action.

Chuan's reign as the longest-serving democratically elected prime minister in Thai history came to an abrupt end when, in May 1995, Chamlong Srimuang's Palang Dharma party withdrew from the ruling coalition, obliging Chuan to dissolve parliament and call a general election. Ironically, considering his squeaky-clean reputation, Chuan lost the support of Palang Dharma over alleged corruption in his **land reform scheme**. Almost 600,000 families, many of them landless peasants, had been given 4.4 million acres since 1993. However, ten people given free land in Phuket, among them relations of Democrat Party MPs, were not poor farmers but rich businessmen, who received land near the seafront suitable for hotel development.

At a time of anxiety over the king's coronary problems, it was feared that the ensuing instability might provoke a military intervention. However, the new army commander, General Wimol Wongwanich, has consistently stressed his intention to steer the military clear of politics since the demonstratons of 1992, and the **election** duly took place on July 2, 1995. Chuam's Democrat Party secured 86 seats, but the largest party turned out to be Chart Thai (formerly led by the disgraced Chatichai Choonhavan), with 92 out of 391 seats. Its new leader, **Banharn Silpa-archa**, immediately began negotiations with other parties to form a coalition – a process which in Thailand can take weeks or even months – and at the time of writing looks set to become prime minister, heading a seven-party block including Palang Dharma. Dubbed by the local press a "walking ATM", a reference to his reputation for buying votes, Banharn is also known as a decisive go-getter and a wily political strategist. Analysts believe that he will largely continue the policies of Chuan and may even speed up economic growth, already running at eight percent a year, by increasing government spending and approving more construction contracts; but there are worries about a correlating rise in corruption as many Chart Thai MPs are themselves involved in construction businesses.

ART AND ARCHITECTURE

Aside from pockets of Hindu-inspired statuary and architecture, the vast majority of historical Thai culture takes its inspiration from Theravada Buddhism, and though the country does have some excellent museums, to understand fully the evolution of Thai art you have to visit its temples. For Thailand's architects and sculptors, the act of creation was an act of merit and a representation of unchanging truths, rather than an act of expression, and thus Thai art history is characterized by broad schools rather than individual names. This section is designed to help you make sense of the most common aspects of Thai art and architecture at their various stages of development.

THE BASICS

To appreciate the plethora of temples and religious images in Thailand, you first need a grasp of the fundamental architectural forms and the iconography of Buddhism and Hinduism. Only then can you begin to appreciate the differences in the creations of different eras.

THE WAT

The **wat** or Buddhist temple complex has a great range of uses, as home to a monastic community, a place of public worship, a shrine for holy images and a shaded meeting place for townspeople and villagers. Wat architecture has evolved in ways as various as its functions,

but there remain several essential components which have stayed constant for some fifteen centuries.

The most important wat building is the **bot** (sometimes known as the *ubosot*), a term most accurately translated as the "ordination hall". It usually stands at the heart of the compound and is the preserve of the monks: lay persons are rarely allowed inside. There's only one bot in any wat complex, and often the only way to distinguish it from other temple buildings is by the eight **sema** or boundary stones which always surround it. Positioned at the four corners of the bot and at the cardinal points of the compass, these stone *sema* define the consecrated ground and usually look something like upright gravestones, though they can take many forms. They are often carved all over with symbolic Buddhist scenes or ideograms, and sometimes are even protected within miniature shrines of their own. (One of the best *sema* collections is housed in the National Museum of Khon Kaen.)

Often almost identical to the bot, the **viharn** or assembly hall is for the lay congregation, and as a tourist this is the building you're most likely to enter, as it usually contains the wat's **principal Buddha image**, and sometimes two or three minor images as well. Large wats may have several viharns, while strict meditation wats, which don't deal with the laity, may not have one at all.

Thirdly, there's the **chedi** or stupa (known as a **that** in the north), a tower which was originally conceived as a monument to enshrine relics of the Buddha, but has since become a place to contain the ashes of royalty – and anyone else who can afford it. Of all Buddhist structures, the chedi has undergone the most changes and as such is often the most characteristic hallmark of each period (see box on p.141).

Less common wat buildings include the small square **mondop**, usually built to house either a Buddha statue or footprint or to contain holy texts, and the **ho trai** or scripture library.

BUDDHIST ICONOGRAPHY

In the early days of Buddhism, image-making was considered inadequate to convey the faith's abstract philosophies, and thus the only approved iconography comprised doctrinal **symbols** such as the *Dharmachakra* (Wheel of Law, also known as Wheel of Doctrine or Wheel of Life). Gradually these symbols were displaced by **images of the Buddha**, construed chiefly as physical embodiments of the Buddha's teachings rather than as portraits of the man (see p.541 for more on the life of the Buddha). Sculptors took their guidance from the Pali texts which ordained the Buddha's most common postures (*asanha*) and gestures (*mudra*).

Of the **four postures** – sitting, standing, walking and reclining – the **seated Buddha**, which represents him in meditation, is the most common in Thailand. A popular variation shows the Buddha seated on a coiled serpent, protected by the serpent's hood – a reference to the story about the Buddha meditating during the rainy season, when a serpent offered to raise him off the wet ground and shelter him from the storms. The **reclining** pose symbolizes the Buddha entering Nirvana at his death, while the **standing** and **walking** images both represent his descent from Tavatimsa heaven.

The most common **hand gestures** include: *Dhyana Mudra* (Meditation), in which the hands rest on the lap, palms upwards; *Bhumisparsa Mudra* (Calling the Earth to Witness, a reference to the Buddha resisting temptation), with the left hand upturned in the lap and the right-hand fingers resting on the right knee and pointing to the earth; *Vitarkha Mudra* (Teaching), with one or both hands held at chest height with the thumb and forefinger touching; and *Abhaya Mudra* (Dispelling Fear), showing the right hand (occasionally both hands) raised in a flat-palmed "stop" gesture.

All three-dimensional Buddha images are objects of reverence, but some are more esteemed than others. Some are alleged to have displayed human attributes or reacted in some way to unusual events, others have performed miracles, or are simply admired for their beauty, their phenomenal size, or even their material value – if made of solid gold or of jade, for example. Most Thais are familiar with these exceptional images, all of which have been given special names, always prefixed by the honorific "Phra", and many of which have spawned thousands of miniaturized copies in the form of amulets. Pilgrimages are made to see the most famous originals.

It was in the Sukhothai era that the craze for producing **Buddha footprints** really took off. Harking back to the time when images were allusive rather than representative, these footprints were generally moulded from stucco to depict the 108 auspicious signs (which included references to the 16 Buddhist heavens, the traditional 4 great continents and 7 great rivers and lakes) and housed in a special mondop. Few of the Sukhothai prints remain, but Ayutthaya-Ratanakosin-era examples are found all over the country, the most famous being Phra Phutthabat near Lopburi, the object of pilgrimages throughout the year.

HINDU ICONOGRAPHY

Hindu images tend to be a lot livelier than Buddhist ones, partly because there is a panoply of gods to choose from, and partly because these gods have mischievous personalities and reappear in all sorts of bizarre incarnations. Central to the Hindu philosophy is the certainty that any object can be viewed as the temporal residence, embodiment or symbol of the deity; thus its iconography includes abstract representations (such as the phallic *lingam* for Shiva) as well as figurative images. Though pure Hinduism receded from Thailand with the collapse of the Khmers, the iconography has endured, as Buddhist Thais have incorporated some Hindu and Brahmin concepts into the national belief system and have continued to create statues of the three chief Hindu deities – Brahma, Vishnu and Shiva – as well as using lesser mythological beasts in modern designs.

Vishnu has always been especially popular: his role of "Preserver" has him embodying the status quo, representing both stability and the notion of altruistic love. He is most often depicted as the deity, but frequently crops up in other human and animal incarnations. There are ten of these manifestations in all, of which **Rama** (number 7) is by far the most popular in Thailand. The epitome of ideal manhood, Rama is the super-hero of the epic story the *Ramayana* (see p.82) and appears in storytelling reliefs and murals in every Hindu temple in Thailand; in painted portraits you can usually recognize him by his green face. Manifestation number eight is **Krishna**, more widely known than Rama in the West, but slightly less common in Thailand. Krishna is usually characterized as a flirtatious, flute-playing, blue-skinned cowherd whose most famous achievement is the lifting of Mount Govadhana (as depicted in relief at Phimai, see overleaf, but he is also a crucial moral figure in

HINDU LEGENDS

Once you've recognized the main characters of the Hindu pantheon, you'll want to know what they're up to in the murals and reliefs that ornament temple walls and ceilings. Of the hundreds of different episodes featured in as many interpretations by painters and sculptors – many taken from the *Ramayana* and *Mahabarata* – the following recur frequently.

The Churning of the Sea of Milk (reproduction of a Khmer lintel in Ayutthaya's Historical Study Centre). A creation myth in which Vishnu appears in his second, tortoise, incarnation. The legend describes how the cosmic ocean (or "milk") was churned with a sacred inverted conical mountain to create the universes and all things in them ("the butter"). A *naga* was used as the churning rope, and the holy tortoise offered his shell to support the mountain – an image which gave rise to the notion of tortoise as the base and foundation stone of the world. The churning also produced a sacred nectar of immortality, which both the gods and the demons were keen to consume. Vishnu craftily encouraged the demons to hold the head end of the *naga* rope while helping to make this nectar, giving the gods the tail-end, and encouraging the demons to drink the liquid at its early, alcoholic stage; the friction of the process caused the *naga* to heat up and breathe fire, burning the demons, who by this stage were so intoxicated that they promptly fell asleep, leaving the distilled nectar for the gods.

Reclining Vishnu Asleep on the Milky Sea of Eternity (the most accessible lintels at Phanom Rung, in the National Museum, Bangkok, and at Wat Phra That Narai Cheng Weng near Sakhon Nakhon). Another common creation myth, this time featuring Vishnu as four-armed deity (sometimes referred to as Phra Narai), sleepily reclining on a *naga*, here representing the Milky Sea of Eternity. Vishnu is dreaming of creating a new universe, shown by the lotus blossoms which spring from his navel, and the four-faced god Brahma who perches atop them; as "Creator", Brahma will be responsible for putting this dream into practice.

Krishna Lifting Mount Govadhana (lintel at Phimai). A story of godly rivalry, in which a community of worshippers suddenly transferred allegiance from the god Indra to the interloping Krishna. Indra, the god of the elements, was so incensed that he attacked the turncoats with a raging storm; they called on Krishna for help, he obliged by lifting up the mighty Mount Govadhana to provide an enormous umbrella.

The Dance of Shiva or Shiva's Dance of Destruction (Phimai, Phanom Rung and at Wat Phra That Narai Cheng Weng near Sakhon Nakhon). A very powerful and highly symbolic image in which the multi-armed Shiva, as Nataraja, performs a wild, ecstatic dance that brings about the total destruction (through fire) of the extant world and replaces it with a new epoch (as represented by a double-sided drum). In the northeastern Khmer temples this dance is a fairly common subject of stone reliefs, nearly always set as a lintel above a major gateway into the sanctuary.

How Ganesh Came to Have an Elephant's Head. At the time of Ganesh's birth, his father, Shiva, happened to be away from home. On returning to his wife's apartments, Shiva was enraged to find a strange young man in Parvati's boudoir and rashly decapitated the youth. Of course, the boy turned out to be Ganesh, Shiva's own son; full of remorse, the god immediately despatched a servant to procure the head of the first living being he encountered so that his son could be restored to life. The servant returned with an elephant's head, which is why this endearing Hindu god has the pot-bellied body of a child and the head of a young elephant. An alternative version of the tale has Shiva overreacting after his baby son's cries woke him from a particularly pleasant daydream.

the *Mahabarata*. Confusingly, Vishnu's ninth avatar is the **Buddha** – a manifestation adopted many centuries ago to minimize defection to the Buddhist faith. When represented as **the deity**, Vishnu is generally shown sporting a crown and four arms, his hands holding a conch shell (whose music wards off demons), a discus (used as a weapon), a club (symbolizing the power of nature and time), and a lotus (symbol of joyful flowering and renewal). The god is often depicted astride a **garuda**, a half-man, half-bird. Even without Vishnu on its back, the garuda is a very important beast – a symbol of strength, it's often shown "supporting" temple buildings.

Statues and representations of **Brahma** (the Creator) are very rare. Confusingly, he too has four arms, but you should recognize him by the fact that he holds no objects, has four faces (sometimes painted red), and is generally borne by a goose-like creature called a *hamsa*.

Shiva (the Destroyer) is the most volatile member of the pantheon. He stands for extreme behaviour, for beginnings and endings (as enacted in his frenzied Dance of Destruction, detailed opposite), and for fertility, and is a symbol of great energy and power. His godlike form typically has four, eight or ten arms, sometimes holding a trident (representing creation, protection and destruction) and a drum (to beat the rhythm of creation). In his most famous role, as **Nataraja**, or Lord of the Dance, he is usually shown in stylized standing position with legs bent into a balletic position, and the full complement of arms outstretched above his head. Three stripes on a figure's forehead also indicate Shiva, or one of his followers. In abstract form, he is represented by a **lingam** or phallic pillar (once found at the heart of every Khmer temple in the northeast). Primarily a symbol of energy and godly power, the lingam also embodies fertility, particularly when set upright in a vulva-shaped vessel known as a **yoni**. The yoni doubles as a receptacle for the holy water that worshippers pour over the lingam.

Close associates of Shiva include **Parvati**, his wife, and **Ganesh**, his elephant-headed son. Depictions of Ganesh abound, both as statues and, because he is the god of knowledge and overcomer of obstacles (in the path of learning), as the symbol of the Fine Arts Department – which crops up on all entrance tickets to museums and historical parks (the origin of his distinguishing physiognomical feature is explained opposite).

The royal, three-headed elephant, **Erawan**, usually only appears as the favourite mount of the god **Indra**, who is rather unremarkable without the beast but generally figures as the king of the gods, with specific power over the elements (particularly rain) – four statues of the god and his mount grace the base of the *prang* at Bangkok's Wat Arun.

Lesser mythological figures, which originated as Hindu symbols but feature frequently

in wats and other Buddhist contexts, include the **yaksha** giants who ward off evil spirits (like the enormous freestanding ones guarding Bangkok's Wat Phra Kaeo); the graceful half-woman, half-bird **kinnari**; and finally, the ubiquitous **naga**, or serpent king of the underworld – often the proud owner of as many as seven heads, whose reptilian body most frequently appears as staircase balustrades in Hindu and Buddhist temples.

THE SCHOOLS

In the 1920s art historians and academics began compiling a classification system for Thai art and architecture which was modelled along the lines of the country's historical periods – these are the guidelines followed below. The following brief overview starts in the sixth century, when Buddhism began to take a hold on the country, a point before which very few examples of art and no known architectural relics have survived.

DVARAVATI
[SIXTH–ELEVENTH CENTURIES]
Centred around Nakhon Pathom, U Thong and Lopburi in the Chao Phraya basin and in the smaller northern enclave of Haripunjaya (modern-day Lamphun), the **Dvaravati** state was populated by Theravada Buddhists who were strongly influenced by Indian culture.

Only one, fairly late, known example of a Dvaravati-era **building** remains standing: the pyramidal laterite chedi in the compound of Lamphun's Wat Kukut, which is divided into five tiers with niches for stucco Buddha images on each row. Dvaravati-era **artefacts** are much more common, and the national museums in Nakhon Pathom and Lamphun both house quite extensive collections of Buddha images from that period. In an effort to combat the defects inherent in the poor-quality limestone at their disposal, sculptors made their Buddhas quite stocky, cleverly dressing the figures in a sheet-like drape that dropped down to ankle level from each raised wrist, forming a U-shaped hemline – a style which they used when casting in bronze as well. Nonetheless many **statues** have cracked, leaving them headless or limbless. Where the faces have survived, Dvaravati statues display some of the most naturalistic features ever produced in Thailand, distinguished by their thick lips, flattened noses and wide cheekbones.

Nakhon Pathom, a target of Buddhist missionaries from India since before the first century AD, has also yielded a substantial hoard of **dharmachakra**, originating in the period when the Buddha could not be directly represented. These metre-high carved stone wheels symbolize the cycles of life and reincarnation, and in Dvaravati examples are often accompanied by a small statue of a deer, which refers to the Buddha preaching his first sermon in a deer park.

SRIVIJAYA
[EIGHTH–THIRTEENTH CENTURIES]

While Dvaravati's Theravada Buddhists were influencing the central plains and, to a limited extent, areas further north, southern Thailand was paying allegiance to the Mahayana Buddhists of the **Srivijayan** empire. The key distinction between Theravada and Mahayana strands of thought is that Mahayanists believe that those who have achieved enlightenment should postpone their entry into Nirvana in order to help others along the way. These stay-behinds, revered like saints both during and after life, are called **bodhisattva**, and **statues** of them were the mainstay of Srivijayan art.

The finest Srivijayan *bodhisattva* statues were cast in bronze and show such grace and sinuosity that they rank among the finest sculpture ever produced in the country. Usually shown in the **tribunga** or hipshot pose, with right hip thrust out and left knee bent, many are lavishly adorned, and some were even bedecked in real jewels when first made. By far the most popular *bodhisattva* subject was **Avalokitesvara**, worshipped as compassion incarnate. Generally shown with four or more arms and with an animal skin over the left shoulder or tied at the waist, Avalokitesvara is also sometimes depicted with his torso covered in tiny Buddha images. Bangkok's National Museum holds the most beautiful Avalokitesvara, found in Chaiya; most of the other best Srivijayan sculptures have been snapped up by Bangkok's curators as well.

As for Srivijayan **temples**, quite a number have been built over, and so are unviewable. The most typical intact example is the Javanese-style chedi at Chaiya's Wat Phra Boromathat, heavily restored but distinguished

from contemporaneous Dvaravati structures by its highly ornamented stepped chedi, with mini chedis at each corner.

KHMER AND LOPBURI
[TENTH–FOURTEENTH CENTURIES]

By the end of the ninth century the **Khmers** of Cambodia were starting to expand from their capital at Angkor into the Dvaravati states, bringing with them the Hindu faith and the cult of the god-king (*devaraja*). As lasting testaments to the sacred power of their kings, the Khmers built hundreds of imposing stone **sanctuaries** across their newly acquired territory: the two top examples are both in southern Isaan, at Phimai and Phanom Rung, though there is also an interesting early one at Muang Singh near Kanchanaburi.

Each magnificent castle-temple – known in Khmer as a **prasat** – was constructed primarily as a shrine of the *shiva lingam*, the phallic representation of the god Shiva. They followed a similar pattern, centred on at least one towering structure, or **prang**, which represented Mount Meru (the gods' heavenly abode), and surrounded by concentric rectangular enclosures, within and beyond which were dug artificial lakes and moats – miniature versions of the primordial ocean dividing heaven from earth.

The prasats' most fascinating and superbly crafted features, however, are the **carvings** that ornament almost every surface. Usually gouged from sandstone, but frequently moulded in stucco, these exuberant reliefs depict Hindu deities, incarnations and stories, especially episodes from the *Ramayana* (see p.82). Towards the end of the twelfth century, the Khmer leadership became Mahayana Buddhist, commissioning Buddhist carvings to be installed alongside the Hindu ones, and simultaneously replacing the *shiva lingam* at the heart of each sanctuary with a Buddha or *bodhisattva* image. (See p.337 for more on the architectural details.)

The temples built in the former Theravada Buddhist principality of **Lopburi** during the Khmer period are much smaller affairs than those in Isaan, and are best represented by the triple-pranged temple of Phra Prang Sam Yot. The Lopburi classification is most usually applied to the Buddha statues that emerged at the tail-end of the Khmer period, picking up the Dvaravati sculptural legacy. Broad-faced and muscular, the classic Lopburi Buddha wears a diadem or ornamental headband – a nod to the Khmers' ideological fusion of earthly and heavenly power – and the *ushnisha* (the sign of enlightenment) becomes distinctly conical rather than a mere bump on the head. Early Lopburi Buddhas come garlanded with necklaces and ornamental belts; later examples eschew the jewels. As you'd expect, Lopburi National Museum houses a good selection.

SUKHOTHAI
[THIRTEENTH–FIFTEENTH CENTURIES]

Capitalizing on the Khmers' weakening hold over central Thailand, two Thai generals established the first real Thai kingdom in **Sukhothai** in 1238, and over the next two hundred years the artists of this realm produced some of Thailand's most refined art. Sukhothai's artistic reputation rests above all on its **sculpture**. More sinuous even than the Srivijayan images, Sukhothai Buddhas tend towards elegant androgyny, with slim oval faces that show little of the humanistic Dvaravati features or the strength of Lopburi statues, and slender curvaceous bodies usually clad in a plain, skintight robe that fastens with a tassle close to the navel (see box on p.189). The sculptors favoured the seated pose, with hands in the *Bhumisparsa Mudra*, most expertly executed in the Phra Buddha Chinnarat image, now housed in Phitsanulok's Wat Si Ratana Mahathat (replicated at Bangkok's Wat Benchamabophit) and in the enormous Phra Sri Sakyamuni, now enshrined in Bangkok's Wat Suthat. They were also the first to represent the **walking Buddha**, a supremely graceful figure with his right leg poised to move forwards and his left arm in the *Vitarkha Mudra*, as seen in the compounds of Sukhothai's Wat Sra Si.

The cities of Sukhothai and nearby Si Satchanalai were already stamped with sturdy relics of the Khmers' presence, but rather than pull down the sacred prangs of their predecessors, Sukhothai builders added bots, viharns and chedis to the existing structures, as well as conceiving quite separate **temple complexes**. Their viharns and bots are the earliest halls of worship still standing in Thailand (the Khmers didn't go in for large public assemblies), but in most cases only the stone pillars and their platforms remain, the wooden roofs having long since disintegrated. The best examples can be seen in the historical park at Sukhothai, with less grandiose structures at the parks in nearby Si Satchanalai and Kamphaeng Phet.

Most of the **chedis**, though, are in much better shape. Many were modelled on the Sri Lankan bell-shaped reliquary tower (symbolizing the Buddha's teachings ringing out far and wide), often set atop a one- or two-tiered square base surrounded by elephant buttresses – Si Satchanalai's Wat Chang Lom is a stylish example. The architects also devised a new type of chedi, as elegant in its way as the images their sculptor colleagues were producing. This was the **lotus-bud chedi**, a slender tower topped with a tapered finial that was to become a hallmark of the Sukhothai era. In Sukhothai both Wat Mahathat and Wat Trapang Ngoen display good samples.

Ancient Sukhothai is also renowned for the skill of its potters, who produced a **ceramic ware** known as Sawankhalok, after the name of one of the nearby kiln towns. Most museum ceramics collections are dominated by Sawankhalok ware, which is distinguished by its grey-green celadon glazes and by the fish and chrysanthemum motifs used to decorate bowls and plates.

LANNA
[THIRTEENTH–SIXTEENTH CENTURIES]

Meanwhile, to the north of Sukhothai, the independent Theravada Buddhist kingdom of Lanna was flourishing. Its art styles – known interchangeably as Chiang Saen and Lanna – evolved from an eclectic range of precursors, building on the Dvaravati heritage of Haripunjaya, copying direct from Indian sources and incorporating Sukhothai and Sri Lankan ideas from the south.

The earliest surviving Lanna **monument** is the Dvaravati-style Chedi Si Liem in Chiang Mai, built to the pyramidical form characteristic of Mon builders in fairly close imitation of the much earlier Wat Kukut in Lampang. Also in Chiang Mai, Wat Jet Yot replicates the temple built at Bodh Gaya in India to commemorate the seven sites where the Buddha meditated in the first seven weeks after attaining enlightenment – hence the symbolic seven pyramidal chedis, and hence also the name, which means "the temple of seven spires".

Lanna **sculpture** also drew some inspiration from Bodh Gaya: the early Lanna images tend to plumpness, with broad shoulders and prominent hair curls, which are all characteristics of the main Buddha at Bodh Gaya. The later works are slimmer, probably as a result of Sukhothai influence, and one of the most famous examples of this type is the Phra Singh Buddha, enshrined in Chiang Mai's Wat Phra Singh. Other good illustrations of both styles are housed in Chiang Mai's National Museum.

AYUTTHAYA
[FOURTEENTH–EIGHTEENTH CENTURIES]

Although the Sukhothai era was artistically fertile, the kingdom had only a short political life and from 1351 Thailand's central plains came under the thrall of a new power centred on **Ayutthaya** and ruled by a former prince of Lopburi. Over the next four centuries, the Ayutthayan capital became one of the most prosperous and ostentatious cities in Asia, its rulers commissioning some four hundred grand wats as symbols of their wealth and power. Though essentially Theravada Buddhists, the kings also adopted some Hindu and Brahmin beliefs from the Khmers – most significantly the concept of *devaraja* or god-kingship, whereby the monarch became a mediator between the people and the Hindu gods. The religious buildings and sculptures of this era reflected this new composite ideology, both by fusing the architectural styles inherited from the Khmers and from Sukhothai and by dressing their Buddhas to look like regents.

Retaining the concentric layout of the typical Khmer **temple complex**, Ayutthayan builders played around with the component structures, most notably the prang, which they refined and elongated into a **corncob-shaped tower**, rounding it off at the top and introducing vertical incisions around its circumference. As a spire they often added a bronze thunderbolt, and into niches within the prang walls they placed Buddha images. In Ayutthaya itself, the ruined complexes of Wat Phra Mahathat and Wat Ratburana both include these corncob prangs, but the most famous example is Bangkok's Wat Arun, which though built during the subsequent Bangkok period is a classic Ayutthayan structure.

Ayutthaya's architects also adapted the Sri Lankan **chedi** so favoured by their Sukhothai predecessors, stretching the bell-shaped base and tapering it into a very graceful conical spire, as at Wat Sri Sanphet in Ayutthaya. The **viharns** of this era are characterized by walls pierced by slit-like windows, designed to foster a mysterious atmosphere by limiting the amount of light inside the building. As with all of Ayutthaya's buildings, few viharns survived the brutal 1767 sacking, with the notable exception of Wat Na Phra Mane. Phitsanulok's Wat Phra Ratana Si Mahathat was built to a similar plan – and in Phetchaburi, Wat Yai Suwannaram has no windows at all.

From Sukhothai's Buddha **sculptures** the Ayutthayans copied the soft oval face, adding an earthlier demeanour to the features and imbuing them with a hauteur in tune with the *devaraja* ideology. Like the Lopburi images, early Ayutthayan statues wear crowns to associate kingship with Buddhahood; as the court became ever more lavish, so these figures became increasingly adorned, until – as in the monumental bronze at Wat Na Phra Mane – they appeared in earrings, armlets, anklets, bandoliers and coronets. The artists justified these luscious portraits of the Buddha – who was, after all, supposed to have given up worldly possessions – by pointing to an episode when the Buddha transformed himself into a well-dressed nobleman to gain the ear of a proud emperor, whereupon he scolded the man into entering the monkhood.

While a couple of wats in Sukhothai show hints of painted decoration, religious **painting** in Thailand really dates from the Ayutthayan era. Unfortunately most of Ayutthaya's own paintings were destroyed in 1767 and others have suffered badly from damp, but several temples in other parts of the country still have some well-preserved murals, in particular Wat Yai Suwannaram in Phetchaburi. By all accounts typical of late seventeenth-century painting, Phetchaburi's murals depict rows of *thep* or divinities paying homage to the Buddha, in scenes presented without shadow or perspective, and mainly executed in dark reds and cream.

RATANAKOSIN
[EIGHTEENTH CENTURY TO THE PRESENT]

When **Bangkok** emerged as Ayutthaya's successor in 1782, the new capital's founder was determined to revive the old city's grandeur, and the **Ratanakosin** (or Bangkok) period began by aping what the Ayutthayans had done.

Since then neither wat architecture nor relig-ious sculpture has evolved much further.

The first Ratanakosin **building** was the bot of Bangkok's Wat Phra Kaeo, built to enshrine the Emerald Buddha. Designed to a typical Ayutthayan plan, it's coated in glittering mirrors and gold leaf, with roofs ranged in multiple tiers and tiled in green and orange. To this day, most newly built bots and viharns follow a more economical version of this para-digm, whitewashing the outside walls but decorating the pediment in gilded ornaments and mosaics of coloured glass. Tiered temple roofs – an Ayutthayan innovation of which few examples remain in that city – still taper off into the slender bird-like finials called *chofa*, and naga staircases – a Khmer feature inherited by Ayutthaya – have become an almost obligatory feature of any major temple. The result is that modern wats are often almost indistinguishable from each other, though Bangkok does have a few exceptions, including Wat Benchamabophit, which uses marble cladding for its walls and incorporates Victorian-style stained-glass windows, and Wat Rajapobhit, which is covered all over in Chinese ceramics. The most dramatic chedi of the Ratanokosin era – the tallest in the world – was constructed in the mid-nineteenth century in Nakhon Pathom to the original Sri Lankan style, but minus the elephant buttresses that you find in Sukhothai.

Early Ratanakosin sculptors produced adorned **Buddha images** very much in the Ayutthayan vein, sometimes adding real jewels to the figures, and more modern images are notable for their ugliness rather than for any radical departure from type. The obsession with size, first apparent in the Sukhothai period, has plumbed new depths, with graceless concrete statues up to 60m high becoming the norm (as in Roi Et's Wat Burapha), a monumentalism made worse by the routine application of browns and dull yellows. Most small images are cast from or patterned on older models, mostly Sukhothai or Ayutthayan in origin.

Painting has fared much better, with the *Ramayana* murals in Bangkok's Wat Phra Kaeo (see p.82) a shining example of how Ayutthayan techniques and traditional subject matters could be adapted into something fantastic, imaginative and beautiful.

Following the democratization of Thailand in the 1930s, artists increasingly became recognized as individuals, and took to signing their work for the first time. In 1933 the first school of fine art (now Bangkok's Silpakorn University) was estab-lished under the Italian sculptor Corrado Feroci, designer of the capital's Democracy Monument, and, as the new generation experimented with secular themes and styles adapted from the Western Impressionist, Post-impressionist and Cubist movements, later embracing Abstraction and Expressionism, Thai art began to look a lot more **"modern"**. Aside from a period during the 1970s, when massive political upheaval forced artists to address issues of social injustice and authoritarian rule, the leading artistic preoccupa-tion of the past 65 years has been Thailand's spiri-tual heritage, with nearly every major figure on the contemporary art scene tackling religious issues at some point. For some artists this has meant a straightforward modernization of Buddhist legends or a reworking of particular symbols, while others have sought to dramatize the moral relevance of their religion in the light of political, social and philosophical trends.

One of the first modern artists to adapt traditional styles and themes was **Angkarn Kalayanapongsa**, whose most public work can be seen in temple murals such as those at Wat Sri Khom Kham in Phayao (see p.278). Characteristic of this aspect of Angkarn's work is the fusion of the elegant, two-dimensional styles of Ayutthayan mural painting (of which few original examples remain) with a surrealis-tic, dreamlike quality. Many of his paintings feature casts of *khon*-like figures and flying *thep* decked out with gilded crowns and orna-mental armlets, anklets and necklaces in a setting studded with symbols from both Buddhism and from contemporary culture.

Aiming for the more secular environments of the gallery and the private home, **Pichai Nirand** rejects the traditional mural style and makes more selective choices of Buddhist imagery, appropriating religious objects and icons and reinterpreting their significance. He's particularly well known for his fine-detail canvases of Buddha footprints, many of which can be seen in Bangkok galleries and public spaces.

Pratuang Emjaroen is probably most famous for his social commentary, as epito-mized by his huge and powerful canvas "Dharma and Adharma; The Days of Disaster", which he painted in response to the vicious clashes between the military and students in 1973. The 5m x 2m picture depicts images of severed limbs, screaming faces and bloody gun-barrels amid shadowy images of the Buddha's face, a spiked *dharmachakra* and other religious symbols. Although it doesn't belong to any public collection, it is occasionally loaned to galleries around Thailand, as are many of Pratuang's other works, many of which discuss the theme of social injustice and display the artist's trademark use of strong shafts of light and bold colour.

The anti-democratic policies which climaxed in the violence of May 1992 (see p.529) have been addressed by **Vasan Sitthiket**, who exhibited a collection of expressionistic, childlike portraits of "sinners" in a show called "Inferno" in June of the same year, disingenuously claiming that his theme was the Buddhist Tosachat. Currently one of Thailand's most outspoken artists, he continues to highlight the tensions of modern Thai life, and his pictures are shown at large and small galleries around the capital.

Longer established, but no less controversial, **Thawan Duchanee** has tended to examine the spiritual tensions of modern life. His juxtaposition of religious icons with fantastical Bosch-like characters and explicitly sexual images prompted a group of fundamentalist students to slash ten of his early paintings in 1971 – an unprecedented reaction to a work of Thai art. Undaunted, Thawan has continued to produce challenging work, including interpretations of the *Ramayana*, the *Jataka* and the *Tri Phum*, in a bid to manifest the individual's struggles against the obstacles that dog the Middle Way, prominent among them lust and violence.

Bangkok has a near monopoly on Thailand's **art galleries**. While the permanent collections at the National Gallery are disappointing, that of the privately owned Visual Dhamma Gallery (see p.106) is far more lively, and regular exhibitions of contemporary work appear at both the Silpakorn University Art Gallery and the Queen Sirikit Convention Centre. The headquarters of Bangkok's major **banks and securities' companies** also display works by modern Thai artists both established and lesser known, and in recent years have made a big show of backing substantial art prizes.

RELIGION: THAI BUDDHISM

Over ninety percent of Thais consider themselves Theravada Buddhists, followers of the teachings of a holy man usually referred to as the Buddha (Enlightened One), though more precisely known as Gautama Buddha to distinguish him from three lesser-known Buddhas who preceded him, and from the fifth and final Buddha who is predicted to arrive in the year 4457 AD. Theravada Buddhism is one of the two main schools of Buddhism practised in Asia, and in Thailand it has absorbed an eclectic assortment of animist and Hindu elements into its beliefs as well. The other ten percent of Thailand's population comprises Mahayana Buddhists, Muslims, Hindus, Sikhs and Christians.

THE BUDDAH: HIS LIFE AND BELIEFS

Buddhists believe that Gautama Buddha was the five-hundredth incarnation of a single being: the stories of these five hundred lives, collectively known as the **Jataka**, provide the inspiration for much Thai art. (Hindus also accept Gautama Buddha into their pantheon, perceiving him as the ninth manifestation of their god Vishnu.)

In his last incarnation he was born in Nepal as **Prince Gautama Siddhartha** in either the sixth or seventh century BC, the son of a king and his hitherto barren wife, who finally became pregnant only after having a dream that a white elephant had entered her womb. At the time of his birth astrologers predicted that Gautama was to become universally respected, either as a worldly king or as a spiritual saviour, depending on which way of life he pursued. Much preferring the former idea, the prince's father forbade anyone to let the boy out of the palace grounds, and took it upon himself to educate Gautama in all aspects of the high life. Most statues of the Buddha depict him with elongated earlobes, which is a reference to this early pampered existence, when he would have worn heavy precious stones in his ears.

The prince married and became a father, but at the age of 29 he flouted his father's authority and sneaked out into the world beyond the palace. On this fateful trip he encountered successively an old man, a sick man, a corpse and a hermit, and thus for the first time was made aware that pain and suffering were intrinsic to human life. Contemplation seemed the only means of discovering why this should be so – and therefore Gautama decided to leave the palace and become a **Hindu ascetic**.

For six or seven years he wandered the countryside leading a life of self-denial and self-mortification, but failed to come any closer to the answer. Eventually concluding that the best course of action must be to follow a "**Middle Way**" – neither indulgent nor overly ascetic – Gautama sat down beneath the famous riverside bodhi tree at **Bodh Gaya** in India, facing the rising sun, to meditate until he achieved enlightenment. For 49 days he sat crosslegged in the "lotus position", contemplating the causes of suffering and wrestling with temptations that materialized to distract him. Most of these were sent by **Mara**, the Evil One, who was finally subdued when Gautama summoned the earth goddess **Mae Toranee** by pointing the fingers of his right hand at the ground – the gesture known as *Bhumisparsa Mudra*, which has been immortalized by hundreds of Thai sculptors. Mae Toranee wrung torrents of water from her hair and engulfed Mara's demonic emissaries in a flood, an episode that also features in several sculptures and paintings, most famously in the statue in Bangkok's Sanam Luang.

Temptations dealt with, Gautama soon came to attain **enlightenment** and so become a Buddha. As the place of his enlightenment, the **bodhi tree** (or bo tree) has assumed special significance for Buddhists: not only does it appear in many Buddhist paintings and a few sculptures, but there's often a real bodhi tree (*ficus religiosa*) planted in temple compounds as well. Furthermore, the bot is nearly always built facing either a body of water or facing east (preferably both).

The Buddha preached his **first sermon** in a deer park in India, where he characterized his *Dharma* (doctrine) as a wheel. From this episode comes the early Buddhist symbol the **Dharmachakra**, known as the Wheel of Law, Wheel of Doctrine or Wheel of Life, which is often accompanied by a statue of a deer. Thais celebrate this first sermon with a public holiday in July known as *Asanha Puja*. On another occasion 1250 people spontaneously gathered to hear the Buddha speak, an event remembered in Thailand as *Maha Puja* and marked by a public holiday in February.

For the next forty-odd years the Buddha travelled the region converting non-believers and performing miracles. One rainy season he even ascended into the Tavatimsa heaven (Heaven of the thirty-three gods) to visit his mother and to preach the doctrine to her. His descent from this heaven is quite a common theme of paintings and sculptures, and the **Standing Buddha** pose of numerous Buddha statues comes from this story. He also went back to his father's palace where he was temporarily reunited with his wife and child: the Khon Kaen museum houses a particularly lovely carving of this event.

The Buddha "died" at the age of eighty on the banks of a river at Kusinari in India – an event often dated to 543 BC, which is why the Thai calendar is 543 years out of synch with the Western one. Lying on his side, propping up his head on his hand, the Buddha passed into **Nirvana** (giving rise to another classic pose, the Reclining Buddha), the unimaginable state of nothingness which knows no suffering and from which there is no reincarnation. Buddhists believe that the day the Buddha entered Nirvana was the same date on which he was born and he achieved enlightenment, a triply significant day that Thais honour with the *Visakha Puja* festival in May.

BUDDHIST DOCTRINE

After the Buddha entered Nirvana, his **doctrine** spread relatively quickly across India, and probably was first promulgated in Thailand in about the third century BC. His teachings, the *Tripitaka*, were written down in the Pali language – a derivative of Sanskrit – in a form that became known as Theravada or "The Doctrine of the Elders".

As taught by the Buddha, **Theravada Buddhism** built on the Hindu theory of perpetual reincarnation in the pursuit of perfection, introducing the notion of life as a cycle of suffering which could only be transcended by enlightened beings able to free themselves from earthly ties and enter into the blissful state of Nirvana. For the well-behaved but unenlightened Buddhist, each reincarnation marks a move up a vague kind of ladder, with animals at the bottom, women figuring lower down than men, and monks coming at the top – a hierarchy complicated by the very pragmatic notion that the more comfortable your lifestyle the higher your spiritual status.

The Buddhist has no hope of enlightenment without acceptance of the **four noble truths**. In encapsulated form, these hold that desire is the root cause of all suffering and can be extinguished only by following the eightfold path or Middle Way. This **Middle Way** is essentially a highly moral mode of life that includes all the usual virtues like compassion, respect and moderation, and eschews vices such as self-indulgence and anti-social behaviour. But the key to it all is an acknowledgement that the physical world is impermanent and ever-changing, and that all things – including the self – are therefore not worth craving. Only by pursuing a condition of complete **detachment** can human beings transcend earthly suffering.

By the beginning of the first millennium, a new movement called **Mahayana** (Great Vehicle) had emerged within the Theravada school, attempting to make Buddhism more accessible by introducing a Hindu-style pantheon of *bodhisattva* or Buddhist saints who, although they had achieved enlightenment, nevertheless postponed entering Nirvana in order to inspire the populace. Mahayana Buddhism subsequently spread north into China, Korea, Vietnam and Japan, also entering the southern Thai kingdom of Srivijaya around the eighth century and parts of Khmer Cambodia in about the eleventh century. Meanwhile Theravada Buddhism (which the Mahayanists disparagingly renamed "Hinayana" or "Lesser Vehicle") established itself most significantly in Sri Lanka, Thailand and Burma.

THE MONKHOOD

In Thailand it's the duty of the 200,000-strong **Sangha** (monkhood) to set an example to the Theravada Buddhist community by living a life as close to the Middle Way as possible and by preaching the *Dharma* to the people. A monk's life is governed by 227 strict rules that include celibacy and the rejection of all personal possessions except gifts.

Each day begins with an alms round in the neighbourhood so that the laity can donate food and thereby gain themselves merit (see over), and then is chiefly spent in meditation, chanting, teaching and study. The stricter of the Thai *Sangha*'s two sects, the **Thammayutika**, places strong emphasis on scholarship and meditation, but the much larger and longer-established **Mahanikai** sect encourages monks to pursue wider activities within the community. Always the most respected members of any community, monks act as teachers, counsellors and arbiters in local disputes and, in rural areas, they often become spokesmen for villagers' rights, particularly on environmental and land ownership issues. Although some Thai women do become nuns, they belong to no official order and aren't respected as much as the monks.

Monkhood doesn't have to be for life: a man may leave the *Sangha* three times without stigma and in fact every Thai male (including royalty) is expected to **enter the monkhood** for a short period at some point in his life, ideally between leaving school and marrying, as a rite of passage into adulthood. So ingrained into the social system is this practice that nearly all Thai companies grant their employees paid leave for their time as a monk. The most popular time for temporary ordination is the three-month Buddhist retreat period – **Pansa**, sometimes referred to as "Buddhist Lent" – which begins in July and lasts for the duration of the rainy season. (The monks' confinement is said to originate from the earliest years of Buddhist history, when farmers complained that perambulating monks were squashing their sprouting rice crops.) **Ordination ceremonies** take place in almost every wat at this time and make spectacular scenes, with the shaven-headed novice usually clad entirely in white and carried about on friends' or relatives' shoulders. The boys' parents donate money, food and necessities such as washing powder and mosquito repellent, processing around the temple compound with their gifts, often joined by dancers or travelling players hired for the occasion.

MONKS IN CONTEMPORARY SOCIETY

In recent years, some monks have extended their role as village spokesmen to become influential activists: monks played a key role in the fierce campaign against the Pak Mun dam in Isaan (see p.353), for example, while the inhabitants of Wat Tham Krabok near Lopburi have successfully turned their temple into an international drug rehabilitation centre, and those of Wat Phai Lom near Bangkok have established the country's largest breeding colony of Asian open-billed storks. However, the increasing involvement of many monks in the secular world has not met with unanimous approval. Ajarn Pongsak's involvement in a reforestation and anti-logging project in the Mae Soi valley of northern Thailand, for example, prompted the accusation "he is a meddlesome monk acting outside his line of duty".

Less heroic, but equally disappointing to the laity, are those monks who **flout the precepts** of the *Sangha* by succumbing to the temptations of a consumer society, flaunting Raybans, Rolexes and Mercedes, chain-smoking and flirting, even making pocket money from predicting lottery results and practising faith healing.

With so much national pride and integrity riding on the sanctity of the *Sangha*, any whiff of a deeper scandal is bound to strike deep into the national psyche, and the recent allegations levelled against the extremely popular **Phra Yantra** have generated widespread public interest. In early 1994, the monk was accused of fathering the child of one of his followers, and of several other affairs and unseemly indulgences; however, his charisma was such that for months the Supreme Sangha Council seemed too scared even to respond to the allegations. The monk's followers (estimated at three million worldwide) have vociferously protested his innocence, and one MP even staked his job on it – resigning in Februray 1995 when Phra Yantra refused for the umpteenth time to take a DNA paternity test. At the time of writing, the case was still unresolved, but whatever the outcome there's no doubt that the protracted debate on the man's personal morality has shaken the stability of Thailand's clerical elitism, and the unwillingness of the government and the Sangha Supreme Council to take any sort of action has damaged the credibility of both.

Interestingly, back in the late 1980s, the similarly charming and influential monk, Phra Bodhirak, was unceremoniously defrocked after criticizing what he saw as a tide of decadence infecting Thai Buddhism and advocating an allround purification of the *Sangha*. He now preaches from his breakaway Santi Asoke sect headquarters on the outskirts of Bangkok, but his ascetic code of behaviour is not sanctioned by the more worldly figures of the Sangha Supreme Council.

BUDDHIST PRACTICE

In practice most Thai Buddhists aim only to be **reborn** higher up the incarnation scale rather than set their sights on the ultimate goal of Nirvana. The rank of the reincarnation is directly related to the good and bad actions performed in the previous life, which accumulate to determine one's **karma** or destiny – hence the Thai obsession with "making merit".

Merit-making (*tham bun*) can be done in all sorts of ways, from giving a monk his breakfast to attending a Buddhist service or donating money to the neighbourhood temple, and most festivals are essentially communal merit-making opportunities. For a Thai man, temporary ordination is a very important way of accruing merit not only for himself but also for his mother and sisters – wealthier citizens might take things a step further by commissioning the casting of a Buddha statue or even paying for the building of a wat. One of the more bizarre but common merit-making activities involves **releasing caged birds**: worshippers buy one or more tiny finches from vendors at wat compounds and, by liberating them from their cage, prove their Buddhist compassion towards all living things. The fact that the birds were free until netted earlier that morning doesn't seem to detract from the ritual at all. In riverside and seaside wats, birds are sometimes replaced by fish or even baby turtles.

SPIRITS AND NON-BUDDHIST DEITIES

The complicated history of the area now known as Thailand has, not surprisingly, made Thai Buddhism a strangely syncretic faith, as you'll realize when you enter a Buddhist temple compound to be confronted by a statue of a Hindu deity. While regular Buddhist merit-making insures a Thai for the next life, there are certain **Hindu gods and animist spirits** that most Thais also cultivate for help with more immediate problems. Sophisticated Bangkokians and illiterate farmers alike will find no inconsistency in these apparently incompatible practices, and as often as not it's a Buddhist monk who is called in to exorcize a malevolent spirit. Even the Buddhist King Bhumibol employs Brahmin priests and astrologers to determine auspicious days and officiate at certain royal ceremonies and, like his royal predecessors of the Chakri dynasty, he also associates himself with the Hindu god Vishnu by assuming the title Rama IX – Rama, hero of the Hindu epic the *Ramayana*, having been Vishnu's seventh manifestation on earth.

If a Thai wants help in achieving a short-term goal, like passing an exam, becoming pregnant or winning the lottery, then he or she will quite likely turn to the **Hindu pantheon**, visiting an enshrined statue of either Brahma, Vishnu, Shiva, Indra or Ganesh, and making offerings of flowers, incense and maybe food. If the outcome is favourable, devotees will probably come back to show thanks, bringing more offerings and maybe even hiring a dance troupe to perform a celebratory *lakhon chatri* as well. Built in honour of Brahma, Bangkok's Erawan Shrine is the most famous place of Hindu-inspired worship in the country.

Whereas Hindu deities tend to be benevolent, **spirits** (or *phi*) are not nearly as reliable and need to be mollified more frequently. They come in hundreds of varieties, some more malign than others, and inhabit everything from trees, rivers and caves to public buildings and private homes – even taking over people if they feel like it. So that these *phi* don't pester human inhabitants, each building has a special **spirit house** in its vicinity, as a dwelling for spirits ousted by the building's construction. Usually raised on a short column and designed to look like a wat or a traditional Thai house, these spirit houses are generally about the size of a dolls'-house, but their ornamentation is supposed to reflect the status of the humans' building – thus if that building is enlarged or refurbished, then the spirit house should be improved accordingly. Daily offerings of incense, lighted candles and garlands of jasmine are placed inside the spirit house to keep the *phi* happy – a disgruntled spirit is a dangerous spirit, liable to cause sickness, accidents and even death.

FLORA, FAUNA AND ENVIRONMENTAL ISSUES

Spanning some 2000km north to south, Thailand lies in the heart of Southeast Asia's tropical zone, its northernmost region just a few degrees south of the Tropic of Cancer, its southern border running less than ten degrees north of the Equator. As with other tropical regions across the world, Thailand's climate is characterized by high humidity and even higher temperatures, a very fertile combination which nourishes a huge diversity of **flora and fauna** in a vast range of habitats: dry tropical **monsoon and deciduous forests** in the mountainous north; wet **tropical rainforests** in the steamy south; flood plains in the central region; **mangrove swamps** along its coasts; and some of the world's most beautiful **coral reefs** off each coastline. The country boasts some 928 species of bird and an estimated 27,000 flower species – some ten percent of the world's total. These statistics, however, mask a situation that has deteriorated rapidly since World War II, as short-sighted economic development has taken a serious toll on Thailand's landscape.

Half of Thailand's forest is protected as **national park**, and it is in these reserves that the kingdom's natural heritage is best appreciated. The most rewarding of the country's national parks, including Khao Yai in the northeast, Doi Inthanon and Doi Suthep in

the north, and Khao Sam Roi Yot and Khao Sok in the south, are described in detail in *The Guide*; general practical information on national parks is given in *Basics* on p.50.

THE GEOGRAPHY OF THAILAND

Northern Thailand, being further from the Equator, has a so-called **monsoon climate**, meaning that rain only falls at certain times of year (during the "rainy season") and the region is otherwise prone to long dry periods. The south has a much more typical **tropical climate**: the land here is almost permanently moist, with rain falling more often and more consistently throughout the year. The north-south divide is generally considered to fall just north of Ranong, at the Kra Isthmus (see p.435).

Thailand's economy is agricultural, and the vast majority of Thais live off the land. Waterlogged rice paddies characterize the central plains, cassava, tapioca and eucalyptus are grown as cash crops on the scrubby plateau of the northeast, and rubber plantations dominate the commercial land-use of the south. Dotted along Thailand's coastline are mangrove swamps and palm forests; the country's coral reefs are discussed under "Wildlife" (see p.550).

MONSOON AND DECIDUOUS FORESTS

Most of Thailand's forest growth is **monsoon forest**, so called because its trees and plants have to be survive long stretches without any significant rainfall. To do this, many trees lose their leaves during the dry periods (which last between 2 months in parts of the south and 6 months in the north) to help conserve water; areas of such trees are known as **tropical deciduous forests**, and are typically light and open, with trees of between 7 and 15m and fairly thick undergrowth.

Teak is perhaps the most precious and sought-after monsoon-forest commodity. This solid timber is rich in silicic acid and oil, a combination which not only deters attacks by insects and fungi but also prevents the wood from warping, making it the ideal material for everything from houses to furniture. Often scraping 40m, teak trees are instantly recognizable, their large, elliptical leaves in situ from May through October or forming crunchy brown carpets beneath the trees for the rest of the year. Teak trees take around two hundred years to attain their full size, but artificial cultivation is becoming increasingly widespread in Thailand, and a teak tree's life-span on a plantation can be as short as fifteen years.

Bamboo thrives in a monsoon climate, shooting up at a remarkable rate during the wet season, but surviving undaunted at other times and often in soils too poor for other species; as a result bamboo often predominates in secondary forests (those where logging or clearing has previously taken place, and a new generation of plants has grown up – the majority of Thailand's forest). The smooth woody hollow stem characteristic of all varieties of bamboo is a fantastically adaptable material, used by the Thais for constructing everything from outside walls to chairs to water pipes (in hill-tribe villages) and musical instruments; and the bamboo shoot is an essential ingredient in Thai-Chinese cuisine.

Monsoon forest is relatively easy to clear, especially with the notorious slash-and-burn technique, and so a significant proportion of Thailand's monsoon forest has been cleared for both small and commercial cultivation purposes.

TROPICAL RAINFORESTS

Lowland tropical rainforests, such as those that cover most of southern Thailand (especially Khao Sok, Thale Ban and Tarutao national parks), some western pockets of the central plains, and the area around Chanthaburi, harbour the highest density of plant and animal species in the world. The biodiversity is such that an area of just one square kilometre can be home to a hundred different species of tree, the vast majority of them evergreen; and there are no naturally occurring single-tree forests. Furthermore, each rainforest boasts two quite distinct climatic zones: the uppermost canopy, which reaches heights of 50 to 80m, is subjected to intense sunlight and a dramatic nightly humidity drop from one hundred down to sixty percent, while the lower canopy is protected from these extremes and enjoys a fairly constant climate.

Characteristic of a lowland rainforest is the multi-layered series of **canopies**, with a church-like dome some 60m above ground level, a middle canopy of trees averaging 25m, and, because of the resultant shade, relatively little growth close to the forest floor. The soil is consequently deficient in nutrients, so many of the massive rainforest trees (some with girths of 2–6m), grow triangular overground buttress roots (see p.469) to absorb food from the forest floor.

Chief among the rainforests' massive inhabitants is the leathery-leaved **dipterocarp** family which tends to dominate their upper canopies. The forty-metre-plus branchless trunks are used for timber and oil, but the family (which embraces over 400 different species found in rainforests and elsewhere) gets its name from its two-winged fruits.

Rainforest trees play host to a plethora of epiphytes, lianas and other plant types of a dependent nature. Thai rainforests are choked with an astonishing variety of **epiphytic orchids**; all have three sepals and three petals, and can absorb moisture and nutrients from the atmosphere (rather than from the host plant) with the aid of specially adapted roots. Some of the most common ephiphytic orchids in Thailand include the gold, spiky petalled *bulbophyllum concinnum*, the bright-yellow *dendrobium trigonopsis*, the ivory-coloured *cymbidium siamensis*, the flame-hued *cattleyas*, and the blue *vanda coerulea*. Lianas such as the **strangling fig** are more of a threat to the rainforest trees, even the towering giants. The seeds of the strangling fig germinate on branches high above the ground and drop surprisingly hardy feeder roots to the forest floor; over time, these roots get tangled into a thick web that encloses the tree and eventually strangles it to death. As the host tree dies, its sap is sucked into the fig tendrils and the fig itself then grows a trunk, transforming itself from a liana into a tree.

MONTANE FORESTS

As the altitude rises above 1000m, the canopy of tall trees gives way to **montane forest** growth of oaks, chestnuts, laurels and other shorter temperate-zone tree families, many with twisted trunks and comparatively small leaves. Rainfall is frequent and often continuous at these elevations, so moss usually covers the forest floor and the undergrowth seems a lot denser, particularly with epiphytes, rhododendrons, and various types of tree fern. These highland forests are exposed to the harshest winds and coolest temperatures, so only the hardiest, sturdiest tree and plant species survive.

Montane forest can occur within areas dominated by either monsoon forest or tropical rainforest. Good examples can be seen in Doi Inthanon and Phu Kradung national parks, and in parts of Doi Suthep and Khao Yai national parks. In the higher areas of the north not protected as national park, a lot of the primary montane forest has been cleared for cultivation, especially by local hill tribespeople who favour the slash-and-burn farming technique.

MANGROVE SWAMPS AND COASTAL FORESTS

Mangrove swamps grow along the 2500km of both southern coasts of Thailand, and are the key to an ecosystem which protects and nourishes an enormous variety of plant and animal species – although like much of Thailand's natural heritage, they have fallen victim to destructive economic policies (see "Environmental Issues", p.553). At high tide only the upper branches of the thirty or so species of mangrove are visible, thick with glossy, dark green leaves, but as the tide recedes, a tangled mass of aerial roots is exposed. These roots not only absorb oxygen, but also trap water-borne debris brought in by the tides, thus gradually extending the swamp area (reclaiming land from the sea) and simultaneously nurturing fertile conditions for the new mangrove seedlings.

Nipa palms share the mangrove's penchant for brackish water, and these stubby-stemmed palm trees grow in abundance in southern **coastal areas**, though commercial plantations are now replacing the natural colonies. Like most other species of palm indigenous to Thailand, the nipa is a versatile plant, its components exploited to the full – alcohol is distilled from its sugary sap, for instance, while roofs, sticky-rice baskets and chair-backs are constructed from its fronds.

Taller and more elegant, **coconut palms** grace some of Thailand's most beautiful beaches. On islands such as Ko Samui, they form the backbone of the local economy, with millions of coconuts harvested every month,

most of them by specially trained pig-tailed macaques (see p.400), for their milk, their oil, their fibrous husks (used in matting and for brushes) and their wood.

Casuarinas also flourish in sandy soils and are common on the beaches of southern Thailand; because they are also fast-growing and attain heights of up to 20m, they are quite often used in afforestation programmes on beaches elsewhere. At first glance, the casuarina's feathery profile makes it look like a pine tree of some kind, but it's actually made up of tiny twigs, not needles.

THE WILDLIFE

Before World War II, Thailand's landscapes were virtually unspoiled and were teeming with wild animals such as elephants, wild boars, rhinoceroses, bears and deer. So numerous were these species, in fact, that they were regarded as little more than an impediment to economic progress, an attitude which resulted in a calamitous reduction of Thailand's wildlife and its habitats.

Nonetheless, in zoogeographical terms, Thailand lies in an exceptionally rich "transition zone" of the Indo-Malayan realm, its forests, mountains and national parks attracting both Indo-Chinese and Sundaic creatures. In all, Thailand is home to 282 species of mammal (of which 40 are considered to be endangered) and 928 species of bird (190 of them endangered).

MAMMALS

In the main national parks of Khao Yai, Doi Inthanon, Khao Sok and the like, the animals you're most likely to encounter – with your ears if not your eyes – are **primates**, particularly macaques and gibbons. Thailand's primates spend much of their time foraging for food in the highest reaches of the rainforests' upper canopies, only descending closer to the ground to rest and to socialize.

The gibbons are responsible for the unmistakable hooting that echoes through the forests of some of the national parks. Chief noise-maker is the **white-handed or lar gibbon**, an appealing beige-bodied, white-faced animal whose appearance, intelligence and dexterity unfortunately make it a popular pet.

Similarly chatty, macaques hang out in gangs of twenty or more. The **long-tailed or**

crab-eating macaque lives in the lowlands, near the rivers, lakes and coasts of Krabi, Ko Tarutao, Ang Thong and Khao Sam Roi Yot, for example. It eats not only crabs, but mussels, other small animals and fruit, transporting and storing food in its big cheek pouch, when swimming and diving – activities at which it excels. The **pig-tailed macaque**, so called because of its short curly tail, spends most of its time scaling the tall trees of Erawan, Doi Inthanon and other national parks; a skill which has many of the males captured and trained to pick coconuts – a practice that's very common in Surat Thani (see p.400).

You're almost certain to see deer in areas of protected forest, especially the **barking deer**, a medium-sized loner happy in pretty much any type of woodland (easily seen in Khao Yai, Phu Kradung, Erawan) and the large, dark-brown **sambar deer**, which prefers the deciduous forests of the same parks. The tiny **mouse deer** is rarer, and at only 20cm from ground to shoulder it's Southeast Asia's smallest hoofed animal. Mouse deer live in the undergrowth of rainforests (Khao Yai, Erawan, Ko Surin) but their reputed tastiness could see them heading for the endangered species list.

Commonly sighted on night treks in Doi Inthanon, Doi Suthep, Khao Yai and Khao Sam Roi Yot national parks, the **civet** – varieties of which include palm, Indian and three-striped palm civets – is a small cat which hunts smaller mammals in trees and on the ground; it's known in the West for the powerful smell released from its anal glands, a scent used commercially as a perfume base. More elusive are the **tiger** (continually under threat both from poachers and the destruction of its habitat by logging interests; for now Khao Yai and Khao Sok are the two likeliest places for sightings) and the very small, arboreal **clouded leopard**. The latter, also on the endangered list, is the size of a large domestic cat and feeds on birds and monkeys but only under the cover of darkness, rarely venturing out in moonlight let alone daylight.

The shy, nocturnal **tapir** lives deep in the forest of peninsular Thailand but is occasionally spotted in daylight. A relative of both the horse and the rhino, the tapir is the size of a pony and has a stubby trunk-like snout and distinctive colouring that serves to confuse predators: the front half of its body and all four

legs are black, while the rear half is white. It's an ungulate, with three-toed hind legs and four-toed front ones. Another unusual ungulate is the **gaur**, recognizable by its brown coat, sharp horns, powerful off-white legs and sheer bulk – the largest member of the cattle family, it measures up to 2m at shoulder height and can weigh over a ton. It feeds mainly at night, and is most frequently spotted at salt licks, for example in Khao Yai.

It's thought there are now as few as two thousand wild **elephants** left in Thailand: small-eared Asian elephants found mainly in Khao Yai and Khao Sok. Elephants can be dangerous if provoked and have caused a number of tourist deaths by trampling and tusking, so keep your distance. (For more on elephants in the wild and in captivity see the boxes on p.251 and p.102.)

BIRDS

Even if you don't see many mammals on a trek through a national park, you're certain to spot a satisfying range of **birds**. Home to upland, lowland and Malaysian species, Thailand also attracts all sorts of migrants, especially water birds – these last are best observed from September to March in Khao Sam Roi Yot, while Khao Yai is a prime year-round site for land birds.

There are said to be twelve species of **hornbill** in Thailand, all equally majestic with massive, powerful wings (the flapping of which can be heard for hundreds of metres) and huge beaks surmounted by bizarre bony casques. Khao Yai is the easiest place to spot at least two of the species: the plain black-and-white **Indian pied hornbill** and the flashier **great hornbill**, whose monochromic body and bill are broken up with jaunty splashes of yellow.

The shyness of the gorgeous **pitta** makes a sighting all the more rewarding. Usually seen fluttering around on the floor of evergreen forests, especially in Doi Inthanon, Doi Suthep and Khao Yai, these plump little birds – varieties of which include the **rusty-naped**, the **blue** and the **eared** – have dazzling markings in iridescent reds, yellows, blues and blacks. The one pitta, you might see outside a rainforest is the **blue-winged** pitta which occasionally migrates to dryer bamboo forests.

The striking orange-breasted and red-headed **trogon** lives mainly in the middle layer of Khao

Yai's tropical forests, as does the **barbet**, a little lime-green relative of the woodpecker. Less dramatic, but more frequently sighted forest residents include the brownish **babbler**, whose short tail and rounded, apparently ineffectual wings mean it spends most of its time on the forest floor; the noisy, fruit-eating, olive-and-brown-hued **bulbul**; and, most likely of all close to human habitats, the **yellow-vented bulbul**, which, as its name suggests, has a yellow flash on the underside of its brown body. The **black-naped oriole**, small groups of which fly from tree to tree in gardens as well as forests, is recognizable by its loud chirping and its yellow body, black head and wing markings and reddish beak.

Thailand's **ricefields** also attract a host of different birds, not only for the seeds and grasses, but also for the insects, rodents and even fish that inhabit the paddies. Some of the most common ricefield visitors are the various species of **munia**, a chubby relative of the finch, whose chunky, conical beak is ideally suited to cracking the unripened seeds of the rice plant – the aptly named **scaly breasted** munia and the **white-headed** munia are the most recognizable members of the family, although all members are an assortment of browns and whites. **Egrets** and **herons** also frequent the fields, wading through the waterlogged furrows or perching on the backs of water buffalos and pecking at cattle insects, while from November to April, thousands of **Asian open-billed storks** – so called because of the gap between the upper and lower mandibles – descend on agricultural land as well, building nests in sugar-palm trees and bamboos and feeding on pira snails – each baby stork polishing off at least half a kilo a day.

Coastal areas also attract storks, egrets and herons, and the mudflats of Khao Sam Roi Yot are a breeding ground for the large, long-necked **purple heron** as well. The magnificent **white-bellied sea eagle** haunts the Thai coast, nesting in the forbidding crags around Krabi, Phang Nga and Ko Tarutao, and preying on fish and sea snakes. The tiny **sea swift** makes its nest – the major ingredient of bird's nest soup and a target for thieves – in the limestone crags, too, though it prefers the caves within these karsts; for more on these swifts and their nests see p.479.

SNAKES

Thailand is home to around 175 different species and sub-species of **snake,** six of them venomous and the rest fairly harmless. Death by snakebite is not common, but all hospitals should keep a stock of serum, produced at the Snake Farm in Bangkok (see p.109 and *Basics* p.21).

Found everywhere and highly venomous, the two-metre, nocturnal, yellow-and-black-striped **banded krait** is one to avoid, as is the shorter but equally poisonous **Thai or monocled cobra**, which lurks in low-lying humid areas and close to human habitation. As its name implies, this particular serpent sports a distinctive eye mark on its hood, the only detail on an otherwise plain brown body. The other most widespread poisonous snake is the sixty-centimetre **Malayan pit viper**, whose dangerousness is compounded by its unnerving ability to change the tone of its pinky-brown and black-marked body according to its surroundings.

The ubiquitous shiny black or brown **common blind snake**, also known as the flowerpot snake, grows to only 17cm, and is as harmless as its worm-like appearance suggests. Also non-venomous but considerably mightier, with an average measurement of 7.5m (maximum 10m) and a top weight of 140kg, the **reticulated python** is Thailand's largest snake, and the second largest in the world after the anaconda. Tan-coloured, with "reticulated" black lines containing whitish oval spots, like eyes, the reticulated python is found near human habitation all over Thailand, especially in the suburbs of Greater Bangkok. It feeds on rats, rabbits, small deer, pigs, cats and dogs which it kills by constriction; if provoked, it can kill humans in the same way.

Other common Thai snakes include the **iridescent earth or sunbeam snake**, named after the sheen of its scales which glisten and change from black to a dark brown in the sunlight. Non-venomous and burrowing, this snake reaches a length of 1.2m and is found all over Thailand. South of Chumphon, the **mangrove snake** lives in the humid swamps that fringe the river banks, estuaries and coastal plains. Arboreal, nocturnal and mildly venomous, it can grow to about 2.5m and is black with thin yellow bands set at fairly wide intervals. Finally, the **golden tree**

snake is the most common of Thailand's flying snakes, so called because they can glide from tree to ground (although not the other way round). Frequently sighted in Greater Bangkok, this mildly venomous tree snake is not golden, but green with a dense pattern of black flecks, and grows to about 1.5m.

Quite a few of Thailand's snakes can swim if they have to, but the country is also home to a number of **sea snakes**, whose tails are flattened to act as an efficient paddle in water. Most sea snakes are venomous though not aggressive. Of the poisonous ones, the commonest and most easily recognized is the **banded sea snake**, which is silvery grey with thirty to fifty black bands and a slightly yellow underside at its front end. It grows to 1.5m and inhabits shallow coastal waters, coming onto land to lay its eggs.

MARINE SPECIES

The Indian Ocean (Andaman Sea) and the South China Sea (Gulf of Thailand) together play host to over 850 species of open-water fish, more than one hundred species of reef fish and some two hundred species of hard coral.

As a result of the destruction of much of Thailand's **coral reef** due to tourism and dynamite fishing (see "Environmental Issues", p.553), the most rewarding places to observe underwater life are the stretches of water conserved as **national marine parks**. The best of these are detailed in *The Guide* and include Ko Similan, Ko Surin, Ko Tarutao and Ang Thong; Thailand's major diving bases have their headquarters on Ko Phuket, and in Pattaya and Chumphon. (See also "Outdoor Pursuits" in *Basics* on p.48.)

Coral reefs are living organisms composed of a huge variety of marine life forms, but the foundation of every reef is its ostensibly inanimate **stony coral** – hard constructions such as boulder, mushroom, bushy staghorn and brain coral. Stony coral is composed of whole colonies of polyps – minuscule inverterbrates which feed on plankton, depend on algae and direct sunlight for photosynthesis, and extract calcium carbonate (limestone) from sea water in order to reproduce. The polyps use this calcium carbonate to build new skeletons outside their bodies – an asexual reproductive process

known as budding – and this is how a reef is formed. It's an extraordinarily slow process, with colony growth averaging somewhere between 0.5cm to 2.8cm a year.

The fleshy plant-like **soft coral**, such as dead man's fingers and elephant's ear, generally establishes itself on and around these banks of stony coral, swaying with the currents and using tentacles to trap all sorts of micro-organisms. Soft coral is also composed of polyps, but a variey with flacccid internal skeletons built from protein rather than calcium. **Horny coral**, like sea whips and intricate sea fans, looks like a cross between the stony and the soft varieties, while **sea anemones** have much the most obvious, and poisonous, tentacles of any member of the coral family, using them to trap fish and other large prey.

The algae and plankton that accumulate around coral colonies attract a whole catalogue of fish known collectively as **reef fish**. Most are small in stature, with vibrant colours which serve as camouflage against the coral, flattened bodies and broad tails for easy manoeuvring around the reef, and specially adapted features to help them poke about for food in the tiniest crannies.

Among the most typical and easily recognizable reef fish is the gorgeously coloured **emperor angel fish**, which boasts spectacular horizontal stripes in bright blue and orange, and an orange tail. The **moorish idol** is another fantastic sight, bizarrely shaped with a trailing streamer – or pennant fin – extending from its dorsal fin, a pronounced snout, and dramatic black, yellow and white bands of colour. Similarly eye-catching, the ovoid **powder-blue surgeon fish** has a light blue body, a bright yellow dorsal fin and a white "chinstrap". The commonly spotted **long-nosed butterfly fish** is named for the butterfly-like movements of its yellow-banded silver body as it darts in and out of crevices looking for food. The bright orange **clown fish**, so called because the thick white stripes across its body resemble a clown's ruff, is more properly known as the anenome fish because of its mutually protective relationship with the sea anemone, near which it can usually be sighted. Equally predictable is the presence of **cleaner fish**, or cleaner wrasse, on the edges of every shoal of reef fish. Streamlined, with a long snout and jaws that act like tweezers, a cleaner fish spends its days picking parasites off the skins of other fish – a symbiotic relationship essential to both parties.

Some reef fish, among them the ubiquitous turquoise and purple **parrot fish**, eat coral. With the help of a bird-like beak, which is in fact several teeth fused together, the parrot fish scrapes away at the coral and then grinds the fragments down with another set of back teeth – a practice reputedly responsible for the erosion of a great deal of Thailand's reef. The magnificent mauve and burgundy **crown-of-thorns starfish** also feeds on coral, laying waste to as much as fifty square centimetres of stony coral in a 24-hour period. Its appearance is as formidable as its eating habits, with a body that measures up to 50cm in diameter protected by "arms" covered in highly venomous spines.

Larger, less frequent visitors to Thailand's offshore reefs include the **moray eel**, whose elongated jaws of viciously pointed teeth make it a deadly predator, and the similarly equipped **barracuda**, the world's fastest-swimming fish. **Sharks** are quite common off the Andaman coast reefs, where it's also sometimes possible to swim with a **manta ray**, whose extraordinary flatness, strange winglike fins, and massive size – up to 6m across and weighing some 1600kg – makes it an astonishing presence. **Turtles** sometimes paddle around reef waters, too, but all four local species – leatherback, Olive Ridley, green and hawksbill – are fast becoming endangered in Thailand, so much so that the Royal Forestry Department has placed several of their egg-laying beaches under national park protection (see p.442), including those at Hat Mai Khao on Phuket, Thai Muang, Ko Surin Tai and Ko Tarutao.

Other commonly spotted creatures are the **sea urchin**, whose evil-looking spines grow up to 35cm in length, and the ugly but harmless **sea cucumber**, which looks like a large slug and lies half-buried on the sea bed. Deceptively slothful in appearance, sea cucumbers are constantly busy ingesting and excreting so much sand and mud that the combined force of those in a three-square-kilometre area can together redistribute one million kilogrammes of sea-bed material a year.

ENVIRONMENTAL ISSUES

Only in the 1970s did some sort of environmental awareness emerge in Thailand, when the politicization of the poor rural areas began to catch up with the powerbrokers in Bangkok. For years farmers had been displaced from land on which they had long established a thriving ecological balance, to be resettled out of the way of the Bangkok-based logging interests. Discontent with this treatment finally led some of the farmers to join the student protests of 1973, and in the subsequent right-wing backlash many political ringleaders fled the capital to seek refuge in the north. Many have since returned under amnesty, and their experiences among the nation's dispossessed have ensured that the environment plays a major role in the mainstream politics of Thailand.

DEFORESTATION

Undoubtedly the biggest crisis facing Thailand's environment is **deforestation**, the effects of which are felt all over the country. As well as providing shelter and sustenance for birds and animals (a single male tiger, for instance, needs about 50 square kilometres of forest to survive), trees prevent water from dispersing and binds the soil together. When they are cut down, water and topsoil are both rapidly lost, as was demonstrated tragically in 1988, when villages in the south were devastated by mudslides that swept down deforested slopes, killing hundreds of people. A formal **ban on most commercial logging** was finally established in the following year, but much illegal activity has continued.

There was little likelihood that the ban would ever be fully observed, as nothing has been done to change the pattern of wood consumption and the government has instituted no supervisory body to ensure the cessation of illegal logging. To make matters worse, there's the endemic problem of "influence": when the big guns from Bangkok want to build a golf course on a forest reserve, it is virtually impossible for a lowly provincial civil servant to resist their money. On top of that, there's the problem of precisely defining a role for the Royal Forestry Department, which was set up early this century to exploit the forest's resources, but now is charged with the maintenance of the trees. In order to boost its profile the RFD classifies as "forest" virtually anything that looks green from an aeroplane –

rubber plantations, eucalyptus farms and even ricefields. Even employing this extraordinary lax criterion, the RFD acknowledges that the percentage of Thailand's territory covered by "forest" has fallen from 53 percent in 1961 to just 28 percent in 1988. Environmental groups think the true figure is even lower.

The timber firms and their financial backers and political protectors have various ways of circumventing the law. Much skulduggery goes on close to the **Burmese border**, where the lawbreakers can claim that the felled timber came from outside the country. Some of it does indeed come from Burma, where the vicious and greedy military regime has set up deals with some of the less scrupulous Thai timber merchants – a racket put in motion by a former chief of the Thai army.

Another favourite trick involves the legal concession granted for the clearance of the hardwood whenever a dam or road condemns an area of forest. Invariably what then happens is that trees are felled outside the designated area and mixed in with the legitimately cut logs. A notorious case concerned the concession to remove trees destroyed by Typhoon Gay in Chumphon and Ranong provinces in 1989 when thousands of healthy trees were felled by the logging company while the local government officials looked on helplessly.

The environmental vandals are not slow to profit from the misfortunes of **Cambodia** either. There the Khmer Rouge has benefited from Thailand's logging ban, which came at the same time as the withdrawal of support from China, previously the Khmer Rouge's chief military backer. When Thailand cast its eye on the tracts of forests controlled by the Khmer Rouge, the Khmers saw a source of funding for its war against the Vietnamese puppet government in Phnom Penh. Secretive deals were done and the result is that a number of Thai logging companies now import untold quantities of hardwood from the Khmer Rouge. Recently, however, Phnom Penh has threatened a total ban on all unprocessed timber exports, complaining in the *Bangkok Post* that "every day three hundred trucks travel to Thailand stocked with our logs".

REFORESTATION SCHEMES

Commercial **reforestation** has actually worsened the situation. Backed by vested interests, the RFD has classified several areas as "degraded" forest, even though some of these are ancient virgin forest. Once thus designated, the hardwood forests are felled and cleared for commercial development. This usually takes the form of the plantation of fast-growing species such as **eucalyptus**, which are vital to the economically important – but grossly polluting – pulp and paper industries, but suck nutrients and water from the soil at a terrible rate, and are also impossible to mix with other crops. Moreover, some ten million people happen to live in these "degraded" forests.

Under the **khor jor kor** plan, part of Thailand's National Forest Policy of 1985, it's intended that some 25 percent of the country's land area is to remain covered with forest (including rubber plantations), with a further fifteen percent set aside for commercial plantation by the private sector and government agencies. The first phase of *khor jor kor* targeted some 250,000 Isaan families – labelled "encroachers" – for relocation from about 2500 villages, thereby reducing their living space by about one third. Some two thousand families have already been uprooted to make way for new plantations. Without warning, soldiers arrived at two villages in Khon Khaen province, ordered their inhabitants to leave and proceeded to demolish their dwellings. Each family was given temporary food rations and a nominal sum of money before being dumped in resettlement sites that had not been finished and had no attached farmland. Villagers were forced to kill their most valuable possessions – their buffalo – for food. As a result of the subsequent furore, the future of the *khor jor kor* plan is in doubt.

INFRASTRUCTURE PROJECTS

Another major cause of deforestation is development of the country's infrastructure. The expanding **road network**, essential to Thailand's emergence as an industrialized nation, has inevitably damaged the ecology of the country, as have the **quarries** that supplied the construction boom of the 1980s. But nothing has stirred as much controversy as Thailand's **hydro-electric schemes**, which might be a lot cleaner than the production and burning of lignite – the low-grade coal that's Thailand's major source of energy – but destroys vast areas and, of course, displaces countless people.

The most recent controversial project was the construction of the **Pak Mun dam** across the River Mun in southern Isaan (see p.353), completed in July 1994 despite vociferous and at times violent protest. Over two thousand local farming families have lost their homes, and scores of fishermen have had their annual incomes severely depleted, demanding compensation to the tune of B35,000 a year for three years; the Electricity Generating Authority of Thailand (EGAT) is offering B10,000 each for a period of two and a half years.

The initiation of this project was somewhat troublesome for the Thai government, which applied to the World Bank for partial funding, more to legitimize the construction than to compensate for financial shortfall. The decision on funding was to be taken at the 1991 annual meeting of the World Bank and International Monetary Fund, held in Bangkok. To the embarrassment of the Thais, the meeting was preceded by the release of an international report showing that the electricity company's environmental impact study on the dam was deficient, and that bacteria likely to multiply in the reservoir would cause disease amongst the local inhabitants.

Protestors used the opening of the meeting – which was Thailand's most prestigious event of the year and inaugurated the much-vaunted Queen Sirikit National Convention Centre – as a platform to voice their opposition, and were temporarily heartened when the World Bank announced a postponement on the decision. In Thailand such "postponements" usually mean cancellation, with face-saving for all. Unfortunately, notwithstanding its new "green image", the Bank approved the loan a few months later, perhaps influenced by the Thai government's defiant announcement that it would press ahead with the dam with or without funding.

MANGROVES AND CORAL REEFS

In the past, **mangrove swamps** were used by rice farmers to raise **prawns**, using the tides to wash the larvae into prepared pools. Some rice farmers even converted their paddies into prawn farms, but generally the scale of this aquaculture was small and sustainable.

Then, in 1972, the Department of Fisheries began to promote modern technology, enticing many people to invest all they could afford – and sometimes more – in this growth sector. It looked like good money, with farmers initially reporting profits of three hundred percent,

which for people used to living on the breadline was a gift from the gods. However, big business swiftly moved in, so that today almost all prawn farming in Thailand is in the hands of a few companies.

This was bad for the local farmers, and disastrous for the ecology of the mangroves. Large-scale prawn farming uses vast amounts of sea water, which salinates the neighbouring land to the extent that rice farmers who used to produce two crops a year are now reduced to one small harvest. Furthermore, the chemicals used to feed the prawns and ward off disease are allowed to wash back into the swamps, damaging not only the mangroves themselves, but also the water used for irrigation, drinking and washing. Pollution also kills the very industry that produces it, forcing farmers to move their breeding pools along the coast, damaging yet more mangrove. This destruction of the mangrove forests to make way for new breeding pools is exemplified by the case of the Wen River National Forest Reserve in Kanchanaburi, where the RFD's own figures show that a mere ten percent of the fertile mangrove forest has survived intact.

Many of Thailand's **coral reefs** – some of which are thought to be around 450 million years old – are being destroyed by factors attributable to tourism, the country's biggest foreign-exchange earner since 1975. The main cause of tourism-related destruction is the pollution generated by the hotels and bungalows which have multiplied unchecked at many of the most beautiful sites on the coasts. The demand for coral souvenirs is exploited by unscrupulous divers and local traders, and many irresponsible dive leaders allow their customers to use harpoon guns, which cause terrible damage to reefs. Still, the destruction of coral by tourists is dwarfed by that wreaked by the practice of **dynamite fishing**, which goes on in areas away from the normal tourist haunts.

ENDANGERED SPECIES AND WILDLIFE TRADE

Having hunted many of its indigenous species to extinction – such as Schomburgk's deer, the Javan rhinoceros and the Sumatran rhinoceros – Thailand now acts as the "wildlife supermarket of the world", to quote the World Wide Fund for Nature, which condemned Thailand as "probably the worst country in the world for the illegal trade in endangered wildlife". Thailand signed the Convention on the International Trade in Endangered Species – **CITES** – in 1973, but for years afterwards the Thais exploited the uncertainty as to whether CITES covered trade in species originating outside the trading country. Even now that it has been established that CITES applies to all commerce in all listed species, Thailand continues to make money out of imported animals and animal products.

Cambodia – not a signatory of CITES – is the major supplier of **live animals**. The main action is focused on border towns such as Aranyaprathet, where Thai middle-merchants can easily acquire monkeys, deer, wildcats, monitor lizards and various other reptiles, secure in the knowledge that official intervention will be minimal. The RFD, which is charged with the suppression of wildlife trade, has a budget for only thirty wildlife officers nationwide, and doesn't have the money to train them properly, so even if they do intercept a transaction in an endangered species, they probably won't know what they're looking at.

Several animal traders deal quite openly in Bangkok, chiefly at the Weekend Market (see p.113), but the capital's trade is weighted towards **animal products**. One of the most serious problems is the business in crocodile skins, many of which come from South America, and are sold in huge numbers in Bangkok and other tourist areas. Another critical area is the trade in ivory, most of which is imported from Burma and Laos, although some is native – despite the fact that the Asian elephant has long been protected by law in Thailand. Tiger body-parts are also traded in Thailand, going to brokers for the black markets of China, Taiwan and Hong Kong, where bones, skin, teeth, whiskers and penis are prized for their "medicinal" properties; it's thought that much of Thailand's dwindling tiger population ends up in such lucrative pieces. The Thai government has come under pressure from CITES to do something about the poaching, and tigers rescued alive from illegal traders are now given **sanctuary** in one of two special enclosures purpose built by the UK-based Tiger Trust and financed by contributions from the Thai government and from private donation.

Thailand's own legislation – the Wild Animals Reservation and Protection Act – is notoriously weak at protecting native Thai species not listed by CITES. For example, the WWF has accused Thailand of showing little interest in protecting its **orchid** species, which grow here in a profusion unmatched anywhere else. And although Thailand's politicians are sensitive to international disapproval when it comes to conservation issues, it seems that there is still a lack of real will to clamp down on the people who profit from the destruction of rare animals. After the WWF made its "supermarket" comment, several highly publicized raids were made on traders who were breeding endangered species for commercial purposes – as well as on a restaurant serving exotic and endangered dishes. The fines, however, were relatively small, and it soon became clear that the raids had served their cosmetic purpose once they had been reported on television.

Contributions by Gavin Lewis

MUSIC

Music is an important part of Thai culture, whether related to Buddhist activities in the local temple (still a focal point for many communities), animist rituals, Brahmin ceremonies, or the wide range of popular song styles. The most interesting types of Thai music, *luk thung* and *mor lam*, are incredibly popular and distinctively Thai in character. But they – and Thai popular music in general – are largely ignored by visitors to the country. The little that tourists do tend to hear are classical or court ensembles at restaurants or the National Theatre, or the discordant pipes and drums that accompany Thai boxing (*muay Thai*).

THE CLASSICAL TRADITION

Thai classical dance and music can be traced back to stone engravings during the Sukhothai period (thirteenth to fifteenth centuries), which show ensembles of musicians playing traditional instruments, called **phipat**. The *phipat* ensembles include a large array of percussion instruments, rather like the Indonesian gamelan – gong circles, xylophones and drums – plus a raucous oboe called the *phinai*. The music was developed to accompany classical dance-drama (*khon* or *lakhon*) or shadow puppet theatre (*nang*), and you can see an ensemble playing for a shadow-puppet show depicted in the magnificent *Ramayana* murals in the Grand Palace complex in Bangkok.

Phipat music sounds strange to Western ears as the seven equal notes of the Thai scale

fall between the cracks of the piano keyboard. But heard in the right environment – in a temple, at a dance performance or at a Thai boxing match – it can be entrancing. As there is no notation, everything is memorized. And, as in all Thai music, elements have been assimilated over the years from diverse sources, and then synthesized into something new.

Despite the country's rapid Westernization, Thai classical music has been undergoing something of a revival in the past few years, partly as a result of royal patronage. There have been recent experiments, too, that attempt to blend Thai classical and Western styles – often jazz or rock; led by avant garde groups like **Kangsadan** and **Fong Naam**, they have been quite a success. There has even been a return to using Thai classical music as backing for popular singers: **Ood Oh-pah Tossaporn** had the *luk thung* hit of the year in 1990 with classical backing, and other singers have followed his lead.

There are regular dance and classical music performances in Bangkok at the National Theatre and the Chalermkrung Royal Theatre. Look out, especially, for concerts by the veteran flautist and pi-player **Chamnian Srithaiphan**, recently made a National Artist. Somewhat lacklustre **temple dancing** can usually be seen at the Erawan Shrine on Rama I Road and the *lak muang* shrine behind the Grand Palace. People pay for the temple musicians and dancers to go through a routine in thanks for their good fortune. A number of restaurants also mount music and dance shows for tourists.

FOLK MUSIC

Thailand's folk musics are often referred to as **pleng phua bahn**, which encompasses styles from any of the country's four distinct regions (central, north, northeast and south), with their 61 languages and dialects. Despite the rapid social change of the past decade, numerous folk styles are still enthusiastically played, from the hilltribe New Year dances in the far north to the all-night singing jousts of northeastern *mor lam glawn*, to the haunting Muslim vocals of *likay wolou* in the deep south.

The most notable folk style to have grown in popularity in recent years is the up-tempo and danceable northeastern instrumental style known as **bong lang** (the name comes from a wooden xylophone that is attached vertically to a tree). *Bong lang* is thought to predate Indian-Thai culture, and while it is clearly an ancient music, the style continues to be refined; as recently as the late 1970s, the *phin hai*, a jar with rubber stretched across the mouth, was introduced, though often only to put a cute young woman at the front of the band. The sound, made by plucking the rubber, is similar to that of a double bass.

The best place to see *bong lang* is upcountry, especially in Kalasin province in Isaan between November and March. In the major northeastern cities – Khon Kaen, Ubon Ratchathani and Udon Thani – check with the TAT offices for details of festivals like *Songkhran* (April), the *Bun Bang Fai* rocket festival (May), and the *Asanha Puja* candle festival (July).

THAI POP

For the last decade or so, the Thai popular music industry has developed at an unprecedented rate, reflecting the high economic growth rates and rapid industrialization, the wider availability of cheap cassette players, and the introduction of the 1979 Copyright Act (which has helped local artists, even if it has had little effect on the piracy of top Western acts). "Happy, No Problem", as the hit song by Asanee & Wasan put it.

The most popular genre to emerge during this period has been **string**, a Westernized form of Thai pop. *String* artists like the nation's top singer, **Thongchai "Bird" Macintyre**, sell hundreds of thousands of cassettes and feature in nationwide advertising campaigns for consumer products. The range of styles within this genre goes from ballads to rock to hard rock to disco and rap; whatever is popular in the US or Britain gets picked up quickly and is reassembled with Thai lyrics, plus a particular local flavour that often favours sweet melodies.

Assimilation of Western styles has been boosted by performances in Thailand by top Western acts like Michael Jackson and INXS. Often these shows are supported by local upcoming national favourites, like new reggae band **T-Bone**, or the "blues" singer **Mama Blues**. Currently popular are lead female singers backed by cute toy-boy dancers, à la Madonna. Nearly every Southeast Asian country has its own version of Madonna or Michael Jackson: in Thailand it's the vampy **Honey** and Jackson soundalike **Tik Shiro**.

SONGS FOR LIFE

Another big genre is **pleng phua chiwit**, or "songs for life", which started as a kind of progressive rock in the early 1970s, with bands like **Caravan** (no relation to the British songsters) blending *pleng phua bahn* (folk songs) with Western folk and rock. Caravan were at the forefront of the left-wing campaign for democracy with songs like "Khon Gap Kwai" (Human with Buffalos):

> *Greed eats our labour and divides people*
> *into classes*
> *The rice farmers fall to the bottom*
> *Insulted as backward and ignorant brutes*
> *With one important and sure thing: death.*

Although an elected government survived from 1973 to 1976, the military returned soon after and Caravan, like many of the student activists, went into hiding in the jungle. There they performed to villagers and hilltribe people and gave the occasional concert. In 1979 the government offered an amnesty and most of the students, and Caravan too, disillusioned with the Communist Party's support for the Khmer Rouge in Cambodia, returned to normal life. The military's predilection for coups, however, continues. The bloody street riots of 1992 (in protest at the then military-installed government) once again brought some "songs for life" artists out to support the pro-democracy protests.

More generally, in the 1980s, the strong social activist stance was replaced by more individual and personal themes, as can be heard in the music of Thailand's most successful rock band, **Carabou**. The band has since splintered into smaller groups and its position as top rock act has been taken by **Zuzu**, one of the more interesting rock groups, who often use regional music and instruments. Individual singer-songwriters in this genre are mostly earnest young men like the hugely popular Pongsit Kamphee, reputedly a former stagehand for Caravan. Interestingly, Caravan often reform for Japanese tours. In May 1990 the band led a "Woodstock-style" benefit gig in Phnom Penh and Angkor Wat, Cambodia, dubbed "Music for Peace: Encore Caravan".

But what is significant is that the generation that has grown up in the 1980s has done so on a diet of mainly Thai pop, in contrast to the 1970s generation, who followed Western pop. This is particularly the case with the growing middle class in Bangkok. Similarly, rural youngsters have also caught on to *string* music, while at the same time enjoying a much wider selection of Thai country music: *luk thung* and *mor lam*.

THAI COUNTRY MUSIC

Go to one of the huge **luk thung** shows held in a temple or local stadium on the outskirts of Bangkok, or to any temple fair in the countryside, and you'll hear one of the great undiscovered popular musics of Asia. The shows, amidst the bright lights, food stalls and fairground games, last several hours and involve dozens of dancers and costume changes.

Like modern Thai pop, *luk thung* has its roots in the development of radio and the influence of the West in the 1940s. Western orchestration for Thai melodies had been introduced in the 1930s and this led to the development of *dontree sakol*, or modern music, in the form of big band and swing, country and Western, Hollywood film music, rock 'n' roll, and so on. In the early days, two distinctive Thai genres developed: *luk grung*, a schmaltzy romantic ballad form; and *luk thung*, country music. Currently the popular music market divides into forty percent *luk thung*, thirty percent *string* and twenty percent *luk grung*.

Luk grung, with its clearly enunciated singing style and romantic fantasies, has long been associated with the rich stratas of Bangkok society; it's the kind of music played by state organs like Radio Thailand. However, it was largely transformed during the 1960s by the popularity of Western stars like Cliff Richard; as musicians started to mimic the new Western music, a new term was coined, *wong shadow* (*wong* means group, and *shadow* came from the British group, The Shadows). This trend led to the development of *string* in the 1980s.

In contrast, **luk thung** (literally, "child of the field") has always been associated with the rural and urban poor, and because of this has gained nationwide popularity over the past forty years. According to *luk thung* DJ Jenpope Jobkrabunwan, the term was first coined by Jamnong Rangsitkuhn in 1962, but he says the first song was "Oh Jow Sow Chao Rai" (Oh, the Vegetable Grower's Bride), recorded in 1937, and the first big singer, **Kamrot Samboonanon**, emerged in the mid-1940s. Originally called *pleng talad* (market songs) or *pleng chiwit* (songs of life), the style blended together folk songs (*pleng pua bahn*), central Thai classical music and Thai folk dances (*ram wong*).

In 1952, a new singer, **Suraphon Sombatjalern**, made his debut with a song entitled "Nam Da Sow Vienne" (Tears of the Laotian [Vientiane] Girl) and became the undisputed king of the style until his untimely murder (for serious womanizing, rumour has it) in 1967. Along with female singer **Pongsri Woranut**, Sombatjalern helped to develop the music into a mature form.

There was initially, says Jenpope, a folk sound but external influences soon changed the music. Malay *string*-band sounds were added in the 1950s, as were Latin brass and rhythms like the chachachá and mambo (Asian tours by Xavier Cugat influenced many Asian pop styles during the 1950s), as well as elements from Hollywood movie music and "yodelling" country and Western vocal styles from the likes of Gene Autry and Hank Williams.

Today, *luk thung* is a mix of Thai folk music and traditional entertainment forms like *likay* (travelling popular theatre), as well as a range of Western styles. There are certainly some strong musical affinities with other regional pop styles like Indonesian *dangdut* and Japanese *enka*, but what is distinctly Thai – quite apart from the spectacular live shows that include upwards of fifty dancers in amazing costumes – are the singing styles and content of the lyrics.

Vocal styles are full of glissando, wavering grace notes and wailing ornamentation. A singer must have a wide vocal range, as *luk thung* megastar **Pompuang Duangjan** explained: "Making the *luk thung* sound is difficult, you must handle well the high and low notes. And because the emotional content is stronger than in *luk grung*, you must also be able to create a strongly charged atmosphere."

Duangjan had the kind of voice that turns the spine to jelly. She rose to prominence during the late 1970s, joining sweet-voiced **Sayan Sanya** as the biggest male and female names in the business. Like Sombatjalern, both came from the rural peasantry, making identification with themes and stories that related directly to the audience much easier. Songs narrate mini-novellas, based around typical characters like the lorry driver, peasant lad or girl, poor farmer, prostitute or maid; and the themes are those of going away to the big city, infidelity, grief, tragedy and sexual pleasure.

Interestingly, it is not always the lyrics that carry the sexual charge of the song (and if lyrics are deemed too risqué by the authorities the song will be strictly censored) but rather the vocal style and the stage presentation, which can be very bawdy indeed.

With the advent of TV and the rise in popularity of string, the number of large up-country *luk thung* shows has declined. It's not easy, said Duangjan, to travel with over a hundred staff, including some fifty dancers in the *hang kruang* (chorus). "We play for over four hours," she said, "but *string* bands, with only a few staff members, play a paltry two hours!" Her response to the advent of string and the increasing importance of promotional videos was to develop a dancefloor-oriented sound – **electronic luk thung**. Few *luk thung* singers are capable of this, but Duangjan had the vocal range to tackle both ballad forms and the up-tempo dance numbers. Her musical diversification increased her popularity enormously.

She died in 1992, aged only 31, and up to 200,000 people, from the country's royalty and elite to the rural poor, made their way to her funeral in her home town of Suphanburi. A massive tribute was staged at the temple with everyone in the *luk thung* business performing her songs. As top TV broadcaster Somkiet Onwimon said: "She was certainly a role model for many poor, rural people. She always had time for everyone and, despite her obvious educational handicap (she was illiterate), she made something of her short life."

MOR LAM

Luk thung has also faced a strong challenge from another area: **mor lam**. This is the folk style from the poor, dry northeastern region of Isaan, an area famed for droughts, hot spicy food, good boxers and great music. Over the last ten years, the modern pop form of this style has risen dramatically, at *luk thung*'s expense.

Traditionally, a *mor lam* is a master of the *lam* singing style (sung in the Isaan dialect, which is actually Laotian), and is accompanied by the *khaen* (bamboo mouth organ), the *phin* (2–4-string guitar) and *ching* (small temple bells).

Modern *mor lam* developed from *mor lam glawn*, a narrative form where all-night singing jousts are held between male and female singers, and from *mor lam soeng*, the group dance form. Both still play an important part in many social events like weddings, births and deaths, festivals and temple fairs. A *mor lam* may sing intricate fixed-metre Laotian epic poems or may relate current affairs in a spontaneous rap. In the large groups, Western instruments like guitar (replacing the *phin*) and synthesizer (for the *khaen*) are used.

The style came to national prominence some fifteen to twenty years ago, when a female mor lam singer, **Banyen Rakgan**, appeared on national TV. In the early 1980s the music was heard not only in Isaan but also in the growing slums of Bangkok, as rural migrants poured into the capital – and continue to do so – in search of work. By the end of the decade stars like **Jintara Poonlarp** (with her hit song "Isaan Woman Far From Home") and **Pornsak Songsaeng** could command the same sell-out concerts as their *luk thung* counterparts.

A show by rising star **Chalermphol Malaikham** is typical of those of the bigger artists and the format is similar to *luk thung* shows – lots of dancers in wild costumes, comedy skits, and a large backing orchestra. Malaikham sings both styles, thus appealing to as wide a group of people as possible. The subject matter is similar in both, but musically they are very different. *Mor lam* has a much faster, relentless rhythm and the vocal delivery is rapid-fire, rather like a rap; it's also sung in Laotian.

You'll immediately recognize a *mor lam* song with its introductory wailing moan "Oh la naw", which means "fortune". *Mor lam* artists, brought up bilingually, can easily switch from *luk thung* to *mor lam*, but *luk thung* artists, who speak only the national central Thai dialect (Siamese), cannot branch out so easily. This is another reason why Pompuang Duangjan moved into a dancefloor sound. Some years ago, Sayan Sanya tried his hand at *mor lam* with Banyen Rakgan and bombed.

LUK THUNG PRAYUK AND MOR LAM SING

One way producers have tried to revitalize *luk thung* has been with **luk thung prayuk** ("applied" *luk thung*), which mixes the two country styles in one song. At the forefront of this innovation is **Pimpa Pornsiri**. She came to prominence in 1985 with the nationwide hit "Nam Da Mia Saud" (Tears of Mrs Saudi), a song about a lonely wife left in Isaan by her husband who is away working in the Middle East.

Pimpa tours throughout the country for as many as forty weeks a year, supported by 133 people and nine trucks. Her band features Western instruments like a drum kit, bass, guitars and a three-horn brass section, in addition to Thai instruments like the *ching* (small cymbals) and *glong kaek* (a pair of barrel drums played with sticks). The latter instruments provide much of the basic rhythmic pulse to Thai music.

Another new and exciting development has been **mor lam sing**, a turbo-charged modern version of *mor lam glawn*, pumped out by the small electric combos that are becoming an increasingly common sight in Isaan. The number of large travelling *luk thung* or *mor lam* shows has declined in recent years, due to high overheads, TV entertainment and the popularity of string bands, so *mor lam sing* satisfies the need for local music with a modern edge.

Mor lam sing is clearly a development of traditional *mor lam glawn*; maybe this is a case of traditions being kept alive, albeit in a racier, more contemporary format. Rural life in Isaan is changing, and *mor lam sing* seems to mirror the times. As motorbikes replace bicycles and the pace of life speeds up, it's interesting to note that the *sing* in *mor lam sing* comes from the Thai slang for a wayward "biker" teenager – *dek sing* (*sing* is short for the English word, racing), literally, a "racing kid". Many of the cassettes featuring this music, which come from places like Khon Kaen and Ubon Ratchatani, have a subtitle something like, "Sing Pet Pet" (Hot, Hot Sing) or "Sing Saeb Saeb" (Spicy Hot Sing).

The music is definitely hot, especially if you see it live, when bands will often play through the night, never missing the groove for a minute, driven on by the relentless *phin* and *khaen* playing. To some people, the fast plucking style of the *phin* gives a West African or Celtic tinge; the *khaen* has a rich sound – over

a bass drone players improvise around the melody, while at the same time vamping the basic rhythm. Male and female singers rotate or duet humorous love songs, which often start with one of the *mor khaen* setting up the beat. They sing about topical issues, bits of news, crack lewd jokes or make fun of the audience. All very tongue-in-cheek.

KANTRUM: THAI-CAMBODIAN POP

"Isaan nua (north) has *mor lam*, Isaan dai (south) has *kantrum*," sings **Darkie**, the first, and so far only star of **kantrum**, Thai-Cambodian pop, in his song, "Isaan Dai Sah Muk Kee" (Southern Isaan Unity). His music is a very specific offshoot, from the southern part of Isaan, where Thai-Cambodians mix with ethnic Laotians and Thais.

At a recent festival in the town of Buriram, organizers explained that the local *kantrum* talent contest was held to try to find a new group to challenge Darkie's position as the style's top singer. The winning group, **Saw In Concert**, combine both *kantrum* and *mor lam* in their show. For the *kantrum* numbers, the music is based around the plaintive melody of the *tro* (a two-stringed homemade fiddle, known in Thai as a *saw duan*) and the thumping rhythm of the conga-like *sko* drums. The rhythm seems harder, faster than *mor lam*, and one band member suggests that this is what people like about the music. A male-female lead vocal team fronts the band – opening songs with a wavering wail, dancing and alternating lead singing – and is supported by a five-woman dancing group, wearing, as is now customary, very short skirts.

Modern *kantrum* has developed from Cambodian folk and classical music, played in a small group consisting of fiddle, small hand drums and *krab* (pieces of hardwood bashed together rather like claves). This traditional style is now quite hard to find in Thailand; some ten or so years ago, musicians started to electrify the music, using both traditional and Western instruments. So far *kantrum* is only popular in Isaan, and that seems unlikely to change, as few people outside the region speak either Cambodian or the Thai-Cambodian dialect, Suay.

John Clewley
(Abridged from the Rough Guide to World Music.)

CDs are now produced in Thailand but feature mainly string artists and a few *luk thung* bands. There are, however, a few excellent discs on Western labels.

There is a lot more variety on local Thai cassettes – which comprise all the non-CD recommendations below. Buying them can be fun. In Bangkok, check out day and night markets, or the tape stores on Charoen Road, and tell the sellers the name of an artist you'd like to hear. Most major *luk thung* or *mor lam* artists release a cassette every three months, which is often given an artist's series number. Old-style recordings of Suraphon Sombatjalern and the like can be found on the ground floor of the *Mah Boon Krong Centre* near Siam Square.

CLASSICAL

Fong Naam *The Hang Hong Suite* (Nimbus, UK). This is the best introduction to the vivacious and glittering sound of classical Thai music, from one of Thailand's very best ensembles. The disc includes some very upbeat funeral music and a series of parodies of the musical languages of neighbouring cultures: Chinese, Cambodian, Laotian, Vietnamese and Burmese. The group's *The Sleeping Angel* (Nimbus, UK) is also a splendid recording while their most recent Thai cassette is a great collaboration with Isaan *mor lam* musicians, notably *khaen* player Sombat Simlao, and US bass player Abraham Laboriel.

Musicians of the National Dance Company of Cambodia *Homrong* (Real World, UK). Some tracks on this disc are strikingly similar to Thai classical music; others are more folk-based and are clearly at the root of present-day Thai-Cambodian pop, *kantrum*. The story of the National Dance Company reviving the traditions of classical Cambodian music after the horrific destruction of the Pol Pot regime is inspiring.

Various *Thailande* (Auvidis/UNESCO, France). An atmospheric disc of three contrasting ensembles from Chiang Mai. Intricate textures that draw you in.

HILLTRIBE MUSIC

Various *Thailand: Musiques et Chants des Peuples du Triangle d'Or* (Globe Music, France). Recordings of the traditional music of Thailand's main hilltribe groups: Meo, Lisu, Shan, Lahu, Yao, Akha and Karen.

LUK THUNG

Pompuang Duangjan *Greatest Hits Vol 2* (BKP, Thailand). A representative selection of *luk thung* hits from the late star of popular country music with a full, rich voice unlike anyone else in the business. In Thailand, the best of many cassettes to go for is called *Pompuang Lai Por Sor* [Pompuang's Many Eras] (Topline, Thailand).

Pimpa Pornsiri *Tee Sud Khong Pimpa* [The Biggest of Pimpa] (Rota, Thailand). All the hits of *luk thung prayuk*'s biggest name.

Suranee Ratchasima *Jeep Dor* [Returning Courtship] (Sure, Thailand). Rising *luk thung* singer from Khorat shows off her pipes on this set of standards.

Ood Oh-pah Tossaporn *Pleng Wan* [Sweet Songs] (Onpa, Thailand). Rock singer Tossaporn made a stunning *luk thung* debut with this 1990 recording, with catchy Thai classical backing.

Sayan Sanya *Luk Thung Talap Thong* [*Luk Thung* from the Golden Tape] (Onpa, Thailand). Heir to Sombatjalern's throne, sweet-voiced Sanya has never sounded better than on this greatest hits collection.

Suraphon Sombatjalern *Mere Mai Pleng Thai* [Mother of Thai Song] (Crown, Thailand). Greatest hits by the king of *luk thung.*

MOR LAM/NORTHEASTERN MUSIC

Isan Sléte *Songs and Music from North East Thailand* (GlobeStyle, UK). Excellent selection of traditional *mor lam*. Vocal and instrumental numbers, played by a band of master musicians.

Various *Instrumental Music of Northeast Thailand* (King, Japan). Wonderful collection of *bong lang* and related instrumental northeastern styles. Lively and fun. Unmissable.

Discography continued

Various Mor Lam Singing of Northeast Thailand (King, Japan). Most mor lam glawn narrative and dance styles, even spirit possession rituals, are included on this, one of the best Thai CDs available.

Banyen Rakgan Luk Thung, Mor Lam Sood Hit [Luk Thung, Mor Lam Top Hits] (Rota, Thailand). Sixteen scorchers from the first national mor lam star. Rakgan's voice is a standout. Good example of the big-band mor lam sound.

Pornsak Songsaeng Gaud Mawn Nawn Pur [Holding the Pillow in My Delirium] (Onpa, Thailand). Selection from mor lam's top male act, a fine singer with a deep, distinctive voice.

Jintara Poonlarp Dam Jai Nam Da [Depends on the Tears] (MGA, Thailand). Poonlarp has conquered mor lam over the past few years with her powerful voice and fast delivery.

Sarm Tone Pong Pong Chung [Sound of the Drum] (Kita, Thailand). An interesting group, founded in 1990, who mix mor lam and luk thung in a humorous urban pop style. Good fun live, too.

KANTRUM

Darkie Kantrum Rock Vols I & II (available on separate cassettes). Benchmark recordings by kantrum's only major star: Darkie's fine wailing voice is featured in rock-kantrum, kantrum and kantrum luk thung. Unfortunately, this cassette is only available in southern Isaan at present.

BOOKS

The following books should be readily available in the UK, US and/or Bangkok. We have given the publishers and prices for most of the in-print titles, though with some Thai titles it's impossible to give an accurate price in baht. The currency indicates the country of publication – where a price appears without a publisher, this means that the book is produced by the publisher previously cited in that listing. The titles listed as being out of print (o/p) should be easy enough to find in secondhand bookstores.

TRAVEL

Carl Bock, *Temples and Elephants* (o/p in UK and US). Nineteenth-century account of a rough journey from Bangkok to the far north, dotted with vivid descriptions of rural life and court ceremonial.

Ian Buruma, *God's Dust* (Vintage, £5.99; Noonday, $11). Modern portraits of various Southeast and East Asian countries, of which only forty pages are devoted to Thailand – worthwhile nevertheless for its sharp, unsentimental and stylish observations.

Karen Connelly, *Touch the Dragon* (Silkworm Books, B250). Evocative and humorous journal of an impressionable Canadian teenager, sent on an exchange programme to Den Chai in northern Thailand for a year.

John R Davies, *Touring Northern Thailand* (Footloose Books, £8.95). Comprehensive listings of places of interest in the north, essentially for travellers with their own transport, with very useful odometer distances given throughout. Stretches as far south as Sukhothai and Mae Sot, though little attention paid to the area around Nan; published in 1991, so some information, especially on accommodation, out of date.

Tristan Jones, *To Venture Further* (Grafton, £5.99; o/p in US). Amazing tale of how the author, a veteran adventurer and an amputee, pioneered the crossing of the Kra Isthmus in a longtail boat staffed by a disabled crew. Unusually forthright perspective on Thailand and its people.

Charles Nicholl, *Borderlines* (Picador, £5.99; Viking Penguin, $8.95). Entertaining adventures and dangerous romance in the "Golden Triangle" form the core of this slightly hackneyed traveller's tale, interwoven with stimulating and well-informed cultural diversions.

James O'Reilly and Larry Habegger (eds.), *Travelers' Tales: Thailand* (Travelers' Tales, B398; $15.95). Perfect background reading for any trip to Thailand: a chunky volume of collected contemporary writings about the kingdom, some from established Thailand experts, social commentators and travel writers, others culled from enthusiastic visitors with unusual and often very funny stories to share. A great idea, thoughtfully and effectively executed.

Alistair Shearer, *Thailand: the Lotus Kingdom* (o/p in UK and US). Amusing, sensitive and well-researched contemporary travelogue: a cut above the competition.

Eric Valli and Diane Summers, *Nest Gatherers of Tiger Cave* (Thames and Hudson, £19.95; o/p in US); published in Thailand under the title *The Shadow Hunters* (Suntree). Beautifully photographed large-format photo-essay on the birds' nest collectors of southern Thailand. The authors spent over a year with the harvesters, scaling the phenomenal heights of the sheer limestone walls with them.

William Warren, *Bangkok's Waterways: An Explorer's Handbook* (Asia Books). A cross between a useful guide and an indulgent coffee-table book: attractively produced survey of the capital's riverine sights, spiced with cultural and historical snippets.

Richard West, *Thailand: The Last Domino* (o/p in UK and US). Worthy attempt to get under the skin of "enigmatic Thailand", with a heady mix of political analysis, travelogue and anecdote. The author focuses on Thailand's relationships with neighbouring countries to show how it failed to become the "last domino" in the spread of communism.

CULTURE AND SOCIETY

Michael Carrithers, *The Buddha* (Oxford University Press, £5.99; $7.95). Clear, accessible account of the life of the Buddha, and the development and significance of his thought.

Robert and Nanthapa Cooper, *Culture Shock! Thailand* (Kuperard, £6.95; $10.95). Widely available but in every respect inferior to Denis Segaller's books on Thai culture (see below) – seems chiefly intended for prospective employers worried about how to deal with the Thai maid.

John R. Davies, *A Trekkers' Guide to the Hilltribes of Northern Thailand* (Footloose Books, B150). Bite-sized but well-informed insight into hilltribe cultures, including some practical information and a small dictionary of hilltribe languages.

Sanitsuda Ekachai, *Behind the Smile* (Thai Development Support Committee, £5; B200). Collected articles of a *Bangkok Post* journalist highlighting the effect of Thailand's sudden economic growth on the country's rural poor.

Jonathan Falla, *True Love and Bartholomew: Rebels on the Burmese Border* (Cambridge University Press, £24.95; $44.95). Well-written and sympathetic first-hand account of a year (1886-87) spent with the Karen inside their self-proclaimed independent state of Kawtulay, about 15km west of the Thai/Burma border. An affectionate, informed and rare portrait of these persecuted people, their political demands, and the minutiae of their daily lives.

Marlane Guelden, *Thailand: Into the Spirit World* (Asia Books). In richly photographed coffee-table format, a wide-ranging, anecdotal account of the role of magic and spirits in Thai life, from tattoos and amulets to the ghosts of the violently dead.

William J Klausner, *Reflections on Thai Culture* (Siam Society, Bangkok). Humorous accounts of an anthropologist living in Thailand since 1955. Entertaining mixture of the academic and the anecdotal; especially good on everyday life and festivals in Isaan villages.

Elaine and Paul Lewis, *Peoples of the Golden Triangle* (Thames and Hudson, £28; $40). Hefty, exhaustive work illustrated with excellent photographs, describing every aspect of hilltribe life.

John McKinnon (ed.), *Highlanders of Thailand* (Oxford University Press, o/p). A rather dry but enlightening collection of essays on the hill tribes.

Trilok Chandra Majupuria, *Erawan Shrine and Brahma Worship in Thailand* (Tecpress, Bangkok). The most concise introduction to the complexities of Thai religion, with a much wider scope than the title implies.

Pasuk Phongpaichit and Sungsidh Piriyarangsan, *Corruption and Democracy in Thailand* (Political Economy Centre, Faculty of Economics, Chulalongkorn University, B200). Fascinating academic study, revealing the nuts and bolts of corruption in Thailand and its links with all levels of political life, and suggesting a route to a stronger society.

Phya Anuman Rajadhon *Some Traditions of the Thai* (DK Books, Bangkok). Meticulously researched essays written by one of Thailand's leading scholars, republished to commemorate the centenary of the author's birth.

Denis Segaller, *Thai Ways* and *More Thai Ways* (Asia Books, Bangkok). Fascinating collections of short pieces on Thai customs and traditions written for the former *Bangkok World* by a long-term English resident of Bangkok.

Pira Sudham, *People of Esarn* (Shire Books, Bangkok). Wry and touching potted life-stories of villagers who live in, leave and return to the poverty-stricken northeast, compiled by a northeastern village lad turned author.

Thanh-Dam Truong, *Sex, Money and Morality: Prostitution and Tourism in South-East Asia* (Zed Books, £12.95; o/p in the US). Hard-hitting analysis of the marketing of Thailand as sex-tourism capital of Asia.

William Warren, *Living in Thailand* (Thames and Hudson, £28). Luscious coffee-table volume of traditional houses and furnishings, with an emphasis on the homes of Thailand's rich and famous; seductively photographed by Luca Invernizzi Tettoni.

HISTORY

Anna Leonowens, *The Original Anna and the King of Siam* (Chalermnit). The mendacious memoirs of the nineteenth-century English governess that inspired the infamous Yul Brunner film *The King and I*; low on accuracy, high on inside-palace gossip.

Michael Smithies, *Old Bangkok* (Oxford University Press, £8.95). Brief, anecdotal history of the capital's early development, emphasizing what remains to be seen of bygone Bangkok.

John Stewart, *To the River Kwai: Two Journeys – 1943, 1979* (Bloomsbury, £3.99). A survivor of the horrific World War II POW camps along the River Kwai, the author returns to the region, interlacing his wartime reminiscences with observations on how he feels and what he sees 36 years later.

William Warren, *Jim Thompson: the Legendary American of Thailand* (Jim Thompson Thai Silk Co, Bangkok). The engrossing biography of the ex-OSS agent, art collector and Thai silk magnate whose disappearance in Malaysia in 1967 has never been satisfactorily resolved.

Joseph J Wright Jr, *The Balancing Act: A History of Modern Thailand* (Asia Books). Detailed analysis of the Thai political scene from the end of the absolute monarchy in 1932 until the February 1991 coup; plenty of anecdotes and wider cultural references make it a far from dry read.

David K Wyatt, *Thailand: A Short History* (Yale University Press, £14; $17). The only comprehensive history of Thailand that's up to date and accurate. An excellent treatment, scholarly but highly readable, with a good eye for witty, telling details. Good chapters on the story of the Thais before they reached what's now Thailand, and on recent (up to 1984) developments.

ART AND ARCHITECTURE

Steve van Beek, *The Arts of Thailand* (Thames and Hudson, £24; $45). Lavishly produced and perfectly pitched introduction to the history of Thai architecture, sculpture and painting, with superb photographs by Luca Invernizzi Tettoni.

Jean Boisselier, *The Heritage of Thai Sculpture* (Asia Books, Bangkok). Weighty but accessible seminal tome by influential French art historian.

Susan Conway, *Thai Textiles* (British Museum Press, £16.95; University of Washington Press, $35). A fascinating, richly illustrated work which draws on the evidence of sculptures and temple murals to trace the evolution of Thai weaving techniques and costume styles, and to examine the functional and ceremonial uses of textiles.

Dorothy H Fickle, *Images of the Buddha in Thailand* (Oxford University Press, £8.95; $16.95). Clear, concise, though rather arid examination of Thai Buddha images of all peri-

ods, and the historical and religious influences which have shaped their development. Well-illustrated, with a short introduction on the life of the Buddha himself.

Betty Gosling, *Sukhothai: Its History, Culture and Art* (Oxford University Press, £30; $49.95). Overpriced but thoroughly researched dissection of the ruins of Sukhothai and the kings who commissioned them.

Sumet Jumsai, *Naga: Cultural Origins in Siam and the West Pacific* (Oxford University Press, £32; $45). Wide-ranging discussion of water symbols in Thailand and other parts of Asia, offering a stimulating mix of art, architecture, mythology and cosmology.

Apinan Poshyananda, *Modern Art In Thailand* (Oxford University Press, £60; $110). Excellent introduction – the only one of its kind – which extends right up to the present day, with very readable discussions on dozens of individual artists, and lots of colour plates.

Smithi Siribhadra and Elizabeth Moore, *Palaces of the Gods: Khmer Art and Architecture in Thailand* (White Mouse, £50; River Books, B1795). Lavishly produced tome covering all known Khmer sites in the country, with detailed but accessible descriptions and artistic assessments, illustrated with stunning photographs by Michael Freeman.

NATURAL HISTORY AND ECOLOGY

Hans-Ulrich Bernard with Marcus Brooke, *Insight Guide to Southeast Asian Wildlife* (APA, £13.99; Prentice Hall, o/p). Adequate introduction to the flora and fauna of the region, with a fairly detailed focus on several of Thailand's national parks. Full of gorgeous photos, but not very useful for identifying species in the field.

Ashley J. Boyd and Collin Piprell, *Diving in Thailand* (Asia Books, B495; Hippocrene $22.50). A thorough guide to 84 dive sites, detailing access, weather conditions, visibility, scenery and marine life for each, slanted towards the underwater photographer; general introductory sections on Thailand's marine life, conservation and photography tips.

Denis Gray, Collin Piprell and Mark Graham, *National Parks of Thailand* (Industrial Finance Corporation of Thailand, B498). Useful and readable handbook for naturalists which covers all the major national parks and details the wildlife and forest types you're likely to come across in each.

Margaret S. Gremli and Helen E. Newman, *Insight Guides Underwater: Marine Life in the South China Sea* (Geocentre, £6.99). Although not extending to the Andaman coast, Thailand's best snorkelling and diving area, this handy, at-a-glance reference guide to reef fish and coral formations covers pretty much everything you'll see there as well as on the Gulf coast. Packed with clear and informative colour photos, yet small enough for a daypack.

Philip Hurst, *Rainforest Politics* (Zed Books, £11.95; $19.95). Case studies of alarming ecological destruction in six Southeast Asian countries, sponsored by Friends of the Earth, which clearly and powerfully assesses the causes and offers pragmatic solutions.

Wilhelm Lotschert, Gerhard Beese, *Collins Guide to Tropical Plants* (Collins, £14.99; Viking Penguin, $24.95). Handy reference book with detailed descriptions of 325 plants, and 274 colour photos.

LITERATURE

Kampoon Boontawee, *A Child of the Northeast* (DK Books). Overly sentimental prize-winning novel set in 1930s Isaan, but well worth reading for its wealth of local colour and insights into northeastern folklore and customs.

A. Dingwall (ed.), *Traveller's Literary Companion: Southeast Asia* (Inprint Publishing, £13.95; Passport Books, NTC, $22.95). An immensely useful, though rather dry, reference source, with a large section on Thailand, including a book list, well-chosen extracts, biographical details of authors and other literary notes.

Kukrit Pramoj, *Si Phaendin: Four Reigns* (DK Books, 2 vols). A kind of historical romance spanning the four reigns of Ramas V to VIII (1892–1946) as experienced by a heroine called Ploi. Written by former prime minister Kukrit Pramoj, the story has become a modern classic in Thailand, made into films, plays and TV dramas, with Ploi as the archetypal feminine role model.

Rama I, *Thai Ramayana* (Chalermnit). Slightly stilted abridged prose translation of King Rama I's version of the epic Hindu narrative, full of gleeful descriptions of bizarre mythological characters and supernatural battles. Essential reading if you want anything like a full appreciation of Thai painting, carving and classical dance.

Nikom Rayawa, *High Banks, Heavy Logs* (Penguin, B349). Gentle tale of a philosophizing woodcarver and his traditional elephant-logging community, which won the Southeast Asian Writers' Award.

J C Shaw, *The Ramayana through Western Eyes* (DK Books). The bare bones of the epic tale are retold between tenuously comparable excerpts from Western poets, including Shakespeare, Shelley and Walt Whitman. Much more helpfully, the text is interspersed with key scenes from the murals at Bangkok's Wat Phra Kaeo.

S P Somtow, *Jasmine Nights* (Hamish Hamilton, £9.95). An engaging and humorous rites-of-passage tale, of an upper-class boy learning what it is to be Thai.

Khamsing Srinawk, *The Politician and Other Stories* (Oxford University Press, £10.99). A collection of brilliantly satiric short stories, full of pithy moral observation and biting irony, which capture the vulnerability of peasant farmers in the north and northeast, as they try to come to grips with the modern world. Written by an insider from a peasant family, who was educated at Chulalongkorn University, became a hero of the left, and joined the communist insurgents after the 1976 clampdown.

THAILAND IN FOREIGN LITERATURE

Botan, *Letters from Thailand* (DK Books). Probably the best introduction to the Chinese community in Bangkok, presented in the form of letters written over a twenty-year period by a Chinese emigrant to his mother. Branded both as anti-Chinese and anti-Thai, this 1969 prizewinning book is now mandatory reading in school social studies' classes.

Pierre Boulle, *The Bridge Over the River Kwai* (Fontana, o/p; Bantam, $4.50). The World War II novel which inspired the David Lean movie and kicked off the Kanchanaburi tourist industry.

Spalding Gray, *Swimming to Cambodia* (Picador, £5.99; Theatre Communications Group, $8.95). Hugely entertaining and politically acute account of the actor and monologuist's time in Thailand on location for the filming of *The Killing Fields*.

FOOD AND COOKERY

Vatcharin Bhumichitr, *The Taste of Thailand* (Pavilion, £12.99; Macmillan, $15). Another glossy introduction to this eminently photogenic country, this time through its food. The author runs a Thai restaurant in London and provides background colour as well as about 150 recipes adapted for Western kitchens.

Jacqueline M Piper, *Fruits of South-East Asia* (Oxford University Press, £6.95). An exploration of the bounteous fruits of the region, tracing their role in cooking, medicine, handicrafts and rituals. Well illustrated with photos, watercolours and early botanical drawings.

LANGUAGE

Thai belongs to one of the oldest families of languages in the world, Austro-Thai, and is radically different from most of the other tongues of Southeast Asia. Being tonal, Thai is extremely difficult for Westerners to master, but by building up from a small core of set phrases, you'll soon get the hang of enough to get by. Most Thais who deal with tourists speak some English, but once you stray off the beaten track you'll probably need at least a few words in Thai. Anywhere you go, you'll impress and get better treatment if you at least make an effort to speak a few words.

Distinct dialects are spoken in the north, the northeast and the south, which can increase the difficulty of comprehending what's said to you. **Thai script** is even more of a problem to Westerners, with 44 consonants to represent 21 consonant sounds and 32 vowels to deal with 48 different vowel sounds. However, street signs in touristed areas are nearly always written in Roman script as well as Thai, and in other circumstances you're better off asking than trying to unscramble the swirling mess of symbols, signs and accents. Transliteration into Roman script leads to many problems – see the note in the *Introduction*.

For the basics, the most useful **language book** on the market is *Thai: A Rough Guide Phrasebook* (Rough Guides, £3.50; $5), which covers the essential phrases and expressions in both Thai script and phonetic equivalents, as well as dipping into grammar and providing a fuller vocabulary in dictionary format (English–Thai and Thai–English). Among pocket dictionaries available in Thailand, G. H. Allison's *Mini English–Thai and Thai–English Dictionary*

(Chalermnit, B60) has the edge over *Robertson's Practical English–Thai Dictionary* (Asia Books, B229), although it's more difficult to find.

The best **teach-yourself course** is *Linguaphone Thai* (£169.90; $250), which includes six cassettes; *Colloquial Thai* (Routledge, book £9.99, book and 2 cassettes £25.99) covers some of the same ground less thoroughly. For a more traditional text book, try *The Fundamentals of the Thai Language* (Marketing Media Associates Co., £12.95), which is comprehensive, though hard going; G.H. Allison's *Easy Thai* (Tuttle, £7.99; $9.95) is best for those who feel the urge to learn the alphabet.

PRONUNCIATION

Mastering **tones** is probably the most difficult part of learning Thai. Five different tones are used – low, middle, high, falling, and rising – by which the meaning of a single syllable can be altered in five different ways. Thus, using four of the five tones, you can make a sentence just from just one syllable: *mái mài mâi mǎi* – "New wood burns, doesn't it?" As well as the natural difficulty in becoming attuned to speaking and listening to these different tones, Western efforts are complicated by our tendency to denote the overall meaning of a sentence by modulating our tones – for example, turning a statement into a question through a shift of stress and tone. Listen to native Thai speakers and you'll soon begin to pick up the different approach to tone.

The pitch of each tone is gauged in relation to your vocal range when speaking, but they should all lie within a narrow band, separated by gaps just big enough to differentiate them. The **low tones** (syllables marked `), **middle tones** (unmarked syllables), and **high tones** (syllables marked ´) should each be pronounced evenly and with no inflection. The **falling tone** (syllables marked ^) is spoken with an obvious drop in pitch, as if you were sharply emphasizing a word in English. The **rising tone** (marked ~) is pronounced as if you were asking an exaggerated question in English.

As well as the unfamiliar tones, you'll find that, despite the best efforts of the transliterators, there is no precise English equivalent to many **vowel and consonant sounds** in the Thai language. The lists that follow give a rough idea of pronunciation.

VOWELS

a as in dad.

aa has no precise equivalent, but is pronounced as it looks, with the vowel elongated.

ae as in there.

ai/ay as in buy.

ao as in now.

aw as in awe.

e as in pen.

eu as in sir, but heavily nasalized.

i as in tip.

ii as in feet.

o as in knock.

oe as in hurt, but more closed.

oh as in toe.

u as in loot.

uu as in pool.

CONSONANTS

r as in rip, but with the tongue flapped quickly against the palate – in everyday speech, it's often pronounced like "l".

kh as in keep.

ph as in put.

th as in time.

k is unaspirated and unvoiced, and closer to "g".

p is also unaspirated and unvoiced, and closer to "b".

t is also unaspirated and unvoiced, and closer to "d".

THAI WORDS AND PHRASES

GREETINGS AND BASIC PHRASES

Whenever you speak to a stranger in Thailand, you should end your sentence in *khráp* if you're a man, *khâ* if you're a woman – these untranslatable politening syllables will gain good will, and should always be used after *sawàt dii* (hello/goodbye) and *khàwp khun* (Thank you). *Khráp* and *khâ* are also often used to answer "yes" to a question, though the most common way is to repeat the verb of the question (precede it with *mâi* for "no"). *Châi* (yes) and *mâi châi* (no) are less frequently used than their English equivalents.

Hello	*sawàt dii*	My name is . . .	*phõm (men)/ diichãn (women) chêu . . .*
Where are you going? (not always meant literally, but used as a general greeting)	*pai nãi*	I come from . . .	*phõm/diichãn maa jàak . . .*
		I don't understand	*mâi khâo jai*
I'm out having fun/I'm travelling (answer to *pai nãi*, almost indefinable pleasantry)	*pai thîaw*	Do you speak English?	*khun phûut phasãa angkrìt dâi mãi?*
		Do you have . . . ?	*mii . . . mãi?*
		Is there . . . ?	*. . . mii mãi?*
Goodbye	*sawàt dii/la kàwn*	Is . . . possible?	*. . . dâi mãi?*
Good luck/cheers	*chôk dii*	Can you help me?	*chûay phõm/diichãn dâi mãi?*
Excuse me	*khãw thâwt*		
Thank you	*khàwp khun*	(I) want . . .	*ao . . .*
It's nothing/it doesn't matter/no problem	*mâi pen rai*	(I) would like to . . .	*yàak jà . . .*
		(I) like . . .	*châwp . . .*
How are you?	*sabai dii reũ ?*	What is this called in Thai?	*níi phasãa thai rîak wâa arai?*
I'm fine	*sabai dii*		
What's your name?	*khun chêu arai ?*		

GETTING AROUND

Where is the . . . ?	*. . . yùu thîi nãi?*	What time does the bus arrive in . . . ?	*rót thẽung . . . kìi mohng?*
How far?	*klai thâo rai?*		
I would like to go to . . .	*yàak jà pai . . .*	Stop here	*jàwt thîi níi*
Where have you been?	*pai nãi maa?*	here	*thîi níi*
Where is this bus going?	*rót níi pai nãi?*	over there	*thîi nâan/thîi nôhn*
When will the bus leave?	*rót jà àwk mêua rai?*	right	*khwãa*
		left	*sái*

GETTING AROUND (cont.)

straight	*trong*	ticket	*tŭa*
north	*něua*	hotel	*rohng raem*
south	*tâi*	post office	*praisanii*
east	*tawan àwk*	restaurant	*raan ahăan*
west	*tawan tòk*	shop	*raan*
near/far	*klâi/klai*	market	*talàat*
street	*thanŏn*	hospital	*rohng phayaabaan*
train station	*sathàanii rót fai*	motorbike	*rót mohtoesai*
bus station	*sathàanii rót meh*	taxi	*rót táksîi*
airport	*sanăam bin*	boat	*reua*

ACCOMMODATION AND SHOPPING

How much is …?	*… thâo rai/kìi bàat?*	Can I store my bag here?	*fàak krapăo wái thîi nîi dâi măi?*
How much is a room here per night?	*hâwng thîi nîi kheun lá thâo rai?*	cheap/expensive	*thùuk/phaeng*
Do you have a cheaper room?	*mii hâwng thùuk kwàa măi?*	air-con room	*hăwng ae*
		ordinary room	*hăwng thammadaa*
Can I/we look at the room?	*duu hâwng dâi măi?*	telephone	*thohrásàp*
I/We'll stay two nights	*jà yùu săwng kheun*	laundry	*sák phâa*
Can you reduce the price?	*lót raakhaa dâi măi?*	blanket	*phâa hòm*
		fan	*phát lom*

GENERAL ADJECTIVES

alone	*khon diaw*	easy	*ngâi*
another	*ìik … nèung*	fun	*sanùk*
bad	*mâi dii*	hot (temperature)	*ráwn*
big	*yài*	hot (spicy)	*pèt*
clean	*sa-àat*	hungry	*hĭu khâo*
closed	*pìt*	ill	*mâi sabai*
cold (object)	*yen*	open	*pòet*
cold (person or weather)	*năo*	pretty	*sŭai*
delicious	*aròi*	small	*lek*
difficult	*yâak*	thirsty	*hĭu nám*
dirty	*sokaprok*	tired	*nèu-ai*
		very	*mâak*

GENERAL NOUNS

Nouns have no plurals or genders, and don't require an article.

bathroom/toilet	*hăwng nám*	friend	*phêuan*
boyfriend or girlfriend	*faen*	money	*ngoen*
foreigner	*fàràng*	water	*nám*
food	*ahăan*		

GENERAL VERBS

Thai verbs do not conjugate at all, and also often double up as nouns and adjectives, which means that foreigners' most unidiomatic attempts to construct sentences are often readily understood.

come	*maa*	give	*hâi*	sleep	*nawn làp*
do	*tham*	go	*pai*	take	*ao*
eat	*kin/thaan khâo*	sit	*nâng*	walk	*doen pai*

NUMBERS

zero	*sǔun*	eight	*pàet*	twenty-two,	*yîi sìp sǎwng, yîi*
one	*nèung*	nine	*kâo*	twenty-three, etc	*sìp sǎam . . .*
two	*sǎwng*	ten	*sìp*	thirty, forty, etc	*sǎam sìp, sìi sìp . .*
three	*sǎam*	eleven	*sìp èt*	one hundred, two	*nèung rói, sǎwng*
four	*sìi*	twelve, thir-	*sìp sǎwng, sìp*	hundred, etc	*rói . . .*
five	*hâa*	teen, etc	*sǎam . . .*	one thousand	*nèung phan*
six	*hòk*	twenty	*yîi sìp/yiip*	ten thousand	*nèung mèun*
seven	*jèt*	twenty-one	*yîi sìp èt*		

TIME

The commonest system for telling the time, as outlined below, is actually a confusing mix of several different systems. The State Railway and government officials use the 24-hour clock (9am is *kâo naalikaa*, 10am *sìp naalikaa*, and so on), which is always worth trying if you get stuck.

1–5am	*tii nèung–tii hâa*	minute	*naathii*
6–11am	*hòk mohng cháo–sìp*	hour	*chûa mohng*
	èt mohng cháo	day	*waan*
noon	*thîang*	week	*aathít*
1pm	*bài mohng*	month	*deuan*
2–4pm	*bài sǎwng mohng–*	year	*pii*
	bài sìi mohng	today	*wan níi*
5–6pm	*hâa mohng yen–hòk*	tomorrow	*phrûng níi*
	mohng yen	yesterday	*mêua wan*
7–11pm	*nèung thûm–hâa*	now	*dǐaw níi*
	thûm	next week	*aathít nâa*
midnight	*thîang kheun*	last week	*aathìt kàwn*
What time is it?	*kìi mohng láew?*	morning	*cháo*
How many hours?	*kìi chûa mohng?*	afternoon	*bài*
How long?	*naan thâo rai?*	evening	*yen*
		night	*kheun*

A THAI GLOSSARY

Amphoe District.

Amphoe muang Provincial capital.

Ao Bay.

Aspara Female deity.

Avalokitesvara Bodhisattava representing compassion.

Avatar Earthly manifestation of a deity.

Ban Village or house.

Bencharong Polychromatic ceramics made in China for the Thai market.

Bhumisparsa mudra Most common gesture of Buddha images; symbolizes the Buddha's victory over temptation.

Bodhisattva In Mahayana Buddhism, an enlightened being who postpones his or her entry into Nirvana.

Bot Main sanctuary of a Buddhist temple.

Brahma One of the Hindu trinity: "the Creator". Usually depicted with four faces and four arms.

Changwat Province.

Chao ley/ Chao nam "Sea gipsies" – nomadic fisherfolk of southern Thailand.

Chedi Reliquary tower in Buddhist temple.

Chofa Finial on temple roof.

Deva Mythical deity.

Devaraja God-king.

Dharma The teachings or doctrine of the Buddha.

Dharmachakra Buddhist Wheel of Law (also known as Wheel of Doctrine or Wheel of Life).

Doi Mountain.

Erawan Mythical three-headed elephant; Indra's vehicle.

Farang A foreigner; a corruption of the word *français*.

Ganesh Hindu elephant-headed deity, remover of obstacles and god of knowledge.

Garuda Mythical Hindu creature – half-man half-bird; Vishnu's vehicle.

Gopura Entrance pavilion to temple precinct (especially Khmer).

Hamsa Sacred mythical goose; Brahma's vehicle.

Hang yao Longtail boat.

Hanuman Monkey god and chief of the monkey army in the *Ramayana*; ally of Rama.

Hat Beach.

Hin Stone.

Hinayana Pejorative term for Theravada school of Buddhism, literally "Lesser Vehicle".

Ho trai A scripture library.

Indra Hindu king of the gods and, in Buddhism, devotee of the Buddha; usually carries a thunderbolt.

Isaan Northeast Thailand.

Jataka Stories of the five hundred lives of the Buddha.

Khaen Reed and wood pipe; the characteristic musical instrument of Isaan.

Khao Hill, mountain.

Khlong Canal.

Khon Classical dance-drama.

Kinnari Mythical creature – half-woman, half-horse.

Kirtimukha Very powerful deity depicted as a lion-head.

Ko Island.

Ku The Laotian word for *prang*; a tower in a temple complex.

Laem Headland or cape.

Lakhon Classical dance-drama.

Lak muang City pillar; revered home for the city's guardian spirit.

Lakshaman/Phra Lak Rama's younger brother.

Lakshana Auspicious signs or "marks of greatness" displayed by the Buddha.

Likay Popular folk theatre.

Longyi Burmese sarong.

Maenam River.

Mahathat Chedi containing relics of the Buddha.

Mahayana School of Buddhism now practised mainly in China, Japan and Korea; literally "the Great Vehicle".

Mara The Evil One; tempter of the Buddha.

Meru/Sineru Mythical mountain at the centre of Hindu and Buddhist cosmologies.

Mondop Small, square temple building to house minor images or religious texts.

Moo Neighbourhood within an *amphoe*.

Muang City or town.

Muay Thai Thai boxing.

Mudra Symbolic gesture of the Buddha.

Mut mee Tie-dyed cotton or silk.

Naga Mythical dragon-headed serpent in Buddhism and Hinduism.

Nakhon Honorific title for a city.

Nam Water.

Nam tok Waterfall.

Nang thalung Shadow puppet entertainment, found in southern Thailand.

Nirvana Final liberation from the cycle of rebirths; state of non-being to which Buddhists aspire.

Pak Tai Southern Thailand.

Pali Language of ancient India; the script of the original Buddhist scriptures.

Phi Animist spirit.

Phra Honorific term for a person – literally "excellent".

Phu Mountain.

Prang Central tower in a Khmer temple.

Prasat Khmer temple complex or central shrine.

Rama Human manifestation of Hindu deity Vishnu; hero of the *Ramayana*.

Ramakien Thai version of the *Ramayana*.

Ramayana Hindu epic of good versus evil: chief characters include Rama, Sita, Ravana, Hanuman.

Ravana Rama's adversary in the *Ramayana*; represents evil. Also known as Totsagan.

Reua Boat.

Reua hang yao Longtail boat.

Rishi Ascetic hermit.

Rot ae/rot tua Air-conditioned bus.

Rot thammada Ordinary bus.

Sala Meeting hall or open-sided pavilion.

Samlor Passenger tricycle; literally "three-wheeled".

Sanskrit Sacred language of Hinduism, also used in Buddhism.

Sanuk Fun.

Sema Boundary stone to mark consecrated ground within temple complex.

Shiva One of the Hindu trinity – "The Destroyer".

Shiva lingam Phallic representation of Shiva.

Soi Alley or side-road.

Songkhran Thai New Year.

Songthaew Pick-up used as public transport; literally "two rows", after the vehicle's two facing benches.

Takraw Game played with a rattan ball.

Talat Market.

Talat nam Floating market.

Talat yen Night market.

Tavatimsa Buddhist heaven.

Tha Pier.

Thale Sea or lake.

Tham Cave.

Thanon Road.

That Chedi.

Thep A divinity.

Theravada Main school of Buddhist thought in Thailand; also known as Hinayana.

Totsagan Rama's evil rival in the *Ramayana*; also known as Ravana.

Tripitaka Buddhist scriptures.

Tuk-tuk Motorized three-wheeled taxi.

Uma Shiva's consort.

Ushnisha Cranial protuberance on Buddha images, signifying an enlightened being.

Viharn Temple assembly hall for the laity; usually contains the principal Buddha image.

Vipassana Buddhist meditation technique; literally " insight".

Vishnu One of the Hindu trinity – "The Preserver". Usually shown with four arms, holding a disc, a conch, a lotus and a club.

Wai Thai greeting expressed by a prayer-like gesture with the hands.

Wang Palace.

Wat Temple.

Wiang Fortified town.

Yaksha Mythical giant.

Yantra Magical combination of numbers and letters, used to ward off danger.

INDEX

HELP US UPDATE

We've gone to a lot of effort to ensure that this second edition of *The Rough Guide to Thailand* is accurate and up-to-date. However, things do change – places get "discovered", opening hours are notoriously fickle, restaurants and rooms raise prices or lower standards, extra buses are laid on or off. If you feel that we've got it wrong or left something out, we'd like to know, and if you can remember the address, the price, the time, the phone number, so much the better.

We'll credit all contributions, and send a copy of the next edition (or any other Rough Guide if you prefer) for the best letters. Please mark all letters " Rough Guide to Thailand Update" and send to:

Rough Guides, 1 Mercer Street, London WC2H 9QJ
or, Rough Guides, 375 Hudson Street, 3rd Floor, New York NY10014

THANKS TO OUR READERS

Thanks to the readers of the last edition who wrote in with helpful comments and suggestions:

Dominique Baldy, Relyn Begnall and Bryan Brazel, Cathy Bove, Wade Brice, Simon Brooksbank, David Brusselen, Moira P Cameron, Toby Charnand, Colin Clark, Kate Cracknell, Andrea Crisp, Susan Dickie, Ted Donovan, Xuela Edwards and Nicky Brown, Philip Elliott, Neil Fosbrooke, David Fountaine, Megan Goldin, A Gough, Gary Harrold, Adrian Harwood, Eddie Hing, Toni and Gordon Johnson, Brett Kellett, Donal L Knipe, Andrew Knowlman, Mark Lewis, Matt and Gail Lewis, Roger Lewis, Ian Lovatt, Andrew Lowrey, Tony Masters, Brian McLelland, Angelo Victor Mercure, Janice, Jock and Rachel Moilliet, John L Morton, John Oldale, Francesco Orecchioni, Alex Ovenden, Penelope Philpott, Laurence Rayner and Maggie Adams, Joannna Rees, Brian Savage, Lorimer Scott, Mike Sheffield, Nicky Simmons and Chris Wilson, Anna Sinclair and Rich Elmes, William Stewart, Annette C Stieber, Nick Stone, Eileen Stuart, Mr and Mrs Thackray, Christopher B Theaker, Anna Wardley, Paul Whitfield, Rona Williams, Pat Yale, Ruth Yearley.

Apologies to anyone whose name has been spelt incorrectly, and to those whose signatures could not be deciphered.

direct orders from

		UK£8.99	US$14.95	CAN$19.99
Amsterdam	1-85828-218-7	UK£8.99	US$14.95	CAN$19.99
Andalucia	1-85828-219-5	9.99	16.95	22.99
Australia	1-85828-220-9	13.99	21.95	29.99
Bali	1-85828-134-2	8.99	14.95	19.99
Barcelona	1-85828-221-7	8.99	14.95	19.99
Berlin	1-85828-129-6	8.99	14.95	19.99
Belgium & Luxembourg	1-85828-222-5	10.99	17.95	23.99
Brazil	1-85828-102-4	9.99	15.95	19.99
Britain	1-85828-208-X	12.99	19.95	25.99
Brittany & Normandy	1-85828-224-1	9.99	16.95	22.99
Bulgaria	1-85828-183-0	9.99	16.95	22.99
California	1-85828-181-4	10.99	16.95	22.99
Canada	1-85828-130-X	10.99	14.95	19.99
China	1-85828-225-X	15.99	24.95	32.99
Corfu	1-85828-226-8	8.99	14.95	19.99
Corsica	1-85828-227-6	9.99	16.95	22.99
Costa Rica	1-85828-136-9	9.99	15.95	21.99
Crete	1-85828-132-6	8.99	14.95	18.99
Cyprus	1-85828-182-2	9.99	16.95	22.99
Czech & Slovak Republics	1-85828-121-0	9.99	16.95	22.99
Egypt	1-85828-188-1	10.99	17.95	23.99
Europe	1-85828-159-8	14.99	19.95	25.99
England	1-85828-160-1	10.99	17.95	23.99
First Time Europe	1-85828-270-5	7.99	9.95	12.99
Florida	1-85828-184-4	10.99	16.95	22.99
France	1-85828-228-4	12.99	19.95	25.99
Germany	1-85828-128-8	11.99	17.95	23.99
Goa	1-85828-275-6	8.99	14.95	19.99
Greece	1-85828-131-8	9.99	16.95	20.99
Greek Islands	1-85828-163-6	8.99	14.95	19.99
Guatemala	1-85828-189-X	10.99	16.95	22.99
Hawaii: Big Island	1-85828-158-X	8.99	12.95	16.99
Hawaii	1-85828-206-3	10.99	16.95	22.99
Holland	1-85828-229-2	10.99	17.95	23.99
Hong Kong	1-85828-187-3	8.99	14.95	19.99
Hungary	1-85828-123-7	8.99	14.95	19.99
India	1-85828-200-4	14.99	23.95	31.99
Ireland	1-85828-179-2	10.99	17.95	23.99
Italy	1-85828-167-9	12.99	19.95	25.99
Jamaica	1-85828-230-6	9.99	16.95	22.99
Kenya	1-85828-192-X	11.99	18.95	24.99
London	1-85828-231-4	9.99	15.95	21.99
Mallorca & Menorca	1-85828-165-2	8.99	14.95	19.99
Malaysia, Singapore & Brunei	1-85828-232-2	11.99	18.95	24.99
Mexico	1-85828-044-3	10.99	16.95	22.99
Morocco	1-85828-040-0	9.99	16.95	21.99
Moscow	1-85828-118-0	8.99	14.95	19.99
Nepal	1-85828-190-3	10.99	17.95	23.99
New York	1-85828-171-7	9.99	15.95	21.99
Norway	1-85828-234-9	10.99	17.95	23.99
Pacific Northwest	1-85828-092-3	9.99	14.95	19.99

In the UK, Rough Guides are available from all good bookstores, but can be obtained from Penguin by contacting: Penguin Direct, Penguin Books Ltd, Bath Road, Harmondsworth, West Drayton, Middlesex UB7 0DA; or telephone the credit line on 0181-899 4036 (9am–5pm) and ask for Penguin Direct. Visa and Access accepted. Delivery will normally be within 14 working days. Penguin Direct ordering facilities are only available in the UK and the USA. The availability and published prices quoted are correct at the time of going to press but are subject to alteration without prior notice.

around the world

Paris	1-85828-235-7	8.99	14.95	19.99
Poland	1-85828-168-7	10.99	17.95	23.99
Portugal	1-85828-180-6	9.99	16.95	22.99
Prague	1-85828-122-9	8.99	14.95	19.99
Provence	1-85828-127-X	9.99	16.95	22.99
Pyrenees	1-85828-093-1	8.99	15.95	19.99
Rhodes & the Dodecanese	1-85828-120-2	8.99	14.95	19.99
Romania	1-85828-097-4	9.99	15.95	21.99
San Francisco	1-85828-185-7	8.99	14.95	19.99
Scandinavia	1-85828-236-5	12.99	20.95	27.99
Scotland	1-85828-166-0	9.99	16.95	22.99
Sicily	1-85828-178-4	9.99	16.95	22.99
Singapore	1-85828-135-0	8.99	14.95	19.99
Soutwest USA	1-85828-239-X	10.99	16.95	22.99
Spain	1-85828-240-3	11.99	18.95	24.99
St Petersburg	1-85828-133-4	8.99	14.95	19.99
Sweden	1-85828-241-1	10.99	17.95	23.99
Thailand	1-85828-140-7	10.99	17.95	24.99
Tunisia	1-85828-139-3	10.99	17.95	24.99
Turkey	1-85828-242-X	12.99	19.95	25.99
Tuscany & Umbria	1-85828-243-8	10.99	17.95	23.99
USA	1-85828-161-X	14.99	19.95	25.99
Venice	1-85828-170-9	8.99	14.95	19.99
Vietnam	1-85828-191-1	9.99	15.95	21.99
Wales	1-85828-245-4	10.99	17.95	23.99
Washington DC	1-85828-246-2	8.99	14.95	19.99
West Africa	1-85828-101-6	15.99	24.95	34.99
More Women Travel	1-85828-098-2	10.99	16.95	22.99
Zimbabwe & Botswana	1-85828-186-5	11.99	18.95	24.99
Phrasebooks				
Czech	1-85828-148-2	3.50	5.00	7.00
French	1-85828-144-X	3.50	5.00	7.00
German	1-85828-146-6	3.50	5.00	7.00
Greek	1-85828-145-8	3.50	5.00	7.00
Italian	1-85828-143-1	3.50	5.00	7.00
Mexican	1-85828-176-8	3.50	5.00	7.00
Portuguese	1-85828-175-X	3.50	5.00	7.00
Polish	1-85828-174-1	3.50	5.00	7.00
Spanish	1-85828-147-4	3.50	5.00	7.00
Thai	1-85828-177-6	3.50	5.00	7.00
Turkish	1-85828-173-3	3.50	5.00	7.00
Vietnamese	1-85828-172-5	3.50	5.00	7.00
Reference				
Classical Music	1-85828-113-X	12.99	19.95	25.99
European Football	1-85828-256-X	14.99	23.95	31.99
Internet	1-85828-198-9	5.00	8.00	10.00
Jazz	1-85828-137-7	16.99	24.95	34.99
Opera	1-85828-138-5	16.99	24.95	34.99
Reggae	1-85828-247-0	12.99	19.95	25.99
Rock	1-85828-201-2	17.99	26.95	35.00
World Music	1-85828-017-6	16.99	22.95	29.99

In the USA, or for international orders, charge your order by Master Card or Visa (US$15.00 minimum order): call 1-800-253-6476; or send orders, with complete name, address and zip code, and list price, plus $2.00 shipping and handling per order to: Consumer Sales, Penguin USA, PO Box 999 – Dept #17109, Bergenfield, NJ 07621. No COD. Prepay foreign orders by international money order, a cheque drawn on a US bank, or US currency. No postage stamps are accepted. All orders are subject to stock availability at the time they are processed. Refunds will be made for books not available at that time. Please allow a minimum of four weeks for delivery.

Stay in touch with us!

ROUGH*NEWS* is Rough Guides' free newsletter.
In three issues a year we give you news, travel
issues, music reviews, readers' letters and the
latest dispatches from authors on the road.

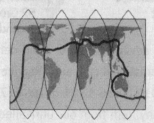

SLEEP EASY
BOOK AHEAD

Italy · Australia · Kenya · Denmark · Canada · Portugal · Norway · Finland · Greece · Malaysia · Czech Republic · Switzerland · Netherlands · South Africa · Japan · Hong Kong · Scotland · Rep of Ireland · France · Indonesia · Chile · Hungary · England & Wales · Luxembourg · New Zealand · Belgium · Spain · United States of America · Russia · Brazil · Austria · Northern Ireland · Sweden · Germany · Taiwan · Thailand

IBN INTERNATIONAL BOOKING NETWORK

Reserve hostels worldwide and secure a good nights sleep...

in more than 36 countries

up to six months ahead

with immediate confirmation

HOSTELLING INTERNATIONAL

*Budget accommodation you can **Trust***

IBN Credit Card Hotlines *NOW* **Available** ✆ Australia (2) 9261 1111 ✆ Canada (1) 800 663 5777 ✆ England and Wales (171) 836 1036 ✆ France (1) 44 89 87 27 ✆ Northern Ireland (1232) 324733 ✆ Republic of Ireland (1) 8301766 ✆ New Zealand (9) 379 4224 ✆ Scotland (141) 3323004 ✆ Switzerland (1) 360 1414 ✆ United States (1) 202 7836161